Relationship Section

Rotated Alphabetical Terms Section

Term Clusters Section

Margin Index: To use, bend pages of book backward and follow margin index to pages with black edge markers.

THESAURUS

of Psychological Index Terms

ELEVENTH EDITION

Lisa Gallagher Tuleya, *Editor*

American Psychological Association
Washington, DC

Published by
American Psychological Association
750 First Street, NE
Washington, DC 20002
www.apa.org

To order
APA Order Department
P.O. Box 92984
Washington, DC 20090-2984
Tel: (800) 374-2721; Direct: (202) 336-5510
Fax: (202) 336-5502; TDD/TTY: (202) 336-6123
Online: www.apa.org/books/
E-mail: order@apa.org

In the U.K., Europe, Africa, and the Middle East, copies may be ordered from
American Psychological Association
3 Henrietta Street
Covent Garden, London
WC2E 8LU England

Typeset by PageCentre, Inc., Tempe, AZ

Printer: Maple-Vail Book Manufacturing Group, York, PA
Cover Designer: Naylor Design, Washington, DC

Library of Congress Cataloging-in-Publication Data

Thesaurus of Psychological index terms. — 11th ed. / Lisa Gallagher Tuleya,
p. cm.
ISBN-13: 978-1-59147-926-0 (pbk. : alk. paper)
ISBN-10: 1-59147-926-6 (pbk. : alk. paper) 1. Subject headings—Psychology. I. Tuyela, Lisa Gallagher. II. American Psychological Association.

Z695.1.PP7T48 2007
025.4'915—dc22 2007005627

British Library Cataloguing-in-Publication Data
A CIP record is available from the British Library.

Printed in the United States of America
Eleventh Edition

Table of Contents

Preface

The *Thesaurus of Psychological Index Terms®* is the controlled vocabulary used by the American Psychological Association's (APA) professional indexers to index all of APA's databases: PsycINFO®, PsycARTICLES®, PsycBOOKS®, PsycEXTRA®, and PsycCRITIQUES®. With the wide variety of concepts and vocabulary used in the psychological literature, search and retrieval about specific concepts is virtually impossible without the controlled vocabulary of the *Thesaurus*. It provides a way of structuring the subject matter in a way that is consistent among users. The *Thesaurus of Psychological Index Terms*, first published in 1974, has an influential role in research because it reflects the most current trends found in the behavioral and social science literature. The *Thesaurus* can help authenticate the use of terms as they become accepted nomenclature.

The *APA Dictionary of Psychology*, published in July 2006, has become an invaluable resource in the research and development of *Thesaurus* terminology. The *Dictionary* was used in the creation of nearly 30 scope notes for this edition. In an effort to eliminate confusion, a task force of vocabulary specialists created 225 new scope notes for existing terms. These changes focused primarily on neuroscience and disorders terminology that needed clarification with a scope note.

The new terms introduced in the 2006 annual update of the *Thesaurus* were added or "mapped back" to all the relevant records in all APA databases to provide users with greater access to historical content. At the same time, the terms introduced during the earlier 2003, 2004, and 2005 updates were also mapped back through all years, and we revised 214 historical notes to reflect the changes. We continued this policy in the 2007 eleventh edition by adding new terms to more than 28,000 records, for a total number of nearly 50,000 records since the publication of the tenth edition of the *Thesaurus*.

Best wishes for your research!

Lisa Gallagher Tuleya
Editor

History of the *Thesaurus*

Psychology has multiple roots in the older disciplines of philosophy, medicine, education, and physics. As a result, the vocabulary of the psychological literature is characterized by considerable diversity. As the field of psychology grew, each new generation of psychologists added to the vocabulary to describe their studies and perceptions of behavioral processes. This early, uncontrolled evolution of the psychological vocabulary contributed to imprecise search results.

In response to these problems, the American Psychological Association developed the first edition of the *Thesaurus of Psychological Index Terms* in 1974. This controlled vocabulary was designed to provide a means of structuring the subject matter of psychology and to serve as an efficient indexing and retrieval tool. Since the publication of the first edition, the PsycINFO indexing staff has charted trends and newly emerging areas of interest reflected in the psychological literature as a way of updating and revising the *Thesaurus*. The present edition of the *Thesaurus* represents a concerted effort to provide a more valuable tool for researchers, practitioners, information science professionals, students, and others interested in the field of psychology.

First Edition (1974)

Term selection was the first step in the development of the 1974 edition. The 800 index terms used by *Psychological Abstracts* (PA) prior to 1973 and a list of the frequencies of the occurrence of single words in titles and abstracts in PA over a 5-year period were taken as the starting points. In addition, phrases and terms were obtained from key-word-in-context (KWIC) lists produced from 10,000 titles of journal articles, books, separates, and dissertations. Inclusion/exclusion rules were developed, with a resulting list of about 3,000 potential terms reviewed by subject matter specialists for final selection. These terms were arranged to express interrelationships, including use, used for, broader, narrower, and related categories.

Second Edition (1977)

The first revision of the *Thesaurus*, which included 204 new terms, was published in 1977. Some 180 never-used terms from the original *Thesaurus* were deleted, and a rotated alphabetical term section was added to make it faster and easier to find index terms.

Third Edition (1982)

The second revision of the *Thesaurus*, which included 240 new terms, was published in 1982. The most significant change introduced in the third edition was the development of scope notes or definitions for more than 1,300 terms. In addition, superscript dates were added to all terms to indicate the date of inclusion in the *Thesaurus* vocabulary.

Fourth Edition (1985)

The third revision of the *Thesaurus* included 247 new terms and 162 new and revised scope notes. Posting notes (PN) were added to each index term to indicate the number of times the terms had been used for indexing. Also, each postable index term was given a unique five-digit subject code (SC) that can be used in online searching as an alternative to entering the term text.

Fifth Edition (1988)

An important change occurred during the fourth revision—the incorporation of all nonpostable terms into the Rotated Alphabetical Terms Section. These terms appeared in nonbold italic print and were marked with a star (★). More than 250 postable terms and 100 nonpostable terms were added to the vocabulary. In addition, more than 100 new scope notes were added and more than 75 scope notes were revised. Because the *Thesaurus* had been in use for many years, an extensive hierarchy reconstruction project was begun with the intention of continuing the process for development of future editions.

Sixth Edition (1991)

The fifth revision of the *Thesaurus* included the addition of 238 new postable terms and 100 new nonpostable terms. More than 50 scope notes were rewritten and 120 new scope notes were added to the vocabulary. In a continuing effort to make the *Thesaurus* more useful, the Relationship Section was enhanced by the addition of down arrows (↓) in each main term's hierarchy next to narrower and related terms that also have narrower terms. Term Clusters were developed to present a collection of index terms based on conceptual similarity to assist users unfamiliar with the *Thesaurus* vocabulary. As in earlier editions, revision of existing hierarchical relationships continued.

Seventh Edition (1994)

The 20-year anniversary edition of the *Thesaurus* was marked with many changes to the Relationship Section. Approximately 220 new postable terms and 115 new nonpostable terms were added. Nearly 110 new scope notes were added to the existing 1,970 scope notes. These included scope notes for terms new to the seventh edition as well as terms from previous editions. Revision of almost 2,000 hierarchies also occurred to increase their accuracy and to ensure consistent relationships. The hierarchies for array terms, conceptually broad terms identified with a slash (/), were reconstructed for the first time since the inception of the *Thesaurus* and the slash was removed. Posting notes were updated to indicate how many times each postable term was used to index a record through June 1993. A new "Neuropsychology and Neurology" cluster was added to the Term Clusters Section complete with seven subclusters. Finally, the Rotated Alphabetical Terms section was completely revised so that nonpostable terms appeared for the first time with their "Use" reference.

Eighth Edition (1997)

The seventh revision of the *Thesaurus* included the addition of 254 new postable terms and 191 new nonpostable terms. More than 200 term hierarchies were revised, and 115 new scope notes were added. The 2,026 existing scope notes were reviewed for clarity, and more than 225 of these were revised or rewritten. In addition, close to 60 terms changed from a postable to a nonpostable status and were referred to a synonymous term or a term of broader scope. Finally, all index terms that contained the word "handicapped" (e.g., Multiply Handicapped) were reviewed and changed to "disabled" (e.g., Multiply Disabled) to reflect the changing terminology in the literature.

Ninth Edition (2001)

The eighth revision of the *Thesaurus* included the addition of 100 new postable terms and 50 nonpostable terms. More than 375 hierarchies were revised, 13 new scope notes were added, and more than 155 scope notes were revised to improve clarity. In addition, approximately 10 terms changed from a nonpostable to postable status, and 26 terms changed from a postable to nonpostable status, with reference to a synonymous term or a term of broader scope. With the 1998 advent of the Population, Geographic/Location, Age Group, Publication Type, Document Type, and Methodology identifier fields, 213 terms with content areas overlapping those fields were deleted from the *Thesaurus* entirely. In an effort to use language that is consistent with that used by the general public, to expand terms that had historically been truncated (because of former system constraints), and to correct spelling errors from previous *Thesaurus* editions, 16 terms received spelling or format modifications. A Computer Cluster with 8 Subclusters was added to the Term Clusters Section, and the Geographic Cluster and its Subclusters were deleted. Lastly, because of insufficient usage or overlap with other terminology, 25 terms were removed from the *Thesaurus* altogether.

Tenth Edition (2004)

The tenth edition of the *Thesaurus* included the addition of 200 new postable and 123 nonpostable terms. Because of insufficient usage or overlap with other terminology, 30 terms were deleted from the *Thesaurus* entirely. The tenth edition introduced two significant changes to the structure of the *Thesaurus*. The first change was the Historical Note feature which contains information about a term's history since its introduction, including changes to a term, the range of years a term was in use, and instructions for searching. The second significant change was the retrospective indexing of new *Thesaurus* terms. In past editions, index terms with posting notes (PN) = 0 were new terms that were added to the *Thesaurus*. These terms had 0 postings because they had not been used in the indexing process as of the publication date and had not accumulated any postings. In addition to these changes, 23 terms changed from a nonpostable to postable status, 23 terms changed from a postable to nonpostable status, and 10 terms became nonpostable to a different postable counterpart. Other changes included adding or revising more than 50 scope notes, revising nearly 40 hierarchies, and changing the text or spelling of nearly 20 terms.

Development of the Eleventh Edition (2007)

NEW POSTABLE TERMS

Since the publication of the tenth edition, 214 new postable index terms have been added to the eleventh edition. The new terms represent concepts and terminology expressed in psychological and behavioral literature as well as the literature found in areas related to psychology (e.g., education, medicine, and business). In addition, new terminology was developed for classical psychological concepts requiring appropriate controlled vocabulary. These additions bring the total number of postable index terms to 5,613, nonpostable to 2,609, and the total number of terms to 8,222.

In determining whether terms should be included, staff considered: (a) the frequency of the term's occurrence in the psychological literature, (b) the term's potential usefulness in providing access to a concept, (c) the term's relationship to or overlap with existing *Thesaurus* terminology, (d) user feedback, and (e) lack of potential application problems by indexing staff. Every term has been researched extensively and integrated into the hierarchies in the Relationship Section. The Rotated Alphabetical Terms Section has been updated with the new terms as well. See Tables 1–5 on pages x–xv for a listing of all new postable index terms, nonpostable index terms, and other significant term changes occurring in this edition.

OTHER CHANGES

Term Hierarchies

Extensive revision of hierarchical relationships occurred during the development of this edition. Hierarchies were examined to ensure accuracy, completeness, and consistency. In a continuation of our efforts to examine hierarchical structures with each edition, 54 hierarchies were revised to minimize any misleading and redundant relationships as well as to maintain a coherent and cohesive vocabulary structure.

Scope Notes

Approximately 225 scope notes were added to existing terms, bringing the total number of scope notes in the *Thesaurus* to 2,632. Scope notes were added to terms with ambiguous meanings, terms that needed to be differentiated from existing terms, or terms with restricted indexing usage. In addition, 21 scope notes were also rewritten or revised to improve clarity, to broaden or restrict the term's range of application, or to accommodate new eleventh edition terms. The *APA Dictionary of Psychology*, published in July 2006, was used in the creation of nearly 30 scope notes for this edition.

Historical Notes

The historical notes feature provides information about changes to a term, the range of years a term was in use, and instructions for searching. Nearly 270 historical notes were added and more than 200 historical notes were revised for this edition.

New Nonpostable Terms

In an effort to provide additional entry points into the *Thesaurus* vocabulary and to direct users more efficiently to terms that are "used for" indexing, 149 new nonpostable terms were added to this edition. See Table 2 on page xii for a complete list of these terms.

Posting Notes

Primarily as an aid to psychologists, researchers, librarians, and students, each postable index term in the Relationship Section appears with a posting note (PN) reference indicating how many times that index term has been used in the indexing process at the time of this publication. These posting notes are based on accumulations of term usage through December 2006.

Retrospective Indexing

For this edition, new terms were mapped to all relevant records in APA's databases spanning all years in an effort to provide users greater access to historical content. Terms introduced in 2003, 2004, 2005, and 2006 were also mapped further back. The number of posting notes for these terms reflects the number of records re-indexed. New terms were mapped to nearly 50,000 records for this edition.

Change in Term Status

Terms with very low postings, obsolete and out-of-date terms, and terms that have undergone change in usage in the field of psychology were identified for a change in status during this revision. In this edition, 34 terms changed from a postable to nonpostable status. Although these discontinued terms appear in the *Thesaurus* as nonpostable and are no longer used in indexing, each is accompanied by a historical note designating the period during which it was used. These 34 discontinued terms were, however, removed from the database records and were replaced with their postable counterparts. In addition, 17 terms changed from a nonpostable to a postable status, and 5 nonpostable terms point to a different postable counterpart. See Table 3 on page xiv for a full listing of these changes.

Deleted Terms

Because of insufficient usage or overlap with other terminology, 24 terms were removed from the *Thesaurus* entirely. Four of the deleted terms were nonpostable, and five of the deleted terms were removed from all records and replaced with a comparable postable term. See Table 4 on page xv for a list of all the deleted terms.

Changes to Spelling or Text of Terms

In an effort to use language that is consistent with that used by the field of psychology, five terms received spelling or format modifications. See Table 5 on page xv for a listing of these changes.

Table 1: New Postable Terms (214)

Accommodation (Cognitive Process)
Accommodation (Disabilities)
Active Living
Adolescent Psychopathology
African Cultural Groups
Aging in Place
Agnosticism
Allied Health Personnel
American Psychological Association
American Psychological Association Divisions
Apoptosis
Armed Services Vocational Aptitude Battery
Assimilation (Cognitive Process)
Assistive Technology
Attachment Theory
Atypical Depression
Atypical Disorders
Awards (Jury)
Awards (Merit)
Banking
Binge Drinking
Bioinformatics
Biotechnology
Bioterrorism
Body Mass Index
Built Environment
Business Investments
Causality
Celebrities
Charter Schools
Child Psychopathology
Clinical Audits
Clinical Governance
Clinical Practice
Cognitive Bias
Collaborative Learning
Collectivism
Commercialization
Communication Barriers
Communities of Practice
Computer Assisted Language Learning
Computer Assisted Therapy
Conflict of Interest
Consumer Education
Criminal Profiling
Criminal Record
Critical Thinking
Cross Examination
Customer Relationship Management
Diathesis Stress Model
Digital Divide
Digital Video
Disease Management
Diversity
Dual Task Performance
Economic Development
Economic Security
Educational Standards
Electronic Commerce
Electronic Retailing
Emergency Preparedness
Emotion Focused Therapy
Emotional Disturbances
Emotional Regulation
Erectile Dysfunction
Evolutionary Economics
Expatriates
Facilities
Faith Based Organizations
False Beliefs
Family Preservation
Family Reunification
Female Attitudes
Female Sexual Dysfunction
Feminist Psychology
Films
Finance
Financial Services
Financial Strain
Fixation (Psychoanalytic)
Fixation (Psychological)
Framing Effects
Fundraising
Geropsychology
Glutamate Receptors
Goal Orientation
Grand Mal Seizures
Gratitude
Group Characteristics
Group Differences
Group Identity
Health Care Economics
Health Care Reform
Heritability
Heroes
Hindsight Bias
Horticulture Therapy
Human Services
Human Trafficking
Hydrocephalus
Hypothalamic Pituitary Adrenal Axis
Immune System
Individual Education Programs
Inductive Logic Programming
Infidelity
Information Dissemination
Information Literacy
Information Processing Model
Information Technology
Innovation
Intelligent Agents
International Students
Internet Addiction
Internet Usage
Internship Programs
Interrogation
Intimate Partner Violence
Knowledge Economy
Knowledge Management
Knowledge Transfer
Labor Market
Left Hemisphere
Locomotion
Male Attitudes
Membership
Mental Health Parity
Mergers and Acquisitions
Metabolic Syndrome
Military Attrition
Military Deployment
Military Duty Status
Mindfulness
Missing Children
Motivational Interviewing
Multinational Corporations
Multiple Intelligences
Museums
Myoclonus
Nanotechnology
Narrative Therapy
National Security
Necrosis
Nepotism
Neurasthenia
Neurocognition
Neurofeedback
Neurotransmitter Uptake Inhibitors
NGOs
Online Social Networks
Ontologies
Ontology (Philosophy)
Outsourcing
Pandemics
Parental Involvement
Passive Smoking
Patents
Pathophysiology
Peacekeeping
Perceptual Learning
Peripheral Neuropathy
Personalization
Petit Mal Seizures
Pharmaceutical Industry
Pharmacoeconomics
Physical Health
Plants (Botanical)
Prescription Privileges
Pretend Play
Prisoner Abuse
Productivity
Professional Recognition
Protective Factors
Psychology of Women
Psychoneuroendocrinology
Range of Motion
Rationality
Readiness to Change
Religious Conversion
Repetition Compulsion
Research and Development
Right Hemisphere
Same Sex Marriage
Scaffolding
Self Expression
Sensitization
Serotonin Norepinephrine Reuptake Inhibitors
Service Learning
Sildenafil
Sleepiness
Small Businesses
Social Justice
Social Marketing
Social Responsibility
Stages of Change
Stem Cells
Student Engagement
Study Abroad
Supply Chain Management

Table 1: New Postable Terms (214)—Cont'd

Supply Chains
Technology Transfer
Terror Management Theory
Traditions
Transportation Safety
Trauma
Treatment Barriers
Tumor Necrosis Factor
Underage Drinking
Utilization Reviews
Venture Capital
Virtual Classrooms
Virtual Teams
Websites
Welfare Reform
Workplace Violence

Table 2: New Nonpostable Terms (149)

Absence Seizure
USE Petit Mal Seizures

Academic Engagement
USE Student Engagement

Academic Standards
USE Educational Standards

Acquisitions (Organizational)
USE Mergers and Acquisitions

Active Duty
USE Military Duty Status

Affect Regulation
USE Emotional Regulation

Afferent Neurons
USE Sensory Neurons

Africans
USE African Cultural Groups

Alcohol Dependence
USE Alcoholism

Alcoholic Korsakoffs Syndrome
USE Korsakoffs Syndrome

Alzheimer Disease
USE Alzheimers Disease

Amygdaloid Nucleus
USE Amygdala

Androgen Insensitivity Syndrome
USE Testicular Feminization Syndrome

APA
USE American Psychological Association

APA Divisions
USE American Psychological Association Divisions

Assistive Devices
USE Assistive Technology

ASVAB
USE Armed Services Vocational Aptitude Battery

Attrition (Military)
USE Military Attrition

Auxiliary Health Workers
USE Allied Health Personnel

Barriers (Treatment)
USE Treatment Barriers

Basal Magnocellular Cholinergic Nucleus
USE Nucleus Basalis Magnocelluaris

Battered Women
USE Battered Females

Behavioral Sensitization
USE Sensitization

Bicycle Accidents
USE Transportation Accidents

Bicycle Safety
USE Transportation Safety

Brain Growth
USE Brain Development

Brain Volume
USE Brain Size

Buildings
USE Facilities

Business Innovation
USE Innovation

CALL
USE Computer Assisted Language Learning

Causation
USE Causality

Cause Effect Relationship
USE Causality

Change Readiness
USE Readiness to Change

Cinema
USE Films

Cochlear Nerve
USE Acoustic Nerve

Collective Hysteria
USE Mass Hysteria

Computer Adaptive Testing
USE Adaptive Testing

Concurrent Tasks
USE Dual Task Performance

Cones (Retina)
USE Cones (Eye)

Contracting Out
USE Outsourcing

Corporate Acquisitions
USE Mergers and Acquisitions

Corticospinal Tracts
USE Pyramidal Tracts

Criminal History
USE Criminal Record

CRM
USE Customer Relationship Management

Customs
USE Traditions

Damage Awards
USE Awards (Jury)

Debt
USE Financial Strain

Deployment (Military
USE Military Deployment

Disaster Planning
USE Emergency Preparedness

Disaster Preparedness
USE Emergency Preparedness

Down Syndrome
USE Downs Syndrome

Drug Dealing
USE Illegal Drug Distribution

Drug Industry
USE Pharmaceutical Industry

Drug Trafficking
USE Illegal Drug Distribution

Dual Reuptake Inhibitors
USE Serotonin Norepinephrine Reuptake Inhibitors

Dual Task Procedure
USE Dual Task Performance

E-Commerce
USE Electronic Commerce

EEG Biofeedback
USE Neurofeedback

Emotionally Focused Therapy
USE Emotion Focused Therapy

Employee Recognition
USE Professional Recognition

End of Life Care
USE Palliative Care

E-tailing
USE Electronic Retailing

Environmental Tobacco Smoke
USE Passive Smoking

Epidemic Hysteria
USE Mass Hysteria

Exchange (Business)
USE Commerce

Executive Dysfunction
USE Cognitive Impairment

Extrapyramidal Motor System
USE Extrapyramidal Tracts

Extrapyramidal System
USE Extrapyramidal Tracts

Extroversion
USE Extraversion

Financial Problems
USE Financial Strain

Financial Security
USE Economic Security

Financial Stress
USE Financial Strain

Gangrene
USE Necrosis

Gardening Therapy
USE Horticulture Therapy

Geriatric Psychology
USE Geropsychology

Table 2: New Nonpostable Terms (149)—Cont'd

Gratefulness
  USE Gratitude

Health Care Barriers
  USE Treatment Barriers

Health Economics
  USE Health Care Economics

Helmets
  USE Safety Devices

Hemianopsia
  USE Hemianopia

Honors
  USE Awards (Merit)

Humanitarian Behavior
  USE Prosocial Behavior

Hypercortisolism
  USE Cushings Syndrome

IEP
  USE Individual Education Programs

ILP
  USE Inductive Logic Programming

Individualized Educational Plans
  USE Individual Education Programs

Insulin Resistance Syndrome
  USE Metabolic Syndrome

International Study
  USE Study Abroad

Internet Shopping
  USE Electronic Commerce

Internet Social Networking
  USE Online Social Networks

Interpersonal Therapy
  USE Interpersonal Psychotherapy

Investments (Business)
  USE Business Investments

Involuntary Smoking
  USE Passive Smoking

Job Duties
  USE Job Characteristics

Job Functions
  USE Job Characteristics

Lateral Geniculate Nucleus
  USE Geniculate Bodies (Thalamus)

MAOs
  USE Monoamine Oxidases

Medial Geniculate Nucleus
  USE Geniculate Bodies (Thalamus)

Medical Audits
  USE Clinical Audits

Mental Health Care Barriers
  USE Treatment Barriers

Metabolic Syndrome X
  USE Metabolic Syndrome

Military Reserves
  USE Military Duty Status

Monetary Contributions
  USE Fundraising

Motivation to Change
  USE Readiness to Change

Multinational Enterprises
  USE Multinational Corporations

Multinational Organizations
  USE Multinational Corporations

Natural Disaster Preparedness
  USE Emergency Preparedness

Neuroreceptors
  USE Neural Receptors

Nongovernmental Organizations
  USE NGOs

Non-governmental Organizations
  USE NGOs

Nucleus Basalis of Meynert
  USE Nucleus Basalis Magnocelluaris

Offender Profiling
  USE Criminal Profiling

Offshoring
  USE Outsourcing

Online Retailing
  USE Electronic Retailing

Online Shopping
  USE Electronic Commerce

Organizational Innovation
  USE Innovation

Parental Participation
  USE Parental Involvement

Part Time Employment
  USE Employment Status

Pensions
  USE Employee Pension Plans

Pharmaceutical Economics
  USE Pharmacoeconomics

Philanthropy
  USE Charitable Behavior

Plasma Donation
  USE Tissue Donation

Prison Record
  USE Criminal Record

Propanolol
  USE Propranolol

PTSD
  USE Posttraumatic Stress Disorder

Rational Thinking
  USE Rationality

Robots
  USE Robotics

Sanitariums
  USE Sanatoriums

Seasonality
  USE Seasonal Variations

School Engagement
  USE Student Engagement

Secondhand Smoking
  USE Passive Smoking

SNRI
  USE Serotonin Norepinephrine Reuptake Inhibitors

Spine
  USE Spinal Column

Synaptic Plasticity
  USE Neural Plasticity

Tabes Dorsalis
  USE Neurosyphilis

Technological Innovation
  USE Innovation

Thankfulness
  USE Gratitude

Time Planning Style
  USE Time Management

Time Scheduling
  USE Time Management

Time Utilization
  USE Time Management

Tonic-Clonic Seizures
  USE Grand Mal Seizures

Trade (Business)
  USE Commerce

Transnational Corporations
  USE Multinational Corporations

Vestibular Disorders
  USE Labyrinth Disorders

Vestibulocochlear Nerve
  USE Acoustic Nerve

Viagra
  USE Sildenafil

Virtual Markets
  USE Electronic Commerce

Web Sites
  USE Websites

Women Centered Psychology
  USE Psychology of Women

Table 3: Change in Term Status (56)

The following 34 terms changed from postable to nonpostable status.

Acquired Immune Deficiency Syndrome
USE AIDS

Anabolism
USE Biosynthesis

Autistic Children
USE Autism

Barbiturate Poisoning
USE Toxic Disorders

Cochran Q Test
USE Nonparametric Statistical Tests

Compulsive Repetition
USE Repetition Compulsion

Convulsions
USE Seizures

Cortical Evoked Potentials
USE Evoked Potentials

Deoxyribonucleic Acid
USE DNA

Early Infantile Autism
USE Autism

Emotionally Disturbed
USE Emotional Disturbances

Family Violence
USE Domestic Violence

Foreign Nationals
USE Expatriates

Foreign Students
USE International Students

Foreign Study
USE Study Abroad

Frigidity
USE Female Sexual Dysfunction

Gilles de la Tourette Disorder
USE Tourette Syndrome

Human Immunodeficiency Virus
USE HIV

Hydrocephaly
USE Hydrocephalus

Hypothalamo Pituitary Adrenal System
USE Hypothalamic Pituitary Adrenal Axis

Impotence
USE Erectile Dysfunction

Left Brain
USE Left Hemisphere

Legal Interrogation
USE Interrogation

Minimal Brain Disorders
USE Attention Deficit Disorder with Hyperactivity

Motion Pictures
USE Films

Multi Infarct Dementia
USE Vascular Dementia

Organizational Mergers
USE Mergers and Acquisitions

Paramedical Personnel
USE Allied Health Personnel

Peripheral Nerve Disorders
USE Peripheral Neuropathy

Poisons
USE Toxins

Process Psychosis
USE Process Schizophrenia

Psychedelic Drugs
USE Hallucinogenic Drugs

Right Brain
USE Right Hemisphere

Trisomy 21
USE Downs Syndrome

The following 17 terms changed from nonpostable to postable status.

AIDS
Brain Development
Chemotherapy
Collaboration
Commerce
DNA
Domestic Violence
HIV
Individualism
Overweight
Physical Activity
Process Schizophrenia
Psychopathy
Seizures
Tourette Syndrome
Toxins
Training

The following 5 nonpostable terms now point to a different postable counterpart.

Criminal Interrogation
USE Interrogation

Drowsiness
USE Sleepiness

Medics
USE Allied Health Personnel

Movies
USE Films

Police Interrogation
USE Interrogation

Table 4: Deleted Terms (24)

Army General Classification Test

Childrens Personality Questionnaire

Chloroform

Climacteric Depression (nonpostable term)

Climacteric Psychosis (nonpostable term)

Columbia Mental Maturity Scale

Cranial Spinal Cord

Edwards Personality Inventory

Film Strips

Gates MacGinitie Reading Tests

Grand Mal Epilepsy

Guilford Zimmerman Temperament Survey

Inadequate Personality

Involutional Depression

Involutional Paranoid Psychosis

Kolmogorov Smirnov Test

Motion Pictures (Educational)

Motion Pictures (Entertainment)

Myoclonia

Neurasthenia Neurosis

Petit Mal Epilepsy

Pyramidotomy

Q Test (nonpostable term)

Teaching Internship (nonpostable term)

Table 5: Changes to Spelling or Text of Terms (5)

DNA
Fomerly
DNA (Deoxyribonucleic Acid)

Ghettos (nonpostable term)
Formerly
Urban Ghettoes

Illegal Drug Distribution
Formerly
Drug Distribution

National Guard Personnel
Formerly
National Guardsmen

Rationalization (Defense Mechanism)
Formerly
Rationalization

User Guide

GENERAL INFORMATION

Word Form Conventions

Conventions dealing with singular and plural word forms, direct and indirect entries, abbreviations, acronyms, homographs, and punctuation have been used to ensure standardization of the *Thesaurus* vocabulary. Noun forms are preferred entries, with the plural form used when the term is a noun that can be qualified, for example, **Films**, **Stem Cells**, or **Websites**. The singular form is used when the entry refers to processes, properties, or conditions, for example, **Cognitive Bias**, **Goal Orientation**, or **Internet Addiction**. Direct entry or natural word order is preferred when a concept is represented by two or more words, for example, **Passive Smoking** vs. "Smoking, Passive" or **Electronic Commerce** vs. "Commerce, Electronic."

In cases where ambiguity may occur and to clarify the meaning of homographs, qualifying expressions are included in parentheses, for example, **Accommodation (Cognitive Process)**, **Accommodation (Disabilities)**, and **Plants (Botanical)**.

Also, a selected number of acronyms are used, such as **AIDS**, **DNA**, and **HIV**.

Term Relationships

The terms in the Relationship Section are displayed to reflect the following relationships:

USE. Directs the user from a term that cannot be used (nonpostable) to a term that can be used (postable) in indexing and searching. The **Use** reference indicates preferred forms of synonyms, abbreviations, spelling, and word sequence:

> Offender Profiling
> **Use** Criminal Profiling

UF (Used For). Reciprocal of the **Use** reference. Terms listed as **UF** references represent some but not all of the most frequently encountered synonyms, abbreviations, alternate spellings, or word sequences:

> **Criminal Profiling** 2007
> **UF** Offender Profiling

B (Broader Term) and **N (Narrower Term)**. Reciprocal designators used to indicate hierarchical relationships:

> **Emotional Trauma** 1967
> **B** Trauma 2006

> **Trauma** 2006
> **N** Emotional Trauma 1967

R (Related Term). Reciprocal designator used to indicate relationships that are semantic or conceptual, but not hierarchical. Related term references indicate to searchers (or indexers) terms that they may not have considered, but might be related to their topic of interest:

> **Critical Thinking** 2006
> **R** Logical Thinking 1967

RELATIONSHIP SECTION

Each *Thesaurus* term is listed alphabetically and, as appropriate, is cross-referenced and displayed with its broader, narrower, and related terms, also called subterms. Since the beginning of the database in 1967, the American Psychological Association's (APA) indexing vocabulary has been updated periodically with new terms. The date of the term's inclusion in the *Thesaurus* appears as a four-digit superscript. Each postable subterm in a main term's hierarchy also has its date of inclusion shown as well. Seventeen dates can be found: 1967, 1971, 1973, 1978, 1982, 1984, 1985, 1988, 1991, 1994, 1997, 2001, 2003, 2004, 2005, 2006, and 2007. Some of these dates do not correspond with a *Thesaurus* publication year.

The subject code **(SC)** gives the unique five-digit code associated with the term and can be used instead of entering the term text to retrieve records on some online search systems.

Each postable index term in the Relationship Section appears with a posting note **(PN)** reference indicating how many times that term has been used in the indexing of records. Posting notes are based on accumulations of term usage through December 2006. Relevant records were retrospectively indexed (re-indexed) with new eleventh edition terms. The number of posting notes for these terms reflects the number of records re-indexed. The historical note for each of these terms also indicates this. In past editions, terms that had an indicator PN = 0 were new terms that had yet to accumulate any postings.

Many terms that have ambiguous meanings have scope notes **(SN)**. In many cases, a scope note provides a definition and/or information on proper use of the term. The scope note always refers to the one term with which it is associated and does not necessarily have implications for the subterms displayed in the term's hierarchy. The following is an example of a scope note found in the Relationship Section:

Definition	**Clinical Audits** 2007 **SN** A systematic evaluation of the effectiveness of diagnostic and treatment procedures.
Usage	**Left Hemisphere** 2005 **SN** Used only when the left hemisphere of the brain is the focus of the document.

The historical note **(HN)** provides information about the historical usage of a term since its introduction to the *Thesaurus*. Specifically, it includes information about changes to a term, the range of years a term was in use, and instructions for searching. In past editions, historical information was captured in the scope note, but with the addition of the historical note, the scope note will be used primarily for definitions of terms.

Change in Usage	**Parental Authoritarianism** **HN** Use PARENTAL PERIMISSIVENESS to access references from 1973 to June 2003.
Change in Status	**Brain Development** 2007 **HN** In April 2007, BRAIN DEVELOPMENT changed status from nonpostable to postable. Relevant records were re-indexed with this term. The posting note reflects the number of records that were re-indexed.

Nonpostable index terms, those not used in the indexing process, are shown in nonbold print with an appropriate **USE** reference. Nonpostable terms are provided as points of entry into the *Thesaurus* vocabulary.

The following example from the Relationship Section illustrates a nonpostable term entry:

Nonpostable Index Term:	Gardening Therapy
Postable Index Term:	**USE** Horticulture Therapy 2007

Finally, the Relationship Section uses down arrows (↓) in front of any narrower **(N)** or related **(R)** terms that have narrower terms themselves. This feature alerts the user to consider another more specific hierarchical level. APA databases are indexed to the level of specificity in a given document. In using the Relationship Section and in choosing index terms, consider following any main term's subterms (**N** and **R** terms only) to the lowest level of specificity by turning to the page in the *Thesaurus* where the narrower **(N)** or related **(R)** subterm appears as a main entry to determine if more specific terminology is available. Below is a sample of an index term entry in the Relationship Section.

HOW TO READ A TERM RECORD

The following example from the Relationship Section illustrates the various components that may be included in the hierarchy of a postable index term:

Postable Index Term (With year of entry)	**Parenting Style** 2003
Posting Note and Subject Code (Number of postings and 5-digit unique indentifier)	**PN** 1392 **SC** 36678
Scope Note	**SN** Characteristic manner in which parents raise their children. Compare CHILDREARING PRACTICES.
Historical Note	**HN** This term was introduced in June 2003. Relevant records were reindexed with this term. The posting note reflects the number of terms that were reindexed.
Used for (Nonpostable terms)	**UF** Authoritarianism (Parental) Parental Authoritarianism
Broader Term	**B** Parental Characteristics 1994
Narrower Terms	**N** Parental Permissiveness 1973
Related Terms (Down arrow indicates more specific terms)	**R** ↓Childrearing Practices 1967 ↓Parent Child Relations 1967

ROTATED ALPHABETICAL TERMS SECTION

Many terms represent concepts not expressed in a single word; therefore, postable and nonpostable *Thesaurus* terms in this section are listed in alphabetical order by each word contained within them. The Rotated Alphabetical Terms Section is useful in finding all *Thesaurus* terms that have a particular word in common. This display groups related terms when they may otherwise be separated in the alphabetical Relationship Section. It is important to note that this section should be used in conjunction with the Relationship Section since hierarchies, scope notes, posting notes, and term dates do not appear in the Rotated Alphabetical Terms Section. A term containing three words will appear in three locations in this section as illustrated below:

		Animal	Courtship	Behavior
		Animal	Courtship	Displays
		Animal	Defensive	Behavior
	Animal	**Courtship**	Behavior	
	Animal	**Courtship**	Displays	
	Human	**Courtship**		
		Displays		
Animal	Courtship	**Displays**		
	Auditory	**Displays**		

Nonpostable index terms (terms not used for indexing) are represented in nonbold print followed by the appropriate "**Use**" term in italics. All words in the term, just like the postable terms above, appear in different locations depending on how many words are contained in the index term as illustrated below:

	Illumination	
	Illumination	Therapy
	USE	*Phototherapy*
Autokinetic	**Illusion**	
Hormone	**Therapy**	
Illumination	Therapy	
	USE	*Phototherapy*
Implosive	**Therapy**	

TERM CLUSTERS SECTION

Clusters are collections of index terms that are related to one another conceptually rather than hierarchically, and are displayed together under broad subject categories. This section is useful for viewing all terms in each cluster collectively.

Clusters provide an entry point into the *Thesaurus* vocabulary by allowing a large group of similar terms to be scanned easily and efficiently, thus helping users translate their search vocabulary into *Thesaurus* vocabulary. In a sense, the clusters present an "index" to some of the indexing vocabulary found in the Relationship Section.

It is important to note that the Clusters Section should not be used alone, but in conjunction with the Relationship Section. Useful details regarding particular index terms can be found in the Relationship Section such as scope notes, posting notes, hierarchies, dates for term inclusion, and links to additional search terms.

Not every index term will appear in the Term Clusters Section. Terms appear under nine broad cluster subject areas. The nine subject areas are meant to present index terms for selected subject areas that are frequented in psychological research, but do not cover all subject areas in psychology. There are approximately 3,751 postable index terms in the Clusters Section. Terms may appear in more than one broad cluster area and also in more than one subcluster under any broad subject area, if appropriate. The Term Clusters and Subclusters are listed in Table 6 on page xix.

Table 6: Term Cluster/Subcluster Subject Areas

Computers Cluster
- Computer Applications
- Computer Automation
- Computers & Communication
- Computers & Media
- Education & Training
- Equipment
- Human Machine Systems & Engineering
- Information

Disorders Cluster
- Antisocial Behavior & Behavior Disorders
- Diagnosis
- Disorder Characteristics
- Learning Disorders & Mental Retardation
- Physical & Psychosomatic Disorders
- Psychological Disorders
- Speech & Language Disorders
- Symptomatology

Educational Cluster
- Academic Learning & Achievement
- Curricula
- Educational Personnel & Administration
- Educational Testing & Counseling
- Schools & Institutions
- Special Education
- Student Characteristics & Academic Environment
- Student Populations
- Teaching & Teaching Methods

Legal Cluster
- Adjudication
- Criminal Groups
- Criminal Offenses
- Criminal Rehabilitation
- Laws
- Legal Issues
- Legal Personnel
- Legal Processes

Neuropsychology & Neurology Cluster
- Assessment & Diagnosis
- Electrophysiology
- Neuroanatomy
- Neurological Disorders
- Neurological Intervention
- Neurosciences
- Neurotransmitters & Neuroregulators

Occupational & Employment Cluster
- Career Areas
- Employee, Occupational & Job Characteristics
- Occupational Groups
- Organizations & Organizational Behavior
- Personnel Management & Professional Personnel Issues

Statistical Cluster
- Design, Analysis & Interpretation
- Statistical Reliability & Validity
- Statistical Theory & Experimentation

Tests & Testing Cluster
- Academic Achievement & Aptitude Measures
- Attitude & Interest Measures
- Developmental Measures
- Intelligence Measures
- Neuropsychological Measures
- Nonprojective Personality Measures
- Perceptual Measures
- Projective Personality Measures
- Testing
- Testing Methods

Treatment Cluster
- Alternative Therapies
- Behavior Modification & Therapy
- Counseling
- Hospitalization & Institutionalization
- Medical & Physical Treatment
- Psychotherapy
- Rehabilitation
- Treatment (General)
- Treatment Facilities

Search Guide

INTRODUCTION

Using the *Thesaurus of Psychological Index Terms* to search the American Psychological Association's (APA) databases can enhance the precision of your retrieved references and guide you to closely related topics that you might otherwise miss. The standardized vocabulary in the *Thesaurus* eliminates the need to worry about phraseology used by authors to describe a concept. For effective searches and development of comprehensive search strategies, follow the steps outlined below:

1. Select a search topic

> **Example:** "I'm interested in high school students and bullying."

2. Specifically define the concepts of the topic and develop a list of synonyms that represent the concepts. This can include independent and/or dependent experimental variables and/or a population. A properly defined concept can result in an efficient search with precise retrieval of highly relevant articles, and will also reduce the need to scan and eliminate irrelevant references. The following example shows a more specific and defined topic:

> **Example:** "I'm interested in bullying intervention and educational programs for high school students."

3. Look up your concepts in the *Thesaurus of Psychological Index Terms*. Start in any of the three sections, choosing terms on the basis of your topic and familiarity with the *Thesaurus* vocabulary. See the User Guide on page xvi for a description of each section of the *Thesaurus*.

No matter which section of the *Thesaurus* you consult first, be sure to check the Relationship Section before finalizing your terms. The Relationship Section includes scope notes that define the terms, historical notes that provide information about the historical usage of terms since their introduction, as well as posting notes, subject codes, term dates, and the critical *used for*, *broader*, *narrower*, and *related* terms.

The most important things to look for in the Relationship Section are the narrower terms and the date for main term entry (for material indexed after that date). It is important to note each descriptor's year of entry in the *Thesaurus* (indicated by a four-digit superscript number appended to each term in the Relationship Section) because before 2003, new terminology was not "mapped back" to older records to which they are conceptually relevant. Beginning with the tenth edition, database records were retrospectively indexed with the new terminology to provide users with the most comprehensive search results. The posting note number of these terms reflects the number of records that have been re-indexed. The historical note for each of these terms also indicates this.

To retrieve articles relevant to terms before their inclusion in the *Thesaurus*, consider their broader concepts as index terms or use free text strategies to find records added to the database before the starting date.

Also, note each entry's posting note, which is a rough guide to the number of articles you can expect to find under that term.

It is important to remember that all records are indexed to the source document's level of specificity. Therefore, all applicable narrower terms should be examined. For example, a document that focuses on "school violence" will be indexed under **School Violence**, not the broader and less specific term **Violence**. A search strategy should be formulated using all applicable narrower terms, and any related terms that may also closely match a search topic.

> **Example:**
>
> a. Bullying
>
> b. School Violence
>
> c. School Based Intervention or Educational Programs (These terms can be used to describe the concept of intervention and educational programs.)
>
> d. High School Students or High Schools or Secondary Education (These terms form the context of high school education.)

Using these terms, your search statement using Boolean logic would be:

> (Bullying OR School Violence) AND (School Based Intervention OR Educational Programs) AND (High School Students OR High Schools OR Secondary Education)

ONLINE SEARCHING

In search systems, *Thesaurus* terms are located in a descriptor or index term field. Each vendor system that carries APA's databases operates differently, yet each has the capability to limit a search to the descriptor or index term field. Online search systems give you the opportunity to manipulate your search statement to provide precision and recall in retrieval. Formulate your topic and refer to the *Thesaurus* for appropriate terminology.

Online systems allow the use of Boolean logic in a search. Use the Boolean logical operators **AND, OR,** and **NOT** to combine terms.

Example of Boolean Logic

(Shaded Areas Indicate Retrieval)

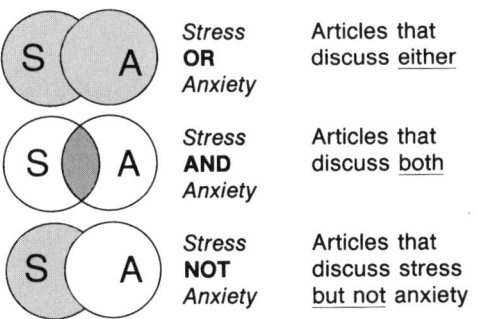

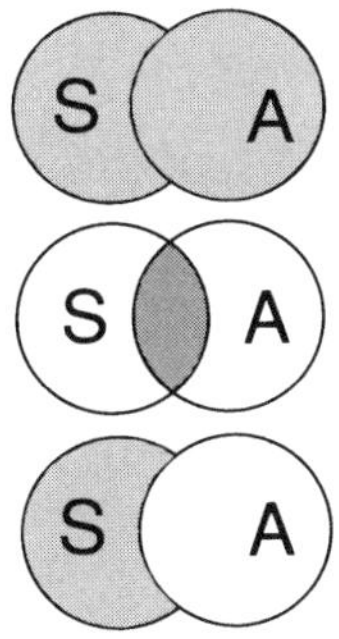

Stress **OR** *Anxiety*	Articles that discuss either
Stress **AND** *Anxiety*	Articles that discuss both
Stress **NOT** *Anxiety*	Articles that discuss stress but not anxiety

Example:

Bullying

OR School Violence

AND (School Based Intervention **OR** Educational Programs)

AND (High School Students **OR** High Schools **OR** Secondary Education)

Online Thesaurus

For added convenience in searching APA's databases, most vendor systems offer an online thesaurus that can automatically display terms along with their broader, narrower, and related concepts. This feature can help reduce typing and enhance the speed of a search, especially when several narrower terms need to be entered, and by allowing users to move from term to term and find new appropriate search terms with ease.

Explode Feature

The Explode feature is available on some search systems. When a search system's explode command is used, the system will automatically search the index term and the first level of its narrower terms. Some terms listed as narrower to an index term may have narrower terms of their own—"narrowers of narrowers." In the *Thesaurus*, narrower terms that have narrower terms of their own are marked with a down-arrow. To achieve comprehensive retrieval, they must be exploded as well.

Major Terms

Index terms applied to records that represent the primary focus of the reference are designated as "major." Many search systems allow for searching of major terms. An example of a PsycINFO record with major index terms applied appears in Appendix B.

ADJUSTING YOUR SEARCH RETRIEVAL

If your search retrieves too many records, try making your search more specific by adding another concept. If nearly all of your records appear relevant, but there are still too many, consider restricting your retrieval to recent publication years or a particular language.

If you retrieve too few records, consider dropping a concept, adding synonymous terms, or eliminating restrictions to specific fields.

Content Classification Code Searching

PsycINFO uses a content classification system that divides the field of psychology into 22 major or broad categories and 135 subcategories. Content classification codes can be searched in most systems. Use of the content classification system in searching can shorten online time and screen out undesired references. Content classification codes are particularly useful to retrieve records from a broad subject area in which many different index terms may have been used. Classification codes will limit a search because only one or two codes are assigned to each record. Keep in mind, however, that a classification code search usually does not retrieve everything in the database that is relevant to a respective topic. A well-constructed search will always include relevant descriptors or index terms.

Search classification codes at their broad level. Using the first two digits of a category retrieves the entire category and enables the search to be executed throughout the entire year range of the database. If more specific information is needed, search one or more four-digit subcategories. Four-digit subcategories were added in 1976; therefore, a search on a four-digit subcategory will limit retrieval to records added in 1976 and later.

A list of the content classification system appears in **Appendix A**.

Age Group Searching

All search systems use identifying tags for the ages of human populations. A record may have more than one age group tag. Search for age groups in the Age Group field. The following table lists the values that are available in the Age Group field. Values that are indented indicate that they are narrower. When the broader value is searched, the narrower values are automatically searched as well.

Age Group Field Values

Childhood (birth–12 yrs)
Neonatal (birth–1 mo)
Infancy (1–23 mo)
Preschool Age (2–5 yrs)
School Age (6–12 yrs)
Adolescence (13–17 yrs)
Adulthood (18 yrs and older)
Young Adulthood (18–29 yrs)
Thirties (30–39 yrs)
Middle Age (40–64 yrs)
Aged (65 yrs and older)
Very Old (85 yrs and older)

Population Group Searching

Search for population group characteristics other than age in the Population Group field. The following table lists the values that are available in the Population Group field. A record may have more than one population group value.

Population Group Field Values

Human
Animal
Female
Male
Inpatient
Outpatient

Publication Type Searching

The Publication Type captures the type of document indexed in the database, such as book, journal, dissertation abstract, and so on. This is, in effect, the top level of description in the database. This field includes values such as peer-reviewed journal, non-peer-reviewed journal, or "peer-review status unknown."

Publication Type Values

Book
Authored Book
Edited Book
Journal
Peer-Reviewed Journal
Non-Peer-Reviewed Journal
Peer-Review Status Unknown
Dissertation Abstract
Electronic Collection (database collection-refers to PsycCRITIQUES)
Encyclopedia

Document Type Searching

Document Type captures what a document *is*, as opposed to what the document is *about*. For example, the types of items found in a journal in addition to "journal article" will be contained in this field, such as journal letters, editorials, and book reviews.

Document Type Field Values

Abstract Collection
Bibliography
Chapter
Column/Opinion
Comment/Reply
Editorial
Encyclopedia Entry
Erratum/Correction
Journal Article
Letter
Obituary
Publication Information
Reprint
Review-Book
Review-Media
Review-Software & Other

Methodology Searching

Methodology Type allows users to limit their searches to records using the precise methodology that is of interest to them. This field contains a set of values such as clinical case report, empirical studies, literature review, and so on, and is very useful to advanced users.

Methodology Field Values

- Clinical Case Study
- Empirical Study
  - Experimental Replication
  - Field Study
  - Longitudinal Study
    - Prospective Study
    - Retrospective Study
- Nonclinical Case Study
- Followup Study
- Literature Review
  - Systematic Review
- Mathematical Modeling
- Meta Analysis
- Qualitative Study
- Quantitative Study
- Treatment Outcome/Clinical Trial

Searching for Auxiliary Materials

This field captures supplemental data or other auxiliary information found appended to the source document or available on the Internet. This field may appear in records for all publication types.

Auxiliary Material Field Values

- 3-D Modeling Images
- Appendices
- Audio
- Data Sets
- DVD/CD
- Tables and Figures
- Video
- Websites
- WorkBook/Study Guide
- Other

Searching for Geographic Locations

In the ninth edition of the *Thesaurus*, all geographical location terms were removed. If you are looking for studies done in a particular country, you should now search for it in the Geographic Location field.

Searching for Tests and Measures

A Tests and Measures field was added in 2003. Originally, this field contained the names of published tests and measures used in a study (up to 10 names), whether they are the focus of the document or not. It does not replace indexing of tests and measures if they are the focus of the original source document. Unpublished tests were added to the field in June 2004.

HOW TO CONTACT US

To contact us, call our toll-free line at 800-374-2722 in North America, 9:00 a.m. to 5:00 p.m., U.S. Eastern time, Monday through Friday.

We can also be contacted at 202-336-5650, FAX 202-336-5633, TTY 202-336-6123 or e-mail at psycinfo@apa.org.

Information on databases, subscriptions, vendor system documentation, journals covered in PsycINFO, and search aids can also be found on PsycINFO's Web site: http://www.apa.org/databases.

APPENDIX A: Content Classification System

Note: This classification code system was designed to describe the content of the PsycINFO database, not the field of psychology.

2100 General Psychology
- **2140** History & Systems

2200 Psychometrics & Statistics & Methodology
- **2220** Tests & Testing
  - **2221** Sensory & Motor Testing
  - **2222** Developmental Scales & Schedules
  - **2223** Personality Scales & Inventories
  - **2224** Clinical Psychological Testing
  - **2225** Neuropsychological Assessment
  - **2226** Health Psychology Testing
  - **2227** Educational Measurement
  - **2228** Occupational & Employment Testing
  - **2229** Consumer Opinion & Attitude Testing
- **2240** Statistics & Mathematics
- **2260** Research Methods & Experimental Design

2300 Human Experimental Psychology
- **2320** Sensory Perception
  - **2323** Visual Perception
  - **2326** Auditory & Speech Perception
- **2330** Motor Processes
- **2340** Cognitive Processes
  - **2343** Learning & Memory
  - **2346** Attention
- **2360** Motivation & Emotion
- **2380** Consciousness States
- **2390** Parapsychology

2400 Animal Experimental & Comparative Psychology
- **2420** Learning & Motivation
- **2440** Social & Instinctive Behavior

2500 Physiological Psychology & Neuroscience
- **2510** Genetics
- **2520** Neuropsychology & Neurology
- **2530** Electrophysiology
- **2540** Physiological Processes
- **2560** Psychophysiology
- **2580** Psychopharmacology

2600 Psychology & the Humanities
- **2610** Literature & Fine Arts
- **2630** Philosophy

2700 Communication Systems
- **2720** Linguistics & Language & Speech
- **2750** Mass Media Communications

2800 Developmental Psychology
- **2820** Cognitive & Perceptual Development
- **2840** Psychosocial & Personality Development
- **2860** Gerontology

2900 Social Processes & Social Issues
- **2910** Social Structure & Organization
- **2920** Religion
- **2930** Culture & Ethnology
- **2950** Marriage & Family
  - **2953** Divorce & Remarriage
  - **2956** Childrearing & Child Care
- **2960** Political Processes & Political Issues
- **2970** Sex Roles & Women's Issues
- **2980** Sexual Behavior & Sexual Orientation
- **2990** Drug & Alcohol Usage (Legal)

3000 Social Psychology
- **3020** Group & Interpersonal Processes
- **3040** Social Perception & Cognition

3100 Personality Psychology
- **3120** Personality Traits & Processes
- **3140** Personality Theory
  - **3143** Psychoanalytic Theory

3200 Psychological & Physical Disorders
- **3210** Psychological Disorders
  - **3211** Affective Disorders
  - **3213** Schizophrenia & Psychotic States
  - **3215** Neuroses & Anxiety Disorders
  - **3217** Personality Disorders
- **3230** Behavior Disorders & Antisocial Behavior
  - **3233** Substance Abuse & Addiction
  - **3236** Criminal Behavior & Juvenile Delinquency
- **3250** Developmental Disorders & Autism
  - **3253** Learning Disorders
  - **3256** Mental Retardation
- **3260** Eating Disorders
- **3270** Speech & Language Disorders
- **3280** Environmental Toxins & Health
- **3290** Physical & Somatoform & Psychogenic Disorders
  - **3291** Immunological Disorders
  - **3293** Cancer
  - **3295** Cardiovascular Disorders
  - **3297** Neurological Disorders & Brain Damage
  - **3299** Vision & Hearing & Sensory Disorders

3300 Health & Mental Health Treatment & Prevention
- **3310** Psychotherapy & Psychotherapeutic Counseling
  - **3311** Cognitive Therapy
  - **3312** Behavior Therapy & Behavior Modification
  - **3313** Group & Family Therapy
  - **3314** Interpersonal & Client Centered & Humanistic Therapy
  - **3315** Psychoanalytic Therapy
- **3340** Clinical Psychopharmacology
- **3350** Specialized Interventions
  - **3351** Clinical Hypnosis
  - **3353** Self Help Groups
  - **3355** Lay & Paraprofessional & Pastoral Counseling
  - **3357** Art & Music & Movement Therapy
- **3360** Health Psychology & Medicine
  - **3361** Behavioral & Psychological Treatment of Physical Illness
  - **3363** Medical Treatment of Physical Illness
  - **3365** Promotion & Maintenance of Health & Wellness
- **3370** Health & Mental Health Services
  - **3371** Outpatient Services
  - **3373** Community & Social Services
  - **3375** Home Care & Hospice
  - **3377** Nursing Homes & Residential Care
  - **3379** Inpatient & Hospital Services
- **3380** Rehabilitation
  - **3383** Drug & Alcohol Rehabilitation
  - **3384** Occupational & Vocational Rehabilitation
  - **3385** Speech & Language Therapy
  - **3386** Criminal Rehabilitation & Penology

3400 Professional Psychological & Health Personnel Issues
- **3410** Professional Education & Training
- **3430** Professional Personnel Attitudes & Characteristics
- **3450** Professional Ethics & Standards & Liability
- **3470** Impaired Professionals

3500 Educational Psychology
- **3510** Educational Administration & Personnel
- **3530** Curriculum & Programs & Teaching Methods
- **3550** Academic Learning & Achievement
- **3560** Classroom Dynamics & Student Adjustment & Attitudes
- **3570** Special & Remedial Education
  - **3575** Gifted & Talented
- **3580** Educational/Vocational Counseling & Student Services

3600 Industrial & Organizational Psychology
- **3610** Occupational Interests & Guidance
- **3620** Personnel Management & Selection & Training
- **3630** Personnel Evaluation & Job Performance
- **3640** Management & Management Training
- **3650** Personnel Attitudes & Job Satisfaction
- **3660** Organizational Behavior
- **3670** Working Conditions & Industrial Safety

3700 Sport Psychology & Leisure
- **3720** Sports
- **3740** Recreation & Leisure

3800 Military Psychology

3900 Consumer Psychology
- **3920** Consumer Attitudes & Behavior
- **3940** Marketing & Advertising

4000 Engineering & Environmental Psychology
- **4010** Human Factors Engineering
- **4030** Lifespace & Institutional Design
- **4050** Community & Environmental Planning
- **4070** Environmental Issues & Attitudes
- **4090** Transportation

4100 Intelligent Systems
- **4120** Artificial Intelligence & Expert Systems
- **4140** Robotics
- **4160** Neural Networks

4200 Forensic Psychology & Legal Issues
- **4210** Civil Rights & Civil Law
- **4230** Criminal Law & Criminal Adjudication
- **4250** Mediation & Conflict Resolution
- **4270** Crime Prevention
- **4290** Police & Legal Personnel

APPENDIX B: Sample PsycINFO Record

PsycINFO: Expanded Record

Send to printer

Unique Identifier
2006-11390-012
Title
Self-efficacy and college students' perceptions and use of online learning systems.
Publication Year
2007
Language
English
Author
Bates, Reid; Khasawneh, Samer
E-Mail
Bates, Reid: rabates@lsu.edu; Khasawneh, Samer: samer@70802.yahoo.com
Correspondence Address
Reid Bates, School of Human Resource Education and Workforce Development, Louisiana State University, 107 Old Forestry, Baton Rouge, LA, US, 70803, rabates@lsu.edu
Affiliation
Bates, Reid: School of Human Resource Education and Workforce Development, Louisiana State University, Baton Rouge, LA, US
Khasawneh, Samer: School of Human Resource Education and Workforce Development, Louisiana State University, Baton Rouge, LA, US
Source
Computers in Human Behavior. 2007 Jan Vol 23(1) 175-191
Publisher
Elsevier Science, Netherlands
ISSN/ISBN
0747-5632 (Print)
Format Availability
Electronic; Print
Format Covered
Electronic
Publication Type
Journal; Peer Reviewed Journal
Document Type
Original Journal Article
Abstract
This research hypothesized a mediated model in which a set of antecedent variables influenced students' online learning self-efficacy which, in turn, affected student outcome expectations, mastery perceptions, and the hours spent per week using online learning technology to complete learning assignments for university courses. The results are consistent with the inference of a partially mediated model in which the block of antecedents had a direct effect on self-efficacy, a direct influence on the outcome measures, and an indirect effect on the outcomes through their influence on self-efficacy. In general, the findings suggest that the relationships between self-efficacy, its antecedents, and several online learning outcomes are more complex than has typically been recognized in the research. (PsycINFO Database Record (c) 2006 APA, all rights reserved)
DOI
10.1016/j.chb.2004.04.004
Keywords
online learning systems; self-efficacy; college students' perceptions; technology
Index Terms
*College Students; *Computer Assisted Instruction; *Internet; *Self Efficacy; *Student Attitudes; Technology
Classification Code
3530 Curriculum & Programs & Teaching Methods; 4000 Engineering & Environmental Psychology
Population
Human; Male; Female
Age Group
Adulthood (18 yrs & older)
Location
US
Methodology
0400 Empirical Study; 1800 Quantitative Study
Release Date
20061106

APPENDIX C: Sample PsycEXTRA Record

PsycEXTRA Record

Unique Identifier	475012006-001
Document Title	Evaluating Substance Abuse Treatment Programs for Adolescent Probationers
Content Owner	RAND Corporation 1200 South Hayes Street Arlington, Virginia, 22202-5050 US http://www.rand.org
Institutional Author	RAND Corporation
Publication Date	2004
Pagination	3 pp
Language Availability	English
Abstract	There is little information on the effectiveness of substance abuse treatment services commonly available to adolescents. In this study, RAND researchers found that one such program helped young probationers reduce substance abuse and improve their psychological functioning. These findings suggest that more research is needed on the relative effectiveness of the types of programs typically available to youths in the community and the specialized services typically found to be effective in rigorous experimental studies of adolescent treatment.
Key Words	substance abuse treatment programs; adolescent probationers; treatment effectiveness; psychological functioning
Index Terms	Drug Abuse; Drug Rehabilitation; Juvenile Delinquency; Mental Health; Probation; Treatment Effectiveness Evaluation
Classification Code	3383 (Drug & Alcohol Rehabilitation)
Population Group	Human; Male; Female
Age Group	Adolescence (13-17 yrs)
Location	US
Document Type	Report
Release Date	20060406

RELATIONSHIP SECTION

Abandonment 1997
PN 168 **SC** 00005
SN Loneliness, anxiety, and emotional and psychological loss of support resulting from desertion or neglect. Used for human populations.
UF Desertion
R Attachment Behavior 1985
↓ Child Abuse 1971
Child Neglect 1988
Dependency (Personality) 1967
↓ Emotional States 1973
Loneliness 1973
↓ Relationship Termination 1997
Separation Anxiety 1973
↓ Separation Reactions 1997

Abdomen 1973
PN 278 **SC** 00010
B Anatomy 1967

Abdominal Wall 1973
PN 16 **SC** 00020
B Muscles 1967

Abducens Nerve 1973
PN 29 **SC** 00030
SN Cranial motor nerve controlling the lateral rectus muscle of the eye.
UF Nerve (Abducens)
B Cranial Nerves 1973

Ability 1967
PN 4329 **SC** 00070
SN Conceptually broad term referring to the skills, talents, or qualities that enable one to perform a task. Use a more specific term if possible.
UF Aptitude
Skills
Talent
N Academic Aptitude 1973
↓ Cognitive Ability 1973
↓ Communication Skills 1973
↓ Employee Skills 1973
Learning Ability 1973
↓ Nonverbal Ability 1988
↓ Reading Skills 1973
Self Care Skills 1978
Social Skills 1978
R Ability Grouping 1973
Ability Level 1978
↓ Achievement Potential 1973
↓ Competence 1982
Creativity 1967
Gifted 1967
↓ Intelligence 1967
↓ Performance 1967

Ability Grouping 1973
PN 442 **SC** 00040
SN Grouping or selection of individuals for instructional or other purposes based on differences in ability or achievement.
R ↓ Ability 1967
Ability Level 1978
Academic Aptitude 1973
↓ Education 1967
Educational Placement 1978
Grade Level 1994
Special Education 1967

Ability Level 1978
PN 2572 **SC** 00050
SN Demonstrated level of performance. Used in academic, cognitive, perceptual, or occupational contexts, as well as an indicator of a patient's level of functioning.
UF Functional Status
Level of Functioning
R ↓ Ability 1967
Ability Grouping 1973
Activities of Daily Living 1991
Adaptive Testing 1985

Ability Tests
Use Aptitude Measures

Ablation
Use Lesions

Abnormal Psychology 2003
PN 783 **SC** 00083
SN Branch of psychology concerned with the study of mental disorders.
HN This term was introduced in June 2003. Relevant records were re-indexed with this term. The posting note reflects the number of records that were re-indexed.
B Psychology 1967
R ↓ Mental Disorders 1967
↓ Psychopathology 1967

Aboriginal Populations
Use Indigenous Populations

Abortion (Induced)
Use Induced Abortion

Abortion (Spontaneous)
Use Spontaneous Abortion

Abortion Laws 1973
PN 131 **SC** 00110
B Laws 1967
R Induced Abortion 1971

Abreaction
Use Catharsis

Absence Seizures
Use Petit Mal Seizures

Absenteeism (Employee)
Use Employee Absenteeism

Absorption (Physiological) 1973
PN 83 **SC** 00140
B Physiology 1967
R Bioavailability 1991
↓ Cells (Biology) 1973
Intestines 1973
Skin (Anatomy) 1967

Abstinence (Drugs)
Use Drug Abstinence

Abstinence (Sexual)
Use Sexual Abstinence

Abstraction 1967
PN 1344 **SC** 00160
SN Process of selecting or isolating a certain conceptual aspect from a concrete whole.

Abstraction — (cont'd)
B Thinking 1967
N ↓ Imagery 1967
R Divergent Thinking 1973

Abuse of Power 1997
PN 92 **SC** 00165
B Power 1967
R Authority 1967
Coercion 1994
↓ Dominance 1967
↓ Leadership 1967
Prisoner Abuse 2007

Abuse Potential (Drugs)
Use Drug Abuse Liability

Abuse Reporting 1997
PN 205 **SC** 00180
N Child Abuse Reporting 1997
R Battered Females 1988
↓ Child Abuse 1971
Duty to Warn 2001
Elder Abuse 1988
Informants 1988
↓ Laws 1967
↓ Partner Abuse 1991
Physical Abuse 1991
Privileged Communication 1973
Professional Ethics 1973
↓ Sexual Abuse 1988

Academic Achievement 1967
PN 25800 **SC** 00190
UF Gradepoint Average
Scholastic Achievement
School Achievement
B Achievement 1967
N Academic Overachievement 1967
Academic Underachievement 1967
College Academic Achievement 1967
Mathematics Achievement 1973
Reading Achievement 1973
Science Achievement 1997
R Academic Achievement Motivation 1973
Academic Achievement Prediction 1967
Academic Aptitude 1973
Academic Failure 1978
Academic Self Concept 1997
↓ Education 1967
Educational Attainment Level 1997
Educational Standards 2007
School Graduation 1991
School Learning 1967
School Transition 1997

Academic Achievement Motivation 1973
PN 2655 **SC** 00200
B Achievement Motivation 1967
R ↓ Academic Achievement 1967
Academic Self Concept 1997

Academic Achievement Prediction 1967
PN 3031 **SC** 00210
SN Prediction of future academic achievement based on results of tests, inventories, or other measures.
B Prediction 1967
R ↓ Academic Achievement 1967

Academic Aptitude 1973
PN 1655 **SC** 00220
SN Potential ability to perform or achieve in scholastic pursuits.

Academic Aptitude — (cont'd)
UF Aptitude (Academic)
Scholastic Aptitude
B Ability 1967
Achievement Potential 1973
R Ability Grouping 1973
↓ Academic Achievement 1967
↓ Education 1967
↓ Nonverbal Ability 1988
Reading Ability 1973
Student Admission Criteria 1973
Verbal Ability 1967

Academic Engagement
Use Student Engagement

Academic Environment 1973
PN 1010 SC 00230
SN Physical setting or emotional climate where formal instruction takes place.
B Social Environments 1973
N Classroom Environment 1973
Same Sex Education 2003
↓ School Environment 1973
R Learning Environment 2004
School Violence 2003
↓ Single Sex Environments 2001

Academic Failure 1978
PN 1190 SC 00233
B Failure 1967
R ↓ Academic Achievement 1967
Academic Underachievement 1967

Academic Grade Level
Use Grade Level

Academic Overachievement 1967
PN 486 SC 00240
SN Academic achievement greater than that anticipated on basis of one's scholastic aptitude score or individual intelligence.
UF Overachievement (Academic)
B Academic Achievement 1967

Academic Records
Use Student Records

Academic Self Concept 1997
PN 658 SC 00248
B Self Concept 1967
R ↓ Academic Achievement 1967
Academic Achievement Motivation 1973
Self Confidence 1994
Self Efficacy 1985
Self Perception 1967

Academic Specialization 1973
PN 2140 SC 00250
SN Concentration of effort or interest in a special area of knowledge or discipline at an institution of learning.
UF College Major
Specialization (Academic)
R Educational Aspirations 1973
Professional Specialization 1991

Academic Standards
Use Educational Standards

Academic Underachievement 1967
PN 1877 SC 00260
SN Academic achievement less than that expected based on one's scholastic aptitude score or individual intelligence.
UF Underachievement (Academic)
B Academic Achievement 1967
R Academic Failure 1978
↓ Failure 1967

Acalculia 1973
PN 180 SC 00270
SN Form of aphasia involving impaired ability to perform simple arithmetic calculations.
UF Dyscalculia
B Aphasia 1967
R ↓ Learning Disabilities 1973

Accelerated Speech
Use Speech Rate

Acceleration Effects 1973
PN 224 SC 00290
SN Behavioral, physiological, or psychological effects resulting from acceleration onset/offset or the effects of changes in acceleration rate. Used for both human and animal populations.
R ↓ Aviation 1967
Decompression Effects 1973
Flight Simulation 1973
↓ Gravitational Effects 1967
Physiological Stress 1967
Spaceflight 1967

Acceptance (Social)
Use Social Acceptance

Accessory Nerve
Use Cranial Nerves

Accident Prevention 1973
PN 749 SC 00330
B Prevention 1973
R ↓ Accidents 1967
Risk Management 1997
↓ Safety 1967
↓ Transportation Accidents 1973
Transportation Safety 2007
Warning Labels 1997
↓ Warnings 1997

Accident Proneness 1973
PN 202 SC 00340
R ↓ Accidents 1967
↓ Safety 1967

Accidents 1967
PN 1250 SC 00350
N Falls 2004
Home Accidents 1973
Industrial Accidents 1973
Pedestrian Accidents 1973
↓ Transportation Accidents 1973
R Accident Prevention 1973
Accident Proneness 1973
↓ Disasters 1973
Driving Under the Influence 1988
↓ Hazardous Materials 1991
Hazards 1973
↓ Injuries 1973
↓ Safety 1967
Warning Labels 1997

Accidents — (cont'd)
↓ Warnings 1997

Acclimatization (Thermal)
Use Thermal Acclimatization

Accommodation (Cognitive Process) 2007
PN 14 SC 00375
SN The adjustment of mental schemas to match information acquired through experience. Consider also OCULAR ACCOMMODATION.
HN This term was introduced in April 2007. Relevant records were re-indexed with this term. The posting note reflects the number of records that were re-indexed.
B Cognitive Processes 1967
R Assimilation (Cognitive Process) 2007
↓ Cognitive Style 1967
Piaget (Jean) 1967
Schema 1988

Accommodation (Disabilities) 2007
PN 10 SC 00376
SN Adjustment or modification of the environment or a task in order to meet the needs of individuals with disabilities. Consider also OCULAR ACCOMMODATION.
HN This term was introduced in April 2007. Relevant records were re-indexed with this term. The posting note reflects the number of records that were re-indexed.
R ↓ Disabilities 2003
Disability Laws 1994
Person Environment Fit 1991

Accomplishment
Use Achievement

Accountability 1988
PN 969 SC 00385
SN Liability and/or responsibility for specified results or outcomes of an activity over which one has authority.
B Responsibility 1973
R Blame 1994
↓ Competence 1982
Consumer Protection 1973
Criminal Responsibility 1991
Duty to Warn 2001
↓ Management 1967
Professional Liability 1985
↓ Professional Standards 1973
Quality Control 1988
Quality of Care 1988

Accountants 1973
PN 392 SC 00390
UF Certified Public Accountants
B White Collar Workers 1973

Accreditation (Education Personnel) 1973
PN 117 SC 00400
SN Professional licensing or certification of teachers, school psychologists, or other educational personnel, usually required for employment.
UF Teacher Accreditation
B Professional Certification 1973
Professional Licensing 1973
R ↓ Education 1967
Educational Quality 1997
Professional Examinations 1994

Accreditation (Educational Programs)
Use Educational Program Accreditation

Acculturation 2003
PN 4394 **SC** 00410
SN Contact of at least two autonomous cultural groups resulting in change in one or the other, or both groups. Includes the process of a minority group giving up its own cultural traits and absorbing those of a dominant society.
HN In June 2003, this term replaced the discontinued term CULTURAL ASSIMILATION. CULTURAL ASSIMILATION was removed from all records and replaced with ACCULTURATION.
UF Assimilation (Cultural)
Cultural Assimilation
B Culture Change 1967
R Cross Cultural Communication 1997
Cross Cultural Psychology 1997
Cultural Sensitivity 1994
Multiculturalism 1997

Acetaldehyde 1982
PN 154 **SC** 00415
SN First oxidation product of primary alcohol metabolism. Acetaldehyde has narcotic properties.
UF Acetic Aldehyde
Ethanal
Ethylaldehyde
R ↓ Alcohols 1967
↓ Carbohydrate Metabolism 1973
↓ Dopamine Metabolites 1982

Acetazolamide 1973
PN 42 **SC** 00420
B Diuretics 1973
Enzyme Inhibitors 1985
R ↓ Anticonvulsive Drugs 1973

Acetic Aldehyde
Use Acetaldehyde

Acetylcholine 1973
PN 1308 **SC** 00430
B Cholinergic Drugs 1973
Cholinomimetic Drugs 1973
Neurotransmitters 1985
R Acetylcholinesterase 1973
↓ Choline 1973
Cholinergic Nerves 1973
Cholinergic Receptors 2003

Acetylcholine Receptors
Use Cholinergic Receptors

Acetylcholinesterase 1973
PN 533 **SC** 00440
B Esterases 1973
R Acetylcholine 1973
Cholinesterase 1973

Acetylsalicylic Acid
Use Aspirin

Aches
Use Pain

Achievement 1967
PN 4669 **SC** 00470
UF Accomplishment
Attainment (Achievement)
Success
N ↓ Academic Achievement 1967
Occupational Success 1978
R ↓ Achievement Measures 1967
Awards (Merit) 2005
↓ Competence 1982
↓ Failure 1967

Achievement — (cont'd)
↓ Performance 1967
↓ Productivity 2007

Achievement Measures 1967
PN 2274 **SC** 00490
SN Tests designed to measure knowledge and/or skills acquired from learning, experience, or training.
UF Tests (Achievement)
B Measurement 1967
N Iowa Tests of Basic Skills 1973
Stanford Achievement Test 1973
Wide Range Achievement Test 1973
Woodcock Johnson Psychoeducational Battery 2001
R ↓ Achievement 1967
Criterion Referenced Tests 1982

Achievement Motivation 1967
PN 3955 **SC** 00500
SN Need that drives an individual to improve, succeed, or excel.
UF NAch
Need Achievement
B Motivation 1967
N Academic Achievement Motivation 1973
R ↓ Achievement Potential 1973
Fear of Success 1978
↓ Needs 1967

Achievement Potential 1973
PN 267 **SC** 00510
SN One's general ability to achieve in any area, including academic.
UF Potential (Achievement)
N Academic Aptitude 1973
R ↓ Ability 1967
↓ Achievement Motivation 1967

Achilles Tendon Reflex 1973
PN 17 **SC** 00520
B Reflexes 1971

Achromatic Color 1973
PN 210 **SC** 00530
SN Visual quality which lacks hue and saturation, consequently varying only in brilliance. Includes variations from black through gray to white.
B Color 1967
R ↓ Chromaticity 1997
Color Saturation 1997

Acids 1973
PN 728 **SC** 00550
N ↓ Amino Acids 1973
Ascorbic Acid 1973
Aspirin 1973
Dihydroxyphenylacetic Acid 1991
↓ Fatty Acids 1973
Heparin 1973
Homovanillic Acid 1978
Hydroxyindoleacetic Acid (5-) 1985
Kainic Acid 1988
Lactic Acid 1991
Lysergic Acid Diethylamide 1967
Nicotinic Acid 1973
↓ Nucleic Acids 1973
Taurine 1982
Uric Acid 1973
R ↓ Drugs 1967
↓ Solvents 1982

Acoustic Nerve 1973
PN 190 **SC** 00570
SN Cranial nerve composed of cochlear and vestibular nerves which connects the inner ear hair cells to the brain. It transmits information on hearing and balance.
UF Auditory Nerve
Cochlear Nerve
Nerve (Acoustic)
Vestibulocochlear Nerve
B Cranial Nerves 1973

Acoustic Reflex 1973
PN 650 **SC** 00580
SN Bilateral contraction of stapedius muscles when a loud sound is presented.
UF Intra Aural Muscle Reflex
Stapedius Reflex
B Reflexes 1971
R Startle Reflex 1967

Acoustic Stimuli
Use Auditory Stimulation

Acoustics 1997
PN 1358 **SC** 00591
SN Structural properties of auditorially perceived stimuli or sounds.
UF Sound Waves
R ↓ Auditory Perception 1967
↓ Auditory Stimulation 1967
Noise Effects 1973
↓ Speech Characteristics 1973
↓ Stimulus Parameters 1967

Acquaintance Rape 1991
PN 360 **SC** 00593
SN Rape perpetrated by a person or persons known to the victim.
UF Date Rape
B Rape 1973
R ↓ Human Courtship 1973
Social Dating 1973

Acquired Immune Deficiency Syndrome
HN In May 2006, this term was discontinued and removed from all records containing it, and was replaced with AIDS, its postable counterpart.
Use AIDS

Acquisitions (Organizational)
Use Mergers and Acquisitions

Acrophobia 1973
PN 67 **SC** 00600
SN Fear of heights.
B Phobias 1967

ACTH (Hormone)
Use Corticotropin

ACTH Releasing Factor
Use Corticotropin Releasing Factor

Acting Out 1967
PN 634 **SC** 00620
SN Behavioral manifestation of those impulses and desires that are unacceptable or irreconcilable with an individual's conscience. When such behavior becomes maladaptive, socially or personally, it is classified as an acting out disorder.
B Symptoms 1967
R ↓ Behavior Disorders 1971
Enactments 1997
Rebelliousness 2003

Active Avoidance
Use Avoidance Conditioning

Active Duty
Use Military Duty Status

Active Living 2007
PN 11 **SC** 00634
SN Integration of physical activity into daily life by focusing on the built environment, including neighborhoods, transportation systems, buildings, parks, and open spaces.
HN This term was introduced in April 2007. Relevant records were re-indexed with this term. The posting note reflects the number of records that were re-indexed.
B Lifestyle 1978
R Daily Activities 1994
↓ Health Behavior 1982
Health Promotion 1991
↓ Physical Activity 2007

Activism 2003
PN 967 **SC** 00635
SN Doctrines or practices emphasizing direct action (usually political) in support of or opposition to one side of a controversial issue.
HN In June 2003, this term was created to replace the discontinued term ACTIVIST MOVEMENTS. ACTIVIST MOVEMENTS was removed from all records containing it and replaced with ACTIVISM.
UF Activist Movements
B Social Behavior 1967
N Student Activism 1973
R Black Power Movement 1973
Civil Rights Movement 1973
Community Involvement 2003
Homosexual Liberation Movement 1973
↓ Political Attitudes 1973
↓ Political Participation 1988
School Integration 1982
Social Change 1967
Social Demonstrations 1973
↓ Social Integration 1982
Womens Liberation Movement 1973

Activism (Student)
Use Student Activism

Activist Movements
HN In June 2003, the term was discontinued and removed from all records containing it, and was replaced with ACTIVISM, its postable counterpart.
Use Activism

Activities of Daily Living 1991
PN 2343 **SC** 00655
SN Basic personal care skills such as eating, bathing, dressing, and other personal hygenic skills used to measure functional ability in the elderly and the emotionally and physically disabled. Compare DAILY ACTIVITIES.
R Ability Level 1978
Activity Level 1982
Assisted Living 2003
Daily Activities 1994
Geriatric Assessment 1997
Habilitation 1991
Hygiene 1994
Independent Living Programs 1991
Physical Mobility 1994
↓ Rehabilitation 1967
Self Care Skills 1978

Activity Level 1982
PN 6795 **SC** 00660
SN General energetic state of an organism, frequently used as a measure of drug effects but not restricted to this application.
B Motor Processes 1967
R Activities of Daily Living 1991
Daily Activities 1994
↓ Motivation 1967
↓ Physical Activity 2007
Physical Mobility 1994
Rotational Behavior 1994

Activity Theory 2003
PN 211 **SC** 00664
SN Theory formulated by early 20th century Russian psychologists analyzing behavior based on an individual's activity in or interaction with his or her environment.
HN This term was introduced in June 2003. Relevant records were re-indexed with this term. The posting note reflects the number of records that were re-indexed.
B Theories 1967
R ↓ Learning 1967
↓ Motivation 1967
↓ Participation 1973
Vygotsky (Lev) 1991

Activity Therapy
Use Recreation Therapy

Actualization (Self)
Use Self Actualization

Acupuncture 1973
PN 545 **SC** 00690
B Alternative Medicine 1997
Physical Treatment Methods 1973

Acute Alcoholic Intoxication 1973
PN 68 **SC** 00700
SN Temporary mental disturbance marked by muscle incoordination and paresis as the result of excessive alcohol ingestion.
B Alcohol Intoxication 1973
Brain Disorders 1967
Toxic Disorders 1973
R Toxic Encephalopathies 1973

Acute Paranoid Disorder
Use Paranoia (Psychosis)

Acute Psychosis 1973
PN 622 **SC** 00710
HN In 1988, this term replaced the discontinued term ACUTE PSYCHOTIC EPISODE. In 2000, ACUTE PSYCHOTIC EPISODE was removed from all records containing it, and replaced with ACUTE PSYCHOSIS.
UF Acute Psychotic Episode
Brief Reactive Psychosis
Psychotic Episode (Acute)
B Psychosis 1967
N Acute Schizophrenia 1973

Acute Psychotic Episode
HN Term was discontinued in 1988. In 2000, the term was removed from all records containing it, and replaced with ACUTE PSYCHOSIS, its postable counterpart.
Use Acute Psychosis

Acute Schizophrenia 1973
PN 688 **SC** 00730
SN An episode of schizophrenia that is marked by sudden onset and short duration.
B Acute Psychosis 1973
Schizophrenia 1967
R Postpartum Psychosis 2003

Acute Stress Disorder 2003
PN 182 **SC** 00733
SN Disorder characterized by the development of anxiety and dissociative symptoms as a result of exposure to a traumatic event. Symptoms last at least two days and no longer than four weeks.
HN This term was introduced in June 2003. Relevant records were re-indexed with this term. The posting note reflects the number of records that were re-indexed.
B Anxiety Disorders 1997
R Debriefing (Psychological) 2004
Emotional Trauma 1967
Posttraumatic Stress Disorder 1985
Stress Reactions 1973

Adaptability (Personality) 1973
PN 838 **SC** 00740
SN Ability to be flexible and to maximize functioning in the face of environmental changes. See ADJUSTMENT for terms relating to the process of adapting.
UF Flexibility (Personality)
B Personality Traits 1967
R ↓ Adjustment 1967
Agreeableness 1997
Coping Behavior 1967
Openness to Experience 1997
Resilience (Psychological) 2003

Adaptation 1967
PN 2726 **SC** 00750
SN Physiological or biological modification of an organism or its morphology in response to the physical environment. For psychological, social, or emotional adaptation, use ADJUSTMENT or one of its narrower or related terms.
UF Readaptation
N Environmental Adaptation 1973
↓ Sensory Adaptation 1967
Thermal Acclimatization 1973

Adaptation (Dark)
Use Dark Adaptation

Adaptation (Environmental)
Use Environmental Adaptation

Adaptation (Light)
Use Light Adaptation

Adaptation (Sensory)
Use Sensory Adaptation

Adaptation (Social)
Use Social Adjustment

Adaptive Behavior 1991
PN 1099 **SC** 00793
SN Behaviors indicating ability to take care of personal needs, function socially, and control problem behavior. Primarily used for disabled or disordered populations.
B Behavior 1967
R ↓ Adjustment 1967
↓ Mental Disorders 1967
↓ Mental Retardation 1967
↓ Rehabilitation 1967

Adaptive Behavior — (cont'd)
Self Care Skills 1978
Social Skills 1978
Special Education 1967

Adaptive Testing 1985
PN 398 **SC** 00795
SN Testing method, usually using a computer, in which test items of varying difficulty levels are selected according to the degree to which the examinee's previous answers were correct.
UF Computer Adaptive Testing
Tailored Testing
B Testing Methods 1967
R Ability Level 1978
Computer Assisted Testing 1988
Item Analysis (Statistical) 1973
↓ Test Construction 1973

Addiction 1973
PN 2420 **SC** 00800
B Behavior Disorders 1971
N ↓ Alcoholism 1967
↓ Drug Addiction 1967
Internet Addiction 2006
Sexual Addiction 1997
R Craving 1997
↓ Drug Abuse 1973
↓ Drug Usage 1971
Pathological Gambling 1988
Workaholism 2004

Addisons Disease 1973
PN 22 **SC** 00810
SN A progressive disorder characterized by a deficiency of adrenal hormones. Symptoms include but are not limited to, weakness, fatigue, loss of weight, and nausea.
B Adrenal Gland Disorders 1973
Syndromes 1973

Adenosine 1973
PN 651 **SC** 00820
B Nucleic Acids 1973

ADHD
Use Attention Deficit Disorder with Hyperactivity

Adjectives 1973
PN 562 **SC** 00830
B Form Classes (Language) 1973

Adjudication 1967
PN 5901 **SC** 00840
SN Process of judicial decision making.
HN Use ADJUDICATION to access references to JURIES from 1967-1984.
UF Courts
Juvenile Court
Sentencing
Verdict Determination
B Law Enforcement 1978
N Court Referrals 1994
R Criminal Conviction 1973
↓ Criminal Justice 1991
Criminal Record 2006
Criminal Responsibility 1991
Juries 1985
Jury Selection 1994
Juvenile Justice 2004

Adjudication — (cont'd)
Legal Decisions 1991
↓ Legal Evidence 1991
Litigation 2003

Adjunctive Behavior 1982
PN 69 **SC** 00845
SN Noncontingent appropriate or inappropriate behavior that is maintained by an event which acquires its reinforcing characteristics as the result of some other ongoing reinforcement contingency.
B Behavior 1967
N Polydipsia 1982
R ↓ Operant Conditioning 1967
Pica 1973

Adjustment 1967
PN 10706 **SC** 00850
SN Conceptually broad term referring to a state of harmony between internal needs and external demands and the processes used in achieving this condition. Use a more specific term if possible. Differentiate from ADAPTATION, which refers to physiological or biological adaptation.
N ↓ Emotional Adjustment 1973
Occupational Adjustment 1973
School Adjustment 1967
Social Adjustment 1973
R Adaptability (Personality) 1973
Adaptive Behavior 1991
Adjustment Disorders 1994
Person Environment Fit 1991
Well Being 1994
Work Adjustment Training 1991

Adjustment Disorders 1994
PN 297 **SC** 00855
SN Maladaptive reaction to psychosocial stressors which impairs social or occupational functioning. Usually a temporary condition that remits after new levels of adaptation are obtained or stressors have been removed.
B Mental Disorders 1967
R ↓ Adjustment 1967
Coping Behavior 1967
↓ Emotional Adjustment 1973
Emotional Trauma 1967
Occupational Adjustment 1973
Posttraumatic Stress Disorder 1985
School Adjustment 1967
Social Adjustment 1973
↓ Stress 1967
Stress Reactions 1973

Adler (Alfred) 1967
PN 538 **SC** 00860
SN Identifies biographical or autobiographical studies and discussions of Adler's works.
R Adlerian Psychotherapy 1997
Individual Psychology 1973
↓ Psychologists 1967

Adlerian Psychotherapy 1997
PN 330 **SC** 00865
UF Individual Psychotherapy (Adlerian)
B Psychoanalysis 1967
Psychotherapy 1967
R Adler (Alfred) 1967
Individual Psychology 1973

Administration (Test)
Use Test Administration

Administrators
Use Management Personnel

Administrators (School)
Use School Administrators

Admission (Hospital)
Use Hospital Admission

Admission (Psychiatric Hospital)
Use Psychiatric Hospital Admission

Admission Criteria (Student)
Use Student Admission Criteria

Adolescent Attitudes 1988
PN 7470 **SC** 00925
SN Attitudes of, not toward, adolescents.
B Attitudes 1967

Adolescent Development 1973
PN 13814 **SC** 00930
SN Process of physical, cognitive, personality, and psychosocial growth occurring from age 13 through 17. Use a more specific term if possible.
B Human Development 1967
R ↓ Childhood Development 1967
Developmental Age Groups 1973
↓ Developmental Stages 1973
↓ Physical Development 1973
↓ Psychogenesis 1973
Sex Linked Developmental Differences 1973
Sexual Development 1973

Adolescent Fathers 1985
PN 257 **SC** 00932
SN Fathers aged 13-17 years.
UF Teenage Fathers
B Fathers 1967
R Adolescent Pregnancy 1988

Adolescent Mothers 1985
PN 1419 **SC** 00935
SN Mothers aged 13-17 years. Consider also UNWED MOTHERS.
UF Teenage Mothers
B Mothers 1967
R Adolescent Pregnancy 1988

Adolescent Pregnancy 1988
PN 1527 **SC** 00936
UF Teenage Pregnancy
B Pregnancy 1967
R Adolescent Fathers 1985
Adolescent Mothers 1985
↓ Social Issues 1991

Adolescent Psychiatry 1985
PN 2046 **SC** 00937
B Psychiatry 1967
R Adolescent Psychopathology 2007
Adolescent Psychotherapy 1994

Adolescent Psychology 1973
PN 1300 **SC** 00940
SN Branch of developmental psychology devoted to the study and treatment of adolescents. Use a more specific term if possible.

Adolescent Psychology — (cont'd)
B Developmental Psychology 1973
R Adolescent Psychopathology 2007

Adolescent Psychopathology 2007
PN 42 SC 00943
SN The study of the causes and processes in the development of mental disorders, emotional problems, or maladaptive behaviors among adolescents. Used for the scientific discipline or for unspecified dysfunctions.
HN This term was introduced in April 2007. Relevant records were re-indexed with this term. The posting note reflects the number of records that were re-indexed.
B Psychopathology 1967
R Adolescent Psychiatry 1985
Adolescent Psychology 1973
Child Psychopathology 2007

Adolescent Psychotherapy 1994
PN 1152 SC 00945
B Psychotherapy 1967
R Adolescent Psychiatry 1985
↓ Child Psychotherapy 1967

Adopted Children 1973
PN 1027 SC 00960
B Adoptees 1985
Family Members 1973
R ↓ Adoption (Child) 1967
Interracial Adoption 1994

Adoptees 1985
PN 445 SC 00965
SN Anyone who has been formally adopted as a dependent. Limited to human populations.
N Adopted Children 1973
R ↓ Adoption (Child) 1967
Interracial Adoption 1994

Adoption (Child) 1967
PN 1503 SC 00970
B Legal Processes 1973
N Interracial Adoption 1994
R Adopted Children 1973
↓ Adoptees 1985
Adoptive Parents 1973
Child Welfare 1988

Adoptive Parents 1973
PN 751 SC 00980
B Parents 1967
R ↓ Adoption (Child) 1967
Interracial Adoption 1994

Adrenal Cortex Hormones 1973
PN 255 SC 00990
B Hormones 1967
N Aldosterone 1973
Corticosterone 1973
Cortisone 1973
Deoxycorticosterone 1973
↓ Glucocorticoids 1982
Hydrocortisone 1973
Prednisolone 1973
R ↓ Adrenal Glands 1973
↓ Adrenal Medulla Hormones 1973
↓ Corticosteroids 1973
↓ Stress 1967

Adrenal Cortex Steroids
Use Corticosteroids

Adrenal Gland Disorders 1973
PN 89 SC 01010
B Endocrine Disorders 1973
N Addisons Disease 1973
Cushings Syndrome 1973
R ↓ Endocrine Sexual Disorders 1973
↓ Pituitary Disorders 1973

Adrenal Gland Secretion 1973
PN 91 SC 01020
B Endocrine Gland Secretion 1973

Adrenal Glands 1973
PN 553 SC 01030
B Endocrine Glands 1973
N Hypothalamic Pituitary Adrenal Axis 2006
R ↓ Adrenal Cortex Hormones 1973

Adrenal Medulla Hormones 1973
PN 64 SC 01040
B Hormones 1967
N Norepinephrine 1973
R ↓ Adrenal Cortex Hormones 1973

Adrenalectomy 1973
PN 418 SC 01050
B Endocrine Gland Surgery 1973

Adrenaline
Use Epinephrine

Adrenaline Receptors
Use Adrenergic Receptors

Adrenergic Blocking Drugs 1973
PN 1179 SC 01070
UF Beta Blockers
B Drugs 1967
N Alpha Methylparatyrosine 1978
Dihydroergotamine 1973
Hydroxydopamine (6-) 1978
Phenoxybenzamine 1973
Propranolol 1973
Yohimbine 1988
R ↓ Antihypertensive Drugs 1973
↓ Ergot Derivatives 1973
↓ Sympathetic Nervous System 1973
↓ Sympatholytic Drugs 1973
↓ Tricyclic Antidepressant Drugs 1997

Adrenergic Drugs 1973
PN 480 SC 01080
HN In 1997, this term replaced the discontinued term ADRENOLYTIC DRUGS. In 2000, ADRENOLYTIC DRUGS was removed from all records containing it, and replaced with ADRENERGIC DRUGS.
UF Adrenolytic Drugs
B Drugs 1967
N ↓ Amphetamine 1967
Dextroamphetamine 1973
Ephedrine 1973
Epinephrine 1967
Methoxamine 1973
Tyramine 1973
R ↓ Catecholamines 1973
Serotonin 1973
↓ Sympathetic Nervous System 1973
↓ Sympathomimetic Drugs 1973

Adrenergic Nerves 1973
PN 404 SC 01090
SN Nerves that release catecholamines at a synapse after an impulse.

Adrenergic Nerves — (cont'd)
UF Nerves (Adrenergic)
B Autonomic Nervous System 1967

Adrenergic Receptors 2003
PN 401 SC 01093
SN Class of neural receptors that are sensitive to the neurotransmitters epinephrine and norepinephrine.
HN This term was introduced in June 2003. Relevant records were re-indexed with this term. The posting note reflects the number of records that were re-indexed.
UF Adrenaline Receptors
Adrenoceptors
Receptors (Adrenergic)
B Neural Receptors 1973
R ↓ Catecholamines 1973
Receptor Binding 1985

Adrenoceptors
Use Adrenergic Receptors

Adrenocorticotropin
Use Corticotropin

Adrenolytic Drugs
HN Term was discontinued in 1997. In 2000, the term was removed from all records containing it, and replaced with ADRENERGIC DRUGS, its postable counterpart.
Use Adrenergic Drugs

Adult Attitudes 1988
PN 8506 SC 01122
SN Attitudes of, not toward, adults.
B Attitudes 1967

Adult Children
Use Adult Offspring

Adult Children of Alcoholics
Use Children of Alcoholics

Adult Day Care 1997
PN 165 SC 01125
SN Home- or center-based care of physically or mentally disabled adults during daytime hours, providing personal, social, and homemaker services.
R Day Care Centers 1973
Elder Care 1994
Home Care 1985
Home Visiting Programs 1973
Long Term Care 1994

Adult Development 1978
PN 4806 SC 01127
SN Process of physical, cognitive, personality, and psychosocial growth occurring from age 18. Use a more specific term if possible.
B Human Development 1967
R Adult Learning 1997
Developmental Age Groups 1973
↓ Developmental Stages 1973
Generativity 2001
Mentor 1985
Physiological Aging 1967
↓ Psychogenesis 1973

Adult Education 1973
PN 1854 SC 01130
SN Formal or informal education for adults, including but not limited to basic education, high school equivalency, vocational education, correspondence courses, continuing education, non-degree coursework, and lifelong learning programs.

Adult Education — (cont'd)
UF High School Equivalency
B Education 1967
N ↓ Continuing Education 1985
R Adult Learning 1997
Literacy Programs 1997
Reentry Students 1985

Adult Learning 1997
PN 470 SC 01133
B Learning 1967
R Adult Development 1978
↓ Adult Education 1973
↓ Continuing Education 1985
Reentry Students 1985

Adult Offspring 1985
PN 3031 SC 01135
SN Ages 18 or older.
UF Adult Children
Grown Children
B Family Members 1973
Offspring 1988
R Empty Nest 1991

Adultery
Use Extramarital Intercourse

Advance Directives 1994
PN 460 SC 01163
SN Declaration of personal wishes through legal documents or written instructions pertaining to future medical care if one becomes incapacitated.
UF Living Wills
R Assisted Suicide 1997
↓ Client Rights 1988
↓ Death and Dying 1967
Euthanasia 1973
↓ Legal Processes 1973
Life Sustaining Treatment 1997
Palliative Care 1991
Terminally Ill Patients 1973
Treatment Refusal 1994
Treatment Withholding 1988

Advance Organizers 1985
PN 198 SC 01165
SN Structural overview of material to be taught to facilitate incorporation of new material into that previously learned or known.
UF Structured Overview
B Instructional Media 1967
Teaching Methods 1967
R ↓ Learning Strategies 1991
Study Habits 1973

Adventitious Disorders 2001
PN 58 SC 01168
SN Disabilities that are accidental or acquired, rather than congenital.
HN The term ADVENTITIOUSLY HANDICAPPED was used to represent the concept from 1973-1996, and ADVENTITIOUSLY DISABLED was used from 1997-2000. In 2001, ADVENTITIOUS DISORDERS was created to replace the discontinued and deleted term ADVENTITIOUSLY DISABLED. ADVENTITIOUSLY DISABLED and ADVENTITIOUSLY HANDICAPPED were removed from all records containing them and replaced with ADVENTITIOUS DISORDERS.

Adventitious Disorders — (cont'd)
UF Adventitiously Handicapped
B Disorders 1967
R ↓ Congenital Disorders 1973

Adventitiously Handicapped
HN The term was discontinued in 1997, when the term ADVENTITIOUSLY DISABLED was created to capture this concept. In 2000, with the deletion of the term ADVENTITIOUSLY DISABLED, ADVENTITIOUSLY HANDICAPPED was made a nonpostable term for the postable term ADVENTITIOUS DISORDERS. ADVENTITIOUSLY DISABLED and ADVENTITIOUSLY HANDICAPPED were removed from all records and replaced with ADVENTITIOUS DISORDERS.
Use Adventitious Disorders

Adverbs 1973
PN 94 SC 01180
B Form Classes (Language) 1973

Advertising 1967
PN 4332 SC 01190
N Television Advertising 1973
R Brand Names 1978
Brand Preferences 1994
↓ Consumer Research 1973
↓ Marketing 1973
↓ Mass Media 1967
Product Design 1997
Public Relations 1973
↓ Quality of Services 1997
↓ Retailing 1991

Advocacy 1985
PN 1490 SC 01195
SN The process of defending or pleading the cause of another individual or group.
UF Child Advocacy
R Child Welfare 1988
↓ Civil Rights 1978
Empowerment 1991
↓ Government Policy Making 1973
Legislative Processes 1973
Public Service Announcements 2004
Right to Treatment 1997

Aerobic Exercise 1988
PN 617 SC 01197
B Exercise 1973
R ↓ Health Behavior 1982
Physical Fitness 1973
Weight Control 1985

Aerospace Personnel 1973
PN 655 SC 01200
UF Aircraft Crew
Aviation Personnel
Flight Attendants
Navigators (Aircraft)
B Professional Personnel 1978
N Aircraft Pilots 1973
Astronauts 1973
R ↓ Business and Industrial Personnel 1967
Engineers 1967
Physicists 1973
Scientists 1967

Aesthetic Preferences 1973
PN 1472 SC 01210
B Preferences 1967
R Aesthetics 1967
Interior Design 1982

Aesthetics 1967
PN 1888 SC 01220
SN Scientific or philosophical study of beauty or judgments of beauty. Also, the aesthetic qualities themselves.
R Aesthetic Preferences 1973
↓ Arts 1973
Interior Design 1982

Aetiology
Use Etiology

Affairs (Sexual)
Use Extramarital Intercourse

Affect Regulation
Use Emotional Regulation

Affection 1973
PN 758 SC 01250
UF Liking
B Emotional States 1973
R ↓ Interpersonal Interaction 1967
Intimacy 1973
Love 1973
Physical Contact 1982
↓ Psychosexual Behavior 1967
Romance 1997
Sexuality 1973

Affective Disorders 2001
PN 8121 SC 01255
SN Mental disorders characterized by a disturbance in mood which is abnormally depressed or elated. Compare EMOTIONAL STABILITY or EMOTIONALLY DISTURBED.
HN Use AFFECTIVE DISTURBANCES to access references from 1967-2000.
UF Affective Disturbances
Mood Disorders
B Mental Disorders 1967
N ↓ Bipolar Disorder 2001
↓ Major Depression 1988
↓ Mania 1967
Seasonal Affective Disorder 1991
R Affective Psychosis 1973
Premenstrual Dysphoric Disorder 2004
Schizoaffective Disorder 1994

Affective Disturbances
HN In 2000, the term was discontinued and removed from all records containing it, and was replaced with AFFECTIVE DISORDERS, its postable counterpart.
Use Affective Disorders

Affective Education 1982
PN 552 SC 01265
SN Curriculum aimed at changing emotional and social behavior of students and enhancing their understanding of such behavior.
UF Humanistic Education
B Curriculum 1967
R Self Actualization 1973
↓ Self Concept 1967
Social Skills 1978

Affective Psychosis 1973
PN 429 SC 01270
SN Any psychosis characterized by severe disturbances in mood.
B Psychosis 1967
R ↓ Affective Disorders 2001
↓ Bipolar Disorder 2001

Afferent Neurons
Use Sensory Neurons

Afferent Pathways 1982
PN 1497 **SC** 01275
SN Collections of fibers that carry neural impulses toward neural processing areas from sensory mechanisms or other processing areas.
UF Sensory Pathways
B Neural Pathways 1982
N ↓ Lemniscal System 1985
Spinothalamic Tracts 1973
R Dorsal Horns 1985
↓ Efferent Pathways 1982
↓ Receptive Fields 1985
↓ Sensory Neurons 1973

Afferent Stimulation 1973
PN 239 **SC** 01280
SN Sensory stimulation causing nerve impulses to be carried toward the brain, spinal cord, or sensory relay and processing areas.
UF Afferentation
B Stimulation 1967
R ↓ Nervous System 1967
↓ Perceptual Stimulation 1973
↓ Stereotaxic Techniques 1973
↓ Surgery 1971

Afferentation
Use Afferent Stimulation

Affiliation Motivation 1967
PN 788 **SC** 01300
SN Need for association with others and formation of friendships.
UF Need for Affiliation
B Motivation 1967
R ↓ Membership 2007
↓ Needs 1967

Affirmative Action 1985
PN 543 **SC** 01305
SN Programs or policies designed to actively recruit females and minority group members for employment or higher education, in an effort to correct underrepresentative distributions of these groups relative to the general population.
R Age Discrimination 1994
↓ Civil Rights 1978
Disability Discrimination 1997
Diversity in the Workplace 2003
Employment Discrimination 1994
↓ Human Resource Management 2003
Minority Groups 1967
↓ Personnel 1967
↓ Personnel Recruitment 1973
↓ Personnel Selection 1967
Race and Ethnic Discrimination 1994
Sex Discrimination 1978
↓ Social Discrimination 1982
Social Equality 1973

African Americans
Use Blacks

African Cultural Groups 2006
PN 99 **SC** 01310
SN Cultural groups from the continent of Africa.
HN This term was introduced in May 2006. Relevant records were re-indexed with this term. The posting note reflects the number of records that were re-indexed.

African Cultural Groups — (cont'd)
UF Africans
B Racial and Ethnic Groups 2001
R Blacks 1982

Africans
Use African Cultural Groups

After School Programs 2003
PN 293 **SC** 01350
HN This term was introduced in June 2003. Relevant records were re-indexed with this term. The posting note reflects the number of records that were re-indexed.
R ↓ Educational Programs 1973
↓ Extracurricular Activities 1973

Aftercare 1973
PN 775 **SC** 01320
SN Continuing program of rehabilitation designed to reinforce and maintain the effects of treatment and to help clients adjust to their environment after hospital release.
B Treatment 1967
R Continuum of Care 2004
Discharge Planning 1994
Maintenance Therapy 1997
Outpatient Commitment 1991
↓ Outpatient Treatment 1967
Partial Hospitalization 1985
Posttreatment Followup 1973
↓ Treatment Planning 1997

Aftereffect (Perceptual)
Use Perceptual Aftereffect

Afterimage 1967
PN 323 **SC** 01340
SN Persistence of sensory excitation, usually visual, after cessation of stimulation. This temporary illusory sensation is due to physiological changes in the receptor cells.
UF Successive Contrast
B Perceptual Aftereffect 1967

Age Differences 1967
PN 48270 **SC** 01360
SN Age comparisons of behavioral, developmental, and cognitive variations between individuals or groups. Used for human or animal subjects.
HN In 1982, this term replaced the discontinued term DEVELOPMENTAL DIFFERENCES. In 2000, DEVELOPMENTAL DIFFERENCES was removed from all records containing it, and replaced with AGE DIFFERENCES.
UF Developmental Differences
R Animal Development 1978
Cohort Analysis 1988
↓ Development 1967
Developmental Age Groups 1973
Diversity in the Workplace 2003
Generation Gap 1973
Grade Level 1994
↓ Group Differences 2007
↓ Human Development 1967
↓ Physical Development 1973
↓ Psychogenesis 1973

Age Discrimination 1994
PN 150 **SC** 01363
HN Use SOCIAL DISCRIMINATION to access references from 1982-1993.

Age Discrimination — (cont'd)
B Social Discrimination 1982
R Affirmative Action 1985
↓ Aged (Attitudes Toward) 1978
Ageism 2003
Aging (Attitudes Toward) 1985
↓ Civil Rights 1978
Employment Discrimination 1994
↓ Prejudice 1967

Age Regression (Hypnotic) 1988
PN 97 **SC** 01365
SN Technique used to recapture early or past life experiences by guiding clients back through their history, usually year by year.
B Hypnosis 1967
Hypnotherapy 1973
R Early Experience 1967
Early Memories 1985
Enactments 1997
False Memory 1997
↓ Life Experiences 1973
↓ Psychotherapeutic Techniques 1967
Repressed Memory 1997

Aged (Attitudes Toward) 1978
PN 1416 **SC** 01372
B Attitudes 1967
N Ageism 2003
R Age Discrimination 1994
↓ Aging 1991
Aging (Attitudes Toward) 1985
Geriatrics 1967
Gerontology 1967
Physiological Aging 1967

Ageism 2003
PN 182 **SC** 01376
HN This term was introduced in June 2003. Relevant records were re-indexed with this term. The posting note reflects the number of records that were re-indexed.
B Aged (Attitudes Toward) 1978
R Age Discrimination 1994
Employment Discrimination 1994
Stereotyped Attitudes 1967

Agencies (Groups)
Use Organizations

Aggressive Behavior 1967
PN 14116 **SC** 01390
UF Agonistic Behavior
Fighting
B Social Behavior 1967
N Aggressive Driving Behavior 2004
↓ Animal Aggressive Behavior 1973
Attack Behavior 1973
Coercion 1994
↓ Conflict 1967
R ↓ Behavior Disorders 1971
Bullying 2003
Conduct Disorder 1991
Cruelty 1973
Retaliation 1991
↓ Social Interaction 1967
Torture 1988

Aggressive Driving Behavior 2004
PN 98 **SC** 01395
HN This term was introduced in June 2004. Relevant records were re-indexed with this term. The posting note reflects the number of records that were re-indexed.

Aggressive Driving Behavior — (cont'd)
UF Road Rage
B Aggressive Behavior 1967
Driving Behavior 1967
R Highway Safety 1973

Aggressiveness 1973
PN 2390 SC 01400
B Personality Traits 1967

Agility (Physical)
Use Physical Agility

Aging 1991
PN 11651 SC 01413
N Aging in Place 2007
Physiological Aging 1967
R ↓ Aged (Attitudes Toward) 1978
Aging (Attitudes Toward) 1985
Developmental Age Groups 1973
↓ Developmental Stages 1973
Generativity 2001
Geriatric Psychiatry 1997
Geriatric Psychotherapy 1973
Geriatrics 1967
Gerontology 1967
Geropsychology 2006
↓ Human Development 1967
Life Changes 2004
Life Expectancy 1982

Aging (Attitudes Toward) 1985
PN 838 SC 01415
SN Attitudes toward the aging process. Includes attitudes toward one's own physical aging and psychological and social maturation.
B Attitudes 1967
R Age Discrimination 1994
↓ Aged (Attitudes Toward) 1978
↓ Aging 1991
Geropsychology 2006
↓ Physical Development 1973
Physiological Aging 1967
↓ Psychosocial Development 1973
Self Perception 1967

Aging (Physiological)
Use Physiological Aging

Aging in Place 2007
PN 8 SC 01417
SN Enabling aging individuals to remain in their homes, retirement communities, or other familiar environments, even as their care needs grow.
HN This term was introduced in April 2007. Relevant records were re-indexed with this term. The posting note reflects the number of records that were re-indexed.
B Aging 1991
R Elder Care 1994
Home Environment 1973
↓ Living Arrangements 1991
Retirement Communities 1997
Self Care Skills 1978

Agitated Depression
Use Major Depression

Agitation 1991
PN 674 SC 01440
SN State usually characterized by restlessness, anxiety, and anguish.
R Akathisia 1991
↓ Anxiety 1967

Agitation — (cont'd)
Distress 1973
Restlessness 1973

Agnosia 1973
PN 548 SC 01450
SN Inability to recognize, understand, or interpret sensory stimuli in the absence of sensory defects. Also, the selective loss of knowledge of specific objects due to emotional disturbance, as seen in schizophrenia, hysteria, or depression.
B Aphasia 1967
Perceptual Disturbances 1973
N Anosognosia 1994
Prosopagnosia 1994

Agnosticism 2007
PN 11 SC 01472
SN A skeptical position holding that the truth or falsity of certain metaphysical ideas or propositions cannot be known. The word is most often used in regard to theological doctrines, especially belief in the existence of God.
HN This term was introduced in April 2007. Relevant records were re-indexed with this term. The posting note reflects the number of records that were re-indexed.
R Atheism 1973
God Concepts 1973
↓ Philosophies 1967
↓ Religious Beliefs 1973
Skepticism 2004

Agonistic Behavior
Use Aggressive Behavior

Agoraphobia 1973
PN 2288 SC 01480
SN Excessive fear of being alone, or being in public places or situations (e.g., in crowds or elevators) from which there is no easy escape or where help cannot be obtained in the event of an incapacitating reaction or panic.
B Phobias 1967

Agrammatism
Use Aphasia

Agraphia 1973
PN 344 SC 01490
SN Inability to write (letters, syllables, words, or phrases) due to an injury to a specific cerebral area or occasionally due to emotional factors.
B Aphasia 1967
R ↓ Learning Disabilities 1973

Agreeableness 1997
PN 273 SC 01495
SN Extent to which an individual is altruistic, sympathetic to others, and eager to help versus being egocentric and skeptical of others' intentions.
B Personality Traits 1967
R Adaptability (Personality) 1973
Cooperation 1967
Cynicism 1973
Egocentrism 1978
Empathy 1967
Five Factor Personality Model 1997
Likability 1988
Openmindedness 1978
↓ Tolerance 1973

Agricultural Extension Workers 1973
PN 68 SC 01500
SN Government employees (usually local, county, or state) who assist with agricultural matters, distribute educational materials, and provide services pertaining to agriculture.
UF County Agricultural Agents
Extension Workers (Agricultural)
B Government Personnel 1973
R ↓ Agricultural Workers 1973

Agricultural Workers 1973
PN 729 SC 01510
UF Farmers
Laborers (Farm)
B Nonprofessional Personnel 1982
N Migrant Farm Workers 1973
R Agricultural Extension Workers 1973
↓ Business and Industrial Personnel 1967

AIDS 2006
PN 8360 SC 01515
HN In May 2006, this term replaced the discontinued term ACQUIRED IMMUNE DEFICIENCY SYNDROME. ACQUIRED IMMUNE DEFICIENCY SYNDROME was removed from all records containing it and replaced with AIDS, its postable counterpart.
UF Acquired Immune Deficiency Syndrome
B HIV 2006
Sexually Transmitted Diseases 2003
Syndromes 1973
R AIDS (Attitudes Toward) 1997
AIDS Dementia Complex 1997
AIDS Prevention 1994
HIV Testing 1997
Safe Sex 2003
Zidovudine 1994

AIDS (Attitudes Toward) 1997
PN 638 SC 01516
B Physical Illness (Attitudes Toward) 1985
R AIDS 2006
AIDS Prevention 1994
↓ HIV 2006

AIDS Dementia Complex 1997
PN 76 SC 01514
SN Decline in mental functioning and cognitive capacity caused by late stage HIV infection.
HN Use AIDS and DEMENTIA to access references from 1988-1996.
B Dementia 1985
R AIDS 2006
↓ HIV 2006

AIDS Prevention 1994
PN 3547 SC 01517
SN Health related programs or services directed toward those at risk for HIV/AIDS. Includes prevention of HIV/AIDS and personal risk through health behavior and lifestyle characteristics.
B Prevention 1973
R AIDS 2006
AIDS (Attitudes Toward) 1997
Condoms 1991
↓ Harm Reduction 2003
↓ Health Behavior 1982
↓ Health Education 1973
Health Promotion 1991
↓ HIV 2006
HIV Testing 1997
Needle Exchange Programs 2001
Safe Sex 2003
Sexual Risk Taking 1997

AIDS Testing
Use HIV Testing

Air Encephalography
Use Pneumoencephalography

Air Force Personnel 1967
PN 1317 **SC** 01530
B Military Personnel 1967
R National Guard Personnel 1973

Air Traffic Accidents 1973
PN 306 **SC** 01540
B Transportation Accidents 1973
R Air Traffic Control 1973
Air Transportation 1973
↓ Aviation Safety 1973

Air Traffic Control 1973
PN 532 **SC** 01550
B Aviation Safety 1973
R Air Traffic Accidents 1973
Air Transportation 1973
↓ Transportation Accidents 1973

Air Transportation 1973
PN 321 **SC** 01560
B Transportation 1973
R Air Traffic Accidents 1973
Air Traffic Control 1973
↓ Aircraft 1973
Public Transportation 1973
Spacecraft 1973

Aircraft 1973
PN 394 **SC** 01570
UF Airplanes
N Helicopters 1973
R Air Transportation 1973
Aircraft Pilots 1973

Aircraft Crew
Use Aerospace Personnel

Aircraft Pilots 1973
PN 1994 **SC** 01580
UF Aviators
Pilots (Aircraft)
B Aerospace Personnel 1973
R ↓ Aircraft 1973
Astronauts 1973
↓ Aviation Safety 1973

Airplanes
Use Aircraft

Akathisia 1991
PN 288 **SC** 01595
SN The inability to remain in a sitting posture or motor restlessness, often resulting from heavy doses of tranquilizing drugs.
R Agitation 1991
Restlessness 1973
↓ Side Effects (Drug) 1973
↓ Symptoms 1967

Akinesia
Use Apraxia

Alanines 1973
PN 51 **SC** 01610
B Amino Acids 1973
N ↓ Phenylalanine 1973

Alanon
Use Alcohol Rehabilitation

Alarm Responses 1973
PN 493 **SC** 01620
SN Behavioral, emotional, or physiological reactions to actual or perceived physical threat. Used primarily for animal populations.
R ↓ Animal Defensive Behavior 1982
Animal Distress Calls 1973
Animal Escape Behavior 1973
↓ Animal Ethology 1967
↓ Fear 1967
Startle Reflex 1967
Tonic Immobility 1978

Alaska Natives 1997
PN 205 **SC** 01635
UF Native Alaskans
B Indigenous Populations 2001
R American Indians 1967
Inuit 2001
Minority Groups 1967
↓ Pacific Islanders 2001
Tribes 1973

Alateen
Use Alcohol Rehabilitation

Albinism 1973
PN 81 **SC** 01640
B Genetic Disorders 1973
R ↓ Eye Disorders 1973
↓ Skin Disorders 1973

Albino Rats
Use Rats

Alcohol (Grain)
Use Ethanol

Alcohol Abstinence
Use Sobriety

Alcohol Abuse 1988
PN 8607 **SC** 01660
HN In 1988, this term replaced the discontinued term PROBLEM DRINKING. In 2000, PROBLEM DRINKING was removed from all records containing it, and replaced with ALCOHOL ABUSE.
UF Problem Drinking
B Alcohol Drinking Patterns 1967
Drug Abuse 1973
N ↓ Alcoholism 1967
Binge Drinking 2006
R ↓ Alcohol Intoxication 1973
Alcohol Withdrawal 1994
Blood Alcohol Concentration 1994
Codependency 1991
Drug Abuse Liability 1994
Polydrug Abuse 1994
Underage Drinking 2007

Alcohol Addiction
Use Alcoholism

Alcohol Dehydrogenases 1973
PN 119 **SC** 01670
B Dehydrogenases 1973
R ↓ Alcohols 1967

Alcohol Dependence
Use Alcoholism

Alcohol Drinking Attitudes 1973
PN 1698 **SC** 01680
SN Attitudes toward the use or abuse of alcohol.
UF Drinking Attitudes
B Drug Usage Attitudes 1973
R Sobriety 1988

Alcohol Drinking Patterns 1967
PN 11677 **SC** 01690
UF Drinking (Alcohol)
B Drinking Behavior 1978
Drug Usage 1971
N ↓ Alcohol Abuse 1988
↓ Alcohol Intoxication 1973
Social Drinking 1973
R ↓ Alcoholism 1967
Binge Drinking 2006
Blood Alcohol Concentration 1994
Underage Drinking 2007

Alcohol Education
Use Drug Education

Alcohol Intoxication 1973
PN 1730 **SC** 01700
UF Drunkenness
Intoxication (Alcohol)
B Alcohol Drinking Patterns 1967
N Acute Alcoholic Intoxication 1973
Chronic Alcoholic Intoxication 1973
R ↓ Alcohol Abuse 1988
↓ Alcoholism 1967
Binge Drinking 2006
Blood Alcohol Concentration 1994
Driving Under the Influence 1988
↓ Toxic Disorders 1973
Toxic Psychoses 1973

Alcohol Rehabilitation 1982
PN 5659 **SC** 01705
SN Treatment for alcoholism or alcohol abuse which may include detoxification, psychotherapy, behavior therapy, Alcoholics Anonymous, and medication.
HN Use DRUG REHABILITATION to access references from 1973-1981.
UF Alanon
Alateen
B Drug Rehabilitation 1973
N Alcoholics Anonymous 1973
Detoxification 1973
R Alcohol Withdrawal 1994
Rehabilitation Counseling 1978
Sobriety 1988

Alcohol Withdrawal 1994
PN 626 **SC** 01707
SN Processes and symptomatic effects resulting from abstinence from alcohol. Used for both human and animal populations.
HN Use DRUG WITHDRAWAL to access references from 1973-1993.
B Drug Withdrawal 1973
R ↓ Alcohol Abuse 1988
↓ Alcohol Rehabilitation 1982
↓ Alcoholic Psychosis 1973
↓ Alcoholism 1967

Alcohol Withdrawal — (cont'd)
Detoxification 1973
Sobriety 1988

Alcoholic Beverages 1973
PN 940 **SC** 01710
UF Beverages (Alcoholic)
N Beer 1973
Liquor 1973
Wine 1973
R Beverages (Nonalcoholic) 1978
↓ Drinking Behavior 1978
Prenatal Exposure 1991

Alcoholic Hallucinosis 1973
PN 53 **SC** 01720
SN Hallucinations caused by cessation of heavy drinking.
B Alcoholic Psychosis 1973
Hallucinosis 1973
N Delirium Tremens 1973
Korsakoffs Psychosis 1973
Wernickes Syndrome 1973

Alcoholic Korsakoffs Syndrome
Use Korsakoffs Psychosis

Alcoholic Offspring
Use Children of Alcoholics

Alcoholic Psychosis 1973
PN 81 **SC** 01730
SN Psychotic condition caused by excessive use of alcohol.
B Alcoholism 1967
Organic Brain Syndromes 1973
Psychosis 1967
N ↓ Alcoholic Hallucinosis 1973
R Alcohol Withdrawal 1994
↓ Nutritional Deficiencies 1973
Toxic Psychoses 1973

Alcoholics Anonymous 1973
PN 750 **SC** 01740
SN A self-supporting, informal, international fellowship whose primary purpose is to help members achieve sobriety.
B Alcohol Rehabilitation 1982
Twelve Step Programs 1997
R ↓ Community Services 1967

Alcoholism 1967
PN 18914 **SC** 01750
UF Alcohol Addiction
Alcohol Dependence
B Addiction 1973
Alcohol Abuse 1988
N ↓ Alcoholic Psychosis 1973
R ↓ Alcohol Drinking Patterns 1967
↓ Alcohol Intoxication 1973
Alcohol Withdrawal 1994
Children of Alcoholics 2003
Fetal Alcohol Syndrome 1985
↓ Nutritional Deficiencies 1973
Sobriety 1988
↓ Toxic Disorders 1973

Alcohols 1967
PN 2555 **SC** 01760
B Drugs 1967
N Ethanol 1973
Isoproterenol 1973
Methanol 1973

Alcohols — (cont'd)
Methoxamine 1973
R Acetaldehyde 1982
Alcohol Dehydrogenases 1973
Blood Alcohol Concentration 1994
↓ Solvents 1982

Aldolases
HN Term was discontinued in 1997. In 2000, the term was removed from all records containing it, and replaced with ENZYMES, its postable counterpart.
Use Enzymes

Aldosterone 1973
PN 105 **SC** 01780
B Adrenal Cortex Hormones 1973
Corticosteroids 1973

Alexia 1982
PN 280 **SC** 01785
SN Inability to read which may be the result of neurological impairment. In a less severe form, often referred to as dyslexia.
UF Word Blindness
B Dysphasia 1978
N Dyslexia 1973
R ↓ Reading Disabilities 1967

Alexithymia 1982
PN 1222 **SC** 01788
SN Affective and cognitive disturbances characterized by impaired fantasy life and an inability to verbalize or differentiate emotions. These disturbances overlap diagnostic categories and appear generally in psychosomatic patients.
B Mental Disorders 1967

Algebra 2003
PN 154 **SC** 01790
SN Branch of mathematics that generalizes arithmetic by representing numbers with variables.
HN Use MATHEMATICS to access references from 1973 to June 2003.
B Mathematics 1982

Algorithms 1973
PN 2958 **SC** 01800
SN Set of well-defined rules established for step-by-step solution of problems in a finite number of steps.
B Mathematics (Concepts) 1967
R Computer Programming 2001
Heuristics 2003
Inductive Logic Programming 2007

Alienation 1971
PN 1663 **SC** 01810
SN Withdrawal or estrangement from persons, objects, or positions of former attachment; feelings of detachment from self or avoidance of emotional experiences.
B Emotional States 1973
R Anomie 1978
Depersonalization 1973
↓ Separation Reactions 1997

Alkaloids 1973
PN 343 **SC** 01820
HN In 1997, this term replaced the discontinued terms HOMATROPINE, QUINIDINE, and RAUWOLFIA. In 2000, these terms were removed from all records containing them, and replaced with ALKALOIDS.
UF Homatropine
Opium Alkaloids

Alkaloids — (cont'd)
Quinidine
Rauwolfia
B Drugs 1967
N Apomorphine 1973
Atropine 1973
Bromocriptine 1988
Caffeine 1973
↓ Cocaine 1973
Codeine 1973
Ephedrine 1973
↓ Gamma Aminobutyric Acid Antagonists 1985
Heroin 1973
Mescaline 1973
Morphine 1973
Nicotine 1973
Papaverine 1973
Peyote 1973
Physostigmine 1973
Pilocarpine 1973
Quinine 1973
Reserpine 1967
Scopolamine 1973
Strychnine 1973
Theophylline 1973
Tubocurarine 1973
R ↓ Anti Inflammatory Drugs 1982
Curare 1973
↓ Ergot Derivatives 1973

Allergens
Use Antigens

Allergic Disorders 1973
PN 311 **SC** 01830
B Immunologic Disorders 1973
N Allergic Skin Disorders 1973
Drug Allergies 1973
Food Allergies 1973
Hay Fever 1973
R Anaphylactic Shock 1973

Allergic Skin Disorders 1973
PN 33 **SC** 01840
B Allergic Disorders 1973
Skin Disorders 1973
R ↓ Dermatitis 1973
Eczema 1973
Neurodermatitis 1973

Allied Health Personnel 2007
PN 393 **SC** 01850
SN Health care personnel that do not include physicians, nurses, or dentists, but require special training and often licensure to assume their supporting roles.
HN In April 2007, this term was created to replace the discontinued term PARAMEDICAL PERSONNEL. PARAMEDICAL PERSONNEL was removed from all records containing it, and was replaced with ALLIED HEALTH PERSONNEL.
UF Auxiliary Health Workers
Medics
Paramedical Personnel
B Health Personnel 1994
N Occupational Therapists 1973
Physical Therapists 1973
Psychiatric Aides 1973
Speech Therapists 1973
R Home Care Personnel 1997

Alligators
Use Crocodilians

Allocation of Resources
Use Resource Allocation

Allport Vernon Lindzey Study Values
HN This term was discontinued in 1997. In 2000, ALLPORT VERNON LINDZEY STUDY VALUES was removed from all records containing it, and replaced with ATTITUDE MEASURES, its postable counterpart.
Use Attitude Measures

Alopecia 1973
PN 120 **SC** 01880
SN Baldness or the loss of hair.
UF Baldness
Hair Loss
B Skin Disorders 1973
R ↓ Genetic Disorders 1973
Hair 1973

Alpha Methylparatyrosine 1978
PN 136 **SC** 01887
UF Alpha Methyltyrosine
B Adrenergic Blocking Drugs 1973
Antihypertensive Drugs 1973
Tyrosine 1973

Alpha Methyltyrosine
Use Alpha Methylparatyrosine

Alpha Rhythm 1973
PN 847 **SC** 01890
SN Electrically measured impulses or waves of low amplitude and a frequency of 8-13 cycles per second usually observable in the electroencephalogram during wakeful rest.
B Electrical Activity 1967
Electroencephalography 1967

Alphabets 1973
PN 234 **SC** 01900
SN Systems for writing a language.
B Written Language 1967
N Initial Teaching Alphabet 1973
↓ Letters (Alphabet) 1973
R Orthography 1973

Alprazolam 1988
PN 605 **SC** 01903
B Benzodiazepines 1978
Minor Tranquilizers 1973
Sedatives 1973

Alternative Medicine 1997
PN 1336 **SC** 01904
SN Treatments, health care practices, or culturally based healing traditions which are not generally used in conventional medical practice.
UF Complementary Medicine
Homeopathic Medicine
B Treatment 1967
N Acupuncture 1973
Faith Healing 1973
Folk Medicine 1973
R Biofeedback Training 1978
Dietary Supplements 2001
Holistic Health 1985
↓ Hypnotherapy 1973
Massage 2001
Medical Treatment (General) 1973
↓ Medicinal Herbs and Plants 2001
Meditation 1973
Osteopathic Medicine 2003
Phototherapy 1991

Alternative Medicine — (cont'd)
↓ Physical Treatment Methods 1973
Preventive Medicine 1973
↓ Shock Therapy 1973
Transcultural Psychiatry 1973

Alternative Schools
Use Nontraditional Education

Altitude Effects 1973
PN 243 **SC** 01910
B Environmental Effects 1973
R ↓ Aviation 1967
↓ Gravitational Effects 1967

Altruism 1973
PN 1780 **SC** 01920
SN Consideration for well being of others as opposed to self-love or egoism. Used for human or animal populations.
B Personality Traits 1967
Prosocial Behavior 1982
R ↓ Assistance (Social Behavior) 1973
Charitable Behavior 1973
Heroes 2007
Sharing (Social Behavior) 1978

Aluminum 1994
PN 66 **SC** 01930
B Metallic Elements 1973

Alzheimer Disease
Use Alzheimers Disease

Alzheimers Disease 1973
PN 16302 **SC** 01940
SN Neurodegenerative disease characterized by the progressive loss of cognitive functioning.
UF Alzheimer Disease
Dementia of Alzheimers Type
B Neurodegenerative Diseases 2004
Organic Brain Syndromes 1973
Presenile Dementia 1973
R ↓ Dementia 1985
Dementia with Lewy Bodies 2001
Picks Disease 1973
↓ Senile Dementia 1973

Amantadine 1978
PN 169 **SC** 01945
UF Amatadine
B Antibiotics 1973
Antitremor Drugs 1973
R Parkinsons Disease 1973

Amatadine
Use Amantadine

Amaurotic Familial Idiocy
HN In June 2003, the term was discontinued and removed from all records containing it, and was replaced with TAY SACHS DISEASE, its postable counterpart.
Use Tay Sachs Disease

Ambidexterity
Use Handedness

Ambiguity (Stimulus)
Use Stimulus Ambiguity

Ambiguity (Tolerance)
Use Tolerance for Ambiguity

Ambition
Use Aspirations

Ambivalence 1973
PN 541 **SC** 01990
B Emotional States 1973

Amblyopia 1973
PN 286 **SC** 02000
SN An optically uncorrectable loss of visual acuity without apparent organic change or defect.
B Eye Disorders 1973
R ↓ Refraction Errors 1973
Strabismus 1973

Ambulatory Care
Use Outpatient Treatment

Amenorrhea 1973
PN 167 **SC** 02010
SN Absence or abnormal cessation of the menses.
B Menstrual Disorders 1973

Amentia
Use Mental Retardation

American Indians 1967
PN 3826 **SC** 02030
UF Indians (American)
Native Americans
B Indigenous Populations 2001
R Alaska Natives 1997
Inuit 2001
Minority Groups 1967
↓ Pacific Islanders 2001
Tribes 1973

American Psychological Association 2007
PN 293 **SC** 02036
SN Used when the activities of the American Psychological Association are the focus of the document.
HN This term was introduced in April 2007. Relevant records were re-indexed with this term. The posting note reflects the number of records that were re-indexed.
UF APA
B Professional Organizations 1973
R American Psychological Association Divisions 2007
↓ Membership 2007
↓ Psychologists 1967
↓ Psychology 1967

American Psychological Association Divisions 2007
PN 23 **SC** 02034
SN Used when the activities of the American Psychological Association's divisions are the focus of the document.
HN This term was introduced in April 2007. Relevant records were re-indexed with this term. The posting note reflects the number of records that were re-indexed.
UF APA Divisions
R American Psychological Association 2007
↓ Professional Organizations 1973
↓ Psychologists 1967
↓ Psychology 1967

Amine Oxidase Inhibitors 1973
PN 16 **SC** 02040
B Enzyme Inhibitors 1985
N ↓ Dopamine Antagonists 1982
Iproniazid 1973
Isocarboxazid 1973

Amine Oxidase Inhibitors — (cont'd)
Lysergic Acid Diethylamide 1967
Nialamide 1973
R ↓ Monoamine Oxidase Inhibitors 1973

Amines 1973
PN 623 **SC** 02060
HN In 1997, this term replaced the discontinued term CHLORISONDAMINE. In 2000, CHLORISONDAMINE was removed from all records containing it, and replaced with AMINES.
UF Chlorisondamine
B Drugs 1967
N Amitriptyline 1973
Atropine 1973
Bufotenine 1973
Chlordiazepoxide 1973
Chlorimipramine 1973
Chlorpromazine 1967
Chlorprothixene 1973
↓ Cocaine 1973
Diphenhydramine 1973
Galanthamine 1973
Guanethidine 1973
Histamine 1973
Imipramine 1973
Mecamylamine 1973
Meperidine 1973
Methylphenidate 1973
Orphenadrine 1973
Phenethylamines 1985
Phenoxybenzamine 1973
Physostigmine 1973
Puromycin 1973
Scopolamine 1973
Serotonin 1973
↓ Sympathomimetic Amines 1973
Thalidomide 1973
Trihexyphenidyl 1973
Tryptamine 1973
R ↓ Amino Acids 1973

Amino Acids 1973
PN 1402 **SC** 02070
SN Organic compounds containing both an amino group and a carboxyl group. Amino acids are the building blocks of proteins.
B Acids 1973
N ↓ Alanines 1973
↓ Aspartic Acid 1973
Cysteine 1973
DOPA 1973
Gamma Aminobutyric Acid 1978
Glutamic Acid 1973
Glutamine 1973
Glycine 1973
Histidine 1973
Leucine 1973
Methionine 1973
Neurokinins 1997
Proline 1982
↓ Tryptophan 1973
↓ Tyrosine 1973
R ↓ Amines 1973
Dietary Supplements 2001
Nerve Growth Factor 1994
↓ Neurotransmitters 1985
↓ Proteins 1973

Aminotransferases
Use Transaminases

Amitriptyline 1973
PN 1141 **SC** 02090
UF Elavil
B Amines 1973
Tranquilizing Drugs 1967
Tricyclic Antidepressant Drugs 1997

Amnesia 1967
PN 3393 **SC** 02120
SN Partial or complete loss of memory caused by organic or psychological factors. The loss may be temporary or permanent, and may involve old or recent memories. Compare FORGETTING and MEMORY DECAY.
B Memory Disorders 1973
N Anterograde Amnesia 2003
Global Amnesia 1997
Retrograde Amnesia 2003
R Dissociation 2001
↓ Dissociative Disorders 2001
False Memory 1997
Forgetting 1973
Korsakoffs Psychosis 1973
↓ Memory 1967
Memory Decay 1973
Repressed Memory 1997

Amniocentesis
Use Prenatal Diagnosis

Amniotic Fluid 1973
PN 56 **SC** 02130
B Body Fluids 1973

Amobarbital 1973
PN 253 **SC** 02140
UF Amobarbital Sodium
Amytal
B Barbiturates 1967
CNS Depressant Drugs 1973
Hypnotic Drugs 1973
Sedatives 1973

Amobarbital Sodium
Use Amobarbital

Amphetamine 1967
PN 3886 **SC** 02160
UF Amphetamine (dl-)
Amphetamine Sulfate
Benzedrine
B Adrenergic Drugs 1973
Appetite Depressing Drugs 1973
CNS Stimulating Drugs 1973
Dopamine Agonists 1985
Sympathomimetic Amines 1973
Vasoconstrictor Drugs 1973
N Dextroamphetamine 1973
Methamphetamine 1973
R Phenethylamines 1985

Amphetamine (d-)
Use Dextroamphetamine

Amphetamine (dl-)
Use Amphetamine

Amphetamine Sulfate
Use Amphetamine

Amphibia 1973
PN 132 **SC** 02200
B Vertebrates 1973
N Frogs 1967
Salamanders 1973
Toads 1973

Amplifiers (Apparatus) 1973
PN 50 **SC** 02210
B Apparatus 1967

Amplitude (Response)
Use Response Amplitude

Amputation 1973
PN 397 **SC** 02230
HN In 2000, this term replaced the discontinued and deleted term AMPUTEES. AMPUTEES was removed from all records containing it and replaced with AMPUTATION.
B Surgery 1971
N Mastectomy 1973
R Phantom Limbs 1973
↓ Prostheses 1973

Amygdala 2003
PN 3638 **SC** 02248
SN Almond-shaped mass of gray matter that is one of the four basal ganglia located in the anterior portion of the temporal lobe, and is part of the limbic system.
HN In June 2003, this term was created to replace the discontinued term AMYGDALOID BODY. AMYGDALOID BODY was removed from all records containing it and replaced with AMYGDALA.
UF Amygdaloid Body
Amygdaloid Nucleus
B Basal Ganglia 1973
Limbic System 1973
R Medial Forebrain Bundle 1982

Amygdaloid Body
HN In June 2003, the term was discontinued and removed from all records containing it, and was replaced with AMYGDALA, its postable counterpart.
Use Amygdala

Amygdaloid Nucleus
Use Amygdala

Amytal
Use Amobarbital

Anabolism
HN In August 2005, the term was discontinued and removed from all records containing it, and was replaced with BIOSYNTHESIS, its postable counterpart.
Use Biosynthesis

Anabolites
Use Metabolites

Anaclitic Depression 1973
PN 50 **SC** 02290
SN Syndrome of withdrawal characterizing infants separated from their mothers for a long period of time.
B Major Depression 1988
R Attachment Behavior 1985
Object Relations 1982
↓ Parental Absence 1973
↓ Separation Reactions 1997

Anagram Problem Solving 1973
PN 314 **SC** 02300
B Problem Solving 1967
R Anagrams 1973

Anagrams 1973
PN 55 **SC** 02310
SN Words or phrases made by rearranging letters of other words or phrases (e.g., leader from dealer).
B Vocabulary 1967
R Anagram Problem Solving 1973

Analeptic Drugs 1973
PN 111 **SC** 02320
UF Antagonists (CNS Depressant Drugs)
CNS Depressant Drug Antagonists
B CNS Stimulating Drugs 1973
N Bemegride 1973
Bicuculline 1994
Picrotoxin 1973
Strychnine 1973
R Caffeine 1973
↓ Cholinomimetic Drugs 1973
↓ Heart Rate Affecting Drugs 1973
Methylphenidate 1973
Pentylenetetrazol 1973
Theophylline 1973

Analgesia 1982
PN 2680 **SC** 02325
SN Pain insensitivity chemically or electrically induced or occurring as a natural phenomenon (e.g., Kiesow's area on the inner cheek).
B Pain Perception 1973
R ↓ Analgesic Drugs 1973
Anesthesia (Feeling) 1973
↓ Endorphins 1982
Enkephalins 1982
Pain Management 1994
Pain Measurement 1997

Analgesic Drugs 1973
PN 1720 **SC** 02330
UF Anodynes
Pain Relieving Drugs
B Drugs 1967
N Aspirin 1973
Atropine 1973
Carbamazepine 1988
Codeine 1973
Dihydroergotamine 1973
Heroin 1973
Meperidine 1973
Methadone 1973
Morphine 1973
Papaverine 1973
Pentazocine 1991
Procaine 1982
Quinine 1973
R Analgesia 1982
↓ Anesthetic Drugs 1973
↓ Anti Inflammatory Drugs 1982
↓ CNS Depressant Drugs 1973
↓ Hypnotic Drugs 1973
↓ Narcotic Drugs 1973
↓ Pain 1967
Pain Management 1994
↓ Sedatives 1973

Analog Computers 1973
PN 26 **SC** 02340
SN Electronic, mechanical, or electromechanical machines that measure continuous electrical or physical magnitudes (e.g., automobile speedometer) rather than operating on discrete digits.
B Computers 1967

Analogy 1991
PN 767 **SC** 02345
R Connotations 1973
↓ Figurative Language 1985
Inference 1973
Logical Thinking 1967
Metaphor 1982
↓ Reasoning 1967

Analysis 1967
PN 2358 **SC** 02370
SN Conceptually broad term referring to the process of examination of a complex problem, its elements, and their relations. Use a more specific term if possible.
N ↓ Behavior Analysis 2001
Causal Analysis 1994
Cohort Analysis 1988
↓ Content Analysis 1978
Content Analysis (Test) 1967
↓ Costs and Cost Analysis 1973
Error Analysis 1973
Item Analysis (Test) 1967
Job Analysis 1967
↓ Statistical Analysis 1967
Systems Analysis 1973
Task Analysis 1967
R Analysis of Covariance 1973
Analysis of Variance 1967
Functional Analysis 2001
Multidimensional Scaling 1982

Analysis of Covariance 1973
PN 708 **SC** 02350
B Variability Measurement 1973
R ↓ Analysis 1967
Analysis of Variance 1967
Multiple Regression 1982
↓ Multivariate Analysis 1982

Analysis of Variance 1967
PN 1549 **SC** 02360
UF ANOVA (Statistics)
B Variability Measurement 1973
R ↓ Analysis 1967
Analysis of Covariance 1973
Homogeneity of Variance 2003
Multiple Regression 1982
↓ Multivariate Analysis 1982
↓ Statistical Regression 1985

Analysts
Use Psychoanalysts

Analytic Psychology
Use Jungian Psychology

Analytical Psychotherapy 1973
PN 943 **SC** 02390
SN Form of psychotherapy based on work of C. G. Jung. The unconscious, personal and collective, is disclosed through free association and dream analysis. Therapeutic goals include integration of conscious and unconscious for growth and personality development and a life of fuller awareness.

Analytical Psychotherapy — (cont'd)
UF Jungian Psychotherapy
B Psychotherapy 1967
R Archetypes 1991
↓ Collective Unconscious 1997
Jung (Carl) 1973
↓ Jungian Psychology 1973

Anankastic Personality
Use Obsessive Compulsive Personality Disorder

Anaphylactic Shock 1973
PN 28 **SC** 02400
SN Immunologic or allergic reaction to antigens such as drugs or foreign proteins to which a hypersensitivity has been established by previous contact.
UF Protein Sensitization
Sensitization (Protein)
B Immunologic Disorders 1973
R ↓ Allergic Disorders 1973
Shock 1967

Anatomical Systems 1973
PN 70 **SC** 02410
SN Conceptually broad term referring to anatomically related structures (e.g., vascular system). Use a more specific term if possible.
B Anatomy 1967
Systems 1967
N ↓ Cardiovascular System 1967
↓ Digestive System 1967
↓ Endocrine System 1973
↓ Immune System 2006
↓ Musculoskeletal System 1973
↓ Nervous System 1967
↓ Respiratory System 1973
↓ Urogenital System 1973

Anatomically Detailed Dolls 1991
PN 78 **SC** 02415
SN Dolls used in a general play setting or for evaluation and assessment purposes in a therapeutic or legal context.
B Toys 1973
R ↓ Child Abuse 1971
↓ Childhood Play Behavior 1978
Clinical Judgment (Not Diagnosis) 1973
Doll Play 1973
↓ Sexual Abuse 1988

Anatomy 1967
PN 1532 **SC** 02420
SN Conceptually broad array term referring both to the science of anatomy and the actual structure or morphology of an organism. Use specific anatomical or neuroanatomical terms if possible.
N Abdomen 1973
↓ Anatomical Systems 1973
Back (Anatomy) 1973
↓ Body Fluids 1973
Breast 1973
↓ Cells (Biology) 1973
Face (Anatomy) 1973
Feet (Anatomy) 1973
Hair 1973
Hand (Anatomy) 1967
Head (Anatomy) 1973
Neck (Anatomy) 1973
Palm (Anatomy) 1973
Scalp (Anatomy) 1973
↓ Sense Organs 1973
Thigh 1973
↓ Tissues (Body) 1973

Anatomy — (cont'd)
R Human Body 2003
Morphology 1973
Neuroanatomy 1967
↓ Physiology 1967

Ancestors 1973
PN 84 SC 02430
UF Great Grandparents
B Family Members 1973
N Grandparents 1973
↓ Parents 1967

Androgen Antagonists
Use Antiandrogens

Androgen Insensitivity Syndrome
Use Testicular Feminization Syndrome

Androgens 1973
PN 891 SC 02440
B Sex Hormones 1973
N Testosterone 1973
R Antiandrogens 1982
Antiestrogens 1982

Androgyny 1982
PN 799 SC 02445
SN Combination of masculine and feminine personality characteristics in one individual.
B Personality Traits 1967
R Femininity 1967
↓ Gender Identity 1985
↓ Human Sex Differences 1967
Masculinity 1967
Sex Roles 1967

Anemia 1973
PN 236 SC 02450
B Blood and Lymphatic Disorders 1973
R ↓ Genetic Disorders 1973
Sickle Cell Disease 1994

Anencephaly 1973
PN 12 SC 02460
SN Congenital disorder that results in the absence of all or a major part of the brain.
B Brain Disorders 1967
Mental Retardation 1967
Neonatal Disorders 1973
R Spina Bifida 1978

Anesthesia (Feeling) 1973
PN 287 SC 02470
R Analgesia 1982
↓ Physical Disorders 1997
↓ Sense Organ Disorders 1973
↓ Tactual Perception 1967

Anesthesiology 1973
PN 180 SC 02480
B Medical Sciences 1967

Anesthetic Drugs 1973
PN 823 SC 02490
B Drugs 1967
N ↓ General Anesthetics 1973
Hexobarbital 1973
Ketamine 1997
↓ Local Anesthetics 1973
Pentobarbital 1973
Phencyclidine 1982
Procaine 1982

Anesthetic Drugs — (cont'd)
R ↓ Analgesic Drugs 1973
↓ Anticonvulsive Drugs 1973
↓ Barbiturates 1967
↓ CNS Depressant Drugs 1973
↓ Hypnotic Drugs 1973
↓ Muscle Relaxing Drugs 1973
↓ Narcotic Drugs 1973
↓ Sedatives 1973

Aneurysms 1973
PN 201 SC 02500
B Cardiovascular Disorders 1967

Anger 1967
PN 4505 SC 02510
UF Rage
B Emotional States 1973
N Hostility 1967
R Anger Control 1997
Hate 1973
Jealousy 1973
Tantrums 1973

Anger Control 1997
PN 449 SC 02520
UF Anger Management
B Emotional Control 1973
R ↓ Anger 1967
↓ Behavior Modification 1973
↓ Behavior Therapy 1967
Explosive Disorder 2001
Self Control 1973

Anger Management
Use Anger Control

Angina Pectoris 1973
PN 210 SC 02530
B Heart Disorders 1973
R Myocardial Infarctions 1973

Angiography 1973
PN 62 SC 02540
B Roentgenography 1973

Angiotensin 1973
PN 553 SC 02550
B Neuropeptides 2003
Peptides 1973
Vasoconstrictor Drugs 1973
R Captopril 1991

Anglos 1988
PN 528 SC 02553
SN Generally applied to English-speaking White populations of non-Hispanic descent.
HN From 2000, used only to reflect author's terminology.
B Whites 1982

Angst
Use Anxiety

Anguish
Use Distress

Anhedonia 1985
PN 361 SC 02575
SN Loss or absence of ability to experience pleasure.
B Symptoms 1967
R Dysthymic Disorder 1988
↓ Neurosis 1967

Anhedonia — (cont'd)
Pleasure 1973
↓ Schizophrenia 1967

Animal Aggressive Behavior 1973
PN 6071 SC 02580
B Aggressive Behavior 1967
Animal Social Behavior 1967
N Animal Predatory Behavior 1978
Attack Behavior 1973
Muricide 1988
Threat Postures 1973
R Animal Dominance 1973
Territoriality 1967

Animal Assisted Therapy 1994
PN 189 SC 02585
SN A type of therapy based on the human-animal companion bond used in an effort to assist in restoring feelings of hope, self worth, responsibility, and communication.
UF Pet Therapy
B Psychotherapeutic Techniques 1967
R ↓ Animals 1967
Geriatric Psychotherapy 1973
Interspecies Interaction 1991
Pets 1982
↓ Rehabilitation 1967

Animal Behavior
Use Animal Ethology

Animal Biological Rhythms 1973
PN 620 SC 02600
SN Rhythmic and periodic variations in behavioral or physiological functions of animals.
HN Use BIOLOGICAL RHYTHMS to access references from 1967-1972.
UF Biological Clocks (Animal)
B Animal Ethology 1967
Biological Rhythms 1967
N Animal Circadian Rhythms 1973
R Animal Sexual Receptivity 1973
Estrus 1973
Hibernation 1973

Animal Breeding 1973
PN 3803 SC 02610
SN Propagation (or reproduction) of a species in its natural environment or in captive settings. Includes birth rate and breeding success. Compare ANIMAL DOMESTICATION, EUGENICS, and SELECTIVE BREEDING.
UF Breeding (Animal)
N Selective Breeding 1973
R Animal Captivity 1994
Animal Domestication 1978
↓ Animal Mating Behavior 1967
↓ Animal Sexual Behavior 1985
Animal Strain Differences 1982
↓ Animals 1967
Assortative Mating 1991
↓ Genetics 1967
Litter Size 1985
↓ Sexual Reproduction 1973

Animal Captivity 1994
PN 823 SC 02615
UF Captivity (Animal)
Zoo Environment
B Animal Environments 1967
R ↓ Animal Breeding 1973
Animal Domestication 1978
Animal Rearing 1991

Animal Captivity — (cont'd)
Animal Welfare 1985

Animal Circadian Rhythms 1973
PN 3239 **SC** 02620
SN Diurnal cyclical variations or patterns of behavioral or physiological functions of animals.
HN Use BIOLOGICAL RHYTHMS to access references from 1967-1972.
UF Circadian Rhythms (Animal)
Daily Biological Rhythms (Animal)
B Animal Biological Rhythms 1973
R Animal Nocturnal Behavior 1973

Animal Coloration 1985
PN 563 **SC** 02625
SN Physical aspect of body color.
R Animal Courtship Displays 1973
↓ Animal Defensive Behavior 1982
↓ Pigments 1973

Animal Communication 1967
PN 2201 **SC** 02630
B Animal Social Behavior 1967
Communication 1967
N Animal Distress Calls 1973
R Animal Scent Marking 1985
↓ Animal Vocalizations 1973
↓ Vocalization 1967

Animal Courtship Behavior 1973
PN 1367 **SC** 02640
UF Courtship (Animal)
B Animal Sexual Behavior 1985
Animal Social Behavior 1967
N Animal Courtship Displays 1973
R Animal Mate Selection 1982
↓ Animal Mating Behavior 1967

Animal Courtship Displays 1973
PN 419 **SC** 02650
UF Courtship Displays (Animal)
B Animal Courtship Behavior 1973
Animal Social Behavior 1967
R Animal Coloration 1985
↓ Animal Mating Behavior 1967
Territoriality 1967

Animal Defensive Behavior 1982
PN 2683 **SC** 02652
SN Innate protective responses that occur in presence of predator or other threatening stimulus.
UF Defensive Behavior (Animal)
B Animal Ethology 1967
N Animal Escape Behavior 1973
Threat Postures 1973
R Alarm Responses 1973
Animal Coloration 1985
Animal Distress Calls 1973
Attack Behavior 1973
Instinctive Behavior 1982
Tonic Immobility 1978

Animal Development 1978
PN 3644 **SC** 02655
SN Conceptually broad term. Use a more specific term if possible.
B Development 1967
R Age Differences 1967
↓ Animals 1967
↓ Motor Development 1973
↓ Neural Development 1985
Perceptual Motor Development 1991

Animal Development — (cont'd)
↓ Physical Development 1973
↓ Prenatal Development 1973

Animal Distress Calls 1973
PN 388 **SC** 02660
UF Distress Calls (Animal)
B Animal Communication 1967
Animal Vocalizations 1973
R Alarm Responses 1973
↓ Animal Defensive Behavior 1982
Instinctive Behavior 1982

Animal Division of Labor 1973
PN 310 **SC** 02670
UF Division of Labor (Animal)
B Animal Social Behavior 1967
Division of Labor 1988
R Animal Dominance 1973

Animal Domestication 1978
PN 242 **SC** 02677
SN Adaptation of wild animals to life and breeding in tame conditions according to the interests of human society. Compare ANIMAL BREEDING, EUGENICS, and SELECTIVE BREEDING.
UF Domestication (Animal)
R ↓ Animal Breeding 1973
Animal Captivity 1994
Pets 1982
Selective Breeding 1973

Animal Dominance 1973
PN 2462 **SC** 02680
UF Dominance (Animal)
Pecking Order
B Animal Social Behavior 1967
Dominance 1967
R ↓ Animal Aggressive Behavior 1973
Animal Division of Labor 1973
Animal Scent Marking 1985
Dominance Hierarchy 1973
Territoriality 1967

Animal Drinking Behavior 1973
PN 2125 **SC** 02690
UF Drinking Behavior (Animal)
B Animal Ethology 1967
Drinking Behavior 1978
R ↓ Ingestion 2001
Licking 1988
Polydipsia 1982
Sucking 1978
Thirst 1967
Water Intake 1967

Animal Emotionality 1978
PN 1334 **SC** 02696
UF Emotionality (Animal)
R Animal Motivation 1967
↓ Emotional Responses 1967

Animal Environments 1967
PN 7639 **SC** 02700
SN Physical and social conditions of an animal's existence or habitat.
UF Habitats (Animal)
B Social Environments 1973
N Animal Captivity 1994
R Animal Rearing 1991
↓ Animals 1967
Place Conditioning 1991
↓ Single Sex Environments 2001

Animal Escape Behavior 1973
PN 961 **SC** 02710
UF Escape Behavior (Animal)
B Animal Defensive Behavior 1982
R Alarm Responses 1973

Animal Ethology 1967
PN 7818 **SC** 02720
SN Study of animal behavior especially in relation to ecology, evolution, neuroanatomy, neurophysiology, and genetics. Used for the discipline or the ethological processes themselves. Use a more specific term if possible.
UF Animal Behavior
Ethology (Animal)
B Behavior 1967
N ↓ Animal Biological Rhythms 1973
↓ Animal Defensive Behavior 1982
Animal Drinking Behavior 1973
Animal Exploratory Behavior 1973
Animal Feeding Behavior 1973
Animal Foraging Behavior 1985
Animal Grooming Behavior 1978
Animal Hoarding Behavior 1973
Animal Homing 1991
Animal Nocturnal Behavior 1973
Animal Open Field Behavior 1973
↓ Animal Parental Behavior 1982
Animal Play 1973
Animal Sex Differences 1967
↓ Animal Sexual Behavior 1985
↓ Animal Social Behavior 1967
↓ Animal Vocalizations 1973
Hibernation 1973
Imprinting 1967
Licking 1988
Migratory Behavior (Animal) 1973
Nest Building 1973
Species Recognition 1985
Territoriality 1967
R Alarm Responses 1973
Animal Motivation 1967
↓ Animals 1967
Echolocation 1973
Instinctive Behavior 1982
Stereotyped Behavior 1973
Tool Use 1991

Animal Exploratory Behavior 1973
PN 2134 **SC** 02730
HN Use EXPLORATORY BEHAVIOR to access references from 1967-1972.
B Animal Ethology 1967
Exploratory Behavior 1967
R Animal Foraging Behavior 1985
Instinctive Behavior 1982
Neophobia 1985
Spontaneous Alternation 1982

Animal Feeding Behavior 1973
PN 6655 **SC** 02740
UF Feeding Behavior (Animal)
B Animal Ethology 1967
R Animal Foraging Behavior 1985
Animal Maternal Behavior 1973
Animal Paternal Behavior 1991
Cannibalism 2003
Food Intake 1967
Hunger 1967
↓ Ingestion 2001
Sucking 1978

Animal Foraging Behavior 1985
PN 2891 **SC** 02743
UF Foraging (Animal)
B Animal Ethology 1967
R Animal Exploratory Behavior 1973
Animal Feeding Behavior 1973
Animal Predatory Behavior 1978

Animal Grooming Behavior 1978
PN 897 **SC** 02745
UF Grooming Behavior (Animal)
B Animal Ethology 1967
R Licking 1988

Animal Hoarding Behavior 1973
PN 314 **SC** 02750
UF Hoarding Behavior (Animal)
B Animal Ethology 1967
Hoarding Behavior 2003

Animal Homing 1991
PN 223 **SC** 02755
SN Returning accurately to one's home or natal area from a distance.
UF Homing (Animal)
B Animal Ethology 1967
R Instinctive Behavior 1982
Migratory Behavior (Animal) 1973
Territoriality 1967

Animal Human Interaction
Use Interspecies Interaction

Animal Innate Behavior
HN Term was discontinued in 1982. In 2000, the term was removed from all records containing it, and replaced with INSTINCTIVE BEHAVIOR, its postable counterpart.
Use Instinctive Behavior

Animal Instinctive Behavior
HN Term was discontinued in 1982. In 2000, the term was removed from all records containing it, and replaced with INSTINCTIVE BEHAVIOR, its postable counterpart.
Use Instinctive Behavior

Animal Learning 2003
PN 1588 **SC** 02772
SN Used for discussions, hypotheses, or theories of learning in animals; includes theories on cognitive processing. Applicable to all nonhuman species. Compare CONDITIONING.
HN This term was introduced in June 2003. Relevant records were re-indexed with this term. The posting note reflects the number of records that were re-indexed.
B Learning 1967
N Cat Learning 1967
Rat Learning 1967
R Comparative Psychology 1967
↓ Conditioning 1967
Learning Ability 1973

Animal Licking Behavior
Use Licking

Animal Locomotion 1982
PN 4205 **SC** 02775
SN Any form of motor activity resulting in bodily propulsion.
B Locomotion 2007
Motor Processes 1967

Animal Mate Selection 1982
PN 2200 **SC** 02778
SN Ethological processes surrounding the choice of mate for sexual reproduction.
UF Mate Selection
R ↓ Animal Courtship Behavior 1973
↓ Animal Mating Behavior 1967
↓ Animal Sexual Behavior 1985
Assortative Mating 1991
↓ Genetics 1967
↓ Sexual Reproduction 1973

Animal Maternal Behavior 1973
PN 3354 **SC** 02780
UF Maternal Behavior (Animal)
B Animal Parental Behavior 1982
R Animal Feeding Behavior 1973
Animal Maternal Deprivation 1988
Animal Paternal Behavior 1991
Animal Rearing 1991
Licking 1988

Animal Maternal Deprivation 1988
PN 333 **SC** 02785
HN Consider using ANIMAL MATERNAL BEHAVIOR prior to 1988.
R Animal Maternal Behavior 1973
Animal Rearing 1991
↓ Social Isolation 1967

Animal Mating Behavior 1967
PN 6679 **SC** 02790
UF Coitus (Animal)
Copulation (Animal)
Mating Behavior (Animal)
B Animal Sexual Behavior 1985
Animal Social Behavior 1967
N Animal Sexual Receptivity 1973
R ↓ Animal Breeding 1973
↓ Animal Courtship Behavior 1973
Animal Courtship Displays 1973
Animal Mate Selection 1982
Assortative Mating 1991
Nest Building 1973
Pheromones 1973
↓ Sexual Reproduction 1973

Animal Models 1988
PN 6945 **SC** 02797
SN Experimentally induced simulations of human conditions in animals designed to investigate the etiology and characteristics of diseases, psychological and psychiatric disorders, or learning processes.
B Models 1967
R ↓ Animals 1967
↓ Experimental Design 1967
↓ Experimentation 1967

Animal Motivation 1967
PN 1661 **SC** 02800
B Motivation 1967
R Animal Emotionality 1978
↓ Animal Ethology 1967
↓ Animals 1967
Instinctive Behavior 1982

Animal Navigation
Use Migratory Behavior (Animal)

Animal Nocturnal Behavior 1973
PN 197 **SC** 02820
UF Nocturnal Behavior (Animal)
B Animal Ethology 1967
R Animal Circadian Rhythms 1973

Animal Open Field Behavior 1973
PN 2180 **SC** 02825
SN Spontaneous animal behavior studied in relatively unrestricted laboratory environments.
HN Prior to 1985 also used for spontaneous animal behavior in natural environments.
UF Open Field Behavior (Animal)
B Animal Ethology 1967

Animal Parental Behavior 1982
PN 1338 **SC** 02828
SN Nurturance and care of offspring performed by male and/or female parents.
UF Parental Behavior (Animal)
B Animal Ethology 1967
Animal Social Behavior 1967
N Animal Maternal Behavior 1973
Animal Paternal Behavior 1991
R Animal Rearing 1991
Parental Investment 1997

Animal Paternal Behavior 1991
PN 401 **SC** 02829
B Animal Parental Behavior 1982
R Animal Feeding Behavior 1973
Animal Maternal Behavior 1973
Animal Rearing 1991

Animal Play 1973
PN 615 **SC** 02830
UF Play (Animal)
B Animal Ethology 1967
R ↓ Animal Social Behavior 1967

Animal Predatory Behavior 1978
PN 2374 **SC** 02834
UF Predatory Behavior (Animal)
B Animal Aggressive Behavior 1973
R Animal Foraging Behavior 1985
Attack Behavior 1973
Instinctive Behavior 1982
Threat Postures 1973

Animal Rearing 1991
PN 979 **SC** 02836
SN Conditions or environment in which animals are bred, nourished, and raised. Compare ANIMAL PARENTAL BEHAVIOR.
R Animal Captivity 1994
↓ Animal Environments 1967
Animal Maternal Behavior 1973
Animal Maternal Deprivation 1988
↓ Animal Parental Behavior 1982
Animal Paternal Behavior 1991

Animal Scent Marking 1985
PN 460 **SC** 02837
UF Scent Marking (Animal)
R ↓ Animal Communication 1967
Animal Dominance 1973
Pheromones 1973
Territoriality 1967

Animal Sex Differences 1967
PN 4833 **SC** 02840
SN Animal behavioral, developmental, and physiological/anatomical differences between the sexes.

Animal Sex Differences — (cont'd)
UF Sex Differences (Animal)
B Animal Ethology 1967
R Sex 1967
Sex Recognition 1997
↓ Single Sex Environments 2001

Animal Sexual Behavior 1985
PN 2897 SC 02845
SN Any form of sexual behavior in animals.
B Animal Ethology 1967
N ↓ Animal Courtship Behavior 1973
↓ Animal Mating Behavior 1967
R ↓ Animal Breeding 1973
Animal Mate Selection 1982
Instinctive Behavior 1982
Sex 1967

Animal Sexual Receptivity 1973
PN 1454 SC 02850
UF Lordosis (Animal)
Sexual Receptivity (Animal)
B Animal Mating Behavior 1967
R ↓ Animal Biological Rhythms 1973
Estrus 1973

Animal Social Behavior 1967
PN 8554 SC 02860
B Animal Ethology 1967
Social Behavior 1967
N ↓ Animal Aggressive Behavior 1973
↓ Animal Communication 1967
↓ Animal Courtship Behavior 1973
Animal Courtship Displays 1973
Animal Division of Labor 1973
Animal Dominance 1973
↓ Animal Mating Behavior 1967
↓ Animal Parental Behavior 1982
R Animal Play 1973
Interspecies Interaction 1991
Physical Contact 1982

Animal Strain Differences 1982
PN 3613 SC 02863
SN Anatomical, physiological, and/or behavioral variations between members of different subspecies or strains. Compare SPECIES DIFFERENCES.
HN Use GENETICS and ANIMAL BREEDING together to access references from 1973-1981.
UF Strain Differences (Animal)
R ↓ Animal Breeding 1973
↓ Genetics 1967

Animal Tool Use
Use Tool Use

Animal Vocalizations 1973
PN 4840 SC 02870
UF Vocalizations (Animal)
B Animal Ethology 1967
Vocalization 1967
N Animal Distress Calls 1973
R ↓ Animal Communication 1967
Echolocation 1973

Animal Welfare 1985
PN 892 SC 02875
R Animal Captivity 1994
Experimental Ethics 1978

Animals 1967
PN 4309 SC 02880
SN Conceptually broad term. Use a more specific term if possible (e.g., VERTEBRATES, MAMMALS, DOGS).
N Female Animals 1973
Infants (Animal) 1978
↓ Invertebrates 1973
Male Animals 1973
↓ Vertebrates 1973
R Animal Assisted Therapy 1994
↓ Animal Breeding 1973
Animal Development 1978
↓ Animal Environments 1967
↓ Animal Ethology 1967
Animal Models 1988
Animal Motivation 1967
Biological Symbiosis 1973
Interspecies Interaction 1991
Pets 1982
Species Differences 1982

Animism 1973
PN 105 SC 02890
SN Ascribing life to inanimate objects. Also, the Piagetian stage of development in which children ascribe emotional attributes and intentions to inanimate objects.
B Philosophies 1967
R Ethnology 1967
Myths 1967
Taboos 1973

Ankle 1973
PN 69 SC 02900
B Joints (Anatomy) 1973
R Feet (Anatomy) 1973
Leg (Anatomy) 1973

Anniversary Events 1994
PN 29 SC 02905
SN Annual occurrence of a specific date that marks a notable event or experience. Includes aspects of both positive or negative reactions to the event or experience.
UF Anniversary Reactions
B Experiences (Events) 1973
R Autobiographical Memory 1994
Early Experience 1967
Early Memories 1985
↓ Life Experiences 1973
Life Review 1991
Reminiscence 1985
Traditions 2007

Anniversary Reactions
Use Anniversary Events

Annual Leave
Use Employee Leave Benefits

Anodynes
Use Analgesic Drugs

Anomie 1978
PN 238 SC 02940
SN Sense of alienation or despair resulting from the loss or weakening of previously held values. Also, a state of lawlessness or a lack of normative standards within groups or societies.

Anomie — (cont'd)
B Social Processes 1967
R Alienation 1971
Personal Values 1973
Social Values 1973

Anonymity 1973
PN 318 SC 02945
SN Unknown, unacknowledged, or concealed personal identity.
R Privileged Communication 1973
Secrecy 1994
Self Disclosure 1973
↓ Social Perception 1967

Anorexia Nervosa 1973
PN 6060 SC 02950
SN Syndrome in which the primary features include excessive fear of becoming overweight, body image disturbance, significant weight loss, refusal to maintain minimal normal weight, and amenorrhea. This disorder occurs most frequently in adolescent females.
B Eating Disorders 1997
Underweight 1973
R ↓ Body Image Disturbances 1973
Bulimia 1985
↓ Nutritional Deficiencies 1973
↓ Somatoform Disorders 2001

Anorexigenic Drugs
Use Appetite Depressing Drugs

Anosmia 1973
PN 231 SC 02970
SN Loss of the sense of smell.
UF Olfactory Impairment
B Sense Organ Disorders 1973
R ↓ Olfactory Perception 1967
Taste Disorders 2001

Anosognosia 1994
PN 140 SC 02975
SN Lack of awareness of, or refusal or failure to deal with or recognize that one has a mental or physical disorder.
B Agnosia 1973
R Coping Behavior 1967
Denial 1973
Illness Behavior 1982

ANOVA (Statistics)
Use Analysis of Variance

Anoxia 1973
PN 823 SC 02990
SN Absence or reduction of oxygen in body tissue.
UF Asphyxia
Hypoxia
Suffocation
B Symptoms 1967
R ↓ Ischemia 1973
↓ Respiratory Distress 1973

Antabuse
Use Disulfiram

Antagonism
Use Hostility

Antagonists (CNS Depressant Drugs)
Use Analeptic Drugs

Anterograde Amnesia 2003
PN 94 **SC** 03015
SN Memory loss for events and experiences that occurred after the incident that produced the amnesia.
HN This term was introduced in June 2003. Relevant records were re-indexed with this term. The posting note reflects the number of records that were re-indexed.
B Amnesia 1967
R Global Amnesia 1997
Retrograde Amnesia 2003

Anthropologists 1973
PN 158 **SC** 03030
B Professional Personnel 1978
R Scientists 1967
Sociologists 1973

Anthropology 1967
PN 1985 **SC** 03040
SN Science dealing with the study of the interrelations of biological, cultural, geographical, and historical characteristics of the human species. Use a more specific term if possible.
B Social Sciences 1967
R Ethnography 1973
Ethnology 1967
Folk Psychology 1997
Museums 2006

Anti Inflammatory Drugs 1982
PN 464 **SC** 03041
SN Agents that reduce inflammation by acting on body mechanisms, without directly antagonizing the causative agent.
UF Antipyretic Drugs
B Drugs 1967
N Aspirin 1973
↓ Glucocorticoids 1982
R ↓ Alkaloids 1973
↓ Analgesic Drugs 1973
↓ Enzymes 1973
↓ Hormones 1967
Hydrocortisone 1973
Neurokinins 1997
Prostaglandins 1982
↓ Steroids 1973

Antiadrenergic Drugs
Use Sympatholytic Drugs

Antiandrogens 1982
PN 140 **SC** 03042
SN Substances capable of preventing the normal effects of androgenic hormones on responsive tissues by antagonistic effects on tissue or by inhibiting androgenic effects.
UF Androgen Antagonists
B Drugs 1967
R ↓ Androgens 1973
↓ Estrogens 1973
↓ Steroids 1973

Antianxiety Drugs
Use Tranquilizing Drugs

Antibiotics 1973
PN 413 **SC** 03050
B Drugs 1967
N Amantadine 1978
Cycloheximide 1973
Penicillins 1973
Puromycin 1973

Antibiotics — (cont'd)
R Antineoplastic Drugs 1982

Antibodies 1973
PN 803 **SC** 03060
B Globulins 1973
Immunologic Factors 2003
R Antigens 1982
Blood Serum 1973
↓ Drugs 1967
Gamma Globulin 1973
↓ Immune System 2006
Immunization 1973
↓ Immunoglobulins 1973
↓ Neurotoxins 1982

Anticholinergic Drugs
Use Cholinergic Blocking Drugs

Anticholinesterase Drugs
Use Cholinesterase Inhibitors

Anticipation (Serial Learning)
Use Serial Anticipation (Learning)

Anticoagulant Drugs 1973
PN 57 **SC** 03100
B Drugs 1967
N Heparin 1973

Anticonvulsive Drugs 1973
PN 2809 **SC** 03110
HN In 1982, this term replaced the discontinued term ANTIEPILEPTIC DRUGS, and in 1997 it replaced PARALDEHYDE. In 2000, these terms were removed from all records containing them, and replaced with ANTICONVULSIVE DRUGS.
UF Antiepileptic Drugs
Paraldehyde
B Drugs 1967
N Carbamazepine 1988
Chloral Hydrate 1973
Clonazepam 1991
Diphenylhydantoin 1973
Nitrazepam 1978
Oxazepam 1978
Pentobarbital 1973
Phenobarbital 1973
Primidone 1973
Valproic Acid 1991
R Acetazolamide 1973
↓ Anesthetic Drugs 1973
↓ Antispasmodic Drugs 1973
↓ Barbiturates 1967
↓ Benzodiazepines 1978
↓ CNS Depressant Drugs 1973
↓ Epilepsy 1967
↓ Hypnotic Drugs 1973
↓ Muscle Relaxing Drugs 1973
↓ Narcotic Drugs 1973
↓ Sedatives 1973
↓ Seizures 2005
↓ Spasms 1973
↓ Tranquilizing Drugs 1967

Antidepressant Drugs 1971
PN 10376 **SC** 03120
HN In 1997, this term replaced the discontinued term DEANOL. In 2000, DEANOL was removed from all records and replaced with ANTIDEPRESSANT DRUGS.

Antidepressant Drugs — (cont'd)
UF Deanol
B Drugs 1967
N Bupropion 1994
Citalopram 1997
Fluoxetine 1991
Fluvoxamine 1994
Iproniazid 1973
Isocarboxazid 1973
Lithium Carbonate 1973
Methylphenidate 1973
Mianserin 1982
Moclobemide 1997
Molindone 1982
Nefazodone 2003
Nialamide 1973
Nomifensine 1982
Paroxetine 1994
Phenelzine 1973
Pheniprazine 1973
Pipradrol 1973
↓ Serotonin Norepinephrine Reuptake Inhibitors 2007
Sertraline 1997
Sulpiride 1973
Tranylcypromine 1973
Trazodone 1988
↓ Tricyclic Antidepressant Drugs 1997
Venlafaxine 2003
Zimeldine 1988
R ↓ CNS Stimulating Drugs 1973
↓ Lithium 1973
↓ Monoamine Oxidase Inhibitors 1973

Antiemetic Drugs 1973
PN 114 **SC** 03140
UF Antinauseant Drugs
B Drugs 1967
N Chlorpromazine 1967
Chlorprothixene 1973
Fluphenazine 1973
Perphenazine 1973
Piracetam 1982
Prochlorperazine 1973
Promethazine 1973
Sulpiride 1973
R ↓ Cholinergic Blocking Drugs 1973
↓ Hypnotic Drugs 1973
Nausea 1973
↓ Sedatives 1973
↓ Tranquilizing Drugs 1967
Vomiting 1973

Antiepileptic Drugs
HN This term was discontinued in 1982. In 2000, ANITEPILEPTIC DRUGS was removed from all records containing it, and replaced with ANTICONVULSIVE DRUGS, its postable counterpart.
Use Anticonvulsive Drugs

Antiestrogens 1982
PN 60 **SC** 03155
SN Substances capable of preventing the normal effects of estrogenic hormones on responsive tissues by antagonistic effects on tissue or by inhibiting estrogenic effects.
UF Estrogen Antagonists
B Drugs 1967
R ↓ Androgens 1973
Antineoplastic Drugs 1982
↓ Estrogens 1973
↓ Steroids 1973

Antigens 1982
PN 372 **SC** 03158
SN Substances such as microorganisms or foreign tissues, cells, proteins, toxoids, or exotoxins having the ability to induce antibody formation.
UF Allergens
Immunogens
B Immunologic Factors 2003
R Antibodies 1973
Blood Groups 1973
↓ Immune System 2006
↓ Immunoglobulins 1973
Interleukins 1994

Antihistaminic Drugs 1973
PN 328 **SC** 03160
B Drugs 1967
N Chlorprothixene 1973
Cimetidine 1985
Diphenhydramine 1973
Mianserin 1982
Orphenadrine 1973
Promethazine 1973
R Histamine 1973
Hydroxyzine 1973
↓ Hypnotic Drugs 1973
↓ Sedatives 1973

Antihypertensive Drugs 1973
PN 320 **SC** 03170
B Drugs 1967
N Alpha Methylparatyrosine 1978
Captopril 1991
Chlorpromazine 1967
Clonidine 1973
Guanethidine 1973
Hexamethonium 1973
Hydralazine 1973
Iproniazid 1973
Mecamylamine 1973
Methyldopa 1973
Pargyline 1973
Pheniprazine 1973
Phenoxybenzamine 1973
Quinpirole 1994
Reserpine 1967
R ↓ Adrenergic Blocking Drugs 1973
↓ Diuretics 1973
↓ Ganglion Blocking Drugs 1973
↓ Heart Rate Affecting Drugs 1973
↓ Hypertension 1973
↓ Hypnotic Drugs 1973
↓ Muscle Relaxing Drugs 1973
↓ Sedatives 1973
↓ Tranquilizing Drugs 1967
↓ Vasodilator Drugs 1973

Antinauseant Drugs
Use Antiemetic Drugs

Antineoplastic Drugs 1982
PN 118 **SC** 03179
SN Drugs used in the prevention of the development, maturation, or spread of neoplastic cells.
B Drugs 1967
R ↓ Antibiotics 1973
Antiestrogens 1982
↓ Hormones 1967
Interferons 1994
↓ Neoplasms 1967
↓ Steroids 1973

Antioxidants 2004
PN 250 **SC** 58079
SN Substances that inhibit oxidation.
HN This term was introduced in June 2004. Relevant records were re-indexed with this term. The posting note reflects the number of records that were re-indexed.
N Ascorbic Acid 1973
R Dietary Supplements 2001
Food Additives 1978
Oxygen 1973
↓ Vitamins 1973

Antiparkinsonian Drugs
Use Antitremor Drugs

Antipathy
Use Aversion

Antipsychotic Drugs
HN Term was discontinued in 1982. In 2000, ANTIPSYCHOTIC DRUGS was removed from all records containing it, and replaced with NEUROLEPTIC DRUGS, its postable counterpart. From 1982, see the specific tranquilizing drugs, neuroleptic drugs, or other appropriate drug classes.
Use Neuroleptic Drugs

Antipyretic Drugs
Use Anti Inflammatory Drugs

Antischizophrenic Drugs
HN Term was discontinued in 1982. In 2000, ANTISCHIZOPHRENIC DRUGS was removed from all records containing it, and replaced with NEUROLEPTIC DRUGS, its postable counterpart. From 1982, see the specific tranquilizing drugs, neuroleptic drugs, or other appropriate drug classes.
Use Neuroleptic Drugs

AntiSemitism 1973
PN 424 **SC** 03220
B Racial and Ethnic Attitudes 1982
Religious Prejudices 1973
R Hate Crimes 2003
Holocaust 1988
Jews 1997
Judaism 1967
↓ Prejudice 1967
Racism 1973

Antisocial Behavior 1971
PN 4942 **SC** 03230
UF Deviant Behavior
Sociopathology
B Behavior 1967
N Child Neglect 1988
↓ Criminal Behavior 2003
Cruelty 1973
Elder Abuse 1988
Emotional Abuse 1991
↓ Harassment 2001
↓ Juvenile Delinquency 1967
↓ Partner Abuse 1991
Patient Abuse 1991
Persecution 1973
Physical Abuse 1991
Recidivism 1973
Runaway Behavior 1973
↓ Sexual Abuse 1988
↓ Terrorism 1982

Antisocial Behavior — (cont'd)
Torture 1988
Verbal Abuse 2003
↓ Violence 1973
R Antisocial Personality Disorder 1973
↓ Behavior Disorders 1971
Bullying 2003
↓ Crime 1967
Erotomania 1997
Explosive Disorder 2001
↓ Impulse Control Disorders 1997
↓ Prosocial Behavior 1982
↓ Psychopathology 1967
Psychopathy 2007
↓ Social Behavior 1967

Antisocial Personality Disorder 1973
PN 2843 **SC** 03240
SN Personality disorder characterized by conflict with others, low frustration tolerance, inadequate conscience development, and rejection of authority and discipline.
UF Psychopath
Sociopath
B Personality Disorders 1967
R ↓ Antisocial Behavior 1971
Autism 1967
↓ Criminals 1967
↓ Juvenile Delinquency 1967
Narcissistic Personality Disorder 1973
Psychopathy 2007

Antispasmodic Drugs 1973
PN 14 **SC** 03250
SN Drugs that prevent or reduce spasms usually by relaxation of smooth muscle.
UF Parasympatholytic Drugs
B Drugs 1967
N Atropine 1973
Chlorprothixene 1973
Meperidine 1973
Orphenadrine 1973
Papaverine 1973
Trihexyphenidyl 1973
R ↓ Anticonvulsive Drugs 1973
↓ Cholinergic Blocking Drugs 1973
↓ Muscle Relaxing Drugs 1973
↓ Spasms 1973

Antitremor Drugs 1973
PN 232 **SC** 03260
SN Drugs that diminish skeletal muscle tone through action on the central nervous system.
UF Antiparkinsonian Drugs
B Drugs 1967
N Amantadine 1978
Diphenhydramine 1973
Levodopa 1973
Nomifensine 1982
Orphenadrine 1973
Trihexyphenidyl 1973
R ↓ Decarboxylase Inhibitors 1982
Parkinsons Disease 1973
Tremor 1973

Antitubercular Drugs 1973
PN 15 **SC** 03270
B Drugs 1967
N Iproniazid 1973
Isoniazid 1973

Antitubercular Drugs — (cont'd)
R ↓ Tuberculosis 1973

Antiviral Drugs 1994
PN 504 SC 03280
B Drugs 1967
N Zidovudine 1994

Antonyms 1973
PN 59 SC 03290
B Semantics 1967
Vocabulary 1967
R Words (Phonetic Units) 1967

Ants 1973
PN 738 SC 03300
B Insects 1967
R Larvae 1973

Anxiety 1967
PN 28111 SC 03310
SN Apprehension or fear of impending actual or imagined danger, vulnerability, or uncertainty.
HN Prior to 1988, also used for anxiety disorders.
UF Angst
Anxiousness
Apprehension
Worry
B Emotional States 1973
N Computer Anxiety 2001
Mathematics Anxiety 1985
Performance Anxiety 1994
Social Anxiety 1985
Speech Anxiety 1985
Test Anxiety 1967
R Agitation 1991
↓ Anxiety Disorders 1997
Anxiety Management 1997
↓ Fear 1967
Fear of Success 1978
Generalized Anxiety Disorder 2004
Guilt 1967
Jealousy 1973
↓ Neurosis 1967
Panic 1973
Panic Attack 2003
Panic Disorder 1988
↓ Phobias 1967
Shame 1994
↓ Stress 1967

Anxiety Disorders 1997
PN 8343 SC 03315
SN Disorders characterized by anxiety or dread without apparent object or cause. Symptoms include irritability, anxious expectations, pangs of conscience, anxiety attacks, or phobias.
HN In 1997, this term was created to replace the discontinued term ANXIETY NEUROSIS. In 2000, ANXIETY NEUROSIS was removed from all records containing it, and replaced with ANXIETY DISORDERS.
UF Anxiety Neurosis
B Mental Disorders 1967
N Acute Stress Disorder 2003
Castration Anxiety 1973
Death Anxiety 1978
Generalized Anxiety Disorder 2004
Obsessive Compulsive Disorder 1985
Panic Disorder 1988
↓ Phobias 1967
Posttraumatic Stress Disorder 1985
Separation Anxiety 1973

Anxiety Disorders — (cont'd)
R ↓ Anxiety 1967
Anxiety Management 1997
Fear of Success 1978
Guilt 1967
Hypochondriasis 1973
Mathematics Anxiety 1985
Panic Attack 2003
Performance Anxiety 1994
Social Anxiety 1985
Speech Anxiety 1985
Test Anxiety 1967

Anxiety Management 1997
PN 262 SC 03318
R ↓ Anxiety 1967
↓ Anxiety Disorders 1997
↓ Behavior Modification 1973
↓ Behavior Therapy 1967
↓ Cognitive Techniques 1985
Cognitive Therapy 1982
↓ Relaxation Therapy 1978
Stress Management 1985

Anxiety Neurosis
HN Term was discontinued in 1997. In 2000, the term was removed from all records containing it, and replaced with ANXIETY DISORDERS, its postable counterpart.
Use Anxiety Disorders

Anxiety Reducing Drugs
Use Tranquilizing Drugs

Anxiolytic Drugs
Use Tranquilizing Drugs

Anxiousness
Use Anxiety

Aorta 1973
PN 46 SC 03360
B Arteries (Anatomy) 1973

APA
Use American Psychological Association

APA Divisions
Use American Psychological Association Divisions

Apathy 1973
PN 316 SC 03380
UF Indifference
B Emotional States 1973
R Hopelessness 1988
↓ Separation Reactions 1997

Apes
Use Primates (Nonhuman)

Aphagia 1973
PN 53 SC 03400
SN Not eating, the refusal to eat, or an inability to swallow foods or fluids.
B Pain 1967
Symptoms 1967
R ↓ Eating Disorders 1997

Aphasia 1967
PN 5309 SC 03410
SN Partial or complete impairment of language comprehension, formulation, or use due to brain damage.
UF Agrammatism
Word Deafness

Aphasia — (cont'd)
B Brain Disorders 1967
Language Disorders 1982
N Acalculia 1973
↓ Agnosia 1973
Agraphia 1973
↓ Dysphasia 1978
R ↓ Learning Disabilities 1973
↓ Perceptual Disturbances 1973

Aphrodisiacs 1973
PN 33 SC 03420
R ↓ Cannabis 1973

Aplysia
Use Snails

Apnea 1973
PN 201 SC 03430
SN Temporary absence of breathing or prolonged respiratory failure.
B Respiratory Distress 1973
Respiratory Tract Disorders 1973
N Sleep Apnea 1991
R ↓ Neonatal Disorders 1973
Sudden Infant Death 1982

Apolipoproteins 2004
PN 566 SC 03435
SN The protein component of lipoproteins.
HN This term was introduced in June 2004. Relevant records were re-indexed with this term. The posting note reflects the number of records that were re-indexed.
B Proteins 1973
R Lipoproteins 1973

Apomorphine 1973
PN 1641 SC 03440
UF Apomorphine Hydrochloride
B Alkaloids 1973
Dopamine Agonists 1985
Emetic Drugs 1973
Hypnotic Drugs 1973
Narcotic Drugs 1973

Apomorphine Hydrochloride
Use Apomorphine

Apoplexy
Use Cerebrovascular Accidents

Apoptosis 2006
PN 125 SC 03465
SN The normal physiological process of programmed cell death that is activated by changes in the nuclei.
HN This term was introduced in May 2006. Relevant records were re-indexed with this term. The posting note reflects the number of records that were re-indexed.
R ↓ Cells (Biology) 1973
Necrosis 2006
↓ Physiology 1967

Apparatus 1967
PN 3923 SC 03480
SN Set of materials, instruments, or equipment designed for specific operation in any setting. Use a more specific term if possible.
HN In 1997, this term replaced the discontinued terms TRANSISTORS (APPARATUS) and VOLT METERS. In 2000, these terms were removed from all records containing them, and replaced with APPARATUS.

Apparatus — (cont'd)
UF Devices (Experimental)
Equipment
Experimental Apparatus
Transistors (Apparatus)
Volt Meters
N Amplifiers (Apparatus) 1973
Audiometers 1973
Cage Apparatus 1973
Cameras 1973
↓ Computer Peripheral Devices 1985
↓ Computers 1967
Electrodes 1967
Generators (Apparatus) 1973
Incubators (Apparatus) 1973
Keyboards 1985
↓ Mazes 1967
Metronomes 1973
Microscopes 1973
Oscilloscopes 1973
Polygraphs 1973
Shuttle Boxes 1973
Skinner Boxes 1973
Sonar 1973
↓ Stimulators (Apparatus) 1973
Tachistoscopes 1973
↓ Tape Recorders 1973
Timers (Apparatus) 1973
Transducers 1973
Vibrators (Apparatus) 1973
R ↓ Augmentative Communication 1994
Polysomnography 2003
↓ Television 1967

Apparent Distance 1973
PN 124 SC 03490
SN Subjective perception of distance as opposed to actual distance, based on comparison of retinal and familiar sizes.
B Distance Perception 1973

Apparent Movement 1967
PN 1102 SC 03500
SN Subjective perception of movement in the absence of real physical movement.
UF Stroboscopic Movement
B Motion Perception 1967
N Autokinetic Illusion 1967

Apparent Size 1973
PN 286 SC 03510
SN Subjective perception of size as opposed to real or actual size.
UF Size (Apparent)
B Size Discrimination 1967

Apperception 1973
PN 130 SC 03520
SN Process of assimilating new perceptions and relating them to existing body of knowledge.
R ↓ Attention 1967
↓ Perception 1967

Appetite 1973
PN 1004 SC 03530
SN Indicates an instinctive or acquired motivation, impulse, or desire stemming from internal physiological conditions. Compare HUNGER.
B Physiology 1967
N Hunger 1967
R ↓ Appetite Depressing Drugs 1973
Craving 1997

Appetite — (cont'd)
Dietary Restraint 1994
Eating Attitudes 1994
↓ Eating Behavior 2004
↓ Eating Disorders 1997
Satiation 1967

Appetite Depressing Drugs 1973
PN 202 SC 03540
UF Anorexigenic Drugs
B Drugs 1967
N ↓ Amphetamine 1967
Dextroamphetamine 1973
Fenfluramine 1973
Phenmetrazine 1973
R ↓ Appetite 1973

Appetite Disorders
HN Term was discontinued in 1997. In 2000, the term was removed from all records containing it, and replaced with EATING DISORDERS, its postable counterpart.
Use Eating Disorders

Applied Psychology 1973
PN 1326 SC 03560
SN Broad discipline in which psychological principles and theories are used to solve practical problems.
B Psychology 1967
N ↓ Clinical Psychology 1967
Community Psychology 1973
Consumer Psychology 1973
Counseling Psychology 1973
↓ Educational Psychology 1967
Engineering Psychology 1967
Environmental Psychology 1982
Industrial and Organizational Psychology 2003
Military Psychology 1967
Political Psychology 1997
Social Psychology 1967
Sport Psychology 1982

Apprehension
Use Anxiety

Apprenticeship 1973
PN 238 SC 03580
B Personnel Training 1967
R ↓ Experiential Learning 1997
Mentor 1985

Approval (Social)
Use Social Approval

Apraxia 1973
PN 914 SC 03600
SN Inability to execute complex coordinated movements resulting from lesions in the motor area of the cortex but involving no sensory impairment or paralysis.
UF Akinesia
B Movement Disorders 1985
Symptoms 1967
R Parkinsonism 1994
↓ Speech Disorders 1967

Aptitude
Use Ability

Aptitude (Academic)
Use Academic Aptitude

Aptitude Measures 1967
PN 2681 SC 03630
SN Tests designed to assess capacities or potential abilities in performing tasks, skills, or other acts which have not yet been learned.
HN In 1997, this term replaced the discontinued term SCHOOL AND COLLEGE ABILITY TEST. In 2000, SCHOOL AND COLLEGE ABILITY TEST was removed from all records containing it, and was replaced with APTITUDE MEASURES, its postable counterpart.
UF Ability Tests
School and College Ability Test
Tests (Aptitude)
B Measurement 1967
N Armed Services Vocational Aptitude Battery 2005
College Entrance Examination Board Scholastic Aptitude Test 2001
Differential Aptitude Tests 1973
General Aptitude Test Battery 1973
Graduate Record Examination 1973

Arabs 1988
PN 929 SC 03635
UF Palestinians
B Racial and Ethnic Groups 2001
R Minority Groups 1967

Arachnida 1973
PN 591 SC 03640
UF Spiders
B Arthropoda 1973

Arachnophobia
Use Phobias

Archetypes 1991
PN 653 SC 03650
SN Unconscious representation of inherited collective experience on which the personality is built. Anima, animus, and the shadow are major archetypes.
HN Consider JUNGIAN PSYCHOLOGY to access references from 1973-1990.
B Collective Unconscious 1997
R Analytical Psychotherapy 1973
↓ Imagery 1967
Jung (Carl) 1973
↓ Jungian Psychology 1973
Myths 1967
Unconscious (Personality Factor) 1967

Architects 1973
PN 102 SC 03670
B Business and Industrial Personnel 1967

Architecture 1973
PN 879 SC 03680
B Arts 1973
N Interior Design 1982
R Built Environment 2007
Computer Assisted Design 1997
↓ Environment 1967
↓ Environmental Planning 1982
Religious Buildings 1973
Urban Planning 1973

Arecoline 1973
PN 81 **SC** 03690
UF Arecoline Hydrobromide
B Cholinomimetic Drugs 1973
R Bromides 1973

Arecoline Hydrobromide
Use Arecoline

Arguments 1973
PN 906 **SC** 03710
B Conflict 1967
Interpersonal Communication 1973
R Debates 1997

Arithmetic
Use Mathematics

Arm (Anatomy) 1973
PN 861 **SC** 03730
B Musculoskeletal System 1973
R Elbow (Anatomy) 1973
Hand (Anatomy) 1967
Shoulder (Anatomy) 1973
Wrist 1973

Armed Services Vocational Aptitude Battery 2005
PN 71 **SC** 03735
HN This term was introduced in August 2005. Relevant records were re-indexed with this term. The posting note reflects the number of records that were re-indexed.
UF ASVAB
B Aptitude Measures 1967

Army Personnel 1967
PN 1529 **SC** 03750
B Military Personnel 1967
R Draftees 1973
National Guard Personnel 1973

Arousal (Physiological)
Use Physiological Arousal

Arousal (Sexual)
Use Sexual Arousal

Arrest (Law)
Use Legal Arrest

Arrhythmias (Heart) 1973
PN 334 **SC** 03790
B Heart Disorders 1973
N Bradycardia 1973
Fibrillation (Heart) 1973
Tachycardia 1973

Arson 1985
PN 267 **SC** 03795
UF Firesetting
B Crime 1967
R ↓ Violent Crime 2003

Art 1967
PN 2480 **SC** 03800
SN Products of aesthetic expression. Not used as a document type identifier.
UF Artwork
B Arts 1973
N Crafts 1973
Drawing 1967
Painting (Art) 1973
Photographic Art 1973

Art — (cont'd)
Sculpturing 1973
R Museums 2006

Art Education 1973
PN 744 **SC** 03810
B Curriculum 1967

Art Therapy 1973
PN 2167 **SC** 03820
SN Therapy that uses the creative work of clients for emotional expression, sublimation, achievement, and to reveal underlying conflicts.
B Creative Arts Therapy 1994
R Educational Therapy 1997
Movement Therapy 1997
Recreation Therapy 1973
Self Expression 2006

Arterial Pulse 1973
PN 426 **SC** 03830
UF Pulse (Arterial)
R Blood Circulation 1973

Arteries (Anatomy) 1973
PN 311 **SC** 03840
UF Coronary Vessels
Retinal Vessels
B Blood Vessels 1973
N Aorta 1973
Carotid Arteries 1973

Arteriosclerosis 1973
PN 54 **SC** 03850
SN A disorder characterized by thickening and hardening of the arterial walls resulting in decreased blood flow.
B Cardiovascular Disorders 1967
N Atherosclerosis 1973
Cerebral Arteriosclerosis 1973
R ↓ Blood Pressure Disorders 1973

Arthritis 1973
PN 906 **SC** 03860
UF Rheumatism
B Joint Disorders 1973
N Rheumatoid Arthritis 1973
R ↓ Infectious Disorders 1973

Arthropoda 1973
PN 60 **SC** 03870
B Invertebrates 1973
N Arachnida 1973
↓ Crustacea 1973
↓ Insects 1967

Articulation (Speech) 1967
PN 1976 **SC** 03880
SN Production of speech sounds resulting from vocal tract movements.
B Speech Characteristics 1973
Verbal Communication 1967
R Phonetics 1967
Pronunciation 1973

Articulation Disorders 1973
PN 473 **SC** 03890
SN Speech disorders involving the substitution, omission, distortion, or addition of phonemes.

Articulation Disorders — (cont'd)
UF Misarticulation
B Speech Disorders 1967
N Dysarthria 1973

Artificial Insemination
Use Reproductive Technology

Artificial Intelligence 1982
PN 3312 **SC** 03895
SN Study and application of computers to simulate and perform functions of human information processing.
B Computer Applications 1973
N ↓ Expert Systems 1991
Knowledge Engineering 2003
↓ Machine Learning 2003
Neural Networks 1991
R Automated Speech Recognition 1994
Automation 1967
Case Based Reasoning 2003
↓ Cognitive Processes 1967
Cognitive Science 2003
↓ Computers 1967
Cybernetics 1967
Decision Support Systems 1997
Fuzzy Logic 2003
Human Machine Systems 1997
↓ Intelligence 1967
Intelligent Agents 2007
Intelligent Tutoring Systems 2003
Robotics 1985

Artificial Limbs
Use Prostheses

Artificial Pacemakers 1973
PN 65 **SC** 03910
UF Pacemakers (Artificial)
B Medical Therapeutic Devices 1973

Artificial Respiration 1973
PN 85 **SC** 03920
UF Lifesaving
B Physical Treatment Methods 1973
R Respiration 1967
↓ Respiratory System 1973
↓ Respiratory Tract Disorders 1973

Artistic Ability 1973
PN 373 **SC** 03930
B Nonverbal Ability 1988
N Musical Ability 1973
R Creativity 1967

Artists 1973
PN 1739 **SC** 03940
B Personnel 1967
N Musicians 1991
Writers 1991

Arts 1973
PN 736 **SC** 03950
SN Conceptually broad term referring to all forms of the arts, including the performing arts. Use a more specific term if possible.
UF Performing Arts
B Humanities 2003
N ↓ Architecture 1973
↓ Art 1967
Dance 1973
↓ Music 1967
↓ Theatre 1973

Arts — (cont'd)
R Aesthetics 1967
Postmodernism 1997

Artwork
Use Art

Asbestos
Use Hazardous Materials

Asceticism 1973
PN 52 **SC** 03970
B Philosophies 1967
Religious Practices 1973
R Religion 1967
↓ Religious Beliefs 1973

Ascorbic Acid 1973
PN 129 **SC** 03980
UF Vitamin C
B Acids 1973
Antioxidants 2004
Vitamins 1973

Asian Americans
HN This term was discontinued in 1982. In 2000, ASIAN AMERICANS was removed from all records containing it, and replaced with ASIANS, its postable counterpart.
Use Asians

Asians 1982
PN 5886 **SC** 04007
HN In 1982, this term was created to replace the discontinued term ASIAN AMERICANS. In 2000, ASIAN AMERICANS was removed from all records and replaced with ASIANS.
UF Asian Americans
B Racial and Ethnic Groups 2001
N Chinese Cultural Groups 1997
Japanese Cultural Groups 1997
Korean Cultural Groups 1997
South Asian Cultural Groups 2004
↓ Southeast Asian Cultural Groups 2004
Vietnamese Cultural Groups 1997
R Minority Groups 1967

Aspartic Acid 1973
PN 507 **SC** 04010
B Amino Acids 1973
Neurotransmitters 1985
N N-Methyl-D-Aspartate 1994

Aspergers Syndrome 1991
PN 999 **SC** 04015
SN Syndrome or disorder usually first diagnosed in childhood, characterized by severe and sustained impairment in social interactions and restricted, repetitive patterns of behaviors, interests, and activities.
UF Autistic Psychopathy
B Pervasive Developmental Disorders 2001
Syndromes 1973
R Autism 1967
Developmental Disabilities 1982
Rett Syndrome 1994

Asphyxia
Use Anoxia

Aspiration Level 1973
PN 320 **SC** 04030
SN Level of expectations for future achievement.

Aspiration Level — (cont'd)
R ↓ Aspirations 1967

Aspirations 1967
PN 930 **SC** 04040
SN Individual desires to achieve goals and ideals. Use a more specific term if possible.
UF Ambition
N Educational Aspirations 1973
Occupational Aspirations 1973
R Aspiration Level 1973
Goal Orientation 2005
Goal Setting 1997
↓ Goals 1967
↓ Motivation 1967

Aspirin 1973
PN 163 **SC** 04050
UF Acetylsalicylic Acid
B Acids 1973
Analgesic Drugs 1973
Anti Inflammatory Drugs 1982

Assassination (Political)
Use Political Assassination

Assertiveness 1973
PN 2059 **SC** 04070
B Personality Traits 1967
R Assertiveness Training 1978
Empowerment 1991
Extraversion 1967
↓ Resistance 1997
Self Expression 2006

Assertiveness Training 1978
PN 1004 **SC** 04072
SN Training in the social skills required to be able to refuse requests; to express both positive and negative feelings; to initiate, engage in, and terminate conversation; and to make personal requests without suffering from excessive stress.
B Human Potential Movement 1982
Training 2006
R Assertiveness 1973
↓ Behavior Modification 1973
Communication Skills Training 1982
Human Relations Training 1978
Social Skills Training 1982

Assessment
Use Measurement

Assessment (Cognitive)
Use Cognitive Assessment

Assessment (Psychological)
Use Psychological Assessment

Assessment Centers 1982
PN 372 **SC** 04082
SN Centers specializing in standardized, systematic behavioral evaluation processes used to make selection, promotion, development, counseling, and career planning personnel decisions.
R ↓ Facilities 2006
Occupational Guidance 1967
↓ Personnel Evaluation 1973
Personnel Placement 1973
Personnel Promotion 1978
↓ Personnel Selection 1967

Assessment Criteria
Use Evaluation Criteria

Assimilation (Cognitive Process) 2007
PN 66 **SC** 04087
SN The process of incorporating information into already existing cognitive structures without modifying those structures. Also refers to judgment-making processes in which similarities are found between the target being judged and features of the context in which it is judged. For cultural assimilation use ACCULTURATION.
HN This term was introduced in April 2007. Relevant records were re-indexed with this term. The posting note reflects the number of records that were re-indexed.
B Cognitive Processes 1967
R Accommodation (Cognitive Process) 2007
↓ Cognitive Style 1967
↓ Judgment 1967
Piaget (Jean) 1967
Schema 1988

Assimilation (Cultural)
Use Acculturation

Assistance (Social Behavior) 1973
PN 2501 **SC** 04100
SN Act of rendering aid or help. Limited to human populations.
UF Helping Behavior
B Interpersonal Interaction 1967
Prosocial Behavior 1982
N Social Support 2004
R Altruism 1973
Charitable Behavior 1973
↓ Help Seeking Behavior 1978
Volunteers 2003

Assistance Seeking (Professional)
Use Health Care Utilization

Assisted Living 2003
PN 202 **SC** 04104
SN Housing and living arrangements for individuals needing a minimal amount of care and supervision.
HN This term was introduced in June 2003. Relevant records were re-indexed with this term. The posting note reflects the number of records that were re-indexed.
B Housing 1973
R Activities of Daily Living 1991
Independent Living Programs 1991
↓ Living Arrangements 1991
↓ Residential Care Institutions 1973

Assisted Suicide 1997
PN 549 **SC** 04105
SN Provision of support and/or means that gives a patient the power to take his or her own life.
B Suicide 1967
R Advance Directives 1994
Bioethics 2003
↓ Death and Dying 1967
Euthanasia 1973
Life Sustaining Treatment 1997
Palliative Care 1991
Professional Ethics 1973
Terminally Ill Patients 1973
Treatment Refusal 1994
Treatment Withholding 1988

Assistive Devices
Use Assistive Technology

Assistive Technology 2007
PN 136 **SC** 04106
SN Devices that assist persons with disabilities in achieving independence by improving functional capabilities.
HN This term was introduced in April 2007. Relevant records were re-indexed with this term. The posting note reflects the number of records that were re-indexed.
UF Assistive Devices
B Technology 1973
R ↓ Augmentative Communication 1994
Mobility Aids 1978

Association (Free)
Use Free Association

Associationism 1973
PN 131 **SC** 04120
SN Theory which holds that learning and mental development consist mainly of combinations and recombinations of irreducible mental elements. Also, the basis for theories that explain learning in terms of stimulus and response.
B History of Psychology 1967
Psychological Theories 2001

Associations (Contextual)
Use Contextual Associations

Associations (Groups)
Use Organizations

Associations (Word)
Use Word Associations

Associative Processes 1967
PN 4088 **SC** 04160
SN Development or maintenance of learned or cognitive connections (associations) between events, sensations, ideas, memories, or behavior as the result of functional relationships, similarity-contrast, or spatial-temporal contiguity.
B Cognitive Processes 1967
N Cognitive Contiguity 1973
Connotations 1973
Contextual Associations 1967
Isolation Effect 1973
R Cognitive Generalization 1967
Connectionism 1994
Cues 1967
Word Associations 1967
Word Recognition 1988

Assortative Mating 1991
PN 142 **SC** 04165
SN Nonrandom mating between unrelated individuals with similar characteristics. Used for human or animal populations.
UF Assortive Mating
R ↓ Animal Breeding 1973
Animal Mate Selection 1982
↓ Animal Mating Behavior 1967
Family Resemblance 1991
↓ Genetics 1967
Human Mate Selection 1988
Phenotypes 1973
Population Genetics 1973
↓ Psychosexual Behavior 1967

Assortive Mating
Use Assortative Mating

Asthenia 1973
PN 65 **SC** 04170
SN Physical weakness, lack of strength and vitality, or a lack of concentration.
B Symptoms 1967
N Myasthenia 1973
R Neurasthenia 2005

Asthenic Personality
HN This term was discontinued in 1997. In 2000, ASTHENIC PERSONALITY was removed from all records containing it, and replaced with PERSONALITY DISORDERS, its postable counterpart.
Use Personality Disorders

Asthma 1967
PN 2102 **SC** 04190
B Dyspnea 1973
R ↓ Immunologic Disorders 1973
↓ Somatoform Disorders 2001

Astrology 1973
PN 127 **SC** 04200
R ↓ Parapsychology 1967
Superstitions 1973

Astronauts 1973
PN 175 **SC** 04210
B Aerospace Personnel 1973
R Aircraft Pilots 1973
↓ Military Personnel 1967
Spacecraft 1973

ASVAB
Use Armed Services Vocational Aptitude Battery

Asylums
Use Psychiatric Hospitals

At Risk Populations 1985
PN 19528 **SC** 04225
SN Groups or individuals considered in danger of developing a physical, mental, emotional, behavioral, or other disorder due to adverse internal or external factors.
UF High Risk Populations
Risk Populations
R Coronary Prone Behavior 1982
↓ Intervention 2003
Predisposition 1973
Premorbidity 1978
Risk Assessment 2004
Risk Factors 2001
Susceptibility (Disorders) 1973

Ataractic Drugs
Use Tranquilizing Drugs

Ataraxic Drugs
Use Tranquilizing Drugs

Ataxia 1973
PN 610 **SC** 04250
SN Loss of coordination of voluntary muscular movement.
UF Dysmetria
B Movement Disorders 1985
Symptoms 1967
R Hyperkinesis 1973

Atheism 1973
PN 58 **SC** 04260
SN Disbelief in the existence of a God or Gods.

Atheism — (cont'd)
B Religious Beliefs 1973
R Agnosticism 2007

Atherosclerosis 1973
PN 236 **SC** 04270
SN A form of arteriosclerosis in which there is an accumulation of plaque deposits in the medium and large sized arteries.
B Arteriosclerosis 1973

Athetosis 1973
PN 32 **SC** 04280
SN Nonprogressive, developmentally-evolving disorder arising from basal ganglia damage in the full term brain characterized by postural reflex impairments, involuntary movements, and dysarthria with preservation of sensation, ocular movement, and frequently, intelligence.
B Brain Disorders 1967
Movement Disorders 1985
R Cerebral Palsy 1967

Athletes 1973
PN 4682 **SC** 04287
N College Athletes 1994
R Athletic Participation 1973
Athletic Performance 1991
Athletic Training 1991
Celebrities 2007
↓ Sports 1967
Sports (Attitudes Toward) 2004

Athletic Participation 1973
PN 1541 **SC** 04290
B Participation 1973
Recreation 1967
R ↓ Athletes 1973
College Athletes 1994
↓ Extracurricular Activities 1973
↓ Sports 1967

Athletic Performance 1991
PN 1869 **SC** 04300
UF Sport Performance
B Performance 1967
R ↓ Athletes 1973
Athletic Training 1991
College Athletes 1994
↓ Sports 1967
↓ Teams 1988

Athletic Training 1991
PN 599 **SC** 04305
UF Sport Training
Training (Athletic)
B Training 2006
R ↓ Athletes 1973
Athletic Performance 1991
Coaches 1988
College Athletes 1994
↓ Education 1967
↓ Extracurricular Activities 1973
↓ Sports 1967
↓ Teams 1988

Atmospheric Conditions 1973
PN 631 **SC** 04310
UF Barometric Pressure
Climate (Meteorological)
Weather
B Environmental Effects 1973
R Pollution 1973
↓ Temperature Effects 1967

Atmospheric Conditions — (cont'd)
Thermal Acclimatization 1973

Atomism
Use Reductionism

Atria (Heart)
Use Heart Auricles

Atrial Fibrillation
Use Fibrillation (Heart)

Atrophy (Cerebral)
Use Cerebral Atrophy

Atrophy (Muscular)
Use Muscular Atrophy

Atropine 1973
PN 542 **SC** 04350
UF Hyoscyamine (dl-)
Methylatropine
B Alkaloids 1973
Amines 1973
Analgesic Drugs 1973
Antispasmodic Drugs 1973
Cholinergic Blocking Drugs 1973
Narcotic Drugs 1973
Sedatives 1973

Attachment Behavior 1985
PN 9133 **SC** 04355
SN Formation of and investment in significant relationships. Usually refers to the emotional and biological attachment of human or animal infants to caretaking figures.
UF Bonding (Emotional)
B Behavior 1967
R Abandonment 1997
Anaclitic Depression 1973
Attachment Disorders 2001
Attachment Theory 2007
Dependency (Personality) 1967
Emotional Development 1973
Erotomania 1997
Fixation (Psychoanalytic) 2007
Fixation (Psychological) 2007
Intimacy 1973
Love 1973
Object Relations 1982
↓ Parent Child Relations 1967
Postpartum Depression 1973
Postpartum Psychosis 2003
Separation Anxiety 1973
Separation Individuation 1982
↓ Separation Reactions 1997
Stranger Reactions 1988

Attachment Disorders 2001
PN 191 **SC** 04357
UF Reactive Attachment Disorder
R Attachment Behavior 1985
↓ Child Abuse 1971
Child Neglect 1988
Failure to Thrive 1988
↓ Parent Child Relations 1967
↓ Relationship Termination 1997
Separation Anxiety 1973
↓ Separation Reactions 1997

Attachment Theory 2007
PN 375 **SC** 04358
SN Theoretical framework for relationships that describes the development of strong emotional bonds with others, particularly parents or other primary caregivers who create feelings of security. Separation from those with whom the bond is formed can lead to feelings of distress and anxiety.
HN This term was introduced in April 2007. Relevant records were re-indexed with this term. The posting note reflects the number of records that were re-indexed.
B Psychological Theories 2001
R Attachment Behavior 1985
Emotional Development 1973
Emotional Security 1973
Object Relations 1982
↓ Parent Child Relations 1967
↓ Psychosocial Development 1973
Separation Anxiety 1973

Attack Behavior 1973
PN 837 **SC** 04360
SN Forceful, assaultive behavior. Used for human or animal populations.
B Aggressive Behavior 1967
Animal Aggressive Behavior 1973
R ↓ Animal Defensive Behavior 1982
Animal Predatory Behavior 1978
Instinctive Behavior 1982
Retaliation 1991

Attainment (Achievement)
Use Achievement

Attainment Level (Education)
Use Educational Attainment Level

Attempted Suicide 1973
PN 5406 **SC** 04380
UF Parasuicide
Suicide (Attempted)
B Behavior Disorders 1971
Self Destructive Behavior 1985
R Suicidal Ideation 1991
↓ Suicide 1967
Suicide Prevention 1973

Attendance (School)
Use School Attendance

Attendants (Institutions) 1973
PN 398 **SC** 04400
UF Hospital Attendants
Residential Care Attendants
R Prison Personnel 1973
↓ Psychiatric Hospital Staff 1973

Attention 1967
PN 16945 **SC** 04410
SN Condition of perceptual or cognitive awareness of or focusing on some aspect of one's environment. Compare ATTENTION SPAN and VIGILANCE.
B Awareness 1967
N Divided Attention 1973
↓ Monitoring 1973
Selective Attention 1973
↓ Sustained Attention 1997
Vigilance 1967
Visual Attention 2004
R Apperception 1973
Attention Span 1973
Concentration 1982

Attention — (cont'd)
Distraction 1978
Human Channel Capacity 1973
Listening (Interpersonal) 1997
↓ Perception 1967
Rotary Pursuit 1967
Signal Detection (Perception) 1967
Time On Task 1988
↓ Tracking 1967

Attention Deficit Disorder 1985
PN 4681 **SC** 04412
SN A disorder characterized by persistent developmentally inappropriate inattention and impulsivity.
N Attention Deficit Disorder with Hyperactivity 2001
R Attention Span 1973
Distractibility 1973
Impulsiveness 1973
↓ Mental Disorders 1967
Oppositional Defiant Disorder 1997

Attention Deficit Disorder with Hyperactivity 2001
PN 5051 **SC** 04414
SN A behavior disorder in which the essential features are signs of developmentally inappropriate inattention, impulsivity, and hyperactivity.
HN Use both ATTENTION DEFICIT DISORDER and HYPERKINESIS to access references prior to 2001. In May 2006, this term replaced the discontinued term MINIMAL BRAIN DISORDERS. MINIMAL BRAIN DISORDERS was removed from all records containing it and replaced with ATTENTION DEFICIT DISORDER WITH HYPERACTIVITY, its postable counterpart.
UF ADHD
Minimal Brain Disorders
B Attention Deficit Disorder 1985
R Attention Span 1973
Distractibility 1973
Hyperkinesis 1973
Impulsiveness 1973
↓ Mental Disorders 1967
Oppositional Defiant Disorder 1997

Attention Span 1973
PN 462 **SC** 04413
SN Temporal duration of concentration or amount of material grasped during exposure to stimuli or information. Compare ATTENTION.
B Sustained Attention 1997
R ↓ Attention 1967
↓ Attention Deficit Disorder 1985
Attention Deficit Disorder with Hyperactivity 2001
Conceptual Tempo 1985
Distraction 1978
Vigilance 1967

Attitude Change 1967
PN 5834 **SC** 04430
SN Significant alteration in individual or group attitudes or opinions.
UF Opinion Change
R ↓ Attitudes 1967
Brainwashing 1982

Attitude Formation 1973
PN 939 **SC** 04440
SN Process of developing an opinion or attitude, especially as influenced by psychological, emotional, social, and experiential factors.

Attitude Formation — (cont'd)
R ↓ Attitudes 1967

Attitude Measurement 1973
PN 1071 SC 04460
SN Projective, physiological, self-report, or other approaches to the assessment of attitudes.
B Measurement 1967
R ↓ Attitude Measures 1967
↓ Attitudes 1967
Likert Scales 1994

Attitude Measures 1967
PN 3348 SC 04470
SN Instruments or devices used in the assessment of attitudes.
HN In 1997, this term replaced the discontinued terms ALLPORT VERNON LINDZEY STUDY VALUES, MINNESOTA TEACHER ATTITUDE INVENTORY, and OPINION ATTITUDE AND INTEREST SURVEY. In 2000, these terms were removed from all records containing them, and replaced with ATTITUDE MEASURES.
UF Allport Vernon Lindzey Study Values
Minnesota Teacher Attitude Inventory
Opinion Attitude and Interest Survey
Opinion Questionnaires
Opinion Surveys
B Measurement 1967
N Wilson Patterson Conservatism Scale 1973
R Attitude Measurement 1973
↓ Attitudes 1967
Likert Scales 1994
↓ Preference Measures 1973
Semantic Differential 1967

Attitude Similarity 1973
PN 1084 SC 04480
R ↓ Attitudes 1967

Attitudes 1967
PN 14490 SC 04500
SN Conceptually broad term referring to a mental position or feeling toward certain ideas, facts, or persons. Use a more specific term if possible.
UF Beliefs (Nonreligious)
Opinions
N Adolescent Attitudes 1988
Adult Attitudes 1988
↓ Aged (Attitudes Toward) 1978
Aging (Attitudes Toward) 1985
Child Attitudes 1988
Childrearing Attitudes 1973
↓ Client Attitudes 1982
Community Attitudes 1973
Computer Attitudes 1988
↓ Consumer Attitudes 1973
Counselor Attitudes 1973
Death Attitudes 1973
↓ Disabled (Attitudes Toward) 1997
↓ Drug Usage Attitudes 1973
Eating Attitudes 1994
↓ Employee Attitudes 1967
Employer Attitudes 1973
Environmental Attitudes 1978
Family Planning Attitudes 1973
Female Attitudes 2006
Health Attitudes 1985
↓ Health Personnel Attitudes 1985
Homosexuality (Attitudes Toward) 1982
Job Applicant Attitudes 1973
Male Attitudes 2006
Marriage Attitudes 1973
Obesity (Attitudes Toward) 1997

Attitudes — (cont'd)
Occupational Attitudes 1973
↓ Parental Attitudes 1973
↓ Physical Illness (Attitudes Toward) 1985
↓ Political Attitudes 1973
Psychologist Attitudes 1991
Public Opinion 1973
↓ Racial and Ethnic Attitudes 1982
↓ Sex Role Attitudes 1978
Sexual Attitudes 1973
↓ Socioeconomic Class Attitudes 1973
Sports (Attitudes Toward) 2004
Stereotyped Attitudes 1967
Student Attitudes 1967
↓ Teacher Attitudes 1967
Work (Attitudes Toward) 1973
R Attitude Change 1967
Attitude Formation 1973
Attitude Measurement 1973
↓ Attitude Measures 1967
Attitude Similarity 1973
Attribution 1973
↓ Cognitions 1985
Hedonism 1973
Impression Formation 1978
Irrational Beliefs 1982
Labeling 1978
Planned Behavior 1997
↓ Prejudice 1967
↓ Religious Beliefs 1973
Stigma 1991
Superstitions 1973
World View 1988

Attorneys 1973
PN 1124 SC 04510
UF Lawyers
B Legal Personnel 1985
R ↓ Law Enforcement Personnel 1973
Law Students 1978

Attraction (Interpersonal)
Use Interpersonal Attraction

Attribution 1973
PN 14001 SC 04525
SN Perception of causes of behavior or events or of dispositional properties of an individual or group.
B Social Perception 1967
R ↓ Attitudes 1967
Blame 1994
Causal Analysis 1994
Impression Formation 1978
Inference 1973
Internal External Locus of Control 1967
Learned Helplessness 1978
Self Fulfilling Prophecies 1997

Attrition (Experimental)
Use Experimental Attrition

Attrition (Military)
Use Military Attrition

Atypical Depression 2005
PN 104 SC 58088
SN A form of depression in which the symptoms are inconsistent with the diagnostic criteria of other affective disorders.
HN This term was introduced in August 2005. Relevant records were re-indexed with this term. The posting note reflects the number of records that were re-indexed.

Atypical Depression — (cont'd)
B Atypical Disorders 2005
R ↓ Major Depression 1988

Atypical Disorders 2005
PN 152 SC 58087
SN Applied to a disorder when it does not meet the full diagnostic criteria of a particular disorder.
HN This term was introduced in August 2005. Relevant records were re-indexed with this term. The posting note reflects the number of records that were re-indexed.
B Disorders 1967
N Atypical Depression 2005

Atypical Paranoid Disorder
Use Paranoia (Psychosis)

Atypical Somatoform Disorder
Use Body Dysmorphic Disorder

Audiences 1967
PN 1060 SC 04530
SN Groups of spectators or listeners.
N Sports Spectators 1997
R Observers 1973

Audiogenic Seizures 1978
PN 116 SC 04536
SN Seizures induced by exposure to high frequency sounds.
B Seizures 2005
R ↓ Auditory Stimulation 1967

Audiology 1973
PN 283 SC 04540
SN Scientific study of hearing, including: anatomical and functional properties of the ear; hearing disorders and their assessment and treatment; and the rehabilitation of hearing-impaired persons. Consider also AUDIOMETRY and SPEECH AND HEARING MEASURES.
B Paramedical Sciences 1973

Audiometers 1973
PN 22 SC 04550
B Apparatus 1967

Audiometry 1967
PN 1142 SC 04560
SN Specific procedures or audiometric tests used to measure hearing acuity and range in the diagnosis and evaluation of hearing impairments. Consider also AUDIOLOGY and SPEECH AND HEARING MEASURES.
UF Bekesy Audiometry
N Bone Conduction Audiometry 1973
R Auditory Acuity 1988
↓ Auditory Stimulation 1967
↓ Perceptual Measures 1973

Audiotapes 1973
PN 443 SC 04570
SN Tape recordings of sound used in both educational and noneducational settings.
B Audiovisual Communications Media 1973

Audiovisual Aids (Educational)
Use Educational Audiovisual Aids

Audiovisual Communications Media 1973
PN 410 SC 04590
B Communications Media 1973
N Audiotapes 1973
Digital Video 2007

Audiovisual Communications Media — (cont'd)
Educational Audiovisual Aids 1973
Films 2005
Photographs 1967
Radio 1973
↓ Television 1967
Television Advertising 1973
Videotapes 1973

Audiovisual Instruction 1973
PN 360 **SC** 04600
B Teaching Methods 1967
N Televised Instruction 1973
Videotape Instruction 1973
R Educational Audiovisual Aids 1973

Audition
Use Auditory Perception

Auditory Acuity 1988
PN 252 **SC** 04615
SN The ability or capacity of a listener to perceive fine detail.
HN Consider AUDITORY THRESHOLDS or AUDITORY DISCRIMINATION to access references prior to 1988.
UF Hearing Acuity
B Auditory Perception 1967
Perceptual Discrimination 1973
R ↓ Audiometry 1967
Auditory Discrimination 1967
Auditory Localization 1973
Auditory Thresholds 1973

Auditory Cortex 1967
PN 1277 **SC** 04620
SN Sensory region of the temporal lobe that receives and processes auditory information.
UF Cortex (Auditory)
B Temporal Lobe 1973

Auditory Discrimination 1967
PN 3958 **SC** 04630
SN Distinguishing between sounds of different intensity, frequency, pattern, complexity, or other characteristics.
B Auditory Perception 1967
Perceptual Discrimination 1973
R Auditory Acuity 1988

Auditory Displays 1973
PN 141 **SC** 04640
SN Presentations of patterned auditory stimulation.
B Auditory Stimulation 1967
Displays 1967

Auditory Evoked Potentials 1973
PN 4218 **SC** 04650
SN Measured electrical responses of the central nervous system to auditory stimulation.
B Evoked Potentials 1967

Auditory Feedback 1973
PN 415 **SC** 04660
SN Return of information on specified behavioral functions or parameters by means of auditory stimulation. Such stimulation may serve to regulate or control subsequent behavior, cognition, perception, or performance. Also, the process of hearing one's own vocalizations, especially as pertains to regulating the parameters of one's speech.
B Auditory Stimulation 1967
Sensory Feedback 1973

Auditory Feedback — (cont'd)
N Delayed Auditory Feedback 1973

Auditory Hallucinations 1973
PN 767 **SC** 04670
B Hallucinations 1967

Auditory Localization 1973
PN 1190 **SC** 04680
SN Subjective determination of the specific spatial location of a sound source or relative locations of sound sources.
UF Localization (Sound)
Sound Localization
B Auditory Perception 1967
Perceptual Localization 1967
R Auditory Acuity 1988

Auditory Masking 1973
PN 1223 **SC** 04690
SN Change in perceptual sensitivity to an auditory stimulus due to the presence of a second stimulus in close temporal proximity.
B Masking 1967
R ↓ Auditory Stimulation 1967

Auditory Nerve
Use Acoustic Nerve

Auditory Neurons 1973
PN 371 **SC** 04710
SN Neurons that conduct auditory impulses to the central nervous system.
B Sensory Neurons 1973

Auditory Perception 1967
PN 10532 **SC** 04720
SN Awareness, detection, or identification of sounds.
UF Audition
Listening
B Perception 1967
N Auditory Acuity 1988
Auditory Discrimination 1967
Auditory Localization 1973
↓ Loudness Perception 1973
Music Perception 1997
↓ Pitch Perception 1973
Speech Perception 1967
R Acoustics 1997
Auditory Thresholds 1973
↓ Ear Disorders 1973
Listening (Interpersonal) 1997
Pattern Discrimination 1967
↓ Rhythm 1991

Auditory Stimulation 1967
PN 10886 **SC** 04730
UF Acoustic Stimuli
Noise (Sound)
Sound
B Perceptual Stimulation 1973
N Auditory Displays 1973
↓ Auditory Feedback 1973
Dichotic Stimulation 1982
Filtered Noise 1973
↓ Loudness 1967
↓ Pitch (Frequency) 1967
White Noise 1973
R Acoustics 1997
Audiogenic Seizures 1978
↓ Audiometry 1967
Auditory Masking 1973
Bone Conduction Audiometry 1973
Silence 2003

Auditory Stimulation — (cont'd)
↓ Speech Processing (Mechanical) 1973

Auditory Thresholds 1973
PN 1912 **SC** 04740
SN The minimal level of auditory stimulation, the minimal difference between any auditory stimuli, or the minimal stimulus change that is perceptually detectable.
B Thresholds 1967
R Auditory Acuity 1988
↓ Auditory Perception 1967
↓ Perceptual Measures 1973

Augmentative Communication 1994
PN 752 **SC** 04750
SN Communication that is supported by keyboards, typewriters, books, gestural systems, or other devices to enable individuals with communication or speech disorders to communicate effectively.
UF Facilitated Communication
B Communication 1967
N ↓ Manual Communication 1978
R ↓ Apparatus 1967
Assistive Technology 2007
↓ Communication Disorders 1982
↓ Medical Therapeutic Devices 1973
↓ Speech Disorders 1967
Speech Therapy 1967

Aura 1973
PN 175 **SC** 04760
SN Sensations experienced immediately prior to the onset of a seizure, migraine headache, or other nervous system disorder symptoms. Also, the patient's recognition of the beginning of an epileptic attack. Use PARAPSYCHOLOGY or PARAPSYCHOLOGICAL PHENOMENA to access references on psychic auras and halos.
B Symptoms 1967
R ↓ Epilepsy 1967

Aurally Handicapped
HN The term was discontinued in 1997, when the term AURALLY DISABLED was created to capture this concept. In 2000, with the deletion of the term AURALLY DISABLED, AURALLY HANDICAPPED was made a nonpostable term for the postable term HEARING DISORDERS. AURALLY DISABLED and AURALLY HANDICAPPED were removed from all records containing them and replaced with HEARING DISORDERS.
Use Hearing Disorders

Auricles (Heart)
Use Heart Auricles

Auricular Fibrillation
Use Fibrillation (Heart)

Authoritarianism 1967
PN 2306 **SC** 04820
SN Complex of personality characteristics expressed as antidemocratic social attitudes, rigid attachment to traditional values, uncritical acceptance of authority, and intolerance of opposing views.
UF Domination
B Personality Traits 1967
R Dogmatism 1978
↓ Dominance 1967
Egalitarianism 1985
Openmindedness 1978

Authoritarianism (Parental)
HN Use PARENTAL PERMISSIVENESS to access references from 1973 to June 2003.
Use Parenting Style

Authoritarianism Rebellion Scale
HN Term was discontinued in 1997. In 2000, the term was removed from all records containing it, and replaced with NONPROJECTIVE PERSONALITY MEASURES, its postable counterpart.
Use Nonprojective Personality Measures

Authority 1967
PN 1262 **SC** 04845
SN Ability or vested power to influence thought, attitudes, and behavior.
R Abuse of Power 1997
Coercion 1994
↓ Dominance 1967
↓ Leadership 1967
Omnipotence 1994
↓ Power 1967
↓ Social Influences 1967
↓ Status 1967

Authors
Use Writers

Autism 1967
PN 10559 **SC** 04850
SN A pervasive developmental disorder diagnosed in early childhood that is characterized by an inability to develop social relationships, impaired language and communication skills, abnormal responses to stimuli, and repetitive patterns of behavior.
HN In August 2005, this term replaced the discontinued terms AUTISTIC CHILDREN and EARLY INFANTILE AUTISM. These terms were removed from all records containing them and replaced with AUTISM.
UF Autistic Children
Early Infantile Autism
B Mental Disorders 1967
Pervasive Developmental Disorders 2001
R Antisocial Personality Disorder 1973
Aspergers Syndrome 1991
Autistic Thinking 1973
Developmental Disabilities 1982
Theory of Mind 2001

Autism Spectrum Disorders
Use Pervasive Developmental Disorders

Autistic Children
HN In August 2005, this term was discontinued and removed from all records containing it, and was replaced with AUTISM, its postable counterpart.
Use Autism

Autistic Psychopathy
Use Aspergers Syndrome

Autistic Thinking 1973
PN 38 **SC** 04870
B Thinking 1967
Thought Disturbances 1973
R Autism 1967

Autobiographical Memory 1994
PN 1262 **SC** 04875
SN Personal memories of past events that have occurred over the course of one's life. Compare REMINISCENCE and LIFE REVIEW.

Autobiographical Memory — (cont'd)
B Memory 1967
R Anniversary Events 1994
Early Experience 1967
Early Memories 1985
↓ Life Experiences 1973
Life Review 1991
Reminiscence 1985

Autobiography 1973
PN 1762 **SC** 04880
SN Recorded account of one's own life.
B Biography 1967

Autoeroticism 1997
PN 27 **SC** 04890
HN Use MASTURBATION to access references from 1973-1996.
R Eroticism 1973
Masturbation 1973
Narcissism 1967
↓ Psychosexual Behavior 1967

Autogenic Training 1973
PN 524 **SC** 04900
SN Physiological form of psychotherapy based on studies of sleep and hypnosis and the application of yoga principles.
B Psychotherapeutic Techniques 1967
Psychotherapy 1967
Training 2006
R Biofeedback Training 1978
↓ Relaxation Therapy 1978

Autohypnosis 1973
PN 313 **SC** 04910
SN Practice, process, or hypnotic state resulting from self-induced hypnosis.
UF Self Hypnosis
B Hypnosis 1967
R Catalepsy 1973

Autoimmune Disorders
Use Immunologic Disorders

Autokinetic Illusion 1967
PN 253 **SC** 04930
SN Apparent movement of a fixated light in a dark field.
UF Illusion (Autokinetic)
B Apparent Movement 1967
Visual Perception 1967

Automated Information Coding 1973
PN 102 **SC** 04940
B Automated Information Processing 1973
R ↓ Computers 1967

Automated Information Processing 1973
PN 890 **SC** 04950
UF Information Processing (Automated)
B Information Technology 2007
N Automated Information Coding 1973
↓ Automated Information Retrieval 1973
Automated Information Storage 1973
R ↓ Communication Systems 1973
↓ Computers 1967
↓ Data Processing 1967
↓ Electronic Communication 2001
↓ Expert Systems 1991
Information 1967
↓ Information Systems 1991
Internet 2001

Automated Information Retrieval 1973
PN 479 **SC** 04960
UF Information Retrieval (Automated)
B Automated Information Processing 1973
N Computer Searching 1991
R Automated Information Storage 1973
↓ Computers 1967
Databases 1991
Information Services 1988
↓ Information Systems 1991

Automated Information Storage 1973
PN 118 **SC** 04970
B Automated Information Processing 1973
R ↓ Automated Information Retrieval 1973
↓ Computers 1967
Databases 1991
↓ Information Systems 1991

Automated Speech Recognition 1994
PN 381 **SC** 04975
SN Machine or other apparatus used in the automatic recognition and understanding of human speech.
UF Automatic Speaker Recognition
B Speech Processing (Mechanical) 1973
R ↓ Artificial Intelligence 1982
↓ Computer Applications 1973
↓ Expert Systems 1991
Speech Perception 1967

Automatic Speaker Recognition
Use Automated Speech Recognition

Automation 1967
PN 745 **SC** 04980
SN Use of mechanical and/or electronic devices to automatically control the operation of an apparatus, system, or process.
R ↓ Artificial Intelligence 1982
↓ Computers 1967

Automatism 1973
PN 337 **SC** 04990
SN An act or movement performed without conscious control.
B Symptoms 1967

Automobile Accidents
Use Motor Traffic Accidents

Automobile Safety
Use Highway Safety

Automobiles 1973
PN 482 **SC** 05020
B Motor Vehicles 1982
R Drivers 1973

Autonomic Ganglia 1973
PN 41 **SC** 05050
SN Clusters of neurons or ganglia within the autonomic nervous system that innervate internal organs.
UF Celiac Plexus
Hypogastric Plexus
Myenteric Plexus
Postganglionic Autonomic Fibers
Preganglionic Autonomic Fibers
Stellate Ganglion
Submucous Plexus
B Autonomic Nervous System 1967
Ganglia 1973

Autonomic Ganglia — (cont'd)
R ↓ Peripheral Nervous System 1973

Autonomic Nervous System 1967
PN 1663 SC 05060
SN The enteric, parasympathetic, and sympathetic nervous systems that regulate key autonomic or involuntary body functions, including the activity of the cardiac muscle, smooth muscles, and glands.
B Peripheral Nervous System 1973
N Adrenergic Nerves 1973
Autonomic Ganglia 1973
Cholinergic Nerves 1973
↓ Parasympathetic Nervous System 1973
↓ Sympathetic Nervous System 1973
R Autonomic Nervous System Disorders 1973

Autonomic Nervous System Disorders 1973
PN 99 SC 05070
B Nervous System Disorders 1967
R ↓ Autonomic Nervous System 1967

Autonomy (Government) 1973
PN 71 SC 05080
R Government 1967

Autonomy (Personality)
Use Independence (Personality)

Autopsy 1973
PN 218 SC 05090
R ↓ Diagnosis 1967
↓ Medical Diagnosis 1973
Psychological Autopsy 1988

Autoregulation
Use Homeostasis

Autoshaping 1978
PN 430 SC 05106
SN Learned behavior or the experimental paradigm involving a Pavlovian pairing of a reinforcer and a stimulus independent of the subject's behavior until the subject makes a response to the stimulus. At that point the reinforcer is made contingent on the acquired response to the stimulus, thereby bringing the response under operant control.
B Conditioning 1967
R Noncontingent Reinforcement 1988
↓ Reinforcement 1967

Autosome Disorders 1973
PN 191 SC 05110
B Chromosome Disorders 1973
N Crying Cat Syndrome 1973
Downs Syndrome 1967
R Autosomes 1973

Autosomes 1973
PN 57 SC 05120
B Chromosomes 1973
R ↓ Autosome Disorders 1973

Autotomy
Use Self Mutilation

Auxiliary Health Workers
Use Allied Health Personnel

Aversion 1967
PN 961 SC 05130
UF Antipathy
Dislike

Aversion — (cont'd)
B Emotional States 1973
N Hate 1973
R Disgust 1994

Aversion Conditioning 1982
PN 2445 SC 05135
SN Conditioning paradigm in which aversive effects are paired with external stimuli resulting in an aversion to the stimuli. Also, the learned aversion itself.
UF Odor Aversion Conditioning
Taste Aversion Conditioning
B Conditioning 1967
N Covert Sensitization 1988
R Aversive Stimulation 1973

Aversion Therapy 1973
PN 535 SC 05140
SN Form of behavior therapy designed to eliminate undesirable behavior patterns through learned associations with unpleasant or painful stimuli. Also known as aversive conditioning therapy.
B Behavior Therapy 1967
N Covert Sensitization 1988
R Counterconditioning 1973
↓ Shock Therapy 1973

Aversive Stimulation 1973
PN 1871 SC 05150
SN Presentation of a noxious stimulus. Also, any noxious stimuli (i.e., stimuli that an organism attempts to avoid or escape from). Compare PUNISHMENT.
B Stimulation 1967
R ↓ Aversion Conditioning 1982
Covert Sensitization 1988

Aviation 1967
PN 930 SC 05160
N Flight Instrumentation 1973
Spaceflight 1967
R Acceleration Effects 1973
Altitude Effects 1973
↓ Aviation Safety 1973
↓ Gravitational Effects 1967

Aviation Personnel
Use Aerospace Personnel

Aviation Safety 1973
PN 311 SC 05170
B Safety 1967
N Air Traffic Control 1973
R Air Traffic Accidents 1973
Aircraft Pilots 1973
↓ Aviation 1967
↓ Transportation Accidents 1973

Aviators
Use Aircraft Pilots

Avoidance 1967
PN 3616 SC 05190
UF Escape
R Avoidance Conditioning 1967
Neophobia 1985
↓ Resistance 1997

Avoidance Conditioning 1967
PN 7177 SC 05200
SN Learned behavior or the operant conditioning procedure in which the subject learns a behavior that prevents the occurrence of an aversive stimulus. Compare ESCAPE CONDITIONING.

Avoidance Conditioning — (cont'd)
UF Active Avoidance
Conditioning (Avoidance)
Passive Avoidance
B Operant Conditioning 1967
R Avoidance 1967

Avoidant Personality Disorder 1994
PN 172 SC 05205
SN Personality disorder characterized by excessive social discomfort, extreme sensitivity to negative perceptions of oneself, pervasive preoccupation with being criticized or rejected in social situations, and low self esteem.
B Personality Disorders 1967
R Social Anxiety 1985
Social Phobia 1985

Awards (Jury) 2005
PN 58 SC 05208
HN This term was introduced in August 2005. Relevant records were re-indexed with this term. The posting note reflects the number of records that were re-indexed.
UF Damage Awards
B Legal Processes 1973
R ↓ Decision Making 1967
Juries 1985
Litigation 2003

Awards (Merit) 2005
PN 956 SC 05209
SN Something given to recognize professional or educational achievement and merit.
HN This term was introduced in August 2005. Relevant records were re-indexed with this term. The posting note reflects the number of records that were re-indexed.
UF Honors
R ↓ Achievement 1967
↓ Incentives 1967
Occupational Success 1978
↓ Performance 1967
Praise 1973
Professional Recognition 2005
↓ Rewards 1967

Awareness 1967
PN 4585 SC 05210
SN Conscious realization, perception, or knowledge.
B Consciousness States 1971
N ↓ Attention 1967
Body Awareness 1982
Phonological Awareness 2004
R Metacognition 1991
Mindfulness 2006
Sensory Gating 1991

Axons 1973
PN 433 SC 05220
SN Long, thread-like outgrowths or extensions of a nerve cell that carry messages away from the main part of the cell. Each nerve cell has one axon, which can travel long distances through the body before passing on its message to other nerve cells or the message's final destination, such as the brain or a muscle. Axons are also referred to as nerve fibers.
B Neurons 1973

Azidothymidine
Use Zidovudine

AZT
Use Zidovudine

Babbling
Use Infant Vocalization

Babinski Reflex 1973
PN 5 **SC** 05250
B Reflexes 1971

Baboons 1973
PN 785 **SC** 05260
B Primates (Nonhuman) 1973

Babysitting
Use Child Care

Back (Anatomy) 1973
PN 195 **SC** 05270
B Anatomy 1967

Back Pain 1982
PN 1602 **SC** 05275
B Pain 1967
R Chronic Pain 1985
↓ Physical Disorders 1997

Background (Family)
Use Family Background

Backward Masking
Use Masking

Baclofen 1991
PN 226 **SC** 05293
B Muscle Relaxing Drugs 1973

Bacteria
Use Microorganisms

Bacterial Disorders 1973
PN 150 **SC** 05300
B Infectious Disorders 1973
N Bacterial Meningitis 1973
Gonorrhea 1973
Pulmonary Tuberculosis 1973
↓ Tuberculosis 1973
R Pneumonia 1973
Rheumatic Fever 1973

Bacterial Meningitis 1973
PN 27 **SC** 05310
SN Bacterial disease in which the membranes covering the brain and spinal cord become inflamed.
B Bacterial Disorders 1973
Meningitis 1973

Balance (Motor Processes)
Use Equilibrium

Baldness
Use Alopecia

Ballet
Use Dance

Banking 2007
PN 79 **SC** 05355
SN Business where monetary transactions such as deposits, withdrawals, and loans take place.
HN This term was introduced in April 2007. Relevant records were re-indexed with this term. The posting note reflects the number of records that were re-indexed.
R Finance 2007
Financial Services 2007
Funding 1988
Money 1967

Bannister Repertory Grid 1973
PN 49 **SC** 05360
B Nonprojective Personality Measures 1973

Baptists
Use Protestants

Barbital 1973
PN 61 **SC** 05380
B Barbiturates 1967
CNS Depressant Drugs 1973
Hypnotic Drugs 1973
Sedatives 1973

Barbiturate Poisoning
HN In August 2005, this term was discontinued and removed from all records containing it, and replaced with TOXIC DISORDERS, its postable counterpart.
Use Toxic Disorders

Barbiturates 1967
PN 278 **SC** 05400
B Drugs 1967
N Amobarbital 1973
Barbital 1973
Hexobarbital 1973
Methohexital 1973
Pentobarbital 1973
Phenobarbital 1973
Secobarbital 1973
Thiopental 1973
R ↓ Anesthetic Drugs 1973
↓ Anticonvulsive Drugs 1973
↓ CNS Depressant Drugs 1973
↓ Hypnotic Drugs 1973
Primidone 1973
↓ Sedatives 1973

Bargaining 1973
PN 965 **SC** 05410
B Negotiation 1973

Barium 1973
PN 10 **SC** 05420
B Metallic Elements 1973

Barometric Pressure
Use Atmospheric Conditions

Baroreceptors 1973
PN 122 **SC** 05440
SN Sensory nerve endings in the vascular system (especially in the large arteries of the carotid sinus and aortic arch) that are sensitive to the stretching of vessel walls in response to changes in blood pressure.
UF Pressoreceptors
B Neural Receptors 1973
Sensory Neurons 1973
Sympathetic Nervous System 1973

Barriers (Treatment)
Use Treatment Barriers

Basal Ganglia 1973
PN 3277 **SC** 05470
SN A group of nuclei that includes the caudate nucleus, putamen, globus pallidus, and substantia nigra, located in the basal regions of the cerebral hemispheres and involved in the control and production of movement.
UF Corpus Striatum
Ventral Striatum
B Ganglia 1973
Telencephalon 1973

Basal Ganglia — (cont'd)
N Amygdala 2003
Caudate Nucleus 1973
Globus Pallidus 1973
Putamen 1985
↓ Striatum 2003
Substantia Nigra 1994
R Extrapyramidal Symptoms 1994
Nucleus Basalis Magnocellularis 1994
Progressive Supranuclear Palsy 1997
↓ Thalamus 1967

Basal Magnocellular Cholinergic Nucleus
Use Nucleus Basalis Magnocellularis

Basal Metabolism 1973
PN 51 **SC** 05480
SN The amount of heat produced by the body to maintain life processes at the lowest level of cell activity in the waking state.
B Metabolism 1967

Basal Readers
Use Reading Materials

Basal Skin Resistance 1973
PN 14 **SC** 05500
SN Baseline or minimum electrical current generated or conducted by the body as measured on the skin surface during a resting state.
B Skin Resistance 1973

Baseball 1973
PN 316 **SC** 05510
B Recreation 1967
Sports 1967

Basic Skills Testing
Use Minimum Competency Tests

Basketball 1973
PN 594 **SC** 05520
B Recreation 1967
Sports 1967

Bass (Fish) 1973
PN 29 **SC** 05530
B Fishes 1967

Bats 1973
PN 452 **SC** 05550
UF Chiroptera
B Mammals 1973

Battered Child Syndrome 1973
PN 43 **SC** 05560
SN Behavioral pattern, including inability to relate to others and feelings of rejection, characteristic of infants and children who have been abused.
B Child Abuse 1971
Syndromes 1973
R Physical Abuse 1991

Battered Females 1988
PN 2173 **SC** 05561
HN Use FAMILY VIOLENCE to access references from 1985-1987.
UF Battered Women
B Human Females 1973
R ↓ Abuse Reporting 1997
Domestic Violence 2006
↓ Partner Abuse 1991
Physical Abuse 1991
Shelters 1991

Battered Women
Use Battered Females

Bayes Theorem
Use Statistical Probability

Bayley Scales of Infant Development 1994
PN 57 **SC** 05575
B Developmental Measures 1994
R ↓ Intelligence Measures 1967

Beavers 1973
PN 21 **SC** 05580
B Rodents 1973

Beck Depression Inventory 1988
PN 454 **SC** 05588
B Nonprojective Personality Measures 1973

Bedwetting
Use Urinary Incontinence

Beer 1973
PN 184 **SC** 05590
B Alcoholic Beverages 1973

Bees 1973
PN 1025 **SC** 05600
B Insects 1967
R Larvae 1973

Beetles 1973
PN 324 **SC** 05610
B Insects 1967
R Larvae 1973

Behavior 1967
PN 13279 **SC** 05670
SN Conceptually broad term referring to any or all aspects of human or animal behavior. Use a more specific term if possible.
N Adaptive Behavior 1991
↓ Adjunctive Behavior 1982
↓ Animal Ethology 1967
↓ Antisocial Behavior 1971
Attachment Behavior 1985
↓ Childhood Play Behavior 1978
Choice Behavior 1967
Classroom Behavior 1973
Conservation (Ecological Behavior) 1978
↓ Consumer Behavior 1967
Coping Behavior 1967
Coronary Prone Behavior 1982
↓ Drinking Behavior 1978
↓ Driving Behavior 1967
↓ Eating Behavior 2004
↓ Exploratory Behavior 1967
↓ Health Behavior 1982
↓ Hoarding Behavior 2003
Illness Behavior 1982
Instinctive Behavior 1982
↓ Psychosexual Behavior 1967
Self Defeating Behavior 1988
↓ Self Destructive Behavior 1985
↓ Social Behavior 1967
Stereotyped Behavior 1973
Voting Behavior 1973
Wandering Behavior 1991
R ↓ Behavior Analysis 2001
Behavior Change 1973
↓ Behavior Disorders 1971
↓ Behavior Modification 1973
↓ Behavior Problems 1967
↓ Behavior Therapy 1967

Behavior — (cont'd)
↓ Behavioral Assessment 1982
Behavioral Contrast 1978
↓ Behavioral Sciences 1997
Behaviorism 1967
Human Nature 1997
Planned Behavior 1997

Behavior Analysis 2001
PN 795 **SC** 05613
SN Field of psychology emphasizing the experimental, conceptual, and applied analysis of behavior in humans and animals.
B Analysis 1967
N ↓ Behavioral Assessment 1982
R ↓ Behavior 1967

Behavior Change 1973
PN 6002 **SC** 05620
SN Detectable changes in behavior due to psychotherapeutic, behavioral, or other intervention, or spontaneous occurrence.
R ↓ Behavior 1967
↓ Behavior Modification 1973
Lifestyle Changes 1997
Motivational Interviewing 2007
Personality Change 1967
Readiness to Change 2007
Stages of Change 2007

Behavior Contracting 1978
PN 296 **SC** 05624
SN Therapeutic technique involving a formal written contract, usually between two parties, which explicitly states the relationship between a particular behavior and its consequences (sanctions). Viewed as a structural means of scheduling reinforcement between the two parties, it is used as a method of controlling contingencies of reinforcement.
R ↓ Behavior Modification 1973
↓ Behavior Therapy 1967

Behavior Disorders 1971
PN 6237 **SC** 05630
SN Disorders characterized by persistent and repetitive patterns of behavior that violate societal norms or rules or that seriously impair a person's functioning. Compare BEHAVIOR PROBLEMS.
B Disorders 1967
N ↓ Addiction 1973
Attempted Suicide 1973
↓ Drug Abuse 1973
↓ Homicide 1967
↓ Juvenile Delinquency 1967
Self Mutilation 1973
R Acting Out 1967
↓ Aggressive Behavior 1967
↓ Antisocial Behavior 1971
↓ Behavior 1967
↓ Behavior Problems 1967
Body Rocking 1973
Conduct Disorder 1991
↓ Crime 1967
↓ Criminal Behavior 2003
Faking 1973
Fecal Incontinence 1973
↓ Mental Disorders 1967
Oppositional Defiant Disorder 1997
Pathological Gambling 1988
↓ Self Destructive Behavior 1985
↓ Symptoms 1967
Thumbsucking 1973
Trichotillomania 2003
Urinary Incontinence 1973

Behavior Modification 1973
PN 8975 **SC** 05640
SN Use of classical conditioning or operant (instrumental) learning techniques to modify behavior.
B Treatment 1967
N ↓ Behavior Therapy 1967
Biofeedback Training 1978
Classroom Behavior Modification 1973
↓ Contingency Management 1973
Fading (Conditioning) 1982
Omission Training 1985
Overcorrection 1985
↓ Self Management 1985
Time Out 1985
R Anger Control 1997
Anxiety Management 1997
Assertiveness Training 1978
↓ Behavior 1967
Behavior Change 1973
Behavior Contracting 1978
↓ Behavioral Assessment 1982
Cognitive Behavior Therapy 2003
Cognitive Restructuring 1985
Cognitive Therapy 1982
Communication Skills Training 1982
Constant Time Delay 1997
Counterconditioning 1973
Functional Analysis 2001
↓ Operant Conditioning 1967
↓ Prompting 1997
Readiness to Change 2007
↓ Relaxation Therapy 1978
↓ Self Help Techniques 1982
Self Monitoring 1982
Social Skills Training 1982
Stages of Change 2007
Stress Management 1985

Behavior Problems 1967
PN 15685 **SC** 05650
SN Disruptive or improper behaviors that generally fall within societal norms and do not seriously impair a person's functioning. Compare BEHAVIOR DISORDERS.
UF Disruptive Behavior
Misbehavior
Misconduct
N Tantrums 1973
R ↓ Behavior 1967
↓ Behavior Disorders 1971
Conduct Disorder 1991
Functional Analysis 2001
Rebelliousness 2003

Behavior Therapy 1967
PN 10535 **SC** 05660
SN Therapeutic approach that may employ classical conditioning, operant learning techniques, or other behavioral techniques, in an attempt to eliminate or modify problem behavior, addressing itself primarily to the client's overt behavior, as opposed to thoughts, feelings, or other cognitive processes.
B Behavior Modification 1973
Psychotherapy 1967
N ↓ Aversion Therapy 1973
↓ Exposure Therapy 1997
Implosive Therapy 1973
Reciprocal Inhibition Therapy 1973
Response Cost 1997
Systematic Desensitization Therapy 1973
R Anger Control 1997
Anxiety Management 1997
↓ Behavior 1967
Behavior Contracting 1978

Behavior Therapy — (cont'd)
Cognitive Behavior Therapy 2003
Counterconditioning 1973
Eye Movement Desensitization Therapy 1997
Paradoxical Techniques 1982

Behavioral Assessment 1982
PN 5330 **SC** 05671
SN Identification and measurement of response units and their controlling environmental and organismic variables for the purposes of understanding and altering human behavior.
B Behavior Analysis 2001
Psychological Assessment 1997
N Functional Analysis 2001
R ↓ Behavior 1967
↓ Behavior Modification 1973
↓ Empirical Methods 1973

Behavioral Contrast 1978
PN 308 **SC** 05674
SN Change in response rate or latency following a change in reinforcement of one component of multiple operant discrimination schedules of reinforcement.
R ↓ Behavior 1967
↓ Reinforcement 1967
Response Frequency 1973
Response Latency 1967
Stimulus Discrimination 1973

Behavioral Ecology 1997
PN 742 **SC** 57450
SN Study, usually based on naturalistic observations, of the interaction between the environment and the behavior of organisms within that environment.
R ↓ Ecological Factors 1973
Ecological Psychology 1994
Ecology 1973
Environmental Psychology 1982
Research Setting 2001

Behavioral Economics 2003
PN 287 **SC** 58057
SN The application of economic principles to human behavior.
HN This term was introduced in June 2003. Relevant records were re-indexed with this term. The posting note reflects the number of records that were re-indexed.
B Economics 1985
R ↓ Consumer Behavior 1967

Behavioral Genetics 1994
PN 1365 **SC** 57405
SN Scientific discipline concerned with the role of genes and gene action in the expression of behavior. Includes analysis of whole populations for specific traits, e.g., intelligence. Used for the scientific discipline or the behavioral genetic processes themselves.
B Genetics 1967
R Biopsychosocial Approach 1991
↓ Genetic Disorders 1973
Genetic Dominance 1973
Genetic Recessiveness 1973
Nature Nurture 1994
Population Genetics 1973
Psychobiology 1982
Sociobiology 1982

Behavioral Health
Use Health Care Psychology

Behavioral Medicine
Use Health Care Psychology

Behavioral Sciences 1997
PN 1059 **SC** 05680
SN Group of scientific disciplines dealing with human and animal action and behavior.
HN Use SOCIAL SCIENCES to access references from 1973-1996.
B Social Sciences 1967
N ↓ Psychology 1967
R ↓ Behavior 1967
↓ Sociology 1967

Behavioral Sensitization
Use Sensitization

Behaviorism 1967
PN 2528 **SC** 05690
B History of Psychology 1967
Psychological Theories 2001
R ↓ Behavior 1967
Positivism (Philosophy) 1997
Skinner (Burrhus Frederic) 1991
Watson (John Broadus) 1991

Bekesy Audiometry
Use Audiometry

Beliefs (Nonreligious)
Use Attitudes

Beliefs (Religion)
Use Religious Beliefs

Bem Sex Role Inventory 1988
PN 77 **SC** 05727
B Nonprojective Personality Measures 1973

Bemegride 1973
PN 20 **SC** 05730
B Analeptic Drugs 1973

Benactyzine 1973
PN 27 **SC** 05740
B Cholinergic Blocking Drugs 1973
Tranquilizing Drugs 1967

Benadryl
Use Diphenhydramine

Bender Gestalt Test 1967
PN 429 **SC** 05770
B Projective Personality Measures 1973
R ↓ Neuropsychological Assessment 1982

Benign Neoplasms 1973
PN 39 **SC** 05800
B Neoplasms 1967

Benton Revised Visual Retention Test 1973
PN 43 **SC** 05810
B Intelligence Measures 1967
R ↓ Neuropsychological Assessment 1982

Benzedrine
Use Amphetamine

Benzodiazepine Agonists 1994
PN 195 **SC** 05821
R ↓ Benzodiazepines 1978

Benzodiazepine Antagonists 1985
PN 444 **SC** 05822
R ↓ Benzodiazepines 1978

Benzodiazepines 1978
PN 3488 **SC** 05824
B Drugs 1967
N Alprazolam 1988
Chlordiazepoxide 1973
Clonazepam 1991
Diazepam 1973
Flunitrazepam 2004
Flurazepam 1982
Lorazepam 1988
Midazolam 1991
Nitrazepam 1978
Oxazepam 1978
R ↓ Anticonvulsive Drugs 1973
Benzodiazepine Agonists 1994
Benzodiazepine Antagonists 1985
↓ Hypnotic Drugs 1973
↓ Minor Tranquilizers 1973
↓ Muscle Relaxing Drugs 1973
↓ Sedatives 1973
↓ Tranquilizing Drugs 1967

Bereavement
Use Grief

Beta Blockers
Use Adrenergic Blocking Drugs

Between Groups Design 1985
PN 90 **SC** 05828
SN Experimental design in which the subjects serve in only one treatment condition. Includes designs of matched or correlated groups and randomized groups.
B Experimental Design 1967

Beverages (Alcoholic)
Use Alcoholic Beverages

Beverages (Nonalcoholic) 1978
PN 316 **SC** 05833
UF Coffee
Tea
R ↓ Alcoholic Beverages 1973
↓ Drinking Behavior 1978
Nutrition 1973

Bias (Experimenter)
Use Experimenter Bias

Bias (Response)
Use Response Bias

Bias Crimes
Use Hate Crimes

Biased Sampling 1973
PN 275 **SC** 05860
SN Inadequate selection of subject samples resulting in an inaccurate representation of the larger population.

Biased Sampling — (cont'd)
B Sampling (Experimental) 1973

Bible 1973
PN 624 SC 05870
B Religious Literature 1973
R ↓ Christianity 1973
Judaism 1967
↓ Religious Beliefs 1973

Bibliotherapy 1973
PN 438 SC 05890
SN Use of reading as adjunct to psychotherapy.
B Treatment 1967
R Poetry Therapy 1994

Bicuculline 1994
PN 168 SC 05895
HN Use GAMMA AMINOBUTYRIC ACID ANTAGONISTS to access references from 1985-1993.
B Analeptic Drugs 1973
Gamma Aminobutyric Acid Antagonists 1985

Bicycle Accidents
Use Transportation Accidents

Bicycle Safety
Use Transportation Safety

Big Five Personality Model
Use Five Factor Personality Model

Bile 1973
PN 27 SC 05900
B Body Fluids 1973
R Taurine 1982

Bilingual Education 1978
PN 850 SC 05907
SN Education in one's native language as well as the majority language of the country in which one is educated, or education in two languages.
B Education 1967
R Bilingualism 1973
English as Second Language 1997
Foreign Language Learning 1967
Foreign Languages 1973
Multicultural Education 1988
↓ Multilingualism 1973
↓ Teaching 1967

Bilingualism 1973
PN 3765 SC 05910
B Multilingualism 1973
R Bilingual Education 1978
Code Switching 1988
Cross Cultural Communication 1997
English as Second Language 1997
↓ Language 1967
Language Proficiency 1988
Native Language 2004

Binge Drinking 2006
PN 180 SC 05914
SN Drinking heavily to the point of intoxication during a period of time set aside for the purpose of drinking.
HN This term was introduced in May 2006. Relevant records were re-indexed with this term. The posting note reflects the number of records that were re-indexed.
B Alcohol Abuse 1988
R ↓ Alcohol Drinking Patterns 1967
↓ Alcohol Intoxication 1973
Social Drinking 1973

Binge Eating 1991
PN 1305 SC 05915
SN Eating excessive quantities of food, often after stressful events. Compare BULIMIA.
B Eating Behavior 2004
R Bulimia 1985
↓ Eating Disorders 1997
Purging (Eating Disorders) 2003
↓ Symptoms 1967

Binocular Vision 1967
PN 1905 SC 05920
B Visual Perception 1967

Binomial Distribution 1973
PN 82 SC 05930
B Statistical Probability 1967
R ↓ Statistical Sample Parameters 1973

Bioavailability 1991
PN 203 SC 05935
SN The degree and rate at which a drug enters the bloodstream and is circulated to specific organs or tissues, as measured by drug concentrations in body fluids or by pharmacologic or therapeutic response.
UF Bioequivalence
R Absorption (Physiological) 1973
↓ Biochemistry 1967
↓ Drug Dosages 1973
↓ Drug Therapy 1967
↓ Drugs 1967
↓ Metabolism 1967
↓ Pharmacology 1973

Biochemical Markers
Use Biological Markers

Biochemistry 1967
PN 4188 SC 05940
SN Study of the biological and physiological chemistry of living organisms. Used for the scientific discipline or the biochemical processes themselves.
B Chemistry 1967
N ↓ Neurochemistry 1973
R Bioavailability 1991
Biological Markers 1991
↓ Physiology 1967

Biodata
Use Biographical Data

Bioequivalence
Use Bioavailability

Bioethics 2003
PN 777 SC 05944
SN Discipline concerned with the ethical and social implications of biological research and medicine.
HN This term was introduced in June 2003. Relevant records were re-indexed with this term. The posting note reflects the number of records that were re-indexed.
UF Medical Ethics
B Ethics 1967
R Assisted Suicide 1997
↓ Biotechnology 2007
↓ Client Rights 1988
Euthanasia 1973
Experimental Ethics 1978
↓ Genetic Engineering 1994
↓ Health Care Delivery 1978
↓ Medical Sciences 1967
Professional Ethics 1973

Biofeedback 1973
PN 1673 SC 05945
SN Provision of immediate ongoing information regarding one's own physiological processes.
B Feedback 1967
N Biofeedback Training 1978
Neurofeedback 2006
R ↓ Biotechnology 2007
↓ Conditioning 1967
↓ Reinforcement 1967
↓ Stimulation 1967

Biofeedback Training 1978
PN 2396 SC 05946
SN Self-directed process by which a person uses biofeedback information to gain voluntary control over processes or functions that are primarily under autonomic control. Used in experimental or treatment settings with human subjects.
B Behavior Modification 1973
Biofeedback 1973
Training 2006
R ↓ Alternative Medicine 1997
Autogenic Training 1973

Biographical Data 1978
PN 1122 SC 05948
SN Information identifying an individual's background, life history, or present status.
UF Biodata
R Biographical Inventories 1973
Demographic Characteristics 1967
↓ Educational Background 1967
↓ Family Background 1973
↓ Life Experiences 1973
Patient History 1973

Biographical Inventories 1973
PN 124 SC 05950
SN Sets of items listing information on an individual's background. Not used as a document type identifier.
B Inventories 1967
R Biographical Data 1978

Biography 1967
PN 1701 SC 05960
SN Recorded account of a person's life.
HN From 1967-2000, the term was also used as a document type identifier; however, this usage has been discontinued due to the advent of Form/Content Type field identifiers. References from 1967-2000 can be accessed using either BIOGRAPHY or the Biography Form/Content Type field identifier.
B Prose 1973
N Autobiography 1973
R Narratives 1997
Psychohistory 1978

Bioinformatics 2007
PN 12 SC 05965
SN Information technology as applied to the life sciences, especially the technology used for the collection, storage, and retrieval of genomic data.
HN This term was introduced in April 2007. Relevant records were re-indexed with this term. The posting note reflects the number of records that were re-indexed.
B Information Technology 2007
R ↓ Biology 1967
Data Collection 1982
Databases 1991
Genome 2003
↓ Information Systems 1991

Biological Clocks (Animal)
Use Animal Biological Rhythms

Biological Family 1988
PN 623 **SC** 05975
SN The genetic family members of a person in contrast to adoptive or foster families.
UF Birth Parents
Natural Family
B Family 1967
Family Members 1973
R Family of Origin 1991

Biological Markers 1991
PN 2287 **SC** 05977
UF Biochemical Markers
Clinical Markers
R ↓ Biochemistry 1967
Interleukins 1994
↓ Medical Diagnosis 1973
Physiological Correlates 1967
Predisposition 1973
Prognosis 1973
↓ Screening 1982
Susceptibility (Disorders) 1973

Biological Psychiatry 1994
PN 256 **SC** 05978
SN A branch of psychiatry focusing on biological, physical, and neurological factors in the etiology and treatment of mental and behavioral disorders.
B Psychiatry 1967
R Neurobiology 1973
Neuropsychiatry 1973
Psychobiology 1982

Biological Rhythms 1967
PN 623 **SC** 05980
SN Rhythmic and periodic variations in physiological and psychological functions. Used for human or animal populations.
N ↓ Animal Biological Rhythms 1973
Human Biological Rhythms 1973
Sleep Wake Cycle 1985
R Lunar Synodic Cycle 1973
Seasonal Variations 1973

Biological Symbiosis 1973
PN 722 **SC** 06000
SN Intimate relationship between organisms of two or more kinds, particularly one in which the symbiont benefits from the host. Includes parasitic behavior. Limited to animal populations.
UF Parasitism
Symbiosis (Biological)
R ↓ Animals 1967
↓ Biology 1967
Interspecies Interaction 1991

Biology 1967
PN 4091 **SC** 06010
SN Branch of science dealing with living organisms. Used for the scientific discipline or the biological processes themselves.
B Sciences 1967
N Botany 1973
Neurobiology 1973
Sociobiology 1982
Zoology 1973
R Bioinformatics 2007
Biological Symbiosis 1973
Biosynthesis 1973
↓ Biotechnology 2007
Phylogenesis 1973

Biology — (cont'd)
Psychobiology 1982

Biopsy 1973
PN 84 **SC** 06020
B Medical Diagnosis 1973
R ↓ Surgery 1971

Biopsychosocial Approach 1991
PN 1702 **SC** 06024
SN A systematic integration of biological, psychological, and social approaches to the study, treatment, and understanding of mental health and mental disorders.
UF Biopsychosocial Model
R Behavioral Genetics 1994
Holistic Health 1985
Interdisciplinary Treatment Approach 1973
Psychobiology 1982
Systems Theory 1988

Biopsychosocial Model
Use Biopsychosocial Approach

Biosynthesis 1973
PN 148 **SC** 06030
SN Formation of chemical compounds of relatively complex structure from nutrients by enzyme-catalyzed reactions in living cells.
HN In August 2005, this term replaced the discontinued term ANABOLISM. ANABOLISM was removed from all records containing it, and was replaced with BIOSYNTHESIS, its postable counterpart.
UF Anabolism
B Metabolism 1967
R ↓ Biology 1967

Biotechnology 2007
PN 51 **SC** 06031
SN The use of biological organisms, processes, or systems to develop or modify products, or perform industrial processes.
HN This term was introduced in April 2007. Relevant records were re-indexed with this term. The posting note reflects the number of records that were re-indexed.
B Technology 1973
N Cloning 2003
Reproductive Technology 1988
R Bioethics 2003
↓ Biofeedback 1973
↓ Biology 1967
↓ Genetic Engineering 1994

Bioterrorism 2007
PN 45 **SC** 06032
SN The use of biological agents or weapons to carry out acts of terrorism.
HN This term was introduced in April 2007. Relevant records were re-indexed with this term. The posting note reflects the number of records that were re-indexed.
B Terrorism 1982
R ↓ War 1967
↓ Weapons 1978

Bipolar Affective Disorder
Use Bipolar Disorder

Bipolar Disorder 2001
PN 10574 **SC** 06034
HN The term MANIC DEPRESSIVE PSYCHOSIS was used to represent this concept from 1967-1988, and MANIC DEPRESSION was used from 1988-

Bipolar Disorder — (cont'd)
2000. In 2001, BIPOLAR DISORDER was created to replace these terms. MANIC DEPRESSIVE PSYCHOSIS and MANIC DEPRESSION were removed from all records containing them and replaced with BIPOLAR DISORDER.
UF Bipolar Affective Disorder
Bipolar Mood Disorder
Manic Depression
Manic Depressive Psychosis
B Affective Disorders 2001
N Cyclothymic Personality 1973
R Affective Psychosis 1973
↓ Major Depression 1988
↓ Mania 1967

Bipolar Mood Disorder
Use Bipolar Disorder

Biracial Children
Use Interracial Offspring

Birds 1967
PN 7831 **SC** 06040
UF Fowl
B Vertebrates 1973
N Blackbirds 1973
Budgerigars 1973
Canaries 1973
Chickens 1967
Doves 1973
Ducks 1973
Geese 1973
Owls 1997
Penguins 1973
Pigeons 1967
Quails 1973
Robins 1973
Sea Gulls 1973

Birth 1967
PN 3043 **SC** 06050
UF Childbirth
Parturition
N Natural Childbirth 1978
Premature Birth 1973
R Birth Injuries 1973
Birth Rites 1973
Birth Trauma 1973
Birth Weight 1985
Childbirth Training 1978
Labor (Childbirth) 1973
Midwifery 1985
Obstetrical Complications 1978
Perinatal Period 1994
↓ Pregnancy 1967
↓ Sexual Reproduction 1973

Birth Control 1971
PN 1696 **SC** 06060
UF Contraception
Population Control
B Family Planning 1973
N ↓ Contraceptive Devices 1973
Rhythm Method 1973
Tubal Ligation 1973
Vasectomy 1973
R Condoms 1991
Induced Abortion 1971
Overpopulation 1973
Premarital Intercourse 1973
Safe Sex 2003
Sexual Abstinence 1973
↓ Sterilization (Sex) 1973

Birth Control Attitudes
Use Family Planning Attitudes

Birth Injuries 1973
PN 107 **SC** 06070
SN Physical injuries (such as brain damage) received during birth, mostly in, but not limited to, breech births, instrument deliveries, neonatal anoxia, or premature births. Used for both human and animal populations.
UF Injuries (Birth)
B Injuries 1973
R ↓ Birth 1967
Birth Trauma 1973
↓ Neonatal Disorders 1973
Obstetrical Complications 1978

Birth Order 1967
PN 1893 **SC** 06080
B Family Structure 1973

Birth Parents
Use Biological Family

Birth Rate 1982
PN 219 **SC** 06087
SN Ratio of the number of live births to the number of individuals in a human population within a specified time period.
R Fertility 1988
↓ Population 1973

Birth Rites 1973
PN 99 **SC** 06090
B Rites of Passage 1973
R ↓ Birth 1967
Circumcision 2001

Birth Trauma 1973
PN 127 **SC** 06100
SN Stress, as experienced by infants, of being born and bombarded with external stimuli that may have negative influences on subsequent psychological development. Limited to human populations.
B Trauma 2006
R ↓ Birth 1967
Birth Injuries 1973

Birth Weight 1985
PN 1213 **SC** 06105
UF Low Birth Weight
B Body Weight 1967
R ↓ Birth 1967
Premature Birth 1973

Bisexuality 1973
PN 2260 **SC** 06110
B Psychosexual Behavior 1967
Sexual Orientation 1997
R Lesbianism 1973
Male Homosexuality 1973
Transsexualism 1973
Transvestism 1973

Bitterness
Use Taste Perception

Black Power Movement 1973
PN 56 **SC** 06130
B Social Movements 1967
R ↓ Activism 2003

Blackbirds 1973
PN 197 **SC** 06140
B Birds 1967

Blacks 1982
PN 27429 **SC** 06150
HN In 1982, this term was created to replace the discontinued term NEGROES. In 2000, NEGROES was removed from all records containing it, and replaced with BLACKS.
UF African Americans
Negroes
B Racial and Ethnic Groups 2001
R African Cultural Groups 2006
Minority Groups 1967

Blacky Pictures Test
HN Term was discontinued in 1997. In 2000, the term was removed from all records containing it, and replaced with PROJECTIVE PERSONALITY MEASURES, its postable counterpart.
Use Projective Personality Measures

Bladder 1973
PN 114 **SC** 06170
B Urogenital System 1973

Blame 1994
PN 650 **SC** 06175
SN To assign fault or responsibility for an event, state, or behavior, or the condition of fault or responsibility for something believed to deserve censure.
R Accountability 1988
Attribution 1973
Guilt 1967
↓ Responsibility 1973
Shame 1994
↓ Social Perception 1967

Blind 1967
PN 3268 **SC** 06180
B Vision Disorders 1982
N Deaf Blind 1991
R Braille 1978

Blink Reflex
Use Eyeblink Reflex

Block Design Test (Kohs)
Use Kohs Block Design Test

Blood 1967
PN 2169 **SC** 06200
B Body Fluids 1973
N ↓ Blood Plasma 1973
R Blood Alcohol Concentration 1994
↓ Blood and Lymphatic Disorders 1973
Blood Groups 1973
Blood Volume 1973
↓ Heart 1967

Blood Alcohol Concentration 1994
PN 292 **SC** 06205
R ↓ Alcohol Abuse 1988
↓ Alcohol Drinking Patterns 1967
↓ Alcohol Intoxication 1973
↓ Alcohols 1967
↓ Blood 1967
Driving Under the Influence 1988

Blood Alcohol Concentration — (cont'd)
Drug Usage Screening 1988

Blood and Lymphatic Disorders 1973
PN 514 **SC** 06210
UF Blood Disorders
Hematologic Disorders
Lymphatic Disorders
B Physical Disorders 1997
N Anemia 1973
Hemophilia 1973
Leukemias 1973
Malaria 1973
Porphyria 1973
Rh Incompatibility 1973
Sickle Cell Disease 1994
R ↓ Blood 1967
Epstein Barr Viral Disorder 1994

Blood Brain Barrier 1994
PN 105 **SC** 06215
SN Functional barrier between brain blood vessels and brain tissues.
R Blood Circulation 1973
↓ Blood Flow 1973
↓ Blood Vessels 1973
↓ Brain 1967
↓ Cardiovascular System 1967
Cerebrospinal Fluid 1973
↓ Neurochemistry 1973

Blood Cells 1973
PN 239 **SC** 06220
B Cells (Biology) 1973
N Erythrocytes 1973
↓ Leucocytes 1973

Blood Circulation 1973
PN 207 **SC** 06230
UF Circulation (Blood)
R Arterial Pulse 1973
Blood Brain Barrier 1994
↓ Blood Flow 1973
Blood Volume 1973
Cerebral Blood Flow 1994

Blood Coagulation 1973
PN 54 **SC** 06240
UF Coagulation (Blood)

Blood Disorders
Use Blood and Lymphatic Disorders

Blood Donation
Use Tissue Donation

Blood Flow 1973
PN 866 **SC** 06270
N Cerebral Blood Flow 1994
R Blood Brain Barrier 1994
Blood Circulation 1973
Blood Volume 1973

Blood Glucose
Use Blood Sugar

Blood Groups 1973
PN 86 **SC** 06300
SN Genetically determined classes of human erythrocytes based on specific antigens for which the groups are named.
R Antigens 1982
↓ Blood 1967
Erythrocytes 1973

Blood Groups — (cont'd)
↓ Genetics 1967

Blood Plasma 1973
PN 4176 **SC** 06310
UF Plasma (Blood)
B Blood 1967
N Blood Serum 1973

Blood Platelets 1973
PN 1237 **SC** 06320
UF Platelets (Blood)

Blood Pressure 1967
PN 3661 **SC** 06330
N Diastolic Pressure 1973
Systolic Pressure 1973
R ↓ Blood Pressure Disorders 1973
Blood Volume 1973
Cardiovascular Reactivity 1994
Cerebral Blood Flow 1994
↓ Vasoconstrictor Drugs 1973
↓ Vasodilator Drugs 1973

Blood Pressure Disorders 1973
PN 42 **SC** 06340
B Cardiovascular Disorders 1967
N ↓ Hypertension 1973
Hypotension 1973
Syncope 1973
R ↓ Arteriosclerosis 1973
↓ Blood Pressure 1967
Vasoconstriction 1973
Vasodilation 1973

Blood Proteins 1973
PN 143 **SC** 06350
B Proteins 1973
N Hemoglobin 1973
↓ Immunoglobulins 1973
Serum Albumin 1973

Blood Serum 1973
PN 1986 **SC** 06360
UF Serum (Blood)
B Blood Plasma 1973
R Antibodies 1973

Blood Sugar 1973
PN 497 **SC** 06370
UF Blood Glucose
B Glucose 1973

Blood Transfusion 1973
PN 64 **SC** 06380
UF Transfusion (Blood)
B Physical Treatment Methods 1973
R Disease Transmission 2004
Hemodialysis 1973
Tissue Donation 1991

Blood Vessels 1973
PN 97 **SC** 06390
B Cardiovascular System 1967
N ↓ Arteries (Anatomy) 1973
Capillaries (Anatomy) 1973
Veins (Anatomy) 1973
R Blood Brain Barrier 1994

Blood Volume 1973
PN 163 **SC** 06400
R ↓ Blood 1967
Blood Circulation 1973

Blood Volume — (cont'd)
↓ Blood Flow 1973
↓ Blood Pressure 1967

Blue Collar Workers 1973
PN 1348 **SC** 06410
SN Employees whose unskilled, semiskilled, or skilled occupations involve physical labor.
UF Laborers (Construction and Industry)
B Business and Industrial Personnel 1967
N Industrial Foremen 1973
Skilled Industrial Workers 1973
Unskilled Industrial Workers 1973
R Technical Service Personnel 1973

Boarding Schools 1988
PN 134 **SC** 06412
SN Elementary or secondary residential educational institutions for students enrolled in an instructional program. Primarily used for non-disordered populations.
B Schools 1967
R Institutional Schools 1978

Boards of Education 1978
PN 117 **SC** 06416
SN Governing bodies responsible for managing public school systems.
R ↓ Education 1967
Educational Administration 1967
↓ School Administrators 1973

Body Art
Use Cosmetic Techniques

Body Awareness 1982
PN 949 **SC** 06425
SN Perception of one's physical self or body at any particular time.
B Awareness 1967
R ↓ Body Image 1967
Human Body 2003
Self Perception 1967
↓ Somesthetic Perception 1967

Body Dysmorphic Disorder 2001
PN 338 **SC** 06427
SN A preoccupation with a slight or imagined defect in appearance that causes significant distress or impairment in social, occupational, or other areas of functioning. Compare BODY IMAGE DISTURBANCES.
HN In 2001, this term was created to replace the discontinued term DYSMORPHOPHOBIA. DYSMORPHOPHOBIA was removed from all records containing it and replaced with BODY DYSMORPHIC DISORDER.
UF Atypical Somatoform Disorder
Dysmorphophobia
B Somatoform Disorders 2001
R ↓ Body Image Disturbances 1973
Obsessive Compulsive Disorder 1985

Body Fluids 1973
PN 130 **SC** 06430
B Anatomy 1967
N Amniotic Fluid 1973
Bile 1973
↓ Blood 1967
Cerebrospinal Fluid 1973
Mucus 1973
Saliva 1973
Sweat 1973

Body Fluids — (cont'd)
Urine 1973
R ↓ Physiology 1967

Body Height 1973
PN 514 **SC** 06440
UF Height (Body)
B Body Size 1985
R Body Mass Index 2006
Physique 1967

Body Image 1967
PN 4710 **SC** 06450
SN Mental representation of one's body according to feedback received from one's body, the environment, and other people.
N ↓ Body Image Disturbances 1973
R Body Awareness 1982
Human Body 2003

Body Image Disturbances 1973
PN 1027 **SC** 06460
SN Distortions in the evaluative picture or mental representation an individual has of his/her body. Compare BODY DYSMORPHIC DISORDER.
B Body Image 1967
N Koro 1994
Phantom Limbs 1973
R Anorexia Nervosa 1973
Body Dysmorphic Disorder 2001
Castration Anxiety 1973

Body Language 1973
PN 481 **SC** 06470
SN Type of nonverbal communication in which thoughts, feelings, etc., are expressed through bodily movement or posture.
UF Kinesics
B Interpersonal Communication 1973
Nonverbal Communication 1971
R Gestures 1973
Posture 1973

Body Mass Index 2006
PN 213 **SC** 06474
SN A measure of relative body weight derived from calculations of one's weight in kilograms and height in inches squared. Often used as an indicator for obesity.
HN This term was introduced in May 2006. Relevant records were re-indexed with this term. The posting note reflects the number of records that were re-indexed.
R Body Height 1973
↓ Body Size 1985
↓ Body Weight 1967
Obesity 1973
↓ Overweight 2007

Body Rocking 1973
PN 65 **SC** 06480
UF Rocking (Body)
B Symptoms 1967
R ↓ Behavior Disorders 1971

Body Rotation
Use Rotational Behavior

Body Size 1985
PN 1600 **SC** 06485
SN Used for human or animal populations. For human populations consider also PHYSIQUE or SOMATOTYPES.

Body Size — (cont'd)
B Size 1973
N Body Height 1973
↓ Body Weight 1967
R Body Mass Index 2006
Physique 1967

Body Sway Testing 1973
PN 88 SC 06490
B Measurement 1967
R ↓ Neuropsychological Assessment 1982

Body Temperature 1973
PN 1828 SC 06500
UF Temperature (Body)
B Physiology 1967
N Skin Temperature 1973
Thermoregulation (Body) 1973
R Hypothermia 1973

Body Types
Use Somatotypes

Body Weight 1967
PN 6553 SC 06520
UF Weight (Body)
B Body Size 1985
N Birth Weight 1985
↓ Overweight 2007
↓ Underweight 1973
R Body Mass Index 2006
Obesity (Attitudes Toward) 1997
Physique 1967
Weight Control 1985

Bombesin 1988
PN 120 SC 06523
B Neuropeptides 2003
Peptides 1973

Bonding (Emotional)
Use Attachment Behavior

Bone Conduction Audiometry 1973
PN 40 SC 06530
B Audiometry 1967
R ↓ Auditory Stimulation 1967
↓ Perceptual Measures 1973

Bone Disorders 1973
PN 169 SC 06540
B Musculoskeletal Disorders 1973
N Osteoporosis 1991

Bone Marrow 1973
PN 305 SC 06550
B Immune System 2006
R Bones 1973

Bones 1973
PN 320 SC 06570
B Connective Tissues 1973
Musculoskeletal System 1973
R Bone Marrow 1973
Jaw 1973
Spinal Column 1973

Bonobos 1997
PN 103 SC 06575
SN Members of the species Pan panicus. Although not members of the chimpanzee species, Bonobos are often referred to as pygmy chimpanzees.

Bonobos — (cont'd)
UF Pygmy Chimpanzees
B Primates (Nonhuman) 1973
R Chimpanzees 1973

Bonuses 1973
PN 50 SC 06580
B Employee Benefits 1973
R Salaries 1973

Books 1973
PN 1519 SC 06600
SN Refers to books as a means of communication, as distinct from the document type identifier BOOK.
B Printed Communications Media 1973
N ↓ Textbooks 1978
R Reading Materials 1973

Borderline Mental Retardation 1973
PN 318 SC 06610
SN IQ 71-84.
HN In 2000, this term replaced the discontinued term SLOW LEARNERS and the discontinued and deleted term BORDERLINE MENTALLY RETARDED. These terms were removed from all records containing them and replaced with BORDERLINE MENTAL RETARDATION.
UF Slow Learners
B Mental Retardation 1967
R Psychosocial Mental Retardation 1973

Borderline Personality Disorder 2001
PN 1389 SC 06622
SN Personality disorder with maladaptive patterns of behavior characterized by impulsive and unpredictable actions, mood instability, and unstable interpersonal relationships.
HN Use BORDERLINE STATES to access references from 1978-2000.
B Personality Disorders 1967
R Borderline States 1978
↓ Self Destructive Behavior 1985

Borderline States 1978
PN 3894 SC 06624
SN State in which individual has not broken with reality but may become psychotic if exposed to unfavorable circumstances.
R Borderline Personality Disorder 2001
↓ Mental Disorders 1967
↓ Neurosis 1967
↓ Psychosis 1967

Boredom 1973
PN 391 SC 06630
B Emotional States 1973
R Monotony 1978

Botany 1973
PN 101 SC 06640
B Biology 1967
R Horticulture Therapy 2007
Phylogenesis 1973
↓ Plants (Botanical) 2007

Bottle Feeding 1973
PN 139 SC 06650
B Eating Behavior 2004

Boundaries (Psychological) 1997
PN 390 SC 06660
SN Psychological barriers that separate or divide, and, in some cases, protect the integrity of individuals or groups.

Boundaries (Psychological) — (cont'd)
R ↓ Group Dynamics 1967
Intergroup Dynamics 1973
↓ Interpersonal Interaction 1967
Personal Space 1973
↓ Personality Processes 1967
Territoriality 1967

Boundary Violations (Sexual)
Use Professional Client Sexual Relations

Bourgeois
Use Middle Class

Bowel Disorders
Use Colon Disorders

Boys
Use Human Males

Brachial Plexus
Use Spinal Nerves

Bradycardia 1973
PN 139 SC 06730
SN Excessively slow heart beat.
B Arrhythmias (Heart) 1973

Bradykinesia 2001
PN 43 SC 06735
SN Abnormal slowness of movement, which is often a symptom of neurological disorders, particularly Parkinson's disease.
UF Hypokinesia
B Dyskinesia 1973
R Hyperkinesis 1973
Parkinsonism 1994
Parkinsons Disease 1973

Braille 1978
PN 187 SC 06737
B Reading 1967
R ↓ Blind 1967
Braille Instruction 1973
Reading Education 1973
Reading Materials 1973
↓ Tactual Perception 1967

Braille Instruction 1973
PN 57 SC 06740
B Curriculum 1967
R Braille 1978
Reading Education 1973

Brain 1967
PN 18032 SC 06750
B Central Nervous System 1967
N ↓ Brain Stem 1973
↓ Forebrain 1985
↓ Hindbrain 1997
↓ Mesencephalon 1973
R Blood Brain Barrier 1994
↓ Brain Disorders 1967
Brain Size 1973
Brain Weight 1973
Cerebral Atrophy 1994
↓ Cerebral Dominance 1973
↓ Lateral Dominance 1967
Left Hemisphere 2005
↓ Neuroimaging 2003
Ocular Dominance 1973
Right Hemisphere 2005

Brain Ablation
Use Brain Lesions

Brain Concussion 1973
PN 318 **SC** 06770
SN A traumatic brain injury resulting from closed head trauma and characterized by transient alterations of neural function, including the loss of consciousness.
UF Concussion (Brain)
B Head Injuries 1973
Traumatic Brain Injury 1997

Brain Damage 1967
PN 13167 **SC** 06780
SN Injury to the brain or degeneration of brain cells that may occur from a number of conditions and may be widespread and diffuse or focal and localized. Common causes include hypoxia, infection, or cerebrovascular disorders. Brain damage may be associated with a behavioral or functional abnormality.
HN In 2000, this term replaced the discontinued and deleted term BRAIN DAMAGED. BRAIN DAMAGED was removed from all records containing it and replaced with BRAIN DAMAGE.
B Brain Disorders 1967
N ↓ Traumatic Brain Injury 1997
R Cerebral Atrophy 1994
Cognitive Impairment 2003
↓ Congenital Disorders 1973
↓ Disorders 1967
↓ Epilepsy 1967
Global Amnesia 1997
↓ Head Injuries 1973
↓ Mental Retardation 1967
↓ Neuropsychological Assessment 1982

Brain Development 2007
PN 765 **SC** 06785
HN In April 2007, BRAIN DEVELOPMENT changed status from nonpostable to postable. Relevant records were re-indexed with this term. The posting note reflects the number of records that were re-indexed.
UF Brain Growth
B Neural Development 1985
R ↓ Cognitive Development 1973

Brain Disorders 1967
PN 2677 **SC** 06800
SN Pathological conditions affecting the intracranial components of the central nervous system.
B Central Nervous System Disorders 1973
N Acute Alcoholic Intoxication 1973
Anencephaly 1973
↓ Aphasia 1967
Athetosis 1973
↓ Brain Damage 1967
Brain Neoplasms 1973
Cerebral Palsy 1967
Cerebrovascular Accidents 1973
Chronic Alcoholic Intoxication 1973
↓ Encephalitis 1973
↓ Encephalopathies 1982
↓ Epilepsy 1967
↓ Epileptic Seizures 1973
General Paresis 1973
Hydrocephalus 2006
Microcephaly 1973
↓ Organic Brain Syndromes 1973
Parkinsons Disease 1973
Tay Sachs Disease 2003

Brain Disorders — (cont'd)
R ↓ Brain 1967
Cerebral Atrophy 1994
↓ Memory Disorders 1973
↓ Mental Disorders 1967
↓ Neuroimaging 2003
Rett Syndrome 1994
↓ Seizures 2005

Brain Growth
Use Brain Development

Brain Injury (Traumatic)
Use Traumatic Brain Injury

Brain Lesions 1967
PN 10756 **SC** 06830
HN Not defined prior to 1982. From 1982, limited to experimentally induced lesions and used primarily for animal populations.
UF Brain Ablation
Cerebral Lesions
Subcortical Lesions
B Lesions 1967
N Hypothalamus Lesions 1973
R Decerebration 1973
Decortication (Brain) 1973

Brain Mapping
Use Stereotaxic Atlas

Brain Maps
Use Stereotaxic Atlas

Brain Metabolism
Use Neurochemistry

Brain Neoplasms 1973
PN 596 **SC** 06860
SN Proliferation of abnormal cells in the brain producing an intracranial mass, or tumor. Primary brain tumors originate in the brain tissue and secondary tumors are metastatic (spread to the brain from another location).
B Brain Disorders 1967
Nervous System Neoplasms 1973

Brain Self Stimulation 1985
PN 524 **SC** 06864
SN Self administered brain stimulation resulting in either positive or negative reinforcement. Intracranial self stimulation activates the brain reward circuitries and is considered to be a measure of brain reward function.
UF Intracranial Self Stimulation
B Brain Stimulation 1967
Self Stimulation 1967

Brain Size 1973
PN 1354 **SC** 06868
UF Brain Volume
B Size 1973
R ↓ Brain 1967
Brain Weight 1973
Cerebral Atrophy 1994

Brain Stem 1973
PN 1782 **SC** 06870
B Brain 1967
N Locus Ceruleus 1982
Medulla Oblongata 1973
↓ Pons 1973
Reticular Formation 1967

Brain Stem — (cont'd)
R ↓ Cerebellum 1973
↓ Hindbrain 1997

Brain Stimulation 1967
PN 2624 **SC** 06880
B Stereotaxic Techniques 1973
Stimulation 1967
N Brain Self Stimulation 1985
Chemical Brain Stimulation 1973
Electrical Brain Stimulation 1973
Spreading Depression 1967
Transcranial Magnetic Stimulation 2003
R Physiological Arousal 1967

Brain Volume
Use Brain Size

Brain Weight 1973
PN 217 **SC** 06882
R ↓ Brain 1967
Brain Size 1973
Cerebral Atrophy 1994

Brainstorming 1982
PN 177 **SC** 06883
SN Group problem solving technique involving spontaneous contribution of ideas from all group members.
B Group Problem Solving 1973
R Choice Shift 1994
↓ Group Dynamics 1967

Brainwashing 1982
PN 110 **SC** 06884
SN Indoctrination of an individual or group by means of physical or psychological duress in order to alter their political, social, religious, or moral beliefs.
UF Thought Control
B Persuasive Communication 1967
R Attitude Change 1967
Coercion 1994
Propaganda 1973

Brand Names 1978
PN 1229 **SC** 06885
B Names 1985
R ↓ Advertising 1967
Brand Preferences 1994
↓ Consumer Behavior 1967
↓ Consumer Research 1973
↓ Marketing 1973
↓ Retailing 1991

Brand Preferences 1994
PN 884 **SC** 06887
SN Includes loyalty to brand name products or product switching.
B Consumer Attitudes 1973
Preferences 1967
R ↓ Advertising 1967
Brand Names 1978
↓ Consumer Behavior 1967
↓ Consumer Research 1973
↓ Marketing 1973

Bravery
Use Courage

Breakthrough (Psychotherapeutic)
Use Psychotherapeutic Breakthrough

Breakup (Relationship)
Use Relationship Termination

Breast 1973
PN 390 SC 06920
B Anatomy 1967

Breast Cancer Screening
Use Cancer Screening

Breast Examination
Use Self Examination (Medical)

Breast Feeding 1973
PN 990 SC 06930
B Eating Behavior 2004
R Lactation 1973
Weaning 1973

Breast Neoplasms 1973
PN 3049 SC 06940
UF Mammary Neoplasms
B Neoplasms 1967
R Mammography 1994
Mastectomy 1973

Breathing
Use Respiration

Breeding (Animal)
Use Animal Breeding

Brief Psychotherapy 1967
PN 3893 SC 06970
SN Short-term or time-limited methods of psychotherapy.
UF Short Term Psychotherapy
Time Limited Psychotherapy
B Psychotherapy 1967
R Solution Focused Therapy 2004

Brief Reactive Psychosis
Use Acute Psychosis

Bright Light Therapy
Use Phototherapy

Brightness Constancy 1985
PN 46 SC 06975
SN The tendency to perceive the brightness of stimuli as stable despite objective changes in illumination.
B Brightness Perception 1973
Perceptual Constancy 1985

Brightness Contrast 1985
PN 267 SC 06977
B Visual Contrast 1985

Brightness Perception 1973
PN 1515 SC 06980
UF Luminance Threshold
B Visual Perception 1967
N Brightness Constancy 1985
R ↓ Illumination 1967
Luminance 1982

Broca's Area 2004
PN 123 SC 06985
SN An area located in the left cerebral hemisphere that is highly involved in speech and language processes.
HN This term was introduced in June 2004. Relevant records were re-indexed with this term. The posting note reflects the number of records that were re-indexed.

Broca's Area — (cont'd)
B Frontal Lobe 1973

Bromides 1973
PN 54 SC 06990
HN In 1997, this term replaced the discontinued term LITHIUM BROMIDE. In 2000, LITHIUM BROMIDE was removed from all records containing it and replaced with BROMIDES.
UF Lithium Bromide
B Drugs 1967
R Arecoline 1973
Neostigmine 1973
Scopolamine 1973

Bromocriptine 1988
PN 245 SC 06995
B Alkaloids 1973
Enzyme Inhibitors 1985
Ergot Derivatives 1973

Bronchi 1973
PN 13 SC 07000
B Respiratory System 1973

Bronchial Disorders 1973
PN 83 SC 07010
B Respiratory Tract Disorders 1973

Brothers 1973
PN 279 SC 07020
B Human Males 1973
Siblings 1967

Bruxism 1985
PN 70 SC 07035
HN Use NOCTURNAL TEETH GRINDING to access references from 1973-1984.
UF Teeth Grinding
N Nocturnal Teeth Grinding 1973
R Myofascial Pain 1991

Buddhism 1973
PN 587 SC 07040
B Religious Affiliation 1973
N Zen Buddhism 1973
R Buddhists 1997

Buddhists 1997
PN 77 SC 07045
B Religious Groups 1997
R ↓ Buddhism 1973

Budgerigars 1973
PN 96 SC 07050
B Birds 1967

Budgets 1997
PN 220 SC 07052
HN Use COSTS AND COST ANALYSIS to access references from 1973-1996.
B Costs and Cost Analysis 1973
R Cost Containment 1991
↓ Economics 1985
↓ Economy 1973
Finance 2007
Funding 1988
Income (Economic) 1973
Money 1967

Bufotenine 1973
PN 19 SC 07060
B Amines 1973
Hallucinogenic Drugs 1967

Bufotenine — (cont'd)
Vasoconstrictor Drugs 1973

Buildings
Use Facilities

Built Environment 2007
PN 19 SC 07072
SN The manmade, artificial surroundings that provide the setting for human activity, ranging from large-scale civic surroundings and buildings to personal places and housing.
HN This term was introduced in April 2007. Relevant records were re-indexed with this term. The posting note reflects the number of records that were re-indexed.
B Environment 1967
R ↓ Architecture 1973
↓ Housing 1973
Urban Planning 1973

Bulimia 1985
PN 5160 SC 07078
SN Disorder characterized primarily by binge eating and often accompanied by self-induced vomiting and/or misuse of laxatives.
B Eating Disorders 1997
R Anorexia Nervosa 1973
Binge Eating 1991
Purging (Eating Disorders) 2003
↓ Somatoform Disorders 2001

Bulls
Use Cattle

Bullying 2003
PN 1037 SC 58064
SN A form of intimidation usually characterized by teasing, threatening, antagonizing, hitting, and victimizing.
HN This term was introduced in June 2003. Relevant records were re-indexed with this term. The posting note reflects the number of records that were re-indexed.
R ↓ Aggressive Behavior 1967
↓ Antisocial Behavior 1971
↓ Conflict 1967
↓ Dominance 1967
Emotional Abuse 1991
↓ Harassment 2001
↓ Perpetrators 1988
Physical Abuse 1991
School Violence 2003
Teasing 2003
Threat 1967
Victimization 1973

Bupropion 1994
PN 426 SC 07081
B Antidepressant Drugs 1971

Burnout
Use Occupational Stress

Burns 1973
PN 482 SC 07090
B Injuries 1973
R Electrical Injuries 1973
↓ Wounds 1973

Buses
Use Motor Vehicles

Bush Babies
Use Lemurs

Business 1967
PN 4118 **SC** 07110
UF Industry
Manufacturing
N ↓ Commerce 2007
Pharmaceutical Industry 2007
Small Businesses 2007
R ↓ Business Investments 2007
Business Management 1973
↓ Business Organizations 1973
Business Students 1973
Commercialization 2007
Entrepreneurship 1991
Globalization 2003
↓ Management 1967
Ownership 1985
↓ Retailing 1991
Self Employment 1994
Supply Chain Management 2007
Supply Chains 2007

Business and Industrial Personnel 1967
PN 6050 **SC** 07120
UF Businessmen
Industrial Personnel
B Personnel 1967
N Architects 1973
↓ Blue Collar Workers 1973
Industrial Psychologists 1973
Sales Personnel 1973
Secretarial Personnel 1973
↓ Service Personnel 1991
Skilled Industrial Workers 1973
↓ Technical Personnel 1978
↓ White Collar Workers 1973
R ↓ Aerospace Personnel 1973
↓ Agricultural Workers 1973
Engineers 1967
↓ Government Personnel 1973
↓ Nonprofessional Personnel 1982
↓ Professional Personnel 1978
Scientists 1967
Technical Service Personnel 1973

Business Education 1973
PN 679 **SC** 07123
B Curriculum 1967
R Business Management 1973
↓ Human Resource Management 2003
Management Training 1973
↓ Personnel Training 1967

Business Innovation
Use Innovation

Business Investments 2007
PN 148 **SC** 07125
SN Assets or items that are acquired with the hope that they will generate income or appreciate in the future.
HN This term was introduced in April 2007. Relevant records were re-indexed with this term. The posting note reflects the number of records that were re-indexed.
UF Investments (Business)
N Venture Capital 2007
R ↓ Business 1967
↓ Economics 1985
Entrepreneurship 1991
Money 1967

Business Management 1973
PN 1621 **SC** 07130
B Management 1967
R ↓ Business 1967
Business Education 1973
Entrepreneurship 1991
↓ Human Resource Management 2003
Knowledge Management 2005
↓ Management Methods 1973
Supply Chain Management 2007

Business Networking
Use Professional Networking

Business Organizations 1973
PN 5770 **SC** 07140
UF Companies
Corporations
B Organizations 1967
Private Sector 1985
N Multinational Corporations 2006
R ↓ Business 1967
Globalization 2003
Organizational Learning 2003

Business Students 1973
PN 899 **SC** 07150
B Students 1967
R ↓ Business 1967

Businessmen
Use Business and Industrial Personnel

Buspirone 1991
PN 580 **SC** 07165
B Minor Tranquilizers 1973
R Serotonin Agonists 1988

Butterflies 1973
PN 183 **SC** 07170
B Insects 1967
R Larvae 1973

Butyrylperazine
HN Term was discontinued in 1997. In 2000, the term was removed from all records containing it, and replaced with PHENOTHIAZINE DERIVATIVES, its nonpostable counterpart.
Use Phenothiazine Derivatives

Buying
Use Consumer Behavior

Cadres
Use Social Groups

Caffeine 1973
PN 1589 **SC** 07210
B Alkaloids 1973
CNS Stimulating Drugs 1973
Diuretics 1973
Heart Rate Affecting Drugs 1973
Respiration Stimulating Drugs 1973
R ↓ Analeptic Drugs 1973

Cage Apparatus 1973
PN 92 **SC** 07220
B Apparatus 1967

Calcium 1973
PN 870 **SC** 07240
B Chemical Elements 1973
Metallic Elements 1973

Calcium — (cont'd)
N Calcium Ions 1973

Calcium Channel Blockers
Use Channel Blockers

Calcium Ions 1973
PN 179 **SC** 07260
B Calcium 1973
Electrolytes 1973

Calculators
Use Digital Computers

Calculus 2003
PN 46 **SC** 07280
SN Branch of mathematics concerned with calculation using special symbolic notation.
HN Use MATHEMATICS to access references from 1973 to June 2003.
B Mathematics 1982

California F Scale 1973
PN 34 **SC** 07290
B Nonprojective Personality Measures 1973

California Psychological Inventory 1967
PN 314 **SC** 07300
B Personality Measures 1967

CALL
Use Computer Assisted Language Learning

Calories 1973
PN 439 **SC** 07330
R Energy Expenditure 1967

Cameras 1973
PN 105 **SC** 07350
B Apparatus 1967

Campaigns (Political)
Use Political Campaigns

Camping 1973
PN 119 **SC** 07370
B Recreation 1967
R Summer Camps (Recreation) 1973
Vacationing 1973

Camps (Therapeutic)
Use Therapeutic Camps

Campuses 1973
PN 260 **SC** 07390
B School Facilities 1973

Canaries 1973
PN 83 **SC** 07410
B Birds 1967

Cancer Screening 1997
PN 943 **SC** 07415
UF Breast Cancer Screening
Prostate Cancer Screening
Skin Cancer Screening
B Health Screening 1997
R Health Promotion 1991
Mammography 1994
Physical Examination 1988
Self Examination (Medical) 1988

Cancers
Use Neoplasms

Candidates (Political)
Use Political Candidates

Canids 1997
PN 31 **SC** 07434
UF Coyotes
B Mammals 1973
N Dogs 1967
Foxes 1973
Wolves 1973

Cannabinoids 1982
PN 770 **SC** 07436
UF Nabilone
N Tetrahydrocannabinol 1973
R ↓ Cannabis 1973

Cannabis 1973
PN 1089 **SC** 07440
UF Hemp (Cannabis)
B Drugs 1967
N Hashish 1973
Marijuana 2003
R Aphrodisiacs 1973
↓ Cannabinoids 1982
↓ Hallucinogenic Drugs 1967
↓ Narcotic Drugs 1973
Tetrahydrocannabinol 1973

Cannibalism 2003
PN 170 **SC** 07443
SN Eating of one's own species. Used for both human and animal populations.
HN This term was introduced in June 2003. Relevant records were re-indexed with this term. The posting note reflects the number of records that were re-indexed.
R Animal Feeding Behavior 1973
Death Rites 1973
Rites (Nonreligious) 1973
Taboos 1973

Canonical Correlation
Use Multivariate Analysis

Capgras Syndrome 1985
PN 251 **SC** 07447
SN Clinical condition in which patient believes an acquaintance, a closely related person, or a close associate has been replaced by a double or an impostor.
B Psychosis 1967
Syndromes 1973
R Delusions 1967
↓ Symptoms 1967

Capillaries (Anatomy) 1973
PN 25 **SC** 07450
B Blood Vessels 1973

Capital Punishment 1973
PN 692 **SC** 07460
UF Death Penalty
Punishment (Capital)

Capitalism 1973
PN 405 **SC** 07470
B Political Economic Systems 1973
R Entrepreneurship 1991
Ownership 1985

Capsaicin 1991
PN 244 **SC** 07475
B Fatty Acids 1973

Captivity (Animal)
Use Animal Captivity

Captopril 1991
PN 43 **SC** 07477
B Antihypertensive Drugs 1973
Enzyme Inhibitors 1985
R Angiotensin 1973

Carbachol 1973
PN 242 **SC** 07480
B Cholinomimetic Drugs 1973

Carbamazepine 1988
PN 996 **SC** 07483
B Analgesic Drugs 1973
Anticonvulsive Drugs 1973

Carbidopa 1988
PN 46 **SC** 07485
HN Use DECARBOXYLASES to access references from 1982-1987.
B Decarboxylase Inhibitors 1982
R DOPA 1973

Carbohydrate Metabolism 1973
PN 93 **SC** 07490
B Metabolism 1967
N Glucose Metabolism 1994
R Acetaldehyde 1982
Guanosine 1985

Carbohydrates 1973
PN 558 **SC** 07510
N Deoxyglucose 1991
↓ Sugars 1973

Carbon 1973
PN 22 **SC** 07520

Carbon Dioxide 1973
PN 403 **SC** 07530
R Respiration 1967

Carbon Monoxide 1973
PN 207 **SC** 07540
R ↓ Toxins 2007

Carbon Monoxide Poisoning 1973
PN 100 **SC** 07550
UF Carboxyhemoglobinemia
B Toxic Disorders 1973

Carbonic Anhydrase
HN Term was discontinued in 1997. In 2000, the term was removed from all records containing it, and replaced with ENZYMES, its postable counterpart.
Use Enzymes

Carboxyhemoglobinemia
Use Carbon Monoxide Poisoning

Carcinogens 1973
PN 59 **SC** 07580
R ↓ Drugs 1967
Passive Smoking 2006
Pollution 1973
↓ Tobacco Smoking 1967

Carcinomas
Use Neoplasms

Cardiac Arrest
Use Heart Disorders

Cardiac Disorders
Use Heart Disorders

Cardiac Rate
Use Heart Rate

Cardiac Surgery
Use Heart Surgery

Cardiography 1973
PN 29 **SC** 07620
B Medical Diagnosis 1973
N Electrocardiography 1967

Cardiology 1973
PN 88 **SC** 07630
B Medical Sciences 1967
R ↓ Cardiovascular System 1967

Cardiotonic Drugs
HN Term was discontinued in 1997. In 2000, the term was removed from all records containing it, and replaced with DRUGS, its postable counterpart.
Use Drugs

Cardiovascular Disorders 1967
PN 3821 **SC** 07640
UF Circulatory Disorders
Coronary Disorders
Raynauds Disease
Vascular Disorders
B Physical Disorders 1997
N Aneurysms 1973
↓ Arteriosclerosis 1973
↓ Blood Pressure Disorders 1973
↓ Cerebrovascular Disorders 1973
Embolisms 1973
↓ Heart Disorders 1973
↓ Hemorrhage 1973
↓ Hypertension 1973
↓ Ischemia 1973
↓ Thromboses 1973
R ↓ Cardiovascular System 1967
Coronary Prone Behavior 1982
↓ Dyspnea 1973
↓ Heart Rate Affecting Drugs 1973
Metabolic Syndrome 2007

Cardiovascular Reactivity 1994
PN 1958 **SC** 07645
SN Cardiovascular system responses to mental, physical, or environmental stress or other states due to intervention or natural occurrence.
R ↓ Blood Pressure 1967
↓ Cardiovascular System 1967
Heart Rate 1967
Physiological Arousal 1967
Physiological Correlates 1967
↓ Psychophysiology 1967
Stress Reactions 1973

Cardiovascular System 1967
PN 1979 **SC** 07650
B Anatomical Systems 1973
N ↓ Blood Vessels 1973
↓ Heart 1967
R Blood Brain Barrier 1994
Cardiology 1973
↓ Cardiovascular Disorders 1967

Cardiovascular System — (cont'd)
Cardiovascular Reactivity 1994
Spleen 1973

Career Aspirations
Use Occupational Aspirations

Career Change 1978
PN 682 **SC** 07666
UF Job Change
R Career Development 1985
Employment History 1978
Job Satisfaction 1967
Life Changes 2004
Occupational Adjustment 1973
Occupational Aspirations 1973
Occupational Choice 1967
Occupational Mobility 1973
↓ Occupations 1967
Professional Development 1982

Career Choice
Use Occupational Choice

Career Counseling
Use Occupational Guidance

Career Development 1985
PN 4212 **SC** 07672
SN Formation of work identity or progression of career decisions and/or events as influenced by life or work experience, education, on-the-job training, or other factors.
UF Career Transitions
Management Development
B Development 1967
Human Resource Management 2003
R Career Change 1978
Employment History 1978
↓ Management 1967
Occupational Choice 1967
↓ Occupations 1967
Personnel Placement 1973
Personnel Promotion 1978
↓ Personnel Training 1967
Professional Development 1982
Professional Identity 1991
Professional Networking 2004
Professional Specialization 1991
↓ Training 2006

Career Education 1978
PN 849 **SC** 07675
SN Comprehensive educational programs focusing on individual career development beginning in childhood and continuing through the adult years.
UF Career Exploration
B Curriculum 1967
R Occupational Guidance 1967
↓ Training 2006

Career Exploration
Use Career Education

Career Goals
Use Occupational Aspirations

Career Guidance
Use Occupational Guidance

Career Maturity
Use Vocational Maturity

Career Preference
Use Occupational Preference

Career Transitions
Use Career Development

Careers
Use Occupations

Caregiver Burden 1994
PN 2617 **SC** 07713
SN Used primarily for family or nonprofessional caregivers and the stress or associated emotional responses experienced when caring for the mentally or physically disabled. Consider OCCUPATIONAL STRESS for professional caregivers, e.g., health care personnel.
R Caregivers 1988
Elder Care 1994
Home Care 1985
Homebound 1988
Respite Care 1988
↓ Stress 1967

Caregivers 1988
PN 9118 **SC** 07715
SN Family members, professionals, or paraprofessionals who provide care to children or to the mentally or physically disabled.
UF Family Caregivers
R Caregiver Burden 1994
↓ Child Care 1991
Elder Care 1994
↓ Health Care Services 1978
Home Care 1985
Home Care Personnel 1997
Quality of Care 1988
Respite Care 1988
↓ Treatment 1967

Carotid Arteries 1973
PN 215 **SC** 07720
B Arteries (Anatomy) 1973

Carp 1973
PN 53 **SC** 07740
B Fishes 1967
N Goldfish 1973

Cartoons (Humor) 1973
PN 327 **SC** 07780
B Humor 1967

Case Based Reasoning 2003
PN 111 **SC** 07783
SN Problem solving technique that matches the current problem to previously encountered problems. Used in artificial intelligence discussions.
HN This term was introduced in June 2003. Relevant records were re-indexed with this term. The posting note reflects the number of records that were re-indexed.
B Reasoning 1967
R ↓ Artificial Intelligence 1982
↓ Expert Systems 1991
↓ Inductive Deductive Reasoning 1973
↓ Problem Solving 1967

Case History
Use Patient History

Case Management 1991
PN 1717 **SC** 07788
SN A system of managing and coordinating the delivery of health care in order to improve the continuity and quality of care as well as reducing costs. Case management is usually a function of a hospital's UTILIZATION REVIEW department.

Case Management — (cont'd)
B Management 1967
N Discharge Planning 1994
R Clinical Audits 2007
Cost Containment 1991
↓ Health Care Administration 1997
Health Care Costs 1994
↓ Health Care Delivery 1978
↓ Health Insurance 1973
Health Service Needs 1997
Intake Interview 1994
Long Term Care 1994
↓ Managed Care 1994
Needs Assessment 1985
Outreach Programs 1997
Social Casework 1967
↓ Treatment 1967
↓ Treatment Duration 1988
↓ Treatment Planning 1997

Case Report 1967
PN 22106 **SC** 07790
SN Used in records discussing issues involved in the process of conducting exploratory studies of single or multiple clinical cases.
HN From 1967-2000, the term was also used as a mandatory document type identifier; however, this usage has been discontinued due to the advent of Form/Content Type field identifiers. References from 1967-2000 can be accessed using either CASE REPORT or the Case Report Form/Content Type field identifier.

Caseworkers
Use Social Workers

Caste System 1973
PN 266 **SC** 07810
B Social Structure 1967
Systems 1967

Castration 1967
PN 351 **SC** 07820
B Endocrine Gland Surgery 1973
Sterilization (Sex) 1973
N Male Castration 1973
Ovariectomy 1973

Castration Anxiety 1973
PN 182 **SC** 07830
SN Anxiety resulting from real or imagined threats to one's genitalia or sexual functions; primarily used in psychoanalytic contexts.
B Anxiety Disorders 1997
R ↓ Body Image Disturbances 1973

Cat Learning 1967
PN 124 **SC** 07840
HN Not defined prior to 1982. Use CAT LEARNING or CATS to access references from 1967-1981. From 1982, used for discussions of hypotheses or theories of learning in cats.
B Animal Learning 2003
Learning 1967

CAT Scan
Use Tomography

Catabolism 1973
PN 36 **SC** 07850
SN Destructive metabolism involving release of energy (heat) and resulting in breakdown of complex materials within the organism.

Catabolism — (cont'd)
B Metabolism 1967

Catabolites
Use Metabolites

Catalepsy 1973
PN 406 **SC** 07860
SN Condition of muscular semirigidity and trance-like postures. Cataleptic persons make no voluntary motor movements and may display waxy flexibility.
B Movement Disorders 1985
Symptoms 1967
R Autohypnosis 1973
↓ Hysteria 1967
↓ Schizophrenia 1967
Suggestibility 1967

Catamnesis
Use Posttreatment Followup

Cataplexy 1973
PN 125 **SC** 07880
SN Temporary loss of muscle tone or weakness following extreme emotion.
B Movement Disorders 1985
Muscular Disorders 1973
Neuromuscular Disorders 1973
R Narcolepsy 1973

Cataracts 1973
PN 125 **SC** 07890
B Eye Disorders 1973

Catatonia 1973
PN 626 **SC** 07900
SN Reaction characterized by muscular rigidity or stupor sometimes punctuated by sudden violent outbursts, panic, or hallucinations.
B Symptoms 1967
R Catatonic Schizophrenia 1973

Catatonic Schizophrenia 1973
PN 183 **SC** 07910
SN A type of schizophrenia characterized by mental and psychomotor disturbances such as muscular rigidity or stupor.
B Schizophrenia 1967
R Catatonia 1973

Catecholamines 1973
PN 2344 **SC** 07920
UF Monoamines (Brain)
B Neurotransmitters 1985
Sympathomimetic Amines 1973
N Dopamine 1973
Epinephrine 1967
Norepinephrine 1973
R ↓ Adrenergic Drugs 1973
Adrenergic Receptors 2003
↓ Decarboxylase Inhibitors 1982
↓ Dopamine Antagonists 1982
Methyldopa 1973

Categorizing
Use Classification (Cognitive Process)

Catharsis 1973
PN 286 **SC** 07940
SN Process of reliving painful experiences and feelings, and the associated emotional responses.

Catharsis — (cont'd)
UF Abreaction
B Personality Processes 1967
R ↓ Psychoanalysis 1967

Catheterization 1973
PN 128 **SC** 07950
B Physical Treatment Methods 1973

Cathexis 1973
PN 132 **SC** 07960
SN Psychoanalytic term designating the attachment of intense emotions to a particular object, person, or oneself.
B Personality Processes 1967

Cathode Ray Tubes
Use Video Display Units

Catholicism (Roman)
Use Roman Catholicism

Catholics 1997
PN 401 **SC** 07975
B Christians 1997
R Roman Catholicism 1973

Cats 1967
PN 7204 **SC** 07980
B Felids 1997

Cattell Culture Fair Intelligence Test
Use Culture Fair Intelligence Test

Cattle 1973
PN 695 **SC** 08010
UF Bulls
Cows
B Mammals 1973

Caucasians
HN Term was discontinued in 1982. In 2000, the term was removed from all records containing it, and replaced with WHITES, its postable counterpart.
Use Whites

Cauda Equina
Use Spinal Nerves

Caudate Nucleus 1973
PN 1121 **SC** 08040
SN An elongated basal ganglion in the corpus striatum that is adjacent to the lateral ventricle and involved with the initiation and control of voluntary movement.
B Basal Ganglia 1973
Striatum 2003
R Nucleus Accumbens 1982

Causal Analysis 1994
PN 1130 **SC** 08045
SN Systematic analysis of causal relationships among variables.
B Analysis 1967
Methodology 1967
R Attribution 1973
Causality 2005
↓ Experimentation 1967
Path Analysis 1991
↓ Statistical Regression 1985
Structural Equation Modeling 1994

Causality 2005
PN 745 **SC** 08042
SN The relationship of causes to their effects.
HN This term was introduced in August 2005. Relevant records were re-indexed with this term. The posting note reflects the number of records that were re-indexed.
UF Causation
Cause Effect Relationships
R Causal Analysis 1994
Etiology 1967
Risk Factors 2001

Causation
Use Causality

Cause Effect Relationships
Use Causality

Cecotrophy
Use Coprophagia

Celebrities 2007
PN 22 **SC** 08049
SN Famous people who attract a high degree of public interest and attention.
HN This term was introduced in April 2007. Relevant records were re-indexed with this term. The posting note reflects the number of records that were re-indexed.
R ↓ Athletes 1973
Fame 1985
Musicians 1991

Celebrity
Use Fame

Celiac Plexus
Use Autonomic Ganglia

Celibacy
Use Sexual Abstinence

Cell Nucleus 1973
PN 96 **SC** 08070
R ↓ Cells (Biology) 1973

Cells (Biology) 1973
PN 1695 **SC** 08080
B Anatomy 1967
N ↓ Blood Cells 1973
↓ Chromosomes 1973
Cones (Eye) 1973
Connective Tissue Cells 1973
Epithelial Cells 1973
↓ Neurons 1973
Sperm 1973
Stem Cells 2006
R Absorption (Physiological) 1973
Apoptosis 2006
Cell Nucleus 1973
Cytology 1973
Cytoplasm 1973
Necrosis 2006
↓ Physiology 1967

Censorship 1978
PN 130 **SC** 08086
R ↓ Civil Rights 1978
↓ Communication 1967
↓ Communications Media 1973
Freedom 1978
Information 1967
↓ Laws 1967
↓ Social Issues 1991

Centering 1991
PN 22 **SC** 08088
SN Focusing of attention and concentration on a particular stimulus or on the whole of the present environment and circumstances. Used primarily in, but not limited to, therapeutic settings.
R ↓ Consciousness States 1971
Meditation 1973
↓ Psychotherapeutic Techniques 1967
↓ Self Management 1985

Central Nervous System 1967
PN 3448 **SC** 08100
SN The largest part of the vertebrate nervous system which consists of the brain, spinal cord, and meninges.
B Nervous System 1967
N ↓ Brain 1967
Extrapyramidal Tracts 1973
Meninges 1973
Neural Analyzers 1973
↓ Neural Pathways 1982
↓ Spinal Cord 1973
R ↓ Central Nervous System Disorders 1973

Central Nervous System Disorders 1973
PN 875 **SC** 08110
B Nervous System Disorders 1967
N ↓ Brain Disorders 1967
↓ Chorea 1973
Dysarthria 1973
↓ Meningitis 1973
↓ Myelitis 1973
Neurosyphilis 1973
Progressive Supranuclear Palsy 1997
R ↓ Central Nervous System 1967
Hemiplegia 1978
Hypothermia 1973
↓ Paralysis 1973
Paraplegia 1978
Quadriplegia 1985
↓ Spinal Cord Injuries 1973

Central Nervous System Drugs
Use CNS Affecting Drugs

Central Tendency Measures 1973
PN 57 **SC** 08130
B Statistical Analysis 1967
Statistical Measurement 1973
N Mean 1973
Median 1973
R ↓ Population (Statistics) 1973
T Test 1973
↓ Variability Measurement 1973

Central Vision
Use Foveal Vision

CER (Conditioning)
Use Conditioned Emotional Responses

Cerebellar Cortex
Use Cerebellum

Cerebellar Nuclei
Use Cerebellum

Cerebellopontile Angle
Use Cerebellum

Cerebellum 1973
PN 2421 **SC** 08180
SN A large, dorsally projecting portion of the brain located above the brain stem and beneath the posterior portion of the cerebrum, which is involved in the coordination of muscular movement, the maintenance of equilibrium and posture, and motor skill learning.
UF Cerebellar Cortex
Cerebellar Nuclei
Cerebellopontile Angle
B Hindbrain 1997
N Purkinje Cells 1994
R ↓ Brain Stem 1973

Cerebral Aqueduct
Use Cerebral Ventricles

Cerebral Arteriosclerosis 1973
PN 52 **SC** 08210
SN Thickening and hardening of the artery walls in the brain.
B Arteriosclerosis 1973
Cerebrovascular Disorders 1973
R Cerebrovascular Accidents 1973
↓ Senile Dementia 1973

Cerebral Atrophy 1994
PN 795 **SC** 08215
SN In brain tissue, a loss of neurons and the connections between them. Atrophy can be focal or generalized, and if the cerebral hemispheres are affected, there may be impairment of consciousness and voluntary processes.
UF Atrophy (Cerebral)
Cortical Atrophy
R ↓ Brain 1967
↓ Brain Damage 1967
↓ Brain Disorders 1967
Brain Size 1973
Brain Weight 1973
↓ Cerebral Cortex 1967
↓ Cerebral Dominance 1973

Cerebral Blood Flow 1994
PN 1613 **SC** 08217
B Blood Flow 1973
R Blood Circulation 1973
↓ Blood Pressure 1967
↓ Cerebral Cortex 1967

Cerebral Cortex 1967
PN 7788 **SC** 08220
SN The outermost layer of the cerebrum, made up of four lobes and responsible for higher mental processes.
UF Cortex (Cerebral)
B Telencephalon 1973
N Cerebral Ventricles 1973
Corpus Callosum 1973
↓ Frontal Lobe 1973
Left Hemisphere 2005
↓ Limbic System 1973
↓ Occipital Lobe 1973
↓ Parietal Lobe 1973
Right Hemisphere 2005
↓ Temporal Lobe 1973
R Cerebral Atrophy 1994
Cerebral Blood Flow 1994
Interhemispheric Interaction 1985

Cerebral Dominance 1973
PN 4725 **SC** 08230
SN The control of lower brain centers by the cerebrum or cerebral cortex. Compare LATERAL DOMINANCE.
B Dominance 1967
N ↓ Lateral Dominance 1967
R ↓ Brain 1967
Cerebral Atrophy 1994
Interhemispheric Interaction 1985
Left Hemisphere 2005
Right Hemisphere 2005

Cerebral Hemorrhage 1973
PN 344 **SC** 08250
SN Intracerebral or subarachnoid bleeding into the brain tissue from a ruptured blood vessel.
B Cerebrovascular Disorders 1973
Hemorrhage 1973
R Cerebrovascular Accidents 1973

Cerebral Ischemia 1973
PN 636 **SC** 08260
SN Reduction of blood flow to brain tissue.
B Cerebrovascular Disorders 1973
Ischemia 1973
R Cerebrovascular Accidents 1973

Cerebral Lesions
Use Brain Lesions

Cerebral Palsy 1967
PN 1533 **SC** 08280
SN A heterogeneous group of motor disorders associated with developmental brain injuries that originate during the prenatal period, birth, or shortly after. Often accompanied by poor coordination, cerebral palsy sometimes involves learning and speech difficulties.
B Brain Disorders 1967
Paralysis 1973
R Athetosis 1973

Cerebral Vascular Disorders
Use Cerebrovascular Disorders

Cerebral Ventricles 1973
PN 860 **SC** 08310
SN Four communicating cavities within the brain that are continuous with the central canal of the spinal cord. The ventricles are filled with cerebrospinal fluid.
UF Cerebral Aqueduct
Choroid Plexus
Ependyma
Ventricles (Cerebral)
B Cerebral Cortex 1967

Cerebrospinal Fluid 1973
PN 1910 **SC** 08320
SN A clear fluid that occupies the brain's subarachnoid space and acts as a buffer for the cerebral cortex.
UF Spinal Fluid
B Body Fluids 1973
R Blood Brain Barrier 1994

Cerebrovascular Accidents 1973
PN 4732 **SC** 08330
SN Sudden death of some brain cells due to an ischemic or hemorrhagic intracranial vascular event (when the blood flow to the brain is impaired by blockage or rupture of an artery to the brain).
UF Apoplexy
Stroke (Cerebrum)

Cerebrovascular Accidents — (cont'd)
B Brain Disorders 1967
Cerebrovascular Disorders 1973
R Cerebral Arteriosclerosis 1973
Cerebral Hemorrhage 1973
Cerebral Ischemia 1973
Coma 1973
Metabolic Syndrome 2007

Cerebrovascular Disorders 1973
PN 806 **SC** 08340
SN Disorders characterized by impaired blood flow in the arteries and veins that supply the brain.
UF Cerebral Vascular Disorders
B Cardiovascular Disorders 1967
N Cerebral Arteriosclerosis 1973
Cerebral Hemorrhage 1973
Cerebral Ischemia 1973
Cerebrovascular Accidents 1973
R Coma 1973
↓ Hypertension 1973
↓ Nervous System Disorders 1967
Vascular Dementia 1997

Certification (Professional)
Use Professional Certification

Certification Examinations
Use Professional Examinations

Certified Public Accountants
Use Accountants

Cervical Plexus
Use Spinal Nerves

Cervical Sprain Syndrome
Use Whiplash

Cervix 1973
PN 305 **SC** 08390
B Uterus 1973

Chance (Fortune) 1973
PN 384 **SC** 08420
SN The possibility of a favorable or unfavorable outcome in an uncertain situation.
UF Luck
B Probability 1967
N ↓ Statistical Probability 1967
R Uncertainty 1991

Change (Organizational)
Use Organizational Change

Change (Social)
Use Social Change

Change Readiness
Use Readiness to Change

Channel Blockers 1991
PN 590 **SC** 08450
UF Calcium Channel Blockers
B Drugs 1967
R ↓ Vasodilator Drugs 1973
Verapamil 1991

Chaos Theory 1997
PN 303 **SC** 09455
B Theories 1967
R ↓ Mathematical Modeling 1973
Predictability (Measurement) 1973
↓ Prediction 1967

Chaos Theory — (cont'd)
↓ Probability 1967
↓ Stochastic Modeling 1973
Uncertainty 1991

Chaplains 1973
PN 90 **SC** 08460
SN Clergymen officially attached to branch of military, hospital, institution, court, or university.
B Clergy 1973
R Lay Religious Personnel 1973
↓ Military Personnel 1967
Ministers (Religion) 1973
Priests 1973
Rabbis 1973

Character
Use Personality

Character Development
Use Personality Development

Character Disorders
Use Personality Disorders

Character Formation
Use Personality Development

Charisma 1988
PN 285 **SC** 08515
B Personality Traits 1967
R Leadership Qualities 1997
Leadership Style 1973
Transformational Leadership 2003

Charismatic Leadership
Use Transformational Leadership

Charitable Behavior 1973
PN 638 **SC** 08520
SN Generous or spontaneous goodness as manifested in actions for the benefit of others, especially for the needy, poor, or helpless.
UF Philanthropy
B Interpersonal Interaction 1967
Prosocial Behavior 1982
R Altruism 1973
↓ Assistance (Social Behavior) 1973
Faith Based Organizations 2007
Fundraising 2007
Sharing (Social Behavior) 1978
Tissue Donation 1991
Volunteers 2003

Charter Schools 2006
PN 25 **SC** 08525
SN Independent public schools that operate outside of the traditional school system, but are held accountable for favorable outcomes by local and/or state school boards.
HN This term was introduced in May 2006. Relevant records were re-indexed with this term. The posting note reflects the number of records that were re-indexed.
B Schools 1967
R ↓ Educational Programs 1973
↓ Nontraditional Education 1982

Cheating 1973
PN 492 **SC** 08530
B Deception 1967
R Dishonesty 1973
Fraud 1994
Test Taking 1985

Chemical Brain Stimulation 1973
PN 1007 **SC** 08540
SN Stimulation of brain structures to elicit different behaviors by injection or microinfusion of brain chemicals (neurotransmitters).
B Brain Stimulation 1967
Stereotaxic Techniques 1973

Chemical Elements 1973
PN 242 **SC** 08550
HN In 1997, this term replaced the discontinued term NONMETALLIC ELEMENTS. In 2000, NONMETALLIC ELEMENTS was removed from all records containing it, and replaced with CHEMICAL ELEMENTS.
UF Nonmetallic Elements
B Chemicals 1991
N ↓ Calcium 1973
R ↓ Electrolytes 1973
Food Additives 1978

Chemicals 1991
PN 744 **SC** 08555
SN May include compounds.
N ↓ Chemical Elements 1973
R ↓ Hazardous Materials 1991

Chemistry 1967
PN 562 **SC** 08560
SN Study of the atomic composition of substances, elements, and their reactions, and the formation, decomposition, and properties of molecules. Used for the scientific discipline or the chemical processes themselves.
B Sciences 1967
N ↓ Biochemistry 1967

Chemoreceptors 1973
PN 528 **SC** 08570
SN A cell or group of cells that transduce a chemical signal into an action potential and which may monitor internal or external stimuli.
B Neural Receptors 1973
Sensory Neurons 1973
R Olfactory Mucosa 1973
Taste Buds 1973
Taste Disorders 2001
Vomeronasal Sense 1982

Chemotherapy 2007
PN 821 **SC** 08580
SN The use of chemical agents (as opposed to radiation therapy) to treat cancer.
HN In April 2007, CHEMOTHERAPY changed status from nonpostable to postable. Relevant records were re-indexed with this term. The posting note reflects the number of records that were re-indexed.
B Drug Therapy 1967

Chess 1973
PN 226 **SC** 08590
B Games 1967

Chest
Use Thorax

Chewing Tobacco
Use Smokeless Tobacco

Chi Square Test 1973
PN 226 **SC** 08620
B Nonparametric Statistical Tests 1967
R Statistical Significance 1973

Chicanos
Use Mexican Americans

Chickens 1967
PN 2339 **SC** 08630
B Birds 1967

Child Abduction
Use Kidnapping

Child Abuse 1971
PN 15792 **SC** 08650
SN Abuse of children or adolescents in a family, institutional, or other setting.
UF Child Maltreatment
B Crime 1967
N Battered Child Syndrome 1973
R Abandonment 1997
↓ Abuse Reporting 1997
Anatomically Detailed Dolls 1991
Attachment Disorders 2001
Child Abuse Reporting 1997
Child Neglect 1988
Child Welfare 1988
Domestic Violence 2006
Emotional Abuse 1991
Failure to Thrive 1988
Munchausen Syndrome by Proxy 1997
Patient Abuse 1991
Pedophilia 1973
Physical Abuse 1991
↓ Sexual Abuse 1988
Verbal Abuse 2003
↓ Violent Crime 2003

Child Abuse Reporting 1997
PN 321 **SC** 08652
SN Reporting of physical abuse, emotional abuse, sexual abuse, verbal abuse, or child neglect by the victim or other individuals.
B Abuse Reporting 1997
R ↓ Child Abuse 1971
Child Neglect 1988
Child Welfare 1988

Child Advocacy
Use Advocacy

Child Attitudes 1988
PN 3421 **SC** 08658
SN Attitudes of, not toward, children.
B Attitudes 1967

Child Behavior Checklist 1994
PN 207 **SC** 08659
B Nonprojective Personality Measures 1973

Child Care 1991
PN 2351 **SC** 08660
SN Care of children of any age in any setting.
UF Babysitting
N Child Day Care 1973
Child Self Care 1988
R Caregivers 1988
↓ Childrearing Practices 1967
Foster Care 1978

Child Care Workers 1978
PN 996 **SC** 08663
SN Mental health, educational, or social services personnel providing day care or residential care for children.
R Child Day Care 1973
Day Care Centers 1973
↓ Nonprofessional Personnel 1982
↓ Service Personnel 1991

Child Custody 1982
PN 1836 **SC** 08665
SN Legal guardianship of a child.
B Legal Processes 1973
R Child Support 1988
Child Visitation 1988
Divorce 1973
Family Reunification 2007
Guardianship 1988
Joint Custody 1988
↓ Living Arrangements 1991
Mediation 1988
↓ Parental Absence 1973
Protective Services 1997

Child Day Care 1973
PN 1870 **SC** 08670
SN Day care that provides for a child's physical needs and often his/her developmental or educational needs. Kinds of day care include day care centers and school-based programs.
UF Day Care (Child)
B Child Care 1991
R Child Care Workers 1978
Child Self Care 1988
Child Welfare 1988
Day Care Centers 1973
Quality of Care 1988

Child Discipline 1973
PN 1193 **SC** 08680
UF Discipline (Child)
B Childrearing Practices 1967
Family Relations 1967
N Parental Permissiveness 1973
R ↓ Parent Child Relations 1967
Parental Role 1973

Child Guidance Clinics 1973
PN 340 **SC** 08690
SN Facilities which exist for the diagnosis and treatment of behavioral and emotional disorders in childhood.
UF Child Psychiatric Clinics
B Clinics 1967
R ↓ Community Facilities 1973
Community Mental Health Centers 1973
↓ Mental Health Programs 1973
↓ Mental Health Services 1978
Psychiatric Clinics 1973

Child Labor 2003
PN 70 **SC** 08691
SN The employment of youth.
HN This term was introduced in June 2003. Relevant records were re-indexed with this term. The posting note reflects the number of records that were re-indexed.
R Child Welfare 1988

Child Maltreatment
Use Child Abuse

Child Molestation
Use Pedophilia

Child Neglect 1988
PN 2090 **SC** 08695
SN Failure of parents or caretakers to provide basic care and emotional support necessary for normal development.

Child Neglect — (cont'd)
B Antisocial Behavior 1971
R Abandonment 1997
Attachment Disorders 2001
↓ Child Abuse 1971
Child Abuse Reporting 1997
Child Welfare 1988
Emotional Abuse 1991
Failure to Thrive 1988
Munchausen Syndrome by Proxy 1997

Child Psychiatric Clinics
Use Child Guidance Clinics

Child Psychiatry 1967
PN 3666 **SC** 08710
SN Branch of psychiatry devoted to the study and treatment of behavioral, mental, and emotional disorders of children. Use a more specific term if possible.
B Psychiatry 1967
R Child Psychopathology 2007
Orthopsychiatry 1973

Child Psychology 1967
PN 2260 **SC** 08720
SN Branch of developmental psychology devoted to the study of behavior, adjustment, and development and the treatment of behavioral, mental, and emotional disorders of children. Use a more specific term if possible.
B Developmental Psychology 1973
R Child Psychopathology 2007

Child Psychopathology 2007
PN 49 **SC** 08725
SN The study of the causes and processes in the development of mental disorders, emotional problems, or maladaptive behaviors among children. Used for the scientific discipline or for unspecified dysfunctions.
HN This term was introduced in April 2007. Relevant records were re-indexed with this term. The posting note reflects the number of records that were re-indexed.
B Psychopathology 1967
R Adolescent Psychopathology 2007
Child Psychiatry 1967
Child Psychology 1967

Child Psychotherapy 1967
PN 3748 **SC** 08730
B Psychotherapy 1967
N Play Therapy 1973
R Adolescent Psychotherapy 1994

Child Self Care 1988
PN 111 **SC** 08733
SN Responsibility for personal care without adult supervision, usually before or after the school day. Primarily used for children under age 14.
UF Latchkey Children
B Child Care 1991
R Child Day Care 1973
Child Welfare 1988
Self Care Skills 1978

Child Support 1988
PN 178 **SC** 08735
SN Legal obligation of parents or guardians to contribute to the economic maintenance of their children including provision of education, clothing, and food.
R Child Custody 1982
Divorce 1973
Joint Custody 1988

Child Support — (cont'd)
↓ Marital Separation 1973

Child Visitation 1988
PN 318 **SC** 08737
SN The right of or court-granted permission to parents, grandparents, or guardians to visit children.
UF Visitation Rights
B Legal Processes 1973
R Child Custody 1982

Child Welfare 1988
PN 2748 **SC** 08738
R ↓ Adoption (Child) 1967
Advocacy 1985
↓ Child Abuse 1971
Child Abuse Reporting 1997
Child Day Care 1973
Child Labor 2003
Child Neglect 1988
Child Self Care 1988
Family Preservation 2007
Foster Care 1978
Juvenile Justice 2004
Protective Services 1997
Social Casework 1967
↓ Social Services 1982
Welfare Reform 2007

Childbirth
Use Birth

Childbirth (Natural)
Use Natural Childbirth

Childbirth Training 1978
PN 197 **SC** 08746
B Prenatal Care 1991
Training 2006
R ↓ Birth 1967
Labor (Childbirth) 1973
Natural Childbirth 1978
↓ Obstetrics 1978
↓ Pregnancy 1967

Childhood Development 1967
PN 22790 **SC** 08760
SN Process of physical, cognitive, personality, and psychosocial growth occurring from birth through age 12. Use a more specific term if possible.
B Human Development 1967
N ↓ Early Childhood Development 1973
R Adolescent Development 1973
Developmental Age Groups 1973
↓ Developmental Stages 1973
↓ Motor Development 1973
Object Relations 1982
↓ Perceptual Development 1973
↓ Physical Development 1973
↓ Psychogenesis 1973
↓ Psychomotor Development 1973
Separation Individuation 1982
Transitional Objects 1985

Childhood Memories
Use Early Memories

Childhood Neurosis 1973
PN 233 **SC** 08770
UF Infantile Neurosis
B Neurosis 1967

Childhood Play Behavior 1978
PN 4413 **SC** 08777
UF Play Behavior (Childhood)
B Behavior 1967
N Pretend Play 2005
R Anatomically Detailed Dolls 1991
Childhood Play Development 1973
Childrens Recreational Games 1973
Doll Play 1973
↓ Games 1967
↓ Recreation 1967
Role Playing 1967
Toy Selection 1973
↓ Toys 1973

Childhood Play Development 1973
PN 899 **SC** 08780
UF Play Development (Childhood)
B Psychosocial Development 1973
R ↓ Childhood Play Behavior 1978
Childrens Recreational Games 1973
Emotional Development 1973
Pretend Play 2005

Childhood Psychosis 1967
PN 663 **SC** 08790
UF Infantile Psychosis
B Psychosis 1967
N Childhood Schizophrenia 1967
Symbiotic Infantile Psychosis 1973

Childhood Schizophrenia 1967
PN 784 **SC** 08800
B Childhood Psychosis 1967
Schizophrenia 1967
R Symbiotic Infantile Psychosis 1973

Childlessness 1982
PN 280 **SC** 08805
SN State of having no children.
B Family Structure 1973
Parenthood Status 1985
R Delayed Parenthood 1985
Family Planning Attitudes 1973

Childrearing Attitudes 1973
PN 1499 **SC** 08810
B Attitudes 1967
R ↓ Family Relations 1967
↓ Parental Attitudes 1973

Childrearing Practices 1967
PN 7042 **SC** 08820
SN Specific methods used by parents to raise children. Compare PARENTING STYLE. Limited to human populations.
B Family Relations 1967
N ↓ Child Discipline 1973
Toilet Training 1973
Weaning 1973
R ↓ Child Care 1991
Father Child Relations 1973
Mother Child Relations 1967
↓ Parent Child Relations 1967
Parent Training 1978
↓ Parental Attitudes 1973
↓ Parental Characteristics 1994
Parental Role 1973
Parenting Skills 1997

Childrearing Practices — (cont'd)
↓ Parenting Style 2003
↓ Sociocultural Factors 1967

Children of Alcoholics 2003
PN 639 **SC** 08830
HN This term was introduced in June 2003. Relevant records were re-indexed with this term. The posting note reflects the number of records that were re-indexed.
UF Adult Children of Alcoholics
Alcoholic Offspring
Offspring of Alcoholics
B Offspring 1988
R ↓ Alcoholism 1967
↓ Family Background 1973
↓ Parent Child Relations 1967
Transgenerational Patterns 1991

Childrens Apperception Test 1973
PN 51 **SC** 08840
B Projective Personality Measures 1973

Childrens Manifest Anxiety Scale 1973
PN 40 **SC** 08850
B Nonprojective Personality Measures 1973

Childrens Recreational Games 1973
PN 96 **SC** 08870
B Games 1967
Recreation 1967
R ↓ Childhood Play Behavior 1978
Childhood Play Development 1973
Pretend Play 2005
↓ Toys 1973

Chimpanzees 1973
PN 1493 **SC** 08890
B Mammals 1973
Primates (Nonhuman) 1973
R Bonobos 1997

Chinchillas 1973
PN 90 **SC** 08900
B Mammals 1973
Rodents 1973

Chinese Cultural Groups 1997
PN 1394 **SC** 08902
HN Use ASIANS to access references from 1982-1996.
B Asians 1982

Chiroptera
Use Bats

Chloral Hydrate 1973
PN 32 **SC** 08910
B Anticonvulsive Drugs 1973
Hypnotic Drugs 1973
Sedatives 1973

Chloralose
HN Term was discontinued in 1997. In 2000, the term was removed from all records containing it, and replaced with HYPNOTIC DRUGS, its postable counterpart.
Use Hypnotic Drugs

Chlordiazepoxide 1973
PN 914 **SC** 08930
UF Librium
B Amines 1973
Benzodiazepines 1978

Chlordiazepoxide — (cont'd)
Minor Tranquilizers 1973

Chloride Ions 1973
PN 75 **SC** 08940
B Electrolytes 1973

Chlorimipramine 1973
PN 1006 **SC** 08950
UF Clomipramine
B Amines 1973
Serotonin Reuptake Inhibitors 1997
Tricyclic Antidepressant Drugs 1997

Chlorisondamine
HN Term was discontinued in 1997. In 2000, the term was removed from all records containing it, and replaced with AMINES, its postable counterpart.
Use Amines

Chlorophenylpiperazine
Use Piperazines

Chlorpromazine 1967
PN 1463 **SC** 08990
UF Thorazine
B Amines 1973
Antiemetic Drugs 1973
Antihypertensive Drugs 1973
CNS Depressant Drugs 1973
Phenothiazine Derivatives 1973
Sedatives 1973

Chlorprothixene 1973
PN 22 **SC** 09000
B Amines 1973
Antiemetic Drugs 1973
Antihistaminic Drugs 1973
Antispasmodic Drugs 1973
Minor Tranquilizers 1973
Phenothiazine Derivatives 1973

Choice Behavior 1967
PN 8696 **SC** 09010
SN Motivational or judgmental processes involved in the decision or tendency to select one alternative over another or others. Also used for the choices themselves. Used for human or animal populations.
B Behavior 1967
Decision Making 1967
R Classification (Cognitive Process) 1967
Framing Effects 2005
Freedom 1978
Human Mate Selection 1988
Psychological Reactance 1978
Social Dilemma 2003
Therapist Selection 1994
Uncertainty 1991
Utility Theory 2004
Volition 1988

Choice Shift 1994
PN 34 **SC** 09013
SN In social psychology, the changes or shifts in choices made by groups during decision making processes that may differ from choices made by each group member acting on their own.
UF Risky Shift
B Group Decision Making 1978
R Brainstorming 1982
Group Discussion 1967
↓ Group Dynamics 1967

Choice Shift — (cont'd)
↓ Group Problem Solving 1973
↓ Risk Taking 1967

Cholecystokinin 1982
PN 960 **SC** 09015
SN Hormone secreted by upper intestinal mucosa on contact with gastric contents, cholecystokini; stimulates contraction of the gallbladder. Also, a neurotransmitter.
UF Pancreozymin
B Hormones 1967
Neuropeptides 2003
Neurotransmitters 1985
Peptides 1973

Cholesterol 1973
PN 861 **SC** 09020
B Steroids 1973

Choline 1973
PN 509 **SC** 09030
UF Choline Chloride
B Vitamins 1973
N Lecithin 1991
R Acetylcholine 1973
Cholinesterase 1973
Succinylcholine 1973

Choline Chloride
Use Choline

Cholinergic Blocking Drugs 1973
PN 928 **SC** 09050
UF Anticholinergic Drugs
Cholinolytic Drugs
B Drugs 1967
N Atropine 1973
Benactyzine 1973
Levodopa 1973
Nicotine 1973
Orphenadrine 1973
Scopolamine 1973
Trihexyphenidyl 1973
R ↓ Antiemetic Drugs 1973
↓ Antispasmodic Drugs 1973
Cholinergic Nerves 1973
Cholinesterase 1973
↓ Cholinomimetic Drugs 1973
↓ Hallucinogenic Drugs 1967
↓ Parasympathetic Nervous System 1973
↓ Phenothiazine Derivatives 1973

Cholinergic Drugs 1973
PN 671 **SC** 09060
UF Muscarinic Drugs
B Drugs 1967
N Acetylcholine 1973
Physostigmine 1973
Pilocarpine 1973
R Cholinergic Receptors 2003
↓ Cholinomimetic Drugs 1973

Cholinergic Nerves 1973
PN 912 **SC** 09070
SN Nerves that activate acetylcholine for parasympathetic and sympathetic fibers.
UF Nerves (Cholinergic)
B Autonomic Nervous System 1967
R Acetylcholine 1973
↓ Cholinergic Blocking Drugs 1973
↓ Cholinomimetic Drugs 1973

Cholinergic Receptors 2003
PN 618 **SC** 09075
SN Class of neural receptors that are sensitive to the neurotransmitter acetylcholine.
HN This term was introduced in June 2003. Relevant records were re-indexed with this term. The posting note reflects the number of records that were re-indexed.
UF Acetylcholine Receptors
Cholinoceptors
Muscarinic Receptors
Nicotinic Receptors
Receptors (Cholinergic)
B Neural Receptors 1973
R Acetylcholine 1973
↓ Cholinergic Drugs 1973
Receptor Binding 1985

Cholinesterase 1973
PN 146 **SC** 09080
B Esterases 1973
R Acetylcholinesterase 1973
↓ Choline 1973
↓ Cholinergic Blocking Drugs 1973
↓ Cholinesterase Inhibitors 1973

Cholinesterase Inhibitors 1973
PN 982 **SC** 09090
UF Anticholinesterase Drugs
B Enzyme Inhibitors 1985
N Galanthamine 1973
Neostigmine 1973
Physostigmine 1973
R Cholinesterase 1973
↓ Cholinomimetic Drugs 1973

Cholinoceptors
Use Cholinergic Receptors

Cholinolytic Drugs
Use Cholinergic Blocking Drugs

Cholinomimetic Drugs 1973
PN 136 **SC** 09100
UF Parasympathomimetic Drugs
B Drugs 1967
N Acetylcholine 1973
Arecoline 1973
Carbachol 1973
Neostigmine 1973
Physostigmine 1973
Pilocarpine 1973
R ↓ Analeptic Drugs 1973
↓ Cholinergic Blocking Drugs 1973
↓ Cholinergic Drugs 1973
Cholinergic Nerves 1973
↓ Cholinesterase Inhibitors 1973
↓ Parasympathetic Nervous System 1973

Chorda Tympani Nerve
Use Facial Nerve

Chorea 1973
PN 142 **SC** 09120
SN Involuntary and disorderly movements; frequently a manifestation of basal ganglia disease.
B Central Nervous System Disorders 1973
Movement Disorders 1985
N Huntingtons Disease 1973
R ↓ Infectious Disorders 1973

Choroid
Use Eye (Anatomy)

Choroid Plexus
Use Cerebral Ventricles

Christianity 1973
PN 2614 **SC** 09150
B Religious Affiliation 1973
N Protestantism 1973
Roman Catholicism 1973
R Bible 1973
↓ Christians 1997

Christians 1997
PN 493 **SC** 09152
B Religious Groups 1997
N Catholics 1997
Protestants 1997
R ↓ Christianity 1973

Chromaticity 1997
PN 321 **SC** 09155
SN The collective aspects of a color stimulus determined by its hue (dominant wavelength of light) and its saturation (purity).
N Color Saturation 1997
Hue 1973
R Achromatic Color 1973
↓ Color 1967
↓ Color Perception 1967
Luminance 1982

Chromosome Disorders 1973
PN 448 **SC** 09160
UF Karyotype Disorders
Mosaicism
B Genetic Disorders 1973
N ↓ Autosome Disorders 1973
Deletion (Chromosome) 1973
↓ Sex Chromosome Disorders 1973
Translocation (Chromosome) 1973
Trisomy 1973
Williams Syndrome 2003
R ↓ Chromosomes 1973

Chromosomes 1973
PN 869 **SC** 09170
B Cells (Biology) 1973
N Autosomes 1973
Sex Chromosomes 1973
R ↓ Chromosome Disorders 1973
↓ Genes 1973
Genetic Linkage 1994
↓ Genetics 1967
Genome 2003
Mutations 1973

Chronic Alcoholic Intoxication 1973
PN 90 **SC** 09180
B Alcohol Intoxication 1973
Brain Disorders 1967
Chronic Illness 1991
R Toxic Encephalopathies 1973

Chronic Fatigue Syndrome 1997
PN 892 **SC** 09181
SN Syndrome thought to be caused by a viral organism resulting in chronic fatigue, fever, pain, sore throat, and, in some cases, depression.
B Chronic Illness 1991
Syndromes 1973
R ↓ Encephalopathies 1982
Epstein Barr Viral Disorder 1994
Fatigue 1967
↓ Muscular Disorders 1973
↓ Viral Disorders 1973

Chronic Illness 1991
PN 3659 **SC** 09183
SN An illness or disorder that persists for a prolonged period of time. Used in conjunction with other specific terms where appropriate.
N Chronic Alcoholic Intoxication 1973
Chronic Fatigue Syndrome 1997
↓ Chronic Mental Illness 1997
Chronic Pain 1985
R Chronic Stress 2004
Chronicity (Disorders) 1982
Disease Management 2007
↓ Disorders 1967
↓ Mental Disorders 1967
↓ Physical Disorders 1997
Severity (Disorders) 1982

Chronic Mental Illness 1997
PN 825 **SC** 09184
SN A mental illness that persists for a prolonged period of time. Use a more specific term if possible.
UF Persistent Mental Illness
B Chronic Illness 1991
Mental Disorders 1967
N Chronic Psychosis 1973
R Chronicity (Disorders) 1982
Prognosis 1973
Severity (Disorders) 1982
↓ Treatment Resistant Disorders 1994

Chronic Pain 1985
PN 4894 **SC** 09185
B Chronic Illness 1991
Pain 1967
R Back Pain 1982
Chronic Stress 2004
Myofascial Pain 1991
Somatoform Pain Disorder 1997

Chronic Psychosis 1973
PN 165 **SC** 09190
B Chronic Mental Illness 1997
Psychosis 1967

Chronic Schizophrenia
HN Term was discontinued in 1988. In 2000, the term was removed from all records containing it, and replaced with SCHIZOPHRENIA, its postable counterpart.
Use Schizophrenia

Chronic Stress 2004
PN 415 **SC** 09202
SN Stress that is continual over a long period of time.
HN This term was introduced in June 2004. Relevant records were re-indexed with this term. The posting note reflects the number of records that were re-indexed.
B Stress 1967
R ↓ Chronic Illness 1991
Chronic Pain 1985
Chronicity (Disorders) 1982
Psychological Stress 1973

Chronicity (Disorders) 1982
PN 2243 **SC** 09203
SN Used only when chronicity itself is a factor, variable, or major focus of the research. Used in conjunction with other specific terms where appropriate.
R ↓ Chronic Illness 1991
↓ Chronic Mental Illness 1997
Chronic Stress 2004
↓ Disorders 1967

Chronicity (Disorders) — (cont'd)
↓ Mental Disorders 1967
↓ Physical Disorders 1997
Severity (Disorders) 1982

Chunking 2004
PN 101 **SC** 09204
SN Process of organizing or grouping information into larger units or "chunks."
HN This term was introduced in June 2004. Relevant records were re-indexed with this term. The posting note reflects the number of records that were re-indexed.
B Cognitive Processes 1967
R ↓ Memory 1967
Mnemonic Learning 1973
↓ Short Term Memory 1967

Churches
Use Religious Buildings

Cichlids 1973
PN 301 **SC** 09210
B Fishes 1967

Cigarette Smoking
Use Tobacco Smoking

Cimetidine 1985
PN 44 **SC** 09225
B Antihistaminic Drugs 1973

Cinema
Use Films

Circadian Rhythms (Animal)
Use Animal Circadian Rhythms

Circadian Rhythms (Human)
Use Human Biological Rhythms

Circulation (Blood)
Use Blood Circulation

Circulatory Disorders
Use Cardiovascular Disorders

Circumcision 2001
PN 151 **SC** 09255
HN From 1973-2000, BIRTH RITES and SURGERY were used together to capture this concept.
UF Female Genital Mutilation
B Surgery 1971
R Birth Rites 1973
↓ Female Genitalia 1973
Gynecology 1978
↓ Male Genitalia 1973
↓ Religious Practices 1973
↓ Rites of Passage 1973

Cirrhosis (Liver) 1973
PN 164 **SC** 09260
B Liver Disorders 1973
R Jaundice 1973

Citalopram 1997
PN 617 **SC** 09265
B Antidepressant Drugs 1971
Serotonin Reuptake Inhibitors 1997

Cities
Use Urban Environments

Citizen Participation
Use Community Involvement

Citizenship 1973
PN 783 **SC** 09280
SN Formal status or social quality of being a member of a community, country, or some other political designation.
R Immigration 1973
↓ Laws 1967
↓ Political Attitudes 1973

Civic Behavior
Use Community Involvement

Civil Law 1994
PN 439 **SC** 09284
B Law (Government) 1973
R ↓ Civil Rights 1978
Disability Laws 1994
↓ Law Enforcement 1978
↓ Legal Processes 1973
Litigation 2003
Same Sex Marriage 2007

Civil Rights 1978
PN 2048 **SC** 09288
SN Rights of personal liberty and equality guaranteed to citizens by constitution and legislation.
B Human Rights 1978
N ↓ Client Rights 1988
Equal Education 1978
R Advocacy 1985
Affirmative Action 1985
Age Discrimination 1994
Censorship 1978
Civil Law 1994
Civil Rights Movement 1973
Democracy 1973
Disability Discrimination 1997
Disability Laws 1994
Empowerment 1991
Freedom 1978
Informed Consent 1985
↓ Justice 1973
↓ Laws 1967
↓ Legal Processes 1973
Race and Ethnic Discrimination 1994
Same Sex Marriage 2007
Sex Discrimination 1978
↓ Social Discrimination 1982
Social Equality 1973
↓ Social Integration 1982
↓ Social Issues 1991
↓ Social Justice 2006
↓ Social Movements 1967

Civil Rights Movement 1973
PN 196 **SC** 09290
SN Social and political effort to gain the constitutional rights of citizens, especially by minority groups whose rights have been denied. See SOCIAL MOVEMENTS for more specific terms.
B Social Movements 1967
R ↓ Activism 2003
↓ Civil Rights 1978

Civil Servants
Use Government Personnel

Clairvoyance 1973
PN 145 **SC** 09310
B Extrasensory Perception 1967
N Precognition 1973

Class Attitudes
Use Socioeconomic Class Attitudes

Class Size 2004
PN 138 **SC** 09325
HN This term was introduced in June 2004. Relevant records were re-indexed with this term. The posting note reflects the number of records that were re-indexed.
B Group Size 1967
R Classroom Environment 1973
↓ Classrooms 1967

Classical Conditioning 1967
PN 4873 **SC** 09330
SN Learned behavior or the experimental paradigm or procedure used to develop and evoke classically conditioned responses.
UF Conditioning (Classical)
Pavlovian Conditioning
Respondent Conditioning
B Conditioning 1967
N ↓ Conditioned Emotional Responses 1967
↓ Conditioned Responses 1967
Eyelid Conditioning 1973
Higher Order Conditioning 1997
Unconditioned Responses 1973
R Conditioned Stimulus 1973
Learning Theory 1967
Orienting Responses 1967
Pavlov (Ivan) 1991
Unconditioned Stimulus 1973

Classical Test Theory 2003
PN 67 **SC** 09335
SN A statistical approach in psychological measurement in which observed scores consist of both the true score and error.
HN This term was introduced in June 2003. Relevant records were re-indexed with this term. The posting note reflects the number of records that were re-indexed.
B Testing 1967
Theories 1967
R Item Response Theory 1985
Psychometrics 1967
↓ Test Scores 1967

Classification (Cognitive Process) 1967
PN 8924 **SC** 09370
UF Categorizing
Sorting (Cognition)
B Cognitive Processes 1967
R Choice Behavior 1967

Classification Systems
Use Taxonomies

Classmates 1973
PN 97 **SC** 09400
B Students 1967

Classroom Behavior 1973
PN 4616 **SC** 09405
B Behavior 1967
R Classroom Behavior Modification 1973
Classroom Discipline 1973
Classroom Environment 1973
↓ Classroom Management 2004

Classroom Behavior Modification 1973
PN 2240 **SC** 09410
B Behavior Modification 1973
R Classroom Behavior 1973
Classroom Discipline 1973
↓ Classroom Management 2004
↓ Education 1967

Classroom Discipline 1973
PN 1414 **SC** 09420
UF Discipline (Classroom)
B Classroom Management 2004
R Classroom Behavior 1973
Classroom Behavior Modification 1973
↓ Education 1967
School Suspension 1973
Teacher Student Interaction 1973

Classroom Environment 1973
PN 5057 **SC** 09430
SN Physical, social, emotional, psychological, or intellectual characteristics of a classroom, especially as they contribute to the learning process. Includes classroom climate and class size.
B Academic Environment 1973
R Class Size 2004
Classroom Behavior 1973
↓ Classroom Management 2004
↓ Classrooms 1967
Learning Environment 2004
↓ School Environment 1973
School Violence 2003
Virtual Classrooms 2007

Classroom Instruction
Use Teaching

Classroom Management 2004
PN 349 **SC** 09445
SN Ways in which teachers organize and manage the classroom environment to ensure order and promote learning.
HN This term was introduced in June 2004. Relevant records were re-indexed with this term. The posting note reflects the number of records that were re-indexed.
B Management 1967
N Classroom Discipline 1973
R Classroom Behavior 1973
Classroom Behavior Modification 1973
Classroom Environment 1973

Classroom Teachers
Use Teachers

Classrooms 1967
PN 2188 **SC** 09460
B School Facilities 1973
N Virtual Classrooms 2007
R Class Size 2004
Classroom Environment 1973

Claustrophobia 1973
PN 100 **SC** 09470
SN Fear of enclosed spaces.
B Phobias 1967

Cleft Palate 1967
PN 229 **SC** 09480
B Congenital Disorders 1973
Neonatal Disorders 1973
R ↓ Speech Disorders 1967

Clergy 1973
PN 775 **SC** 09490
B Religious Personnel 1973
N Chaplains 1973
Ministers (Religion) 1973
Priests 1973
Rabbis 1973
R Evangelists 1973
Lay Religious Personnel 1973

Clergy — (cont'd)
Missionaries 1973
↓ Religious Groups 1997

Clerical Personnel 1973
PN 577 **SC** 09500
UF Keypunch Operators
Typists
B White Collar Workers 1973
R Secretarial Personnel 1973

Clerical Secretarial Skills 1973
PN 209 **SC** 09510
UF Secretarial Skills
B Employee Skills 1973
R Proofreading 1988
Typing 1991
Word Processing 1991

Client Abuse
Use Patient Abuse

Client Attitudes 1982
PN 8493 **SC** 09527
SN Attitudes of clients that may affect compliance with a particular treatment modality, or preferences for a particular type of treatment. May include attitudes toward health care professionals.
UF Patient Attitudes
B Attitudes 1967
Client Characteristics 1973
N Client Satisfaction 1994
R Clients 1973
Therapist Selection 1994
Treatment Barriers 2005
Treatment Compliance 1982

Client Centered Therapy 1967
PN 1246 **SC** 09530
UF Nondirective Therapy
Person Centered Psychotherapy
Rogerian Therapy
B Humanistic Psychotherapy 2003
Psychotherapy 1967
R ↓ Humanistic Psychology 1985
↓ Psychotherapeutic Techniques 1967
Rogers (Carl) 1991

Client Characteristics 1973
PN 13015 **SC** 09540
SN Physical, psychological, emotional, and other traits of individual clients or patients influencing the outcome of the therapeutic process.
UF Patient Characteristics
N ↓ Client Attitudes 1982
↓ Health Behavior 1982
Illness Behavior 1982
Patient Violence 1994
R Client Participation 1997
Client Treatment Matching 1997
Clients 1973
↓ Cross Cultural Treatment 1994
Patient History 1973
Patient Selection 1997
↓ Treatment Planning 1997

Client Compliance
Use Treatment Compliance

Client Counselor Interaction
Use Psychotherapeutic Processes

Client Dropouts
Use Treatment Dropouts

Client Education 1985
PN 2096 **SC** 09555
SN Informing or instructing patients or clients on the specifics of their disorder and/or its treatment. For client educational level use EDUCATIONAL BACKGROUND.
UF Patient Education
Pretraining (Therapy)
B Education 1967
R Disease Management 2007
↓ Health Education 1973
Health Knowledge 1994
Health Promotion 1991
Psychoeducation 1994
↓ Therapeutic Processes 1978
Treatment Compliance 1982

Client Participation 1997
PN 648 **SC** 09556
UF Patient Participation
B Participation 1973
R ↓ Client Characteristics 1973
↓ Client Rights 1988
Clients 1973
↓ Patients 1967
Treatment Barriers 2005
Treatment Compliance 1982

Client Records 1997
PN 289 **SC** 57455
UF Patient Records
B Medical Records 1978
R Patient History 1973
Privileged Communication 1973

Client Rights 1988
PN 1136 **SC** 09557
SN Right of patient or client to be fully informed of benefits or risks of treatment procedures and to make informed decisions to accept or reject treatment.
UF Patient Rights
B Civil Rights 1978
N Right to Treatment 1997
R Advance Directives 1994
Bioethics 2003
Client Participation 1997
Clients 1973
Empowerment 1991
Guardianship 1988
↓ Human Rights 1978
Informed Consent 1985
Involuntary Treatment 1994
Life Sustaining Treatment 1997
Quality of Care 1988
↓ Treatment 1967
Treatment Compliance 1982
Treatment Refusal 1994
Treatment Withholding 1988

Client Satisfaction 1994
PN 2232 **SC** 09558
UF Patient Satisfaction
B Client Attitudes 1982
Satisfaction 1973
R Clients 1973

Client Transfer 1997
PN 66 **SC** 57465
SN Transfer of client or patient care within or between treatment settings, therapists, or other health care providers.
UF Patient Transfer
R ↓ Facility Discharge 1988
↓ Hospital Discharge 1973

Client Transfer — (cont'd)
Patient Selection 1997
Professional Referral 1973
Psychiatric Hospital Discharge 1978
↓ Treatment 1967
Treatment Refusal 1994
Treatment Termination 1982

Client Treatment Matching 1997
PN 586 **SC** 57470
SN Treatment selection based on matching the client's characteristics and needs with appropriate treatment modalities.
UF Patient Treatment Matching
Treatment Client Matching
R ↓ Client Characteristics 1973
Clinical Judgment (Not Diagnosis) 1973
Patient Selection 1997
↓ Treatment 1967
Treatment Guidelines 2001
↓ Treatment Outcomes 1982
↓ Treatment Planning 1997

Client Violence
Use Patient Violence

Clients 1973
PN 3247 **SC** 09560
SN Persons receiving psychotherapy, counseling, or other mental health or social service. Consider also PATIENTS or one of its narrower terms.
UF Counselees
R ↓ Client Attitudes 1982
↓ Client Characteristics 1973
Client Participation 1997
↓ Client Rights 1988
Client Satisfaction 1994
Patient Selection 1997

Climate (Meteorological)
Use Atmospheric Conditions

Climate (Organizational)
Use Organizational Climate

Climax (Sexual)
Use Orgasm

Clinical Audits 2007
PN 49 **SC** 09605
SN A systematic evaluation of the effectiveness of diagnostic and treatment procedures.
HN This term was introduced in April 2007. Relevant records were re-indexed with this term. The posting note reflects the number of records that were re-indexed.
UF Medical Audits
B Evaluation 1967
R ↓ Case Management 1991
Clinical Governance 2007
↓ Health Care Administration 1997
Quality Control 1988
Quality of Care 1988
Treatment Effectiveness Evaluation 1973

Clinical Governance 2007
PN 28 **SC** 09608
SN Structure or guidelines most commonly used by the United Kingdom's National Health Service (NHS) to measure, monitor, and improve the quality of health care.
HN This term was introduced in April 2007. Relevant records were re-indexed with this term. The posting note reflects the number of records that were re-indexed.

Clinical Governance — (cont'd)
R Clinical Audits 2007
↓ Health Care Administration 1997
↓ Health Care Policy 1994
Quality Control 1988
Quality of Care 1988
↓ Quality of Services 1997
Treatment Guidelines 2001

Clinical Judgment (Medical Diagnosis)
Use Medical Diagnosis

Clinical Judgment (Not Diagnosis) 1973
PN 3919 **SC** 09620
SN Analysis, evaluation, or prediction of disordered or abnormal behavior, symptoms, or other aspects of psychological functioning. Includes assessing the appropriateness of a particular treatment and the degree or likelihood of clinical improvement.
B Judgment 1967
R Anatomically Detailed Dolls 1991
Client Treatment Matching 1997
↓ Diagnosis 1967
Geriatric Assessment 1997
Intake Interview 1994
↓ Measurement 1967
Prognosis 1973
↓ Psychiatric Evaluation 1997
↓ Psychodiagnosis 1967
↓ Psychodiagnostic Typologies 1967
↓ Psychological Assessment 1997
↓ Treatment Planning 1997

Clinical Judgment (Psychodiagnosis)
Use Psychodiagnosis

Clinical Markers
Use Biological Markers

Clinical Methods Training 1973
PN 2855 **SC** 09640
SN Instruction and skills training in methods for management and treatment of mental and behavior disorders. Includes training of populations such as parents, teachers, clergy, and administrators as well as mental health or medical personnel.
UF Training (Clinical Methods)
B Training 2006
N ↓ Clinical Psychology Graduate Training 2001
Clinical Psychology Internship 1973
↓ Community Mental Health Training 1973
Psychiatric Training 1973
Psychoanalytic Training 1973
Psychotherapy Training 1973
R Counselor Education 1973
Microcounseling 1978
Personal Therapy 1991
Practicum Supervision 1978
Theoretical Orientation 1982

Clinical Practice 2007
PN 634 **SC** 09645
SN The exercise of the profession of clinical psychologist or therapist, who work directly with clients or patients to assess, diagnose, and treat emotional and behavioral problems. Clinical practice typically refers to work in health and mental health clinics or in group or independent practice.
HN This term was introduced in April 2007. Relevant records were re-indexed with this term. The posting note reflects the number of records that were re-indexed.

Clinical Practice — (cont'd)
R Clinicians 1973
↓ Health Care Delivery 1978
↓ Mental Health Services 1978

Clinical Psychologists 1973
PN 1800 **SC** 09650
B Mental Health Personnel 1967
Psychologists 1967
R Clinicians 1973
Hypnotherapists 1973
↓ Psychotherapists 1973

Clinical Psychology 1967
PN 4408 **SC** 09660
B Applied Psychology 1973
Psychology 1967
N Medical Psychology 1973

Clinical Psychology Graduate Training 2001
PN 1571 **SC** 09675
HN In 2000, the truncated term CLINICAL PSYCHOLOGY GRAD TRAINING (which was used from 1973-2000) was deleted, removed from all records containing it, and replaced with its expanded form, CLINICAL PSYCHOLOGY GRADUATE TRAINING.
UF Training (Clinical Psychology Graduate)
B Clinical Methods Training 1973
Graduate Psychology Education 1967
Postgraduate Training 1973
N Clinical Psychology Internship 1973
R Practicum Supervision 1978

Clinical Psychology Internship 1973
PN 540 **SC** 09680
B Clinical Methods Training 1973
Clinical Psychology Graduate Training 2001
Internship Programs 2006
Postgraduate Training 1973
R Practicum Supervision 1978

Clinical Supervision
Use Professional Supervision

Clinical Trials 2004
PN 1231 **SC** 09687
SN Systematic, planned studies to evaluate the safety and efficacy of drugs, devices, or diagnostic or therapeutic practices. Used only when the methodology is the focus of discussion.
HN This term was introduced in June 2004. Relevant records were re-indexed with this term. The posting note reflects the number of records that were re-indexed.
B Experimental Design 1967
R ↓ Drug Therapy 1967
Evidence Based Practice 2004
Treatment Effectiveness Evaluation 1973

Clinicians 1973
PN 2341 **SC** 09690
SN Medical or mental health care professionals who are directly involved in the care and treatment of patients, as distinguished from those working in other areas such as research or administration.
B Professional Personnel 1978
R Clinical Practice 2007
Clinical Psychologists 1973
Counseling Psychologists 1988
↓ Medical Personnel 1967
↓ Mental Health Personnel 1967
↓ Physicians 1967

Clinicians — (cont'd)
Psychiatrists 1967
↓ Therapists 1967

Clinics 1967
PN 1518 **SC** 09700
B Treatment Facilities 1973
N Child Guidance Clinics 1973
Psychiatric Clinics 1973
Walk In Clinics 1973
R Community Mental Health Centers 1973
↓ Crisis Intervention Services 1973
↓ Hospitals 1967
↓ Treatment 1967

Cliques
Use Social Groups

Clomipramine
Use Chlorimipramine

Clonazepam 1991
PN 227 **SC** 09735
B Anticonvulsive Drugs 1973
Benzodiazepines 1978
Minor Tranquilizers 1973

Clonidine 1973
PN 1119 **SC** 09740
B Antihypertensive Drugs 1973

Cloning 2003
PN 82 **SC** 09742
SN Process of asexually reproducing an organism from a single cell of the original organism.
HN This term was introduced in June 2003. Relevant records were re-indexed with this term. The posting note reflects the number of records that were re-indexed.
B Biotechnology 2007
Genetic Engineering 1994
R DNA 2006
Reproductive Technology 1988

Closed Circuit Television 1973
PN 98 **SC** 09750
B Television 1967

Closed Head Injuries
Use Head Injuries

Closedmindedness
Use Openmindedness

Closure (Perceptual)
Use Perceptual Closure

Clothing 1967
PN 1092 **SC** 09770
HN Use CLOTHING FASHIONS to access references prior to 1991.
B Fads and Fashions 1973
R ↓ Physical Appearance 1982

Clozapine 1991
PN 2780 **SC** 09775
B Neuroleptic Drugs 1973
Sedatives 1973

Cloze Testing 1973
PN 272 **SC** 09780
SN Tests or procedures assessing comprehension (e.g., reading or listening) in which the person being tested is required to provide missing components.

Cloze Testing — (cont'd)
B Testing Methods 1967
R Sentence Completion Tests 1991

Clubs (Social Organizations) 1973
PN 197 SC 09790
B Recreation 1967

Cluster Analysis 1973
PN 1381 SC 09800
UF Clustering
B Statistical Analysis 1967

Clustering
Use Cluster Analysis

CNS Affecting Drugs 1973
PN 211 SC 09840
UF Central Nervous System Drugs
B Drugs 1967
N ↓ CNS Depressant Drugs 1973
↓ CNS Stimulating Drugs 1973
R ↓ Heart Rate Affecting Drugs 1973

CNS Depressant Drug Antagonists
Use Analeptic Drugs

CNS Depressant Drugs 1973
PN 113 SC 09860
B CNS Affecting Drugs 1973
N Amobarbital 1973
Barbital 1973
Chlorpromazine 1967
Glutethimide 1973
Haloperidol 1973
Scopolamine 1973
R ↓ Analgesic Drugs 1973
↓ Anesthetic Drugs 1973
↓ Anticonvulsive Drugs 1973
↓ Barbiturates 1967
↓ Dopamine Antagonists 1982
Flurazepam 1982
↓ Hypnotic Drugs 1973
↓ Muscle Relaxing Drugs 1973
↓ Narcotic Drugs 1973
↓ Sedatives 1973

CNS Stimulating Drugs 1973
PN 1372 SC 09870
UF Psychostimulant Drugs
Stimulants of CNS
B CNS Affecting Drugs 1973
N ↓ Amphetamine 1967
↓ Analeptic Drugs 1973
Caffeine 1973
Dextroamphetamine 1973
Ephedrine 1973
Methamphetamine 1973
Methylphenidate 1973
Pemoline 1978
Pentylenetetrazol 1973
Pipradrol 1973
Piracetam 1982
R ↓ Antidepressant Drugs 1971
↓ Emetic Drugs 1973
↓ Heart Rate Affecting Drugs 1973
Smokeless Tobacco 1994

Coaches 1988
PN 825 SC 09880
HN Use TEACHERS to access references from 1973-1987.
R Athletic Training 1991
↓ Sports 1967

Coagulation (Blood)
Use Blood Coagulation

Coalition Formation 1973
PN 429 SC 09910
SN Temporary alliance of distinct parties, persons, or states for joint action.
B Social Processes 1967
R ↓ Social Movements 1967

Coast Guard Personnel 1988
PN 22 SC 00915
B Military Personnel 1967

Cobalt 1973
PN 22 SC 09920
B Metallic Elements 1973

Cocaine 1973
PN 7290 SC 09930
B Alkaloids 1973
Amines 1973
Local Anesthetics 1973
N Crack Cocaine 2003

Cochlea 1973
PN 727 SC 09940
UF Organ of Corti
B Labyrinth (Anatomy) 1973
R Cochlear Implants 1994

Cochlear Implants 1994
PN 534 SC 09945
B Hearing Aids 1973
Prostheses 1973
Surgery 1971
R Cochlea 1973
↓ Deaf 1967
↓ Hearing Disorders 1982
Partially Hearing Impaired 1973

Cochlear Nerve
Use Acoustic Nerve

Cochran Q Test
HN In August 2005, this term was discontinued and removed from all records containing it, and was replaced with NONPARAMETRIC STATISTICAL TESTS, its postable counterpart.
Use Nonparametric Statistical Tests

Cockroaches 1973
PN 198 SC 09960
B Insects 1967
R Larvae 1973

Code Switching 1988
PN 283 SC 09965
SN Alternating use of languages, dialects, or language styles in speech.
UF Language Alternation
B Oral Communication 1985
R Bilingualism 1973
Sociolinguistics 1985

Codeine 1973
PN 121 SC 09970
UF Codeine Sulfate
Methylmorphine
B Alkaloids 1973
Analgesic Drugs 1973
Hypnotic Drugs 1973
Opiates 1973

Codeine Sulfate
Use Codeine

Codependency 1991
PN 308 SC 09985
R ↓ Alcohol Abuse 1988
Dependency (Personality) 1967
Dependent Personality Disorder 1994
↓ Drug Abuse 1973
Dysfunctional Family 1991
↓ Emotional Adjustment 1973
Enabling 1997
↓ Family 1967
↓ Family Relations 1967
↓ Interpersonal Interaction 1967
↓ Marital Relations 1967
↓ Parent Child Relations 1967
↓ Personality Traits 1967

Coeds
Use College Students

Coeducation 1973
PN 185 SC 10000
SN Education of male and female students at the same institution.
R ↓ Education 1967
Same Sex Education 2003
↓ Single Sex Environments 2001

Coercion 1994
PN 725 SC 10020
B Aggressive Behavior 1967
Social Influences 1967
R Abuse of Power 1997
Authority 1967
Brainwashing 1982
↓ Dominance 1967
Obedience 1973
↓ Persuasive Communication 1967
↓ Power 1967
↓ Punishment 1967
↓ Resistance 1997
Threat 1967
Torture 1988
↓ Violence 1973

Coffee
Use Beverages (Nonalcoholic)

Cognition 1967
PN 9570 SC 10040
SN Act or process of knowing, which includes awareness and judgment, perceiving, reasoning, and conceiving.
R ↓ Cognitive Development 1973
Cognitive Impairment 2003
↓ Cognitive Processes 1967
Cognitive Science 2003
Information Processing Model 2007
Intuition 1973
Metacognition 1991
Need for Cognition 1997

Cognition Enhancing Drugs
Use Nootropic Drugs

Cognitions 1985
PN 5161 SC 10045
SN The content of cognitive or thinking processes.
UF Thought Content
N ↓ Expectations 1967
Irrational Beliefs 1982

Cognitions — (cont'd)
R ↓ Attitudes 1967
Concepts 1967
False Beliefs 2007
Mind 1991
Rumination (Cognitive Process) 2001
Schema 1988
Thought Suppression 2003

Cognitive Ability 1973
PN 26961 **SC** 10050
SN Level of functioning in intellectual tasks.
UF Cognitive Functioning
Executive Functioning
Intellectual Functioning
B Ability 1967
N Mathematical Ability 1973
Reading Ability 1973
↓ Spatial Ability 1982
Verbal Ability 1967
R Cognitive Assessment 1997
Cognitive Impairment 2003
Cognitive Processing Speed 1997
Metacognition 1991

Cognitive Appraisal 2004
PN 396 **SC** 10051
SN Evaluation of an event or situation leading to an emotional response.
HN This term was introduced in June 2004. Relevant records were re-indexed with this term. The posting note reflects the number of records that were re-indexed.
B Cognitive Processes 1967
R ↓ Emotional Responses 1967

Cognitive Assessment 1997
PN 1654 **SC** 10053
SN Used only for references that focus on the assessment process or the particular assessment itself.
UF Assessment (Cognitive)
B Psychological Assessment 1997
R ↓ Cognitive Ability 1973
↓ Cognitive Processes 1967
↓ Intelligence 1967
↓ Intelligence Measures 1967
Intelligence Quotient 1967
↓ Neuropsychological Assessment 1982
↓ Psychiatric Evaluation 1997

Cognitive Behavior Therapy 2003
PN 2832 **SC** 10055
SN An integrated approach to psychotherapy that combines the techniques of cognitive and behavior therapy.
HN Use COGNITIVE THERAPY to access references from 1982 to June 2003.
B Psychotherapy 1967
R ↓ Behavior Modification 1973
↓ Behavior Therapy 1967
Cognitive Restructuring 1985
Cognitive Therapy 1982

Cognitive Bias 2006
PN 136 **SC** 10057
SN Cognitive distortions that are common to all human beings and skew perception, judgment, and decision making.
HN This term was introduced in May 2006. Relevant records were re-indexed with this term. The posting note reflects the number of records that were re-indexed.

Cognitive Bias — (cont'd)
B Cognitive Processes 1967
N Hindsight Bias 2006

Cognitive Complexity 1973
PN 1209 **SC** 10060
SN Conceptual, behavioral, or perceptual dimensions of thinking style that characterize an individual's differentiation or processing of stimuli.
UF Complexity (Cognitive)
B Cognitive Style 1967

Cognitive Contiguity 1973
PN 64 **SC** 10070
SN View of memory organization which holds that events that are experienced together tend to become associated with each other in memory.
UF Contiguity (Cognitive)
B Associative Processes 1967

Cognitive Deficits
Use Cognitive Impairment

Cognitive Development 1973
PN 19464 **SC** 10080
SN Acquisition of conscious thought, reasoning, symbol manipulation, and problem solving abilities beginning in infancy and following an orderly sequence. Compare INTELLECTUAL DEVELOPMENT.
B Psychogenesis 1973
N ↓ Intellectual Development 1973
↓ Language Development 1967
↓ Perceptual Development 1973
R Brain Development 2007
Cognition 1967
↓ Concept Formation 1967
Conservation (Concept) 1973
Constructivism 1994
Egocentrism 1978
Object Permanence 1985
Piaget (Jean) 1967
↓ Speech Development 1973
Theory of Mind 2001

Cognitive Discrimination 1973
PN 1236 **SC** 10090
SN Ability to distinguish between examples vs nonexamples of a concept, based on the presence or absence of its defining attributes.
UF Discrimination (Cognitive)
B Cognitive Processes 1967
Concept Formation 1967
Discrimination 1967
R False Beliefs 2007
↓ Lexical Access 1988
Lexical Decision 1988
Stroop Effect 1988
Visual Search 1982

Cognitive Dissonance 1967
PN 1509 **SC** 10100
SN Psychological conflict resulting from incongruous beliefs or attitudes held simultaneously, or from inconsistency between belief and behavior.
UF Dissonance (Cognitive)
R ↓ Cognitive Processes 1967
Psychological Reactance 1978

Cognitive Dysfunction
Use Cognitive Impairment

Cognitive Functioning
Use Cognitive Ability

Cognitive Generalization 1967
PN 718 **SC** 10110
SN Ability to evaluate the equivalence of an example of a concept or object across different contexts or modalities.
UF Generalization (Cognitive)
B Cognitive Processes 1967
Concept Formation 1967
R ↓ Associative Processes 1967
False Beliefs 2007
Semantic Generalization 1973

Cognitive Hypothesis Testing 1982
PN 616 **SC** 10112
SN Problem solving behavior in which the individual derives a set of rules (hypotheses) that are then sampled and tested until the one rule is discovered that consistently results in correct responding to the problem.
HN Use HYPOTHESIS TESTING or other appropriate terms to access references prior to 1982.
UF Hypothesis Testing (Cognitive)
Rule Learning
B Learning 1967
Problem Solving 1967
R ↓ Concept Formation 1967
Heuristics 2003
↓ Reasoning 1967

Cognitive Impairment 2003
PN 6198 **SC** 10113
SN Impaired mental or intellectual functioning.
HN This term was introduced in June 2003. Relevant records were re-indexed with this term. The posting note reflects the number of records that were re-indexed.
UF Cognitive Deficits
Cognitive Dysfunction
Executive Dysfunction
R ↓ Brain Damage 1967
Cognition 1967
↓ Cognitive Ability 1973
↓ Dementia 1985
↓ Memory Disorders 1973
↓ Mental Retardation 1967
↓ Thought Disturbances 1973

Cognitive Load
Use Human Channel Capacity

Cognitive Maps 1982
PN 1570 **SC** 10117
SN Mental representations of spatial environments that allow for the planning and execution of movement within them.
B Cognitive Processes 1967
R Direction Perception 1997
Mental Models 2003
Schema 1988
Spatial Imagery 1982
↓ Spatial Memory 1988
Spatial Organization 1973
Spatial Orientation (Perception) 1973

Cognitive Mediation 1967
PN 1287 **SC** 10120
SN Intervention of cognitive processes between observable stimuli and responses, resulting in a change in subsequent behavior.

Cognitive Mediation — (cont'd)
UF Mediation (Cognitive)
B Cognitive Processes 1967
R Naming 1988

Cognitive Processes 1967
PN 45070 SC 10130
SN Mental processes involved in the acquisition, processing, and utilization of knowledge or information.
UF Human Information Processes
Information Processes (Human)
N Accommodation (Cognitive Process) 2007
Assimilation (Cognitive Process) 2007
↓ Associative Processes 1967
Chunking 2004
Classification (Cognitive Process) 1967
Cognitive Appraisal 2004
↓ Cognitive Bias 2006
Cognitive Discrimination 1973
Cognitive Generalization 1967
Cognitive Maps 1982
Cognitive Mediation 1967
↓ Comprehension 1967
Concentration 1982
↓ Concept Formation 1967
↓ Decision Making 1967
False Beliefs 2007
↓ Fantasy 1997
↓ Ideation 1973
Imagination 1967
Intuition 1973
Mental Rotation 1991
Metacognition 1991
Naming 1988
↓ Problem Solving 1967
Rumination (Cognitive Process) 2001
Schema 1988
Semantic Generalization 1973
Social Cognition 1994
↓ Thinking 1967
Thought Suppression 2003
Transposition (Cognition) 1973
R ↓ Artificial Intelligence 1982
Cognition 1967
Cognitive Assessment 1997
Cognitive Dissonance 1967
Cognitive Processing Speed 1997
Cognitive Psychology 1985
↓ Conflict Resolution 1982
Connectionism 1994
Declarative Knowledge 1997
Generation Effect (Learning) 1991
Human Information Storage 1973
Information Processing Model 2007
↓ Learning 1967
↓ Learning Strategies 1991
↓ Memory 1967
Mind 1991
Neurocognition 2006
Procedural Knowledge 1997
Questioning 1982
Reality Testing 1973
↓ Spatial Ability 1982
↓ Strategies 1967
Word Associations 1967

Cognitive Processing Speed 1997
PN 1006 SC 10133
UF Information Processing Speed
R ↓ Cognitive Ability 1973
↓ Cognitive Processes 1967

Cognitive Processing Speed — (cont'd)
↓ Cognitive Style 1967
Conceptual Tempo 1985
Human Channel Capacity 1973
Reaction Time 1967
Response Latency 1967

Cognitive Psychology 1985
PN 3512 SC 10135
SN Branch of psychology concerned with aspects of behavior as they relate to mental processes.
B Psychology 1967
R ↓ Cognitive Processes 1967
Cognitive Science 2003
Connectionism 1994

Cognitive Rehabilitation 1985
PN 1245 SC 10136
SN Procedures used to restore or enhance the cognitive functioning level of individuals with mental disability, injury, or disease (e.g., brain damaged stroke patients).
B Neuropsychological Rehabilitation 1997
Rehabilitation 1967
R Memory Training 1994

Cognitive Restructuring 1985
PN 516 SC 10137
SN Cognitive technique for altering self-defeating thought patterns by first identifying and analyzing negative self-statements and then developing adaptive self-statements.
B Cognitive Techniques 1985
R ↓ Behavior Modification 1973
Cognitive Behavior Therapy 2003
Cognitive Therapy 1982

Cognitive Science 2003
PN 1107 SC 10139
SN Study of cognition from a multidisciplinary approach involving the disciplines of psychology, linguistics, computer science, and artificial intelligence.
HN This term was introduced in June 2003. Relevant records were re-indexed with this term. The posting note reflects the number of records that were re-indexed.
B Sciences 1967
R ↓ Artificial Intelligence 1982
Cognition 1967
Cognitive Psychology 1985
↓ Linguistics 1973
↓ Neurosciences 1973

Cognitive Style 1967
PN 7504 SC 10140
SN Preferred or habitual style of learning or thinking.
UF Learning Style
B Personality Traits 1967
N Cognitive Complexity 1973
Conceptual Tempo 1985
Field Dependence 1973
Impulsiveness 1973
Reflectiveness 1997
R Accommodation (Cognitive Process) 2007
Assimilation (Cognitive Process) 2007
Cognitive Processing Speed 1997
↓ Learning Strategies 1991
Multiple Intelligences 2007
Neurolinguistic Programming 2001
Perceptual Style 1973
↓ Personality 1967
Schema 1988

Cognitive Techniques 1985
PN 1274 SC 10142
SN Methods directed at producing change in thought patterns that may result in changes in affect and behavior.
B Treatment 1967
N Cognitive Restructuring 1985
Cognitive Therapy 1982
Self Instructional Training 1985
R Anxiety Management 1997
Stress Management 1985

Cognitive Therapy 1982
PN 9538 SC 10144
SN Directive therapy based on the belief that the way one perceives and structures the world determines one's feelings and behavior. Treatment aims at altering cognitive schema and hence permitting the patient to change his/her distorted self-view and world view.
B Cognitive Techniques 1985
R Anxiety Management 1997
↓ Behavior Modification 1973
Cognitive Behavior Therapy 2003
Cognitive Restructuring 1985
↓ Psychotherapy 1967
Rational Emotive Behavior Therapy 2003
Self Instructional Training 1985
↓ Self Management 1985

Cohabitation 1973
PN 634 SC 10150
SN Primarily, but not exclusively, used for unmarried couples living together.
B Living Arrangements 1991
R Couples 1982
↓ Family 1967
Living Alone 1994
Roommates 1973

Cohesion (Group)
Use Group Cohesion

Cohort Analysis 1988
PN 620 SC 10165
SN Analysis of the effects attributed to being a member of a group sharing a particular characteristic, experience, or event. Use AGE DIFFERENCES for effects attributable to normal biological, cognitive, or psychosocial maturation.
B Analysis 1967
Experimental Design 1967
Methodology 1967
R Age Differences 1967
Generation Gap 1973

Coitus
Use Sexual Intercourse (Human)

Coitus (Animal)
Use Animal Mating Behavior

Cold Effects 1973
PN 775 SC 10200
B Temperature Effects 1967

Colitis 1973
PN 61 SC 10220
SN Inflammation of the colon.
B Colon Disorders 1973
N Ulcerative Colitis 1973
R Gastrointestinal Ulcers 1967
Irritable Bowel Syndrome 1991

Collaboration 2007
PN 1068 **SC** 10240
SN The act or process of two or more people working together in order to obtain an outcome desired by all. Also refers to an interpersonal relationship in which the parties show cooperation and sensitivity to the others' needs.
HN In April 2007, COLLABORATION changed status from nonpostable to postable. Relevant records were re-indexed with this term. The posting note reflects the number of records that were re-indexed.
B Interpersonal Interaction 1967
R Collaborative Learning 2007
Cooperation 1967

Collaborative Learning 2007
PN 152 **SC** 10245
SN Learning that occurs when two or more individuals work together to solve a common problem.
HN This term was introduced in April 2007. Relevant records were re-indexed with this term. The posting note reflects the number of records that were re-indexed.
B Learning 1967
R Collaboration 2007
Cooperative Learning 1994
Group Discussion 1967
Group Instruction 1973
Peer Tutoring 1973
↓ Teaching Methods 1967
↓ Teams 1988

Collective Behavior 1967
PN 3518 **SC** 10250
SN Behaviors which characterize groups or individuals acting in groups, usually working toward or achieving a specific goal. Used for human or animal populations.
B Interpersonal Interaction 1967
N Riots 1973
R Collectivism 2007
Contagion 1988
Entrapment Games 1973
↓ Group Dynamics 1967
Group Participation 1973
Mass Hysteria 1973
Social Demonstrations 1973
↓ Sociometry 1991

Collective Hysteria
Use Mass Hysteria

Collective Unconscious 1997
PN 130 **SC** 10255
SN Genetically determined part of the unconscious shared by all members of a species or race of people.
HN Consider JUNGIAN PSYCHOLOGY to access references prior to 1997.
B Jungian Psychology 1973
N Archetypes 1991
R Analytical Psychotherapy 1973
Jung (Carl) 1973

Collectivism 2007
PN 294 **SC** 10257
SN Political, economic, or social philosophy in which the needs and goals of a collective group are emphasized over those of its individual members.
HN This term was introduced in April 2007. Relevant records were re-indexed with this term. The posting note reflects the number of records that were re-indexed.
B Philosophies 1967
R ↓ Collective Behavior 1967
Ingroup Outgroup 1997

Collectivism — (cont'd)
↓ Political Economic Systems 1973

College Academic Achievement 1967
PN 5338 **SC** 10260
B Academic Achievement 1967

College Athletes 1994
PN 657 **SC** 10270
B Athletes 1973
College Students 1967
R Athletic Participation 1973
Athletic Performance 1991
Athletic Training 1991
↓ Sports 1967
↓ Teams 1988

College Degrees
Use Educational Degrees

College Dropouts 1973
PN 461 **SC** 10290
B School Dropouts 1967

College Education
Use Undergraduate Education

College Entrance Examination Board Scholastic Aptitude Test 2001
PN 407 **SC** 10235
HN In 2001, the truncated term COLL ENT EXAM BD SCHOLASTIC APT TEST (which was used from 1973-2000) was deleted, removed from all records containing it, and replaced with its expanded form, COLLEGE ENTRANCE EXAMINATION BOARD SCHOLASTIC APTITUDE TEST.
UF Preliminary Scholastic Aptitude Test
SAT
Scholastic Aptitude Test
B Aptitude Measures 1967
Entrance Examinations 1973

College Environment 1973
PN 1513 **SC** 10300
SN Social or emotional climate or physical setting of a college or university.
B School Environment 1973
R ↓ Colleges 1967
Community Colleges 1978

College Graduates 1982
PN 467 **SC** 10304
R ↓ College Students 1967
Educational Degrees 1973
School Graduation 1991
School to Work Transition 1994

College Major
Use Academic Specialization

College Students 1967
PN 36169 **SC** 10320
SN Students attending an institution of higher education.
UF Coeds
Undergraduates
B Students 1967
N College Athletes 1994
Community College Students 1973
Education Students 1982
Junior College Students 1973
Nursing Students 1973
ROTC Students 1973

College Students — (cont'd)
R College Graduates 1982
Graduate Students 1967
Postgraduate Students 1973
Preservice Teachers 1982
Reentry Students 1985

College Teachers 1973
PN 4670 **SC** 10330
UF Professors
B Teachers 1967

Colleges 1967
PN 4377 **SC** 10350
UF Junior Colleges
Universities
B Schools 1967
N Community Colleges 1978
R College Environment 1973
↓ Higher Education 1973
Military Schools 1973

Colon Disorders 1973
PN 462 **SC** 10370
UF Bowel Disorders
B Gastrointestinal Disorders 1973
N ↓ Colitis 1973
Constipation 1973
Diarrhea 1973
Fecal Incontinence 1973
Irritable Bowel Syndrome 1991

Color 1967
PN 3413 **SC** 10380
SN Property of matter or light sources that corresponds to the relative reflectance or absorption of incident light and the wavelength of the incident light or light source. Color is described perceptually by the dimensions of hue, lightness, brightness, and saturation. Compare HUE.
N Achromatic Color 1973
Eye Color 1991
Hue 1973
R ↓ Chromaticity 1997
Color Saturation 1997
↓ Pigments 1973
↓ Visual Stimulation 1973

Color Blindness 1973
PN 350 **SC** 10390
B Eye Disorders 1973
R ↓ Color Perception 1967
↓ Genetic Disorders 1973

Color Constancy 1985
PN 172 **SC** 10395
SN The tendency to perceive hue, brightness, and saturation as stable despite objective changes in context and illumination.
B Color Perception 1967
Perceptual Constancy 1985

Color Contrast 1985
PN 262 **SC** 10397
B Color Perception 1967
Visual Contrast 1985

Color Perception 1967
PN 4710 **SC** 10400
UF Spectral Sensitivity
B Visual Perception 1967
N Color Constancy 1985
Color Contrast 1985

Color Perception — (cont'd)
R ↓ Chromaticity 1997
Color Blindness 1973
Color Saturation 1997
Prismatic Stimulation 1973

Color Pyramid Test
HN Term was discontinued in 1997. In 2000, the term was removed from all records containing it, and replaced with PROJECTIVE PERSONALITY MEASURES, its postable counterpart.
Use Projective Personality Measures

Color Saturation 1997
PN 32 SC 10420
SN The degree of purity or richness of a color.
UF Saturation (Color)
B Chromaticity 1997
R Achromatic Color 1973
↓ Color 1967
↓ Color Perception 1967
Hue 1973
Luminance 1982

Colostomy 1973
PN 44 SC 10430
B Surgery 1971

Coma 1973
PN 450 SC 10450
B Symptoms 1967
R Cerebrovascular Accidents 1973
↓ Cerebrovascular Disorders 1973
↓ Consciousness Disturbances 1973
↓ Epileptic Seizures 1973
↓ Injuries 1973
Insulin Shock Therapy 1973

Combat Experience 1991
PN 1085 SC 10452
SN Direct participation in war.
R ↓ Experiences (Events) 1973
↓ Military Personnel 1967
Posttraumatic Stress Disorder 1985
↓ War 1967

Comfort (Physical)
Use Physical Comfort

Commerce 2007
PN 677 SC 10460
SN An agreed upon exchange of goods and/or services, either for money or for other goods or services.
HN In April 2007, COMMERCE changed status from nonpostable to postable. Relevant records were re-indexed with this term. The posting note reflects the number of records that were re-indexed.
UF Exchange (Business)
Trade (Business)
B Business 1967
N ↓ Electronic Commerce 2006

Commercialization 2007
PN 55 SC 10463
SN The phase of product development where a new product goes into full-scale production and distribution.
HN This term was introduced in April 2007. Relevant records were re-indexed with this term. The posting note reflects the number of records that were re-indexed.

Commercialization — (cont'd)
R ↓ Business 1967

Commercials
Use Television Advertising

Commissioned Officers 1973
PN 327 SC 10470
SN Military officers who have received a formal certificate granting rank and authority and who thereby hold a position of command.
UF Military Officers
Officers (Commissioned)
B Military Personnel 1967
R ↓ Management Personnel 1973
Volunteer Military Personnel 1973

Commissurotomy 1985
PN 342 SC 10475
SN Surgical disconnection of the corpus callosum and the major commissure of the brain.
UF Split Brain
B Neurosurgery 1973
R Corpus Callosum 1973

Commitment 1985
PN 2140 SC 10478
SN The process or extent of devoting one's efforts or resources to an activity, task, or interpersonal relationship.
N Organizational Commitment 1991
R ↓ Involvement 1973
↓ Motivation 1967

Commitment (Outpatient)
Use Outpatient Commitment

Commitment (Psychiatric) 1973
PN 1339 SC 10480
SN Confinement to a mental institution by court order following certification by appropriate psychiatric or other mental health authorities. The process may be voluntary but is generally involuntary.
B Hospitalization 1967
Legal Processes 1973
N Outpatient Commitment 1991
R Court Referrals 1994
Guardianship 1988
Health Care Seeking Behavior 1997
↓ Institutional Release 1978
Involuntary Treatment 1994
↓ Psychiatric Hospital Admission 1973
Psychiatric Hospital Discharge 1978
↓ Psychiatric Hospitalization 1973
Right to Treatment 1997
Self Referral 1991

Communes 1973
PN 117 SC 10510
B Communities 1967
N Kibbutz 1973

Communicable Diseases
Use Infectious Disorders

Communication 1967
PN 8234 SC 10570
SN Conceptually broad term referring to the transmission of verbal or nonverbal information. Use a more specific term if possible.
UF Information Exchange
N ↓ Animal Communication 1967
↓ Augmentative Communication 1994
↓ Electronic Communication 2001

Communication — (cont'd)
↓ Interpersonal Communication 1973
↓ Nonverbal Communication 1971
↓ Persuasive Communication 1967
Scientific Communication 1973
↓ Verbal Communication 1967
R Censorship 1978
↓ Communication Skills 1973
Communication Skills Training 1982
↓ Communication Systems 1973
Communication Theory 1973
↓ Communications Media 1973
↓ Content Analysis 1978
Emotional Content 1973
Information 1967
Information Dissemination 2005
Knowledge Transfer 2007
Messages 1973
Privileged Communication 1973
Rhetoric 1991
Symbolism 1967
↓ Vocalization 1967
↓ Voice 1973

Communication (Privileged)
Use Privileged Communication

Communication (Professional)
Use Scientific Communication

Communication Apprehension
Use Speech Anxiety

Communication Barriers 2006
PN 113 SC 58090
SN A broad term used to describe anything that deters one from communicating.
HN This term was introduced in May 2006. Relevant records were re-indexed with this term. The posting note reflects the number of records that were re-indexed.
R ↓ Communication Skills 1973
↓ Interpersonal Communication 1973
Speech Anxiety 1985

Communication Disorders 1982
PN 1132 SC 10533
SN Impaired ability to communicate, usually due to speech, language, or hearing disorders.
B Disorders 1967
N ↓ Hearing Disorders 1982
↓ Language Disorders 1982
↓ Speech Disorders 1967
R ↓ Augmentative Communication 1994
↓ Communication Skills 1973
Communication Skills Training 1982
Developmental Disabilities 1982
↓ Mental Disorders 1967
↓ Physical Disorders 1997
Speech Anxiety 1985
Speech Therapy 1967

Communication Skills 1973
PN 4117 SC 10540
SN Individual ability or competency in any type of communication. Limited to human populations.
UF Communicative Competence
B Ability 1967
N Language Proficiency 1988
Rhetoric 1991
Writing Skills 1985
R ↓ Communication 1967
Communication Barriers 2006
↓ Communication Disorders 1982

Communication Skills — (cont'd)
Communication Skills Training 1982
Pragmatics 1985
Social Cognition 1994
↓ Verbal Communication 1967

Communication Skills Training 1982
PN 1563 **SC** 10542
SN Instruction, usually group oriented, to increase quality and capability of interpersonal communication.
B Training 2006
R Assertiveness Training 1978
↓ Behavior Modification 1973
↓ Communication 1967
↓ Communication Disorders 1982
↓ Communication Skills 1973
Human Relations Training 1978
Sensitivity Training 1973
↓ Skill Learning 1973
Social Skills Training 1982

Communication Systems 1973
PN 1151 **SC** 10550
SN Organized schemes for transmitting and receiving information.
B Systems 1967
N Internet 2001
Telephone Systems 1973
R ↓ Automated Information Processing 1973
↓ Communication 1967
↓ Electronic Communication 2001
↓ Information Systems 1991
Knowledge Economy 2007

Communication Theory 1973
PN 613 **SC** 10560
B Theories 1967
R ↓ Communication 1967
Cybernetics 1967
Information Theory 1967

Communications Media 1973
PN 1329 **SC** 10580
UF Media (Communications)
N ↓ Audiovisual Communications Media 1973
↓ Mass Media 1967
↓ Telecommunications Media 1973
R Censorship 1978
↓ Communication 1967
Computer Mediated Communication 2003
↓ Electronic Communication 2001

Communicative Competence
Use Communication Skills

Communism 1973
PN 777 **SC** 10590
UF Marxism
B Political Economic Systems 1973

Communities 1967
PN 7070 **SC** 10600
B Social Environments 1973
N ↓ Communes 1973
Communities of Practice 2007
↓ Neighborhoods 1973
Retirement Communities 1997
R Community Development 1997
Community Involvement 2003

Communities of Practice 2007
PN 88 **SC** 10605
SN Groups or associations of professionals who share a common interest or skill and come together to collectively learn and solve problems.
HN This term was introduced in April 2007. Relevant records were re-indexed with this term. The posting note reflects the number of records that were re-indexed.
B Communities 1967
R Group Participation 1973
Organizational Learning 2003
↓ Problem Solving 1967
Professional Networking 2004
↓ Social Interaction 1967
↓ Social Learning 1973

Community Attitudes 1973
PN 1658 **SC** 10620
SN Attitudes which characterize a group of individuals living in close proximity and organized into a social structure, however tenuous.
B Attitudes 1967
R Public Opinion 1973

Community College Students 1973
PN 1253 **SC** 10627
SN Students attending public postsecondary institutions offering 2-year degree programs and transfer components.
B College Students 1967
R Junior College Students 1973

Community Colleges 1978
PN 510 **SC** 10630
B Colleges 1967
R College Environment 1973
↓ Community Facilities 1973

Community Development 1997
PN 504 **SC** 10635
UF Rural Development
Urban Development
B Development 1967
R ↓ Communities 1967
Community Involvement 2003
↓ Community Services 1967
Economic Development 2007
Modernization 2003
Rural Environments 1967
Urban Environments 1967
Urban Planning 1973

Community Facilities 1973
PN 757 **SC** 10640
B Facilities 2006
N Community Mental Health Centers 1973
↓ Housing 1973
Public Transportation 1973
Shopping Centers 1973
Suicide Prevention Centers 1973
R Child Guidance Clinics 1973
Community Colleges 1978
↓ Community Services 1967
Day Care Centers 1973
Group Homes 1982
Halfway Houses 1973
↓ Libraries 1982
↓ Recreation Areas 1973
↓ Rehabilitation Centers 1973
Religious Buildings 1973
↓ Schools 1967
Sheltered Workshops 1967

Community Facilities — (cont'd)
Shelters 1991
Urban Planning 1973

Community Involvement 2003
PN 700 **SC** 10644
SN Involvement of an individual in community activities.
HN This term was introduced in June 2003. Relevant records were re-indexed with this term. The posting note reflects the number of records that were re-indexed.
UF Citizen Participation
Civic Behavior
B Involvement 1973
R ↓ Activism 2003
↓ Communities 1967
Community Development 1997
↓ Community Services 1967
↓ Prosocial Behavior 1982
Service Learning 2007
Volunteers 2003

Community Mental Health 1973
PN 980 **SC** 10647
SN General psychological well being or adjustment of persons in a given area.
B Mental Health 1967
R Community Mental Health Centers 1973
Community Mental Health Services 1978
↓ Community Mental Health Training 1973
Community Psychiatry 1973
Community Psychology 1973
Deinstitutionalization 1982
↓ Mental Health Programs 1973

Community Mental Health Centers 1973
PN 2026 **SC** 10650
UF Mental Health Centers (Community)
B Community Facilities 1973
Treatment Facilities 1973
R Child Guidance Clinics 1973
↓ Clinics 1967
Community Mental Health 1973
Community Mental Health Services 1978
↓ Crisis Intervention Services 1973
Day Care Centers 1973
Hot Line Services 1973
↓ Mental Health Programs 1973
↓ Mental Health Services 1978
Psychiatric Clinics 1973
Suicide Prevention Centers 1973

Community Mental Health Services 1978
PN 5120 **SC** 10656
B Community Services 1967
Mental Health Services 1978
R Community Mental Health 1973
Community Mental Health Centers 1973
Community Psychiatry 1973
Community Psychology 1973
Deinstitutionalization 1982
Group Homes 1982
↓ Mental Health 1967
↓ Mental Health Programs 1973
Outreach Programs 1997
Supported Employment 1994

Community Mental Health Training 1973
PN 382 **SC** 10660
UF Mental Health Training (Community)
Training (Community Mental Health)

Community Mental Health Training — (cont'd)
B Clinical Methods Training 1973
N Mental Health Inservice Training 1973
R Community Mental Health 1973
↓ Mental Health Programs 1973

Community Psychiatry 1973
PN 547 SC 10670
SN Branch of psychiatry concerned with the provision and delivery of community health care needs such as diagnosis; treatment; primary, secondary, and tertiary prevention; rehabilitation; and aftercare. Such services are usually delivered at community mental health centers.
B Psychiatry 1967
R Community Mental Health 1973
Community Mental Health Services 1978
Community Psychology 1973
↓ Mental Health 1967
↓ Mental Health Programs 1973

Community Psychology 1973
PN 1258 SC 10680
SN Branch of psychology that emphasizes the analysis of social processes and interactions and design of social interventions within groups and the community.
B Applied Psychology 1973
R Community Mental Health 1973
Community Mental Health Services 1978
Community Psychiatry 1973
↓ Mental Health Programs 1973

Community Services 1967
PN 8493 SC 10690
B Social Services 1982
N Community Mental Health Services 1978
Community Welfare Services 1973
↓ Crisis Intervention Services 1973
Home Visiting Programs 1973
Public Health Services 1973
R Alcoholics Anonymous 1973
Community Development 1997
↓ Community Facilities 1973
Community Involvement 2003
↓ Health Care Services 1978
Human Services 2007
Independent Living Programs 1991
Integrated Services 1997
↓ Mental Health Programs 1973
↓ Mental Health Services 1978
Outreach Programs 1997
↓ Self Help Techniques 1982
Shelters 1991
↓ Support Groups 1991

Community Welfare Services 1973
PN 552 SC 10700
UF Public Welfare Services
B Community Services 1967
R Welfare Reform 2007
Welfare Services (Government) 1973

Commuting (Travel) 1985
PN 140 SC 10705
R Geographical Mobility 1978
Telecommuting 2003
↓ Transportation 1973
Traveling 1973

Comorbidity 1991
PN 10389 SC 10707
SN Coexistence of two or more physical and/or mental disorders.

Comorbidity — (cont'd)
R ↓ Diagnosis 1967
Differential Diagnosis 1967
↓ Disorders 1967
Dual Diagnosis 1991
↓ Mental Disorders 1967
Mental Disorders due to General Medical Conditions 2001
↓ Physical Disorders 1997
↓ Psychopathology 1967

Companies
Use Business Organizations

Comparative Psychiatry
Use Transcultural Psychiatry

Comparative Psychology 1967
PN 1742 SC 10720
SN Branch of psychology devoted to the study of behavioral differences between organisms of different species. Use SPECIES DIFFERENCES for comparative studies.
HN Prior to 1982, also used for comparative studies. From 1982, limited to the scientific discipline.
B Psychology 1967
R ↓ Animal Learning 2003

Compatibility (Interpersonal)
Use Interpersonal Compatibility

Compensation (Defense Mechanism) 1973
PN 114 SC 10740
SN Defense mechanism of covering up or making up for conscious or unconscious insecurity or feelings of failure.
B Defense Mechanisms 1967

Compensatory Education 1973
PN 269 SC 10745
SN Education designed to enhance intellectual and social skills of disadvantaged students, and to compensate for environmental, experiential, cultural, or economic deficits. Compare REMEDIAL EDUCATION.
B Curriculum 1967
R ↓ Educational Programs 1973
Project Follow Through 1973
Project Head Start 1973
↓ Remedial Education 1985
Upward Bound 1973

Competence 1982
PN 5841 SC 10747
SN Possession of sufficient skills, knowledge, or qualities as required in a given situation.
N Professional Competence 1997
R ↓ Ability 1967
Accountability 1988
↓ Achievement 1967
Competency to Stand Trial 1985
Minimum Competency Tests 1985
↓ Performance 1967
Social Skills 1978

Competence (Social)
Use Social Skills

Competency to Stand Trial 1985
PN 598 SC 10749
B Legal Processes 1973
R ↓ Competence 1982
Criminal Responsibility 1991
Forensic Evaluation 1994

Competency to Stand Trial — (cont'd)
Mentally Ill Offenders 1985

Competition 1967
PN 5109 SC 10750
SN Used for human and animal populations.
B Social Behavior 1967
R Rivalry 1973

Complementary Medicine
Use Alternative Medicine

Complexity (Cognitive)
Use Cognitive Complexity

Complexity (Stimulus)
Use Stimulus Complexity

Complexity (Task)
Use Task Complexity

Compliance 1973
PN 2328 SC 10810
SN Limited to human populations.
B Social Behavior 1967
N Treatment Compliance 1982
R Obedience 1973
↓ Resistance 1997

Comprehension 1967
PN 5913 SC 10820
SN Knowledge or understanding of communications, objects, events, or situations as relates to their meaning, significance, relationships, or general principles.
UF Understanding
B Cognitive Processes 1967
N Number Comprehension 1973
↓ Verbal Comprehension 1985
R Intuition 1973
↓ Meaning 1967
Meaningfulness 1967
Metacognition 1991
Theory of Mind 2001

Comprehension Tests 1973
PN 86 SC 10830
B Measurement 1967

Compressed Speech 1973
PN 165 SC 10840
B Speech Processing (Mechanical) 1973

Compulsions 1973
PN 991 SC 10850
SN Repetitive behaviors, usually of an irrational and uncontrollable nature.
N Repetition Compulsion 2005
R ↓ Hoarding Behavior 2003
Obsessions 1967
Obsessive Compulsive Disorder 1985
Obsessive Compulsive Personality Disorder 1973
Perfectionism 1988

Compulsive Gambling
Use Pathological Gambling

Compulsive Neurosis
Use Obsessive Compulsive Disorder

Compulsive Personality Disorder
Use Obsessive Compulsive Personality Disorder

Compulsive Repetition
HN In August 2005, this term was discontinued and removed from all records containing it, and was replaced with REPETITION COMPULSION, its postable counterpart.
Use Repetition Compulsion

Compulsivity (Sexual)
Use Sexual Addiction

Computer Adaptive Testing
Use Adaptive Testing

Computer Anxiety 2001
PN 89 **SC** 10897
B Anxiety 1967
R Computer Attitudes 1988
Computer Literacy 1991

Computer Applications 1973
PN 9108 **SC** 10900
SN Application of computers, computer technology, or software to any area.
N ↓ Artificial Intelligence 1982
Computer Assisted Design 1997
Computer Assisted Diagnosis 1973
↓ Computer Assisted Instruction 1973
Computer Assisted Testing 1988
Computer Assisted Therapy 2007
↓ Computer Simulation 1973
Groupware 2003
Hypermedia 1997
Hypertext 1997
R Automated Speech Recognition 1994
Computer Assisted Language Learning 2007
Computer Mediated Communication 2003
↓ Computer Peripheral Devices 1985
Computer Searching 1991
↓ Computers 1967
Databases 1991
Decision Support Systems 1997
Digital Divide 2007
Digital Video 2007
↓ Electronic Communication 2001
↓ Information Systems 1991
Intelligent Agents 2007
Internet 2001
Microcomputers 1985
Online Therapy 2003
Virtual Reality 1997
Word Processing 1991

Computer Assisted Design 1997
PN 176 **SC** 10905
SN Use of a computer system to design a product so that it can be displayed, manipulated, and revised or modified quickly and easily.
B Computer Applications 1973
R ↓ Architecture 1973
↓ Computer Simulation 1973
↓ Computer Software 1967
↓ Computers 1967
↓ Environmental Planning 1982
Human Factors Engineering 1973
Human Machine Systems Design 1997
Product Design 1997

Computer Assisted Diagnosis 1973
PN 1269 **SC** 10910
B Computer Applications 1973
Diagnosis 1967
R Computer Assisted Therapy 2007
Magnetic Resonance Imaging 1994

Computer Assisted Diagnosis — (cont'd)
↓ Medical Diagnosis 1973
↓ Neuroimaging 2003
↓ Psychodiagnosis 1967
Telemedicine 2003
↓ Tomography 1988

Computer Assisted Instruction 1973
PN 7456 **SC** 10920
SN Use of computers to present instructional materials to students and to assess performance. Compare TEACHING MACHINES.
UF Computer Based Training
Instruction (Computer Assisted)
B Computer Applications 1973
Teaching Methods 1967
N Computer Assisted Language Learning 2007
Intelligent Tutoring Systems 2003
R Individualized Instruction 1973
Programmed Instruction 2001
Teaching Machines 1973

Computer Assisted Language Learning 2007
PN 126 **SC** 58099
SN The use of computer technology in language learning.
HN This term was introduced in April 2007. Relevant records were re-indexed with this term. The posting note reflects the number of records that were re-indexed.
UF CALL
B Computer Assisted Instruction 1973
R ↓ Computer Applications 1973
Foreign Language Learning 1967
↓ Language Arts Education 1973
↓ Language Development 1967

Computer Assisted Testing 1988
PN 1513 **SC** 10921
SN Use of computers in test construction or administration, usually in an educational or employment setting. Not used for diagnosis.
B Computer Applications 1973
Testing 1967
R Adaptive Testing 1985

Computer Assisted Therapy 2007
PN 17 **SC** 58100
SN Adjunctive use of computers in the treatment of disease.
HN This term was introduced in April 2007. Relevant records were re-indexed with this term. The posting note reflects the number of records that were re-indexed.
B Computer Applications 1973
Treatment 1967
R Computer Assisted Diagnosis 1973
↓ Computer Software 1967
↓ Computers 1967
Online Therapy 2003
Telemedicine 2003

Computer Attitudes 1988
PN 1124 **SC** 10922
B Attitudes 1967
R Computer Anxiety 2001
↓ Computers 1967

Computer Based Training
Use Computer Assisted Instruction

Computer Conferencing
Use Teleconferencing

Computer Games 1988
PN 850 **SC** 10923
UF Video Games
B Computers 1967
Games 1967
R ↓ Computer Simulation 1973
↓ Recreation 1967
Simulation Games 1973
↓ Toys 1973

Computer Literacy 1991
PN 299 **SC** 10924
B Literacy 1973
R Computer Anxiety 2001
Computer Searching 1991
Computer Training 1994
↓ Computers 1967
Digital Divide 2007

Computer Mediated Communication 2003
PN 1079 **SC** 58071
SN Use of computer technologies to support human communication. Examples include email, chat, and Internet or local computer network forums.
HN This term was introduced in June 2003. Relevant records were re-indexed with this term. The posting note reflects the number of records that were re-indexed.
UF Electronic Mail
Email
B Electronic Communication 2001
R ↓ Communications Media 1973
↓ Computer Applications 1973
↓ Computer Peripheral Devices 1985
Distance Education 2003
Groupware 2003
↓ Human Computer Interaction 1997
↓ Information Technology 2007
Internet 2001
↓ Internet Usage 2007
Messages 1973
Online Social Networks 2007
Online Therapy 2003
Telemedicine 2003
Virtual Classrooms 2007
Virtual Teams 2007

Computer Peripheral Devices 1985
PN 266 **SC** 10925
SN Computer peripheral components and hand-held microcomputer devices used for entering data, and collecting, displaying, receiving, and communicating information.
B Apparatus 1967
N Video Display Units 1985
R ↓ Computer Applications 1973
Computer Mediated Communication 2003
↓ Computers 1967
Data Collection 1982
↓ Electronic Communication 2001
↓ Human Computer Interaction 1997
Human Machine Systems 1997
Keyboards 1985
↓ Visual Displays 1973

Computer Programming 2001
PN 498 **SC** 10928
HN In 2000, this term was created to update the spelling from the discontinued term COMPUTER PROGRAMING. COMPUTER PROGRAMING was removed from all records containing it and replaced with COMPUTER PROGRAMMING.

Computer Programming — (cont'd)
UF Programming (Computer)
R Algorithms 1973
Computer Programming Languages 1973
↓ Computer Software 1967
↓ Computers 1967
↓ Data Processing 1967
Inductive Logic Programming 2007
Systems Analysis 1973
↓ Systems Design 2003

Computer Programming Languages 1973
PN 821 **SC** 10930
HN In 2000, this term was created to update the spelling from the discontinued term COMPUTER PROGRAMING LANGUAGES. COMPUTER PROGRAMING LANGUAGES was removed from all records containing it and replaced with COMPUTER PROGRAMMING LANGUAGES.
UF FORTRAN
Programming Languages (Computer)
R Computer Programming 2001
Computer Training 1994
↓ Computers 1967
↓ Data Processing 1967

Computer Programs
Use Computer Software

Computer Searching 1991
PN 609 **SC** 10945
SN Use of computerized interactive communication system to access and retrieve information.
UF Online Searching
B Automated Information Retrieval 1973
R ↓ Computer Applications 1973
Computer Literacy 1991
↓ Computers 1967
Databases 1991
↓ Electronic Communication 2001
Human Machine Systems 1997
Information 1967
Information Seeking 1973
Information Services 1988
↓ Internet Usage 2007

Computer Simulation 1973
PN 2931 **SC** 10950
B Computer Applications 1973
Simulation 1967
N Neural Networks 1991
Virtual Reality 1997
R Computer Assisted Design 1997
Computer Games 1988
Decision Support Systems 1997
Simulation Games 1973

Computer Software 1967
PN 5885 **SC** 10960
UF Computer Programs
N Decision Support Systems 1997
Groupware 2003
Word Processing 1991
R Computer Assisted Design 1997
Computer Assisted Therapy 2007
Computer Programming 2001
↓ Computers 1967
↓ Data Processing 1967
Databases 1991
Hypermedia 1997
Hypertext 1997
Intelligent Agents 2007
↓ Systems 1967

Computer Supported Cooperative Work
Use Groupware

Computer Training 1994
PN 277 **SC** 10963
B Training 2006
R Computer Literacy 1991
Computer Programming Languages 1973
↓ Curriculum 1967

Computerized Databases
Use Databases

Computers 1967
PN 4714 **SC** 10970
B Apparatus 1967
N Analog Computers 1973
Computer Games 1988
Digital Computers 1973
Microcomputers 1985
R ↓ Artificial Intelligence 1982
Automated Information Coding 1973
↓ Automated Information Processing 1973
↓ Automated Information Retrieval 1973
Automated Information Storage 1973
Automation 1967
↓ Computer Applications 1973
Computer Assisted Design 1997
Computer Assisted Therapy 2007
Computer Attitudes 1988
Computer Literacy 1991
↓ Computer Peripheral Devices 1985
Computer Programming 2001
Computer Programming Languages 1973
Computer Searching 1991
↓ Computer Software 1967
Cybernetics 1967
↓ Data Processing 1967
Databases 1991
Digital Divide 2007
↓ Expert Systems 1991
↓ Human Computer Interaction 1997
Robotics 1985
↓ Systems 1967

Concentration 1982
PN 571 **SC** 10977
SN Cognitive effort directed to one object or area of study.
B Cognitive Processes 1967
Sustained Attention 1997
R ↓ Attention 1967
Distraction 1978
Rumination (Cognitive Process) 2001
Selective Attention 1973

Concentration Camps 1973
PN 422 **SC** 10980
R Holocaust 1988
Prisons 1967

Concept Formation 1967
PN 7266 **SC** 11000
SN Developmental or learning process involving identification of common properties of objects, events, or qualities, usually represented by words or symbols, and generalization of those properties to all appropriate objects, events, or qualities.
HN In 1982, this term replaced the discontinued term CONCEPT LEARNING. In 2000, CONCEPT LEARNING was removed from all records containing it and replaced with CONCEPT FORMATION.
UF Concept Learning
Conceptualization

Concept Formation — (cont'd)
B Cognitive Processes 1967
N Cognitive Discrimination 1973
Cognitive Generalization 1967
R ↓ Cognitive Development 1973
Cognitive Hypothesis Testing 1982
Concepts 1967
Conservation (Concept) 1973
↓ Discrimination Learning 1982
↓ Generalization (Learning) 1982
↓ Learning 1967

Concept Learning
HN Term was discontinued in 1982. In 2000, the term was removed from all records containing it, and replaced with CONCEPT FORMATION, its postable counterpart.
Use Concept Formation

Concept Validity
HN Use STATISTICAL VALIDITY to access references from 1982 to June 2003.
Use Test Validity

Concepts 1967
PN 4246 **SC** 11030
SN Generic ideas or categories derived from common properties of objects, events, or qualities, usually represented by words or symbols.
R ↓ Cognitions 1985
↓ Concept Formation 1967
Information 1967
↓ Mathematics (Concepts) 1967
↓ Terminology 1991

Conceptual Imagery 1973
PN 603 **SC** 11040
SN Mental representation of concepts or conceptual relationships.
UF Imagery (Conceptual)
B Imagery 1967
R Imagination 1967
Schema 1988

Conceptual Tempo 1985
PN 54 **SC** 11045
SN The dimension of cognitive style often measured by response latency or the time required to solve a problem.
B Cognitive Style 1967
R Attention Span 1973
Cognitive Processing Speed 1997
Impulsiveness 1973
Perceptual Style 1973
Reaction Time 1967
Reflectiveness 1997

Conceptualization
Use Concept Formation

Concurrent Reinforcement Schedules 1988
PN 259 **SC** 11057
SN Simultaneous use of two or more reinforcement schedules.
B Reinforcement Schedules 1967

Concurrent Tasks
Use Dual Task Performance

Concurrent Validity
HN Use STATISTICAL VALIDITY to access references from 1988 to June 2003.
Use Test Validity

Concussion (Brain)
Use Brain Concussion

Conditioned Emotional Responses 1967
PN 706 **SC** 11070
UF CER (Conditioning)
B Classical Conditioning 1967
Conditioned Responses 1967
Emotional Responses 1967
Operant Conditioning 1967
N Conditioned Fear 2003

Conditioned Fear 2003
PN 555 **SC** 11072
HN This term was introduced in June 2003. Relevant records were re-indexed with this term. The posting note reflects the number of records that were re-indexed.
B Conditioned Emotional Responses 1967
R ↓ Fear 1967

Conditioned Inhibition
Use Conditioned Suppression

Conditioned Place Preference
Use Place Conditioning

Conditioned Reflex
Use Conditioned Responses

Conditioned Responses 1967
PN 4118 **SC** 11090
UF Conditioned Reflex
B Classical Conditioning 1967
Operant Conditioning 1967
Responses 1967
N ↓ Conditioned Emotional Responses 1967
Conditioned Suppression 1973

Conditioned Stimulus 1973
PN 2670 **SC** 11100
SN In classical conditioning, that stimulus (e.g., a light) that acquires the capacity to elicit a conditioned response (e.g., salivation) as a result of that stimulus having been paired consistently with an unconditioned stimulus (e.g., food). In operant conditioning, those stimuli (S+,S-) which differentially signal the presence or absence of reinforcement. Compare CUES.
UF Discriminative Stimulus
B Conditioning 1967
R ↓ Classical Conditioning 1967
↓ Latent Inhibition 1997
↓ Operant Conditioning 1967
Preconditioning 1994
Secondary Reinforcement 1967
↓ Stimulation 1967

Conditioned Suppression 1973
PN 1159 **SC** 11110
SN Learned behavior or the conditioning procedure in which the pairing of a neutral stimulus with an aversive stimulus, presented during the performance of a positively-reinforced behavior, results in a decrease of that behavior.
UF Conditioned Inhibition
Suppression (Conditioned)
B Conditioned Responses 1967
R Prepulse Inhibition 1997

Conditioning 1967
PN 3938 **SC** 11120
SN A process or procedure used to modify or change behavior.

Conditioning — (cont'd)
B Learning 1967
N Autoshaping 1978
↓ Aversion Conditioning 1982
↓ Classical Conditioning 1967
Conditioned Stimulus 1973
Counterconditioning 1973
↓ Operant Conditioning 1967
Place Conditioning 1991
Preconditioning 1994
Unconditioned Stimulus 1973
R ↓ Animal Learning 2003
↓ Biofeedback 1973
↓ Latent Inhibition 1997
Primary Reinforcement 1973
↓ Reinforcement 1967
Spontaneous Recovery (Learning) 1973
↓ Stimulation 1967

Conditioning (Avoidance)
Use Avoidance Conditioning

Conditioning (Classical)
Use Classical Conditioning

Conditioning (Escape)
Use Escape Conditioning

Conditioning (Eyelid)
Use Eyelid Conditioning

Conditioning (Operant)
Use Operant Conditioning

Conditioning (Verbal)
Use Verbal Learning

Condoms 1991
PN 1712 **SC** 11185
B Contraceptive Devices 1973
R AIDS Prevention 1994
↓ Birth Control 1971
↓ Family Planning 1973
↓ Prevention 1973
Safe Sex 2003
↓ Sexually Transmitted Diseases 2003

Conduct Disorder 1991
PN 2172 **SC** 11187
SN Repetitive and persistent aggressive or nonaggressive behavior in which basic rights of others or social norms are violated. Self esteem is generally low, and an inability to develop social relationships and lack of concern for others may or may not be present.
HN Consider using BEHAVIOR DISORDERS prior to 1991.
R ↓ Aggressive Behavior 1967
↓ Behavior Disorders 1971
↓ Behavior Problems 1967
Explosive Disorder 2001
↓ Impulse Control Disorders 1997
↓ Mental Disorders 1967
Oppositional Defiant Disorder 1997

Cones (Eye) 1973
PN 654 **SC** 11190
SN Photoreceptor cells in the retina that function in relatively bright light and detect fine detail and color.
UF Cones (Retina)
B Cells (Biology) 1973
Photoreceptors 1973
Retina 1967

Cones (Eye) — (cont'd)
R Fovea 1982

Cones (Retina)
Use Cones (Eye)

Confabulation 1973
PN 167 **SC** 11200
SN Giving untruthful answers to questions about situations or events that are not recalled due to loss of memory. Confabulation is not a conscious attempt to deceive.
B Thought Disturbances 1973
R False Memory 1997
Korsakoffs Psychosis 1973

Confession (Legal)
Use Legal Confession

Confession (Religion) 1973
PN 25 **SC** 11220
B Religious Practices 1973

Confidence (Self)
Use Self Confidence

Confidence Limits (Statistics) 1973
PN 310 **SC** 11230
B Statistical Analysis 1967
R Effect Size (Statistical) 1985
↓ Hypothesis Testing 1973
Predictability (Measurement) 1973
↓ Statistical Measurement 1973
↓ Statistical Sample Parameters 1973
Statistical Significance 1973
↓ Statistical Tests 1973

Confidentiality of Information
Use Privileged Communication

Confirmatory Factor Analysis
Use Factor Analysis

Conflict 1967
PN 8486 **SC** 11250
SN Hostile encounter or antagonistic state or action.
B Aggressive Behavior 1967
Interpersonal Interaction 1967
N Arguments 1973
↓ Family Conflict 2003
Riots 1973
↓ Violence 1973
↓ War 1967
R Bullying 2003

Conflict of Interest 2005
PN 102 **SC** 11253
SN A situation in which an individual or organization (either private or governmental) is in a position to exploit a professional or official capacity in some way for their personal, corporate, or political benefit.
HN This term was introduced in August 2005. Relevant records were re-indexed with this term. The posting note reflects the number of records that were re-indexed.
R ↓ Conflict Resolution 1982
Professional Ethics 1973
Role Conflicts 1973

Conflict Resolution 1982
PN 4023 **SC** 11255
SN Process of reducing or removing antagonisms among individuals, groups, organizations, or political entities.

Conflict Resolution — (cont'd)
N Mediation 1988
R ↓ Cognitive Processes 1967
Conflict of Interest 2005
Forgiveness 1988
Litigation 2003
↓ Negotiation 1973
↓ Social Interaction 1967

Conformity (Personality) 1967
PN 1469 SC 11270
B Personality Traits 1967
Social Behavior 1967
R Nonconformity (Personality) 1973
Openness to Experience 1997

Confusion (Mental)
Use Mental Confusion

Congenital Disorders 1973
PN 1300 SC 11290
HN The term CONGENITALLY HANDICAPPED was also used to capture this concept from 1973-1996, and CONGENITALLY DISABLED was used from 1997-2000. In 2001, CONGENITAL DISORDERS replaced the discontinued and deleted term CONGENITALLY DISABLED. CONGENITALLY DISABLED and CONGENITALLY HANDICAPPED were removed from all records containing them and replaced with CONGENITAL DISORDERS.
UF Congenitally Handicapped
B Disorders 1967
N Cleft Palate 1967
↓ Drug Induced Congenital Disorders 1973
Hermaphroditism 1973
Microcephaly 1973
Prader Willi Syndrome 1991
Spina Bifida 1978
R Adventitious Disorders 2001
↓ Brain Damage 1967
Cystic Fibrosis 1985
Deaf Blind 1991
Developmental Disabilities 1982
↓ Genetic Disorders 1973
Hydrocephalus 2006
↓ Mental Disorders 1967
Myotonia 1973
↓ Neonatal Disorders 1973
↓ Physical Disorders 1997
Prenatal Diagnosis 1988
↓ Syphilis 1973
Teratogens 1988

Congenitally Handicapped
HN The term was discontinued in 1997, when the term CONGENITALLY DISABLED was created to capture this concept. In 2000, with the deletion of the term CONGENITALLY DISABLED, CONGENITALLY HANDICAPPED was made a nonpostable term for the postable term CONGENITAL DISORDERS. CONGENITALLY DISABLED and CONGENITALLY HANDICAPPED were removed from all records containing them and replaced with CONGENITAL DISORDERS.
Use Congenital Disorders

Conjoined Twins 2003
PN 12 SC 11305
HN In July 2003, this term was created to replace the discontinued term SIAMESE TWINS. SIAMESE TWINS was removed from all records containing it and replaced with CONJOINED TWINS, its postable counterpart.

Conjoined Twins — (cont'd)
UF Siamese Twins
B Neonatal Disorders 1973
Twins 1967

Conjoint Measurement 1994
PN 66 SC 11307
SN Statistical measurement of a variable that is composed of two or more components which affect the variable being measured.
B Statistical Measurement 1973
R ↓ Experimental Design 1967
Psychometrics 1967
↓ Statistical Analysis 1967

Conjoint Therapy 1973
PN 458 SC 11310
SN Type of marriage or family therapy in which partners or family members are seen in joint sessions.
UF Triadic Therapy
B Family Therapy 1967
Marriage Counseling 1973
R Couples Therapy 1994
↓ Group Psychotherapy 1967
↓ Psychotherapeutic Techniques 1967

Connectionism 1994
PN 1056 SC 11315
SN Theoretical principles that characterize all learning and behavior as connected to the stimulus-response paradigm and the theory that neural linkages, whether inherited or acquired, bond these behaviors.
R ↓ Associative Processes 1967
↓ Cognitive Processes 1967
Cognitive Psychology 1985
↓ Learning 1967
Learning Theory 1967
Neural Networks 1991

Connective Tissue Cells 1973
PN 21 SC 11320
B Cells (Biology) 1973
R ↓ Connective Tissues 1973

Connective Tissues 1973
PN 44 SC 11330
B Tissues (Body) 1973
N Bones 1973
R Connective Tissue Cells 1973

Connotations 1973
PN 257 SC 11340
B Associative Processes 1967
R Analogy 1991
↓ Figurative Language 1985
Semantic Generalization 1973
Word Meaning 1973

Consanguineous Marriage 1973
PN 53 SC 11350
B Endogamous Marriage 1973

Conscience 1967
PN 275 SC 11360
SN Cognitive and affective processes which govern the individual's standards of behavior, performance, and morality.
B Psychoanalytic Personality Factors 1973
Superego 1973

Conscientiousness 1997
PN 427 SC 11365
SN Extent to which an individual is purposeful, well-organized, strong-willed, and determined.
B Personality Traits 1967
R Five Factor Personality Model 1997
Perfectionism 1988
Persistence 1973
↓ Responsibility 1973
Self Monitoring (Personality) 1985

Conscious (Personality Factor) 1973
PN 825 SC 11370
SN That portion of personal mental functioning which is known to the individual or is observable by introspection.
HN Use CONSCIOUS (PERSONALITY FACTORS) prior to 1988.
B Psychoanalytic Personality Factors 1973

Consciousness Disturbances 1973
PN 290 SC 11380
N Delirium 1973
↓ Hypnosis 1967
Place Disorientation 1973
↓ Sleep Disorders 1973
Sleep Talking 1973
Suggestibility 1967
Time Disorientation 1973
R Coma 1973
↓ Consciousness States 1971
Dissociation 2001
↓ Dissociative Disorders 2001
↓ Mental Disorders 1967
↓ Sleep 1967

Consciousness Raising Groups 1978
PN 141 SC 11387
SN Disciplined interaction of a small group of people whose exchange of feelings and experiences results in an increased awareness of social issues such as discriminatory social practices and stereotyped thinking.
B Human Potential Movement 1982
R ↓ Encounter Group Therapy 1973
↓ Group Dynamics 1967
↓ Group Psychotherapy 1967
Sensitivity Training 1973

Consciousness States 1971
PN 6552 SC 11390
SN Conceptually broad term referring to variations in the degree and type of mental awareness. Use a more specific term if possible.
UF Deja Vu
N ↓ Awareness 1967
Sleepiness 2007
Wakefulness 1973
R Centering 1991
↓ Consciousness Disturbances 1973
Dissociation 2001
Mind 1991
Physiological Arousal 1967
↓ Sleep 1967

Conservation (Concept) 1973
PN 1224 SC 11400
SN Knowledge of constancy of size, volume, or amount in spite of changed distance or shape; used as measure of cognitive development.
R ↓ Cognitive Development 1973
↓ Concept Formation 1967
Object Permanence 1985
↓ Perceptual Development 1973

Conservation (Concept) — (cont'd)
Piaget (Jean) 1967

Conservation (Ecological Behavior) 1978
PN 916 **SC** 11403
UF Recycling
B Behavior 1967
R Ecology 1973
Environmental Attitudes 1978
Environmental Education 1994

Conservatism 1973
PN 676 **SC** 11405
UF Traditionalism
B Personality Traits 1967
R Political Conservatism 1973
Religious Fundamentalism 2003

Conservatism (Political)
Use Political Conservatism

Conservatorship
Use Guardianship

Consistency (Measurement) 1973
PN 385 **SC** 11420
B Statistical Analysis 1967
R Error of Measurement 1985
↓ Prediction Errors 1973
Statistical Reliability 1973
Statistical Validity 1973

Consonants 1973
PN 1204 **SC** 11430
B Letters (Alphabet) 1973
Phonemes 1973
R Syllables 1973
Words (Phonetic Units) 1967

Conspecifics 2003
PN 570 **SC** 11433
SN An organism that is a member of the same species as another organism.
HN This term was introduced in June 2003. Relevant records were re-indexed with this term. The posting note reflects the number of records that were re-indexed.
R Species Recognition 1985

Constant Time Delay 1997
PN 34 **SC** 11435
SN Instruction involving a prompting technique in which dependence on the prompting is faded by a fixed time delay between the presentation of a target stimulus and the delivery of the controlling prompt.
B Prompting 1997
R ↓ Behavior Modification 1973
↓ Learning Strategies 1991
Task Analysis 1967
↓ Teaching Methods 1967

Constipation 1973
PN 112 **SC** 11440
B Colon Disorders 1973

Construct Validity
HN Use STATISTICAL VALIDITY to access references from 1982 to June 2003.
Use Test Validity

Constructionism
Use Constructivism

Constructivism 1994
PN 2576 **SC** 11448
SN Theoretical perspective that characterizes perceptual experience and reality as constructed by the mind in the observation of the effects of independent actions on objects.
UF Constructionism
B Theories 1967
R ↓ Cognitive Development 1973
↓ Learning 1967
↓ Perception 1967
Phenomenology 1967
Piaget (Jean) 1967

Consultation (Professional)
Use Professional Consultation

Consultation Liaison Psychiatry 1991
PN 780 **SC** 11465
B Professional Consultation 1973
Psychiatry 1967

Consumer Attitudes 1973
PN 5104 **SC** 11470
SN Attitudes of, not toward, consumers.
B Attitudes 1967
N Brand Preferences 1994
Consumer Satisfaction 1994
R ↓ Consumer Research 1973
Consumer Surveys 1973
Customer Relationship Management 2007
Public Relations 1973
↓ Quality of Services 1997

Consumer Behavior 1967
PN 8166 **SC** 11480
UF Buying
B Behavior 1967
N Shopping 1997
R Behavioral Economics 2003
Brand Names 1978
Brand Preferences 1994
Consumer Education 2007
↓ Consumer Research 1973
Consumer Satisfaction 1994
Consumer Surveys 1973
Customer Relationship Management 2007
↓ Electronic Commerce 2006
↓ Retailing 1991
Shopping Centers 1973
Supply and Demand 2004

Consumer Education 2007
PN 61 **SC** 11483
SN Methods of informing or educating consumers about the evaluation of goods and services.
HN This term was introduced in April 2007. Relevant records were re-indexed with this term. The posting note reflects the number of records that were re-indexed.
B Education 1967
R ↓ Consumer Behavior 1967
Consumer Protection 1973
Fraud 1994

Consumer Fraud
Use Fraud

Consumer Product Design
Use Product Design

Consumer Protection 1973
PN 198 **SC** 11490
R Accountability 1988
Consumer Education 2007
↓ Laws 1967
↓ Legal Processes 1973
Product Design 1997
Warning Labels 1997
↓ Warnings 1997

Consumer Psychology 1973
PN 656 **SC** 11500
SN Subdiscipline in psychology that has as its emphasis the behavioral and psychological aspects of consumer behavior.
B Applied Psychology 1973

Consumer Research 1973
PN 1747 **SC** 11510
SN Marketing and advertising research assessing consumer needs, competition, and methods of sale for a product.
B Experimentation 1967
N Consumer Surveys 1973
R ↓ Advertising 1967
Brand Names 1978
Brand Preferences 1994
↓ Consumer Attitudes 1973
↓ Consumer Behavior 1967
Consumer Satisfaction 1994
Customer Relationship Management 2007
Mail Surveys 1994
↓ Marketing 1973
Product Design 1997
Telephone Surveys 1994

Consumer Satisfaction 1994
PN 1240 **SC** 11515
UF Customer Satisfaction
B Consumer Attitudes 1973
Satisfaction 1973
R ↓ Consumer Behavior 1967
↓ Consumer Research 1973
Consumer Surveys 1973
Customer Relationship Management 2007
Quality Control 1988
↓ Quality of Services 1997

Consumer Surveys 1973
PN 301 **SC** 11520
SN Surveys assessing consumer needs, product usage, and effectiveness of marketing and advertising.
B Consumer Research 1973
Surveys 1967
R ↓ Consumer Attitudes 1973
↓ Consumer Behavior 1967
Consumer Satisfaction 1994
Mail Surveys 1994
Product Design 1997
Telephone Surveys 1994

Contact Lenses 1973
PN 50 **SC** 11540
B Optical Aids 1973

Contagion 1988
PN 227 **SC** 11544
SN Transmission of behavior, attitudes, or emotions to other persons through suggestions, verbal communication, imitation, or gestures. Not used for infectious disorders.

Contagion — (cont'd)
B Social Behavior 1967
R ↓ Collective Behavior 1967
Mass Hysteria 1973

Content Analysis 1978
PN 2780 **SC** 11548
SN Systematic, objective, quantitative, or qualitative description of the manifest or latent content of communications.
B Analysis 1967
Methodology 1967
N Discourse Analysis 1997
R ↓ Communication 1967

Content Analysis (Test) 1967
PN 278 **SC** 11550
SN Systematic examination of a test, primarily to determine whether the test items constitute an adequate sample of the domain or subject matter to be tested.
B Analysis 1967
Test Construction 1973
Testing 1967

Content Validity
Use Test Validity

Contextual Associations 1967
PN 5989 **SC** 11560
SN In learning and memory, associations made to environmental or internal conditions during learning or memorization. In perception and communication, environmental conditions that affect such aspects as perceptual accuracy, comprehension, or meaning.
UF Associations (Contextual)
B Associative Processes 1967
R Place Conditioning 1991
↓ Priming 1988
Semantic Priming 1994
Word Frequency 1973
Word Meaning 1973

Contiguity (Cognitive)
Use Cognitive Contiguity

Contingency Management 1973
PN 1215 **SC** 11580
SN Behavior modification technique in which the stimuli and reinforcers that control a given behavior are manipulated to increase the likelihood of occurrence of the desired behavior.
B Behavior Modification 1973
N Token Economy Programs 1973
R Noncontingent Reinforcement 1988

Contingent Negative Variation 1982
PN 390 **SC** 11583
SN Cortical evoked potential of slow negativity recorded in the period between stimulus-presentation and responses, and which is associated with states of attention or expectancy.
UF Readiness Potential
B Evoked Potentials 1967

Continuing Education 1985
PN 750 **SC** 11590
SN Formal or informal courses, educational programs or services, usually at the postsecondary level, designed to advance or update adult learning for personal, academic, or occupational and professional purposes.

Continuing Education — (cont'd)
B Adult Education 1973
N ↓ Inservice Training 1985
R Adult Learning 1997
Distance Education 2003
↓ Higher Education 1973
Individualized Instruction 1973
Professional Development 1982
Reentry Students 1985
↓ Training 2006

Continuity of Care
Use Continuum of Care

Continuous Reinforcement
Use Reinforcement Schedules

Continuum of Care 2004
PN 279 **SC** 11605
SN Provision of continuous, comprehensive, and integrated care that involves health, mental health, and/or social services.
HN This term was introduced in June 2004. Relevant records were re-indexed with this term. The posting note reflects the number of records that were re-indexed.
UF Continuity of Care
B Health Care Services 1978
R Aftercare 1973
↓ Health Care Delivery 1978
Quality of Care 1988

Contour
Use Form and Shape Perception

Contour Perception
Use Form and Shape Perception

Contraception
Use Birth Control

Contraceptive Devices 1973
PN 341 **SC** 11630
B Birth Control 1971
N Condoms 1991
Diaphragms (Birth Control) 1973
Intrauterine Devices 1973
Oral Contraceptives 1973

Contracting Out
Use Outsourcing

Contracts (Psychological)
Use Psychological Contracts

Control (Emotional)
Use Emotional Control

Control (Locus of)
Use Internal External Locus of Control

Control (Self)
Use Self Control

Control (Social)
Use Social Control

Control Groups
Use Experiment Controls

Controls (Instrument)
Use Instrument Controls

Convergent Thinking
Use Inductive Deductive Reasoning

Convergent Validity
Use Test Validity

Conversation 1973
PN 4603 **SC** 11710
B Interpersonal Communication 1973
Verbal Communication 1967
R Listening (Interpersonal) 1997

Conversion Disorder 2001
PN 638 **SC** 11717
HN In 2001, this term replaced the discontinued term CONVERSION NEUROSIS. CONVERSION NEUROSIS was removed from all records containing it and replaced with CONVERSION DISORDER.
UF Conversion Hysteria
Conversion Neurosis
Hysterical Neurosis (Conversion)
B Somatoform Disorders 2001
N Hysterical Paralysis 1973
Hysterical Vision Disturbances 1973
Pseudocyesis 1973
R ↓ Defense Mechanisms 1967
Histrionic Personality Disorder 1991
Hypochondriasis 1973
↓ Hysteria 1967
Somatization 1994
Somatoform Pain Disorder 1997

Conversion Hysteria
Use Conversion Disorder

Conversion Neurosis
HN In 2001, the term was discontinued and removed from all records containing it, and replaced with CONVERSION DISORDER, its postable counterpart.
Use Conversion Disorder

Conviction (Criminal)
Use Criminal Conviction

Convulsions
HN In August 2005, this term was discontinued and removed from all records containing it, and was replaced with SEIZURES, its postable counterpart.
Use Seizures

Cooperating Teachers 1978
PN 147 **SC** 11756
SN Experienced elementary or secondary teachers employed to supervise student teachers or teacher interns in schools which, although not integral parts of teacher education institutions, provide experiences for the student teachers and teacher interns.
UF Supervising Teachers
B Teachers 1967
R Practicum Supervision 1978
Student Teachers 1973
Student Teaching 1973
↓ Teacher Education 1967

Cooperation 1967
PN 7689 **SC** 11760
SN The process of working together toward the attainment of a goal. Used for human or animal populations.
B Interpersonal Interaction 1967
Prosocial Behavior 1982
R Agreeableness 1997
Collaboration 2007
Cooperative Learning 1994
Groupware 2003
Volunteers 2003

Cooperative Education 1982
PN 160 **SC** 11765
SN Combined complementary work and study experience or program coordinated by a teacher and designed by the school and the employer to achieve some occupational goal. Not to be confused with work study programs which serve as means for financial assistance.
B Vocational Education 1973
R Curricular Field Experience 1982
↓ Educational Programs 1973
↓ Experiential Learning 1997

Cooperative Learning 1994
PN 1351 **SC** 11766
SN Learning in small groups where cooperation among group members determines rewards and performance.
B Learning 1967
R Collaborative Learning 2007
Cooperation 1967
Group Instruction 1973
Individualized Instruction 1973
Peer Tutoring 1973
School Learning 1967
↓ Teaching 1967
↓ Teaching Methods 1967
↓ Teams 1988

Cooperative Therapy
Use Cotherapy

Coordination (Motor)
Use Motor Coordination

Coordination (Perceptual Motor)
Use Perceptual Motor Coordination

Coping Behavior 1967
PN 25310 **SC** 11790
SN Use of conscious or unconscious strategies or mechanisms in adapting to stress, various disorders, or environmental demands.
B Behavior 1967
R Adaptability (Personality) 1973
Adjustment Disorders 1994
Anosognosia 1994
↓ Emotional Adjustment 1973
↓ Emotional Control 1973
↓ Helplessness 1997
Illness Behavior 1982
Resilience (Psychological) 2003

Copper 1973
PN 128 **SC** 11800
B Metallic Elements 1973

Coprophagia 2001
PN 4 **SC** 11805
SN Eating of feces. Used for both human and animal populations.
UF Cecotrophy
B Ingestion 2001
R Defecation 1967
↓ Eating Disorders 1997
Fetishism 1973
Pica 1973

Copulation
Use Sexual Intercourse (Human)

Copulation (Animal)
Use Animal Mating Behavior

Cornea 1973
PN 66 **SC** 11830
B Eye (Anatomy) 1967

Coronary Disorders
Use Cardiovascular Disorders

Coronary Heart Disease
Use Heart Disorders

Coronary Prone Behavior 1982
PN 2405 **SC** 11855
SN Constellation of behaviors or attitudes constituting a risk factor for coronary heart disease. Traits can include ambition, competitiveness, sense of time urgency, devotion to work over relaxation, positive attitude toward pressure, aggressiveness, impatience, need for recognition, and tendency toward hostility.
UF Type A Personality
Type B Personality
B Behavior 1967
R At Risk Populations 1985
↓ Cardiovascular Disorders 1967
Illness Behavior 1982
↓ Personality 1967
↓ Personality Traits 1967
Predisposition 1973
Stress Reactions 1973
Susceptibility (Disorders) 1973

Coronary Thromboses 1973
PN 10 **SC** 11860
B Heart Disorders 1973
Thromboses 1973
R Myocardial Infarctions 1973

Coronary Vessels
Use Arteries (Anatomy)

Corporal Punishment
Use Punishment

Corporate Acquisitions
Use Mergers and Acquisitions

Corporations
Use Business Organizations

Corpus Callosum 1973
PN 1110 **SC** 11900
SN A large bundle of nerve fibers that interconnect the right and left cerebral hemispheres in a reciprocal manner.
B Cerebral Cortex 1967
Neural Pathways 1982
R Commissurotomy 1985
Interhemispheric Interaction 1985
Left Hemisphere 2005
Right Hemisphere 2005

Corpus Striatum
Use Basal Ganglia

Correctional Institutions 1973
PN 1460 **SC** 11910
UF Institutions (Correctional)
B Facilities 2006
N Prisons 1967
Reformatories 1973
R Criminal Rehabilitation 2004
Halfway Houses 1973
Incarceration 1973

Correctional Institutions — (cont'd)
Institution Visitation 1973
Institutional Schools 1978
Maximum Security Facilities 1985
Penology 1973

Corrective Lenses
Use Optical Aids

Correlation (Statistical)
Use Statistical Correlation

Cortex (Auditory)
Use Auditory Cortex

Cortex (Cerebral)
Use Cerebral Cortex

Cortex (Motor)
Use Motor Cortex

Cortex (Somatosensory)
Use Somatosensory Cortex

Cortex (Visual)
Use Visual Cortex

Cortical Atrophy
Use Cerebral Atrophy

Cortical Evoked Potentials
HN In May 2006, this term was discontinued and removed from all records containing it, and was replaced with EVOKED POTENTIALS, its postable counterpart.
Use Evoked Potentials

Corticoids
Use Corticosteroids

Corticospinal Tracts
Use Pyramidal Tracts

Corticosteroids 1973
PN 689 **SC** 12000
UF Adrenal Cortex Steroids
Corticoids
B Steroids 1973
N Aldosterone 1973
Corticosterone 1973
Cortisone 1973
Deoxycorticosterone 1973
Hydrocortisone 1973
Prednisolone 1973
R ↓ Adrenal Cortex Hormones 1973

Corticosterone 1973
PN 1627 **SC** 12010
B Adrenal Cortex Hormones 1973
Corticosteroids 1973

Corticotropin 1973
PN 1671 **SC** 12020
UF ACTH (Hormone)
Adrenocorticotropin
B Neuropeptides 2003
Pituitary Hormones 1973
R Corticotropin Releasing Factor 1994

Corticotropin Releasing Factor 1994
PN 768 **SC** 12025
UF ACTH Releasing Factor
B Hormones 1967
Neuropeptides 2003
Peptides 1973

Corticotropin Releasing Factor — (cont'd)
R Corticotropin 1973

Cortisol
Use Hydrocortisone

Cortisone 1973
PN 89 **SC** 12040
B Adrenal Cortex Hormones 1973
Corticosteroids 1973

Cosmetic Techniques 2001
PN 147 **SC** 12035
UF Body Art
Piercings
Tattoos
R ↓ Fads and Fashions 1973
Initiation Rites 1973
↓ Physical Appearance 1982
Plastic Surgery 1973
Rites (Nonreligious) 1973
Self Expression 2006
Self Mutilation 1973
Skin (Anatomy) 1967
Subculture (Anthropological) 1973

Cost Containment 1991
PN 310 **SC** 12041
SN Policies or procedures to restrain or control expenses in any setting.
R Budgets 1997
↓ Case Management 1991
↓ Costs and Cost Analysis 1973
Diagnosis Related Groups 1988
↓ Economics 1985
Fee for Service 1994
Health Care Costs 1994
↓ Health Care Services 1978
Health Maintenance Organizations 1982
↓ Managed Care 1994
Money 1967
↓ Professional Fees 1978
Resource Allocation 1997
↓ Treatment 1967

Cost Effectiveness
Use Costs and Cost Analysis

Costs and Cost Analysis 1973
PN 6484 **SC** 12045
SN Applied to any subject and includes prices, expenses, or payments; also attachment of dollar estimates to the costs of an operation and its alternatives.
UF Cost Effectiveness
Price
B Analysis 1967
N Budgets 1997
Health Care Costs 1994
R Cost Containment 1991
↓ Economics 1985
↓ Economy 1973
Finance 2007
Funding 1988
Health Care Economics 2007
Money 1967
Pharmacoeconomics 2007
↓ Professional Fees 1978
Resource Allocation 1997
Risk Management 1997

Cotherapy 1982
PN 223 **SC** 12047
SN Psychotherapeutic process in which a client or a group of clients are treated by more than one therapist.
HN Use CONJOINT THERAPY to access references from 1973-1981.
UF Cooperative Therapy
Multiple Therapy
B Psychotherapeutic Techniques 1967
R Psychiatric Training 1973
↓ Psychotherapy 1967
Psychotherapy Training 1973

Counselees
Use Clients

Counseling 1967
PN 12455 **SC** 12080
SN Conceptually broad term referring to a form of helping process which involves giving advice and information, in order to assist individuals or groups in coping with their problems. Use a more specific term if possible.
N Cross Cultural Counseling 2003
Educational Counseling 1967
Genetic Counseling 1978
Group Counseling 1973
↓ Marriage Counseling 1973
Microcounseling 1978
Occupational Guidance 1967
Pastoral Counseling 1967
Peer Counseling 1978
Premarital Counseling 1973
↓ Psychotherapeutic Counseling 1973
Rehabilitation Counseling 1978
School Counseling 1982
R Counseling Psychology 1973
↓ Counselors 1967
Employee Assistance Programs 1985
↓ Family Therapy 1967
Feminist Therapy 1994
↓ Health Care Services 1978
↓ Mental Health Services 1978
Social Casework 1967
Student Personnel Services 1978
↓ Support Groups 1991
↓ Treatment 1967

Counseling (Group)
Use Group Counseling

Counseling Psychologists 1988
PN 413 **SC** 12065
B Psychologists 1967
R Clinicians 1973
Counseling Psychology 1973

Counseling Psychology 1973
PN 1694 **SC** 12070
B Applied Psychology 1973
R ↓ Counseling 1967
Counseling Psychologists 1988

Counselor Attitudes 1973
PN 1362 **SC** 12090
SN Attitudes of, not toward, counselors.
B Attitudes 1967
Counselor Characteristics 1973
R Counselor Role 1973
↓ Counselors 1967
↓ Health Personnel Attitudes 1985

Counselor Attitudes — (cont'd)
Psychologist Attitudes 1991

Counselor Characteristics 1973
PN 2868 **SC** 12100
UF Counselor Effectiveness
Counselor Personality
N Counselor Attitudes 1973
R ↓ Counselors 1967

Counselor Client Interaction
Use Psychotherapeutic Processes

Counselor Education 1973
PN 4281 **SC** 12120
B Education 1967
R ↓ Clinical Methods Training 1973
Counselor Trainees 1973
Microcounseling 1978
Practicum Supervision 1978
↓ Psychology Education 1978
Psychotherapy Training 1973
Rehabilitation Education 1997

Counselor Effectiveness
Use Counselor Characteristics

Counselor Personality
Use Counselor Characteristics

Counselor Role 1973
PN 1115 **SC** 12150
UF Role (Counselor)
B Roles 1967
R Counselor Attitudes 1973
↓ Counselors 1967
Therapist Role 1978

Counselor Trainees 1973
PN 2065 **SC** 12160
R Counselor Education 1973
↓ Counselors 1967
Therapist Trainees 1973

Counselors 1967
PN 4246 **SC** 12170
B Professional Personnel 1978
N Rehabilitation Counselors 1978
School Counselors 1973
Vocational Counselors 1973
R ↓ Counseling 1967
Counselor Attitudes 1973
↓ Counselor Characteristics 1973
Counselor Role 1973
Counselor Trainees 1973
↓ Health Personnel 1994
↓ Mental Health Personnel 1967
↓ Psychologists 1967
↓ Social Workers 1973
Sociologists 1973
↓ Therapists 1967

Counterconditioning 1973
PN 96 **SC** 12180
SN Technique used to extinguish a response to a certain stimulus by conditioning an alternative, often incompatible response to that stimulus.
B Conditioning 1967
R ↓ Aversion Therapy 1973
↓ Behavior Modification 1973
↓ Behavior Therapy 1967
Reciprocal Inhibition Therapy 1973

Countertransference 1973
PN 4112 **SC** 12190
SN Conscious or unconscious emotional reaction of the therapist to the patient, which may interfere with the treatment.
B Psychotherapeutic Processes 1967
R Enactments 1997
Negative Therapeutic Reaction 1997
Professional Client Sexual Relations 1994
Psychotherapeutic Transference 1967

Countries 1967
PN 2960 **SC** 12195
SN Applies to cross-national studies when individual countries are not mentioned or are too numerous to list.
N Developed Countries 1985
Developing Countries 1985
R Geography 1973

County Agricultural Agents
Use Agricultural Extension Workers

Couples 1982
PN 5495 **SC** 12205
SN Two individuals in an intimate relationship.
R Cohabitation 1973
Dyads 1973
↓ Family 1967
Romance 1997
Significant Others 1991
Social Dating 1973
↓ Spouses 1973

Couples Therapy 1994
PN 1641 **SC** 12207
SN Used specifically for unmarried couples. Use MARRIAGE COUNSELING for married couples.
R Conjoint Therapy 1973
↓ Marriage Counseling 1973
↓ Psychotherapy 1967
Sex Therapy 1978

Courage 1973
PN 165 **SC** 12210
UF Bravery
B Personality Traits 1967
R Heroes 2007

Course Evaluation 1978
PN 641 **SC** 12215
SN Procedures, materials, or the process involved in the assessment of quality or effectiveness of an academic or vocational course or program by its students or participants. Evaluation may include content, structure, or method of material presentation.
B Evaluation 1967
R ↓ Curriculum 1967
Educational Program Evaluation 1973
Educational Quality 1997
Teacher Effectiveness Evaluation 1978
↓ Teaching 1967

Course Objectives
Use Educational Objectives

Course of Illness
Use Disease Course

Court Ordered Treatment
Use Court Referrals

Court Referrals 1994
PN 389 **SC** 12219
SN Court ordered assessment, treatment, consultation, or other services for defendants, plaintiffs, or criminals.
UF Court Ordered Treatment
B Adjudication 1967
R ↓ Commitment (Psychiatric) 1973
↓ Criminal Justice 1991
↓ Criminals 1967
Defendants 1985
Forensic Evaluation 1994
Insanity Defense 1985
Involuntary Treatment 1994
Mediation 1988
Mentally Ill Offenders 1985
Probation 1973
Professional Referral 1973
↓ Treatment 1967

Courts
Use Adjudication

Courtship (Animal)
Use Animal Courtship Behavior

Courtship (Human)
Use Human Courtship

Courtship Displays (Animal)
Use Animal Courtship Displays

Cousins 1973
PN 23 **SC** 12260
B Family Members 1973

Covert Sensitization 1988
PN 45 **SC** 12265
SN Form of aversion conditioning in which noxious mental images, thoughts, or feelings are associated with undesirable behavior by verbal cues. Frequently used in therapeutic settings.
B Aversion Conditioning 1982
Aversion Therapy 1973
R Aversive Stimulation 1973

Cows
Use Cattle

Coyotes
Use Canids

Crabs 1973
PN 399 **SC** 12300
B Crustacea 1973

Crack Cocaine 2003
PN 246 **SC** 12305
SN A highly addictive form of alkaloidal cocaine that is smoked.
HN This term was introduced in June 2003. Relevant records were re-indexed with this term. The posting note reflects the number of records that were re-indexed.
B Cocaine 1973

Crafts 1973
PN 73 **SC** 12310
UF Handicrafts
B Art 1967

Cramps (Muscle)
Use Muscular Disorders

Cranial Nerves 1973
PN 237 **SC** 12330
UF Accessory Nerve
Glossopharyngeal Nerve
Hypoglossal Nerve
Nerve (Accessory)
Nerves (Cranial)
Oculomotor Nerve
Trochlear Nerve
B Peripheral Nervous System 1973
N Abducens Nerve 1973
Acoustic Nerve 1973
Facial Nerve 1973
Olfactory Nerve 1973
Optic Nerve 1973
Trigeminal Nerve 1973
Vagus Nerve 1973

Craving 1997
PN 788 **SC** 12350
R ↓ Addiction 1973
↓ Appetite 1973
↓ Drug Abuse 1973
↓ Drug Usage 1971
↓ Emotional States 1973
Food 1978
↓ Needs 1967

Crayfish 1973
PN 169 **SC** 12360
B Crustacea 1973

Creative Arts Therapy 1994
PN 207 **SC** 12365
SN Therapeutic use of the arts in medicine, mental health, or education.
B Treatment 1967
N Art Therapy 1973
Dance Therapy 1973
Music Therapy 1973
Poetry Therapy 1994
Recreation Therapy 1973
R Improvisation 2004
Movement Therapy 1997
↓ Psychotherapeutic Techniques 1967

Creative Writing 1994
PN 499 **SC** 12370
HN Use LITERATURE to access references from 1973-1993.
UF Writing (Creative)
B Written Communication 1985
R ↓ Literature 1967
Narratives 1997
Poetry 1973
↓ Prose 1973
Rhetoric 1991
Self Expression 2006
Storytelling 1988

Creativity 1967
PN 11418 **SC** 12380
SN Ability to perceive new relationships, and to derive new ideas and solve problems by pursuing nontraditional patterns of thinking. Compare DIVERGENT THINKING.
UF Innovativeness
Originality
B Personality Traits 1967
R ↓ Ability 1967
↓ Artistic Ability 1973
Divergent Thinking 1973
Gifted 1967
Improvisation 2004

Creativity — (cont'd)
Innovation 2007
↓ Intelligence 1967
Openness to Experience 1997
Pretend Play 2005
Self Expression 2006

Creativity Measurement 1973
PN 451 **SC** 12390
B Measurement 1967

Credibility 1973
PN 1182 **SC** 12400
R ↓ Interpersonal Communication 1973
Reputation 1997
↓ Social Perception 1967

Creutzfeldt Jakob Syndrome 1994
PN 223 **SC** 12410
SN A rare, difficult-to-diagnose, transmissable spongiform encephalopathy recognized to exist in sporadic, familial, iatrogenic, and variant forms.
B Encephalopathies 1982
Presenile Dementia 1973
Syndromes 1973
R ↓ Dementia 1985
↓ Proteins 1973

Cri du Chat Syndrome
Use Crying Cat Syndrome

Crib Death
Use Sudden Infant Death

Crime 1967
PN 7388 **SC** 12430
UF Felonies
Misdemeanors
B Social Issues 1991
N Arson 1985
↓ Child Abuse 1971
Driving Under the Influence 1988
Hate Crimes 2003
Human Trafficking 2007
Illegal Drug Distribution 1997
Kidnapping 1988
↓ Sex Offenses 1982
↓ Theft 1973
Vandalism 1978
↓ Violent Crime 2003
R ↓ Antisocial Behavior 1971
↓ Behavior Disorders 1971
Crime Prevention 1985
↓ Crime Victims 1982
↓ Criminal Behavior 2003
↓ Criminal Justice 1991
Criminal Responsibility 1991
↓ Criminals 1967
Fraud 1994
Informants 1988
↓ Perpetrators 1988
Self Defense 1985
Stalking 2001
↓ Terrorism 1982
Victimization 1973

Crime Prevention 1985
PN 1184 **SC** 12432
SN Measures aimed at deterring the occurrence of crime or delinquent behavior.
B Prevention 1973
R ↓ Crime 1967
↓ Criminal Justice 1991

Crime Prevention — (cont'd)
↓ Juvenile Delinquency 1967
↓ Law Enforcement 1978

Crime Victims 1982
PN 2014 **SC** 12434
SN Individuals subjected to and adversely affected by criminal activity.
HN Use VICTIMIZATION to access references from 1973-1981.
N Hostages 1988
R ↓ Crime 1967
Self Defense 1985
Victimization 1973

Criminal Behavior 2003
PN 1772 **SC** 12437
HN This term was introduced in June 2003. Relevant records were re-indexed with this term. The posting note reflects the number of records that were re-indexed.
UF Criminality
B Antisocial Behavior 1971
N ↓ Juvenile Delinquency 1967
R ↓ Behavior Disorders 1971
↓ Crime 1967
Criminal Profiling 2007
Criminal Record 2006
Criminal Rehabilitation 2004
↓ Criminals 1967

Criminal Conviction 1973
PN 626 **SC** 12440
SN Declaration made by a court finding a person guilty and responsible for a criminal offense.
UF Conviction (Criminal)
B Criminal Justice 1991
R ↓ Adjudication 1967
Criminal Record 2006
↓ Criminals 1967
Legal Decisions 1991

Criminal History
Use Criminal Record

Criminal Interrogation
Use Interrogation

Criminal Justice 1991
PN 2307 **SC** 12445
SN Used for the system, discipline, or the actual process itself.
B Justice 1973
Legal Processes 1973
N Criminal Conviction 1973
Juvenile Justice 2004
R ↓ Adjudication 1967
Court Referrals 1994
↓ Crime 1967
Crime Prevention 1985
Criminal Law 1973
Forensic Psychiatry 1973
Forensic Psychology 1985
↓ Law Enforcement 1978
Legal Decisions 1991
Litigation 2003
Penology 1973

Criminal Law 1973
PN 671 **SC** 12450
B Law (Government) 1973
R ↓ Criminal Justice 1991
Litigation 2003

Criminal Profiling 2007
PN 102 **SC** 58101
SN Methods used to identify characteristics of likely perpetrators of a crime based on a systematic evaluation of the crime scene together with other information, such as the background of the victim or victims.
HN This term was introduced in April 2007. Relevant records were re-indexed with this term. The posting note reflects the number of records that were re-indexed.
UF Offender Profiling
R ↓ Criminal Behavior 2003
↓ Discrimination 1967
Victimization 1973

Criminal Record 2006
PN 25 **SC** 12451
SN An official record of criminal arrests, convictions, and correctional information.
HN This term was introduced in May 2006. Relevant records were re-indexed with this term. The posting note reflects the number of records that were re-indexed.
UF Criminal History
Prison Record
R ↓ Adjudication 1967
↓ Criminal Behavior 2003
Criminal Conviction 1973
↓ Criminals 1967
Incarceration 1973
Legal Arrest 1973
Recidivism 1973

Criminal Rehabilitation 2004
PN 550 **SC** 12452
HN This term was introduced in June 2004. Relevant records were re-indexed with this term. The posting note reflects the number of records that were re-indexed.
B Rehabilitation 1967
R ↓ Correctional Institutions 1973
↓ Criminal Behavior 2003
↓ Criminals 1967
Parole 1973
↓ Prisoners 1967
Prisons 1967
Probation 1973

Criminal Responsibility 1991
PN 480 **SC** 12453
SN State of mind that permits one to be held accountable for criminal acts.
B Responsibility 1973
R Accountability 1988
↓ Adjudication 1967
Competency to Stand Trial 1985
↓ Crime 1967
↓ Criminals 1967
Defendants 1985
Insanity Defense 1985
↓ Perpetrators 1988

Criminality
Use Criminal Behavior

Criminally Insane
Use Mentally Ill Offenders

Criminals 1967
PN 6285 **SC** 12460
UF Offenders (Adult)
B Perpetrators 1988
N Female Criminals 1973
Male Criminals 1973

Criminals — (cont'd)
Mentally Ill Offenders 1985
R Antisocial Personality Disorder 1973
Court Referrals 1994
↓ Crime 1967
↓ Criminal Behavior 2003
Criminal Conviction 1973
Criminal Record 2006
Criminal Rehabilitation 2004
Criminal Responsibility 1991
Defendants 1985
Forensic Evaluation 1994
↓ Juvenile Delinquency 1967
↓ Prisoners 1967
Recidivism 1973

Criminology 1973
PN 820 **SC** 12470
R Penology 1973

Crises 1971
PN 1713 **SC** 12490
N Family Crises 1973
Identity Crisis 1973
Organizational Crises 1973
R ↓ Crisis Intervention 1973
↓ Crisis Intervention Services 1973
↓ Disasters 1973
↓ Experiences (Events) 1973
↓ Stress 1967

Crisis (Reactions to)
Use Stress Reactions

Crisis Intervention 1973
PN 2287 **SC** 12510
SN Brief therapeutic approach which is ameliorative rather than curative of acute psychiatric emergencies. Used in such contexts as emergency rooms of psychiatric or general hospitals, or in the home or place of crisis occurrence, this treatment approach focuses on interpersonal and intrapsychic factors and environmental modification of behavior.
B Intervention 2003
N Debriefing (Psychological) 2004
Suicide Prevention 1973
R ↓ Crises 1971
↓ Crisis Intervention Services 1973
Family Intervention 2003

Crisis Intervention Services 1973
PN 987 **SC** 12520
SN Community organizations, programs, or mental health personnel which provide crisis care.
B Community Services 1967
Mental Health Programs 1973
Treatment 1967
N Hot Line Services 1973
Suicide Prevention Centers 1973
R ↓ Clinics 1967
Community Mental Health Centers 1973
↓ Crises 1971
↓ Crisis Intervention 1973
Emergency Services 1973
↓ Intervention 2003
↓ Treatment Facilities 1973
Walk In Clinics 1973

Criterion Referenced Tests 1982
PN 357 **SC** 12525
SN Tests in which scores are measured against explicitly stated objectives rather than a group norm.
UF Mastery Tests
Objective Referenced Tests

Criterion Referenced Tests — (cont'd)
B Measurement 1967
R ↓ Achievement Measures 1967
Performance Tests 1973

Criterion Related Validity
Use Test Validity

Critical Flicker Fusion Threshold 1967
PN 447 **SC** 12530
UF Flicker Fusion Frequency
B Visual Thresholds 1973
R ↓ Perceptual Measures 1973

Critical Incident Debriefing
Use Debriefing (Psychological)

Critical Period 1988
PN 181 **SC** 12533
R ↓ Development 1967
Imprinting 1967

Critical Scores
Use Cutting Scores

Critical Thinking 2006
PN 719 **SC** 12537
SN A higher-level cognitive process that involves purposeful and reflective evaluation of information to form a judgment or create a solution.
HN This term was introduced in May 2006. Relevant records were re-indexed with this term. The posting note reflects the number of records that were re-indexed.
B Thinking 1967
R ↓ Decision Making 1967
Divergent Thinking 1973
Logical Thinking 1967
Metacognition 1991
↓ Problem Solving 1967
↓ Reasoning 1967

Criticism 1973
PN 765 **SC** 12540
B Social Behavior 1967
Social Influences 1967
N Self Criticism 2003
R Skepticism 2004
Social Approval 1967

CRM
Use Customer Relationship Management

Crocodilians 1973
PN 25 **SC** 12570
UF Alligators
B Reptiles 1967

Cross Cultural Communication 1997
PN 832 **SC** 12580
UF Intercultural Communication
Interethnic Communication
B Interpersonal Communication 1973
R Acculturation 2003
Bilingualism 1973
Cross Cultural Counseling 2003
Cross Cultural Differences 1967
Cross Cultural Psychology 1997
↓ Cross Cultural Treatment 1994
Cultural Sensitivity 1994
Multicultural Education 1988
Multiculturalism 1997
Racial and Ethnic Differences 1982
↓ Racial and Ethnic Groups 2001

Cross Cultural Communication — (cont'd)
Racial and Ethnic Relations 1982

Cross Cultural Counseling 2003
PN 358 **SC** 12585
SN Counseling relationship where the cultural background of the client differs from the counselor or therapist.
HN This term was introduced in June 2003. Relevant records were re-indexed with this term. The posting note reflects the number of records that were re-indexed.
B Counseling 1967
Cross Cultural Treatment 1994
R Cross Cultural Communication 1997
Cultural Sensitivity 1994
↓ Psychotherapeutic Processes 1967

Cross Cultural Differences 1967
PN 24480 **SC** 12590
SN Used for comparisons between populations with different psychological, sociological, or cultural mores. Used for comparisons both within and across countries. Compare REGIONAL DIFFERENCES and RACIAL AND ETHNIC DIFFERENCES.
UF Cultural Differences
B Sociocultural Factors 1967
R Cross Cultural Communication 1997
Cross Cultural Psychology 1997
↓ Cross Cultural Treatment 1994
Cultural Sensitivity 1994
Diversity 2007
Diversity in the Workplace 2003
Ethnology 1967
Multiculturalism 1997
Racial and Ethnic Differences 1982
↓ Racial and Ethnic Groups 2001
Regional Differences 2001

Cross Cultural Psychology 1997
PN 1248 **SC** 12591
SN Branch of psychology that studies members of various cultural groups and their specific cultural experiences resulting in similarities and differences in human behavior.
B Psychology 1967
R Acculturation 2003
Cross Cultural Communication 1997
Cross Cultural Differences 1967
↓ Culture (Anthropological) 1967
↓ Culture Bound Syndromes 2004
Ethnocentrism 1973
Ethnology 1967
Racial and Ethnic Differences 1982
↓ Racial and Ethnic Groups 2001
↓ Sociocultural Factors 1967
Transcultural Psychiatry 1973

Cross Cultural Treatment 1994
PN 1311 **SC** 12593
SN Treatment, in any context, where the racial, ethnic, or cultural background of the patient or client is different from that of the health care provider, e.g., therapist, counselor, or physician. Used primarily when the cultural or racial aspects of the treatment paradigm are the major focus.
B Treatment 1967
N Cross Cultural Counseling 2003
R ↓ Client Characteristics 1973
Cross Cultural Communication 1997
Cross Cultural Differences 1967
Cultural Sensitivity 1994
Racial and Ethnic Differences 1982
↓ Racial and Ethnic Groups 2001

Cross Cultural Treatment — (cont'd)
↓ Therapist Characteristics 1973
Transcultural Psychiatry 1973

Cross Disciplinary Research
Use Interdisciplinary Research

Cross Examination 2005
PN 41 **SC** 12597
SN In a court of law, questioning of a witness called by the opposing side.
HN This term was introduced in August 2005. Relevant records were re-indexed with this term. The posting note reflects the number of records that were re-indexed.
R Expert Testimony 1973
Interrogation 2005
↓ Legal Evidence 1991
↓ Legal Testimony 1982
Witnesses 1985

Crossed Eyes
Use Strabismus

Crowding 1978
PN 628 **SC** 12610
SN Conditions of high population density for a given area. Used for animal or human populations.
R Environmental Stress 1973
Overpopulation 1973
Personal Space 1973
Social Density 1978

CRT
Use Video Display Units

Cruelty 1973
PN 144 **SC** 12620
B Antisocial Behavior 1971
Personality Traits 1967
R ↓ Aggressive Behavior 1967

Crustacea 1973
PN 406 **SC** 12630
B Arthropoda 1973
N Crabs 1973
Crayfish 1973

Crying 1973
PN 730 **SC** 12640
B Vocalization 1967
Voice 1973
R Infant Vocalization 1973

Crying Cat Syndrome 1973
PN 38 **SC** 12650
SN A rare infantile syndrome resulting from a missing piece of chromosome 5. The name of the disorder is based on the infant's high-pitched cat-like cry. The cause of the syndrome is unknown and the main symptoms include failure to thrive, microcephaly, mental retardation, and tiny external genitalia.
UF Cri du Chat Syndrome
B Autosome Disorders 1973
Mental Retardation 1967
Neonatal Disorders 1973
Syndromes 1973

Cuban Americans
Use Hispanics

Cued Recall 1994
PN 579 **SC** 12678
B Recall (Learning) 1967
R Cues 1967
Forgetting 1973
Free Recall 1973
↓ Memory 1967
↓ Prompting 1997

Cues 1967
PN 11900 **SC** 12680
SN Internal or external verbal or nonverbal signals which influence learning, performance, or behavior. Cues are often only obscure secondary stimuli which, though not fully detected, serve to facilitate learning, performance, or behavior. Compare CONDITIONED STIMULUS.
R ↓ Associative Processes 1967
Cued Recall 1994
Isolation Effect 1973
↓ Memory 1967
Mnemonic Learning 1973
↓ Priming 1988
↓ Prompting 1997
Semantic Priming 1994

Cultism 1973
PN 710 **SC** 12690
R Ethnology 1967
Myths 1967
Occultism 1978
↓ Religious Beliefs 1973
Religious Experiences 1997
Shamanism 1973
↓ Sociocultural Factors 1967

Cultural Assimilation
HN In June 2003, the term was discontinued and removed from all records containing it, and was replaced with ACCULTURATION, its postable counterpart.
Use Acculturation

Cultural Deprivation 1973
PN 236 **SC** 12710
SN Inability of individuals to participate in their society's cultural achievements because of poverty, social discrimination, or other disadvantage. Consider also SOCIAL DEPRIVATION.
UF Culturally Disadvantaged
B Deprivation 1967
Sociocultural Factors 1967
R Disadvantaged 1967
Multiculturalism 1997
Poverty Areas 1973
↓ Social Deprivation 1973
↓ Social Environments 1973

Cultural Differences
Use Cross Cultural Differences

Cultural Factors
Use Sociocultural Factors

Cultural Familial Mental Retardation
Use Psychosocial Mental Retardation

Cultural Pluralism
Use Multiculturalism

Cultural Psychiatry
Use Transcultural Psychiatry

Cultural Sensitivity 1994
PN 2834 **SC** 12728
SN Awareness and appreciation of the values, norms, and beliefs unique to a particular cultural, minority, ethnic, or racial group.
UF Ethnic Sensitivity
R Acculturation 2003
Cross Cultural Communication 1997
Cross Cultural Counseling 2003
Cross Cultural Differences 1967
↓ Cross Cultural Treatment 1994
↓ Culture (Anthropological) 1967
Ethnic Identity 1973
Ethnic Values 1973
Minority Groups 1967
Multicultural Education 1988
Multiculturalism 1997
↓ Racial and Ethnic Attitudes 1982
Racial and Ethnic Differences 1982
↓ Racial and Ethnic Groups 2001
Racial and Ethnic Relations 1982
Sensitivity Training 1973
↓ Sociocultural Factors 1967

Cultural Test Bias 1973
PN 869 **SC** 12730
SN Any significant differential performance on tests by different populations (e.g., Hispanics vs Blacks) as a result of test characteristics that are sensitive to cultural, subcultural, racial, or ethnic factors but that are irrelevant to the variable or construct being measured.
UF Test Bias (Cultural)
B Test Bias 1985
R Response Bias 1967
Test Interpretation 1985

Culturally Disadvantaged
Use Cultural Deprivation

Culture (Anthropological) 1967
PN 10609 **SC** 12750
N ↓ Society 1967
Subculture (Anthropological) 1973
R Cross Cultural Psychology 1997
Cultural Sensitivity 1994
Ethnology 1967
↓ Family Structure 1973
Multiculturalism 1997
Popular Culture 2003
↓ Racial and Ethnic Groups 2001
↓ Sociocultural Factors 1967
Traditions 2007

Culture Bound Syndromes 2004
PN 126 **SC** 12755
SN A pathological behavior pattern that is specific to a particular geographic, ethnic, or cultural group.
HN In June 2004, this term was created to replace the deleted term ETHNOSPECIFIC DISORDERS. ETHNOSPECIFIC DISORDERS was removed from all records containing it and replaced with CULTURE BOUND SYNDROMES.
UF Culture Specific Syndromes
B Syndromes 1973
N Koro 1994
R Cross Cultural Psychology 1997
↓ Racial and Ethnic Groups 2001
↓ Sociocultural Factors 1967
Transcultural Psychiatry 1973

Culture Change 1967
PN 796 **SC** 12760
SN Modification in behavior, values, customs, or artifacts over time or as the result of migration to a different cultural environment.
B Sociocultural Factors 1967
N Acculturation 2003
R Culture Shock 1973
Ethnology 1967
Modernization 2003
Multiculturalism 1997

Culture Fair Intelligence Test 1973
PN 36 **SC** 12770
UF Cattell Culture Fair Intelligence Test
B Intelligence Measures 1967

Culture Shock 1973
PN 230 **SC** 12780
SN Social, psychological, or emotional difficulties in adapting to a new culture or similar difficulties in adapting to one's own culture as the result of rapid social or cultural changes.
R ↓ Culture Change 1967
Ethnology 1967

Culture Specific Syndromes
Use Culture Bound Syndromes

Curare 1973
PN 30 **SC** 12790
B Muscle Relaxing Drugs 1973
R ↓ Alkaloids 1973
Tubocurarine 1973

Curiosity 1967
PN 448 **SC** 12800
UF Inquisitiveness
B Personality Traits 1967
R ↓ Exploratory Behavior 1967
Openness to Experience 1997
Questioning 1982

Curricular Field Experience 1982
PN 543 **SC** 12805
SN Organizationally or institutionally supervised educational activities, restricted primarily to high school and college, usually undertaken outside the classroom or campus in order to promote practical experience in a specific discipline.
UF Field Instruction
Field Work (Educational)
B Experiential Learning 1997
R Cooperative Education 1982
↓ Curriculum 1967
Educational Field Trips 1973
↓ Educational Programs 1973
↓ Practice 1967

Curriculum 1967
PN 9588 **SC** 12810
SN Set of courses constituting a framework for education in a given subject area.
B Education 1967
N Affective Education 1982
Art Education 1973
Braille Instruction 1973
Business Education 1973
Career Education 1978
Compensatory Education 1973
Driver Education 1973
Foreign Language Education 1973
↓ Health Education 1973

Curriculum — (cont'd)
Home Economics 1985
↓ Language Arts Education 1973
Mathematics Education 1973
Music Education 1973
Physical Education 1967
↓ Psychology Education 1978
Science Education 1973
Social Studies Education 1978
↓ Vocational Education 1973
R Computer Training 1994
Course Evaluation 1978
Curricular Field Experience 1982
Curriculum Based Assessment 1994
Curriculum Development 1973
Educational Objectives 1978
Educational Program Accreditation 1994
Educational Standards 2007
Home Schooling 1994
↓ Nontraditional Education 1982

Curriculum Based Assessment 1994
PN 353 **SC** 12815
B Educational Measurement 1967
R ↓ Curriculum 1967
Individual Education Programs 2006

Curriculum Development 1973
PN 3585 **SC** 12820
SN Initiating, designing, implementing, and testing of activities designed to create new curricula or to change existing ones.
B Development 1967
R ↓ Curriculum 1967
Educational Program Planning 1973
↓ Program Development 1991

Cursive Writing 1973
PN 68 **SC** 12830
UF Writing (Cursive)
B Handwriting 1967
R Orthography 1973

Cushings Syndrome 1973
PN 106 **SC** 12840
SN A metabolic disorder caused by increased production of cortisol and characterized by central obesity, muscle weakness, florid complexion, hirutism in women, and diminished libido or impotence in men.
UF Hypercortisolism
B Adrenal Gland Disorders 1973
Metabolism Disorders 1973
Syndromes 1973

Customer Relationship Management 2007
PN 66 **SC** 12841
SN The practice by companies of anticipating the future needs of their customers based on knowledge of past purchasing behaviors.
HN This term was introduced in April 2007. Relevant records were re-indexed with this term. The posting note reflects the number of records that were re-indexed.
UF CRM
B Management 1967
R ↓ Consumer Attitudes 1973
↓ Consumer Behavior 1967
↓ Consumer Research 1973
Consumer Satisfaction 1994

Customer Satisfaction
Use Consumer Satisfaction

Customs
Use Traditions

Cutaneous Receptive Fields 1985
PN 83 **SC** 12845
SN The area of skin being supplied by specific peripheral nerves and localized synaptic distribution in the CNS.
UF Dermatomes
B Receptive Fields 1985

Cutaneous Sense 1967
PN 1616 **SC** 12850
SN Any of the senses, such as pressure, pain, warmth, cold, and touch, whose receptors lie within or beneath the skin or in the mucous membrane.
UF Haptic Perception
B Somesthetic Perception 1967
N ↓ Tactual Perception 1967

Cutting Scores 1985
PN 183 **SC** 12855
SN Points at which a continuum of scores may be divided into groups for such purposes as pass/fail decisions or test interpretations.
UF Critical Scores
B Scoring (Testing) 1973
Test Scores 1967
R Score Equating 1985
Test Interpretation 1985

Cybercounseling
Use Online Therapy

Cybernetics 1967
PN 631 **SC** 12860
SN Study of control and communication between humans, machines, animals, and organizations and the parallels between information processing machines and human or animal intellectual or brain function.
R ↓ Artificial Intelligence 1982
Communication Theory 1973
↓ Computers 1967
↓ Expert Systems 1991
Human Machine Systems 1997
Robotics 1985

Cyclic Adenosine Monophosphate 1978
PN 355 **SC** 12875
B Nucleotides 1978
R Guanosine 1985

Cycloheximide 1973
PN 167 **SC** 12880
B Antibiotics 1973

Cyclothymic Disorder
Use Cyclothymic Personality

Cyclothymic Personality 1973
PN 148 **SC** 12890
SN Affective disorder characterized by alternating and recurring periods of depression and elation, similar to manic depressive disorder but of a less severe nature.
UF Cyclothymic Disorder
B Bipolar Disorder 2001
R Hypomania 1973

Cynicism 1973
PN 222 **SC** 12900
B Personality Traits 1967
R Agreeableness 1997
Fatalism 1973

Cynicism — (cont'd)
Hopelessness 1988
Negativism 1973
Pessimism 1973
Skepticism 2004

Cysteine 1973
PN 125 **SC** 12910
B Amino Acids 1973

Cystic Fibrosis 1985
PN 378 **SC** 12915
SN A genetic metabolic disorder characterized by abnormally thick, sticky mucus that clogs the lungs and leads to life-threatening lung infections.
B Digestive System Disorders 1973
Lung Disorders 1973
Metabolism Disorders 1973
R ↓ Congenital Disorders 1973

Cytochrome Oxidase 1973
PN 175 **SC** 12920
B Oxidases 1973

Cytokines 2003
PN 421 **SC** 12925
SN Non-antibody proteins secreted by various cell types that act as intercellular mediators.
HN This term was introduced in June 2003. Relevant records were re-indexed with this term. The posting note reflects the number of records that were re-indexed.
B Immunologic Factors 2003
N Interferons 1994
Interleukins 1994
Tumor Necrosis Factor 2006

Cytology 1973
PN 175 **SC** 12930
R ↓ Cells (Biology) 1973

Cytoplasm 1973
PN 36 **SC** 12940
R ↓ Cells (Biology) 1973

Daily Activities 1994
PN 1269 **SC** 12955
SN Daily patterns of behavior that are not reflective of functional ability. Compare ACTIVITIES OF DAILY LIVING.
R Active Living 2007
Activities of Daily Living 1991
Activity Level 1982
Hobbies 1988
↓ Interests 1967
Leisure Time 1973
↓ Lifestyle 1978
↓ Recreation 1967
Self Care Skills 1978

Daily Biological Rhythms (Animal)
Use Animal Circadian Rhythms

Damage Awards
Use Awards (Jury)

Dance 1973
PN 626 **SC** 12970
UF Ballet
B Arts 1973
Recreation 1967
R Dance Therapy 1973
Improvisation 2004
Self Expression 2006

Dance Therapy 1973
PN 401 **SC** 12980
B Creative Arts Therapy 1994
R Dance 1973
Movement Therapy 1997
Recreation Therapy 1973
Self Expression 2006

Dangerousness 1988
PN 846 **SC** 12985
R Patient Violence 1994
↓ Violence 1973

Dark Adaptation 1973
PN 471 **SC** 12990
UF Adaptation (Dark)
B Sensory Adaptation 1967
Visual Perception 1967
R Light Adaptation 1982
↓ Perceptual Measures 1973
↓ Visual Thresholds 1973

Darwinism 1973
PN 612 **SC** 13000
SN Biological theory of evolution formulated by C. Darwin, including the fundamental tenet of natural selection as the operating principle of organic change.
B Theories 1967
N Natural Selection 1997
R Evolutionary Economics 2007
Evolutionary Psychology 2003
Theory of Evolution 1967

Data Collection 1982
PN 2744 **SC** 13005
SN Systematic accumulation, generation, or assembly of information. Compare EXPERIMENTAL METHODS.
B Methodology 1967
R Bioinformatics 2007
↓ Computer Peripheral Devices 1985
↓ Data Processing 1967
Information 1967
↓ Medical Records 1978
Qualitative Research 2003
Quantitative Methods 2003
↓ Sampling (Experimental) 1973
Statistical Data 1982
↓ Statistical Measurement 1973
↓ Surveys 1967

Data Pooling
Use Meta Analysis

Data Processing 1967
PN 563 **SC** 13020
N Word Processing 1991
R ↓ Automated Information Processing 1973
Computer Programming 2001
Computer Programming Languages 1973
↓ Computer Software 1967
↓ Computers 1967
Data Collection 1982
↓ Expert Systems 1991
Information 1967
↓ Information Systems 1991
↓ Medical Records 1978

Databases 1991
PN 965 **SC** 13024
SN Collection of computerized data stored in a computer or on magnetic tape or disks from which information can be accessed and retrieved.

Databases — (cont'd)
UF Computerized Databases
Online Databases
R ↓ Automated Information Retrieval 1973
Automated Information Storage 1973
Bioinformatics 2007
↓ Computer Applications 1973
Computer Searching 1991
↓ Computer Software 1967
↓ Computers 1967
Decision Support Systems 1997
↓ Electronic Communication 2001
↓ Expert Systems 1991
Human Machine Systems 1997
Information 1967
Information Services 1988
↓ Information Systems 1991

Date Rape
Use Acquaintance Rape

Dating (Social)
Use Social Dating

Daughters 1973
PN 2123 **SC** 13040
B Family Members 1973
Human Females 1973
Offspring 1988

Day Camps (Recreation)
Use Summer Camps (Recreation)

Day Care (Child)
Use Child Day Care

Day Care (Treatment)
Use Partial Hospitalization

Day Care Centers 1973
PN 747 **SC** 13070
SN Facilities for day care of individuals of any age.
R Adult Day Care 1997
Child Care Workers 1978
Child Day Care 1973
↓ Community Facilities 1973
Community Mental Health Centers 1973
↓ Facilities 2006

Day Hospital
Use Partial Hospitalization

Daydreaming 1973
PN 336 **SC** 13080
R ↓ Fantasy 1997
Fantasy (Defense Mechanism) 1967

DDT (Insecticide) 1973
PN 8 **SC** 13090
B Insecticides 1973

Deaf 1967
PN 6319 **SC** 13100
SN Profoundly or severely hearing impaired. Consider also PARTIALLY HEARING IMPAIRED for severely hearing impaired.
B Hearing Disorders 1982
N Deaf Blind 1991
R Cochlear Implants 1994
Lipreading 1973
Partially Hearing Impaired 1973

Deaf Blind 1991
PN 144 **SC** 13103
B Blind 1967
Deaf 1967
Multiple Disabilities 2001
R ↓ Congenital Disorders 1973
Developmental Disabilities 1982

Deanol
HN Term was discontinued in 1997. In 2000, the term was removed from all records containing it, and replaced with ANTIDEPRESSANT DRUGS, its postable counterpart.
Use Antidepressant Drugs

Death and Dying 1967
PN 11532 **SC** 13110
UF Dying
Mortality
N Euthanasia 1973
Parental Death 2003
R Advance Directives 1994
Assisted Suicide 1997
Death Anxiety 1978
Death Attitudes 1973
Death Education 1982
Death Rites 1973
Grief 1973
Mortality Rate 1973
Near Death Experiences 1985
Palliative Care 1991
Psychological Autopsy 1988
Sudden Infant Death 1982
↓ Suicide 1967
Terminal Cancer 1973
Terminally Ill Patients 1973
Terror Management Theory 2006
Treatment Withholding 1988

Death Anxiety 1978
PN 1135 **SC** 13115
B Anxiety Disorders 1997
R ↓ Death and Dying 1967
Death Attitudes 1973

Death Attitudes 1973
PN 2501 **SC** 13120
B Attitudes 1967
R ↓ Death and Dying 1967
Death Anxiety 1978
Euthanasia 1973
↓ Religious Beliefs 1973

Death Education 1982
PN 392 **SC** 13124
SN Education in the process of death and dying. Applies to patients or students of any age including helping professionals.
UF Thanatology
B Education 1967
R ↓ Death and Dying 1967
↓ Treatment 1967

Death Instinct 1988
PN 323 **SC** 13127
UF Thanatos
B Psychoanalytic Personality Factors 1973
R Self Preservation 1997
Unconscious (Personality Factor) 1967

Death Penalty
Use Capital Punishment

Death Rate
Use Mortality Rate

Death Rites 1973
PN 276 **SC** 13150
UF Funerals
B Rites of Passage 1973
R Cannibalism 2003
↓ Death and Dying 1967

Debates 1997
PN 398 **SC** 13153
UF Political Debates
Presidential Debates
R Arguments 1973
Group Discussion 1967
↓ Persuasive Communication 1967
Political Campaigns 1973
Political Candidates 1973
Political Elections 1973
↓ Political Processes 1973
Public Speaking 1973
Rhetoric 1991

Debriefing (Experimental) 1991
PN 40 **SC** 13154
SN At the conclusion of an experiment, the process that removes any deception and discloses the facts to subjects participating in the research by giving full details of the research purpose and procedures.
UF Disclosure (Experimental)
R ↓ Experimental Design 1967
Experimental Ethics 1978
Experimental Subjects 1985
↓ Experimentation 1967
Informed Consent 1985

Debriefing (Psychological) 2004
PN 152 **SC** 13155
SN Psychological intervention used to reduce distress from psychological trauma.
HN This term was introduced in June 2004. Relevant records were re-indexed with this term. The posting note reflects the number of records that were re-indexed.
UF Critical Incident Debriefing
Psychological Debriefing
B Crisis Intervention 1973
R Acute Stress Disorder 2003
Emotional Trauma 1967
Posttraumatic Stress Disorder 1985

Debt
Use Financial Strain

Decarboxylase Inhibitors 1982
PN 63 **SC** 13157
B Enzyme Inhibitors 1985
N Carbidopa 1988
R ↓ Antitremor Drugs 1973
↓ Catecholamines 1973
↓ Dopamine Antagonists 1982
↓ Enzymes 1973
↓ Serotonin Antagonists 1973

Decarboxylases 1973
PN 120 **SC** 13160
B Enzymes 1973

Decentralization 1978
PN 108 **SC** 13166
SN Process of distributing or allocating administrative control over organizational functions to authorities that are more local.

Decentralization — (cont'd)
R Educational Administration 1967
Hospital Administration 1978
↓ Organizational Change 1973
Organizational Development 1973
Organizational Objectives 1973
Organizational Structure 1967

Deception 1967
PN 2876 **SC** 13170
UF Lying
N Cheating 1973
Faking 1973
Fraud 1994
Malingering 1973
R Dishonesty 1973
Secrecy 1994
Sincerity 1973

Decerebration 1973
PN 125 **SC** 13180
SN Elimination of cerebral functioning by transecting the brain stem or by cutting off the cerebral blood supply.
B Neurosurgery 1973
R ↓ Brain Lesions 1967

Decision Making 1967
PN 21549 **SC** 13190
SN Cognitive process involving evaluation of the incentives, goals, and outcomes of alternative actions.
B Cognitive Processes 1967
N Choice Behavior 1967
↓ Group Decision Making 1978
Management Decision Making 1973
R Awards (Jury) 2005
Critical Thinking 2006
Decision Support Systems 1997
Decision Theory 2003
↓ Expert Systems 1991
Framing Effects 2005
Heuristics 2003
↓ Judgment 1967
↓ Problem Solving 1967
Risk Assessment 2004
Uncertainty 1991
Utility Theory 2004
Volition 1988

Decision Support Systems 1997
PN 921 **SC** 13193
SN Computer-based planning and decision making systems that provide data on the outcomes or results of alternative decision choices.
B Computer Software 1967
Expert Systems 1991
R ↓ Artificial Intelligence 1982
↓ Computer Applications 1973
↓ Computer Simulation 1973
Databases 1991
↓ Decision Making 1967
Decision Theory 2003
↓ Information Systems 1991
Knowledge Engineering 2003

Decision Theory 2003
PN 263 **SC** 58062
SN Analytic techniques for modeling decision making in light of possible consequences or outcomes.
HN This term was introduced in June 2003. Relevant records were re-indexed with this term. The posting note reflects the number of records that were re-indexed.

Decision Theory — (cont'd)
B Theories 1967
R ↓ Decision Making 1967
Decision Support Systems 1997
↓ Mathematical Modeling 1973

Declarative Knowledge 1997
PN 524 SC 13194
SN Knowledge about "how" and "what" things are, which can be modified due to new experiences or internal thought processes. Compare PROCEDURAL KNOWLEDGE.
UF Factual Knowledge
R ↓ Cognitive Processes 1967
Divergent Thinking 1973
Heuristics 2003
Information 1967
↓ Knowledge Level 1978
↓ Memory 1967
Metacognition 1991
↓ Problem Solving 1967
Procedural Knowledge 1997
↓ Reasoning 1967

Decoding
Use Human Information Storage

Decompression Effects 1973
PN 49 SC 13200
R Acceleration Effects 1973
↓ Gravitational Effects 1967
Physiological Stress 1967
Spaceflight 1967
Underwater Effects 1973

Decortication (Brain) 1973
PN 126 SC 13210
SN Functional deactivation or physical removal of all or portions of the cortical substance of the brain. Primarily used for experimental contexts.
B Neurosurgery 1973
R ↓ Brain Lesions 1967

Deductive Reasoning
Use Inductive Deductive Reasoning

Deer 1973
PN 272 SC 13230
B Mammals 1973

Defecation 1967
PN 258 SC 13240
B Excretion 1967
R Coprophagia 2001

Defendants 1985
PN 704 SC 13245
SN Persons who are being sued or prosecuted in a court of law.
R Court Referrals 1994
Criminal Responsibility 1991
↓ Criminals 1967
↓ Law (Government) 1973

Defense Mechanisms 1967
PN 3840 SC 13250
SN Any intrapsychic strategies that serve to provide relief from emotional conflict or frustration or from unreasonable or undesirable thoughts which lead to anxiety, distress, or depression.
B Personality Processes 1967
N Compensation (Defense Mechanism) 1973
Denial 1973

Defense Mechanisms — (cont'd)
Displacement (Defense Mechanism) 1973
Fantasy (Defense Mechanism) 1967
Grandiosity 1994
Identification (Defense Mechanism) 1973
Intellectualization 1973
Introjection 1973
Isolation (Defense Mechanism) 1973
Projection (Defense Mechanism) 1967
Projective Identification 1994
Rationalization (Defense Mechanism) 1973
Reaction Formation 1973
Regression (Defense Mechanism) 1967
Repression (Defense Mechanism) 1967
Sublimation 1973
Suppression (Defense Mechanism) 1973
Withdrawal (Defense Mechanism) 1973
R ↓ Conversion Disorder 2001
Externalization 1973
↓ Internalization 1997
↓ Mental Disorders 1967
↓ Personality Disorders 1967
↓ Psychopathology 1967

Defensive Behavior (Animal)
Use Animal Defensive Behavior

Defensiveness 1967
PN 699 SC 13260
B Personality Traits 1967

Deformity
Use Physical Disfigurement

Degrees (Educational)
Use Educational Degrees

Dehydration 1988
PN 115 SC 13285
SN State of excessively reduced body water or water deficit.
R Homeostasis 1973
Water Deprivation 1967
Water Intake 1967

Dehydrogenases 1973
PN 137 SC 13290
B Enzymes 1973
N Alcohol Dehydrogenases 1973
Lactate Dehydrogenase 1973

Deinstitutionalization 1982
PN 1496 SC 13293
SN Programs emphasizing out-of-hospital treatment and community residence of clients, usually chronic psychiatric or handicapped patients, including those who may never have been hospitalized or who may or may not have experienced normal community life.
B Mental Health Programs 1973
R Community Mental Health 1973
Community Mental Health Services 1978
Discharge Planning 1994
Habilitation 1991
↓ Homeless 1988
Homeless Mentally Ill 1997
↓ Institutional Release 1978
↓ Mainstreaming 1991
Partial Hospitalization 1985
↓ Rehabilitation 1967
Right to Treatment 1997

Deja Vu
Use Consciousness States

Delay of Gratification 1978
PN 370 SC 13297
SN Voluntary postponement of need satisfaction or fulfillment of desires.
R ↓ Impulse Control Disorders 1997
↓ Motivation 1967
↓ Reinforcement 1967
Reinforcement Delay 1985
↓ Rewards 1967

Delayed Alternation 1994
PN 62 SC 13298
SN Alternation of rewards, usually in maze learning, with a delay between successive trials, forcing experimental subject to also alternate responses in order to receive the reward.
B Operant Conditioning 1967
R ↓ Learning 1967
Reinforcement Delay 1985
Response Variability 1973
↓ Rewards 1967
Spontaneous Alternation 1982

Delayed Auditory Feedback 1973
PN 152 SC 13300
B Auditory Feedback 1973
Delayed Feedback 1973

Delayed Development 1973
PN 2014 SC 13310
SN Delays in any or all areas including cognitive, social, language, sensory, and emotional development.
B Development 1967
N Failure to Thrive 1988
Language Delay 1988
Retarded Speech Development 1973
R Developmental Age Groups 1973
Developmental Disabilities 1982
↓ Human Development 1967
↓ Physical Development 1973
↓ Psychogenesis 1973

Delayed Feedback 1973
PN 191 SC 13320
B Feedback 1967
Perceptual Stimulation 1973
N Delayed Auditory Feedback 1973

Delayed Parenthood 1985
PN 58 SC 13325
SN Voluntary decision to postpone parenthood, usually for reasons involving personal development or career interests.
R Childlessness 1982
↓ Family Planning 1973
Family Planning Attitudes 1973
Parental Role 1973

Delayed Reinforcement
Use Reinforcement Delay

Delayed Speech
Use Retarded Speech Development

Deletion (Chromosome) 1973
PN 100 SC 13340
B Chromosome Disorders 1973

Delinquency (Juvenile)
Use Juvenile Delinquency

Delirium 1973
PN 1275 **SC** 13360
B Consciousness Disturbances 1973
Symptoms 1967
R Hyperthermia 1973

Delirium Tremens 1973
PN 160 **SC** 13370
SN Acute alcoholic, psychotic condition characterized by intense tremors, anxiety, hallucinations, and delusions.
B Alcoholic Hallucinosis 1973
Syndromes 1973

Delta Rhythm 1973
PN 141 **SC** 13380
SN Electrically measured impulses or waves of high amplitude and low frequency (1-3 cycles per second) observable in the electroencephalogram during sleep stages 3 and 4 (moderate to deep sleep).
B Electrical Activity 1967
Electroencephalography 1967

Delusions 1967
PN 2856 **SC** 13390
SN False personal beliefs held despite contradictory evidence and common sense.
B Thought Disturbances 1973
R Capgras Syndrome 1985
Erotomania 1997
Grandiosity 1994
↓ Schizophrenia 1967

Dementia 1985
PN 12818 **SC** 13395
SN An acquired mental disorder characterized by progressive decline in cognitive function due to brain damage or disease.
B Mental Disorders 1967
Organic Brain Syndromes 1973
N AIDS Dementia Complex 1997
Dementia with Lewy Bodies 2001
↓ Presenile Dementia 1973
↓ Senile Dementia 1973
Vascular Dementia 1997
R Alzheimers Disease 1973
Cognitive Impairment 2003
Creutzfeldt Jakob Syndrome 1994
↓ Neurodegenerative Diseases 2004
Parkinsons Disease 1973
Picks Disease 1973
Pseudodementia 1985

Dementia (Multi Infarct)
Use Vascular Dementia

Dementia (Presenile)
Use Presenile Dementia

Dementia (Senile)
Use Senile Dementia

Dementia of Alzheimers Type
Use Alzheimers Disease

Dementia Paralytica
Use General Paresis

Dementia Praecox
Use Schizophrenia

Dementia with Lewy Bodies 2001
PN 399 **SC** 13435
SN Neurodegenerative disease marked by the presence of Lewy body cells in the cerebral cortex and brain stem. Symptoms often include dementia, parkinsonism, and striking fluctuations in cognitive performance.
UF Lewy Body Disease
B Dementia 1985
Neurodegenerative Diseases 2004
R Alzheimers Disease 1973
Parkinsonism 1994
Parkinsons Disease 1973

Democracy 1973
PN 1019 **SC** 13440
B Political Economic Systems 1973
R ↓ Civil Rights 1978

Democratic Party
Use Political Parties

Demographic Characteristics 1967
PN 21319 **SC** 13460
UF Population Characteristics
R Biographical Data 1978
↓ Population 1973
Psychosocial Factors 1988

Demonic Possession
Use Spirit Possession

Demonstrations (Social)
Use Social Demonstrations

Dendrites 1973
PN 470 **SC** 13490
SN Branched or branching extensions of a nerve cell or neuron that receive stimuli from other neurons.
B Neurons 1973

Denial 1973
PN 1086 **SC** 13500
SN Exclusion from conscious awareness of unpleasant realities, which would produce anxiety if acknowledged.
B Defense Mechanisms 1967
R Anosognosia 1994

Density (Social)
Use Social Density

Dental Education 1973
PN 83 **SC** 13520
B Graduate Education 1973

Dental Students 1973
PN 149 **SC** 13530
B Students 1967
R Graduate Students 1967

Dental Surgery 1973
PN 106 **SC** 13540
B Dental Treatment 1973
Surgery 1971

Dental Treatment 1973
PN 819 **SC** 13550
B Physical Treatment Methods 1973
N Dental Surgery 1973

Dentist Patient Interaction
Use Therapeutic Processes

Dentistry 1973
PN 220 **SC** 13560
B Medical Sciences 1967

Dentists 1973
PN 246 **SC** 13570
B Medical Personnel 1967

Deoxycorticosterone 1973
PN 38 **SC** 13580
B Adrenal Cortex Hormones 1973
Corticosteroids 1973

Deoxyglucose 1991
PN 110 **SC** 13585
B Carbohydrates 1973

Deoxyribonucleic Acid
HN In May 2006, this term was discontinued and removed from all records containing it, and was replaced with DNA, its postable counterpart.
Use DNA

Dependency (Drug)
Use Drug Dependency

Dependency (Personality) 1967
PN 2249 **SC** 13620
SN Lack of self-reliance, reflecting need for security, love, and protection from others.
B Personality Traits 1967
R Abandonment 1997
Attachment Behavior 1985
Codependency 1991
Dependent Personality Disorder 1994
Enabling 1997

Dependent Personality Disorder 1994
PN 113 **SC** 13625
SN Personality disorder characterized by pervasive patterns of dependent, passive, and submissive behavior.
B Personality Disorders 1967
R Codependency 1991
Dependency (Personality) 1967

Dependent Variables 1973
PN 166 **SC** 13630
SN Statistical or experimental parameters whose values change as a consequence of changes in one or more other independent variables.
B Statistical Variables 1973

Depersonalization 1973
PN 492 **SC** 13640
SN State in which an individual perceives or experiences a sensation of unreality concerning himself or his environment; seen in disorders such as schizophrenia, affective disorders, organic mental disorders, and personality disorders.
B Dissociative Disorders 2001
Symptoms 1967
R Alienation 1971

Deployment (Military)
Use Military Deployment

Depression (Emotion) 1967
PN 18543 **SC** 13650
SN Mild depression that is not considered clinical depression. For clinical depression, use MAJOR DEPRESSION.
HN Prior to 1988, also used for major depression in clinical populations.

Depression (Emotion) — (cont'd)
B Emotional States 1973
R ↓ Major Depression 1988
Sadness 1973
↓ Separation Reactions 1997

Depressive Reaction (Neurotic)
Use Major Depression

Deprivation 1967
PN 1367 **SC** 13680
SN Removal, denial, or lack of something needed or desired.
N Cultural Deprivation 1973
Food Deprivation 1967
REM Dream Deprivation 1973
Sleep Deprivation 1967
↓ Stimulus Deprivation 1973
Water Deprivation 1967
R Environmental Stress 1973
↓ Motivation 1967
Physiological Stress 1967
Psychological Stress 1973
↓ Stress 1967

Depth Perception 1967
PN 2292 **SC** 13690
B Spatial Perception 1967
N Stereoscopic Vision 1973
R Eye Convergence 1982
Linear Perspective 1982
Motion Parallax 1997
Ocular Accommodation 1982

Depth Psychology 1973
PN 365 **SC** 13700
SN Any of the psychological theories which study the unconscious processes of the personality.
B Psychology 1967

Dermatitis 1973
PN 152 **SC** 13710
B Skin Disorders 1973
N Eczema 1973
Neurodermatitis 1973
R Allergic Skin Disorders 1973
↓ Infectious Disorders 1973
↓ Toxic Disorders 1973

Dermatomes
Use Cutaneous Receptive Fields

Desegregation
Use Social Integration

Desensitization (Systematic)
Use Systematic Desensitization Therapy

Desertion
Use Abandonment

Design (Experimental)
Use Experimental Design

Design (Man Machine Systems)
Use Human Machine Systems Design

Desipramine 1973
PN 1022 **SC** 13760
B Tricyclic Antidepressant Drugs 1997

Desirability (Social)
Use Social Desirability

Desires
Use Motivation

Detection (Signal)
Use Signal Detection (Perception)

Detention (Legal)
Use Legal Detention

Determinism 1997
PN 229 **SC** 13815
SN A doctrine that assumes events or objects have antecedent causes that determine their nature.
B Philosophies 1967
R Epistemology 1973
Idealism 1973
Positivism 1973
Volition 1988

Detoxification 1973
PN 1079 **SC** 13820
B Alcohol Rehabilitation 1982
Drug Rehabilitation 1973
R Alcohol Withdrawal 1994
↓ Drug Abstinence 1994
↓ Drug Therapy 1967
↓ Drug Withdrawal 1973
Sobriety 1988

Developed Countries 1985
PN 358 **SC** 13823
B Countries 1967

Developing Countries 1985
PN 1529 **SC** 13825
UF Third World Countries
Underdeveloped Countries
B Countries 1967
R Economic Development 2007
Modernization 2003

Development 1967
PN 3035 **SC** 13830
UF Growth
Ontogeny
N Animal Development 1978
Career Development 1985
Community Development 1997
Curriculum Development 1973
↓ Delayed Development 1973
↓ Human Development 1967
Organizational Development 1973
↓ Physical Development 1973
Precocious Development 1973
Professional Development 1982
↓ Program Development 1991
↓ Psychogenesis 1973
R Age Differences 1967
Critical Period 1988
Developmental Age Groups 1973
↓ Developmental Stages 1973
Life Span 2004
Sex Linked Developmental Differences 1973

Developmental Age Groups 1973
PN 761 **SC** 13840
SN Groups defined by a chronological age span, and characterized by certain physical, behavioral, psychological, and social attributes. Use AGE DIFFERENCES for age comparisons within or between groups.
R Adolescent Development 1973
Adult Development 1978
Age Differences 1967

Developmental Age Groups — (cont'd)
↓ Aging 1991
↓ Childhood Development 1967
↓ Delayed Development 1973
↓ Development 1967
↓ Developmental Stages 1973
Emotional Development 1973
↓ Human Development 1967
Mental Age 1973
↓ Motor Development 1973
↓ Physical Development 1973
Precocious Development 1973
↓ Psychogenesis 1973

Developmental Differences
HN Term was discontinued in 1982. In 2000, the term was removed from all records containing it, and replaced with AGE DIFFERENCES, its postable counterpart.
Use Age Differences

Developmental Disabilities 1982
PN 6586 **SC** 13853
SN As encompassed in federal legislation for educational assistance to handicapped children, includes disabilities originating before age 18 that constitute substantial barriers to normal functioning. Use a more specific term if possible.
B Disabilities 2003
R Aspergers Syndrome 1991
Autism 1967
↓ Communication Disorders 1982
↓ Congenital Disorders 1973
Deaf Blind 1991
↓ Delayed Development 1973
↓ Genetic Disorders 1973
↓ Human Development 1967
↓ Learning Disorders 1967
↓ Mental Retardation 1967
↓ Nervous System Disorders 1967
↓ Pervasive Developmental Disorders 2001

Developmental Measures 1994
PN 305 **SC** 13857
N Bayley Scales of Infant Development 1994

Developmental Psychology 1973
PN 3818 **SC** 13860
B Psychology 1967
N Adolescent Psychology 1973
Child Psychology 1967
Gerontology 1967
R ↓ Human Development 1967

Developmental Stages 1973
PN 3323 **SC** 13870
SN Phases in an individual's development characterized by certain physical, behavioral, mental, or social attributes, e.g., the latency stage of psychosexual development or the sensorimotor intelligence stage of cognitive development.
N Menopause 1973
↓ Prenatal Developmental Stages 1973
Puberty 1973
R Adolescent Development 1973
Adult Development 1978
↓ Aging 1991
↓ Childhood Development 1967
↓ Development 1967
Developmental Age Groups 1973
Erikson (Erik) 1991
Fixation (Psychoanalytic) 2007
Generativity 2001
↓ Human Development 1967

Developmental Stages — (cont'd)
Life Changes 2004
Object Permanence 1985
↓ Perceptual Development 1973
↓ Physical Development 1973
Piaget (Jean) 1967
↓ Psychogenesis 1973
↓ Rites of Passage 1973

Deviant Behavior
Use Antisocial Behavior

Deviation IQ
Use Standard Scores

Deviations (Sexual)
Use Paraphilias

Devices (Experimental)
Use Apparatus

Dexamethasone 1985
PN 832 **SC** 13905
SN A synthetic analogue of cortisol.
B Glucocorticoids 1982
R Dexamethasone Suppression Test 1988

Dexamethasone Suppression Test 1988
PN 699 **SC** 13907
SN Laboratory analysis of hypersecretion of cortisol and the body's failure to suppress cortisol after the administration of dexamethasone. Used primarily for diagnosis of major depressive disorders.
B Medical Diagnosis 1973
R Dexamethasone 1985

Dexamphetamine
Use Dextroamphetamine

Dexedrine
Use Dextroamphetamine

Dexterity (Physical)
Use Physical Dexterity

Dextroamphetamine 1973
PN 1817 **SC** 13940
UF Amphetamine (d-)
Dexamphetamine
Dexedrine
B Adrenergic Drugs 1973
Amphetamine 1967
Appetite Depressing Drugs 1973
CNS Stimulating Drugs 1973
Sympathomimetic Amines 1973

Diabetes 1973
PN 2698 **SC** 13950
B Endocrine Disorders 1973
Metabolism Disorders 1973
N Diabetes Insipidus 1973
Diabetes Mellitus 1973
R Metabolic Syndrome 2007

Diabetes Insipidus 1973
PN 109 **SC** 13960
SN A rare disease characterized by frequent urination, dilute urine, and increased thirst. The condition may be temporary or permanent.

Diabetes Insipidus — (cont'd)
B Diabetes 1973
R ↓ Genetic Disorders 1973

Diabetes Mellitus 1973
PN 1723 **SC** 13970
SN A medical disease characterized by decreased production of insulin (Type 1) or insulin resistance (Type 2).
B Diabetes 1973

Diacetylmorphine
Use Heroin

Diagnosis 1967
PN 13741 **SC** 13990
N Computer Assisted Diagnosis 1973
Differential Diagnosis 1967
Educational Diagnosis 1978
Galvanic Skin Response 1967
↓ Medical Diagnosis 1973
↓ Psychodiagnosis 1967
R Autopsy 1973
Clinical Judgment (Not Diagnosis) 1973
Comorbidity 1991
Diagnosis Related Groups 1988
↓ Disorders 1967
Dual Diagnosis 1991
General Health Questionnaire 1991
Geriatric Assessment 1997
Intake Interview 1994
International Classification of Diseases 2001
Labeling 1978
↓ Measurement 1967
↓ Mental Disorders 1967
Misdiagnosis 1997
↓ Neuropsychological Assessment 1982
Pain Measurement 1997
Patient History 1973
↓ Physical Disorders 1997
Prognosis 1973
Research Diagnostic Criteria 1994
↓ Screening 1982
Severity (Disorders) 1982
Symptom Checklists 1991

Diagnosis Related Groups 1988
PN 88 **SC** 13985
UF DRGs
R Cost Containment 1991
↓ Diagnosis 1967
Health Care Costs 1994
↓ Health Insurance 1973
Misdiagnosis 1997
↓ Professional Fees 1978

Diagnostic and Statistical Manual 1994
PN 2321 **SC** 13988
SN Used when the current Diagnostic and Statistical Manual or its revisions is the primary focus of the reference. Not used for specific psychodiagnostic categories.
HN Use PSYCHODIAGNOSTIC TYPOLOGIES to access references prior to 1994.
UF DSM
B Psychodiagnostic Typologies 1967
R International Classification of Diseases 2001
↓ Mental Disorders 1967
↓ Psychodiagnosis 1967
Research Diagnostic Criteria 1994
Subtypes (Disorders) 2004

Diagnostic Interview Schedule 1991
PN 152 **SC** 13900
B Interview Schedules 2001
Psychodiagnostic Interview 1973
R ↓ Psychodiagnostic Typologies 1967
↓ Screening 1982

Dialect 1973
PN 499 **SC** 14000
SN A variety of language characteristic of a geographical region or ethnic, occupational, socioeconomic, or other group.
B Language 1967
N Nonstandard English 1973
R Ethnolinguistics 1973

Dialectics 1973
PN 684 **SC** 14010
SN Intellectual investigation through deductive reasoning and juxtaposition of opposing or contradictory ideas.
R ↓ Reasoning 1967

Dialysis 1973
PN 308 **SC** 14020
B Physical Treatment Methods 1973
N Hemodialysis 1973

Diaphragm (Anatomy) 1973
PN 22 **SC** 14030
B Muscles 1967
Respiratory System 1973
R Thorax 1973

Diaphragms (Birth Control) 1973
PN 15 **SC** 14040
B Contraceptive Devices 1973

Diarrhea 1973
PN 121 **SC** 14050
B Colon Disorders 1973
R Fecal Incontinence 1973

Diastolic Pressure 1973
PN 274 **SC** 14060
B Blood Pressure 1967

Diathesis Stress Model 2005
PN 81 **SC** 14065
SN A theory that suggests that stress can precipitate and facilitate some physical and mental disorders to which a person is already predisposed.
HN This term was introduced in August 2005. Relevant records were re-indexed with this term. The posting note reflects the number of records that were re-indexed.
R Predisposition 1973
↓ Stress 1967
Susceptibility (Disorders) 1973

Diazepam 1973
PN 2279 **SC** 14070
UF Valium
B Benzodiazepines 1978
Minor Tranquilizers 1973
Muscle Relaxing Drugs 1973

Dichoptic Stimulation 1982
PN 155 **SC** 14075
SN Simultaneous presentation of different stimuli to each eye independently.

Dichoptic Stimulation — (cont'd)
B Visual Stimulation 1973

Dichotic Stimulation 1982
PN 919 SC 14077
SN Simultaneous presentation of different sounds to the two ears.
B Auditory Stimulation 1967

Dieldrin
HN Term was discontinued in 1997. In 2000, the term was removed from all records containing it, and replaced with INSECTICIDES, its postable counterpart.
Use Insecticides

Diencephalon 1973
PN 321 SC 14110
SN The region of the brain that includes the epithalamus, hypothalamus, and thalamus.
B Forebrain 1985
N ↓ Hypothalamus 1967
Optic Chiasm 1973
↓ Thalamus 1967

Dietary Restraint 1994
PN 731 SC 14112
B Eating Behavior 2004
R ↓ Appetite 1973
Diets 1978
Food Intake 1967

Dietary Supplements 2001
PN 307 SC 14113
SN Orally ingested products intended as supplements to the diet, including vitamins, herbs, amino acids, and concentrates, metabolites, and extracts of these substances.
UF Nutritional Supplements
R ↓ Alternative Medicine 1997
↓ Amino Acids 1973
↓ Antioxidants 2004
Diets 1978
↓ Medicinal Herbs and Plants 2001
Nutrition 1973
↓ Vitamins 1973

Diets 1978
PN 4597 SC 14114
SN Food and drink regularly consumed or prescribed for a special reason. Used for human or animal populations.
R Dietary Restraint 1994
Dietary Supplements 2001
↓ Drinking Behavior 1978
↓ Eating Behavior 2004
Food 1978
Food Additives 1978
Food Allergies 1973
Food Deprivation 1967
Food Preferences 1973
↓ Health Behavior 1982
Nutrition 1973
↓ Nutritional Deficiencies 1973
Obesity 1973
↓ Underweight 1973
Weight Control 1985

Differential Aptitude Tests 1973
PN 72 SC 14150
B Aptitude Measures 1967

Differential Diagnosis 1967
PN 5922 SC 14160
SN Diagnosis aimed at distinguishing between physical and/or mental disorders of similar character by comparison of symptoms.
B Diagnosis 1967
R Comorbidity 1991
Dual Diagnosis 1991
Educational Diagnosis 1978
↓ Medical Diagnosis 1973
↓ Psychodiagnosis 1967

Differential Limen
Use Thresholds

Differential Personality Inventory
HN In 1997 this term was discontinued. In 2000, the term was removed from all records containing it, and was replaced with NONPROJECTIVE PERSONALITY MEASURES, its postable counterpart.
Use Nonprojective Personality Measures

Differential Reinforcement 1973
PN 979 SC 14190
SN Selective reinforcement of one response in a defined category (response class) of responses to the exclusion of any other members (responses) of that category. Has application in treatment as well as in experimental contexts.
B Reinforcement 1967
R ↓ Discrimination Learning 1982
Omission Training 1985

Difficulty Level (Test) 1973
PN 349 SC 14200
UF Test Difficulty
B Test Construction 1973
Testing 1967
R Item Response Theory 1985

Digestion 1973
PN 109 SC 14210
B Physiology 1967
R ↓ Digestive System 1967
↓ Ingestion 2001
Salivation 1973
Swallowing 1988

Digestive System 1967
PN 393 SC 14220
B Anatomical Systems 1973
N Esophagus 1973
↓ Gastrointestinal System 1973
Liver 1973
Mouth (Anatomy) 1967
Pharynx 1973
Teeth (Anatomy) 1973
↓ Tongue 1973
R Digestion 1973
↓ Digestive System Disorders 1973
Salivary Glands 1973

Digestive System Disorders 1973
PN 129 SC 14230
B Physical Disorders 1997
N Cystic Fibrosis 1985
↓ Gastrointestinal Disorders 1973

Digestive System Disorders — (cont'd)
Jaundice 1973
↓ Liver Disorders 1973
R ↓ Digestive System 1967
↓ Infectious Disorders 1973
↓ Neoplasms 1967
↓ Symptoms 1967
↓ Toxic Disorders 1973

Digit Span Testing 1973
PN 289 SC 14240
SN Test of immediate recall involving presentation of a random series of numerals which the subject repeats after the series has been presented.
B Measurement 1967

Digital Computers 1973
PN 271 SC 14250
SN Electronic or electromechanical machines that operate directly on binary digits when executing programs and manipulating data (e.g., calculators).
UF Calculators
B Computers 1967
R Digital Video 2007

Digital Divide 2007
PN 82 SC 14253
SN Disparities in access to and use of information and communication technologies due to linguistic, economic, educational, social, or geographic reasons.
HN This term was introduced in April 2007. Relevant records were re-indexed with this term. The posting note reflects the number of records that were re-indexed.
R ↓ Computer Applications 1973
Computer Literacy 1991
↓ Computers 1967
Disadvantaged 1967
Information Literacy 2007
↓ Internet Usage 2007
↓ Technology 1973

Digital Video 2007
PN 33 SC 14257
SN The capturing, manipulation, and storage of video using a digital, rather than analog format.
HN This term was introduced in April 2007. Relevant records were re-indexed with this term. The posting note reflects the number of records that were re-indexed.
B Audiovisual Communications Media 1973
R ↓ Computer Applications 1973
Digital Computers 1973
Videotapes 1973

Digits (Mathematics)
Use Numbers (Numerals)

Dihydroergotamine 1973
PN 31 SC 14270
B Adrenergic Blocking Drugs 1973
Analgesic Drugs 1973
Ergot Derivatives 1973
Vasoconstrictor Drugs 1973

Dihydroxyphenylacetic Acid 1991
PN 156 SC 14273
UF DOPAC
B Acids 1973
Dopamine Metabolites 1982

Dihydroxytryptamine 1991
PN 55 **SC** 14275
B Serotonin Antagonists 1973

Dilantin
Use Diphenylhydantoin

Dilation (Pupil)
Use Pupil Dilation

Diphenhydramine 1973
PN 89 **SC** 14310
UF Benadryl
B Amines 1973
Antihistaminic Drugs 1973
Antitremor Drugs 1973

Diphenylhydantoin 1973
PN 245 **SC** 14320
UF Dilantin
Diphenylhydantoin Sodium
Phenytoin
B Anticonvulsive Drugs 1973

Diphenylhydantoin Sodium
Use Diphenylhydantoin

Diptera 1973
PN 413 **SC** 14350
UF Flies
B Insects 1967
N Drosophila 1973
R Larvae 1973

Directed Discussion Method 1973
PN 124 **SC** 14360
B Teaching Methods 1967
R Lecture Method 1973

Directed Reverie Therapy
HN Term discontinued in 2000. Use DIRECTED REVERIE THERAPY to access references from 1978-2000.
Use Guided Imagery

Direction Perception 1997
PN 680 **SC** 14365
B Spatial Perception 1967
R Cognitive Maps 1982
↓ Motion Perception 1967
↓ Perceptual Localization 1967
↓ Spatial Memory 1988
Spatial Organization 1973

Disabilities 2003
PN 3139 **SC** 14366
HN Use DISORDERS to access references from 2001 to June 2003.
UF Handicaps
N Developmental Disabilities 1982
↓ Learning Disabilities 1973
↓ Multiple Disabilities 2001
↓ Reading Disabilities 1967
R Accommodation (Disabilities) 2007
Disability Discrimination 1997
Disability Laws 1994
↓ Disabled (Attitudes Toward) 1997
↓ Disorders 1967

Disability Discrimination 1997
PN 195 **SC** 57480
B Social Discrimination 1982
R Affirmative Action 1985
↓ Civil Rights 1978

Disability Discrimination — (cont'd)
↓ Disabilities 2003
Disability Laws 1994
↓ Disabled (Attitudes Toward) 1997
↓ Disorders 1967
↓ Mental Disorders 1967
Mental Illness (Attitudes Toward) 1967
↓ Physical Illness (Attitudes Toward) 1985
↓ Prejudice 1967
Sensory Disabilities (Attitudes Toward) 2001

Disability Evaluation 1988
PN 230 **SC** 14367
SN Evaluation of one's ability to work in order to determine the need for insurance or health benefits.
R ↓ Employee Benefits 1973
↓ Insurance 1973
Social Security 1988

Disability Laws 1994
PN 710 **SC** 57410
SN Rules declared by federal or state governments and enacted by legislative bodies that affect populations with mental or physical disabilities or disorders. Used for the laws themselves, or the interpretation or application of the laws.
B Laws 1967
R Accommodation (Disabilities) 2007
Civil Law 1994
↓ Civil Rights 1978
↓ Disabilities 2003
Disability Discrimination 1997
Disabled Personnel 1997

Disability Management 1991
PN 187 **SC** 14368
SN Process of returning an impaired or disabled worker to the workplace. Includes evaluation, assessment, early intervention, and rehabilitation.
B Management 1967
R Disabled Personnel 1997
Employee Assistance Programs 1985
↓ Prevention 1973
↓ Rehabilitation 1967
Vocational Evaluation 1991
↓ Vocational Rehabilitation 1967

Disabled (Attitudes Toward) 1997
PN 2033 **SC** 14373
HN In 1997, this term replaced the discontinued term HANDICAPPED (ATTITUDES TOWARD). In 2000, HANDICAPPED (ATTITUDES TOWARD) was removed from all records containing it, and replaced with DISABLED (ATTITUDES TOWARD).
UF Handicapped (Attitudes Toward)
B Attitudes 1967
N Mental Illness (Attitudes Toward) 1967
Mental Retardation (Attitudes Toward) 2001
Physical Disabilities (Attitudes Toward) 2001
Sensory Disabilities (Attitudes Toward) 2001
R ↓ Disabilities 2003
Disability Discrimination 1997
↓ Physical Illness (Attitudes Toward) 1985
Stereotyped Attitudes 1967

Disabled Personnel 1997
PN 397 **SC** 14369
SN Employees with physical or mental disabilities or injuries resulting from work-related activities.
B Personnel 1967
R Disability Laws 1994
Disability Management 1991
↓ Disorders 1967
Impaired Professionals 1985

Disabled Personnel — (cont'd)
Supported Employment 1994
Workers' Compensation Insurance 2003
↓ Working Conditions 1973

Disadvantaged 1967
PN 4248 **SC** 14370
SN Individuals deprived of equal access to society's resources, especially as regards education, culture, and employment.
UF Economically Disadvantaged
Socially Disadvantaged
Underprivileged
R Cultural Deprivation 1973
Digital Divide 2007
↓ Homeless 1988
Poverty 1973
↓ Social Class 1967
↓ Social Deprivation 1973
↓ Socioeconomic Status 1967

Disappointment 1973
PN 128 **SC** 14380
B Emotional States 1973
R Dissatisfaction 1973
↓ Separation Reactions 1997

Disaster Planning
Use Emergency Preparedness

Disaster Preparedness
Use Emergency Preparedness

Disasters 1973
PN 1485 **SC** 14390
N Natural Disasters 1973
R ↓ Accidents 1967
↓ Crises 1971
Emergency Preparedness 2007
↓ Stress 1967

Discharge Planning 1994
PN 141 **SC** 14395
B Case Management 1991
Treatment Planning 1997
R Aftercare 1973
Deinstitutionalization 1982
↓ Facility Discharge 1988
↓ Hospital Discharge 1973
↓ Institutional Release 1978
Posttreatment Followup 1973
Psychiatric Hospital Discharge 1978
Treatment Termination 1982

Discipline (Child)
Use Child Discipline

Discipline (Classroom)
Use Classroom Discipline

Disclosure (Experimental)
Use Debriefing (Experimental)

Disclosure (Self)
Use Self Disclosure

Discourse Analysis 1997
PN 2874 **SC** 14425
SN Analysis of written and spoken language.
B Content Analysis 1978
R ↓ Grammar 1967
↓ Language 1967
↓ Linguistics 1973
Morphology (Language) 1973

Discourse Analysis — (cont'd)
Pragmatics 1985
Rhetoric 1991
↓ Semantics 1967
↓ Syntax 1971
Text Structure 1982
↓ Verbal Communication 1967

Discovery Teaching Method 1973
PN 157 **SC** 14430
SN Unstructured or guided instruction which encourages independent exploration or discovery.
B Teaching Methods 1967
R ↓ Experiential Learning 1997
Montessori Method 1973
Nondirected Discussion Method 1973
Open Classroom Method 1973
Self Regulated Learning 2003

Discriminant Validity
Use Test Validity

Discrimination 1967
PN 2981 **SC** 14450
SN Conceptually broad term referring to the general process of differentiation between qualities, entities, or people. Use a more specific term if possible.
N Cognitive Discrimination 1973
Drug Discrimination 1985
↓ Perceptual Discrimination 1973
↓ Social Discrimination 1982
Stimulus Discrimination 1973
R Criminal Profiling 2007
↓ Discrimination Learning 1982
↓ Perception 1967
Stereotyped Attitudes 1967

Discrimination (Cognitive)
Use Cognitive Discrimination

Discrimination (Social)
Use Social Discrimination

Discrimination Learning 1982
PN 3106 **SC** 14445
SN Learning paradigm in which responses to one stimulus (S+) are reinforced while responses to another stimulus (S-) are either not reinforced or are punished. Also, the learned discriminative responses themselves.
UF Discriminative Learning
B Learning 1967
Operant Conditioning 1967
N Drug Discrimination 1985
Matching to Sample 1994
Nonreversal Shift Learning 1973
Reversal Shift Learning 1967
R ↓ Concept Formation 1967
Differential Reinforcement 1973
↓ Discrimination 1967
Extinction (Learning) 1967
Fading (Conditioning) 1982
↓ Generalization (Learning) 1982
Kinship Recognition 1988
Stimulus Control 1967
Stimulus Discrimination 1973

Discriminative Learning
Use Discrimination Learning

Discriminative Stimulus
Use Conditioned Stimulus

Discussion (Group)
Use Group Discussion

Disease Course 1991
PN 5282 **SC** 14470
SN Stages or progression of physical or mental disorders. Compare PROGNOSIS.
UF Course of Illness
Disorder Course
R Disease Management 2007
↓ Disorders 1967
↓ Mental Disorders 1967
↓ Physical Disorders 1997
Prognosis 1973

Disease Management 2007
PN 244 **SC** 14473
SN Integrated treatment approach that seeks to improve the health of patients over the entire course of the illness through disease-specific management, education, and patient support. Health care costs are reduced by preventing or minimizing the effects of the disease through integrative care.
HN This term was introduced in April 2007. Relevant records were re-indexed with this term. The posting note reflects the number of records that were re-indexed.
B Treatment 1967
R ↓ Chronic Illness 1991
Client Education 1985
Disease Course 1991
Health Care Costs 1994
↓ Managed Care 1994
Treatment Compliance 1982
↓ Treatment Planning 1997

Disease Outbreaks
Use Epidemics

Disease Transmission 2004
PN 508 **SC** 14480
SN Transmission of disease from one individual to another.
HN This term was introduced in June 2004. Relevant records were re-indexed with this term. The posting note reflects the number of records that were re-indexed.
R Blood Transfusion 1973
Etiology 1967
↓ Infectious Disorders 1973
Intravenous Drug Usage 1994
Pandemics 2007
↓ Sexual Intercourse (Human) 1973
↓ Sexually Transmitted Diseases 2003

Diseases (Venereal)
Use Sexually Transmitted Diseases

Disgust 1994
PN 249 **SC** 14495
B Emotional States 1973
R ↓ Aversion 1967

Dishonesty 1973
PN 236 **SC** 14500
B Personality Traits 1967
R Cheating 1973
↓ Deception 1967
Fraud 1994
Sincerity 1973

Dislike
Use Aversion

Disorder Course
Use Disease Course

Disorders 1967
PN 18287 **SC** 14520
SN Conceptually broad term referring primarily to physical illness. Also used when particular disorders are not specified. Use a more specific term if possible. For general discussions of health impairment consider also the term HEALTH.
HN The term HANDICAPPED was also used to represent this concept from 1967-1996, and DISABLED was used from 1997-2000. In 2000, DISORDERS replaced the discontinued and deleted terms DISABLED and HANDICAPPED. DISABLED and HANDICAPPED were removed from all records containing them and replaced with DISORDERS.
UF Exceptional Children (Handicapped)
N Adventitious Disorders 2001
↓ Atypical Disorders 2005
↓ Behavior Disorders 1971
↓ Communication Disorders 1982
↓ Congenital Disorders 1973
↓ Learning Disorders 1967
↓ Mental Disorders 1967
↓ Physical Disorders 1997
R ↓ Brain Damage 1967
↓ Chronic Illness 1991
Chronicity (Disorders) 1982
Comorbidity 1991
↓ Diagnosis 1967
↓ Disabilities 2003
Disability Discrimination 1997
Disabled Personnel 1997
Disease Course 1991
Etiology 1967
Health Complaints 1997
Illness Behavior 1982
↓ Injuries 1973
International Classification of Diseases 2001
↓ Mental Retardation 1967
Onset (Disorders) 1973
Predisposition 1973
Premorbidity 1978
Prenatal Exposure 1991
Prognosis 1973
Recovery (Disorders) 1973
Relapse (Disorders) 1973
↓ Remission (Disorders) 1973
Severity (Disorders) 1982
Special Needs 1994
Subtypes (Disorders) 2004
Susceptibility (Disorders) 1973
↓ Symptoms 1967
↓ Syndromes 1973

Disorientation (Place)
Use Place Disorientation

Disorientation (Time)
Use Time Disorientation

Displacement (Defense Mechanism) 1973
PN 77 **SC** 14550
B Defense Mechanisms 1967

Displays 1967
PN 426 **SC** 14560
SN Physical arrangements of stimuli to form a desired pattern; temporal, spatial, or otherwise.
N Auditory Displays 1973
Graphical Displays 1985
Tactual Displays 1973
↓ Visual Displays 1973

Displays — (cont'd)
R ↓ Instrument Controls 1985

Disposition
Use Personality

Disruptive Behavior
Use Behavior Problems

Dissatisfaction 1973
PN 614 SC 14590
B Emotional States 1973
R Disappointment 1973
Frustration 1967
↓ Satisfaction 1973

Dissociation 2001
PN 1167 SC 14592
SN Used generally to describe the process whereby thoughts, attitudes, emotions, or a coordinated set of activities becomes separated from one's personality or mental processes. Compare DISSOCIATIVE DISORDERS.
HN Consider DISSOCIATIVE PATTERNS from 1973-2000.
R ↓ Amnesia 1967
↓ Consciousness Disturbances 1973
↓ Consciousness States 1971
↓ Dissociative Disorders 2001
↓ Neurosis 1967

Dissociative Disorders 2001
PN 1740 SC 14593
SN Mental disorders characterized by disruptions and/or alterations in the normally integrated functions of consciousness, memory, or identity. Compare DISSOCIATION.
HN Consider DISSOCIATIVE PATTERNS to access records from 1973-2000.
UF Dissociative Neurosis
Dissociative Patterns
Hysterical Neurosis (Dissociation)
B Mental Disorders 1967
N Depersonalization 1973
Dissociative Identity Disorder 1997
Fugue Reaction 1973
R ↓ Amnesia 1967
↓ Consciousness Disturbances 1973
Dissociation 2001
↓ Personality Disorders 1967

Dissociative Identity Disorder 1997
PN 1641 SC 14595
HN In 1997, this term was created to replace the discontinued term MULTIPLE PERSONALITY. In 2000, MULTIPLE PERSONALITY was removed from all records and replaced with DISSOCIATIVE IDENTITY DISORDER.
UF Multiple Personality
Split Personality
B Dissociative Disorders 2001

Dissociative Neurosis
HN Term discontinued in 1997.
Use Dissociative Disorders

Dissociative Patterns
HN Term discontinued in 2000. Use DISSOCIATIVE PATTERNS to access references from 1973-2000.
Use Dissociative Disorders

Dissonance (Cognitive)
Use Cognitive Dissonance

Distance Discrimination
Use Distance Perception

Distance Education 2003
PN 586 SC 14633
SN Type of education where students work at home or at the office and communicate with faculty via various forms of communications media.
HN This term was introduced in June 2003. Relevant records were re-indexed with this term. The posting note reflects the number of records that were re-indexed.
UF Distance Learning
B Education 1967
R Computer Mediated Communication 2003
↓ Continuing Education 1985
↓ Electronic Communication 2001
Individualized Instruction 1973
↓ Nontraditional Education 1982
↓ Telecommunications Media 1973
Virtual Classrooms 2007

Distance Learning
Use Distance Education

Distance Perception 1973
PN 1141 SC 14640
UF Distance Discrimination
B Spatial Perception 1967
N Apparent Distance 1973
Motion Parallax 1997
R Eye Convergence 1982
Linear Perspective 1982

Distortion (Perceptual)
Use Perceptual Distortion

Distractibility 1973
PN 408 SC 14660
B Symptoms 1967
R ↓ Attention Deficit Disorder 1985
Attention Deficit Disorder with Hyperactivity 2001
Distraction 1978

Distraction 1978
PN 1861 SC 14663
SN Process or potential cause of interruption of attention.
R ↓ Attention 1967
Attention Span 1973
Concentration 1982
Distractibility 1973
Divided Attention 1973
Selective Attention 1973

Distress 1973
PN 8163 SC 14670
SN Negative emotional state characterized by physical and/or emotional discomfort, pain, or anguish. Compare STRESS.
UF Anguish
B Emotional States 1973
R Agitation 1991
↓ Separation Reactions 1997
↓ Stress 1967
Suffering 1973

Distress Calls (Animal)
Use Animal Distress Calls

Distributed Practice 1973
PN 161 SC 14690
SN Practice schedule in which relatively short periods of practice are spaced with intermittent rest or periods of activity unrelated to the practiced task. Compare MASSED PRACTICE.
B Learning Schedules 1967
Practice 1967

Distribution (Frequency)
Use Frequency Distribution

Distributive Justice 2003
PN 131 SC 14705
SN The fairness of resource allocation, responsibility distribution, and other decision outcomes.
HN Use JUSTICE to access references from 1988 to June 2003.
B Social Justice 2006
R Equity (Payment) 1978
↓ Equity (Social) 1978
↓ Organizational Behavior 1978
Resource Allocation 1997

Distrust
Use Suspicion

Disulfiram 1978
PN 218 SC 14725
UF Antabuse
B Emetic Drugs 1973

Diuresis 1973
PN 32 SC 14730
SN Increased flow of urine.
B Urination 1967
R ↓ Diuretics 1973

Diuretics 1973
PN 131 SC 14740
B Drugs 1967
N Acetazolamide 1973
Caffeine 1973
Theophylline 1973
R ↓ Antihypertensive Drugs 1973
Diuresis 1973
Probenecid 1982
Purging (Eating Disorders) 2003
↓ Urination 1967

Diurnal Variations
Use Human Biological Rhythms

Divergent Thinking 1973
PN 763 SC 14760
SN Component of intelligence which is manifested in the ability to generate a wide variety of original ideas or solutions to a particular problem. Compare CREATIVITY.
B Thinking 1967
R ↓ Abstraction 1967
Creativity 1967
Critical Thinking 2006
Declarative Knowledge 1997
↓ Inductive Deductive Reasoning 1973
↓ Intelligence 1967
Procedural Knowledge 1997

Diversity 2007
PN 1042 SC 14761
SN In people, characteristics such as ability, age, education, ethnicity, gender, marital status, parental status, race, religion, sexual orientation, or socioeconomic status that make individuals different from

Diversity — (cont'd)
each other. In general terms, the relative uniqueness or variation in the qualities or attributes under discussion.
HN This term was introduced in April 2007. Relevant records were re-indexed with this term. The posting note reflects the number of records that were re-indexed.
R Cross Cultural Differences 1967
↓ Group Differences 2007
Individual Differences 1967
Multiculturalism 1997
Racial and Ethnic Differences 1982

Diversity in the Workplace 2003
PN 624 **SC** 14763
SN All forms of variation among individuals in the workplace, including but not limited to, ethnicity, gender, age, sexual orientation, religious affiliation, ability, financial status, and personality.
HN This term was introduced in June 2003. Relevant records were re-indexed with this term. The posting note reflects the number of records that were re-indexed.
UF Workforce Diversity
Workplace Diversity
R Affirmative Action 1985
Age Differences 1967
Cross Cultural Differences 1967
↓ Employee Characteristics 1988
↓ Human Sex Differences 1967
Individual Differences 1967
Multiculturalism 1997
↓ Organizational Characteristics 1997
Organizational Climate 1973
Racial and Ethnic Differences 1982

Divided Attention 1973
PN 954 **SC** 14765
SN Simultaneous attending to two or more stimuli or through two or more perceptual modalities. Compare SELECTIVE ATTENTION.
B Attention 1967
R Distraction 1978
Selective Attention 1973

Division of Labor 1988
PN 691 **SC** 14767
N Animal Division of Labor 1973
R ↓ Economics 1985
Household Management 1985
↓ Occupations 1967
Sex Roles 1967
Work Load 1982

Division of Labor (Animal)
Use Animal Division of Labor

Divorce 1973
PN 5580 **SC** 14780
B Marital Separation 1973
R Child Custody 1982
Child Support 1988
Divorced Persons 1973
↓ Family 1967
Joint Custody 1988
Life Changes 2004
Mediation 1988
Remarriage 1985

Divorced Persons 1973
PN 850 **SC** 14790
R Divorce 1973
↓ Family 1967

Divorced Persons — (cont'd)
↓ Marital Separation 1973
↓ Marital Status 1973
↓ Parental Absence 1973

Dizygotic Twins
Use Heterozygotic Twins

Dizziness
Use Vertigo

DNA 2006
PN 624 **SC** 14810
HN In May 2006, this term replaced the discontinued term DEOXYRIBONUCLEIC ACID. DEOXYRIBONUCLEIC ACID was removed from all records containing it and replaced with DNA, its postable counterpart.
UF Deoxyribonucleic Acid
B Nucleic Acids 1973
R Cloning 2003
Genome 2003

Doctors
Use Physicians

Dogmatism 1978
PN 570 **SC** 14830
B Personality Traits 1967
R Authoritarianism 1967
Openmindedness 1978
Relativism 1997

Dogs 1967
PN 2489 **SC** 14840
B Canids 1997

Doll Play 1973
PN 118 **SC** 14850
B Recreation 1967
R Anatomically Detailed Dolls 1991
↓ Childhood Play Behavior 1978

Dolphins 1973
PN 327 **SC** 14860
B Whales 1985
R Porpoises 1973

Domestic Service Personnel 1973
PN 71 **SC** 14870
UF Maids
B Service Personnel 1991
R ↓ Nonprofessional Personnel 1982

Domestic Violence 2006
PN 5737 **SC** 14872
SN Injurious or abusive behavior in family or other domestic interpersonal situations.
HN In May 2006, this term replaced the discontinued term FAMILY VIOLENCE. FAMILY VIOLENCE was removed from all records containing it and replaced with DOMESTIC VIOLENCE, its postable counterpart.
UF Family Violence
B Violence 1973
Violent Crime 2003
R Battered Females 1988
↓ Child Abuse 1971
Elder Abuse 1988
Emotional Abuse 1991
↓ Family Conflict 2003
↓ Family Relations 1967
Intimate Partner Violence 2007
Marital Conflict 1973

Domestic Violence — (cont'd)
↓ Partner Abuse 1991
Physical Abuse 1991
↓ Sexual Abuse 1988
Shelters 1991

Domestication (Animal)
Use Animal Domestication

Dominance 1967
PN 1250 **SC** 14900
SN Conceptually broad term referring to relative positions of objects, persons, things, or processes. Use a more specific term if possible.
N Animal Dominance 1973
↓ Cerebral Dominance 1973
Dominance Hierarchy 1973
Genetic Dominance 1973
R Abuse of Power 1997
Authoritarianism 1967
Authority 1967
Bullying 2003
Coercion 1994
Emotional Superiority 1973
Obedience 1973
↓ Power 1967
↓ Status 1967

Dominance (Animal)
Use Animal Dominance

Dominance Hierarchy 1973
PN 1374 **SC** 14890
SN Social structure of a group as it relates to the relative social rank or dominance status of its members. Used for human or animal populations.
B Dominance 1967
R Animal Dominance 1973
↓ Social Behavior 1967
↓ Social Structure 1967

Domination
Use Authoritarianism

DOPA 1973
PN 114 **SC** 14940
B Amino Acids 1973
R Carbidopa 1988
Dopamine 1973
Levodopa 1973
Methyldopa 1973

DOPAC
Use Dihydroxyphenylacetic Acid

Dopamine 1973
PN 9291 **SC** 14950
B Catecholamines 1973
R DOPA 1973
↓ Dopamine Metabolites 1982
↓ Heart Rate Affecting Drugs 1973
Homovanillic Acid 1978
Levodopa 1973
Methyldopa 1973
Methylphenyltetrahydropyridine 1994

Dopamine Agonists 1985
PN 1461 **SC** 14951
B Drugs 1967
N ↓ Amphetamine 1967
Apomorphine 1973
Morphine 1973
Quinpirole 1994

Dopamine Antagonists 1982
PN 1490 **SC** 14952
- **B** Amine Oxidase Inhibitors 1973
- **N** Sulpiride 1973
- **R** ↓ Catecholamines 1973
  - ↓ CNS Depressant Drugs 1973
  - ↓ Decarboxylase Inhibitors 1982
  - ↓ Narcotic Drugs 1973
  - ↓ Tranquilizing Drugs 1967

Dopamine Metabolites 1982
PN 272 **SC** 14955
SN Molecules generated from the metabolism of dopamine.
- **B** Metabolites 1973
- **N** Dihydroxyphenylacetic Acid 1991
  - Homovanillic Acid 1978
- **R** Acetaldehyde 1982
  - Dopamine 1973
  - ↓ Metabolism 1967

Dormitories 1973
PN 481 **SC** 14960
- **UF** Residence Halls
- **B** Housing 1973
  - School Facilities 1973

Dorsal Horns 1985
PN 301 **SC** 14965
SN Longitudinal columns of gray matter (i.e., neuronal cell bodies) in the posterior spinal cord mainly serving sensory mechanisms.
- **B** Spinal Cord 1973
- **R** ↓ Afferent Pathways 1982
  - Dorsal Roots 1973

Dorsal Roots 1973
PN 238 **SC** 14970
SN The sensory root, generally afferent, of a spinal nerve, having a dorsal root ganglion which contains the neuron cell bodies of the nerve fibers conveyed by the root in its distal end.
- **B** Spinal Cord 1973
- **R** Dorsal Horns 1985

Double Bind Interaction 1973
PN 128 **SC** 14990
SN Simultaneous communication of conflicting messages in which the response to either message evokes rejection or disapproval.
- **B** Interpersonal Communication 1973
- **R** Dysfunctional Family 1991
  - Schizophrenogenic Family 1967
  - Schizophrenogenic Mothers 1973

Doubt 1973
PN 113 **SC** 15000
- **B** Emotional States 1973
- **R** Mental Confusion 1973
  - Suspicion 1973
  - Uncertainty 1991

Doves 1973
PN 205 **SC** 15010
- **B** Birds 1967

Down Syndrome
Use Downs Syndrome

Downs Syndrome 1967
PN 3541 **SC** 15020
SN A chromosome disorder caused by the presence of an extra chromosome 21. One of the most common genetic birth defects, and the most frequent genetic cause of mild to moderate mental retardation and associated medical disorders or conditions.
HN In August 2005, this term replaced the discontinued term TRISOMY 21. TRISOMY 21 was removed from all records containing it, and replaced with DOWNS SYNDROME.
- **UF** Down Syndrome
  - Mongolism
  - Trisomy 21
- **B** Autosome Disorders 1973
  - Mental Retardation 1967
  - Neonatal Disorders 1973
  - Syndromes 1973
- **R** Moderate Mental Retardation 2001

Downsizing 2003
PN 244 **SC** 15017
SN Reduction in workforce within an organization through terminations, retirements, or buyouts.
HN This term was introduced in June 2003. Relevant records were re-indexed with this term. The posting note reflects the number of records that were re-indexed.
- **B** Organizational Change 1973
- **R** Employee Turnover 1973
  - Job Security 1978
  - Personnel Termination 1973

Doxepin 1994
PN 36 **SC** 15025
HN Use ANTIDEPRESSANT DRUGS or TRANQUILIZING DRUGS to access references from 1973-1993.
- **B** Tranquilizing Drugs 1967
  - Tricyclic Antidepressant Drugs 1997

Draftees 1973
PN 71 **SC** 15030
SN Military personnel conscripted for service.
- **B** Enlisted Military Personnel 1973
- **R** Army Personnel 1967
  - Navy Personnel 1967

Drama 1973
PN 1191 **SC** 15040
- **B** Theatre 1973
- **R** Improvisation 2004
  - ↓ Literature 1967
  - Writers 1991

Drama Therapy
Use Psychodrama

Draw A Man Test
HN Prior to 1988, use Goodenough Harris Draw A Person Test.
Use Human Figures Drawing

Drawing 1967
PN 3243 **SC** 15050
- **B** Art 1967

Dream Analysis 1973
PN 2168 **SC** 15060
- **UF** Dream Interpretation
- **B** Psychoanalysis 1967
  - Psychotherapeutic Techniques 1967
- **R** ↓ Dreaming 1967
  - ↓ Parapsychology 1967

Dream Content 1973
PN 1721 **SC** 15070
- **R** ↓ Dreaming 1967
  - Nightmares 1973
  - ↓ Sleep 1967

Dream Interpretation
Use Dream Analysis

Dream Recall 1973
PN 423 **SC** 15090
- **R** ↓ Dreaming 1967
  - Lucid Dreaming 1994

Dreaming 1967
PN 2570 **SC** 15100
- **N** Lucid Dreaming 1994
  - Nightmares 1973
  - REM Dreams 1973
- **R** Dream Analysis 1973
  - Dream Content 1973
  - Dream Recall 1973
  - ↓ Sleep 1967

DRGs
Use Diagnosis Related Groups

Drinking (Alcohol)
Use Alcohol Drinking Patterns

Drinking Attitudes
Use Alcohol Drinking Attitudes

Drinking Behavior 1978
PN 472 **SC** 15127
- **B** Behavior 1967
- **N** ↓ Alcohol Drinking Patterns 1967
  - Animal Drinking Behavior 1973
  - Water Intake 1967
- **R** ↓ Alcoholic Beverages 1973
  - Beverages (Nonalcoholic) 1978
  - Diets 1978
  - Driving Under the Influence 1988
  - ↓ Fluid Intake 1985
  - ↓ Ingestion 2001
  - Sucking 1978
  - Thirst 1967

Drinking Behavior (Animal)
Use Animal Drinking Behavior

Drive
Use Motivation

Driver Education 1973
PN 240 **SC** 15150
- **B** Curriculum 1967
- **R** Drivers 1973

Driver Safety
Use Highway Safety

Drivers 1973
PN 2207 **SC** 15170
- **R** Automobiles 1973
  - Driver Education 1973
  - ↓ Driving Behavior 1967
  - Highway Safety 1973
  - Motor Traffic Accidents 1973
  - ↓ Motor Vehicles 1982

Driving Behavior 1967
PN 4026 **SC** 15180
SN Manner in which one operates a motor vehicle.

Driving Behavior — (cont'd)
B Behavior 1967
N Aggressive Driving Behavior 2004
Driving Under the Influence 1988
R Drivers 1973
Highway Safety 1973
Motor Traffic Accidents 1973
Pedestrian Accidents 1973
Safety Belts 1973

Driving Under the Influence 1988
PN 1149 SC 15185
UF Drunk Driving
B Crime 1967
Driving Behavior 1967
R ↓ Accidents 1967
↓ Alcohol Intoxication 1973
Blood Alcohol Concentration 1994
↓ Drinking Behavior 1978
↓ Drug Usage 1971
Highway Safety 1973

Dropouts 1973
PN 323 SC 15190
N Potential Dropouts 1973
↓ School Dropouts 1967
Treatment Dropouts 1978
R ↓ Education 1967
Experimental Attrition 1994
↓ School Enrollment 1973

Drosophila 1973
PN 972 SC 15200
UF Fruit Fly
B Diptera 1973
R Larvae 1973

Drowsiness
Use Sleepiness

Drug Abstinence 1994
PN 1036 SC 15215
SN Voluntary or involuntary abstinence from drugs. For alcohol abstinence, use SOBRIETY.
UF Abstinence (Drugs)
N Sobriety 1988
R Detoxification 1973
↓ Drug Abuse 1973
↓ Drug Rehabilitation 1973
↓ Drug Usage 1971
↓ Drug Withdrawal 1973
Recovery (Disorders) 1973
Smoking Cessation 1988

Drug Abuse 1973
PN 21464 SC 15220
UF Substance Abuse
B Behavior Disorders 1971
Drug Usage 1971
N ↓ Alcohol Abuse 1988
↓ Drug Dependency 1973
↓ Inhalant Abuse 1985
Polydrug Abuse 1994
R ↓ Addiction 1973
Codependency 1991
Craving 1997
↓ Drug Abstinence 1994
Drug Abuse Liability 1994
Drug Abuse Prevention 1994
↓ Drug Addiction 1967
↓ Drug Legalization 1997
Drug Overdoses 1978

Drug Abuse — (cont'd)
Drug Usage Screening 1988
↓ Drugs 1967
Illegal Drug Distribution 1997
Intravenous Drug Usage 1994
Needle Exchange Programs 2001
Needle Sharing 1994
↓ Social Issues 1991

Drug Abuse Liability 1994
PN 194 SC 15225
SN Properties of any psychoactive drug or substance which lead to self administration and potential for abuse, dependence, and addiction.
UF Abuse Potential (Drugs)
R ↓ Alcohol Abuse 1988
↓ Drug Abuse 1973
↓ Drug Addiction 1967
↓ Drug Dependency 1973
↓ Pharmacology 1973
Psychopharmacology 1967

Drug Abuse Prevention 1994
PN 2151 SC 15227
UF Substance Abuse Prevention
B Prevention 1973
R ↓ Drug Abuse 1973
Drug Education 1973
Early Intervention 1982
↓ Harm Reduction 2003
Preventive Medicine 1973
Primary Mental Health Prevention 1973

Drug Addiction 1967
PN 6345 SC 15230
SN Physical and emotional dependence on a chemical substance. Compare DRUG DEPENDENCY.
B Addiction 1973
Drug Dependency 1973
Side Effects (Drug) 1973
N Heroin Addiction 1973
R ↓ Drug Abuse 1973
Drug Abuse Liability 1994
Drug Overdoses 1978
↓ Drug Withdrawal 1973
Intravenous Drug Usage 1994
Methadone Maintenance 1978
Polydrug Abuse 1994

Drug Administration Methods 1973
PN 2895 SC 15240
SN Techniques, procedures, and routes (e.g., oral, intravenous) of administration of drugs (in experimental or therapeutic contexts) including dosage forms (e.g., liquids, tablets), frequency, and duration of drug administration. Used only when methodological aspects of administering drugs are discussed.
N Drug Self Administration 2004
↓ Injections 1973
R ↓ Drug Dosages 1973
↓ Drugs 1967

Drug Adverse Reactions
HN Term was discontinued in 1982. In 2000, the term was removed from all records containing it, and replaced with SIDE EFFECTS (DRUG), its postable counterpart.
Use Side Effects (Drug)

Drug Allergies 1973
PN 28 SC 15260
B Allergic Disorders 1973
Side Effects (Drug) 1973

Drug Allergies — (cont'd)
R Drug Sensitivity 1973

Drug Augmentation 2004
PN 404 SC 15263
SN To increase or supplement any drug treatment.
HN This term was introduced in June 2004. Relevant records were re-indexed with this term. The posting note reflects the number of records that were re-indexed.
R ↓ Drug Dosages 1973
↓ Drug Therapy 1967

Drug Dealing
Use Illegal Drug Distribution

Drug Dependency 1973
PN 6734 SC 15270
SN Psychological craving for or habituation to the use of a chemical substance which may or may not be accompanied by physical dependency. Used for animal or human populations. Compare DRUG ADDICTION.
UF Dependency (Drug)
B Drug Abuse 1973
Side Effects (Drug) 1973
N ↓ Drug Addiction 1967
R Drug Abuse Liability 1994
Drug Usage Screening 1988
Polydrug Abuse 1994

Drug Discrimination 1985
PN 1410 SC 15272
SN A discrimination learning paradigm used to study psychopharmacological and neuropharmacological phenomena. Also, the organism's ability to discriminate the presence, absence, or other qualitative aspects of a chemical substance.
B Discrimination 1967
Discrimination Learning 1982
R ↓ Drugs 1967

Drug Dissociation
Use State Dependent Learning

Drug Dosages 1973
PN 6436 SC 15280
N Drug Overdoses 1978
R Bioavailability 1991
↓ Drug Administration Methods 1973
Drug Augmentation 2004
Drug Self Administration 2004
↓ Drugs 1967

Drug Education 1973
PN 1733 SC 15290
UF Alcohol Education
B Health Education 1973
R Drug Abuse Prevention 1994
↓ Drugs 1967

Drug Effects
HN Term discontinued in 1982. Prior to 1982, a mandatory term applied to all studies involving any use of chemical substances administered for nontreatment purposes to human or animal subjects. From 1982, use specific drug classes or names, or terms referring to the chemical substance introduced for nontreatment purposes. In 2000, the term was removed from all records containing it, and replaced with DRUGS, its postable counterpart.
Use Drugs

Drug Induced Congenital Disorders 1973
PN 98 **SC** 15310
B Congenital Disorders 1973
Toxic Disorders 1973
N Fetal Alcohol Syndrome 1985
R Thalidomide 1973

Drug Induced Hallucinations 1973
PN 76 **SC** 15320
B Hallucinations 1967
R Psychedelic Experiences 1973

Drug Industry
Use Pharmaceutical Industry

Drug Interactions 1982
PN 5314 **SC** 15325
SN Chemical and/or pharmacological reactions of drugs in combination, including agonistic and antagonistic interactions.
HN In 1982, this term was created to replace the discontinued terms DRUG POTENTIATION and DRUG SYNERGISM. In 2000, these terms were removed from all records containing them, and replaced with DRUG INTERACTIONS.
UF Drug Potentiation
Drug Synergism
Potentiation (Drugs)
R ↓ Drugs 1967
↓ Neurotoxins 1982
Polydrug Abuse 1994
Polypharmacy 2004

Drug Laws 1973
PN 665 **SC** 15330
B Laws 1967
N ↓ Marijuana Laws 1973
R ↓ Drug Legalization 1997
↓ Drugs 1967
Illegal Drug Distribution 1997

Drug Legalization 1997
PN 49 **SC** 15333
N Marijuana Legalization 1973
R ↓ Drug Abuse 1973
↓ Drug Laws 1973
↓ Drug Usage 1971
↓ Harm Reduction 2003
Illegal Drug Distribution 1997

Drug Overdoses 1978
PN 665 **SC** 15335
B Drug Dosages 1973
R ↓ Drug Abuse 1973
↓ Drug Addiction 1967
↓ Drug Therapy 1967
↓ Drug Usage 1971

Drug Potentiation
HN Term was discontinued in 1982. In 2000, the term was removed from all records containing it, and replaced with DRUG INTERACTIONS, its postable counterpart.
Use Drug Interactions

Drug Rehabilitation 1973
PN 12678 **SC** 15350
UF Rehabilitation (Drug)
B Rehabilitation 1967
N ↓ Alcohol Rehabilitation 1982
Detoxification 1973

Drug Rehabilitation — (cont'd)
R ↓ Drug Abstinence 1994
Drug Usage Screening 1988
↓ Drugs 1967
Employee Assistance Programs 1985
Methadone Maintenance 1978
↓ Psychosocial Rehabilitation 1973
Rehabilitation Counseling 1978
Smoking Cessation 1988
Sobriety 1988
↓ Twelve Step Programs 1997

Drug Self Administration 2004
PN 312 **SC** 15355
SN Administration of drugs or chemicals by one's self. Used clinically or experimentally for humans or animals. Not to be confused with SELF MEDICATION.
HN This term was introduced in June 2004. Relevant records were re-indexed with this term. The posting note reflects the number of records that were re-indexed.
UF Self Administration (Drugs)
B Drug Administration Methods 1973
R ↓ Drug Dosages 1973
↓ Drug Usage 1971
↓ Injections 1973

Drug Sensitivity 1973
PN 2070 **SC** 15360
SN Behavioral or physical sensitivity, resistance, or reactivity to a particular chemical substance.
UF Sensitivity (Drugs)
B Side Effects (Drug) 1973
R Drug Allergies 1973
Drug Tolerance 1973
Sensitization 2005

Drug Synergism
HN Term was discontinued in 1982. In 2000, the term was removed from all records containing it, and replaced with DRUG INTERACTIONS, its postable counterpart.
Use Drug Interactions

Drug Testing
Use Drug Usage Screening

Drug Therapy 1967
PN 66205 **SC** 15380
SN Mandatory term applied to studies dealing with the use of drugs in the clinical treatment of diseases or psychological disorders. Used for human or animal populations. For the use of drugs in non-clinical contexts, use PHARMACOLOGY or PSYCHOPHARMACOLOGY.
UF Medication
Pharmacotherapy
Therapy (Drug)
B Physical Treatment Methods 1973
N Chemotherapy 2007
Hormone Therapy 1994
↓ Narcoanalysis 1973
Polypharmacy 2004
Vitamin Therapy 1978
R Bioavailability 1991
Clinical Trials 2004
Detoxification 1973
Drug Augmentation 2004
Drug Overdoses 1978
↓ Drugs 1967
Maintenance Therapy 1997
Neuroleptic Malignant Syndrome 1988
↓ Outpatient Treatment 1967

Drug Therapy — (cont'd)
Pharmaceutical Industry 2007
Pharmacoeconomics 2007
↓ Prescribing (Drugs) 1991
Prescription Drugs 1991
Self Medication 1991
↓ Side Effects (Drug) 1973
Sleep Treatment 1973
Tardive Dyskinesia 1988
Treatment Resistant Depression 1994

Drug Tolerance 1973
PN 2989 **SC** 15390
SN Condition in which, after repeated administration, a drug produces a decreased effect and must be administered in larger doses to produce the effect of the original dose.
UF Tolerance (Drug)
R Drug Sensitivity 1973
↓ Drugs 1967
↓ Side Effects (Drug) 1973

Drug Trafficking
Use Illegal Drug Distribution

Drug Usage 1971
PN 9835 **SC** 15400
SN Act, amount, or mode of using any type of drug. Applies only to humans and should be used when neither abuse nor addiction are the subject matter, regardless of the legality of the particular drug.
N ↓ Alcohol Drinking Patterns 1967
↓ Drug Abuse 1973
Intravenous Drug Usage 1994
Marijuana Usage 1973
↓ Tobacco Smoking 1967
R ↓ Addiction 1973
Craving 1997
Driving Under the Influence 1988
↓ Drug Abstinence 1994
↓ Drug Legalization 1997
Drug Overdoses 1978
Drug Self Administration 2004
Drug Usage Screening 1988
↓ Drugs 1967
Illegal Drug Distribution 1997
Needle Sharing 1994

Drug Usage Attitudes 1973
PN 1574 **SC** 15410
B Attitudes 1967
N Alcohol Drinking Attitudes 1973
R Health Attitudes 1985
Marijuana Legalization 1973

Drug Usage Screening 1988
PN 623 **SC** 15415
SN Procedures used to measure or detect prevalence of drug use through analysis of blood, urine, or other body fluids. Not used for measuring the clinical efficacy of therapeutic drugs.
UF Drug Testing
B Screening 1982
R Blood Alcohol Concentration 1994
↓ Drug Abuse 1973
↓ Drug Dependency 1973
↓ Drug Rehabilitation 1973
↓ Drug Usage 1971
↓ Drugs 1967
↓ Health Screening 1997
↓ Medical Diagnosis 1973
Physical Examination 1988
Urinalysis 1973

Drug Withdrawal 1973
PN 4153 **SC** 15420
SN Processes and symptomatic effects resulting from abstinence from a chemical agent or medication. Used for human or animal populations.
HN In 1982, this term replaced the discontinued term DRUG WITHDRAWAL EFFECTS. In 2000, DRUG WITHDRAWAL EFFECTS was removed from all records containing it and replaced with DRUG WITHDRAWAL.
UF Drug Withdrawal Effects
Withdrawal (Drug)
N Alcohol Withdrawal 1994
Nicotine Withdrawal 1997
R Detoxification 1973
↓ Drug Abstinence 1994
↓ Drug Addiction 1967

Drug Withdrawal Effects
HN Term was discontinued in 1982. In 2000, the term was removed from all records containing it, and replaced with DRUG WITHDRAWAL, its postable counterpart.
Use Drug Withdrawal

Drugs 1967
PN 21287 **SC** 15440
SN Conceptually broad term referring to any substance other than food administered for experimental or treatment purposes. Use specific drug classes or names if possible.
HN In 1982, this term replaced the discontinued term DRUG EFFECTS, and in 1997 it replaced CARDIOTONIC DRUGS and NARCOANALYTIC DRUGS. In 2000, these terms were removed from all records containing them, and replaced with DRUGS.
UF Cardiotonic Drugs
Drug Effects
Narcoanalytic Drugs
Psychoactive Drugs
Psychotropic Drugs
N ↓ Adrenergic Blocking Drugs 1973
↓ Adrenergic Drugs 1973
↓ Alcohols 1967
↓ Alkaloids 1973
↓ Amines 1973
↓ Analgesic Drugs 1973
↓ Anesthetic Drugs 1973
↓ Anti Inflammatory Drugs 1982
Antiandrogens 1982
↓ Antibiotics 1973
↓ Anticoagulant Drugs 1973
↓ Anticonvulsive Drugs 1973
↓ Antidepressant Drugs 1971
↓ Antiemetic Drugs 1973
Antiestrogens 1982
↓ Antihistaminic Drugs 1973
↓ Antihypertensive Drugs 1973
Antineoplastic Drugs 1982
↓ Antispasmodic Drugs 1973
↓ Antitremor Drugs 1973
↓ Antitubercular Drugs 1973
↓ Antiviral Drugs 1994
↓ Appetite Depressing Drugs 1973
↓ Barbiturates 1967
↓ Benzodiazepines 1978
Bromides 1973
↓ Cannabis 1973
Channel Blockers 1991
↓ Cholinergic Blocking Drugs 1973
↓ Cholinergic Drugs 1973
↓ Cholinomimetic Drugs 1973
↓ CNS Affecting Drugs 1973

Drugs — (cont'd)
↓ Diuretics 1973
↓ Dopamine Agonists 1985
↓ Emetic Drugs 1973
↓ Enzyme Inhibitors 1985
↓ Enzymes 1973
↓ Ergot Derivatives 1973
↓ Ganglion Blocking Drugs 1973
↓ Hallucinogenic Drugs 1967
↓ Heart Rate Affecting Drugs 1973
↓ Hypnotic Drugs 1973
↓ Muscle Relaxing Drugs 1973
↓ Narcotic Agonists 1988
↓ Narcotic Antagonists 1973
↓ Narcotic Drugs 1973
↓ Neurotransmitter Uptake Inhibitors 2007
Nonprescription Drugs 1991
↓ Nootropic Drugs 1991
Prescription Drugs 1991
↓ Psychotomimetic Drugs 1973
↓ Respiration Stimulating Drugs 1973
↓ Sedatives 1973
Serotonin Agonists 1988
↓ Serotonin Antagonists 1973
↓ Steroids 1973
↓ Sympatholytic Drugs 1973
↓ Sympathomimetic Drugs 1973
↓ Tranquilizing Drugs 1967
↓ Vasoconstrictor Drugs 1973
↓ Vasodilator Drugs 1973
R ↓ Acids 1973
Antibodies 1973
Bioavailability 1991
Carcinogens 1973
↓ Drug Abuse 1973
↓ Drug Administration Methods 1973
Drug Discrimination 1985
↓ Drug Dosages 1973
Drug Education 1973
Drug Interactions 1982
↓ Drug Laws 1973
↓ Drug Rehabilitation 1973
↓ Drug Therapy 1967
Drug Tolerance 1973
↓ Drug Usage 1971
Drug Usage Screening 1988
↓ Hormones 1967
↓ Insecticides 1973
↓ Peptides 1973
Placebo 1973
Prenatal Exposure 1991
↓ Prescribing (Drugs) 1991
↓ Proteins 1973
Self Medication 1991
↓ Side Effects (Drug) 1973
Teratogens 1988
↓ Toxicity 1973
↓ Vitamins 1973

Drunk Driving
Use Driving Under the Influence

Drunkenness
Use Alcohol Intoxication

DSM
Use Diagnostic and Statistical Manual

Dual Careers 1982
PN 947 **SC** 15455
SN Situation in which both partners or spouses in a family pursue careers.

Dual Careers — (cont'd)
R ↓ Family 1967
↓ Family Structure 1973
Family Work Relationship 1997
Working Women 1978

Dual Diagnosis 1991
PN 1162 **SC** 15457
SN Diagnosis based on the coexistence of two or more DSM disorders.
R Comorbidity 1991
↓ Diagnosis 1967
Differential Diagnosis 1967
↓ Psychodiagnostic Typologies 1967

Dual Relationships 2003
PN 145 **SC** 15458
SN Occurs when individuals in a helping profession take on more than one role with their client, student, or patient.
HN This term was introduced in June 2003. Relevant records were re-indexed with this term. The posting note reflects the number of records that were re-indexed.
R ↓ Interpersonal Interaction 1967
Professional Client Sexual Relations 1994
Professional Ethics 1973
↓ Therapeutic Processes 1978

Dual Reuptake Inhibitors
Use Serotonin Norepinephrine Reuptake Inhibitors

Dual Task Performance 2006
PN 113 **SC** 15459
SN Experimental procedure in which participants are asked to perform two tasks simultaneously. Used only when a dual task paradigm is the focus of the study.
HN This term was introduced in May 2006. Relevant records were re-indexed with this term. The posting note reflects the number of records that were re-indexed.
UF Concurrent Tasks
Dual Task Procedure
R Task Complexity 1973

Dual Task Procedure
Use Dual Task Performance

Dualism 1973
PN 1541 **SC** 15460
SN Theory viewing mind and body as two separate and irreducible entities.
UF Mind Body
B Philosophies 1967
R Mind 1991

Duchennes Disease
Use Muscular Disorders

Ducks 1973
PN 364 **SC** 15480
B Birds 1967

Duodenum
Use Intestines

Duration (Response)
Use Response Duration

Duration (Stimulus)
Use Stimulus Duration

Duty to Warn 2001
PN 79 **SC** 15525
SN A health care professional's legal and ethical obligation to warn third parties of danger, violence, or the possibility of contracting a serious illness.
R ↓ Abuse Reporting 1997
Accountability 1988
Informants 1988
Informed Consent 1985
Privileged Communication 1973
Professional Ethics 1973
Professional Liability 1985
↓ Professional Standards 1973

Dwarfism (Pituitary)
Use Hypopituitarism

Dyads 1973
PN 2937 **SC** 15540
B Social Groups 1973
R Couples 1982

Dying
Use Death and Dying

Dying Patients
Use Terminally Ill Patients

Dynamics (Group)
Use Group Dynamics

Dynorphins 1985
PN 164 **SC** 15575
B Endogenous Opiates 1985
Pituitary Hormones 1973

Dysarthria 1973
PN 420 **SC** 15580
SN Articulation disorder resulting from central nervous system disease, especially brain damage.
B Articulation Disorders 1973
Central Nervous System Disorders 1973
R Muscular Dystrophy 1973
↓ Paralysis 1973

Dyscalculia
Use Acalculia

Dysfunctional Family 1991
PN 624 **SC** 15590
SN A family system in which relationships or communication are impaired.
R Codependency 1991
Double Bind Interaction 1973
↓ Family 1967
↓ Family Relations 1967
↓ Family Structure 1973
Marital Conflict 1973
Schizophrenogenic Family 1967

Dyskinesia 1973
PN 893 **SC** 15600
SN Abnormal involuntary motor processes that occur due to underlying disease processes.
B Movement Disorders 1985
Symptoms 1967
N Bradykinesia 2001
Myoclonus 2006
Tardive Dyskinesia 1988

Dyskinesia — (cont'd)
R ↓ Neuromuscular Disorders 1973

Dyslexia 1973
PN 3497 **SC** 15610
SN Reading disorder involving an inability to understand what is read. Less severe than alexia.
B Alexia 1982
Learning Disabilities 1973
Reading Disabilities 1967
R Educational Diagnosis 1978
↓ Reading 1967

Dysmenorrhea 1973
PN 125 **SC** 15620
SN Difficult and painful menstruation.
B Menstrual Disorders 1973

Dysmetria
Use Ataxia

Dysmorphophobia
HN In 2000, the term was discontinued and removed from all records containing it. DYSMORPHOPHOBIA was replaced with BODY DYSMORPHIC DISORDER, its postable counterpart.
Use Body Dysmorphic Disorder

Dyspareunia 1973
PN 117 **SC** 15650
SN A woman's sensation of painful sexual intercourse.
B Sexual Function Disturbances 1973
Sexual Intercourse (Human) 1973
R Female Sexual Dysfunction 2005
Vaginismus 1973

Dysphagia 2003
PN 113 **SC** 15654
SN Difficulty swallowing.
HN This term was introduced in June 2003. Relevant records were re-indexed with this term. The posting note reflects the number of records that were re-indexed.
R Esophagus 1973
Pharyngeal Disorders 1973
Swallowing 1988

Dysphasia 1978
PN 286 **SC** 15655
SN Impairment of language comprehension, formulation, or use due to brain damage. Used only for partial impairments.
B Aphasia 1967
N ↓ Alexia 1982

Dysphonia 1973
PN 352 **SC** 15660
SN Any speech disorder involving problems of voice quality, pitch, or intensity.
UF Voice Disorders
B Speech Disorders 1967
R Laryngeal Disorders 1973

Dysphoria
Use Major Depression

Dyspnea 1973
PN 132 **SC** 15680
SN Difficulty in breathing which may or may not have an organic cause.
B Respiratory Distress 1973
Respiratory Tract Disorders 1973

Dyspnea — (cont'd)
Symptoms 1967
N Asthma 1967
R ↓ Cardiovascular Disorders 1967
↓ Lung Disorders 1973
↓ Somatoform Disorders 2001

Dyspraxia
Use Movement Disorders

Dysthymia
Use Dysthymic Disorder

Dysthymic Disorder 1988
PN 1163 **SC** 15693
SN Chronic affective disorder characterized by either relatively mild depressive symptoms or marked loss of pleasure in usual activities.
HN Consider DEPRESSION (EMOTION) to access references prior to 1988.
UF Dysthymia
B Major Depression 1988
R Anhedonia 1985

Dystonia
Use Muscular Disorders

Dystrophy (Muscular)
Use Muscular Dystrophy

E-Commerce
Use Electronic Commerce

E-Tailing
Use Electronic Retailing

E-Therapy
Use Online Therapy

Eagerness
Use Enthusiasm

Ear (Anatomy) 1967
PN 601 **SC** 15720
B Sense Organs 1973
N External Ear 1973
↓ Labyrinth (Anatomy) 1973
Middle Ear 1973
↓ Vestibular Apparatus 1967
R ↓ Ear Disorders 1973

Ear Canal
Use External Ear

Ear Disorders 1973
PN 382 **SC** 15740
SN Disorders of the external, middle, or inner ear. Use HEARING DISORDERS for pathology involving auditory neural pathways beyond the inner ear.
HN In 1997, this term replaced the discontinued term OTOSCLEROSIS. In 2000, OTOSCLEROSIS was removed from all records and replaced with EAR DISORDERS.
UF Otosclerosis
B Sense Organ Disorders 1973
N ↓ Labyrinth Disorders 1973
Tinnitus 1973
R ↓ Auditory Perception 1967
↓ Ear (Anatomy) 1967
↓ Hearing Disorders 1982

Ear Ossicles
Use Middle Ear

Early Childhood Development 1973
PN 4762 **SC** 15770
SN Process of physical, cognitive, personality, and psychosocial growth occurring from birth through age 5. Use a more specific term if possible.
B Childhood Development 1967
N ↓ Infant Development 1973
R Early Experience 1967
Early Memories 1985
↓ Physical Development 1973
↓ Psychogenesis 1973

Early Experience 1967
PN 9856 **SC** 15780
SN Any occurrences early in an individual's life. Used for human or animal populations.
B Experiences (Events) 1973
R Age Regression (Hypnotic) 1988
Anniversary Events 1994
Autobiographical Memory 1994
↓ Early Childhood Development 1973
Early Memories 1985
Enactments 1997
Life Review 1991

Early Infantile Autism
HN In August 2005, this term was discontinued and removed from all records containing it, and was replaced with AUTISM, its postable counterpart.
Use Autism

Early Intervention 1982
PN 5114 **SC** 15793
SN Action taken utilizing medical, family, school, social, or mental health resources and aimed at infants and children at risk for, or in the early stages of mental, physical, learning, or other disorders.
B Intervention 2003
R Drug Abuse Prevention 1994
↓ Prenatal Care 1991
↓ Prevention 1973
Primary Mental Health Prevention 1973
School Based Intervention 2003
Special Education 1967
Special Needs 1994
↓ Treatment 1967

Early Memories 1985
PN 1190 **SC** 15796
SN Memories of events that occurred early in an individual's life.
UF Childhood Memories
B Memory 1967
R Age Regression (Hypnotic) 1988
Anniversary Events 1994
Autobiographical Memory 1994
↓ Early Childhood Development 1973
Early Experience 1967
False Memory 1997
Life Review 1991
Reminiscence 1985
Repressed Memory 1997

Earthworms 1973
PN 38 **SC** 15800
B Worms 1967

Eating
HN In 2000, the term was discontinued and removed from all records containing it, and replaced with INGESTION, its postable counterpart. In 2004, EATING BEHAVIOR replaced INGESTION as the postable counterpart to EATING. Consider using INGESTION to access references from 1967 to June 2004.
Use Eating Behavior

Eating Attitudes 1994
PN 913 **SC** 15823
B Attitudes 1967
R ↓ Appetite 1973
↓ Eating Behavior 2004
Food Preferences 1973
Obesity (Attitudes Toward) 1997

Eating Behavior 2004
PN 2260 **SC** 15824
SN Used for human populations only.
HN In June 2004, this term was created to replace the discontinued term FEEDING PRACTICES. FEEDING PRACTICES was removed from all records containing it and replaced with EATING BEHAVIOR.
UF Eating
Eating Habits
Eating Patterns
Feeding Practices
B Behavior 1967
N Binge Eating 1991
Bottle Feeding 1973
Breast Feeding 1973
Dietary Restraint 1994
Weaning 1973
R ↓ Appetite 1973
Diets 1978
Eating Attitudes 1994
↓ Eating Disorders 1997
Food Intake 1967
Mealtimes 2004

Eating Disorders 1997
PN 6459 **SC** 15825
HN In 1997, this term was created to replace the discontinued term APPETITE DISORDERS. In 2000, APPETITE DISORDERS was removed from all records and replaced with EATING DISORDERS.
UF Appetite Disorders
B Mental Disorders 1967
N Anorexia Nervosa 1973
Bulimia 1985
Hyperphagia 1973
Kleine Levin Syndrome 2001
Pica 1973
Purging (Eating Disorders) 2003
R Aphagia 1973
↓ Appetite 1973
Binge Eating 1991
Coprophagia 2001
↓ Eating Behavior 2004
Nausea 1973
↓ Nutritional Deficiencies 1973
↓ Physical Disorders 1997
Rumination (Eating) 2001
↓ Symptoms 1967
↓ Underweight 1973

Eating Habits
Use Eating Behavior

Eating Patterns
HN This term was discontinued in 1982.
Use Eating Behavior

Echinodermata 1973
PN 45 **SC** 15840
UF Starfish
B Invertebrates 1973

Echoencephalography 1973
PN 9 **SC** 15850
SN A noninvasive diagnostic procedure that uses ultrasound to study anatomical structures and pathological processes in the brain.
B Encephalography 1973
Medical Diagnosis 1973

Echolalia 1973
PN 119 **SC** 15870
B Language Disorders 1982
R Tourette Syndrome 2006

Echolocation 1973
PN 263 **SC** 15880
R ↓ Animal Ethology 1967
↓ Animal Vocalizations 1973

Eclectic Psychology
Use Theoretical Orientation

Eclectic Psychotherapy 1994
PN 195 **SC** 15887
SN An approach to psychotherapy that utilizes various therapeutic techniques without concern for theoretical orientation.
B Psychotherapy 1967
R Integrative Psychotherapy 2003
Interdisciplinary Treatment Approach 1973
Multimodal Treatment Approach 1991

Ecological Factors 1973
PN 1478 **SC** 15890
SN Elements involved in relations between organisms and their natural environments.
N Pollution 1973
Topography 1973
R Behavioral Ecology 1997
Ecological Psychology 1994
Ecology 1973
↓ Environmental Effects 1973

Ecological Psychology 1994
PN 500 **SC** 15895
SN Branch of psychology that studies the frequency or nature of psychological processes or behavior as they occur in natural settings. Compare ENVIRONMENTAL PSYCHOLOGY.
B Psychology 1967
R Behavioral Ecology 1997
↓ Ecological Factors 1973
Environmental Psychology 1982

Ecology 1973
PN 1328 **SC** 15900
R Behavioral Ecology 1997
Conservation (Ecological Behavior) 1978
↓ Ecological Factors 1973
↓ Environment 1967
Environmental Attitudes 1978
Environmental Education 1994
Pollution 1973

Economic Development 2007
PN 226 **SC** 15907
SN A process that aims to enhance the well-being of inhabitants or regions, countries, or communities through a number of related goals, including wealth

Economic Development — (cont'd)
creation, poverty reduction, better education, improved health, effective resource utilization, and a cleaner environment.
HN This term was introduced in April 2007. Relevant records were re-indexed with this term. The posting note reflects the number of records that were re-indexed.
R Community Development 1997
Developing Countries 1985
↓ Economy 1973
Industrialization 1973
Poverty Areas 1973

Economic Security 2007
PN 34 **SC** 15908
SN The protection of an individual or entity's economic status, and the prediction of future cash-flow or economic well-being.
HN This term was introduced in April 2007. Relevant records were re-indexed with this term. The posting note reflects the number of records that were re-indexed.
UF Financial Security
R Income (Economic) 1973
Job Security 1978
Salaries 1973
↓ Socioeconomic Status 1967

Economically Disadvantaged
Use Disadvantaged

Economics 1985
PN 5555 **SC** 15915
SN Social science dealing with the production, distribution, and consumption of goods and services. Used for the discipline or economic factors themselves.
B Social Sciences 1967
N Behavioral Economics 2003
Evolutionary Economics 2007
Health Care Economics 2007
Pharmacoeconomics 2007
R Budgets 1997
↓ Business Investments 2007
Cost Containment 1991
↓ Costs and Cost Analysis 1973
↓ Division of Labor 1988
↓ Economy 1973
Globalization 2003
Health Care Costs 1994
Human Capital 2003
Money 1967
↓ Political Economic Systems 1973
Resource Allocation 1997
Supply and Demand 2004

Economy 1973
PN 1669 **SC** 15920
N Knowledge Economy 2007
R Budgets 1997
↓ Costs and Cost Analysis 1973
Economic Development 2007
↓ Economics 1985
Globalization 2003
Money 1967
↓ Political Economic Systems 1973
Taxation 1985

ECS Therapy
Use Electroconvulsive Shock Therapy

Ecstasy (Drug)
Use Methylenedioxymethamphetamine

ECT (Therapy)
Use Electroconvulsive Shock Therapy

Eczema 1973
PN 58 **SC** 15950
B Dermatitis 1973
R Allergic Skin Disorders 1973

Educable Mentally Retarded
HN In 2000, EDUCABLE MENTALLY RETARDED was discontinued, and removed from all records containing it. The term was replaced with MILD MENTAL RETARDATION, its postable counterpart.
Use Mild Mental Retardation

Education 1967
PN 12864 **SC** 16000
SN Conceptually broad term referring to the process of imparting or obtaining knowledge, skills, and values. Use a more specific term if possible.
UF Educational Process
N ↓ Adult Education 1973
Bilingual Education 1978
Client Education 1985
Consumer Education 2007
Counselor Education 1973
↓ Curriculum 1967
Death Education 1982
Distance Education 2003
Elementary Education 1973
↓ Family Life Education 1997
High School Education 2003
↓ Higher Education 1973
Middle School Education 1985
Multicultural Education 1988
↓ Nontraditional Education 1982
Nursing Education 1973
Paraprofessional Education 1973
↓ Personnel Training 1967
Preschool Education 1973
Private School Education 1973
Public School Education 1973
Religious Education 1973
↓ Remedial Education 1985
Secondary Education 1973
Social Work Education 1973
Special Education 1967
↓ Teacher Education 1967
R Ability Grouping 1973
↓ Academic Achievement 1967
Academic Aptitude 1973
Accreditation (Education Personnel) 1973
Athletic Training 1991
Boards of Education 1978
Classroom Behavior Modification 1973
Classroom Discipline 1973
Coeducation 1973
↓ Dropouts 1973
Educational Administration 1967
Educational Aspirations 1973
↓ Educational Background 1967
Educational Counseling 1967
Educational Degrees 1973
Educational Diagnosis 1978
Educational Financial Assistance 1973
Educational Incentives 1973
↓ Educational Laboratories 1973
↓ Educational Measurement 1967
Educational Objectives 1978
↓ Educational Personnel 1973
Educational Placement 1978
Educational Program Accreditation 1994
↓ Educational Programs 1973

Education — (cont'd)
↓ Educational Psychology 1967
Educational Quality 1997
Educational Reform 1997
Educational Television 1967
Environmental Education 1994
Equal Education 1978
↓ Extracurricular Activities 1973
Grade Level 1994
Home Schooling 1994
Mainstreaming (Educational) 1978
Psychoeducation 1994
Questioning 1982
School Adjustment 1967
School Attendance 1973
School Counseling 1982
↓ School Dropouts 1967
↓ School Enrollment 1973
↓ School Environment 1973
↓ School Facilities 1973
School Graduation 1991
School Integration 1982
School Learning 1967
School Readiness 1973
School to Work Transition 1994
School Transition 1997
School Truancy 1973
↓ Schools 1967
Student Admission Criteria 1973
Student Attitudes 1967
↓ Student Characteristics 1982
Student Personnel Services 1978
Student Records 1978
↓ Students 1967
Study Habits 1973
↓ Teacher Characteristics 1973
Teacher Student Interaction 1973
Teacher Tenure 1973
↓ Teaching 1967
↓ Teaching Methods 1967
Theories of Education 1973
↓ Training 2006

Education Students 1982
PN 624 **SC** 15995
SN Students enrolled in a school or department of education.
B College Students 1967
R Preservice Teachers 1982
Student Teachers 1973
↓ Teacher Education 1967

Educational Administration 1967
PN 3028 **SC** 16010
UF School Administration
School Organization
B Management 1967
R Boards of Education 1978
Decentralization 1978
↓ Education 1967
Educational Reform 1997

Educational Administrators
Use School Administrators

Educational Aspirations 1973
PN 1218 **SC** 16020
SN Personal desire for achievement in a certain educational field or to a certain level or degree.
B Aspirations 1967
R Academic Specialization 1973
↓ Education 1967
Educational Objectives 1978

Educational Attainment Level 1997
PN 1934 **SC** 16025
SN Completion of a course of study or reaching a specific educational level.
UF Attainment Level (Education)
B Educational Background 1967
R ↓ Academic Achievement 1967
Educational Degrees 1973
School Graduation 1991
School to Work Transition 1994

Educational Audiovisual Aids 1973
PN 379 **SC** 16030
UF Audiovisual Aids (Educational)
B Audiovisual Communications Media 1973
Instructional Media 1967
R ↓ Audiovisual Instruction 1973
Educational Television 1967
Televised Instruction 1973
Videotape Instruction 1973

Educational Background 1967
PN 4420 **SC** 16040
N Educational Attainment Level 1997
Parent Educational Background 1973
R Biographical Data 1978
↓ Education 1967
School Leavers 1988

Educational Background (Parents)
Use Parent Educational Background

Educational Counseling 1967
PN 2823 **SC** 16060
SN Assistance offered to school or college students on school program planning, course selection, or academic specialization. Compare SCHOOL COUNSELING.
UF Educational Guidance
Guidance (Educational)
B Counseling 1967
R ↓ Education 1967
Occupational Guidance 1967
Student Personnel Services 1978

Educational Degrees 1973
PN 994 **SC** 16070
UF College Degrees
Degrees (Educational)
Graduate Degrees
Undergraduate Degrees
R College Graduates 1982
↓ Education 1967
Educational Attainment Level 1997
Educational Program Accreditation 1994
High School Graduates 1978
↓ Higher Education 1973
School Graduation 1991

Educational Diagnosis 1978
PN 2897 **SC** 16075
SN Identification of cognitive, perceptual, emotional, and other factors which influence academic performance or school adjustment, usually for such purposes as placement of students in curricula or programs suited to their needs, and referral.
B Diagnosis 1967
R Differential Diagnosis 1967
Dyslexia 1973
↓ Education 1967
↓ Educational Measurement 1967
Educational Placement 1978
↓ Learning Disabilities 1973

Educational Diagnosis — (cont'd)
↓ Learning Disorders 1967
↓ Psychodiagnosis 1967
Psychological Report 1988
↓ Reading Disabilities 1967
Woodcock Johnson Psychoeducational Battery 2001

Educational Environment
Use School Environment

Educational Field Trips 1973
PN 91 **SC** 16080
UF Field Trips (Educational)
B Teaching Methods 1967
R Curricular Field Experience 1982
↓ Experiential Learning 1997

Educational Financial Assistance 1973
PN 333 **SC** 16090
UF Financial Assistance (Educational)
Scholarships
School Federal Aid
School Financial Assistance
Stipends
R ↓ Education 1967
Funding 1988
Student Personnel Services 1978

Educational Guidance
Use Educational Counseling

Educational Incentives 1973
PN 142 **SC** 16120
SN Any type of incentive used or experienced in a school, classroom, or other educational context.
B Incentives 1967
Motivation 1967
R ↓ Education 1967

Educational Inequality
Use Equal Education

Educational Intervention
Use School Based Intervention

Educational Laboratories 1973
PN 209 **SC** 16130
UF Laboratories (Educational)
B School Facilities 1973
N Language Laboratories 1973
R ↓ Education 1967

Educational Measurement 1967
PN 7383 **SC** 16140
SN Practices, procedures, methods, and tests used in the assessment of student characteristics or performance, such as academic achievement and school adjustment.
B Testing 1967
N Curriculum Based Assessment 1994
↓ Entrance Examinations 1973
Grading (Educational) 1973
Minimum Competency Tests 1985
R ↓ Education 1967
Educational Diagnosis 1978
↓ Screening 1982

Educational Objectives 1978
PN 1823 **SC** 16145
SN Specific educational goals toward which one's efforts are directed, or goals proposed or established by educational authorities.

Educational Objectives — (cont'd)
UF Course Objectives
Instructional Objectives
B Goals 1967
R ↓ Curriculum 1967
↓ Education 1967
Educational Aspirations 1973
Educational Quality 1997
Educational Reform 1997
Mastery Learning 1985

Educational Personnel 1973
PN 3951 **SC** 16150
UF Faculty
B Professional Personnel 1978
N ↓ School Administrators 1973
School Counselors 1973
School Nurses 1973
Teacher Aides 1973
↓ Teachers 1967
R ↓ Education 1967
↓ Educational Psychologists 1973
↓ Mental Health Personnel 1967
Missionaries 1973
Professional Supervision 1988
Speech Therapists 1973

Educational Placement 1978
PN 2074 **SC** 16155
SN Assignment of students to classes, programs, or schools according to their abilities and readiness.
UF Placement (Educational)
R Ability Grouping 1973
↓ Education 1967
Educational Diagnosis 1978
Grade Level 1994
↓ Mainstreaming 1991
Mainstreaming (Educational) 1978
Remedial Reading 1973
↓ Screening 1982
Special Education 1967

Educational Process
Use Education

Educational Program Accreditation 1994
PN 247 **SC** 16165
SN Recognition and approval of educational programs or institution's maintenance of standards to qualify graduates for professional practice or admission to higher or more specialized educational institutions.
UF Accreditation (Educational Programs)
School Accreditation
R ↓ Curriculum 1967
↓ Education 1967
Educational Degrees 1973
↓ Educational Programs 1973
Educational Quality 1997
Educational Standards 2007
↓ Graduate Psychology Education 1967
↓ Higher Education 1973
↓ Psychology Education 1978

Educational Program Evaluation 1973
PN 3882 **SC** 16170
SN Techniques, materials, or process of determining the worth or effectiveness of an educational program in relation to its goals or other criteria.
UF Program Evaluation (Educational)
B Program Evaluation 1985
R Course Evaluation 1978
↓ Educational Programs 1973
Educational Quality 1997

Educational Program Evaluation — (cont'd)
Educational Standards 2007

Educational Program Planning 1973
PN 1561 SC 16180
UF Program Planning (Educational)
B Program Development 1991
R Curriculum Development 1973
↓ Educational Programs 1973

Educational Programs 1973
PN 10000 SC 16190
UF Work Study Programs
N Individual Education Programs 2006
Literacy Programs 1997
Project Follow Through 1973
Project Head Start 1973
Special Education 1967
Study Abroad 2007
Upward Bound 1973
R After School Programs 2003
Charter Schools 2006
Compensatory Education 1973
Cooperative Education 1982
Curricular Field Experience 1982
↓ Education 1967
Educational Program Accreditation 1994
Educational Program Evaluation 1973
Educational Program Planning 1973
Educational Reform 1997
↓ Internship Programs 2006
Multicultural Education 1988
↓ Nontraditional Education 1982
↓ Program Development 1991
School Based Intervention 2003

Educational Psychologists 1973
PN 637 SC 16200
SN Psychologists conducting research and formulating policies in areas of diagnosis and measurement, school adjustment, school learning, and special education.
B Psychologists 1967
N School Psychologists 1973
R ↓ Educational Personnel 1973

Educational Psychology 1967
PN 3092 SC 16210
SN Branch of psychology that emphasizes the application of psychological theories and research findings to educational processes, especially in the areas of learning and motivation.
B Applied Psychology 1973
N School Psychology 1973
R ↓ Education 1967

Educational Quality 1997
PN 596 SC 16205
UF Quality of Education
R Accreditation (Education Personnel) 1973
Course Evaluation 1978
↓ Education 1967
Educational Objectives 1978
Educational Program Accreditation 1994
Educational Program Evaluation 1973
Educational Reform 1997
Educational Standards 2007
Equal Education 1978
Teacher Effectiveness Evaluation 1978

Educational Reform 1997
PN 1629 SC 16217
R ↓ Education 1967
Educational Administration 1967
Educational Objectives 1978
↓ Educational Programs 1973
Educational Quality 1997
↓ Policy Making 1988

Educational Standards 2007
PN 97 SC 16218
SN Expected levels of proficiency in academic knowledge and performance for a particular developmental stage or grade level. Standards can be set at the local, state, or federal levels.
HN This term was introduced in April 2007. Relevant records were re-indexed with this term. The posting note reflects the number of records that were re-indexed.
UF Academic Standards
R ↓ Academic Achievement 1967
↓ Curriculum 1967
Educational Program Accreditation 1994
Educational Program Evaluation 1973
Educational Quality 1997
Standardized Tests 1985

Educational Supervision
Use Professional Supervision

Educational Television 1967
PN 265 SC 16220
B Television 1967
R ↓ Education 1967
Educational Audiovisual Aids 1973
Televised Instruction 1973

Educational Theory
Use Theories of Education

Educational Therapy 1997
PN 59 SC 16225
HN Use SCHOOL COUNSELING to access references from 1982-1996.
R Art Therapy 1973
Music Therapy 1973
Psychoeducation 1994
↓ Psychotherapy 1967
↓ Remedial Education 1985
School Counseling 1982
Special Education 1967
↓ Teaching Methods 1967

Educational Toys 1973
PN 47 SC 16230
B Toys 1973

Edwards Personal Preference Schedule 1967
PN 123 SC 16240
B Nonprojective Personality Measures 1973

Edwards Social Desirability Scale 1973
PN 14 SC 16260
B Nonprojective Personality Measures 1973

EEG (Electrophysiology)
Use Electroencephalography

EEG Biofeedback
Use Neurofeedback

Effect Size (Statistical) 1985
PN 600 SC 16272
SN A statistical estimate that represents the magnitude of a statistically significant result.
UF Magnitude of Effect (Statistical)
B Statistical Analysis 1967
R Confidence Limits (Statistics) 1973
Statistical Significance 1973

Efferent Pathways 1982
PN 500 SC 16275
SN Collections of fibers that typically carry neural impulses away from central nervous system connections toward muscular and glandular innervations.
UF Motor Pathways
B Neural Pathways 1982
Parasympathetic Nervous System 1973
N Extrapyramidal Tracts 1973
Pyramidal Tracts 1973
R ↓ Afferent Pathways 1982
Motor Neurons 1973
↓ Motor Processes 1967

Efficacy Expectations
Use Self Efficacy

Efficiency (Employee)
Use Employee Efficiency

Effort
Use Energy Expenditure

Egalitarianism 1985
PN 241 SC 16287
B Personality Traits 1967
R Authoritarianism 1967
↓ Equity (Social) 1978
Resource Allocation 1997

Ego 1967
PN 4737 SC 16290
B Psychoanalytic Personality Factors 1973
R ↓ Ego Development 1991
Ego Identity 1991

Ego Development 1991
PN 879 SC 16294
SN Gradual development of a part of the id into the ego or an awareness of a child that he or she is a real distinct and separate entity.
B Personality Development 1967
N Ego Identity 1991
R Ego 1967
↓ Psychoanalytic Theory 1967

Ego Identity 1991
PN 613 SC 16297
SN The experience of the self as a recognizable entity resulting from one's ego ideal, behavior and social roles, and adjustments to reality.
B Ego Development 1991
R Ego 1967
Erikson (Erik) 1991
Identity Formation 2004
↓ Personality Development 1967
↓ Self Concept 1967

Egocentrism 1978
PN 801 SC 16300
SN Self-centered preoccupation or concern regarding one's own needs, wishes, desires, or preferences and usually accompanied by a disregard for the con-

Egocentrism — (cont'd)
cerns of others. Also, in cognitive development, the inclination to believe that others maintain the same experiential perspective as oneself.
HN Use EGOCENTRISM to access references to role taking or perspective taking from 1978-1981.
R Agreeableness 1997
↓ Cognitive Development 1973
Narcissism 1967
↓ Personality 1967
↓ Personality Traits 1967
Role Taking 1982

Egotism 1973
PN 193 **SC** 16310
B Personality Traits 1967
R Emotional Superiority 1973
Grandiosity 1994

Eidetic Imagery 1973
PN 155 **SC** 16320
SN Clear and detailed memory for objects or events perceived, usually visually.
UF Photographic Memory
B Memory 1967
R Episodic Memory 1988
↓ Spatial Memory 1988
↓ Visual Memory 1994

Ejaculation
Use Male Orgasm

EKG (Electrophysiology)
Use Electrocardiography

Elavil
Use Amitriptyline

Elbow (Anatomy) 1973
PN 111 **SC** 16360
B Joints (Anatomy) 1973
R Arm (Anatomy) 1973

Elder Abuse 1988
PN 666 **SC** 16363
SN Abuse or neglect of elderly persons in a family, institutional, or other setting.
B Antisocial Behavior 1971
R ↓ Abuse Reporting 1997
Domestic Violence 2006
Emotional Abuse 1991
Patient Abuse 1991
Physical Abuse 1991
↓ Sexual Abuse 1988
Verbal Abuse 2003

Elder Care 1994
PN 1519 **SC** 16364
SN Informal or formal support systems or programs for the care of the elderly or assistance to the families who have responsibilities for their care.
R Adult Day Care 1997
Aging in Place 2007
Caregiver Burden 1994
Caregivers 1988
Employee Assistance Programs 1985
↓ Employee Benefits 1973
Home Care 1985
Home Care Personnel 1997
Home Visiting Programs 1973
Homebound 1988
Protective Services 1997

Elected Government Officials
Use Government Personnel

Elections (Political)
Use Political Elections

Elective Abortion
Use Induced Abortion

Elective Mutism 1973
PN 296 **SC** 16390
UF Selective Mutism
B Mental Disorders 1967
Mutism 1973

Electra Complex 1973
PN 25 **SC** 16400
B Psychoanalytic Personality Factors 1973

Electric Fishes 1973
PN 148 **SC** 16410
B Fishes 1967

Electrical Activity 1967
PN 10561 **SC** 16420
SN Electrically measured responses or response patterns, usually of individual units (i.e., cells) or groups of cells, in any part of the nervous system. Includes neural or neuron impulses; neural depolarization or hyperpolarization; spike, resting, action, generator, graded, presynaptic, or postsynaptic potentials. Compare ELECTROPHYSIOLOGY.
B Electrophysiology 1973
N Alpha Rhythm 1973
Delta Rhythm 1973
↓ Evoked Potentials 1967
Kindling 1985
Postactivation Potentials 1985
Theta Rhythm 1973
R Electrocardiography 1967
↓ Electroencephalography 1967
Polysomnography 2003

Electrical Brain Stimulation 1973
PN 4021 **SC** 16430
B Brain Stimulation 1967
Electrical Stimulation 1973
Electrophysiology 1973
Stereotaxic Techniques 1973
R ↓ Evoked Potentials 1967
Kindling 1985
Postactivation Potentials 1985
↓ Self Stimulation 1967

Electrical Injuries 1973
PN 49 **SC** 16440
B Injuries 1973
R Burns 1973
Shock 1967
↓ Wounds 1973

Electrical Stimulation 1973
PN 2350 **SC** 16460
B Stimulation 1967
N Electrical Brain Stimulation 1973
↓ Electroconvulsive Shock 1967
R Experimental Epilepsy 1978
Shock 1967

Electro Oculography 1973
PN 162 **SC** 16470
UF EOG (Electrophysiology)
B Electrophysiology 1973
Medical Diagnosis 1973
Ophthalmologic Examination 1973
R Electroretinography 1967

Electrocardiography 1967
PN 415 **SC** 16480
UF EKG (Electrophysiology)
B Cardiography 1973
Electrophysiology 1973
R ↓ Electrical Activity 1967

Electroconvulsive Shock 1967
PN 982 **SC** 16490
B Electrical Stimulation 1973
N Electroconvulsive Shock Therapy 1967
R Shock 1967

Electroconvulsive Shock Therapy 1967
PN 3627 **SC** 16500
UF ECS Therapy
ECT (Therapy)
Electroshock Therapy
B Electroconvulsive Shock 1967
Shock Therapy 1973

Electrodermal Response
Use Galvanic Skin Response

Electrodes 1967
PN 391 **SC** 16520
B Apparatus 1967
R ↓ Stimulators (Apparatus) 1973

Electroencephalography 1967
PN 10473 **SC** 16530
SN Method of graphically recording the electrical activity (potentials) of the brain by means of intracranial electrodes or electrodes applied to the scalp. Used both for the method as well as the resulting electroencephalogram or the electrophysiological activity itself.
UF EEG (Electrophysiology)
B Electrophysiology 1973
Encephalography 1973
Medical Diagnosis 1973
N Alpha Rhythm 1973
Delta Rhythm 1973
Theta Rhythm 1973
R ↓ Electrical Activity 1967
Magnetoencephalography 1985
Neurofeedback 2006
Rheoencephalography 1973

Electrolytes 1973
PN 331 **SC** 16540
UF Ions
N Calcium Ions 1973
Chloride Ions 1973
Magnesium Ions 1973
Potassium Ions 1973
Sodium Ions 1973
Zinc 1985
R ↓ Chemical Elements 1973

Electromyography 1967
PN 2600 **SC** 16550
UF EMG (Electrophysiology)
B Electrophysiology 1973
Medical Diagnosis 1973

Electronic Commerce 2006
PN 137 **SC** 16553
SN Business and commercial transactions conducted using telecommunications and the Internet. Transactions include marketing, buying, selling, and servicing products.
HN This term was introduced in May 2006. Relevant records were re-indexed with this term. The posting note reflects the number of records that were re-indexed.
UF E-Commerce
Internet Shopping
Online Shopping
Virtual Markets
B Commerce 2007
N Electronic Retailing 2007
R ↓ Consumer Behavior 1967
Internet 2001
↓ Marketing 1973
↓ Retailing 1991
Shopping 1997

Electronic Communication 2001
PN 1051 **SC** 16555
SN Conceptually broad term referring to the transmission or telecommunication of verbal or audiovisual information including, but not limited to electronic mail or email, Internet or local computer network Forums, Bulletin Boards, or other electronic messaging systems.
B Communication 1967
N Computer Mediated Communication 2003
R ↓ Automated Information Processing 1973
↓ Communication Systems 1973
↓ Communications Media 1973
↓ Computer Applications 1973
↓ Computer Peripheral Devices 1985
Computer Searching 1991
Databases 1991
Distance Education 2003
Groupware 2003
Information 1967
↓ Information Systems 1991
Internet 2001
Messages 1973
↓ Technology 1973
Virtual Teams 2007

Electronic Mail
Use Computer Mediated Communication

Electronic Retailing 2007
PN 20 **SC** 16558
SN The sale of retail goods via the Internet.
HN This term was introduced in April 2007. Relevant records were re-indexed with this term. The posting note reflects the number of records that were re-indexed.
UF E-Tailing
Online Retailing
B Electronic Commerce 2006
Retailing 1991
R Internet 2001
↓ Marketing 1973
Shopping 1997

Electronystagmography 1973
PN 9 **SC** 16560
B Electrophysiology 1973
Medical Diagnosis 1973

Electrophysiology 1973
PN 2803 **SC** 16570
SN Branch of physiology concerned with the study of electrical phenomena within the living organism (i.e., nerve and muscle tissue). Used for the scientific discipline or the electrophysiological processes themselves. Compare ELECTRICAL ACTIVITY.
B Physiology 1967
N ↓ Electrical Activity 1967
Electrical Brain Stimulation 1973
Electro Oculography 1973
Electrocardiography 1967
↓ Electroencephalography 1967
Electromyography 1967
Electronystagmography 1973
Electroplethysmography 1973
Electroretinography 1967
Galvanic Skin Response 1967
↓ Skin Electrical Properties 1973
Skin Potential 1973
R ↓ Medical Diagnosis 1973

Electroplethysmography 1973
PN 7 **SC** 16580
B Electrophysiology 1973
Medical Diagnosis 1973
Plethysmography 1973

Electroretinography 1967
PN 238 **SC** 16590
B Electrophysiology 1973
Medical Diagnosis 1973
Ophthalmologic Examination 1973
R Electro Oculography 1973

Electroshock Therapy
Use Electroconvulsive Shock Therapy

Electrosleep Treatment 1978
PN 15 **SC** 16605
SN Therapeutic application of a low intensity, intermittent electrical current to the skull, often producing a state of relaxation, but not necessarily sleep.
B Physical Treatment Methods 1973
R ↓ Shock Therapy 1973
Sleep Treatment 1973

Elementarism
Use Reductionism

Elementary Education 1973
PN 1521 **SC** 16620
B Education 1967
R Elementary Schools 1973

Elementary School Students 1967
PN 32602 **SC** 16630
SN Students in grades 1-6.
B Students 1967
N Intermediate School Students 1973
Primary School Students 1973
R Grade Level 1994
Middle School Students 1985

Elementary School Teachers 1973
PN 5897 **SC** 16640
B Teachers 1967

Elementary Schools 1973
PN 1771 **SC** 16650
UF Grammar Schools
Primary Schools

Elementary Schools — (cont'd)
B Schools 1967
R Elementary Education 1973

Elephants 1973
PN 104 **SC** 16660
B Mammals 1973

Elimination (Excretion)
Use Excretion

Ellis (Albert) 1991
PN 89 **SC** 16680
SN Identifies biographical or autobiographical studies and discussions of Ellis's works.
R ↓ Psychologists 1967
Rational Emotive Behavior Therapy 2003
Self Talk 1988

Email
Use Computer Mediated Communication

Embarrassment 1973
PN 349 **SC** 16690
B Emotional States 1973
R Shame 1994

Embedded Figures Testing 1967
PN 183 **SC** 16700
B Nonprojective Personality Measures 1973

Embolisms 1973
PN 77 **SC** 16710
B Cardiovascular Disorders 1967
R ↓ Thromboses 1973

Embryo 1973
PN 411 **SC** 16720
B Prenatal Developmental Stages 1973
R Stem Cells 2006

EMDR
Use Eye Movement Desensitization Therapy

Emergency Preparedness 2007
PN 52 **SC** 16727
SN Governmental, institutional, or individual planning for and responses to both natural and human-made disasters.
HN This term was introduced in April 2007. Relevant records were re-indexed with this term. The posting note reflects the number of records that were re-indexed.
UF Disaster Planning
Disaster Preparedness
Natural Disaster Preparedness
R ↓ Disasters 1973
Emergency Services 1973
Natural Disasters 1973
Risk Management 1997
↓ Terrorism 1982

Emergency Services 1973
PN 2677 **SC** 16730
R ↓ Crisis Intervention Services 1973
Emergency Preparedness 2007
Natural Disasters 1973

Emetic Drugs 1973
PN 90 **SC** 16740
UF Vomit Inducing Drugs
B Drugs 1967
N Apomorphine 1973
Disulfiram 1978

Emetic Drugs — (cont'd)
R ↓ CNS Stimulating Drugs 1973
↓ Narcotic Drugs 1973
Vomiting 1973

EMG (Electrophysiology)
Use Electromyography

Emotion Focused Therapy 2007
PN 73 SC 16753
SN An integrative individual therapy that focuses on emotion as the key determinant of personality development and of psychotherapeutic change. In sessions, the therapist helps the client to become aware of, accept, make sense of, and regulate emotions as a way of resolving problems and promoting growth.
HN This term was introduced in April 2007. Relevant records were re-indexed with this term. The posting note reflects the number of records that were re-indexed.
UF Emotionally Focused Therapy
B Psychotherapy 1967
R ↓ Emotional Control 1973
↓ Emotions 1967
Individual Psychotherapy 1973
Integrative Psychotherapy 2003

Emotional Abuse 1991
PN 1146 SC 16755
UF Psychological Abuse
B Antisocial Behavior 1971
R Bullying 2003
↓ Child Abuse 1971
Child Neglect 1988
Domestic Violence 2006
Elder Abuse 1988
Erotomania 1997
↓ Partner Abuse 1991
Patient Abuse 1991
Physical Abuse 1991
Verbal Abuse 2003

Emotional Adjustment 1973
PN 11421 SC 16760
SN Personal acceptance, adaptation, and relation to one's inner self and environment.
UF Emotional Maladjustment
Maladjustment (Emotional)
Personal Adjustment
Psychological Adjustment
B Adjustment 1967
N ↓ Emotional Control 1973
Identity Crisis 1973
R Adjustment Disorders 1994
Codependency 1991
Coping Behavior 1967
Emotional Disturbances 2007
↓ Emotions 1967
↓ Mental Disorders 1967
↓ Mental Health 1967
↓ Personality 1967
↓ Psychopathology 1967
Resilience (Psychological) 2003

Emotional Content 1973
PN 2423 SC 16765
SN Emotional themes, substance, form, or characteristics of feelings, especially as they are portrayed in various forms of communication (e.g., reading material, motion pictures) or as manifested in specific situations.
R ↓ Communication 1967
↓ Emotions 1967

Emotional Control 1973
PN 1737 SC 16770
SN Self-regulation of the influence that one's emotions have on one's thoughts and behavior.
UF Control (Emotional)
Emotional Restraint
B Emotional Adjustment 1973
N Anger Control 1997
R Coping Behavior 1967
Emotion Focused Therapy 2007
Emotional Regulation 2007
Internal External Locus of Control 1967
Self Control 1973
Social Control 1988
Tantrums 1973

Emotional Development 1973
PN 3885 SC 16780
B Psychogenesis 1973
R Attachment Behavior 1985
Attachment Theory 2007
Childhood Play Development 1973
Developmental Age Groups 1973
Emotional Intelligence 2003
↓ Emotions 1967
Object Relations 1982
↓ Personality Development 1967
↓ Physical Development 1973
Psychosexual Development 1982
↓ Psychosocial Development 1973

Emotional Disturbances 2007
PN 5993 SC 16785
SN Persistent maladjustive emotional responses considered inappropriate to the situation.
HN In April 2007, this term was created to replace the discontinued term EMOTIONALLY DISTURBED. EMOTIONALLY DISTURBED was removed from all records containing it, and was replaced with EMOTIONAL DISTURBANCES.
UF Emotionally Disturbed
R ↓ Emotional Adjustment 1973
↓ Emotional States 1973
↓ Mental Disorders 1967

Emotional Expressiveness
Use Emotionality (Personality)

Emotional Immaturity 1973
PN 68 SC 16800
SN Tendency to exhibit emotional reactions considered inappropriate for one's age.
UF Immaturity (Emotional)
B Personality Traits 1967
R Emotional Maturity 1973

Emotional Inferiority 1973
PN 108 SC 16810
SN Conscious or unconscious feelings of insecurity, insignificance, and inadequacy and of being unable to cope with life's demands.
UF Inferiority (Emotional)
B Personality Traits 1967
R Neuroticism 1973

Emotional Insecurity
Use Emotional Security

Emotional Instability 1973
PN 279 SC 16830
SN Tendency to display unpredictable and rapidly changing emotions or moods.

Emotional Instability — (cont'd)
UF Instability (Emotional)
B Personality Traits 1967
R Emotional Stability 1973
Neuroticism 1973

Emotional Intelligence 2003
PN 872 SC 16833
SN Ability to monitor and appraise one's own and others' feelings and emotions, and to use this information to guide thinking and action.
HN This term was introduced in June 2003. Relevant records were re-indexed with this term. The posting note reflects the number of records that were re-indexed.
B Intelligence 1967
R Emotional Development 1973
Emotional Maturity 1973
↓ Emotional Responses 1967
↓ Emotions 1967
Multiple Intelligences 2007

Emotional Maladjustment
Use Emotional Adjustment

Emotional Maturity 1973
PN 661 SC 16850
SN Attainment of a level of emotional development and exhibition of emotional patterns commonly associated with persons of a specific age level. Not to be confused with EMOTIONAL CONTROL, which involves the suppression or control of direction of one's emotions.
UF Maturity (Emotional)
B Personality Traits 1967
R Emotional Immaturity 1973
Emotional Intelligence 2003

Emotional Needs
Use Psychological Needs

Emotional Regulation 2007
PN 494 SC 16858
SN The ability of an individual to modulate an emotion or set of emotions.
HN This term was introduced in April 2007. Relevant records were re-indexed with this term. The posting note reflects the number of records that were re-indexed.
UF Affect Regulation
R ↓ Emotional Control 1973
Self Control 1973
Self Regulation 2003

Emotional Responses 1967
PN 9957 SC 16860
SN Use ANIMAL EMOTIONALITY for nonhuman subjects.
HN From 1982, limited to human populations.
B Responses 1967
N ↓ Conditioned Emotional Responses 1967
R Animal Emotionality 1978
Cognitive Appraisal 2004
Emotional Intelligence 2003
↓ Emotions 1967
Laughter 1978
Stranger Reactions 1988

Emotional Restraint
Use Emotional Control

Emotional Security 1973
PN 774 **SC** 16880
SN Possession of inner resources enabling one to cope with unfamiliar or threatening situations, especially as engendered through early nurturance.
UF Emotional Insecurity
Insecurity (Emotional)
Security (Emotional)
B Personality Traits 1967
R Attachment Theory 2007
Emotional Stability 1973

Emotional Stability 1973
PN 610 **SC** 16890
SN Resistance to affective disruption or tendency toward evenness of feelings.
UF Stability (Emotional)
B Personality Traits 1967
R Emotional Instability 1973
Emotional Security 1973
Neuroticism 1973
Resilience (Psychological) 2003

Emotional States 1973
PN 18079 **SC** 16900
UF Moods
B Emotions 1967
N Affection 1973
Alienation 1971
Ambivalence 1973
↓ Anger 1967
↓ Anxiety 1967
Apathy 1973
↓ Aversion 1967
Boredom 1973
Depression (Emotion) 1967
Disappointment 1973
Disgust 1994
Dissatisfaction 1973
Distress 1973
Doubt 1973
Embarrassment 1973
Emotional Trauma 1967
Enthusiasm 1973
Euphoria 1973
↓ Fear 1967
Frustration 1967
Gratitude 2006
Grief 1973
Guilt 1967
Happiness 1973
↓ Helplessness 1997
Homesickness 1994
Hope 1991
Hopelessness 1988
Jealousy 1973
Loneliness 1973
Love 1973
↓ Mania 1967
Mental Confusion 1973
Optimism 1973
Pessimism 1973
Pleasure 1973
Pride 1973
Restlessness 1973
Sadness 1973
Shame 1994
Suffering 1973
Suspicion 1973
Sympathy 1973
R Abandonment 1997
Craving 1997
Emotional Disturbances 2007
Irritability 1988

Emotional States — (cont'd)
Learned Helplessness 1978
Morale 1978
↓ Personality 1967

Emotional Superiority 1973
PN 59 **SC** 16910
SN Feeling that one is better than others in ability, virtue, or worth.
UF Superiority (Emotional)
B Personality Traits 1967
R ↓ Dominance 1967
Egotism 1973
Grandiosity 1994

Emotional Trauma 1967
PN 9994 **SC** 16920
UF Trauma (Emotional)
B Emotional States 1973
Trauma 2006
R Acute Stress Disorder 2003
Adjustment Disorders 1994
Debriefing (Psychological) 2004
False Memory 1997
Posttraumatic Stress Disorder 1985
Repressed Memory 1997
↓ Separation Reactions 1997

Emotionality (Animal)
Use Animal Emotionality

Emotionality (Personality) 1973
PN 2072 **SC** 16930
SN Personality trait characteristic of a person who tends to react strongly or excessively to emotional situations.
UF Emotional Expressiveness
B Personality Traits 1967
R ↓ Emotions 1967
Neuroticism 1973

Emotionally Disturbed
HN In April 2007, this term was discontinued and removed from all records containing it, and was replaced with EMOTIONAL DISTURBANCES, its postable counterpart.
Use Emotional Disturbances

Emotionally Focused Therapy
Use Emotion Focused Therapy

Emotions 1967
PN 15670 **SC** 16960
SN Conceptually broad term referring to the affective aspects of human consciousness. Use a more specific term if possible. Use ANIMAL EMOTIONALITY for nonhuman subjects.
UF Feelings
N ↓ Emotional States 1973
R Emotion Focused Therapy 2007
↓ Emotional Adjustment 1973
Emotional Content 1973
Emotional Development 1973
Emotional Intelligence 2003
↓ Emotional Responses 1967
Emotionality (Personality) 1973
Expressed Emotion 1991
Human Nature 1997
Morale 1978
↓ Personality 1967

Empathy 1967
PN 5251 **SC** 16970
B Personality Traits 1967
R Agreeableness 1997

Emphysema (Pulmonary)
Use Pulmonary Emphysema

Empirical Methods 1973
PN 1987 **SC** 16990
SN Scientific methodology based on experimentation, systematic observation, or measurement, rather than theoretical formulation.
B Methodology 1967
N ↓ Experimental Methods 1967
Observation Methods 1967
R ↓ Behavioral Assessment 1982
Positivism (Philosophy) 1997
Qualitative Research 2003
Quantitative Methods 2003

Employability 1973
PN 646 **SC** 17000
SN Potential usefulness of an individual as judged on the basis of job skills, functional literacy, emotional or social maturity, intellectual development, or personal values (e.g., personal responsibility).
R ↓ Employee Skills 1973
↓ Employment Status 1982
↓ Personnel 1967
Supported Employment 1994
Vocational Evaluation 1991

Employee Absenteeism 1973
PN 1125 **SC** 17010
UF Absenteeism (Employee)
R ↓ Personnel 1967
Tardiness 2003

Employee Assistance Programs 1985
PN 1539 **SC** 17015
SN Programs or services provided by the employer to help employees with personal or other matters, including retirement planning or alcohol rehabilitation.
B Employee Benefits 1973
R ↓ Counseling 1967
Disability Management 1991
↓ Drug Rehabilitation 1973
Elder Care 1994
↓ Program Development 1991
↓ Support Groups 1991

Employee Attitudes 1967
PN 8164 **SC** 17020
SN Attitudes of, not toward, employees.
B Attitudes 1967
Employee Characteristics 1988
N Job Satisfaction 1967
R Employee Motivation 1973
Job Involvement 1978
↓ Job Performance 1967
Organizational Commitment 1991
Work (Attitudes Toward) 1973

Employee Benefits 1973
PN 633 **SC** 17030
SN Benefits provided by an employer that may be voluntary or mandated by federal or state law.
N Bonuses 1973
Employee Assistance Programs 1985
↓ Employee Health Insurance 1973
Employee Leave Benefits 1973
Employee Pension Plans 1973

Employee Benefits — (cont'd)
Workers' Compensation Insurance 2003
R Disability Evaluation 1988
Elder Care 1994
↓ Personnel 1967
Salaries 1973

Employee Characteristics 1988
PN 2011 SC 17035
N ↓ Employee Attitudes 1967
Employee Efficiency 1973
Employee Motivation 1973
Employee Productivity 1973
↓ Employee Skills 1973
Job Experience Level 1973
Job Knowledge 1997
R Diversity in the Workplace 2003
Organizational Commitment 1991
↓ Personnel 1967
Professional Competence 1997
Professional Identity 1991
Professionalism 2003
Workaholism 2004

Employee Efficiency 1973
PN 288 SC 17040
UF Efficiency (Employee)
B Employee Characteristics 1988
Job Performance 1967
R Employee Productivity 1973

Employee Health Insurance 1973
PN 101 SC 17050
B Employee Benefits 1973
Health Insurance 1973
N Workers' Compensation Insurance 2003

Employee Interaction 1988
PN 1732 SC 17055
SN Dynamics of interpersonal interactions between employees.
B Interpersonal Interaction 1967
Organizational Behavior 1978
N Supervisor Employee Interaction 1997
R Groupware 2003
↓ Personnel 1967

Employee Leave Benefits 1973
PN 262 SC 17060
UF Annual Leave
Sick Leave
Vacation Benefits
B Employee Benefits 1973

Employee Motivation 1973
PN 1997 SC 17080
B Employee Characteristics 1988
Motivation 1967
R ↓ Employee Attitudes 1967
Job Involvement 1978
Professional Recognition 2005

Employee Pension Plans 1973
PN 81 SC 17090
UF Pension Plans (Employee)
Pensions
B Employee Benefits 1973

Employee Productivity 1973
PN 1824 SC 17110
UF Productivity (Employee)
B Employee Characteristics 1988
Job Performance 1967
Productivity 2007

Employee Productivity — (cont'd)
R Employee Efficiency 1973
Professional Recognition 2005

Employee Recognition
Use Professional Recognition

Employee Selection
Use Personnel Selection

Employee Skills 1973
PN 812 SC 17130
B Ability 1967
Employee Characteristics 1988
N Clerical Secretarial Skills 1973
R Employability 1973
Job Knowledge 1997
Professional Competence 1997
Supported Employment 1994
Vocational Evaluation 1991

Employee Supervisor Interaction
Use Supervisor Employee Interaction

Employee Termination
Use Personnel Termination

Employee Turnover 1973
PN 1917 SC 17140
UF Personnel Turnover
Turnover
R Downsizing 2003
Employment History 1978
Job Security 1978
↓ Occupational Tenure 1973
↓ Personnel 1967

Employees
Use Personnel

Employer Attitudes 1973
PN 766 SC 17160
SN Attitudes of, not toward, employers.
B Attitudes 1967
R Organizational Commitment 1991
↓ Personnel 1967
Work (Attitudes Toward) 1973

Employment
Use Employment Status

Employment Discrimination 1994
PN 526 SC 17173
SN Prejudiced and differential treatment of employees or job applicants based on factors other than performance or qualifications.
UF Job Discrimination
B Social Discrimination 1982
R Affirmative Action 1985
Age Discrimination 1994
Ageism 2003
↓ Human Resource Management 2003
Job Applicant Screening 1973
↓ Personnel Evaluation 1973
↓ Personnel Selection 1967
↓ Prejudice 1967
Race and Ethnic Discrimination 1994
Racism 1973
Sex Discrimination 1978
Sexism 1988

Employment History 1978
PN 471 SC 17174
SN Past record of an individual's working life, including periods of unemployment.
R Career Change 1978
Career Development 1985
Employee Turnover 1973
↓ Employment Status 1982
Job Experience Level 1973
Occupational Mobility 1973
Occupational Success 1978
↓ Occupational Tenure 1973
↓ Occupations 1967
↓ Personnel 1967
Personnel Promotion 1978
Personnel Termination 1973
Professional Development 1982
Retirement 1973
Unemployment 1967

Employment Interviews
Use Job Applicant Interviews

Employment Processes
Use Personnel Recruitment

Employment Status 1982
PN 5906 SC 17196
SN Condition of employment including full- or part-time, temporary or permanent, and unemployment.
HN Use OCCUPATIONS to access references from 1967-1981.
UF Employment
Part Time Employment
N Self Employment 1994
Unemployment 1967
R Employability 1973
Employment History 1978
Job Applicants 1985
↓ Occupational Tenure 1973
Reemployment 1991
Retirement 1973
Supported Employment 1994
Working Women 1978

Employment Tests 1973
PN 656 SC 17200
SN Tests used in personnel selection to measure the suitability of an applicant for a given occupation.
B Measurement 1967
R Job Applicant Screening 1973

Empowerment 1991
PN 2496 SC 17203
SN Promotion or attainment of autonomy and freedom of choice for individuals or groups.
R Advocacy 1985
Assertiveness 1973
↓ Civil Rights 1978
↓ Client Rights 1988
↓ Helplessness 1997
Independence (Personality) 1973
↓ Involvement 1973
↓ Power 1967
Self Determination 1994

Empty Nest 1991
PN 47 SC 17205
SN Home environment after children have reached maturity and left home. Also, includes the concept of adult children returning to the home.
UF Return to Home
R Adult Offspring 1985
↓ Family 1967

Empty Nest — (cont'd)
↓ Family Relations 1967
Family Size 1973
↓ Family Structure 1973
Home Environment 1973
Intergenerational Relations 1988
↓ Living Arrangements 1991
↓ Parent Child Relations 1967

Enabling 1997
PN 47 **SC** 17207
B Social Influences 1967
R Codependency 1991
Dependency (Personality) 1967
↓ Social Reinforcement 1967

Enactments 1997
PN 241 **SC** 17209
SN Regressive or defensive interactions between a therapist and client or interaction between two or more people that reenacts past experiences or emotional conflicts of one or more of the persons involved.
UF Reenactments
R Acting Out 1967
Age Regression (Hypnotic) 1988
Countertransference 1973
Early Experience 1967
↓ Interpersonal Interaction 1967
Projective Identification 1994
↓ Psychotherapeutic Processes 1967
Psychotherapeutic Transference 1967
Reminiscence 1985
Repetition Compulsion 2005

Encephalitis 1973
PN 451 **SC** 17210
SN Inflammation of the brain due to a viral infection. A rare disease, it is severe and potentially life-threatening. May also be caused by autoimmune processes, toxins, or other conditions.
B Brain Disorders 1967
Viral Disorders 1973
N Encephalomyelitis 1973
R ↓ Infectious Disorders 1973

Encephalography 1973
PN 45 **SC** 17220
SN Broad term used to describe radiographic examination of the brain. Use a more specific term if possible.
B Medical Diagnosis 1973
Neuroimaging 2003
N Echoencephalography 1973
↓ Electroencephalography 1967
Pneumoencephalography 1973
Rheoencephalography 1973
R ↓ Roentgenography 1973

Encephalography (Air)
Use Pneumoencephalography

Encephalomyelitis 1973
PN 74 **SC** 17240
SN An inflammation of the brain and spinal cord, often used to indicate an infectious process but also applicable to a variety of autoimmune and toxic-metabolic processes.
B Encephalitis 1973
Myelitis 1973

Encephalomyelitis — (cont'd)
R ↓ Infectious Disorders 1973

Encephalopathies 1982
PN 609 **SC** 17247
SN Degenerative diseases of the brain.
B Brain Disorders 1967
N Creutzfeldt Jakob Syndrome 1994
Toxic Encephalopathies 1973
Wernickes Syndrome 1973
R Chronic Fatigue Syndrome 1997
Thyrotoxicosis 1973

Encoding
Use Human Information Storage

Encopresis
Use Fecal Incontinence

Encounter Group Therapy 1973
PN 280 **SC** 17270
SN Goal-oriented unstructured groups whose members seek heightened self-awareness and fulfillment of their human potential. The group leader (not necessarily a clinically trained therapist) participates freely in the group activity. Techniques used include role playing, sensory awareness, and physical contact.
B Group Psychotherapy 1967
Human Potential Movement 1982
N Marathon Group Therapy 1973
R Consciousness Raising Groups 1978
Human Relations Training 1978
Sensitivity Training 1973

Encouragement 1973
PN 233 **SC** 17290
B Social Interaction 1967
R ↓ Social Reinforcement 1967

End of Life Care
Use Palliative Care

Endocrine Disorders 1973
PN 278 **SC** 17300
B Physical Disorders 1997
N ↓ Adrenal Gland Disorders 1973
↓ Diabetes 1973
Endocrine Neoplasms 1973
↓ Endocrine Sexual Disorders 1973
Parathyroid Disorders 1973
↓ Pituitary Disorders 1973
↓ Thyroid Disorders 1973
R ↓ Endocrine System 1973
Hypothermia 1973
Migraine Headache 1973
↓ Secretion (Gland) 1973
↓ Somatoform Disorders 2001

Endocrine Gland Secretion 1973
PN 127 **SC** 17310
B Secretion (Gland) 1973
N Adrenal Gland Secretion 1973
R ↓ Endocrine Glands 1973

Endocrine Gland Surgery 1973
PN 10 **SC** 17320
B Surgery 1971
N Adrenalectomy 1973
↓ Castration 1967
Hypophysectomy 1973
Pinealectomy 1973
Thyroidectomy 1973

Endocrine Glands 1973
PN 74 **SC** 17330
B Endocrine System 1973
Glands 1967
N ↓ Adrenal Glands 1973
↓ Gonads 1973
Parathyroid Glands 1973
Pineal Body 1973
↓ Pituitary Gland 1973
Thyroid Gland 1973
R ↓ Endocrine Gland Secretion 1973
↓ Hormones 1967
Pancreas 1973

Endocrine Neoplasms 1973
PN 28 **SC** 17340
B Endocrine Disorders 1973
Neoplasms 1967

Endocrine Sexual Disorders 1973
PN 106 **SC** 17350
UF Ovary Disorders
Testes Disorders
B Endocrine Disorders 1973
Genital Disorders 1967
N ↓ Hypogonadism 1973
Testicular Feminization Syndrome 1973
R ↓ Adrenal Gland Disorders 1973
↓ Gynecological Disorders 1973
Hermaphroditism 1973
↓ Infertility 1973
↓ Male Genital Disorders 1973
↓ Pituitary Disorders 1973
↓ Thyroid Disorders 1973

Endocrine System 1973
PN 491 **SC** 17360
B Anatomical Systems 1973
N ↓ Endocrine Glands 1973
R ↓ Endocrine Disorders 1973
Pancreas 1973
Psychoneuroendocrinology 2007

Endocrinology 1973
PN 341 **SC** 17370
SN Scientific discipline dealing with the study of endocrine glands and internal secretions.
B Medical Sciences 1967
N ↓ Neuroendocrinology 1985
R Psychoneuroimmunology 1991

Endogamous Marriage 1973
PN 25 **SC** 17380
B Marriage 1967
N Consanguineous Marriage 1973

Endogenous Depression 1978
PN 1208 **SC** 17384
B Major Depression 1988

Endogenous Opiates 1985
PN 556 **SC** 17385
UF Opioids (Endogenous)
B Opiates 1973
Peptides 1973
N Dynorphins 1985
↓ Endorphins 1982

Endorphins 1982
PN 922 **SC** 17386
SN Endogenous morphine-like brain polypeptides that can bind to opiate receptors.
B Endogenous Opiates 1985
Neurotransmitters 1985

Endorphins — (cont'd)
Proteins 1973
N Enkephalins 1982
R Analgesia 1982
↓ Neuropeptides 2003

Endurance 1973
PN 148 **SC** 17390
SN Ability to withstand hardship, adversity, or stress. Used for human or animal populations.
N Physical Endurance 1973
Psychological Endurance 1973
R ↓ Stress 1967

Energy Expenditure 1967
PN 2191 **SC** 17400
SN Expenditure of mental or physical effort.
UF Effort
R Calories 1973
Metabolic Rates 1973

Engineering Psychology 1967
PN 662 **SC** 17410
SN Branch of applied psychology that emphasizes the study of machine design, the relationship between humans and machines, and the effects of machines on human behavior. Use a more specific term if possible.
B Applied Psychology 1973
R Human Factors Engineering 1973

Engineers 1967
PN 882 **SC** 17420
B Professional Personnel 1978
R ↓ Aerospace Personnel 1973
↓ Business and Industrial Personnel 1967
Scientists 1967

English as Second Language 1997
PN 1500 **SC** 17450
UF ESL
R Bilingual Education 1978
Bilingualism 1973
Foreign Language Education 1973
Foreign Languages 1973
↓ Language 1967
↓ Language Arts Education 1973
Language Proficiency 1988
↓ Multilingualism 1973
Native Language 2004

Enjoyment
Use Pleasure

Enkephalins 1982
PN 557 **SC** 17475
SN Endogenous morphine-like brain polypeptides closely related to endorphins.
B Endorphins 1982
R Analgesia 1982
↓ Neuropeptides 2003
↓ Peptides 1973

Enlisted Military Personnel 1973
PN 273 **SC** 17480
SN Military personnel ranking below commissioned officers.
B Military Personnel 1967
N Draftees 1973
Noncommissioned Officers 1973
R Volunteer Military Personnel 1973

Enlistment (Military)
Use Military Enlistment

Enrollment (School)
Use School Enrollment

Enteropeptidase
Use Kinases

Enthusiasm 1973
PN 95 **SC** 17530
UF Eagerness
B Emotional States 1973
R Morale 1978
↓ Motivation 1967

Entrance Examinations 1973
PN 298 **SC** 17540
B Educational Measurement 1967
N College Entrance Examination Board Scholastic Aptitude Test 2001
R Student Admission Criteria 1973

Entrapment Games 1973
PN 25 **SC** 17550
B Games 1967
R ↓ Collective Behavior 1967
Game Theory 1967
Non Zero Sum Games 1973
Prisoners Dilemma Game 1973

Entrepreneurship 1991
PN 726 **SC** 17555
SN Initiation, organization, management, and assumption of the attendant risks of a business or enterprise.
R ↓ Business 1967
↓ Business Investments 2007
Business Management 1973
Capitalism 1973
↓ Leadership 1967
↓ Management 1967
Ownership 1985
↓ Private Sector 1985
Self Employment 1994
Small Businesses 2007
Venture Capital 2007

Enuresis
Use Urinary Incontinence

Environment 1967
PN 9035 **SC** 17570
SN Totality of physical, social, psychological, or cultural conditions surrounding an organism.
N Built Environment 2007
↓ Facility Environment 1988
Learning Environment 2004
↓ Single Sex Environments 2001
↓ Social Environments 1973
↓ Therapeutic Environment 2001
R ↓ Architecture 1973
Ecology 1973
Environmental Adaptation 1973
Environmental Attitudes 1978
Environmental Education 1994
↓ Environmental Planning 1982
Environmental Stress 1973
Geography 1973
↓ Hazardous Materials 1991
Nature Nurture 1994
Person Environment Fit 1991
Physical Comfort 1982
Research Setting 2001
Urban Planning 1973

Environmental Adaptation 1973
PN 604 **SC** 17590
SN Physiological or biological adaptation to conditions in the physical environment. For psychological, social, or emotional adaptation use ADJUSTMENT or one of its related terms.
UF Adaptation (Environmental)
B Adaptation 1967
R ↓ Environment 1967
Mimicry (Biology) 2003
Person Environment Fit 1991

Environmental Attitudes 1978
PN 2259 **SC** 17594
SN Perceptions of or beliefs regarding the physical environment, including factors affecting its quality (e.g., overpopulation, pollution).
B Attitudes 1967
R Conservation (Ecological Behavior) 1978
Ecology 1973
↓ Environment 1967
Environmental Education 1994

Environmental Design
Use Environmental Planning

Environmental Education 1994
PN 313 **SC** 17598
SN Used for educational and noneducational settings.
R Conservation (Ecological Behavior) 1978
Ecology 1973
↓ Education 1967
↓ Environment 1967
Environmental Attitudes 1978
Pollution 1973

Environmental Effects 1973
PN 2625 **SC** 17600
SN Used for the effects of meterological or climatic phenomena, as well as for any effect of a surrounding physical environment on an organism's physical, behavioral, or emotional functioning.
N Altitude Effects 1973
Atmospheric Conditions 1973
↓ Gravitational Effects 1967
Noise Effects 1973
Seasonal Variations 1973
↓ Temperature Effects 1967
Underwater Effects 1973
R ↓ Ecological Factors 1973
Environmental Stress 1973
Home Environment 1973
Lunar Synodic Cycle 1973
Occupational Exposure 1988
Physiological Stress 1967
Prenatal Exposure 1991
↓ Social Environments 1973

Environmental Planning 1982
PN 889 **SC** 17607
SN Planning and design of environment with goals of efficient human-environment interaction and minimal ecological disruption.
UF Environmental Design
N Interior Design 1982
Urban Planning 1973
R ↓ Architecture 1973
Computer Assisted Design 1997
↓ Environment 1967
Person Environment Fit 1991
↓ Recreation Areas 1973

Environmental Psychology 1982
PN 909 **SC** 17609
SN Branch of psychology that studies the relationship between environmental variables and behavior, including manipulation of one by the other.
B Applied Psychology 1973
R Behavioral Ecology 1997
Ecological Psychology 1994

Environmental Stress 1973
PN 955 **SC** 17610
SN Naturally occurring or experimentally manipulated qualities of the physical environment which result in strain or disequilibrium. Consider also other specific terms (e.g., CROWDING, NOISE EFFECTS).
B Stress 1967
R Crowding 1978
↓ Deprivation 1967
↓ Environment 1967
↓ Environmental Effects 1973
Overpopulation 1973
Physiological Stress 1967
Thermal Acclimatization 1973

Environmental Therapy
Use Milieu Therapy

Environmental Tobacco Smoke
Use Passive Smoking

Envy
Use Jealousy

Enzyme Inhibitors 1985
PN 468 **SC** 17625
SN Any agent that slows or otherwise disrupts the activity of an enzyme, such as antienzymes or enzyme antibodies.
B Drugs 1967
N Acetazolamide 1973
↓ Amine Oxidase Inhibitors 1973
Bromocriptine 1988
Captopril 1991
↓ Cholinesterase Inhibitors 1973
↓ Decarboxylase Inhibitors 1982
Hydroxylase Inhibitors 1985
↓ Monoamine Oxidase Inhibitors 1973
Sildenafil 2006
Theophylline 1973
R ↓ Enzymes 1973

Enzymes 1973
PN 1542 **SC** 17630
HN In 1997, this term replaced the discontinued terms ALDOLASES and CARBONIC ANHYDRASE. In 2000, these terms were removed from all records containing them, and replaced with ENZYMES.
UF Aldolases
Carbonic Anhydrase
B Drugs 1967
N Decarboxylases 1973
↓ Dehydrogenases 1973
↓ Esterases 1973
Hydroxylases 1973
Isozymes 1973
Kinases 1982
↓ Oxidases 1973
Phosphatases 1973
Phosphorylases 1973
Proteinases 1973
↓ Transferases 1973

Enzymes — (cont'd)
R ↓ Anti Inflammatory Drugs 1982
↓ Decarboxylase Inhibitors 1982
↓ Enzyme Inhibitors 1985
↓ Proteins 1973

EOG (Electrophysiology)
Use Electro Oculography

Ependyma
Use Cerebral Ventricles

Ephedrine 1973
PN 74 **SC** 17660
B Adrenergic Drugs 1973
Alkaloids 1973
CNS Stimulating Drugs 1973
Sympathomimetic Amines 1973
Vasoconstrictor Drugs 1973
R ↓ Local Anesthetics 1973

Epidemic Hysteria
Use Mass Hysteria

Epidemics 2001
PN 425 **SC** 17665
SN Sudden increase in the incidence of a disease, injury, or other health-related event.
UF Disease Outbreaks
B Public Health 1988
N Pandemics 2007
R Epidemiology 1973
Hygiene 1994
↓ Infectious Disorders 1973
↓ Injuries 1973
↓ Syndromes 1973

Epidemiology 1973
PN 18534 **SC** 17670
SN Study of the occurrence, distribution, and containment of disease or mental disorders. Used for the scientific discipline as a whole or for specific epidemiological factors or findings (e.g., disease incidence or prevalence statistics).
B Medical Sciences 1967
R ↓ Epidemics 2001

Epilepsy 1967
PN 8088 **SC** 17680
SN Neurological condition characterized by recurrent seizures of any type that result from abnormal electrical excitation in the brain. Epilepsy is marked by convulsions; involuntary movements; altered consciousness; and disturbed sensation, perception, behavior, or mood.
B Brain Disorders 1967
N ↓ Epileptic Seizures 1973
Experimental Epilepsy 1978
R ↓ Anticonvulsive Drugs 1973
Aura 1973
↓ Brain Damage 1967
Fugue Reaction 1973
Grand Mal Seizures 2006
Petit Mal Seizures 2006

Epileptic Seizures 1973
PN 1689 **SC** 17690
SN Recurrent seizures symptomatic of epilepsy.
B Brain Disorders 1967
Epilepsy 1967
Seizures 2005

Epileptic Seizures — (cont'd)
N Experimental Epilepsy 1978
R Coma 1973

Epinephrine 1967
PN 972 **SC** 17700
UF Adrenaline
B Adrenergic Drugs 1973
Catecholamines 1973
Heart Rate Affecting Drugs 1973
Hormones 1967
R Vasoconstriction 1973
Vasodilation 1973

Episcopalians
Use Protestants

Episodic Memory 1988
PN 1383 **SC** 17705
B Memory 1967
R Eidetic Imagery 1973

Epistemology 1973
PN 2835 **SC** 17710
SN Philosophical study of knowledge, including its origin, nature, and limits.
B Philosophies 1967
R Determinism 1997
Hermeneutics 1991
↓ Metaphysics 1973
Positivism (Philosophy) 1997
Relativism 1997

Epithelial Cells 1973
PN 41 **SC** 17720
B Cells (Biology) 1973
R Skin (Anatomy) 1967

Epithelium
Use Skin (Anatomy)

Epstein Barr Viral Disorder 1994
PN 28 **SC** 17740
SN The infection of human B lymphocytes by human herpes virus 4; thought to be the causative agent of infectious mononucleosis and facilitator of various lympho-proliferative disorders.
B Infectious Disorders 1973
Viral Disorders 1973
R ↓ Blood and Lymphatic Disorders 1973
Chronic Fatigue Syndrome 1997
Lymphocytes 1973

Equal Education 1978
PN 529 **SC** 17745
SN Provision of comparable educational opportunities to all individuals irrespective of race, national origin, religion, sex, socioeconomic status, or ability.
UF Educational Inequality
B Civil Rights 1978
R ↓ Education 1967
Educational Quality 1997
School Integration 1982
Social Equality 1973

Equality (Social)
Use Social Equality

Equilibrium 1973
PN 1001 **SC** 17760
SN Maintenance of postural balance. For physiological equilibrium consider HOMEOSTASIS.

Equilibrium — (cont'd)
UF Balance (Motor Processes)
R Falls 2004
↓ Labyrinth Disorders 1973
↓ Perceptual Motor Processes 1967
Spatial Orientation (Perception) 1973

Equipment
Use Apparatus

Equity (Payment) 1978
PN 768 **SC** 17784
SN In society, group, or other interpersonal situations, the process of equal allocation of economic resources, rewards, or payoffs.
B Equity (Social) 1978
R Distributive Justice 2003
↓ Justice 1973
Money 1967
Resource Allocation 1997
Salaries 1973
↓ Social Behavior 1967
↓ Social Processes 1967

Equity (Social) 1978
PN 1198 **SC** 17786
SN In society, group, or other interpersonal situations, the maintenance of relationships in which the proportions of each member's societal and cultural contributions or benefits are approximately equal.
N Equity (Payment) 1978
R Distributive Justice 2003
Egalitarianism 1985
↓ Justice 1973
Resource Allocation 1997
↓ Social Behavior 1967
↓ Social Processes 1967

Erectile Dysfunction 2006
PN 700 **SC** 17788
SN The inability to achieve and/or maintain an erection.
HN In May 2006, this term was created to replace the discontinued term IMPOTENCE. IMPOTENCE was removed from all records containing it and replaced with ERECTILE DYSFUNCTION, its postable counterpart.
UF Impotence
B Sexual Function Disturbances 1973
R Erection (Penis) 1973
↓ Male Orgasm 1973

Erection (Penis) 1973
PN 806 **SC** 17790
B Psychosexual Behavior 1967
R Erectile Dysfunction 2006

Ergonomics
Use Human Factors Engineering

Ergot Derivatives 1973
PN 169 **SC** 17810
B Drugs 1967
N Bromocriptine 1988
Dihydroergotamine 1973
R ↓ Adrenergic Blocking Drugs 1973
↓ Alkaloids 1973
Lysergic Acid Diethylamide 1967
Tyramine 1973

Erikson (Erik) 1991
PN 311 **SC** 17815
SN Identifies biographical or autobiographical studies and discussions of Erikson's works.

Erikson (Erik) — (cont'd)
R ↓ Developmental Stages 1973
Ego Identity 1991
Generativity 2001
↓ Neopsychoanalytic School 1973
↓ Psychoanalysis 1967
↓ Psychoanalytic Theory 1967
↓ Psychologists 1967
↓ Psychosocial Development 1973

Eroticism 1973
PN 829 **SC** 17820
B Sexual Arousal 1978
R Autoeroticism 1997
Inhibited Sexual Desire 1997

Erotomania 1997
PN 58 **SC** 17823
SN A person's false belief that others are sexually attracted to and/or in love with him or her. Also used to describe an abnormally strong sexual desire.
R ↓ Antisocial Behavior 1971
Attachment Behavior 1985
Delusions 1967
Emotional Abuse 1991
Grandiosity 1994
Hypersexuality 1973
Love 1973
Obsessions 1967
↓ Partner Abuse 1991
↓ Psychosexual Behavior 1967
Sexual Fantasy 1997
Victimization 1973

Error Analysis 1973
PN 910 **SC** 17830
SN Collection, classification, and/or analysis of mistakes, especially in task or test performance.
B Analysis 1967
R ↓ Errors 1967
Human Machine Systems 1997

Error of Measurement 1985
PN 690 **SC** 17835
SN Observed differences in obtained scores or measures due to chance variance.
UF Error Variance
Measurement Error
Standard Error of Measurement
B Errors 1967
Statistical Analysis 1967
R Consistency (Measurement) 1973
Least Squares 1985
↓ Scoring (Testing) 1973
Standard Deviation 1973
↓ Statistical Estimation 1985
↓ Statistical Measurement 1973
↓ Test Bias 1985
Test Reliability 1973
↓ Test Scores 1967

Error Variance
Use Error of Measurement

Errors 1967
PN 4607 **SC** 17840
SN Inappropriate, inaccurate, or incorrect responses or performance. Also, factual errors or other informational inaccuracies and performance errors on the part of others to which a subject reacts.
UF Mistakes
N Error of Measurement 1985
↓ Prediction Errors 1973
↓ Refraction Errors 1973

Errors — (cont'd)
R Error Analysis 1973
Halo Effect 1982
Proofreading 1988

Erythroblastosis Fetalis
Use Rh Incompatibility

Erythrocytes 1973
PN 416 **SC** 17860
UF Red Blood Cells
B Blood Cells 1973
R Blood Groups 1973

Escape
Use Avoidance

Escape Behavior (Animal)
Use Animal Escape Behavior

Escape Conditioning 1973
PN 467 **SC** 17890
SN Learned behavior or the operant conditioning procedure in which the subject learns a specific behavior that results in the termination of an ongoing aversive stimulus. Consider also NEGATIVE REINFORCEMENT. Compare AVOIDANCE CONDITIONING.
UF Conditioning (Escape)
B Operant Conditioning 1967

Eserine
Use Physostigmine

Eskimos
HN In 2000, the term was discontinued and removed from all records containing it, and replaced with INUIT, its postable counterpart.
Use Inuit

ESL
Use English as Second Language

Esophagus 1973
PN 152 **SC** 17920
B Digestive System 1967
R Dysphagia 2003

ESP (Parapsychology)
Use Extrasensory Perception

Essay Testing 1973
PN 142 **SC** 17940
B Testing Methods 1967

Essential Hypertension 1973
PN 395 **SC** 17950
SN High blood pressure with no identifiable cause. Also referred to as primary hypertension.
B Hypertension 1973

Esterases 1973
PN 64 **SC** 17970
B Enzymes 1973
N Acetylcholinesterase 1973
Cholinesterase 1973
R Hydroxylases 1973
Phosphatases 1973

Estimation 1967
PN 2090 **SC** 17980
SN Subjective judgment or inference about the character, quality, or nature of a person, process, or thing which may or may not involve the inspection or availability of data or pertinent information.

Estimation — (cont'd)
N ↓ Statistical Estimation 1985
Time Estimation 1967
R ↓ Expectations 1967
↓ Prediction 1967

Estradiol 1973
PN 1530 SC 18000
B Estrogens 1973

Estrogen Antagonists
Use Antiestrogens

Estrogen Replacement Therapy
Use Hormone Therapy

Estrogens 1973
PN 1686 SC 18010
B Sex Hormones 1973
N Estradiol 1973
Estrone 1973
R Antiandrogens 1982
Antiestrogens 1982

Estrone 1973
PN 19 SC 18020
B Estrogens 1973

Estrus 1973
PN 809 SC 18030
R ↓ Animal Biological Rhythms 1973
Animal Sexual Receptivity 1973
↓ Menstrual Cycle 1973
↓ Menstruation 1973

Ethanal
Use Acetaldehyde

Ethanol 1973
PN 6688 SC 18040
UF Alcohol (Grain)
Ethyl Alcohol
B Alcohols 1967
R Fetal Alcohol Syndrome 1985

Ether (Anesthetic) 1973
PN 52 SC 18050
UF Ethyl Ether (Anesthetic)
B General Anesthetics 1973

Ethics 1967
PN 4354 SC 18060
SN For ethics in social or cultural situations, consider MORALITY.
N Bioethics 2003
Experimental Ethics 1978
Professional Ethics 1973
R Euthanasia 1973
Evil 2003
Integrity 1997
Morality 1967
↓ Religious Beliefs 1973
↓ Social Influences 1967
Social Responsibility 2007
↓ Values 1967

Ethnic Differences
Use Racial and Ethnic Differences

Ethnic Discrimination
Use Race and Ethnic Discrimination

Ethnic Groups
HN In 2000, the term was discontinued and removed from all records containing it. ETHNIC GROUPS was replaced with RACIAL AND ETHNIC GROUPS, its postable counterpart.
Use Racial and Ethnic Groups

Ethnic Identity 1973
PN 5391 SC 18090
SN Feelings, ties, or associations that an individual experiences as a member of a particular ethnic group.
UF Ethnicity
B Sociocultural Factors 1967
R Cultural Sensitivity 1994
Group Identity 2007
Identity Formation 2004
Ingroup Outgroup 1997
Reference Groups 1994
↓ Self Concept 1967
↓ Social Identity 1988

Ethnic Sensitivity
Use Cultural Sensitivity

Ethnic Values 1973
PN 700 SC 18100
B Social Influences 1967
Sociocultural Factors 1967
Values 1967
R Cultural Sensitivity 1994
↓ Racial and Ethnic Groups 2001

Ethnicity
Use Ethnic Identity

Ethnocentrism 1973
PN 484 SC 18110
SN Exaggerated tendency to identify with one's own ethnic group, or the inclination to judge others in terms of standards and values of one's own group.
B Racial and Ethnic Attitudes 1982
R Cross Cultural Psychology 1997
↓ Social Identity 1988

Ethnography 1973
PN 2068 SC 18120
SN Descriptive study of cultures and societies. Used for the scientific discipline or the descriptive analyses themselves. Consider also ETHNOLOGY.
R Anthropology 1967
Ethnology 1967
Folk Psychology 1997
Kinship Structure 1973
Race (Anthropological) 1973
↓ Rites of Passage 1973
↓ Sociocultural Factors 1967
Traditions 2007

Ethnolinguistics 1973
PN 312 SC 18130
SN A part of anthropological linguistics concerned with the interrelation between a language and the cultural behavior of those who speak it.
B Linguistics 1973
R ↓ Dialect 1973
Ethnology 1967
Metalinguistics 1994
Psycholinguistics 1967
Slang 1973
Sociolinguistics 1985

Ethnology 1967
PN 1759 SC 18140
SN Conceptually broad term referring to the study of the origin, distribution, characteristics, and relations of the cultures or ethnic groups of the world. Also, a branch of anthropology dealing with the comparative or analytical study of human culture or societies. Use a more specific term if possible. Consider also ETHNOGRAPHY.
R Animism 1973
Anthropology 1967
Cross Cultural Differences 1967
Cross Cultural Psychology 1997
Cultism 1973
↓ Culture (Anthropological) 1967
↓ Culture Change 1967
Culture Shock 1973
Ethnography 1973
Ethnolinguistics 1973
Folk Medicine 1973
Folk Psychology 1997
Folklore 1991
Kinship 1985
Kinship Structure 1973
Myths 1967
Race (Anthropological) 1973
↓ Racial and Ethnic Attitudes 1982
Racial and Ethnic Differences 1982
↓ Racial and Ethnic Groups 2001
Racial and Ethnic Relations 1982
Shamanism 1973
↓ Sociocultural Factors 1967
Taboos 1973
Transcultural Psychiatry 1973
Witchcraft 1973

Ethology (Animal)
Use Animal Ethology

Ethyl Alcohol
Use Ethanol

Ethyl Ether (Anesthetic)
Use Ether (Anesthetic)

Ethylaldehyde
Use Acetaldehyde

Etiology 1967
PN 16200 SC 18190
SN Study of the causes and origins of psychological or physical conditions. Used for the science itself or the specific etiological findings and processes.
UF Aetiology
Etiopathogenesis
Pathogenesis
R Causality 2005
Disease Transmission 2004
↓ Disorders 1967
↓ Mental Disorders 1967
Patient History 1973
↓ Physical Disorders 1997

Etiopathogenesis
Use Etiology

Etymology 1973
PN 91 SC 18200
SN Branch of linguistic science which traces the origin of words and morphemes to their earliest determinable base in a given language group and describes historical changes in words. Used for the discipline or specific etymological aspects of given words.

Etymology — (cont'd)
UF Word Origins
B Linguistics 1973
R Words (Phonetic Units) 1967

Eugenics 1973
PN 208 SC 18210
SN Applied science or the biosocial movement which advocates the use of practices aimed at improving the genetic composition of a population. Usually refers to human populations. Compare ANIMAL BREEDING, ANIMAL DOMESTICATION, and SELECTIVE BREEDING.
B Genetic Engineering 1994
Genetics 1967
Sciences 1967
R ↓ Family Planning 1973
Genetic Counseling 1978
Reproductive Technology 1988
Selective Breeding 1973
↓ Sterilization (Sex) 1973

Euphoria 1973
PN 177 SC 18230
B Emotional States 1973
R Happiness 1973
Pleasure 1973

Eustachian Tube
Use Middle Ear

Euthanasia 1973
PN 807 SC 18255
SN Allowing an incurably ill person to die, usually for reasons of mercy.
UF Mercy Killing
B Death and Dying 1967
R Advance Directives 1994
Assisted Suicide 1997
Bioethics 2003
Death Attitudes 1973
↓ Ethics 1967
Professional Ethics 1973
↓ Treatment 1967
Treatment Withholding 1988

Evaluation 1967
PN 8105 SC 18260
SN Conceptually broad term referring to the appraisal of the characteristics, significance, importance, or relative value of a person, organization, or thing.
N Clinical Audits 2007
Course Evaluation 1978
Forensic Evaluation 1994
Geriatric Assessment 1997
Needs Assessment 1985
Peer Evaluation 1982
↓ Personnel Evaluation 1973
↓ Program Evaluation 1985
↓ Psychiatric Evaluation 1997
Risk Assessment 2004
Self Evaluation 1967
Treatment Effectiveness Evaluation 1973
Vocational Evaluation 1991
R Evaluation Criteria 2001
Intake Interview 1994
↓ Measurement 1967
↓ Psychological Assessment 1997
Psychological Report 1988

Evaluation (Psychiatric)
Use Psychiatric Evaluation

Evaluation (Treatment Effectiveness)
Use Treatment Effectiveness Evaluation

Evaluation Criteria 2001
PN 375 SC 18270
SN Specifications that may be used to appraise individuals, organizations, tests, values, or processes.
UF Assessment Criteria
R ↓ Evaluation 1967

Evangelists 1973
PN 101 SC 18320
B Religious Personnel 1973
R ↓ Clergy 1973
Lay Religious Personnel 1973
Missionaries 1973

Event Related Potentials
Use Evoked Potentials

Evidence Based Medicine
Use Evidence Based Practice

Evidence Based Practice 2004
PN 2080 SC 18326
SN Basing clinical practice and decision making on the appraisal of systematic research findings.
HN This term was introduced in June 2004. Relevant records were re-indexed with this term. The posting note reflects the number of records that were re-indexed.
UF Evidence Based Medicine
R Clinical Trials 2004
↓ Experimentation 1967
↓ Health Care Delivery 1978

Evil 2003
PN 270 SC 18327
HN This term was introduced in June 2003. Relevant records were re-indexed with this term. The posting note reflects the number of records that were re-indexed.
R ↓ Ethics 1967
Morality 1967
↓ Religious Beliefs 1973
Sin 1973
Social Values 1973

Evoked Potentials 1967
PN 8065 SC 18330
SN In the brain and central nervous system, a neuroelectrical response that is evoked by external somatosensory, auditory, or visual stimulation.
HN In May 2006, this term replaced the discontinued term CORTICAL EVOKED POTENTIALS. CORTICAL EVOKED POTENTIALS was removed from all records containing it and replaced with EVOKED POTENTIALS, its postable counterpart.
UF Cortical Evoked Potentials
Event Related Potentials
B Electrical Activity 1967
N Auditory Evoked Potentials 1973
Contingent Negative Variation 1982
Olfactory Evoked Potentials 1973
Somatosensory Evoked Potentials 1973
Visual Evoked Potentials 1973
R Electrical Brain Stimulation 1973
↓ Neuroimaging 2003
Sensory Gating 1991

Evolution (Theory of)
Use Theory of Evolution

Evolutionary Economics 2007
PN 6 SC 18341
SN A methodology applying evolutionary concepts to the study of the economy, with emphasis on dynamics, changing structures and technologies, resource constraints, and disequilibrium processes.
HN This term was introduced in April 2007. Relevant records were re-indexed with this term. The posting note reflects the number of records that were re-indexed.
B Economics 1985
R ↓ Darwinism 1973
Evolutionary Psychology 2003
Natural Selection 1997
Theory of Evolution 1967

Evolutionary Psychology 2003
PN 965 SC 18343
SN A branch of psychology that applies concepts from evolutionary theory to behavior.
HN This term was introduced in June 2003. Relevant records were re-indexed with this term. The posting note reflects the number of records that were re-indexed.
B Psychology 1967
R ↓ Darwinism 1973
Evolutionary Economics 2007
Sociobiology 1982
Theory of Evolution 1967

Exceptional Children (Gifted)
Use Gifted

Exceptional Children (Handicapped)
Use Disorders

Exchange (Business)
Use Commerce

Excitation (Physiological)
Use Physiological Arousal

Excretion 1967
PN 654 SC 18370
UF Elimination (Excretion)
B Physiology 1967
N Defecation 1967
↓ Urination 1967

Executive Dysfunction
Use Cognitive Impairment

Executive Functioning
Use Cognitive Ability

Executives
Use Top Level Managers

Exercise 1973
PN 7256 SC 18390
UF Physical Exercise
B Physical Activity 2007
N Aerobic Exercise 1988
Weightlifting 1994
Yoga 1973
R ↓ Health Behavior 1982
Movement Therapy 1997
Physical Fitness 1973
Weight Control 1985

Exhaustion
Use Fatigue

Exhibitionism 1973
PN 242 **SC** 18420
B Paraphilias 1988
R Voyeurism 1973

Existential Therapy 1973
PN 488 **SC** 18430
SN Form of psychotherapy that deals with the here and now of the patient's total situation rather than with his/her past; it emphasizes emotional experiences rather than rational thinking, and stresses a person's responsibility for his/her own existence.
B Psychotherapy 1967
R ↓ Humanistic Psychotherapy 2003
Logotherapy 1973

Existentialism 1967
PN 1448 **SC** 18440
SN Philosophy based on the analysis of the individual's existence in the world which holds that human existence cannot be completely described in scientific terms. Existentialism also stresses the freedom and responsibility of the individual as well as the uniqueness of religious and ethical experiences and the analysis of subjective phenomena such as anxiety, guilt, and suffering.
B Philosophies 1967
R Relativism 1997
↓ Religious Beliefs 1973

Exogamous Marriage 1973
PN 135 **SC** 18450
UF Interethnic Marriage
Intermarriage
B Marriage 1967
N Interfaith Marriage 1973
Interracial Marriage 1973

Expatriates 2007
PN 304 **SC** 18452
SN Persons living in a country other than their own, generally with the intent to return to their home country.
HN In April 2007, this term was created to replace the discontinued term FOREIGN NATIONALS. FOREIGN NATIONALS was removed from all records containing it, and was replaced with EXPATRIATES.
UF Foreign Nationals
N Foreign Workers 1985
R Immigration 1973
International Students 2007

Expectant Fathers 1985
PN 123 **SC** 18455
B Expectant Parents 1985
R ↓ Fathers 1967

Expectant Mothers 1985
PN 412 **SC** 18456
B Expectant Parents 1985
R ↓ Mothers 1967

Expectant Parents 1985
PN 123 **SC** 18457
N Expectant Fathers 1985
Expectant Mothers 1985
R ↓ Parents 1967

Expectations 1967
PN 12245 **SC** 18460
SN Anticipation of future behavior or events. Also refers to investigations of the effects of that anticipation on behavior.

Expectations — (cont'd)
B Cognitions 1985
N Experimenter Expectations 1973
Parental Expectations 1997
Role Expectations 1973
Teacher Expectations 1978
R ↓ Estimation 1967
Future 1991
Halo Effect 1982
Hope 1991
Self Efficacy 1985
Self Fulfilling Prophecies 1997

Experience (Practice)
Use Practice

Experience Level 1988
PN 4228 **SC** 18495
SN Amount of practical knowledge, skill, or practice as a result of direct participation in a particular activity.
UF Expertise
N Job Experience Level 1973
R ↓ Knowledge Level 1978
↓ Practice 1967

Experience Level (Job)
Use Job Experience Level

Experiences (Events) 1973
PN 9100 **SC** 18510
SN Perceptual, emotional, and/or cognitive consequences associated with specific events or contexts. Compare LIFE EXPERIENCES.
N Anniversary Events 1994
Early Experience 1967
↓ Life Experiences 1973
Vicarious Experiences 1973
R Combat Experience 1991
↓ Crises 1971
Familiarity 1967
Homesickness 1994
Near Death Experiences 1985

Experiences (Life)
Use Life Experiences

Experiential Learning 1997
PN 561 **SC** 18517
B Learning 1967
Teaching Methods 1967
N Curricular Field Experience 1982
↓ Internship Programs 2006
Service Learning 2007
R Apprenticeship 1973
Cooperative Education 1982
Discovery Teaching Method 1973
Educational Field Trips 1973
On the Job Training 1973
School Learning 1967

Experiential Psychotherapy 1973
PN 431 **SC** 18520
SN Psychotherapeutic approach, having some roots in existentialism, that emphasizes the concrete, lived, and felt experience of the client.
B Psychotherapy 1967

Experiment Controls 1973
PN 412 **SC** 18530
UF Control Groups
R ↓ Experimental Design 1967
Experimental Subjects 1985
↓ Experimentation 1967

Experiment Controls — (cont'd)
↓ Methodology 1967

Experiment Volunteers
HN In July 2003, the term was discontinued and removed from all records containing it, and replaced with EXPERIMENTAL SUBJECTS, its postable counterpart.
Use Experimental Subjects

Experimental Apparatus
Use Apparatus

Experimental Attrition 1994
PN 171 **SC** 18555
SN Reduction in the number of experimental subjects over time as a result of resignation or other factors.
UF Attrition (Experimental)
Research Dropouts
R ↓ Dropouts 1973
Experimental Subjects 1985
↓ Experimentation 1967

Experimental Design 1967
PN 6492 **SC** 18560
SN General procedural plan for conducting an experiment or other research study in view of the specific data desired. This may include identification of the independent and dependent variables; selection of subjects and their assignment to specific experimental conditions/treatments; the sequence of experimental conditions/treatments; and a method of analysis. Consider also EXPERIMENTAL METHODS.
UF Design (Experimental)
Research Design
N Between Groups Design 1985
Clinical Trials 2004
Cohort Analysis 1988
Followup Studies 1973
↓ Hypothesis Testing 1973
↓ Longitudinal Studies 1973
Repeated Measures 1985
R Animal Models 1988
Conjoint Measurement 1994
Debriefing (Experimental) 1991
Experiment Controls 1973
↓ Experimental Methods 1967
↓ Experimentation 1967
↓ Methodology 1967
↓ Population (Statistics) 1973
Psychometrics 1967
Qualitative Research 2003
Quantitative Methods 2003
Quasi Experimental Methods 2003
Research Setting 2001
↓ Sampling (Experimental) 1973
↓ Statistical Analysis 1967
↓ Statistical Variables 1973
↓ Test Construction 1973

Experimental Environment
Use Research Setting

Experimental Epilepsy 1978
PN 221 **SC** 18564
SN Paroxysmal transient disruption of normal electrical activity in the brain induced by chemical, electrical, or physical stimulation of the brain or by repetitive sensory stimulation.
B Epilepsy 1967
Epileptic Seizures 1973

Experimental Epilepsy — (cont'd)
R ↓ Electrical Stimulation 1973
Kindling 1985
↓ Seizures 2005

Experimental Ethics 1978
PN 1926 SC 18566
B Ethics 1967
R Animal Welfare 1985
Bioethics 2003
Debriefing (Experimental) 1991
↓ Experimentation 1967
Fraud 1994
Informed Consent 1985
Professional Ethics 1973

Experimental Instructions 1967
PN 2852 SC 18570
SN Directions given to a subject participating in an experiment.
UF Instructions (Experimental)
R ↓ Experimentation 1967
↓ Methodology 1967

Experimental Laboratories 1973
PN 583 SC 18580
UF Laboratories (Experimental)
R ↓ Experimentation 1967
↓ Methodology 1967
Research Setting 2001

Experimental Methods 1967
PN 6792 SC 18590
SN System of scientific investigation, usually based on a design and carried out under controlled conditions with the aim of testing a hypothesis, in which one or more variables is manipulated.
UF Scientific Methods
B Empirical Methods 1973
N Quasi Experimental Methods 2003
↓ Stimulus Presentation Methods 1973
R ↓ Experimental Design 1967
Quantitative Methods 2003

Experimental Neurosis 1973
PN 66 SC 18600
SN Acute neurotic-like state produced experimentally by requiring discrimination or problem solving responses which are beyond the subject's ability or level of learning. Such states are induced by the repeated delivery of aversive stimulation following failure.
B Neurosis 1967
R Experimental Psychosis 1973
Learned Helplessness 1978

Experimental Psychologists 1973
PN 168 SC 18610
B Psychologists 1967

Experimental Psychology 1967
PN 1844 SC 18620
B Psychology 1967
R ↓ Experimentation 1967

Experimental Psychosis 1973
PN 22 SC 18630
SN Experimentally induced psychotic-like state or condition usually achieved through drug administration. Not to be confused with inadvertent induction of psychotic conditions resulting from toxic side effects in drug therapy. Compare TOXIC PSYCHOSES.

Experimental Psychosis — (cont'd)
B Psychosis 1967
R Experimental Neurosis 1973
↓ Hallucinogenic Drugs 1967
↓ Psychotomimetic Drugs 1973

Experimental Replication 1973
PN 3691 SC 18640
SN Used in records discussing issues involved in the process of conducting a replication of an experiment.
HN From 1973-2000, the term was also used as a mandatory document type identifier; however, this usage has been discontinued due to the advent of Form/Content Type field identifiers. References from 1973-2000 can be accessed using either EXPERIMENTAL REPLICATION or the Experimental Replication Form/Content Type field identifier.
UF Replication (Experimental)
R ↓ Experimentation 1967
↓ Methodology 1967

Experimental Setting
Use Research Setting

Experimental Subjects 1985
PN 2191 SC 18645
SN Any individual who is, knowingly or unknowingly, a member of an experiment or research population. Used only when methodological or procedural aspects are discussed regarding research subjects. Used primarily for human populations.
HN In June 2003, this term replaced the discontinued term EXPERIMENT VOLUNTEERS. EXPERIMENT VOLUNTEERS was removed from all records containing it and replaced with EXPERIMENTAL SUBJECTS.
UF Experiment Volunteers
Research Subjects
Volunteers (Experiment)
R Debriefing (Experimental) 1991
Experiment Controls 1973
Experimental Attrition 1994
↓ Experimentation 1967

Experimentation 1967
PN 30554 SC 18650
SN Conceptually broad term referring to any or all aspects of scientific research. Use a more specific term if possible.
UF Investigation
Research
N ↓ Consumer Research 1973
Interdisciplinary Research 1985
Qualitative Research 2003
Quantitative Methods 2003
Research Setting 2001
R Animal Models 1988
Causal Analysis 1994
Debriefing (Experimental) 1991
Evidence Based Practice 2004
Experiment Controls 1973
Experimental Attrition 1994
↓ Experimental Design 1967
Experimental Ethics 1978
Experimental Instructions 1967
Experimental Laboratories 1973
Experimental Psychology 1967
Experimental Replication 1973
Experimental Subjects 1985
Experimenters 1973
↓ Measurement 1967
↓ Methodology 1967
↓ Population (Statistics) 1973
Psychometrics 1967

Experimentation — (cont'd)
Psychophysics 1967
↓ Sampling (Experimental) 1973
↓ Statistical Analysis 1967
↓ Statistical Correlation 1967
Statistical Reliability 1973
Statistical Validity 1973
↓ Statistical Variables 1973
↓ Theories 1967

Experimenter Bias 1967
PN 632 SC 18660
SN Potential and unintentional influence on experimental outcomes caused by the experimenter.
UF Bias (Experimenter)
R Experimenter Expectations 1973
Experimenters 1973
Halo Effect 1982

Experimenter Expectations 1973
PN 164 SC 18670
SN Results from experimentation which are anticipated or desired by the researcher in order to confirm a hypothesis and which may serve as a potential factor in experimenter bias.
B Expectations 1967
R Experimenter Bias 1967
Experimenters 1973

Experimenters 1973
PN 743 SC 18680
R ↓ Experimentation 1967
Experimenter Bias 1967
Experimenter Expectations 1973

Expert Systems 1991
PN 1586 SC 18685
UF Knowledge Based Systems
B Artificial Intelligence 1982
Systems 1967
N Decision Support Systems 1997
R ↓ Automated Information Processing 1973
Automated Speech Recognition 1994
Case Based Reasoning 2003
↓ Computers 1967
Cybernetics 1967
↓ Data Processing 1967
Databases 1991
↓ Decision Making 1967
Heuristics 2003
Human Machine Systems 1997
↓ Information Systems 1991
Intelligent Agents 2007
Intelligent Tutoring Systems 2003
Knowledge Engineering 2003
Knowledge Management 2005
↓ Machine Learning 2003
↓ Problem Solving 1967
Robotics 1985

Expert Testimony 1973
PN 1871 SC 18690
SN Legal testimony by persons, who by virtue of their training, skills, or expertise, are qualified to give evidence concerning some scientific, technical, or professional matter.
UF Testimony (Expert)
B Legal Testimony 1982
R Cross Examination 2005
Forensic Evaluation 1994
Forensic Psychiatry 1973
Forensic Psychology 1985
Litigation 2003

Expertise
Use Experience Level

Explicit Memory 1997
PN 553 **SC** 18695
SN Memory of events where one is also aware of learning or experiencing the event.
B Memory 1967
R Implicit Memory 2003

Exploratory Behavior 1967
PN 840 **SC** 18700
SN Locomotor activity or perceptual processes involved in investigating and/or orienting oneself to an environment.
HN From 1973, limited to human populations. From 1973, use ANIMAL EXPLORATORY BEHAVIOR to access references to nonhumans.
B Behavior 1967
N Animal Exploratory Behavior 1973
R Curiosity 1967
Information Seeking 1973
↓ Motivation 1967

Explosive Disorder 2001
PN 82 **SC** 18705
SN Disorder characterized by discrete episodes of loss of control of aggressive impulses that may result in serious assault or destruction of property.
HN In 2000, this term was created to replace the discontinued term EXPLOSIVE PERSONALITY. EXPLOSIVE PERSONALITY was removed from all records containing it and replaced with EXPLOSIVE DISORDER.
UF Explosive Personality
Intermittent Explosive Disorder
B Impulse Control Disorders 1997
R Anger Control 1997
↓ Antisocial Behavior 1971
Conduct Disorder 1991
↓ Personality Disorders 1967

Explosive Personality
HN In 2000, EXPLOSIVE PERSONALITY was discontinued and removed from all records containing it. The term was replaced with EXPLOSIVE DISORDER, its postable counterpart.
Use Explosive Disorder

Exposure Therapy 1997
PN 687 **SC** 18715
B Behavior Therapy 1967
N Implosive Therapy 1973
Systematic Desensitization Therapy 1973

Exposure Time (Stimulus)
Use Stimulus Duration

Expressed Emotion 1991
PN 756 **SC** 18725
SN Frequency and quality of negative emotions, e.g., anger or hostility, expressed by family members or significant others, that often lead to a high relapse rate, especially in schizophrenic patients.
R ↓ Emotions 1967
Relapse (Disorders) 1973
↓ Schizophrenia 1967

Expressions (Facial)
Use Facial Expressions

Expressive Psychotherapy 1973
PN 144 **SC** 18740
SN Psychotherapeutic method used to promote more effective personality functioning through uninhibited expression of feelings and open discussion of personal problems.
B Psychotherapy 1967
R Improvisation 2004
Supportive Psychotherapy 1997

Expulsion (School)
Use School Expulsion

Extended Family 1973
PN 332 **SC** 18760
B Family 1967
Family Structure 1973

Extension Workers (Agricultural)
Use Agricultural Extension Workers

External Ear 1973
PN 75 **SC** 18780
UF Ear Canal
B Ear (Anatomy) 1967

External Rewards 1973
PN 379 **SC** 18790
SN Tangible or overtly identifiable rewards given in return for service or attainment which may act as reinforcement for the activity rewarded. Compare PRIMARY REINFORCEMENT.
UF Extrinsic Rewards
B Rewards 1967
R Extrinsic Motivation 1973
Internal External Locus of Control 1967

Externalization 1973
PN 846 **SC** 18800
B Personality Processes 1967
R ↓ Defense Mechanisms 1967
↓ Internalization 1997
↓ Personality Development 1967

Extinction (Learning) 1967
PN 3883 **SC** 18810
SN Learned behavior or the experimental paradigm involving withholding reinforcement for a conditioned response and resulting in a gradual reduction and eventual elimination of responding or a return to a rate of responding comparable to levels prior to conditioning. Term may be used in either classical (Pavlovian) or operant (instrumental) conditioning contexts.
B Learning 1967
R ↓ Discrimination Learning 1982
↓ Reinforcement 1967

Extracurricular Activities 1973
PN 747 **SC** 18820
N Fraternity Membership 1973
School Club Membership 1973
Sorority Membership 1973
R After School Programs 2003
Athletic Participation 1973
Athletic Training 1991
↓ Education 1967

Extradimensional Shift Learning
Use Nonreversal Shift Learning

Extramarital Intercourse 1973
PN 454 **SC** 18830
UF Adultery
Affairs (Sexual)

Extramarital Intercourse — (cont'd)
Mate Swapping
B Psychosexual Behavior 1967
Sexual Intercourse (Human) 1973
R Infidelity 2006
↓ Marital Relations 1967
Monogamy 1997
Promiscuity 1973

Extrapyramidal Motor System
Use Extrapyramidal Tracts

Extrapyramidal Symptoms 1994
PN 620 **SC** 18835
SN Neurological side effects of pharmacological agents, most often neuroleptics, that are manifested as tremors, involuntary movements, rigidity, or muscle contractions. These symptoms may also be seen in Parkinsons, Alzheimers, or other degenerative neurological diseases.
B Symptoms 1967
R ↓ Basal Ganglia 1973
Extrapyramidal Tracts 1973
↓ Nervous System Disorders 1967

Extrapyramidal System
Use Extrapyramidal Tracts

Extrapyramidal Tracts 1973
PN 128 **SC** 18840
SN Polysynaptic descending nerve pathways found outside of the pyramidal tract that are comprised of cortical and subcortical structures, including the basal ganglia, reticular formation, cerebellum, and spinal cord. This network of neurons plays an important role in motor behavior and control.
UF Extrapyramidal Motor System
Extrapyramidal System
B Central Nervous System 1967
Efferent Pathways 1982
Spinal Cord 1973
R Extrapyramidal Symptoms 1994
Pyramidal Tracts 1973

Extrasensory Perception 1967
PN 825 **SC** 18850
UF ESP (Parapsychology)
B Parapsychological Phenomena 1973
Perception 1967
N ↓ Clairvoyance 1973
Psychokinesis 1973
R Telepathy 1973

Extraversion 1967
PN 3169 **SC** 18854
SN Personality trait which reflects the extent to which an individual likes people and prefers large gatherings; is assertive, active, and talkative; enjoys excitement and stimulation; and tends to have a cheerful disposition.
UF Extroversion
B Personality Traits 1967
R Assertiveness 1973
Five Factor Personality Model 1997
Gregariousness 1973
Introversion 1967
Sensation Seeking 1978
Sociability 1973

Extrinsic Motivation 1973
PN 617 **SC** 18860
SN Need or desire arising from outside the individual which causes action toward some goal.

Extrinsic Motivation — (cont'd)
B Motivation 1967
R External Rewards 1973
↓ Goals 1967
Internal External Locus of Control 1967
↓ Needs 1967

Extrinsic Rewards
Use External Rewards

Extroversion
Use Extraversion

Eye (Anatomy) 1967
PN 1421 **SC** 18890
UF Choroid
Sclera
B Sense Organs 1973
N Cornea 1973
Eye Color 1991
Fovea 1982
Iris (Eye) 1973
Lens (Eye) 1973
Pupil (Eye) 1973
↓ Retina 1967
R ↓ Eye Disorders 1973
↓ Eye Movements 1967
Ocular Dominance 1973
Pupil Dilation 1973
Retinal Image 1973
↓ Visual Perception 1967

Eye Accommodation
Use Ocular Accommodation

Eye Color 1991
PN 33 **SC** 18895
B Color 1967
Eye (Anatomy) 1967
R Iris (Eye) 1973
↓ Pigments 1973

Eye Contact 1973
PN 681 **SC** 18900
SN Form of nonverbal communication in which two individuals meet each other's glance.
B Interpersonal Communication 1973
Nonverbal Communication 1971
R ↓ Social Reinforcement 1967

Eye Convergence 1982
PN 335 **SC** 18902
SN Turning the eyes toward or away from each other when fixating on distal objects.
UF Vergence Movements
B Eye Movements 1967
R ↓ Depth Perception 1967
↓ Distance Perception 1973
Strabismus 1973

Eye Disorders 1973
PN 515 **SC** 18910
SN Diseases or defects of the eye. Use VISION DISORDERS for other pathology involving visual neural pathways.
B Vision Disorders 1982
N Amblyopia 1973
Cataracts 1973
Color Blindness 1973
Glaucoma 1973
Nystagmus 1973
↓ Refraction Errors 1973
Strabismus 1973
Tunnel Vision 1973

Eye Disorders — (cont'd)
R Albinism 1973
↓ Eye (Anatomy) 1967
Hysterical Vision Disturbances 1973
↓ Visual Perception 1967

Eye Dominance
Use Ocular Dominance

Eye Examination
Use Ophthalmologic Examination

Eye Fixation 1982
PN 2172 **SC** 18924
SN Orienting one's eye(s) toward and stabilizing one's gaze on a specified visual stimulus.
UF Gazing
Ocular Fixation
Visual Fixation
B Visual Perception 1967
R Visual Attention 2004
Visual Field 1967

Eye Movement Desensitization Therapy 1997
PN 427 **SC** 18927
SN Treatment methodology used in the reduction of the emotional impact of trauma-based symptomatology associated with anxiety, nightmares, flashbacks, or intrusive thought processes.
UF EMDR
B Psychotherapy 1967
R ↓ Behavior Therapy 1967
↓ Eye Movements 1967

Eye Movements 1967
PN 7940 **SC** 18930
UF Oculomotor Response
Saccadic Eye Movements
N Eye Convergence 1982
Nystagmus 1973
Rapid Eye Movement 1971
R ↓ Eye (Anatomy) 1967
Eye Movement Desensitization Therapy 1997
REM Dreams 1973
REM Sleep 1973
Visual Search 1982

Eyeblink Reflex 1973
PN 986 **SC** 18940
UF Blink Reflex
B Reflexes 1971
R Startle Reflex 1967

Eyelid Conditioning 1973
PN 789 **SC** 18950
SN Conditioned eye blinking or the classical conditioning paradigm resulting in conditioned eye blinking.
UF Conditioning (Eyelid)
B Classical Conditioning 1967

Eyewitnesses
Use Witnesses

Eysenck Personality Inventory 1973
PN 521 **SC** 18960
B Nonprojective Personality Measures 1973

F Test 1973
PN 107 **SC** 18970
B Parametric Statistical Tests 1973
R ↓ Variability Measurement 1973

Face (Anatomy) 1973
PN 1017 **SC** 18980
B Anatomy 1967
R Facial Features 1973
Head (Anatomy) 1973

Face Perception 1985
PN 4214 **SC** 18985
SN Used for human or animal populations.
UF Face Recognition
B Visual Perception 1967
R ↓ Facial Expressions 1967
Facial Features 1973
Prosopagnosia 1994
↓ Social Perception 1967

Face Recognition
Use Face Perception

Facial Expressions 1967
PN 3735 **SC** 18990
UF Expressions (Facial)
B Nonverbal Communication 1971
N Grimaces 1973
Smiles 1973
R Face Perception 1985
Facial Features 1973

Facial Features 1973
PN 1132 **SC** 18993
R Face (Anatomy) 1973
Face Perception 1985
↓ Facial Expressions 1967
↓ Physical Appearance 1982
Physical Attractiveness 1973

Facial Muscles 1973
PN 352 **SC** 19000
B Muscles 1967

Facial Nerve 1973
PN 197 **SC** 19010
UF Chorda Tympani Nerve
Nerve (Facial)
B Cranial Nerves 1973

Facilitated Communication
Use Augmentative Communication

Facilitation (Social)
Use Social Facilitation

Facilities 2006
PN 170 **SC** 19022
SN Use a more specific term if possible.
HN This term was introduced in May 2006. Relevant records were re-indexed with this term. The posting note reflects the number of records that were re-indexed.
UF Buildings
N ↓ Community Facilities 1973
↓ Correctional Institutions 1973
↓ Libraries 1982
Maximum Security Facilities 1985
Museums 2006

Facilities — (cont'd)
Religious Buildings 1973
↓ Residential Care Institutions 1973
↓ School Facilities 1973
↓ Treatment Facilities 1973
R Assessment Centers 1982
Day Care Centers 1973
↓ Facility Environment 1988

Facility Admission 1988
PN 191 **SC** 19024
UF Facility Readmission
N ↓ Hospital Admission 1973
R ↓ Facility Discharge 1988
↓ Institutionalization 1967
↓ Treatment Facilities 1973

Facility Discharge 1988
PN 106 **SC** 19026
N ↓ Hospital Discharge 1973
R Client Transfer 1997
Discharge Planning 1994
↓ Facility Admission 1988
↓ Institutionalization 1967
↓ Treatment Facilities 1973

Facility Environment 1988
PN 572 **SC** 19028
B Environment 1967
Therapeutic Environment 2001
N Hospital Environment 1982
R ↓ Facilities 2006
↓ Treatment Facilities 1973

Facility Readmission
Use Facility Admission

Factitious Disorders 1988
PN 381 **SC** 19035
SN A general term for any physical or psychological disorder whose symptoms are voluntarily produced, without any apparent aim or purpose. Compare MALINGERING.
UF Ganser Syndrome
B Mental Disorders 1967
N Munchausen Syndrome 1994
R Malingering 1973
Pseudodementia 1985

Factor Analysis 1967
PN 7176 **SC** 19040
HN Use FACTOR ANALYSIS to access references to the factor structure of psychometric measures from 1967-1984.
UF Confirmatory Factor Analysis
B Multivariate Analysis 1982
N Item Analysis (Statistical) 1973
↓ Statistical Rotation 1973
R Factor Structure 1985
Goodness of Fit 1988
Path Analysis 1991
↓ Statistical Correlation 1967
Statistical Significance 1973
Structural Equation Modeling 1994

Factor Structure 1985
PN 5876 **SC** 19045
SN The internal correlational structure of a set of variables said to measure a given construct.
HN Use FACTOR ANALYSIS to access references prior to 1985.
R ↓ Factor Analysis 1967
↓ Statistical Rotation 1973
Structural Equation Modeling 1994

Factorial Validity
HN In 2000, FACTORIAL VALIDITY was discontinued and removed from all records containing it. The term was replaced with STATISTICAL VALIDITY, its postable counterpart.
Use Statistical Validity

Factory Environments
Use Working Conditions

Factual Knowledge
Use Declarative Knowledge

Faculty
Use Educational Personnel

Fading (Conditioning) 1982
PN 152 **SC** 19087
SN Gradual attenuation of dissimilarity of stimuli dimensions contingent on the subject's mastery of difference between those stimuli. The fading technique is used to facilitate errorless discrimination learning.
B Behavior Modification 1973
Operant Conditioning 1967
R ↓ Discrimination Learning 1982
Stimulus Attenuation 1973
Stimulus Discrimination 1973

Fads and Fashions 1973
PN 191 **SC** 19090
N Clothing 1967
R Cosmetic Techniques 2001
Popular Culture 2003
Social Change 1967
Trends 1991

Failure 1967
PN 2215 **SC** 19100
N Academic Failure 1978
R Academic Underachievement 1967
↓ Achievement 1967

Failure to Thrive 1988
PN 258 **SC** 19105
SN Growth disorder of infants and children due to nutritional and/or emotional deprivation and resulting in loss of weight and delayed physical, emotional, and social development.
B Delayed Development 1973
R Attachment Disorders 2001
↓ Child Abuse 1971
Child Neglect 1988
↓ Nutritional Deficiencies 1973

Fainting
Use Syncope

Fairbairnian Theory
Use Object Relations

Fairy Tales
Use Folklore

Faith Based Organizations 2007
PN 14 **SC** 19117
SN Charitable or nonprofit organizations aligned with religious groups that provide social and community services to the public.
HN This term was introduced in April 2007. Relevant records were re-indexed with this term. The posting note reflects the number of records that were re-indexed.

Faith Based Organizations — (cont'd)
B Religious Organizations 1991
R Charitable Behavior 1973
Human Services 2007
Nonprofit Organizations 1973
↓ Prosocial Behavior 1982
↓ Social Services 1982

Faith Healing 1973
PN 597 **SC** 19120
UF Psychic Healing
B Alternative Medicine 1997
Religious Practices 1973
R Folk Medicine 1973
Shamanism 1973
Witchcraft 1973

Faking 1973
PN 572 **SC** 19130
B Deception 1967
R ↓ Behavior Disorders 1971

Falls 2004
PN 316 **SC** 19132
HN This term was introduced in June 2004. Relevant records were re-indexed with this term. The posting note reflects the number of records that were re-indexed.
B Accidents 1967
R Equilibrium 1973
↓ Injuries 1973

False Beliefs 2007
PN 153 **SC** 19133
SN Internal cognitive representations that have no basis in reality.
HN This term was introduced in April 2007. Relevant records were re-indexed with this term. The posting note reflects the number of records that were re-indexed.
B Cognitive Processes 1967
R ↓ Cognitions 1985
Cognitive Discrimination 1973
Cognitive Generalization 1967
Irrational Beliefs 1982
Theory of Mind 2001

False Memory 1997
PN 1011 **SC** 19135
UF Pseudomemory
B Memory 1967
R Age Regression (Hypnotic) 1988
↓ Amnesia 1967
Confabulation 1973
Early Memories 1985
Emotional Trauma 1967
↓ Hypnosis 1967
↓ Hypnotherapy 1973
Repressed Memory 1997
Source Monitoring 2004
Suggestibility 1967

False Pregnancy
Use Pseudocyesis

Fame 1985
PN 181 **SC** 19145
UF Celebrity
R Celebrities 2007
Reputation 1997
↓ Social Perception 1967
↓ Status 1967

Familial Idiocy (Amaurotic)
Use Tay Sachs Disease

Familiarity 1967
PN 4617 **SC** 19160
SN Knowledge of, or close acquaintance with, an object, stimulus, person, environment, situation, or act.
R ↓ Experiences (Events) 1973
↓ Practice 1967
Stranger Reactions 1988

Family 1967
PN 15239 **SC** 19300
SN Conceptually broad term. Use a more specific term if possible.
N Biological Family 1988
Extended Family 1973
Family of Origin 1991
Interethnic Family 1988
Interracial Family 1988
Nuclear Family 1973
Schizophrenogenic Family 1967
Stepfamily 1991
R Codependency 1991
Cohabitation 1973
Couples 1982
Divorce 1973
Divorced Persons 1973
Dual Careers 1982
Dysfunctional Family 1991
Empty Nest 1991
↓ Family Background 1973
Family Crises 1973
↓ Family Life Education 1997
↓ Family Members 1973
↓ Family Planning 1973
↓ Family Relations 1967
Family Resemblance 1991
↓ Family Structure 1973
Kinship 1985
↓ Living Arrangements 1991
↓ Marital Separation 1973
↓ Marital Status 1973
↓ Marriage 1967
Transgenerational Patterns 1991
Widowers 1973
Widows 1973
Working Women 1978

Family Background 1973
PN 4898 **SC** 19170
UF Background (Family)
N Family Socioeconomic Level 1973
Parent Educational Background 1973
Parental Occupation 1973
R Biographical Data 1978
Children of Alcoholics 2003
↓ Family 1967
Family of Origin 1991
↓ Marital Status 1973

Family Caregivers
Use Caregivers

Family Conflict 2003
PN 540 **SC** 19178
HN This term was introduced in June 2003. Relevant records were re-indexed with this term. The posting note reflects the number of records that were re-indexed.

Family Conflict — (cont'd)
B Conflict 1967
Family Relations 1967
N Marital Conflict 1973
R Domestic Violence 2006
Family Intervention 2003
Home Environment 1973
↓ Parent Child Relations 1967
↓ Partner Abuse 1991

Family Counseling
Use Family Therapy

Family Crises 1973
PN 616 **SC** 19190
B Crises 1971
R ↓ Family 1967
Family Intervention 2003
Family Reunification 2007
↓ Stress 1967

Family Dynamics
Use Family Relations

Family Environment
Use Home Environment

Family Intervention 2003
PN 720 **SC** 19195
SN Interventions that involve the family as a whole, or individual family members; includes interventions that are provided by family members on behalf of another family member.
HN This term was introduced in June 2003. Relevant records were re-indexed with this term. The posting note reflects the number of records that were re-indexed.
B Intervention 2003
R ↓ Crisis Intervention 1973
↓ Family Conflict 2003
Family Crises 1973
Family Preservation 2007
↓ Family Relations 1967
↓ Family Therapy 1967

Family Life
Use Family Relations

Family Life Education 1997
PN 157 **SC** 19203
UF Marriage and Family Education
B Education 1967
N Parent Training 1978
Sex Education 1973
R ↓ Family 1967
↓ Family Relations 1967
↓ Family Therapy 1967
Household Management 1985

Family Medicine 1988
PN 502 **SC** 19205
B Medical Sciences 1967
R Family Physicians 1973
General Practitioners 1973

Family Members 1973
PN 10239 **SC** 19210
N Adopted Children 1973
Adult Offspring 1985
↓ Ancestors 1973
Biological Family 1988
Cousins 1973

Family Members — (cont'd)
Daughters 1973
Foster Children 1973
Grandchildren 1973
Grandparents 1973
Illegitimate Children 1973
Inlaws 1997
Orphans 1973
↓ Parents 1967
↓ Siblings 1967
Sons 1973
↓ Spouses 1973
Stepchildren 1973
R ↓ Family 1967
Family of Origin 1991
Family Resemblance 1991
Nepotism 2005
↓ Offspring 1988
Only Children 1982
Significant Others 1991

Family of Origin 1991
PN 701 **SC** 19215
SN Family in which an individual was raised. Compare BIOLOGICAL FAMILY.
B Family 1967
R Biological Family 1988
↓ Family Background 1973
↓ Family Members 1973
Family Reunification 2007
↓ Family Structure 1973
Stepfamily 1991

Family Physicians 1973
PN 986 **SC** 19220
B Physicians 1967
R Family Medicine 1988
General Practitioners 1973

Family Planning 1973
PN 817 **SC** 19230
N ↓ Birth Control 1971
R Condoms 1991
Delayed Parenthood 1985
Eugenics 1973
↓ Family 1967
Fertility Enhancement 1973
Induced Abortion 1971
↓ Sterilization (Sex) 1973

Family Planning Attitudes 1973
PN 1009 **SC** 19240
UF Birth Control Attitudes
B Attitudes 1967
R Childlessness 1982
Delayed Parenthood 1985
↓ Family Relations 1967

Family Preservation 2007
PN 176 **SC** 19244
SN Efforts made by state and county social workers to enable a family to stay together.
HN This term was introduced in April 2007. Relevant records were re-indexed with this term. The posting note reflects the number of records that were re-indexed.
R Child Welfare 1988
Family Intervention 2003
Family Reunification 2007
Family Systems Theory 2003
↓ Family Therapy 1967

Family Relations 1967
PN 25241 **SC** 19250
SN Dynamics of interpersonal interaction and developmental processes taking place between and among members of a biological or socially defined family unit. See FAMILY MEMBERS for references to biological relatives in a family.
UF Family Dynamics
Family Life
B Interpersonal Relationships 2004
N ↓ Child Discipline 1973
↓ Childrearing Practices 1967
↓ Family Conflict 2003
↓ Marital Relations 1967
↓ Parent Child Relations 1967
Parental Role 1973
Sibling Relations 1973
R Childrearing Attitudes 1973
Codependency 1991
Domestic Violence 2006
Dysfunctional Family 1991
Empty Nest 1991
↓ Family 1967
Family Intervention 2003
↓ Family Life Education 1997
Family Planning Attitudes 1973
Family Systems Theory 2003
Family Work Relationship 1997
Intergenerational Relations 1988
Marriage Attitudes 1973
↓ Relationship Satisfaction 2001
Social Support 2004
Transgenerational Patterns 1991

Family Resemblance 1991
PN 103 **SC** 19255
R Assortative Mating 1991
↓ Family 1967
↓ Family Members 1973
↓ Genetics 1967
Transgenerational Patterns 1991
↓ Twins 1967

Family Reunification 2007
PN 68 **SC** 19257
SN Family services that attempt to reunite children in out-of-home care with their birth or extended families of origin. Also refers to efforts to reunite families separated as a result of migration, war, conflict, or disaster.
HN This term was introduced in April 2007. Relevant records were re-indexed with this term. The posting note reflects the number of records that were re-indexed.
R Child Custody 1982
Family Crises 1973
Family of Origin 1991
Family Preservation 2007
Foster Care 1978
Home Environment 1973

Family Size 1973
PN 938 **SC** 19260
B Family Structure 1973
Size 1973
R Empty Nest 1991
↓ Parenthood Status 1985

Family Socioeconomic Level 1973
PN 1130 **SC** 19270
B Family Background 1973
Socioeconomic Status 1967

Family Socioeconomic Level — (cont'd)
R Parent Educational Background 1973
Parental Occupation 1973

Family Structure 1973
PN 4333 **SC** 19280
N Birth Order 1967
Childlessness 1982
Extended Family 1973
Family Size 1973
Matriarchy 1973
Monogamy 1997
Nuclear Family 1973
↓ Parental Absence 1973
Patriarchy 1973
Polygamy 1973
Schizophrenogenic Family 1967
Stepfamily 1991
R ↓ Culture (Anthropological) 1967
Dual Careers 1982
Dysfunctional Family 1991
Empty Nest 1991
↓ Family 1967
Family of Origin 1991
Homosexual Parents 1994
Kinship Structure 1973
Living Alone 1994
↓ Living Arrangements 1991
Only Children 1982
↓ Parenthood Status 1985
↓ Single Parents 1978
↓ Sociocultural Factors 1967
Stepchildren 1973
Stepparents 1973

Family Systems Model
Use Family Systems Theory

Family Systems Theory 2003
PN 627 **SC** 19284
SN An approach that utilizes the principles of systems theory to understand and treat families.
HN This term was introduced in June 2003. Relevant records were re-indexed with this term. The posting note reflects the number of records that were re-indexed.
UF Family Systems Model
R Family Preservation 2007
↓ Family Relations 1967
↓ Family Therapy 1967

Family Therapy 1967
PN 14563 **SC** 19290
UF Family Counseling
B Psychotherapeutic Counseling 1973
N Conjoint Therapy 1973
R ↓ Counseling 1967
Family Intervention 2003
↓ Family Life Education 1997
Family Preservation 2007
Family Systems Theory 2003
Social Casework 1967

Family Violence
HN In May 2006, this term was discontinued and removed from all records containing it, and was replaced with DOMESTIC VIOLENCE, its postable counterpart.
Use Domestic Violence

Family Work Relationship 1997
PN 1654 **SC** 19297
UF Job Family Relationship
Work Family Relationship

Family Work Relationship — (cont'd)
R Dual Careers 1982
↓ Family Relations 1967
Role Conflicts 1973
Work (Attitudes Toward) 1973
↓ Working Conditions 1973
Working Women 1978

Fans (Sports)
Use Sports Spectators

Fantasies (Thought Disturbances) 1967
PN 513 **SC** 19310
SN Thinking that severely distorts reality.
B Thought Disturbances 1973
R ↓ Fantasy 1997
Magical Thinking 1973

Fantasy 1997
PN 956 **SC** 19315
HN Use IMAGINATION to access references from 1982-1996.
B Cognitive Processes 1967
N Sexual Fantasy 1997
R Daydreaming 1973
Fantasies (Thought Disturbances) 1967
Fantasy (Defense Mechanism) 1967
↓ Ideation 1973
Imagination 1967
Magical Thinking 1973

Fantasy (Defense Mechanism) 1967
PN 845 **SC** 19320
SN Daydreaming dominated by unconscious material and primary processes for the purpose of wish fulfillment or to alleviate social isolation.
B Defense Mechanisms 1967
R Daydreaming 1973
↓ Fantasy 1997
Sexual Fantasy 1997

Farmers
Use Agricultural Workers

Fascism 1973
PN 502 **SC** 19342
UF Nazism
B Political Economic Systems 1973
R Holocaust 1988

Fat Metabolism
Use Lipid Metabolism

Fatalism 1973
PN 120 **SC** 19360
B Philosophies 1967
R Cynicism 1973
Nihilism 1973
Pessimism 1973

Father Absence 1973
PN 743 **SC** 19370
SN For animals consider ANIMAL PARENTAL BEHAVIOR.
HN From 1982, limited to human populations.
B Parental Absence 1973
R Matriarchy 1973

Father Child Communication 1985
PN 143 **SC** 19375
SN Verbal or nonverbal communication between father and child.

Father Child Communication — (cont'd)
B Parent Child Communication 1973
R Father Child Relations 1973

Father Child Relations 1973
PN 3100 SC 19380
SN For animals consider ANIMAL PARENTAL BEHAVIOR.
HN From 1982, limited to human populations.
B Parent Child Relations 1967
R ↓ Childrearing Practices 1967
Father Child Communication 1985
↓ Parental Attitudes 1973
Parental Permissiveness 1973
Parental Role 1973

Fathers 1967
PN 5055 SC 19390
SN For animals consider ANIMAL PARENTAL BEHAVIOR.
HN From 1982, limited to human populations.
B Human Males 1973
Parents 1967
N Adolescent Fathers 1985
Single Fathers 1994
R Expectant Fathers 1985

Fatigue 1967
PN 2932 SC 19400
SN A usually transient state of discomfort and loss of efficiency as a normal reaction to emotional strain, physical exertion, boredom, or lack of rest.
UF Exhaustion
Tiredness
B Symptoms 1967
R Chronic Fatigue Syndrome 1997
Hypersomnia 1994
Sleepiness 2007

Fatty Acids 1973
PN 680 SC 19410
B Acids 1973
Lipids 1973
N Capsaicin 1991
↓ Phosphatides 1973
R Prostaglandins 1982

Fear 1967
PN 8165 SC 19420
B Emotional States 1973
N Fear of Success 1978
Panic 1973
R Alarm Responses 1973
↓ Anxiety 1967
Conditioned Fear 2003
Neophobia 1985
↓ Neurosis 1967
Panic Attack 2003
↓ Phobias 1967
Shame 1994
Social Anxiety 1985
Stranger Reactions 1988

Fear of Public Speaking
Use Speech Anxiety

Fear of Strangers
Use Stranger Reactions

Fear of Success 1978
PN 425 SC 19424
SN Need to inhibit maximum utilization of one's abilities in achievement situations due to expected negative consequences.

Fear of Success — (cont'd)
B Fear 1967
Motivation 1967
R ↓ Achievement Motivation 1967
↓ Anxiety 1967
↓ Anxiety Disorders 1997
Self Handicapping Strategy 1988

Fear Survey Schedule 1973
PN 65 SC 19430
B Nonprojective Personality Measures 1973

Fecal Incontinence 1973
PN 421 SC 19440
UF Encopresis
Incontinence (Fecal)
B Colon Disorders 1973
R ↓ Behavior Disorders 1971
Diarrhea 1973
↓ Symptoms 1967

Fee for Service 1994
PN 134 SC 19450
SN Payment for health related services in which the health care provider is reimbursed for services by the client or health insurance carrier.
B Health Insurance 1973
Professional Fees 1978
R Cost Containment 1991
↓ Health Care Delivery 1978
↓ Health Care Services 1978
Health Maintenance Organizations 1982
↓ Managed Care 1994

Feedback 1967
PN 8039 SC 19460
SN General concept denoting the return of information that may regulate or control subsequent behavior, cognition, perception, or performance. Use a more specific term if possible.
N ↓ Biofeedback 1973
↓ Delayed Feedback 1973
Knowledge of Results 1967
↓ Sensory Feedback 1973
R Intelligent Tutoring Systems 2003
↓ Learning 1967
↓ Reinforcement 1967
↓ Stimulation 1967

Feeding Behavior (Animal)
Use Animal Feeding Behavior

Feeding Practices
HN In June 2004, this term was discontinued and removed from all records containing it, and replaced with EATING BEHAVIOR, its postable counterpart.
Use Eating Behavior

Feelings
Use Emotions

Feet (Anatomy) 1973
PN 325 SC 19500
UF Heels (Anatomy)
Toes (Anatomy)
B Anatomy 1967
Musculoskeletal System 1973
R Ankle 1973
Leg (Anatomy) 1973

Felids 1997
PN 54 SC 19505
UF Lions
Tigers

Felids — (cont'd)
B Mammals 1973
N Cats 1967

Felonies
Use Crime

Female Animals 1973
PN 4391 SC 19520
B Animals 1967

Female Attitudes 2006
PN 509 SC 19525
SN Attitudes of females. Used when females are the focus of discussion.
HN This term was introduced in May 2006. Relevant records were re-indexed with this term. The posting note reflects the number of records that were re-indexed.
B Attitudes 1967
R ↓ Human Females 1973

Female Criminals 1973
PN 762 SC 19530
B Criminals 1967
Human Females 1973

Female Delinquency 2001
PN 407 SC 19535
HN In 2000, this term was created to replace the discontinued term FEMALE DELINQUENTS. FEMALE DELINQUENTS was removed from all records containing it and replaced with FEMALE DELINQUENCY.
B Juvenile Delinquency 1967
R ↓ Human Females 1973
Male Delinquency 2001

Female Genital Mutilation
Use Circumcision

Female Genitalia 1973
PN 423 SC 19550
SN Used for both human and animal populations.
UF Genitalia (Female)
B Urogenital System 1973
N Ovaries 1973
↓ Uterus 1973
Vagina 1973
R Circumcision 2001

Female Homosexuality
Use Lesbianism

Female Only Environments
Use Single Sex Environments

Female Orgasm 1973
PN 341 SC 19560
SN Used for both human and animal populations.
B Orgasm 1973
R Female Sexual Dysfunction 2005
Masturbation 1973
↓ Sexual Intercourse (Human) 1973

Female Sexual Dysfunction 2005
PN 183 SC 19565
SN Refers to a female's lack of sexual desire or an inability to enjoy or complete sexual intercourse or achieve orgasm.
HN In August 2005, this term replaced the discontinued term FRIGIDITY. FRIGIDITY was removed from all records containing it, and was replaced with FEMALE SEXUAL DYSFUNCTION, its postable counterpart.

Female Sexual Dysfunction — (cont'd)
UF Frigidity
B Sexual Function Disturbances 1973
R Dyspareunia 1973
Female Orgasm 1973
Inhibited Sexual Desire 1997
Libido 1973
↓ Orgasm 1973
↓ Symptoms 1967
Vaginismus 1973

Females (Human)
Use Human Females

Femininity 1967
PN 2749 SC 19580
B Personality Traits 1967
R Androgyny 1982
↓ Gender Identity 1985
Masculinity 1967
Sex Roles 1967

Feminism 1978
PN 5719 SC 19585
R Feminist Psychology 2007
Feminist Therapy 1994
↓ Sex Role Attitudes 1978
Womens Liberation Movement 1973

Feminist Psychology 2007
PN 163 SC 19586
SN An approach to psychological issues that emphasizes the role of the female perspective in thought, action, and emotion in the life of the individual and in society.
HN This term was introduced in April 2007. Relevant records were re-indexed with this term. The posting note reflects the number of records that were re-indexed.
B Psychology 1967
R Feminism 1978
Psychology of Women 2007

Feminist Therapy 1994
PN 479 SC 19587
SN An approach to psychotherapy, counseling, or consultation based on the assumptions and tenets of feminism.
B Psychotherapy 1967
R ↓ Counseling 1967
Feminism 1978

Feminization Syndrome (Testicular)
Use Testicular Feminization Syndrome

Femoral Nerve
Use Spinal Nerves

Fenfluramine 1973
PN 636 SC 19610
B Appetite Depressing Drugs 1973
Sympathomimetic Drugs 1973

Fentanyl 1985
PN 221 SC 19613
SN Synthetic opiate frequently used illicitly.
B Opiates 1973

Fertility 1988
PN 650 SC 19618
SN The quality or state of being capable of breeding or reproducing. Used for human and animal populations.

Fertility — (cont'd)
B Sexual Reproduction 1973
R Birth Rate 1982
Fertility Enhancement 1973
↓ Infertility 1973

Fertility Enhancement 1973
PN 47 SC 19620
R ↓ Family Planning 1973
Fertility 1988
↓ Hormones 1967
Oral Contraceptives 1973

Fertilization 1973
PN 188 SC 19630
R ↓ Pregnancy 1967
Reproductive Technology 1988
↓ Sexual Reproduction 1973

Fetal Alcohol Syndrome 1985
PN 566 SC 19635
SN A cluster of abnormalities characteristic of children born to mothers who drank heavily during pregnancy. Features include mental deficiency, motor dysfunction, and abnormal physical development.
B Drug Induced Congenital Disorders 1973
Syndromes 1973
R ↓ Alcoholism 1967
Ethanol 1973
↓ Mental Retardation 1967
↓ Prenatal Development 1973

Fetal Exposure
Use Prenatal Exposure

Fetishism 1973
PN 297 SC 19640
UF Sexual Fetishism
B Paraphilias 1988
R Coprophagia 2001
Sexual Masochism 1973
Sexual Sadism 1973
Transvestism 1973

Fetus 1967
PN 1097 SC 19650
B Prenatal Developmental Stages 1973

Fever
Use Hyperthermia

Fibrillation (Heart) 1973
PN 77 SC 19680
UF Atrial Fibrillation
Auricular Fibrillation
Ventricular Fibrillation
B Arrhythmias (Heart) 1973

Fibromyalgia 2004
PN 285 SC 19685
SN A common nonarticular rheumatic condition that is characterized by muscle pain, tenderness, and stiffness.
HN Use MUSCULAR DISORDERS to access references from 1994 to June 2004.
B Muscular Disorders 1973
R ↓ Pain 1967

Fiction
Use Literature

Field Dependence 1973
PN 2147 SC 19710
SN Aspect of cognitive style as seen in relative lack of autonomy from external referents, the inability to overcome embedding contexts, or the reliance on visual rather than gravitational cues in perception of the upright. Used also for reciprocal concept of field independence.
B Cognitive Style 1967

Field Experiment
Use Observation Methods

Field Instruction
Use Curricular Field Experience

Field Trips (Educational)
Use Educational Field Trips

Field Work (Educational)
Use Curricular Field Experience

Fighting
Use Aggressive Behavior

Figurative Language 1985
PN 557 SC 19736
SN Verbal expressions that signify one concept by using words that would normally be used to signify some other concept as a result of a conceptual analogy or qualitative similarity between the concepts.
UF Figures of Speech
Simile
B Language 1967
N Metaphor 1982
R Analogy 1991
Connotations 1973
Symbolism 1967
↓ Verbal Meaning 1973

Figure Ground Discrimination 1973
PN 788 SC 19740
SN Discrimination of a portion of a visual configuration as a coherent figure distinct from the background.
B Perceptual Discrimination 1973
R Form and Shape Perception 1967
Pattern Discrimination 1967
↓ Spatial Perception 1967

Figures of Speech
Use Figurative Language

Films 2005
PN 3035 SC 19751
SN Includes films produced for entertainment, educational, or training purposes.
HN In August 2005, this term was created to replace the discontinued term MOTION PICTURES and the deleted terms MOTION PICTURES (EDUCATIONAL), MOTION PICTURES (ENTERTAINMENT), and FILM STRIPS. These terms were removed from all records containing them, and replaced with FILMS.
UF Cinema
Motion Pictures
Movies
B Audiovisual Communications Media 1973
Mass Media 1967

Filtered Noise 1973
PN 86 **SC** 19760
B Auditory Stimulation 1967

Filtered Speech 1973
PN 54 **SC** 19770
B Speech Processing (Mechanical) 1973

Finance 2007
PN 197 **SC** 19775
SN The management of money and assets. It also includes money or credit to make purchases.
HN This term was introduced in April 2007. Relevant records were re-indexed with this term. The posting note reflects the number of records that were re-indexed.
R Banking 2007
Budgets 1997
↓ Costs and Cost Analysis 1973
Financial Services 2007
Financial Strain 2005
Funding 1988
Income (Economic) 1973
Money 1967
Resource Allocation 1997
Venture Capital 2007

Financial Assistance (Educational)
Use Educational Financial Assistance

Financial Problems
Use Financial Strain

Financial Security
Use Economic Security

Financial Services 2007
PN 96 **SC** 19781
SN Services that provide money management assistance.
HN This term was introduced in April 2007. Relevant records were re-indexed with this term. The posting note reflects the number of records that were re-indexed.
R Banking 2007
Finance 2007
Funding 1988

Financial Strain 2005
PN 201 **SC** 19783
HN This term was introduced in August 2005. Relevant records were re-indexed with this term. The posting note reflects the number of records that were re-indexed.
UF Debt
Financial Problems
Financial Stress
B Stress 1967
R Finance 2007
Income (Economic) 1973
↓ Income Level 1973

Financial Stress
Use Financial Strain

Fine Motor Skill Learning 1973
PN 186 **SC** 19790
B Perceptual Motor Learning 1967
Skill Learning 1973

Finger Tapping 1973
PN 490 **SC** 19800
B Motor Performance 1973

Fingers (Anatomy) 1973
PN 782 **SC** 19820
B Musculoskeletal System 1973
N Thumb 1973
R Hand (Anatomy) 1967

Fingerspelling 1973
PN 92 **SC** 19830
B Manual Communication 1978
R Sign Language 1973

Fire Fighters 1991
PN 277 **SC** 19845
R Fire Prevention 1973
↓ Government Personnel 1973

Fire Prevention 1973
PN 70 **SC** 19850
B Prevention 1973
R Fire Fighters 1991
↓ Safety 1967

Firearms 2003
PN 165 **SC** 19855
HN Use WEAPONS to access references from 1973 to June 2003.
UF Guns
B Weapons 1978
R Gun Control Laws 1973

Firesetting
Use Arson

FIRO-B
Use Fundamental Interpersonal Relation Orientation Behavior Ques

First Experiences 2004
PN 108 **SC** 19867
SN Initial experience of an event in an individual's life.
HN This term was introduced in June 2004. Relevant records were re-indexed with this term. The posting note reflects the number of records that were re-indexed.
R ↓ Life Experiences 1973

First Language
Use Native Language

Fishes 1967
PN 3024 **SC** 19870
B Vertebrates 1973
N Bass (Fish) 1973
↓ Carp 1973
Cichlids 1973
Electric Fishes 1973
Salmon 1973
Sticklebacks 1973
R Larvae 1973

Five Factor Personality Model 1997
PN 1265 **SC** 19875
SN A model of personality dimensions that encompass five broad factors: neuroticism, extraversion, openness to experience, agreeableness, and conscientiousness.

Five Factor Personality Model — (cont'd)
UF Big Five Personality Model
B Personality Theory 1967
R Agreeableness 1997
Conscientiousness 1997
Extraversion 1967
NEO Personality Inventory 1997
Neuroticism 1973
Openness to Experience 1997
↓ Personality 1967
↓ Personality Development 1967
↓ Personality Traits 1967

Fixation (Psychoanalytic) 2007
PN 65 **SC** 19878
SN In psychoanalytic theory, the persistence of an early psychosexual stage or inappropriate attachment to an early psychosexual object or mode of gratification, such as anal or oral activity.
HN This term was introduced in April 2007. Relevant records were re-indexed with this term. The posting note reflects the number of records that were re-indexed.
R Attachment Behavior 1985
↓ Developmental Stages 1973
↓ Psychoanalytic Theory 1967

Fixation (Psychological) 2007
PN 34 **SC** 19877
SN An obsessive preoccupation with a single idea, impulse, or aim.
HN This term was introduced in April 2007. Relevant records were re-indexed with this term. The posting note reflects the number of records that were re-indexed.
R Attachment Behavior 1985
Obsessions 1967

Fixed Interval Reinforcement 1973
PN 825 **SC** 19880
UF Interval Reinforcement
B Reinforcement Schedules 1967

Fixed Ratio Reinforcement 1973
PN 862 **SC** 19890
UF Ratio Reinforcement
B Reinforcement Schedules 1967

Flashbacks
Use Hallucinations

Flexibility (Personality)
Use Adaptability (Personality)

Flexion Reflex 1973
PN 186 **SC** 19910
B Reflexes 1971

Flextime
Use Work Scheduling

Flicker Fusion Frequency
Use Critical Flicker Fusion Threshold

Flies
Use Diptera

Flight Attendants
Use Aerospace Personnel

Flight Instrumentation 1973
PN 210 **SC** 19930
UF Instrumentation (Flight)
B Aviation 1967
Instrument Controls 1985

Flight Simulation 1973
PN 723 **SC** 19940
B Simulation 1967
R Acceleration Effects 1973
↓ Gravitational Effects 1967

Flooding Therapy
Use Implosive Therapy

Fluency
Use Verbal Fluency

Fluid Intake 1985
PN 1086 **SC** 19965
SN Ingestion of liquids or solutions. Frequently used as an objective measure of physiological or motivational state or learning. Used for human or animal populations.
B Ingestion 2001
N Water Intake 1967
R ↓ Drinking Behavior 1978
Thirst 1967

Flunitrazepam 2004
PN 106 **SC** 19966
SN A benzodiazepine with sedative and hypnotic properties.
HN This term was introduced in June 2004. Relevant records were re-indexed with this term. The posting note reflects the number of records that were re-indexed.
UF Rohypnol
B Benzodiazepines 1978

Fluoxetine 1991
PN 2482 **SC** 19967
UF Prozac
B Antidepressant Drugs 1971
Serotonin Reuptake Inhibitors 1997

Fluphenazine 1973
PN 504 **SC** 19970
UF Prolixin
B Antiemetic Drugs 1973
Phenothiazine Derivatives 1973

Flurazepam 1982
PN 100 **SC** 19974
SN Organic heterocyclic compound, used as a benzodiazepine tranquilizer and a nonbarbiturate sedative.
B Benzodiazepines 1978
Hypnotic Drugs 1973
Sedatives 1973
R ↓ CNS Depressant Drugs 1973

Fluvoxamine 1994
PN 631 **SC** 19975
B Antidepressant Drugs 1971
Serotonin Reuptake Inhibitors 1997

Focusing (Visual)
Use Ocular Accommodation

Folic Acid 1973
PN 198 **SC** 19980
B Vitamins 1973

Folie A Deux 1973
PN 123 **SC** 19990
SN A condition in which two closely related people, usually in the same family; share the same paranoid delusions. Generally, there is a dominant partner with fixed delusions who influences the development of similar delusions in a dependent or suggestible partner.
UF Shared Paranoid Disorder
B Paranoia (Psychosis) 1967
R Paranoid Schizophrenia 1967

Folk Medicine 1973
PN 724 **SC** 20000
B Alternative Medicine 1997
R Ethnology 1967
Faith Healing 1973
↓ Medical Sciences 1967
Shamanism 1973
Transcultural Psychiatry 1973

Folk Psychology 1997
PN 199 **SC** 20005
SN Branch of psychology that deals with legends, beliefs, folklore, and customs of a race or people, especially primitive societies.
B Psychology 1967
R Anthropology 1967
Ethnography 1973
Ethnology 1967
Folklore 1991
Social Psychology 1967
Transcultural Psychiatry 1973

Folklore 1991
PN 422 **SC** 20010
HN Use MYTHS to access references from 1973-1990.
UF Fairy Tales
Folktales
R Ethnology 1967
Folk Psychology 1997
↓ Literature 1967
Myths 1967
Storytelling 1988
Traditions 2007

Folktales
Use Folklore

Follicle Stimulating Hormone 1991
PN 47 **SC** 20025
B Gonadotropic Hormones 1973

Followup (Posttreatment)
Use Posttreatment Followup

Followup Studies 1973
PN 12329 **SC** 20040
SN Used in records discussing issues involved in the process of conducting studies with individuals or groups who are followed and reexamined to assess and compare present findings with the original observations or measurements.
HN From 1973-2000, the term was also used as a mandatory document type identifier; however, this usage has been discontinued due to the advent of Form/Content Type field identifiers. References from 1973-2000 can be accessed using either FOLLOWUP STUDIES or the Followup Studies Form/Content Type field identifier.
UF Studies (Followup)
B Experimental Design 1967
R ↓ Longitudinal Studies 1973

Food 1978
PN 3241 **SC** 20045
R Craving 1997
Diets 1978
Food Additives 1978
Food Allergies 1973
Food Intake 1967
Food Preferences 1973
Nutrition 1973

Food Additives 1978
PN 139 **SC** 20047
R ↓ Antioxidants 2004
↓ Chemical Elements 1973
Diets 1978
Food 1978
Nutrition 1973

Food Allergies 1973
PN 93 **SC** 20050
B Allergic Disorders 1973
R Diets 1978
Food 1978

Food Deprivation 1967
PN 2296 **SC** 20060
SN Absence of ad libitum food access. In experimental settings, food deprivation is used to achieve a definable level of motivation within the organism.
B Deprivation 1967
Stimulus Deprivation 1973
R Diets 1978
Hunger 1967
↓ Nutritional Deficiencies 1973
Starvation 1973

Food Intake 1967
PN 8190 **SC** 20070
SN Ingestion of food. Frequently used as an objective measure of physiological or motivational state or learning. Used for human or animal populations.
B Ingestion 2001
R Animal Feeding Behavior 1973
Dietary Restraint 1994
↓ Eating Behavior 2004
Food 1978
Rumination (Eating) 2001
Sucking 1978
Weight Control 1985

Food Preferences 1973
PN 2240 **SC** 20080
B Preferences 1967
R Diets 1978
Eating Attitudes 1994
Food 1978

Football 1973
PN 345 **SC** 20090
B Recreation 1967
Sports 1967

Foraging (Animal)
Use Animal Foraging Behavior

Forced Choice (Testing Method) 1967
PN 324 **SC** 20100
SN Assessment method requiring a choice between equally unlikely or undesirable alternatives, designed to reduce the effects of social desirability on the selection of test answers.
UF True False Tests
B Testing Methods 1967

Forebrain 1985
PN 1079 **SC** 20105
SN Of the three major divisions of the brain (forebrain, midbrain, and hindbrain), the forebrain is the most rostral part, and is comprised of the telencephalon and diencephalon. Responsible for voluntary motor functions, as well as sensory and associative information processing.
UF Prosencephalon
B Brain 1967
N ↓ Diencephalon 1973
Nucleus Basalis Magnocellularis 1994
↓ Telencephalon 1973

Foreign Language Education 1973
PN 1598 **SC** 20110
SN Curriculum, teaching methods, and educational programs used in the instruction of a language that is not native to the learner.
UF Immersion Programs
Second Language Education
B Curriculum 1967
R English as Second Language 1997

Foreign Language Learning 1967
PN 3833 **SC** 20120
B Learning 1967
R Bilingual Education 1978
Computer Assisted Language Learning 2007
Foreign Languages 1973
↓ Language Development 1967
Language Laboratories 1973
Language Proficiency 1988

Foreign Language Translation 1973
PN 4400 **SC** 20130
SN Rendering from one language to another. Use with foreign language test translations.
R Foreign Languages 1973

Foreign Languages 1973
PN 1703 **SC** 20140
SN Second or nonnative languages.
B Language 1967
R Bilingual Education 1978
English as Second Language 1997
Foreign Language Learning 1967
Foreign Language Translation 1973

Foreign Nationals
HN In April 2007, this term was discontinued and removed from all records containing it, and was replaced with EXPATRIATES, its postable counterpart.
Use Expatriates

Foreign Organizations 1973
PN 82 **SC** 20150
SN Organizations located in or originating from a foreign country.

Foreign Organizations — (cont'd)
B Organizations 1967
R International Organizations 1973

Foreign Policy Making 1973
PN 384 **SC** 20160
UF Policy Making (Foreign)
B Government Policy Making 1973
R Government 1967
International Relations 1967
National Security 2006
Peace 1988
Peacekeeping 2005
↓ War 1967

Foreign Students
HN In April 2007, this term was discontinued and removed from all records containing it, and was replaced with INTERNATIONAL STUDENTS, its postable counterpart.
Use International Students

Foreign Study
HN In April 2007, this term was discontinued and removed from all records containing it, and was replaced with STUDY ABROAD, its postable counterpart.
Use Study Abroad

Foreign Workers 1985
PN 319 **SC** 20175
SN Persons employed in a country other than their own, generally with intent to return to their home country.
UF Guest Workers
B Expatriates 2007
R Migrant Farm Workers 1973

Foremen (Industrial)
Use Industrial Foremen

Forensic Evaluation 1994
PN 1378 **SC** 20185
B Evaluation 1967
Legal Processes 1973
Psychiatric Evaluation 1997
R Competency to Stand Trial 1985
Court Referrals 1994
↓ Criminals 1967
Expert Testimony 1973
Forensic Psychiatry 1973
Forensic Psychology 1985
Insanity Defense 1985
Mentally Ill Offenders 1985
↓ Psychodiagnosis 1967
↓ Psychological Assessment 1997
Psychological Report 1988

Forensic Psychiatry 1973
PN 2035 **SC** 20190
SN Branch of psychiatry devoted to legal issues relating to disordered behavior and mental disorders, including legal responsibility, competency to stand trial, and commitment issues.
B Psychiatry 1967
R ↓ Criminal Justice 1991
Expert Testimony 1973
Forensic Evaluation 1994
Forensic Psychology 1985
Insanity Defense 1985

Forensic Psychology 1985
PN 1774 **SC** 20195
UF Legal Psychology
B Psychology 1967
R ↓ Criminal Justice 1991
Expert Testimony 1973
Forensic Evaluation 1994
Forensic Psychiatry 1973
Psychological Autopsy 1988

Forgetting 1973
PN 1352 **SC** 20200
SN Inability to recall, recollect, or reproduce previously learned material, behavior, or experience. Compare AMNESIA and MEMORY DECAY.
R ↓ Amnesia 1967
Cued Recall 1994
Free Recall 1973
Fugue Reaction 1973
↓ Interference (Learning) 1967
↓ Latent Inhibition 1997
↓ Learning 1967
↓ Memory 1967
Memory Decay 1973
Memory Training 1994
Reminiscence 1985
↓ Retention 1967
Serial Recall 1994
Suppression (Defense Mechanism) 1973

Forgiveness 1988
PN 768 **SC** 20205
R ↓ Conflict Resolution 1982
↓ Religious Beliefs 1973
↓ Social Interaction 1967

Form and Shape Perception 1967
PN 5531 **SC** 20210
SN Perception of the physical form or shape of objects through any of the senses, usually haptic or visual.
UF Contour
Contour Perception
Form Perception
Shape Perception
B Perception 1967
R Figure Ground Discrimination 1973
Motion Parallax 1997
Object Recognition 1997
Pattern Discrimination 1967

Form Classes (Language) 1973
PN 548 **SC** 20220
UF Words (Form Classes)
B Language 1967
Syntax 1971
N Adjectives 1973
Adverbs 1973
Nouns 1973
Pronouns 1973
Verbs 1973

Form Perception
Use Form and Shape Perception

Fornix 1982
PN 290 **SC** 20234
SN Arched white fiber tract extending from the hippocampal formation to the septum, anterior nucleus of the thalamus, and mammillary body.
UF Hippocampal Commissure
Trigonum Cerebrale
B Limbic System 1973
Neural Pathways 1982

Fornix — (cont'd)
R Medial Forebrain Bundle 1982
Septal Nuclei 1982

FORTRAN
Use Computer Programming Languages

Forward Masking
Use Masking

Foster Care 1978
PN 2104 **SC** 20245
SN Family care provided by persons other than the natural or adoptive parents.
UF Foster Homes
R ↓ Child Care 1991
Child Welfare 1988
Family Reunification 2007
Foster Children 1973
Foster Parents 1973
Protective Services 1997

Foster Children 1973
PN 807 **SC** 20250
B Family Members 1973
R Foster Care 1978

Foster Homes
Use Foster Care

Foster Parents 1973
PN 542 **SC** 20260
B Parents 1967
R Foster Care 1978
Surrogate Parents (Humans) 1973

Fovea 1982
PN 226 **SC** 20265
SN Centrally located and depressed portion of the retina containing only cone photoreceptors.
B Eye (Anatomy) 1967
R Cones (Eye) 1973
Foveal Vision 1988
Visual Field 1967

Foveal Vision 1988
PN 373 **SC** 20267
UF Central Vision
B Visual Perception 1967
R Fovea 1982

Fowl
Use Birds

Foxes 1973
PN 116 **SC** 20290
B Canids 1997

Fragile X Syndrome 1994
PN 425 **SC** 20295
SN Mutation of a gene on the X chromosome, most often resulting in mental retardation as well as a cluster of characteristic physical and behavioral abnormalities, including hyperactivity, seizures, language delay, and enlarged ears, head, and testes.
B Sex Linked Hereditary Disorders 1973
Syndromes 1973
R ↓ Mental Retardation 1967
↓ Sex Chromosome Disorders 1973

Fragmentation (Schizophrenia) 1973
PN 17 **SC** 20300
SN Used in general to refer to the separation of words from meaning, thought from emotion, perceptions from reality, and actions from motives that is often characteristic of schizophrenia. Fragmentation often specifically refers to the use of disorganized, unconnected words.
UF Loosening of Associations
B Thought Disturbances 1973
R ↓ Schizophrenia 1967

Frail
Use Health Impairments

Framing Effects 2005
PN 85 **SC** 20310
SN Occurs when the description of a situation or a problem is framed or described in either a positive (gains) or negative (losses) way.
HN This term was introduced in August 2005. Relevant records were re-indexed with this term. The posting note reflects the number of records that were re-indexed.
R Choice Behavior 1967
↓ Decision Making 1967

Frankness
Use Honesty

Fraternal Twins
Use Heterozygotic Twins

Fraternity Membership 1973
PN 229 **SC** 20340
SN Belonging to a club traditionally restricted to males. Used also for fraternity organizations.
B Extracurricular Activities 1973
Membership 2007

Fraud 1994
PN 171 **SC** 20345
UF Consumer Fraud
B Deception 1967
R Cheating 1973
Consumer Education 2007
↓ Crime 1967
Dishonesty 1973
Experimental Ethics 1978

Free Association 1994
PN 215 **SC** 20347
SN Spontaneous association of ideas or mental images restricted by consciousness. Primarily used in, but not restricted to, psychoanalysis or Jungian analysis as a method to gain access to the organization and content of a patient's mind.
UF Association (Free)
R ↓ Jungian Psychology 1973
↓ Psychoanalysis 1967
↓ Psychoanalytic Theory 1967
↓ Psychotherapeutic Techniques 1967
Unconscious (Personality Factor) 1967

Free Recall 1973
PN 2227 **SC** 20350
SN Method of measuring the retention of learned material in which a subject is asked to recall as much of the material as possible, in any order, without the aid of external cues. Compare SERIAL ANTICIPATION (LEARNING) and RECONSTRUCTION (LEARNING).

Free Recall — (cont'd)
B Recall (Learning) 1967
R Cued Recall 1994
Forgetting 1973
↓ Memory 1967
Serial Recall 1994

Free Will
Use Volition

Freedom 1978
PN 886 **SC** 20354
R Censorship 1978
Choice Behavior 1967
↓ Civil Rights 1978
Individualism 2007
↓ Justice 1973
↓ Political Processes 1973
Psychological Reactance 1978
Volition 1988

Frequency (Pitch)
Use Pitch (Frequency)

Frequency (Response)
Use Response Frequency

Frequency (Stimulus)
Use Stimulus Frequency

Frequency Distribution 1973
PN 560 **SC** 20380
UF Distribution (Frequency)
B Statistical Analysis 1967
Statistical Measurement 1973
N Normal Distribution 1973
Skewed Distribution 1973
R Standard Deviation 1973

Freud (Sigmund) 1967
PN 6192 **SC** 20390
SN Identifies biographical or autobiographical studies and discussions of Freud's works.
R Freudian Psychoanalytic School 1973
↓ Neopsychoanalytic School 1973
↓ Psychoanalysis 1967
↓ Psychoanalytic Theory 1967
↓ Psychologists 1967

Freudian Psychoanalytic School 1973
PN 1104 **SC** 20400
UF Psychoanalytic School (Freudian)
B History of Psychology 1967
Psychoanalytic Theory 1967
Psychological Theories 2001
R Freud (Sigmund) 1967
Metapsychology 1994
↓ Neopsychoanalytic School 1973
Psychoanalytic Interpretation 1967

Friendship 1967
PN 4632 **SC** 20410
B Interpersonal Relationships 2004
R Interpersonal Compatibility 1973
Peer Pressure 1994
↓ Peer Relations 1967
Relationship Quality 2004
↓ Relationship Satisfaction 2001
↓ Relationship Termination 1997
Significant Others 1991
Social Dating 1973
Social Support 2004

Frigidity
HN In August 2005, this term was discontinued and removed from all records containing it, and was replaced with FEMALE SEXUAL DYSFUNCTION, its postable counterpart.
Use Female Sexual Dysfunction

Frogs 1967
PN 1046 **SC** 20430
B Amphibia 1973
R Larvae 1973

Frontal Lobe 1973
PN 5606 **SC** 20440
SN The anterior division of the cerebral cortex that is involved in planning, problem solving, organizing, reasoning, attention, and personality.
B Cerebral Cortex 1967
N Broca's Area 2004
Gyrus Cinguli 1973
Motor Cortex 1973
Prefrontal Cortex 1994

Frostig Developmental Test of Visual Perception 2001
PN 34 **SC** 20455
HN In 2001, the truncated term FROSTIG DEVELOPMENT TEST VIS PERCEPT (which was used from 1973-2000) was deleted, removed from all records containing it, and replaced with its expanded form FROSTIG DEVELOPMENTAL TEST OF VISUAL PERCEPTION.
B Intelligence Measures 1967

Fruit Fly
Use Drosophila

Frustration 1967
PN 1557 **SC** 20470
B Emotional States 1973
R Dissatisfaction 1973
Mental Confusion 1973

Fugue Reaction 1973
PN 55 **SC** 20480
SN Dissociative reaction characterized by extensive amnesia and a sudden change in one's lifestyle. Upon recovery, prefugue events are remembered but those that occurred during the fugue are forgotten.
B Dissociative Disorders 2001
R ↓ Epilepsy 1967
Forgetting 1973

Fulfillment
Use Satisfaction

Functional Analysis 2001
PN 376 **SC** 20496
SN A part of behavioral assessment concerned with the experimental manipulation of environmental events that are maintaining or suppressing a target behavior.
B Behavioral Assessment 1982
R ↓ Analysis 1967
↓ Behavior Modification 1973
↓ Behavior Problems 1967
↓ Methodology 1967

Functional Knowledge
Use Procedural Knowledge

Functional Status
Use Ability Level

Functionalism 1973
PN 336 **SC** 20500
SN Doctrine or system of psychology which holds (contrary to structural psychology) that mental processes are the proper subject matter of psychology and that an essential feature of all psychological processes is the part they play in the adaptive functions of an organism.
B History of Psychology 1967
Psychological Theories 2001
R James (William) 1991

Fundamental Interpersonal Relation Orientation Behavior Ques 2001
PN 58 **SC** 20515
HN In 2001, the truncated term FUND INTERPER RELA ORIENTAT BEH QUES (which was used from 1973-2000) was deleted, removed from all records containing it, and mapped to its expanded form FUNDAMENTAL INTERPERSONAL RELATION ORIENTATION BEHAVIOR QUES.
UF FIRO-B
B Nonprojective Personality Measures 1973

Fundamentalism (Religious)
HN In July 2003, the text was updated from FUNDAMENTALISM to FUNDAMENTALISM (RELIGIOUS). The term was also discontinued and removed from all records containing it, and was replaced with RELIGIOUS FUNDAMENTALISM, its postable counterpart.
Use Religious Fundamentalism

Funding 1988
PN 1362 **SC** 20524
R Banking 2007
Budgets 1997
↓ Costs and Cost Analysis 1973
Educational Financial Assistance 1973
Finance 2007
Financial Services 2007
Fundraising 2007
↓ Government Policy Making 1973
↓ Government Programs 1973
Money 1967
Resource Allocation 1997
Venture Capital 2007

Fundraising 2007
PN 22 **SC** 20525
SN The process of soliciting and raising money via donations from individuals, organizations, businesses, or other institutions.
HN This term was introduced in April 2007. Relevant records were re-indexed with this term. The posting note reflects the number of records that were re-indexed.
UF Monetary Contributions
R Charitable Behavior 1973
Funding 1988
Money 1967

Funerals
Use Death Rites

Furniture 1985
PN 52 **SC** 20527
R Human Factors Engineering 1973
Interior Design 1982
Physical Comfort 1982

Future 1991
PN 1331 **SC** 20528
R ↓ Expectations 1967
↓ History 1973
↓ Prediction 1967
Social Change 1967
↓ Time 1967
Trends 1991

Fuzzy Logic 2003
PN 119 **SC** 58067
SN A mathematical technique used to deal with imprecise data and problems.
HN This term was introduced in June 2003. Relevant records were re-indexed with this term. The posting note reflects the number of records that were re-indexed.
R ↓ Artificial Intelligence 1982
Fuzzy Set Theory 1991
↓ Mathematical Modeling 1973

Fuzzy Set Theory 1991
PN 293 **SC** 20529
SN Mathematical theory of sets in which membership is a matter of degree and boundaries are indistinct.
B Statistical Analysis 1967
Theories 1967
R Fuzzy Logic 2003
↓ Mathematical Modeling 1973
↓ Psychophysical Measurement 1967
↓ Statistical Probability 1967

GABA Agonists
Use Gamma Aminobutyric Acid Agonists

GABA Antagonists
Use Gamma Aminobutyric Acid Antagonists

Galanin
Use Peptides

Galantamine
Use Galanthamine

Galanthamine 1973
PN 120 **SC** 20530
UF Galantamine
B Amines 1973
Cholinesterase Inhibitors 1973

Galvanic Skin Response 1967
PN 2004 **SC** 20550
SN Means of assessing sympathetic nervous system activity (i.e., arousal) by measuring onset of palmar sweat gland response.
UF Electrodermal Response
GSR (Electrophysiology)
Psychogalvanic Reflex
B Diagnosis 1967
Electrophysiology 1973
Medical Diagnosis 1973
R Skin Potential 1973
↓ Skin Resistance 1973

Gamblers Anonymous
Use Twelve Step Programs

Gambling 1973
PN 1190 **SC** 20560
B Recreation 1967
Risk Taking 1967
Social Behavior 1967

Gambling — (cont'd)
N Pathological Gambling 1988
R ↓ Games 1967

Game Theory 1967
PN 1181 SC 20570
SN Mathematical theory which attempts to analyze and model the decision making process involved in gain-loss situations.
B Theories 1967
R Entrapment Games 1973
↓ Games 1967
Non Zero Sum Games 1973
Prisoners Dilemma Game 1973
↓ Simulation 1967

Games 1967
PN 2898 SC 20580
N Chess 1973
Childrens Recreational Games 1973
Computer Games 1988
Entrapment Games 1973
Non Zero Sum Games 1973
Prisoners Dilemma Game 1973
Simulation Games 1973
R ↓ Childhood Play Behavior 1978
↓ Gambling 1973
Game Theory 1967
↓ Recreation 1967
↓ Toys 1973

Gamma Aminobutyric Acid 1978
PN 2155 SC 20585
B Amino Acids 1973
Neurotransmitters 1985
R ↓ Gamma Aminobutyric Acid Agonists 1985
↓ Gamma Aminobutyric Acid Antagonists 1985

Gamma Aminobutyric Acid Agonists 1985
PN 523 SC 20587
UF GABA Agonists
N Muscimol 1994
R Gamma Aminobutyric Acid 1978

Gamma Aminobutyric Acid Antagonists 1985
PN 386 SC 20589
UF GABA Antagonists
B Alkaloids 1973
N Bicuculline 1994
Picrotoxin 1973
R Gamma Aminobutyric Acid 1978

Gamma Globulin 1973
PN 14 SC 20590
B Immunoglobulins 1973
R Antibodies 1973

Ganglia 1973
PN 337 SC 20600
SN A grouping of neural cell bodies located outside of the central nervous system.
B Nervous System 1967
N Autonomic Ganglia 1973
↓ Basal Ganglia 1973
Spinal Ganglia 1973
R ↓ Peripheral Nervous System 1973

Ganglion Blocking Drugs 1973
PN 16 SC 20610
B Drugs 1967
N Hexamethonium 1973
Mecamylamine 1973

Ganglion Blocking Drugs — (cont'd)
Nicotine 1973
R ↓ Antihypertensive Drugs 1973

Ganglion Cells (Retina) 1985
PN 315 SC 20615
SN Retinal cells that receive information from bipolar cells and carry visual information to the brain. The axons of such cells give rise to the optic nerve.
UF Retinal Ganglion Cells
B Neurons 1973
Retina 1967

Gangrene
Use Necrosis

Gangs (Juvenile)
Use Juvenile Gangs

Ganser Syndrome
Use Factitious Disorders

Gardening Therapy
Use Horticulture Therapy

Gastrointestinal Disorders 1973
PN 807 SC 20630
B Digestive System Disorders 1973
N ↓ Colon Disorders 1973
Gastrointestinal Ulcers 1967
Vomiting 1973
R Influenza 1973
↓ Neoplasms 1967
↓ Somatoform Disorders 2001
↓ Toxic Disorders 1973

Gastrointestinal System 1973
PN 439 SC 20640
B Digestive System 1967
N Intestines 1973
Stomach 1973
R Pancreas 1973

Gastrointestinal Ulcers 1967
PN 637 SC 20650
UF Peptic Ulcers
Ulcers (Gastrointestinal)
B Gastrointestinal Disorders 1973
R ↓ Colitis 1973

Gastropods
Use Mollusca

Gating (Sensory)
Use Sensory Gating

Gaussian Distribution
Use Normal Distribution

Gay Liberation Movement
Use Homosexual Liberation Movement

Gay Males
Use Male Homosexuality

Gay Parents
Use Homosexual Parents

Gazing
Use Eye Fixation

Geese 1973
PN 126 SC 20710
B Birds 1967

Gender Differences
Use Human Sex Differences

Gender Identity 1985
PN 3162 SC 20717
SN Inner conviction that one is male or female or inner sense of being masculine or feminine.
UF Sexual Identity (Gender)
N Transsexualism 1973
R Androgyny 1982
Femininity 1967
↓ Gender Identity Disorder 1997
Masculinity 1967
↓ Personality 1967
Psychosexual Development 1982
↓ Self Concept 1967
Sex Roles 1967
↓ Sexual Orientation 1997

Gender Identity Disorder 1997
PN 253 SC 20719
HN Consider GENDER IDENTITY to access references from 1985-1996.
B Mental Disorders 1967
N Transsexualism 1973
R ↓ Gender Identity 1985
Hermaphroditism 1973
↓ Sexual Orientation 1997
Transvestism 1973

Gender Role Attitudes
Use Sex Role Attitudes

Gender Roles
Use Sex Roles

Gene Expression 2004
PN 907 SC 20726
SN Process by which messenger RNA is transcribed and then translated into proteins.
HN This term was introduced in June 2004. Relevant records were re-indexed with this term. The posting note reflects the number of records that were re-indexed.
R ↓ Genes 1973
↓ Genetics 1967
Quantitative Trait Loci 2004
Ribonucleic Acid 1973

General Anesthetics 1973
PN 185 SC 20720
B Anesthetic Drugs 1973
N Ether (Anesthetic) 1973
Methohexital 1973
Thiopental 1973

General Aptitude Test Battery 1973
PN 63 SC 20730
B Aptitude Measures 1967

General Health Questionnaire 1991
PN 190 SC 20740
B Personality Measures 1967
Questionnaires 1967
R ↓ Diagnosis 1967
↓ Health 1973
↓ Screening Tests 1982

General Paresis 1973
PN 83 **SC** 20750
SN Progressive dementia, muscular weakness, and paralysis occurring in the late stages of syphilis.
UF Dementia Paralytica
Paresis (General)
B Brain Disorders 1967
R Neurosyphilis 1973
↓ Paralysis 1973
↓ Syphilis 1973

General Practitioners 1973
PN 2362 **SC** 20760
B Physicians 1967
R Family Medicine 1988
Family Physicians 1973

Generalization (Cognitive)
Use Cognitive Generalization

Generalization (Learning) 1982
PN 1696 **SC** 20775
SN Responding in a similar manner to different stimuli that have some common property as the result of a conditioned or learned similarity. Also known as secondary generalization. Also includes generalization of any learned behavior to a new context or setting. Compare TRANSFER (LEARNING) or STIMULUS GENERALIZATION.
B Learning 1967
N Response Generalization 1973
Stimulus Generalization 1967
R ↓ Concept Formation 1967
↓ Discrimination Learning 1982
↓ Transfer (Learning) 1967

Generalization (Response)
Use Response Generalization

Generalization (Semantic)
Use Semantic Generalization

Generalization (Stimulus)
Use Stimulus Generalization

Generalized Anxiety Disorder 2004
PN 356 **SC** 20801
SN An anxiety disorder characterized by free-floating, persistent, and excessive worry for at least six months.
HN Use ANXIETY DISORDERS to access references from 1994 to June 2004.
B Anxiety Disorders 1997
R ↓ Anxiety 1967

Generation Effect (Learning) 1991
PN 131 **SC** 20802
SN In learning or memory contexts, the effect of generating a stimuli oneself rather than having it presented by external sources.
B Learning 1967
R ↓ Cognitive Processes 1967
↓ Memory 1967

Generation Gap 1973
PN 303 **SC** 20805
SN Differences in values, morals, attitudes, and behavior of young adults and older adults in contemporary society.
R Age Differences 1967
Cohort Analysis 1988
Intergenerational Relations 1988
↓ Parent Child Relations 1967
Transgenerational Patterns 1991

Generativity 2001
PN 121 **SC** 20807
SN The concern with passing on to the next generation knowledge and guidance which will outlive oneself. The conflict between generativity vs self-absorption is the seventh of E. Erikson's eight stages of man, and often occurs during middle adulthood.
R Adult Development 1978
↓ Aging 1991
↓ Developmental Stages 1973
Erikson (Erik) 1991
Intergenerational Relations 1988
↓ Prosocial Behavior 1982
↓ Psychosocial Development 1973

Generators (Apparatus) 1973
PN 33 **SC** 20810
B Apparatus 1967

Genes 1973
PN 5593 **SC** 20820
N Quantitative Trait Loci 2004
R ↓ Chromosomes 1973
Gene Expression 2004
Genetic Linkage 1994
↓ Genetics 1967
Genome 2003

Genetic Counseling 1978
PN 738 **SC** 20826
SN Presentation and discussion, usually with prospective parents, of factors involved in potential inheritance of disorders.
B Counseling 1967
R Eugenics 1973
↓ Genetic Disorders 1973
↓ Genetic Engineering 1994
Genetic Testing 2003
↓ Genetics 1967

Genetic Disorders 1973
PN 1532 **SC** 20830
UF Hereditary Disorders
B Physical Disorders 1997
N Albinism 1973
↓ Chromosome Disorders 1973
Huntingtons Disease 1973
Phenylketonuria 1973
Porphyria 1973
Rh Incompatibility 1973
↓ Sex Linked Hereditary Disorders 1973
Sickle Cell Disease 1994
Tay Sachs Disease 2003
Williams Syndrome 2003
R Alopecia 1973
Anemia 1973
Behavioral Genetics 1994
Color Blindness 1973
↓ Congenital Disorders 1973
Developmental Disabilities 1982
Diabetes Insipidus 1973
Genetic Counseling 1978
↓ Genetic Engineering 1994
Genetic Testing 2003
↓ Genetics 1967
Hypopituitarism 1973
Mutations 1973
Picks Disease 1973
Prenatal Diagnosis 1988
↓ Refraction Errors 1973

Genetic Dominance 1973
PN 76 **SC** 20840
B Dominance 1967
R Behavioral Genetics 1994
Genetic Recessiveness 1973
↓ Genetics 1967

Genetic Engineering 1994
PN 176 **SC** 20845
N Cloning 2003
Eugenics 1973
R Bioethics 2003
↓ Biotechnology 2007
Genetic Counseling 1978
↓ Genetic Disorders 1973
Genetic Linkage 1994
↓ Genetics 1967
Population Genetics 1973
Reproductive Technology 1988
Selective Breeding 1973

Genetic Linkage 1994
PN 985 **SC** 20847
SN Linkage of genes at different loci on the same chromosome and analysis of how genes are inherited together.
UF Linkage Analysis
R ↓ Chromosomes 1973
↓ Genes 1973
↓ Genetic Engineering 1994
↓ Genetics 1967
Genotypes 1973
Quantitative Trait Loci 2004

Genetic Recessiveness 1973
PN 48 **SC** 20850
UF Recessiveness (Genetic)
R Behavioral Genetics 1994
Genetic Dominance 1973
↓ Genetics 1967

Genetic Screening
Use Genetic Testing

Genetic Testing 2003
PN 347 **SC** 20855
SN Screening for presence or predisposition to a particular trait or disease that may be passed on to one's offspring.
HN This term was introduced in June 2003. Relevant records were re-indexed with this term. The posting note reflects the number of records that were re-indexed.
UF Genetic Screening
B Health Screening 1997
R Genetic Counseling 1978
↓ Genetic Disorders 1973
↓ Medical Diagnosis 1973
Preventive Medicine 1973

Genetics 1967
PN 17855 **SC** 20860
SN Conceptually broad term referring both to the science of heredity and the biological process of transmission of characteristics from progenitor to offspring.
UF Heredity
N Behavioral Genetics 1994
Eugenics 1973
Genome 2003
Population Genetics 1973
R ↓ Animal Breeding 1973
Animal Mate Selection 1982
Animal Strain Differences 1982

Genetics — (cont'd)
Assortative Mating 1991
Blood Groups 1973
↓ Chromosomes 1973
Family Resemblance 1991
Gene Expression 2004
↓ Genes 1973
Genetic Counseling 1978
↓ Genetic Disorders 1973
Genetic Dominance 1973
↓ Genetic Engineering 1994
Genetic Linkage 1994
Genetic Recessiveness 1973
Genotypes 1973
Heritability 2005
Hybrids (Biology) 1973
Instinctive Behavior 1982
Mutations 1973
Natural Selection 1997
Nature Nurture 1994
↓ Nucleic Acids 1973
Phenotypes 1973
Polymorphism 2003
Predisposition 1973
Quantitative Trait Loci 2004
Reproductive Technology 1988
Selective Breeding 1973
↓ Sexual Reproduction 1973
Species Differences 1982
Translocation (Chromosome) 1973
↓ Twins 1967

Geniculate Bodies (Thalamus) 1973
PN 558 **SC** 20870
SN Small nuclei located in the thalamus that transmit visual and auditory information to the cortex.
UF Lateral Geniculate Nucleus
Medial Geniculate Nucleus
B Thalamus 1967
R Visual Receptive Fields 1982

Genital Disorders 1967
PN 305 **SC** 20880
UF Sex Differentiation Disorders
Sexual Disorders (Physiological)
B Urogenital Disorders 1973
N ↓ Endocrine Sexual Disorders 1973
↓ Gynecological Disorders 1973
Hermaphroditism 1973
↓ Infertility 1973
↓ Male Genital Disorders 1973
R Sex 1967

Genital Herpes
Use Herpes Genitalis

Genitalia (Female)
Use Female Genitalia

Genitalia (Male)
Use Male Genitalia

Geniuses
Use Gifted

Genocide 1988
PN 301 **SC** 20915
SN Deliberate and systematic destruction of a racial, political, or cultural group.

Genocide — (cont'd)
B Homicide 1967
N Holocaust 1988

Genome 2003
PN 306 **SC** 20917
SN An organism's complete gene complement contained in a set of chromosomes.
HN This term was introduced in June 2003. Relevant records were re-indexed with this term. The posting note reflects the number of records that were re-indexed.
UF Human Genome
B Genetics 1967
R Bioinformatics 2007
↓ Chromosomes 1973
DNA 2006
↓ Genes 1973
Quantitative Trait Loci 2004

Genotypes 1973
PN 1775 **SC** 20920
R Genetic Linkage 1994
↓ Genetics 1967
Phenotypes 1973
Polymorphism 2003

Genuineness
Use Sincerity

Geographic Regions
Use Geography

Geographical Differences
Use Regional Differences

Geographical Mobility 1978
PN 558 **SC** 20924
SN Capacity or facility of individuals to move from one geographic region to another. Includes job- or study-related commuting.
UF Mobility (Geographical)
R Commuting (Travel) 1985
↓ Human Migration 1973

Geography 1973
PN 1369 **SC** 20925
SN Science dealing with the description of the topographical features of the earth and the distribution of life on earth. Also, geographic areas or their features.
UF Geographic Regions
Physical Divisions (Geographic)
Physical Geography
Political Divisions (Geographic)
B Sciences 1967
R ↓ Countries 1967
↓ Environment 1967
Regional Differences 2001

Geomagnetism
Use Magnetism

Geometry 2003
PN 252 **SC** 20930
SN Branch of mathematics concerned with the relationships of points, lines, angles, curves, space, and surfaces.
HN Use MATHEMATICS to access references from 1973 to June 2003.

Geometry — (cont'd)
B Mathematics 1982

Gerbils 1973
PN 769 **SC** 20940
B Rodents 1973

Geriatric Assessment 1997
PN 524 **SC** 20945
B Evaluation 1967
R Activities of Daily Living 1991
Clinical Judgment (Not Diagnosis) 1973
↓ Diagnosis 1967
Geriatric Patients 1973
Geriatric Psychiatry 1997
Geriatrics 1967
Gerontology 1967
↓ Measurement 1967
Needs Assessment 1985
↓ Psychiatric Evaluation 1997
↓ Psychological Assessment 1997
↓ Screening 1982

Geriatric Patients 1973
PN 6589 **SC** 20950
SN Older persons suffering from mental or physical diseases and disabilities and under some form of treatment.
B Patients 1967
R Geriatric Assessment 1997

Geriatric Psychiatry 1997
PN 731 **SC** 20955
B Psychiatry 1967
R ↓ Aging 1991
Geriatric Assessment 1997
Geriatric Psychotherapy 1973
Geriatrics 1967
Gerontology 1967

Geriatric Psychology
Use Geropsychology

Geriatric Psychotherapy 1973
PN 364 **SC** 20960
B Psychotherapy 1967
R ↓ Aging 1991
Animal Assisted Therapy 1994
Geriatric Psychiatry 1997
Geriatrics 1967
Gerontology 1967
Physiological Aging 1967

Geriatrics 1967
PN 2823 **SC** 20970
SN Medical subdiscipline which deals with the problems of old age and aging.
HN Use GERIATRICS or GERONTOLOGY to access references on the aged (elderly) from 1967-1972.
B Medical Sciences 1967
R ↓ Aged (Attitudes Toward) 1978
↓ Aging 1991
Geriatric Assessment 1997
Geriatric Psychiatry 1997
Geriatric Psychotherapy 1973
Gerontology 1967
Geropsychology 2006
Physiological Aging 1967

German Measles
Use Rubella

Gerontology 1967
PN 3472 **SC** 21000
SN Scientific study of old age and the phenomena associated with old age.
HN Use GERONTOLOGY or GERIATRICS to access references to the aged (elderly) from 1967-1972.
B Developmental Psychology 1973
R ↓ Aged (Attitudes Toward) 1978
↓ Aging 1991
Geriatric Assessment 1997
Geriatric Psychiatry 1997
Geriatric Psychotherapy 1973
Geriatrics 1967
Geropsychology 2006
Life Review 1991

Geropsychology 2006
PN 72 **SC** 21005
SN Specialized field of psychology concerned with the psychological and behavioral aspects of aging.
HN This term was introduced in May 2006. Relevant records were re-indexed with this term. The posting note reflects the number of records that were re-indexed.
UF Geriatric Psychology
B Psychology 1967
R ↓ Aging 1991
Aging (Attitudes Toward) 1985
Geriatrics 1967
Gerontology 1967

Gestalt Psychology 1967
PN 1222 **SC** 21010
SN School of psychology concerned with the study of the individual's perception of and response to configurational wholes.
B History of Psychology 1967
Psychological Theories 2001

Gestalt Therapy 1973
PN 1170 **SC** 21020
SN Type of psychotherapy which emphasizes treatment of the individual as a whole and focuses on sensory awareness of present experience.
B Human Potential Movement 1982
Psychotherapy 1967
R ↓ Humanistic Psychotherapy 2003

Gestation
Use Pregnancy

Gestures 1973
PN 1521 **SC** 21040
B Nonverbal Communication 1971
R Body Language 1973

Ghettoes 1973
PN 135 **SC** 21050
UF Ghettos
B Neighborhoods 1973
R Poverty Areas 1973
Race and Ethnic Discrimination 1994
Urban Environments 1967

Ghettos
Use Ghettoes

Gifted 1967
PN 6895 **SC** 21060
UF Exceptional Children (Gifted)
Geniuses
Intellectually Gifted

Gifted — (cont'd)
Talented
R ↓ Ability 1967
Creativity 1967
↓ Intelligence 1967
Savants 2001

Gilles de la Tourette Disorder
HN In May 2006, this term was discontinued and removed from all records containing it, and was replaced with TOURETTE SYNDROME, its postable counterpart.
Use Tourette Syndrome

Gipsies
Use Gypsies

Girls
Use Human Females

Glands 1967
PN 718 **SC** 21080
N ↓ Endocrine Glands 1973
Mammary Glands 1973
Pancreas 1973
Salivary Glands 1973
R Pheromones 1973

Glaucoma 1973
PN 103 **SC** 21090
B Eye Disorders 1973

Global Amnesia 1997
PN 80 **SC** 21095
SN A profound memory disorder that features both retrograde and anterograde types. The disorder is marked by confusion and impaired thought processes. Often results from cerebral lesions or other forms of brain damage.
HN Use AMNESIA to access references from 1967-1996.
B Amnesia 1967
R Anterograde Amnesia 2003
↓ Brain Damage 1967
Retrograde Amnesia 2003

Globalization 2003
PN 1092 **SC** 21098
SN Refers to the emergence of a global cultural system brought about by advances in communications technology; the internationalization of consumerism; the world-wide influence of popular culture; and the increasing development, activism, connectivity, and interdependence of the world's markets and businesses.
HN This term was introduced in June 2003. Relevant records were re-indexed with this term. The posting note reflects the number of records that were re-indexed.
R ↓ Business 1967
↓ Business Organizations 1973
↓ Economics 1985
↓ Economy 1973
Modernization 2003
Multinational Corporations 2006
Popular Culture 2003

Globulins 1973
PN 189 **SC** 21100
UF Glycoproteins
B Proteins 1973
N Antibodies 1973
↓ Immunoglobulins 1973

Globus Pallidus 1973
PN 490 **SC** 21110
SN A nucleus of the basal ganglia that is implicated in complex motor processes.
B Basal Ganglia 1973
R ↓ Striatum 2003

Glossolalia 1973
PN 59 **SC** 21130
SN Unintelligible speech occurring in hypnotic or mediumistic trances, religious experiences, or some mental disorders.
R ↓ Mental Disorders 1967
↓ Religious Practices 1973

Glossopharyngeal Nerve
Use Cranial Nerves

Glucagon 1973
PN 85 **SC** 21150
B Hormones 1967
Neuropeptides 2003

Glucocorticoids 1982
PN 837 **SC** 21155
SN Any steroid-like compound capable of significantly influencing intermediary metabolism. Glucocorticoids are also clinically useful anti-inflammatory agents.
B Adrenal Cortex Hormones 1973
Anti Inflammatory Drugs 1982
N Dexamethasone 1985

Glucose 1973
PN 1496 **SC** 21160
B Sugars 1973
N Blood Sugar 1973
R Glucose Metabolism 1994
Glycogen 1973

Glucose Metabolism 1994
PN 618 **SC** 21165
B Carbohydrate Metabolism 1973
R ↓ Glucose 1973
↓ Neurochemistry 1973

Glue Sniffing 1973
PN 63 **SC** 21170
B Inhalant Abuse 1985

Glutamate
Use Glutamic Acid

Glutamate Receptors 2007
PN 346 **SC** 21178
SN Any of various receptors that bind and respond to the excitatory neurotransmitter glutamate. Glutamate receptors are found on the surface of most neurons.
HN This term was introduced in April 2007. Relevant records were re-indexed with this term. The posting note reflects the number of records that were re-indexed.
B Neural Receptors 1973
R Glutamic Acid 1973
N-Methyl-D-Aspartate 1994
↓ Neurotransmitters 1985

Glutamic Acid 1973
PN 1654 **SC** 21180
UF Glutamate
B Amino Acids 1973
Neurotransmitters 1985

Glutamic Acid — (cont'd)
R Glutamate Receptors 2007
Kainic Acid 1988

Glutamine 1973
PN 245 SC 21190
B Amino Acids 1973

Glutethimide 1973
PN 17 SC 21210
B CNS Depressant Drugs 1973
Hypnotic Drugs 1973
Sedatives 1973

Glycine 1973
PN 293 SC 21220
B Amino Acids 1973
Neurotransmitters 1985

Glycogen 1973
PN 98 SC 21230
R ↓ Glucose 1973

Glycoproteins
Use Globulins

Goal Orientation 2005
PN 498 SC 21236
SN Orienting oneself toward achieving a goal.
HN This term was introduced in August 2005. Relevant records were re-indexed with this term. The posting note reflects the number of records that were re-indexed.
R ↓ Aspirations 1967
Goal Setting 1997
↓ Goals 1967
Occupational Aspirations 1973

Goal Setting 1997
PN 981 SC 21237
R ↓ Aspirations 1967
Goal Orientation 2005
↓ Goals 1967
↓ Motivation 1967

Goals 1967
PN 6376 SC 21240
SN Aims toward which an individual or a group aspire or toward which effort is directed. Use a more specific term if possible.
UF Objectives
N Educational Objectives 1978
Organizational Objectives 1973
R ↓ Aspirations 1967
Extrinsic Motivation 1973
Goal Orientation 2005
Goal Setting 1997
↓ Incentives 1967
Intention 1988
Intrinsic Motivation 1973
↓ Motivation 1967
↓ Needs 1967

Goats 1973
PN 193 SC 21250
B Mammals 1973

God Concepts 1973
PN 900 SC 21260
B Religious Beliefs 1973
R Agnosticism 2007
Theology 2003

Goiters 1973
PN 21 SC 21270
B Thyroid Disorders 1973
R Hyperthyroidism 1973
Hypothyroidism 1973

Goldfish 1973
PN 552 SC 21280
B Carp 1973

Gonadotropic Hormones 1973
PN 494 SC 21300
UF Gonadotropin
B Hormones 1967
N Follicle Stimulating Hormone 1991
Luteinizing Hormone 1978
Prolactin 1973
R ↓ Pituitary Hormones 1973
↓ Sex Hormones 1973

Gonadotropin
Use Gonadotropic Hormones

Gonads 1973
PN 189 SC 21320
B Endocrine Glands 1973
Urogenital System 1973
N Ovaries 1973
Testes 1973

Gonorrhea 1973
PN 72 SC 21330
B Bacterial Disorders 1973
Sexually Transmitted Diseases 2003

Goodenough Harris Draw A Person Test 1967
PN 132 SC 21340
B Intelligence Measures 1967
R Human Figures Drawing 1973

Goodness of Fit 1988
PN 470 SC 21350
B Statistical Analysis 1967
R ↓ Factor Analysis 1967
↓ Mathematical Modeling 1973
Maximum Likelihood 1985
Statistical Significance 1973

Gorillas 1973
PN 337 SC 21370
B Primates (Nonhuman) 1973

Gossip 1982
PN 204 SC 21375
SN Idle personal talk or communication of unsubstantiated information.
UF Rumors
B Interpersonal Communication 1973
R Messages 1973

Gough Adjective Check List 1973
PN 25 SC 21380
B Nonprojective Personality Measures 1973

Government 1967
PN 1667 SC 21390
UF Government Bureaucracy
B Public Sector 1985
R Autonomy (Government) 1973
Foreign Policy Making 1973
Government Agencies 1973
↓ Government Personnel 1973
↓ Government Policy Making 1973

Government — (cont'd)
↓ Government Programs 1973
Gun Control Laws 1973
Job Corps 1973
↓ Law (Government) 1973
↓ Law Enforcement 1978
↓ Laws 1967
↓ Legal Processes 1973
Legislative Processes 1973
↓ Marijuana Laws 1973
Marijuana Legalization 1973
Peace Corps 1973
↓ Political Economic Systems 1973
↓ Politics 1967
Project Follow Through 1973
Project Head Start 1973
Taxation 1985
Upward Bound 1973
Welfare Services (Government) 1973

Government Agencies 1973
PN 1054 SC 21400
B Organizations 1967
Public Sector 1985
R Government 1967

Government Bureaucracy
Use Government

Government Personnel 1973
PN 1688 SC 21420
UF Civil Servants
Elected Government Officials
B Personnel 1967
N Agricultural Extension Workers 1973
↓ Law Enforcement Personnel 1973
↓ Military Personnel 1967
Police Personnel 1973
Public Health Service Nurses 1973
R ↓ Business and Industrial Personnel 1967
Fire Fighters 1991
Government 1967

Government Policy Making 1973
PN 8371 SC 21430
UF Policy Making (Government)
Public Policy
B Policy Making 1988
N Foreign Policy Making 1973
↓ Laws 1967
Legislative Processes 1973
Welfare Reform 2007
R Advocacy 1985
Funding 1988
Government 1967
↓ Health Care Policy 1994
↓ Legal Processes 1973
National Security 2006
↓ War 1967

Government Programs 1973
PN 1558 SC 21440
UF Programs (Government)
N Job Corps 1973
Medicaid 1994
Medicare 1988
Peace Corps 1973
Project Follow Through 1973
Project Head Start 1973
Social Security 1988
Upward Bound 1973
Welfare Services (Government) 1973
R Funding 1988
Government 1967

Government Programs — (cont'd)
↓ Program Development 1991
Shelters 1991
↓ Social Services 1982

Grade Level 1994
PN 649 **SC** 21445
UF Academic Grade Level
R Ability Grouping 1973
Age Differences 1967
↓ Education 1967
Educational Placement 1978
↓ Elementary School Students 1967
High School Students 1967
Junior High School Students 1971
Kindergarten Students 1973
School Transition 1997
Special Education Students 1973
Transfer Students 1973

Gradepoint Average
Use Academic Achievement

Grading (Educational) 1973
PN 776 **SC** 21460
SN Rating of achievement level by means of established scales or standards. Consider also SCORING (TESTING) or TEST SCORES.
B Educational Measurement 1967
R ↓ Scoring (Testing) 1973

Graduate Degrees
Use Educational Degrees

Graduate Education 1973
PN 1100 **SC** 21480
B Higher Education 1973
N Dental Education 1973
↓ Graduate Psychology Education 1967
↓ Medical Education 1973
Rehabilitation Education 1997

Graduate Psychology Education 1967
PN 3511 **SC** 21490
UF Training (Graduate Psychology)
B Graduate Education 1973
Psychology Education 1978
N ↓ Clinical Psychology Graduate Training 2001
R Educational Program Accreditation 1994

Graduate Record Examination 1973
PN 175 **SC** 21500
B Aptitude Measures 1967

Graduate Schools 1973
PN 190 **SC** 21510
B Schools 1967
R ↓ Higher Education 1973

Graduate Students 1967
PN 4257 **SC** 21520
SN Students pursuing academic studies past the college level.
B Students 1967
R ↓ College Students 1967
Dental Students 1973
Law Students 1978
Medical Students 1967
Postgraduate Students 1973

Graduation (School)
Use School Graduation

Grammar 1967
PN 3993 **SC** 21530
SN Science of the structure of language including universal grammar, descriptive and prescriptive grammar, and the rules and principles of syntax, phonology, and semantics applied in verbal communication. Compare SYNTAX.
B Linguistics 1973
N Morphology (Language) 1973
↓ Phonology 1973
↓ Semantics 1967
↓ Syntax 1971
Transformational Generative Grammar 1973
R Discourse Analysis 1997
↓ Language 1967
↓ Verbal Communication 1967
Words (Phonetic Units) 1967

Grammar Schools
Use Elementary Schools

Grand Mal Seizures 2006
PN 34 **SC** 21551
SN Type of seizure characterized by tonic and clonic convulsions and loss of consciousness.
HN This term was introduced in May 2006. Relevant records were re-indexed with this term. The posting note reflects the number of records that were re-indexed.
UF Tonic-Clonic Seizures
B Seizures 2005
R ↓ Epilepsy 1967

Grandchildren 1973
PN 519 **SC** 21560
B Family Members 1973

Grandiosity 1994
PN 58 **SC** 21565
B Defense Mechanisms 1967
R Delusions 1967
Egotism 1973
Emotional Superiority 1973
Erotomania 1997
Narcissism 1967
Omnipotence 1994

Grandparents 1973
PN 1208 **SC** 21570
B Ancestors 1973
Family Members 1973

Graphical Displays 1985
PN 1209 **SC** 21575
SN Pictorial rendering of data (e.g., bar graphs, continuous line graphs, and data plots).
HN Consider VISUAL DISPLAYS to access references from 1973-1984.
B Displays 1967
R Statistical Data 1982
↓ Statistical Measurement 1973

Graphology
Use Handwriting

Grasping 1997
PN 471 **SC** 21585
B Motor Processes 1967

Grasshoppers 1973
PN 110 **SC** 21590
B Insects 1967
R Larvae 1973

Gratefulness
Use Gratitude

Gratitude 2006
PN 75 **SC** 21595
SN A feeling of thankfulness or appreciation.
HN This term was introduced in May 2006. Relevant records were re-indexed with this term. The posting note reflects the number of records that were re-indexed.
UF Gratefulness
Thankfulness
B Emotional States 1973

Gravitational Effects 1967
PN 355 **SC** 21600
B Environmental Effects 1973
N Weightlessness 1967
R Acceleration Effects 1973
Altitude Effects 1973
↓ Aviation 1967
Decompression Effects 1973
Flight Simulation 1973
Spaceflight 1967
Underwater Effects 1973

Great Grandparents
Use Ancestors

Gregariousness 1973
PN 50 **SC** 21660
B Personality Traits 1967
R Extraversion 1967
Sociability 1973

Grief 1973
PN 7096 **SC** 21680
UF Bereavement
Mourning
B Emotional States 1973
R ↓ Death and Dying 1967
↓ Separation Reactions 1997
Suffering 1973

Grimaces 1973
PN 14 **SC** 21690
B Facial Expressions 1967

Grooming Behavior (Animal)
Use Animal Grooming Behavior

Gross Motor Skill Learning 1973
PN 200 **SC** 21700
B Perceptual Motor Learning 1967
Skill Learning 1973

Ground Transportation 1973
PN 181 **SC** 21710
B Transportation 1973
N ↓ Motor Vehicles 1982
Railroad Trains 1973

Ground Transportation — (cont'd)
R Highway Safety 1973

Grounded Theory 2004
PN 343 SC 21715
SN Methodological approach to constructing theories based on systematically analyzing qualitative data.
HN This term was introduced in June 2004. Relevant records were re-indexed with this term. The posting note reflects the number of records that were re-indexed.
B Methodology 1967
R Qualitative Research 2003
Theory Formulation 1973

Group Characteristics 2007
PN 117 SC 21720
SN Descriptive characteristics of a group.
HN This term was introduced in April 2007. Relevant records were re-indexed with this term. The posting note reflects the number of records that were re-indexed.
N ↓ Group Size 1967
Group Structure 1967
R ↓ Group Differences 2007
↓ Group Dynamics 1967
Group Identity 2007

Group Cohesion 1973
PN 1563 SC 21730
SN Mutual bonds formed among the members of a group as a consequence of their combined efforts toward a common goal or purpose.
UF Cohesion (Group)
B Group Dynamics 1967
R Group Development 1997

Group Counseling 1973
PN 4111 SC 21740
UF Counseling (Group)
B Counseling 1967
R ↓ Self Help Techniques 1982
↓ Support Groups 1991
↓ Twelve Step Programs 1997

Group Decision Making 1978
PN 2060 SC 21745
SN Process of arriving at a decision or judgment by a group.
B Decision Making 1967
N Choice Shift 1994
R Management Decision Making 1973

Group Development 1997
PN 336 SC 21747
SN Used in treatment and nontreatment settings.
B Group Dynamics 1967
R Group Cohesion 1973
Group Participation 1973
↓ Group Psychotherapy 1967
↓ Group Size 1967
Group Structure 1967

Group Differences 2007
PN 431 SC 21748
SN Characteristics or attributes setting one collection of persons apart from another.
HN This term was introduced in April 2007. Relevant records were re-indexed with this term. The posting note reflects the number of records that were re-indexed.

Group Differences — (cont'd)
N Racial and Ethnic Differences 1982
R Age Differences 1967
Diversity 2007
↓ Group Characteristics 2007
↓ Group Dynamics 1967
↓ Human Sex Differences 1967
Regional Differences 2001

Group Discussion 1967
PN 2528 SC 21750
UF Discussion (Group)
B Group Dynamics 1967
Interpersonal Communication 1973
R Choice Shift 1994
Collaborative Learning 2007
Debates 1997

Group Dynamics 1967
PN 10634 SC 21760
UF Dynamics (Group)
N Group Cohesion 1973
Group Development 1997
Group Discussion 1967
Group Participation 1973
Group Performance 1967
Intergroup Dynamics 1973
R Boundaries (Psychological) 1997
Brainstorming 1982
Choice Shift 1994
↓ Collective Behavior 1967
Consciousness Raising Groups 1978
↓ Group Characteristics 2007
↓ Group Differences 2007
Group Identity 2007
Group Instruction 1973
↓ Group Problem Solving 1973
↓ Group Psychotherapy 1967
Human Relations Training 1978
Ingroup Outgroup 1997
↓ Organizational Behavior 1978
Peer Pressure 1994
Reference Groups 1994
Sensitivity Training 1973
↓ Sociometry 1991
↓ Teams 1988

Group Health Plans
Use Health Maintenance Organizations

Group Homes 1982
PN 818 SC 21767
SN Housing for groups of patients, children, or others who need or desire emotional and physical support.
B Housing 1973
R ↓ Community Facilities 1973
Community Mental Health Services 1978
↓ Residential Care Institutions 1973
Retirement Communities 1997
Shelters 1991

Group Identity 2007
PN 295 SC 21768
SN Associating oneself strongly with a group and its members and its distinctive features, including actions, beliefs, objectives, and standards. Group identity can be constructed based on shared religion, ethnicity, political or social values, or language.
HN This term was introduced in April 2007. Relevant records were re-indexed with this term. The posting note reflects the number of records that were re-indexed.

Group Identity — (cont'd)
R Ethnic Identity 1973
↓ Group Characteristics 2007
↓ Group Dynamics 1967
Ingroup Outgroup 1997
↓ Membership 2007
Reference Groups 1994
↓ Social Identity 1988

Group Instruction 1973
PN 1007 SC 21770
B Teaching Methods 1967
R Collaborative Learning 2007
Cooperative Learning 1994
↓ Group Dynamics 1967

Group Participation 1973
PN 1927 SC 21780
SN Involvement in a group's purpose or activities.
B Group Dynamics 1967
Interpersonal Interaction 1967
Participation 1973
R ↓ Collective Behavior 1967
Communities of Practice 2007
Group Development 1997
↓ Membership 2007
Social Loafing 2003

Group Performance 1967
PN 2473 SC 21790
SN Process and effectiveness of a group in accomplishing an intended goal.
B Group Dynamics 1967
Interpersonal Interaction 1967
Performance 1967

Group Problem Solving 1973
PN 1437 SC 21800
SN Dynamics of group interaction during the process of analyzing, defining, and attaining the solution to a problem.
B Problem Solving 1967
N Brainstorming 1982
R Choice Shift 1994
↓ Group Dynamics 1967

Group Psychotherapy 1967
PN 12850 SC 21810
UF Group Therapy
B Psychotherapy 1967
N ↓ Encounter Group Therapy 1973
Therapeutic Community 1967
R Conjoint Therapy 1973
Consciousness Raising Groups 1978
Group Development 1997
↓ Group Dynamics 1967
↓ Human Potential Movement 1982
Psychodrama 1967
Sensitivity Training 1973
↓ Support Groups 1991
Transactional Analysis 1973
↓ Twelve Step Programs 1997

Group Size 1967
PN 1789 SC 21820
UF Size (Group)
B Group Characteristics 2007
Size 1973

Group Size — (cont'd)
N Class Size 2004
R Group Development 1997

Group Structure 1967
PN 1272 SC 21830
SN Patterns of organization, behavior, and communication of a group that determine the interpersonal relations of its members.
B Group Characteristics 2007
R Group Development 1997

Group Testing 1973
PN 270 SC 21840
B Measurement 1967
R Test Administration 1973

Group Therapy
Use Group Psychotherapy

Groups (Organizations)
Use Organizations

Groups (Social)
Use Social Groups

Groupware 2003
PN 96 SC 21892
SN Computer software and other technology designed to enable communication and foster productivity both within and among groups of people working together on a task.
HN This term was introduced in June 2003. Relevant records were re-indexed with this term. The posting note reflects the number of records that were re-indexed.
UF Computer Supported Cooperative Work
B Computer Applications 1973
Computer Software 1967
R Computer Mediated Communication 2003
Cooperation 1967
↓ Electronic Communication 2001
↓ Employee Interaction 1988
Supervisor Employee Interaction 1997
↓ Technology 1973
Teleconferencing 1997
↓ Work Teams 2001
↓ Working Conditions 1973

Grown Children
Use Adult Offspring

Growth
Use Development

Growth Centers
Use Human Potential Movement

Growth Hormone
Use Somatotropin

Growth Hormone Inhibitor
Use Somatostatin

GSR (Electrophysiology)
Use Galvanic Skin Response

Guanethidine 1973
PN 38 SC 21930
B Amines 1973
Antihypertensive Drugs 1973

Guanethidine — (cont'd)
R Norepinephrine 1973

Guanosine 1985
PN 100 SC 21929
R ↓ Carbohydrate Metabolism 1973
Cyclic Adenosine Monophosphate 1978
↓ Nucleic Acids 1973

Guardianship 1988
PN 224 SC 21932
SN Court appointment of an individual to act as a guardian or conservator and to legally act and speak in the interest of a minor or a physically or mentally disabled adult.
UF Conservatorship
B Legal Processes 1973
R Child Custody 1982
↓ Client Rights 1988
↓ Commitment (Psychiatric) 1973
Informed Consent 1985
Protective Services 1997

Guessing 1973
PN 308 SC 21933
SN Responding to questions or test items on the basis of little or no knowledge of the correct answer.
R Intuition 1973
Questioning 1982
↓ Strategies 1967
Test Taking 1985

Guest Workers
Use Foreign Workers

Guidance (Educational)
Use Educational Counseling

Guidance (Occupational)
Use Occupational Guidance

Guidance Counseling
Use School Counseling

Guided Fantasy
Use Guided Imagery

Guided Imagery 2001
PN 431 SC 21957
SN Mind-body technique involving the deliberate prompting of mental images, used in the treatment of mental disorders, for performance enhancement, and in helping patients cope with diseases and their symptoms.
UF Directed Reverie Therapy
Guided Fantasy
B Psychotherapeutic Techniques 1967
Psychotherapy 1967
R ↓ Hypnotherapy 1973
↓ Imagery 1967
Relaxation 1973
↓ Relaxation Therapy 1978

Guilt 1967
PN 2512 SC 21970
B Emotional States 1973
R ↓ Anxiety 1967
↓ Anxiety Disorders 1997
Blame 1994
Shame 1994

Guinea Pigs 1967
PN 1073 SC 21980
B Rodents 1973

Gulls
Use Sea Gulls

Gun Control Laws 1973
PN 119 SC 22000
B Laws 1967
R Firearms 2003
Government 1967

Guns
Use Firearms

Gustatory Perception
Use Taste Perception

Gymnastic Therapy
Use Recreation Therapy

Gynecological Disorders 1973
PN 289 SC 22040
B Genital Disorders 1967
Urogenital Disorders 1973
N ↓ Menstrual Disorders 1973
R ↓ Endocrine Sexual Disorders 1973
Hermaphroditism 1973
↓ Hypogonadism 1973
↓ Infertility 1973
Pseudocyesis 1973
Sterility 1973

Gynecologists 1973
PN 114 SC 22050
B Physicians 1967
R Obstetricians 1978
Surgeons 1973

Gynecology 1978
PN 286 SC 22053
SN Medical specialty dealing with the female endocrine system, reproductive physiology, and diseases of the genital tract. Used for the medical specialty or the specific gynecological issues or findings.
B Medical Sciences 1967
R Circumcision 2001
↓ Obstetrics 1978

Gypsies 1973
PN 107 SC 22055
UF Gipsies
B Racial and Ethnic Groups 2001
R ↓ Human Migration 1973
Minority Groups 1967

Gyrus Cinguli 1973
PN 882 SC 22060
SN A long curved structure or convolution on the medial surface of the cerebral hemispheres that forms part of the limbic system.
B Frontal Lobe 1973
Limbic System 1973

Habilitation 1991
PN 98 SC 22065
SN Establishment, not restoration, of fundamental capabilities, knowledge, experiences, and attitudes before or along with the usual rehabilitation procedures as a means of increasing patient awareness and developing their potential. Used primarily for physically or mentally disabled populations. Compare REHABILITATION.

Habilitation — (cont'd)
R Activities of Daily Living 1991
Deinstitutionalization 1982
Independent Living Programs 1991
↓ Mainstreaming 1991
↓ Rehabilitation 1967
↓ Skill Learning 1973

Habitat Selection
Use Territoriality

Habitats (Animal)
Use Animal Environments

Habits 1967
PN 1000 **SC** 22080
UF Mannerisms
N Nail Biting 1973
Thumbsucking 1973
↓ Tobacco Smoking 1967
Trichotillomania 2003
R ↓ Learning 1967

Habituation 1967
PN 2793 **SC** 22090
SN Progressive attenuation of a response elicited by repetitive stimulation.
R ↓ Sensory Adaptation 1967

Hair 1973
PN 309 **SC** 22100
B Anatomy 1967
R Alopecia 1973
Scalp (Anatomy) 1973
Skin (Anatomy) 1967

Hair Loss
Use Alopecia

Hair Pulling
HN In 2003, the term was discontinued and removed from all records containing it, and was replaced with TRICHOTILLOMANIA, its postable counterpart.
Use Trichotillomania

Halcion
Use Triazolam

Halfway Houses 1973
PN 257 **SC** 22140
SN Facilities for psychiatric, drug, or alcohol rehabilitation patients or mentally retarded individuals who no longer need hospitalization or institutionalization, but who are not yet fully prepared to return to their communities.
B Residential Care Institutions 1973
Treatment Facilities 1973
R ↓ Community Facilities 1973
↓ Correctional Institutions 1973
↓ Psychiatric Hospital Programs 1967
Psychiatric Hospitals 1967

Hallucinations 1967
PN 1606 **SC** 22150
SN Perceptions through any sense modality in the absence of an appropriate stimulus. (Usually indicative of abnormality but may be experienced occasionally by normal persons.)
UF Flashbacks
B Perceptual Disturbances 1973
N Auditory Hallucinations 1973
Drug Induced Hallucinations 1973
Hypnagogic Hallucinations 1973
Visual Hallucinations 1973

Hallucinations — (cont'd)
R ↓ Hallucinogenic Drugs 1967
↓ Hallucinosis 1973
Near Death Experiences 1985

Hallucinogenic Drugs 1967
PN 755 **SC** 22160
HN In April 2007, this term replaced the discontinued term PSYCHEDELIC DRUGS. PSYCHEDELIC DRUGS was removed from all records containing it, and was replaced with HALLUCINOGENIC DRUGS.
UF Psychedelic Drugs
B Drugs 1967
N Bufotenine 1973
Lysergic Acid Diethylamide 1967
Mescaline 1973
Peyote 1973
Phencyclidine 1982
Psilocybin 1973
R ↓ Cannabis 1973
↓ Cholinergic Blocking Drugs 1973
Experimental Psychosis 1973
↓ Hallucinations 1967
↓ Psychotomimetic Drugs 1973
Tetrahydrocannabinol 1973

Hallucinosis 1973
PN 72 **SC** 22170
SN Mental disorder characterized by hallucinations occurring in a normal state of consciousness and attributable to specific organic factors.
B Psychosis 1967
N ↓ Alcoholic Hallucinosis 1973
R ↓ Hallucinations 1967

Halo Effect 1982
PN 165 **SC** 22177
SN Tendency to rate individuals too high or too low on the basis of one outstanding trait or an erroneous overall impression. Often the source of error in rating scales.
R ↓ Errors 1967
↓ Expectations 1967
Experimenter Bias 1967
Rating 1967
↓ Social Perception 1967

Haloperidol 1973
PN 3850 **SC** 22180
B CNS Depressant Drugs 1973
Sedatives 1973
Tranquilizing Drugs 1967

Halstead Reitan Neuropsychological Battery 2001
PN 135 **SC** 22185
HN In 2000, the truncated term HALSTEAD REITAN NEUROPSYCH BATTERY (which was used from 1991-2000) was deleted, removed from all records containing it, and replaced with its expanded form HALSTEAD REITAN NEUROPSYCHOLOGICAL BATTERY. Use NEUROPSYCHOLOGICAL ASSESSMENT to access references from 1982-1990.
B Neuropsychological Assessment 1982

Hamsters 1973
PN 1710 **SC** 22190
B Rodents 1973

Hand (Anatomy) 1967
PN 1664 **SC** 22200
B Anatomy 1967
Musculoskeletal System 1973

Hand (Anatomy) — (cont'd)
R Arm (Anatomy) 1973
↓ Fingers (Anatomy) 1973
Palm (Anatomy) 1973
Wrist 1973

Handedness 1978
PN 3281 **SC** 22210
SN Learned or spontaneous differential dexterity with and tendency to use one hand rather than the other.
UF Ambidexterity
B Lateral Dominance 1967

Handicapped (Attitudes Toward)
HN Term was discontinued in 1997. In 2000, the term was removed from all records containing it, and replaced with DISABLED (ATTITUDES TOWARD), its postable counterpart.
Use Disabled (Attitudes Toward)

Handicaps
HN Use DISORDERS to access references from 2001 to June 2003.
Use Disabilities

Handicrafts
Use Crafts

Handwriting 1967
PN 1188 **SC** 22250
UF Graphology
Writing (Handwriting)
B Verbal Communication 1967
Written Language 1967
N Cursive Writing 1973
Handwriting Legibility 1973
Printing (Handwriting) 1973

Handwriting Legibility 1973
PN 85 **SC** 22260
UF Legibility (Handwriting)
B Handwriting 1967
Legibility 1978

Happiness 1973
PN 1898 **SC** 22270
UF Joy
B Emotional States 1973
R Euphoria 1973
Pleasure 1973

Haptic Perception
Use Cutaneous Sense

Harassment 2001
PN 238 **SC** 22282
B Antisocial Behavior 1971
N Sexual Harassment 1985
Stalking 2001
R Bullying 2003
Hate Crimes 2003
↓ Perpetrators 1988
Threat 1967
Victimization 1973

Harassment (Sexual)
Use Sexual Harassment

Hardiness
HN In June 2003, the term was discontinued and removed from all records containing it, and was replaced with RESILIENCE (PSYCHOLOGICAL), its postable counterpart. Use PSYCHOLOGICAL ENDURANCE to access references from 1991-1996.
Use Resilience (Psychological)

Harm Reduction 2003
PN 522 **SC** 22287
SN Pragmatic approach concerned with reducing potential harm to individuals participating in high risk behaviors.
HN This term was introduced in June 2003. Relevant records were re-indexed with this term. The posting note reflects the number of records that were re-indexed.
N Needle Exchange Programs 2001
R AIDS Prevention 1994
Drug Abuse Prevention 1994
↓ Drug Legalization 1997
Risk Management 1997

Hashish 1973
PN 90 **SC** 22290
B Cannabis 1973
R Marijuana 2003
Tetrahydrocannabinol 1973

Hate 1973
PN 488 **SC** 22300
B Aversion 1967
R ↓ Anger 1967
Hate Crimes 2003
Hostility 1967

Hate Crimes 2003
PN 137 **SC** 22301
SN A crime committed against an individual, a small group, or a large population in which the perpetrator is motivated by a bias against the victim because of his or her race, ethnicity, religion, sex, national origin, or sexual orientation.
HN This term was introduced in June 2003. Relevant records were re-indexed with this term. The posting note reflects the number of records that were re-indexed.
UF Bias Crimes
B Crime 1967
R AntiSemitism 1973
↓ Harassment 2001
Hate 1973
↓ Prejudice 1967
↓ Racial and Ethnic Attitudes 1982
Racism 1973
↓ Religious Prejudices 1973
↓ Sexual Orientation 1997
Victimization 1973
↓ Violence 1973

Hawaii Natives 2001
PN 42 **SC** 22315
UF Native Hawaiians
B Pacific Islanders 2001
R Minority Groups 1967

Hay Fever 1973
PN 18 **SC** 22320
B Allergic Disorders 1973
Respiratory Tract Disorders 1973

Hay Fever — (cont'd)
R ↓ Somatoform Disorders 2001

Hazardous Materials 1991
PN 361 **SC** 22325
UF Asbestos
Toxic Waste
N ↓ Insecticides 1973
Teratogens 1988
↓ Toxins 2007
R ↓ Accidents 1967
↓ Chemicals 1991
↓ Environment 1967
Occupational Exposure 1988
Pollution 1973
↓ Safety 1967
↓ Toxicity 1973

Hazards 1973
PN 525 **SC** 22330
R ↓ Accidents 1967
Risk Perception 1997
↓ Safety 1967
↓ Safety Devices 1973
Warning Labels 1997
↓ Warnings 1997

Head (Anatomy) 1973
PN 878 **SC** 22340
B Anatomy 1967
R Face (Anatomy) 1973
Scalp (Anatomy) 1973
Skin (Anatomy) 1967

Head Banging 1973
PN 59 **SC** 22350
B Self Destructive Behavior 1985

Head Injuries 1973
PN 3293 **SC** 22360
UF Closed Head Injuries
B Injuries 1973
N Brain Concussion 1973
R ↓ Brain Damage 1967
↓ Traumatic Brain Injury 1997
Whiplash 1997
↓ Wounds 1973

Head Start
Use Project Head Start

Headache 1973
PN 1725 **SC** 22380
B Pain 1967
Symptoms 1967
N Migraine Headache 1973
Muscle Contraction Headache 1973
R ↓ Somatoform Disorders 2001

Health 1973
PN 19619 **SC** 22390
UF Wellness
N Holistic Health 1985
↓ Mental Health 1967
Physical Health 2007
↓ Public Health 1988
R General Health Questionnaire 1991
Health Attitudes 1985
↓ Health Behavior 1982
Health Complaints 1997
Health Knowledge 1994
Hygiene 1994
Preventive Medicine 1973
Public Health Services 1973

Health — (cont'd)
Well Being 1994

Health Attitudes 1985
PN 5425 **SC** 22391
UF Health Locus of Control
B Attitudes 1967
R ↓ Drug Usage Attitudes 1973
↓ Health 1973
↓ Health Behavior 1982
Health Knowledge 1994
Health Promotion 1991
Lifestyle Changes 1997
Obesity (Attitudes Toward) 1997
↓ Physical Illness (Attitudes Toward) 1985
Treatment Barriers 2005

Health Behavior 1982
PN 8588 **SC** 22392
SN Individual lifestyle and behavior which may or may not enhance or maintain good health.
B Behavior 1967
Client Characteristics 1973
N Safe Sex 2003
R Active Living 2007
Aerobic Exercise 1988
AIDS Prevention 1994
Diets 1978
↓ Exercise 1973
↓ Health 1973
Health Attitudes 1985
Health Knowledge 1994
Health Promotion 1991
Holistic Health 1985
Hygiene 1994
↓ Lifestyle 1978
Lifestyle Changes 1997
↓ Physical Activity 2007
↓ Prenatal Care 1991
Preventive Medicine 1973
Self Examination (Medical) 1988
Self Referral 1991
Weight Control 1985

Health Care Administration 1997
PN 497 **SC** 57485
B Management 1967
N Hospital Administration 1978
R ↓ Case Management 1991
Clinical Audits 2007
Clinical Governance 2007
↓ Health Care Delivery 1978
Health Care Economics 2007
↓ Health Care Policy 1994
↓ Health Care Services 1978
↓ Mental Health Programs 1973
↓ Mental Health Services 1978
↓ Treatment Facilities 1973
Utilization Reviews 2007

Health Care Barriers
Use Treatment Barriers

Health Care Costs 1994
PN 2772 **SC** 22393
UF Medical Care Costs
Mental Health Care Costs
B Costs and Cost Analysis 1973
R ↓ Case Management 1991
Cost Containment 1991
Diagnosis Related Groups 1988
Disease Management 2007
↓ Economics 1985
↓ Health Care Delivery 1978

Health Care Costs — (cont'd)
Health Care Economics 2007
Health Care Reform 2006
↓ Health Care Services 1978
Health Care Utilization 1985
↓ Health Insurance 1973
Health Maintenance Organizations 1982
↓ Managed Care 1994
↓ Mental Health Services 1978
Pharmacoeconomics 2007
↓ Professional Fees 1978
↓ Treatment 1967
Utilization Reviews 2007

Health Care Delivery 1978
PN 10281 **SC** 22394
SN Practices, policies, or referral processes that contribute to making mental and/or medical health care personnel, services, or facilities available to persons in need of such care.
N Home Care 1985
Hospice 1982
↓ Managed Care 1994
Telemedicine 2003
R Bioethics 2003
↓ Case Management 1991
Clinical Practice 2007
Continuum of Care 2004
Evidence Based Practice 2004
Fee for Service 1994
↓ Health Care Administration 1997
Health Care Costs 1994
Health Care Economics 2007
↓ Health Care Policy 1994
Health Care Reform 2006
↓ Health Care Services 1978
Health Care Utilization 1985
Health Maintenance Organizations 1982
Health Service Needs 1997
↓ Mental Health Programs 1973
↓ Mental Health Services 1978
Needs Assessment 1985
Outreach Programs 1997
Palliative Care 1991
↓ Prevention 1973
Primary Health Care 1988
Private Practice 1978
Quality of Care 1988
↓ Quality of Services 1997
↓ Treatment 1967
Treatment Barriers 2005
↓ Treatment Planning 1997

Health Care Economics 2007
PN 67 **SC** 58105
SN Analysis of the costs, benefits, management, and outcomes of health care and efficient use of available resources in its planning and delivery.
HN This term was introduced in April 2007. Relevant records were re-indexed with this term. The posting note reflects the number of records that were re-indexed.
UF Health Economics
B Economics 1985
R ↓ Costs and Cost Analysis 1973
↓ Health Care Administration 1997
Health Care Costs 1994
↓ Health Care Delivery 1978
↓ Health Care Policy 1994
↓ Health Care Services 1978
↓ Health Insurance 1973

Health Care Policy 1994
PN 2682 **SC** 57415
UF Mental Health Care Policy
B Policy Making 1988
N Health Care Reform 2006
R Clinical Governance 2007
↓ Government Policy Making 1973
↓ Health Care Administration 1997
↓ Health Care Delivery 1978
Health Care Economics 2007
↓ Health Care Services 1978
↓ Health Insurance 1973
Medicaid 1994
Medicare 1988
Mental Health Parity 2007
↓ Mental Health Services 1978

Health Care Professionals
HN Use MEDICAL PERSONNEL or MENTAL HEALTH PERSONNEL to access references prior to 1994.
Use Health Personnel

Health Care Psychology 1985
PN 2626 **SC** 22398
UF Behavioral Health
Behavioral Medicine
Health Psychology
N Medical Psychology 1973
R Interdisciplinary Treatment Approach 1973
Psychosomatic Medicine 1978

Health Care Reform 2006
PN 113 **SC** 58093
SN The effort of government to improve health care access, advance quality of care, and control health care costs.
HN This term was introduced in May 2006. Relevant records were re-indexed with this term. The posting note reflects the number of records that were re-indexed.
B Health Care Policy 1994
R Health Care Costs 1994
↓ Health Care Delivery 1978
↓ Health Care Services 1978
Health Care Utilization 1985
↓ Health Insurance 1973

Health Care Seeking Behavior 1997
PN 1354 **SC** 22399
HN Consider HELP SEEKING BEHAVIOR or HEALTH CARE UTILIZATION to access references from 1978-1984 and 1985-1996, respectively.
UF Treatment Seeking Behavior
B Help Seeking Behavior 1978
R ↓ Commitment (Psychiatric) 1973
↓ Health Care Services 1978
Health Care Utilization 1985
Health Service Needs 1997
↓ Hospital Admission 1973
↓ Mental Health Services 1978
Online Therapy 2003
Self Referral 1991
↓ Treatment 1967
Treatment Barriers 2005

Health Care Services 1978
PN 10099 **SC** 22396
B Treatment 1967
N Continuum of Care 2004
Long Term Care 1994
↓ Mental Health Services 1978
Palliative Care 1991
Primary Health Care 1988

Health Care Services — (cont'd)
R Caregivers 1988
↓ Community Services 1967
Cost Containment 1991
↓ Counseling 1967
Fee for Service 1994
↓ Health Care Administration 1997
Health Care Costs 1994
↓ Health Care Delivery 1978
Health Care Economics 2007
↓ Health Care Policy 1994
Health Care Reform 2006
Health Care Seeking Behavior 1997
Health Care Utilization 1985
Health Maintenance Organizations 1982
Health Service Needs 1997
Human Services 2007
Integrated Services 1997
↓ Managed Care 1994
↓ Mental Health Programs 1973
Outreach Programs 1997
↓ Prenatal Care 1991
↓ Prevention 1973
Quality of Care 1988
↓ Quality of Services 1997
↓ Rehabilitation 1967
Self Referral 1991
Social Casework 1967
↓ Social Services 1982
Telemedicine 2003

Health Care Utilization 1985
PN 7299 **SC** 22397
SN Processes involved in or factors affecting usage of professional or nonprofessional health services or programs. Use HEALTH CARE SEEKING BEHAVIOR for factors involved in seeking treatment.
HN Use HELP SEEKING BEHAVIOR to access references from 1978-1984.
UF Assistance Seeking (Professional)
Health Service Utilization
Utilization (Health Care)
R Health Care Costs 1994
↓ Health Care Delivery 1978
Health Care Reform 2006
Health Care Seeking Behavior 1997
↓ Health Care Services 1978
↓ Help Seeking Behavior 1978
Self Referral 1991
Treatment Barriers 2005
Utilization Reviews 2007

Health Complaints 1997
PN 371 **SC** 22402
R ↓ Disorders 1967
↓ Health 1973
Symptom Checklists 1991
↓ Symptoms 1967

Health Economics
Use Health Care Economics

Health Education 1973
PN 5467 **SC** 22400
SN Instruction or programs in school, institutional, or community settings which present material about factors affecting health behavior and attitudes.
B Curriculum 1967
N Drug Education 1973
Sex Education 1973
R AIDS Prevention 1994
Client Education 1985
Health Knowledge 1994
Health Promotion 1991

Health Education — (cont'd)
↓ Prenatal Care 1991
↓ Prevention 1973
Psychoeducation 1994

Health Impairments 2001
PN 851 **SC** 22415
HN In 2001, this term was created to replace the discontinued and deleted term HEALTH IMPAIRED. HEALTH IMPAIRED was removed from all records containing it and replaced with HEALTH IMPAIRMENTS.
UF Frail
B Physical Disorders 1997
R Homebound 1988

Health Insurance 1973
PN 1466 **SC** 22420
B Insurance 1973
N ↓ Employee Health Insurance 1973
Fee for Service 1994
Health Maintenance Organizations 1982
Medicaid 1994
Medicare 1988
R ↓ Case Management 1991
Diagnosis Related Groups 1988
Health Care Costs 1994
Health Care Economics 2007
↓ Health Care Policy 1994
Health Care Reform 2006
↓ Hospitalization 1967
↓ Managed Care 1994
Mental Health Parity 2007
Utilization Reviews 2007

Health Knowledge 1994
PN 2548 **SC** 22421
SN Knowledge or understanding of illness, health, or mental health and health related issues.
B Knowledge Level 1978
R Client Education 1985
↓ Health 1973
Health Attitudes 1985
↓ Health Behavior 1982
↓ Health Education 1973
Health Promotion 1991
Mental Illness (Attitudes Toward) 1967
↓ Physical Illness (Attitudes Toward) 1985
Telemedicine 2003

Health Locus of Control
Use Health Attitudes

Health Maintenance Organizations 1982
PN 641 **SC** 22425
SN Organizations providing comprehensive, coordinated medical services to voluntarily enrolled members on a prepaid basis.
UF Group Health Plans
HMO
B Health Insurance 1973
Managed Care 1994
Organizations 1967
R Cost Containment 1991
Fee for Service 1994
Health Care Costs 1994
↓ Health Care Delivery 1978
↓ Health Care Services 1978
Health Promotion 1991
Preventive Medicine 1973

Health Personnel 1994
PN 4223 **SC** 57420
SN Personnel working in a medical or mental health profession. Used for unspecified health care professionals or when both medical and mental health professionals are discussed. Use a more specific term if possible.
HN Consider MEDICAL PERSONNEL or MENTAL HEALTH PERSONNEL to access references prior to 1994.
UF Health Care Professionals
B Professional Personnel 1978
N ↓ Allied Health Personnel 2007
↓ Medical Personnel 1967
↓ Mental Health Personnel 1967
R ↓ Counselors 1967
Home Care Personnel 1997
↓ Social Workers 1973
↓ Therapists 1967

Health Personnel Attitudes 1985
PN 6906 **SC** 22426
SN Attitudes of persons working in health or medical professions.
B Attitudes 1967
N ↓ Therapist Attitudes 1978
R Counselor Attitudes 1973
Psychologist Attitudes 1991

Health Promotion 1991
PN 5171 **SC** 22423
SN Education or other types of interventions used to improve and encourage both physical and mental health.
HN Consider using HEALTH EDUCATION to access references from 1973-1990.
R Active Living 2007
AIDS Prevention 1994
Cancer Screening 1997
Client Education 1985
Health Attitudes 1985
↓ Health Behavior 1982
↓ Health Education 1973
Health Knowledge 1994
Health Maintenance Organizations 1982
↓ Health Screening 1997
Lifestyle Changes 1997
↓ Prevention 1973
Preventive Medicine 1973
↓ Public Health 1988
Public Service Announcements 2004
↓ Screening 1982
Social Marketing 2007

Health Psychology
Use Health Care Psychology

Health Screening 1997
PN 627 **SC** 22431
HN Consider PHYSICAL EXAMINATION to access references from 1988-1996.
B Screening 1982
N Cancer Screening 1997
Genetic Testing 2003
HIV Testing 1997
Physical Examination 1988
R Drug Usage Screening 1988
Health Promotion 1991
Mammography 1994
↓ Medical Diagnosis 1973
Preventive Medicine 1973
↓ Public Health 1988

Health Service Needs 1997
PN 1892 **SC** 22432
UF Mental Health Service Needs
B Needs 1967
R ↓ Case Management 1991
↓ Health Care Delivery 1978
Health Care Seeking Behavior 1997
↓ Health Care Services 1978
Intake Interview 1994
↓ Mental Health Services 1978
Needs Assessment 1985
Treatment Barriers 2005

Health Service Utilization
Use Health Care Utilization

Hearing Acuity
Use Auditory Acuity

Hearing Aids 1973
PN 720 **SC** 22430
B Medical Therapeutic Devices 1973
N Cochlear Implants 1994

Hearing Disorders 1982
PN 3476 **SC** 22435
SN Disorders involving the hearing mechanisms, specifically the sensorineural pathways.
HN The term AURALLY HANDICAPPED was also used to represent this concept from 1973-1996, and AURALLY DISABLED was used from 1997-2000. In 2000, HEARING DISORDERS replaced the discontinued and deleted term AURALLY DISABLED. AURALLY DISABLED and AURALLY HANDICAPPED were removed from all records containing them and replaced with HEARING DISORDERS.
UF Aurally Handicapped
Sensorineural Hearing Loss
B Communication Disorders 1982
N ↓ Deaf 1967
R Cochlear Implants 1994
↓ Ear Disorders 1973

Hearing Impaired (Partially)
Use Partially Hearing Impaired

Hearing Measures
Use Speech and Hearing Measures

Heart 1967
PN 658 **SC** 22460
B Cardiovascular System 1967
N Heart Auricles 1973
Heart Valves 1973
Heart Ventricles 1973
Myocardium 1973
R ↓ Blood 1967
Vagus Nerve 1973

Heart Attacks
Use Heart Disorders

Heart Auricles 1973
PN 18 **SC** 22470
UF Atria (Heart)
Auricles (Heart)
B Heart 1967

Heart Beat
Use Heart Rate

Heart Disorders 1973
PN 3286 **SC** 22480
UF Cardiac Arrest
Cardiac Disorders

Heart Disorders — (cont'd)
Coronary Heart Disease
Heart Attacks
B Cardiovascular Disorders 1967
N Angina Pectoris 1973
↓ Arrhythmias (Heart) 1973
Coronary Thromboses 1973
Myocardial Infarctions 1973
R Rheumatic Fever 1973
Williams Syndrome 2003

Heart Rate 1967
PN 7279 SC 22490
UF Cardiac Rate
Heart Beat
Heartbeat
R Cardiovascular Reactivity 1994

Heart Rate Affecting Drugs 1973
PN 77 SC 22500
B Drugs 1967
N Caffeine 1973
Epinephrine 1967
Theophylline 1973
Verapamil 1991
R ↓ Analeptic Drugs 1973
↓ Antihypertensive Drugs 1973
↓ Cardiovascular Disorders 1967
↓ CNS Affecting Drugs 1973
↓ CNS Stimulating Drugs 1973
Dopamine 1973
↓ Muscle Relaxing Drugs 1973
↓ Vasoconstrictor Drugs 1973
↓ Vasodilator Drugs 1973

Heart Surgery 1973
PN 770 SC 22510
UF Cardiac Surgery
B Surgery 1971
R Organ Transplantation 1973

Heart Transplants
Use Organ Transplantation

Heart Valves 1973
PN 54 SC 22530
UF Valves (Heart)
B Heart 1967

Heart Ventricles 1973
PN 71 SC 22540
UF Ventricles (Heart)
B Heart 1967

Heartbeat
Use Heart Rate

Heat Effects 1973
PN 771 SC 22560
B Temperature Effects 1967

Hebephrenic Schizophrenia
HN In 2000, HEBEPHRENIC SCHIZOPHRENIA was discontinued and removed from all records containing it. The term was replaced with SCHIZOPHRENIA (DISORGANIZED TYPE), its postable counterpart.
Use Schizophrenia (Disorganized Type)

Hedonism 1973
PN 241 SC 22580
R ↓ Attitudes 1967
↓ Philosophies 1967

Heels (Anatomy)
Use Feet (Anatomy)

Height (Body)
Use Body Height

Helicopters 1973
PN 84 SC 22610
B Aircraft 1973

Helium 1973
PN 30 SC 22620

Helmets
Use Safety Devices

Help Seeking Behavior 1978
PN 2331 SC 22624
SN Searching for or requesting help from others through formal or informal mechanisms.
HN From 1978-1984 used primarily for the seeking or utilization of professional care or services. From 1997, use HEALTH CARE SEEKING BEHAVIOR to access references on help seeking in a treatment context.
B Social Behavior 1967
N Health Care Seeking Behavior 1997
R ↓ Assistance (Social Behavior) 1973
Health Care Utilization 1985
Self Referral 1991

Helping Behavior
Use Assistance (Social Behavior)

Helplessness 1997
PN 239 SC 22627
B Emotional States 1973
N Learned Helplessness 1978
R Coping Behavior 1967
Empowerment 1991
Hopelessness 1988
Internal External Locus of Control 1967
↓ Power 1967
Self Control 1973
Self Determination 1994
Self Efficacy 1985

Helplessness (Learned)
Use Learned Helplessness

Hematologic Disorders
Use Blood and Lymphatic Disorders

Hematoma 1973
PN 83 SC 22640
B Hemorrhage 1973
Symptoms 1967
R ↓ Injuries 1973

Hemianopia 1973
PN 191 SC 22650
SN Blindness affecting either the right or left half of the visual field, usually resulting from a stroke or brain injury.
UF Hemianopsia
Hemiopia
B Vision Disorders 1982
R ↓ Nervous System Disorders 1967

Hemianopsia
Use Hemianopia

Hemiopia
Use Hemianopia

Hemiplegia 1978
PN 389 SC 22675
SN Paralysis of one side of the body resulting from disease or injury to the brain or spinal cord.
B Paralysis 1973
R ↓ Central Nervous System Disorders 1973
↓ Injuries 1973
↓ Musculoskeletal Disorders 1973
Paraplegia 1978
Quadriplegia 1985
↓ Spinal Cord Injuries 1973

Hemispherectomy 1973
PN 152 SC 22680
SN Surgical removal or resection of a cerebral hemisphere, usually as treatment for intractable epilepsy.
B Neurosurgery 1973

Hemispheric Specialization
HN Use CEREBRAL DOMINANCE to access references from 1973-1990.
Use Lateral Dominance

Hemodialysis 1973
PN 624 SC 22690
B Dialysis 1973
R Blood Transfusion 1973

Hemoglobin 1973
PN 159 SC 22700
B Blood Proteins 1973
Pigments 1973

Hemophilia 1973
PN 262 SC 22710
B Blood and Lymphatic Disorders 1973
Sex Linked Hereditary Disorders 1973

Hemorrhage 1973
PN 127 SC 22720
B Cardiovascular Disorders 1967
Symptoms 1967
N Cerebral Hemorrhage 1973
Hematoma 1973

Hemp (Cannabis)
Use Cannabis

Henmon Nelson Tests of Mental Ability
HN Term was discontinued in 1997. In 2000, the term was removed from all records containing it, and replaced with INTELLIGENCE MEASURES, its postable counterpart.
Use Intelligence Measures

Heparin 1973
PN 30 SC 22750
B Acids 1973
Anticoagulant Drugs 1973

Hepatic Disorders
Use Liver Disorders

Hepatitis 1973
PN 683 SC 22770
B Liver Disorders 1973
N Toxic Hepatitis 1973
R ↓ Infectious Disorders 1973
Jaundice 1973

Hereditary Disorders
Use Genetic Disorders

Heredity
Use Genetics

Heritability 2005
PN 305 **SC** 22795
SN The proportion of phenotypic variance that can be attributed to genetic factors.
HN This term was introduced in August 2005. Relevant records were re-indexed with this term. The posting note reflects the number of records that were re-indexed.
R ↓ Genetics 1967

Hermaphroditism 1973
PN 181 **SC** 22800
SN The presence of both ovarian and testicular tissue and secondary sex characteristics in one individual.
UF Intersexuality
Pseudohermaphroditism
B Congenital Disorders 1973
Genital Disorders 1967
R ↓ Endocrine Sexual Disorders 1973
↓ Gender Identity Disorder 1997
↓ Gynecological Disorders 1973
Klinefelters Syndrome 1973
↓ Male Genital Disorders 1973
Sterility 1973
Testicular Feminization Syndrome 1973
Turners Syndrome 1973

Hermeneutics 1991
PN 718 **SC** 22805
SN Theory and method of interpreting meaning. Originally, the term referred to interpretation of the scriptures.
B Philosophies 1967
R Epistemology 1973
↓ Metaphysics 1973
Phenomenology 1967
Positivism (Philosophy) 1997
Rhetoric 1991
↓ Semiotics 1985

Heroes 2007
PN 157 **SC** 22807
HN This term was introduced in April 2007. Relevant records were re-indexed with this term. The posting note reflects the number of records that were re-indexed.
R Altruism 1973
Courage 1973
Myths 1967
Role Models 1982

Heroin 1973
PN 1268 **SC** 22810
UF Diacetylmorphine
B Alkaloids 1973
Analgesic Drugs 1973
Opiates 1973
Sedatives 1973
R Heroin Addiction 1973

Heroin Addiction 1973
PN 1789 **SC** 22820
B Drug Addiction 1967
R Heroin 1973
Methadone Maintenance 1978

Herpes Genitalis 1988
PN 99 **SC** 22825
UF Genital Herpes
B Sexually Transmitted Diseases 2003
Viral Disorders 1973

Herpes Simplex 1973
PN 339 **SC** 22830
B Skin Disorders 1973
Viral Disorders 1973

Heterogeneity of Variance
Use Homogeneity of Variance

Heterosexism
Use Homosexuality (Attitudes Toward)

Heterosexual Interaction
Use Male Female Relations

Heterosexuality 1973
PN 2182 **SC** 22840
B Psychosexual Behavior 1967
Sexual Orientation 1997
R Lesbianism 1973
Male Female Relations 1988
Male Homosexuality 1973
Sex Linked Developmental Differences 1973
Sexual Development 1973

Heterozygotic Twins 1973
PN 925 **SC** 22850
UF Dizygotic Twins
Fraternal Twins
B Twins 1967

Heuristic Modeling 1973
PN 555 **SC** 22860
B Simulation 1967
R Heuristics 2003
↓ Mathematical Modeling 1973

Heuristics 2003
PN 818 **SC** 22862
SN Informal techniques for problem solving based on simple rules or prior experience.
HN This term was introduced in June 2003. Relevant records were re-indexed with this term. The posting note reflects the number of records that were re-indexed.
B Problem Solving 1967
R Algorithms 1973
Cognitive Hypothesis Testing 1982
↓ Decision Making 1967
Declarative Knowledge 1997
↓ Expert Systems 1991
Heuristic Modeling 1973
↓ Inductive Deductive Reasoning 1973
↓ Reasoning 1967
↓ Strategies 1967

Hexamethonium 1973
PN 34 **SC** 22870
B Antihypertensive Drugs 1973
Ganglion Blocking Drugs 1973

Hexobarbital 1973
PN 30 **SC** 22880
B Anesthetic Drugs 1973
Barbiturates 1967
Hypnotic Drugs 1973
Sedatives 1973

Hibernation 1973
PN 97 **SC** 22890
B Animal Ethology 1967
R ↓ Animal Biological Rhythms 1973

High Risk Populations
Use At Risk Populations

High School Education 2003
PN 357 **SC** 22921
SN Education for grades 9 through 12.
HN This term was introduced in June 2003. Relevant records were re-indexed with this term. The posting note reflects the number of records that were re-indexed.
B Education 1967
R High Schools 1973
Secondary Education 1973

High School Equivalency
Use Adult Education

High School Graduates 1978
PN 348 **SC** 22924
R Educational Degrees 1973
High School Students 1967
School Graduation 1991
School to Work Transition 1994

High School Personality Questionnaire 2001
PN 34 **SC** 22927
HN In 2000, the truncated term HIGH SCH PERSONALITY QUESTIONNAIRE (which was used from 1973-2000) was deleted, removed from all records containing it, and replaced with its expanded form HIGH SCHOOL PERSONALITY QUESTIONNAIRE.
B Nonprojective Personality Measures 1973

High School Students 1967
PN 20766 **SC** 22930
SN Students in grades 9-12.
B Students 1967
R Grade Level 1994
High School Graduates 1978
Reentry Students 1985

High School Teachers 1973
PN 2848 **SC** 22940
B Teachers 1967

High Schools 1973
PN 1517 **SC** 22950
B Schools 1967
R High School Education 2003
Military Schools 1973
Secondary Education 1973

Higher Education 1973
PN 2993 **SC** 22960
SN College or university education beyond the successful completion of high school or grammar school, or the attainment of an approved equivalent.
B Education 1967
N ↓ Graduate Education 1973
↓ Postgraduate Training 1973
Undergraduate Education 1978
R ↓ Colleges 1967
↓ Continuing Education 1985
Educational Degrees 1973
Educational Program Accreditation 1994
Graduate Schools 1973
Professional Specialization 1991
School Graduation 1991

Higher Order Conditioning 1997
PN 34 **SC** 22970
SN A classical conditioning method in which the original conditioned stimulus is used as the unconditioned stimulus in a new experimental setting.

Higher Order Conditioning — (cont'd)
UF Second Order Conditioning
B Classical Conditioning 1967

Highway Safety 1973
PN 1378 SC 22980
UF Automobile Safety
Driver Safety
B Safety 1967
R Aggressive Driving Behavior 2004
Drivers 1973
↓ Driving Behavior 1967
Driving Under the Influence 1988
↓ Ground Transportation 1973
Motor Traffic Accidents 1973
↓ Transportation Accidents 1973

Hindbrain 1997
PN 40 SC 22985
SN The posterior division of the three primary divisions of the developing vertebrate brain, and the corresponding part of the adult brain that includes the cerebellum, medulla oblongata, and pons. These parts function collectively to control autonomic functions and equilibrium.
UF Rhombencephalon
B Brain 1967
N ↓ Cerebellum 1973
Medulla Oblongata 1973
↓ Pons 1973
R ↓ Brain Stem 1973
Raphe Nuclei 1982

Hindsight Bias 2006
PN 99 SC 22987
SN The tendency to believe that one could have predicted a past event after the outcome is known.
HN This term was introduced in May 2006. Relevant records were re-indexed with this term. The posting note reflects the number of records that were re-indexed.
B Cognitive Bias 2006
R ↓ Memory 1967

Hinduism 1973
PN 363 SC 22990
B Religious Affiliation 1973
R Hindus 1997

Hindus 1997
PN 112 SC 22995
B Religious Groups 1997
R Hinduism 1973

Hippies
Use Subculture (Anthropological)

Hippocampal Commissure
Use Fornix

Hippocampus 1967
PN 10191 SC 23010
SN A curved, elongated ridge found in the temporal lobe of the forebrain that constitutes an important part of the limbic system, and is involved in the forming, storing, and processing of memory.
B Limbic System 1973
R Medial Forebrain Bundle 1982
Septal Nuclei 1982

Hips 1973
PN 323 SC 23020
B Musculoskeletal System 1973

Hiring
Use Personnel Selection

Hispanics 1982
PN 8789 SC 23035
UF Cuban Americans
Latinos/Latinas
Puerto Rican Americans
Spanish Americans
B Racial and Ethnic Groups 2001
N Mexican Americans 1973
R Minority Groups 1967

Histamine 1973
PN 368 SC 23050
B Amines 1973
Neurotransmitters 1985
R ↓ Antihistaminic Drugs 1973
Histidine 1973

Histidine 1973
PN 44 SC 23060
B Amino Acids 1973
R Histamine 1973

Histology 1973
PN 206 SC 23070
SN Branch of anatomy dealing with the structure of cells, tissues, and organs in relation to their functions. Used for the scientific discipline or the organic structure itself.
R Morphology 1973
↓ Physiology 1967
↓ Tissues (Body) 1973

History 1973
PN 14452 SC 23075
SN Recording and/or explanation of previous events, experiences, trends, and treatments.
N ↓ History of Psychology 1967
R Future 1991
Museums 2006
Psychohistory 1978
Trends 1991

History of Psychology 1967
PN 11733 SC 23080
B History 1973
N Associationism 1973
Behaviorism 1967
Freudian Psychoanalytic School 1973
Functionalism 1973
Gestalt Psychology 1967
↓ Neopsychoanalytic School 1973
Structuralism 1973
R Phenomenology 1967
↓ Psychological Theories 2001
↓ Psychology 1967
↓ Theories 1967

Histrionic Personality Disorder 1991
PN 320 SC 23082
SN Personality disorder characterized by emotional instability, excitability, overreaction, self-dramatization, self-centeredness, and over-dependence on others.
HN In 2000, this term replaced the discontinued term HYSTERICAL PERSONALITY. HYSTERICAL PERSONALITY was removed from all records containing it, and replaced with HISTRIONIC PERSONALITY DISORDER.
UF Hysterical Personality
B Personality Disorders 1967
R ↓ Conversion Disorder 2001
↓ Hysteria 1967

HIV 2006
PN 12580 SC 23083
HN In May 2006, this term replaced the discontinued term HUMAN IMMUNODEFICIENCY VIRUS. HUMAN IMMUNODEFICIENCY VIRUS was removed from all records containing it and replaced with HIV, its postable counterpart.
UF Human Immunodeficiency Virus
B Immunologic Disorders 1973
Sexually Transmitted Diseases 2003
Viral Disorders 1973
N AIDS 2006
R AIDS (Attitudes Toward) 1997
AIDS Dementia Complex 1997
AIDS Prevention 1994
HIV Testing 1997
Safe Sex 2003
Zidovudine 1994

HIV Testing 1997
PN 449 SC 23084
UF AIDS Testing
B Health Screening 1997
Medical Diagnosis 1973
R AIDS 2006
AIDS Prevention 1994
↓ HIV 2006

HMO
Use Health Maintenance Organizations

Hoarding Behavior 2003
PN 87 SC 23089
SN Accumulating and storing things for a possible future need. Often considered a compulsive behavior.
HN This term was introduced in June 2003. Relevant records were re-indexed with this term. The posting note reflects the number of records that were re-indexed.
B Behavior 1967
N Animal Hoarding Behavior 1973
R ↓ Compulsions 1973
Obsessive Compulsive Disorder 1985

Hoarding Behavior (Animal)
Use Animal Hoarding Behavior

Hobbies 1988
PN 83 SC 23100
HN Use RECREATION to access references from 1973-1988.
R Daily Activities 1994
↓ Interests 1967
Leisure Time 1973
↓ Recreation 1967

Hoffmanns Reflex 1973
PN 54 **SC** 23110
SN Flexing of the thumb and some other finger resulting from a sudden tapping of the nail of the index, middle, or ring finger. Also known as digital reflex, finger flexion reflex, snapping reflex, H reflex, or Hoffmann's (H) response.
B Reflexes 1971

Holidays 1988
PN 117 **SC** 23113
SN Days marked by general suspension of work in commemoration or celebration of an event.
R Leisure Time 1973
↓ Recreation 1967
Tourism 2003
Traditions 2007
Vacationing 1973

Holistic Health 1985
PN 887 **SC** 23115
SN Personal practices or medical or psychological diagnosis and treatment based on the concept that humans are composed of body, mind, and spirit. An observed disorder or dysfunction in one component implies the need for treatment of the whole organism to restore health.
UF Wholistic Health
B Health 1973
R ↓ Alternative Medicine 1997
Biopsychosocial Approach 1991
↓ Health Behavior 1982
↓ Lifestyle 1978
Meditation 1973
↓ Physical Treatment Methods 1973
Preventive Medicine 1973
↓ Psychotherapy 1967

Holocaust 1988
PN 673 **SC** 23117
SN Nazi persecution and genocide of Jews and others in Europe between 1933 and 1945.
B Genocide 1988
R AntiSemitism 1973
Concentration Camps 1973
Fascism 1973
Holocaust Survivors 1988
Jews 1997
Judaism 1967

Holocaust Survivors 1988
PN 698 **SC** 23118
B Survivors 1994
R Holocaust 1988
Jews 1997

Holtzman Inkblot Technique 1967
PN 161 **SC** 23120
B Projective Personality Measures 1973
Projective Techniques 1967

Homatropine
HN Term was discontinued in 1997. In 2000, the term was removed from all records containing it, and replaced with ALKALOIDS, its postable counterpart.
Use Alkaloids

Home Accidents 1973
PN 74 **SC** 23140
B Accidents 1967

Home Birth
Use Midwifery

Home Care 1985
PN 2296 **SC** 23145
SN Health and personal care provided in the home environment, usually by family members.
B Health Care Delivery 1978
R Adult Day Care 1997
Caregiver Burden 1994
Caregivers 1988
Elder Care 1994
Home Care Personnel 1997
Home Visiting Programs 1973
Homebound 1988
Hospice 1982
Long Term Care 1994
↓ Outpatient Treatment 1967
Quality of Care 1988
Respite Care 1988

Home Care Personnel 1997
PN 151 **SC** 23146
SN Personnel providing personal care, nursing services, medical treatment, or followup care to patients in their homes.
UF Home Health Aides
B Paraprofessional Personnel 1973
R ↓ Allied Health Personnel 2007
Caregivers 1988
Elder Care 1994
↓ Health Personnel 1994
Home Care 1985
Home Visiting Programs 1973

Home Economics 1985
PN 103 **SC** 23147
B Curriculum 1967
R Household Management 1985

Home Environment 1973
PN 5744 **SC** 23150
UF Family Environment
B Social Environments 1973
R Aging in Place 2007
Empty Nest 1991
↓ Environmental Effects 1973
↓ Family Conflict 2003
Family Reunification 2007
Learning Environment 2004
Living Alone 1994
↓ Living Arrangements 1991
↓ Single Sex Environments 2001

Home Health Aides
Use Home Care Personnel

Home Reared Mentally Retarded 1973
PN 50 **SC** 23160
B Mental Retardation 1967
R Institutionalized Mentally Retarded 1973

Home Schooling 1994
PN 79 **SC** 23165
SN Provision of compulsory education in the home.
B Nontraditional Education 1982
R ↓ Curriculum 1967
↓ Education 1967
↓ Teaching Methods 1967

Home Visiting Programs 1973
PN 838 **SC** 23170
SN Planned educational, health, or counseling procedures or activities that take place in the home.

Home Visiting Programs — (cont'd)
B Community Services 1967
Mental Health Programs 1973
R Adult Day Care 1997
Elder Care 1994
Home Care 1985
Home Care Personnel 1997
Homebound 1988
↓ Program Development 1991

Homebound 1988
PN 75 **SC** 23173
SN Individuals restricted to place of residence for health or disability reasons.
R Caregiver Burden 1994
Elder Care 1994
Health Impairments 2001
Home Care 1985
Home Visiting Programs 1973

Homeless 1988
PN 2886 **SC** 23174
B Social Issues 1991
N Homeless Mentally Ill 1997
R Deinstitutionalization 1982
Disadvantaged 1967
Poverty 1973
Shelters 1991
↓ Social Deprivation 1973

Homeless Mentally Ill 1997
PN 392 **SC** 23171
UF Mentally Ill Homeless
B Homeless 1988
R Deinstitutionalization 1982
↓ Mental Disorders 1967
↓ Psychopathology 1967

Homemakers 2003
PN 465 **SC** 23176
HN In June 2003, this term was created to replace the discontinued term HOUSEWIVES. HOUSEWIVES was removed from all records containing it and replaced with HOMEMAKERS.
UF Housewives
R Household Management 1985

Homemaking
Use Household Management

Homeopathic Medicine
Use Alternative Medicine

Homeostasis 1973
PN 661 **SC** 23180
SN Tendency of an organism to maintain a state of physiological equilibrium and the processes by which such a stable internal environment is maintained.
UF Autoregulation
B Physiology 1967
R Dehydration 1988
Instinctive Behavior 1982

Homesickness 1994
PN 59 **SC** 23183
B Emotional States 1973
R ↓ Experiences (Events) 1973
↓ Life Experiences 1973
Loneliness 1973
Reminiscence 1985
Sadness 1973
↓ Separation Reactions 1997

Homework 1988
PN 456 **SC** 23185
SN Assignment given to students or clients to be completed outside regular classroom period or therapeutic setting.
R Note Taking 1991
↓ Psychotherapeutic Techniques 1967
Study Habits 1973

Homicide 1967
PN 3237 **SC** 23190
UF Murder
B Behavior Disorders 1971
Violent Crime 2003
N ↓ Genocide 1988
Infanticide 1978
Serial Homicide 2003

Homing (Animal)
Use Animal Homing

Homogeneity of Variance 2003
PN 188 **SC** 23198
SN Extent to which the variance in two or more statistical samples is similar or different.
HN In June 2003, this term was created to replace the discontinued term VARIANCE HOMOGENEITY. VARIANCE HOMOGENEITY was removed from all records containing it and replaced with HOMOGENEITY of VARIANCE.
UF Heterogeneity of Variance
Variance Homogeneity
B Statistical Measurement 1973
R Analysis of Variance 1967
Standard Deviation 1973

Homographs 1973
PN 122 **SC** 23200
SN Words identical in spelling but different in derivation, pronunciation, and meaning.
B Vocabulary 1967
R Homonyms 1973
Orthography 1973
Words (Phonetic Units) 1967

Homonyms 1973
PN 117 **SC** 23210
B Semantics 1967
Vocabulary 1967
R Homographs 1973
Words (Phonetic Units) 1967

Homophobia
Use Homosexuality (Attitudes Toward)

Homosexual Liberation Movement 1973
PN 116 **SC** 23220
UF Gay Liberation Movement
B Social Movements 1967
R ↓ Activism 2003

Homosexual Parents 1994
PN 298 **SC** 23225
UF Gay Parents
Lesbian Parents
B Parents 1967
R ↓ Family Structure 1973
Lesbianism 1973
Male Homosexuality 1973
Significant Others 1991

Homosexuality 1967
PN 3675 **SC** 23230
B Psychosexual Behavior 1967
Sexual Orientation 1997
N Lesbianism 1973
Male Homosexuality 1973
R Homosexuality (Attitudes Toward) 1982
Same Sex Marriage 2007
Transsexualism 1973
Transvestism 1973

Homosexuality (Attitudes Toward) 1982
PN 2167 **SC** 23233
SN Attitudes regarding sexual contact between persons of the same sex.
UF Heterosexism
Homophobia
B Attitudes 1967
R ↓ Homosexuality 1967
↓ Sexual Orientation 1997
Stereotyped Attitudes 1967

Homovanillic Acid 1978
PN 665 **SC** 23235
SN Excretion product of dopamine metabolism.
B Acids 1973
Dopamine Metabolites 1982
R Dopamine 1973

Honesty 1973
PN 569 **SC** 23240
UF Frankness
B Personality Traits 1967
R Integrity 1997

Honors
Use Awards (Merit)

Hope 1991
PN 912 **SC** 23247
B Emotional States 1973
R ↓ Expectations 1967
Hopelessness 1988
Optimism 1973
Positivism 1973
Trust (Social Behavior) 1967

Hopelessness 1988
PN 984 **SC** 23250
SN Feeling that one's physical, emotional, or social state is beyond improvement.
B Emotional States 1973
R Apathy 1973
Cynicism 1973
↓ Helplessness 1997
Hope 1991
Pessimism 1973

Hormone Therapy 1994
PN 910 **SC** 23255
UF Estrogen Replacement Therapy
B Drug Therapy 1967
R ↓ Hormones 1967

Hormones 1967
PN 4061 **SC** 23260
N ↓ Adrenal Cortex Hormones 1973
↓ Adrenal Medulla Hormones 1973
Cholecystokinin 1982
Corticotropin Releasing Factor 1994
Epinephrine 1967
Glucagon 1973
↓ Gonadotropic Hormones 1973

Hormones — (cont'd)
Insulin 1973
Leptin 2004
Melatonin 1973
Parathyroid Hormone 1973
↓ Pituitary Hormones 1973
↓ Progestational Hormones 1985
↓ Sex Hormones 1973
↓ Thyroid Hormones 1973
R ↓ Anti Inflammatory Drugs 1982
Antineoplastic Drugs 1982
↓ Drugs 1967
↓ Endocrine Glands 1973
Fertility Enhancement 1973
Hormone Therapy 1994
Pheromones 1973
Prostaglandins 1982
Psychoneuroendocrinology 2007
Somatostatin 1991
↓ Steroids 1973

Horses 1973
PN 397 **SC** 23270
B Mammals 1973

Horticulture Therapy 2007
PN 13 **SC** 23273
SN The use of gardening as an auxiliary intervention for therapeutic or rehabilitational purposes. It is typically used for individuals with physical or mental illness or disability but may also be used to improve the social, educational, psychological, and physical well-being of older adults, as well as those recovering from injury.
HN This term was introduced in April 2007. Relevant records were re-indexed with this term. The posting note reflects the number of records that were re-indexed.
UF Gardening Therapy
R Botany 1973
↓ Plants (Botanical) 2007
Recreation Therapy 1973

Hospice 1982
PN 1203 **SC** 23275
SN Supportive palliative care of terminally ill patients, usually in their own home, by a treatment team and family members; sometimes involves residential care.
B Health Care Delivery 1978
R Home Care 1985
Palliative Care 1991
Terminally Ill Patients 1973

Hospital Accreditation 1973
PN 33 **SC** 23280
SN Recognition of a hospital as maintaining standards set by a government agency.
R ↓ Hospitals 1967

Hospital Addiction Syndrome
Use Munchausen Syndrome

Hospital Administration 1978
PN 406 **SC** 23286
B Health Care Administration 1997
R Decentralization 1978
↓ Hospitals 1967
↓ Medical Records 1978

Hospital Admission 1973
PN 777 **SC** 23290
UF Admission (Hospital)
Readmission (Hospital)

Hospital Admission — (cont'd)
B Facility Admission 1988
Hospitalization 1967
N ↓ Psychiatric Hospital Admission 1973
R Health Care Seeking Behavior 1997
↓ Hospital Discharge 1973
↓ Institutional Release 1978
↓ Psychiatric Hospitalization 1973

Hospital Attendants
Use Attendants (Institutions)

Hospital Discharge 1973
PN 745 **SC** 23303
B Facility Discharge 1988
Hospitalization 1967
Institutional Release 1978
N Psychiatric Hospital Discharge 1978
R Client Transfer 1997
Discharge Planning 1994
↓ Hospital Admission 1973
↓ Psychiatric Hospital Admission 1973
Psychiatric Hospital Readmission 1973
↓ Psychiatric Hospitalization 1973
Treatment Termination 1982

Hospital Environment 1982
PN 1104 **SC** 23304
SN Physical, organizational, or psychological characteristics of a hospital, and their potential impact on hospital staff and patients.
B Facility Environment 1988
R ↓ Hospitals 1967
Intensive Care 1988

Hospital Programs 1978
PN 1683 **SC** 23306
SN Organized plans for care, including psychiatric treatment, or training in general medical hospital settings.
N ↓ Psychiatric Hospital Programs 1967
R Intensive Care 1988
Partial Hospitalization 1985
↓ Program Development 1991
Psychiatric Units 1991

Hospital Psychiatric Units
Use Psychiatric Units

Hospital Staff
Use Medical Personnel

Hospitalization 1967
PN 2601 **SC** 23320
B Institutionalization 1967
N ↓ Commitment (Psychiatric) 1973
↓ Hospital Admission 1973
↓ Hospital Discharge 1973
↓ Psychiatric Hospitalization 1973
R ↓ Health Insurance 1973
Long Term Care 1994
Patient Seclusion 1994
Psychiatric Units 1991

Hospitalized Patients 1973
PN 7110 **SC** 23330
B Patients 1967

Hospitals 1967
PN 3468 **SC** 23340
UF Infirmaries
B Residential Care Institutions 1973
Treatment Facilities 1973

Hospitals — (cont'd)
N Psychiatric Hospitals 1967
Sanatoriums 1973
R ↓ Clinics 1967
Hospital Accreditation 1973
Hospital Administration 1978
Hospital Environment 1982
Intensive Care 1988
Maximum Security Facilities 1985
Nursing Homes 1973
Psychiatric Clinics 1973
Psychiatric Units 1991

Hostages 1988
PN 119 **SC** 23347
HN Use CRIME VICTIMS to access references from 1982-1987.
B Crime Victims 1982
R Kidnapping 1988
Prisoners of War 1973
↓ Terrorism 1982

Hostility 1967
PN 3212 **SC** 23350
UF Antagonism
Resentment
B Anger 1967
R Hate 1973
Retaliation 1991

Hot Line Services 1973
PN 596 **SC** 23360
SN Telephone information, counseling, and crisis intervention services.
UF Telephone Hot Lines
B Crisis Intervention Services 1973
Mental Health Programs 1973
R Community Mental Health Centers 1973
Information Services 1988
Suicide Prevention Centers 1973

Household Management 1985
PN 999 **SC** 23365
SN Activities carried out for the regular maintenance of home and personal belongings.
UF Homemaking
Housework
B Management 1967
R ↓ Division of Labor 1988
↓ Family Life Education 1997
Home Economics 1985
Homemakers 2003

Household Structure
Use Living Arrangements

Housewives
HN In June 2003, this term was discontinued and removed from all records containing it, and replaced with HOMEMAKERS, its postable counterpart.
Use Homemakers

Housework
Use Household Management

Housing 1973
PN 1926 **SC** 23380
B Community Facilities 1973
N Assisted Living 2003
Dormitories 1973
Group Homes 1982
Retirement Communities 1997
Shelters 1991

Housing — (cont'd)
R Built Environment 2007
↓ Living Arrangements 1991
↓ Social Programs 1973

Hue 1973
PN 365 **SC** 23390
SN One of the perceived dimensions of color corresponding to the wavelength of the light. Compare COLOR.
B Chromaticity 1997
Color 1967
R Color Saturation 1997

Human Animal Interaction
Use Interspecies Interaction

Human Biological Rhythms 1973
PN 3199 **SC** 23400
SN Periodic variations in human physiological and psychological functions.
HN Use BIOLOGICAL RHYTHMS to access references from 1967-1972.
UF Circadian Rhythms (Human)
Diurnal Variations
B Biological Rhythms 1967

Human Body 2003
PN 1058 **SC** 23402
SN The body as an artistic, cultural, sociological, or physical concept.
HN This term was introduced in June 2003. Relevant records were re-indexed with this term. The posting note reflects the number of records that were re-indexed.
R ↓ Anatomy 1967
Body Awareness 1982
↓ Body Image 1967
Physique 1967
Soul 2004

Human Capital 2003
PN 276 **SC** 23405
SN Investment of resources including time, money, education, and training to increase productivity and profits.
HN This term was introduced in June 2003. Relevant records were re-indexed with this term. The posting note reflects the number of records that were re-indexed.
R ↓ Economics 1985
Labor Market 2007
↓ Personnel Supply 1973
Resource Allocation 1997
Social Capital 2004

Human Channel Capacity 1973
PN 1876 **SC** 23410
SN Number of signals or information volume which can be processed simultaneously.
UF Cognitive Load
Mental Load
R ↓ Attention 1967
Cognitive Processing Speed 1997
Human Information Storage 1973
Work Load 1982

Human Computer Interaction 1997
PN 2720 **SC** 23415
UF Human Computer Interface
N ↓ Internet Usage 2007
R Computer Mediated Communication 2003
↓ Computer Peripheral Devices 1985
↓ Computers 1967

Human Computer Interaction — (cont'd)
Human Factors Engineering 1973
Human Machine Systems 1997
Human Machine Systems Design 1997
Keyboards 1985

Human Computer Interface
Use Human Computer Interaction

Human Courtship 1973
PN 364 **SC** 23420
UF Courtship (Human)
B Psychosexual Behavior 1967
N Social Dating 1973
R Acquaintance Rape 1991
Human Mate Selection 1988
Male Female Relations 1988
Monogamy 1997
↓ Relationship Termination 1997
Romance 1997

Human Development 1967
PN 5793 **SC** 23430
SN Conceptually broad term. Use a more specific term if possible.
UF Maturation
B Development 1967
N Adolescent Development 1973
Adult Development 1978
↓ Childhood Development 1967
R Age Differences 1967
↓ Aging 1991
↓ Delayed Development 1973
Developmental Age Groups 1973
Developmental Disabilities 1982
↓ Developmental Psychology 1973
↓ Developmental Stages 1973
Life Expectancy 1982
Nature Nurture 1994
↓ Physical Development 1973
↓ Psychogenesis 1973

Human Factors Engineering 1973
PN 3510 **SC** 23440
UF Ergonomics
Usability (Systems)
R Computer Assisted Design 1997
Engineering Psychology 1967
Furniture 1985
↓ Human Computer Interaction 1997
Human Machine Systems 1997
↓ Instrument Controls 1985
Quality Control 1988
↓ Working Conditions 1973

Human Females 1973
PN 44219 **SC** 23450
SN Used for all-female populations when sex is pertinent to the focus of the study. For comparison of sexes use HUMAN SEX DIFFERENCES.
UF Females (Human)
Girls
Women
N Battered Females 1988
Daughters 1973
Female Criminals 1973
↓ Mothers 1967
Sisters 1973
Widows 1973
Wives 1973
Working Women 1978
R Female Attitudes 2006
Female Delinquency 2001
↓ Human Sex Differences 1967

Human Females — (cont'd)
Sex Linked Developmental Differences 1973

Human Figures Drawing 1973
PN 742 **SC** 23460
SN Projective measures or techniques designed to yield information from drawings of human figures and responses to questions about the drawings.
UF Draw A Man Test
B Projective Personality Measures 1973
R Goodenough Harris Draw A Person Test 1967
Mirror Image 1991

Human Genome
Use Genome

Human Immunodeficiency Virus
HN In May 2006, this term was discontinued and removed from all records containing it, and was replaced with HIV, its postable counterpart.
Use HIV

Human Information Processes
Use Cognitive Processes

Human Information Storage 1973
PN 9694 **SC** 23480
SN Process of information perception, encoding, or storage, and retrieval of material from memory.
UF Decoding
Encoding
Information Storage (Human)
R ↓ Cognitive Processes 1967
Human Channel Capacity 1973
Information 1967
Information Processing Model 2007
↓ Lexical Access 1988
Lexical Decision 1988
↓ Memory 1967
Word Recognition 1988

Human Machine Systems 1997
PN 2329 **SC** 23485
SN Systems based on the human engineering concept that views human operators and the machines they operate as functionally integrated parts of a larger goal-oriented system.
HN In 1997, this term was created to replace the discontinued term MAN MACHINE SYSTEMS. In 2000, MAN MACHINE SYSTEMS was removed from all records containing it, and replaced with HUMAN MACHINE SYSTEMS.
UF Man Machine Systems
B Systems 1967
R ↓ Artificial Intelligence 1982
↓ Computer Peripheral Devices 1985
Computer Searching 1991
Cybernetics 1967
Databases 1991
Error Analysis 1973
↓ Expert Systems 1991
↓ Human Computer Interaction 1997
Human Factors Engineering 1973
Human Machine Systems Design 1997
Systems Analysis 1973
Virtual Reality 1997

Human Machine Systems Design 1997
PN 2762 **SC** 23487
HN In 1997, this term was created to replace the discontinued term MAN MACHINE SYSTEMS DESIGN. In 2000, MAN MACHINE SYSTEMS DESIGN was removed from all records containing it, and replaced with HUMAN MACHINE SYSTEMS DESIGN.

Human Machine Systems Design — (cont'd)
UF Design (Man Machine Systems)
Man Machine Systems Design
B Systems Design 2003
R Computer Assisted Design 1997
↓ Human Computer Interaction 1997
Human Machine Systems 1997
↓ Instrument Controls 1985
↓ Systems 1967
Systems Analysis 1973

Human Males 1973
PN 14533 **SC** 23490
SN Used for all-male populations when sex is pertinent to the focus of the study. For comparison of sexes use HUMAN SEX DIFFERENCES.
UF Boys
Males (Human)
Men
N Brothers 1973
↓ Fathers 1967
Husbands 1973
Male Criminals 1973
Sons 1973
Widowers 1973
R ↓ Human Sex Differences 1967
Male Attitudes 2006
Male Delinquency 2001
Sex Linked Developmental Differences 1973

Human Mate Selection 1988
PN 833 **SC** 23495
UF Mate Selection
R Assortative Mating 1991
Choice Behavior 1967
↓ Human Courtship 1973
↓ Interpersonal Attraction 1967
Interpersonal Compatibility 1973
↓ Psychosexual Behavior 1967
Romance 1997

Human Migration 1973
PN 1894 **SC** 23500
SN Movement of residence from one place to another. Includes nomadism; labor or seasonal migration; patterns of rural, urban, or suburban migration; or voluntary or forced relocation.
UF Migration (Human)
Population Shifts
B Social Processes 1967
N Refugees 1988
R Geographical Mobility 1978
Gypsies 1973
Immigration 1973
Migrant Farm Workers 1973

Human Nature 1997
PN 1187 **SC** 23502
R ↓ Behavior 1967
↓ Emotions 1967
Instinctive Behavior 1982
Mind 1991
↓ Personality 1967

Human Potential Movement 1982
PN 261 **SC** 23504
SN Movement aimed at the enhancement of personal psychological growth. Formats used include Gestalt therapy, sensory awakening, sensory awareness, meditation, encounter groups, transactional analysis, assertiveness training, and humanistic psychology.

Human Potential Movement — (cont'd)
UF Growth Centers
Personal Growth Techniques
N Assertiveness Training 1978
Consciousness Raising Groups 1978
↓ Encounter Group Therapy 1973
Gestalt Therapy 1973
Human Relations Training 1978
Sensitivity Training 1973
Transactional Analysis 1973
R ↓ Group Psychotherapy 1967
Humanism 1973
↓ Humanistic Psychology 1985
Maslow (Abraham Harold) 1991
Meditation 1973
Self Actualization 1973

Human Relations Training 1978
PN 548 **SC** 23506
SN Techniques aimed at promoting awareness of feelings and needs of others in order to facilitate positive interpersonal interactions.
UF T Groups
B Human Potential Movement 1982
Training 2006
R Assertiveness Training 1978
Communication Skills Training 1982
↓ Encounter Group Therapy 1973
↓ Group Dynamics 1967
Marathon Group Therapy 1973
Parent Training 1978
↓ Personnel Training 1967
Sensitivity Training 1973
Social Skills Training 1982

Human Resource Management 2003
PN 3444 **SC** 58070
HN In June 2003, this term was created to replace the discontinued term PERSONNEL MANAGEMENT. PERSONNEL MANAGEMENT was removed from all records containing it and replaced with HUMAN RESOURCE MANAGEMENT.
UF Human Resources
Personnel Management
N Career Development 1985
Job Analysis 1967
Labor Management Relations 1967
↓ Personnel Evaluation 1973
↓ Personnel Recruitment 1973
↓ Personnel Selection 1967
Personnel Termination 1973
R Affirmative Action 1985
Business Education 1973
Business Management 1973
Employment Discrimination 1994
Labor Market 2007
Outsourcing 2007
↓ Personnel 1967
Supervisor Employee Interaction 1997
Supported Employment 1994

Human Resources
Use Human Resource Management

Human Rights 1978
PN 1389 **SC** 23508
SN Fundamental rights of every human being to life, freedom, and equality. Often used for freedom from arbitrary governmental interference.

Human Rights — (cont'd)
B Social Issues 1991
N ↓ Civil Rights 1978
R ↓ Client Rights 1988
Human Trafficking 2007
Social Equality 1973
↓ Social Movements 1967
↓ Social Processes 1967
Treatment Withholding 1988

Human Services 2007
PN 639 **SC** 23509
HN This term was introduced in April 2007. Relevant records were re-indexed with this term. The posting note reflects the number of records that were re-indexed.
R ↓ Community Services 1967
Faith Based Organizations 2007
↓ Health Care Services 1978
Integrated Services 1997
↓ Social Programs 1973
↓ Social Services 1982
Welfare Services (Government) 1973

Human Sex Differences 1967
PN 63045 **SC** 23510
UF Gender Differences
Sex Differences (Human)
N Sex Linked Developmental Differences 1973
R Androgyny 1982
Diversity in the Workplace 2003
↓ Group Differences 2007
↓ Human Females 1973
↓ Human Males 1973
Sex 1967
Sex Recognition 1997
↓ Single Sex Environments 2001

Human Trafficking 2007
PN 17 **SC** 23515
SN The buying and selling of human beings for the purposes of forced labor and/or sexual exploitation. Victims are physically forced, intimidated, deceived, or coerced into their situations.
HN This term was introduced in April 2007. Relevant records were re-indexed with this term. The posting note reflects the number of records that were re-indexed.
B Crime 1967
R ↓ Human Rights 1978
Kidnapping 1988
Prostitution 1973
Victimization 1973

Humanism 1973
PN 1096 **SC** 23520
SN Philosophy that asserts commitment to the use of reason and observation to serve human need and interest.
B Philosophies 1967
R ↓ Human Potential Movement 1982
↓ Humanistic Psychology 1985
↓ Humanistic Psychotherapy 2003

Humanistic Education
Use Affective Education

Humanistic Psychology 1985
PN 983 **SC** 23527
SN School of psychology emphasizing a holistic approach including self-actualization, creativity, and free choice.

Humanistic Psychology — (cont'd)
B Psychology 1967
N Transpersonal Psychology 1988
R Client Centered Therapy 1967
↓ Human Potential Movement 1982
Humanism 1973
↓ Humanistic Psychotherapy 2003
Maslow (Abraham Harold) 1991
Neurolinguistic Programming 2001
Rogers (Carl) 1991
Self Psychology 1988

Humanistic Psychotherapy 2003
PN 72 **SC** 23528
SN Approach to psychotherapy based on humanistic philosophy that focuses on the client as a whole and recognizes the individual's capacity for self-healing.
HN This term was introduced in June 2003. Relevant records were re-indexed with this term. The posting note reflects the number of records that were re-indexed.
B Psychotherapy 1967
N Client Centered Therapy 1967
R Existential Therapy 1973
Gestalt Therapy 1973
Humanism 1973
↓ Humanistic Psychology 1985
Rogers (Carl) 1991

Humanitarian Behavior
Use Prosocial Behavior

Humanities 2003
PN 234 **SC** 23535
SN Branches of learning such as literature, art, and philosophy that are concerned with human thought and culture.
HN This term was introduced in June 2003. Relevant records were re-indexed with this term. The posting note reflects the number of records that were re-indexed.
N ↓ Arts 1973
↓ Literature 1967
↓ Philosophies 1967
Theology 2003

Humor 1967
PN 2362 **SC** 23540
N Cartoons (Humor) 1973
Jokes 1973
R Laughter 1978

Hunger 1967
PN 718 **SC** 23560
SN Need or desire for food. May also be defined operationally in experimental settings as the duration of food deprivation or the organism's percentage of normal body weight following food deprivation. Compare APPETITE.
B Appetite 1973
Motivation 1967
R Animal Feeding Behavior 1973
Food Deprivation 1967
Starvation 1973

Huntingtons Chorea
HN Term was discontinued in 1997. In 2000, the term was removed from all records containing it, and replaced with HUNTINGTONS DISEASE, its postable counterpart.
Use Huntingtons Disease

Huntingtons Disease 1973
PN 1158 **SC** 23570
SN A hereditary, degenerative brain disorder for which there is no known treatment or cure, resulting in uncontrolled movements, loss of intellectual faculties, and emotional disturbance.
HN In 1997, this term replaced the discontinued term HUNTINGTONS CHOREA. In 2000, HUNTINGTONS CHOREA was removed from all records containing it, and replaced with HUNTINGTONS DISEASE.
UF Huntingtons Chorea
B Chorea 1973
Genetic Disorders 1973

Husbands 1973
PN 1653 **SC** 23590
B Human Males 1973
Spouses 1973

Hybrids (Biology) 1973
PN 129 **SC** 23600
R ↓ Genetics 1967

Hydralazine 1973
PN 10 **SC** 23620
B Antihypertensive Drugs 1973
Sympatholytic Drugs 1973

Hydrocephalus 2006
PN 364 **SC** 23629
SN The abnormal buildup of cerebrospinal fluid in the ventricles of the brain and the cranial cavity, accompanied by enlargement of the skull and brain atrophy.
HN In May 2006, this term was created to replace the discontinued term HYDROCEPHALY. HYDROCEPHALY was removed from all records containing it and replaced with HYDROCEPHALUS, its postable counterpart.
UF Hydrocephaly
B Brain Disorders 1967
R ↓ Congenital Disorders 1973
↓ Infectious Disorders 1973
↓ Mental Retardation 1967
↓ Neonatal Disorders 1973
↓ Seizures 2005

Hydrocephaly
HN In May 2006, this term was discontinued and removed from all records containing it, and was replaced with HYDROCEPHALUS, its postable counterpart.
Use Hydrocephalus

Hydrocortisone 1973
PN 3498 **SC** 23640
UF Cortisol
B Adrenal Cortex Hormones 1973
Corticosteroids 1973
R ↓ Anti Inflammatory Drugs 1982

Hydrogen 1973
PN 24 **SC** 23650

Hydroxydopamine (6-) 1978
PN 706 **SC** 23656
UF Oxidopamine
B Adrenergic Blocking Drugs 1973

Hydroxyindoleacetic Acid (5-) 1985
PN 488 **SC** 23658
SN Major metabolic product of serotonin.

Hydroxyindoleacetic Acid (5-) — (cont'd)
B Acids 1973
Serotonin Metabolites 1978

Hydroxylase Inhibitors 1985
PN 32 **SC** 23665
B Enzyme Inhibitors 1985
R Hydroxylases 1973

Hydroxylases 1973
PN 434 **SC** 23670
B Enzymes 1973
R ↓ Esterases 1973
Hydroxylase Inhibitors 1985
Phosphatases 1973

Hydroxytryptamine (5-)
Use Serotonin

Hydroxytryptophan (5-) 1991
PN 123 **SC** 23685
B Tryptophan 1973

Hydroxyzine 1973
PN 35 **SC** 23690
B Minor Tranquilizers 1973
R ↓ Antihistaminic Drugs 1973

Hygiene 1994
PN 298 **SC** 23700
HN Use HEALTH to access references from 1973-1993.
R Activities of Daily Living 1991
↓ Epidemics 2001
↓ Health 1973
↓ Health Behavior 1982
Self Care Skills 1978

Hyoscine
Use Scopolamine

Hyoscyamine (dl-)
Use Atropine

Hyperactivity
Use Hyperkinesis

Hyperalgesia
Use Somatosensory Disorders

Hypercholesterolemia
Use Metabolism Disorders

Hypercortisolism
Use Cushings Syndrome

Hyperesthesia
Use Somatosensory Disorders

Hyperglycemia 1985
PN 142 **SC** 23745
B Metabolism Disorders 1973
Symptoms 1967

Hypericum Perforatum 2003
PN 165 **SC** 23747
HN This term was introduced in June 2003. Relevant records were re-indexed with this term. The posting note reflects the number of records that were re-indexed.
UF Saint John's Wort
St. John's Wort

Hypericum Perforatum — (cont'd)
B Medicinal Herbs and Plants 2001

Hyperkinesis 1973
PN 6214 **SC** 23760
SN Excessive and usually inappropriate motor activity accompanied by poor attention span and restlessness. Consider also ATTENTION DEFICIT DISORDER.
UF Hyperactivity
B Nervous System Disorders 1967
Symptoms 1967
R Ataxia 1973
Attention Deficit Disorder with Hyperactivity 2001
Bradykinesia 2001
↓ Neuromuscular Disorders 1973
Oppositional Defiant Disorder 1997
Restlessness 1973

Hypermedia 1997
PN 419 **SC** 23780
SN Computerized multimedia that contain images, video clips, and sounds in addition to or instead of text, and include highlighted elements that, when selected by the user, instruct the computer program to retrieve one or more of the computerized media.
B Computer Applications 1973
R ↓ Computer Software 1967
Hypertext 1997

Hyperparathyroidism
Use Parathyroid Disorders

Hyperphagia 1973
PN 363 **SC** 23800
UF Polyphagia
B Eating Disorders 1997
Symptoms 1967
R Kleine Levin Syndrome 2001
Obesity 1973
↓ Somatoform Disorders 2001

Hypersensitivity (Immunologic)
Use Immunologic Disorders

Hypersexuality 1973
PN 133 **SC** 23820
UF Nymphomania
B Psychosexual Behavior 1967
R Erotomania 1997
Promiscuity 1973
Sex Drive 1973
Sexual Addiction 1997

Hypersomnia 1994
PN 102 **SC** 23825
SN Excessive sleepiness.
B Sleep Disorders 1973
R Fatigue 1967
Kleine Levin Syndrome 2001
Narcolepsy 1973
↓ Symptoms 1967

Hypertension 1973
PN 2728 **SC** 23830
B Blood Pressure Disorders 1973
Cardiovascular Disorders 1967
N Essential Hypertension 1973
R ↓ Antihypertensive Drugs 1973
↓ Cerebrovascular Disorders 1973

Hypertext 1997
PN 221 **SC** 23835
SN Computer-readable text that contains highlighted words or phrases that, when selected by the user, instruct the computer program to retrieve one or more similar documents.
B Computer Applications 1973
R ↓ Computer Software 1967
Hypermedia 1997

Hyperthermia 1973
PN 418 **SC** 23840
UF Fever
B Symptoms 1967
R Delirium 1973
Thermoregulation (Body) 1973

Hyperthyroidism 1973
PN 169 **SC** 23850
B Thyroid Disorders 1973
R Goiters 1973
Tachycardia 1973
Thyrotoxicosis 1973
↓ Underweight 1973

Hyperventilation 1973
PN 353 **SC** 23860
B Respiratory Distress 1973
Respiratory Tract Disorders 1973
Symptoms 1967
R ↓ Somatoform Disorders 2001

Hypesthesia
Use Somatosensory Disorders

Hypnagogic Hallucinations 1973
PN 47 **SC** 23870
SN False sensory perceptions without actual appropriate stimuli, occurring while falling asleep.
B Hallucinations 1967
R ↓ Sleep Disorders 1973

Hypnoanalysis
Use Hypnotherapy

Hypnosis 1967
PN 4890 **SC** 23890
SN Trance-like state induced by effective suggestion and characterized by increased suggestibility to the hypnotist. For hypnosis used in treatment, use HYPNOTHERAPY.
B Consciousness Disturbances 1973
N Age Regression (Hypnotic) 1988
Autohypnosis 1973
R False Memory 1997
↓ Hypnotherapy 1973
Posthypnotic Suggestions 1994

Hypnotherapists 1973
PN 70 **SC** 23900
SN Persons conducting treatment by means of hypnosis.
B Hypnotists 1973
Psychotherapists 1973
R Clinical Psychologists 1973
Psychiatrists 1967
Psychoanalysts 1973

Hypnotherapy 1973
PN 3475 **SC** 23910
SN Use of hypnosis in treatment.
UF Hypnoanalysis
B Psychotherapy 1967
N Age Regression (Hypnotic) 1988
R ↓ Alternative Medicine 1997
False Memory 1997
Guided Imagery 2001
↓ Hypnosis 1967
Posthypnotic Suggestions 1994
Progressive Relaxation Therapy 1978
↓ Psychoanalysis 1967
↓ Relaxation Therapy 1978

Hypnotic Drugs 1973
PN 942 **SC** 23920
HN In 1973, this term replaced the discontinued term CHLORALOSE. In 2000, CHLORALOSE was removed from all records containing it, and replaced with HYPNOTIC DRUGS.
UF Chloralose
Sleep Inducing Drugs
B Drugs 1967
N Amobarbital 1973
Apomorphine 1973
Barbital 1973
Chloral Hydrate 1973
Codeine 1973
Flurazepam 1982
Glutethimide 1973
Hexobarbital 1973
Meprobamate 1973
Methaqualone 1973
Nitrazepam 1978
Pentobarbital 1973
Phenobarbital 1973
Secobarbital 1973
Thalidomide 1973
Thiopental 1973
Triazolam 1988
R ↓ Analgesic Drugs 1973
↓ Anesthetic Drugs 1973
↓ Anticonvulsive Drugs 1973
↓ Antiemetic Drugs 1973
↓ Antihistaminic Drugs 1973
↓ Antihypertensive Drugs 1973
↓ Barbiturates 1967
↓ Benzodiazepines 1978
↓ CNS Depressant Drugs 1973
↓ Narcotic Drugs 1973
↓ Sedatives 1973

Hypnotic Susceptibility 1973
PN 1706 **SC** 23930
SN Personal characteristic or state of being receptive to hypnosis.
UF Susceptibility (Hypnotic)
B Personality Traits 1967
R Openness to Experience 1997
Posthypnotic Suggestions 1994

Hypnotists 1973
PN 51 **SC** 23940
SN Persons conducting scientific experiments by means of hypnosis.

Hypnotists — (cont'd)
B Personnel 1967
N Hypnotherapists 1973

Hypoactive Sexual Desire Disorder
Use Inhibited Sexual Desire

Hypochondriasis 1973
PN 803 **SC** 23950
B Somatoform Disorders 2001
R ↓ Anxiety Disorders 1997
↓ Conversion Disorder 2001
Somatization 1994
Somatoform Pain Disorder 1997

Hypogastric Plexus
Use Autonomic Ganglia

Hypoglossal Nerve
Use Cranial Nerves

Hypoglycemia 1973
PN 312 **SC** 23980
B Metabolism Disorders 1973
Symptoms 1967

Hypogonadism 1973
PN 84 **SC** 24000
B Endocrine Sexual Disorders 1973
N Klinefelters Syndrome 1973
Turners Syndrome 1973
R ↓ Gynecological Disorders 1973
Hypopituitarism 1973
↓ Male Genital Disorders 1973
Sterility 1973

Hypokinesia
Use Bradykinesia

Hypomania 1973
PN 397 **SC** 24010
SN Mild form of mania.
B Mania 1967
R Cyclothymic Personality 1973

Hyponatremia 1997
PN 104 **SC** 24015
SN Abnormally low blood sodium level.
B Metabolism Disorders 1973
R Polydipsia 1982
↓ Sodium 1973
↓ Toxic Disorders 1973

Hypoparathyroidism
Use Parathyroid Disorders

Hypophysectomy 1973
PN 123 **SC** 24030
UF Pituitary Gland Surgery
B Endocrine Gland Surgery 1973

Hypophysis Disorders
Use Pituitary Disorders

Hypopituitarism 1973
PN 84 **SC** 24050
UF Dwarfism (Pituitary)
Pituitary Dwarfism
B Pituitary Disorders 1973
R ↓ Genetic Disorders 1973
↓ Hypogonadism 1973

Hypotension 1973
PN 178 **SC** 24060
B Blood Pressure Disorders 1973

Hypothalamic Pituitary Adrenal Axis 2006
PN 1202 **SC** 24065
SN An integral part of the neuroendocrine system that controls reactions to stress and is involved in the regulation of various physical processes such as digestion, the immune system, and energy usage.
HN In May 2006, this term was created to replace the discontinued term HYPOTHALAMO PITUITARY ADRENAL SYSTEM. HYPOTHALAMO PITUITARY ADRENAL SYSTEM was removed from all records containing it and replaced with HYPOTHALAMIC PITUITARY ADRENAL AXIS, its postable counterpart.
UF Hypothalamo Pituitary Adrenal System
B Adrenal Glands 1973
Hypothalamus 1967
Pituitary Gland 1973
R Hypothalamo Hypophyseal System 1973

Hypothalamo Hypophyseal System 1973
PN 428 **SC** 24070
SN A neuroendocrine system of neurons, fiber tracts, endocrine tissue, and blood vessels in the hypothalamus and the pituitary gland which produces and releases pituitary hormones into the systemic circulation to maintain homeostasis.
B Hypothalamus 1967
Pituitary Gland 1973
R Hypothalamic Pituitary Adrenal Axis 2006
↓ Pituitary Hormones 1973

Hypothalamo Pituitary Adrenal System
HN In May 2006, this term was discontinued and removed from all records containing it, and was replaced with HYPOTHALAMIC PITUITARY ADRENAL AXIS, its postable counterpart.
Use Hypothalamic Pituitary Adrenal Axis

Hypothalamus 1967
PN 5264 **SC** 24080
SN A region of the brain located below the thalamus, forming the major portion of the ventral region of the diencephalon and functioning to regulate certain metabolic and autonomic processes, including body temperature, hunger, thirst, and circadian cycles.
UF Mammillary Bodies (Hypothalamic)
B Diencephalon 1973
N Hypothalamic Pituitary Adrenal Axis 2006
Hypothalamo Hypophyseal System 1973
Preoptic Area 1994
R Medial Forebrain Bundle 1982

Hypothalamus Lesions 1973
PN 927 **SC** 24090
HN Not defined prior to 1982. From 1982, limited to experimentally induced lesions and used primarily for animal populations.
B Brain Lesions 1967

Hypothermia 1973
PN 558 **SC** 24100
B Symptoms 1967
R ↓ Body Temperature 1973
↓ Central Nervous System Disorders 1973
↓ Endocrine Disorders 1973
Thermoregulation (Body) 1973

Hypothesis Testing 1973
PN 1324 **SC** 24110
SN Application of statistical tests to determine whether a research hypothesis should be accepted or rejected.
HN From 1982, limited to discussions of statistical procedures. Use HYPOTHESIS TESTING or other appropriate terms to access references to COGNITIVE HYPOTHESIS TESTING prior to 1982.
B Experimental Design 1967
N Null Hypothesis Testing 1973
R Confidence Limits (Statistics) 1973
Predictability (Measurement) 1973
↓ Prediction Errors 1973
↓ Probability 1967
↓ Statistical Analysis 1967
Statistical Power 1991
Statistical Significance 1973
↓ Theories 1967
Theory Formulation 1973
Theory Verification 1973

Hypothesis Testing (Cognitive)
Use Cognitive Hypothesis Testing

Hypothyroidism 1973
PN 337 **SC** 24120
UF Myxedema
B Thyroid Disorders 1973
R Goiters 1973
↓ Infertility 1973
↓ Metabolism Disorders 1973
Thyrotropin 1973
Thyroxine 1973

Hypoxia
Use Anoxia

Hysterectomy 1973
PN 290 **SC** 24150
B Sterilization (Sex) 1973
Surgery 1971
R Ovariectomy 1973

Hysteria 1967
PN 1302 **SC** 24160
SN A neurosis characterized by a physical deficit without an organic cause, marked by emotional excitability, amnesia, and disturbances of sensory and motor functions. This diagnosis is no longer used in contemporary practice.
B Mental Disorders 1967
N Mass Hysteria 1973
R Catalepsy 1973
↓ Conversion Disorder 2001
Histrionic Personality Disorder 1991
↓ Neurosis 1967
Suggestibility 1967

Hysterical Blindness
Use Hysterical Vision Disturbances

Hysterical Neurosis (Conversion)
Use Conversion Disorder

Hysterical Neurosis (Dissociation)
Use Dissociative Disorders

Hysterical Paralysis 1973
PN 36 **SC** 24220
SN Transient psychogenic loss of motor function in the absence of an organic cause, often precipitated by a traumatic event.

Hysterical Paralysis — (cont'd)
UF Paralysis (Hysterical)
B Conversion Disorder 2001
R Somatization 1994

Hysterical Personality
HN In 2000, the term was discontinued and removed from all records containing it, and replaced with HISTRIONIC PERSONALITY DISORDER, its postable counterpart.
Use Histrionic Personality Disorder

Hysterical Vision Disturbances 1973
PN 31 **SC** 24240
SN Loss of vision caused by conversion hysteria or highly traumatic event, or blindness occurring without sight organ disorder.
UF Hysterical Blindness
Vision Disturbances (Hysterical)
B Conversion Disorder 2001
R ↓ Eye Disorders 1973

Iatrogenic Effects
Use Side Effects (Treatment)

Ibotenic Acid 1991
PN 102 **SC** 24245
B Insecticides 1973
Neurotoxins 1982
N Muscimol 1994

ICD
Use International Classification of Diseases

Iconic Memory 1985
PN 111 **SC** 24248
SN Brief sensory memory, usually lasting only fractions of a second.
B Short Term Memory 1967

Id 1973
PN 121 **SC** 24250
B Psychoanalytic Personality Factors 1973
R Unconscious (Personality Factor) 1967

Ideal Self
Use Self Concept

Idealism 1973
PN 274 **SC** 24260
B Philosophies 1967
R Determinism 1997

Ideation 1973
PN 533 **SC** 24270
SN Process of idea or image formation.
B Cognitive Processes 1967
N Imagination 1967
Suicidal Ideation 1991
R ↓ Fantasy 1997

Identical Twins
Use Monozygotic Twins

Identification (Defense Mechanism) 1973
PN 915 **SC** 24290
B Defense Mechanisms 1967
R Introjection 1973
Projective Identification 1994

Identity (Personal)
Use Self Concept

Identity (Professional)
Use Professional Identity

Identity Crisis 1973
PN 397 **SC** 24320
B Crises 1971
Emotional Adjustment 1973
R ↓ Personality Development 1967
↓ Self Concept 1967
↓ Stress 1967

Identity Formation 2004
PN 1021 **SC** 24322
SN The process of developing one's identity based on early influences and experiences.
HN This term was introduced in June 2004. Relevant records were re-indexed with this term. The posting note reflects the number of records that were re-indexed.
R Ego Identity 1991
Ethnic Identity 1973
↓ Personality Development 1967
↓ Self Concept 1967
↓ Social Identity 1988

Idiot Savants
HN In 2000, the term was discontinued and removed from all records containing it, and replaced with SAVANTS, its postable counterpart.
Use Savants

IEP
Use Individual Education Programs

Ileum
Use Intestines

Illegal Drug Distribution 1997
PN 218 **SC** 15277
UF Drug Dealing
Drug Trafficking
B Crime 1967
R ↓ Drug Abuse 1973
↓ Drug Laws 1973
↓ Drug Legalization 1997
↓ Drug Usage 1971

Illegitimate Children 1973
PN 57 **SC** 24380
B Family Members 1973

Illinois Test of Psycholinguistic Abilities 2001
PN 174 **SC** 24391
HN In 2000, the truncated term ILLINOIS TEST PSYCHOLINGUIST ABIL (which was used from 1973-2000) was deleted, removed from all records containing it, and replaced with its expanded form ILLINOIS TEST OF PSYCHOLINGUISTIC ABILITIES.
B Intelligence Measures 1967

Illiteracy
Use Literacy

Illness (Physical)
Use Physical Disorders

Illness Behavior 1982
PN 2091 **SC** 24415
SN Adaptive or nonadaptive behaviors exhibited by an individual during the course of an illness or dysfunction.
B Behavior 1967
Client Characteristics 1973
R Anosognosia 1994
Coping Behavior 1967
Coronary Prone Behavior 1982

Illness Behavior — (cont'd)
↓ Disorders 1967
↓ Physical Disorders 1997
↓ Physical Illness (Attitudes Toward) 1985
Recovery (Disorders) 1973
Somatization 1994
↓ Somatoform Disorders 2001
Treatment Compliance 1982

Illumination 1967
PN 5462 **SC** 24420
SN Visible portion of the electromagnetic radiation spectrum but may include ultraviolet and infrared light. May also refer more generally to ambient light. Compare LUMINANCE.
UF Light
Photic Threshold
B Visual Stimulation 1973
N Photopic Stimulation 1973
Scotopic Stimulation 1973
R ↓ Brightness Perception 1973
Light Adaptation 1982
↓ Light Refraction 1982
Luminance 1982

Illumination Therapy
Use Phototherapy

Illusion (Autokinetic)
Use Autokinetic Illusion

Illusions (Perception) 1967
PN 3715 **SC** 24440
SN Misperception or alteration of reality in subjective perception.
UF Optical Illusions
B Perception 1967
N Mueller Lyer Illusion 1988
↓ Perceptual Aftereffect 1967
Spatial Distortion 1973
R ↓ Perceptual Distortion 1982
↓ Perceptual Disturbances 1973

ILP
Use Inductive Logic Programming

Image (Retinal)
Use Retinal Image

Imagery 1967
PN 8208 **SC** 24470
UF Visualization
B Abstraction 1967
N Conceptual Imagery 1973
Spatial Imagery 1982
R Archetypes 1991
Guided Imagery 2001
Imagination 1967

Imagery (Conceptual)
Use Conceptual Imagery

Imagination 1967
PN 3005 **SC** 24490
SN Process of forming mental images of objects, qualities, situations, or relationships, which are not immediately apparent to the senses.
B Cognitive Processes 1967
Ideation 1973
R Conceptual Imagery 1973
↓ Fantasy 1997
↓ Imagery 1967
Magical Thinking 1973
Pretend Play 2005

Imagination — (cont'd)
Vicarious Experiences 1973

Imaginativeness
Use Openness to Experience

Imipramine 1973
PN 2078 **SC** 24520
UF Tofranil
B Amines 1973
Tricyclic Antidepressant Drugs 1997

Imitation (Learning) 1967
PN 4357 **SC** 24530
SN Imitation by human or animal subjects to learn a model's behavior or responses.
UF Modeling Behavior
B Social Learning 1973
R Observational Learning 1973
Role Models 1982

Immaturity (Emotional)
Use Emotional Immaturity

Immersion Programs
Use Foreign Language Education

Immigrants
Use Immigration

Immigration 1973
PN 5691 **SC** 24560
SN Permanent resettlement in a country other than the country of one's origin.
UF Immigrants
B Social Processes 1967
R Citizenship 1973
↓ Expatriates 2007
↓ Human Migration 1973
Refugees 1988

Immune System 2006
PN 158 **SC** 24565
SN Body system concerned with defending the body against infection and foreign organisms, substances, and cells.
HN This term was introduced in May 2006. Relevant records were re-indexed with this term. The posting note reflects the number of records that were re-indexed.
B Anatomical Systems 1973
N Bone Marrow 1973
R Antibodies 1973
Antigens 1982
↓ Immunologic Disorders 1973
↓ Immunologic Factors 2003
Immunoreactivity 1994

Immunization 1973
PN 744 **SC** 24570
UF Vaccination
B Physical Treatment Methods 1973
R Antibodies 1973

Immunogens
Use Antigens

Immunoglobulins 1973
PN 358 **SC** 24580
B Blood Proteins 1973
Globulins 1973
Immunologic Factors 2003
N Gamma Globulin 1973
R Antibodies 1973
Antigens 1982

Immunoglobulins — (cont'd)
↓ Immunologic Disorders 1973
Immunoreactivity 1994
Interferons 1994

Immunologic Disorders 1973
PN 696 **SC** 24590
UF Autoimmune Disorders
Hypersensitivity (Immunologic)
B Physical Disorders 1997
N ↓ Allergic Disorders 1973
Anaphylactic Shock 1973
↓ HIV 2006
Rh Incompatibility 1973
R Asthma 1967
↓ Immune System 2006
↓ Immunoglobulins 1973

Immunologic Factors 2003
PN 105 **SC** 24594
SN Substances that affect the functioning of the immune system.
HN This term was introduced in June 2003. Relevant records were re-indexed with this term. The posting note reflects the number of records that were re-indexed.
N Antibodies 1973
Antigens 1982
↓ Cytokines 2003
↓ Immunoglobulins 1973
R ↓ Immune System 2006
↓ Immunology 1973
Immunoreactivity 1994

Immunology 1973
PN 2680 **SC** 24600
SN Medical science dealing with the study of immunity. Used for the scientific discipline or the immunological processes themselves.
UF Immunopathology
B Medical Sciences 1967
N Psychoneuroimmunology 1991
R ↓ Immunologic Factors 2003
Immunoreactivity 1994

Immunopathology
Use Immunology

Immunoreactivity 1994
PN 1559 **SC** 24613
HN Use IMMUNOLOGY to access references from 1973-1993.
R ↓ Immune System 2006
↓ Immunoglobulins 1973
↓ Immunologic Factors 2003
↓ Immunology 1973
Interleukins 1994

Impaired Professionals 1985
PN 362 **SC** 24615
SN Professional personnel who are physically or psychologically disordered to the extent that such disorders interfere with the performance of professional duties or conflict with professional standards. Does not include handicaps that do not interfere with professional performance.
R Disabled Personnel 1997
↓ Medical Personnel 1967
↓ Mental Health Personnel 1967
Personal Therapy 1991
Professional Ethics 1973
Professional Liability 1985
↓ Professional Personnel 1978
↓ Professional Standards 1973

Implicit Learning 2004
PN 337 **SC** 24617
SN Learning that occurs without awareness of how the knowledge or skills were acquired. Not to be confused with INCIDENTAL LEARNING.
HN This term was introduced in June 2004. Relevant records were re-indexed with this term. The posting note reflects the number of records that were re-indexed.
B Learning 1967
R Implicit Memory 2003

Implicit Memory 2003
PN 575 **SC** 24618
SN Memory of events without specific awareness of learning or experiencing the event.
HN This term was introduced in June 2003. Relevant records were re-indexed with this term. The posting note reflects the number of records that were re-indexed.
B Memory 1967
R Explicit Memory 1997
Implicit Learning 2004

Implosive Therapy 1973
PN 399 **SC** 24620
SN Behavioral therapy involving flooding the client with anxiety through intense or prolonged real-life or imagined exposure to feared objects or situations, thereby demonstrating that they cause no harm. The aim is gradual extinction of anxiety or phobic responses.
UF Flooding Therapy
B Behavior Therapy 1967
Exposure Therapy 1997

Impotence
HN In May 2006, this term was discontinued and removed from all records containing it, and replaced with ERECTILE DYSFUNCTION, its postable counterpart.
Use Erectile Dysfunction

Impression Formation 1978
PN 1791 **SC** 24634
SN Process by which an individual transforms various perceptions and observations about another person or group into an overall impression or set of attitudes toward or about that person or group.
B Social Perception 1967
R ↓ Attitudes 1967
Attribution 1973
Impression Management 1978

Impression Management 1978
PN 1172 **SC** 24636
SN Techniques of image cultivation or impression formation designed to obtain good evaluations of one's self and to win approval from others. Used for both individuals and groups.
UF Ingratiation
R Impression Formation 1978
Self Monitoring (Personality) 1985
↓ Social Behavior 1967
↓ Social Perception 1967
Uncertainty 1991

Imprinting 1967
PN 531 **SC** 24640
SN Rapid learning process that takes place during early critical periods of development. Establishes the basis for patterns of social behavior. Used for both human and animal populations.
B Animal Ethology 1967
Social Learning 1973

Imprinting — (cont'd)
R Critical Period 1988
Species Recognition 1985

Improvisation 2004
PN 234 **SC** 24642
SN Creating dialogue, movement, or music in a spontaneous, unscripted fashion. Used in clinical and nonclinical settings.
HN This term was introduced in June 2004. Relevant records were re-indexed with this term. The posting note reflects the number of records that were re-indexed.
R ↓ Creative Arts Therapy 1994
Creativity 1967
Dance 1973
Drama 1973
Expressive Psychotherapy 1973
Psychodrama 1967
↓ Psychotherapeutic Techniques 1967

Impulse Control Disorders 1997
PN 214 **SC** 24645
SN Mental disorders characterized by an intense need to gratify one's immediate desires and failure to resist the impulse or temptation.
B Mental Disorders 1967
N Explosive Disorder 2001
R ↓ Antisocial Behavior 1971
Conduct Disorder 1991
Delay of Gratification 1978
Impulsiveness 1973
Internet Addiction 2006
Kleptomania 1973
↓ Paraphilias 1988
Pathological Gambling 1988
Pyromania 1973
Self Control 1973

Impulsiveness 1973
PN 3208 **SC** 24650
B Cognitive Style 1967
R ↓ Attention Deficit Disorder 1985
Attention Deficit Disorder with Hyperactivity 2001
Conceptual Tempo 1985
↓ Impulse Control Disorders 1997
Kleptomania 1973
Pathological Gambling 1988
Pyromania 1973
Reflectiveness 1997

In Vitro Fertilization
Use Reproductive Technology

Incarceration 1973
PN 1570 **SC** 24670
B Institutionalization 1967
Law Enforcement 1978
R ↓ Correctional Institutions 1973
Criminal Record 2006
Institution Visitation 1973
↓ Institutional Release 1978

Incentives 1967
PN 1613 **SC** 24680
SN Events or objects which increase or induce drives or determination. Popularly described as one's expectation of reward. May be used for human or animal populations. Compare REWARDS and REINFORCEMENT.
B Motivation 1967
N Educational Incentives 1973
Monetary Incentives 1973

Incentives — (cont'd)
R Awards (Merit) 2005
↓ Goals 1967
↓ Needs 1967
↓ Rewards 1967
Temptation 1973

Incest 1973
PN 2182 SC 24690
B Paraphilias 1988
Sexual Abuse 1988
Sexual Intercourse (Human) 1973
R Pedophilia 1973
↓ Perpetrators 1988
↓ Sex Offenses 1982

Incidental Learning 1967
PN 982 SC 24700
SN Learning that occurs unintentionally, usually as a result of some other unrelated activity. Not to be confused with IMPLICIT LEARNING. Use LATENT LEARNING for animal populations.
HN From 1982, limited to human populations.
B Learning 1967
N Latent Learning 1973

Inclusion (Educational)
Use Mainstreaming (Educational)

Income (Economic) 1973
PN 972 SC 24710
SN Monetary gain (such as wages, interest, dividends, profits) received by individuals or nations within a given period for labor or services rendered or from capital resources.
R Budgets 1997
Economic Security 2007
Finance 2007
Financial Strain 2005
↓ Income Level 1973
Poverty 1973
Salaries 1973
↓ Socioeconomic Status 1967
Taxation 1985

Income Level 1973
PN 1869 SC 24720
SN Total amount of monetary gain received within a given period that is associated with socioeconomic status.
B Socioeconomic Status 1967
N Lower Income Level 1973
Middle Income Level 1973
Upper Income Level 1973
R Financial Strain 2005
Income (Economic) 1973
Salaries 1973
↓ Social Class 1967

Incompatibility (Rh)
Use Rh Incompatibility

Incontinence (Fecal)
Use Fecal Incontinence

Incontinence (Urinary)
Use Urinary Incontinence

Incorporation (Psychological)
Use Internalization

Incubators (Apparatus) 1973
PN 13 SC 24780
B Apparatus 1967

Independence (Personality) 1973
PN 2791 SC 24790
UF Autonomy (Personality)
B Personality Traits 1967
R Empowerment 1991
Internal External Locus of Control 1967
↓ Resistance 1997
Self Determination 1994

Independent Living
Use Self Care Skills

Independent Living Programs 1991
PN 263 SC 24798
SN Community-based programs or services to assist disabled individuals in performing all or most of their daily functions, thus increasing self sufficiency and self determination and eliminating a need to depend on others.
R Activities of Daily Living 1991
Assisted Living 2003
↓ Community Services 1967
Habilitation 1991
↓ Mainstreaming 1991
↓ Program Development 1991
↓ Rehabilitation 1967
Self Care Skills 1978
Supported Employment 1994

Independent Party (Political)
Use Political Parties

Independent Study
Use Individualized Instruction

Independent Variables 1973
PN 175 SC 24810
SN Statistical or experimental parameters that are manipulated in an attempt to analyze their relative effect on specified dependent variables.
B Statistical Variables 1973

Indians (American)
Use American Indians

Indifference
Use Apathy

Indigenous Populations 2001
PN 855 SC 24845
UF Aboriginal Populations
Maori
Natives
B Racial and Ethnic Groups 2001
N Alaska Natives 1997
American Indians 1967
Inuit 2001
↓ Pacific Islanders 2001
R Minority Groups 1967

Individual Counseling
Use Individual Psychotherapy

Individual Differences 1967
PN 12526 SC 24860
SN Any specific characteristic or quantitative difference in a quality or trait that can serve to distinguish one individual from another. Used for both human and animal populations.
R Diversity 2007
Diversity in the Workplace 2003

Individual Differences — (cont'd)
↓ Personality 1967
Personality Correlates 1967
↓ Personality Theory 1967
Self Expression 2006

Individual Education Programs 2006
PN 40 SC 24863
SN Written plans of instruction that are designed to meet the individual student's special learning needs and are agreed upon by the teacher, parents, school officials, and the student (when appropriate).
HN This term was introduced in May 2006. Relevant records were re-indexed with this term. The posting note reflects the number of records that were re-indexed.
UF IEP
Individualized Educational Plans
B Educational Programs 1973
R Curriculum Based Assessment 1994
Individualized Instruction 1973
Special Education 1967
Special Needs 1994

Individual Problem Solving
Use Problem Solving

Individual Psychology 1973
PN 1276 SC 24880
SN Theory and practice of Adlerian psychology, stressing the unique wholeness of the individual and viewing the striving to overcome and master obstacles as the primary motivating force.
B Neopsychoanalytic School 1973
R Adler (Alfred) 1967
Adlerian Psychotherapy 1997

Individual Psychotherapy 1973
PN 2081 SC 24890
SN Psychotherapy occurring on a one-on-one basis as compared to a group setting or environment. Use ADLERIAN PSYCHOTHERAPY to access references on Adlerian individual psychotherapy.
UF Individual Counseling
Individual Therapy
Psychotherapy (Individual)
B Psychotherapy 1967
R Emotion Focused Therapy 2007

Individual Psychotherapy (Adlerian)
Use Adlerian Psychotherapy

Individual Testing 1973
PN 125 SC 24900
B Measurement 1967
R Test Administration 1973

Individual Therapy
Use Individual Psychotherapy

Individualism 2007
PN 403 SC 24920
SN A political and social philosophy that stresses the priority of individual needs over group needs.
HN In April 2007, INDIVIDUALISM changed status from nonpostable to postable. Relevant records were re-indexed with this term. The posting note reflects the number of records that were re-indexed.
B Philosophies 1967
R Freedom 1978
Individuality 1973
Self Determination 1994
Self Expression 2006
Social Values 1973

Individuality 1973
PN 2160 **SC** 24930
B Personality Traits 1967
R Individualism 2007
Nonconformity (Personality) 1973
Self Determination 1994
Self Expression 2006

Individualized Educational Plans
Use Individual Education Programs

Individualized Instruction 1973
PN 2323 **SC** 24940
SN Instruction adapted to individual needs or instruction in which a student works alone or only with a teacher. Also, self-initiated study with or without formal academic guidance or involvement.
UF Independent Study
Instruction (Individualized)
Self Directed Learning
Self Instruction
B Teaching Methods 1967
R ↓ Computer Assisted Instruction 1973
↓ Continuing Education 1985
Cooperative Learning 1994
Distance Education 2003
Individual Education Programs 2006
↓ Learning 1967
Open Classroom Method 1973
Programmed Instruction 2001
Self Regulated Learning 2003
↓ Tutoring 1973

Induced Abortion 1971
PN 1519 **SC** 24950
UF Abortion (Induced)
Elective Abortion
Therapeutic Abortion
B Surgery 1971
R Abortion Laws 1973
↓ Birth Control 1971
↓ Family Planning 1973
Spontaneous Abortion 1971

Inductive Deductive Reasoning 1973
PN 1789 **SC** 24960
UF Convergent Thinking
Deductive Reasoning
Syllogistic Reasoning
B Reasoning 1967
N Inference 1973
R Case Based Reasoning 2003
Divergent Thinking 1973
Heuristics 2003
Logical Thinking 1967
↓ Problem Solving 1967

Inductive Logic Programming 2007
PN 17 **SC** 24964
SN An area of research in machine learning that provides a framework and algorithms for learning relational descriptions in the form of logic problems. ILP systems address relations rule induction and other basic tasks underlying data mining.
HN This term was introduced in April 2007. Relevant records were re-indexed with this term. The posting note reflects the number of records that were re-indexed.
UF ILP
B Machine Learning 2003
R Algorithms 1973
Computer Programming 2001

Inductive Logic Programming — (cont'd)
Knowledge Engineering 2003

Industrial Accidents 1973
PN 717 **SC** 24970
B Accidents 1967
R Occupational Exposure 1988
Occupational Safety 1973
Work Related Illnesses 1994

Industrial and Organizational Psychology 2003
PN 2846 **SC** 25012
HN In June 2003, this term was created to replace the discontinued term INDUSTRIAL PSYCHOLOGY. INDUSTRIAL PSYCHOLOGY was removed from all records and replaced with INDUSTRIAL and ORGANIZATIONAL PSYCHOLOGY.
UF Industrial Psychology
Organizational Psychology
B Applied Psychology 1973

Industrial Arts Education
Use Vocational Education

Industrial Foremen 1973
PN 67 **SC** 24980
UF Foremen (Industrial)
B Blue Collar Workers 1973
R ↓ Management Personnel 1973

Industrial Personnel
Use Business and Industrial Personnel

Industrial Psychologists 1973
PN 167 **SC** 25000
B Business and Industrial Personnel 1967
Psychologists 1967
R Social Psychologists 1973

Industrial Psychology
HN In June 2003, the term was discontinued and removed from all records containing it, and was replaced with INDUSTRIAL and ORGANIZATIONAL PSYCHOLOGY, its postable counterpart.
Use Industrial and Organizational Psychology

Industrial Safety
Use Occupational Safety

Industrialization 1973
PN 549 **SC** 25030
B Social Processes 1967
R Economic Development 2007
Modernization 2003
↓ Technology 1973
Urbanization 1973

Industry
Use Business

Infant Development 1973
PN 7634 **SC** 25060
B Early Childhood Development 1973
N Neonatal Development 1973
R ↓ Physical Development 1973
↓ Psychogenesis 1973

Infant Vocalization 1973
PN 736 **SC** 25080
UF Babbling
Vocalization (Infant)

Infant Vocalization — (cont'd)
B Voice 1973
R Crying 1973

Infanticide 1978
PN 484 **SC** 25085
UF Neonaticide
B Homicide 1967

Infantile Neurosis
Use Childhood Neurosis

Infantile Paralysis
Use Poliomyelitis

Infantile Psychosis
Use Childhood Psychosis

Infantilism 1973
PN 66 **SC** 25120
SN Individuals who have matured beyond the stage of infancy, who retain childish physical, mental, or emotional qualities, often involving infantile objects and/or role playing. Also considered an infantile regression marked by early memories and fantasies of regressive dependencies.
R ↓ Mental Disorders 1967

Infants (Animal) 1978
PN 5908 **SC** 25134
UF Neonates (Animal)
B Animals 1967

Infarctions (Myocardial)
Use Myocardial Infarctions

Infections
Use Infectious Disorders

Infectious Disorders 1973
PN 1213 **SC** 25160
UF Communicable Diseases
Infections
Neuroinfections
B Physical Disorders 1997
N ↓ Bacterial Disorders 1973
Epstein Barr Viral Disorder 1994
↓ Parasitic Disorders 1973
↓ Sexually Transmitted Diseases 2003
↓ Viral Disorders 1973
R ↓ Arthritis 1973
↓ Chorea 1973
↓ Dermatitis 1973
↓ Digestive System Disorders 1973
Disease Transmission 2004
↓ Encephalitis 1973
Encephalomyelitis 1973
↓ Epidemics 2001
↓ Hepatitis 1973
Hydrocephalus 2006
Jaundice 1973
↓ Liver Disorders 1973
↓ Myelitis 1973

Inference 1973
PN 3498 **SC** 25180
B Inductive Deductive Reasoning 1973
R Analogy 1991
Attribution 1973

Inferior Colliculus 1973
PN 338 **SC** 25190
SN Neuroanatomical structure situated next to the pons that serves as the midbrain auditory center.

Inferior Colliculus — (cont'd)
B Mesencephalon 1973

Inferiority (Emotional)
Use Emotional Inferiority

Infertility 1973
PN 1023 **SC** 25210
B Genital Disorders 1967
N Sterility 1973
R ↓ Endocrine Sexual Disorders 1973
Fertility 1988
↓ Gynecological Disorders 1973
Hypothyroidism 1973
Klinefelters Syndrome 1973
↓ Male Genital Disorders 1973

Infidelity 2006
PN 150 **SC** 25215
SN Sexual relationship or intimacy with someone outside of a committed relationship.
HN This term was introduced in May 2006. Relevant records were re-indexed with this term. The posting note reflects the number of records that were re-indexed.
R Extramarital Intercourse 1973
Male Female Relations 1988
↓ Marital Relations 1967
Monogamy 1997
Promiscuity 1973

Infirmaries
Use Hospitals

Inflammation 2004
PN 446 **SC** 25225
SN Local response to injury or irritation characterized by swelling, redness, pain, heat, and/or loss of function.
HN This term was introduced in June 2004. Relevant records were re-indexed with this term. The posting note reflects the number of records that were re-indexed.
R ↓ Injuries 1973
↓ Pathology 1973
↓ Symptoms 1967

Inflection 1973
PN 579 **SC** 25230
SN A grammatically functional change in the pitch or loudness of the voice. Also, the syntactic change in words to designate such factors as case, gender, or tense.
B Prosody 1991
R ↓ Phonology 1973
↓ Speech Characteristics 1973
↓ Syntax 1971

Influence (Interpersonal)
Use Interpersonal Influences

Influences (Social)
Use Social Influences

Influenza 1973
PN 245 **SC** 25260
B Viral Disorders 1973
R ↓ Gastrointestinal Disorders 1973
↓ Nervous System Disorders 1967
↓ Respiratory Tract Disorders 1973

Informants 1988
PN 180 **SC** 25270
SN Persons who provide information against another person who is suspected of committing a violation.

Informants — (cont'd)
UF Whistleblowing
R ↓ Abuse Reporting 1997
↓ Crime 1967
Duty to Warn 2001
Labor Management Relations 1967
↓ Organizational Behavior 1978
↓ Social Behavior 1967

Information 1967
PN 6411 **SC** 25360
SN Conceptually broad term referring to a body of knowledge. Use a more specific term if possible. Differentiate from KNOWLEDGE LEVEL which is the amount of information acquired or received by an individual or group.
R ↓ Automated Information Processing 1973
Censorship 1978
↓ Communication 1967
Computer Searching 1991
Concepts 1967
Data Collection 1982
↓ Data Processing 1967
Databases 1991
Declarative Knowledge 1997
↓ Electronic Communication 2001
Human Information Storage 1973
Information Seeking 1973
Information Services 1988
↓ Information Specialists 1988
↓ Information Systems 1991
Information Theory 1967
↓ Knowledge Level 1978
↓ Libraries 1982
Messages 1973
Privileged Communication 1973
Procedural Knowledge 1997

Information (Messages)
Use Messages

Information Dissemination 2005
PN 308 **SC** 25285
SN The process of distributing information.
HN This term was introduced in August 2005. Relevant records were re-indexed with this term. The posting note reflects the number of records that were re-indexed.
R ↓ Communication 1967
Information Literacy 2007
Information Services 1988
↓ Information Systems 1991
↓ Information Technology 2007
Information Theory 1967
Knowledge Transfer 2007
↓ Libraries 1982
Technology Transfer 2007
Websites 2007

Information Exchange
HN Term discontinued in 2000. From 1973-1999, the term was used to refer to a myriad of communicative and other exchanges.
Use Communication

Information Literacy 2007
PN 28 **SC** 25295
SN Skills needed to locate, retrieve, evaluate, and use information.
HN This term was introduced in April 2007. Relevant records were re-indexed with this term. The posting note reflects the number of records that were re-indexed.

Information Literacy — (cont'd)
R Digital Divide 2007
Information Dissemination 2005
Information Seeking 1973
Information Services 1988
↓ Information Systems 1991

Information Processes (Human)
Use Cognitive Processes

Information Processing (Automated)
Use Automated Information Processing

Information Processing Model 2007
PN 267 **SC** 25313
SN A model concerned with the basic mental operations of attention, perception, and memory. These processes are similar to the input, processing, and output functions of a computer.
HN This term was introduced in April 2007. Relevant records were re-indexed with this term. The posting note reflects the number of records that were re-indexed.
B Models 1967
R Cognition 1967
↓ Cognitive Processes 1967
Human Information Storage 1973
↓ Memory 1967

Information Processing Speed
Use Cognitive Processing Speed

Information Retrieval (Automated)
Use Automated Information Retrieval

Information Seeking 1973
PN 1853 **SC** 25330
R Computer Searching 1991
↓ Exploratory Behavior 1967
Information 1967
Information Literacy 2007
Questioning 1982

Information Services 1988
PN 364 **SC** 25335
R ↓ Automated Information Retrieval 1973
Computer Searching 1991
Databases 1991
Hot Line Services 1973
Information 1967
Information Dissemination 2005
Information Literacy 2007
↓ Information Systems 1991
↓ Information Technology 2007
↓ Libraries 1982
Technology Transfer 2007

Information Specialists 1988
PN 30 **SC** 25338
B Professional Personnel 1978
N Librarians 1988
R Information 1967

Information Storage (Human)
Use Human Information Storage

Information Systems 1991
PN 1937 **SC** 25345
SN Collection, organization, and storage of data or the operational functions used to process information.

Information Systems — (cont'd)
UF Management Information Systems
B Systems 1967
N Internet 2001
R ↓ Automated Information Processing 1973
↓ Automated Information Retrieval 1973
Automated Information Storage 1973
Bioinformatics 2007
↓ Communication Systems 1973
↓ Computer Applications 1973
↓ Data Processing 1967
Databases 1991
Decision Support Systems 1997
↓ Electronic Communication 2001
↓ Expert Systems 1991
Information 1967
Information Dissemination 2005
Information Literacy 2007
Information Services 1988
↓ Information Technology 2007
Intelligent Agents 2007
Knowledge Economy 2007
Knowledge Engineering 2003
Knowledge Management 2005
Word Processing 1991

Information Technology 2007
PN 932 **SC** 25347
SN The use of computers, electronics, and telecommunications technology to process or disseminate information.
HN This term was introduced in April 2007. Relevant records were re-indexed with this term. The posting note reflects the number of records that were re-indexed.
B Technology 1973
N ↓ Automated Information Processing 1973
Bioinformatics 2007
R Computer Mediated Communication 2003
Information Dissemination 2005
Information Services 1988
↓ Information Systems 1991

Information Theory 1967
PN 678 **SC** 25350
SN Branch of science that deals statistically with the transmission of information and its measurable characteristics. Used for the scientific discipline or for application of information theory to specific areas of investigation.
B Theories 1967
R Communication Theory 1973
Information 1967
Information Dissemination 2005
↓ Stochastic Modeling 1973

Informed Consent 1985
PN 1893 **SC** 25363
SN Process of making rational decisions regarding one's treatment or participation in experimental procedures.
R ↓ Civil Rights 1978
↓ Client Rights 1988
Debriefing (Experimental) 1991
Duty to Warn 2001
Experimental Ethics 1978
Guardianship 1988
Involuntary Treatment 1994
↓ Legal Processes 1973
Professional Ethics 1973
Treatment Compliance 1982
Treatment Refusal 1994
Treatment Withholding 1988

Ingestion 2001
PN 2767 **SC** 25364
SN Oral intake of food, liquids, medicine, etc. Used for both human and animal populations.
HN In 2001, this term was created to replace the discontinued term EATING. EATING was removed from all records containing it and replaced with INGESTION. In June 2004, EATING became nonpostable to EATING BEHAVIOR.
B Physiology 1967
N Coprophagia 2001
↓ Fluid Intake 1985
Food Intake 1967
R Animal Drinking Behavior 1973
Animal Feeding Behavior 1973
Digestion 1973
↓ Drinking Behavior 1978
Pica 1973
Swallowing 1988

Ingratiation
Use Impression Management

Ingroup Outgroup 1997
PN 1571 **SC** 25366
UF Outgroup Ingroup
B Social Groups 1973
R Collectivism 2007
Ethnic Identity 1973
↓ Group Dynamics 1967
Group Identity 2007
Intergroup Dynamics 1973
Self Perception 1967
↓ Social Identity 1988
↓ Social Networks 1994
↓ Social Perception 1967

Inhalant Abuse 1985
PN 331 **SC** 25367
SN Inhalation of vapors from volatile chemical substances (such as aerosol sprays, solvents, and anesthetics) in order to produce mind-altering effects.
UF Solvent Abuse
B Drug Abuse 1973
N Glue Sniffing 1973
R ↓ Solvents 1982

Inhibited Sexual Desire 1997
PN 104 **SC** 25370
SN Lack of sexual interest or feelings.
UF Hypoactive Sexual Desire Disorder
B Sexual Function Disturbances 1973
R Eroticism 1973
Female Sexual Dysfunction 2005
Libido 1973
Sex Drive 1973
↓ Sexual Arousal 1978

Inhibition (Personality) 1973
PN 1172 **SC** 25380
B Personality Processes 1967

Inhibition (Proactive)
Use Proactive Inhibition

Inhibition (Retroactive)
Use Retroactive Inhibition

Initial Teaching Alphabet 1973
PN 17 **SC** 25410
SN A system developed in England in 1959 that uses a phoneme-grapheme correspondence to stress consistency between symbol and sound for beginning reading instruction.

Initial Teaching Alphabet — (cont'd)
B Alphabets 1973
R ↓ Language Arts Education 1973
Phonics 1973
↓ Reading 1967
Reading Education 1973
↓ Teaching Methods 1967

Initiation Rites 1973
PN 94 **SC** 25420
B Rites of Passage 1973
R Cosmetic Techniques 2001

Initiative 1973
PN 264 **SC** 25430
B Personality Traits 1967

Injections 1973
PN 746 **SC** 25440
B Drug Administration Methods 1973
N Intramuscular Injections 1973
Intraperitoneal Injections 1973
Intravenous Injections 1973
Subcutaneous Injections 1973
R Drug Self Administration 2004

Injuries 1973
PN 4050 **SC** 25450
UF Physical Trauma
Trauma (Physical)
B Trauma 2006
N Birth Injuries 1973
Burns 1973
Electrical Injuries 1973
↓ Head Injuries 1973
↓ Spinal Cord Injuries 1973
↓ Wounds 1973
R ↓ Accidents 1967
Coma 1973
↓ Disorders 1967
↓ Epidemics 2001
Falls 2004
Hematoma 1973
Hemiplegia 1978
Inflammation 2004
Paraplegia 1978
Physical Disfigurement 1978
↓ Physical Disorders 1997
Quadriplegia 1985
↓ Safety 1967
Shock 1967

Injuries (Birth)
Use Birth Injuries

Inlaws 1997
PN 42 **SC** 25465
B Family Members 1973
R ↓ Parents 1967
↓ Spouses 1973

Inmates (Prison)
Use Prisoners

Innate Behavior (Animal)
Use Instinctive Behavior

Inner City
Use Urban Environments

Inner Ear
Use Labyrinth (Anatomy)

Inner Speech
Use Self Talk

Innovation 2007
PN 825 **SC** 25499
SN Generation of an idea or introduction of a new technology, product, process, or service.
HN This term was introduced in April 2007. Relevant records were re-indexed with this term. The posting note reflects the number of records that were re-indexed.
UF Business Innovation
Organizational Innovation
Technological Innovation
R Creativity 1967
↓ Organizational Behavior 1978
Organizational Development 1973
Research and Development 2007
↓ Technology 1973

Innovativeness
Use Creativity

Inquisitiveness
Use Curiosity

Insanity
Use Mental Disorders

Insanity Defense 1985
PN 756 **SC** 25525
SN Legal defense designed to invoke an exemption from criminal responsibility on the basis of a mental disorder at the time of the alleged criminal offense.
B Legal Processes 1973
R Court Referrals 1994
Criminal Responsibility 1991
Forensic Evaluation 1994
Forensic Psychiatry 1973
↓ Mental Disorders 1967
Mentally Ill Offenders 1985

Insecticides 1973
PN 268 **SC** 25530
HN In 1997, this term replaced the discontinued term DIELDRIN. In 2000, DIELDRIN was removed from all records containing it, and replaced with INSECTICIDES.
UF Dieldrin
Pesticides
B Hazardous Materials 1991
N DDT (Insecticide) 1973
↓ Ibotenic Acid 1991
Parathion 1973
R ↓ Drugs 1967
↓ Insects 1967
↓ Neurotoxins 1982
Nicotine 1973
↓ Toxins 2007

Insects 1967
PN 1895 **SC** 25540
B Arthropoda 1973
N Ants 1973
Bees 1973
Beetles 1973
Butterflies 1973
Cockroaches 1973
↓ Diptera 1973
Grasshoppers 1973
Larvae 1973
Mantis 1973
Moths 1973

Insects — (cont'd)
Wasps 1982
R ↓ Insecticides 1973

Insecurity (Emotional)
Use Emotional Security

Insensitivity (Personality)
Use Sensitivity (Personality)

Inservice Teacher Education 1973
PN 1555 **SC** 25570
SN Course or program designed to provide teachers with growth in job-related competencies or skills. Usually school sponsored.
B Inservice Training 1985
Teacher Education 1967
R On the Job Training 1973
Professional Development 1982

Inservice Training 1985
PN 466 **SC** 25575
B Continuing Education 1985
Personnel Training 1967
N Inservice Teacher Education 1973
Mental Health Inservice Training 1973
R On the Job Training 1973
Professional Development 1982

Inservice Training (Mental Health)
Use Mental Health Inservice Training

Insight 1973
PN 1143 **SC** 25590
B Personality Processes 1967
R Intuition 1973
Perceptiveness (Personality) 1973

Insight (Psychotherapeutic Process) 1973
PN 268 **SC** 25600
B Psychotherapeutic Processes 1967

Insight Therapy 1973
PN 173 **SC** 25610
SN Psychotherapeutic method which seeks to uncover the causes of the client's conflicts through conscious awareness (i.e., insight) into unconscious dynamics of feelings, responses, and behavior.
B Psychotherapy 1967

Insomnia 1973
PN 2097 **SC** 25620
UF Sleeplessness
B Sleep Disorders 1973
Symptoms 1967

Instability (Emotional)
Use Emotional Instability

Instinctive Behavior 1982
PN 1743 **SC** 25638
SN Stereotyped, unlearned, largely stimulus-bound, adaptive behavior limited in its expression by the inherent properties of the nervous system and genetic factors. Used for human or animal populations.
HN In 1982, this term was created to replace the discontinued terms ANIMAL INNATE BEHAVIOR and ANIMAL INSTINCTIVE BEHAVIOR. In 2000, these terms were removed from all records containing them, and replaced with INSTINCTIVE BEHAVIOR.
UF Animal Innate Behavior
Animal Instinctive Behavior
Innate Behavior (Animal)

Instinctive Behavior — (cont'd)
B Behavior 1967
R ↓ Animal Defensive Behavior 1982
Animal Distress Calls 1973
↓ Animal Ethology 1967
Animal Exploratory Behavior 1973
Animal Homing 1991
Animal Motivation 1967
Animal Predatory Behavior 1978
↓ Animal Sexual Behavior 1985
Attack Behavior 1973
↓ Genetics 1967
Homeostasis 1973
Human Nature 1997
↓ Motivation 1967
Neophobia 1985
↓ Physiology 1967
↓ Reflexes 1971
Self Preservation 1997
Species Recognition 1985
Spontaneous Alternation 1982

Institution Visitation 1973
PN 151 **SC** 25650
SN Visiting a patient or convict in an institution (e.g., hospital, prison, or nursing home) by someone from outside the institution (e.g., friends or family).
UF Visitation (Institution)
R ↓ Correctional Institutions 1973
Incarceration 1973
↓ Residential Care Institutions 1973

Institutional Release 1978
PN 247 **SC** 25664
SN Discharge or release of an individual from any type of correctional or therapeutic residential facility.
B Institutionalization 1967
N ↓ Hospital Discharge 1973
R ↓ Commitment (Psychiatric) 1973
Deinstitutionalization 1982
Discharge Planning 1994
↓ Hospital Admission 1973
Incarceration 1973
↓ Psychiatric Hospital Admission 1973
↓ Psychiatric Hospitalization 1973

Institutional Schools 1978
PN 251 **SC** 25666
SN Schools that are part of larger residential institutions such as hospitals or prisons.
B Schools 1967
R Boarding Schools 1988
↓ Correctional Institutions 1973
↓ Residential Care Institutions 1973
↓ Treatment Facilities 1973

Institutionalization 1967
PN 2267 **SC** 25670
N ↓ Hospitalization 1967
Incarceration 1973
↓ Institutional Release 1978
R ↓ Facility Admission 1988
↓ Facility Discharge 1988
Orphanages 1973

Institutionalized Mentally Retarded 1973
PN 1393 **SC** 25680
B Mental Retardation 1967
R Home Reared Mentally Retarded 1973
↓ Residential Care Institutions 1973

Institutions (Correctional)
Use Correctional Institutions

Institutions (Residential Care)
Use Residential Care Institutions

Instruction
Use Teaching

Instruction (Computer Assisted)
Use Computer Assisted Instruction

Instruction (Individualized)
Use Individualized Instruction

Instruction (Programmed)
Use Programmed Instruction

Instructional Media 1967
PN 1569 **SC** 25740
SN Formats or technologies for conveyance of didactic content, including print, film, computers, phonographic records, and magnetic tape.
B Teaching 1967
N Advance Organizers 1985
Educational Audiovisual Aids 1973
Reading Materials 1973
Teaching Machines 1973
↓ Textbooks 1978

Instructional Objectives
Use Educational Objectives

Instructions (Experimental)
Use Experimental Instructions

Instructors
Use Teachers

Instrument Controls 1985
PN 139 **SC** 25765
SN May include knobs, handles, levers, latches, dials, switches, buttons, and any other mechanism used to control the operation of machines and instruments.
HN Consider VISUAL DISPLAYS to access references from 1973-1984.
UF Controls (Instrument)
N Flight Instrumentation 1973
R ↓ Displays 1967
Human Factors Engineering 1973
Human Machine Systems Design 1997
Keyboards 1985

Instrumental Conditioning
Use Operant Conditioning

Instrumental Learning
Use Operant Conditioning

Instrumentality 1991
PN 178 **SC** 25785
R ↓ Motivation 1967
↓ Personality Traits 1967
Self Efficacy 1985

Instrumentation (Flight)
Use Flight Instrumentation

Insulin 1973
PN 1149 **SC** 25800
B Hormones 1967
R Insulin Shock Therapy 1973

Insulin Resistance Syndrome
Use Metabolic Syndrome

Insulin Shock Therapy 1973
PN 47 **SC** 25820
B Shock Therapy 1973
R Coma 1973
Insulin 1973

Insurance 1973
PN 293 **SC** 25830
N ↓ Health Insurance 1973
Life Insurance 1973
Social Security 1988
R Disability Evaluation 1988
Risk Management 1997

Insurance Agents
Use Sales Personnel

Intake Interview 1994
PN 206 **SC** 25845
SN Initial evaluation, assessment, or screening of clients or patients to determine needs and appropriate health, mental health, rehabilitation, or other services.
B Interviews 1967
R ↓ Case Management 1991
Clinical Judgment (Not Diagnosis) 1973
↓ Diagnosis 1967
↓ Evaluation 1967
Health Service Needs 1997
↓ Interview Schedules 2001
Needs Assessment 1985
↓ Psychiatric Evaluation 1997
↓ Psychodiagnostic Interview 1973
↓ Screening 1982

Integrated Services 1997
PN 1238 **SC** 25847
SN Collaboration and cooperation among social service, education, health, or community service providers.
UF Interagency Services
R ↓ Community Services 1967
↓ Health Care Services 1978
Human Services 2007
Interdisciplinary Treatment Approach 1973
↓ Mental Health Programs 1973
↓ Mental Health Services 1978
Multimodal Treatment Approach 1991
Public Health Services 1973
↓ Social Programs 1973
↓ Social Services 1982

Integration (Racial)
Use Social Integration

Integrative Psychotherapy 2003
PN 376 **SC** 25853
SN Integration of two or more theoretical approaches and clinical methods of psychotherapy.
HN This term was introduced in June 2003. Relevant records were re-indexed with this term. The posting note reflects the number of records that were re-indexed.
B Psychotherapy 1967
R Eclectic Psychotherapy 1994
Emotion Focused Therapy 2007
Interdisciplinary Treatment Approach 1973
Multimodal Treatment Approach 1991

Integrity 1997
PN 286 **SC** 25855
B Personality Traits 1967
R ↓ Ethics 1967
Honesty 1973

Integrity — (cont'd)
Morality 1967
↓ Values 1967

Intellectual Development 1973
PN 2074 **SC** 25860
SN Acquisition of factual knowledge. Consider COGNITIVE DEVELOPMENT for acquisition of reasoning, thought, and problem solving abilities.
B Cognitive Development 1973
N ↓ Language Development 1967
R ↓ Intelligence 1967

Intellectual Functioning
Use Cognitive Ability

Intellectualism 1973
PN 99 **SC** 25870
SN Doctrine which attempts to explain emotion and volition in terms of cognitive processes.
B Philosophies 1967

Intellectualization 1973
PN 23 **SC** 25880
SN Defense mechanism in which distressful emotional content of a painful situation is avoided by focusing on intellectual (cognitive) aspects of the situation or by engaging in abstract thinking.
B Defense Mechanisms 1967
R Isolation (Defense Mechanism) 1973

Intellectually Gifted
Use Gifted

Intelligence 1967
PN 11912 **SC** 25900
SN General ability to think, reason, learn, apply knowledge, or deal effectively with the environment. Consider also INTELLIGENCE QUOTIENT.
N Emotional Intelligence 2003
Multiple Intelligences 2007
R ↓ Ability 1967
↓ Artificial Intelligence 1982
Cognitive Assessment 1997
Creativity 1967
Divergent Thinking 1973
Gifted 1967
↓ Intellectual Development 1973
Intelligence Quotient 1967
Mental Age 1973
↓ Reasoning 1967
↓ Thinking 1967
Wisdom 1994

Intelligence Age
Use Mental Age

Intelligence Measures 1967
PN 5438 **SC** 25910
HN In 1997, this term replaced the discontinued terms HENMON NELSON TESTS OF MENTAL ABILITY, LEITER ADULT INTELLIGENCE SCALE, TEMPORAL SPATIAL CONCEPT SCALE, and VANE KINDERGARTEN TEST. In 2000, these terms were removed from all records containing them, and replaced with INTELLIGENCE MEASURES.
UF Henmon Nelson Tests of Mental Ability
Leiter Adult Intelligence Scale
Temporal Spatial Concept Scale
Tests (Intelligence)
Vane Kindergarten Test
B Measurement 1967
N Benton Revised Visual Retention Test 1973
Culture Fair Intelligence Test 1973

Intelligence Measures — (cont'd)
Frostig Developmental Test of Visual Perception 2001
Goodenough Harris Draw A Person Test 1967
Illinois Test of Psycholinguistic Abilities 2001
Kaufman Assessment Battery for Children 2001
Kohs Block Design Test 1973
Miller Analogies Test 1973
Peabody Picture Vocabulary Test 1973
Porteus Maze Test 1973
Raven Coloured Progressive Matrices 1973
Raven Progressive Matrices 1978
Slosson Intelligence Test 2001
Stanford Binet Intelligence Scale 1967
Wechsler Adult Intelligence Scale 1967
Wechsler Bellevue Intelligence Scale 1967
Wechsler Intelligence Scale for Children 2001
Wechsler Preschool Primary Scale 1988
R Bayley Scales of Infant Development 1994
Cognitive Assessment 1997

Intelligence Quotient 1967
PN 4781 **SC** 25920
SN Relative intelligence of an individual expressed as a score on a standardized test of intelligence. Consider also INTELLIGENCE.
B Test Scores 1967
R Cognitive Assessment 1997
↓ Intelligence 1967
Mental Age 1973

Intelligent Agents 2007
PN 52 **SC** 25925
SN Specialized software applications that enable users to better find information or to achieve specified goals. An essential feature of such agents is that they may adapt and learn.
HN This term was introduced in April 2007. Relevant records were re-indexed with this term. The posting note reflects the number of records that were re-indexed.
R ↓ Artificial Intelligence 1982
↓ Computer Applications 1973
↓ Computer Software 1967
↓ Expert Systems 1991
↓ Information Systems 1991

Intelligent Tutoring Systems 2003
PN 140 **SC** 25930
SN Systems which provide individualized instruction and performance assessment in response to a learner's actions. Used in artificial intelligence discussions.
HN This term was introduced in June 2003. Relevant records were re-indexed with this term. The posting note reflects the number of records that were re-indexed.
B Computer Assisted Instruction 1973
R ↓ Artificial Intelligence 1982
↓ Expert Systems 1991
↓ Feedback 1967
↓ Learning 1967

Intensity (Stimulus)
Use Stimulus Intensity

Intensive Care 1988
PN 838 **SC** 25942
R Hospital Environment 1982
↓ Hospital Programs 1978
↓ Hospitals 1967

Intention 1988
PN 4407 **SC** 25945
SN Determination to act in a certain manner.
R ↓ Goals 1967
↓ Motivation 1967
Planned Behavior 1997

Intentional Learning 1973
PN 383 **SC** 25950
SN Purposive or motivated learning.
B Learning 1967

Interaction (Interpersonal)
Use Interpersonal Interaction

Interaction (Social)
Use Social Interaction

Interaction Analysis (Statistics) 1973
PN 170 **SC** 25990
B Statistical Analysis 1967
R Interaction Variance 1973

Interaction Variance 1973
PN 46 **SC** 26000
B Variability Measurement 1973
R Interaction Analysis (Statistics) 1973

Interagency Services
Use Integrated Services

Intercourse (Sexual)
Use Sexual Intercourse (Human)

Intercultural Communication
Use Cross Cultural Communication

Interdisciplinary Research 1985
PN 1174 **SC** 26025
SN Any research effort coordinated or executed by members of two or more specialties, disciplines, or theoretical orientations.
UF Cross Disciplinary Research
Multidisciplinary Research
B Experimentation 1967
R Interdisciplinary Treatment Approach 1973

Interdisciplinary Treatment Approach 1973
PN 4382 **SC** 26030
SN Combination of two or more disciplines in the prevention, diagnosis, treatment, or rehabilitation of mental or physical disorders.
UF Multidisciplinary Treatment Approach
B Treatment 1967
R Biopsychosocial Approach 1991
Eclectic Psychotherapy 1994
↓ Health Care Psychology 1985
Integrated Services 1997
Integrative Psychotherapy 2003
Interdisciplinary Research 1985
Multimodal Treatment Approach 1991
Partial Hospitalization 1985
↓ Teams 1988

Interest Inventories 1973
PN 537 **SC** 26040
B Inventories 1967

Interest Patterns
HN Term was discontinued in 1982. In 2000, the term was removed from all records containing it, and replaced with INTERESTS, its postable counterpart.
Use Interests

Interests 1967
PN 2227 **SC** 26080
HN In 1982, this term replaced the discontinued term INTEREST PATTERNS. In 2000, INTEREST PATTERNS was removed from all records containing it, and replaced with INTERESTS.
UF Interest Patterns
N Occupational Interests 1967
R Daily Activities 1994
Hobbies 1988

Interethnic Communication
Use Cross Cultural Communication

Interethnic Family 1988
PN 36 **SC** 26070
B Family 1967
R Interracial Adoption 1994
Interracial Family 1988
Racial and Ethnic Differences 1982

Interethnic Marriage
Use Exogamous Marriage

Interfaith Marriage 1973
PN 71 **SC** 26090
B Exogamous Marriage 1973

Interference (Learning) 1967
PN 3890 **SC** 26100
SN Inhibition of learning due to negative transfer effects of competing memories, thoughts, or learned behavior. Effects include slower learning and poorer memory.
B Learning 1967
N ↓ Latent Inhibition 1997
Proactive Inhibition 1973
Retroactive Inhibition 1973
R Forgetting 1973
↓ Memory 1967
↓ Retention 1967
Stroop Effect 1988

Interferons 1994
PN 317 **SC** 26103
B Cytokines 2003
Proteins 1973
R Antineoplastic Drugs 1982
↓ Immunoglobulins 1973

Intergenerational Relations 1988
PN 1955 **SC** 26105
SN Contact between related or nonrelated persons of different generational age groups.
R Empty Nest 1991
↓ Family Relations 1967
Generation Gap 1973
Generativity 2001
Transgenerational Patterns 1991

Intergenerational Transmission
Use Transgenerational Patterns

Intergroup Dynamics 1973
PN 2067 **SC** 26110
B Group Dynamics 1967
R Boundaries (Psychological) 1997
Ingroup Outgroup 1997

Interhemispheric Interaction 1985
PN 1076 **SC** 26112
SN Any neurophysiological, electrophysiological, or neurochemical exchange occurring between the cerebral hemispheres.

Interhemispheric Interaction — (cont'd)
UF Interhemispheric Transfer
R ↓ Cerebral Cortex 1967
↓ Cerebral Dominance 1973
Corpus Callosum 1973
Left Hemisphere 2005
Right Hemisphere 2005

Interhemispheric Transfer
Use Interhemispheric Interaction

Interior Design 1982
PN 299 **SC** 26115
SN Practice or resultant product of planning and implementing the design of architectural interiors and furnishings.
B Architecture 1973
Environmental Planning 1982
R Aesthetic Preferences 1973
Aesthetics 1967
Furniture 1985

Interleukins 1994
PN 750 **SC** 26117
SN Compounds produced by lymphocytes that regulate immune system functioning and individual cell mediated immunity.
B Cytokines 2003
R Antigens 1982
Biological Markers 1991
Immunoreactivity 1994
Lymphocytes 1973

Intermarriage
Use Exogamous Marriage

Intermediate School Students 1973
PN 79 **SC** 26130
SN Includes the middle and/or upper elementary school grades, usually grades 4, 5, and 6. Use ELEMENTARY SCHOOL STUDENTS unless specific reference is made to population as intermediate school students.
B Elementary School Students 1967

Intermittent Explosive Disorder
Use Explosive Disorder

Intermittent Reinforcement
Use Reinforcement Schedules

Internal Consistency
Use Test Reliability

Internal External Locus of Control 1967
PN 11420 **SC** 26150
UF Control (Locus of)
Locus of Control
B Personality Traits 1967
R Attribution 1973
↓ Emotional Control 1973
External Rewards 1973
Extrinsic Motivation 1973
↓ Helplessness 1997
Independence (Personality) 1973
Internal Rewards 1973
Intrinsic Motivation 1973
Self Control 1973
Self Determination 1994

Internal Rewards 1973
PN 148 **SC** 26160
SN Satisfaction of a personal value or intrinsic criteria of behavior through action or attainment. Compare SECONDARY REINFORCEMENT.

Internal Rewards — (cont'd)
UF Intrinsic Rewards
B Rewards 1967
R Internal External Locus of Control 1967
Intrinsic Motivation 1973

Internalization 1997
PN 932 **SC** 26165
UF Incorporation (Psychological)
B Personality Processes 1967
N Introjection 1973
R ↓ Defense Mechanisms 1967
Externalization 1973
Object Permanence 1985
Object Relations 1982
↓ Personality Development 1967
↓ Psychotherapeutic Processes 1967

International Classification of Diseases 2001
PN 380 **SC** 26168
SN Used when the International Classification of Diseases or its revisions is the primary focus of the reference. Not used for specific psychodiagnostic categories.
HN Consider PSYCHODIAGNOSTIC TYPOLOGIES to access references prior to 1997. In 2000, the truncated term INTERNATIONAL CLASS OF DISEASES was deleted and removed from all records containing it, and replaced with INTERNATIONAL CLASSIFICATION OF DISEASES, its expanded form.
UF ICD
B Psychodiagnostic Typologies 1967
R ↓ Diagnosis 1967
Diagnostic and Statistical Manual 1994
↓ Disorders 1967
↓ Mental Disorders 1967
↓ Psychodiagnosis 1967
Research Diagnostic Criteria 1994

International Organizations 1973
PN 1112 **SC** 26170
SN Used for intergovernmental or nongovernmental, nonprofit, international organizations. For multinational for-profit organizations use MULTINATIONAL CORPORATIONS.
B Organizations 1967
R Foreign Organizations 1973
NGOs 2006

International Relations 1967
PN 1745 **SC** 26180
R Foreign Policy Making 1973
National Security 2006
Peace 1988
Peacekeeping 2005

International Students 2007
PN 1163 **SC** 26182
SN Persons attending school or a training program in a country other than their own, generally with the intent to return to their home country.
HN In April 2007, this term was created to replace the discontinued term FOREIGN STUDENTS. FOREIGN STUDENTS was removed from all records containing it, and was replaced with INTERNATIONAL STUDENTS.
UF Foreign Students
B Students 1967
R ↓ Expatriates 2007
Study Abroad 2007

International Study
Use Study Abroad

Internet 2001
PN 6296 **SC** 26185
SN A global system of linked computer networks that facilitates information retrieval and international communication.
UF World Wide Web (WWW)
B Communication Systems 1973
Information Systems 1991
R ↓ Automated Information Processing 1973
↓ Computer Applications 1973
Computer Mediated Communication 2003
↓ Electronic Commerce 2006
↓ Electronic Communication 2001
Electronic Retailing 2007
Internet Addiction 2006
Online Therapy 2003
↓ Telecommunications Media 1973
Telemedicine 2003
Websites 2007

Internet Addiction 2006
PN 67 **SC** 26186
SN An excessive and pathological pattern of Internet use.
HN This term was introduced in May 2006. Relevant records were re-indexed with this term. The posting note reflects the number of records that were re-indexed.
B Addiction 1973
Internet Usage 2007
R ↓ Impulse Control Disorders 1997
Internet 2001

Internet Counseling
Use Online Therapy

Internet Shopping
Use Electronic Commerce

Internet Social Networking
Use Online Social Networks

Internet Usage 2007
PN 358 **SC** 58106
HN This term was introduced in April 2007. Relevant records were re-indexed with this term. The posting note reflects the number of records that were re-indexed.
B Human Computer Interaction 1997
N Internet Addiction 2006
Online Social Networks 2007
R Computer Mediated Communication 2003
Computer Searching 1991
Digital Divide 2007

Internists 1973
PN 168 **SC** 26190
B Physicians 1967

Internship (Medical)
Use Medical Internship

Internship Programs 2006
PN 242 **SC** 26202
SN Supervised programs offering practical and professional experience to students and recent graduates.
HN This term was introduced in May 2006. Relevant records were re-indexed with this term. The posting note reflects the number of records that were re-indexed.

Internship Programs — (cont'd)
B Experiential Learning 1997
N Clinical Psychology Internship 1973
Medical Internship 1973
R ↓ Educational Programs 1973

Interobserver Reliability
Use Interrater Reliability

Interocular Transfer 1985
PN 141 **SC** 26207
SN Any neurophysiological, electrophysiological, or perceptual interaction between the two eyes.
B Visual Perception 1967
R Ocular Dominance 1973
↓ Perceptual Aftereffect 1967
↓ Sensory Adaptation 1967

Interpersonal Attraction 1967
PN 2894 **SC** 26210
UF Attraction (Interpersonal)
B Interpersonal Interaction 1967
N Sexual Attraction 2003
R Human Mate Selection 1988
↓ Interpersonal Relationships 2004
Likability 1988
Physical Attractiveness 1973

Interpersonal Communication 1973
PN 10326 **SC** 26220
B Communication 1967
Interpersonal Interaction 1967
N Arguments 1973
Body Language 1973
Conversation 1973
Cross Cultural Communication 1997
Double Bind Interaction 1973
Eye Contact 1973
Gossip 1982
Group Discussion 1967
Interviewing 1973
↓ Interviews 1967
Job Applicant Interviews 1973
Listening (Interpersonal) 1997
↓ Negotiation 1973
↓ Parent Child Communication 1973
R Communication Barriers 2006
Credibility 1973
Neurolinguistic Programming 2001
Pragmatics 1985
Scientific Communication 1973
Self Disclosure 1973
Self Expression 2006
Self Reference 1994
Speech Anxiety 1985

Interpersonal Compatibility 1973
PN 456 **SC** 26230
UF Compatibility (Interpersonal)
B Interpersonal Interaction 1967
R Friendship 1967
Human Mate Selection 1988
↓ Interpersonal Relationships 2004

Interpersonal Competence
Use Social Skills

Interpersonal Distance
Use Personal Space

Interpersonal Influences 1967
PN 4327 **SC** 26240
SN Effect one individual has on another with or without apparent intention or direct exercise of command.

Interpersonal Influences — (cont'd)
UF Influence (Interpersonal)
B Interpersonal Interaction 1967
Social Influences 1967
N Peer Pressure 1994
R ↓ Persuasive Communication 1967
Reference Groups 1994
Suggestibility 1967

Interpersonal Interaction 1967
PN 23888 **SC** 26250
UF Interaction (Interpersonal)
Rapport
B Social Interaction 1967
N ↓ Assistance (Social Behavior) 1973
Charitable Behavior 1973
Collaboration 2007
↓ Collective Behavior 1967
↓ Conflict 1967
Cooperation 1967
↓ Employee Interaction 1988
Group Participation 1973
Group Performance 1967
↓ Interpersonal Attraction 1967
↓ Interpersonal Communication 1973
Interpersonal Compatibility 1973
↓ Interpersonal Influences 1967
Male Female Relations 1988
↓ Participation 1973
↓ Peer Relations 1967
Persecution 1973
Rivalry 1973
Social Dating 1973
Stranger Reactions 1988
R Affection 1973
Boundaries (Psychological) 1997
Codependency 1991
Dual Relationships 2003
Enactments 1997
↓ Interpersonal Relationships 2004
Intimacy 1973
Mentor 1985
Mirroring 1997
Popularity 1988
↓ Relationship Satisfaction 2001
Retaliation 1991
Social Cognition 1994
↓ Social Networks 1994

Interpersonal Perception
Use Social Perception

Interpersonal Psychotherapy 1997
PN 498 **SC** 26263
SN Technique formulated by H. S. Sullivan based on the study of the patient's interpersonal relationships both within and outside of the psychotherapeutic situation.
UF Interpersonal Therapy
B Psychotherapy 1967
R ↓ Psychotherapeutic Techniques 1967

Interpersonal Relationship Satisfaction
Use Relationship Satisfaction

Interpersonal Relationships 2004
PN 3552 **SC** 58084
HN This term was introduced in June 2004. Relevant records were re-indexed with this term. The posting note reflects the number of records that were re-indexed.
UF Personal Relationships
N ↓ Family Relations 1967
Friendship 1967

Interpersonal Relationships — (cont'd)
Kinship 1985
↓ Marital Relations 1967
R ↓ Interpersonal Attraction 1967
Interpersonal Compatibility 1973
↓ Interpersonal Interaction 1967
Relationship Quality 2004
↓ Relationship Satisfaction 2001

Interpersonal Therapy
Use Interpersonal Psychotherapy

Interracial Adoption 1994
PN 156 **SC** 26265
UF Transracial Adoption
B Adoption (Child) 1967
R Adopted Children 1973
↓ Adoptees 1985
Adoptive Parents 1973
Interethnic Family 1988
Interracial Family 1988

Interracial Family 1988
PN 67 **SC** 26270
B Family 1967
R Interethnic Family 1988
Interracial Adoption 1994
Interracial Marriage 1973
Interracial Offspring 1988
Racial and Ethnic Differences 1982
Racial and Ethnic Relations 1982

Interracial Marriage 1973
PN 243 **SC** 26280
UF Miscegenous Marriage
B Exogamous Marriage 1973
R Interracial Family 1988
Interracial Offspring 1988
Racial and Ethnic Relations 1982

Interracial Offspring 1988
PN 269 **SC** 26282
UF Biracial Children
B Offspring 1988
R Interracial Family 1988
Interracial Marriage 1973
Racial and Ethnic Differences 1982
Racial and Ethnic Relations 1982

Interrater Reliability 1982
PN 2139 **SC** 26284
SN Statistically measured correspondence between judgments by observers of a common event.
UF Interobserver Reliability
R Observation Methods 1967
Rating 1967
Statistical Reliability 1973
Test Reliability 1973

Interresponse Time 1973
PN 307 **SC** 26290
SN Interval between successive responses.
B Response Parameters 1973
Time 1967
R Response Frequency 1973

Interrogation 2005
PN 400 **SC** 26291
HN In August 2005, this term was created to replace the discontinued term LEGAL INTERROGATION. LEGAL INTERROGATION was removed from all records containing it and replaced with INTERROGATION.

Interrogation — (cont'd)
UF Criminal Interrogation
Legal Interrogation
Police Interrogation
R Cross Examination 2005
Interviewing 1973
↓ Law Enforcement 1978
Legal Confession 2003
Legal Detention 1973
↓ Legal Testimony 1982
Polygraphs 1973
Questioning 1982

Intersensory Integration
Use Sensory Integration

Intersensory Processes 1978
PN 1409 **SC** 26295
B Perception 1967
N Sensory Integration 1991
Synesthesia 2003
R Perceptual Motor Development 1991
↓ Perceptual Motor Processes 1967

Intersexuality
Use Hermaphroditism

Interspecies Interaction 1991
PN 1420 **SC** 26297
SN Social behavior involving members of two or more animal species including humans and animals.
UF Animal Human Interaction
Human Animal Interaction
B Social Behavior 1967
R Animal Assisted Therapy 1994
↓ Animal Social Behavior 1967
↓ Animals 1967
Biological Symbiosis 1973
Pets 1982
Species Differences 1982

Interstimulus Interval 1967
PN 2354 **SC** 26300
SN In conditioning contexts, the temporal interval separating the conditioned stimulus and unconditioned stimulus or the temporal interval between the elements of a multiple component (i.e., compound) stimulus.
B Stimulus Intervals 1973
R Reinforcement Delay 1985

Intertrial Interval 1973
PN 1050 **SC** 26310
SN Temporal interval between successive discrete trials in conditioning or learning contexts.
B Stimulus Intervals 1973

Interval Reinforcement
Use Fixed Interval Reinforcement AND Variable Interval Reinforcement

Intervention 2003
PN 6548 **SC** 26323
SN Intervening on the behalf of one or more individuals. Use a more specific term if possible.
HN This term was introduced in June 2003. Relevant records were re-indexed with this term. The posting note reflects the number of records that were re-indexed.
N ↓ Crisis Intervention 1973
Early Intervention 1982
Family Intervention 2003
School Based Intervention 2003

Intervention — (cont'd)
R At Risk Populations 1985
↓ Crisis Intervention Services 1973
↓ Prevention 1973
↓ Rehabilitation 1967
↓ Treatment 1967

Interview Schedules 2001
PN 52 **SC** 26325
SN Precoded questionnaires for gathering data, which are completed during interviews.
B Interviews 1967
N Diagnostic Interview Schedule 1991
Structured Clinical Interview 2001
R Intake Interview 1994
↓ Psychiatric Evaluation 1997
↓ Psychological Assessment 1997

Interviewers 1988
PN 410 **SC** 26330
R Interviewing 1973
↓ Interviews 1967

Interviewing 1973
PN 2218 **SC** 26340
SN Used for the methods, techniques, principles, and practice of interviewing.
B Interpersonal Communication 1973
R Interrogation 2005
Interviewers 1988
↓ Interviews 1967
Microcounseling 1978
Questioning 1982

Interviews 1967
PN 3828 **SC** 26350
B Interpersonal Communication 1973
N Intake Interview 1994
↓ Interview Schedules 2001
Job Applicant Interviews 1973
↓ Psychodiagnostic Interview 1973
R Interviewers 1988
Interviewing 1973
↓ Measurement 1967
Qualitative Research 2003
Questioning 1982

Intestines 1973
PN 211 **SC** 26360
UF Duodenum
Ileum
B Gastrointestinal System 1973
R Absorption (Physiological) 1973

Intimacy 1973
PN 4006 **SC** 26370
R Affection 1973
Attachment Behavior 1985
↓ Interpersonal Interaction 1967
Love 1973
Physical Contact 1982
Romance 1997

Intimate Partner Violence 2007
PN 506 **SC** 26373
SN Actual or threatened physical or sexual violence, or psychological and emotional abuse, directed toward a current or former spouse, boyfriend, girlfriend, or dating partner.
HN This term was introduced in April 2007. Relevant records were re-indexed with this term. The posting note reflects the number of records that were re-indexed.

Intimate Partner Violence — (cont'd)
B Partner Abuse 1991
Violence 1973
R Domestic Violence 2006

Intoxication
Use Toxic Disorders

Intoxication (Alcohol)
Use Alcohol Intoxication

Intra Aural Muscle Reflex
Use Acoustic Reflex

Intracranial Self Stimulation
Use Brain Self Stimulation

Intramuscular Injections 1973
PN 89 **SC** 26400
B Injections 1973

Intraperitoneal Injections 1973
PN 86 **SC** 26410
B Injections 1973

Intrauterine Devices 1973
PN 32 **SC** 26420
B Contraceptive Devices 1973

Intravenous Drug Usage 1994
PN 1776 **SC** 26425
UF IV Drug Usage
B Drug Usage 1971
R Disease Transmission 2004
↓ Drug Abuse 1973
↓ Drug Addiction 1967
Intravenous Injections 1973
Needle Exchange Programs 2001
Needle Sharing 1994

Intravenous Injections 1973
PN 681 **SC** 26430
B Injections 1973
R Intravenous Drug Usage 1994
Needle Sharing 1994

Intrinsic Motivation 1973
PN 1852 **SC** 26440
SN Need or desire which arises from within the individual and causes action toward some goal.
B Motivation 1967
R ↓ Goals 1967
Internal External Locus of Control 1967
Internal Rewards 1973
Need for Cognition 1997
↓ Needs 1967

Intrinsic Rewards
Use Internal Rewards

Introjection 1973
PN 177 **SC** 26460
B Defense Mechanisms 1967
Internalization 1997
R Identification (Defense Mechanism) 1973

Introspection 1973
PN 459 **SC** 26470
B Personality Processes 1967
R Reflectiveness 1997
Self Monitoring (Personality) 1985
Self Perception 1967

Introversion 1967
PN 1329 **SC** 26480
B Personality Traits 1967
R Extraversion 1967

Intuition 1973
PN 973 **SC** 26485
B Cognitive Processes 1967
R Cognition 1967
↓ Comprehension 1967
Guessing 1973
Insight 1973

Inuit 2001
PN 295 **SC** 26487
HN In 2001, this term was created to replace the discontinued term ESKIMOS. ESKIMOS was removed from all records containing it and replaced with INUIT.
UF Eskimos
B Indigenous Populations 2001
R Alaska Natives 1997
American Indians 1967
Minority Groups 1967
↓ Pacific Islanders 2001

Inventories 1967
PN 5621 **SC** 26490
B Measurement 1967
N Biographical Inventories 1973
Interest Inventories 1973

Invertebrates 1973
PN 338 **SC** 26540
B Animals 1967
N ↓ Arthropoda 1973
Echinodermata 1973
↓ Mollusca 1973
↓ Worms 1967
R ↓ Vertebrates 1973

Investigation
Use Experimentation

Investments (Business)
Use Business Investments

Involuntary Smoking
Use Passive Smoking

Involuntary Treatment 1994
PN 587 **SC** 26555
SN The treatment of people diagnosed with a mental illness against their will.
B Treatment 1967
R ↓ Client Rights 1988
↓ Commitment (Psychiatric) 1973
Court Referrals 1994
Informed Consent 1985
Right to Treatment 1997
Treatment Compliance 1982
Treatment Dropouts 1978
Treatment Refusal 1994

Involvement 1973
PN 3294 **SC** 26575
B Social Behavior 1967
N Community Involvement 2003
Job Involvement 1978
Parental Involvement 2005
R ↓ Commitment 1985
Empowerment 1991
↓ Participation 1973

Involvement — (cont'd)
Student Engagement 2006

Ions
Use Electrolytes

Iowa Tests of Basic Skills 1973
PN 55 **SC** 26590
B Achievement Measures 1967

Iproniazid 1973
PN 17 **SC** 26600
B Amine Oxidase Inhibitors 1973
Antidepressant Drugs 1971
Antihypertensive Drugs 1973
Antitubercular Drugs 1973
Monoamine Oxidase Inhibitors 1973

Iris (Eye) 1973
PN 57 **SC** 26630
B Eye (Anatomy) 1967
R Eye Color 1991

Iron 1973
PN 231 **SC** 26640
B Metallic Elements 1973

Irradiation
Use Radiation

Irrational Beliefs 1982
PN 920 **SC** 26654
SN Erroneous or distorted convictions or ideas firmly held despite objective and obvious contradictory proof or evidence.
B Cognitions 1985
R ↓ Attitudes 1967
False Beliefs 2007
Superstitions 1973

Irritability 1988
PN 333 **SC** 26658
SN Used for human or animal populations.
B Personality Traits 1967
R ↓ Emotional States 1973

Irritable Bowel Syndrome 1991
PN 405 **SC** 26659
SN Functional disorder of the colon that is generally psychosomatic.
B Colon Disorders 1973
Syndromes 1973
R ↓ Colitis 1973
↓ Somatoform Disorders 2001

Ischemia 1973
PN 557 **SC** 26660
SN A decrease in blood supply to a bodily organ, tissue, or part caused by vasoconstriction or obstruction of the inflow of arterial blood.
B Cardiovascular Disorders 1967
N Cerebral Ischemia 1973
R Anoxia 1973

Islam 1973
PN 727 **SC** 26670
B Religious Affiliation 1973
R Muslims 1997

Isocarboxazid 1973
PN 33 **SC** 26680
B Amine Oxidase Inhibitors 1973
Antidepressant Drugs 1971
Monoamine Oxidase Inhibitors 1973

Isoenzymes
Use Isozymes

Isolation (Defense Mechanism) 1973
PN 156 **SC** 26700
SN Unconscious separation of an unacceptable impulse, idea, or act from its original memory source, removing the emotional charge associated with the original memory.
B Defense Mechanisms 1967
R Intellectualization 1973

Isolation (Social)
Use Social Isolation

Isolation Effect 1973
PN 248 **SC** 26720
SN Facilitating effect of isolation of distinctive features of an item (e.g., type face, color) in learning.
B Associative Processes 1967
R Cues 1967
Stimulus Salience 1973
↓ Verbal Learning 1967

Isoniazid 1973
PN 32 **SC** 26730
B Antitubercular Drugs 1973

Isoproterenol 1973
PN 157 **SC** 26740
B Alcohols 1967
Sympathomimetic Drugs 1973

Isozymes 1973
PN 67 **SC** 26750
UF Isoenzymes
B Enzymes 1973

Itching
Use Pruritus

Item Analysis (Statistical) 1973
PN 1154 **SC** 26800
SN Quantitative analysis of a test item, especially regarding its difficulty level and validity.
B Factor Analysis 1967
R Adaptive Testing 1985
Item Response Theory 1985
Statistical Weighting 1985
Test Items 1973

Item Analysis (Test) 1967
PN 1617 **SC** 26810
SN Qualitative analysis of a test item, especially regarding its content and form.
B Analysis 1967
Test Construction 1973
Testing 1967
R Item Content (Test) 1973
Test Items 1973

Item Bias
Use Test Bias

Item Content (Test) 1973
PN 526 **SC** 26820
SN Topics or subject matter covered in test questions, units, or tasks.
B Test Construction 1973
Testing 1967
R Item Analysis (Test) 1967
Test Forms 1988
Test Items 1973

Item Response Theory 1985
PN 2187 **SC** 26825
SN A statistical approach in psychological measurement. Also known as item characteristic curve theory.
UF Latent Trait Theory
Logistic Models
Rasch Model
B Testing 1967
Theories 1967
R Classical Test Theory 2003
Difficulty Level (Test) 1973
Item Analysis (Statistical) 1973
Psychometrics 1967
↓ Test Scores 1967

IV Drug Usage
Use Intravenous Drug Usage

Jails
Use Prisons

James (William) 1991
PN 355 **SC** 26855
SN Identifies biographical or autobiographical studies and discussions of James's works.
R Functionalism 1973
↓ Psychologists 1967

Japanese Americans 1973
PN 75 **SC** 26863

Japanese Cultural Groups 1997
PN 433 **SC** 26865
HN Use ASIANS to access references from 1982-1996.
B Asians 1982

Jaundice 1973
PN 44 **SC** 26870
B Digestive System Disorders 1973
Liver Disorders 1973
R Cirrhosis (Liver) 1973
↓ Hepatitis 1973
↓ Infectious Disorders 1973

Jaw 1973
PN 346 **SC** 26880
UF Mandibula
Maxilla
B Musculoskeletal System 1973
R Bones 1973

Jealousy 1973
PN 901 **SC** 26890
UF Envy
B Emotional States 1973
R ↓ Anger 1967
↓ Anxiety 1967

Jews 1997
PN 906 **SC** 26900
HN Use JUDAISM to access references prior to 1997.
B Religious Groups 1997
R AntiSemitism 1973
Holocaust 1988
Holocaust Survivors 1988
Judaism 1967
Minority Groups 1967

Job Analysis 1967
PN 1765 **SC** 26910
SN Analysis specifying job duties, responsibilities, and technical components.
B Analysis 1967
Human Resource Management 2003
R ↓ Job Characteristics 1985
Task Analysis 1967
Work Load 1982

Job Applicant Attitudes 1973
PN 329 **SC** 26920
SN Attitudes of, not toward, job applicants.
B Attitudes 1967
R Job Applicants 1985
Job Search 1985
Occupational Attitudes 1973
↓ Personnel 1967

Job Applicant Interviews 1973
PN 904 **SC** 26930
UF Employment Interviews
B Interpersonal Communication 1973
Interviews 1967
Personnel Selection 1967
R Job Search 1985
↓ Personnel Evaluation 1973
↓ Personnel Recruitment 1973

Job Applicant Screening 1973
PN 883 **SC** 26940
UF Testing (Job Applicants)
B Personnel Selection 1967
Screening 1982
R Employment Discrimination 1994
Employment Tests 1973
Job Search 1985
↓ Personnel Evaluation 1973
↓ Personnel Recruitment 1973

Job Applicants 1985
PN 764 **SC** 26953
SN Persons seeking employment.
R ↓ Employment Status 1982
Job Applicant Attitudes 1973
Job Search 1985
↓ Personnel 1967

Job Change
Use Career Change

Job Characteristics 1985
PN 3121 **SC** 26957
SN Responsibilities or tasks that characterize a specific job.
UF Job Duties
Job Functions
N Work Load 1982
R Job Analysis 1967
↓ Occupations 1967
Quality of Work Life 1988

Job Corps 1973
PN 36 **SC** 26960
SN U.S. Government program of vocational and psychosocial training and counseling for disadvantaged adolescents and adults.
B Government Programs 1973
R Government 1967

Job Discrimination
Use Employment Discrimination

Job Duties
Use Job Characteristics

Job Enrichment 1973
PN 150 **SC** 26980
SN Formal or informal programs or techniques used to enhance the quality of a job or to further challenge the employee.
B Working Conditions 1973
R Job Experience Level 1973
Job Satisfaction 1967
Occupational Guidance 1967
Occupational Mobility 1973
↓ Personnel Training 1967

Job Experience Level 1973
PN 2414 **SC** 26990
UF Experience Level (Job)
B Employee Characteristics 1988
Experience Level 1988
R Employment History 1978
Job Enrichment 1973
Job Knowledge 1997
Occupational Status 1978

Job Family Relationship
Use Family Work Relationship

Job Functions
Use Job Characteristics

Job Involvement 1978
PN 1412 **SC** 26994
B Involvement 1973
R ↓ Employee Attitudes 1967
Employee Motivation 1973
↓ Job Performance 1967
Job Satisfaction 1967
Organizational Commitment 1991
Participative Management 1988
Work (Attitudes Toward) 1973

Job Knowledge 1997
PN 457 **SC** 26996
B Employee Characteristics 1988
Knowledge Level 1978
R ↓ Employee Skills 1973
Job Experience Level 1973
↓ Job Performance 1967
Knowledge Management 2005

Job Mobility
Use Occupational Mobility

Job Performance 1967
PN 10384 **SC** 27010
B Performance 1967
N Employee Efficiency 1973
Employee Productivity 1973
R ↓ Employee Attitudes 1967
Job Involvement 1978
Job Knowledge 1997
Organizational Commitment 1991
↓ Personnel 1967
↓ Personnel Evaluation 1973
Personnel Promotion 1978
Work Load 1982

Job Promotion
Use Personnel Promotion

Job Reentry
Use Reemployment

Job Satisfaction 1967
PN 10902 **SC** 27040
SN Positive attitudes toward one's work when tangible and/or intangible rewards fulfill expectations.
UF Work Satisfaction
B Employee Attitudes 1967
Satisfaction 1973
R Career Change 1978
Job Enrichment 1973
Job Involvement 1978
Organizational Commitment 1991
Quality of Work Life 1988
Role Satisfaction 1994

Job Search 1985
PN 645 **SC** 27043
SN Process of seeking employment. For consideration of career alternatives use CAREER EDUCATION.
R Job Applicant Attitudes 1973
Job Applicant Interviews 1973
Job Applicant Screening 1973
Job Applicants 1985
Reemployment 1991
Unemployment 1967

Job Security 1978
PN 360 **SC** 27045
SN Probable assurance of continued employment.
R Downsizing 2003
Economic Security 2007
Employee Turnover 1973
↓ Occupational Tenure 1973
Personnel Termination 1973
Retirement 1973
Unemployment 1967

Job Selection
Use Occupational Choice

Job Status
Use Occupational Status

Job Stress
Use Occupational Stress

Job Training
Use Personnel Training

Jobs
Use Occupations

Joint Custody 1988
PN 123 **SC** 27065
R Child Custody 1982
Child Support 1988
Divorce 1973

Joint Disorders 1973
PN 128 **SC** 27070
B Musculoskeletal Disorders 1973
N ↓ Arthritis 1973
R ↓ Joints (Anatomy) 1973

Joints (Anatomy) 1973
PN 253 **SC** 27080
B Musculoskeletal System 1973
N Ankle 1973
Elbow (Anatomy) 1973
Knee 1973
Shoulder (Anatomy) 1973
Wrist 1973
R ↓ Joint Disorders 1973
Range of Motion 2007

Jokes 1973
PN 339 **SC** 27090
B Humor 1967
R Teasing 2003

Journalists 1973
PN 338 **SC** 27100
B Professional Personnel 1978
R ↓ News Media 1997

Joy
Use Happiness

Judaism 1967
PN 1785 **SC** 27130
B Religious Affiliation 1973
R AntiSemitism 1973
Bible 1973
Holocaust 1988
Jews 1997
Rabbis 1973

Judges 1985
PN 525 **SC** 27135
B Legal Personnel 1985

Judgment 1967
PN 9051 **SC** 27140
SN Mental act of comparing or evaluating choices within a given set of values frequently with the purpose of choosing a course of action.
N Clinical Judgment (Not Diagnosis) 1973
Probability Judgment 1978
R Assimilation (Cognitive Process) 2007
↓ Decision Making 1967
Judgment Disturbances 1973
Uncertainty 1991
Wisdom 1994

Judgment Disturbances 1973
PN 17 **SC** 27150
SN Maladaptive judgment resulting from wish-fulfilling, impulsive decisions based on need for immediate infantile gratification.
B Thought Disturbances 1973
R ↓ Judgment 1967

Judo 1973
PN 60 **SC** 27160
B Recreation 1967
Sports 1967
R Martial Arts 1985

Jumping 1973
PN 159 **SC** 27170
B Motor Performance 1973
Motor Processes 1967

Jung (Carl) 1973
PN 1192 **SC** 27180
SN Identifies biographical or autobiographical studies and discussions of Jung's works.
R Analytical Psychotherapy 1973
Archetypes 1991
↓ Collective Unconscious 1997
↓ Jungian Psychology 1973
↓ Psychologists 1967

Jungian Psychology 1973
PN 2695 **SC** 27190
SN Analytical psychology characterized by theories of the collective unconscious, the archetype, the complex, and psychological types.

Jungian Psychology — (cont'd)
UF Analytic Psychology
B Neopsychoanalytic School 1973
N ↓ Collective Unconscious 1997
R Analytical Psychotherapy 1973
Archetypes 1991
Free Association 1994
Jung (Carl) 1973

Jungian Psychotherapy
Use Analytical Psychotherapy

Junior College Students 1973
PN 212 **SC** 27200
SN Students in two-year colleges.
B College Students 1967
R Community College Students 1973

Junior Colleges
Use Colleges

Junior High School Students 1971
PN 10879 **SC** 27220
SN Students in 7th and 8th grade. Sometimes includes students in 9th grade.
B Students 1967
R Grade Level 1994
Middle School Students 1985

Junior High School Teachers 1973
PN 1557 **SC** 27230
B Teachers 1967
R Middle School Teachers 2003

Junior High Schools 1973
PN 380 **SC** 27240
B Schools 1967
R Middle Schools 2003
Secondary Education 1973

Juries 1985
PN 1338 **SC** 27245
SN Bodies of persons sworn to give a verdict in a court of law. Also used for mock and simulated juries.
HN Use ADJUDICATION to access references from 1973-1984.
R ↓ Adjudication 1967
Awards (Jury) 2005
Jury Selection 1994
↓ Legal Personnel 1985

Jury Selection 1994
PN 74 **SC** 27252
HN Use JURIES to access references from 1985-1993.
R ↓ Adjudication 1967
Juries 1985

Justice 1973
PN 3123 **SC** 27260
SN Used for the impartial and fair settlement of conflict and differences, or the designation of rewards or punishment.
N ↓ Criminal Justice 1991
Procedural Justice 2003
↓ Social Justice 2006
R ↓ Civil Rights 1978
Equity (Payment) 1978
↓ Equity (Social) 1978
Freedom 1978
↓ Law (Government) 1973
↓ Law Enforcement 1978
Morality 1967
Reward Allocation 1988

Justice — (cont'd)
Social Equality 1973
↓ Social Issues 1991

Juvenile Court
Use Adjudication

Juvenile Delinquency 1967
PN 9902 **SC** 27280
SN Behavior of children or adolescents that is antisocial, dangerous, or criminal, and usually subject to legal action. The age at which juveniles become adults varies across countries and cultures, but usually ranges from 15-18 years.
HN In 2000, this term became the postable counterpart for the discontinued term JUVENILE DELINQUENTS. JUVENILE DELINQUENTS was removed from all records containing it and replaced with JUVENILE DELINQUENCY.
UF Delinquency (Juvenile)
Offenders (Juvenile)
B Antisocial Behavior 1971
Behavior Disorders 1971
Criminal Behavior 2003
N Female Delinquency 2001
Male Delinquency 2001
R Antisocial Personality Disorder 1973
Crime Prevention 1985
↓ Criminals 1967
Juvenile Gangs 1973
Juvenile Justice 2004
Predelinquent Youth 1978

Juvenile Gangs 1973
PN 689 **SC** 27300
UF Gangs (Juvenile)
R ↓ Juvenile Delinquency 1967
Juvenile Justice 2004

Juvenile Justice 2004
PN 582 **SC** 27303
SN Conceptually broad term referring to the laws, legal services and programs, and judicial institutions that deal with delinquent and/or exploited children and adolescents.
HN This term was introduced in June 2004. Relevant records were re-indexed with this term. The posting note reflects the number of records that were re-indexed.
B Criminal Justice 1991
R ↓ Adjudication 1967
Child Welfare 1988
↓ Juvenile Delinquency 1967
Juvenile Gangs 1973
Predelinquent Youth 1978

Kainic Acid 1988
PN 238 **SC** 27305
B Acids 1973
R Glutamic Acid 1973
↓ Neurotoxins 1982

Kangaroos 1973
PN 23 **SC** 27310
B Marsupials 1973

Karate
Use Martial Arts

Karyotype Disorders
Use Chromosome Disorders

Kaufman Assessment Battery for Children 2001
PN 189 **SC** 27323
HN In 2000, the truncated term KAUFMAN ASSESSMENT BATTERY CHILDREN (which was used from 1988-2000) was deleted, removed from all records containing it, and replaced with its expanded form KAUFMAN ASSESSMENT BATTERY FOR CHILDREN.
B Intelligence Measures 1967

Ketamine 1997
PN 372 **SC** 27327
B Anesthetic Drugs 1973

Keyboards 1985
PN 129 **SC** 27328
B Apparatus 1967
R ↓ Computer Peripheral Devices 1985
↓ Human Computer Interaction 1997
↓ Instrument Controls 1985
Typing 1991

Keypunch Operators
Use Clerical Personnel

Kibbutz 1973
PN 401 **SC** 27340
B Communes 1973

Kidnapping 1988
PN 155 **SC** 27345
UF Child Abduction
B Crime 1967
R Hostages 1988
Human Trafficking 2007
Missing Children 2007
↓ Violent Crime 2003

Kidney Diseases 1988
PN 665 **SC** 27347
UF Renal Diseases
B Urogenital Disorders 1973

Kidney Transplants
Use Organ Transplantation

Kidneys 1973
PN 357 **SC** 27360
B Urogenital System 1973

Kinases 1982
PN 997 **SC** 27366
SN Enzymes that catalyze the conversion of proenzymes to active enzymes or the transfer of phosphate groups to form triphosphates (ATP).
UF Enteropeptidase
B Enzymes 1973

Kindergarten Students 1973
PN 3836 **SC** 27370
SN Students in kindergarten.
B Students 1967
R Grade Level 1994
↓ Preschool Students 1982

Kindergartens 1973
PN 542 **SC** 27380
B Schools 1967

Kindling 1985
PN 409 **SC** 27385
SN Afterdischarges and generalized convulsions produced by repeated brain stimulation, usually electrical. Often used as an experimental model of epilepsy.
B Electrical Activity 1967
R Electrical Brain Stimulation 1973
Experimental Epilepsy 1978

Kinesics
Use Body Language

Kinesthetic Perception 1967
PN 1294 **SC** 27390
SN Sensory modality involving awareness of body movement, position, and posture, and movement of body parts, such as muscles, tendons, and joints. Used for human or animal populations.
B Somesthetic Perception 1967
R Spatial Orientation (Perception) 1973

Kinship 1985
PN 837 **SC** 27395
SN The state of being related such as by birth, common ancestry, or marriage. Used for human or animal populations.
B Interpersonal Relationships 2004
R Ethnology 1967
↓ Family 1967
Kinship Recognition 1988
Kinship Structure 1973

Kinship Recognition 1988
PN 437 **SC** 27399
R ↓ Discrimination Learning 1982
Kinship 1985
Species Recognition 1985

Kinship Structure 1973
PN 227 **SC** 27400
R Ethnography 1973
Ethnology 1967
↓ Family Structure 1973
Kinship 1985
↓ Sociocultural Factors 1967

Kirton Adaption Innovation Inventory 2001
PN 12 **SC** 27411
HN In 2000, the truncated term KIRTON ADAPTION INNOVATION INVEN (which was used from 1997-2000) was deleted, removed from all records containing it, and replaced with its expanded form KIRTON ADAPTION INNOVATION INVENTORY.
B Personality Measures 1967

Kleine Levin Syndrome 2001
PN 15 **SC** 27415
SN A condition characterized by recurrent hypersomnia and hyperphagia and marked by such symptoms as mental confusion, excessive sleep requirements, restlessness, and hallucinations.
B Eating Disorders 1997
Sleep Disorders 1973
Syndromes 1973
R Hyperphagia 1973
Hypersomnia 1994

Kleptomania 1973
PN 113 **SC** 27420
R ↓ Impulse Control Disorders 1997
Impulsiveness 1973
↓ Personality Disorders 1967

Klinefelters Syndrome 1973
PN 105 **SC** 27430
SN A condition in males caused by the abnormal presence of two X chromosomes and one Y chromosome resulting in small testes, infertility, and underdevelopment of secondary sex characteristics.
B Hypogonadism 1973
Male Genital Disorders 1973
Neonatal Disorders 1973
Sex Chromosome Disorders 1973
Syndromes 1973
R Hermaphroditism 1973
↓ Infertility 1973
↓ Mental Retardation 1967

Knee 1973
PN 245 **SC** 27440
B Joints (Anatomy) 1973
R Leg (Anatomy) 1973

Knowledge Based Systems
Use Expert Systems

Knowledge Economy 2007
PN 33 **SC** 58107
SN An economy that utilizes knowledge-intensive activities for the production of goods and services. Such an economy is characterized by reliance on science, research, technology, innovation, computers, and the Internet.
HN This term was introduced in April 2007. Relevant records were re-indexed with this term. The posting note reflects the number of records that were re-indexed.
B Economy 1973
R ↓ Communication Systems 1973
↓ Information Systems 1991
Knowledge Management 2005

Knowledge Engineering 2003
PN 124 **SC** 27444
SN The process of creating intelligent systems. Used in artificial intelligence discussions.
HN This term was introduced in June 2003. Relevant records were re-indexed with this term. The posting note reflects the number of records that were re-indexed.
B Artificial Intelligence 1982
R Decision Support Systems 1997
↓ Expert Systems 1991
Inductive Logic Programming 2007
↓ Information Systems 1991

Knowledge Level 1978
PN 13558 **SC** 27446
SN Range of received or acquired information, understanding, or awareness. Limited to human populations.
N Health Knowledge 1994
Job Knowledge 1997
R Declarative Knowledge 1997
↓ Experience Level 1988
Information 1967
Knowledge Management 2005
Procedural Knowledge 1997
Wisdom 1994

Knowledge Management 2005
PN 393 **SC** 27448
SN The development, management, and dissemination of an organization's intellectual and knowledge-based assets, generally through the use of computer technology.
HN This term was introduced in August 2005. Relevant records were re-indexed with this term. The posting note reflects the number of records that were re-indexed.
R Business Management 1973
↓ Expert Systems 1991
↓ Information Systems 1991
Job Knowledge 1997
Knowledge Economy 2007
↓ Knowledge Level 1978
Knowledge Transfer 2007
Ontologies 2007
Technology Transfer 2007

Knowledge of Results 1967
PN 638 **SC** 27450
B Feedback 1967

Knowledge Transfer 2007
PN 165 **SC** 27452
SN Transferring or sharing knowledge, ideas, skills, information, or experience from one individual or organization to another.
HN This term was introduced in April 2007. Relevant records were re-indexed with this term. The posting note reflects the number of records that were re-indexed.
R ↓ Communication 1967
Information Dissemination 2005
Knowledge Management 2005
Research and Development 2007

Kohlberg (Lawrence) 1991
PN 132 **SC** 27455
SN Identifies biographical or autobiographical studies and discussions of Kohlberg's works.
R Moral Development 1973
↓ Psychologists 1967

Kohs Block Design Test 1973
PN 42 **SC** 27460
UF Block Design Test (Kohs)
B Intelligence Measures 1967

Korean Cultural Groups 1997
PN 458 **SC** 27483
HN Use ASIANS to access references from 1982-1996.
B Asians 1982

Koro 1994
PN 46 **SC** 27485
SN A mental disorder characterized by fear or delusions of the shrinkage of the penis, labia, or breasts into the abdomen or chest. Observed primarily in Southern Chinese and some African cultures.
B Body Image Disturbances 1973
Culture Bound Syndromes 2004
Mental Disorders 1967

Korsakoffs Psychosis 1973
PN 528 **SC** 27490
SN In chronic alcoholism, a form of amnesia with loss of short term memory, often characterized by disorientation, delirium, and hallucinations. The individual may confabulate to conceal the condition.

Korsakoffs Psychosis — (cont'd)
UF Alcoholic Korsakoffs Syndrome
B Alcoholic Hallucinosis 1973
R ↓ Amnesia 1967
Confabulation 1973
Wernickes Syndrome 1973

Kuder Occupational Interest Survey 1973
PN 49 **SC** 27510
B Occupational Interest Measures 1973

Kuder Preference Record 1973
PN 27 **SC** 27520
B Preference Measures 1973

Kupfer Detre Self Rating Scale
HN Term was discontinued in 1997. In 2000, the term was removed from all records containing it, and replaced with NONPROJECTIVE PERSONALITY MEASURES, its postable counterpart.
Use Nonprojective Personality Measures

Kwashiorkor 1973
PN 9 **SC** 27550
SN Protein deficiency in children resulting in retarded growth, changes in skin and hair pigment, edema, and pathologic changes in the liver.
B Protein Deficiency Disorders 1973

L Dopa
Use Levodopa

Labeling 1978
PN 1560 **SC** 27565
SN In social or therapeutic settings, designating the condition of an individual or group by a simplistic word or phrase which may serve to indicate status, stigma, or other characteristics.
R ↓ Attitudes 1967
↓ Diagnosis 1967
↓ Names 1985
↓ Psychodiagnostic Typologies 1967
↓ Social Perception 1967
Stereotyped Attitudes 1967
Stigma 1991

Labor (Childbirth) 1973
PN 522 **SC** 27570
R ↓ Birth 1967
Childbirth Training 1978
Midwifery 1985
Obstetrical Complications 1978

Labor Management Relations 1967
PN 983 **SC** 27580
UF Labor Relations
B Human Resource Management 2003
R Informants 1988
Labor Unions 1973
↓ Management 1967
Mediation 1988
↓ Organizational Behavior 1978
Psychological Contracts 2003
Strikes 1973
Supervisor Employee Interaction 1997

Labor Market 2007
PN 514 **SC** 27583
SN The market where labor supply and demand interact; workers compete for jobs and employers compete for workers.
HN This term was introduced in April 2007. Relevant records were re-indexed with this term. The posting note reflects the number of records that were re-indexed.
R Human Capital 2003
↓ Human Resource Management 2003
Outsourcing 2007
↓ Personnel 1967
↓ Personnel Supply 1973
Supply and Demand 2004

Labor Relations
Use Labor Management Relations

Labor Union Members 1973
PN 295 **SC** 27600
R ↓ Personnel 1967

Labor Unions 1973
PN 642 **SC** 27610
B Organizations 1967
R Labor Management Relations 1967

Laboratories (Educational)
Use Educational Laboratories

Laboratories (Experimental)
Use Experimental Laboratories

Laborers (Construction and Industry)
Use Blue Collar Workers

Laborers (Farm)
Use Agricultural Workers

Labyrinth (Anatomy) 1973
PN 181 **SC** 27660
SN The bony structure of the inner ear that houses the membranous labyrinth (i.e., the cochlea, vestibule, semicircular canals, utricle, and saccule). May also refer to these latter membranous structures.
UF Inner Ear
B Ear (Anatomy) 1967
N Cochlea 1973
R ↓ Vestibular Apparatus 1967

Labyrinth (Apparatus)
Use Mazes

Labyrinth Disorders 1973
PN 101 **SC** 27680
SN Balance disorders caused by disruptions in the labyrinth, an organ in the inner ear that is part of the vestibular system and which is responsible for maintaining balance and orienting the body in the environment.
UF Vestibular Disorders
B Ear Disorders 1973
N Menieres Disease 1973
Motion Sickness 1973
R Equilibrium 1973
↓ Somesthetic Perception 1967
Vertigo 1973
↓ Vestibular Apparatus 1967

Lactate Dehydrogenase 1973
PN 27 **SC** 27690
B Dehydrogenases 1973

Lactation 1973
PN 821 **SC** 27700
B Secretion (Gland) 1973
R Breast Feeding 1973
Postnatal Period 1973

Lactic Acid 1991
PN 110 **SC** 27720
UF Sodium Lactate
B Acids 1973

Language 1967
PN 15574 **SC** 27740
N ↓ Dialect 1973
↓ Figurative Language 1985
Foreign Languages 1973
↓ Form Classes (Language) 1973
Native Language 2004
Phrases 1973
Profanity 1991
Rhetoric 1991
Sentences 1967
Sign Language 1973
Spelling 1973
↓ Vocabulary 1967
↓ Written Language 1967
R Bilingualism 1973
Discourse Analysis 1997
English as Second Language 1997
↓ Grammar 1967
↓ Language Development 1967
↓ Linguistics 1973
↓ Literacy 1973
Metalinguistics 1994
Monolingualism 1973
↓ Multilingualism 1973
Neurolinguistics 1991
Ontologies 2007
Symbolism 1967
↓ Verbal Communication 1967

Language Alternation
Use Code Switching

Language Arts Education 1973
PN 2433 **SC** 27750
SN Education in subjects aimed at development of comprehension and use of written and oral language.
B Curriculum 1967
N Phonics 1973
Reading Education 1973
Spelling 1973
R Computer Assisted Language Learning 2007
English as Second Language 1997
Initial Teaching Alphabet 1973
↓ Literacy 1973
Literacy Programs 1997

Language Delay 1988
PN 514 **SC** 27755
B Delayed Development 1973
Language Development 1967
R ↓ Language Disorders 1982
Retarded Speech Development 1973

Language Development 1967
PN 15092 **SC** 27760
SN Acquisition of the rules governing the structure of language (e.g., syntax) and meaning. Use SPEECH DEVELOPMENT for acquisition of speech sound production. Compare VERBAL LEARNING.
B Cognitive Development 1973
Intellectual Development 1973
N Language Delay 1988
R Computer Assisted Language Learning 2007
Foreign Language Learning 1967
↓ Language 1967
↓ Language Disorders 1982
Metalinguistics 1994
Reading Development 1997
↓ Speech Development 1973
↓ Verbal Communication 1967
Vygotsky (Lev) 1991

Language Disorders 1982
PN 4212 **SC** 27763
SN Disorders, usually due to cognitive or neurological dysfunction, resulting in problems in symbolization or in delays in language and speech development.
B Communication Disorders 1982
N ↓ Aphasia 1967
Echolalia 1973
↓ Mutism 1973
R Language Delay 1988
↓ Language Development 1967
Neurolinguistics 1991
↓ Speech Disorders 1967

Language Laboratories 1973
PN 10 **SC** 27770
B Educational Laboratories 1973
R Foreign Language Learning 1967
Learning Centers (Educational) 1973

Language Proficiency 1988
PN 1707 **SC** 27773
SN Accuracy and fluency of verbal communication in a second language learning or bilingual context. Includes concept of Limited English Proficiency, which is knowledge of English without sufficient proficiency to communicate or participate in an English-speaking society. Consider VERBAL FLUENCY for other contexts.
UF Limited English Proficiency
B Communication Skills 1973
Verbal Communication 1967
R Bilingualism 1973
English as Second Language 1997
Foreign Language Learning 1967
Verbal Ability 1967
Verbal Fluency 1973

Larvae 1973
PN 412 **SC** 27780
B Insects 1967
R Ants 1973
Bees 1973
Beetles 1973
Butterflies 1973
Cockroaches 1973
↓ Diptera 1973
Drosophila 1973
↓ Fishes 1967
Frogs 1967
Grasshoppers 1973
Mantis 1973
Moths 1973
Salamanders 1973

Larvae — (cont'd)
Toads 1973
Wasps 1982

Laryngeal Disorders 1973
PN 132 **SC** 27790
SN Disorders of the larynx that affect normal breathing, swallowing, and speaking. Damage to the larynx or its tissues can result in interference with any or all of these functions.
B Respiratory Tract Disorders 1973
R Dysphonia 1973

Larynx 1973
PN 213 **SC** 27800
B Respiratory System 1973
N Vocal Cords 1973

Laser Irradiation 1973
PN 51 **SC** 27810
B Radiation 1967

Latchkey Children
Use Child Self Care

Latency (Response)
Use Response Latency

Lateness
Use Tardiness

Latent Inhibition 1997
PN 477 **SC** 27825
B Interference (Learning) 1967
N Proactive Inhibition 1973
Retroactive Inhibition 1973
R Conditioned Stimulus 1973
↓ Conditioning 1967
Forgetting 1973
↓ Memory 1967
Prepulse Inhibition 1997

Latent Learning 1973
PN 138 **SC** 27830
SN Learning that is not immediately manifested in performance but which remains dormant until activated by some contingency. Use INCIDENTAL LEARNING for human populations.
HN From 1982, limited to animal populations.
B Incidental Learning 1967

Latent Trait Theory
Use Item Response Theory

Lateral Dominance 1967
PN 8637 **SC** 27840
SN The tendency for the right or left hemisphere to be dominant over the other for most functions, leading to a differential primacy, functional asymmetry, or preference for one side of the body. Compare CEREBRAL DOMINANCE.
UF Hemispheric Specialization
B Cerebral Dominance 1973
N Handedness 1978
Ocular Dominance 1973
R ↓ Brain 1967
Left Hemisphere 2005
Right Hemisphere 2005

Lateral Geniculate Nucleus
Use Geniculate Bodies (Thalamus)

Latinos/Latinas
Use Hispanics

Laughter 1978
PN 460 **SC** 27855
B Vocalization 1967
R ↓ Emotional Responses 1967
↓ Humor 1967
↓ Nonverbal Communication 1971
Smiles 1973

Law (Government) 1973
PN 466 **SC** 27860
SN Science and philosophy of law as sanctioned by governmental authority. For specific laws or statutes, use LAWS.
N Civil Law 1994
Criminal Law 1973
R Defendants 1985
Government 1967
↓ Justice 1973
↓ Law Enforcement 1978
↓ Laws 1967
Political Psychology 1997

Law Enforcement 1978
PN 1388 **SC** 27865
B Legal Processes 1973
N ↓ Adjudication 1967
Incarceration 1973
Legal Arrest 1973
Legal Detention 1973
R Civil Law 1994
Crime Prevention 1985
↓ Criminal Justice 1991
Government 1967
Interrogation 2005
↓ Justice 1973
↓ Law (Government) 1973
↓ Laws 1967
↓ Legal Evidence 1991
Parole 1973
Probation 1973

Law Enforcement Personnel 1973
PN 553 **SC** 27870
B Government Personnel 1973
Legal Personnel 1985
N Parole Officers 1973
Police Personnel 1973
Prison Personnel 1973
Probation Officers 1973
R Attorneys 1973
↓ Social Workers 1973

Law Students 1978
PN 241 **SC** 27875
B Students 1967
R Attorneys 1973
Graduate Students 1967

Laws 1967
PN 6861 **SC** 27880
SN Rules of conduct made obligatory by some legal or controlling authority; includes statutes enacted by a legislative body.
B Government Policy Making 1973
N Abortion Laws 1973
Disability Laws 1994
↓ Drug Laws 1973
Gun Control Laws 1973
R ↓ Abuse Reporting 1997
Censorship 1978
Citizenship 1973
↓ Civil Rights 1978
Consumer Protection 1973

Laws — (cont'd)
Government 1967
↓ Law (Government) 1973
↓ Law Enforcement 1978
Legal Decisions 1991
↓ Legal Processes 1973
Legislative Processes 1973
Litigation 2003

Lawsuits
Use Litigation

Lawyers
Use Attorneys

Lay Religious Personnel 1973
PN 87 **SC** 27900
SN Participants or members of a religious group or organization who perform various functional and ceremonial tasks not requiring a member of the clergy.
B Religious Personnel 1973
R Chaplains 1973
↓ Clergy 1973
Evangelists 1973
Missionaries 1973

Lead (Metal) 1973
PN 300 **SC** 27910
B Metallic Elements 1973

Lead Poisoning 1973
PN 392 **SC** 27920
B Toxic Disorders 1973
R Pica 1973

Leadership 1967
PN 8090 **SC** 27930
B Social Behavior 1967
N Leadership Qualities 1997
Leadership Style 1973
Transformational Leadership 2003
R Abuse of Power 1997
Authority 1967
Entrepreneurship 1991
↓ Management 1967

Leadership Qualities 1997
PN 660 **SC** 27935
B Leadership 1967
R Charisma 1988
Leadership Style 1973
↓ Management 1967
↓ Personality Traits 1967

Leadership Style 1973
PN 3468 **SC** 27940
B Leadership 1967
Social Behavior 1967
R Charisma 1988
Leadership Qualities 1997
Transformational Leadership 2003

Learned Helplessness 1978
PN 1726 **SC** 27945
SN Learned expectation that one's responses are independent of reward and, hence, do not predict or control the occurrence of rewards. Learned helplessness derives from a history, experimentally induced or naturally occurring, of having received punishment/aversive stimulation regardless of responses made. Such circumstances result in an impaired ability to learn. Used for human or animal populations.

Learned Helplessness — (cont'd)
UF Helplessness (Learned)
B Helplessness 1997
R Attribution 1973
↓ Emotional States 1973
Experimental Neurosis 1973

Learning 1967
PN 23831 SC 28030
SN Conceptually broad term referring to the process of acquiring knowledge, skills, or behaviors by instruction, study, or experience. Use a more specific term if possible.
N Adult Learning 1997
↓ Animal Learning 2003
Cat Learning 1967
Cognitive Hypothesis Testing 1982
Collaborative Learning 2007
↓ Conditioning 1967
Cooperative Learning 1994
↓ Discrimination Learning 1982
↓ Experiential Learning 1997
Extinction (Learning) 1967
Foreign Language Learning 1967
↓ Generalization (Learning) 1982
Generation Effect (Learning) 1991
Implicit Learning 2004
↓ Incidental Learning 1967
Intentional Learning 1973
↓ Interference (Learning) 1967
Mastery Learning 1985
Maze Learning 1967
Mnemonic Learning 1973
Nonverbal Learning 1973
Observational Learning 1973
Organizational Learning 2003
Overlearning 1967
↓ Perceptual Learning 2006
Probability Learning 1967
Rat Learning 1967
Relearning 1973
School Learning 1967
Self Regulated Learning 2003
Sequential Learning 1973
↓ Serial Learning 1967
↓ Skill Learning 1973
↓ Social Learning 1973
Spatial Learning 1994
Spontaneous Recovery (Learning) 1973
State Dependent Learning 1982
↓ Transfer (Learning) 1967
Trial and Error Learning 1973
↓ Verbal Learning 1967
R Activity Theory 2003
↓ Cognitive Processes 1967
↓ Concept Formation 1967
Connectionism 1994
Constructivism 1994
Delayed Alternation 1994
↓ Feedback 1967
Forgetting 1973
↓ Habits 1967
Individualized Instruction 1973
Intelligent Tutoring Systems 2003
Learning Ability 1973
↓ Learning Disorders 1967
Learning Environment 2004
Learning Rate 1973
↓ Learning Schedules 1967
↓ Learning Strategies 1991
Learning Theory 1967
↓ Machine Learning 2003
↓ Memory 1967

Learning — (cont'd)
Metacognition 1991
Primacy Effect 1973
↓ Prompting 1997
Recency Effect 1973
↓ Reinforcement 1967
↓ Retention 1967
↓ Serial Position Effect 1982
Spontaneous Alternation 1982
↓ Strategies 1967
Time On Task 1988

Learning Ability 1973
PN 1677 SC 27960
SN Capacity to acquire a behavior, skill, or knowledge from experience, formal instruction, or conditioning. Used for animal or human populations.
B Ability 1967
R ↓ Animal Learning 2003
↓ Learning 1967

Learning Centers (Educational) 1973
PN 109 SC 27970
B School Facilities 1973
R Language Laboratories 1973

Learning Disabilities 1973
PN 15417 SC 27980
SN According to U.S. federal legislation, disabilities involved in understanding or using language, manifested in impaired listening, thinking, talking, reading, writing, or arithmetic skills. Includes perceptual handicaps, brain injury, minimal brain dysfunction, and developmental aphasia. Compare LEARNING DISORDERS.
B Disabilities 2003
Learning Disorders 1967
N Dyslexia 1973
R Acalculia 1973
Agraphia 1973
↓ Aphasia 1967
Educational Diagnosis 1978
↓ Perceptual Disturbances 1973

Learning Disorders 1967
PN 1708 SC 27990
SN According to U.S. federal legislation, learning problems that are due to visual, hearing, or motor handicaps, mental retardation, emotional disturbance or environmental, cultural, or economic disadvantage. Compare LEARNING DISABILITIES.
B Disorders 1967
N ↓ Learning Disabilities 1973
↓ Reading Disabilities 1967
R Developmental Disabilities 1982
Educational Diagnosis 1978
↓ Learning 1967
↓ Mental Disorders 1967
↓ Physical Disorders 1997

Learning Environment 2004
PN 1384 SC 27991
SN Used for any environment where learning can occur. Not limited to educational settings.
HN This term was introduced in June 2004. Relevant records were re-indexed with this term. The posting note reflects the number of records that were re-indexed.
B Environment 1967
R ↓ Academic Environment 1973
Classroom Environment 1973
Home Environment 1973
↓ Learning 1967
↓ Learning Strategies 1991

Learning Environment — (cont'd)
↓ School Environment 1973
Virtual Classrooms 2007

Learning Organizations
Use Organizational Learning

Learning Rate 1973
PN 633 SC 28000
R ↓ Learning 1967
↓ Serial Position Effect 1982

Learning Schedules 1967
PN 121 SC 28010
UF Schedules (Learning)
N Distributed Practice 1973
Massed Practice 1973
R ↓ Learning 1967

Learning Strategies 1991
PN 3574 SC 28013
SN Techniques, methods, or tactics used for learning.
UF Strategies (Learning)
B Strategies 1967
N Mnemonic Learning 1973
Observational Learning 1973
↓ Social Learning 1973
Trial and Error Learning 1973
R Advance Organizers 1985
↓ Cognitive Processes 1967
↓ Cognitive Style 1967
Constant Time Delay 1997
↓ Learning 1967
Learning Environment 2004
Memory Training 1994
Metacognition 1991
Note Taking 1991
↓ Prompting 1997
Self Regulated Learning 2003
Service Learning 2007
Study Habits 1973
Time Management 1994

Learning Style
Use Cognitive Style

Learning Theory 1967
PN 2846 SC 28020
B Theories 1967
R ↓ Classical Conditioning 1967
Connectionism 1994
↓ Learning 1967
Multiple Intelligences 2007
↓ Operant Conditioning 1967

Least Preferred Coworker Scale 1973
PN 62 SC 28050
B Preference Measures 1973

Least Squares 1985
PN 271 SC 28055
SN Method of estimating the curve-of-best-fit or regression line of a set of points representing statistical data.
B Statistical Estimation 1985
R Error of Measurement 1985
↓ Statistical Regression 1985

Lecithin 1991
PN 11 SC 28058
B Choline 1973
Phosphatides 1973

Lecture Method 1973
PN 742 **SC** 28060
B Teaching Methods 1967
R Directed Discussion Method 1973

Left Brain
HN In August 2005, this term was discontinued and removed from all records containing it, and was replaced with LEFT HEMISPHERE, its postable counterpart.
Use Left Hemisphere

Left Hemisphere 2005
PN 852 **SC** 28073
SN Used only when the left hemisphere of the brain is the focus of the document.
HN In August 2005, this term was created to replace the discontinued term LEFT BRAIN. LEFT BRAIN was removed from all records containing it, and was replaced with LEFT HEMISPHERE, its postable counterpart.
UF Left Brain
B Cerebral Cortex 1967
R ↓ Brain 1967
↓ Cerebral Dominance 1973
Corpus Callosum 1973
Interhemispheric Interaction 1985
↓ Lateral Dominance 1967
Ocular Dominance 1973
Right Hemisphere 2005

Leg (Anatomy) 1973
PN 499 **SC** 28080
B Musculoskeletal System 1973
R Ankle 1973
Feet (Anatomy) 1973
Knee 1973
Thigh 1973

Legal Arrest 1973
PN 659 **SC** 28090
SN Taking custody, under legal authority, of a person for the purpose of holding or detaining him/her to answer criminal charges or civil demands.
UF Arrest (Law)
B Law Enforcement 1978
R Criminal Record 2006

Legal Confession 2003
PN 111 **SC** 28093
SN Disclosure of information that could be considered damaging to the person confessing.
HN This term was introduced in June 2003. Relevant records were re-indexed with this term. The posting note reflects the number of records that were re-indexed.
UF Confession (Legal)
B Legal Processes 1973
R Interrogation 2005
↓ Legal Evidence 1991
↓ Legal Testimony 1982
Self Disclosure 1973

Legal Decisions 1991
PN 1135 **SC** 28095
SN Used for discussions of the implications or the effects of specific judicial decisions. Not used for the actual process of judicial decision making.
R ↓ Adjudication 1967
Criminal Conviction 1973
↓ Criminal Justice 1991
↓ Laws 1967
↓ Legal Processes 1973

Legal Decisions — (cont'd)
Legislative Processes 1973
Litigation 2003

Legal Detention 1973
PN 193 **SC** 28100
SN Being detained (e.g., in jail) by law enforcers for having committed or for being suspected of having committed a crime, especially immediately prior to a legal court disposition.
UF Detention (Legal)
B Law Enforcement 1978
R Interrogation 2005

Legal Evidence 1991
PN 535 **SC** 28103
SN Testimony, records, documents, objects, and diagrams submitted to a court during a hearing or trial.
B Legal Processes 1973
N ↓ Legal Testimony 1982
R ↓ Adjudication 1967
Cross Examination 2005
↓ Law Enforcement 1978
Legal Confession 2003
Litigation 2003
Witnesses 1985

Legal Interrogation
HN In August 2005, the term was discontinued and removed from all records containing it, and was replaced with INTERROGATION, its postable counterpart.
Use Interrogation

Legal Liability (Professional)
Use Professional Liability

Legal Personnel 1985
PN 308 **SC** 28107
UF Paralegal Personnel
B Professional Personnel 1978
N Attorneys 1973
Judges 1985
↓ Law Enforcement Personnel 1973
R Juries 1985

Legal Processes 1973
PN 9078 **SC** 28110
SN Broad concept encompassing psychological and behavioral aspects of the law—its formation, enforcement, impact, and implications. Also includes reference to the legal justice system and legislative processes as they relate to psychology.
N ↓ Adoption (Child) 1967
Awards (Jury) 2005
Child Custody 1982
Child Visitation 1988
↓ Commitment (Psychiatric) 1973
Competency to Stand Trial 1985
↓ Criminal Justice 1991
Forensic Evaluation 1994
Guardianship 1988
Insanity Defense 1985
↓ Law Enforcement 1978
Legal Confession 2003
↓ Legal Evidence 1991
↓ Legal Testimony 1982
Legislative Processes 1973
Litigation 2003
Parole 1973
Probation 1973
R Advance Directives 1994
Civil Law 1994

Legal Processes — (cont'd)
↓ Civil Rights 1978
Consumer Protection 1973
Government 1967
↓ Government Policy Making 1973
Informed Consent 1985
↓ Laws 1967
Legal Decisions 1991
Professional Liability 1985
Protective Services 1997
Risk Management 1997
↓ Social Issues 1991

Legal Psychology
Use Forensic Psychology

Legal Testimony 1982
PN 1160 **SC** 28115
SN Evidence presented by a witness under oath or affirmation (as distinguished from evidence derived from other sources) either orally or written as a deposition or an affidavit.
B Legal Evidence 1991
Legal Processes 1973
N Expert Testimony 1973
R Cross Examination 2005
Interrogation 2005
Legal Confession 2003
Litigation 2003
Witnesses 1985

Legalization (Marihuana)
Use Marijuana Legalization

Legibility 1978
PN 68 **SC** 28127
N Handwriting Legibility 1973
R Readability 1978
↓ Written Language 1967

Legibility (Handwriting)
Use Handwriting Legibility

Legislative Processes 1973
PN 1009 **SC** 28140
B Government Policy Making 1973
Legal Processes 1973
R Advocacy 1985
Government 1967
↓ Laws 1967
Legal Decisions 1991

Leisure Time 1973
PN 2591 **SC** 28150
R Daily Activities 1994
Hobbies 1988
Holidays 1988
↓ Recreation 1967
Relaxation 1973

Leiter Adult Intelligence Scale
HN Term was discontinued in 1997. In 2000, the term was removed from all records containing it, and replaced with INTELLIGENCE MEASURES, its postable counterpart.
Use Intelligence Measures

Lemniscal System 1985
PN 20 **SC** 28165
SN Long ascending sensory neural pathways projecting to the diencephalon. This system includes the medial lemniscus, lateral lemniscus, spinothalamic tracts, and secondary trigeminal projections.

Lemniscal System — (cont'd)
B Afferent Pathways 1982
N Spinothalamic Tracts 1973
R Reticular Formation 1967

Lemurs 1973
PN 425 SC 28170
UF Bush Babies
B Mammals 1973

Length of Stay
Use Treatment Duration

Lens (Eye) 1973
PN 88 SC 28180
B Eye (Anatomy) 1967
R ↓ Light Refraction 1982
Ocular Accommodation 1982

Leptin 2004
PN 253 SC 28182
SN A peptide hormone that regulates food intake and energy balance.
HN This term was introduced in June 2004. Relevant records were re-indexed with this term. The posting note reflects the number of records that were re-indexed.
B Hormones 1967
Peptides 1973

Lesbian Parents
Use Homosexual Parents

Lesbianism 1973
PN 4509 SC 28190
UF Female Homosexuality
B Homosexuality 1967
R Bisexuality 1973
Heterosexuality 1973
Homosexual Parents 1994
Male Homosexuality 1973

Lesions 1967
PN 2435 SC 28200
HN Not defined prior to 1982. From 1982, limited to experimentally induced lesions and used primarily for animal populations.
UF Ablation
Sectioning (Lesion)
N ↓ Brain Lesions 1967
Neural Lesions 1973
R ↓ Surgery 1971

Lesson Plans 1973
PN 362 SC 28220
B Teaching Methods 1967

Letters (Alphabet) 1973
PN 2225 SC 28230
B Alphabets 1973
N Consonants 1973
Vowels 1973

Leucine 1973
PN 59 SC 28240
B Amino Acids 1973

Leucocytes 1973
PN 476 SC 28250
UF Leukocytes
White Blood Cells
B Blood Cells 1973
N Lymphocytes 1973
Natural Killer Cells 2003

Leukemias 1973
PN 497 SC 28260
B Blood and Lymphatic Disorders 1973
Neoplasms 1967

Leukocytes
Use Leucocytes

Leukotomy
Use Psychosurgery

Level of Functioning
Use Ability Level

Levodopa 1973
PN 1119 SC 28290
UF L Dopa
B Antitremor Drugs 1973
Cholinergic Blocking Drugs 1973
R DOPA 1973
Dopamine 1973

Lewy Body Disease
Use Dementia with Lewy Bodies

Lexical Access 1988
PN 2511 SC 29293
N Lexical Decision 1988
R Cognitive Discrimination 1973
Human Information Storage 1973
Semantic Memory 1988
↓ Verbal Memory 1994
Word Meaning 1973
Words (Phonetic Units) 1967

Lexical Decision 1988
PN 2355 SC 29296
B Lexical Access 1988
R Cognitive Discrimination 1973
Human Information Storage 1973
Semantic Memory 1988
↓ Verbal Memory 1994
Word Meaning 1973
Words (Phonetic Units) 1967

Liberalism 1973
PN 318 SC 28298
B Personality Traits 1967
R Political Liberalism 1973

Liberalism (Political)
Use Political Liberalism

Libido 1973
PN 370 SC 28310
B Psychoanalytic Personality Factors 1973
R Female Sexual Dysfunction 2005
Inhibited Sexual Desire 1997
Sex Drive 1973

Librarians 1988
PN 79 SC 28314
B Information Specialists 1988
R ↓ Professional Personnel 1978

Libraries 1982
PN 238 SC 28317
B Facilities 2006
N School Libraries 1973
R ↓ Community Facilities 1973
Information 1967
Information Dissemination 2005
Information Services 1988

Libraries (School)
Use School Libraries

Librium
Use Chlordiazepoxide

Licensing (Professional)
Use Professional Licensing

Licensure Examinations
Use Professional Examinations

Licking 1988
PN 250 SC 28345
SN Used for human or animal populations.
UF Animal Licking Behavior
B Animal Ethology 1967
Motor Processes 1967
R Animal Drinking Behavior 1973
Animal Grooming Behavior 1978
Animal Maternal Behavior 1973

Lidocaine 1973
PN 246 SC 28350
UF Xylocaine
B Local Anesthetics 1973

Life Changes 2004
PN 534 SC 28351
SN Changes in one's life that may be considered significant and may have an effect on lifestyle, health, or well-being.
HN Use LIFE EXPERIENCES to access references from 1985 to June 2004.
UF Life Transitions
B Life Experiences 1973
R ↓ Aging 1991
Career Change 1978
↓ Developmental Stages 1973
Divorce 1973
Life Span 2004
Lifestyle Changes 1997
↓ Marriage 1967
Menopause 1973
Parental Death 2003
↓ Parenthood Status 1985
↓ Pregnancy 1967
↓ Quality of Life 1985
Well Being 1994

Life Course
Use Life Span

Life Expectancy 1982
PN 1039 SC 28352
SN Anticipated number of years of life for an individual, based on statistical probability. Used for both human and animal populations.
HN Use AGED and PHYSIOLOGICAL AGING together to access references from 1973-1981.
UF Longevity
R ↓ Aging 1991
↓ Human Development 1967
Life Span 2004
Physiological Aging 1967

Life Experiences 1973
PN 10032 SC 28355
SN Specific events that are commonly considered noteworthy or memorable (e.g., college graduation, wedding) or are considered unusual or otherwise significant (e.g., life change due to illness). Compare EXPERIENCES (EVENTS).

Life Experiences — (cont'd)
UF Experiences (Life)
B Experiences (Events) 1973
N Life Changes 2004
R Age Regression (Hypnotic) 1988
Anniversary Events 1994
Autobiographical Memory 1994
Biographical Data 1978
First Experiences 2004
Homesickness 1994
Life Review 1991
Life Satisfaction 1985
Life Span 2004

Life Insurance 1973
PN 33 SC 28360
B Insurance 1973

Life Review 1991
PN 399 SC 28361
SN Reflection on and return to past life experiences in order to think about and reintegrate them into present life circumstances. Usually performed in a treatment or intervention setting. Not limited to elderly populations.
HN Consider using REMINISCENCE to access references from 1985-1990.
R Anniversary Events 1994
Autobiographical Memory 1994
Early Experience 1967
Early Memories 1985
Gerontology 1967
↓ Life Experiences 1973
Narratives 1997
Reminiscence 1985
↓ Treatment 1967

Life Satisfaction 1985
PN 3655 SC 28362
B Satisfaction 1973
R ↓ Life Experiences 1973
Lifestyle Changes 1997
↓ Quality of Life 1985
Role Satisfaction 1994
Well Being 1994

Life Span 2004
PN 1043 SC 28365
HN Use LIFE EXPECTANCY to access references from 1982 to June 2004.
UF Life Course
R ↓ Development 1967
Life Changes 2004
Life Expectancy 1982
↓ Life Experiences 1973

Life Sustaining Treatment 1997
PN 241 SC 28368
B Treatment 1967
R Advance Directives 1994
Assisted Suicide 1997
↓ Client Rights 1988
Medical Treatment (General) 1973
Palliative Care 1991
Terminally Ill Patients 1973
Treatment Refusal 1994
Treatment Withholding 1988

Life Transitions
Use Life Changes

Lifesaving
Use Artificial Respiration

Lifestyle 1978
PN 3589 SC 28375
SN Typical way of life or manner of living characteristic of an individual or groups.
N Active Living 2007
Lifestyle Changes 1997
R Daily Activities 1994
↓ Health Behavior 1982
Holistic Health 1985
↓ Personality 1967
↓ Personality Processes 1967
↓ Quality of Life 1985

Lifestyle Changes 1997
PN 420 SC 28380
B Lifestyle 1978
R Behavior Change 1973
Health Attitudes 1985
↓ Health Behavior 1982
Health Promotion 1991
Life Changes 2004
Life Satisfaction 1985
↓ Quality of Life 1985
Readiness to Change 2007
Stages of Change 2007
Well Being 1994

Light
Use Illumination

Light Adaptation 1982
PN 352 SC 28393
SN Change in the general level of sensitivity of the photoreceptors as a result of exposure to light.
UF Adaptation (Light)
B Sensory Adaptation 1967
R Dark Adaptation 1973
↓ Illumination 1967
↓ Visual Thresholds 1973

Light Refraction 1982
PN 57 SC 28395
SN Deflection of light from a straight path when passing obliquely through the interface of two media that have different densities.
N ↓ Refraction Errors 1973
R ↓ Illumination 1967
Lens (Eye) 1973

Light Therapy
Use Phototherapy

Likability 1988
PN 166 SC 28387
B Personality Traits 1967
R Agreeableness 1997
↓ Interpersonal Attraction 1967
Peer Pressure 1994
Social Approval 1967
↓ Social Perception 1967

Likert Scales 1994
PN 138 SC 28388
B Rating Scales 1967
R Attitude Measurement 1973
↓ Attitude Measures 1967
Self Report 1982

Likert Scales — (cont'd)
Semantic Differential 1967
↓ Surveys 1967

Liking
Use Affection

Limbic System 1973
PN 1729 SC 28410
SN A system of interconnected brain structures associated with emotion, motivation, attention, memory, and various autonomic functions.
B Cerebral Cortex 1967
Neural Pathways 1982
N Amygdala 2003
Fornix 1982
Gyrus Cinguli 1973
Hippocampus 1967
Medial Forebrain Bundle 1982
Olfactory Bulb 1973
Septal Nuclei 1982
R Nucleus Accumbens 1982
Raphe Nuclei 1982

Limen
Use Thresholds

Limited English Proficiency
Use Language Proficiency

Linear Perspective 1982
PN 271 SC 28427
SN Apparent convergence of parallel contours that are projected into the plane of sight of the observer.
UF Visual Perspective
B Vision 1967
R ↓ Depth Perception 1967
↓ Distance Perception 1973
↓ Size Discrimination 1967
↓ Visual Stimulation 1973

Linear Regression 1973
PN 467 SC 28430
B Statistical Correlation 1967
Statistical Regression 1985
R Multiple Regression 1982

Linguistics 1973
PN 5925 SC 28450
N Ethnolinguistics 1973
Etymology 1973
↓ Grammar 1967
Metalinguistics 1994
Neurolinguistics 1991
Orthography 1973
Psycholinguistics 1967
Sociolinguistics 1985
R Cognitive Science 2003
Discourse Analysis 1997
↓ Language 1967
Pragmatics 1985
↓ Prosody 1991
↓ Semiotics 1985
↓ Verbal Communication 1967

Linkage Analysis
Use Genetic Linkage

Lions
Use Felids

Lipid Metabolism 1973
PN 240 **SC** 28460
UF Fat Metabolism
B Metabolism 1967
R ↓ Lipids 1973

Lipid Metabolism Disorders 1973
PN 72 **SC** 28470
B Metabolism Disorders 1973
N Tay Sachs Disease 2003

Lipids 1973
PN 1095 **SC** 28480
N ↓ Fatty Acids 1973
R Lipid Metabolism 1973
↓ Steroids 1973

Lipoproteins 1973
PN 458 **SC** 28490
R Apolipoproteins 2004
↓ Proteins 1973

Lipreading 1973
PN 377 **SC** 28500
UF Speechreading
R ↓ Deaf 1967
Speech Perception 1967
↓ Visual Perception 1967

Lips (Face) 1973
PN 167 **SC** 28510
R Mouth (Anatomy) 1967

Liquor 1973
PN 66 **SC** 28520
B Alcoholic Beverages 1973

Listening
Use Auditory Perception

Listening (Interpersonal) 1997
PN 315 **SC** 28535
B Interpersonal Communication 1973
R ↓ Attention 1967
↓ Auditory Perception 1967
Conversation 1973
Listening Comprehension 1973
Social Skills 1978

Listening Comprehension 1973
PN 1592 **SC** 28540
B Verbal Comprehension 1985
R Listening (Interpersonal) 1997

Literacy 1973
PN 4227 **SC** 28550
UF Illiteracy
N Computer Literacy 1991
R ↓ Language 1967
↓ Language Arts Education 1973
Literacy Programs 1997
Phonological Awareness 2004
Reading Development 1997
Reading Education 1973
↓ Reading Skills 1973
Writing Skills 1985

Literacy Programs 1997
PN 470 **SC** 28555
B Educational Programs 1973
R ↓ Adult Education 1973
↓ Language Arts Education 1973
↓ Literacy 1973
Reading Education 1973
↓ Reading Skills 1973
↓ Social Services 1982
Writing Skills 1985

Literature 1967
PN 6882 **SC** 28560
UF Fiction
B Humanities 2003
N Poetry 1973
↓ Prose 1973
R Creative Writing 1994
Drama 1973
Folklore 1991
Metaphor 1982
Myths 1967
Narratives 1997
Postmodernism 1997
↓ Religious Literature 1973
Writers 1991

Literature Review 1967
PN 22078 **SC** 28580
SN Used in records discussing issues involved in the process of conducting surveys of previously published material.
HN From 1967-2000, the term was also used as a mandatory document type identifier; however, this usage has been discontinued due to the advent of Form/Content Type field identifiers. References from 1967-2000 can be accessed using either LITERATURE REVIEW or the Literature Review Form/Content Type field identifier. In 1973, this term replaced the discontinued term REVIEW (OF LITERATURE). In 2000, REVIEW (OF LITERATURE) was removed from all records containing it, and replaced with LITERATURE REVIEW.
UF Review (of Literature)
R Meta Analysis 1985

Lithium 1973
PN 3887 **SC** 28590
SN Used for documents that do not specify the type of lithium used, e.g., carbonate, chloride, or bromide. Use a more specific term if possible.
B Metallic Elements 1973
N Lithium Carbonate 1973
R ↓ Antidepressant Drugs 1971
↓ Tricyclic Antidepressant Drugs 1997

Lithium Bromide
HN Term was discontinued in 1997. In 2000, the term was removed from all records containing it, and replaced with BROMIDES, its postable counterpart.
Use Bromides

Lithium Carbonate 1973
PN 756 **SC** 28610
B Antidepressant Drugs 1971
Lithium 1973

Litigation 2003
PN 516 **SC** 28612
SN A lawsuit or formal court action intended to resolve disputes between two parties.
HN This term was introduced in June 2003. Relevant records were re-indexed with this term. The posting note reflects the number of records that were re-indexed.
UF Lawsuits
B Legal Processes 1973
R ↓ Adjudication 1967
Awards (Jury) 2005
Civil Law 1994
↓ Conflict Resolution 1982
↓ Criminal Justice 1991
Criminal Law 1973
Expert Testimony 1973
↓ Laws 1967
Legal Decisions 1991
↓ Legal Evidence 1991
↓ Legal Testimony 1982

Litter Size 1985
PN 142 **SC** 28615
SN Used for animal populations only.
B Size 1973
R ↓ Animal Breeding 1973

Liver 1973
PN 508 **SC** 28620
B Digestive System 1967

Liver Disorders 1973
PN 406 **SC** 28630
UF Hepatic Disorders
B Digestive System Disorders 1973
N Cirrhosis (Liver) 1973
↓ Hepatitis 1973
Jaundice 1973
R ↓ Infectious Disorders 1973
↓ Neoplasms 1967
↓ Toxic Disorders 1973

Living Alone 1994
PN 95 **SC** 28633
HN Use LIVING ARRANGEMENTS to access references from 1991-1993.
B Living Arrangements 1991
R Cohabitation 1973
↓ Family Structure 1973
Home Environment 1973
↓ Marital Status 1973
Single Persons 1973

Living Arrangements 1991
PN 1329 **SC** 28635
UF Household Structure
N Cohabitation 1973
Living Alone 1994
R Aging in Place 2007
Assisted Living 2003
Child Custody 1982
Empty Nest 1991
↓ Family 1967
↓ Family Structure 1973
Home Environment 1973
↓ Housing 1973
↓ Marital Status 1973
Retirement Communities 1997
Roommates 1973
Shelters 1991
↓ Single Sex Environments 2001

Living Wills
Use Advance Directives

Lizards 1973
PN 631 **SC** 28640
B Reptiles 1967

Lobectomy
Use Psychosurgery

Lobotomy
Use Psychosurgery

Local Anesthetics 1973
PN 125 **SC** 28660
B Anesthetic Drugs 1973
N ↓ Cocaine 1973
Lidocaine 1973
Quinine 1973
R Ephedrine 1973
Methoxamine 1973

Localization (Perceptual)
Use Perceptual Localization

Localization (Sound)
Use Auditory Localization

Locomotion 2007
PN 333 **SC** 28683
SN The ability to move from one place to another.
HN This term was introduced in April 2007. Relevant records were re-indexed with this term. The posting note reflects the number of records that were re-indexed.
B Motor Processes 1967
N Animal Locomotion 1982
R ↓ Physical Activity 2007
Physical Mobility 1994

Locus Ceruleus 1982
PN 510 **SC** 28687
SN Pigmented nucleus in the brain stem that synthesizes norepinephrine.
B Brain Stem 1973
R Reticular Formation 1967

Locus of Control
Use Internal External Locus of Control

Logic (Philosophy) 1973
PN 566 **SC** 28700
B Philosophies 1967

Logical Thinking 1967
PN 2125 **SC** 28710
UF Ratiocination
B Thinking 1967
R Analogy 1991
Critical Thinking 2006
↓ Inductive Deductive Reasoning 1973
Rationality 2005

Logistic Models
Use Item Response Theory

Logistic Regression 2003
PN 176 **SC** 28718
SN A type of regression analysis used to predict whether or not something will happen. Most often used when the dependent variable is dichotomous or categorical.
HN This term was introduced in June 2003. Relevant records were re-indexed with this term. The posting note reflects the number of records that were re-indexed.
B Statistical Correlation 1967
Statistical Regression 1985
R Multiple Regression 1982

Logotherapy 1973
PN 431 **SC** 28720
SN Existential analysis based on spiritual values and emphasizing search for the meaning of human existence.

Logotherapy — (cont'd)
B Psychotherapy 1967
R Existential Therapy 1973

Loneliness 1973
PN 1905 **SC** 28730
B Emotional States 1973
R Abandonment 1997
Homesickness 1994

Long Term Care 1994
PN 1488 **SC** 28735
SN Delivery of health or mental health services over a prolonged or extended period. Care can be in an institutional setting or in the community, e.g., at home, and delivered by health care professionals, family, or friends.
B Health Care Services 1978
Treatment Duration 1988
R Adult Day Care 1997
↓ Case Management 1991
Home Care 1985
↓ Hospitalization 1967
↓ Mental Health Services 1978
Nursing Homes 1973
Palliative Care 1991

Long Term Memory 1973
PN 2486 **SC** 28740
SN Retention of events or learned material for relatively long periods, presumed to be based on permanent encoding and storage of information transferred from short term memory. Consider also RETENTION.
B Memory 1967

Long Term Potentiation
Use Postactivation Potentials

Longevity
Use Life Expectancy

Longitudinal Studies 1973
PN 14228 **SC** 28760
SN Used in records discussing issues involved in the process of conducting observations or measurements of the same individual or group over an extended period.
HN From 1973-2000, the term was also used as a mandatory document type identifier; however, this usage has been discontinued due to the advent of Form/Content Type field identifiers. References from 1973-2000 can be accessed using either LONGITUDINAL STUDIES or the Longitudinal Studies Form/Content Type field identifier.
UF Studies (Longitudinal)
B Experimental Design 1967
N Prospective Studies 1997
R Followup Studies 1973
Retrospective Studies 1997

Loosening of Associations
Use Fragmentation (Schizophrenia)

Lorazepam 1988
PN 487 **SC** 28765
B Benzodiazepines 1978
Minor Tranquilizers 1973

Lordosis (Animal)
Use Animal Sexual Receptivity

Loudness 1967
PN 606 **SC** 28780
UF Sound Pressure Level
B Auditory Stimulation 1967
N Noise Levels (Work Areas) 1973

Loudness Discrimination 1973
PN 191 **SC** 28790
B Loudness Perception 1973

Loudness Perception 1973
PN 349 **SC** 28800
B Auditory Perception 1967
N Loudness Discrimination 1973

Love 1973
PN 2938 **SC** 28830
B Emotional States 1973
R Affection 1973
Attachment Behavior 1985
Erotomania 1997
Intimacy 1973
Romance 1997

Low Birth Weight
Use Birth Weight

Lower Class 1973
PN 1005 **SC** 28850
B Social Class 1967
Socioeconomic Status 1967

Lower Class Attitudes 1973
PN 74 **SC** 28860
SN Attitudes of, not toward, the lower class.
B Socioeconomic Class Attitudes 1973

Lower Income Level 1973
PN 3144 **SC** 28870
B Income Level 1973
R Poverty 1973

Loxapine 1982
PN 58 **SC** 28875
SN Organic heterocyclic compound used as a tranquilizing agent.
UF Oxilapine
B Minor Tranquilizers 1973

Loyalty 1973
PN 502 **SC** 28880
B Personality Traits 1967

LSD (Drug)
Use Lysergic Acid Diethylamide

Lucid Dreaming 1994
PN 62 **SC** 28893
B Dreaming 1967
R Dream Recall 1973
REM Dreams 1973
REM Sleep 1973
↓ Sleep 1967

Luck
Use Chance (Fortune)

Lumbar Spinal Cord 1973
PN 207 **SC** 28900
B Spinal Cord 1973

Lumbrosacral Plexus
Use Spinal Nerves

Luminance 1982
PN 1694 **SC** 28930
SN Product of multiplying the physical intensity of a light wave by the spectral sensitivity of the typical observer's visual system for that specific wavelength. Compare ILLUMINATION.
R ↓ Brightness Perception 1973
↓ Chromaticity 1997
Color Saturation 1997
↓ Illumination 1967
Stimulus Intensity 1967
↓ Visual Thresholds 1973

Luminance Threshold
Use Brightness Perception AND Visual Thresholds

Lunar Synodic Cycle 1973
PN 127 **SC** 28950
SN Successive phases of the moon reflecting its motion around the earth.
R ↓ Biological Rhythms 1967
↓ Environmental Effects 1973

Lung 1973
PN 236 **SC** 28960
B Respiratory System 1973

Lung Disorders 1973
PN 685 **SC** 28970
UF Pulmonary Disorders
B Respiratory Tract Disorders 1973
N Cystic Fibrosis 1985
Pneumonia 1973
Pulmonary Emphysema 1973
Pulmonary Tuberculosis 1973
R ↓ Dyspnea 1973

Lupus 1973
PN 360 **SC** 28980
SN A chronic inflammatory autoimmune disease affecting various parts of the body, especially the skin, joints, blood, and kidneys. Individuals with lupus will produce antibodies that attack their own body tissues.
B Skin Disorders 1973
R ↓ Tuberculosis 1973

Luria Nebraska Neuropsychological Battery 2001
PN 92 **SC** 28983
HN In 2000, the truncated term LURIA NEBRASKA NEUROPSYCH BATTERY (which was used from 1991-2000) was deleted, removed from all records containing it, and replaced with its expanded form LURIA NEBRASKA NEUROPSYCHOLOGICAL BATTERY. Use NEUROPSYCHOLOGICAL ASSESSMENT to access references from 1982-1990.
B Neuropsychological Assessment 1982

Luteinizing Hormone 1978
PN 518 **SC** 28985
B Gonadotropic Hormones 1973
R ↓ Pituitary Hormones 1973
↓ Sex Hormones 1973

Lutherans
Use Protestants

Lying
Use Deception

Lymphatic Disorders
Use Blood and Lymphatic Disorders

Lymphocytes 1973
PN 837 **SC** 29060
B Leucocytes 1973
R Epstein Barr Viral Disorder 1994
Interleukins 1994

Lysergic Acid Diethylamide 1967
PN 922 **SC** 29070
UF LSD (Drug)
B Acids 1973
Amine Oxidase Inhibitors 1973
Hallucinogenic Drugs 1967
Psychotomimetic Drugs 1973
Serotonin Antagonists 1973
R ↓ Ergot Derivatives 1973

Machiavellianism 1973
PN 428 **SC** 29087
SN Extent to which an individual feels that any means, however unscrupulous, can justifiably be used to achieve power.
B Personality Traits 1967

Machine Learning 2003
PN 329 **SC** 29088
SN Changes in systems that perform tasks associated with artificial intelligence.
HN This term was introduced in June 2003. Relevant records were re-indexed with this term. The posting note reflects the number of records that were re-indexed.
B Artificial Intelligence 1982
N Inductive Logic Programming 2007
R ↓ Expert Systems 1991
↓ Learning 1967
Neural Networks 1991

Magazines 1973
PN 703 **SC** 29090
B Printed Communications Media 1973

Magical Thinking 1973
PN 214 **SC** 29100
SN Belief that one's utterances, thoughts, or behavior can have a controlling influence on specific events or prevent their occurrence by means that operate beyond the normal laws of cause and effect.
B Thinking 1967
Thought Disturbances 1973
R Fantasies (Thought Disturbances) 1967
↓ Fantasy 1997
Imagination 1967
Omnipotence 1994

Magnesium 1973
PN 214 **SC** 29110
B Metallic Elements 1973
N Magnesium Ions 1973

Magnesium Ions 1973
PN 18 **SC** 29120
B Electrolytes 1973
Magnesium 1973

Magnet Schools
Use Nontraditional Education

Magnetic Resonance Imaging 1994
PN 3192 **SC** 29133
SN Non-invasive imaging technique that creates in vivo images that measure variation in the brain or other bodily structures.

Magnetic Resonance Imaging — (cont'd)
UF MRI
B Neuroimaging 2003
Tomography 1988
R Computer Assisted Diagnosis 1973
Magnetoencephalography 1985

Magnetism 1985
PN 803 **SC** 29135
UF Geomagnetism
R Magnetoencephalography 1985
Physics 1973
Transcranial Magnetic Stimulation 2003

Magnetoencephalography 1985
PN 509 **SC** 29136
SN A procedure that measures the magnetic fields produced by electrical activity in the brain. The method has various research and clinical applications, including the localization of dysfunctional brain areas.
R ↓ Electroencephalography 1967
Magnetic Resonance Imaging 1994
Magnetism 1985

Magnitude Estimation 1991
PN 229 **SC** 29138
SN Unidimensional scaling method used in statistics and psychophysics for quantitative judgment and ratio estimation.
B Psychophysical Measurement 1967
Statistical Estimation 1985
R Scaling (Testing) 1967

Magnitude of Effect (Statistical)
Use Effect Size (Statistical)

Maids
Use Domestic Service Personnel

Mail Surveys 1994
PN 190 **SC** 29141
B Surveys 1967
R ↓ Consumer Research 1973
Consumer Surveys 1973
↓ Methodology 1967
↓ Questionnaires 1967
Telephone Surveys 1994

Mainstreaming 1991
PN 391 **SC** 29144
SN Integration or transition into society of individuals who have been considered for institutionalization or other type of isolation, but are now considered able to learn from education or community involvement.
N Mainstreaming (Educational) 1978
R Deinstitutionalization 1982
Educational Placement 1978
Habilitation 1991
Independent Living Programs 1991
↓ Rehabilitation 1967
School to Work Transition 1994
↓ Social Integration 1982
Special Education 1967
Special Needs 1994

Mainstreaming (Educational) 1978
PN 3765 **SC** 29145
SN Integration of students with special education needs into classes or schools with regular students.
UF Inclusion (Educational)
B Mainstreaming 1991
R ↓ Education 1967
Educational Placement 1978

Mainstreaming (Educational) — (cont'd)
School Integration 1982
Special Education 1967

Maintenance Therapy 1997
PN 481 **SC** 29142
SN Treatment or therapy that is designed to maintain patients in a stable condition and to promote either gradual healing or to prevent the relapse of a disorder or condition. Used primarily, but not exclusively, in drug therapy settings.
R Aftercare 1973
↓ Drug Therapy 1967
Methadone Maintenance 1978
↓ Outpatient Treatment 1967
Relapse Prevention 1994
↓ Treatment Duration 1988

Major Depression 1988
PN 49234 **SC** 29143
SN Affective disorder marked by dysphoric mood, inactivity, lack of interest, insomnia, feelings of worthlessness, diminished ability to think, and thoughts of suicide. Use DEPRESSION (EMOTION) for nonclinical depression.
HN Consider DEPRESSION (EMOTION) to access references prior to 1988. In 1988, this term replaced the discontinued term PSYCHOTIC DEPRESSIVE REACTION, and in 2000 it replaced the term NEUROTIC DEPRESSIVE REACTION. In 2000, these terms were removed from all records containing them, and replaced with MAJOR DEPRESSION.
UF Agitated Depression
Depressive Reaction (Neurotic)
Dysphoria
Melancholia
Neurotic Depressive Reaction
Psychotic Depressive Reaction
Unipolar Depression
B Affective Disorders 2001
N Anaclitic Depression 1973
Dysthymic Disorder 1988
Endogenous Depression 1978
Postpartum Depression 1973
Reactive Depression 1973
Recurrent Depression 1994
Treatment Resistant Depression 1994
R Atypical Depression 2005
↓ Bipolar Disorder 2001
Depression (Emotion) 1967
↓ Neurosis 1967
Pseudodementia 1985
Seasonal Affective Disorder 1991

Major Tranquilizers
Use Neuroleptic Drugs

Maladjustment (Emotional)
Use Emotional Adjustment

Maladjustment (Social)
Use Social Adjustment

Malaria 1973
PN 112 **SC** 29180
B Blood and Lymphatic Disorders 1973
Parasitic Disorders 1973

Malaria — (cont'd)
R ↓ Nervous System Disorders 1967

Male Animals 1973
PN 4621 **SC** 29190
B Animals 1967

Male Attitudes 2006
PN 126 **SC** 29195
SN Attitudes of males. Used only when males are the focus of discussion.
HN This term was introduced in May 2006. Relevant records were re-indexed with this term. The posting note reflects the number of records that were re-indexed.
B Attitudes 1967
R ↓ Human Males 1973

Male Castration 1973
PN 714 **SC** 29200
SN Used for both human and animal populations.
B Castration 1967

Male Criminals 1973
PN 1391 **SC** 29210
B Criminals 1967
Human Males 1973

Male Delinquency 2001
PN 1225 **SC** 29215
HN In 2001, this term was created to replace the discontinued term MALE DELINQUENTS. MALE DELINQUENTS was removed from all records containing it and replaced with MALE DELINQUENCY.
B Juvenile Delinquency 1967
R Female Delinquency 2001
↓ Human Males 1973

Male Female Relations 1988
PN 2617 **SC** 29225
SN Relationships or interactions between the sexes. Limited to human populations.
UF Heterosexual Interaction
B Interpersonal Interaction 1967
R Heterosexuality 1973
↓ Human Courtship 1973
Infidelity 2006
↓ Marital Relations 1967
↓ Relationship Satisfaction 2001
↓ Relationship Termination 1997
Social Dating 1973
Social Skills 1978

Male Genital Disorders 1973
PN 54 **SC** 29230
B Genital Disorders 1967
N Klinefelters Syndrome 1973
Testicular Feminization Syndrome 1973
R ↓ Endocrine Sexual Disorders 1973
Hermaphroditism 1973
↓ Hypogonadism 1973
↓ Infertility 1973
Sterility 1973

Male Genitalia 1973
PN 226 **SC** 29240
SN Used for both human and animal populations.
UF Genitalia (Male)
B Urogenital System 1973
N Penis 1973
Prostate 1973

Male Genitalia — (cont'd)
Testes 1973
R Circumcision 2001

Male Homosexuality 1973
PN 6323 **SC** 29250
UF Gay Males
B Homosexuality 1967
R Bisexuality 1973
Heterosexuality 1973
Homosexual Parents 1994
Lesbianism 1973

Male Only Environments
Use Single Sex Environments

Male Orgasm 1973
PN 377 **SC** 29260
SN Used for both human and animal populations.
UF Ejaculation
B Orgasm 1973
N Nocturnal Emission 1973
Premature Ejaculation 1973
R Erectile Dysfunction 2006
Masturbation 1973
↓ Sexual Intercourse (Human) 1973

Males (Human)
Use Human Males

Malignant Neoplasms
Use Neoplasms

Malingering 1973
PN 1138 **SC** 29290
SN Feigning or exaggerating illness or symptoms, usually in order to escape work, evoke sympathy, or gain compensation.
B Deception 1967
R ↓ Factitious Disorders 1988
↓ Mental Disorders 1967
Munchausen Syndrome 1994
↓ Physical Disorders 1997
↓ Somatoform Disorders 2001

Malnutrition
Use Nutritional Deficiencies

Malpractice
Use Professional Liability

Mammals 1973
PN 2077 **SC** 29310
B Vertebrates 1973
N Bats 1973
↓ Canids 1997
Cattle 1973
Chimpanzees 1973
Chinchillas 1973
Deer 1973
Elephants 1973
↓ Felids 1997
Goats 1973
Horses 1973
Lemurs 1973
↓ Marsupials 1973
↓ Primates (Nonhuman) 1973
Rabbits 1967
↓ Rodents 1973
Seals (Animal) 1973
Sheep 1973
↓ Whales 1985

Mammary Glands 1973
PN 24 **SC** 29320
B Glands 1967

Mammary Neoplasms
Use Breast Neoplasms

Mammillary Bodies (Hypothalamic)
Use Hypothalamus

Mammography 1994
PN 459 **SC** 29345
B Roentgenography 1973
R Breast Neoplasms 1973
Cancer Screening 1997
↓ Health Screening 1997
↓ Medical Diagnosis 1973
Physical Examination 1988
Preventive Medicine 1973

Man Machine Systems
HN Term was discontinued in 1997. In 2000, the term was removed from all records containing it, and replaced with HUMAN MACHINE SYSTEMS, its postable counterpart.
Use Human Machine Systems

Man Machine Systems Design
HN Term was discontinued in 1997. In 2000, the term was removed from all records containing it, and replaced with HUMAN MACHINE SYSTEMS DESIGN, its postable counterpart.
Use Human Machine Systems Design

Managed Care 1994
PN 2168 **SC** 29365
SN Competitive prepaid plan of health care delivery to contain costs and provide access to quality health care.
HN Use CASE MANAGEMENT to access references from 1991-1993.
B Health Care Delivery 1978
N Health Maintenance Organizations 1982
R ↓ Case Management 1991
Cost Containment 1991
Disease Management 2007
Fee for Service 1994
Health Care Costs 1994
↓ Health Care Services 1978
↓ Health Insurance 1973
Quality of Care 1988
↓ Treatment Planning 1997
Utilization Reviews 2007

Management 1967
PN 3571 **SC** 29420
SN Conceptually broad term referring to the process of manipulation of human or material resources to accomplish given goals. Use a more specific term if possible.
N Business Management 1973
↓ Case Management 1991
↓ Classroom Management 2004
Customer Relationship Management 2007
Disability Management 1991
Educational Administration 1967
↓ Health Care Administration 1997
Household Management 1985
Risk Management 1997
↓ Self Management 1985
Stress Management 1985

Management — (cont'd)
Time Management 1994
R Accountability 1988
↓ Business 1967
Career Development 1985
Entrepreneurship 1991
Labor Management Relations 1967
↓ Leadership 1967
Leadership Qualities 1997
Management Decision Making 1973
↓ Management Methods 1973
↓ Management Personnel 1973
Management Planning 1973
Management Training 1973
Transformational Leadership 2003
↓ Work Teams 2001

Management Decision Making 1973
PN 2057 **SC** 29370
B Decision Making 1967
R ↓ Group Decision Making 1978
↓ Management 1967
↓ Management Methods 1973
Management Planning 1973
Participative Management 1988

Management Development
Use Career Development

Management Information Systems
Use Information Systems

Management Methods 1973
PN 4389 **SC** 29380
N Participative Management 1988
Self Managing Work Teams 2001
R Business Management 1973
↓ Management 1967
Management Decision Making 1973
Management Planning 1973
Supervisor Employee Interaction 1997
↓ Teams 1988
Work Scheduling 1973
↓ Work Teams 2001

Management Personnel 1973
PN 10591 **SC** 29390
UF Administrators
Supervisors
B White Collar Workers 1973
N Middle Level Managers 1973
Top Level Managers 1973
R Commissioned Officers 1973
Industrial Foremen 1973
↓ Management 1967
↓ School Administrators 1973
Supervisor Employee Interaction 1997

Management Planning 1973
PN 620 **SC** 29400
UF Planning (Management)
R ↓ Management 1967
Management Decision Making 1973
↓ Management Methods 1973
↓ Marketing 1973

Management Training 1973
PN 1730 **SC** 29410
B Personnel Training 1967
R Business Education 1973
↓ Management 1967

Management Training — (cont'd)
Wilderness Experience 1991

Manager Employee Interaction
Use Supervisor Employee Interaction

Mandibula
Use Jaw

Mania 1967
PN 3110 **SC** 29450
SN Excitement of psychotic origins characterized by mental and physical hyperactivity, elevated mood, agitation, and disorganization of behavior.
B Affective Disorders 2001
Emotional States 1973
N Hypomania 1973
R ↓ Bipolar Disorder 2001

Manic Depression
HN In 2000, the term was discontinued and removed from all records containing it, and replaced with BIPOLAR DISORDER, its postable counterpart.
Use Bipolar Disorder

Manic Depressive Psychosis
HN This term was discontinued in 1988, when the term MANIC DEPRESSION was created to capture this concept. In 2000, MANIC DEPRESSION was discontinued and made nonpostable for the new term BIPOLAR DISORDER. MANIC DEPRESSIVE PSYCHOSIS and MANIC DEPRESSION were removed from all records containing them and replaced with BIPOLAR DISORDER.
Use Bipolar Disorder

Mann Whitney U Test 1973
PN 19 **SC** 29470
B Nonparametric Statistical Tests 1967

Mannerisms
Use Habits

Manpower
HN Use PERSONNEL to access references from 1967-1981.
Use Personnel Supply

Mantis 1973
PN 32 **SC** 29500
UF Praying Mantis
B Insects 1967
R Larvae 1973

Manual Communication 1978
PN 171 **SC** 29505
SN Form of communication used by the deaf in which sign language and finger spelling are substituted for speech. Also, an unsystematic or informal method of communication with gestures.
B Augmentative Communication 1994
Nonverbal Communication 1971
Verbal Communication 1967
N Fingerspelling 1973
Sign Language 1973

Manufacturing
Use Business

Maori
Use Indigenous Populations

MAOs
Use Monoamine Oxidases

Maprotiline 1982
PN 215 **SC** 29527
B Tricyclic Antidepressant Drugs 1997

Marathon Group Therapy 1973
PN 143 **SC** 29540
SN Encounter group that meets for extended sessions and that aims to develop the ability to express oneself emotionally and to initiate intimate interpersonal interactions.
B Encounter Group Therapy 1973
R Human Relations Training 1978
Sensitivity Training 1973

Marihuana
HN In June 2003, the term was discontinued and removed from all records containing it, and was replaced with MARIJUANA, its postable counterpart.
Use Marijuana

Marijuana 2003
PN 1228 **SC** 29590
HN In June 2003, this term replaced the discontinued term MARIHUANA. MARIHUANA was removed from all records and replaced with MARIJUANA.
UF Marihuana
B Cannabis 1973
R Hashish 1973
↓ Marijuana Laws 1973
Marijuana Usage 1973
Tetrahydrocannabinol 1973

Marijuana Laws 1973
PN 40 **SC** 29560
B Drug Laws 1973
N Marijuana Legalization 1973
R Government 1967
Marijuana 2003
Marijuana Usage 1973

Marijuana Legalization 1973
PN 62 **SC** 29570
UF Legalization (Marihuana)
B Drug Legalization 1997
Marijuana Laws 1973
R ↓ Drug Usage Attitudes 1973
Government 1967

Marijuana Usage 1973
PN 1473 **SC** 29580
B Drug Usage 1971
R Marijuana 2003
↓ Marijuana Laws 1973

Marine Personnel 1973
PN 248 **SC** 29600
B Military Personnel 1967

Marital Adjustment
Use Marital Relations

Marital Conflict 1973
PN 2194 **SC** 29620
B Family Conflict 2003
Marital Relations 1967
R Domestic Violence 2006
Dysfunctional Family 1991
↓ Relationship Termination 1997

Marital Fidelity
Use Monogamy

Marital Relations 1967
PN 8723 **SC** 29640
UF Marital Adjustment
B Family Relations 1967
Interpersonal Relationships 2004
N Marital Conflict 1973
Marital Satisfaction 1988
R Codependency 1991
Extramarital Intercourse 1973
Infidelity 2006
Male Female Relations 1988
↓ Relationship Termination 1997
Romance 1997

Marital Satisfaction 1988
PN 2190 **SC** 29645
B Marital Relations 1967
Relationship Satisfaction 2001
Satisfaction 1973
R Relationship Quality 2004
↓ Relationship Termination 1997
Role Satisfaction 1994

Marital Separation 1973
PN 1073 **SC** 29650
UF Separation (Marital)
B Relationship Termination 1997
N Divorce 1973
R Child Support 1988
Divorced Persons 1973
↓ Family 1967
↓ Marital Status 1973
↓ Parental Absence 1973

Marital Status 1973
PN 2595 **SC** 29660
N Never Married 1994
R Divorced Persons 1973
↓ Family 1967
↓ Family Background 1973
Living Alone 1994
↓ Living Arrangements 1991
↓ Marital Separation 1973
↓ Marriage 1967
Remarriage 1985
↓ Single Parents 1978
Single Persons 1973
Widowers 1973
Widows 1973

Marital Therapy
Use Marriage Counseling

Marketing 1973
PN 5578 **SC** 29670
N Social Marketing 2007
R ↓ Advertising 1967
Brand Names 1978
Brand Preferences 1994
↓ Consumer Research 1973
↓ Electronic Commerce 2006
Electronic Retailing 2007
Management Planning 1973
Personalization 2007
Product Design 1997
↓ Quality of Services 1997
↓ Retailing 1991

Markov Chains 1973
PN 375 **SC** 29680
SN Statistical model representing conditional and sequential probabilities to determine the future values of a random variable.

Markov Chains — (cont'd)
B Simulation 1967
Stochastic Modeling 1973

Marlowe Crowne Social Desirability Scale 2001
PN 60 **SC** 29691
HN In 2001, the truncated term MARLOWE CROWNE SOC DESIRABIL SCALE (which was used from 1973-2000) was deleted, removed from all records containing it, and replaced with its expanded form MARLOWE CROWNE SOCIAL DESIRABILITY SCALE.
B Nonprojective Personality Measures 1973

Marriage 1967
PN 3450 **SC** 29700
N ↓ Endogamous Marriage 1973
↓ Exogamous Marriage 1973
Monogamy 1997
Polygamy 1973
Remarriage 1985
Same Sex Marriage 2007
R ↓ Family 1967
Life Changes 2004
↓ Marital Status 1973
Marriage Rites 1973
Romance 1997

Marriage and Family Education
Use Family Life Education

Marriage Attitudes 1973
PN 934 **SC** 29710
SN General attitudes toward marriage and divorce, or attitudes toward a specific marital relationship.
B Attitudes 1967
R ↓ Family Relations 1967

Marriage Counseling 1973
PN 3802 **SC** 29720
UF Marital Therapy
Marriage Therapy
B Counseling 1967
N Conjoint Therapy 1973
R Couples Therapy 1994
↓ Psychotherapeutic Counseling 1973
↓ Psychotherapy 1967
Sex Therapy 1978

Marriage Rites 1973
PN 69 **SC** 29730
B Rites of Passage 1973
R ↓ Marriage 1967
Traditions 2007

Marriage Therapy
Use Marriage Counseling

Married Couples
Use Spouses

Marsupials 1973
PN 75 **SC** 29760
B Mammals 1973
N Kangaroos 1973
Opossums 1973

Martial Arts 1985
PN 202 **SC** 29765
UF Karate
B Recreation 1967
Sports 1967

Martial Arts — (cont'd)
R Judo 1973
Meditation 1973
Self Defense 1985

Marxism
Use Communism

Masculinity 1967
PN 3660 SC 29780
B Personality Traits 1967
R Androgyny 1982
Femininity 1967
↓ Gender Identity 1985
Sex Roles 1967

Masking 1967
PN 836 SC 29790
SN Changes in perceptual sensitivity to a stimulus due to the presence of a second stimulus in close temporal proximity.
UF Backward Masking
Forward Masking
N Auditory Masking 1973
Visual Masking 1973
R ↓ Perceptual Stimulation 1973

Maslow (Abraham Harold) 1991
PN 114 SC 29795
SN Identifies biographical or autobiographical studies and discussions of Maslow's works.
R ↓ Human Potential Movement 1982
↓ Humanistic Psychology 1985
↓ Psychologists 1967
Self Actualization 1973

Masochism 1973
PN 420 SC 29800
SN Pleasure derived from being physically or psychologically abused.
B Sadomasochism 1973
N Sexual Masochism 1973
R Masochistic Personality 1973
↓ Sadism 1973
↓ Self Destructive Behavior 1985

Masochistic Personality 1973
PN 73 SC 29810
SN Personality marked by self-destructiveness or self-defeating behavior, a conscious or unconscious need to suffer, and seeking out opportunities for suffering or self-injury.
B Sadomasochistic Personality 1973
R ↓ Masochism 1973
↓ Self Destructive Behavior 1985
Sexual Masochism 1973

Mass Culture
Use Popular Culture

Mass Hysteria 1973
PN 93 SC 29820
SN Spontaneous development of physical or emotional symptoms, such as anxiety or agitation, among a large group of people. The behavior can be in reaction to puzzling or frightening events.
UF Collective Hysteria
Epidemic Hysteria
B Hysteria 1967
R ↓ Collective Behavior 1967
Contagion 1988

Mass Media 1967
PN 4037 SC 29830
B Communications Media 1973
N Films 2005
↓ News Media 1997
↓ Printed Communications Media 1973
Radio 1973
↓ Television 1967
R ↓ Advertising 1967
Popular Culture 2003
Public Service Announcements 2004

Massage 2001
PN 111 SC 29835
SN Systematic manipulation of body tissues. Used in both therapeutic and non-therapeutic situations.
B Tactual Stimulation 1973
R ↓ Alternative Medicine 1997
Physical Contact 1982
Physical Therapy 1973
↓ Physical Treatment Methods 1973

Massed Practice 1973
PN 162 SC 29840
SN Practice schedule with trials that are closely spaced and continuous over a long period. Compare DISTRIBUTED PRACTICE.
B Learning Schedules 1967
Practice 1967

Mastectomy 1973
PN 296 SC 29850
B Amputation 1973
R Breast Neoplasms 1973

Mastery Learning 1985
PN 296 SC 29855
SN Educational approach involving specification of educational objectives and success criteria and individual pacing in attaining them.
B Learning 1967
R Educational Objectives 1978
School Learning 1967
Sequential Learning 1973
↓ Teaching Methods 1967

Mastery Tests
Use Criterion Referenced Tests

Masticatory Muscles 1973
PN 63 SC 29860
B Muscles 1967

Masturbation 1973
PN 471 SC 29870
B Psychosexual Behavior 1967
R Autoeroticism 1997
Female Orgasm 1973
↓ Male Orgasm 1973

Matching Test
Use Matching to Sample

Matching to Sample 1994
PN 724 SC 29873
UF Matching Test
B Discrimination Learning 1982
R ↓ Memory 1967
↓ Recognition (Learning) 1967

Mate Selection
Use Animal Mate Selection AND Human Mate Selection

Mate Swapping
Use Extramarital Intercourse

Materialism 1973
PN 511 SC 29890
B Philosophies 1967

Maternal Behavior (Animal)
Use Animal Maternal Behavior

Maternal Behavior (Human)
Use Mother Child Relations

Maternal Investment
Use Parental Investment

Mates (Humans)
Use Spouses

Mathematical Ability 1973
PN 2948 SC 29930
UF Numerical Ability
B Cognitive Ability 1973
Nonverbal Ability 1988
R ↓ Mathematics (Concepts) 1967
Mathematics Anxiety 1985

Mathematical Modeling 1973
PN 6246 SC 29940
SN Use of mathematical formulas or equations to analyze or systematize data for description in quantitative terms.
B Simulation 1967
N Structural Equation Modeling 1994
R Chaos Theory 1997
Decision Theory 2003
Fuzzy Logic 2003
Fuzzy Set Theory 1991
Goodness of Fit 1988
Heuristic Modeling 1973
↓ Stochastic Modeling 1973

Mathematical Psychology 1973
PN 299 SC 29950
SN Discipline that attempts to systematize the data of psychology by means of mathematical and statistical models and applications.
B Psychology 1967

Mathematicians 1973
PN 90 SC 29960
B Professional Personnel 1978
R Physicists 1973
Scientists 1967

Mathematics 1982
PN 2890 SC 29965
SN Science of numbers and the operations performed on them. Compare MATHEMATICS (CONCEPTS).
UF Arithmetic
B Sciences 1967
N Algebra 2003
Calculus 2003
Geometry 2003
Statistics 1982
R Mathematics Anxiety 1985

Mathematics (Concepts) 1967
PN 3003 SC 29970
SN Specific principles that are cognitively internalized or are to be learned concerning numbers, their relations, and mathematical operations performed on them. Compare MATHEMATICS.

Mathematics (Concepts) — (cont'd)
N Algorithms 1973
Number Systems 1973
Numbers (Numerals) 1967
R Concepts 1967
Mathematical Ability 1973
Mathematics Achievement 1973
Mathematics Education 1973
↓ Statistical Analysis 1967

Mathematics Achievement 1973
PN 4484 **SC** 29980
B Academic Achievement 1967
R ↓ Mathematics (Concepts) 1967
Mathematics Anxiety 1985
Mathematics Education 1973
Science Achievement 1997

Mathematics Anxiety 1985
PN 348 **SC** 29985
SN Fear or tension associated with the study or performance of arithmetic and mathematical tasks.
B Anxiety 1967
R ↓ Anxiety Disorders 1997
Mathematical Ability 1973
↓ Mathematics 1982
Mathematics Achievement 1973

Mathematics Education 1973
PN 4978 **SC** 29990
B Curriculum 1967
R ↓ Mathematics (Concepts) 1967
Mathematics Achievement 1973
Science Achievement 1997

Mating Behavior (Animal)
Use Animal Mating Behavior

Matriarchy 1973
PN 50 **SC** 30010
B Family Structure 1973
R Father Absence 1973
Patriarchy 1973
↓ Sex Role Attitudes 1978
Sex Roles 1967

Matriculation
Use School Enrollment

Maturation
Use Human Development

Maturity (Emotional)
Use Emotional Maturity

Maturity (Physical)
Use Physical Maturity

Maturity (Vocational)
Use Vocational Maturity

Maxilla
Use Jaw

Maximum Likelihood 1985
PN 516 **SC** 30075
SN Method of estimating population parameters from sample data by selecting parameter values that maximize the likelihood of the occurrence of the observed sample results.

Maximum Likelihood — (cont'd)
B Statistical Estimation 1985
R Goodness of Fit 1988

Maximum Security Facilities 1985
PN 186 **SC** 30077
B Facilities 2006
R ↓ Correctional Institutions 1973
↓ Hospitals 1967

Maze Learning 1967
PN 2745 **SC** 30080
SN Learning the correct route through a maze to obtain reinforcement. Used for human or animal populations.
B Learning 1967
R Spatial Learning 1994

Maze Pathways 1973
PN 151 **SC** 30090
SN Use when specifically referring to pathway choice, discrimination, or spatial organization of pathway. Used for human or animal populations. When comparing types of mazes, use MAZES.
UF Runways (Maze)
B Mazes 1967

Mazes 1967
PN 677 **SC** 30110
SN System of pathways consisting of a number of blind alleys and one or more correct paths leading to a goal/reinforcement. Used to study learning and motivation in humans and animals.
UF Labyrinth (Apparatus)
B Apparatus 1967
N Maze Pathways 1973
T Mazes 1973

MCPP
Use Piperazines

MDMA
Use Methylenedioxymethamphetamine

Mealtimes 2004
PN 53 **SC** 30150
SN Use for human populations only.
HN Use FEEDING PRACTICES to access references from 1973 to June 2004.
R ↓ Eating Behavior 2004

Mean 1973
PN 366 **SC** 30160
B Central Tendency Measures 1973
R Standard Scores 1985

Meaning 1967
PN 4751 **SC** 30170
SN Generally refers to the significance, sense, connotation, or denotation conveyed by any form of information.
N Nonverbal Meaning 1973
↓ Verbal Meaning 1973
R ↓ Comprehension 1967
Meaningfulness 1967

Meaningfulness 1967
PN 1412 **SC** 30180
R ↓ Comprehension 1967
↓ Meaning 1967

Measles 1973
PN 48 **SC** 30190
B Viral Disorders 1973
R Rubella 1973

Measurement 1967
PN 26994 **SC** 30200
SN Conceptually broad term referring to the process and tools used in assessment of human subjects. Use specific test names or procedures if possible.
UF Assessment
Tests
N ↓ Achievement Measures 1967
↓ Aptitude Measures 1967
Attitude Measurement 1973
↓ Attitude Measures 1967
Body Sway Testing 1973
Comprehension Tests 1973
Creativity Measurement 1973
Criterion Referenced Tests 1982
Digit Span Testing 1973
Employment Tests 1973
Group Testing 1973
Individual Testing 1973
↓ Intelligence Measures 1967
↓ Inventories 1967
Multidimensional Scaling 1982
Needs Assessment 1985
↓ Occupational Interest Measures 1973
Pain Measurement 1997
↓ Perceptual Measures 1973
Performance Tests 1973
↓ Personality Measures 1967
Posttesting 1973
↓ Preference Measures 1973
Pretesting 1973
Professional Examinations 1994
Profiles (Measurement) 1973
Projective Testing Technique 1973
↓ Psychiatric Evaluation 1997
↓ Psychological Assessment 1997
Psychometrics 1967
↓ Questionnaires 1967
↓ Rating Scales 1967
↓ Reading Measures 1973
↓ Retention Measures 1973
↓ Screening 1982
↓ Screening Tests 1982
↓ Selection Tests 1973
Sensorimotor Measures 1973
Sociometric Tests 1967
Speech and Hearing Measures 1973
Standardized Tests 1985
↓ Statistical Measurement 1973
Subtests 1973
↓ Surveys 1967
Symptom Checklists 1991
↓ Testing 1967
Verbal Tests 1973
R Clinical Judgment (Not Diagnosis) 1973
↓ Diagnosis 1967
↓ Evaluation 1967
↓ Experimentation 1967
Geriatric Assessment 1997
↓ Interviews 1967
↓ Methodology 1967
Piagetian Tasks 1973
↓ Prediction Errors 1973
Response Bias 1967
Semantic Differential 1967
Sociograms 1973
↓ Statistical Analysis 1967
↓ Test Construction 1973

Measurement — (cont'd)
Test Norms 1973
↓ Test Scores 1967
↓ Testing Methods 1967
Testwiseness 1978

Measurement Error
Use Error of Measurement

Mecamylamine 1973
PN 207 **SC** 30220
B Amines 1973
Antihypertensive Drugs 1973
Ganglion Blocking Drugs 1973

Mechanical Aptitude 1973
PN 90 **SC** 30230
B Nonverbal Ability 1988

Mechanoreceptors 1973
PN 257 **SC** 30250
SN A specialized set of neural receptor cells whose functions are to transduce mechanical stimuli and convey the information to the central nervous system.
B Neural Receptors 1973
Sensory Neurons 1973

Media (Communications)
Use Communications Media

Medial Forebrain Bundle 1982
PN 216 **SC** 30286
SN Complex group of nerve fibers arising from basal olfactory regions, the periamygdaloid region, and the septal nuclei passing to, and through, the lateral preoptic and hypothalamic regions. This bundle provides the chief pathway for reciprocal connections between the hypothalamus and the biogenic amine systems of the brain stem.
B Limbic System 1973
R Amygdala 2003
Fornix 1982
Hippocampus 1967
↓ Hypothalamus 1967
Septal Nuclei 1982

Medial Geniculate Nucleus
Use Geniculate Bodies (Thalamus)

Median 1973
PN 38 **SC** 30290
B Central Tendency Measures 1973

Median Nerve
Use Spinal Nerves

Mediated Responses 1967
PN 138 **SC** 30310
SN Intervening or anticipatory responses aroused by stimuli and subsequently responsible for the initiation of behavior.
B Responses 1967

Mediation 1988
PN 1669 **SC** 30315
SN Intervention by independent and impartial third party or parties to promote reconciliation, settlement, or compromise between conflicting parties.
B Conflict Resolution 1982
R Child Custody 1982
Court Referrals 1994
Divorce 1973
Labor Management Relations 1967
↓ Negotiation 1973

Mediation (Cognitive)
Use Cognitive Mediation

Medicaid 1994
PN 518 **SC** 30323
SN Government health care program for impoverished citizens administered by most local public assistance offices. Compare MEDICARE.
B Government Programs 1973
Health Insurance 1973
R ↓ Health Care Policy 1994
Medicare 1988
Social Security 1988
Welfare Services (Government) 1973

Medical Audits
Use Clinical Audits

Medical Care Costs
Use Health Care Costs

Medical Diagnosis 1973
PN 4066 **SC** 30330
SN Diagnosis of mental or physical disorders through use of medical methods or tests. Compare PSYCHODIAGNOSIS.
UF Clinical Judgment (Medical Diagnosis)
B Diagnosis 1967
N Biopsy 1973
↓ Cardiography 1973
Dexamethasone Suppression Test 1988
Echoencephalography 1973
Electro Oculography 1973
↓ Electroencephalography 1967
Electromyography 1967
Electronystagmography 1973
Electroplethysmography 1973
Electroretinography 1967
↓ Encephalography 1973
Galvanic Skin Response 1967
HIV Testing 1997
↓ Ophthalmologic Examination 1973
↓ Plethysmography 1973
Pneumoencephalography 1973
Prenatal Diagnosis 1988
Rheoencephalography 1973
↓ Roentgenography 1973
↓ Tomography 1988
Urinalysis 1973
R Autopsy 1973
Biological Markers 1991
Computer Assisted Diagnosis 1973
Differential Diagnosis 1967
Drug Usage Screening 1988
↓ Electrophysiology 1973
Genetic Testing 2003
↓ Health Screening 1997
Mammography 1994
Patient History 1973
Physical Examination 1988
Prognosis 1973
Psychological Report 1988

Medical Education 1973
PN 5233 **SC** 30340
B Graduate Education 1973
N Medical Internship 1973
Medical Residency 1973
Psychiatric Training 1973
R Nursing Education 1973

Medical Ethics
Use Bioethics

Medical History
Use Patient History

Medical Internship 1973
PN 203 **SC** 30350
UF Internship (Medical)
B Internship Programs 2006
Medical Education 1973
Postgraduate Training 1973

Medical Model 1978
PN 910 **SC** 30355
SN Conceptual approach to disorders originally applied to the study and treatment of physical illness. Also known as the disease or faulty mechanism model.
B Models 1967

Medical Patients 1973
PN 4924 **SC** 30360
B Patients 1967

Medical Personnel 1967
PN 3479 **SC** 30370
UF Hospital Staff
B Health Personnel 1994
N Dentists 1973
Military Medical Personnel 1973
↓ Nurses 1967
Optometrists 1973
Pharmacists 1991
Physical Therapists 1973
↓ Physicians 1967
↓ Psychiatric Hospital Staff 1973
R Clinicians 1973
Impaired Professionals 1985
↓ Medical Sciences 1967
↓ Mental Health Personnel 1967
Scientists 1967

Medical Personnel Supply 1973
PN 32 **SC** 30380
SN Manpower needs and availability of medical personnel.
B Personnel Supply 1973

Medical Psychology 1973
PN 434 **SC** 30390
SN Subspecialty of clinical psychology concerned with physical health and illness.
B Clinical Psychology 1967
Health Care Psychology 1985
R ↓ Medical Sciences 1967

Medical Records 1978
PN 706 **SC** 30395
HN Use MEDICAL RECORDS KEEPING to access references from 1978-1996.
N Client Records 1997
R Data Collection 1982
↓ Data Processing 1967
Hospital Administration 1978
Patient History 1973
↓ Treatment 1967

Medical Regimen Compliance
Use Treatment Compliance

Medical Residency 1973
PN 2092 **SC** 30400
SN Required hospital training in a medical specialty for a medical graduate and licensed physician.
UF Psychiatric Residency
Residency (Medical)

Medical Residency — (cont'd)
B Medical Education 1973
Postgraduate Training 1973

Medical Sciences 1967
PN 2656 SC 30410
UF Medicine (Science of)
B Sciences 1967
N Anesthesiology 1973
Cardiology 1973
Dentistry 1973
↓ Endocrinology 1973
Epidemiology 1973
Family Medicine 1988
Geriatrics 1967
Gynecology 1978
↓ Immunology 1973
Neurology 1967
↓ Obstetrics 1978
Ophthalmology 1973
Osteopathic Medicine 2003
↓ Pathology 1973
Pediatrics 1973
↓ Psychiatry 1967
Psychosomatic Medicine 1978
Radiology 1973
↓ Surgery 1971
Veterinary Medicine 1973
R Bioethics 2003
Folk Medicine 1973
↓ Medical Personnel 1967
Medical Psychology 1973
↓ Neurosciences 1973
↓ Paramedical Sciences 1973

Medical Students 1967
PN 4924 SC 30420
B Students 1967
R Graduate Students 1967

Medical Therapeutic Devices 1973
PN 654 SC 30430
SN Equipment designed for rehabilitation or treatment of abnormal or undesirable conditions.
UF Therapeutic Devices (Medical)
N Artificial Pacemakers 1973
↓ Hearing Aids 1973
↓ Optical Aids 1973
↓ Prostheses 1973
R ↓ Augmentative Communication 1994
Mobility Aids 1978

Medical Treatment (General) 1973
PN 3115 SC 30440
SN Use for medical treatment as a broad topic.
B Treatment 1967
R ↓ Alternative Medicine 1997
Life Sustaining Treatment 1997
↓ Physical Treatment Methods 1973

Medicare 1988
PN 445 SC 30445
SN Government health care program for the aged administered through the Social Security Administration or the Health Care Financing Administration. Compare MEDICAID.
B Government Programs 1973
Health Insurance 1973
R ↓ Health Care Policy 1994
Medicaid 1994
Social Security 1988

Medication
Use Drug Therapy

Medicinal Herbs and Plants 2001
PN 544 SC 30455
SN Herbs and plants whose roots, leaves, seeds, bark, or other constituents possess therapeutic qualities when administered in a treatment capacity.
B Plants (Botanical) 2007
N Hypericum Perforatum 2003
R ↓ Alternative Medicine 1997
Dietary Supplements 2001

Medicine (Science of)
Use Medical Sciences

Medics
HN Term was discontinued in 1997. In 2000, the term was removed from all records containing it, and replaced with PARAMEDICAL PERSONNEL, its postable counterpart. In April 2007, PARAMEDICAL PERSONNEL was discontinued and removed from all records containing it, and replaced with ALLIED HEALTH PERSONNEL, its postable counterpart.
Use Allied Health Personnel

Meditation 1973
PN 1640 SC 30480
SN Family of contemplative techniques, all of which involve a conscious attempt to focus one's attention in a nonanalytical way and to refrain from ruminating, discursive thought. Sometimes considered a spiritual or religious practice.
B Religious Practices 1973
R ↓ Alternative Medicine 1997
Centering 1991
Holistic Health 1985
↓ Human Potential Movement 1982
Martial Arts 1985
Mindfulness 2006
Prayer 1973
↓ Relaxation Therapy 1978

Medulla Oblongata 1973
PN 530 SC 30490
SN Lowest subdivision of the brain stem, adjacent to the spinal cord. Controls autonomic functions including respiration and circulation.
B Brain Stem 1973
Hindbrain 1997

Melancholia
HN Use DEPRESSION (EMOTION) to access references from 1973-1987.
Use Major Depression

Melancholy
Use Sadness

Melanin 1973
PN 70 SC 30530
B Pigments 1973
R Melanocyte Stimulating Hormone 1985
Melatonin 1973
↓ Tyrosine 1973

Melanocyte Stimulating Hormone 1985
PN 123 SC 30535
UF Melanotropin
B Peptides 1973
Pituitary Hormones 1973
R Melanin 1973
Melatonin 1973

Melanotropin
Use Melanocyte Stimulating Hormone

Melatonin 1973
PN 1039 SC 30540
B Hormones 1967
R Melanin 1973
Melanocyte Stimulating Hormone 1985
Pineal Body 1973

Mellaril
Use Thioridazine

Membership 2007
PN 686 SC 30555
SN Belonging to a particular group or organization.
HN This term was introduced in April 2007. Relevant records were re-indexed with this term. The posting note reflects the number of records that were re-indexed.
N Fraternity Membership 1973
School Club Membership 1973
Sorority Membership 1973
R Affiliation Motivation 1967
American Psychological Association 2007
Group Identity 2007
Group Participation 1973
Organizational Commitment 1991
↓ Organizations 1967
↓ Religious Affiliation 1973
Social Acceptance 1967

Membranes 1973
PN 402 SC 30560
B Tissues (Body) 1973
N Meninges 1973
↓ Nasal Mucosa 1973
Nictitating Membrane 1973

Memory 1967
PN 34177 SC 30570
N Autobiographical Memory 1994
Early Memories 1985
Eidetic Imagery 1973
Episodic Memory 1988
Explicit Memory 1997
False Memory 1997
Implicit Memory 2003
Long Term Memory 1973
Memory Decay 1973
Memory Trace 1973
Reminiscence 1985
Repressed Memory 1997
↓ Short Term Memory 1967
↓ Spatial Memory 1988
Spontaneous Recovery (Learning) 1973
↓ Verbal Memory 1994
↓ Visual Memory 1994
R ↓ Amnesia 1967
Chunking 2004
↓ Cognitive Processes 1967
Cued Recall 1994
Cues 1967
Declarative Knowledge 1997
Forgetting 1973
Free Recall 1973
Generation Effect (Learning) 1991
Hindsight Bias 2006
Human Information Storage 1973
Information Processing Model 2007
↓ Interference (Learning) 1967
↓ Latent Inhibition 1997
↓ Learning 1967
Matching to Sample 1994
↓ Memory Disorders 1973
Memory Training 1994
Metacognition 1991

Memory — (cont'd)
Note Taking 1991
Procedural Knowledge 1997
↓ Prompting 1997
↓ Recall (Learning) 1967
Relearning 1973
↓ Retention 1967
Rote Learning 1973
Serial Recall 1994
Source Monitoring 2004

Memory Decay 1973
PN 545 **SC** 30580
SN Fading of memory traces over time. Compare FORGETTING and AMNESIA.
B Memory 1967
R ↓ Amnesia 1967
Forgetting 1973
Memory Training 1994

Memory Disorders 1973
PN 2148 **SC** 30590
B Thought Disturbances 1973
N ↓ Amnesia 1967
R ↓ Brain Disorders 1967
Cognitive Impairment 2003
↓ Memory 1967
Memory Training 1994
↓ Mental Disorders 1967
↓ Physical Disorders 1997

Memory Enhancing Drugs
Use Nootropic Drugs

Memory for Designs Test 1973
PN 34 **SC** 30610
B Nonprojective Personality Measures 1973
R ↓ Neuropsychological Assessment 1982

Memory Trace 1973
PN 514 **SC** 30620
SN Hypothetical change in nerve cells or brain activity that accompanies the storage of information.
B Memory 1967

Memory Training 1994
PN 379 **SC** 30623
B Training 2006
R Cognitive Rehabilitation 1985
Forgetting 1973
↓ Learning Strategies 1991
↓ Memory 1967
Memory Decay 1973
↓ Memory Disorders 1973
Mnemonic Learning 1973
↓ Neuropsychological Rehabilitation 1997
↓ Practice 1967
↓ Recall (Learning) 1967
↓ Recognition (Learning) 1967
↓ Retention 1967

Men
Use Human Males

Menarche 1973
PN 254 **SC** 30630
B Menstruation 1973
R Puberty 1973

Menieres Disease 1973
PN 78 **SC** 30640
SN A disease of the labyrinth of the inner ear causing symptoms including vertigo, tinnitus, fluctuating hearing loss, and a sensation of fullness or pain in the affected ear.
B Labyrinth Disorders 1973
Syndromes 1973
R Vertigo 1973

Meninges 1973
PN 42 **SC** 30650
SN Collection of three protective membranes covering the brain and spinal cord: pia mater (in direct contact with the CNS), arachnoid (innermost), and dura mater (outermost and attached to the skull).
B Central Nervous System 1967
Membranes 1973

Meningitis 1973
PN 103 **SC** 30660
SN Inflammation of the meninges covering the brain and spinal cord. May have viral, bacterial, or fungal causes.
B Central Nervous System Disorders 1973
N Bacterial Meningitis 1973

Meningomyelocele
Use Spina Bifida

Menopause 1973
PN 1646 **SC** 30670
B Developmental Stages 1973
R Life Changes 2004
↓ Menstrual Cycle 1973

Menstrual Cycle 1973
PN 1472 **SC** 30680
N ↓ Menstruation 1973
Ovulation 1973
R Estrus 1973
Menopause 1973
Premenstrual Dysphoric Disorder 2004
Premenstrual Syndrome 2003

Menstrual Disorders 1973
PN 252 **SC** 30690
B Gynecological Disorders 1973
N Amenorrhea 1973
Dysmenorrhea 1973
Premenstrual Dysphoric Disorder 2004
R Premenstrual Syndrome 2003

Menstruation 1973
PN 459 **SC** 30700
B Menstrual Cycle 1973
N Menarche 1973
R Estrus 1973

Mental Age 1973
PN 377 **SC** 30710
SN Intelligence level expressed in units of chronological age and determined by comparison with other individuals of the same age using intelligence test scores.
UF Intelligence Age
R Developmental Age Groups 1973
↓ Intelligence 1967
Intelligence Quotient 1967

Mental Confusion 1973
PN 545 **SC** 30720
UF Confusion (Mental)
B Emotional States 1973
R Doubt 1973
Frustration 1967
↓ Thought Disturbances 1973
Wandering Behavior 1991

Mental Deficiency
Use Mental Retardation

Mental Disorders 1967
PN 39903 **SC** 30740
SN Conceptually broad term referring to all forms of psychopathology. Use a more specific term if possible.
UF Insanity
Mental Illness
Nervous Breakdown
Psychiatric Disorders
B Disorders 1967
N Adjustment Disorders 1994
↓ Affective Disorders 2001
Alexithymia 1982
↓ Anxiety Disorders 1997
Autism 1967
↓ Chronic Mental Illness 1997
↓ Dementia 1985
↓ Dissociative Disorders 2001
↓ Eating Disorders 1997
Elective Mutism 1973
↓ Factitious Disorders 1988
↓ Gender Identity Disorder 1997
↓ Hysteria 1967
↓ Impulse Control Disorders 1997
Koro 1994
Mental Disorders due to General Medical Conditions 2001
↓ Neurosis 1967
↓ Paraphilias 1988
↓ Personality Disorders 1967
↓ Pervasive Developmental Disorders 2001
Pseudodementia 1985
↓ Psychosis 1967
Schizoaffective Disorder 1994
R Abnormal Psychology 2003
Adaptive Behavior 1991
↓ Attention Deficit Disorder 1985
Attention Deficit Disorder with Hyperactivity 2001
↓ Behavior Disorders 1971
Borderline States 1978
↓ Brain Disorders 1967
↓ Chronic Illness 1991
Chronicity (Disorders) 1982
↓ Communication Disorders 1982
Comorbidity 1991
Conduct Disorder 1991
↓ Congenital Disorders 1973
↓ Consciousness Disturbances 1973
↓ Defense Mechanisms 1967
↓ Diagnosis 1967
Diagnostic and Statistical Manual 1994
Disability Discrimination 1997
Disease Course 1991
↓ Emotional Adjustment 1973
Emotional Disturbances 2007
Etiology 1967
Glossolalia 1973
Homeless Mentally Ill 1997
Infantilism 1973
Insanity Defense 1985
International Classification of Diseases 2001

Mental Disorders — (cont'd)
↓ Learning Disorders 1967
Malingering 1973
↓ Memory Disorders 1973
Mental Illness (Attitudes Toward) 1967
↓ Mental Retardation 1967
Mentally Ill Offenders 1985
Microcephaly 1973
Narcissism 1967
Onset (Disorders) 1973
↓ Organic Brain Syndromes 1973
↓ Perceptual Disturbances 1973
↓ Personality Processes 1967
↓ Physical Disorders 1997
Porphyria 1973
Predisposition 1973
Premorbidity 1978
Prognosis 1973
Psychiatric Patients 1967
Psychiatric Symptoms 1997
↓ Psychodiagnosis 1967
↓ Psychological Assessment 1997
↓ Psychopathology 1967
Recovery (Disorders) 1973
Relapse (Disorders) 1973
↓ Remission (Disorders) 1973
Research Diagnostic Criteria 1994
Rett Syndrome 1994
↓ Sadomasochism 1973
Savants 2001
Schizophrenogenic Family 1967
Severity (Disorders) 1982
↓ Sexual Function Disturbances 1973
↓ Sleep Disorders 1973
Special Needs 1994
Structured Clinical Interview 2001
↓ Suicide 1967
Susceptibility (Disorders) 1973
↓ Symptoms 1967
↓ Syndromes 1973
↓ Thought Disturbances 1973
↓ Toxic Disorders 1973
↓ Treatment Resistant Disorders 1994
Work Related Illnesses 1994

Mental Disorders due to General Medical Conditions 2001
PN 42 **SC** 30745
SN Used for disorders characterized by the presence of mental symptoms judged to be the direct physiological consequence of a general medical condition. Use only for disorders described by this or more specific phraseology. This could include "Catatonic Disorder due to a General Medical Condition," "Dementia due to a General Medical Condition," etc. For a more specific disorder, also use a term for the symptom (e.g., CATATONIA, DEMENTIA). Compare COMORBIDITY.
B Mental Disorders 1967
R Comorbidity 1991

Mental Health 1967
PN 17866 **SC** 30750
B Health 1973
N Community Mental Health 1973
R Community Mental Health Services 1978
Community Psychiatry 1973
↓ Emotional Adjustment 1973
↓ Mental Health Personnel 1967
↓ Mental Health Programs 1973
↓ Mental Health Services 1978
Primary Mental Health Prevention 1973
Well Being 1994

Mental Health Care Barriers
Use Treatment Barriers

Mental Health Care Costs
Use Health Care Costs

Mental Health Care Policy
Use Health Care Policy

Mental Health Centers (Community)
Use Community Mental Health Centers

Mental Health Consultation
HN Term was discontinued in 1982. In 2000, the term was removed from all records containing it, and replaced with PROFESSIONAL CONSULTATION, its postable counterpart.
Use Professional Consultation

Mental Health Inservice Training 1973
PN 529 **SC** 30780
UF Inservice Training (Mental Health)
Training (Mental Health Inservice)
B Community Mental Health Training 1973
Inservice Training 1985
R ↓ Mental Health Programs 1973
Professional Development 1982

Mental Health Parity 2007
PN 21 **SC** 30785
SN Refers to equal provisions of insurance coverage between standard health care services and mental health services.
HN This term was introduced in April 2007. Relevant records were re-indexed with this term. The posting note reflects the number of records that were re-indexed.
R ↓ Health Care Policy 1994
↓ Health Insurance 1973
↓ Mental Health Services 1978

Mental Health Personnel 1967
PN 7459 **SC** 30790
B Health Personnel 1994
N Clinical Psychologists 1973
↓ Psychiatric Hospital Staff 1973
Psychiatric Nurses 1973
Psychiatric Social Workers 1973
Psychiatrists 1967
↓ Psychotherapists 1973
School Psychologists 1973
R Clinicians 1973
↓ Counselors 1967
↓ Educational Personnel 1973
Impaired Professionals 1985
↓ Medical Personnel 1967
↓ Mental Health 1967
Mental Health Personnel Supply 1973
Occupational Therapists 1973
↓ Paraprofessional Personnel 1973
Personal Therapy 1991
Professional Supervision 1988
↓ Psychologists 1967
↓ Social Workers 1973
↓ Therapists 1967

Mental Health Personnel Supply 1973
PN 139 **SC** 30800
B Personnel Supply 1973
R ↓ Mental Health Personnel 1967

Mental Health Program Evaluation 1973
PN 1615 **SC** 30810
SN Methodology or procedures for assessment of any mental health program in relation to previously established goals or other criteria. Also used for the formal evaluations themselves. For effectiveness of particular treatment modes, use the specific type of treatment (e.g., DRUG THERAPY). For efficacy of treatment for a particular disorder, use the specific disorder (e.g., MANIA).
UF Program Evaluation (Mental Health)
B Program Evaluation 1985
R ↓ Mental Health Programs 1973
Psychotherapeutic Outcomes 1973
↓ Treatment 1967
Treatment Effectiveness Evaluation 1973
↓ Treatment Outcomes 1982

Mental Health Programs 1973
PN 3112 **SC** 30820
SN Programs for the maintenance of mental health.
UF Programs (Mental Health)
N ↓ Crisis Intervention Services 1973
Deinstitutionalization 1982
Home Visiting Programs 1973
Hot Line Services 1973
Suicide Prevention Centers 1973
R Child Guidance Clinics 1973
Community Mental Health 1973
Community Mental Health Centers 1973
Community Mental Health Services 1978
↓ Community Mental Health Training 1973
Community Psychiatry 1973
Community Psychology 1973
↓ Community Services 1967
↓ Health Care Administration 1997
↓ Health Care Delivery 1978
↓ Health Care Services 1978
Integrated Services 1997
↓ Mental Health 1967
Mental Health Inservice Training 1973
Mental Health Program Evaluation 1973
↓ Mental Health Services 1978
Outreach Programs 1997
Partial Hospitalization 1985
Primary Mental Health Prevention 1973
↓ Program Development 1991
Psychiatric Clinics 1973
Public Health Services 1973

Mental Health Service Needs
Use Health Service Needs

Mental Health Services 1978
PN 15627 **SC** 30825
SN Services available for maintenance of mental health and treatment of mental disorders.
B Health Care Services 1978
N Community Mental Health Services 1978
R Child Guidance Clinics 1973
Clinical Practice 2007
Community Mental Health Centers 1973
↓ Community Services 1967
↓ Counseling 1967
↓ Health Care Administration 1997
Health Care Costs 1994
↓ Health Care Delivery 1978
↓ Health Care Policy 1994
Health Care Seeking Behavior 1997

Mental Health Services — (cont'd)
Health Service Needs 1997
Integrated Services 1997
Long Term Care 1994
↓ Mental Health 1967
Mental Health Parity 2007
↓ Mental Health Programs 1973
Outreach Programs 1997
↓ Prevention 1973
↓ Psychiatric Hospital Programs 1967
Quality of Care 1988
↓ Quality of Services 1997
School Counseling 1982
Social Casework 1967
↓ Social Services 1982
Student Personnel Services 1978
↓ Support Groups 1991
↓ Twelve Step Programs 1997

Mental Health Training (Community)
Use Community Mental Health Training

Mental Hospitals
Use Psychiatric Hospitals

Mental Illness
Use Mental Disorders

Mental Illness (Attitudes Toward) 1967
PN 2197 **SC** 30860
B Disabled (Attitudes Toward) 1997
R Disability Discrimination 1997
Health Knowledge 1994
↓ Mental Disorders 1967

Mental Load
Use Human Channel Capacity

Mental Models 2003
PN 683 **SC** 30867
SN Mental representations of real, imaginary, or hypothetical situations. The structure of the model corresponds to the structure it represents.
HN This term was introduced in June 2003. Relevant records were re-indexed with this term. The posting note reflects the number of records that were re-indexed.
B Models 1967
R Cognitive Maps 1982
Schema 1988

Mental Retardation 1967
PN 19131 **SC** 30870
SN Impaired intellectual (IQ below 70) and adaptive functioning manifested during the developmental period. Use a more specific term if possible. Use for both the concept of the disorder itself and for populations of mentally retarded persons.
HN In 2000, this term replaced the discontinued and deleted term MENTALLY RETARDED. MENTALLY RETARDED was removed from all records containing it and replaced with MENTAL RETARDATION.
UF Amentia
Mental Deficiency
Oligophrenia
Retardation (Mental)
N Anencephaly 1973
Borderline Mental Retardation 1973
Crying Cat Syndrome 1973
Downs Syndrome 1967
Home Reared Mentally Retarded 1973
Institutionalized Mentally Retarded 1973

Mental Retardation — (cont'd)
Mild Mental Retardation 2001
Moderate Mental Retardation 2001
Profound Mental Retardation 2001
Psychosocial Mental Retardation 1973
Severe Mental Retardation 2001
Tay Sachs Disease 2003
R Adaptive Behavior 1991
↓ Brain Damage 1967
Cognitive Impairment 2003
Developmental Disabilities 1982
↓ Disorders 1967
Fetal Alcohol Syndrome 1985
Fragile X Syndrome 1994
Hydrocephalus 2006
Klinefelters Syndrome 1973
↓ Mental Disorders 1967
Mental Retardation (Attitudes Toward) 2001
Microcephaly 1973
Phenylketonuria 1973
Prader Willi Syndrome 1991
Rett Syndrome 1994
Savants 2001
Williams Syndrome 2003

Mental Retardation (Attitudes Toward) 2001
PN 672 **SC** 30881
HN In 2000, the truncated term MENTAL RETARDATION (ATTIT TOWARD) (which was used from 1973-2000) was deleted, removed from all records containing it, and replaced with its expanded form MENTAL RETARDATION (ATTITUDES TOWARD).
B Disabled (Attitudes Toward) 1997
R ↓ Mental Retardation 1967

Mental Rotation 1991
PN 588 **SC** 30883
B Cognitive Processes 1967
R Mirror Image 1991
↓ Spatial Ability 1982
Spatial Imagery 1982
Spatial Organization 1973
↓ Spatial Perception 1967

Mentally Ill Homeless
Use Homeless Mentally Ill

Mentally Ill Offenders 1985
PN 2278 **SC** 30885
UF Criminally Insane
B Criminals 1967
R Competency to Stand Trial 1985
Court Referrals 1994
Forensic Evaluation 1994
Insanity Defense 1985
↓ Mental Disorders 1967

Mentor 1985
PN 1633 **SC** 30895
SN An individual who befriends and facilitates the development of a less experienced individual, especially within a profession, business, trade, or academic environment.
R Adult Development 1978
Apprenticeship 1973
↓ Interpersonal Interaction 1967
Occupational Aspirations 1973
Occupational Guidance 1967
Peer Counseling 1978
Professional Development 1982
Significant Others 1991
↓ Social Influences 1967

Mentor — (cont'd)
Supervisor Employee Interaction 1997
Vocational Counselors 1973

Meperidine 1973
PN 75 **SC** 30900
B Amines 1973
Analgesic Drugs 1973
Antispasmodic Drugs 1973
Narcotic Drugs 1973
Sedatives 1973

Mephenesin
HN Term was discontinued in 1997. In 2000, the term was removed from all records containing it, and replaced with MUSCLE RELAXING DRUGS, its postable counterpart.
Use Muscle Relaxing Drugs

Meprobamate 1973
PN 68 **SC** 30920
B Hypnotic Drugs 1973
Muscle Relaxing Drugs 1973
Sedatives 1973
Tranquilizing Drugs 1967

Mercury (Metal) 1973
PN 121 **SC** 30930
B Metallic Elements 1973

Mercury Poisoning 1973
PN 109 **SC** 30940
B Toxic Disorders 1973

Mercy Killing
Use Euthanasia

Mergers and Acquisitions 2007
PN 317 **SC** 30942
SN The combination and/or purchase of one or more businesses.
HN In April 2007, this term was created to replace the discontinued term ORGANIZATIONAL MERGER. ORGANIZATIONAL MERGER was removed from all records containing it, and was replaced with MERGERS AND ACQUISITIONS.
UF Acquisitions (Organizational)
Corporate Acquisitions
Organizational Merger
B Organizational Change 1973
R Organizational Structure 1967

Mescaline 1973
PN 122 **SC** 30950
B Alkaloids 1973
Hallucinogenic Drugs 1967
Psychotomimetic Drugs 1973
R Peyote 1973

Mesencephalon 1973
PN 1847 **SC** 30960
SN Most rostral portion of the brain stem that connects the pons and cerebellum with the thalamencephalon and cerebral hemispheres. Involved with a variety of sensory and motor processes.
UF Midbrain
Red Nucleus
B Brain 1967
N Inferior Colliculus 1973
Optic Lobe 1973
Substantia Nigra 1994
Superior Colliculus 1973
↓ Tegmentum 1991

Mesoridazine 1973
PN 35 **SC** 30970
B Phenothiazine Derivatives 1973

Messages 1973
PN 2129 **SC** 30980
SN Informational content of communications transmitted between persons or systems.
UF Information (Messages)
R ↓ Communication 1967
Computer Mediated Communication 2003
↓ Electronic Communication 2001
Gossip 1982
Information 1967

Meta Analysis 1985
PN 2683 **SC** 30985
SN Used in records discussing issues involved in the process of conducting a statistical analysis of a large collection of integrated findings.
HN From 1985-2000, the term was also used as a document type identifier; however, this usage has been discontinued due to the advent of Form/Content Type field identifiers. References from 1985-2000 can be accessed using either META ANALYSIS or the Meta Analysis Form/Content Type field identifier.
UF Data Pooling
B Methodology 1967
Statistical Analysis 1967
R Literature Review 1967

Metabolic Rates 1973
PN 330 **SC** 30990
R Energy Expenditure 1967
↓ Metabolism 1967
↓ Physiology 1967

Metabolic Syndrome 2007
PN 107 **SC** 30993
SN A collection of conditions that increase an individual's risk for cardiovascular disease, stroke, and diabetes. These conditions include increased blood pressure, elevated insulin levels, excess body fat around and in the abdomen, abnormal cholesterol levels, prothrombotic state, and proinflammatory state.
HN This term was introduced in April 2007. Relevant records were re-indexed with this term. The posting note reflects the number of records that were re-indexed.
UF Insulin Resistance Syndrome
Metabolic Syndrome X
B Syndromes 1973
R ↓ Cardiovascular Disorders 1967
Cerebrovascular Accidents 1973
↓ Diabetes 1973
↓ Metabolism Disorders 1973
Risk Factors 2001
↓ Symptoms 1967

Metabolic Syndrome X
Use Metabolic Syndrome

Metabolism 1967
PN 3288 **SC** 31000
SN Biochemical changes in the cells, digestive system, and body tissues by which energy is provided, new material is incorporated, and substances, such as drugs, are disposed.
B Physiology 1967
N Basal Metabolism 1973
Biosynthesis 1973
↓ Carbohydrate Metabolism 1973
Catabolism 1973

Metabolism — (cont'd)
Lipid Metabolism 1973
↓ Metabolites 1973
Protein Metabolism 1973
R Bioavailability 1991
↓ Dopamine Metabolites 1982
Metabolic Rates 1973
↓ Metabolism Disorders 1973
↓ Norepinephrine Metabolites 1982
Thermoregulation (Body) 1973

Metabolism Disorders 1973
PN 651 **SC** 31020
UF Hypercholesterolemia
B Physical Disorders 1997
N Cushings Syndrome 1973
Cystic Fibrosis 1985
↓ Diabetes 1973
Hyperglycemia 1985
Hypoglycemia 1973
Hyponatremia 1997
↓ Lipid Metabolism Disorders 1973
Phenylketonuria 1973
Porphyria 1973
R Hypothyroidism 1973
Metabolic Syndrome 2007
↓ Metabolism 1967
↓ Nutritional Deficiencies 1973

Metabolites 1973
PN 1279 **SC** 31030
SN Biochemical products of metabolism.
UF Anabolites
Catabolites
B Metabolism 1967
N ↓ Dopamine Metabolites 1982
↓ Norepinephrine Metabolites 1982
↓ Serotonin Metabolites 1978

Metacognition 1991
PN 2399 **SC** 31040
SN Awareness, monitoring, and knowledge of one's own cognitive processes and activities, including memory and comprehension.
UF Metamemory
B Cognitive Processes 1967
R ↓ Awareness 1967
Cognition 1967
↓ Cognitive Ability 1973
↓ Comprehension 1967
Critical Thinking 2006
Declarative Knowledge 1997
↓ Learning 1967
↓ Learning Strategies 1991
↓ Memory 1967
Metalinguistics 1994
Procedural Knowledge 1997
School Learning 1967

Metalinguistics 1994
PN 219 **SC** 31045
SN Branch of linguistics concerned with how language is used, the role of language in culture, and the use of particular linguistic forms.
B Linguistics 1973
R Ethnolinguistics 1973
↓ Language 1967
↓ Language Development 1967
Metacognition 1991
Pragmatics 1985
Psycholinguistics 1967
Sociolinguistics 1985
Verbal Ability 1967

Metalinguistics — (cont'd)
↓ Verbal Communication 1967

Metallic Elements 1973
PN 339 **SC** 31050
B Metals 1991
N Aluminum 1994
Barium 1973
↓ Calcium 1973
Cobalt 1973
Copper 1973
Iron 1973
Lead (Metal) 1973
↓ Lithium 1973
↓ Magnesium 1973
Mercury (Metal) 1973
↓ Potassium 1973
↓ Sodium 1973
Zinc 1985

Metals 1991
PN 85 **SC** 31052
SN May include alloys.
N ↓ Metallic Elements 1973

Metamemory
Use Metacognition

Metaphor 1982
PN 2730 **SC** 31057
SN Figures of speech used to suggest an analogy between one kind of object or idea and another.
B Figurative Language 1985
R Analogy 1991
↓ Literature 1967
Myths 1967
↓ Semantics 1967
Symbolism 1967

Metaphysics 1973
PN 675 **SC** 31060
SN Branch of philosophy concerned with the fundamental nature of things and existence.
B Philosophies 1967
N Ontology (Philosophy) 2007
R Epistemology 1973
Hermeneutics 1991
Reality 1973
Relativism 1997

Metapsychology 1994
PN 325 **SC** 31070
B Psychology 1967
R Freudian Psychoanalytic School 1973
Object Relations 1982
↓ Psychoanalytic Theory 1967

Methadone 1973
PN 952 **SC** 31080
B Analgesic Drugs 1973
Narcotic Drugs 1973
R Methadone Maintenance 1978

Methadone Maintenance 1978
PN 2151 **SC** 31083
SN Rehabilitation of heroin addicts by substituting methadone for heroin, enabling the addict to lead a relatively normal life. Methadone maintenance does not actually treat the addiction.
R ↓ Drug Addiction 1967
↓ Drug Rehabilitation 1973
Heroin Addiction 1973
Maintenance Therapy 1997
Methadone 1973

Methamphetamine 1973
PN 1110 **SC** 31090
UF Methedrine
B Amphetamine 1967
CNS Stimulating Drugs 1973
Vasoconstrictor Drugs 1973
R Methylenedioxymethamphetamine 1991

Methanol 1973
PN 45 **SC** 31100
UF Methyl Alcohol
B Alcohols 1967

Methaqualone 1973
PN 46 **SC** 31110
UF Quaalude
B Hypnotic Drugs 1973
Sedatives 1973

Methedrine
Use Methamphetamine

Methionine 1973
PN 154 **SC** 31130
B Amino Acids 1973

Methodists
Use Protestants

Methodology 1967
PN 21399 **SC** 31140
SN Conceptually broad term that refers generally to strategies, techniques, or procedures used in applied, descriptive, or empirical studies. Compare EXPERIMENTAL METHODS.
UF Research Methods
N Causal Analysis 1994
Cohort Analysis 1988
↓ Content Analysis 1978
Data Collection 1982
↓ Empirical Methods 1973
Grounded Theory 2004
Meta Analysis 1985
Qualitative Research 2003
Quantitative Methods 2003
Self Report 1982
R Experiment Controls 1973
↓ Experimental Design 1967
Experimental Instructions 1967
Experimental Laboratories 1973
Experimental Replication 1973
↓ Experimentation 1967
Functional Analysis 2001
Mail Surveys 1994
↓ Measurement 1967
↓ Surveys 1967
Telephone Surveys 1994
Theory Formulation 1973
Theory Verification 1973

Methohexital 1973
PN 53 **SC** 31150
B Barbiturates 1967
General Anesthetics 1973

Methoxamine 1973
PN 24 **SC** 31160
B Adrenergic Drugs 1973
Alcohols 1967
Sympathomimetic Amines 1973
Vasoconstrictor Drugs 1973

Methoxamine — (cont'd)
R ↓ Local Anesthetics 1973

Methoxyhydroxyphenylglycol (3,4) 1991
PN 180 **SC** 31165
UF MHPG
B Norepinephrine Metabolites 1982

Methyl Alcohol
Use Methanol

Methylatropine
Use Atropine

Methyldiphenylhydramine
Use Orphenadrine

Methyldopa 1973
PN 55 **SC** 31190
B Antihypertensive Drugs 1973
R ↓ Catecholamines 1973
DOPA 1973
Dopamine 1973

Methylenedioxymethamphetamine 1991
PN 860 **SC** 31195
UF Ecstasy (Drug)
MDMA
R Methamphetamine 1973

Methylmorphine
Use Codeine

Methylphenidate 1973
PN 1796 **SC** 31210
UF Ritalin
B Amines 1973
Antidepressant Drugs 1971
CNS Stimulating Drugs 1973
R ↓ Analeptic Drugs 1973

Methylphenyltetrahydropyridine 1994
PN 104 **SC** 31213
UF MPTP
B Neurotoxins 1982
R Dopamine 1973

Methysergide
Use Serotonin Antagonists

Metrazole
Use Pentylenetetrazol

Metronomes 1973
PN 34 **SC** 31230
B Apparatus 1967

Metropolitan Readiness Tests 1978
PN 41 **SC** 31240
HN Use METROPOLITAN READING READINESS TEST to access references from 1973-1977.
B Reading Measures 1973

Mexican Americans 1973
PN 3788 **SC** 31250
SN Populations of Mexican descent residing permanently in the U.S.
UF Chicanos
B Hispanics 1982

MHPG
Use Methoxyhydroxyphenylglycol (3,4)

Mianserin 1982
PN 331 **SC** 31266
SN Organic heterocyclic compound having antiserotonin properties and used as an antihistamine.
B Antidepressant Drugs 1971
Antihistaminic Drugs 1973
Serotonin Antagonists 1973

Mice 1973
PN 16807 **SC** 31270
B Rodents 1973

Microcephaly 1973
PN 79 **SC** 31280
SN Smallness of the head produced by incomplete development of the brain, often associated with below normal mental and cognitive development.
B Brain Disorders 1967
Congenital Disorders 1973
R ↓ Mental Disorders 1967
↓ Mental Retardation 1967
↓ Neonatal Disorders 1973

Microcomputers 1985
PN 1029 **SC** 31282
UF Personal Computers
B Computers 1967
R ↓ Computer Applications 1973

Microcounseling 1978
PN 104 **SC** 31284
SN Short-term technique for teaching basic interviewing skills using role playing, videotape analysis, and feedback in prepracticum training.
B Counseling 1967
R ↓ Clinical Methods Training 1973
Counselor Education 1973
Interviewing 1973
Paraprofessional Education 1973

Microorganisms 1985
PN 197 **SC** 31287
SN Single-celled microscopic or ultramicroscopic organisms.
UF Bacteria
Single Cell Organisms
N Protozoa 1973

Microscopes 1973
PN 24 **SC** 31290
B Apparatus 1967

Micturition
Use Urination

Midazolam 1991
PN 304 **SC** 31303
B Benzodiazepines 1978
Minor Tranquilizers 1973

Midbrain
Use Mesencephalon

Middle Class 1973
PN 999 **SC** 31320
UF Bourgeois
B Social Class 1967

Middle Class Attitudes 1973
PN 72 **SC** 31330
SN Attitudes of, not toward, the middle class.

Middle Class Attitudes — (cont'd)
B Socioeconomic Class Attitudes 1973

Middle Ear 1973
PN 184 SC 31340
UF Ear Ossicles
Eustachian Tube
Tympanic Membrane
B Ear (Anatomy) 1967

Middle Income Level 1973
PN 127 SC 31350
B Income Level 1973

Middle Level Managers 1973
PN 793 SC 31360
SN Second-line managers or supervisors primarily responsible for daily work flow and production in a business or industrial organization.
B Management Personnel 1973
R Top Level Managers 1973

Middle School Education 1985
PN 322 SC 31364
SN Education for grades six through eight (sometimes five through eight) using methods and materials specifically focusing on the needs and characteristics of early adolescents.
B Education 1967
R Middle Schools 2003

Middle School Students 1985
PN 3052 SC 31367
SN Students in 6th, 7th, and 8th grades. Sometimes may include students in 5th grade. Use ELEMENTARY SCHOOL STUDENTS or JUNIOR HIGH SCHOOL STUDENTS, as appropriate, unless specific reference is made to the population as middle school students.
R ↓ Elementary School Students 1967
Junior High School Students 1971

Middle School Teachers 2003
PN 148 SC 31366
HN This term was introduced in June 2003. Relevant records were re-indexed with this term. The posting note reflects the number of records that were re-indexed.
B Teachers 1967
R Junior High School Teachers 1973

Middle Schools 2003
PN 312 SC 31365
HN This term was introduced in June 2003. Relevant records were re-indexed with this term. The posting note reflects the number of records that were re-indexed.
B Schools 1967
R Junior High Schools 1973
Middle School Education 1985

Midwifery 1985
PN 210 SC 31368
UF Home Birth
B Obstetrics 1978
R ↓ Birth 1967
Labor (Childbirth) 1973

Migraine Headache 1973
PN 2191 SC 31370
B Headache 1973
R ↓ Endocrine Disorders 1973
Nausea 1973
↓ Somatoform Disorders 2001

Migrant Farm Workers 1973
PN 165 SC 31380
B Agricultural Workers 1973
R Foreign Workers 1985
↓ Human Migration 1973

Migration (Human)
Use Human Migration

Migratory Behavior (Animal) 1973
PN 923 SC 31400
UF Animal Navigation
B Animal Ethology 1967
R Animal Homing 1991

Mild Mental Retardation 2001
PN 3627 SC 31405
SN IQ 50-70.
HN In 2000, this term was created to replace the discontinued term EDUCABLE MENTALLY RETARDED and the discontinued and deleted term MILDLY MENTALLY RETARDED. These terms were removed from all records containing them and replaced with MILD MENTAL RETARDATION.
UF Educable Mentally Retarded
B Mental Retardation 1967

Milieu Therapy 1988
PN 291 SC 31420
SN Modification or manipulation of patient's personal life circumstances or environment through controlled and stimulatory environments. Treatment setting can be a hospital, therapeutic community, or home.
HN Use THERAPEUTIC COMMUNITY to access references from 1973-1987.
UF Environmental Therapy
Socioenvironmental Therapy
B Treatment 1967
R Sociotherapy 1973
Therapeutic Community 1967
↓ Therapeutic Environment 2001

Militancy 1973
PN 92 SC 31430
B Social Behavior 1967

Military Attrition 2005
PN 52 SC 31435
SN Reduction in the number of military personnel as a result of resignation or other factors.
HN This term was introduced in August 2005. Relevant records were re-indexed with this term. The posting note reflects the number of records that were re-indexed.
UF Attrition (Military)
R ↓ Military Personnel 1967

Military Deployment 2005
PN 138 SC 31437
SN The movement of military forces into areas of operation.
HN This term was introduced in August 2005. Relevant records were re-indexed with this term. The posting note reflects the number of records that were re-indexed.
UF Deployment (Military)
R ↓ Military Personnel 1967

Military Duty Status 2005
PN 140 SC 31438
HN This term was introduced in August 2005. Relevant records were re-indexed with this term. The posting note reflects the number of records that were re-indexed.

Military Duty Status — (cont'd)
UF Active Duty
Military Reserves
R ↓ Military Personnel 1967

Military Enlistment 1973
PN 296 SC 31440
UF Enlistment (Military)
R Military Recruitment 1973

Military Medical Personnel 1973
PN 224 SC 31450
B Medical Personnel 1967
Military Personnel 1967

Military Officers
Use Commissioned Officers

Military Personnel 1967
PN 4265 SC 31470
UF Servicemen
B Government Personnel 1973
N Air Force Personnel 1967
Army Personnel 1967
Coast Guard Personnel 1988
Commissioned Officers 1973
↓ Enlisted Military Personnel 1973
Marine Personnel 1973
Military Medical Personnel 1973
Military Psychologists 1997
National Guard Personnel 1973
Navy Personnel 1967
ROTC Students 1973
Volunteer Military Personnel 1973
R Astronauts 1973
Chaplains 1973
Combat Experience 1991
Military Attrition 2005
Military Deployment 2005
Military Duty Status 2005
Military Veterans 1973

Military Psychologists 1997
PN 35 SC 31475
B Military Personnel 1967
Psychologists 1967
R Military Psychology 1967

Military Psychology 1967
PN 958 SC 31480
B Applied Psychology 1973
R Military Psychologists 1997

Military Recruitment 1973
PN 300 SC 31490
UF Recruitment (Military)
B Personnel Recruitment 1973
R Military Enlistment 1973

Military Reserves
Use Military Duty Status

Military Schools 1973
PN 185 SC 31500
B Schools 1967
R ↓ Colleges 1967
High Schools 1973

Military Training 1973
PN 1502 **SC** 31510
B Training 2006

Military Veterans 1973
PN 4155 **SC** 31520
UF Veterans (Military)
R ↓ Military Personnel 1967
↓ Personnel 1967

Miller Analogies Test 1973
PN 17 **SC** 31530
B Intelligence Measures 1967

Millon Clinical Multiaxial Inventory 1988
PN 500 **SC** 31540
B Nonprojective Personality Measures 1973

Mimicry (Biology) 2003
PN 159 **SC** 31543
SN Evolutionary process by which one species mimics the appearance or characteristics of another species. Use only for animal populations. Consider also IMITATION (LEARNING).
HN This term was introduced in June 2003. Relevant records were re-indexed with this term. The posting note reflects the number of records that were re-indexed.
R Environmental Adaptation 1973
↓ Physical Appearance 1982
Theory of Evolution 1967

Mind 1991
PN 4367 **SC** 31550
SN Conceptually broad term referring to the organized totality of conscious and unconscious mental processes or psychic activities of an individual.
UF Psyche
R ↓ Cognitions 1985
↓ Cognitive Processes 1967
↓ Consciousness States 1971
Dualism 1973
Human Nature 1997
↓ Perception 1967
Soul 2004
Theory of Mind 2001
Unconscious (Personality Factor) 1967

Mind Blindness
Use Theory of Mind

Mind Body
Use Dualism

Mindfulness 2006
PN 319 **SC** 58094
SN Awareness of one's own actions and thoughts.
HN This term was introduced in May 2006. Relevant records were re-indexed with this term. The posting note reflects the number of records that were re-indexed.
R ↓ Awareness 1967
Meditation 1973
↓ Psychotherapeutic Techniques 1967

Mini Mental State Examination 1994
PN 340 **SC** 31548
B Neuropsychological Assessment 1982

Minimal Brain Disorders
HN In 2000, this term replaced the discontinued and deleted term MINIMALLY BRAIN DAMAGED. MINIMALLY BRAIN DAMAGED was removed from all records containing it and replaced with MINIMAL BRAIN DISORDERS. In May 2006, this term was discontinued and removed from all records containing it, and was replaced with ATTENTION DEFICIT DISORDER WITH HYPERACTIVITY, its postable counterpart.
Use Attention Deficit Disorder with Hyperactivity

Minimum Competency Tests 1985
PN 135 **SC** 31585
UF Basic Skills Testing
B Educational Measurement 1967
R ↓ Competence 1982

Ministers (Religion) 1973
PN 643 **SC** 31590
UF Pastors
B Clergy 1973
R Chaplains 1973
Missionaries 1973

Minks 1973
PN 55 **SC** 31600
B Rodents 1973

Minnesota Multiphasic Personality Inventory 2001
PN 4929 **SC** 31611
HN In 2000, the truncated term MINN MULTIPHASIC PERSONALITY INVEN (which was used from 1967-2000) was deleted, removed from all records containing it, and replaced with its expanded form MINNESOTA MULTIPHASIC PERSONALITY INVENTORY.
UF MMPI
B Nonprojective Personality Measures 1973

Minnesota Teacher Attitude Inventory
HN Term was discontinued in 1997. In 2000, the term was removed from all records containing it, and replaced with ATTITUDE MEASURES, its postable counterpart.
Use Attitude Measures

Minor Tranquilizers 1973
PN 183 **SC** 31630
B Tranquilizing Drugs 1967
N Alprazolam 1988
Buspirone 1991
Chlordiazepoxide 1973
Chlorprothixene 1973
Clonazepam 1991
Diazepam 1973
Hydroxyzine 1973
Lorazepam 1988
Loxapine 1982
Midazolam 1991
Oxazepam 1978
R ↓ Benzodiazepines 1978

Minority Group Discrimination
HN Term was discontinued in 1982. From 1982-1993, SOCIAL DISCRIMINATION was used to capture this concept, and then in 1994, RACE AND ETHNIC DISCRIMINATION was created as the new postable terminology. In 2000, MINORITY GROUP DISCRIMINATION was removed from all records containing it, and replaced with RACE AND ETHNIC DISCRIMINATION, its postable counterpart.
Use Race and Ethnic Discrimination

Minority Groups 1967
PN 5721 **SC** 31640
SN Includes ethnic and linguistic minority groups and in/out social groups.
B Social Groups 1973
R Affirmative Action 1985
Alaska Natives 1997
American Indians 1967
Arabs 1988
↓ Asians 1982
Blacks 1982
Cultural Sensitivity 1994
Gypsies 1973
Hawaii Natives 2001
↓ Hispanics 1982
↓ Indigenous Populations 2001
Inuit 2001
Jews 1997
Multiculturalism 1997
↓ Pacific Islanders 2001
Race and Ethnic Discrimination 1994
↓ Racial and Ethnic Groups 2001
↓ Social Identity 1988

Mirror Image 1991
PN 352 **SC** 31645
R Human Figures Drawing 1973
Mental Rotation 1991
↓ Perceptual Discrimination 1973
Self Perception 1967
↓ Visual Perception 1967

Mirroring 1997
PN 67 **SC** 31647
SN Reflecting or emulating another person's behavior or other qualities in interactional or psychotherapeutic contexts. Also a technique in psychodrama.
B Psychotherapeutic Techniques 1967
R ↓ Interpersonal Interaction 1967
Psychodrama 1967
↓ Psychotherapeutic Processes 1967
Self Psychology 1988

Misanthropy 1973
PN 74 **SC** 31650
UF Misogyny
B Personality Traits 1967

Misarticulation
Use Articulation Disorders

Misbehavior
Use Behavior Problems

Miscarriage
Use Spontaneous Abortion

Miscegenous Marriage
Use Interracial Marriage

Misconduct
Use Behavior Problems

Misdemeanors
Use Crime

Misdiagnosis 1997
PN 176 **SC** 31705
R ↓ Diagnosis 1967
Diagnosis Related Groups 1988
Patient History 1973
Professional Liability 1985
↓ Psychodiagnostic Typologies 1967
↓ Screening 1982

Misogyny
Use Misanthropy

Missing Children 2007
PN 13 **SC** 31715
SN Children whose whereabouts are unknown.
HN This term was introduced in April 2007. Relevant records were re-indexed with this term. The posting note reflects the number of records that were re-indexed.
R Kidnapping 1988
Runaway Behavior 1973

Missionaries 1973
PN 193 **SC** 31720
B Religious Personnel 1973
R ↓ Clergy 1973
↓ Educational Personnel 1973
Evangelists 1973
Lay Religious Personnel 1973
Ministers (Religion) 1973
Nuns 1973
Priests 1973
Religious Conversion 2006

Mistakes
Use Errors

MMPI
Use Minnesota Multiphasic Personality Inventory

Mnemonic Learning 1973
PN 1045 **SC** 31750
SN Use of artificial ways (e.g., imagery) to facilitate learning, memory, recognition, and recall of material learned.
B Learning 1967
Learning Strategies 1991
R Chunking 2004
Cues 1967
Memory Training 1994
Note Taking 1991

Mobility (Geographical)
Use Geographical Mobility

Mobility (Occupational)
Use Occupational Mobility

Mobility (Social)
Use Social Mobility

Mobility Aids 1978
PN 381 **SC** 31774
UF Seeing Eye Dogs
Tactual Maps
Wheelchairs
R Assistive Technology 2007
↓ Medical Therapeutic Devices 1973
Physical Mobility 1994

Moclobemide 1997
PN 145 **SC** 31780
B Antidepressant Drugs 1971
Monoamine Oxidase Inhibitors 1973

Modeling
Use Simulation

Modeling Behavior
Use Imitation (Learning)

Models 1967
PN 39745 **SC** 31805
SN Quantitative or descriptive representations of how systems function, or criteria used for comparison purposes. Not to be used for role models.
N Animal Models 1988
Information Processing Model 2007
Medical Model 1978
Mental Models 2003

Moderate Mental Retardation 2001
PN 1796 **SC** 31807
SN IQ 35-49.
HN In 2000, this term was created to replace the discontinued term TRAINABLE MENTALLY RETARDED and the discontinued and deleted term MODERATELY MENTALLY RETARDED. These terms were removed from all records containing them and replaced with MODERATE MENTAL RETARDATION.
UF Trainable Mentally Retarded
B Mental Retardation 1967
R Downs Syndrome 1967

Modernization 2003
PN 393 **SC** 31822
SN Process of change in which the most current ways or ideas are adopted.
HN This term was introduced in June 2003. Relevant records were re-indexed with this term. The posting note reflects the number of records that were re-indexed.
B Social Processes 1967
R Community Development 1997
↓ Culture Change 1967
Developing Countries 1985
Globalization 2003
Industrialization 1973
Social Change 1967
Urbanization 1973

Molindone 1982
PN 37 **SC** 31833
SN Organic heterocyclic indole having antiserotonin properties and used as an antidepressant, sedative, and tranquilizer.
B Antidepressant Drugs 1971
Neuroleptic Drugs 1973
Sedatives 1973
Serotonin Antagonists 1973

Mollusca 1973
PN 457 **SC** 31840
UF Gastropods
B Invertebrates 1973
N Octopus 1973
Snails 1973

Monetary Contributions
Use Fundraising

Monetary Incentives 1973
PN 767 **SC** 31850
SN Money expected or promised in return for service or attainment which may encourage the continued occurrence of the activity being rewarded.
B Incentives 1967
Motivation 1967
R Monetary Rewards 1973
↓ Needs 1967

Monetary Rewards 1973
PN 561 **SC** 31860
SN Money given in return for service or attainment which may act as reinforcement for the activity being rewarded.
B Rewards 1967
R Monetary Incentives 1973

Money 1967
PN 2033 **SC** 31870
R Banking 2007
Budgets 1997
↓ Business Investments 2007
Cost Containment 1991
↓ Costs and Cost Analysis 1973
↓ Economics 1985
↓ Economy 1973
Equity (Payment) 1978
Finance 2007
Funding 1988
Fundraising 2007
↓ Professional Fees 1978
Resource Allocation 1997

Mongolism
Use Downs Syndrome

Monitoring 1973
PN 2014 **SC** 31890
SN Systematic observation or recording of events, processes, or individuals.
B Attention 1967
N Polysomnography 2003
Self Monitoring 1982
Source Monitoring 2004
Vigilance 1967
R Selective Attention 1973
↓ Tracking 1967

Monkeys 1967
PN 13725 **SC** 31900
B Primates (Nonhuman) 1973

Monoamine Oxidase Inhibitors 1973
PN 1133 **SC** 31920
B Enzyme Inhibitors 1985
N Iproniazid 1973
Isocarboxazid 1973
Moclobemide 1997
Nialamide 1973
Pargyline 1973
Phenelzine 1973
Pheniprazine 1973
Tranylcypromine 1973
R ↓ Amine Oxidase Inhibitors 1973
↓ Antidepressant Drugs 1971
Monoamine Oxidases 1973
↓ Tricyclic Antidepressant Drugs 1997

Monoamine Oxidases 1973
PN 779 **SC** 31930
SN Enzymes that break down the catecholamines norepinephrine, dopamine, serotonin, and epinephrine.
UF MAOs
B Oxidases 1973
R ↓ Monoamine Oxidase Inhibitors 1973

Monoamines (Brain)
Use Catecholamines

Monocular Vision 1973
PN 869 **SC** 31940
B Visual Perception 1967
R Motion Parallax 1997

Monogamy 1997
PN 224 **SC** 31945
SN Used for human or animal populations.
UF Marital Fidelity
B Family Structure 1973
Marriage 1967
Psychosexual Behavior 1967
R Extramarital Intercourse 1973
↓ Human Courtship 1973
Infidelity 2006
Polygamy 1973

Monolingualism 1973
PN 275 **SC** 31950
R ↓ Language 1967

Monotony 1978
PN 95 **SC** 31955
SN Quality of task or stimulation characterized by tedious or wearisome sameness and uniformity.
R Boredom 1973

Monozygotic Twins 1973
PN 1397 **SC** 31960
UF Identical Twins
B Twins 1967

Montessori Method 1973
PN 116 **SC** 31970
SN Method of early childhood education developed by M. Montessori, stressing individual instruction and guidance and emphasizing practical life activities.
B Teaching Methods 1967
R Discovery Teaching Method 1973
Open Classroom Method 1973

Mood Disorders
Use Affective Disorders

Moodiness 1973
PN 71 **SC** 31980
B Personality Traits 1967

Moods
Use Emotional States

Mooney Problem Check List 1973
PN 13 **SC** 32000
B Nonprojective Personality Measures 1973

Moral Development 1973
PN 4282 **SC** 32006
SN Process of acquiring ethical judgment.
B Psychogenesis 1973
R Kohlberg (Lawrence) 1991
Morality 1967
↓ Personality Development 1967
↓ Psychosocial Development 1973

Morale 1978
PN 949 **SC** 32008
SN Prevailing spirit or attitude of an individual or group characterized by self confidence and motivation and sense of purpose.
R ↓ Emotional States 1973
↓ Emotions 1967
Enthusiasm 1973

Morality 1967
PN 6741 **SC** 32010
SN Subjective or objective standards of right or wrong, based on societal norms or ethical principles.
HN In 1982, this term replaced the discontinued term MORALS. In 2000, MORALS was removed from all records and replaced with MORALITY.
UF Morals
R ↓ Ethics 1967
Evil 2003
Integrity 1997
↓ Justice 1973
Moral Development 1973
Personal Values 1973
↓ Religious Beliefs 1973
Reputation 1997
Shame 1994
Social Values 1973
↓ Values 1967

Morals
HN Term was discontinued in 1982. In 2000, the term was removed from all records containing it, and replaced with MORALITY, its postable counterpart.
Use Morality

Mores
Use Values

Morita Therapy 1994
PN 44 **SC** 32035
B Psychotherapeutic Techniques 1967

Morphemes 1973
PN 456 **SC** 32050
SN Minimum meaningful linguistic units that contain no smaller meaningful units.
R Morphology (Language) 1973
Phonetics 1967

Morphine 1973
PN 4621 **SC** 32060
B Alkaloids 1973
Analgesic Drugs 1973
Dopamine Agonists 1985
Opiates 1973

Morphology 1973
PN 1770 **SC** 32070
SN Branch of biology that deals with the structure and form of plants and animals. Used for the scientific discipline or the morphological structure itself.
R ↓ Anatomy 1967
Histology 1973
↓ Physiology 1967
Polymorphism 2003

Morphology (Language) 1973
PN 1229 **SC** 32080
SN Study of morphemes, including both their phonology and semantics. Used for the linguistic discipline or the specific morphological principles or characteristics of words. Compare MORPHEMES.
B Grammar 1967
R Discourse Analysis 1997
Morphemes 1973
↓ Phonology 1973
↓ Prosody 1991
↓ Semantics 1967
↓ Syntax 1971
Words (Phonetic Units) 1967

Mortality
Use Death and Dying

Mortality Rate 1973
PN 2969 **SC** 32100
UF Death Rate
R ↓ Death and Dying 1967
↓ Population 1973

Mosaicism
Use Chromosome Disorders

Moslems
Use Muslims

Mother Absence 1973
PN 315 **SC** 32120
SN For animals use ANIMAL MATERNAL DEPRIVATION.
HN From 1982, limited to human populations.
B Parental Absence 1973
R Patriarchy 1973

Mother Child Communication 1985
PN 1555 **SC** 32125
SN Verbal or nonverbal communication between mother and child.
B Parent Child Communication 1973
R Mother Child Relations 1967

Mother Child Relations 1967
PN 13157 **SC** 32130
SN For animals consider ANIMAL MATERNAL BEHAVIOR.
HN From 1982, limited to human populations.
UF Maternal Behavior (Human)
B Parent Child Relations 1967
R ↓ Childrearing Practices 1967
Mother Child Communication 1985
↓ Parental Attitudes 1973
Parental Permissiveness 1973
Parental Role 1973
Postpartum Depression 1973
Postpartum Psychosis 2003
Schizophrenogenic Mothers 1973
Separation Individuation 1982
Symbiotic Infantile Psychosis 1973

Mothers 1967
PN 18837 **SC** 32140
SN For animals consider ANIMAL MATERNAL BEHAVIOR.
HN From 1982, limited to human populations.
B Human Females 1973
Parents 1967
N Adolescent Mothers 1985
Schizophrenogenic Mothers 1973
Single Mothers 1994
Unwed Mothers 1973
R Expectant Mothers 1985
Primipara 2001

Moths 1973
PN 210 **SC** 32150
B Insects 1967
R Larvae 1973

Motion Parallax 1997
PN 98 **SC** 32155
SN Monocular distance cues for motion perception based on observer movements and the resultant movements of objects in the visual field.
B Distance Perception 1973
Motion Perception 1967
R ↓ Depth Perception 1967
Form and Shape Perception 1967
Monocular Vision 1973

Motion Perception 1967
PN 6697 **SC** 32160
UF Movement Perception
B Spatial Perception 1967
N ↓ Apparent Movement 1967
Motion Parallax 1997
R Direction Perception 1997

Motion Pictures
HN In August 2005, the term was discontinued and removed from all records containing it, and was replaced with FILMS, its postable counterpart.
Use Films

Motion Sickness 1973
PN 428 **SC** 32200
B Labyrinth Disorders 1973

Motivation 1967
PN 20136 **SC** 32210
UF Desires
Drive
N ↓ Achievement Motivation 1967
Affiliation Motivation 1967
Animal Motivation 1967
Educational Incentives 1973
Employee Motivation 1973
Extrinsic Motivation 1973
Fear of Success 1978
Hunger 1967
↓ Incentives 1967
Intrinsic Motivation 1973
Monetary Incentives 1973
Procrastination 1985
Sex Drive 1973
Temptation 1973
Thirst 1967
R Activity Level 1982
Activity Theory 2003
↓ Aspirations 1967
↓ Commitment 1985
Delay of Gratification 1978
↓ Deprivation 1967
Enthusiasm 1973
↓ Exploratory Behavior 1967
Goal Setting 1997
↓ Goals 1967
Instinctive Behavior 1982
Instrumentality 1991
Intention 1988
Motivation Training 1973
↓ Needs 1967
Persistence 1973
Planned Behavior 1997
↓ Reinforcement 1967
Satiation 1967

Motivation to Change
Use Readiness to Change

Motivation Training 1973
PN 201 **SC** 32220
UF Training (Motivation)
B Training 2006
R ↓ Motivation 1967

Motivational Interviewing 2007
PN 274 **SC** 32215
SN A client-centered therapeutic technique used to encourage and strengthen the client's desire and commitment to change an unwanted behavior.
HN This term was introduced in April 2007. Relevant records were re-indexed with this term. The posting note reflects the number of records that were re-indexed.
B Psychotherapeutic Techniques 1967
R Behavior Change 1973
Readiness to Change 2007
Stages of Change 2007

Motor Coordination 1973
PN 2062 **SC** 32230
UF Coordination (Motor)
B Motor Processes 1967
R ↓ Motor Performance 1973
Motor Skills 1973
↓ Perceptual Motor Coordination 1973
↓ Physical Agility 1973

Motor Cortex 1973
PN 1727 **SC** 32240
SN Region of the frontal lobe concerned with primary motor control.
UF Cortex (Motor)
B Frontal Lobe 1973

Motor Development 1973
PN 2323 **SC** 32250
B Physical Development 1973
N Perceptual Motor Development 1991
↓ Psychomotor Development 1973
R Animal Development 1978
↓ Childhood Development 1967
Developmental Age Groups 1973
↓ Motor Processes 1967
Physical Mobility 1994

Motor Disorders
Use Nervous System Disorders

Motor Evoked Potentials
Use Somatosensory Evoked Potentials

Motor Neurons 1973
PN 895 **SC** 32290
SN Neurons that activate the muscles.
B Neurons 1973
R ↓ Efferent Pathways 1982

Motor Pathways
Use Efferent Pathways

Motor Performance 1973
PN 6394 **SC** 32300
B Motor Processes 1967
Performance 1967
N Finger Tapping 1973
Jumping 1973
Running 1973
Walking 1973

Motor Performance — (cont'd)
R Motor Coordination 1973

Motor Processes 1967
PN 14770 **SC** 32310
N Activity Level 1982
Animal Locomotion 1982
Grasping 1997
Jumping 1973
Licking 1988
↓ Locomotion 2007
Motor Coordination 1973
↓ Motor Performance 1973
Motor Skills 1973
↓ Physical Activity 2007
↓ Physical Agility 1973
Physical Mobility 1994
Range of Motion 2007
Rotational Behavior 1994
Sucking 1978
Swallowing 1988
Swimming 1973
Tonic Immobility 1978
Tool Use 1991
Wandering Behavior 1991
R ↓ Efferent Pathways 1982
↓ Motor Development 1973
Muscle Tone 1985
↓ Perceptual Motor Processes 1967
Physical Restraint 1982
Posture 1973

Motor Skill Learning
Use Perceptual Motor Learning

Motor Skills 1973
PN 1980 **SC** 32330
B Motor Processes 1967
Nonverbal Ability 1988
R Motor Coordination 1973
↓ Tracking 1967

Motor Traffic Accidents 1973
PN 2467 **SC** 32340
UF Automobile Accidents
Traffic Accidents (Motor)
B Transportation Accidents 1973
R Drivers 1973
↓ Driving Behavior 1967
Highway Safety 1973
Pedestrian Accidents 1973

Motor Vehicles 1982
PN 644 **SC** 32350
SN Automotive vehicles not operated on rails.
UF Buses
Motorcycles
Trucks
B Ground Transportation 1973
N Automobiles 1973
R Drivers 1973

Motorcycles
Use Motor Vehicles

Mourning
Use Grief

Mouse Killing
Use Muricide

Mouth (Anatomy) 1967
PN 536 **SC** 32370
B Digestive System 1967
R Lips (Face) 1973
Salivary Glands 1973
Teeth (Anatomy) 1973
↓ Tongue 1973

Movement Disorders 1985
PN 1257 **SC** 32375
SN Physically- or psychologically-based abnormalities in motor processes relating primarily to posture, coordination, or locomotion.
UF Dyspraxia
B Nervous System Disorders 1967
N Apraxia 1973
Ataxia 1973
Athetosis 1973
Catalepsy 1973
Cataplexy 1973
↓ Chorea 1973
↓ Dyskinesia 1973
Myasthenia Gravis 1973
↓ Paralysis 1973
↓ Spasms 1973
Tics 1973
Torticollis 1973
Tremor 1973
R ↓ Muscular Disorders 1973
↓ Musculoskeletal Disorders 1973
↓ Neuromuscular Disorders 1973
↓ Symptoms 1967

Movement Perception
Use Motion Perception

Movement Therapy 1997
PN 268 **SC** 32385
SN Therapeutic technique utilizing bodily movements and rhythmic exercises to improve psychological and/or physical functioning of patients or clients.
B Treatment 1967
R Art Therapy 1973
↓ Creative Arts Therapy 1994
Dance Therapy 1973
↓ Exercise 1973
Music Therapy 1973
Recreation Therapy 1973

Movies
Use Films

MPTP
Use Methylphenyltetrahydropyridine

MRI
Use Magnetic Resonance Imaging

Mucus 1973
PN 31 **SC** 32440
B Body Fluids 1973

Mueller Lyer Illusion 1988
PN 121 **SC** 32439
B Illusions (Perception) 1967

Multi Infarct Dementia
HN In August 2005, this term was discontinued and removed from all records containing it, and replaced with VASCULAR DEMENTIA, its postable counterpart.
Use Vascular Dementia

Multicultural Education 1988
PN 955 **SC** 32441
SN Educational program involving two or more ethnic or cultural groups designed to help participants define their own ethnic or cultural identity and to appreciate that of others. The primary purposes are to reduce prejudice and stereotyping, and to promote cultural pluralism.
B Education 1967
R Bilingual Education 1978
Cross Cultural Communication 1997
Cultural Sensitivity 1994
↓ Educational Programs 1973
Multiculturalism 1997

Multiculturalism 1997
PN 2308 **SC** 57500
UF Cultural Pluralism
R Acculturation 2003
Cross Cultural Communication 1997
Cross Cultural Differences 1967
Cultural Deprivation 1973
Cultural Sensitivity 1994
↓ Culture (Anthropological) 1967
↓ Culture Change 1967
Diversity 2007
Diversity in the Workplace 2003
Minority Groups 1967
Multicultural Education 1988
↓ Racial and Ethnic Attitudes 1982
Racial and Ethnic Differences 1982
↓ Racial and Ethnic Groups 2001
Racial and Ethnic Relations 1982
↓ Sociocultural Factors 1967

Multidimensional Scaling 1982
PN 861 **SC** 32443
SN Set of psychological data analysis techniques that represent perceived stimuli in multidimensional spatial or pictorial configurations.
B Measurement 1967
R ↓ Analysis 1967
↓ Rating Scales 1967
Scaling (Testing) 1967

Multidisciplinary Research
Use Interdisciplinary Research

Multidisciplinary Treatment Approach
Use Interdisciplinary Treatment Approach

Multidrug Abuse
Use Polydrug Abuse

Multilingualism 1973
PN 337 **SC** 32450
N Bilingualism 1973
R Bilingual Education 1978
English as Second Language 1997
↓ Language 1967

Multimodal Treatment Approach 1991
PN 1222 **SC** 32455
SN Use of different therapeutic techniques based on the theoretical principles from one medical or psychological specialty or discipline. Compare INTERDISCIPLINARY TREATMENT APPROACH.
B Treatment 1967
R Eclectic Psychotherapy 1994
Integrated Services 1997
Integrative Psychotherapy 2003
Interdisciplinary Treatment Approach 1973

Multinational Corporations 2006
PN 74 **SC** 32457
SN Companies that maintain operations in multiple countries.
HN This term was introduced in May 2006. Relevant records were re-indexed with this term. The posting note reflects the number of records that were re-indexed.
UF Multinational Enterprises
Multinational Organizations
Transnational Corporations
B Business Organizations 1973
R Globalization 2003

Multinational Enterprises
Use Multinational Corporations

Multinational Organizations
Use Multinational Corporations

Multiple Births 1973
PN 70 **SC** 32460
SN Birth of more than one child at the same time to the same parents. Also used to refer to the children themselves. Use a more specific term if possible. Limited to human populations.
B Siblings 1967
N Triplets 1973
↓ Twins 1967

Multiple Choice (Testing Method) 1973
PN 869 **SC** 32470
B Testing Methods 1967

Multiple Disabilities 2001
PN 1102 **SC** 32473
HN The term MULTIPLY HANDICAPPED was used to represent this concept from 1973-1996, and MULTIPLY DISABLED was used from 1997-2000. In 2000, MULTIPLE DISABILITIES was created to replace the discontinued and deleted term MULTIPLY DISABLED. MULTIPLY DISABLED and MULTIPLY HANDICAPPED were removed from all records containing them and replaced with MULTIPLE DISABILITIES.
UF Multiply Handicapped
B Disabilities 2003
N Deaf Blind 1991

Multiple Intelligences 2007
PN 172 **SC** 32475
SN Theory by Howard Gardner in 1983 that suggests that there are at least seven types of intelligence, including musical, logical-mathematical, linguistic, spatial, bodily-kinesthetic, interpersonal, and intrapersonal.
HN This term was introduced in April 2007. Relevant records were re-indexed with this term. The posting note reflects the number of records that were re-indexed.
B Intelligence 1967
R ↓ Cognitive Style 1967
Emotional Intelligence 2003
Learning Theory 1967

Multiple Personality
HN Term was discontinued in 1997. In 2000, the term was removed from all records containing it, and replaced with DISSOCIATIVE IDENTITY DISORDER, its postable counterpart.
Use Dissociative Identity Disorder

Multiple Regression 1982
PN 473 **SC** 32485
SN Method of analyzing the collective and separate influences of two or more independent variables on the variation of a criterion variable.
B Multivariate Analysis 1982
Statistical Regression 1985
R Analysis of Covariance 1973
Analysis of Variance 1967
Linear Regression 1973
Logistic Regression 2003
Nonlinear Regression 1973
Path Analysis 1991
↓ Statistical Correlation 1967

Multiple Sclerosis 1973
PN 2036 **SC** 32490
SN Chronic, progressive nervous system disorder of unknown etiology in which the body's immune system attacks the myelin of the brain and spinal cord. Symptoms include muscle weakness, loss of coordination, and speech and vision disturbances.
B Sclerosis (Nervous System) 1973
R ↓ Myelitis 1973

Multiple Therapy
Use Cotherapy

Multiply Handicapped
HN The term was discontinued in 1997, when the term MULTIPLY DISABLED was created to capture this concept. In 2000, with the deletion of the term MULTIPLY DISABLED, MULTIPLY HANDICAPPED was made a nonpostable term for the new postable term MULTIPLE DISABILITIES. MULTIPLY HANDICAPPED and MULTIPLY DISABLED were removed from all records containing them and replaced with MULTIPLE DISABILITIES.
Use Multiple Disabilities

Multivariate Analysis 1982
PN 1509 **SC** 32513
SN Any statistical technique designed to measure the influence of many independent variables acting simultaneously on more than one dependent variable.
UF Canonical Correlation
B Statistical Analysis 1967
N ↓ Factor Analysis 1967
Multiple Regression 1982
Path Analysis 1991
R Analysis of Covariance 1973
Analysis of Variance 1967
↓ Statistical Correlation 1967
↓ Statistical Regression 1985

Munchausen Syndrome 1994
PN 83 **SC** 32517
SN A disorder characterized by plausible presentations of physical symptoms or an acute illness that are under the individual's control, and often resulting in multiple, unnecessary hospitalizations.
HN Use FACTITIOUS DISORDERS to access references from 1988-1993.
UF Hospital Addiction Syndrome
B Factitious Disorders 1988
R Malingering 1973
Munchausen Syndrome by Proxy 1997
↓ Somatoform Disorders 2001

Munchausen Syndrome by Proxy 1997
PN 151 **SC** 32519
SN A phenomenon in which symptoms of an acute illness are fabricated by an individual other than the patient (e.g., a caregiver or parent) resulting in habitual seeking of medical care.
R ↓ Child Abuse 1971
Child Neglect 1988
Munchausen Syndrome 1994

Murder
Use Homicide

Muricide 1988
PN 43 **SC** 32523
UF Mouse Killing
B Animal Aggressive Behavior 1973

Muscarinic Drugs
Use Cholinergic Drugs

Muscarinic Receptors
Use Cholinergic Receptors

Muscimol 1994
PN 216 **SC** 32525
HN Use GAMMA AMINOBUTYRIC ACID AGONISTS to access references from 1985-1993.
UF Pantherine
B Gamma Aminobutyric Acid Agonists 1985
Ibotenic Acid 1991

Muscle Contraction Headache 1973
PN 640 **SC** 32530
UF Tension Headache
B Headache 1973

Muscle Contractions 1973
PN 786 **SC** 32540
UF Rigidity (Muscles)
R Muscle Relaxation 1973
Muscle Tone 1985
↓ Muscles 1967
Parkinsonism 1994
↓ Reflexes 1971

Muscle Cramps
Use Muscular Disorders

Muscle Relaxation 1973
PN 519 **SC** 32557
R Muscle Contractions 1973
↓ Muscles 1967
Progressive Relaxation Therapy 1978
Relaxation 1973
↓ Relaxation Therapy 1978

Muscle Relaxation Therapy
Use Relaxation Therapy

Muscle Relaxing Drugs 1973
PN 186 **SC** 32560
HN In 1997, this term replaced the discontinued term MEPHENESIN. In 2000, MEPHENESIN was removed from all records and replaced with MUSCLE RELAXING DRUGS.
UF Mephenesin
Neuromuscular Blocking Drugs
B Drugs 1967
N Baclofen 1991
Curare 1973
Diazepam 1973
Meprobamate 1973
Orphenadrine 1973
Papaverine 1973

Muscle Relaxing Drugs — (cont'd)
Succinylcholine 1973
Theophylline 1973
Tubocurarine 1973
R ↓ Anesthetic Drugs 1973
↓ Anticonvulsive Drugs 1973
↓ Antihypertensive Drugs 1973
↓ Antispasmodic Drugs 1973
↓ Benzodiazepines 1978
↓ CNS Depressant Drugs 1973
↓ Heart Rate Affecting Drugs 1973
↓ Tranquilizing Drugs 1967
Vasodilation 1973

Muscle Spasms 1973
PN 97 **SC** 32570
B Spasms 1973
R ↓ Muscles 1967

Muscle Tone 1985
PN 129 **SC** 32575
R ↓ Motor Processes 1967
Muscle Contractions 1973
↓ Reflexes 1971

Muscles 1967
PN 2426 **SC** 32580
B Musculoskeletal System 1973
N Abdominal Wall 1973
Diaphragm (Anatomy) 1973
Facial Muscles 1973
Masticatory Muscles 1973
Oculomotor Muscles 1973
R Muscle Contractions 1973
Muscle Relaxation 1973
Muscle Spasms 1973
↓ Tissues (Body) 1973

Muscular Atrophy 1973
PN 63 **SC** 32590
UF Atrophy (Muscular)
B Muscular Disorders 1973

Muscular Disorders 1973
PN 1230 **SC** 32600
UF Cramps (Muscle)
Duchennes Disease
Dystonia
Muscle Cramps
B Musculoskeletal Disorders 1973
N Cataplexy 1973
Fibromyalgia 2004
Muscular Atrophy 1973
Muscular Dystrophy 1973
Myasthenia Gravis 1973
Myofascial Pain 1991
Myotonia 1973
Torticollis 1973
R Chronic Fatigue Syndrome 1997
↓ Movement Disorders 1985
↓ Neuromuscular Disorders 1973

Muscular Dystrophy 1973
PN 250 **SC** 32610
SN A heterogeneous group of genetic progressive muscle disorders marked by deterioration and weakness of skeletal muscles.
UF Dystrophy (Muscular)
B Muscular Disorders 1973
Neuromuscular Disorders 1973
R Dysarthria 1973
↓ Peripheral Neuropathy 2006

Musculocutaneous Nerve
Use Spinal Nerves

Musculoskeletal Disorders 1973
PN 876 **SC** 32630
UF Skeletomuscular Disorders
Temporomandibular Joint Syndrome
B Physical Disorders 1997
N ↓ Bone Disorders 1973
↓ Joint Disorders 1973
↓ Muscular Disorders 1973
R Hemiplegia 1978
↓ Movement Disorders 1985
↓ Musculoskeletal System 1973
↓ Neuromuscular Disorders 1973
↓ Paralysis 1973
Paraplegia 1978
Poliomyelitis 1973
Quadriplegia 1985
↓ Tuberculosis 1973

Musculoskeletal System 1973
PN 252 **SC** 32640
B Anatomical Systems 1973
N Arm (Anatomy) 1973
Bones 1973
Feet (Anatomy) 1973
↓ Fingers (Anatomy) 1973
Hand (Anatomy) 1967
Hips 1973
Jaw 1973
↓ Joints (Anatomy) 1973
Leg (Anatomy) 1973
↓ Muscles 1967
Skull 1973
Spinal Column 1973
Tendons 1973
Thorax 1973
R ↓ Musculoskeletal Disorders 1973
↓ Nose 1973
Osteopathic Medicine 2003

Museums 2006
PN 232 **SC** 32645
SN Buildings or institutions that exhibit, collect, and archive historic, scientific, artistic, or literary objects and artifacts that are deemed of value.
HN This term was introduced in May 2006. Relevant records were re-indexed with this term. The posting note reflects the number of records that were re-indexed.
B Facilities 2006
R Anthropology 1967
↓ Art 1967
↓ History 1973

Music 1967
PN 6155 **SC** 32650
UF Songs
B Arts 1973
N Musical Instruments 1973
Rock Music 1991
R Music Perception 1997
Musicians 1991
↓ Rhythm 1991
Singing 1997
Tempo 1997

Music Education 1973
PN 1447 **SC** 32660
B Curriculum 1967

Music Perception 1997
PN 986 **SC** 32665
B Auditory Perception 1967
R ↓ Music 1967
Musical Ability 1973
↓ Pitch Perception 1973
↓ Rhythm 1991
Singing 1997
Tempo 1997

Music Therapy 1973
PN 1738 **SC** 32670
B Creative Arts Therapy 1994
R Educational Therapy 1997
Movement Therapy 1997
Recreation Therapy 1973

Musical Ability 1973
PN 1162 **SC** 32680
B Artistic Ability 1973
R Music Perception 1997

Musical Instruments 1973
PN 405 **SC** 32690
UF Piano
B Music 1967

Musicians 1991
PN 973 **SC** 32695
B Artists 1973
R Celebrities 2007
↓ Music 1967

Muslims 1997
PN 481 **SC** 32700
HN Use ISLAM to access references prior to 1997.
UF Moslems
B Religious Groups 1997
R Islam 1973

Mutations 1973
PN 1660 **SC** 32710
SN Individual, strain, or species genetic variation resulting from an abrupt or unusual change in gene structure. Also, an externally induced or naturally occurring change in gene characteristics that is propagated in subsequent divisions of the cell.
R ↓ Chromosomes 1973
↓ Genetic Disorders 1973
↓ Genetics 1967
Translocation (Chromosome) 1973

Mutilation (Self)
Use Self Mutilation

Mutism 1973
PN 271 **SC** 32730
B Language Disorders 1982
N Elective Mutism 1973

Mutual Storytelling Technique 1973
PN 66 **SC** 32740
UF Storytelling Technique
B Psychotherapeutic Techniques 1967

Myasthenia 1973
PN 10 **SC** 32750
SN Anomaly of the muscles, resulting in muscular debility, weakness, lack of tone, fatigue, or exhaustion.

Myasthenia — (cont'd)
B Asthenia 1973

Myasthenia Gravis 1973
PN 81 **SC** 32760
SN A neuromuscular disorder marked by chronic muscle weakness and being prone to fatigue easily.
B Movement Disorders 1985
Muscular Disorders 1973
Neuromuscular Disorders 1973

Myelin Sheath 1973
PN 163 **SC** 32780
SN An insulated sheath that surrounds the axons in the peripheral nervous system.
B Nerve Tissues 1973

Myelitis 1973
PN 13 **SC** 32790
SN An inflammation of bone marrow of the spinal cord characterized by weakness, localized pain, incontinence, sensory loss, or other signs of autonomic dysfunction.
B Central Nervous System Disorders 1973
N Encephalomyelitis 1973
Poliomyelitis 1973
R ↓ Infectious Disorders 1973
Multiple Sclerosis 1973

Myelomeningocele
Use Spina Bifida

Myenteric Plexus
Use Autonomic Ganglia

Myers Briggs Type Indicator 1973
PN 580 **SC** 32810
B Nonprojective Personality Measures 1973

Myocardial Infarctions 1973
PN 1410 **SC** 32820
UF Infarctions (Myocardial)
B Heart Disorders 1973
R Angina Pectoris 1973
Coronary Thromboses 1973

Myocardium 1973
PN 38 **SC** 32830
B Heart 1967

Myoclonus 2006
PN 294 **SC** 32840
SN Involuntary spasms and shock-like contractions in a muscle or group of muscles.
HN In May 2006, this term replaced the deleted term MYOCLONIA. MYOCLONIA was removed from all records and replaced with MYOCLONUS.
B Dyskinesia 1973

Myofascial Pain 1991
PN 155 **SC** 32845
B Muscular Disorders 1973
Pain 1967
R ↓ Bruxism 1985
Chronic Pain 1985
↓ Somatoform Disorders 2001
↓ Syndromes 1973

Myopia 1973
PN 188 **SC** 32850
UF Nearsightedness
B Refraction Errors 1973

Myotonia 1973
PN 68 **SC** 32860
B Muscular Disorders 1973
R ↓ Congenital Disorders 1973

Mysticism 1967
PN 708 **SC** 32870
UF Visions (Mysticism)
B Philosophies 1967
R Occultism 1978
↓ Parapsychology 1967
↓ Religious Beliefs 1973
Religious Experiences 1997
↓ Religious Practices 1973
Witchcraft 1973

Myths 1967
PN 2240 **SC** 32890
R Animism 1973
Archetypes 1991
Cultism 1973
Ethnology 1967
Folklore 1991
Heroes 2007
↓ Literature 1967
Metaphor 1982
Storytelling 1988
Transcultural Psychiatry 1973

Myxedema
Use Hypothyroidism

N-Methyl-D-Aspartate 1994
PN 2480 **SC** 32905
UF NMDA
B Aspartic Acid 1973
R Glutamate Receptors 2007

Nabilone
Use Cannabinoids

NAch
Use Achievement Motivation

Nail Biting 1973
PN 95 **SC** 32920
B Habits 1967

Nalorphine 1973
PN 47 **SC** 32940
B Narcotic Antagonists 1973

Naloxone 1978
PN 2065 **SC** 32944
B Narcotic Antagonists 1973

Naltrexone 1988
PN 1027 **SC** 32945
B Narcotic Antagonists 1973

Names 1985
PN 752 **SC** 32947
N Brand Names 1978
R Labeling 1978
Nouns 1973

Naming 1988
PN 2629 **SC** 32948
SN Process of identifying an object or concept with a word or phrase.
B Cognitive Processes 1967
R Cognitive Mediation 1967
Object Recognition 1997

Nanotechnology 2007
PN 15 **SC** 58108
SN A form of technology in which materials are manipulated at the atomic or molecular level to create novel products used in industry, medicine, or other sectors.
HN This term was introduced in April 2007. Relevant records were re-indexed with this term. The posting note reflects the number of records that were re-indexed.
B Technology 1973
R ↓ Sciences 1967

Napping 1994
PN 123 **SC** 32949
B Sleep 1967
R Sleep Onset 1973
Sleep Wake Cycle 1985

Narcissism 1967
PN 2562 **SC** 32950
SN Self-love in which all sources of pleasure are unrealistically believed to emanate from within oneself, resulting in a false sense of omnipotence, and in which the libido is no longer attached to external love objects, but is redirected to one's self.
B Personality Traits 1967
R Autoeroticism 1997
Egocentrism 1978
Grandiosity 1994
↓ Mental Disorders 1967
Narcissistic Personality Disorder 1973
Selfishness 1973

Narcissistic Personality Disorder 1973
PN 1148 **SC** 32960
SN Personality disorder characterized by excessive self-love, egocentrism, grandiosity, exhibitionism, excessive needs for attention, and sensitivity to criticism.
B Personality Disorders 1967
R Antisocial Personality Disorder 1973
Narcissism 1967

Narcoanalysis 1973
PN 24 **SC** 32970
SN Sleep-like state induced by medication or hypnosis and used in the treatment of mental disorders.
B Drug Therapy 1967
Physical Treatment Methods 1973
N Sleep Treatment 1973

Narcoanalytic Drugs
HN Term was discontinued in 1997. In 2000, the term was removed from all records containing it, and replaced with DRUGS, its postable counterpart.
Use Drugs

Narcolepsy 1973
PN 536 **SC** 32990
SN Neurological condition marked by sudden, recurrent, and uncontrollable compulsions to sleep, cataplexy (flaccid paralysis), hallucinations, or sleep-onset REM.

Narcolepsy — (cont'd)
UF Paroxysmal Sleep
B Sleep Disorders 1973
R Cataplexy 1973
Hypersomnia 1994

Narcosis 1973
PN 79 **SC** 33000
B Toxic Disorders 1973
R ↓ Narcotic Drugs 1973

Narcotic Agonists 1988
PN 978 **SC** 32995
UF Opiate Agonists
B Drugs 1967
N Pentazocine 1991
R ↓ Narcotic Drugs 1973

Narcotic Antagonists 1973
PN 1105 **SC** 33010
UF Opiate Antagonists
Opioid Antagonists
B Drugs 1967
N Nalorphine 1973
Naloxone 1978
Naltrexone 1988
R ↓ Narcotic Drugs 1973

Narcotic Drugs 1973
PN 543 **SC** 33020
B Drugs 1967
N Apomorphine 1973
Atropine 1973
Meperidine 1973
Methadone 1973
↓ Opiates 1973
R ↓ Analgesic Drugs 1973
↓ Anesthetic Drugs 1973
↓ Anticonvulsive Drugs 1973
↓ Cannabis 1973
↓ CNS Depressant Drugs 1973
↓ Dopamine Antagonists 1982
↓ Emetic Drugs 1973
↓ Hypnotic Drugs 1973
Narcosis 1973
↓ Narcotic Agonists 1988
↓ Narcotic Antagonists 1973
↓ Tranquilizing Drugs 1967

Narcotics Anonymous
Use Twelve Step Programs

Narrative Therapy 2006
PN 108 **SC** 33024
SN An approach to psychotherapy that emphasizes the clients' use of written narratives to convey their personal stories.
HN This term was introduced in May 2006. Relevant records were re-indexed with this term. The posting note reflects the number of records that were re-indexed.
B Psychotherapy 1967
R Narratives 1997
Storytelling 1988

Narratives 1997
PN 5125 **SC** 33025
SN Construction or reconstruction of an event or story.
B Verbal Communication 1967
R ↓ Biography 1967
Creative Writing 1994
Life Review 1991
↓ Literature 1967

Narratives — (cont'd)
Narrative Therapy 2006
Storytelling 1988

Nasal Mucosa 1973
PN 68 **SC** 33030
B Membranes 1973
Nose 1973
N Olfactory Mucosa 1973

National Guard Personnel 1973
PN 68 **SC** 33040
B Military Personnel 1967
R Air Force Personnel 1967
Army Personnel 1967
Volunteer Military Personnel 1973

National Security 2006
PN 34 **SC** 33045
SN The protection of the nation-state through the use of intelligence, and diplomatic, military, economic, and political power. May also refer to the actual condition of the nation, in terms of safety from threat.
HN This term was introduced in May 2006. Relevant records were re-indexed with this term. The posting note reflects the number of records that were re-indexed.
R Foreign Policy Making 1973
↓ Government Policy Making 1973
International Relations 1967
↓ War 1967

Nationalism 1967
PN 746 **SC** 33050
B Political Attitudes 1973

Native Alaskans
Use Alaska Natives

Native Americans
Use American Indians

Native Hawaiians
Use Hawaii Natives

Native Language 2004
PN 331 **SC** 58074
HN This term was introduced in June 2004. Relevant records were re-indexed with this term. The posting note reflects the number of records that were re-indexed.
UF First Language
B Language 1967
R Bilingualism 1973
English as Second Language 1997

Natives
Use Indigenous Populations

Natural Childbirth 1978
PN 65 **SC** 33056
UF Childbirth (Natural)
B Birth 1967
R Childbirth Training 1978

Natural Disaster Preparedness
Use Emergency Preparedness

Natural Disasters 1973
PN 1193 **SC** 33060
SN Calamity caused by natural forces resulting in substantial damage, loss, and distress.

Natural Disasters — (cont'd)
B Disasters 1973
R Emergency Preparedness 2007
Emergency Services 1973
↓ Stress 1967

Natural Family
Use Biological Family

Natural Killer Cells 2003
PN 155 **SC** 33072
SN White blood cells that kill tumor- and virus-infected cells as part of the body's immune system.
HN This term was introduced in June 2003. Relevant records were re-indexed with this term. The posting note reflects the number of records that were re-indexed.
B Leucocytes 1973

Natural Selection 1997
PN 394 **SC** 33073
SN Natural evolutionary process that results in the survival of organisms best suited to changing living conditions through the perpetuation of desirable genetic qualities and the elimination of undesirable ones.
HN Consider DARWINISM to access references from 1973-1996.
B Darwinism 1973
R Evolutionary Economics 2007
↓ Genetics 1967
Theory of Evolution 1967

Naturalistic Observation
Use Observation Methods

Nature Nurture 1994
PN 1037 **SC** 33075
SN Debatable issue concerning the controversial role of genetics or heredity versus environment or experience in normal or abnormal developmental processes.
R Behavioral Genetics 1994
↓ Environment 1967
↓ Genetics 1967
↓ Human Development 1967
Predisposition 1973
↓ Psychogenesis 1973

Nausea 1973
PN 388 **SC** 33080
B Symptoms 1967
R ↓ Antiemetic Drugs 1973
↓ Eating Disorders 1997
Migraine Headache 1973
Vomiting 1973

Navigators (Aircraft)
Use Aerospace Personnel

Navy Personnel 1967
PN 1327 **SC** 33100
B Military Personnel 1967
R Draftees 1973

Nazism
Use Fascism

Near Death Experiences 1985
PN 466 **SC** 33105
SN Psychological and sensory phenomena reported by persons who were near clinical death.
B Parapsychological Phenomena 1973
R ↓ Death and Dying 1967
↓ Experiences (Events) 1973

Near Death Experiences — (cont'd)
↓ Hallucinations 1967
Out of Body Experiences 1988

Nearsightedness
Use Myopia

Neck (Anatomy) 1973
PN 353 **SC** 33120
B Anatomy 1967

Necrosis 2006
PN 20 **SC** 33125
SN The pathological process of cell death resulting from lack of blood supply.
HN This term was introduced in May 2006. Relevant records were re-indexed with this term. The posting note reflects the number of records that were re-indexed.
UF Gangrene
R Apoptosis 2006
↓ Cells (Biology) 1973
↓ Pathology 1973

Need Achievement
Use Achievement Motivation

Need for Affiliation
Use Affiliation Motivation

Need for Approval 1997
PN 54 **SC** 33160
B Personality Traits 1967
R ↓ Needs 1967
Social Acceptance 1967
Social Approval 1967
Social Desirability 1967

Need for Cognition 1997
PN 149 **SC** 33167
B Personality Traits 1967
R Cognition 1967
Intrinsic Motivation 1973
↓ Needs 1967

Need Satisfaction 1973
PN 694 **SC** 33170
B Satisfaction 1973
R ↓ Needs 1967
Psychological Needs 1997

Needle Exchange Programs 2001
PN 149 **SC** 33173
B Harm Reduction 2003
Social Programs 1973
R AIDS Prevention 1994
↓ Drug Abuse 1973
Intravenous Drug Usage 1994
Needle Sharing 1994
Outreach Programs 1997

Needle Sharing 1994
PN 295 **SC** 33175
R ↓ Drug Abuse 1973
↓ Drug Usage 1971
Intravenous Drug Usage 1994
Intravenous Injections 1973
Needle Exchange Programs 2001
Sharing (Social Behavior) 1978

Needs 1967
PN 4941 **SC** 33180
N Health Service Needs 1997
Psychological Needs 1997

Needs — (cont'd)
R ↓ Achievement Motivation 1967
Affiliation Motivation 1967
Craving 1997
Extrinsic Motivation 1973
↓ Goals 1967
↓ Incentives 1967
Intrinsic Motivation 1973
Monetary Incentives 1973
↓ Motivation 1967
Need for Approval 1997
Need for Cognition 1997
Need Satisfaction 1973
Needs Assessment 1985
Nurturance 1985
Special Needs 1994

Needs Assessment 1985
PN 2201 **SC** 33185
SN Systematic identification of needs of an individual or a group.
B Evaluation 1967
Measurement 1967
R ↓ Case Management 1991
Geriatric Assessment 1997
↓ Health Care Delivery 1978
Health Service Needs 1997
Intake Interview 1994
↓ Needs 1967
↓ Psychological Assessment 1997
Psychological Needs 1997
Special Needs 1994
↓ Surveys 1967
↓ Treatment Planning 1997
Utilization Reviews 2007

Nefazodone 2003
PN 246 **SC** 33188
HN This term was introduced in June 2003. Relevant records were re-indexed with this term. The posting note reflects the number of records that were re-indexed.
B Antidepressant Drugs 1971

Negative and Positive Symptoms
Use Positive and Negative Symptoms

Negative Reinforcement 1973
PN 479 **SC** 33200
SN A stimulus or stimulus situation that, when withdrawn or discontinued following a response, increases the probability of occurrence of that response. Consider also ESCAPE CONDITIONING.
B Reinforcement 1967

Negative Therapeutic Reaction 1997
PN 47 **SC** 33205
SN In psychoanalysis, after a period of successful and constructive treatment, the worsening of a patient's symptoms and neurotic behavior.
B Psychotherapeutic Processes 1967
R Countertransference 1973
↓ Psychoanalysis 1967
Psychotherapeutic Resistance 1973
Psychotherapeutic Transference 1967

Negative Transfer 1973
PN 209 **SC** 33210
SN Previous learning or practice that hinders the acquisition of new material or skills as the result of dissimilar characteristics of the prior and current learning situation.

Negative Transfer — (cont'd)
B Transfer (Learning) 1967

Negativism 1973
PN 584 **SC** 33220
SN State of mind or behavior characterized by extreme skepticism and persistent opposition or resistance to outside suggestions or advice.
B Personality Traits 1967
R Cynicism 1973
Pessimism 1973
Skepticism 2004

Negotiation 1973
PN 2380 **SC** 33230
B Interpersonal Communication 1973
N Bargaining 1973
R ↓ Conflict Resolution 1982
Mediation 1988

Negroes
HN Term was discontinued in 1982. In 2000, the term was removed from all records containing it, and replaced with BLACKS, its postable counterpart.
Use Blacks

Neighborhoods 1973
PN 1772 **SC** 33260
B Communities 1967
N Ghettoes 1973

Nembutal
Use Pentobarbital

NEO Personality Inventory 1997
PN 241 **SC** 33275
B Personality Measures 1967
R Five Factor Personality Model 1997

NeoFreudian School
Use Neopsychoanalytic School

Neologisms 1973
PN 56 **SC** 33290
B Vocabulary 1967
R Words (Phonetic Units) 1967

Neonatal Development 1973
PN 1063 **SC** 33320
SN Process of physical, cognitive, personality, and psychosocial growth occurring during the first month of life. Use a more specific term if possible.
B Infant Development 1973
R Neonatal Period 2001
↓ Physical Development 1973
↓ Psychogenesis 1973

Neonatal Disorders 1973
PN 209 **SC** 33330
B Physical Disorders 1997
N Anencephaly 1973
Cleft Palate 1967
Conjoined Twins 2003
Crying Cat Syndrome 1973
Downs Syndrome 1967
Klinefelters Syndrome 1973
Phenylketonuria 1973
Tay Sachs Disease 2003
Turners Syndrome 1973
R ↓ Apnea 1973
Birth Injuries 1973
↓ Congenital Disorders 1973
Hydrocephalus 2006

Neonatal Disorders — (cont'd)
Microcephaly 1973
Rh Incompatibility 1973
Sleep Apnea 1991

Neonatal Period 2001
PN 364 **SC** 33340
SN Usually the period from age 0 through 1 month. Compare PERINATAL PERIOD. Used for both human and animal populations.
R Neonatal Development 1973

Neonates (Animal)
Use Infants (Animal)

Neonaticide
Use Infanticide

Neophobia 1985
PN 189 **SC** 33368
SN Fearful or cautious exploration or reaction to novel objects, situations, or stimuli. Usually examined in subhuman species.
R Animal Exploratory Behavior 1973
Avoidance 1967
↓ Fear 1967
Instinctive Behavior 1982
Stimulus Novelty 1973

Neoplasms 1967
PN 10072 **SC** 33370
UF Cancers
Carcinomas
Malignant Neoplasms
Sarcomas
Tumors
B Physical Disorders 1997
N Benign Neoplasms 1973
Breast Neoplasms 1973
Endocrine Neoplasms 1973
Leukemias 1973
↓ Nervous System Neoplasms 1973
Terminal Cancer 1973
R Antineoplastic Drugs 1982
↓ Digestive System Disorders 1973
↓ Gastrointestinal Disorders 1973
↓ Liver Disorders 1973

Neopsychoanalytic School 1973
PN 64 **SC** 33380
SN School of psychoanalysis, originating with Jung and Adler which differs from Freudian psychoanalysis in emphasizing the importance of social and cultural factors in the development of an individual's personality.
UF NeoFreudian School
B History of Psychology 1967
Psychological Theories 2001
N Individual Psychology 1973
↓ Jungian Psychology 1973
R Erikson (Erik) 1991
Freud (Sigmund) 1967
Freudian Psychoanalytic School 1973
↓ Psychoanalytic Theory 1967

Neostigmine 1973
PN 50 **SC** 33390
UF Proserine
B Cholinesterase Inhibitors 1973
Cholinomimetic Drugs 1973
R Bromides 1973

Neostriatum
Use Striatum

Nepotism 2005
PN 20 **SC** 33395
SN Demonstrating favoritism to family members, usually by appointing them to a desired job.
HN This term was introduced in August 2005. Relevant records were re-indexed with this term. The posting note reflects the number of records that were re-indexed.
R ↓ Family Members 1973
Personnel Promotion 1978
↓ Personnel Recruitment 1973
↓ Personnel Selection 1967
Professional Ethics 1973

Nerve (Abducens)
Use Abducens Nerve

Nerve (Accessory)
Use Cranial Nerves

Nerve (Acoustic)
Use Acoustic Nerve

Nerve (Facial)
Use Facial Nerve

Nerve Cells
Use Neurons

Nerve Endings 1973
PN 55 **SC** 33450
B Nervous System 1967
N ↓ Neural Receptors 1973
Proprioceptors 1973
Synapses 1973
Thermoreceptors 1973

Nerve Growth Factor 1994
PN 565 **SC** 33455
SN Polypeptide proteins that stimulate growth and development of peripheral, sympathetic, and sensory neurons.
B Peptides 1973
R ↓ Amino Acids 1973
↓ Nervous System 1967
↓ Neural Development 1985
↓ Neurons 1973

Nerve Tissues 1973
PN 191 **SC** 33460
B Nervous System 1967
Tissues (Body) 1973
N Myelin Sheath 1973
R ↓ Neurons 1973

Nerves (Adrenergic)
Use Adrenergic Nerves

Nerves (Cholinergic)
Use Cholinergic Nerves

Nerves (Cranial)
Use Cranial Nerves

Nerves (Peripheral)
Use Peripheral Nervous System

Nerves (Spinal)
Use Spinal Nerves

Nervous Breakdown
Use Mental Disorders

Nervous System 1967
PN 1527 **SC** 33530
SN System of cells, tissues, and organs that regulate the body's responses to stimuli.
B Anatomical Systems 1973
N ↓ Central Nervous System 1967
↓ Ganglia 1973
↓ Nerve Endings 1973
↓ Nerve Tissues 1973
↓ Neurons 1973
↓ Peripheral Nervous System 1973
↓ Receptive Fields 1985
R Afferent Stimulation 1973
Nerve Growth Factor 1994
↓ Nervous System Disorders 1967
↓ Neural Development 1985
Neural Networks 1991
Neural Plasticity 1994
↓ Stereotaxic Techniques 1973

Nervous System Disorders 1967
PN 6962 **SC** 33540
UF Motor Disorders
Neuroinfections
Neurological Disorders
Neuropathy
B Physical Disorders 1997
N Autonomic Nervous System Disorders 1973
↓ Central Nervous System Disorders 1973
Hyperkinesis 1973
↓ Movement Disorders 1985
↓ Nervous System Neoplasms 1973
↓ Neurodegenerative Diseases 2004
↓ Neuromuscular Disorders 1973
↓ Peripheral Neuropathy 2006
↓ Sclerosis (Nervous System) 1973
↓ Seizures 2005
R ↓ Cerebrovascular Disorders 1973
Developmental Disabilities 1982
Extrapyramidal Symptoms 1994
Hemianopia 1973
Influenza 1973
Malaria 1973
↓ Nervous System 1967
Nystagmus 1973
Parkinsonism 1994
Somatosensory Disorders 2001
↓ Symptoms 1967
↓ Tuberculosis 1973

Nervous System Neoplasms 1973
PN 33 **SC** 33550
B Neoplasms 1967
Nervous System Disorders 1967
N Brain Neoplasms 1973

Nervous System Plasticity
Use Neural Plasticity

Nervousness 1973
PN 119 **SC** 33560
B Personality Traits 1967

Nest Building 1973
PN 835 **SC** 33570
B Animal Ethology 1967
R ↓ Animal Mating Behavior 1967

Networks (Social)
Use Social Networks

Neural Analyzers 1973
PN 39 **SC** 33600
SN The peripheral sensory receptors or nerve endings (e.g., visual analyzer, acoustic analyzer) that select and transform stimuli and their associated projections and terminations in the central nervous system where synthesis of the transformations occurs.
B Central Nervous System 1967

Neural Development 1985
PN 4016 **SC** 33605
SN Functional and morphological development of central and peripheral nervous systems and supportive tissue.
UF Neural Regeneration
Reinnervation
B Physical Development 1973
N Brain Development 2007
R Animal Development 1978
Nerve Growth Factor 1994
↓ Nervous System 1967
Neural Plasticity 1994
Neural Transplantation 1985

Neural Lesions 1973
PN 1066 **SC** 33610
HN Not defined prior to 1982. From 1982, limited to experimentally induced neural lesions and used primarily for animal populations.
B Lesions 1967

Neural Networks 1991
PN 4940 **SC** 33612
SN Computer simulation that duplicates the neural structure and cognitive processes of the human or animal brain.
B Artificial Intelligence 1982
Computer Simulation 1973
R Connectionism 1994
↓ Machine Learning 2003
↓ Nervous System 1967
Neuroanatomy 1967

Neural Pathways 1982
PN 2664 **SC** 33615
SN Collections of central or peripheral neural fibers having a common neurological function and serving to connect neuroanatomical systems such as sensory or motor mechanisms or central nervous system nuclei.
B Central Nervous System 1967
Peripheral Nervous System 1973
N ↓ Afferent Pathways 1982
Corpus Callosum 1973
↓ Efferent Pathways 1982
Fornix 1982
↓ Limbic System 1973
Optic Chiasm 1973
Optic Tract 1982
Reticular Formation 1967

Neural Plasticity 1994
PN 2470 **SC** 33617
SN Change in reactivity of the nervous system and its components as a result of constant successive activations.
UF Nervous System Plasticity
Synaptic Plasticity
R ↓ Nervous System 1967
↓ Neural Development 1985
Postactivation Potentials 1985
↓ Receptive Fields 1985

Neural Receptors 1973
PN 9793 **SC** 33620
SN Specialized receptors sensitive to a specific type of stimulation that act as a communication relay located in the neuron or its membrane.
UF Neuroreceptors
Receptors (Neural)
B Nerve Endings 1973
N Adrenergic Receptors 2003
Baroreceptors 1973
Chemoreceptors 1973
Cholinergic Receptors 2003
Glutamate Receptors 2007
Mechanoreceptors 1973
Nociceptors 1985
↓ Photoreceptors 1973
Proprioceptors 1973
Thermoreceptors 1973
R Receptor Binding 1985

Neural Regeneration
Use Neural Development

Neural Transmission
Use Neurotransmission

Neural Transplantation 1985
PN 404 **SC** 33628
SN The grafting of nerve cells taken from one site to another within the same subject or from one subject to another. Used in the treatment of neurodegenerative diseases.
B Neurosurgery 1973
R ↓ Neural Development 1985
Organ Transplantation 1973
Tissue Donation 1991

Neuralgia 1973
PN 171 **SC** 33630
SN Intense or aching pain occurring along a nerve or group of nerves. It is frequently a result of trauma, chemical irritation, or inflammation, or due to causes that cannot be identified with any organic syndrome.
B Pain 1967
Peripheral Neuropathy 2006
N Trigeminal Neuralgia 1973

Neurasthenia 2005
PN 196 **SC** 33639
SN A mental disorder characterized by weakness and fatigue.
HN In August 2005, this term was created to replace the deleted term NEURASTHENIC NEUROSIS. NEURASTHENIC NEUROSIS was removed from all records containing it and replaced with NEURASTHENIA.
B Somatoform Disorders 2001
R ↓ Asthenia 1973

Neuroanatomy 1967
PN 4658 **SC** 33660
SN Branch of neurology concerned with the anatomy of the nervous system. Used for the scientific discipline or the anatomical structures themselves.
B Neurosciences 1973
R ↓ Anatomy 1967
Neural Networks 1991

Neurobiology 1973
PN 3847 **SC** 33670
SN Biology of the nervous system. Used for the scientific discipline or the neurobiological processes themselves.
B Biology 1967
Neurosciences 1973

Neurobiology — (cont'd)
R Biological Psychiatry 1994

Neurochemistry 1973
PN 10644 **SC** 33680
SN Chemical makeup and metabolism of nervous tissue. Used for the scientific discipline or the neurochemical processes themselves.
UF Brain Metabolism
B Biochemistry 1967
Neurosciences 1973
N ↓ Neuroendocrinology 1985
Receptor Binding 1985
R Blood Brain Barrier 1994
Glucose Metabolism 1994

Neurocognition 2006
PN 108 **SC** 33685
SN Refers to the neurophysiological bases underlying cognitive functions.
HN This term was introduced in May 2006. Relevant records were re-indexed with this term. The posting note reflects the number of records that were re-indexed.
R ↓ Cognitive Processes 1967
Neuropsychology 1973

Neurodegenerative Diseases 2004
PN 494 **SC** 33692
SN Neurologic disorders characterized by progressive nervous system dysfunction and loss of neural tissue.
HN This term was introduced in June 2004. Relevant records were re-indexed with this term. The posting note reflects the number of records that were re-indexed.
B Nervous System Disorders 1967
N Alzheimers Disease 1973
Dementia with Lewy Bodies 2001
Parkinsons Disease 1973
R ↓ Dementia 1985
Neuropathology 1973

Neurodermatitis 1973
PN 33 **SC** 33690
SN Skin inflammation associated with emotional disorders; often appears following periods of stress.
B Dermatitis 1973
Somatoform Disorders 2001
R Allergic Skin Disorders 1973

Neuroendocrinology 1985
PN 1754 **SC** 33695
SN Study of the biological, chemical, and physical relations between the nervous system and endocrine glands. Used for the scientific discipline or neuroendocrinological processes themselves.
B Endocrinology 1973
Neurochemistry 1973
Neurophysiology 1973
N Psychoneuroendocrinology 2007

Neurofeedback 2006
PN 107 **SC** 33696
SN Feedback provided about one's brain wave activity through use of electrodes on the scalp. This information is used for training individuals to control the electrical activity in their brains. Specifically used to manage some behavioral and physiological disorders.
HN This term was introduced in May 2006. Relevant records were re-indexed with this term. The posting note reflects the number of records that were re-indexed.

Neurofeedback — (cont'd)
UF EEG Biofeedback
B Biofeedback 1973
R ↓ Electroencephalography 1967

Neuroimaging 2003
PN 1552 **SC** 33698
SN Conceptually broad term referring to techniques that provide in-depth portraits of regional brain structure, activity, and function. The techniques involve extensive computer analysis and are often used for the assessment and diagnosis of brain impairment.
HN This term was introduced in June 2003. Relevant records were re-indexed with this term. The posting note reflects the number of records that were re-indexed.
N ↓ Encephalography 1973
Magnetic Resonance Imaging 1994
↓ Roentgenography 1973
↓ Tomography 1988
R ↓ Brain 1967
↓ Brain Disorders 1967
Computer Assisted Diagnosis 1973
↓ Evoked Potentials 1967

Neuroinfections
Use Infectious Disorders AND Nervous System Disorders

Neurokinins 1997
PN 133 **SC** 33705
SN Ten amino acid neuropeptides found in mammalian cells.
B Amino Acids 1973
Neuropeptides 2003
Neurotransmitters 1985
R ↓ Anti Inflammatory Drugs 1982
Substance P 1985

Neuroleptic Drugs 1973
PN 11448 **SC** 33710
HN In 1982, this term replaced the discontinued terms ANTIPSYCHOTIC DRUGS and ANTISCHIZOPHRENIC DRUGS. In 2000, these terms were removed from all records containing them, and replaced with NEUROLEPTIC DRUGS.
UF Antipsychotic Drugs
Antischizophrenic Drugs
Major Tranquilizers
B Tranquilizing Drugs 1967
N Clozapine 1991
Molindone 1982
Nialamide 1973
Olanzapine 2003
Quetiapine 2004
Reserpine 1967
Risperidone 1997
Spiroperidol 1991
Sulpiride 1973
Tetrabenazine 1973
R Neuroleptic Malignant Syndrome 1988
Prostaglandins 1982
Tardive Dyskinesia 1988

Neuroleptic Malignant Syndrome 1988
PN 614 **SC** 33715
SN Life-threatening neurological disorder most often caused by an adverse reaction to neuroleptic or antipsychotic drugs.
B Syndromes 1973
Toxic Disorders 1973
R ↓ Drug Therapy 1967
↓ Neuroleptic Drugs 1973
↓ Side Effects (Drug) 1973

Neurolinguistic Programming 2001
PN 126 **SC** 33718
SN R. Bandler's model of techniques and strategies for interpersonal communication based on elements of transformational grammar and preferred sensory representations for learning and self expression. Also, self intervention method in humanistic psychology aimed at personal growth and human potential.
HN In 2000, this term was created to update the spelling from the discontinued term NEUROLINGUISTIC PROGRAMING. NEUROLINGUISTIC PROGRAMING was removed from all records containing it and replaced with NEUROLINGUISTIC PROGRAMMING.
R ↓ Cognitive Style 1967
↓ Humanistic Psychology 1985
↓ Interpersonal Communication 1973
Neurolinguistics 1991
Perceptual Style 1973

Neurolinguistics 1991
PN 420 **SC** 33719
SN Study of the neurological mechanisms involved in the development, acquisition, and use of language. Used for the scientific discipline or the neurolinguistic processes themselves.
B Linguistics 1973
R ↓ Language 1967
↓ Language Disorders 1982
Neurolinguistic Programming 2001
Psycholinguistics 1967
↓ Verbal Communication 1967

Neurological Disorders
Use Nervous System Disorders

Neurologists 1973
PN 259 **SC** 33730
UF Neuropathologists
B Physicians 1967
R Surgeons 1973

Neurology 1967
PN 7756 **SC** 33740
SN Scientific discipline dealing with the anatomy, physiology, and organic diseases of the nervous system. Used for the scientific discipline or the neurological findings themselves.
B Medical Sciences 1967
Neurosciences 1973
R Neuropathology 1973
↓ Neurosurgery 1973

Neuromuscular Blocking Drugs
Use Muscle Relaxing Drugs

Neuromuscular Disorders 1973
PN 339 **SC** 33760
SN Any impairment in the structure or function of the nerves and muscles.
B Nervous System Disorders 1967
N Cataplexy 1973
Muscular Dystrophy 1973
Myasthenia Gravis 1973
↓ Paralysis 1973
Tourette Syndrome 2006
R ↓ Dyskinesia 1973
Hyperkinesis 1973
↓ Movement Disorders 1985
↓ Muscular Disorders 1973
↓ Musculoskeletal Disorders 1973
↓ Sclerosis (Nervous System) 1973
↓ Spinal Cord Injuries 1973

Neurons 1973
PN 9259 **SC** 33770
SN Nerve cells; basic functional units of the nervous system.
UF Nerve Cells
B Cells (Biology) 1973
Nervous System 1967
N Axons 1973
Dendrites 1973
Ganglion Cells (Retina) 1985
Motor Neurons 1973
Purkinje Cells 1994
↓ Sensory Neurons 1973
R Nerve Growth Factor 1994
↓ Nerve Tissues 1973
Visual Receptive Fields 1982

Neuropathologists
Use Neurologists

Neuropathology 1973
PN 4731 **SC** 33790
SN Branch of medicine dealing with morphological and other aspects of nervous system disorders. Used for the scientific discipline or the neuropathological findings themselves.
B Neurosciences 1973
Pathology 1973
R ↓ Neurodegenerative Diseases 2004
Neurology 1967

Neuropathy
Use Nervous System Disorders

Neuropeptide Y 2004
PN 411 **SC** 33804
SN A 36-amino acid peptide located in the nervous system that is associated with feeding behavior.
HN This term was introduced in June 2004. Relevant records were re-indexed with this term. The posting note reflects the number of records that were re-indexed.
B Neuropeptides 2003

Neuropeptides 2003
PN 333 **SC** 33805
SN Peptides located in neural tissue.
HN Use PEPTIDES to access references from 1994 to June 2003.
B Peptides 1973
N Angiotensin 1973
Bombesin 1988
Cholecystokinin 1982
Corticotropin 1973
Corticotropin Releasing Factor 1994
Glucagon 1973
Neurokinins 1997
Neuropeptide Y 2004
Neurotensin 1985
Oxytocin 1973
Prolactin 1973
Somatostatin 1991
Somatotropin 1973
Substance P 1985
Thyrotropin 1973
Vasopressin 1973
R ↓ Endorphins 1982
Enkephalins 1982
↓ Neurotransmitters 1985
↓ Proteins 1973

Neurophysiology 1973
PN 7289 **SC** 33810
SN Physiology of the nervous system. Used for the scientific discipline, the neurophysiological processes, or neurophysiological structures themselves.
B Neurosciences 1973
Physiology 1967
N ↓ Neuroendocrinology 1985
Neurotransmission 2003
Receptor Binding 1985

Neuropsychiatrists
Use Psychiatrists

Neuropsychiatry 1973
PN 1657 **SC** 33830
SN Medical specialty that combines psychiatry and neurology. Used for the scientific discipline or the neuropsychiatric findings themselves.
B Neurosciences 1973
Psychiatry 1967
R Biological Psychiatry 1994

Neuropsychological Assessment 1982
PN 8285 **SC** 33835
SN Use of tests, including intelligence, motor, and lateralization measures, to diagnose brain damage or other neurological dysfunction.
B Psychological Assessment 1997
N Halstead Reitan Neuropsychological Battery 2001
Luria Nebraska Neuropsychological Battery 2001
Mini Mental State Examination 1994
Wechsler Memory Scale 1988
Wisconsin Card Sorting Test 1994
R Bender Gestalt Test 1967
Benton Revised Visual Retention Test 1973
Body Sway Testing 1973
↓ Brain Damage 1967
Cognitive Assessment 1997
↓ Diagnosis 1967
Memory for Designs Test 1973
↓ Neuropsychological Rehabilitation 1997
↓ Testing 1967
↓ Traumatic Brain Injury 1997

Neuropsychological Rehabilitation 1997
PN 644 **SC** 33837
B Rehabilitation 1967
N Cognitive Rehabilitation 1985
R Memory Training 1994
↓ Neuropsychological Assessment 1982

Neuropsychology 1973
PN 10979 **SC** 33840
SN Branch of clinical psychology emphasizing the relationship between brain and behavior, including the diagnosis of brain pathology using cognitive or psychological tests. Used for the discipline or the neuropsychological functions themselves.
B Neurosciences 1973
Physiological Psychology 1967
R Neurocognition 2006
Psychoneuroimmunology 1991

Neuroreceptors
Use Neural Receptors

Neurosciences 1973
PN 2759 **SC** 33850
SN Scientific disciplines concerned with the development, structure, function, chemistry, and pathology of the nervous system.

Neurosciences — (cont'd)
B Sciences 1967
N Neuroanatomy 1967
Neurobiology 1973
↓ Neurochemistry 1973
Neurology 1967
Neuropathology 1973
↓ Neurophysiology 1973
Neuropsychiatry 1973
Neuropsychology 1973
R Cognitive Science 2003
↓ Medical Sciences 1967

Neurosis 1967
PN 5689 **SC** 33860
SN Psychoanalytic term referring to mental conditions characterized primarily by anxiety, fears, obsessive thoughts, compulsions, dissociation, and depression. Neuroses have no organic origins and are believed to be a product of unconscious processes resulting from internal conflicts. Compare PSYCHOSIS.
UF Psychoneurosis
B Mental Disorders 1967
N Childhood Neurosis 1973
Experimental Neurosis 1973
Occupational Neurosis 1973
Traumatic Neurosis 1973
R Anhedonia 1985
↓ Anxiety 1967
Borderline States 1978
Dissociation 2001
↓ Fear 1967
↓ Hysteria 1967
↓ Major Depression 1988
Obsessive Compulsive Disorder 1985

Neurosurgeons
Use Surgeons

Neurosurgery 1973
PN 1186 **SC** 33890
SN Specialized field of surgery concerned with the treatment of diseases or disorders of the nervous system.
B Surgery 1971
N Commissurotomy 1985
Decerebration 1973
Decortication (Brain) 1973
Hemispherectomy 1973
Neural Transplantation 1985
↓ Psychosurgery 1973
Sympathectomy 1973
Tractotomy 1973
Vagotomy 1973
R Neurology 1967

Neurosyphilis 1973
PN 62 **SC** 33900
SN Late phase of the syphilis infection that affects the central nervous system.
UF Tabes Dorsalis
B Central Nervous System Disorders 1973
Syphilis 1973
R General Paresis 1973

Neurotensin 1985
PN 220 **SC** 33905
SN Neuropeptide containing thirteen amino acids that is found in the central nervous system and is involved in neuroendocrine and vascular processes.
B Neuropeptides 2003
Neurotransmitters 1985
Peptides 1973

Neurotic Depressive Reaction
HN In 2000, the term was discontinued, and removed from all records containing it, and replaced with MAJOR DEPRESSION, its postable counterpart.
Use Major Depression

Neuroticism 1973
PN 2714 **SC** 33915
SN Personality trait that contrasts adjustment or emotional stability with maladjustment. Experience of anxiety, anger, disgust, sadness, embarrassment, and a variety of other negative emotions.
B Personality Traits 1967
R Emotional Inferiority 1973
Emotional Instability 1973
Emotional Stability 1973
Emotionality (Personality) 1973
Five Factor Personality Model 1997

Neurotoxicity 2003
PN 593 **SC** 33918
SN Toxicity to nerves and/or nervous tissues.
HN This term was introduced in June 2003. Relevant records were re-indexed with this term. The posting note reflects the number of records that were re-indexed.
B Toxicity 1973
R ↓ Neurotoxins 1982

Neurotoxins 1982
PN 1551 **SC** 33920
SN Bacterial, chemical, or pharmacological substances that are destructive to nerve tissue.
B Toxins 2007
N ↓ Ibotenic Acid 1991
Methylphenyltetrahydropyridine 1994
R Antibodies 1973
Drug Interactions 1982
↓ Insecticides 1973
Kainic Acid 1988
Neurotoxicity 2003
↓ Toxic Disorders 1973
↓ Toxicity 1973

Neurotransmission 2003
PN 1345 **SC** 33923
SN The transmission of nerve impulses across a synapse via chemical substances or electrical signals.
HN This term was introduced in June 2003. Relevant records were re-indexed with this term. The posting note reflects the number of records that were re-indexed.
UF Neural Transmission
Synaptic Transmission
B Neurophysiology 1973
R ↓ Neurotransmitters 1985
Synapses 1973

Neurotransmitter Uptake Inhibitors 2007
PN 1 **SC** 33922
SN Drugs that inhibit the uptake of neurotransmitters and prolong the activity of the neurotransmitter targeted.
HN This term was introduced in April 2007. Relevant records were re-indexed with this term. The posting note reflects the number of records that were re-indexed.
B Drugs 1967
N ↓ Serotonin Norepinephrine Reuptake Inhibitors 2007
↓ Serotonin Reuptake Inhibitors 1997

Neurotransmitters 1985
PN 2142 **SC** 33924
SN Chemical substances, synthesized and released by nerve cells, or glandular hormones that excite or inhibit other nerve, muscle, or gland cells by producing a brief alteration in the postsynaptic membrane of the receiving cell. Use a more specific term if possible.
N Acetylcholine 1973
↓ Aspartic Acid 1973
↓ Catecholamines 1973
Cholecystokinin 1982
↓ Endorphins 1982
Gamma Aminobutyric Acid 1978
Glutamic Acid 1973
Glycine 1973
Histamine 1973
Neurokinins 1997
Neurotensin 1985
Serotonin 1973
Substance P 1985
R ↓ Amino Acids 1973
Glutamate Receptors 2007
↓ Neuropeptides 2003
Neurotransmission 2003
Nitric Oxide 2003
↓ Peptides 1973

Neutrality (Psychotherapeutic)
Use Psychotherapeutic Neutrality

Never Married 1994
PN 94 **SC** 33926
B Marital Status 1973
R ↓ Single Parents 1978
Single Persons 1973
Unwed Mothers 1973

News Media 1997
PN 822 **SC** 33945
B Mass Media 1967
N Newspapers 1973
R Journalists 1973
Radio 1973
↓ Television 1967

Newsletters (Professional)
Use Scientific Communication

Newspapers 1973
PN 931 **SC** 33960
B News Media 1997
Printed Communications Media 1973

NGOs 2006
PN 34 **SC** 33965
SN Nonprofit organizations that operate independently of the government.
HN This term was introduced in May 2006. Relevant records were re-indexed with this term. The posting note reflects the number of records that were re-indexed.
UF Non-governmental Organizations
Nongovernmental Organizations
R International Organizations 1973

Niacin
Use Nicotinic Acid

Niacinamide
Use Nicotinamide

Nialamide 1973
PN 40 **SC** 33990
B Amine Oxidase Inhibitors 1973
Antidepressant Drugs 1971
Monoamine Oxidase Inhibitors 1973
Neuroleptic Drugs 1973

Nicotinamide 1973
PN 46 **SC** 34000
UF Niacinamide
Nicotinic Acid Amide
B Vitamins 1973
R Nicotinic Acid 1973
Pellagra 1973

Nicotine 1973
PN 4161 **SC** 34010
UF Tobacco (Drug)
B Alkaloids 1973
Cholinergic Blocking Drugs 1973
Ganglion Blocking Drugs 1973
R ↓ Insecticides 1973
Nicotine Withdrawal 1997
Smokeless Tobacco 1994
↓ Tobacco Smoking 1967

Nicotine Withdrawal 1997
PN 253 **SC** 34015
B Drug Withdrawal 1973
R Nicotine 1973
Smokeless Tobacco 1994
Smoking Cessation 1988
↓ Tobacco Smoking 1967

Nicotinic Acid 1973
PN 91 **SC** 34020
UF Niacin
B Acids 1973
Vasodilator Drugs 1973
Vitamins 1973
R Nicotinamide 1973

Nicotinic Acid Amide
Use Nicotinamide

Nicotinic Receptors
Use Cholinergic Receptors

Nictitating Membrane 1973
PN 342 **SC** 34040
SN Fold of transparent or semitransparent mucous membrane present in many vertebrates that can be drawn over the eye like a third eyelid. This membrane cleans and moistens the cornea without occluding light.
B Membranes 1973

Night Terrors
Use Sleep Disorders

Nightmares 1973
PN 514 **SC** 34050
B Dreaming 1967
R Dream Content 1973

Nihilism 1973
PN 39 **SC** 34060
B Philosophies 1967
R Fatalism 1973
Pessimism 1973

Nitrazepam 1978
PN 61 **SC** 34066
B Anticonvulsive Drugs 1973
Benzodiazepines 1978
Hypnotic Drugs 1973
Sedatives 1973

Nitric Oxide 2003
PN 689 **SC** 34068
SN Free radical gas produced by catalyzed nitric oxide synthase that acts like a neurotransmitter. Not to be confused with Nitrous Oxide, which acts as an anesthetic.
HN This term was introduced in June 2003. Relevant records were re-indexed with this term. The posting note reflects the number of records that were re-indexed.
R ↓ Neurotransmitters 1985
Nitrogen 1973
Oxygen 1973

Nitrogen 1973
PN 374 **SC** 34070
R Nitric Oxide 2003

NMDA
Use N-Methyl-D-Aspartate

Nociception
Use Pain Perception

Nociceptors 1985
PN 568 **SC** 34080
SN Sensory receptors that respond to pain stimuli.
UF Pain Receptors
B Neural Receptors 1973
Sensory Neurons 1973

Nocturnal Behavior (Animal)
Use Animal Nocturnal Behavior

Nocturnal Emission 1973
PN 9 **SC** 34100
B Male Orgasm 1973

Nocturnal Teeth Grinding 1973
PN 51 **SC** 34110
HN Use NOCTURNAL TEETH GRINDING to access references to BRUXISM from 1973-1984.
B Bruxism 1985
R ↓ Sleep 1967

Noise (Sound)
Use Auditory Stimulation

Noise Effects 1973
PN 1893 **SC** 34150
SN Behavioral, physiological, or psychological effects of environmental or experimentally manipulated noise on an organism.
B Environmental Effects 1973
R Acoustics 1997
Pollution 1973

Noise Levels (Work Areas) 1973
PN 281 **SC** 34160
B Loudness 1967
Working Conditions 1973

Nomenclature (Psychological)
Use Psychological Terminology

Nomifensine 1982
PN 141 **SC** 34175
SN Organic heterocyclic compound used as an antiparkinson agent and antidepressive agent.
B Antidepressant Drugs 1971
Antitremor Drugs 1973

Non Zero Sum Games 1973
PN 48 **SC** 34180
SN Quantitative games in which all players may win points as opposed to zero sum games in which points won by one player must be lost by another or others.
B Games 1967
R Entrapment Games 1973
Game Theory 1967
Prisoners Dilemma Game 1973

Non-governmental Organizations
Use NGOs

Noncommissioned Officers 1973
PN 48 **SC** 34200
SN Subordinate military officers (e.g., sergeants) appointed from enlisted personnel.
UF Officers (Noncommissioned)
B Enlisted Military Personnel 1973

Nonconformity (Personality) 1973
PN 114 **SC** 34210
B Personality Traits 1967
R Conformity (Personality) 1967
Individuality 1973
Rebelliousness 2003

Noncontingent Reinforcement 1988
PN 146 **SC** 34215
SN Presentation of reinforcement (punishment or positive rewards) independently of behavior.
B Reinforcement 1967
R Autoshaping 1978
↓ Contingency Management 1973

Nondirected Discussion Method 1973
PN 25 **SC** 34220
SN Teaching method which encourages students' spontaneity and restricts the leader's role to that of a moderator.
B Teaching Methods 1967
R Discovery Teaching Method 1973

Nondirective Therapy
Use Client Centered Therapy

Nongovernmental Organizations
Use NGOs

Nongraded Schools 1973
PN 11 **SC** 34250
SN Schools that group students according to such characteristics as academic achievement, mental and physical ability, or emotional development, rather than by age or grade level.
B Schools 1967

Nonlinear Regression 1973
PN 97 **SC** 34260
B Statistical Correlation 1967
Statistical Regression 1985

Nonlinear Regression — (cont'd)
R Multiple Regression 1982

Nonmetallic Elements
HN Term was discontinued in 1997. In 2000, the term was removed from all records containing it, and replaced with CHEMICAL ELEMENTS, its postable counterpart.
Use Chemical Elements

Nonparametric Statistical Tests 1967
PN 453 **SC** 34280
HN In August 2005, this term replaced the discontinued term COCHRAN Q TEST. COCHRAN Q TEST was removed from all records containing it and replaced with NONPARAMETRIC STATISTICAL TESTS.
UF Cochran Q Test
B Statistical Tests 1973
N Chi Square Test 1973
Mann Whitney U Test 1973
Sign Test 1973
Wilcoxon Sign Rank Test 1973

Nonprescription Drugs 1991
PN 187 **SC** 34285
SN Drugs or medication sold legally without prescription.
UF Over the Counter Drugs
B Drugs 1967
R Pharmaceutical Industry 2007
Prescription Drugs 1991
Self Medication 1991

Nonprofessional Personnel 1982
PN 144 **SC** 34290
SN Conceptually broad term. Use a more specific term if possible.
HN Use PARAPROFESSIONAL PERSONNEL to access references from 1973-1981.
B Personnel 1967
N ↓ Agricultural Workers 1973
R ↓ Business and Industrial Personnel 1967
Child Care Workers 1978
Domestic Service Personnel 1973
↓ Paraprofessional Personnel 1973
↓ Professional Personnel 1978
↓ Service Personnel 1991
Technical Service Personnel 1973

Nonprofit Organizations 1973
PN 498 **SC** 34300
B Organizations 1967
R Faith Based Organizations 2007

Nonprojective Personality Measures 1973
PN 1318 **SC** 34304
SN Direct assessment of personality traits through scoring of a subject's responses to questions on structured, standardized tests. Use a more specific term if possible.
HN In 1997, this term replaced the discontinued terms AUTHORITARIANISM REBELLION SCALE, DIFFERENTIAL PERSONALITY INVENTORY, KUPFER DETRE SELF RATING SCALE, and WHITE BETZ A B SCALE. In 2000, these terms were removed from all records containing them, and replaced with NONPROJECTIVE PERSONALITY MEASURES.

Nonprojective Personality Measures — (cont'd)
UF Authoritarianism Rebellion Scale
Differential Personality Inventory
Kupfer Detre Self Rating Scale
White Betz A B Scale
B Personality Measures 1967
N Bannister Repertory Grid 1973
Beck Depression Inventory 1988
Bem Sex Role Inventory 1988
California F Scale 1973
Child Behavior Checklist 1994
Childrens Manifest Anxiety Scale 1973
Edwards Personal Preference Schedule 1967
Edwards Social Desirability Scale 1973
Embedded Figures Testing 1967
Eysenck Personality Inventory 1973
Fear Survey Schedule 1973
Fundamental Interpersonal Relation Orientation Behavior Ques 2001
Gough Adjective Check List 1973
High School Personality Questionnaire 2001
Marlowe Crowne Social Desirability Scale 2001
Memory for Designs Test 1973
Millon Clinical Multiaxial Inventory 1988
Minnesota Multiphasic Personality Inventory 2001
Mooney Problem Check List 1973
Myers Briggs Type Indicator 1973
Personal Orientation Inventory 1973
Psychological Screening Inventory 1973
Repression Sensitization Scale 1973
Rod and Frame Test 1973
Rokeach Dogmatism Scale 1973
Rotter Internal External Locus of Control Scale 2001
Sixteen Personality Factors Questionnaire 2001
State Trait Anxiety Inventory 1973
Taylor Manifest Anxiety Scale 1973
Tennessee Self Concept Scale 1973
Vineland Social Maturity Scale 1973
Zungs Self Rating Depression Scale 1973

Nonrapid Eye Movement Sleep
Use NREM Sleep

NonREM Sleep
Use NREM Sleep

Nonreversal Shift Learning 1973
PN 52 **SC** 34330
SN Experimental technique used for the demonstration of mediating processes in concept formation that assesses the ability to shift dimensions in stimulus discrimination tasks, as, for example, from size to color.
UF Extradimensional Shift Learning
B Discrimination Learning 1982

Nonsense Syllable Learning 1967
PN 193 **SC** 34340
SN Verbal learning paradigm in which collections or lists of letters, which have no obvious meaning (e.g., XAB, GZL), are used as stimulus items. Also, the actual acquisition, retention, and retrieval of such stimulus items.

Nonsense Syllable Learning — (cont'd)
B Verbal Learning 1967

Nonstandard English 1973
PN 307 **SC** 34350
B Dialect 1973
R Slang 1973

Nontraditional Careers 1985
PN 376 **SC** 34352
SN Occupations in which certain groups (usually males or females) have traditionally been underrepresented.
B Occupations 1967
R Occupational Choice 1967
Sex Roles 1967

Nontraditional Education 1982
PN 762 **SC** 34355
SN Alternative educational programs within or outside of the formal educational system that provide flexible and innovative teaching, curriculum, grading, or degree requirements.
UF Alternative Schools
Magnet Schools
Open Universities
B Education 1967
N Home Schooling 1994
R Charter Schools 2006
↓ Curriculum 1967
Distance Education 2003
↓ Educational Programs 1973
Service Learning 2007
↓ Teaching Methods 1967
Virtual Classrooms 2007

Nonverbal Ability 1988
PN 450 **SC** 34357
SN Ability in nonlanguage areas such as spatial relations, mathematics, or music.
B Ability 1967
N ↓ Artistic Ability 1973
Mathematical Ability 1973
Mechanical Aptitude 1973
Motor Skills 1973
↓ Spatial Ability 1982
R Academic Aptitude 1973
↓ Nonverbal Communication 1971

Nonverbal Communication 1971
PN 4289 **SC** 34360
B Communication 1967
N Body Language 1973
Eye Contact 1973
↓ Facial Expressions 1967
Gestures 1973
↓ Manual Communication 1978
R Laughter 1978
↓ Nonverbal Ability 1988
Silence 2003

Nonverbal Learning 1973
PN 292 **SC** 34370
SN Acquisition, retention, and retrieval of knowledge or skills that do not involve verbally presented information or language, such as perceptual responses or motor activities.

Nonverbal Learning — (cont'd)
B Learning 1967

Nonverbal Meaning 1973
PN 76 SC 34380
B Meaning 1967

Nonverbal Reinforcement 1973
PN 32 SC 34390
B Social Reinforcement 1967

Nonviolence 1991
PN 104 SC 34393
B Social Interaction 1967
R Pacifism 1973
↓ Political Attitudes 1973
↓ Violence 1973

Nootropic Drugs 1991
PN 395 SC 34395
UF Cognition Enhancing Drugs
Memory Enhancing Drugs
B Drugs 1967
N Piracetam 1982

Noradrenaline
Use Norepinephrine

Norepinephrine 1973
PN 3913 SC 34410
UF Noradrenaline
B Adrenal Medulla Hormones 1973
Catecholamines 1973
Vasoconstrictor Drugs 1973
R Guanethidine 1973
↓ Norepinephrine Metabolites 1982

Norepinephrine Metabolites 1982
PN 303 SC 34413
SN Molecules generated from the metabolism of norepinephrine.
B Metabolites 1973
N Methoxyhydroxyphenylglycol (3,4) 1991
R ↓ Metabolism 1967
Norepinephrine 1973

Normal Distribution 1973
PN 288 SC 34420
UF Gaussian Distribution
B Frequency Distribution 1973
R ↓ Statistical Sample Parameters 1973

Normalization (Test)
Use Test Standardization

Norms (Social)
Use Social Norms

Norms (Statistical)
Use Statistical Norms

Norms (Test)
Use Test Norms

Nortriptyline 1994
PN 237 SC 34485
HN Use ANTIDEPRESSANT DRUGS to access references from 1978-1993.

Nortriptyline — (cont'd)
B Tricyclic Antidepressant Drugs 1997

Norway Rats 1973
PN 157 SC 34500
B Rats 1967

Nose 1973
PN 141 SC 34510
B Respiratory System 1973
N ↓ Nasal Mucosa 1973
R ↓ Musculoskeletal System 1973

Note Taking 1991
PN 167 SC 34515
R Homework 1988
↓ Learning Strategies 1991
↓ Memory 1967
Mnemonic Learning 1973
↓ Strategies 1967
Study Habits 1973
↓ Written Communication 1985

Nouns 1973
PN 1299 SC 34520
B Form Classes (Language) 1973
R ↓ Names 1985

Novel Stimuli
Use Stimulus Novelty

Novelty Seeking
Use Sensation Seeking

Novocaine
HN Term was discontinued in 1982. In 2000, the term was removed from all records containing it, and replaced with PROCAINE, its postable counterpart.
Use Procaine

NREM Sleep 1973
PN 925 SC 34550
UF Nonrapid Eye Movement Sleep
NonREM Sleep
Slow Wave Sleep
B Sleep 1967

Nuclear Family 1973
PN 278 SC 34560
B Family 1967
Family Structure 1973

Nuclear Technology 1985
PN 529 SC 34565
B Technology 1973

Nuclear War 1985
PN 584 SC 34567
B War 1967

Nucleic Acids 1973
PN 75 SC 34570
B Acids 1973
N Adenosine 1973
DNA 2006
↓ Nucleotides 1978
Ribonucleic Acid 1973
R ↓ Genetics 1967
Guanosine 1985

Nucleotides 1978
PN 381 SC 34573
B Nucleic Acids 1973
N Cyclic Adenosine Monophosphate 1978

Nucleus Accumbens 1982
PN 2111 SC 34574
SN One of the largest nuclei in the septal region lying anteriorly and medially to the junction of the caudate nucleus and putamen and laterally to the septal nuclei.
R Caudate Nucleus 1973
↓ Limbic System 1973
Septal Nuclei 1982

Nucleus Basalis Magnocellularis 1994
PN 180 SC 57425
SN Cholinergic nerve cells in the forebrain, connected to areas of the cerebral cortex.
UF Basal Magnocellular Cholinergic Nucleus
Nucleus Basalis of Meynert
B Forebrain 1985
R ↓ Basal Ganglia 1973

Nucleus Basalis of Meynert
Use Nucleus Basalis Magnocellularis

Nudity 1973
PN 78 SC 34575
R Obscenity 1978
↓ Physical Appearance 1982
Pornography 1973

Null Hypothesis Testing 1973
PN 348 SC 34580
SN Application of statistical tests to determine whether a null hypothesis should be accepted or rejected. Limited to discussions of statistical procedures.
B Hypothesis Testing 1973

Number Comprehension 1973
PN 699 SC 34590
SN Knowledge or understanding of the meaning, significance, and relationships symbolized by numerals.
B Comprehension 1967

Number Systems 1973
PN 110 SC 34600
B Mathematics (Concepts) 1967
Systems 1967
R Numbers (Numerals) 1967

Numbers (Numerals) 1967
PN 1550 SC 34610
SN Symbol of a member of an abstract mathematical system which is subject to rules of succession, addition, and multiplication.
UF Digits (Mathematics)
B Mathematics (Concepts) 1967
Written Language 1967
R Number Systems 1973
Numerosity Perception 1967

Numerical Ability
Use Mathematical Ability

Numerosity Perception 1967
PN 642 SC 34630
SN Perception of quantities in stimulus sets in visual, auditory, or other perceptual modes.

Numerosity Perception — (cont'd)
B Perception 1967
R Numbers (Numerals) 1967

Nuns 1973
PN 172 SC 34640
B Religious Personnel 1973
R Missionaries 1973

Nurse Patient Interaction
Use Therapeutic Processes

Nursery School Students 1973
PN 447 SC 34650
SN Students attending a nursery school, usually ages 2, 3, and 4.
B Preschool Students 1982

Nursery Schools 1973
PN 216 SC 34660
B Schools 1967

Nurses 1967
PN 8065 SC 34670
B Medical Personnel 1967
N Psychiatric Nurses 1973
Public Health Service Nurses 1973
School Nurses 1973

Nursing 1973
PN 4969 SC 34680
B Paramedical Sciences 1973

Nursing Education 1973
PN 1670 SC 34690
B Education 1967
R ↓ Medical Education 1973

Nursing Homes 1973
PN 4269 SC 34700
SN Establishments where maintenance and personal or nursing care are provided for persons (as the aged or chronically ill) who are unable to care for themselves.
B Residential Care Institutions 1973
Treatment Facilities 1973
R ↓ Hospitals 1967
Long Term Care 1994
Psychiatric Units 1991
Retirement Communities 1997
Sanatoriums 1973

Nursing Students 1973
PN 1833 SC 34710
B College Students 1967

Nurturance 1985
PN 391 SC 34714
SN Need, tendency, or process of providing care and support to others. For animal populations, use ANIMAL MATERNAL BEHAVIOR or ANIMAL PARENTAL BEHAVIOR.
B Personality Traits 1967
Social Behavior 1967
R ↓ Needs 1967
↓ Parent Child Relations 1967

Nutrition 1973
PN 3015 SC 34720
R Beverages (Nonalcoholic) 1978
Dietary Supplements 2001
Diets 1978
Food 1978

Nutrition — (cont'd)
Food Additives 1978
↓ Nutritional Deficiencies 1973
↓ Physiology 1967

Nutritional Deficiencies 1973
PN 1357 SC 34730
UF Malnutrition
B Physical Disorders 1997
N ↓ Protein Deficiency Disorders 1973
Starvation 1973
↓ Vitamin Deficiency Disorders 1973
R ↓ Alcoholic Psychosis 1973
↓ Alcoholism 1967
Anorexia Nervosa 1973
Diets 1978
↓ Eating Disorders 1997
Failure to Thrive 1988
Food Deprivation 1967
↓ Metabolism Disorders 1973
Nutrition 1973
↓ Underweight 1973

Nutritional Supplements
Use Dietary Supplements

Nymphomania
Use Hypersexuality

Nystagmus 1973
PN 744 SC 34760
SN Eye movement reflex stabilizing the retinal image of a visual stimulus to compensate for head or stimulus movement. Also, eye movement defects resulting from neurological, muscular, or genetic disorders.
UF Optokinetic Nystagmus
Vestibular Nystagmus
B Eye Disorders 1973
Eye Movements 1967
Reflexes 1971
R ↓ Nervous System Disorders 1967

Obedience 1973
PN 468 SC 34770
SN Limited to human populations.
UF Submissiveness
B Personality Traits 1967
R Coercion 1994
↓ Compliance 1973
↓ Dominance 1967
↓ Resistance 1997

Obesity 1973
PN 6103 SC 34780
B Overweight 2007
R Body Mass Index 2006
Diets 1978
Hyperphagia 1973
Obesity (Attitudes Toward) 1997
↓ Somatoform Disorders 2001

Obesity (Attitudes Toward) 1997
PN 127 SC 34783
B Attitudes 1967
R ↓ Body Weight 1967
Eating Attitudes 1994
Health Attitudes 1985
Obesity 1973
Weight Control 1985

Object Permanence 1985
PN 296 SC 34788
SN Knowledge of the continued existence of an object even when it is not directly perceived.

Object Permanence — (cont'd)
R ↓ Cognitive Development 1973
Conservation (Concept) 1973
↓ Developmental Stages 1973
↓ Internalization 1997
↓ Perceptual Constancy 1985

Object Recognition 1997
PN 2269 SC 34789
B Perception 1967
Recognition (Learning) 1967
R Form and Shape Perception 1967
Naming 1988
↓ Perceptual Discrimination 1973

Object Relations 1982
PN 4790 SC 34786
SN Psychoanalytic description of emotional attachments formed with other persons, as opposed to interest and love for oneself; individual's mode of relation to others and self.
UF Fairbairnian Theory
Winnicottian Theory
R Anaclitic Depression 1973
Attachment Behavior 1985
Attachment Theory 2007
↓ Childhood Development 1967
Emotional Development 1973
↓ Internalization 1997
Metapsychology 1994
↓ Psychoanalytic Theory 1967
↓ Psychosocial Development 1973
Self Psychology 1988
Separation Individuation 1982
Transitional Objects 1985

Objective Referenced Tests
Use Criterion Referenced Tests

Objectives
Use Goals

Objectives (Organizational)
Use Organizational Objectives

Objectivity 1973
PN 750 SC 34810
B Personality Traits 1967
R Subjectivity 1994

Oblique Rotation 1973
PN 75 SC 34820
B Statistical Rotation 1973

Obscenity 1978
PN 112 SC 34826
R Nudity 1973
Pornography 1973
Profanity 1991

Observation Methods 1967
PN 3234 SC 34830
SN In research, any techniques used in the intentional examination of persons or processes in natural or manipulated settings for the purpose of obtaining facts or reporting conclusions.
UF Field Experiment
Naturalistic Observation
B Empirical Methods 1973
R Interrater Reliability 1982
Qualitative Research 2003
Self Monitoring 1982

Observational Learning 1973
PN 940 **SC** 34840
SN Learning by observation of others by human or animal subjects or learning by visualization of behavior without actually performing an act and experiencing its consequences. Compare SOCIAL LEARNING.
B Learning 1967
Learning Strategies 1991
R Imitation (Learning) 1967
↓ Social Learning 1973

Observers 1973
PN 922 **SC** 34850
SN Individuals who examine, record, or rate specified events, behaviors, or processes in experimental, social, or therapeutic situations.
R ↓ Audiences 1967

Obsessions 1967
PN 1058 **SC** 34860
B Thought Disturbances 1973
R ↓ Compulsions 1973
Erotomania 1997
Fixation (Psychological) 2007
Obsessive Compulsive Disorder 1985
Obsessive Compulsive Personality Disorder 1973

Obsessive Compulsive Disorder 1985
PN 6020 **SC** 34865
SN Disorder characterized by recurrent obsessions or compulsions that may interfere with the individual's daily functioning or serve as a source of distress.
HN In 2000, this term replaced the discontinued term OBSESSIVE COMPULSIVE NEUROSIS. OBSESSIVE COMPULSIVE NEUROSIS was removed from all records containing it and replaced with OBSESSIVE COMPULSIVE DISORDER.
UF Compulsive Neurosis
Obsessive Compulsive Neurosis
Obsessive Neurosis
B Anxiety Disorders 1997
R Body Dysmorphic Disorder 2001
↓ Compulsions 1973
↓ Hoarding Behavior 2003
↓ Neurosis 1967
Obsessions 1967
Obsessive Compulsive Personality Disorder 1973

Obsessive Compulsive Neurosis
HN In 2000, the term was discontinued, and removed from all records containing it, and replaced with OBSESSIVE COMPULSIVE DISORDER, its postable counterpart.
Use Obsessive Compulsive Disorder

Obsessive Compulsive Personality Disorder 1973
PN 389 **SC** 34880
SN Personality disorder characterized by perfectionism, indecisiveness, excessive devotion to work, inability to express warm emotions, and insistence that things be done in accord with one's own preferences.
UF Anankastic Personality
Compulsive Personality Disorder
B Personality Disorders 1967
R ↓ Compulsions 1973
Obsessions 1967
Obsessive Compulsive Disorder 1985

Obsessive Neurosis
Use Obsessive Compulsive Disorder

Obstetrical Complications 1978
PN 822 **SC** 34895
R ↓ Birth 1967
Birth Injuries 1973
Labor (Childbirth) 1973
↓ Obstetrics 1978
Postsurgical Complications 1973
↓ Pregnancy 1967
Premature Birth 1973

Obstetricians 1978
PN 104 **SC** 34900
B Physicians 1967
R Gynecologists 1973
Surgeons 1973

Obstetrics 1978
PN 357 **SC** 34910
HN Use OBSTETRICS GYNECOLOGY to access references from 1973-1977.
B Medical Sciences 1967
N Midwifery 1985
R Childbirth Training 1978
Gynecology 1978
Obstetrical Complications 1978
↓ Prenatal Care 1991

Obturator Nerve
Use Spinal Nerves

Occipital Lobe 1973
PN 824 **SC** 34930
SN Located at the rear of the cerebral hemisphere; activity in the occipital lobe is generally associated with visual perception and visual imagery.
B Cerebral Cortex 1967
N Visual Cortex 1967

Occultism 1978
PN 184 **SC** 34935
R Cultism 1973
Mysticism 1967
↓ Parapsychological Phenomena 1973
↓ Parapsychology 1967
↓ Religious Beliefs 1973
Spirit Possession 1997
Witchcraft 1973

Occupation (Parental)
Use Parental Occupation

Occupational Adjustment 1973
PN 1410 **SC** 34950
SN Personal adaptation to one's vocation.
UF Vocational Adjustment
B Adjustment 1967
R Adjustment Disorders 1994
Career Change 1978
Occupational Neurosis 1973
↓ Occupations 1967
School to Work Transition 1994
Work Adjustment Training 1991

Occupational Aspirations 1973
PN 2583 **SC** 34960
UF Career Aspirations
Career Goals
Vocational Aspirations
B Aspirations 1967
R Career Change 1978
Goal Orientation 2005
Mentor 1985
↓ Occupations 1967

Occupational Aspirations — (cont'd)
Professional Development 1982

Occupational Attitudes 1973
PN 2159 **SC** 34970
SN Attitudes toward specific occupations or careers.
B Attitudes 1967
R Job Applicant Attitudes 1973
↓ Occupations 1967
Vocational Maturity 1978
Work (Attitudes Toward) 1973

Occupational Choice 1967
PN 4899 **SC** 34980
UF Career Choice
Job Selection
Vocational Choice
R Career Change 1978
Career Development 1985
Nontraditional Careers 1985
Occupational Preference 1973
↓ Occupations 1967
Professional Specialization 1991
Reemployment 1991
Vocational Maturity 1978

Occupational Exposure 1988
PN 572 **SC** 34985
SN Exposure to conditions, substances, or apparatus in the workplace that may be harmful to health.
R ↓ Environmental Effects 1973
↓ Hazardous Materials 1991
Industrial Accidents 1973
Occupational Safety 1973
↓ Occupations 1967
Work Related Illnesses 1994
↓ Working Conditions 1973

Occupational Guidance 1967
PN 5772 **SC** 34990
SN Assistance in career selection or development; assessment of interests, abilities, or aptitude; compilation of occupational and economic information; and referral to placement services.
UF Career Counseling
Career Guidance
Guidance (Occupational)
Vocational Counseling
Vocational Guidance
B Counseling 1967
R Assessment Centers 1982
Career Education 1978
Educational Counseling 1967
Job Enrichment 1973
Mentor 1985
Occupational Success Prediction 1973
↓ Occupations 1967
Student Personnel Services 1978
Vocational Counselors 1973

Occupational Interest Measures 1973
PN 817 **SC** 35000
B Measurement 1967
N Kuder Occupational Interest Survey 1973
Strong Vocational Interest Blank 1967

Occupational Interests 1967
PN 2067 **SC** 35010
UF Vocational Interests
B Interests 1967
R ↓ Occupations 1967
Vocational Maturity 1978

Occupational Mobility 1973
PN 669 **SC** 35020
SN The capacity or actual tendency toward upward progression in occupational status or occupational attainment.
UF Job Mobility
Mobility (Occupational)
Vocational Mobility
R Career Change 1978
Employment History 1978
Job Enrichment 1973
↓ Occupational Tenure 1973
↓ Occupations 1967

Occupational Neurosis 1973
PN 26 **SC** 35030
SN Neurotic disorder developed as a consequence of occupational stress, inappropriate occupational choice, overwork, job dissatisfaction, or other job-related stress.
B Neurosis 1967
R Occupational Adjustment 1973
Occupational Stress 1973

Occupational Preference 1973
PN 1082 **SC** 35040
UF Career Preference
Vocational Preference
B Preferences 1967
R Occupational Choice 1967
↓ Occupations 1967
Professional Specialization 1991
Vocational Maturity 1978

Occupational Safety 1973
PN 1282 **SC** 35050
UF Industrial Safety
B Safety 1967
Working Conditions 1973
R Industrial Accidents 1973
Occupational Exposure 1988
↓ Occupations 1967
Work Related Illnesses 1994

Occupational Status 1978
PN 2165 **SC** 35056
SN Occupational rank or position achieved by employee, usually based on abilities or competence. Also, social prestige attributed to specific occupations.
UF Job Status
Prestige (Occupational)
B Status 1967
R Job Experience Level 1973
↓ Occupational Tenure 1973
↓ Occupations 1967
Personnel Promotion 1978
Professional Recognition 2005

Occupational Stress 1973
PN 9985 **SC** 35060
UF Burnout
Job Stress
Work Stress
B Stress 1967
R Occupational Neurosis 1973
↓ Occupations 1967
Quality of Work Life 1988
Work Related Illnesses 1994
Workaholism 2004

Occupational Success 1978
PN 1757 **SC** 35067
B Achievement 1967
R Awards (Merit) 2005
Employment History 1978
Occupational Success Prediction 1973
↓ Occupations 1967
Personnel Promotion 1978
Professional Recognition 2005

Occupational Success Prediction 1973
PN 791 **SC** 35070
B Personnel Evaluation 1973
Prediction 1967
R Occupational Guidance 1967
Occupational Success 1978

Occupational Tenure 1973
PN 613 **SC** 35080
UF Tenure (Occupational)
N Teacher Tenure 1973
R Employee Turnover 1973
Employment History 1978
↓ Employment Status 1982
Job Security 1978
Occupational Mobility 1973
Occupational Status 1978
↓ Occupations 1967
Personnel Termination 1973

Occupational Therapists 1973
PN 956 **SC** 35090
B Allied Health Personnel 2007
Therapists 1967
R ↓ Mental Health Personnel 1967
↓ Paraprofessional Personnel 1973
↓ Psychiatric Hospital Staff 1973

Occupational Therapy 1967
PN 2803 **SC** 35100
SN Method of treatment for physical or mental disorders that involves engagement of patients in useful or creative activities or work as a means of improving functional skills in the areas of work, daily living, or vocational activities.
B Rehabilitation 1967
R Physical Therapy 1973

Occupations 1967
PN 4749 **SC** 35110
SN Conceptually broad term referring to work specialties as defined by duties and required skills. Use a more specific term if possible.
HN Use OCCUPATIONS to access references on employment status from 1967-1981.
UF Careers
Jobs
Vocations
N Nontraditional Careers 1985
R Career Change 1978
Career Development 1985
↓ Division of Labor 1988
Employment History 1978
↓ Job Characteristics 1985
Occupational Adjustment 1973
Occupational Aspirations 1973
Occupational Attitudes 1973
Occupational Choice 1967
Occupational Exposure 1988
Occupational Guidance 1967
Occupational Interests 1967
Occupational Mobility 1973
Occupational Preference 1973
Occupational Safety 1973

Occupations — (cont'd)
Occupational Status 1978
Occupational Stress 1973
Occupational Success 1978
↓ Occupational Tenure 1973
↓ Personnel 1967
↓ Professional Personnel 1978
↓ Vocational Education 1973
Vocational Maturity 1978
Working Women 1978

Octopus 1973
PN 70 **SC** 35120
B Mollusca 1973

Ocular Accommodation 1982
PN 410 **SC** 35127
SN Process of focusing an image on the retina by means of a flattening or bulging of the lens.
UF Eye Accommodation
Focusing (Visual)
B Reflexes 1971
R ↓ Depth Perception 1967
Lens (Eye) 1973
↓ Refraction Errors 1973

Ocular Dominance 1973
PN 422 **SC** 35130
UF Eye Dominance
B Lateral Dominance 1967
R ↓ Brain 1967
↓ Eye (Anatomy) 1967
Interocular Transfer 1985
Left Hemisphere 2005
Right Hemisphere 2005

Ocular Fixation
Use Eye Fixation

Oculomotor Muscles 1973
PN 173 **SC** 35140
B Muscles 1967

Oculomotor Nerve
Use Cranial Nerves

Oculomotor Response
Use Eye Movements

Odor Aversion Conditioning
Use Aversion Conditioning

Odor Discrimination 1973
PN 1597 **SC** 35170
B Olfactory Perception 1967
Perceptual Discrimination 1973
R Olfactory Thresholds 1973

Oedipal Complex 1973
PN 1445 **SC** 35180
SN In psychoanalytic theory, the attachment of a child to the parent of the opposite sex. It is theorized that the child harbors erotic feelings toward the parent of the opposite sex while exhibiting hostility and aggression to the parent of the same sex.
B Psychoanalytic Personality Factors 1973

Offender Profiling
Use Criminal Profiling

Offenders (Adult)
Use Criminals

Offenders (Juvenile)
Use Juvenile Delinquency

Office Environment
Use Working Conditions

Officers (Commissioned)
Use Commissioned Officers

Officers (Noncommissioned)
Use Noncommissioned Officers

Offshoring
Use Outsourcing

Offspring 1988
PN 2698 **SC** 35230
SN Used specifically for children, regardless of age, whose parents had significant experiences or conditions, e.g., alcoholism, fame, or political persecution. Limited to human populations.
N Adult Offspring 1985
Children of Alcoholics 2003
Daughters 1973
Interracial Offspring 1988
Sons 1973
R ↓ Family Members 1973

Offspring of Alcoholics
Use Children of Alcoholics

Olanzapine 2003
PN 1592 **SC** 35236
HN This term was introduced in June 2003. Relevant records were re-indexed with this term. The posting note reflects the number of records that were re-indexed.
B Neuroleptic Drugs 1973

Olfactory Bulb 1973
PN 944 **SC** 35247
SN Comprised of the main olfactory bulb and the accessory olfactory bulb, this structure is integral to the sense of smell.
B Limbic System 1973
R Olfactory Nerve 1973

Olfactory Evoked Potentials 1973
PN 141 **SC** 35250
SN Electrical potentials within the brain that are evoked by or correlated to olfaction (olfactory perception). Includes the actual electrical phenomena as well as the measurement of such phenomena.
B Evoked Potentials 1967

Olfactory Impairment
Use Anosmia

Olfactory Mucosa 1973
PN 79 **SC** 35260
B Nasal Mucosa 1973
R Chemoreceptors 1973

Olfactory Nerve 1973
PN 155 **SC** 35270
SN A cranial nerve, the olfactory nerve is the bundle of nerve fibers that transduces signals between the olfactory chemoreceptors in the olfactory mucosa and the olfactory bulb.
B Cranial Nerves 1973
R Olfactory Bulb 1973

Olfactory Perception 1967
PN 3252 **SC** 35280
UF Smell Perception
B Perception 1967
N Odor Discrimination 1973
Olfactory Thresholds 1973

Olfactory Perception — (cont'd)
R Anosmia 1973
Taste Perception 1967
Vomeronasal Sense 1982

Olfactory Stimulation 1978
PN 1360 **SC** 35285
B Perceptual Stimulation 1973

Olfactory Thresholds 1973
PN 281 **SC** 35290
B Olfactory Perception 1967
Thresholds 1967
R Odor Discrimination 1973
↓ Perceptual Measures 1973

Oligophrenia
Use Mental Retardation

Oligophrenia (Phenylpyruvic)
Use Phenylketonuria

Omission Training 1985
PN 21 **SC** 35315
SN Removal of positive reinforcement upon occurrence of undesirable behavior. Has applications in both therapeutic and experimental contexts.
B Behavior Modification 1973
Operant Conditioning 1967
R Differential Reinforcement 1973
Time Out 1985

Omnipotence 1994
PN 60 **SC** 35325
B Personality Traits 1967
R Authority 1967
Grandiosity 1994
Magical Thinking 1973
↓ Power 1967

On the Job Training 1973
PN 279 **SC** 35330
B Personnel Training 1967
R ↓ Experiential Learning 1997
Inservice Teacher Education 1973
↓ Inservice Training 1985

Online Databases
Use Databases

Online Retailing
Use Electronic Retailing

Online Searching
Use Computer Searching

Online Shopping
Use Electronic Commerce

Online Social Networks 2007
PN 2 **SC** 58109
SN The use of Internet applications to make connections or to network with individuals or groups who share common interests, contacts, knowledge, or resources.
HN This term was introduced in April 2007. Relevant records were re-indexed with this term. The posting note reflects the number of records that were re-indexed.
UF Internet Social Networking
B Internet Usage 2007
Social Networks 1994
R Computer Mediated Communication 2003
Professional Networking 2004

Online Therapy 2003
PN 303 **SC** 35334
SN Therapy in which clinician and client are geographically separated and communicate via computer or other telecommunications media.
HN This term was introduced in June 2003. Relevant records were re-indexed with this term. The posting note reflects the number of records that were re-indexed.
UF Cybercounseling
E-Therapy
Internet Counseling
Teletherapy
Web Based Mental Health Services
B Treatment 1967
R ↓ Computer Applications 1973
Computer Assisted Therapy 2007
Computer Mediated Communication 2003
Health Care Seeking Behavior 1997
Internet 2001
↓ Psychotherapy 1967
↓ Telecommunications Media 1973

Only Children 1982
PN 141 **SC** 35335
SN Children having no siblings.
R ↓ Family Members 1973
↓ Family Structure 1973

Onomatopoeia and Images Test
HN Term was discontinued in 1997. In 2000, the term was removed from all records containing it, and replaced with PROJECTIVE PERSONALITY MEASURES, its postable counterpart.
Use Projective Personality Measures

Onset (Disorders) 1973
PN 5134 **SC** 35350
SN Beginning or first appearance of a mental or physical disorder.
R ↓ Disorders 1967
↓ Mental Disorders 1967
↓ Physical Disorders 1997
Premorbidity 1978
Prodrome 2004

Ontogeny
Use Development

Ontologies 2007
PN 32 **SC** 35365
SN Used to describe concepts and the relationships that can exist between them, usually within a given field or domain.
HN This term was introduced in April 2007. Relevant records were re-indexed with this term. The posting note reflects the number of records that were re-indexed.
R Knowledge Management 2005
↓ Language 1967
Taxonomies 1973
↓ Terminology 1991

Ontology (Philosophy) 2007
PN 62 **SC** 35366
SN A branch of metaphysics concerned with the nature of being and existence.
HN This term was introduced in April 2007. Relevant records were re-indexed with this term. The posting note reflects the number of records that were re-indexed.
B Metaphysics 1973
Philosophies 1967

Open Classroom Method 1973
PN 381 **SC** 35370
SN Approach to teaching and learning emphasizing the student's right to make decisions and viewing the teacher as a facilitator of learning rather than a transmitter of knowledge. May include grouping of students across grades, independent study, individualized rates of progression, open-plan schools without interior walls, or unstructured time and curricula.
B Teaching Methods 1967
R Discovery Teaching Method 1973
Individualized Instruction 1973
Montessori Method 1973
Team Teaching Method 1973

Open Field Behavior (Animal)
Use Animal Open Field Behavior

Open Universities
Use Nontraditional Education

Openmindedness 1978
PN 218 **SC** 35376
SN Willingness to consider new and unconventional ideas, and readiness to reexamine social, political, and religious values.
UF Closedmindedness
B Personality Traits 1967
R Agreeableness 1997
Authoritarianism 1967
Dogmatism 1978

Openness to Experience 1997
PN 284 **SC** 35378
SN A broad experiential trait manifested in active imagination, aesthetic sensitivity, attentiveness to inner feelings, preference for variety, intellectual curiosity, and independence of judgment.
UF Imaginativeness
B Personality Traits 1967
R Adaptability (Personality) 1973
Conformity (Personality) 1967
Creativity 1967
Curiosity 1967
Five Factor Personality Model 1997
Hypnotic Susceptibility 1973
Rigidity (Personality) 1967
↓ Tolerance 1973

Operant Conditioning 1967
PN 7639 **SC** 35380
SN Learned behavior or the experimental paradigm in which reinforcers (positive or negative) or punishers immediately and contingently follow the performance of some behavior, the frequency of which changes as a direct consequence of such contingent reinforcement.
UF Conditioning (Operant)
Instrumental Conditioning
Instrumental Learning
B Conditioning 1967
N Avoidance Conditioning 1967
↓ Conditioned Emotional Responses 1967
↓ Conditioned Responses 1967
Delayed Alternation 1994
↓ Discrimination Learning 1982
Escape Conditioning 1973
Fading (Conditioning) 1982
Omission Training 1985
Time Out 1985
R ↓ Adjunctive Behavior 1982
↓ Behavior Modification 1973
Conditioned Stimulus 1973

Operant Conditioning — (cont'd)
Learning Theory 1967
Polydipsia 1982
↓ Reinforcement 1967
↓ Self Stimulation 1967
Skinner (Burrhus Frederic) 1991
Unconditioned Stimulus 1973

Operation (Surgery)
Use Surgery

Ophidiophobia 1973
PN 269 **SC** 35400
SN Fear of snakes.
UF Snake Phobia
B Phobias 1967

Ophthalmologic Examination 1973
PN 96 **SC** 35410
UF Eye Examination
B Medical Diagnosis 1973
N Electro Oculography 1973
Electroretinography 1967

Ophthalmology 1973
PN 73 **SC** 35420
B Medical Sciences 1967
R Optometry 1973

Opiate Agonists
Use Narcotic Agonists

Opiate Antagonists
Use Narcotic Antagonists

Opiates 1973
PN 4783 **SC** 35430
UF Opioids
Opium Alkaloids
Opium Derivatives
B Narcotic Drugs 1973
N Codeine 1973
↓ Endogenous Opiates 1985
Fentanyl 1985
Heroin 1973
Morphine 1973
Papaverine 1973

Opinion (Public)
Use Public Opinion

Opinion Attitude and Interest Survey
HN Term was discontinued in 1997. In 2000, the term was removed from all records containing it, and replaced with ATTITUDE MEASURES, its postable counterpart.
Use Attitude Measures

Opinion Change
Use Attitude Change

Opinion Questionnaires
Use Attitude Measures

Opinion Surveys
Use Attitude Measures

Opinions
Use Attitudes

Opioid Antagonists
Use Narcotic Antagonists

Opioids
Use Opiates

Opioids (Endogenous)
Use Endogenous Opiates

Opium Alkaloids
Use Alkaloids AND Opiates

Opium Derivatives
Use Opiates

Opossums 1973
PN 105 **SC** 35530
B Marsupials 1973

Oppositional Defiant Disorder 1997
PN 594 **SC** 35535
SN A psychopathological disorder, usually beginning in childhood, consisting of negativism, disobedience, and hostile behavior toward authority figures.
R ↓ Attention Deficit Disorder 1985
Attention Deficit Disorder with Hyperactivity 2001
↓ Behavior Disorders 1971
Conduct Disorder 1991
Hyperkinesis 1973

Optic Chiasm 1973
PN 90 **SC** 35540
SN The structure at the base of the brain where the optic nerves partially cross, and neural activity from the right eye and left eye is split between connections on both sides of the brain.
B Diencephalon 1973
Neural Pathways 1982
R Optic Nerve 1973

Optic Lobe 1973
PN 144 **SC** 35550
SN In invertebrates and some non-mammalian vertebrates, neural activity flows directly from the photoreceptors in or on the eye into this brain structure for visual processing. In mammals, the optic lobe consists of two quadrigeminal bodies of the midbrain.
B Mesencephalon 1973

Optic Nerve 1973
PN 293 **SC** 35560
SN The bundle of nerve fibers that transmits information from the retina, through the optic tract, to visual processing areas in the brain.
B Cranial Nerves 1973
R Optic Chiasm 1973

Optic Tract 1982
PN 92 **SC** 35563
SN Portion of the optic pathway that extends posteriorly from the optic chiasm in two nerve fiber bundles to synapse near the superior colliculi and in the lateral geniculate body of the thalamus.
B Neural Pathways 1982

Optical Aids 1973
PN 223 **SC** 35565
UF Corrective Lenses
B Medical Therapeutic Devices 1973
N Contact Lenses 1973

Optical Illusions
Use Illusions (Perception)

Optimism 1973
PN 1600 **SC** 35580
SN Attitude characterized by a positive and cheerful disposition and inclination to anticipate the most favorable outcome of events or actions.

Optimism — (cont'd)
B Emotional States 1973
Personality Traits 1967
R Hope 1991
Pessimism 1973
Positive Psychology 2003
Positivism 1973

Optokinetic Nystagmus
Use Nystagmus

Optometrists 1973
PN 64 **SC** 35590
B Medical Personnel 1967

Optometry 1973
PN 228 **SC** 35600
B Paramedical Sciences 1973
R Ophthalmology 1973

Oral Communication 1985
PN 7517 **SC** 35610
SN Expression of information in oral form.
HN Use VERBAL COMMUNICATION to access references from 1967-1984.
UF Speech
Verbalization
B Verbal Communication 1967
N Code Switching 1988
Oral Reading 1973
Public Speaking 1973
Self Talk 1988
Singing 1997
↓ Speech Characteristics 1973
R Rhetoric 1991
Verbal Ability 1967
Verbal Fluency 1973
↓ Vocalization 1967
↓ Voice 1973

Oral Contraceptives 1973
PN 412 **SC** 35620
B Contraceptive Devices 1973
R Fertility Enhancement 1973

Oral Reading 1973
PN 1376 **SC** 35630
SN Reading aloud by individuals or groups or the condition of being read to by others.
UF Reading Aloud
B Oral Communication 1985
Reading 1967

Organ Donation
Use Tissue Donation

Organ of Corti
Use Cochlea

Organ Transplantation 1973
PN 1312 **SC** 35660
UF Heart Transplants
Kidney Transplants
Renal Transplantation
Transplants (Organ)
B Surgery 1971
R Heart Surgery 1973
Neural Transplantation 1985
Tissue Donation 1991

Organic Brain Syndromes 1973
PN 825 **SC** 35670
SN Syndromes of impaired brain tissue function that result in mental and cognitive decline. Symptoms include delirium, confusion, agitation, and dementia; etiology is unknown.
B Brain Disorders 1967
Syndromes 1973
N ↓ Alcoholic Psychosis 1973
Alzheimers Disease 1973
↓ Dementia 1985
Toxic Psychoses 1973
R ↓ Mental Disorders 1967
Postpartum Depression 1973
Postpartum Psychosis 2003

Organic Therapies
HN In 2000, the term was discontinued, and removed from all records containing it, and replaced with PHYSICAL TREATMENT METHODS, its postable counterpart.
Use Physical Treatment Methods

Organizational Behavior 1978
PN 12263 **SC** 35695
SN Behavior of organizations and of individuals within organizational settings.
B Social Behavior 1967
N ↓ Employee Interaction 1988
Organizational Effectiveness 1985
R Distributive Justice 2003
↓ Group Dynamics 1967
Informants 1988
Innovation 2007
Labor Management Relations 1967
↓ Organizational Characteristics 1997
Organizational Commitment 1991
Organizational Learning 2003
Organizational Structure 1967
↓ Organizations 1967
Procedural Justice 2003
Professional Networking 2004
Psychological Contracts 2003
↓ Sociometry 1991

Organizational Change 1973
PN 4750 **SC** 35700
UF Change (Organizational)
N Downsizing 2003
Mergers and Acquisitions 2007
R Decentralization 1978
Organizational Climate 1973
Organizational Crises 1973
Organizational Development 1973
Organizational Learning 2003

Organizational Characteristics 1997
PN 1631 **SC** 35705
N Organizational Climate 1973
Organizational Structure 1967
R Diversity in the Workplace 2003
↓ Organizational Behavior 1978
Organizational Commitment 1991
Organizational Learning 2003
Organizational Objectives 1973
Quality of Work Life 1988

Organizational Climate 1973
PN 5181 **SC** 35710
SN Social or environmental characteristics of an organization which affect the behavior or performance of its members.

Organizational Climate — (cont'd)
UF Climate (Organizational)
Organizational Culture
B Organizational Characteristics 1997
R Diversity in the Workplace 2003
↓ Organizational Change 1973
Organizational Crises 1973
Organizational Structure 1967
Quality of Work Life 1988
↓ Working Conditions 1973

Organizational Commitment 1991
PN 2400 **SC** 35715
SN Commitment of organizations and of individuals within organizational settings.
B Commitment 1985
R ↓ Employee Attitudes 1967
↓ Employee Characteristics 1988
Employer Attitudes 1973
Job Involvement 1978
↓ Job Performance 1967
Job Satisfaction 1967
↓ Membership 2007
↓ Organizational Behavior 1978
↓ Organizational Characteristics 1997
Organizational Effectiveness 1985
Organizational Objectives 1973
Psychological Contracts 2003

Organizational Crises 1973
PN 286 **SC** 35720
B Crises 1971
R ↓ Organizational Change 1973
Organizational Climate 1973
↓ Stress 1967

Organizational Culture
Use Organizational Climate

Organizational Development 1973
PN 2761 **SC** 35730
SN Application of behavioral, management, or other techniques to organizations in order to integrate individuals' or members' needs with organizational goals and objectives.
B Development 1967
R Decentralization 1978
Innovation 2007
↓ Organizational Change 1973
Organizational Learning 2003
Organizational Objectives 1973
Organizational Structure 1967

Organizational Effectiveness 1985
PN 3234 **SC** 35735
SN Measure of the ability of an organization to meet the needs of its environment, including personnel needs.
UF Organizational Performance
B Organizational Behavior 1978
R Organizational Commitment 1991
Organizational Learning 2003
Organizational Objectives 1973
Quality Control 1988

Organizational Goals
Use Organizational Objectives

Organizational Innovation
Use Innovation

Organizational Learning 2003
PN 800 **SC** 35748
SN Conceptually broad term referring to the ability of an organization to adapt, learn, and change with its environment, and to the process of obtaining, sharing, and utilizing knowledge in an organizational setting.
HN This term was introduced in June 2003. Relevant records were re-indexed with this term. The posting note reflects the number of records that were re-indexed.
UF Learning Organizations
B Learning 1967
R ↓ Business Organizations 1973
Communities of Practice 2007
↓ Organizational Behavior 1978
↓ Organizational Change 1973
↓ Organizational Characteristics 1997
Organizational Development 1973
Organizational Effectiveness 1985

Organizational Merger
HN In April 2007, this term was discontinued and removed from all records containing it, and was replaced with MERGERS AND ACQUISITIONS, its postable counterpart.
Use Mergers and Acquisitions

Organizational Objectives 1973
PN 940 **SC** 35760
UF Objectives (Organizational)
Organizational Goals
B Goals 1967
R Decentralization 1978
↓ Organizational Characteristics 1997
Organizational Commitment 1991
Organizational Development 1973
Organizational Effectiveness 1985
Quality Control 1988

Organizational Performance
Use Organizational Effectiveness

Organizational Policy Making
Use Policy Making

Organizational Psychology
Use Industrial and Organizational Psychology

Organizational Structure 1967
PN 4160 **SC** 35770
B Organizational Characteristics 1997
R Decentralization 1978
Mergers and Acquisitions 2007
↓ Organizational Behavior 1978
Organizational Climate 1973
Organizational Development 1973
↓ Organizations 1967
Self Managing Work Teams 2001
↓ Work Teams 2001

Organizations 1967
PN 5849 **SC** 35780
UF Agencies (Groups)
Associations (Groups)
Groups (Organizations)
N ↓ Business Organizations 1973
Foreign Organizations 1973
Government Agencies 1973
Health Maintenance Organizations 1982
International Organizations 1973
Labor Unions 1973
Nonprofit Organizations 1973
↓ Professional Organizations 1973
↓ Religious Organizations 1991

Organizations — (cont'd)
R ↓ Membership 2007
↓ Organizational Behavior 1978
Organizational Structure 1967

Orgasm 1973
PN 170 **SC** 35790
UF Climax (Sexual)
B Psychosexual Behavior 1967
N Female Orgasm 1973
↓ Male Orgasm 1973
R Female Sexual Dysfunction 2005
Sexual Satisfaction 1994

Orientation (Perceptual)
Use Perceptual Orientation

Orientation (Spatial)
Use Spatial Orientation (Perception)

Orienting Reflex 1967
PN 926 **SC** 35820
SN Innate physiological responses, such as pupil dilation, galvanic skin response, and EEG activity, to novel stimuli.
B Reflexes 1971
Sensory Adaptation 1967

Orienting Responses 1967
PN 1184 **SC** 35830
SN Behavioral reactions in an organism, such as arrest of movement or head turning, to novel stimuli; behavioral correlate of orienting reflex.
B Responses 1967
Sensory Adaptation 1967
R ↓ Classical Conditioning 1967

Originality
Use Creativity

Orphanages 1973
PN 131 **SC** 35850
B Residential Care Institutions 1973
R ↓ Institutionalization 1967
Orphans 1973

Orphans 1973
PN 240 **SC** 35860
B Family Members 1973
R Orphanages 1973

Orphenadrine 1973
PN 14 **SC** 35870
UF Methyldiphenylhydramine
B Amines 1973
Antihistaminic Drugs 1973
Antispasmodic Drugs 1973
Antitremor Drugs 1973
Cholinergic Blocking Drugs 1973
Muscle Relaxing Drugs 1973

Orthogonal Rotation 1973
PN 126 **SC** 35880
B Statistical Rotation 1973
N Varimax Rotation 1973

Orthography 1973
PN 1794 **SC** 35890
SN Art and formal rules of writing and spelling according to accepted usage. Also used to refer to the representation of the sounds of a language by written symbols.

Orthography — (cont'd)
B Linguistics 1973
R ↓ Alphabets 1973
Cursive Writing 1973
Homographs 1973
Proofreading 1988
Spelling 1973
↓ Written Language 1967

Orthopedically Handicapped
Use Physical Disorders

Orthopsychiatry 1973
PN 33 **SC** 35910
SN Interdisciplinary approach combining psychiatry, psychology, pediatrics, and other related fields for prevention and early treatment of mental disorders, particularly in children and adolescents.
B Psychiatry 1967
R Child Psychiatry 1967

Oscilloscopes 1973
PN 27 **SC** 35920
B Apparatus 1967

Osteopathic Medicine 2003
PN 26 **SC** 35928
SN A system of therapy and medicine based on the theory that diseases are chiefly due to a loss of structural integrity, which can be restored by manipulation of the skeleton and muscles.
HN This term was introduced in June 2003. Relevant records were re-indexed with this term. The posting note reflects the number of records that were re-indexed.
UF Osteopathy
B Medical Sciences 1967
R ↓ Alternative Medicine 1997
↓ Musculoskeletal System 1973
↓ Physical Treatment Methods 1973

Osteopathy
Use Osteopathic Medicine

Osteoporosis 1991
PN 294 **SC** 35930
B Bone Disorders 1973

Otosclerosis
HN Term discontinued in 1997. In 2000, the term was removed from all records containing it, and replaced with EAR DISORDERS, its postable counterpart.
Use Ear Disorders

Out of Body Experiences 1988
PN 143 **SC** 35945
B Parapsychological Phenomena 1973
R Near Death Experiences 1985

Outcomes (Psychotherapeutic)
Use Psychotherapeutic Outcomes

Outcomes (Treatment)
Use Treatment Outcomes

Outgroup Ingroup
Use Ingroup Outgroup

Outpatient Commitment 1991
PN 120 **SC** 35957
SN Legally mandated psychiatric or psychological treatment on an outpatient basis.

Outpatient Commitment — (cont'd)
UF Commitment (Outpatient)
B Commitment (Psychiatric) 1973
Outpatient Treatment 1967
R Aftercare 1973
Partial Hospitalization 1985

Outpatient Psychiatric Clinics
Use Psychiatric Clinics

Outpatient Treatment 1967
PN 3920 **SC** 35970
SN Treatment in private practice, clinic, or hospital for ambulatory, non-hospitalized patients. Compare PARTIAL HOSPITALIZATION.
UF Ambulatory Care
B Treatment 1967
N Outpatient Commitment 1991
R Aftercare 1973
↓ Drug Therapy 1967
Home Care 1985
Maintenance Therapy 1997
Outpatients 1973
Psychiatric Clinics 1973

Outpatients 1973
PN 2941 **SC** 35980
B Patients 1967
R ↓ Outpatient Treatment 1967

Outreach Programs 1997
PN 451 **SC** 35983
B Social Programs 1973
Social Services 1982
R ↓ Case Management 1991
Community Mental Health Services 1978
↓ Community Services 1967
↓ Health Care Delivery 1978
↓ Health Care Services 1978
↓ Mental Health Programs 1973
↓ Mental Health Services 1978
Needle Exchange Programs 2001
Social Casework 1967
↓ Support Groups 1991

Outsourcing 2007
PN 65 **SC** 35984
SN Acquiring services or products from an outside company or organization.
HN This term was introduced in April 2007. Relevant records were re-indexed with this term. The posting note reflects the number of records that were re-indexed.
UF Contracting Out
Offshoring
R ↓ Human Resource Management 2003
Labor Market 2007

Outward Bound
Use Wilderness Experience

Ovariectomy 1973
PN 1010 **SC** 35990
B Castration 1967
R Hysterectomy 1973

Ovaries 1973
PN 278 **SC** 36000
B Female Genitalia 1973
Gonads 1973

Ovary Disorders
Use Endocrine Sexual Disorders

Over the Counter Drugs
Use Nonprescription Drugs

Overachievement (Academic)
Use Academic Overachievement

Overcorrection 1985
PN 46 **SC** 36025
SN Therapeutic technique involving restitution and/or intensive practice of appropriate behavior following the occurrence of disruptive or inappropriate behavior.
B Behavior Modification 1973
R Overlearning 1967
↓ Practice 1967

Overlearning 1967
PN 248 **SC** 36030
SN Learning in which practice continues beyond the point of mastery of the material or task.
B Learning 1967
R Overcorrection 1985

Overpopulation 1973
PN 209 **SC** 36040
B Population 1973
R ↓ Birth Control 1971
Crowding 1978
Environmental Stress 1973
Social Density 1978

Overweight 2007
PN 403 **SC** 36050
HN In April 2007, OVERWEIGHT changed status from nonpostable to postable. Relevant records were re-indexed with this term. The posting note reflects the number of records that were re-indexed.
B Body Weight 1967
N Obesity 1973
R Body Mass Index 2006
Physique 1967
Somatotypes 1973

Ovulation 1973
PN 193 **SC** 36060
B Menstrual Cycle 1973

Owls 1997
PN 96 **SC** 36063
B Birds 1967

Ownership 1985
PN 702 **SC** 36065
UF Possession
Property
R ↓ Business 1967
Capitalism 1973
Entrepreneurship 1991
Patents 2007
↓ Private Sector 1985
Self Employment 1994
Small Businesses 2007

Oxazepam 1978
PN 127 **SC** 36075
B Anticonvulsive Drugs 1973
Benzodiazepines 1978
Minor Tranquilizers 1973

Oxidases 1973
PN 148 **SC** 36080
B Enzymes 1973
N Cytochrome Oxidase 1973
Monoamine Oxidases 1973

Oxidopamine
Use Hydroxydopamine (6-)

Oxilapine
Use Loxapine

Oxygen 1973
PN 535 **SC** 36090
R ↓ Antioxidants 2004
Nitric Oxide 2003

Oxygenation 1973
PN 178 **SC** 36100
B Physiology 1967

Oxytocin 1973
PN 586 **SC** 36120
SN Naturally secreted pituitary gland hormone that stimulates uterine contractions during labor and milk flow during lactation.
B Neuropeptides 2003
Pituitary Hormones 1973

Pacemakers (Artificial)
Use Artificial Pacemakers

Pacific Islanders 2001
PN 140 **SC** 36133
B Indigenous Populations 2001
N Hawaii Natives 2001
R Alaska Natives 1997
American Indians 1967
Inuit 2001
Minority Groups 1967

Pacifism 1973
PN 51 **SC** 36140
B Philosophies 1967
R Nonviolence 1991

Pain 1967
PN 8615 **SC** 36150
UF Aches
B Symptoms 1967
N Aphagia 1973
Back Pain 1982
Chronic Pain 1985
↓ Headache 1973
Myofascial Pain 1991
↓ Neuralgia 1973
Somatoform Pain Disorder 1997
R ↓ Analgesic Drugs 1973
Fibromyalgia 2004
Pain Management 1994
Pain Measurement 1997
↓ Pain Perception 1973
Pain Thresholds 1973
↓ Physical Disorders 1997
↓ Spasms 1973
Suffering 1973

Pain (Psychogenic)
Use Somatoform Pain Disorder

Pain Disorder
Use Somatoform Pain Disorder

Pain Management 1994
PN 3424 **SC** 36165
B Treatment 1967
R Analgesia 1982
↓ Analgesic Drugs 1973
↓ Pain 1967
Pain Measurement 1997

Pain Management — (cont'd)
↓ Pain Perception 1973
Pain Thresholds 1973
Palliative Care 1991
↓ Physical Treatment Methods 1973
Somatoform Pain Disorder 1997

Pain Measurement 1997
PN 512 **SC** 36167
SN Tests, scales, or other techniques used to assess or evaluate pain in human or animal populations. Used only when the methodology is the focus of the reference.
B Measurement 1967
R Analgesia 1982
↓ Diagnosis 1967
↓ Pain 1967
Pain Management 1994
↓ Pain Perception 1973
Pain Thresholds 1973
↓ Perceptual Measures 1973

Pain Perception 1973
PN 5975 **SC** 36170
UF Nociception
B Somesthetic Perception 1967
N Analgesia 1982
Pain Thresholds 1973
R ↓ Pain 1967
Pain Management 1994
Pain Measurement 1997
Somatosensory Disorders 2001

Pain Receptors
Use Nociceptors

Pain Relieving Drugs
Use Analgesic Drugs

Pain Thresholds 1973
PN 1320 **SC** 36190
B Pain Perception 1973
Thresholds 1967
R ↓ Pain 1967
Pain Management 1994
Pain Measurement 1997
↓ Perceptual Measures 1973

Painting (Art) 1973
PN 837 **SC** 36200
B Art 1967

Paired Associate Learning 1967
PN 2887 **SC** 36210
B Verbal Learning 1967
R Word Associations 1967

Palestinians
Use Arabs

Palliative Care 1991
PN 2401 **SC** 36219
UF End of Life Care
B Health Care Services 1978
R Advance Directives 1994
Assisted Suicide 1997
↓ Death and Dying 1967
↓ Health Care Delivery 1978
Hospice 1982
Life Sustaining Treatment 1997
Long Term Care 1994
Pain Management 1994
Terminally Ill Patients 1973

Palm (Anatomy) 1973
PN 51 **SC** 36220
B Anatomy 1967
R Hand (Anatomy) 1967

Palsy
Use Paralysis

Pancreas 1973
PN 168 **SC** 36240
B Glands 1967
R ↓ Endocrine Glands 1973
↓ Endocrine System 1973
↓ Gastrointestinal System 1973

Pancreozymin
Use Cholecystokinin

Pandemics 2007
PN 58 **SC** 36255
SN Epidemics that occur over a wide geographic area and impact a substantial percentage of the population.
HN This term was introduced in April 2007. Relevant records were re-indexed with this term. The posting note reflects the number of records that were re-indexed.
B Epidemics 2001
R Disease Transmission 2004

Panic 1973
PN 1385 **SC** 36260
HN Prior to 1988, also used for PANIC DISORDER.
B Fear 1967
R ↓ Anxiety 1967
Panic Attack 2003
Panic Disorder 1988

Panic Attack 2003
PN 389 **SC** 36261
SN An episode of intense fear and anxiety that may be accompanied by one or more of the following symptoms: heart palpitations, sweating, shortness of breath, chest pain, nausea, dizziness, and trembling. Generally, attacks are unexpected and last no longer than 15 minutes.
HN This term was introduced in June 2003. Relevant records were re-indexed with this term. The posting note reflects the number of records that were re-indexed.
R ↓ Anxiety 1967
↓ Anxiety Disorders 1997
↓ Fear 1967
Panic 1973
Panic Disorder 1988

Panic Disorder 1988
PN 5356 **SC** 36265
HN Consider PANIC to access references from 1973-1987.
B Anxiety Disorders 1997
R ↓ Anxiety 1967
Panic 1973
Panic Attack 2003

Pantherine
Use Muscimol

Papaverine 1973
PN 36 **SC** 36270
B Alkaloids 1973
Analgesic Drugs 1973
Antispasmodic Drugs 1973
Muscle Relaxing Drugs 1973

Papaverine — (cont'd)
Opiates 1973

Parachlorophenylalanine 1978
PN 188 **SC** 36275
B Phenylalanine 1973
Serotonin Antagonists 1973

Paradigmatic Techniques
Use Paradoxical Techniques

Paradoxical Sleep
Use REM Sleep

Paradoxical Techniques 1982
PN 513 **SC** 36282
SN Techniques designed to disrupt dysfunctional behavior patterns through systematically encouraging them, thus allaying anticipatory anxiety, creating resistance to the symptomatic behavior, or enabling clients to achieve voluntary control over this behavior.
UF Paradigmatic Techniques
Reframing
Symptom Prescription
B Psychotherapeutic Techniques 1967
R ↓ Behavior Therapy 1967
↓ Psychotherapy 1967

Paragraphs 1973
PN 75 **SC** 36300
B Written Language 1967

Paraldehyde
HN Term discontinued in 1997. In 2000, the term was removed from all records containing it, and replaced with ANTICONVULSIVE DRUGS, its postable counterpart.
Use Anticonvulsive Drugs

Paralegal Personnel
Use Legal Personnel

Paralysis 1973
PN 484 **SC** 36320
SN Loss of motor function.
UF Palsy
B Movement Disorders 1985
Neuromuscular Disorders 1973
N Cerebral Palsy 1967
Hemiplegia 1978
Paraplegia 1978
Quadriplegia 1985
R ↓ Central Nervous System Disorders 1973
Dysarthria 1973
General Paresis 1973
↓ Musculoskeletal Disorders 1973
Parkinsons Disease 1973
↓ Peripheral Neuropathy 2006
Poliomyelitis 1973
↓ Sclerosis (Nervous System) 1973
↓ Spinal Cord Injuries 1973

Paralysis (Hysterical)
Use Hysterical Paralysis

Paralysis (Infantile)
Use Poliomyelitis

Paralysis Agitans
Use Parkinsons Disease

Paramedical Personnel
HN In 1997, this term replaced the discontinued term MEDICS. In 2000, MEDICS was removed from all records containing it and replaced with PARAMEDI-

Paramedical Personnel — (cont'd)
CAL PERSONNEL. In April 2007, this term was discontinued and removed from all records containing it, and was replaced with ALLIED HEALTH PERSONNEL, its postable counterpart.
Use Allied Health Personnel

Paramedical Sciences 1973
PN 23 **SC** 36370
N Audiology 1973
Nursing 1973
Optometry 1973
↓ Pharmacology 1973
Physical Therapy 1973
R ↓ Medical Sciences 1967

Parameter Estimation
Use Statistical Estimation

Parameters (Response)
Use Response Parameters

Parameters (Stimulus)
Use Stimulus Parameters

Parametric Statistical Tests 1973
PN 189 **SC** 36400
B Statistical Tests 1973
N F Test 1973
T Test 1973

Paranoia 1988
PN 408 **SC** 36410
SN Mild paranoia in nonpsychotic persons.
B Personality Traits 1967
R Paranoid Personality Disorder 1973

Paranoia (Psychosis) 1967
PN 996 **SC** 36420
SN Gradual development of an elaborate and complex delusional system, usually involving persecutory or grandiose delusions with few other signs of personality or thought disturbance.
UF Acute Paranoid Disorder
Atypical Paranoid Disorder
Paranoid Disorder
B Psychosis 1967
N Folie A Deux 1973
R Paranoid Personality Disorder 1973
Paranoid Schizophrenia 1967

Paranoid Disorder
Use Paranoia (Psychosis)

Paranoid Personality Disorder 1973
PN 214 **SC** 36430
SN Nonpsychotic personality disorder marked by hypersensitivity, jealousy, and unwarranted suspicion with tendency to blame others for one's shortcomings.
B Personality Disorders 1967
R Paranoia 1988
↓ Paranoia (Psychosis) 1967
Paranoid Schizophrenia 1967

Paranoid Schizophrenia 1967
PN 1569 **SC** 36440
SN Type of schizophrenia characterized by grandiosity, suspiciousness, and delusions of persecution, often with hallucinations.
B Schizophrenia 1967
R Folie A Deux 1973
↓ Paranoia (Psychosis) 1967
Paranoid Personality Disorder 1973
↓ Psychosis 1967

Paraphilias 1988
PN 1710 **SC** 36443
SN Sexual urges, fantasies, or behaviors generally involving themes of suffering, humiliation, sexual activity with non-consenting partners, or an orientation toward non-human objects for sexual arousal.
HN In 2000, the term's status changed from non-postable to postable. SEXUAL DEVIATIONS was removed from all records containing it and replaced with PARAPHILIAS.
UF Deviations (Sexual)
Perversions (Sexual)
Sexual Deviations
B Mental Disorders 1967
Psychosexual Behavior 1967
N Exhibitionism 1973
Fetishism 1973
Incest 1973
Pedophilia 1973
Sexual Masochism 1973
Sexual Sadism 1973
Transvestism 1973
Voyeurism 1973
R ↓ Impulse Control Disorders 1997
Pornography 1973
↓ Sex Offenses 1982
↓ Sexual Abuse 1988
Sexual Addiction 1997

Paraplegia 1978
PN 197 **SC** 36446
SN Paralysis of the lower limbs and trunk.
B Paralysis 1973
R ↓ Central Nervous System Disorders 1973
Hemiplegia 1978
↓ Injuries 1973
↓ Musculoskeletal Disorders 1973
Quadriplegia 1985
↓ Spinal Cord Injuries 1973

Paraprofessional Education 1973
PN 615 **SC** 36450
SN Training or education of aides, such as paramedical and paralegal personnel, who assist professional persons.
B Education 1967
R Microcounseling 1978

Paraprofessional Personnel 1973
PN 1215 **SC** 36460
SN Persons with minimal or special training in a profession working as aides or assistants to professionals.
HN Use PARAPROFESSIONAL PERSONNEL to access references to nonprofessional personnel from 1973-1981.
B Personnel 1967
N Home Care Personnel 1997
Teacher Aides 1973
R ↓ Mental Health Personnel 1967
↓ Nonprofessional Personnel 1982
Occupational Therapists 1973
↓ Professional Personnel 1978

Parapsychological Phenomena 1973
PN 1767 **SC** 36470
B Parapsychology 1967
N ↓ Extrasensory Perception 1967
Near Death Experiences 1985
Out of Body Experiences 1988
Telepathy 1973
R Occultism 1978
Religious Experiences 1997
Spirit Possession 1997

Parapsychological Phenomena — (cont'd)
Superstitions 1973

Parapsychology 1967
PN 1333 **SC** 36480
N ↓ Parapsychological Phenomena 1973
R Astrology 1973
Dream Analysis 1973
Mysticism 1967
Occultism 1978
Witchcraft 1973

Parasitic Disorders 1973
PN 178 **SC** 36490
B Infectious Disorders 1973
N Malaria 1973

Parasitism
Use Biological Symbiosis

Parasuicide
Use Attempted Suicide

Parasympathetic Nervous System 1973
PN 128 **SC** 36500
SN Part of the nervous system responsible for conserving resources and restoring homeostasis. Specifically, it slows heart rate, increases intestinal and gland activity, and relaxes sphincter muscles.
B Autonomic Nervous System 1967
N ↓ Efferent Pathways 1982
Vagus Nerve 1973
R ↓ Cholinergic Blocking Drugs 1973
↓ Cholinomimetic Drugs 1973

Parasympatholytic Drugs
HN Use CHOLINERGIC BLOCKING DRUGS to access references from 1973 to June 2004.
Use Antispasmodic Drugs

Parasympathomimetic Drugs
Use Cholinomimetic Drugs

Parathion 1973
PN 9 **SC** 36530
B Insecticides 1973

Parathyroid Disorders 1973
PN 69 **SC** 36540
UF Hyperparathyroidism
Hypoparathyroidism
B Endocrine Disorders 1973

Parathyroid Glands 1973
PN 9 **SC** 36550
B Endocrine Glands 1973
R Parathyroid Hormone 1973

Parathyroid Hormone 1973
PN 21 **SC** 36560
B Hormones 1967
R Parathyroid Glands 1973

Parent Child Communication 1973
PN 2479 **SC** 36580
SN For animals consider ANIMAL PARENTAL BEHAVIOR or ANIMAL MATERNAL BEHAVIOR.
HN From 1982, limited to human populations.
B Interpersonal Communication 1973
N Father Child Communication 1985
Mother Child Communication 1985
R ↓ Parent Child Relations 1967
↓ Parental Characteristics 1994

Parent Child Relations 1967
PN 16718 **SC** 36590
SN For animals consider ANIMAL PARENTAL BEHAVIOR, ANIMAL MATERNAL BEHAVIOR, or ANIMAL PATERNAL BEHAVIOR.
HN From 1982, limited to human populations.
UF Parental Influence
B Family Relations 1967
N Father Child Relations 1973
Mother Child Relations 1967
↓ Parental Attitudes 1973
Parental Permissiveness 1973
R Attachment Behavior 1985
Attachment Disorders 2001
Attachment Theory 2007
↓ Child Discipline 1973
↓ Childrearing Practices 1967
Children of Alcoholics 2003
Codependency 1991
Empty Nest 1991
↓ Family Conflict 2003
Generation Gap 1973
Nurturance 1985
↓ Parent Child Communication 1973
Parent School Relationship 1982
Parent Training 1978
↓ Parental Characteristics 1994
Parental Expectations 1997
Parental Investment 1997
Parental Involvement 2005
Parental Role 1973
Parenting Skills 1997
↓ Parenting Style 2003
Transgenerational Patterns 1991

Parent Educational Background 1973
PN 1004 **SC** 36600
UF Educational Background (Parents)
B Educational Background 1967
Family Background 1973
Parental Characteristics 1994
R Family Socioeconomic Level 1973
Parental Occupation 1973

Parent Effectiveness Training
Use Parent Training

Parent School Relationship 1982
PN 1774 **SC** 36605
SN Interactions between parents and school and/or educational personnel, such as parent-teacher conferences.
UF PTA
R ↓ Parent Child Relations 1967
Parent Training 1978
Parental Involvement 2005
↓ Teacher Attitudes 1967

Parent Training 1978
PN 4059 **SC** 36606
SN Educational materials, information, or instruction for parents.
UF Parent Effectiveness Training
B Family Life Education 1997
Training 2006
R ↓ Childrearing Practices 1967
Human Relations Training 1978
↓ Parent Child Relations 1967
Parent School Relationship 1982
Parental Role 1973
Parenting Skills 1997

Parental Absence 1973
PN 658 **SC** 36610
SN For animals consider ANIMAL PARENTAL BEHAVIOR or ANIMAL MATERNAL BEHAVIOR.
HN From 1982, limited to human populations.
B Family Structure 1973
N Father Absence 1973
Mother Absence 1973
R Anaclitic Depression 1973
Child Custody 1982
Divorced Persons 1973
↓ Marital Separation 1973
↓ Parental Characteristics 1994
Parental Death 2003
↓ Single Parents 1978
Widowers 1973
Widows 1973

Parental Attitudes 1973
PN 10363 **SC** 36620
SN Attitudes of, not toward, parents.
B Attitudes 1967
Parent Child Relations 1967
Parental Characteristics 1994
N Parental Expectations 1997
R Childrearing Attitudes 1973
↓ Childrearing Practices 1967
Father Child Relations 1973
Mother Child Relations 1967
Parental Involvement 2005
Parental Permissiveness 1973
Parental Role 1973

Parental Authoritarianism
HN Use PARENTAL PERMISSIVENESS to access references from 1973 to June 2003.
Use Parenting Style

Parental Behavior (Animal)
Use Animal Parental Behavior

Parental Characteristics 1994
PN 3734 **SC** 36637
N Parent Educational Background 1973
↓ Parental Attitudes 1973
Parental Occupation 1973
Parental Permissiveness 1973
Parental Role 1973
Parenting Skills 1997
↓ Parenting Style 2003
R ↓ Childrearing Practices 1967
↓ Parent Child Communication 1973
↓ Parent Child Relations 1967
↓ Parental Absence 1973
Parental Investment 1997
↓ Parents 1967

Parental Death 2003
PN 185 **SC** 36638
SN Death of parents.
HN This term was introduced in June 2003. Relevant records were re-indexed with this term. The posting note reflects the number of records that were re-indexed.
B Death and Dying 1967
R Life Changes 2004
↓ Parental Absence 1973
↓ Parents 1967

Parental Expectations 1997
PN 305 **SC** 36639
SN Expectations or aspirations for a level of behavior, achievement, or performance (e.g., in school, life, or career) that parents have for their children.

Parental Expectations — (cont'd)
B Expectations 1967
Parental Attitudes 1973
R ↓ Parent Child Relations 1967
Parental Investment 1997
Parental Role 1973
↓ Parents 1967

Parental Influence
Use Parent Child Relations

Parental Investment 1997
PN 671 **SC** 36645
SN Parental provision of resources and/or care to offspring. Used for both human and animal populations.
UF Maternal Investment
Paternal Investment
R ↓ Animal Parental Behavior 1982
↓ Parent Child Relations 1967
↓ Parental Characteristics 1994
Parental Expectations 1997
Parental Involvement 2005

Parental Involvement 2005
PN 791 **SC** 36647
SN The involvement of parents in the care and education of their children.
HN This term was introduced in August 2005. Relevant records were re-indexed with this term. The posting note reflects the number of records that were re-indexed.
UF Parental Participation
B Involvement 1973
R ↓ Parent Child Relations 1967
Parent School Relationship 1982
↓ Parental Attitudes 1973
Parental Investment 1997
Parental Role 1973

Parental Occupation 1973
PN 438 **SC** 36650
UF Occupation (Parental)
B Family Background 1973
Parental Characteristics 1994
R Family Socioeconomic Level 1973
Parent Educational Background 1973

Parental Participation
Use Parental Involvement

Parental Permissiveness 1973
PN 535 **SC** 36660
UF Permissiveness (Parental)
B Child Discipline 1973
Parent Child Relations 1967
Parental Characteristics 1994
Parenting Style 2003
R Father Child Relations 1973
Mother Child Relations 1967
↓ Parental Attitudes 1973
Parental Role 1973

Parental Role 1973
PN 3600 **SC** 36670
SN Descriptions, perceptions, and attitudes about the social, psychological, behavioral, or emotional role of parents.
B Family Relations 1967
Parental Characteristics 1994
Roles 1967
R ↓ Child Discipline 1973
↓ Childrearing Practices 1967
Delayed Parenthood 1985

Parental Role — (cont'd)
Father Child Relations 1973
Mother Child Relations 1967
↓ Parent Child Relations 1967
Parent Training 1978
↓ Parental Attitudes 1973
Parental Expectations 1997
Parental Involvement 2005
Parental Permissiveness 1973

Parenthood Status 1985
PN 1149 **SC** 36675
SN State of having or not having children, or the number of children one has.
N Childlessness 1982
R Family Size 1973
↓ Family Structure 1973
Life Changes 2004

Parenting Skills 1997
PN 1452 **SC** 36677
B Parental Characteristics 1994
R ↓ Childrearing Practices 1967
↓ Parent Child Relations 1967
Parent Training 1978

Parenting Style 2003
PN 1392 **SC** 36678
SN Characteristic manner in which parents raise their children. Compare CHILDREARING PRACTICES.
HN This term was introduced in June 2003. Relevant records were re-indexed with this term. The posting note reflects the number of records that were re-indexed.
UF Authoritarianism (Parental)
Parental Authoritarianism
B Parental Characteristics 1994
N Parental Permissiveness 1973
R ↓ Childrearing Practices 1967
↓ Parent Child Relations 1967

Parents 1967
PN 17894 **SC** 36680
SN For animals consider ANIMAL PARENTAL BEHAVIOR or ANIMAL MATERNAL BEHAVIOR.
HN From 1982, limited to human populations.
B Ancestors 1973
Family Members 1973
N Adoptive Parents 1973
↓ Fathers 1967
Foster Parents 1973
Homosexual Parents 1994
↓ Mothers 1967
↓ Single Parents 1978
Stepparents 1973
Surrogate Parents (Humans) 1973
R ↓ Expectant Parents 1985
Inlaws 1997
↓ Parental Characteristics 1994
Parental Death 2003
Parental Expectations 1997
↓ Spouses 1973

Paresis (General)
Use General Paresis

Paresthesia
Use Somatosensory Disorders

Pargyline 1973
PN 81 **SC** 36700
B Antihypertensive Drugs 1973
Monoamine Oxidase Inhibitors 1973

Parietal Lobe 1973
PN 2048 **SC** 36710
SN Section of the cerebral hemisphere that lies beneath the parietal bone. The parietal lobe is involved with motor function. It is also the location for visual attention, touch perception, goal directed movement, object manipulation, and integration of different senses that allows for single concept understanding.
B Cerebral Cortex 1967
N Somatosensory Cortex 1973

Parkinsonism 1994
PN 867 **SC** 36715
SN Clinical state, usually drug induced, characterized by tremors, muscle rigidity, postural reflex dysfunction, and akinesia. Compare PARKINSONS DISEASE.
R Apraxia 1973
Bradykinesia 2001
Dementia with Lewy Bodies 2001
Muscle Contractions 1973
↓ Nervous System Disorders 1967
Parkinsons Disease 1973
↓ Reflexes 1971
↓ Symptoms 1967
Tremor 1973

Parkinsons Disease 1973
PN 5403 **SC** 36720
SN A disease characterized as a progressive motor disability manifested by tremors, shaking, muscular rigidity, and lack of postural reflexes.
UF Paralysis Agitans
B Brain Disorders 1967
Neurodegenerative Diseases 2004
R Amantadine 1978
↓ Antitremor Drugs 1973
Bradykinesia 2001
↓ Dementia 1985
Dementia with Lewy Bodies 2001
↓ Paralysis 1973
Parkinsonism 1994
Tremor 1973

Parks (Recreational)
Use Recreation Areas

Parochial School Education
Use Private School Education

Parole 1973
PN 406 **SC** 36750
SN Conditional release of a prisoner serving an indeterminate or unexpired sentence.
UF Parolees
B Legal Processes 1973
R Criminal Rehabilitation 2004
↓ Law Enforcement 1978
Probation 1973

Parole Officers 1973
PN 65 **SC** 36760
B Law Enforcement Personnel 1973
R Probation Officers 1973

Parolees
Use Parole

Paroxetine 1994
PN 1162 **SC** 36770
B Antidepressant Drugs 1971
Serotonin Reuptake Inhibitors 1997

Paroxysmal Sleep
Use Narcolepsy

Part Time Employment
Use Employment Status

Partial Hospitalization 1985
PN 1447 **SC** 36775
SN Ambulatory treatment program of intensive, multidisciplinary care. Involves stabilization, rehabilitation, and/or maintenance of patients through more comprehensive treatment than is possible in an outpatient setting. Compare OUTPATIENT TREATMENT.
UF Day Care (Treatment)
Day Hospital
B Treatment 1967
R Aftercare 1973
Deinstitutionalization 1982
↓ Hospital Programs 1978
Interdisciplinary Treatment Approach 1973
↓ Mental Health Programs 1973
Outpatient Commitment 1991
↓ Rehabilitation 1967

Partial Reinforcement
Use Reinforcement Schedules

Partially Hearing Impaired 1973
PN 2787 **SC** 36790
UF Hearing Impaired (Partially)
R Cochlear Implants 1994
↓ Deaf 1967

Partially Sighted 1973
PN 140 **SC** 36800

Participation 1973
PN 3792 **SC** 36810
SN Taking part in an activity. Use a more specific term if possible.
B Interpersonal Interaction 1967
N Athletic Participation 1973
Client Participation 1997
Group Participation 1973
Participative Management 1988
R Activity Theory 2003
↓ Involvement 1973
Student Engagement 2006

Participative Management 1988
PN 560 **SC** 36820
SN Management technique permitting nonmanagement personnel to be involved in the governance, management, or policy-making processes of an institution or organization.
UF Quality Circles
B Management Methods 1973
Participation 1973
R Job Involvement 1978
Management Decision Making 1973
Quality Control 1988
Self Managing Work Teams 2001

Partner Abuse 1991
PN 3182 **SC** 36825
SN Includes married and unmarried persons.
UF Spouse Abuse
B Antisocial Behavior 1971
N Intimate Partner Violence 2007
R ↓ Abuse Reporting 1997
Battered Females 1988
Domestic Violence 2006
Emotional Abuse 1991

Partner Abuse — (cont'd)
Erotomania 1997
↓ Family Conflict 2003
Physical Abuse 1991
↓ Sexual Abuse 1988
Verbal Abuse 2003
↓ Violence 1973

Parturition
Use Birth

Passive Aggressive Personality Disorder 1973
PN 61 **SC** 36850
SN Personality disorder marked by the tendency to passively resist the demands of others, often accompanied by feelings of anger and resentment.
B Personality Disorders 1967

Passive Avoidance
Use Avoidance Conditioning

Passive Smoking 2006
PN 106 **SC** 36865
SN Involuntary inhalation of tobacco smoke.
HN This term was introduced in May 2006. Relevant records were re-indexed with this term. The posting note reflects the number of records that were re-indexed.
UF Environmental Tobacco Smoke
Involuntary Smoking
Secondhand Smoking
B Tobacco Smoking 1967
R Carcinogens 1973
Pollution 1973

Passiveness 1973
PN 307 **SC** 36870
B Personality Traits 1967

Pastoral Counseling 1967
PN 1635 **SC** 36880
SN Provision of counseling by religious personnel.
B Counseling 1967
R ↓ Psychotherapy 1967

Pastors
Use Ministers (Religion)

Patents 2007
PN 81 **SC** 36892
SN Exclusive ownership rights of inventions granted to inventors by the government.
HN This term was introduced in April 2007. Relevant records were re-indexed with this term. The posting note reflects the number of records that were re-indexed.
R Ownership 1985

Paternal Investment
Use Parental Investment

Path Analysis 1991
PN 216 **SC** 36895
SN Quantification of the causal relationships that exist among variables.
B Multivariate Analysis 1982
R Causal Analysis 1994
↓ Factor Analysis 1967
Multiple Regression 1982

Pathogenesis
Use Etiology

Pathological Gambling 1988
PN 1237 **SC** 36905
UF Compulsive Gambling
B Gambling 1973
R ↓ Addiction 1973
↓ Behavior Disorders 1971
↓ Impulse Control Disorders 1997
Impulsiveness 1973

Pathologists 1973
PN 102 **SC** 36920
B Physicians 1967
R Surgeons 1973

Pathology 1973
PN 1889 **SC** 36930
SN The study of the structural and functional changes of diseases.
B Medical Sciences 1967
N Neuropathology 1973
↓ Psychopathology 1967
R Inflammation 2004
Necrosis 2006
Pathophysiology 2005

Pathophysiology 2005
PN 611 **SC** 36932
SN The physiology of the functional and biochemical disturbances of diseases.
HN This term was introduced in August 2005. Relevant records were re-indexed with this term. The posting note reflects the number of records that were re-indexed.
B Physiology 1967
R ↓ Pathology 1973
↓ Psychophysiology 1967

Patient Abuse 1991
PN 134 **SC** 36935
UF Client Abuse
B Antisocial Behavior 1971
R ↓ Child Abuse 1971
Elder Abuse 1988
Emotional Abuse 1991
Patient Violence 1994
↓ Patients 1967
Physical Abuse 1991
Professional Client Sexual Relations 1994
Professional Liability 1985
↓ Professional Standards 1973
↓ Sexual Abuse 1988
↓ Therapeutic Processes 1978
↓ Treatment 1967
Verbal Abuse 2003

Patient Attitudes
Use Client Attitudes

Patient Care Planning
Use Treatment Planning

Patient Characteristics
Use Client Characteristics

Patient Dropouts
Use Treatment Dropouts

Patient Education
Use Client Education

Patient History 1973
PN 3704 **SC** 36955
UF Case History
Medical History

Patient History — (cont'd)
Psychiatric History
R Biographical Data 1978
↓ Client Characteristics 1973
Client Records 1997
↓ Diagnosis 1967
Etiology 1967
↓ Medical Diagnosis 1973
↓ Medical Records 1978
Misdiagnosis 1997
Premorbidity 1978
Prognosis 1973
↓ Psychodiagnosis 1967
↓ Treatment 1967

Patient Participation
Use Client Participation

Patient Records
Use Client Records

Patient Rights
Use Client Rights

Patient Satisfaction
Use Client Satisfaction

Patient Seclusion 1994
PN 179 **SC** 36959
UF Seclusion (Patient)
B Social Isolation 1967
R ↓ Hospitalization 1967
Patient Violence 1994
↓ Patients 1967
↓ Psychiatric Hospitalization 1973
Psychiatric Hospitals 1967
Psychiatric Units 1991

Patient Selection 1997
PN 78 **SC** 57505
SN Selection of patients or clients for participation in research studies or for specific treatment modalities.
R ↓ Client Characteristics 1973
Client Transfer 1997
Client Treatment Matching 1997
Clients 1973
↓ Patients 1967
Therapist Selection 1994

Patient Therapist Interaction
Use Psychotherapeutic Processes

Patient Therapist Sexual Relations
Use Professional Client Sexual Relations

Patient Transfer
Use Client Transfer

Patient Treatment Matching
Use Client Treatment Matching

Patient Violence 1994
PN 699 **SC** 36965
SN Violence or behavioral disruptions by psychiatric or medical patients directed toward other patients, institutional staff, or themselves.
UF Client Violence
B Client Characteristics 1973
Violence 1973
R Dangerousness 1988
Patient Abuse 1991
Patient Seclusion 1994
↓ Patients 1967
Physical Restraint 1982
↓ Therapeutic Processes 1978

Patients 1967
PN 5659 **SC** 36970
SN Persons under medical care. Use a more specific term if possible. Consider also CLIENTS.
N Geriatric Patients 1973
Hospitalized Patients 1973
Medical Patients 1973
Outpatients 1973
Psychiatric Patients 1967
Surgical Patients 1973
Terminally Ill Patients 1973
R Client Participation 1997
Patient Abuse 1991
Patient Seclusion 1994
Patient Selection 1997
Patient Violence 1994

Patriarchy 1973
PN 348 **SC** 36980
B Family Structure 1973
R Matriarchy 1973
Mother Absence 1973
↓ Sex Role Attitudes 1978
Sex Roles 1967

Pattern Discrimination 1967
PN 3611 **SC** 37000
SN Distinguishing temporal, spatial, or pictorial/symbolic regularities (patterns) of visual, auditory, or other types of stimuli. Includes the concept of pattern perception.
B Perceptual Discrimination 1973
R ↓ Auditory Perception 1967
Figure Ground Discrimination 1973
Form and Shape Perception 1967
Perceptual Closure 1973
↓ Rhythm 1991
Texture Perception 1982
Visual Acuity 1982
Visual Search 1982

Pavlov (Ivan) 1991
PN 156 **SC** 37005
SN Identifies biographical or autobiographical studies and discussions of Pavlov's works.
R ↓ Classical Conditioning 1967
↓ Psychologists 1967

Pavlovian Conditioning
Use Classical Conditioning

Pay
Use Salaries

PCP
Use Phencyclidine

Peabody Picture Vocabulary Test 1973
PN 303 **SC** 37030
B Intelligence Measures 1967

Peace 1988
PN 925 **SC** 37038
B Social Interaction 1967
Social Issues 1991
R Foreign Policy Making 1973
International Relations 1967
Peacekeeping 2005
↓ Social Movements 1967

Peace — (cont'd)
↓ War 1967

Peace Corps 1973
PN 35 **SC** 37040
B Government Programs 1973
R Government 1967

Peacekeeping 2005
PN 111 **SC** 37045
SN Act of preserving peace between hostile groups or nations usually by military forces.
HN This term was introduced in August 2005. Relevant records were re-indexed with this term. The posting note reflects the number of records that were re-indexed.
R Foreign Policy Making 1973
International Relations 1967
Peace 1988

Pearson Product Moment Correlation Coefficient
Use Statistical Correlation

Pecking Order
Use Animal Dominance

Pedagogy
Use Teaching

Pederasty
Use Pedophilia

Pedestrian Accidents 1973
PN 156 **SC** 37090
B Accidents 1967
R ↓ Driving Behavior 1967
Motor Traffic Accidents 1973
Pedestrians 1973

Pedestrians 1973
PN 279 **SC** 37100
R Pedestrian Accidents 1973

Pediatricians 1973
PN 633 **SC** 37110
B Physicians 1967

Pediatrics 1973
PN 3642 **SC** 37120
B Medical Sciences 1967

Pedophilia 1973
PN 904 **SC** 37130
UF Child Molestation
Pederasty
B Paraphilias 1988
R ↓ Child Abuse 1971
Incest 1973
↓ Sex Offenses 1982
↓ Sexual Abuse 1988

Peer Counseling 1978
PN 773 **SC** 37135
SN Supervised performance of limited counselor functions by a person of approximately the same age or status as the counselee.
B Counseling 1967
R Mentor 1985
↓ Peer Relations 1967

Peer Counseling — (cont'd)
Peer Tutoring 1973
Peers 1978

Peer Evaluation 1982
PN 1345 **SC** 37137
SN Appraisal by one's peers.
UF Peer Review
B Evaluation 1967
R ↓ Peer Relations 1967
↓ Personnel Evaluation 1973
Professional Competence 1997
↓ Professional Fees 1978
↓ Professional Standards 1973

Peer Pressure 1994
PN 328 **SC** 37138
B Interpersonal Influences 1967
Peer Relations 1967
R Friendship 1967
↓ Group Dynamics 1967
Likability 1988
Peers 1978
↓ Persuasive Communication 1967
Social Acceptance 1967
Social Approval 1967
Temptation 1973
Underage Drinking 2007

Peer Relations 1967
PN 10190 **SC** 37140
B Interpersonal Interaction 1967
N Peer Pressure 1994
R Friendship 1967
Peer Counseling 1978
Peer Evaluation 1982
Peers 1978
Reference Groups 1994
↓ Relationship Termination 1997
↓ Sociometry 1991
Teasing 2003

Peer Review
Use Peer Evaluation

Peer Tutoring 1973
PN 956 **SC** 37150
SN Teaching method in which students provide individual instruction for other students, not necessarily of the same age or grade level.
B Tutoring 1973
R Collaborative Learning 2007
Cooperative Learning 1994
Peer Counseling 1978
Peers 1978

Peers 1978
PN 2904 **SC** 37154
R Peer Counseling 1978
Peer Pressure 1994
↓ Peer Relations 1967
Peer Tutoring 1973
Significant Others 1991

Pellagra 1973
PN 13 **SC** 37160
SN A disorder in which a person does not receive enough niacin (a B complex vitamin). Symptoms include dermatitis, weakness, confusion, and disorientation.

Pellagra — (cont'd)
B Vitamin Deficiency Disorders 1973
R Nicotinamide 1973

Pemoline 1978
PN 103 SC 37175
B CNS Stimulating Drugs 1973

Penguins 1973
PN 81 SC 37180
B Birds 1967

Penicillins 1973
PN 84 SC 37190
B Antibiotics 1973

Penis 1973
PN 322 SC 37200
B Male Genitalia 1973

Penis Envy 1973
PN 85 SC 37210
R ↓ Psychoanalytic Personality Factors 1973

Penitentiaries
Use Prisons

Penology 1973
PN 351 SC 37230
R ↓ Correctional Institutions 1973
↓ Criminal Justice 1991
Criminology 1973

Pension Plans (Employee)
Use Employee Pension Plans

Pensions
Use Employee Pension Plans

Pentazocine 1991
PN 34 SC 37245
B Analgesic Drugs 1973
Narcotic Agonists 1988

Pentobarbital 1973
PN 754 SC 37250
UF Nembutal
Sodium Pentobarbital
B Anesthetic Drugs 1973
Anticonvulsive Drugs 1973
Barbiturates 1967
Hypnotic Drugs 1973
Sedatives 1973

Pentothal
Use Thiopental

Pentylenetetrazol 1973
PN 332 SC 37270
UF Metrazole
Pentylenetetrazole
B CNS Stimulating Drugs 1973
R ↓ Analeptic Drugs 1973

Pentylenetetrazole
Use Pentylenetetrazol

Peptic Ulcers
Use Gastrointestinal Ulcers

Peptides 1973
PN 3555 SC 37330
SN Amides derived from two or more amino acids.

Peptides — (cont'd)
UF Galanin
N Angiotensin 1973
Bombesin 1988
Cholecystokinin 1982
Corticotropin Releasing Factor 1994
↓ Endogenous Opiates 1985
Leptin 2004
Melanocyte Stimulating Hormone 1985
Nerve Growth Factor 1994
↓ Neuropeptides 2003
Neurotensin 1985
Somatostatin 1991
R ↓ Drugs 1967
Enkephalins 1982
↓ Neurotransmitters 1985
↓ Proteins 1973

Perception 1967
PN 8876 SC 37350
SN Conceptually broad term referring to the process of obtaining cognitive or sensory information about the environment. Use a more specific term if possible.
UF Sensation
N ↓ Auditory Perception 1967
↓ Extrasensory Perception 1967
Form and Shape Perception 1967
↓ Illusions (Perception) 1967
↓ Intersensory Processes 1978
Numerosity Perception 1967
Object Recognition 1997
↓ Olfactory Perception 1967
Perceptual Closure 1973
↓ Perceptual Constancy 1985
↓ Perceptual Discrimination 1973
↓ Perceptual Distortion 1982
↓ Perceptual Learning 2006
↓ Perceptual Localization 1967
↓ Perceptual Motor Processes 1967
↓ Perceptual Orientation 1973
Perceptual Style 1973
Risk Perception 1997
Role Perception 1973
Self Perception 1967
Sensory Gating 1991
↓ Social Perception 1967
↓ Somesthetic Perception 1967
↓ Spatial Perception 1967
Subliminal Perception 1973
Taste Perception 1967
↓ Time Perception 1967
↓ Visual Perception 1967
R Apperception 1973
↓ Attention 1967
Constructivism 1994
↓ Discrimination 1967
Mind 1991
↓ Perceptual Development 1973
↓ Perceptual Disturbances 1973
↓ Perceptual Measures 1973
↓ Perceptual Stimulation 1973
↓ Priming 1988
↓ Rhythm 1991
Sensory Neglect 1994
Signal Detection (Perception) 1967

Perceptiveness (Personality) 1973
PN 53 SC 37360
SN Demonstrating insight or sympathetic understanding or keen powers of observation.

Perceptiveness (Personality) — (cont'd)
B Personality Traits 1967
R Insight 1973
Sensitivity (Personality) 1967
↓ Social Perception 1967

Perceptual Aftereffect 1967
PN 1253 SC 37370
SN Subjective perceptual alterations resulting from prolonged exposure to preceding sensory stimulation.
UF Aftereffect (Perceptual)
B Illusions (Perception) 1967
N Afterimage 1967
R Interocular Transfer 1985

Perceptual Closure 1973
PN 202 SC 37380
SN Perception of units which together form a closed unit or whole, being organized together and perceived as a whole.
UF Closure (Perceptual)
Perceptual Fill
B Perception 1967
R Pattern Discrimination 1967

Perceptual Constancy 1985
PN 175 SC 37385
SN Stable perception of a stimulus in any sensory modality despite changes in its objective properties.
B Perception 1967
N Brightness Constancy 1985
Color Constancy 1985
Size Constancy 1985
R Object Permanence 1985

Perceptual Development 1973
PN 3579 SC 37390
SN The acquisition of sensory skills or abilities in the natural course of physical and psychological maturation.
B Cognitive Development 1973
N Perceptual Motor Development 1991
R ↓ Childhood Development 1967
Conservation (Concept) 1973
↓ Developmental Stages 1973
↓ Perception 1967
↓ Perceptual Learning 2006
↓ Physical Development 1973
↓ Psychomotor Development 1973

Perceptual Discrimination 1973
PN 1384 SC 37400
B Discrimination 1967
Perception 1967
N Auditory Acuity 1988
Auditory Discrimination 1967
Figure Ground Discrimination 1973
Odor Discrimination 1973
Pattern Discrimination 1967
Visual Discrimination 1967
R Mirror Image 1991
Object Recognition 1997
Stroop Effect 1988

Perceptual Distortion 1982
PN 298 SC 37410
SN Lack of correspondence between the common perception of a stimulus and the perception by an individual. Perceptual distortion does not involve hallucinatory or illusory components, but rather is a function of individual differences.

Perceptual Distortion — (cont'd)
UF Distortion (Perceptual)
B Perception 1967
N Spatial Distortion 1973
R ↓ Illusions (Perception) 1967
↓ Perceptual Disturbances 1973
Sensory Neglect 1994

Perceptual Disturbances 1973
PN 633 SC 37420
N ↓ Agnosia 1973
↓ Hallucinations 1967
R ↓ Aphasia 1967
↓ Illusions (Perception) 1967
↓ Learning Disabilities 1973
↓ Mental Disorders 1967
↓ Perception 1967
↓ Perceptual Distortion 1982
Sensory Neglect 1994

Perceptual Fill
Use Perceptual Closure

Perceptual Learning 2006
PN 298 SC 37436
SN Learning to perceive relationships between stimuli and objects in the environment. Used for human and animal populations.
HN This term was introduced in May 2006. Relevant records were re-indexed with this term. The posting note reflects the number of records that were re-indexed.
B Learning 1967
Perception 1967
N ↓ Perceptual Motor Learning 1967
R ↓ Perceptual Development 1973
↓ Skill Learning 1973
↓ Tracking 1967

Perceptual Localization 1967
PN 1129 SC 37440
SN Discrimination of the physical displacement or spatial location of a stimulus in any sensory modality.
UF Localization (Perceptual)
B Perception 1967
N Auditory Localization 1973
R Direction Perception 1997
↓ Tracking 1967

Perceptual Measures 1973
PN 818 SC 37450
B Measurement 1967
N Rod and Frame Test 1973
Stroop Color Word Test 1973
R ↓ Audiometry 1967
Auditory Thresholds 1973
Bone Conduction Audiometry 1973
Critical Flicker Fusion Threshold 1967
Dark Adaptation 1973
Olfactory Thresholds 1973
Pain Measurement 1997
Pain Thresholds 1973
↓ Perception 1967
↓ Psychophysical Measurement 1967
Sensorimotor Measures 1973
Speech and Hearing Measures 1973
↓ Thresholds 1967
Vibrotactile Thresholds 1973
↓ Visual Thresholds 1973

Perceptual Motor Coordination 1973
PN 1694 SC 37460
UF Coordination (Perceptual Motor)
B Perceptual Motor Processes 1967
N Physical Dexterity 1973
R Motor Coordination 1973
Perceptual Motor Development 1991

Perceptual Motor Development 1991
PN 520 SC 37470
HN Use MOTOR DEVELOPMENT and PERCEPTUAL DEVELOPMENT to access references from 1973-1990.
UF Sensorimotor Development
B Motor Development 1973
Perceptual Development 1973
R Animal Development 1978
↓ Intersensory Processes 1978
↓ Perceptual Motor Coordination 1973
↓ Perceptual Motor Learning 1967
↓ Perceptual Motor Processes 1967
↓ Psychomotor Development 1973

Perceptual Motor Learning 1967
PN 2351 SC 37480
UF Motor Skill Learning
B Perceptual Learning 2006
N Fine Motor Skill Learning 1973
Gross Motor Skill Learning 1973
R Perceptual Motor Development 1991
↓ Skill Learning 1973
↓ Tracking 1967

Perceptual Motor Measures
Use Sensorimotor Measures

Perceptual Motor Processes 1967
PN 8359 SC 37490
UF Psychomotor Processes
Sensorimotor Processes
B Perception 1967
N ↓ Perceptual Motor Coordination 1973
Sensory Integration 1991
↓ Tracking 1967
R Equilibrium 1973
↓ Intersensory Processes 1978
↓ Motor Processes 1967
Perceptual Motor Development 1991

Perceptual Neglect
Use Sensory Neglect

Perceptual Orientation 1973
PN 1122 SC 37500
SN Awareness of one's position in time and space.
UF Orientation (Perceptual)
B Perception 1967
N Spatial Orientation (Perception) 1973
R Time Perspective 1978

Perceptual Stimulation 1973
PN 672 SC 37510
B Stimulation 1967
N ↓ Auditory Stimulation 1967
↓ Delayed Feedback 1973
Olfactory Stimulation 1978
↓ Sensory Feedback 1973
↓ Somesthetic Stimulation 1973
Taste Stimulation 1967
↓ Visual Stimulation 1973
R Afferent Stimulation 1973
↓ Masking 1967

Perceptual Stimulation — (cont'd)
↓ Perception 1967
Sensory Gating 1991

Perceptual Style 1973
PN 583 SC 37520
SN Manner in which sensory information or stimuli are organized meaningfully by an individual.
B Perception 1967
R ↓ Cognitive Style 1967
Conceptual Tempo 1985
Neurolinguistic Programming 2001
Schema 1988

Perfectionism 1988
PN 686 SC 37523
B Personality Traits 1967
R ↓ Compulsions 1973
Conscientiousness 1997
Self Criticism 2003

Performance 1967
PN 9597 SC 37525
SN Conceptually broad term, having application across broad disciplines and subject matter contexts in which execution or accomplishment of a specified task or objective is of concern. Use terms describing specific activity or performance when possible.
N Athletic Performance 1991
Group Performance 1967
↓ Job Performance 1967
↓ Motor Performance 1973
R ↓ Ability 1967
↓ Achievement 1967
Awards (Merit) 2005
↓ Competence 1982
Performance Anxiety 1994
↓ Productivity 2007

Performance Anxiety 1994
PN 250 SC 37527
B Anxiety 1967
R ↓ Anxiety Disorders 1997
↓ Performance 1967

Performance Tests 1973
PN 1131 SC 37530
SN Tests requiring nonverbal responses, for example, the manipulation of objects or the performance of motor skills.
B Measurement 1967
R Criterion Referenced Tests 1982

Performing Arts
Use Arts

Periaqueductal Gray 1985
PN 469 SC 37550
SN Mesencephalic cells in the gray area surrounding the cerebral aqueduct important for visceral and limbic mechanisms.
B Tegmentum 1991

Perinatal Period 1994
PN 750 SC 37555
SN Usually the period just preceding or just following birth. Compare NEONATAL PERIOD. Used for both human and animal populations.
R ↓ Birth 1967
Postnatal Period 1973
↓ Pregnancy 1967
↓ Prenatal Development 1973

Peripheral Nerve Disorders
HN In May 2006, this term was discontinued and removed from all records containing it, and was replaced with PERIPHERAL NEUROPATHY, its postable counterpart.
Use Peripheral Neuropathy

Peripheral Nervous System 1973
PN 551 **SC** 37570
SN Anatomical systems of structures that are composed of neural tissue outside the brain and spinal cord.
HN Use PERIPHERAL NERVES to access references from 1973-1993.
UF Nerves (Peripheral)
B Nervous System 1967
N ↓ Autonomic Nervous System 1967
↓ Cranial Nerves 1973
↓ Neural Pathways 1982
Spinal Nerves 1973
R Autonomic Ganglia 1973
↓ Ganglia 1973
↓ Peripheral Neuropathy 2006

Peripheral Neuropathy 2006
PN 172 **SC** 37575
SN Disease or degenerative state of the peripheral nerves in which motor, sensory, or vasomotor nerve fibers may be affected.
HN In May 2006, this term was created to replace the discontinued term PERIPHERAL NERVE DISORDERS. PERIPHERAL NERVE DISORDERS was removed from all records containing it and replaced with PERIPHERAL NEUROPATHY, its postable counterpart.
UF Peripheral Nerve Disorders
B Nervous System Disorders 1967
N ↓ Neuralgia 1973
R Muscular Dystrophy 1973
↓ Paralysis 1973
↓ Peripheral Nervous System 1973

Peripheral Vision 1988
PN 490 **SC** 37580
B Visual Perception 1967
R Visual Field 1967

Permissiveness (Parental)
Use Parental Permissiveness

Perpetrators 1988
PN 3324 **SC** 37595
N ↓ Criminals 1967
R Bullying 2003
↓ Crime 1967
Criminal Responsibility 1991
↓ Harassment 2001
Incest 1973
Stalking 2001
Victimization 1973

Perphenazine 1973
PN 148 **SC** 37600
B Antiemetic Drugs 1973
Phenothiazine Derivatives 1973

Persecution 1973
PN 216 **SC** 37610
B Antisocial Behavior 1971
Interpersonal Interaction 1967
R Torture 1988
Victimization 1973

Perseverance
Use Persistence

Perseveration 1967
PN 347 **SC** 37630
SN Persistent repetition of a response to different and perhaps inappropriate stimuli which may be due to a refusal or an inability to interrupt one's behavior or to change from one task to another. Also, pathological repetition of thoughts, acts, or verbalizations.
B Thought Disturbances 1973

Persistence 1973
PN 1350 **SC** 37640
SN Maintenance of particular behavior despite effort, opposition, or cessation of initiating stimulus. Used for human or animal populations.
UF Perseverance
B Personality Traits 1967
R Conscientiousness 1997
↓ Motivation 1967

Persistent Mental Illness
Use Chronic Mental Illness

Person Centered Psychotherapy
Use Client Centered Therapy

Person Environment Fit 1991
PN 863 **SC** 37645
SN Compatibility between individuals and their surroundings.
R Accommodation (Disabilities) 2007
↓ Adjustment 1967
↓ Environment 1967
Environmental Adaptation 1973
↓ Environmental Planning 1982
↓ Personality 1967
↓ Systems 1967
↓ Working Conditions 1973

Personal Adjustment
Use Emotional Adjustment

Personal Computers
Use Microcomputers

Personal Construct Theory
Use Personality Theory

Personal Defense
Use Self Defense

Personal Growth Techniques
Use Human Potential Movement

Personal Orientation Inventory 1973
PN 121 **SC** 37670
B Nonprojective Personality Measures 1973

Personal Relationships
Use Interpersonal Relationships

Personal Space 1973
PN 1260 **SC** 37680
SN Minimal spatial distance preferred by an individual in his/her relations with others.
UF Interpersonal Distance
R Boundaries (Psychological) 1997
Crowding 1978
Physical Contact 1982
↓ Social Behavior 1967
Social Density 1978

Personal Therapy 1991
PN 126 **SC** 37685
SN Therapy for professionals working in the mental health field, for example, psychologists, psychiatrists, or social workers.
B Treatment 1967
R ↓ Clinical Methods Training 1973
Impaired Professionals 1985
↓ Mental Health Personnel 1967
↓ Professional Consultation 1973
Professional Supervision 1988
Psychoanalytic Training 1973
Self Analysis 1994

Personal Values 1973
PN 2851 **SC** 37690
SN Set of ideals that an individual deems worthwhile and that influence his/her behavior.
B Values 1967
R Anomie 1978
Morality 1967

Personality 1967
PN 15118 **SC** 37870
SN Conceptually broad term referring to the totality of an individual's behavioral or emotional characteristics. Use a more specific term if possible.
UF Character
Disposition
Temperament
N ↓ Personality Traits 1967
↓ Psychoanalytic Personality Factors 1973
R ↓ Cognitive Style 1967
Coronary Prone Behavior 1982
Egocentrism 1978
↓ Emotional Adjustment 1973
↓ Emotional States 1973
↓ Emotions 1967
Five Factor Personality Model 1997
↓ Gender Identity 1985
Human Nature 1997
Individual Differences 1967
↓ Lifestyle 1978
Person Environment Fit 1991
Personality Change 1967
Personality Correlates 1967
↓ Personality Development 1967
↓ Personality Disorders 1967
↓ Personality Processes 1967
↓ Personality Theory 1967
Predisposition 1973
Psychodynamics 1973
Self Actualization 1973
↓ Self Concept 1967
Self Disclosure 1973
Self Evaluation 1967
Self Monitoring (Personality) 1985
Self Perception 1967
Somatotypes 1973
Teacher Personality 1973

Personality Assessment
Use Personality Measures

Personality Change 1967
PN 1703 **SC** 37720
SN Process or fact of change associated with development and maturity, or resulting from stress, illness, treatment, or other factors.
B Personality Processes 1967
R Behavior Change 1973
↓ Personality 1967
↓ Personality Development 1967

Personality Correlates 1967
PN 5266 **SC** 37740
SN Description of numerous or unspecified personality traits which bear a mutual or reciprocal relationship to a particular phenomenon or behavior.
R Individual Differences 1967
↓ Personality 1967

Personality Development 1967
PN 7299 **SC** 37750
UF Character Development
Character Formation
B Psychosocial Development 1973
N ↓ Ego Development 1991
Separation Individuation 1982
R Ego Identity 1991
Emotional Development 1973
Externalization 1973
Five Factor Personality Model 1997
Identity Crisis 1973
Identity Formation 2004
↓ Internalization 1997
Moral Development 1973
↓ Personality 1967
Personality Change 1967
↓ Personality Theory 1967

Personality Disorders 1967
PN 6523 **SC** 37760
HN In 1997, this term replaced the discontinued term ASTHENIC PERSONALITY. In 2000, ASTHENIC PERSONALITY was removed from all records containing it, and replaced with PERSONALITY DISORDERS.
UF Asthenic Personality
Character Disorders
B Mental Disorders 1967
N Antisocial Personality Disorder 1973
Avoidant Personality Disorder 1994
Borderline Personality Disorder 2001
Dependent Personality Disorder 1994
Histrionic Personality Disorder 1991
Narcissistic Personality Disorder 1973
Obsessive Compulsive Personality Disorder 1973
Paranoid Personality Disorder 1973
Passive Aggressive Personality Disorder 1973
↓ Sadomasochistic Personality 1973
Schizoid Personality Disorder 1973
Schizotypal Personality Disorder 1991
R ↓ Defense Mechanisms 1967
↓ Dissociative Disorders 2001
Explosive Disorder 2001
Kleptomania 1973
↓ Personality 1967
↓ Personality Processes 1967
↓ Personality Theory 1967
Pyromania 1973

Personality Factors
Use Personality Traits

Personality Factors (Psychoanalytic)
Use Psychoanalytic Personality Factors

Personality Measures 1967
PN 10793 **SC** 37790
UF Personality Assessment
Personality Tests
Tests (Personality)
B Measurement 1967
N California Psychological Inventory 1967
General Health Questionnaire 1991
Kirton Adaption Innovation Inventory 2001

Personality Measures — (cont'd)
NEO Personality Inventory 1997
↓ Nonprojective Personality Measures 1973
↓ Projective Personality Measures 1973
Rokeach Dogmatism Scale 1973
Sensation Seeking Scale 1973
Sentence Completion Tests 1991

Personality Processes 1967
PN 1778 **SC** 37800
SN Conceptually broad term referring to the interaction among personality structures (e.g., ego, id) or pattern of characteristic tendencies, often but not exclusively from a psychoanalytic perspective. Use a more specific term if possible.
N Catharsis 1973
Cathexis 1973
↓ Defense Mechanisms 1967
Externalization 1973
Inhibition (Personality) 1973
Insight 1973
↓ Internalization 1997
Introspection 1973
Personality Change 1967
R Boundaries (Psychological) 1997
↓ Lifestyle 1978
↓ Mental Disorders 1967
↓ Personality 1967
↓ Personality Disorders 1967
↓ Psychoanalytic Personality Factors 1973
↓ Psychoanalytic Theory 1967
Reality Testing 1973

Personality Tests
Use Personality Measures

Personality Theory 1967
PN 4525 **SC** 37850
UF Personal Construct Theory
N Five Factor Personality Model 1997
R Individual Differences 1967
↓ Personality 1967
↓ Personality Development 1967
↓ Personality Disorders 1967
Self Perception 1967
Self Psychology 1988

Personality Traits 1967
PN 28704 **SC** 37860
UF Personality Factors
B Personality 1967
N Adaptability (Personality) 1973
Aggressiveness 1973
Agreeableness 1997
Altruism 1973
Androgyny 1982
Assertiveness 1973
Authoritarianism 1967
Charisma 1988
↓ Cognitive Style 1967
Conformity (Personality) 1967
Conscientiousness 1997
Conservatism 1973
Courage 1973
Creativity 1967
Cruelty 1973
Curiosity 1967
Cynicism 1973
Defensiveness 1967
Dependency (Personality) 1967
Dishonesty 1973
Dogmatism 1978
Egalitarianism 1985
Egotism 1973

Personality Traits — (cont'd)
Emotional Immaturity 1973
Emotional Inferiority 1973
Emotional Instability 1973
Emotional Maturity 1973
Emotional Security 1973
Emotional Stability 1973
Emotional Superiority 1973
Emotionality (Personality) 1973
Empathy 1967
Extraversion 1967
Femininity 1967
Gregariousness 1973
Honesty 1973
Hypnotic Susceptibility 1973
Independence (Personality) 1973
Individuality 1973
Initiative 1973
Integrity 1997
Internal External Locus of Control 1967
Introversion 1967
Irritability 1988
Liberalism 1973
Likability 1988
Loyalty 1973
Machiavellianism 1973
Masculinity 1967
Misanthropy 1973
Moodiness 1973
Narcissism 1967
Need for Approval 1997
Need for Cognition 1997
Negativism 1973
Nervousness 1973
Neuroticism 1973
Nonconformity (Personality) 1973
Nurturance 1985
Obedience 1973
Objectivity 1973
Omnipotence 1994
Openmindedness 1978
Openness to Experience 1997
Optimism 1973
Paranoia 1988
Passiveness 1973
Perceptiveness (Personality) 1973
Perfectionism 1988
Persistence 1973
Pessimism 1973
Positivism 1973
Psychoticism 1978
Rebelliousness 2003
Repression Sensitization 1973
Resilience (Psychological) 2003
Rigidity (Personality) 1967
↓ Risk Taking 1967
Self Control 1973
Selfishness 1973
Sensation Seeking 1978
Sensitivity (Personality) 1967
Seriousness 1973
Sexuality 1973
Sincerity 1973
Sociability 1973
Subjectivity 1994
Suggestibility 1967
Timidity 1973
↓ Tolerance 1973
R Codependency 1991
Coronary Prone Behavior 1982
Egocentrism 1978
Five Factor Personality Model 1997
Instrumentality 1991

Personality Traits — (cont'd)
Leadership Qualities 1997

Personalization 2007
PN 175 **SC** 37875
SN The alteration or adaptation of something to make it specific to or more meaningful or appropriate for a particular person, as in changing the content of material on a web page or in a magazine to address a particular individual.
HN This term was introduced in April 2007. Relevant records were re-indexed with this term. The posting note reflects the number of records that were re-indexed.
R ↓ Marketing 1973

Personnel 1967
PN 5726 **SC** 37980
SN Conceptually broad term referring to the body of persons employed by a given organization or associated with a particular occupation. Use a more specific term if possible.
UF Employees
Workers
N ↓ Artists 1973
↓ Business and Industrial Personnel 1967
Disabled Personnel 1997
↓ Government Personnel 1973
↓ Hypnotists 1973
↓ Nonprofessional Personnel 1982
↓ Paraprofessional Personnel 1973
↓ Professional Personnel 1978
↓ Religious Personnel 1973
↓ Social Workers 1973
R Affirmative Action 1985
Employability 1973
Employee Absenteeism 1973
↓ Employee Benefits 1973
↓ Employee Characteristics 1988
↓ Employee Interaction 1988
Employee Turnover 1973
Employer Attitudes 1973
Employment History 1978
↓ Human Resource Management 2003
Job Applicant Attitudes 1973
Job Applicants 1985
↓ Job Performance 1967
Labor Market 2007
Labor Union Members 1973
Military Veterans 1973
↓ Occupations 1967
↓ Personnel Supply 1973
↓ Personnel Training 1967
Reemployment 1991
Retirement 1973
↓ Teams 1988
Unemployment 1967
Work (Attitudes Toward) 1973
↓ Working Conditions 1973
Working Women 1978

Personnel Development
Use Personnel Training

Personnel Evaluation 1973
PN 3310 **SC** 37900
B Evaluation 1967
Human Resource Management 2003
N Occupational Success Prediction 1973
Teacher Effectiveness Evaluation 1978
R Assessment Centers 1982
Employment Discrimination 1994
Job Applicant Interviews 1973

Personnel Evaluation — (cont'd)
Job Applicant Screening 1973
↓ Job Performance 1967
Peer Evaluation 1982
Personnel Promotion 1978
↓ Personnel Selection 1967
Professional Competence 1997

Personnel Management
HN In June 2003, the term was discontinued and removed from all records containing it, and was replaced with HUMAN RESOURCE MANAGEMENT, its postable counterpart.
Use Human Resource Management

Personnel Placement 1973
PN 442 **SC** 37920
UF Placement (Personnel)
R Assessment Centers 1982
Career Development 1985

Personnel Promotion 1978
PN 599 **SC** 37925
UF Job Promotion
R Assessment Centers 1982
Career Development 1985
Employment History 1978
↓ Job Performance 1967
Nepotism 2005
Occupational Status 1978
Occupational Success 1978
↓ Personnel Evaluation 1973
Professional Recognition 2005

Personnel Recruitment 1973
PN 870 **SC** 37930
UF Employment Processes
Recruitment (Personnel)
B Human Resource Management 2003
N Military Recruitment 1973
Teacher Recruitment 1973
R Affirmative Action 1985
Job Applicant Interviews 1973
Job Applicant Screening 1973
Nepotism 2005

Personnel Selection 1967
PN 4274 **SC** 37940
UF Employee Selection
Hiring
Selection (Personnel)
B Human Resource Management 2003
N Job Applicant Interviews 1973
Job Applicant Screening 1973
R Affirmative Action 1985
Assessment Centers 1982
Employment Discrimination 1994
Nepotism 2005
↓ Personnel Evaluation 1973
↓ Screening 1982

Personnel Supply 1973
PN 187 **SC** 37950
SN Availability of manpower or human resources required for an occupation or service in order to meet demands.
UF Manpower
N Medical Personnel Supply 1973
Mental Health Personnel Supply 1973
R Human Capital 2003
Labor Market 2007
↓ Personnel 1967

Personnel Termination 1973
PN 617 **SC** 37960
UF Employee Termination
B Human Resource Management 2003
R Downsizing 2003
Employment History 1978
Job Security 1978
↓ Occupational Tenure 1973
Retirement 1973
Unemployment 1967

Personnel Training 1967
PN 5331 **SC** 37970
UF Job Training
Personnel Development
Training (Personnel)
B Education 1967
Training 2006
N Apprenticeship 1973
↓ Inservice Training 1985
Management Training 1973
On the Job Training 1973
R Business Education 1973
Career Development 1985
Human Relations Training 1978
Job Enrichment 1973
↓ Personnel 1967
Sensitivity Training 1973

Personnel Turnover
Use Employee Turnover

Perspective Taking
Use Role Taking

Perspiration
Use Sweat

Persuasion Therapy 1973
PN 18 **SC** 38000
SN Limited directive therapy in which the client is encouraged to follow the therapist's advice to deal with current crises.
B Psychotherapy 1967

Persuasive Communication 1967
PN 3391 **SC** 38010
SN Communication, in written or oral form, aimed at influencing others to accept a position, belief, or course of action.
B Communication 1967
N Brainwashing 1982
R Coercion 1994
Debates 1997
↓ Interpersonal Influences 1967
Peer Pressure 1994
Propaganda 1973
Public Service Announcements 2004
Rhetoric 1991

Pervasive Developmental Disorders 2001
PN 878 **SC** 38016
SN Broad term for disorders, usually first diagnosed in children prior to age 4, characterized by severe and profound impairment in social interaction, communication, and the presence of stereotyped behaviors, interests, and activities. Compare DEVELOPMENTAL DISABILITIES.
UF Autism Spectrum Disorders
B Mental Disorders 1967
N Aspergers Syndrome 1991
Autism 1967
Rett Syndrome 1994

Pervasive Developmental Disorders — (cont'd)
R Developmental Disabilities 1982
Stereotyped Behavior 1973

Perversions (Sexual)
Use Paraphilias

Pessimism 1973
PN 643 **SC** 38020
SN Attitude characterized by a gloomy and desperate temperament and inclination to emphasize and expect the worst possible outcome of events and actions.
B Emotional States 1973
Personality Traits 1967
R Cynicism 1973
Fatalism 1973
Hopelessness 1988
Negativism 1973
Nihilism 1973
Optimism 1973
Skepticism 2004

Pesticides
Use Insecticides

Pet Therapy
Use Animal Assisted Therapy

Petit Mal Seizures 2006
PN 52 **SC** 38031
SN Type of seizure characterized by a sudden, brief lapse of consciousness without the presence of convulsions.
HN This term was introduced in May 2006. Relevant records were re-indexed with this term. The posting note reflects the number of records that were re-indexed.
UF Absence Seizures
B Seizures 2005
R ↓ Epilepsy 1967

Pets 1982
PN 745 **SC** 38035
SN Domesticated animals kept primarily for pleasure rather than utility.
R Animal Assisted Therapy 1994
Animal Domestication 1978
↓ Animals 1967
Interspecies Interaction 1991

Peyote 1973
PN 15 **SC** 38050
B Alkaloids 1973
Hallucinogenic Drugs 1967
Psychotomimetic Drugs 1973
R Mescaline 1973

Phantom Limbs 1973
PN 240 **SC** 38060
SN A condition in which a person feels that an amputated limb or body part is still present. Frequently, painful or tingling sensations appear to originate from the amputated extremity.
B Body Image Disturbances 1973
R ↓ Amputation 1973

Pharmaceutical Economics
Use Pharmacoeconomics

Pharmaceutical Industry 2007
PN 159 **SC** 38062
SN An industry that is authorized to develop, manufacture, market, and sell drugs.
HN This term was introduced in April 2007. Relevant records were re-indexed with this term. The posting note reflects the number of records that were re-indexed.
UF Drug Industry
B Business 1967
R ↓ Drug Therapy 1967
Nonprescription Drugs 1991
Pharmacoeconomics 2007
↓ Pharmacology 1973
Prescription Drugs 1991

Pharmacists 1991
PN 250 **SC** 38065
B Medical Personnel 1967

Pharmacoeconomics 2007
PN 68 **SC** 38067
SN Economic evaluation of costs and clinical outcomes of drug therapy and its impact on health care costs.
HN This term was introduced in April 2007. Relevant records were re-indexed with this term. The posting note reflects the number of records that were re-indexed.
UF Pharmaceutical Economics
B Economics 1985
R ↓ Costs and Cost Analysis 1973
↓ Drug Therapy 1967
Health Care Costs 1994
Pharmaceutical Industry 2007
↓ Pharmacology 1973

Pharmacology 1973
PN 3080 **SC** 38070
SN The study of the chemistry, actions, and effects of drugs on living organisms or tissues. Used for intended effects of drugs; for adverse or undesired effects of drugs, use SIDE EFFECTS (DRUG). For the use of drugs in a treatment capacity, use DRUG THERAPY.
B Paramedical Sciences 1973
N Psychopharmacology 1967
R Bioavailability 1991
Drug Abuse Liability 1994
Pharmaceutical Industry 2007
Pharmacoeconomics 2007

Pharmacotherapy
Use Drug Therapy

Pharyngeal Disorders 1973
PN 42 **SC** 38090
B Respiratory Tract Disorders 1973
R Dysphagia 2003

Pharynx 1973
PN 58 **SC** 38100
B Digestive System 1967
Respiratory System 1973

Phenaglycodol
HN Term discontinued in 1997. In 2000, the term was removed from all records containing it, and replaced with SEDATIVES, its postable counterpart.
Use Sedatives

Phencyclidine 1982
PN 883 **SC** 38125
SN Piperadine having hallucinogenic and anesthetic properties.

Phencyclidine — (cont'd)
UF PCP
B Anesthetic Drugs 1973
Hallucinogenic Drugs 1967

Phenelzine 1973
PN 314 **SC** 38130
B Antidepressant Drugs 1971
Monoamine Oxidase Inhibitors 1973

Phenethylamines 1985
PN 135 **SC** 38135
UF Phenylethylamines
B Amines 1973
R ↓ Amphetamine 1967

Pheniprazine 1973
PN 6 **SC** 38140
B Antidepressant Drugs 1971
Antihypertensive Drugs 1973
Monoamine Oxidase Inhibitors 1973

Phenmetrazine 1973
PN 14 **SC** 38150
B Appetite Depressing Drugs 1973
Sympathomimetic Amines 1973

Phenobarbital 1973
PN 364 **SC** 38160
B Anticonvulsive Drugs 1973
Barbiturates 1967
Hypnotic Drugs 1973
Sedatives 1973

Phenomenology 1967
PN 3862 **SC** 38180
B Philosophies 1967
R Constructivism 1994
Hermeneutics 1991
↓ History of Psychology 1967

Phenothiazine Derivatives 1973
PN 229 **SC** 38190
HN In 1997, this term replaced the discontinued terms BUTYRYLPERAZINE and TRIFLUPROMAZINE. In 2000, these terms were removed from all records containing them, and replaced with PHENOTHIAZINE DERIVATIVES.
UF Butyrylperazine
Triflupromazine
B Tranquilizing Drugs 1967
N Chlorpromazine 1967
Chlorprothixene 1973
Fluphenazine 1973
Mesoridazine 1973
Perphenazine 1973
Prochlorperazine 1973
Promazine 1973
Thioridazine 1973
Trifluoperazine 1973
R ↓ Cholinergic Blocking Drugs 1973

Phenotypes 1973
PN 1880 **SC** 38200
R Assortative Mating 1991
↓ Genetics 1967
Genotypes 1973
Polymorphism 2003

Phenoxybenzamine 1973
PN 73 **SC** 38210
B Adrenergic Blocking Drugs 1973
Amines 1973
Antihypertensive Drugs 1973

Phenylalanine 1973
PN 216 **SC** 38220
B Alanines 1973
N Parachlorophenylalanine 1978

Phenylethylamines
Use Phenethylamines

Phenylketonuria 1973
PN 257 **SC** 38230
SN A hereditary metabolic disorder in which the patient cannot process the amino acid phylalnine. It is treatable by diet but results in mental retardation if it goes untreated.
UF Oligophrenia (Phenylpyruvic)
PKU (Hereditary Disorder)
B Genetic Disorders 1973
Metabolism Disorders 1973
Neonatal Disorders 1973
R ↓ Mental Retardation 1967

Phenytoin
Use Diphenylhydantoin

Pheromones 1973
PN 1053 **SC** 38240
SN Chemical substances released by an organism that may influence the behavior of other organisms of the same species in characteristic ways.
R ↓ Animal Mating Behavior 1967
Animal Scent Marking 1985
↓ Glands 1967
↓ Hormones 1967

Phi Coefficient 1973
PN 25 **SC** 38250
B Statistical Correlation 1967

Philanthropy
Use Charitable Behavior

Philosophies 1967
PN 8769 **SC** 38270
B Humanities 2003
N Animism 1973
Asceticism 1973
Collectivism 2007
Determinism 1997
Dualism 1973
Epistemology 1973
Existentialism 1967
Fatalism 1973
Hermeneutics 1991
Humanism 1973
Idealism 1973
Individualism 2007
Intellectualism 1973
Logic (Philosophy) 1973
Materialism 1973
↓ Metaphysics 1973
Mysticism 1967
Nihilism 1973
Ontology (Philosophy) 2007
Pacifism 1973
Phenomenology 1967
Positivism (Philosophy) 1997
Postmodernism 1997
Pragmatism 1973
Realism (Philosophy) 1973
Reductionism 1973
Relativism 1997
R Agnosticism 2007
Hedonism 1973

Philosophy of Life
Use World View

Phobias 1967
PN 3472 **SC** 38280
SN Disorders characterized by persistent, unrealistic, intense fear of an object, activity, or situation.
HN In 1988, this term replaced the discontinued term PHOBIC NEUROSIS. In 2000, PHOBIC NEUROSIS was removed from all records containing it, and replaced with PHOBIAS.
UF Arachnophobia
Phobic Neurosis
Spider Phobia
B Anxiety Disorders 1997
N Acrophobia 1973
Agoraphobia 1973
Claustrophobia 1973
Ophidiophobia 1973
School Phobia 1973
Social Phobia 1985
R ↓ Anxiety 1967
↓ Fear 1967

Phobic Neurosis
HN Term discontinued in 1988. In 2000, the term was removed from all records containing it, and replaced with PHOBIAS, its postable counterpart.
Use Phobias

Phonemes 1973
PN 1804 **SC** 38300
SN Members of the set of the smallest units of speech that serve to distinguish one utterance from another, such as the p of pat and the f of fat. Used both for the concept of phonemes as well as the discipline of phonemics. Compare PHONOLOGY.
B Phonology 1973
N Consonants 1973
R Phonetics 1967
Phonological Awareness 2004
↓ Prosody 1991
Vowels 1973

Phonemic Awareness
Use Phonological Awareness

Phonetics 1967
PN 1705 **SC** 38310
SN Science, study, analysis, and classification of sounds including their production in speech, transmission and perception. Used for the linguistic discipline or the specific phonetic characteristics of utterances themselves.
B Phonology 1973
R Articulation (Speech) 1967
Morphemes 1973
↓ Phonemes 1973
Syllables 1973

Phonics 1973
PN 310 **SC** 38320
SN Science of sound. Also, a method of teaching beginners to read and pronounce words by hearing the phonetic value of letters, letter groups, and especially syllables.
B Language Arts Education 1973
R Initial Teaching Alphabet 1973
Reading Education 1973

Phonological Awareness 2004
PN 802 **SC** 38327
SN Ability to recognize various speech sounds including, syllables, rhymes, and phonemes.
HN This term was introduced in June 2004. Relevant records were re-indexed with this term. The posting note reflects the number of records that were re-indexed.
UF Phonemic Awareness
B Awareness 1967
R ↓ Literacy 1973
↓ Phonemes 1973
↓ Phonology 1973
Reading Development 1997
Reading Readiness 1973
Rhyme 2004
Word Recognition 1988

Phonology 1973
PN 5086 **SC** 38330
SN Study of the ways in which speech sounds (phonemes) and phonetic features form systems and patterns at a given point in time or from a historical perspective. Used for the linguistic discipline or the specific phonological processes or factors themselves. Compare PHONEMES.
B Grammar 1967
N ↓ Phonemes 1973
Phonetics 1967
↓ Prosody 1991
Syllables 1973
Vowels 1973
R Inflection 1973
Morphology (Language) 1973
Phonological Awareness 2004
Rhyme 2004
↓ Semantics 1967
↓ Syntax 1971

Phosphatases 1973
PN 209 **SC** 38340
B Enzymes 1973
R ↓ Esterases 1973
Hydroxylases 1973

Phosphatides 1973
PN 358 **SC** 38350
UF Phospholipids
B Fatty Acids 1973
N Lecithin 1991

Phospholipids
Use Phosphatides

Phosphorus 1973
PN 99 **SC** 38370

Phosphorylases 1973
PN 128 **SC** 38380
B Enzymes 1973

Photic Threshold
Use Illumination AND Visual Thresholds

Photographic Art 1973
PN 98 **SC** 38400
B Art 1967

Photographic Memory
Use Eidetic Imagery

Photographs 1967
PN 1215 **SC** 38410
SN Use for photographs as stimuli.

Photographs — (cont'd)
B Audiovisual Communications Media 1973
R Pictorial Stimuli 1978

Photopic Stimulation 1973
PN 315 SC 38420
SN Presentation of light at intensity levels characteristic of daylight illumination, activating cone photoreceptors in the retina.
B Illumination 1967
R Scotopic Stimulation 1973

Photoreceptors 1973
PN 533 SC 38430
SN Specialized cells for light stimuli.
B Neural Receptors 1973
Sensory Neurons 1973
N Cones (Eye) 1973
Rods (Eye) 1973
R Visual Receptive Fields 1982

Phototherapy 1991
PN 498 SC 38435
UF Bright Light Therapy
Illumination Therapy
Light Therapy
B Physical Treatment Methods 1973
R ↓ Alternative Medicine 1997
↓ Psychotherapy 1967
Seasonal Affective Disorder 1991

Phrases 1973
PN 488 SC 38440
SN Groups of words that function as an element in grammatical structure.
B Language 1967
R ↓ Syntax 1971

Phrenic Nerve
Use Spinal Nerves

Phylogenesis 1973
PN 355 SC 38460
R ↓ Biology 1967
Botany 1973

Physical Abuse 1991
PN 3269 SC 38465
B Antisocial Behavior 1971
Violent Crime 2003
R ↓ Abuse Reporting 1997
Battered Child Syndrome 1973
Battered Females 1988
Bullying 2003
↓ Child Abuse 1971
Domestic Violence 2006
Elder Abuse 1988
Emotional Abuse 1991
↓ Partner Abuse 1991
Patient Abuse 1991
Prisoner Abuse 2007
↓ Sexual Abuse 1988
Verbal Abuse 2003
↓ Violence 1973

Physical Activity 2007
PN 1718 SC 38467
HN In April 2007, PHYSICAL ACTIVITY changed status from nonpostable to postable. Relevant records were re-indexed with this term. The posting note reflects the number of records that were re-indexed.

Physical Activity — (cont'd)
B Motor Processes 1967
N ↓ Exercise 1973
R Active Living 2007
Activity Level 1982
↓ Health Behavior 1982
↓ Locomotion 2007
Physical Fitness 1973

Physical Agility 1973
PN 139 SC 38470
UF Agility (Physical)
B Motor Processes 1967
N Physical Dexterity 1973
R Motor Coordination 1973
Physical Mobility 1994

Physical Appearance 1982
PN 1187 SC 38473
SN Externally visible characteristics or features of a person.
N Physique 1967
R Clothing 1967
Cosmetic Techniques 2001
Facial Features 1973
Mimicry (Biology) 2003
Nudity 1973
Physical Attractiveness 1973
Somatotypes 1973

Physical Attractiveness 1973
PN 2199 SC 38475
R Facial Features 1973
↓ Interpersonal Attraction 1967
↓ Physical Appearance 1982
Sexual Attraction 2003

Physical Comfort 1982
PN 308 SC 38477
SN Perceived degree of physical well-being in response to internal or environmental conditions.
UF Comfort (Physical)
R ↓ Environment 1967
Furniture 1985
↓ Satisfaction 1973

Physical Contact 1982
PN 1171 SC 38478
SN Bodily contact. Used for human or animal populations.
UF Touching
B Social Interaction 1967
R Affection 1973
↓ Animal Social Behavior 1967
Intimacy 1973
Massage 2001
Personal Space 1973
↓ Tactual Perception 1967

Physical Development 1973
PN 2319 SC 38480
UF Physical Growth
B Development 1967
N ↓ Motor Development 1973
↓ Neural Development 1985
↓ Prenatal Development 1973
Sexual Development 1973
R Adolescent Development 1973
Age Differences 1967
Aging (Attitudes Toward) 1985
Animal Development 1978
↓ Childhood Development 1967
↓ Delayed Development 1973
Developmental Age Groups 1973

Physical Development — (cont'd)
↓ Developmental Stages 1973
↓ Early Childhood Development 1973
Emotional Development 1973
↓ Human Development 1967
↓ Infant Development 1973
Neonatal Development 1973
↓ Perceptual Development 1973
Physical Maturity 1973
Precocious Development 1973
↓ Psychogenesis 1973
Sex Linked Developmental Differences 1973

Physical Dexterity 1973
PN 241 SC 38490
UF Dexterity (Physical)
B Perceptual Motor Coordination 1973
Physical Agility 1973
R Physical Mobility 1994

Physical Disabilities (Attitudes Toward) 2001
PN 803 SC 38485
HN In 2000, the truncated terms PHYSICAL DISABILITIES (ATTIT TOWARD) (which was used from 1997-2000) and PHYSICAL HANDICAPS (ATTIT TOWARD) (which was used from 1973-1996) were deleted, removed from all records containing them, and replaced with the expanded form PHYSICAL DISABILITIES (ATTITUDES TOWARD).
UF Physical Handicaps (Attitudes Toward)
B Disabled (Attitudes Toward) 1997

Physical Disfigurement 1978
PN 301 SC 38492
UF Deformity
R ↓ Injuries 1973
↓ Physical Disorders 1997

Physical Disorders 1997
PN 6073 SC 38493
HN Consider DISORDERS to access references prior to 1997. The term PHYSICALLY HANDICAPPED was also used to represent this concept from 1967-1996, and PHYSICALLY DISABLED was used from 1997-2000. In 2000, PHYSICAL DISORDERS replaced the discontinued and deleted term PHYSICALLY DISABLED. PHYSICALLY DISABLED and PHYSICALLY HANDICAPPED were removed from all records containing them and replaced with PHYSICAL DISORDERS.
UF Illness (Physical)
Orthopedically Handicapped
Physical Illness
Physically Handicapped
B Disorders 1967
N ↓ Blood and Lymphatic Disorders 1973
↓ Cardiovascular Disorders 1967
↓ Digestive System Disorders 1973
↓ Endocrine Disorders 1973
↓ Genetic Disorders 1973
Health Impairments 2001
↓ Immunologic Disorders 1973
↓ Infectious Disorders 1973
↓ Metabolism Disorders 1973
↓ Musculoskeletal Disorders 1973
↓ Neonatal Disorders 1973
↓ Neoplasms 1967
↓ Nervous System Disorders 1967
↓ Nutritional Deficiencies 1973
↓ Respiratory Tract Disorders 1973
↓ Sense Organ Disorders 1973
↓ Sensory System Disorders 2001
↓ Skin Disorders 1973

Physical Disorders — (cont'd)
↓ Toxic Disorders 1973
↓ Urogenital Disorders 1973
↓ Vision Disorders 1982
R Anesthesia (Feeling) 1973
Back Pain 1982
↓ Chronic Illness 1991
Chronicity (Disorders) 1982
↓ Communication Disorders 1982
Comorbidity 1991
↓ Congenital Disorders 1973
↓ Diagnosis 1967
Disease Course 1991
↓ Eating Disorders 1997
Etiology 1967
Illness Behavior 1982
↓ Injuries 1973
↓ Learning Disorders 1967
Malingering 1973
↓ Memory Disorders 1973
↓ Mental Disorders 1967
Onset (Disorders) 1973
↓ Pain 1967
Physical Disfigurement 1978
Predisposition 1973
Premorbidity 1978
Prenatal Exposure 1991
Prognosis 1973
Recovery (Disorders) 1973
Relapse (Disorders) 1973
↓ Remission (Disorders) 1973
Rett Syndrome 1994
Severity (Disorders) 1982
↓ Sexual Function Disturbances 1973
↓ Sleep Disorders 1973
Special Needs 1994
Susceptibility (Disorders) 1973
↓ Symptoms 1967
↓ Syndromes 1973
↓ Treatment Resistant Disorders 1994
Work Related Illnesses 1994

Physical Divisions (Geographic)
Use Geography

Physical Education 1967
PN 1898 **SC** 38500
B Curriculum 1967

Physical Endurance 1973
PN 331 **SC** 38510
B Endurance 1973
R Physical Fitness 1973
Physical Strength 1973
Physiological Stress 1967

Physical Examination 1988
PN 574 **SC** 38515
SN Examination or screening of an individual's overall physical health.
B Health Screening 1997
R Cancer Screening 1997
Drug Usage Screening 1988
Mammography 1994
↓ Medical Diagnosis 1973
Preventive Medicine 1973
Self Examination (Medical) 1988

Physical Exercise
Use Exercise

Physical Fitness 1973
PN 1819 **SC** 38530
R Aerobic Exercise 1988
↓ Exercise 1973
↓ Physical Activity 2007
Physical Endurance 1973
Physical Strength 1973

Physical Geography
Use Geography

Physical Growth
Use Physical Development

Physical Handicaps (Attitudes Toward)
HN The term was discontinued in 1997, when the term PHYSICAL DISABILITIES (ATTIT TOWARD) was created to capture this concept. In 2000, these two truncated terms were deleted and mapped to their expanded forms: PHYSICAL HANDICAPS (ATTITUDES TOWARD) and PHYSICAL DISABILITIES (ATTITUDES TOWARD). The truncated versions of the terms were removed from all records containing them, and replaced with PHYSICAL DISABILITIES (ATTITUDES TOWARD), the valid postable version of the term.
Use Physical Disabilities (Attitudes Toward)

Physical Health 2007
PN 500 **SC** 38552
HN This term was introduced in April 2007. Relevant records were re-indexed with this term. The posting note reflects the number of records that were re-indexed.
B Health 1973

Physical Illness
Use Physical Disorders

Physical Illness (Attitudes Toward) 1985
PN 1869 **SC** 38557
SN Attitudes toward one's own or other's physical illness.
B Attitudes 1967
N AIDS (Attitudes Toward) 1997
R Disability Discrimination 1997
↓ Disabled (Attitudes Toward) 1997
Health Attitudes 1985
Health Knowledge 1994
Illness Behavior 1982

Physical Maturity 1973
PN 137 **SC** 38560
SN Attainment of a stage of physical development commonly associated with persons of a given age level.
UF Maturity (Physical)
R ↓ Physical Development 1973

Physical Mobility 1994
PN 496 **SC** 38563
SN Ability to move within one's environment. May be used for mobility problems associated with aging or handicapping conditions. Used for human populations only.
B Motor Processes 1967
R Activities of Daily Living 1991
Activity Level 1982
↓ Locomotion 2007
Mobility Aids 1978
↓ Motor Development 1973
↓ Physical Agility 1973
Physical Dexterity 1973

Physical Restraint 1982
PN 1256 **SC** 38566
SN Use of any physical means to restrict the movement of a client or subject, human or animal.
UF Restraint (Physical)
R ↓ Motor Processes 1967
Patient Violence 1994
↓ Physical Treatment Methods 1973
↓ Treatment 1967

Physical Strength 1973
PN 649 **SC** 38570
UF Strength (Physical)
R Physical Endurance 1973
Physical Fitness 1973

Physical Therapists 1973
PN 170 **SC** 38580
B Allied Health Personnel 2007
Medical Personnel 1967
Therapists 1967

Physical Therapy 1973
PN 810 **SC** 38590
SN Treatment of disorder or injury by physical means, such as light, heat, cold, water, electricity, or by mechanical apparatus or kinesitherapy.
UF Physiotherapy
B Paramedical Sciences 1973
Rehabilitation 1967
R Massage 2001
Occupational Therapy 1967

Physical Trauma
Use Injuries

Physical Treatment Methods 1973
PN 1062 **SC** 38610
HN In 2000, this term became the postable counterpart for the discontinued term ORGANIC THERAPIES. ORGANIC THERAPIES was removed from all records containing it and replaced with PHYSICAL TREATMENT METHODS.
UF Organic Therapies
Treatment Methods (Physical)
B Treatment 1967
N Acupuncture 1973
Artificial Respiration 1973
Blood Transfusion 1973
Catheterization 1973
↓ Dental Treatment 1973
↓ Dialysis 1973
↓ Drug Therapy 1967
Electrosleep Treatment 1978
Immunization 1973
↓ Narcoanalysis 1973
Phototherapy 1991
↓ Psychosurgery 1973
Radiation Therapy 1973
↓ Shock Therapy 1973
↓ Surgery 1971
Transcranial Magnetic Stimulation 2003
R ↓ Alternative Medicine 1997
Holistic Health 1985
Massage 2001
Medical Treatment (General) 1973
Osteopathic Medicine 2003
Pain Management 1994
Physical Restraint 1982

Physically Handicapped
HN The term was discontinued in 1997, when the term PHYSICALLY DISABLED was created to capture this concept. In 2000, with the deletion of the

Physically Handicapped — (cont'd)
term PHYSICALLY DISABLED, PHYSICALLY HANDICAPPED was made a nonpostable term for the postable term PHYSICAL DISORDERS. PHYSICALLY DISABLED and PHYSICALLY HANDICAPPED were removed from all records containing them and replaced with PHYSICAL DISORDERS.
Use Physical Disorders

Physician Patient Interaction
Use Therapeutic Processes

Physicians 1967
PN 8586 **SC** 38640
UF Doctors
B Medical Personnel 1967
N Family Physicians 1973
General Practitioners 1973
Gynecologists 1973
Internists 1973
Neurologists 1973
Obstetricians 1978
Pathologists 1973
Pediatricians 1973
Psychiatrists 1967
Surgeons 1973
R Clinicians 1973

Physicists 1973
PN 49 **SC** 38650
B Professional Personnel 1978
R ↓ Aerospace Personnel 1973
Mathematicians 1973
Scientists 1967

Physics 1973
PN 1228 **SC** 38660
B Sciences 1967
R Magnetism 1985
Relativism 1997

Physiological Aging 1967
PN 4110 **SC** 38670
SN Biological changes which occur in an organism with the passage of time.
UF Aging (Physiological)
B Aging 1991
R Adult Development 1978
↓ Aged (Attitudes Toward) 1978
Aging (Attitudes Toward) 1985
Geriatric Psychotherapy 1973
Geriatrics 1967
Life Expectancy 1982
↓ Physiology 1967
↓ Senile Dementia 1973

Physiological Arousal 1967
PN 4722 **SC** 38680
SN Condition of alertness and readiness to respond as evidenced by physiological signs such as heart rate or blood pressure.
UF Arousal (Physiological)
Excitation (Physiological)
R ↓ Brain Stimulation 1967
Cardiovascular Reactivity 1994
↓ Consciousness States 1971
Physiological Stress 1967
↓ Physiology 1967
↓ Sexual Arousal 1978

Physiological Correlates 1967
PN 8989 **SC** 38690
SN Numerous or unspecified physiological processes which accompany a particular psychological or physical action, state, or characteristic.
R Biological Markers 1991
Cardiovascular Reactivity 1994
Physiological Stress 1967
↓ Physiology 1967
↓ Symptoms 1967

Physiological Psychology 1967
PN 826 **SC** 38700
SN Branch of psychology concerned with the physiological correlates of cognitive, emotional, and behavioral processes. Use PHYSIOLOGY, PSYCHOPHYSIOLOGY, or a more specific term for the specific physiological processes themselves.
B Psychology 1967
N Neuropsychology 1973
R ↓ Psychophysiology 1967

Physiological Stress 1967
PN 2362 **SC** 38710
B Stress 1967
R Acceleration Effects 1973
Decompression Effects 1973
↓ Deprivation 1967
↓ Environmental Effects 1973
Environmental Stress 1973
Physical Endurance 1973
Physiological Arousal 1967
Physiological Correlates 1967
↓ Physiology 1967
Pollution 1973
Thermal Acclimatization 1973

Physiology 1967
PN 3992 **SC** 38720
SN Conceptually broad term referring both to a branch of biological science and to the functions and processes of living organisms. Use a more specific term if possible.
N Absorption (Physiological) 1973
↓ Appetite 1973
↓ Body Temperature 1973
Digestion 1973
↓ Electrophysiology 1973
↓ Excretion 1967
Homeostasis 1973
↓ Ingestion 2001
↓ Metabolism 1967
↓ Neurophysiology 1973
Oxygenation 1973
Pathophysiology 2005
↓ Psychophysiology 1967
↓ Reflexes 1971
↓ Secretion (Gland) 1973
↓ Sexual Reproduction 1973
Thermal Acclimatization 1973
R ↓ Anatomy 1967
Apoptosis 2006
↓ Biochemistry 1967
↓ Body Fluids 1973
↓ Cells (Biology) 1973
Histology 1973
Instinctive Behavior 1982
Metabolic Rates 1973
Morphology 1973
Nutrition 1973
Physiological Aging 1967
Physiological Arousal 1967
Physiological Correlates 1967
Physiological Stress 1967

Physiotherapy
Use Physical Therapy

Physique 1967
PN 1001 **SC** 38740
SN Overall body structure and appearance, including size, musculature, and posture. Limited primarily to human populations. Consider also BODY SIZE or SOMATOTYPES.
B Physical Appearance 1982
R Body Height 1973
↓ Body Size 1985
↓ Body Weight 1967
Human Body 2003
↓ Overweight 2007
Posture 1973
Somatotypes 1973

Physostigmine 1973
PN 591 **SC** 38750
UF Eserine
B Alkaloids 1973
Amines 1973
Cholinergic Drugs 1973
Cholinesterase Inhibitors 1973
Cholinomimetic Drugs 1973

Piaget (Jean) 1967
PN 1678 **SC** 38755
SN Identifies biographical or autobiographical studies and discussions of Piaget's works.
R Accommodation (Cognitive Process) 2007
Assimilation (Cognitive Process) 2007
↓ Cognitive Development 1973
Conservation (Concept) 1973
Constructivism 1994
↓ Developmental Stages 1973
Piagetian Tasks 1973
↓ Psychologists 1967

Piagetian Tasks 1973
PN 857 **SC** 38757
SN In measurement context, tasks used to assess children's cognitive abilities, based on Piaget's theory of cognitive development.
R ↓ Measurement 1967
Piaget (Jean) 1967

Piano
Use Musical Instruments

Pica 1973
PN 155 **SC** 38770
SN An eating disorder in which a patient ingests unnatural and nonnutritive substances, such as paper or dirt, for at least one month. It is most commonly found in young children and pregnant women.
B Eating Disorders 1997
R ↓ Adjunctive Behavior 1982
Coprophagia 2001
↓ Ingestion 2001
Lead Poisoning 1973
Toxicomania 1973

Picketing
Use Social Demonstrations

Picks Disease 1973
PN 181 **SC** 38790
SN A degenerative disease of the brain, possibly hereditary, that usually occurs between the ages of 45-50 years. Symptoms include intellectual decline, emotional instability, and loss of social adjustment.

Picks Disease — (cont'd)
B Presenile Dementia 1973
R Alzheimers Disease 1973
↓ Dementia 1985
↓ Genetic Disorders 1973

Picrotoxin 1973
PN 249 SC 38800
B Analeptic Drugs 1973
Gamma Aminobutyric Acid Antagonists 1985

Pictorial Stimuli 1978
PN 4519 SC 38805
SN Drawings, pictures, or other visual stimuli not composed of letters or digits.
R Photographs 1967
↓ Stimulus Presentation Methods 1973
↓ Visual Displays 1973
↓ Visual Stimulation 1973

Piercings
Use Cosmetic Techniques

Pigeons 1967
PN 5557 SC 38810
B Birds 1967

Pigments 1973
PN 331 SC 38820
N Hemoglobin 1973
Melanin 1973
Rhodopsin 1985
R Animal Coloration 1985
↓ Color 1967
Eye Color 1991

Pigs 1973
PN 904 SC 38830
B Vertebrates 1973

Pilocarpine 1973
PN 198 SC 38840
B Alkaloids 1973
Cholinergic Drugs 1973
Cholinomimetic Drugs 1973

Pilots (Aircraft)
Use Aircraft Pilots

Pimozide 1973
PN 467 SC 38860
B Tranquilizing Drugs 1967

Pineal Body 1973
PN 292 SC 38870
B Endocrine Glands 1973
R Melatonin 1973

Pinealectomy 1973
PN 87 SC 38880
B Endocrine Gland Surgery 1973

Piperazines 1994
PN 177 SC 38885
UF Chlorophenylpiperazine
MCPP
N Trazodone 1988

Pipradrol 1973
PN 16 SC 38890
B Antidepressant Drugs 1971
CNS Stimulating Drugs 1973

Piracetam 1982
PN 175 SC 38900
B Antiemetic Drugs 1973
CNS Stimulating Drugs 1973
Nootropic Drugs 1991

Pitch (Frequency) 1967
PN 3076 SC 38910
SN Perceived changes in auditory stimuli that are a function of the sound's frequency usually measured in hertz. Also, in linguistics, a phonetic element marking the fundamental frequency of a component of speech.
UF Frequency (Pitch)
Tone (Frequency)
B Auditory Stimulation 1967
N Speech Pitch 1973
Ultrasound 1973

Pitch Discrimination 1973
PN 715 SC 38920
B Pitch Perception 1973

Pitch Perception 1973
PN 665 SC 38930
B Auditory Perception 1967
N Pitch Discrimination 1973
R Music Perception 1997

Pituitary Disorders 1973
PN 64 SC 38940
UF Hypophysis Disorders
B Endocrine Disorders 1973
N Hypopituitarism 1973
R ↓ Adrenal Gland Disorders 1973
↓ Endocrine Sexual Disorders 1973
↓ Thyroid Disorders 1973

Pituitary Dwarfism
Use Hypopituitarism

Pituitary Gland 1973
PN 455 SC 38960
B Endocrine Glands 1973
N Hypothalamic Pituitary Adrenal Axis 2006
Hypothalamo Hypophyseal System 1973

Pituitary Gland Surgery
Use Hypophysectomy

Pituitary Hormones 1973
PN 304 SC 38980
B Hormones 1967
N Corticotropin 1973
Dynorphins 1985
Melanocyte Stimulating Hormone 1985
Oxytocin 1973
Somatotropin 1973
Thyrotropin 1973
Vasopressin 1973
R ↓ Gonadotropic Hormones 1973
Hypothalamo Hypophyseal System 1973
Luteinizing Hormone 1978

PKU (Hereditary Disorder)
Use Phenylketonuria

Place Conditioning 1991
PN 951 SC 39005
SN Learned behavior or the conditioning procedure in which a stimulus is paired with an environment, location, or physical position.

Place Conditioning — (cont'd)
UF Conditioned Place Preference
B Conditioning 1967
R ↓ Animal Environments 1967
Contextual Associations 1967

Place Disorientation 1973
PN 79 SC 39010
SN Impaired awareness of place, often characteristic of organic mental disorders.
UF Disorientation (Place)
B Consciousness Disturbances 1973
R Wandering Behavior 1991

Placebo 1973
PN 1672 SC 39020
SN Any effect of therapeutic intervention that cannot be attributed to the specific action of a drug or the treatment. Also, the specific substance used as a control in experiments testing the effect of a particular drug. Term is used selectively for studies of the placebo effect or other methodological issues.
R ↓ Drugs 1967

Placement (Educational)
Use Educational Placement

Placement (Personnel)
Use Personnel Placement

Placenta 1973
PN 96 SC 39040
R ↓ Pregnancy 1967
↓ Uterus 1973

Planarians 1973
PN 44 SC 39060
B Worms 1967

Planned Behavior 1997
PN 933 SC 39065
SN Based on I. Ajzen's theory that behavioral intentions are determined by one's perceived control over the behavior, attitude toward the behavior, and subjective norms.
R ↓ Attitudes 1967
↓ Behavior 1967
Intention 1988
↓ Motivation 1967

Planning (Management)
Use Management Planning

Plants (Botanical) 2007
PN 250 SC 39075
HN This term was introduced in April 2007. Relevant records were re-indexed with this term. The posting note reflects the number of records that were re-indexed.
N ↓ Medicinal Herbs and Plants 2001
R Botany 1973
Horticulture Therapy 2007

Plasma (Blood)
Use Blood Plasma

Plasma Donation
Use Tissue Donation

Plastic Surgery 1973
PN 232 **SC** 39090
B Surgery 1971
R Cosmetic Techniques 2001

Platelets (Blood)
Use Blood Platelets

Play
Use Recreation

Play (Animal)
Use Animal Play

Play Behavior (Childhood)
Use Childhood Play Behavior

Play Development (Childhood)
Use Childhood Play Development

Play Therapy 1973
PN 1627 **SC** 39150
B Child Psychotherapy 1967

Playgrounds 1973
PN 197 **SC** 39160
B Recreation Areas 1973
R ↓ School Facilities 1973

Pleasure 1973
PN 1329 **SC** 39170
UF Enjoyment
B Emotional States 1973
R Anhedonia 1985
Euphoria 1973
Happiness 1973

Plethysmography 1973
PN 98 **SC** 39180
B Medical Diagnosis 1973
N Electroplethysmography 1973

PMS
Use Premenstrual Syndrome

Pneumoencephalography 1973
PN 29 **SC** 39190
SN Radiography of the brain after injection of air into the ventricles.
UF Air Encephalography
Encephalography (Air)
B Encephalography 1973
Medical Diagnosis 1973
Roentgenography 1973

Pneumonia 1973
PN 130 **SC** 39200
B Lung Disorders 1973
R ↓ Bacterial Disorders 1973
↓ Viral Disorders 1973

Poetry 1973
PN 1402 **SC** 39210
B Literature 1967
R Creative Writing 1994
Rhyme 2004

Poetry Therapy 1994
PN 59 **SC** 39215
B Creative Arts Therapy 1994
R Bibliotherapy 1973
↓ Psychotherapeutic Techniques 1967

Point Biserial Correlation 1973
PN 21 **SC** 39220
B Statistical Correlation 1967

Poisoning
Use Toxic Disorders

Poisons
HN In April 2007, this term was discontinued and removed from all records containing it, and was replaced with TOXINS, its postable counterpart.
Use Toxins

Poisson Distribution
Use Skewed Distribution

Police Interrogation
Use Interrogation

Police Personnel 1973
PN 3683 **SC** 39270
B Government Personnel 1973
Law Enforcement Personnel 1973

Policy Making 1988
PN 4065 **SC** 39278
UF Organizational Policy Making
N ↓ Government Policy Making 1973
↓ Health Care Policy 1994
R Educational Reform 1997

Policy Making (Foreign)
Use Foreign Policy Making

Policy Making (Government)
Use Government Policy Making

Poliomyelitis 1973
PN 86 **SC** 39300
SN A viral disorder of the central nervous system that affects nerve cells and muscles, and may result in paralysis.
UF Infantile Paralysis
Paralysis (Infantile)
B Myelitis 1973
Viral Disorders 1973
R ↓ Musculoskeletal Disorders 1973
↓ Paralysis 1973
↓ Respiratory Tract Disorders 1973

Political Assassination 1973
PN 100 **SC** 39320
UF Assassination (Political)
B Violent Crime 2003

Political Attitudes 1973
PN 3686 **SC** 39330
B Attitudes 1967
Politics 1967
N Nationalism 1967
Political Conservatism 1973
Political Liberalism 1973
Political Radicalism 1973
R ↓ Activism 2003
Citizenship 1973
Nonviolence 1991

Political Attitudes — (cont'd)
Political Socialization 1988
Voting Behavior 1973

Political Campaigns 1973
PN 498 **SC** 39340
UF Campaigns (Political)
B Political Processes 1973
R Debates 1997
Political Candidates 1973
Political Elections 1973
Political Issues 1973
Political Parties 1973
Politicians 1978

Political Candidates 1973
PN 631 **SC** 39350
UF Candidates (Political)
B Politics 1967
R Debates 1997
Political Campaigns 1973
Political Elections 1973
Politicians 1978

Political Conservatism 1973
PN 375 **SC** 39360
UF Conservatism (Political)
B Political Attitudes 1973
R Conservatism 1973

Political Debates
Use Debates

Political Divisions (Geographic)
Use Geography

Political Economic Systems 1973
PN 603 **SC** 39370
B Systems 1967
N Capitalism 1973
Communism 1973
Democracy 1973
Fascism 1973
Socialism 1973
Totalitarianism 1973
R Collectivism 2007
↓ Economics 1985
↓ Economy 1973
Government 1967
Political Psychology 1997

Political Elections 1973
PN 735 **SC** 39380
UF Elections (Political)
B Political Processes 1973
R Debates 1997
Political Campaigns 1973
Political Candidates 1973
Political Parties 1973
Politicians 1978
Voting Behavior 1973

Political Involvement
Use Political Participation

Political Issues 1973
PN 1213 **SC** 39390
B Politics 1967
R Political Campaigns 1973
↓ Social Issues 1991
Voting Behavior 1973

Political Liberalism 1973
PN 284 **SC** 39400
UF Liberalism (Political)
B Political Attitudes 1973
R Liberalism 1973

Political Participation 1988
PN 678 **SC** 39405
UF Political Involvement
B Politics 1967
N Voting Behavior 1973
R ↓ Activism 2003
Political Psychology 1997
Social Demonstrations 1973
↓ Social Movements 1967

Political Parties 1973
PN 534 **SC** 39410
UF Democratic Party
Independent Party (Political)
Republican Party
B Politics 1967
R Political Campaigns 1973
Political Elections 1973

Political Processes 1973
PN 1912 **SC** 39420
B Politics 1967
N Political Campaigns 1973
Political Elections 1973
Voting Behavior 1973
R Debates 1997
Freedom 1978
Political Psychology 1997
Political Revolution 1973
↓ Social Processes 1967

Political Psychology 1997
PN 358 **SC** 39425
B Applied Psychology 1973
R ↓ Law (Government) 1973
↓ Political Economic Systems 1973
↓ Political Participation 1988
↓ Political Processes 1973
↓ Politics 1967
Public Opinion 1973
Voting Behavior 1973

Political Radicalism 1973
PN 185 **SC** 39430
UF Radicalism (Political)
B Political Attitudes 1973

Political Refugees
Use Refugees

Political Revolution 1973
PN 214 **SC** 39440
UF Revolutions (Political)
B Radical Movements 1973
R ↓ Political Processes 1973
↓ Terrorism 1982

Political Socialization 1988
PN 215 **SC** 39443
SN Transmission of political norms through social agents, e.g., school, parents, peers, or mass media.
B Socialization 1967
R ↓ Political Attitudes 1973

Politicians 1978
PN 1143 **SC** 39445
R Political Campaigns 1973
Political Candidates 1973

Politicians — (cont'd)
Political Elections 1973
↓ Politics 1967

Politics 1967
PN 4300 **SC** 39450
N ↓ Political Attitudes 1973
Political Candidates 1973
Political Issues 1973
↓ Political Participation 1988
Political Parties 1973
↓ Political Processes 1973
R Government 1967
Political Psychology 1997
Politicians 1978

Pollution 1973
PN 491 **SC** 39460
B Ecological Factors 1973
R Atmospheric Conditions 1973
Carcinogens 1973
Ecology 1973
Environmental Education 1994
↓ Hazardous Materials 1991
Noise Effects 1973
Passive Smoking 2006
Physiological Stress 1967
↓ Temperature Effects 1967

Polydipsia 1982
PN 470 **SC** 39465
SN Noncontingent excessive drinking behavior usually produced and maintained by operant schedules of reinforcement involving food as a reinforcer. Also used for disordered human populations.
B Adjunctive Behavior 1982
R Animal Drinking Behavior 1973
Hyponatremia 1997
↓ Operant Conditioning 1967

Polydrug Abuse 1994
PN 368 **SC** 39467
UF Multidrug Abuse
B Drug Abuse 1973
R ↓ Alcohol Abuse 1988
↓ Drug Addiction 1967
↓ Drug Dependency 1973
Drug Interactions 1982

Polygamy 1973
PN 196 **SC** 39470
SN Used for human or animal populations.
B Family Structure 1973
Marriage 1967
R Monogamy 1997

Polygraphs 1973
PN 375 **SC** 39480
B Apparatus 1967
R Interrogation 2005

Polymorphism 2003
PN 1693 **SC** 39485
SN Expression of more than one morphologic type.
HN This term was introduced in June 2003. Relevant records were re-indexed with this term. The posting note reflects the number of records that were re-indexed.
R ↓ Genetics 1967
Genotypes 1973
Morphology 1973
Phenotypes 1973

Polyphagia
Use Hyperphagia

Polypharmacy 2004
PN 266 **SC** 39492
SN Simultaneous administration of multiple medications to treat the same illness.
HN This term was introduced in June 2004. Relevant records were re-indexed with this term. The posting note reflects the number of records that were re-indexed.
B Drug Therapy 1967
R Drug Interactions 1982
↓ Prescribing (Drugs) 1991

Polysomnography 2003
PN 158 **SC** 39495
SN Simultaneous recording of electrophysiologic activity during sleep.
HN This term was introduced in June 2003. Relevant records were re-indexed with this term. The posting note reflects the number of records that were re-indexed.
UF Sleep Monitoring
B Monitoring 1973
R ↓ Apparatus 1967
↓ Electrical Activity 1967
↓ Sleep 1967
↓ Sleep Disorders 1973

Pons 1973
PN 644 **SC** 39510
SN Broad mass of chiefly transverse nerve fibers in the mammalian brain stem lying ventral to the cerebellum at the anterior end of the medulla oblongata, and responsible for relaying sensory information between the cerebrum and cerebellum.
B Brain Stem 1973
Hindbrain 1997
N Raphe Nuclei 1982

Popular Culture 2003
PN 258 **SC** 39515
SN Expressions or characteristics from art, literature, film, television, sports, or fashion that are widely disseminated and commercialized through the media and society.
HN This term was introduced in June 2003. Relevant records were re-indexed with this term. The posting note reflects the number of records that were re-indexed.
UF Mass Culture
R ↓ Culture (Anthropological) 1967
↓ Fads and Fashions 1973
Globalization 2003
↓ Mass Media 1967
↓ Society 1967
Subculture (Anthropological) 1973
Trends 1991

Popularity 1988
PN 401 **SC** 39520
HN Use SOCIAL APPROVAL to access references from 1973-1987.
R ↓ Interpersonal Interaction 1967
Reputation 1997
Social Acceptance 1967
Social Approval 1967
↓ Social Influences 1967
↓ Social Perception 1967

Population 1973
PN 780 **SC** 39530
SN Total number of organisms (human or animal) inhabiting a given locality.

Population — (cont'd)
N Overpopulation 1973
↓ Population (Statistics) 1973
R Birth Rate 1982
Demographic Characteristics 1967
Mortality Rate 1973
Social Density 1978

Population (Statistics) 1973
PN 812 **SC** 39540
SN All the objects or people of a given class.
B Population 1973
N ↓ Statistical Samples 1973
R ↓ Central Tendency Measures 1973
↓ Experimental Design 1967
↓ Experimentation 1967
↓ Sampling (Experimental) 1973
↓ Statistical Analysis 1967
Statistical Reliability 1973
↓ Statistical Variables 1973

Population Characteristics
Use Demographic Characteristics

Population Control
Use Birth Control

Population Density
Use Social Density

Population Genetics 1973
PN 197 **SC** 39570
SN Study of the genetic composition of human or animal populations; gene interactions and alterations that promote population changes and evolution.
B Genetics 1967
R Assortative Mating 1991
Behavioral Genetics 1994
↓ Genetic Engineering 1994

Population Shifts
Use Human Migration

Pornography 1973
PN 758 **SC** 39580
UF X Rated Materials
R Nudity 1973
Obscenity 1978
↓ Paraphilias 1988
↓ Psychosexual Behavior 1967
Sex 1967
↓ Sex Offenses 1982

Porphyria 1973
PN 51 **SC** 39590
SN A metabolic disorder in which abnormal or excessive porphyrins (nitrogen-containing substances) are found in the blood. The disorder causes abdominal pain, nausea, and neurological changes. Psychiatric symptoms include irritability, depression, agitation, and delirium.
B Blood and Lymphatic Disorders 1973
Genetic Disorders 1973
Metabolism Disorders 1973

Porphyria — (cont'd)
R ↓ Mental Disorders 1967

Porpoises 1973
PN 13 **SC** 39600
B Whales 1985
R Dolphins 1973

Porteus Maze Test 1973
PN 33 **SC** 39610
B Intelligence Measures 1967

Positive and Negative Symptoms 1997
PN 1442 **SC** 39618
UF Negative and Positive Symptoms
B Symptoms 1967
R ↓ Schizophrenia 1967

Positive Psychology 2003
PN 533 **SC** 39619
SN Approach to psychology that emphasizes optimism and positive human functioning instead of focusing on psychopathology and dysfunction.
HN This term was introduced in June 2003. Relevant records were re-indexed with this term. The posting note reflects the number of records that were re-indexed.
B Psychology 1967
R Optimism 1973
Positivism 1973
Well Being 1994

Positive Reinforcement 1973
PN 1090 **SC** 39620
SN Presentation of a positive reinforcer contingent on the performance of some behavior. Also, the positively reinforcing object or event itself which, when made to follow the performance of some behavior, results in an increase in the frequency of occurrence of that behavior. Compare REWARDS.
B Reinforcement 1967
N Praise 1973

Positive Transfer 1973
PN 184 **SC** 39630
SN Previous learning or practice which aids the acquisition of new material or skills as the result of common characteristics shared by the prior and current learning situation.
B Transfer (Learning) 1967

Positivism 1973
PN 539 **SC** 39640
SN Personal quality or state of being positive or confident. Compare OPTIMISM.
B Personality Traits 1967
R Determinism 1997
Hope 1991
Optimism 1973
Positive Psychology 2003

Positivism (Philosophy) 1997
PN 100 **SC** 39642
SN Philosophical view that scientific knowledge comes only from direct observation and application of empirical methods.
B Philosophies 1967
R Behaviorism 1967
↓ Empirical Methods 1973
Epistemology 1973
Hermeneutics 1991
Reductionism 1973

Positron Emission Tomography
Use Tomography

Possession
Use Ownership

Postactivation Potentials 1985
PN 1084 **SC** 39650
SN Enhancement of synaptic and cellular responses induced by brief high frequency electrical stimulation.
UF Long Term Potentiation
Short Term Potentiation
B Electrical Activity 1967
R Electrical Brain Stimulation 1973
Neural Plasticity 1994

Postganglionic Autonomic Fibers
Use Autonomic Ganglia

Postgraduate Students 1973
PN 241 **SC** 39684
SN Students involved in study or research after having completed a master's or doctoral degree. Such students are not necessarily pursuing a degree.
B Students 1967
R ↓ College Students 1967
Graduate Students 1967

Postgraduate Training 1973
PN 583 **SC** 39685
SN Studies or research beyond master's or doctoral degree.
B Higher Education 1973
N ↓ Clinical Psychology Graduate Training 2001
Clinical Psychology Internship 1973
Medical Internship 1973
Medical Residency 1973
R Professional Specialization 1991

Posthypnotic Suggestions 1994
PN 120 **SC** 39687
R ↓ Hypnosis 1967
↓ Hypnotherapy 1973
Hypnotic Susceptibility 1973
↓ Relaxation Therapy 1978
Suggestibility 1967

Postmodernism 1997
PN 1114 **SC** 39689
B Philosophies 1967
R ↓ Arts 1973
↓ Literature 1967

Postnatal Depression
Use Postpartum Depression

Postnatal Dysphoria
Use Postpartum Depression

Postnatal Period 1973
PN 2333 **SC** 39690
R Lactation 1973
Perinatal Period 1994
Postpartum Depression 1973
Postpartum Psychosis 2003
↓ Pregnancy 1967

Postpartum Depression 1973
PN 1615 **SC** 39700
UF Postnatal Depression
Postnatal Dysphoria
Puerperal Depression
B Major Depression 1988
R Attachment Behavior 1985
Mother Child Relations 1967

Postpartum Depression — (cont'd)
↓ Organic Brain Syndromes 1973
Postnatal Period 1973
Postpartum Psychosis 2003

Postpartum Psychosis 2003
PN 66 **SC** 39705
SN Psychotic reaction occurring after childbirth.
HN Use POSTPARTUM DEPRESSION to access references from 1988 to June 2003.
UF Puerperal Psychosis
B Psychosis 1967
R Acute Schizophrenia 1973
Attachment Behavior 1985
Mother Child Relations 1967
↓ Organic Brain Syndromes 1973
Postnatal Period 1973
Postpartum Depression 1973

Postsurgical Complications 1973
PN 362 **SC** 39710
UF Surgical Complications
R Obstetrical Complications 1978
Recovery (Disorders) 1973
Relapse (Disorders) 1973
↓ Surgery 1971
↓ Treatment Outcomes 1982

Posttesting 1973
PN 122 **SC** 39720
SN Measurement performed after experimental manipulation, treatment, or program intervention. Comparison of pretest and posttest scores gives a measure of effectiveness of independent variables such as treatments or programs.
B Measurement 1967
R Repeated Measures 1985
↓ Testing Methods 1967

Posttraumatic Stress Disorder 1985
PN 10916 **SC** 39727
SN Acute, chronic, or delayed reactions to traumatic events such as military combat, assault, or natural disaster.
HN Use TRAUMATIC NEUROSIS or STRESS REACTIONS to access references from 1973-1984.
UF PTSD
B Anxiety Disorders 1997
R Acute Stress Disorder 2003
Adjustment Disorders 1994
Combat Experience 1991
Debriefing (Psychological) 2004
Emotional Trauma 1967
Stress Reactions 1973
↓ Trauma 2006
Traumatic Neurosis 1973

Posttreatment Followup 1973
PN 909 **SC** 39730
SN Periodic check-ups of patients. Usually part of a comprehensive aftercare treatment.
UF Catamnesis
Followup (Posttreatment)
R Aftercare 1973
Discharge Planning 1994
↓ Treatment 1967
↓ Treatment Planning 1997

Posture 1973
PN 2030 **SC** 39740
R Body Language 1973
↓ Motor Processes 1967
Physique 1967

Potassium 1973
PN 331 **SC** 39750
B Metallic Elements 1973
N Potassium Ions 1973

Potassium Ions 1973
PN 102 **SC** 39770
B Electrolytes 1973
Potassium 1973

Potential (Achievement)
Use Achievement Potential

Potential Dropouts 1973
PN 155 **SC** 39790
B Dropouts 1973

Potentiation (Drugs)
Use Drug Interactions

Poverty 1973
PN 2552 **SC** 39820
B Social Issues 1991
R Disadvantaged 1967
↓ Homeless 1988
Income (Economic) 1973
Lower Income Level 1973
↓ Socioeconomic Status 1967

Poverty Areas 1973
PN 191 **SC** 39830
UF Slums
B Social Environments 1973
R Cultural Deprivation 1973
Economic Development 2007
Ghettoes 1973

Power 1967
PN 5818 **SC** 39840
SN Social control an individual has over others.
B Social Influences 1967
N Abuse of Power 1997
R Authority 1967
Coercion 1994
↓ Dominance 1967
Empowerment 1991
↓ Helplessness 1997
Omnipotence 1994

Practical Knowledge
Use Procedural Knowledge

Practice 1967
PN 5677 **SC** 39850
HN In 1982, this term replaced the discontinued term PRACTICE EFFECTS. In 2000, PRACTICE EFFECTS was removed from all records and replaced with PRACTICE.
UF Experience (Practice)
Practice Effects
Rehearsal
N Distributed Practice 1973
Massed Practice 1973
R Curricular Field Experience 1982
↓ Experience Level 1988

Practice — (cont'd)
Familiarity 1967
Memory Training 1994
Overcorrection 1985
Test Coaching 1997

Practice Effects
HN Term discontinued in 1982. In 2000, the term was removed from all records containing it, and replaced with PRACTICE, its postable counterpart.
Use Practice

Practicum Supervision 1978
PN 955 **SC** 39865
SN Supervision of students involved in practical application of learned material.
R ↓ Clinical Methods Training 1973
↓ Clinical Psychology Graduate Training 2001
Clinical Psychology Internship 1973
Cooperating Teachers 1978
Counselor Education 1973
↓ Teacher Education 1967

Prader Willi Syndrome 1991
PN 222 **SC** 39867
SN A congenital disorder that results from the deletion of a gene on chromosome 15. The syndrome is characterized by mental retardation, compact body build, obesity, muscular hypotonia, and hypogonadism.
B Congenital Disorders 1973
Syndromes 1973
R ↓ Mental Retardation 1967

Pragmatics 1985
PN 1647 **SC** 39868
SN Study of the rules governing the use of language in context. Also used for the actual social interaction aspects of communication.
B Semiotics 1985
Verbal Communication 1967
R ↓ Communication Skills 1973
Discourse Analysis 1997
↓ Interpersonal Communication 1973
↓ Linguistics 1973
Metalinguistics 1994

Pragmatism 1973
PN 370 **SC** 39870
B Philosophies 1967

Praise 1973
PN 606 **SC** 39880
B Positive Reinforcement 1973
Verbal Reinforcement 1973
R Awards (Merit) 2005

Prayer 1973
PN 324 **SC** 39890
B Religious Practices 1973
R Meditation 1973

Praying Mantis
Use Mantis

Precocious Development 1973
PN 152 **SC** 39910
B Development 1967
R Developmental Age Groups 1973
↓ Physical Development 1973
↓ Psychogenesis 1973

Precognition 1973
PN 167 **SC** 39920
B Clairvoyance 1973

Preconditioning 1994
PN 60 **SC** 39923
SN Presentation of two stimuli in a consecutive manner without reinforcement to determine if a subject will respond to both stimuli in a conditioning paradigm.
UF Sensory Preconditioning
B Conditioning 1967
R Conditioned Stimulus 1973

Predatory Behavior (Animal)
Use Animal Predatory Behavior

Predelinquent Youth 1978
PN 139 **SC** 39927
SN Children considered at risk for developing delinquent behavior because their sociocultural and family backgrounds and early behavior patterns parallel those of juvenile delinquents.
R ↓ Juvenile Delinquency 1967
Juvenile Justice 2004

Predictability (Measurement) 1973
PN 415 **SC** 39930
SN Statistical procedures used to forecast the value of the criterion variables (such as behavior, performance, or outcomes) on the basis of selected predictor variables.
B Statistical Analysis 1967
Statistical Measurement 1973
R Chaos Theory 1997
Confidence Limits (Statistics) 1973
↓ Hypothesis Testing 1973
↓ Prediction 1967
↓ Prediction Errors 1973
↓ Probability 1967
↓ Statistical Estimation 1985

Prediction 1967
PN 12382 **SC** 39940
N Academic Achievement Prediction 1967
Occupational Success Prediction 1973
R Chaos Theory 1997
↓ Estimation 1967
Future 1991
Predictability (Measurement) 1973
↓ Prediction Errors 1973
Prognosis 1973
Self Fulfilling Prophecies 1997

Prediction Errors 1973
PN 126 **SC** 39950
B Errors 1967
N Type I Errors 1973
Type II Errors 1973
R Consistency (Measurement) 1973
↓ Hypothesis Testing 1973
↓ Measurement 1967
Predictability (Measurement) 1973
↓ Prediction 1967
↓ Statistical Analysis 1967
Statistical Power 1991
Statistical Reliability 1973
Statistical Validity 1973
↓ Statistical Variables 1973

Predictive Validity
HN In 2000, the term was discontinued, and removed from all records containing it, and replaced with STATISTICAL VALIDITY, its postable counterpart.
Use Statistical Validity

Predisposition 1973
PN 2909 **SC** 39970
SN Proneness toward disorders or propensity toward certain behaviors due to physical, psychological, social, or situational factors. Consider also SUSCEPTIBILITY (DISORDERS).
R At Risk Populations 1985
Biological Markers 1991
Coronary Prone Behavior 1982
Diathesis Stress Model 2005
↓ Disorders 1967
↓ Genetics 1967
↓ Mental Disorders 1967
Nature Nurture 1994
↓ Personality 1967
↓ Physical Disorders 1997
Premorbidity 1978
Response Bias 1967
Risk Factors 2001
Susceptibility (Disorders) 1973

Prednisolone 1973
PN 58 **SC** 39980
B Adrenal Cortex Hormones 1973
Corticosteroids 1973

Preference Measures 1973
PN 735 **SC** 39990
B Measurement 1967
N Kuder Preference Record 1973
Least Preferred Coworker Scale 1973
R ↓ Attitude Measures 1967
↓ Preferences 1967

Preferences 1967
PN 9426 **SC** 39995
N Aesthetic Preferences 1973
Brand Preferences 1994
Food Preferences 1973
Occupational Preference 1973
R ↓ Preference Measures 1973
Preferred Rewards 1973

Preferred Rewards 1973
PN 169 **SC** 40030
B Rewards 1967
R ↓ Preferences 1967

Prefrontal Cortex 1994
PN 3788 **SC** 40035
B Frontal Lobe 1973

Preganglionic Autonomic Fibers
Use Autonomic Ganglia

Pregnancy 1967
PN 7852 **SC** 40050
UF Gestation
N Adolescent Pregnancy 1988
R ↓ Birth 1967
Childbirth Training 1978
Fertilization 1973
Life Changes 2004
Obstetrical Complications 1978
Perinatal Period 1994
Placenta 1973

Pregnancy — (cont'd)
Postnatal Period 1973
↓ Prenatal Care 1991
Primipara 2001
Reproductive Technology 1988
Safe Sex 2003
↓ Sexual Reproduction 1973
Sexual Risk Taking 1997

Pregnancy (False)
Use Pseudocyesis

Prejudice 1967
PN 2898 **SC** 40070
B Social Influences 1967
N ↓ Religious Prejudices 1973
R Age Discrimination 1994
AntiSemitism 1973
↓ Attitudes 1967
Disability Discrimination 1997
Employment Discrimination 1994
Hate Crimes 2003
Race and Ethnic Discrimination 1994
↓ Racial and Ethnic Attitudes 1982
Racial and Ethnic Relations 1982
Racism 1973
Sex Discrimination 1978
Sexism 1988
Stereotyped Attitudes 1967
Stigma 1991

Preliminary Scholastic Aptitude Test
Use College Entrance Examination Board Scholastic Aptitude Test

Premarital Counseling 1973
PN 212 **SC** 40090
B Counseling 1967
R ↓ Psychotherapeutic Counseling 1973

Premarital Intercourse 1973
PN 387 **SC** 40100
B Sexual Intercourse (Human) 1973
R ↓ Birth Control 1971
Promiscuity 1973
Social Dating 1973
Unwed Mothers 1973
Virginity 1973

Premature Birth 1973
PN 2176 **SC** 40110
B Birth 1967
R Birth Weight 1985
Obstetrical Complications 1978

Premature Ejaculation 1973
PN 221 **SC** 40120
B Male Orgasm 1973
Sexual Function Disturbances 1973

Premenstrual Dysphoric Disorder 2004
PN 194 **SC** 40113
SN A more severe and disabling form of premenstrual syndrome in which mood symptoms are the primary characteristic.
HN This term was introduced in June 2004. Relevant records were re-indexed with this term. The posting note reflects the number of records that were re-indexed.
B Menstrual Disorders 1973
R ↓ Affective Disorders 2001
↓ Menstrual Cycle 1973
Premenstrual Syndrome 2003

Premenstrual Syndrome 2003
PN 1197 **SC** 40115
SN Physiological, emotional, and mental stress related to the period of time immediately preceding menstruation.
HN In June 2003, this term replaced the discontinued term PREMENSTRUAL TENSION. PREMENSTRUAL TENSION was removed from all records containing it and replaced with PREMENSTRUAL SYNDROME.
UF PMS
Premenstrual Tension
B Syndromes 1973
R ↓ Menstrual Cycle 1973
↓ Menstrual Disorders 1973
Premenstrual Dysphoric Disorder 2004

Premenstrual Tension
HN In June 2003, the term was discontinued and removed from all records containing it, and was replaced with PREMENSTRUAL SYNDROME, its postable counterpart.
Use Premenstrual Syndrome

Premorbidity 1978
PN 1075 **SC** 40135
SN Condition of an individual before onset of illness or disorder.
R At Risk Populations 1985
↓ Disorders 1967
↓ Mental Disorders 1967
Onset (Disorders) 1973
Patient History 1973
↓ Physical Disorders 1997
Predisposition 1973
Susceptibility (Disorders) 1973

Prenatal Care 1991
PN 615 **SC** 40137
SN Medical, health, and educational services provided or obtained during pregnancy. Includes maternal health behavior affecting prenatal development.
N Childbirth Training 1978
R Early Intervention 1982
↓ Health Behavior 1982
↓ Health Care Services 1978
↓ Health Education 1973
↓ Obstetrics 1978
↓ Pregnancy 1967
↓ Prenatal Development 1973
Prenatal Diagnosis 1988
↓ Prevention 1973
Preventive Medicine 1973

Prenatal Development 1973
PN 2776 **SC** 40140
SN Development of an organism prior to birth. Used for human or animal populations.
B Physical Development 1973
N ↓ Prenatal Developmental Stages 1973
R Animal Development 1978
Fetal Alcohol Syndrome 1985
Perinatal Period 1994
↓ Prenatal Care 1991
Prenatal Diagnosis 1988
Prenatal Exposure 1991
↓ Psychogenesis 1973
Teratogens 1988

Prenatal Developmental Stages 1973
PN 68 **SC** 40150
B Developmental Stages 1973
Prenatal Development 1973
N Embryo 1973
Fetus 1967

Prenatal Diagnosis 1988
PN 332 **SC** 40152
SN Techniques or procedures used to detect or identify specific abnormalities or characteristics of the fetus.
UF Amniocentesis
B Medical Diagnosis 1973
R ↓ Congenital Disorders 1973
↓ Genetic Disorders 1973
↓ Prenatal Care 1991
↓ Prenatal Development 1973
Reproductive Technology 1988

Prenatal Exposure 1991
PN 2989 **SC** 40156
SN Exposure to chemicals or other environmental factors prior to birth. Used for human and animal populations.
UF Fetal Exposure
R ↓ Alcoholic Beverages 1973
↓ Disorders 1967
↓ Drugs 1967
↓ Environmental Effects 1973
↓ Physical Disorders 1997
↓ Prenatal Development 1973
Teratogens 1988
Thalidomide 1973
↓ Tobacco Smoking 1967
↓ Toxins 2007

Preoptic Area 1994
PN 309 **SC** 40158
SN Brain region situated immediately below the anterior commissure, above the optic chiasm, and anterior to the hypothalamus. The preoptic area regulates certain autonomic activities in connection with the hypothalamus.
HN Consider HYPOTHALAMUS to access references prior to 1994.
B Hypothalamus 1967

Prepulse Inhibition 1997
PN 630 **SC** 40159
SN Markedly reduced startle response resulting from a weaker stimulus preceding a stronger startle-inducing stimulus.
R Conditioned Suppression 1973
↓ Latent Inhibition 1997
Sensory Gating 1991
Startle Reflex 1967

Presbyterians
Use Protestants

Preschool Education 1973
PN 2087 **SC** 40170
B Education 1967
R Project Head Start 1973

Preschool Students 1982
PN 4000 **SC** 40173
SN Students from infancy to entrance in kindergarten or 1st grade.

Preschool Students — (cont'd)
B Students 1967
N Nursery School Students 1973
R Kindergarten Students 1973

Preschool Teachers 1985
PN 687 **SC** 40176
B Teachers 1967

Prescribing (Drugs) 1991
PN 1511 **SC** 40177
N Prescription Privileges 2005
R ↓ Drug Therapy 1967
↓ Drugs 1967
Polypharmacy 2004
↓ Treatment 1967

Prescription Drugs 1991
PN 760 **SC** 40178
B Drugs 1967
R ↓ Drug Therapy 1967
Nonprescription Drugs 1991
Pharmaceutical Industry 2007
Self Medication 1991

Prescription Privileges 2005
PN 65 **SC** 40179
SN The authority to prescribe medication.
HN This term was introduced in August 2005. Relevant records were re-indexed with this term. The posting note reflects the number of records that were re-indexed.
B Prescribing (Drugs) 1991

Presenile Dementia 1973
PN 238 **SC** 40180
SN A disorder in which deterioration of the brain leads to dementia, with onset ocurring before the age of 65. The disease is marked by loss of memory and a decline in other cognitive and intellectual skills.
UF Dementia (Presenile)
B Dementia 1985
N Alzheimers Disease 1973
Creutzfeldt Jakob Syndrome 1994
Picks Disease 1973
R ↓ Senile Dementia 1973

Preservice Teachers 1982
PN 1457 **SC** 40205
SN Education students or graduates prior to employment as teachers.
B Teachers 1967
R ↓ College Students 1967
Education Students 1982
Student Teachers 1973
Student Teaching 1973
↓ Teacher Education 1967

Presidential Debates
Use Debates

Pressoreceptors
Use Baroreceptors

Pressors (Drugs)
Use Vasoconstrictor Drugs

Pressure Sensation 1973
PN 148 **SC** 40270
R Somatosensory Disorders 2001
↓ Somesthetic Perception 1967

Prestige (Occupational)
Use Occupational Status

Pretend Play 2005
PN 179 **SC** 40277
SN A form of childhood play behavior that involves make-believe activities.
HN This term was introduced in August 2005. Relevant records were re-indexed with this term. The posting note reflects the number of records that were re-indexed.
B Childhood Play Behavior 1978
R Childhood Play Development 1973
Childrens Recreational Games 1973
Creativity 1967
Imagination 1967

Pretesting 1973
PN 186 **SC** 40280
SN Running preliminary trials to establish a baseline. Comparison of pretest and posttest scores gives a measure of effectiveness of independent variables such as treatments or programs.
B Measurement 1967
R Repeated Measures 1985
↓ Testing Methods 1967

Pretraining (Therapy)
Use Client Education

Prevention 1973
PN 11947 **SC** 40290
SN Conceptually broad term referring to any process that acts to deter undesirable occurrences. Use a more specific term if possible.
N Accident Prevention 1973
AIDS Prevention 1994
Crime Prevention 1985
Drug Abuse Prevention 1994
Fire Prevention 1973
Preventive Medicine 1973
Primary Mental Health Prevention 1973
Relapse Prevention 1994
Suicide Prevention 1973
R Condoms 1991
Disability Management 1991
Early Intervention 1982
↓ Health Care Delivery 1978
↓ Health Care Services 1978
↓ Health Education 1973
Health Promotion 1991
↓ Intervention 2003
↓ Mental Health Services 1978
↓ Prenatal Care 1991
Protective Factors 2007
Public Service Announcements 2004
Risk Management 1997
Risk Perception 1997
↓ Safety 1967
Suicide Prevention Centers 1973
↓ Treatment 1967

Preventive Medicine 1973
PN 1057 **SC** 40300
B Prevention 1973
Treatment 1967
R ↓ Alternative Medicine 1997
Drug Abuse Prevention 1994
Genetic Testing 2003
↓ Health 1973
↓ Health Behavior 1982
Health Maintenance Organizations 1982
Health Promotion 1991
↓ Health Screening 1997

Preventive Medicine — (cont'd)
Holistic Health 1985
Mammography 1994
Physical Examination 1988
↓ Prenatal Care 1991
Relapse Prevention 1994

Price
Use Costs and Cost Analysis

Pride 1973
PN 231 **SC** 40310
B Emotional States 1973

Priests 1973
PN 319 **SC** 40320
B Clergy 1973
R Chaplains 1973
Missionaries 1973

Primacy Effect 1973
PN 281 **SC** 40328
SN Component of the serial position effect which is manifested by a greater ease in learning items that occur at the beginning of a series rather than those toward the middle. Compare RECENCY EFFECT.
B Serial Position Effect 1982
R ↓ Learning 1967
Recency Effect 1973

Primal Therapy 1978
PN 58 **SC** 40329
SN Combination of intensive individual therapy and group psychotherapy with emphasis on experiencing and expression of blocked traumatic events or feelings (primals) and their integration into total life functioning.
B Psychotherapy 1967
R ↓ Psychotherapeutic Techniques 1967

Primary Health Care 1988
PN 5337 **SC** 40331
SN Health care provided by a medical professional with whom a patient has initial contact when entering the health care system and by whom a patient may be referred to a specialist.
B Health Care Services 1978
R ↓ Health Care Delivery 1978

Primary Mental Health Prevention 1973
PN 1949 **SC** 40330
SN Mental health programs designed to prevent onset or occurrence of mental illness in high risk or target populations.
B Prevention 1973
R Drug Abuse Prevention 1994
Early Intervention 1982
↓ Mental Health 1967
↓ Mental Health Programs 1973
Relapse Prevention 1994

Primary Reinforcement 1973
PN 71 **SC** 40340
SN Presentation of a primary reinforcer. Also, objects or events which do not require prior pairing with other reinforcers in order to maintain reinforcing properties. Also known as unconditioned reinforcers or unconditioned stimuli. Compare EXTERNAL REWARDS.
B Reinforcement 1967
R ↓ Conditioning 1967
Unconditioned Stimulus 1973

Primary School Students 1973
PN 1020 **SC** 40350
SN Students in kindergarten through 3rd grade. Use ELEMENTARY SCHOOL STUDENTS or KINDERGARTEN STUDENTS unless specific reference is made to population as primary school students.
B Elementary School Students 1967

Primary Schools
Use Elementary Schools

Primates (Nonhuman) 1973
PN 2787 **SC** 40370
UF Apes
B Mammals 1973
N Baboons 1973
Bonobos 1997
Chimpanzees 1973
Gorillas 1973
Monkeys 1967

Primidone 1973
PN 23 **SC** 40380
B Anticonvulsive Drugs 1973
R ↓ Barbiturates 1967

Priming 1988
PN 3620 **SC** 40385
N Semantic Priming 1994
R Contextual Associations 1967
Cues 1967
↓ Perception 1967
↓ Prompting 1997
↓ Semantics 1967

Primipara 2001
PN 37 **SC** 40325
SN Pregnant with, or having borne, only one child or offspring.
R ↓ Mothers 1967
↓ Pregnancy 1967

Printed Communications Media 1973
PN 1001 **SC** 40390
B Mass Media 1967
N ↓ Books 1973
Magazines 1973
Newspapers 1973

Printing (Handwriting) 1973
PN 57 **SC** 40400
B Handwriting 1967

Prismatic Stimulation 1973
PN 246 **SC** 40410
SN Visual stimulation technique in which special lenses are used to spatially distort or invert visual images or the visual field. Also includes prisms that differentially refract light of different wavelengths to produce an array or spectrum of colors.
B Visual Stimulation 1973
R ↓ Color Perception 1967
Spatial Distortion 1973

Prison Personnel 1973
PN 699 **SC** 40420
B Law Enforcement Personnel 1973
R Attendants (Institutions) 1973

Prison Record
Use Criminal Record

Prisoner Abuse 2007
PN 3 **SC** 40427
SN Mistreatment of incarcerated individuals.
HN This term was introduced in April 2007. Relevant records were re-indexed with this term. The posting note reflects the number of records that were re-indexed.
R Abuse of Power 1997
Physical Abuse 1991
↓ Prisoners 1967
Torture 1988

Prisoners 1967
PN 5571 **SC** 40430
UF Inmates (Prison)
N Prisoners of War 1973
R Criminal Rehabilitation 2004
↓ Criminals 1967
Prisoner Abuse 2007

Prisoners Dilemma Game 1973
PN 512 **SC** 40440
SN Nonzero-sum game in which individual outcomes are determined by joint actions of two players. Incentives for both cooperation and competition exist, and no communication is permitted between the two players.
B Games 1967
R Entrapment Games 1973
Game Theory 1967
Non Zero Sum Games 1973
Social Dilemma 2003

Prisoners of War 1973
PN 261 **SC** 40450
B Prisoners 1967
R Hostages 1988

Prisons 1967
PN 2377 **SC** 40460
UF Jails
Penitentiaries
B Correctional Institutions 1973
R Concentration Camps 1973
Criminal Rehabilitation 2004
Reformatories 1973

Privacy 1973
PN 872 **SC** 40467
R Privileged Communication 1973
Secrecy 1994
↓ Social Behavior 1967

Private Practice 1978
PN 807 **SC** 40469
SN Employment of professional personnel in independent for-profit practices (as opposed to public offices or nonprofit settings) in which there is direct contact with clients and payment for services rendered. Private practitioners may function in individual practices, partnerships, or incorporated business settings.
R ↓ Health Care Delivery 1978

Private School Education 1973
PN 632 **SC** 40470
SN Schools or formal education in schools supported and administered by organizations not affiliated with the government.

Private School Education — (cont'd)
UF Parochial School Education
B Education 1967
R Religious Education 1973

Private Sector 1985
PN 752 **SC** 40475
SN Any type of non-government organization, service, or sphere of involvement.
N ↓ Business Organizations 1973
R Entrepreneurship 1991
Ownership 1985

Privileged Communication 1973
PN 1513 **SC** 40480
SN Confidential communication between doctors, lawyers, or therapists and their clients which, by legal sanction, may not be revealed to others. Also, any documents or recorded statements of such communication which can be legally withheld from public inspection.
UF Communication (Privileged)
Confidentiality of Information
R ↓ Abuse Reporting 1997
Anonymity 1973
Client Records 1997
↓ Communication 1967
Duty to Warn 2001
Information 1967
Privacy 1973
Professional Ethics 1973
↓ Psychotherapeutic Processes 1967

Proactive Inhibition 1973
PN 796 **SC** 40490
SN The theory that previous learning of material can interfere with the retention of newly-learned material. Also, the actual proactive interference itself.
UF Inhibition (Proactive)
B Interference (Learning) 1967
Latent Inhibition 1997

Probability 1967
PN 2418 **SC** 40500
SN The likelihood of the chance occurrence of specific events. May include the mathematical study of probability theory.
N ↓ Chance (Fortune) 1973
Response Probability 1973
↓ Statistical Probability 1967
R Chaos Theory 1997
↓ Hypothesis Testing 1973
Predictability (Measurement) 1973
Probability Judgment 1978
Probability Learning 1967

Probability Judgment 1978
PN 1288 **SC** 40505
SN Process of ascertaining or estimating the degree of likelihood that certain specified conditions or events have, can, or will occur.
B Judgment 1967
R ↓ Probability 1967
Probability Learning 1967

Probability Learning 1967
PN 639 **SC** 40510
SN Experimental paradigm in which subjects are asked to guess or estimate whether an experimentally controlled event will occur or choose which of various alternative events will occur. As learning

Probability Learning — (cont'd)
occurs, the proportion of correct responses tends to approach the actual probability proportion of event occurrences. Used for the experimental paradigm or task as well as the learned behavior itself.
B Learning 1967
R ↓ Probability 1967
Probability Judgment 1978

Probation 1973
PN 672 **SC** 40520
SN Period of suspended sentence of a convicted offender following good behavior and during which the offender is not incarcerated but is under the supervision of a probation officer.
B Legal Processes 1973
R Court Referrals 1994
Criminal Rehabilitation 2004
↓ Law Enforcement 1978
Parole 1973

Probation Officers 1973
PN 273 **SC** 40530
B Law Enforcement Personnel 1973
R Parole Officers 1973

Probenecid 1982
PN 17 **SC** 40535
SN Agent that promotes the urinary excretion of uric acid.
R ↓ Diuretics 1973

Problem Drinking
HN Term discontinued in 1988. In 2000, the term was removed from all records containing it, and replaced with ALCOHOL ABUSE, its postable counterpart.
Use Alcohol Abuse

Problem Solving 1967
PN 15926 **SC** 40550
SN Process of determining a correct sequence of alternatives leading to a desired goal or to successful completion or performance of a task.
UF Individual Problem Solving
B Cognitive Processes 1967
N Anagram Problem Solving 1973
Cognitive Hypothesis Testing 1982
↓ Group Problem Solving 1973
Heuristics 2003
R Case Based Reasoning 2003
Communities of Practice 2007
Critical Thinking 2006
↓ Decision Making 1967
Declarative Knowledge 1997
↓ Expert Systems 1991
↓ Inductive Deductive Reasoning 1973
↓ Reasoning 1967
Solution Focused Therapy 2004

Procaine 1982
PN 96 **SC** 40560
HN In 1982, this term replaced the discontinued term NOVOCAINE. In 2000, NOVOCAINE was removed from all records and replaced with PROCAINE.
UF Novocaine
B Analgesic Drugs 1973
Anesthetic Drugs 1973

Procedural Justice 2003
PN 392 **SC** 40563
SN The perceived fairness of the process by which decisions are made and outcomes are determined.
HN This term was introduced in June 2003. Relevant records were re-indexed with this term. The posting note reflects the number of records that were re-indexed.
B Justice 1973
R ↓ Organizational Behavior 1978

Procedural Knowledge 1997
PN 618 **SC** 40565
SN Knowledge regarding how to do things. Compare DECLARATIVE KNOWLEDGE.
UF Functional Knowledge
Practical Knowledge
R ↓ Cognitive Processes 1967
Declarative Knowledge 1997
Divergent Thinking 1973
Information 1967
↓ Knowledge Level 1978
↓ Memory 1967
Metacognition 1991
↓ Reasoning 1967

Process Psychosis
HN In August 2005, the term was discontinued and removed from all records containing it, and replaced with PROCESS SCHIZOPHRENIA, its postable counterpart.
Use Process Schizophrenia

Process Schizophrenia 2005
PN 68 **SC** 40580
SN A form of schizophrenia that begins early in life, develops gradually, and is attributed to endogenous causes.
HN In August 2005, this term replaced the discontinued term PROCESS PSYCHOSIS. PROCESS PSYCHOSIS was removed from all records containing it, and replaced with PROCESS SCHIZOPHRENIA, its postable counterpart.
UF Process Psychosis
B Schizophrenia 1967

Prochlorperazine 1973
PN 18 **SC** 40640
B Antiemetic Drugs 1973
Phenothiazine Derivatives 1973

Procrastination 1985
PN 295 **SC** 40645
SN Habitual, often counterproductive postponing.
HN Use STUDY HABITS to access references in educational contexts from 1973-1984.
B Motivation 1967

Prodrome 2004
PN 123 **SC** 40646
SN A premonitory symptom or early warning sign of a mental or physical disorder.
HN This term was introduced in June 2004. Relevant records were re-indexed with this term. The posting note reflects the number of records that were re-indexed.
B Symptoms 1967
R Onset (Disorders) 1973

Product Design 1997
PN 914 **SC** 40647
SN Process of conceptualizing, planning, researching, developing, and field testing products or goods.

Product Design — (cont'd)
UF Consumer Product Design
R ↓ Advertising 1967
Computer Assisted Design 1997
Consumer Protection 1973
↓ Consumer Research 1973
Consumer Surveys 1973
↓ Marketing 1973
Research and Development 2007
Supply Chains 2007

Productivity 2007
PN 648 **SC** 40649
SN Conceptually broad term, having application across broad disciplines, and dealing with the measurement of output in relationship to input.
HN This term was introduced in April 2007. Relevant records were re-indexed with this term. The posting note reflects the number of records that were re-indexed.
N Employee Productivity 1973
R ↓ Achievement 1967
↓ Performance 1967

Productivity (Employee)
Use Employee Productivity

Profanity 1991
PN 25 **SC** 40655
B Language 1967
R Obscenity 1978

Professional Certification 1973
PN 1015 **SC** 40660
SN In general, certification constitutes permission to use a particular professional title contingent on fulfilling requisite educational and training programs.
UF Certification (Professional)
N Accreditation (Education Personnel) 1973
R Professional Development 1982
Professional Examinations 1994
↓ Professional Licensing 1973
↓ Professional Personnel 1978

Professional Client Sexual Relations 1994
PN 423 **SC** 40665
SN Sexual relations, intimacy, or affectionate behavior between a professional (e.g., therapist, lawyer, religious personnel, or educator) and his or her clients or patients.
UF Boundary Violations (Sexual)
Patient Therapist Sexual Relations
Sexual Boundary Violations
Therapist Patient Sexual Relations
R Countertransference 1973
Dual Relationships 2003
Patient Abuse 1991
Professional Ethics 1973
↓ Professional Standards 1973
↓ Psychosexual Behavior 1967
↓ Psychotherapeutic Processes 1967
Psychotherapeutic Transference 1967
↓ Sexual Abuse 1988
Sexual Harassment 1985
↓ Therapeutic Processes 1978

Professional Communication
Use Scientific Communication

Professional Competence 1997
PN 1817 **SC** 40675
SN Possessing the knowledge and qualifications of a particular profession.

Professional Competence — (cont'd)
B Competence 1982
R ↓ Employee Characteristics 1988
↓ Employee Skills 1973
Peer Evaluation 1982
↓ Personnel Evaluation 1973
Professional Development 1982
Professional Liability 1985
↓ Professional Standards 1973
Professionalism 2003

Professional Consultation 1973
PN 5293 **SC** 40680
SN Advisory services offered by specialists in a particular field which may be client or colleague oriented or focus on policy setting, planning, and programs of an organization.
HN In 1982, this term replaced the discontinued term MENTAL HEALTH CONSULTATION. In 2000, MENTAL HEALTH CONSULTATION was removed from all records containing it and replaced with PROFESSIONAL CONSULTATION.
UF Consultation (Professional)
Mental Health Consultation
N Consultation Liaison Psychiatry 1991
R Personal Therapy 1991
↓ Professional Personnel 1978
Professional Supervision 1988

Professional Development 1982
PN 4631 **SC** 40715
SN Participation in activities that promote professional career development.
B Development 1967
R Career Change 1978
Career Development 1985
↓ Continuing Education 1985
Employment History 1978
Inservice Teacher Education 1973
↓ Inservice Training 1985
Mental Health Inservice Training 1973
Mentor 1985
Occupational Aspirations 1973
↓ Professional Certification 1973
Professional Competence 1997
Professional Identity 1991
↓ Professional Personnel 1978
Professional Recognition 2005
Professional Specialization 1991
↓ Professional Standards 1973

Professional Ethics 1973
PN 9978 **SC** 40720
SN Moral principles of conducting professional research or practices.
B Ethics 1967
R ↓ Abuse Reporting 1997
Assisted Suicide 1997
Bioethics 2003
Conflict of Interest 2005
Dual Relationships 2003
Duty to Warn 2001
Euthanasia 1973
Experimental Ethics 1978
Impaired Professionals 1985
Informed Consent 1985
Nepotism 2005
Privileged Communication 1973
Professional Client Sexual Relations 1994
Professional Liability 1985
↓ Professional Personnel 1978
↓ Professional Standards 1973

Professional Examinations 1994
PN 291 **SC** 40723
SN Required examinations for licensure or certification in order to practice a profession.
UF Certification Examinations
Licensure Examinations
State Board Examinations
B Measurement 1967
R Accreditation (Education Personnel) 1973
↓ Professional Certification 1973
↓ Professional Licensing 1973

Professional Fees 1978
PN 392 **SC** 40724
N Fee for Service 1994
R Cost Containment 1991
↓ Costs and Cost Analysis 1973
Diagnosis Related Groups 1988
Health Care Costs 1994
Money 1967
Peer Evaluation 1982
↓ Professional Personnel 1978
Salaries 1973

Professional Identity 1991
PN 1320 **SC** 40725
SN Concept of self and role within a professional domain.
UF Identity (Professional)
B Social Identity 1988
R Career Development 1985
↓ Employee Characteristics 1988
Professional Development 1982
↓ Professional Personnel 1978
Professionalism 2003
Role Perception 1973
↓ Self Concept 1967

Professional Liability 1985
PN 1355 **SC** 40727
SN Legal liabilities relating to the conduct of one's profession.
UF Legal Liability (Professional)
Malpractice
B Professional Standards 1973
R Accountability 1988
Duty to Warn 2001
Impaired Professionals 1985
↓ Legal Processes 1973
Misdiagnosis 1997
Patient Abuse 1991
Professional Competence 1997
Professional Ethics 1973
↓ Responsibility 1973
Risk Management 1997

Professional Licensing 1973
PN 802 **SC** 40730
SN Permission from an authority (e.g., government review board) to use a particular professional title as well as to practice the profession. Professional licensing laws also specify what activities constitute the legal or legitimate practice of the profession. One does not necessarily need to be certified (professionally) in order to be licensed.
UF Licensing (Professional)
N Accreditation (Education Personnel) 1973
R ↓ Professional Certification 1973
Professional Examinations 1994
↓ Professional Personnel 1978

Professional Networking 2004
PN 154 **SC** 40740
SN A linkage, association, or partnership of individuals or groups who collaborate to achieve professional goals or objectives.
HN This term was introduced in June 2004. Relevant records were re-indexed with this term. The posting note reflects the number of records that were re-indexed.
UF Business Networking
R Career Development 1985
Communities of Practice 2007
Online Social Networks 2007
↓ Organizational Behavior 1978
↓ Social Networks 1994

Professional Newsletters
Use Scientific Communication

Professional Organizations 1973
PN 5008 **SC** 40760
B Organizations 1967
N American Psychological Association 2007
R American Psychological Association Divisions 2007
↓ Professional Personnel 1978

Professional Orientation
Use Theoretical Orientation

Professional Personnel 1978
PN 2843 **SC** 40765
SN Conceptually broad term referring to members of professions requiring prolonged and specialized training. Use a more specific term if possible.
B Personnel 1967
N ↓ Aerospace Personnel 1973
Anthropologists 1973
Clinicians 1973
↓ Counselors 1967
↓ Educational Personnel 1973
Engineers 1967
↓ Health Personnel 1994
↓ Information Specialists 1988
Journalists 1973
↓ Legal Personnel 1985
Mathematicians 1973
Physicists 1973
↓ Psychologists 1967
Scientists 1967
Sociologists 1973
↓ Therapists 1967
R ↓ Business and Industrial Personnel 1967
Impaired Professionals 1985
Librarians 1988
↓ Nonprofessional Personnel 1982
↓ Occupations 1967
↓ Paraprofessional Personnel 1973
↓ Professional Certification 1973
↓ Professional Consultation 1973
Professional Development 1982
Professional Ethics 1973
↓ Professional Fees 1978
Professional Identity 1991
↓ Professional Licensing 1973
↓ Professional Organizations 1973
Professional Referral 1973
Professional Specialization 1991
↓ Professional Standards 1973
Professional Supervision 1988
↓ Religious Personnel 1973

Professional Recognition 2005
PN 331 **SC** 40767
SN Acknowledgement of one's professional performance and qualities.
HN This term was introduced in August 2005. Relevant records were re-indexed with this term. The posting note reflects the number of records that were re-indexed.
UF Employee Recognition
R Awards (Merit) 2005
Employee Motivation 1973
Employee Productivity 1973
Occupational Status 1978
Occupational Success 1978
Personnel Promotion 1978
Professional Development 1982
↓ Rewards 1967

Professional Referral 1973
PN 2360 **SC** 40770
SN Act of directing a client to a professional or agency for assessment, treatment, or consultation.
UF Referral (Professional)
R Client Transfer 1997
Court Referrals 1994
↓ Professional Personnel 1978
Self Referral 1991

Professional Specialization 1991
PN 776 **SC** 40775
SN Training in or choice of a speciality within a profession.
UF Specialization (Professional)
R Academic Specialization 1973
Career Development 1985
↓ Higher Education 1973
Occupational Choice 1967
Occupational Preference 1973
↓ Postgraduate Training 1973
Professional Development 1982
↓ Professional Personnel 1978

Professional Standards 1973
PN 4435 **SC** 40780
SN Minimally acceptable levels of quality professional care or services maintained in order to promote the welfare of those who make use of such services.
UF Standards (Professional)
N Professional Liability 1985
R Accountability 1988
Duty to Warn 2001
Impaired Professionals 1985
Patient Abuse 1991
Peer Evaluation 1982
Professional Client Sexual Relations 1994
Professional Competence 1997
Professional Development 1982
Professional Ethics 1973
↓ Professional Personnel 1978
Professionalism 2003
↓ Quality of Services 1997
Treatment Guidelines 2001

Professional Supervision 1988
PN 3124 **SC** 40785
SN Processes or techniques of supervision of fully trained educational or mental health personnel.
UF Clinical Supervision
Educational Supervision
Supervision (Professional)
R ↓ Educational Personnel 1973
↓ Mental Health Personnel 1967
Personal Therapy 1991

Professional Supervision — (cont'd)
↓ Professional Consultation 1973
↓ Professional Personnel 1978

Professionalism 2003
PN 475 **SC** 40788
SN Conduct, attitudes, and methods attributed to professionals.
HN This term was introduced in June 2003. Relevant records were re-indexed with this term. The posting note reflects the number of records that were re-indexed.
R ↓ Employee Characteristics 1988
Professional Competence 1997
Professional Identity 1991
↓ Professional Standards 1973
Work (Attitudes Toward) 1973

Professors
Use College Teachers

Profiles (Measurement) 1973
PN 1847 **SC** 40800
SN Usually a composite of scores obtained through psychological testing utilizing instruments which yield separate measures and which comprises a picture or profile of the individual's characteristics across several areas.
B Measurement 1967

Profound Mental Retardation 2001
PN 1468 **SC** 40805
SN IQ below 20.
HN In 2000, this term replaced the discontinued and deleted term PROFOUNDLY MENTALLY RETARDED. PROFOUNDLY MENTALLY RETARDED was removed from all records containing it and replaced with PROFOUND MENTAL RETARDATION.
B Mental Retardation 1967

Progestational Hormones 1985
PN 148 **SC** 40815
UF Progestins
B Hormones 1967
N Progesterone 1973

Progesterone 1973
PN 1259 **SC** 40820
B Progestational Hormones 1985
Sex Hormones 1973
Steroids 1973

Progestins
Use Progestational Hormones

Prognosis 1973
PN 3689 **SC** 40830
SN Prediction of the course, duration, and outcome of a disorder. Compare DISEASE COURSE.
R Biological Markers 1991
↓ Chronic Mental Illness 1997
Clinical Judgment (Not Diagnosis) 1973
↓ Diagnosis 1967
Disease Course 1991
↓ Disorders 1967
↓ Medical Diagnosis 1973
↓ Mental Disorders 1967
Patient History 1973
↓ Physical Disorders 1997
↓ Prediction 1967
↓ Psychodiagnosis 1967
Severity (Disorders) 1982
↓ Treatment 1967

Program Development 1991
PN 2930 **SC** 40832
SN Formulation and/or implementation of programs in any setting.
UF Program Planning
B Development 1967
N Educational Program Planning 1973
R Curriculum Development 1973
↓ Educational Programs 1973
Employee Assistance Programs 1985
↓ Government Programs 1973
Home Visiting Programs 1973
↓ Hospital Programs 1978
Independent Living Programs 1991
↓ Mental Health Programs 1973
↓ Program Evaluation 1985
↓ Psychiatric Hospital Programs 1967
↓ Social Programs 1973

Program Evaluation 1985
PN 6868 **SC** 40835
SN Assessment of programs in any setting.
B Evaluation 1967
N Educational Program Evaluation 1973
Mental Health Program Evaluation 1973
R ↓ Program Development 1991

Program Evaluation (Educational)
Use Educational Program Evaluation

Program Evaluation (Mental Health)
Use Mental Health Program Evaluation

Program Planning
Use Program Development

Program Planning (Educational)
Use Educational Program Planning

Programmed Instruction 2001
PN 1043 **SC** 40870
HN In 2000, this term was created to update the spelling from the discontinued term PROGRAMED INSTRUCTION. PROGRAMED INSTRUCTION was removed from all records containing it and replaced with PROGRAMMED INSTRUCTION.
UF Instruction (Programmed)
B Teaching Methods 1967
R ↓ Computer Assisted Instruction 1973
Individualized Instruction 1973
Programmed Textbooks 2001
↓ Prompting 1997
Teaching Machines 1973

Programmed Textbooks 2001
PN 48 **SC** 40900
SN Textbooks prepared for use with programmed instruction. Not used as a document type identifier.
HN In 2000, this term was created to update the spelling from the discontinued term PROGRAMED TEXTBOOKS. PROGRAMED TEXTBOOKS was removed from all records containing it and replaced with PROGRAMMED TEXTBOOKS.
B Textbooks 1978
R Programmed Instruction 2001

Programming (Computer)
HN Use COMPUTER SOFTWARE to access references from 1973-1993.
Use Computer Programming

Programming Languages (Computer)
Use Computer Programming Languages

Programs (Government)
Use Government Programs

Programs (Mental Health)
Use Mental Health Programs

Progressive Relaxation Therapy 1978
PN 613 **SC** 40945
SN Therapeutic procedures which teach clients to tense and relax muscle groups, focusing on the sensations involved in relaxation. This method provides clients with practice in recognizing the sensation of tension which will serve as a cue to produce a state of muscle relaxation.
B Relaxation Therapy 1978
R ↓ Hypnotherapy 1973
Muscle Relaxation 1973
Systematic Desensitization Therapy 1973

Progressive Supranuclear Palsy 1997
PN 97 **SC** 40947
SN A progressive neurological disorder characterized by ophthalmoplegia, dystonia, memory impairment, personality disorders, and dementia. Etiology is unknown.
B Central Nervous System Disorders 1973
R ↓ Basal Ganglia 1973
↓ Senile Dementia 1973

Project Follow Through 1973
PN 42 **SC** 40950
SN U.S. Government educational program for disadvantaged elementary school students to supplement Project Head Start and encourage academic and psychosocial growth.
B Educational Programs 1973
Government Programs 1973
R Compensatory Education 1973
Government 1967

Project Head Start 1973
PN 790 **SC** 40960
SN U.S. Government program for disadvantaged 3-5 yr olds aimed at improving children's educational potential by encouraging their psychosocial development and by providing economic assistance to their families.
UF Head Start
B Educational Programs 1973
Government Programs 1973
R Compensatory Education 1973
Government 1967
Preschool Education 1973
School Readiness 1973

Projection (Defense Mechanism) 1967
PN 567 **SC** 40970
B Defense Mechanisms 1967
R Projective Identification 1994

Projective Identification 1994
PN 441 **SC** 40975
B Defense Mechanisms 1967
R Enactments 1997
Identification (Defense Mechanism) 1973
Projection (Defense Mechanism) 1967

Projective Personality Measures 1973
PN 1060 **SC** 40980
SN Tests which derive an indirect and global assessment of personality through the analysis of meaning or structure freely imposed by the subject upon

Projective Personality Measures — (cont'd)
unstructured or ambiguous materials. Use a more specific term if possible. Compare NONPROJECTIVE PERSONALITY MEASURES.
HN In 1997, this term replaced the discontinued terms BLACKY PICTURES TEST, COLOR PYRAMID TEST, and ONOMATOPOEIA AND IMAGES TEST. In 2000, these terms were removed from all records containing them, and replaced with PROJECTIVE PERSONALITY MEASURES.
UF Blacky Pictures Test
Color Pyramid Test
Onomatopoeia and Images Test
B Personality Measures 1967
Projective Techniques 1967
N Bender Gestalt Test 1967
Childrens Apperception Test 1973
Holtzman Inkblot Technique 1967
Human Figures Drawing 1973
Rorschach Test 1967
Rosenzweig Picture Frustration Study 1967
Rotter Incomplete Sentences Blank 1973
Sentence Completion Tests 1991
Szondi Test 1973
Thematic Apperception Test 1967
Zulliger Z Test 1973
R Psychoanalytic Interpretation 1967

Projective Techniques 1967
PN 1821 **SC** 40990
SN Utilization of ambiguous or unstructured stimuli designed to elicit responses which are believed to reveal an individual's attitudes, defense modes or motivations, and personality structure. Also, the specific tests or techniques themselves. Use a more specific term if possible.
UF Projective Tests
N Holtzman Inkblot Technique 1967
↓ Projective Personality Measures 1973
R Psychoanalytic Interpretation 1967

Projective Testing Technique 1973
PN 386 **SC** 41000
SN Administration, construction, scoring, and interpretation of projective tests.
B Measurement 1967

Projective Tests
Use Projective Techniques

Prolactin 1973
PN 1831 **SC** 41020
B Gonadotropic Hormones 1973
Neuropeptides 2003

Proline 1982
PN 26 **SC** 41027
B Amino Acids 1973

Prolixin
Use Fluphenazine

Promazine 1973
PN 26 **SC** 41040
B Phenothiazine Derivatives 1973

Promethazine 1973
PN 53 **SC** 41050
B Antiemetic Drugs 1973
Antihistaminic Drugs 1973
Sedatives 1973

Promiscuity 1973
PN 184 **SC** 41060
UF Sexual Delinquency
B Psychosexual Behavior 1967
R Extramarital Intercourse 1973
Hypersexuality 1973
Infidelity 2006
Premarital Intercourse 1973
Prostitution 1973
Sexual Addiction 1997

Prompting 1997
PN 174 **SC** 41065
N Constant Time Delay 1997
R ↓ Behavior Modification 1973
Cued Recall 1994
Cues 1967
↓ Learning 1967
↓ Learning Strategies 1991
↓ Memory 1967
↓ Priming 1988
Programmed Instruction 2001
↓ Teaching Methods 1967

Pronouns 1973
PN 555 **SC** 41070
B Form Classes (Language) 1973

Pronunciation 1973
PN 621 **SC** 41080
B Speech Characteristics 1973
R Articulation (Speech) 1967

Proofreading 1988
PN 68 **SC** 41085
R Clerical Secretarial Skills 1973
↓ Errors 1967
Orthography 1973
↓ Reading 1967
Verbal Ability 1967
↓ Written Communication 1985

Propaganda 1973
PN 176 **SC** 41090
B Social Influences 1967
R Brainwashing 1982
↓ Persuasive Communication 1967

Propanolol
Use Propranolol

Property
Use Ownership

Propranolol 1973
PN 634 **SC** 41100
UF Propanolol
B Adrenergic Blocking Drugs 1973

Proprioceptors 1973
PN 256 **SC** 41110
SN Sensory receptors located deep in the tissues that are sensitive to body movement and position.
B Nerve Endings 1973
Neural Receptors 1973
Sensory Neurons 1973

Prose 1973
PN 958 **SC** 41120
B Literature 1967
N ↓ Biography 1967
R Creative Writing 1994
Text Structure 1982

Prosencephalon
Use Forebrain

Proserine
Use Neostigmine

Prosocial Behavior 1982
PN 2117 **SC** 41133
SN Positive social behavior generally concerned with promotion of the welfare of others. Limited to human populations.
UF Humanitarian Behavior
B Social Behavior 1967
N Altruism 1973
↓ Assistance (Social Behavior) 1973
Charitable Behavior 1973
Cooperation 1967
Sharing (Social Behavior) 1978
Trust (Social Behavior) 1967
R ↓ Antisocial Behavior 1971
Community Involvement 2003
Faith Based Organizations 2007
Generativity 2001
Volunteers 2003

Prosody 1991
PN 820 **SC** 41134
SN Physical characteristics of speech that indicate linguistic features such as stress, intonation, intensity, and duration of speech sounds.
HN Use INFLECTION to access references from 1988-1990.
B Phonology 1973
N Inflection 1973
R ↓ Linguistics 1973
Morphology (Language) 1973
↓ Phonemes 1973
Sentence Structure 1973
↓ Speech Characteristics 1973

Prosopagnosia 1994
PN 179 **SC** 41135
SN A visual agnosia usually due to brain damage and characterized by an inability to recognize familiar faces, and in some cases, one's own face.
B Agnosia 1973
R Face Perception 1985

Prospective Studies 1997
PN 280 **SC** 41137
SN Used in records discussing issues involved in the process of conducting studies of observations of the same individual or group over an extended period of time, usually to generate prognostic data or incidence rates related to a particular disorder, event, or behavior.
HN From 1997-2000, the term was also used as a mandatory document type identifier; however, this usage has been discontinued due to the advent of Form/Content Type field identifiers. References from 1997-2000 can be accessed using either PROSPECTIVE STUDIES or the Prospective Studies Form/Content Type field identifier.
B Longitudinal Studies 1973
R Retrospective Studies 1997

Prostaglandins 1982
PN 282 **SC** 41136
SN Physiologically potent compounds of ubiquitous occurrence formed from essential fatty acids and affecting the nervous system, female reproductive organs, and metabolism.
R ↓ Anti Inflammatory Drugs 1982
↓ Fatty Acids 1973
↓ Hormones 1967

Prostaglandins — (cont'd)
↓ Neuroleptic Drugs 1973
↓ Sympathomimetic Drugs 1973

Prostate 1973
PN 412 **SC** 41140
B Male Genitalia 1973

Prostate Cancer Screening
Use Cancer Screening

Prostheses 1973
PN 315 **SC** 41150
UF Artificial Limbs
B Medical Therapeutic Devices 1973
N Cochlear Implants 1994
R ↓ Amputation 1973

Prostitution 1973
PN 1157 **SC** 41160
B Psychosexual Behavior 1967
R Human Trafficking 2007
Promiscuity 1973

Protective Factors 2007
PN 908 **SC** 41167
SN Factors that increase or enhance resistance to risk and make less likely the development of problems, problem behavior, or disorders.
HN This term was introduced in April 2007. Relevant records were re-indexed with this term. The posting note reflects the number of records that were re-indexed.
R ↓ Prevention 1973
Resilience (Psychological) 2003
Risk Factors 2001
Risk Management 1997
↓ Safety 1967

Protective Services 1997
PN 859 **SC** 41170
B Social Services 1982
R Child Custody 1982
Child Welfare 1988
Elder Care 1994
Foster Care 1978
Guardianship 1988
↓ Legal Processes 1973
Shelters 1991
Social Casework 1967

Protein Deficiency Disorders 1973
PN 48 **SC** 41180
B Nutritional Deficiencies 1973
N Kwashiorkor 1973

Protein Metabolism 1973
PN 217 **SC** 41190
B Metabolism 1967

Protein Sensitization
Use Anaphylactic Shock

Proteinases 1973
PN 82 **SC** 41210
B Enzymes 1973

Proteins 1973
PN 4813 **SC** 41220
N Apolipoproteins 2004
↓ Blood Proteins 1973
↓ Endorphins 1982

Proteins — (cont'd)
↓ Globulins 1973
Interferons 1994
R ↓ Amino Acids 1973
Creutzfeldt Jakob Syndrome 1994
↓ Drugs 1967
↓ Enzymes 1973
Lipoproteins 1973
↓ Neuropeptides 2003
↓ Peptides 1973

Protest (Student)
Use Student Activism

Protestantism 1973
PN 539 **SC** 41250
B Christianity 1973
R Protestants 1997

Protestants 1997
PN 333 **SC** 41253
UF Baptists
Episcopalians
Lutherans
Methodists
Presbyterians
B Christians 1997
R Protestantism 1973

Protozoa 1973
PN 34 **SC** 41255
B Microorganisms 1985

Prozac
Use Fluoxetine

Pruritus 1973
PN 83 **SC** 41260
SN Intense sensation of itchiness.
UF Itching
B Skin Disorders 1973
Symptoms 1967
R Scratching 1973

Pseudocyesis 1973
PN 91 **SC** 41270
SN False pregnancy; symptoms of pregnancy are experienced without being pregnant.
UF False Pregnancy
Pregnancy (False)
Pseudopregnancy
B Conversion Disorder 2001
R ↓ Gynecological Disorders 1973

Pseudodementia 1985
PN 116 **SC** 41280
SN Dementia-like disorder in the absence of organic brain disease.
B Mental Disorders 1967
R ↓ Dementia 1985
↓ Factitious Disorders 1988
↓ Major Depression 1988

Pseudohermaphroditism
Use Hermaphroditism

Pseudomemory
Use False Memory

Pseudopregnancy
Use Pseudocyesis

Pseudopsychopathic Schizophrenia
HN Term discontinued in 1988. In 2000, the term was removed from all records containing it, and replaced with SCHIZOPHRENIA, its postable counterpart.
Use Schizophrenia

Psilocybin 1973
PN 66 **SC** 41310
B Hallucinogenic Drugs 1967

Psyche
Use Mind

Psychedelic Drugs
HN In April 2007, this term was discontinued and removed from all records containing it, and was replaced with HALLUCINOGENIC DRUGS, its postable counterpart.
Use Hallucinogenic Drugs

Psychedelic Experiences 1973
PN 92 **SC** 41330
R Drug Induced Hallucinations 1973

Psychiatric Aides 1973
PN 100 **SC** 41340
B Allied Health Personnel 2007
Psychiatric Hospital Staff 1973

Psychiatric Classifications (Taxonomies)
Use Psychodiagnostic Typologies

Psychiatric Clinics 1973
PN 797 **SC** 41370
UF Outpatient Psychiatric Clinics
B Clinics 1967
R Child Guidance Clinics 1973
Community Mental Health Centers 1973
↓ Hospitals 1967
↓ Mental Health Programs 1973
↓ Outpatient Treatment 1967
Walk In Clinics 1973

Psychiatric Disorders
Use Mental Disorders

Psychiatric Evaluation 1997
PN 795 **SC** 41385
UF Evaluation (Psychiatric)
B Evaluation 1967
Measurement 1967
N Forensic Evaluation 1994
R Clinical Judgment (Not Diagnosis) 1973
Cognitive Assessment 1997
Geriatric Assessment 1997
Intake Interview 1994
↓ Interview Schedules 2001
↓ Psychodiagnosis 1967
↓ Psychodiagnostic Interview 1973
↓ Psychological Assessment 1997
Psychological Report 1988
↓ Screening 1982
↓ Screening Tests 1982

Psychiatric History
Use Patient History

Psychiatric Hospital Admission 1973
PN 1292 **SC** 41390
UF Admission (Psychiatric Hospital)
B Hospital Admission 1973
Psychiatric Hospitalization 1973

Psychiatric Hospital Admission — (cont'd)
N Psychiatric Hospital Readmission 1973
R ↓ Commitment (Psychiatric) 1973
↓ Hospital Discharge 1973
↓ Institutional Release 1978
Psychiatric Hospital Discharge 1978

Psychiatric Hospital Discharge 1978
PN 872 SC 41395
B Hospital Discharge 1973
Psychiatric Hospitalization 1973
R Client Transfer 1997
↓ Commitment (Psychiatric) 1973
Discharge Planning 1994
↓ Psychiatric Hospital Admission 1973
Psychiatric Hospital Readmission 1973
Treatment Termination 1982

Psychiatric Hospital Programs 1967
PN 1823 SC 41400
SN Organized plans for care or training in psychiatric hospitals.
B Hospital Programs 1978
N Therapeutic Community 1967
R Halfway Houses 1973
↓ Mental Health Services 1978
↓ Program Development 1991
Token Economy Programs 1973

Psychiatric Hospital Readmission 1973
PN 748 SC 41410
UF Readmission (Psychiatric Hospital)
B Psychiatric Hospital Admission 1973
Psychiatric Hospitalization 1973
R ↓ Hospital Discharge 1973
Psychiatric Hospital Discharge 1978

Psychiatric Hospital Staff 1973
PN 922 SC 41420
B Medical Personnel 1967
Mental Health Personnel 1967
N Psychiatric Aides 1973
R Attendants (Institutions) 1973
Occupational Therapists 1973
Psychiatric Nurses 1973
Psychiatrists 1967

Psychiatric Hospitalization 1973
PN 5128 SC 41430
B Hospitalization 1967
N ↓ Psychiatric Hospital Admission 1973
Psychiatric Hospital Discharge 1978
Psychiatric Hospital Readmission 1973
R ↓ Commitment (Psychiatric) 1973
↓ Hospital Admission 1973
↓ Hospital Discharge 1973
↓ Institutional Release 1978
Patient Seclusion 1994

Psychiatric Hospitals 1967
PN 4879 SC 41440
UF Asylums
Mental Hospitals
State Hospitals
B Hospitals 1967
R Halfway Houses 1973
Patient Seclusion 1994
Psychiatric Units 1991
Sanatoriums 1973

Psychiatric Nurses 1973
PN 1671 SC 41450
B Mental Health Personnel 1967
Nurses 1967

Psychiatric Nurses — (cont'd)
R ↓ Psychiatric Hospital Staff 1973

Psychiatric Patients 1967
PN 23297 SC 41460
B Patients 1967
R ↓ Mental Disorders 1967
Psychiatric Symptoms 1997
↓ Psychopathology 1967

Psychiatric Report
Use Psychological Report

Psychiatric Residency
Use Medical Residency AND Psychiatric Training

Psychiatric Social Workers 1973
PN 101 SC 41470
B Mental Health Personnel 1967
Social Workers 1973

Psychiatric Symptoms 1997
PN 5697 SC 41475
UF Psychotic Symptoms
B Symptoms 1967
R ↓ Mental Disorders 1967
Psychiatric Patients 1967
↓ Psychopathology 1967
Symptom Checklists 1991
Symptom Remission 1973

Psychiatric Training 1973
PN 2715 SC 41480
UF Psychiatric Residency
Training (Psychiatric)
B Clinical Methods Training 1973
Medical Education 1973
R Cotherapy 1982
Psychoanalytic Training 1973
Psychotherapy Training 1973

Psychiatric Units 1991
PN 913 SC 41485
SN Units in a general hospital or inpatient care facility specializing in psychiatric care of acutely disturbed patients.
UF Hospital Psychiatric Units
R ↓ Hospital Programs 1978
↓ Hospitalization 1967
↓ Hospitals 1967
Nursing Homes 1973
Patient Seclusion 1994
Psychiatric Hospitals 1967
↓ Residential Care Institutions 1973

Psychiatrists 1967
PN 6281 SC 41490
UF Neuropsychiatrists
B Mental Health Personnel 1967
Physicians 1967
R Clinicians 1973
Hypnotherapists 1973
↓ Psychiatric Hospital Staff 1973
Psychoanalysts 1973
↓ Psychologists 1967
↓ Psychotherapists 1973

Psychiatry 1967
PN 11910 SC 41500
B Medical Sciences 1967
N Adolescent Psychiatry 1985
Biological Psychiatry 1994
Child Psychiatry 1967
Community Psychiatry 1973

Psychiatry — (cont'd)
Consultation Liaison Psychiatry 1991
Forensic Psychiatry 1973
Geriatric Psychiatry 1997
Neuropsychiatry 1973
Orthopsychiatry 1973
Social Psychiatry 1967
Transcultural Psychiatry 1973
R ↓ Psychology 1967
↓ Treatment 1967

Psychic Healing
Use Faith Healing

Psychoactive Drugs
Use Drugs

Psychoanalysis 1967
PN 29707 SC 41520
UF Psychoanalytic Therapy
B Psychotherapy 1967
N Adlerian Psychotherapy 1997
Dream Analysis 1973
Self Analysis 1994
R Catharsis 1973
Erikson (Erik) 1991
Free Association 1994
Freud (Sigmund) 1967
↓ Hypnotherapy 1973
Negative Therapeutic Reaction 1997
↓ Psychoanalytic Theory 1967
Psychodynamic Psychotherapy 2003
Psychotherapeutic Neutrality 1997
↓ Psychotherapeutic Processes 1967
Transactional Analysis 1973

Psychoanalysts 1973
PN 4563 SC 41530
UF Analysts
B Psychotherapists 1973
R Hypnotherapists 1973
Psychiatrists 1967

Psychoanalytic Interpretation 1967
PN 8536 SC 41540
SN Description or formulation of the meaning or significance of any particular event, condition, or process (e.g., patient's productions, art, literature, or historical biographies) from a psychoanalytic perspective.
B Theoretical Interpretation 1988
R Freudian Psychoanalytic School 1973
↓ Projective Personality Measures 1973
↓ Projective Techniques 1967
↓ Psychoanalytic Theory 1967
Psychohistory 1978

Psychoanalytic Personality Factors 1973
PN 668 SC 41550
UF Personality Factors (Psychoanalytic)
B Personality 1967
N Conscience 1967
Conscious (Personality Factor) 1973
Death Instinct 1988
Ego 1967
Electra Complex 1973
Id 1973
Libido 1973
Oedipal Complex 1973
Subconscious 1973
↓ Superego 1973
Unconscious (Personality Factor) 1967
R Penis Envy 1973
↓ Personality Processes 1967

Psychoanalytic School (Freudian)
Use Freudian Psychoanalytic School

Psychoanalytic Theory 1967
PN 19467 **SC** 41570
N Freudian Psychoanalytic School 1973
R ↓ Ego Development 1991
Erikson (Erik) 1991
Fixation (Psychoanalytic) 2007
Free Association 1994
Freud (Sigmund) 1967
Metapsychology 1994
↓ Neopsychoanalytic School 1973
Object Relations 1982
↓ Personality Processes 1967
↓ Psychoanalysis 1967
Psychoanalytic Interpretation 1967
Self Psychology 1988

Psychoanalytic Therapy
Use Psychoanalysis

Psychoanalytic Training 1973
PN 1129 **SC** 41590
UF Training (Psychoanalytic)
B Clinical Methods Training 1973
R Personal Therapy 1991
Psychiatric Training 1973
Psychotherapy Training 1973
Self Analysis 1994

Psychoanalytically Oriented Psychotherapy
Use Psychodynamic Psychotherapy

Psychobiology 1982
PN 1556 **SC** 41595
SN Scientific discipline emphasizing the holistic functioning of the individual in the environment in relation to normal or abnormal behavior.
B Sciences 1967
R Behavioral Genetics 1994
Biological Psychiatry 1994
↓ Biology 1967
Biopsychosocial Approach 1991
↓ Psychology 1967

Psychodiagnosis 1967
PN 17506 **SC** 41600
SN Diagnosis of mental disorders through the use of psychological methods or tests. Compare MEDICAL DIAGNOSIS.
UF Clinical Judgment (Psychodiagnosis)
B Diagnosis 1967
N ↓ Psychodiagnostic Interview 1973
R Clinical Judgment (Not Diagnosis) 1973
Computer Assisted Diagnosis 1973
Diagnostic and Statistical Manual 1994
Differential Diagnosis 1967
Educational Diagnosis 1978
Forensic Evaluation 1994
International Classification of Diseases 2001
↓ Mental Disorders 1967
Patient History 1973
Prognosis 1973
↓ Psychiatric Evaluation 1997
↓ Psychodiagnostic Typologies 1967
↓ Psychological Assessment 1997
Psychological Report 1988
Research Diagnostic Criteria 1994
Structured Clinical Interview 2001

Psychodiagnostic Interview 1973
PN 1959 **SC** 41630
B Interviews 1967
Psychodiagnosis 1967
N Diagnostic Interview Schedule 1991
Structured Clinical Interview 2001
R Intake Interview 1994
↓ Psychiatric Evaluation 1997
↓ Psychological Assessment 1997

Psychodiagnostic Typologies 1967
PN 6596 **SC** 41640
SN Systematic classification of mental, cognitive, emotional, or behavioral disorders.
UF Psychiatric Classifications (Taxonomies)
Typologies (Psychodiagnostic)
N Diagnostic and Statistical Manual 1994
International Classification of Diseases 2001
Research Diagnostic Criteria 1994
R Clinical Judgment (Not Diagnosis) 1973
Diagnostic Interview Schedule 1991
Dual Diagnosis 1991
Labeling 1978
Misdiagnosis 1997
↓ Psychodiagnosis 1967
Structured Clinical Interview 2001
Subtypes (Disorders) 2004
Taxonomies 1973

Psychodrama 1967
PN 1175 **SC** 41650
SN Projective technique and method of group psychotherapy in which personality make-up, interpersonal relations, conflicts, and emotional problems are explored through dramatization of meaningful situations.
UF Drama Therapy
B Psychotherapeutic Techniques 1967
Psychotherapy 1967
R ↓ Group Psychotherapy 1967
Improvisation 2004
Mirroring 1997
Role Playing 1967

Psychodynamic Psychotherapy 2003
PN 797 **SC** 41657
SN An approach to psychotherapy that emphasizes inner conflict and ongoing intense psychological processes within the individual. Therapy is generally not as lengthy or intensive as psychoanalysis.
HN This term was introduced in June 2003. Relevant records were re-indexed with this term. The posting note reflects the number of records that were re-indexed.
UF Psychoanalytically Oriented Psychotherapy
B Psychotherapy 1967
R ↓ Psychoanalysis 1967

Psychodynamics 1973
PN 8956 **SC** 41660
SN Human behavior and emotions in terms of conscious and unconscious motivations.
UF Psychological Correlates
R ↓ Personality 1967
Psychosocial Factors 1988
↓ Social Behavior 1967
↓ Social Interaction 1967

Psychoeducation 1994
PN 1729 **SC** 41665
R Client Education 1985
↓ Education 1967
Educational Therapy 1997

Psychoeducation — (cont'd)
↓ Health Education 1973
↓ Treatment 1967

Psychogalvanic Reflex
Use Galvanic Skin Response

Psychogenesis 1973
PN 1513 **SC** 41670
SN Development of mental functions, traits, or states.
UF Psychological Development
B Development 1967
N ↓ Cognitive Development 1973
Emotional Development 1973
Moral Development 1973
↓ Psychosocial Development 1973
R Adolescent Development 1973
Adult Development 1978
Age Differences 1967
↓ Childhood Development 1967
↓ Delayed Development 1973
Developmental Age Groups 1973
↓ Developmental Stages 1973
↓ Early Childhood Development 1973
↓ Human Development 1967
↓ Infant Development 1973
Nature Nurture 1994
Neonatal Development 1973
↓ Physical Development 1973
Precocious Development 1973
↓ Prenatal Development 1973
Sex Linked Developmental Differences 1973
Sexual Development 1973

Psychogenic Pain
HN Term discontinued in 1997. In 2000, the term was removed from all records containing it, and replaced with SOMATOFORM PAIN DISORDER, its postable counterpart.
Use Somatoform Pain Disorder

Psychohistory 1978
PN 1426 **SC** 41685
SN Psychological, often psychoanalytical, interpretation of historical events and personalities. Includes psychobiographies, historical group fantasies and processes, studies of childhood from an historical perspective, and historical psychodynamics.
R ↓ Biography 1967
↓ History 1973
Psychoanalytic Interpretation 1967

Psychoimmunology
Use Psychoneuroimmunology

Psychokinesis 1973
PN 286 **SC** 41690
UF Telekinesis
B Extrasensory Perception 1967

Psycholinguistics 1967
PN 3087 **SC** 41700
SN Discipline that combines the techniques of linguistics and psychology in the study of the relationship of language and behavior and cognitive processes. Used for the discipline as well as specific psycholinguistic processes themselves.
B Linguistics 1973
R Ethnolinguistics 1973
Metalinguistics 1994
Neurolinguistics 1991
Vygotsky (Lev) 1991

Psychological Abuse
Use Emotional Abuse

Psychological Adjustment
Use Emotional Adjustment

Psychological Assessment 1997
PN 5025 **SC** 41706
SN Assessment of a patient/client by interviews, observations, or psychological tests to evaluate personality, adjustment, abilities, interests, cognitive functioning, or functioning in other areas of life. Used for references that focus on the assessment process or the assessment itself.
UF Assessment (Psychological)
B Measurement 1967
N ↓ Behavioral Assessment 1982
Cognitive Assessment 1997
↓ Neuropsychological Assessment 1982
R Clinical Judgment (Not Diagnosis) 1973
↓ Evaluation 1967
Forensic Evaluation 1994
Geriatric Assessment 1997
↓ Interview Schedules 2001
↓ Mental Disorders 1967
Needs Assessment 1985
↓ Psychiatric Evaluation 1997
↓ Psychodiagnosis 1967
↓ Psychodiagnostic Interview 1973
Psychological Report 1988
↓ Psychopathology 1967
Structured Clinical Interview 2001

Psychological Autopsy 1988
PN 179 **SC** 41705
SN Psychological profile developed after an individual's death by examination of personal letters or by interviewing acquaintances and relatives. Such autopsies are usually done following suicidal deaths and suspicious cases of death.
R Autopsy 1973
↓ Death and Dying 1967
Forensic Psychology 1985
↓ Suicide 1967

Psychological Contracts 2003
PN 212 **SC** 58068
SN An implicit agreement between two individuals, an individual and an organization, or members of a group that represents the expectations that both parties have regarding the relationship.
HN This term was introduced in June 2003. Relevant records were re-indexed with this term. The posting note reflects the number of records that were re-indexed.
UF Contracts (Psychological)
R Labor Management Relations 1967
↓ Organizational Behavior 1978
Organizational Commitment 1991
Supervisor Employee Interaction 1997

Psychological Correlates
Use Psychodynamics

Psychological Debriefing
Use Debriefing (Psychological)

Psychological Development
Use Psychogenesis

Psychological Endurance 1973
PN 575 **SC** 41710
B Endurance 1973
R Psychological Stress 1973
Resilience (Psychological) 2003
Stress Reactions 1973

Psychological Interpretation
Use Theoretical Interpretation

Psychological Needs 1997
PN 597 **SC** 41715
UF Emotional Needs
B Needs 1967
R Need Satisfaction 1973
Needs Assessment 1985

Psychological Reactance 1978
PN 396 **SC** 41716
SN Decrease in the attractiveness of an activity, behavior, or attitude as a result of having been forced or induced by external sources to engage in the activity or behavior, or to maintain the attitude. Such reactions may appear as emotional dissatisfaction, involvement and performance decrements, or negative attitude.
UF Reactance
R Choice Behavior 1967
Cognitive Dissonance 1967
Freedom 1978

Psychological Report 1988
PN 204 **SC** 41718
UF Psychiatric Report
R Educational Diagnosis 1978
↓ Evaluation 1967
Forensic Evaluation 1994
↓ Medical Diagnosis 1973
↓ Psychiatric Evaluation 1997
↓ Psychodiagnosis 1967
↓ Psychological Assessment 1997

Psychological Screening Inventory 1973
PN 55 **SC** 41720
B Nonprojective Personality Measures 1973
Screening Tests 1982
Selection Tests 1973

Psychological Stress 1973
PN 5587 **SC** 41730
B Stress 1967
R Chronic Stress 2004
↓ Deprivation 1967
Psychological Endurance 1973
Resilience (Psychological) 2003

Psychological Terminology 1973
PN 1636 **SC** 41740
SN Definitions, analysis, evaluation, or review of individual terms or nomenclature in the field of psychology. Compare GLOSSARY.
UF Nomenclature (Psychological)
Terminology (Psychological)
B Terminology 1991
R Scientific Communication 1973

Psychological Testing
Use Psychometrics

Psychological Theories 2001
PN 2443 **SC** 41746
B Theories 1967
N Associationism 1973
Attachment Theory 2007
Behaviorism 1967
Freudian Psychoanalytic School 1973
Functionalism 1973
Gestalt Psychology 1967
↓ Neopsychoanalytic School 1973
Structuralism 1973
R ↓ History of Psychology 1967
↓ Psychology 1967

Psychologist Attitudes 1991
PN 747 **SC** 41747
SN Attitudes of, not toward, psychologists.
B Attitudes 1967
R Counselor Attitudes 1973
↓ Health Personnel Attitudes 1985
↓ Psychologists 1967
↓ Therapist Attitudes 1978

Psychologists 1967
PN 12390 **SC** 41750
B Professional Personnel 1978
N Clinical Psychologists 1973
Counseling Psychologists 1988
↓ Educational Psychologists 1973
Experimental Psychologists 1973
Industrial Psychologists 1973
Military Psychologists 1997
Social Psychologists 1973
R Adler (Alfred) 1967
American Psychological Association 2007
American Psychological Association Divisions 2007
↓ Counselors 1967
Ellis (Albert) 1991
Erikson (Erik) 1991
Freud (Sigmund) 1967
James (William) 1991
Jung (Carl) 1973
Kohlberg (Lawrence) 1991
Maslow (Abraham Harold) 1991
↓ Mental Health Personnel 1967
Pavlov (Ivan) 1991
Piaget (Jean) 1967
Psychiatrists 1967
Psychologist Attitudes 1991
↓ Psychotherapists 1973
Rogers (Carl) 1991
Scientists 1967
Skinner (Burrhus Frederic) 1991
↓ Social Workers 1973
Vygotsky (Lev) 1991
Watson (John Broadus) 1991

Psychology 1967
PN 16564 **SC** 41760
B Behavioral Sciences 1997
N Abnormal Psychology 2003
↓ Applied Psychology 1973
↓ Clinical Psychology 1967
Cognitive Psychology 1985
Comparative Psychology 1967
Cross Cultural Psychology 1997
Depth Psychology 1973
↓ Developmental Psychology 1973
Ecological Psychology 1994
Evolutionary Psychology 2003
Experimental Psychology 1967
Feminist Psychology 2007
Folk Psychology 1997
Forensic Psychology 1985
Geropsychology 2006
↓ Humanistic Psychology 1985
Mathematical Psychology 1973
Metapsychology 1994
↓ Physiological Psychology 1967
Positive Psychology 2003

Psychology — (cont'd)
Psychology of Women 2007
Self Psychology 1988
R American Psychological Association 2007
American Psychological Association Divisions 2007
↓ History of Psychology 1967
↓ Psychiatry 1967
Psychobiology 1982
↓ Psychological Theories 2001
↓ Psychophysiology 1967

Psychology Education 1978
PN 4981 **SC** 41765
B Curriculum 1967
N ↓ Graduate Psychology Education 1967
R Counselor Education 1973
Educational Program Accreditation 1994
Theoretical Orientation 1982

Psychology of Women 2007
PN 238 **SC** 41767
SN An approach to psychology that emphasizes the physical, psychological, and social experiences that are particularly characteristic of women.
HN This term was introduced in April 2007. Relevant records were re-indexed with this term. The posting note reflects the number of records that were re-indexed.
UF Women Centered Psychology
B Psychology 1967
R Feminist Psychology 2007

Psychometrics 1967
PN 11449 **SC** 41770
SN Subdiscipline within psychology dealing with the development and application of statistical techniques to the analysis of psychological data. Also, psychological measurement in which numerical estimates are obtained of a specific aspect of performance.
UF Psychological Testing
B Measurement 1967
R Classical Test Theory 2003
Conjoint Measurement 1994
↓ Experimental Design 1967
↓ Experimentation 1967
Item Response Theory 1985
Psychophysics 1967
↓ Statistical Analysis 1967
Test Interpretation 1985
↓ Testing 1967

Psychomotor Development 1973
PN 438 **SC** 41780
B Motor Development 1973
N ↓ Speech Development 1973
R ↓ Childhood Development 1967
↓ Perceptual Development 1973
Perceptual Motor Development 1991

Psychomotor Processes
Use Perceptual Motor Processes

Psychoneuroendocrinology 2007
PN 90 **SC** 41793
SN The study of the relations among psychological factors, the nervous system, and the endocrine system in determining behavior and health. It includes the effects of psychological stress on neuroendocrine systems and how changes in these systems affect behavior in normal and psychopathological states.
HN This term was introduced in April 2007. Relevant records were re-indexed with this term. The posting note reflects the number of records that were re-indexed.
B Neuroendocrinology 1985
R ↓ Endocrine System 1973
↓ Hormones 1967

Psychoneuroimmunology 1991
PN 786 **SC** 41795
SN Study of the interrelationship among immune responses, psychological processes, and the nervous system. Used for the scientific discipline or the psychoneuroimmunologic processes themselves.
UF Psychoimmunology
B Immunology 1973
Psychophysiology 1967
R ↓ Endocrinology 1973
Neuropsychology 1973

Psychoneurosis
Use Neurosis

Psychopath
Use Antisocial Personality Disorder

Psychopathology 1967
PN 16342 **SC** 41820
SN Study of mental disorders, emotional problems, or maladaptive behaviors. Used for the scientific discipline or for unspecified dysfunctions.
B Pathology 1973
N Adolescent Psychopathology 2007
Child Psychopathology 2007
R Abnormal Psychology 2003
↓ Antisocial Behavior 1971
Comorbidity 1991
↓ Defense Mechanisms 1967
↓ Emotional Adjustment 1973
Homeless Mentally Ill 1997
↓ Mental Disorders 1967
Psychiatric Patients 1967
Psychiatric Symptoms 1997
↓ Psychological Assessment 1997

Psychopathy 2007
PN 779 **SC** 41830
SN A former term for a personality trait marked by egocentricity, impulsivity, and lack of such emotions as guilt and remorse, which is particularly prevalent among repeat offenders diagnosed with antisocial personality disorder.
HN Term discontinued in 1997. In 2000, the term was removed from all records containing it, and replaced with ANTISOCIAL PERSONALITY DISORDER, its postable counterpart. In April 2007, PSYCHOPATHY changed status from nonpostable to postable. Relevant records were re-indexed with this term. The posting note reflects the number of records that were re-indexed.
R ↓ Antisocial Behavior 1971
Antisocial Personality Disorder 1973

Psychopharmacology 1967
PN 4976 **SC** 41840
SN The study of the effect of drugs on behavior or other psychological processes. For the use of drugs in a treatment capacity, use DRUG THERAPY.
B Pharmacology 1973
R Drug Abuse Liability 1994

Psychophysical Measurement 1967
PN 2033 **SC** 41850
SN Techniques or methodology used to assess perceptual sensitivities and functions of any sensory modality as related to the parameters of stimulation.
N Magnitude Estimation 1991
R Fuzzy Set Theory 1991
↓ Perceptual Measures 1973
Signal Detection (Perception) 1967
Threshold Determination 1973

Psychophysics 1967
PN 1449 **SC** 41860
R ↓ Experimentation 1967
Psychometrics 1967

Psychophysiologic Disorders
Use Somatoform Disorders

Psychophysiology 1967
PN 4642 **SC** 41880
SN Study of the physiological correlates of mental, somatic, and behavioral processes.
B Physiology 1967
N Psychoneuroimmunology 1991
R Cardiovascular Reactivity 1994
Pathophysiology 2005
↓ Physiological Psychology 1967
↓ Psychology 1967

Psychosexual Behavior 1967
PN 13324 **SC** 41890
SN Human sexual behavior which includes both mental and somatic aspects of sexuality.
UF Sexual Behavior
B Behavior 1967
N Bisexuality 1973
Erection (Penis) 1973
Extramarital Intercourse 1973
Heterosexuality 1973
↓ Homosexuality 1967
↓ Human Courtship 1973
Hypersexuality 1973
Masturbation 1973
Monogamy 1997
↓ Orgasm 1973
↓ Paraphilias 1988
Promiscuity 1973
Prostitution 1973
Safe Sex 2003
Seduction 1994
Sex Roles 1967
Sexual Abstinence 1973
↓ Sexual Arousal 1978
↓ Sexual Function Disturbances 1973
↓ Sexual Intercourse (Human) 1973
Sexual Risk Taking 1997
Transsexualism 1973
Transvestism 1973
Virginity 1973
R Affection 1973
Assortative Mating 1991
Autoeroticism 1997
Erotomania 1997
Human Mate Selection 1988
Pornography 1973
Professional Client Sexual Relations 1994
Psychosexual Development 1982
Romance 1997
Sex 1967

Psychosexual Behavior — (cont'd)
Sex Linked Developmental Differences 1973
Sexual Addiction 1997
Sexual Attitudes 1973
Sexual Attraction 2003
Sexual Development 1973
Sexual Fantasy 1997
↓ Sexual Orientation 1997
Sexual Partners 2003
Sexual Satisfaction 1994

Psychosexual Development 1982
PN 2178 **SC** 41895
SN Psychological maturation and development of sexual identity, desires, beliefs, and attitudes throughout the life cycle.
B Psychosocial Development 1973
R Emotional Development 1973
↓ Gender Identity 1985
↓ Psychosexual Behavior 1967
Sex 1967
Sexual Attitudes 1973
Sexual Development 1973
Sexuality 1973

Psychosis 1967
PN 11776 **SC** 41910
SN Serious mental disorder characterized by hallucinations, delusions, incoherent speech, disorganized behavior, and loss of contact with reality.
B Mental Disorders 1967
N ↓ Acute Psychosis 1973
Affective Psychosis 1973
↓ Alcoholic Psychosis 1973
Capgras Syndrome 1985
↓ Childhood Psychosis 1967
Chronic Psychosis 1973
Experimental Psychosis 1973
↓ Hallucinosis 1973
↓ Paranoia (Psychosis) 1967
Postpartum Psychosis 2003
Reactive Psychosis 1973
↓ Schizophrenia 1967
Senile Psychosis 1973
Toxic Psychoses 1973
R Borderline States 1978
Paranoid Schizophrenia 1967

Psychosocial Development 1973
PN 11163 **SC** 41920
SN Process of psychological and social maturation occurring at any time during the life cycle.
UF Social Development
B Psychogenesis 1973
N Childhood Play Development 1973
↓ Personality Development 1967
Psychosexual Development 1982
R Aging (Attitudes Toward) 1985
Attachment Theory 2007
Emotional Development 1973
Erikson (Erik) 1991
Generativity 2001
Moral Development 1973
Object Relations 1982

Psychosocial Factors 1988
PN 17855 **SC** 41925
R Demographic Characteristics 1967
Psychodynamics 1973
Risk Factors 2001
↓ Social Influences 1967
↓ Sociocultural Factors 1967

Psychosocial Mental Retardation 1973
PN 53 **SC** 41930
SN Reversible mental retardation due to environmental and/or social factors with no organic etiological component.
UF Cultural Familial Mental Retardation
B Mental Retardation 1967
R Borderline Mental Retardation 1973

Psychosocial Readjustment 1973
PN 1425 **SC** 41940
SN Attainment of attitudes and skills which will facilitate an individual's reintegration or functioning in society, usually following traumatic or unusual personal experiences.
HN In 1982, this term replaced the discontinued term PSYCHOSOCIAL RESOCIALIZATION. In 2000, PSYCHOSOCIAL RESOCIALIZATION was removed from all records and replaced with PSYCHOSOCIAL READJUSTMENT.
UF Psychosocial Resocialization
Readjustment (Psychosocial)
Resocialization (Psychosocial)
R ↓ Psychosocial Rehabilitation 1973
↓ Treatment 1967

Psychosocial Rehabilitation 1973
PN 2531 **SC** 41950
SN Programs, techniques, or processes of treatment by which individuals, institutionalized or otherwise removed from normal community life (e.g., prisoners), acquire psychological and social skills and attitudes which facilitate community reentry.
UF Rehabilitation (Psychosocial)
B Rehabilitation 1967
N Therapeutic Social Clubs 1973
↓ Vocational Rehabilitation 1967
R ↓ Drug Rehabilitation 1973
Psychosocial Readjustment 1973
Rehabilitation Counseling 1978

Psychosocial Resocialization
HN Term was discontinued in 1982. In 2000, the term was removed from all records containing it, and replaced with PSYCHOSOCIAL READJUSTMENT, its postable counterpart.
Use Psychosocial Readjustment

Psychosomatic Disorders
HN Term discontinued in 2000. Use PSYCHOSOMATIC DISORDERS to access records from 1967-2000.
Use Somatoform Disorders

Psychosomatic Medicine 1978
PN 883 **SC** 41975
SN Medical specialty dealing with the diagnosis and treatment of psychosomatic disorders.
B Medical Sciences 1967
R ↓ Health Care Psychology 1985
Somatization Disorder 2001
↓ Somatoform Disorders 2001

Psychostimulant Drugs
Use CNS Stimulating Drugs

Psychosurgery 1973
PN 467 **SC** 41980
SN Cerebral surgery to treat severe mental illness.
UF Leukotomy
Lobectomy
Lobotomy
B Neurosurgery 1973
Physical Treatment Methods 1973

Psychosurgery — (cont'd)
N Thalamotomy 1973
R Sympathectomy 1973
Tractotomy 1973

Psychotherapeutic Breakthrough 1973
PN 81 **SC** 41990
UF Breakthrough (Psychotherapeutic)
B Psychotherapeutic Processes 1967

Psychotherapeutic Counseling 1973
PN 1159 **SC** 42000
B Counseling 1967
Psychotherapy 1967
N ↓ Family Therapy 1967
R ↓ Marriage Counseling 1973
Premarital Counseling 1973

Psychotherapeutic Methods
Use Psychotherapeutic Techniques

Psychotherapeutic Neutrality 1997
PN 58 **SC** 42025
UF Neutrality (Psychotherapeutic)
R ↓ Psychoanalysis 1967
↓ Psychotherapeutic Processes 1967
↓ Psychotherapeutic Techniques 1967

Psychotherapeutic Outcomes 1973
PN 3722 **SC** 42030
SN Limited to treatment results that are a direct function of specific characteristics of clients or therapists or a function of unique or specifically-described circumstances of the treatment itself.
UF Outcomes (Psychotherapeutic)
B Treatment Outcomes 1982
R Mental Health Program Evaluation 1973
Treatment Dropouts 1978
Treatment Effectiveness Evaluation 1973

Psychotherapeutic Processes 1967
PN 24501 **SC** 42040
SN Experiential, attitudinal, emotional, or behavioral phenomena occurring during the course of psychotherapy. Applies to the client or psychotherapist individually or to their interaction.
UF Client Counselor Interaction
Counselor Client Interaction
Patient Therapist Interaction
Therapist Patient Interaction
B Therapeutic Processes 1978
N Countertransference 1973
Insight (Psychotherapeutic Process) 1973
Negative Therapeutic Reaction 1997
Psychotherapeutic Breakthrough 1973
Psychotherapeutic Resistance 1973
Psychotherapeutic Transference 1967
Therapeutic Alliance 1994
R Cross Cultural Counseling 2003
Enactments 1997
↓ Internalization 1997
Mirroring 1997
Privileged Communication 1973
Professional Client Sexual Relations 1994
↓ Psychoanalysis 1967
Psychotherapeutic Neutrality 1997
↓ Psychotherapy 1967
↓ Treatment Outcomes 1982

Psychotherapeutic Resistance 1973
PN 1056 **SC** 42050
SN Conscious or unconscious defensive attempts by the client to prevent repressed material from coming to consciousness.

Psychotherapeutic Resistance — (cont'd)
UF Resistance (Psychotherapeutic)
B Psychotherapeutic Processes 1967
Resistance 1997
R Negative Therapeutic Reaction 1997
Treatment Refusal 1994

Psychotherapeutic Techniques 1967
PN 14578 SC 42060
UF Psychotherapeutic Methods
Therapeutic Techniques (Psychotherapy)
B Treatment 1967
N Animal Assisted Therapy 1994
Autogenic Training 1973
Cotherapy 1982
Dream Analysis 1973
Guided Imagery 2001
Mirroring 1997
Morita Therapy 1994
Motivational Interviewing 2007
Mutual Storytelling Technique 1973
Paradoxical Techniques 1982
Psychodrama 1967
R Age Regression (Hypnotic) 1988
Centering 1991
Client Centered Therapy 1967
Conjoint Therapy 1973
↓ Creative Arts Therapy 1994
Free Association 1994
Homework 1988
Improvisation 2004
Interpersonal Psychotherapy 1997
Mindfulness 2006
Poetry Therapy 1994
Primal Therapy 1978
Psychotherapeutic Neutrality 1997
↓ Psychotherapy 1967
Rational Emotive Behavior Therapy 2003
Reality Therapy 1973
↓ Relaxation Therapy 1978
Role Playing 1967
↓ Self Help Techniques 1982
Self Talk 1988
↓ Twelve Step Programs 1997
Wilderness Experience 1991

Psychotherapeutic Transference 1967
PN 4411 SC 42070
SN Unconscious projection of feelings, thoughts, and wishes to the therapist that were originally associated with important figures from the client's past.
UF Transference (Psychotherapeutic)
B Psychotherapeutic Processes 1967
R Countertransference 1973
Enactments 1997
Negative Therapeutic Reaction 1997
Professional Client Sexual Relations 1994
Therapeutic Alliance 1994

Psychotherapist Attitudes 1973
PN 995 SC 42080
SN Attitudes of, not toward, psychotherapists.
B Therapist Attitudes 1978
R ↓ Psychotherapists 1973
Therapist Role 1978

Psychotherapist Trainees
Use Therapist Trainees

Psychotherapists 1973
PN 4838 SC 42100
B Mental Health Personnel 1967
Therapists 1967

Psychotherapists — (cont'd)
N Hypnotherapists 1973
Psychoanalysts 1973
R Clinical Psychologists 1973
Psychiatrists 1967
↓ Psychologists 1967
Psychotherapist Attitudes 1973

Psychotherapy 1967
PN 28484 SC 42110
UF Reconstructive Psychotherapy
B Treatment 1967
N Adlerian Psychotherapy 1997
Adolescent Psychotherapy 1994
Analytical Psychotherapy 1973
Autogenic Training 1973
↓ Behavior Therapy 1967
Brief Psychotherapy 1967
↓ Child Psychotherapy 1967
Client Centered Therapy 1967
Cognitive Behavior Therapy 2003
Eclectic Psychotherapy 1994
Emotion Focused Therapy 2007
Existential Therapy 1973
Experiential Psychotherapy 1973
Expressive Psychotherapy 1973
Eye Movement Desensitization Therapy 1997
Feminist Therapy 1994
Geriatric Psychotherapy 1973
Gestalt Therapy 1973
↓ Group Psychotherapy 1967
Guided Imagery 2001
↓ Humanistic Psychotherapy 2003
↓ Hypnotherapy 1973
Individual Psychotherapy 1973
Insight Therapy 1973
Integrative Psychotherapy 2003
Interpersonal Psychotherapy 1997
Logotherapy 1973
Narrative Therapy 2006
Persuasion Therapy 1973
Primal Therapy 1978
↓ Psychoanalysis 1967
Psychodrama 1967
Psychodynamic Psychotherapy 2003
↓ Psychotherapeutic Counseling 1973
Rational Emotive Behavior Therapy 2003
Reality Therapy 1973
Relationship Therapy 1973
Solution Focused Therapy 2004
Supportive Psychotherapy 1997
Transactional Analysis 1973
R Cognitive Therapy 1982
Cotherapy 1982
Couples Therapy 1994
Educational Therapy 1997
Holistic Health 1985
↓ Marriage Counseling 1973
Online Therapy 2003
Paradoxical Techniques 1982
Pastoral Counseling 1967
Phototherapy 1991
↓ Psychotherapeutic Processes 1967
↓ Psychotherapeutic Techniques 1967
Recreation Therapy 1973
Spontaneous Remission 1973
Theoretical Orientation 1982

Psychotherapy (Individual)
Use Individual Psychotherapy

Psychotherapy Training 1973
PN 1994 SC 42120
UF Training (Psychotherapy)
B Clinical Methods Training 1973
R Cotherapy 1982
Counselor Education 1973
Psychiatric Training 1973
Psychoanalytic Training 1973

Psychotic Depressive Reaction
HN Term was discontinued in 1988. In 2000, the term was removed from all records containing it, and replaced with MAJOR DEPRESSION, its postable counterpart.
Use Major Depression

Psychotic Episode (Acute)
Use Acute Psychosis

Psychotic Symptoms
Use Psychiatric Symptoms

Psychoticism 1978
PN 671 SC 42145
B Personality Traits 1967

Psychotomimetic Drugs 1973
PN 68 SC 42150
B Drugs 1967
N Lysergic Acid Diethylamide 1967
Mescaline 1973
Peyote 1973
R Experimental Psychosis 1973
↓ Hallucinogenic Drugs 1967

Psychotropic Drugs
Use Drugs

PTA
Use Parent School Relationship

PTSD
Use Posttraumatic Stress Disorder

Puberty 1973
PN 987 SC 42160
B Developmental Stages 1973
R Menarche 1973

Pubescence
Use Sexual Development

Public Attitudes
Use Public Opinion

Public Health 1988
PN 2869 SC 42185
B Health 1973
N ↓ Epidemics 2001
R Health Promotion 1991
↓ Health Screening 1997
Public Health Services 1973
Public Service Announcements 2004

Public Health Service Nurses 1973
PN 269 SC 42190
B Government Personnel 1973
Nurses 1967
R Public Health Services 1973

Public Health Services 1973
PN 1395 SC 42200
B Community Services 1967
R ↓ Health 1973
Integrated Services 1997

Public Health Services — (cont'd)
↓ Mental Health Programs 1973
↓ Public Health 1988
Public Health Service Nurses 1973

Public Opinion 1973
PN 3432 **SC** 42210
UF Opinion (Public)
Public Attitudes
B Attitudes 1967
R Community Attitudes 1973
Political Psychology 1997
Public Relations 1973

Public Policy
Use Government Policy Making

Public Relations 1973
PN 599 **SC** 42220
SN The business of attempting to influence or persuade individuals or the public to have an understanding or concern for, or positive disposition toward, a particular person, organization, idea, policy, practice, or activity.
R ↓ Advertising 1967
↓ Consumer Attitudes 1973
Public Opinion 1973

Public School Education 1973
PN 1681 **SC** 42230
SN Education in free tax-supported schools controlled by a local governmental authority.
B Education 1967

Public Sector 1985
PN 1183 **SC** 42235
SN Any type of government-related or public organization, service, or sphere of involvement.
N Government 1967
Government Agencies 1973

Public Service Announcements 2004
PN 55 **SC** 42232
HN This term was introduced in June 2004. Relevant records were re-indexed with this term. The posting note reflects the number of records that were re-indexed.
R Advocacy 1985
Health Promotion 1991
↓ Mass Media 1967
↓ Persuasive Communication 1967
↓ Prevention 1973
↓ Public Health 1988
Television Advertising 1973

Public Speaking 1973
PN 696 **SC** 42240
SN Formal or informal speech in a group or public setting.
B Oral Communication 1985
R Debates 1997
Speech Anxiety 1985

Public Transportation 1973
PN 179 **SC** 42250
B Community Facilities 1973
Transportation 1973
R Air Transportation 1973
Railroad Trains 1973

Public Welfare Services
Use Community Welfare Services

Puerperal Depression
Use Postpartum Depression

Puerperal Psychosis
Use Postpartum Psychosis

Puerto Rican Americans
Use Hispanics

Pulmonary Disorders
Use Lung Disorders

Pulmonary Emphysema 1973
PN 51 **SC** 42290
UF Emphysema (Pulmonary)
B Lung Disorders 1973

Pulmonary Tuberculosis 1973
PN 19 **SC** 42300
B Bacterial Disorders 1973
Lung Disorders 1973
Tuberculosis 1973

Pulse (Arterial)
Use Arterial Pulse

Punishment 1967
PN 3617 **SC** 42320
SN Presentation of a punisher contingent on the performance of some behavior. Also, the punishing event or object itself which, when following the performance of some behavior, results in a reduction in the occurrence or frequency of that behavior. Compare AVERSIVE STIMULATION. Used for both human and animal populations.
UF Corporal Punishment
B Reinforcement 1967
N Response Cost 1997
R Coercion 1994
Threat 1967

Punishment (Capital)
Use Capital Punishment

Pupil (Eye) 1973
PN 187 **SC** 42340
B Eye (Anatomy) 1967

Pupil Dilation 1973
PN 377 **SC** 42360
UF Dilation (Pupil)
R ↓ Eye (Anatomy) 1967

Purging (Eating Disorders) 2003
PN 130 **SC** 42383
SN Compensatory behaviors including self-induced vomiting, misuse of laxatives, diuretics, or enemas for the purpose of preventing weight gain.
HN This term was introduced in June 2003. Relevant records were re-indexed with this term. The posting note reflects the number of records that were re-indexed.
B Eating Disorders 1997
R Binge Eating 1991
Bulimia 1985
↓ Diuretics 1973
Vomiting 1973

Purkinje Cells 1994
PN 241 **SC** 42385
SN Nerve cells that occupy the middle layer of the cerebral cortex and convey signals away from the cerebellum.
B Cerebellum 1973
Neurons 1973

Puromycin 1973
PN 37 **SC** 42390
B Amines 1973
Antibiotics 1973

Putamen 1985
PN 375 **SC** 42405
SN The largest and most lateral part of the basal ganglia which, together with the caudate nucleus and globus pallidus, forms the corpus striatum.
B Basal Ganglia 1973
Striatum 2003

Pygmalion Effect
Use Self Fulfilling Prophecies

Pygmy Chimpanzees
Use Bonobos

Pyramidal Tracts 1973
PN 204 **SC** 42410
SN Pathway of the central nervous system, originating in the sensorimotor area of the cerebral cortex and generally descending through the spinal cord. Pyramidal tract fibers transmit motor impulses that function in voluntary movement control.
UF Corticospinal Tracts
B Efferent Pathways 1982
Spinal Cord 1973
R Extrapyramidal Tracts 1973

Pyromania 1973
PN 60 **SC** 42430
R ↓ Impulse Control Disorders 1997
Impulsiveness 1973
↓ Personality Disorders 1967

Q Sort Testing Technique 1967
PN 211 **SC** 42440
B Testing Methods 1967

Quaalude
Use Methaqualone

Quadriplegia 1985
PN 118 **SC** 42470
SN Paralysis of both arms and both legs.
B Paralysis 1973
R ↓ Central Nervous System Disorders 1973
Hemiplegia 1978
↓ Injuries 1973
↓ Musculoskeletal Disorders 1973
Paraplegia 1978
↓ Spinal Cord Injuries 1973

Quails 1973
PN 495 **SC** 42480
B Birds 1967

Qualitative Methods
Use Qualitative Research

Qualitative Research 2003
PN 1213 **SC** 42481
SN A type of research methodology that produces descriptive data, with little emphasis given to numerical quantification. Used only when the methodology or research itself is the focus of discussion.
HN This term was introduced in June 2003. Relevant records were re-indexed with this term. The posting note reflects the number of records that were re-indexed.
UF Qualitative Methods
B Experimentation 1967
Methodology 1967

Qualitative Research — (cont'd)
R Data Collection 1982
↓ Empirical Methods 1973
↓ Experimental Design 1967
Grounded Theory 2004
↓ Interviews 1967
Observation Methods 1967

Quality Circles
Use Participative Management

Quality Control 1988
PN 653 SC 42483
SN Efforts or techniques directed at the detection of imperfections or shortcomings in products or services.
R Accountability 1988
Clinical Audits 2007
Clinical Governance 2007
Consumer Satisfaction 1994
Human Factors Engineering 1973
Organizational Effectiveness 1985
Organizational Objectives 1973
Participative Management 1988
↓ Quality of Services 1997

Quality of Care 1988
PN 3645 SC 42484
SN Quality of medical or mental health care.
B Quality of Services 1997
R Accountability 1988
Caregivers 1988
Child Day Care 1973
↓ Client Rights 1988
Clinical Audits 2007
Clinical Governance 2007
Continuum of Care 2004
↓ Health Care Delivery 1978
↓ Health Care Services 1978
Home Care 1985
↓ Managed Care 1994
↓ Mental Health Services 1978
↓ Treatment 1967
Utilization Reviews 2007

Quality of Education
Use Educational Quality

Quality of Life 1985
PN 11116 SC 42485
N Quality of Work Life 1988
R Life Changes 2004
Life Satisfaction 1985
↓ Lifestyle 1978
Lifestyle Changes 1997
Well Being 1994

Quality of Services 1997
PN 1598 SC 57510
SN Used for health care and non-health care services. Consider QUALITY of CARE for health care services.
UF Service Quality
N Quality of Care 1988
R ↓ Advertising 1967
Clinical Governance 2007
↓ Consumer Attitudes 1973
Consumer Satisfaction 1994
↓ Health Care Delivery 1978
↓ Health Care Services 1978
↓ Marketing 1973
↓ Mental Health Services 1978
↓ Professional Standards 1973
Quality Control 1988

Quality of Services — (cont'd)
↓ Retailing 1991
Treatment Guidelines 2001

Quality of Work Life 1988
PN 627 SC 42487
SN Includes aspects such as salary, benefits, safety, and efficiency, as well as variety and challenge, responsibility, contribution, and recognition.
B Quality of Life 1985
R ↓ Job Characteristics 1985
Job Satisfaction 1967
Occupational Stress 1973
↓ Organizational Characteristics 1997
Organizational Climate 1973
↓ Working Conditions 1973

Quantitative Methods 2003
PN 470 SC 42488
SN Form of research methodology in which experimental variables and relationships are assigned numerical value. Used only when the methodology or research itself is the focus of discussion.
HN This term was introduced in June 2003. Relevant records were re-indexed with this term. The posting note reflects the number of records that were re-indexed.
UF Quantitative Research
B Experimentation 1967
Methodology 1967
R Data Collection 1982
↓ Empirical Methods 1973
↓ Experimental Design 1967
↓ Experimental Methods 1967
↓ Statistical Analysis 1967
Statistical Data 1982
↓ Statistical Measurement 1973

Quantitative Research
Use Quantitative Methods

Quantitative Trait Loci 2004
PN 122 SC 58075
SN Locations of genes that control variation in quantitative traits.
HN This term was introduced in June 2004. Relevant records were re-indexed with this term. The posting note reflects the number of records that were re-indexed.
B Genes 1973
R Gene Expression 2004
Genetic Linkage 1994
↓ Genetics 1967
Genome 2003

Quasi Experimental Methods 2003
PN 66 SC 42492
SN Research conducted in settings or environments where normal or traditional controls are not, or cannot be, applied.
HN This term was introduced in June 2003. Relevant records were re-indexed with this term. The posting note reflects the number of records that were re-indexed.
B Experimental Methods 1967
R ↓ Experimental Design 1967

Questioning 1982
PN 1837 SC 42495
R ↓ Cognitive Processes 1967
Curiosity 1967
↓ Education 1967
Guessing 1973
Information Seeking 1973

Questioning — (cont'd)
Interrogation 2005
Interviewing 1973
↓ Interviews 1967
↓ Teaching Methods 1967

Questionnaires 1967
PN 8893 SC 42500
B Measurement 1967
N General Health Questionnaire 1991
R Mail Surveys 1994
↓ Surveys 1967
Telephone Surveys 1994

Quetiapine 2004
PN 585 SC 42510
HN This term was introduced in June 2004. Relevant records were re-indexed with this term. The posting note reflects the number of records that were re-indexed.
B Neuroleptic Drugs 1973

Quinidine
HN Term was discontinued in 1997. In 2000, the term was removed from all records containing it, and replaced with ALKALOIDS, its postable counterpart.
Use Alkaloids

Quinine 1973
PN 206 SC 42560
B Alkaloids 1973
Analgesic Drugs 1973
Local Anesthetics 1973

Quinpirole 1994
PN 176 SC 42570
B Antihypertensive Drugs 1973
Dopamine Agonists 1985

Rabbis 1973
PN 70 SC 42580
B Clergy 1973
R Chaplains 1973
Judaism 1967

Rabbits 1967
PN 3070 SC 42590
B Mammals 1973

Race (Anthropological) 1973
PN 1116 SC 42600
R Ethnography 1973
Ethnology 1967
↓ Racial and Ethnic Attitudes 1982
Racial and Ethnic Differences 1982
↓ Racial and Ethnic Groups 2001
↓ Sociocultural Factors 1967
↓ Whites 1982

Race and Ethnic Discrimination 1994
PN 1474 SC 42605
HN Use SOCIAL DISCRIMINATION to access references from 1982-1993. In 1994, this term replaced the discontinued terms MINORITY GROUP DISCRIMINATION and RACIAL DISCRIMINATION. In 2000, these terms were removed from all records containing them, and replaced with RACE AND ETHNIC DISCRIMINATION.
UF Ethnic Discrimination
Minority Group Discrimination
Racial Discrimination
B Social Discrimination 1982
R Affirmative Action 1985
↓ Civil Rights 1978

Race and Ethnic Discrimination — (cont'd)
Employment Discrimination 1994
Ghettoes 1973
Minority Groups 1967
↓ Prejudice 1967
↓ Racial and Ethnic Attitudes 1982
Racial and Ethnic Differences 1982
Racism 1973

Race Attitudes
HN Term was discontinued in 1982. In 2000, the term was removed from all records containing it, and replaced with RACIAL AND ETHNIC ATTITUDES, its postable counterpart.
Use Racial and Ethnic Attitudes

Race Relations
HN Term was discontinued in 1982. In 2000, the term was removed from all records containing it, and replaced with RACIAL AND EHNIC RELATIONS, its postable counterpart.
Use Racial and Ethnic Relations

Racial and Ethnic Attitudes 1982
PN 4587 **SC** 42617
SN Attitudes about race or ethnicity or toward members of a given racial or ethnic group. Not to be used for the general attitudes of individuals of a specific racial or ethnic group.
HN In 1982, this term was created to replace the discontinued term RACE ATTITUDES. In 2000, RACE ATTITUDES was removed from all records containing it and replaced with RACIAL AND ETHNIC ATTITUDES.
UF Race Attitudes
B Attitudes 1967
N AntiSemitism 1973
Ethnocentrism 1973
Racism 1973
R Cultural Sensitivity 1994
Ethnology 1967
Hate Crimes 2003
Multiculturalism 1997
↓ Prejudice 1967
Race (Anthropological) 1973
Race and Ethnic Discrimination 1994
↓ Racial and Ethnic Groups 2001
Racial and Ethnic Relations 1982
Stereotyped Attitudes 1967

Racial and Ethnic Differences 1982
PN 18505 **SC** 42618
SN Differences between two or more racial or ethnic groups. Use CROSS CULTURAL DIFFERENCES for cultural comparisons, and use REGIONAL DIFFERENCES for geographical comparisons.
HN In 1982, this term replaced the discontinued term RACIAL DIFFERENCES. In 2000, RACIAL DIFFERENCES was removed from all records containing it, and replaced with RACIAL AND ETHNIC DIFFERENCES.
UF Ethnic Differences
Racial Differences
B Group Differences 2007
R Cross Cultural Communication 1997
Cross Cultural Differences 1967
Cross Cultural Psychology 1997
↓ Cross Cultural Treatment 1994
Cultural Sensitivity 1994
Diversity 2007
Diversity in the Workplace 2003
Ethnology 1967
Interethnic Family 1988

Racial and Ethnic Differences — (cont'd)
Interracial Family 1988
Interracial Offspring 1988
Multiculturalism 1997
Race (Anthropological) 1973
Race and Ethnic Discrimination 1994
↓ Racial and Ethnic Groups 2001
Racism 1973

Racial and Ethnic Groups 2001
PN 6565 **SC** 42616
HN In 2000, this term was created to replace the discontinued term ETHNIC GROUPS. ETHNIC GROUPS was removed from all records and replaced with RACIAL AND ETHNIC GROUPS.
UF Ethnic Groups
N African Cultural Groups 2006
Arabs 1988
↓ Asians 1982
Blacks 1982
Gypsies 1973
↓ Hispanics 1982
↓ Indigenous Populations 2001
↓ Whites 1982
R Cross Cultural Communication 1997
Cross Cultural Differences 1967
Cross Cultural Psychology 1997
↓ Cross Cultural Treatment 1994
Cultural Sensitivity 1994
↓ Culture (Anthropological) 1967
↓ Culture Bound Syndromes 2004
Ethnic Values 1973
Ethnology 1967
Minority Groups 1967
Multiculturalism 1997
Race (Anthropological) 1973
↓ Racial and Ethnic Attitudes 1982
Racial and Ethnic Differences 1982
↓ Religious Groups 1997
↓ Sociocultural Factors 1967
Tribes 1973

Racial and Ethnic Relations 1982
PN 1956 **SC** 42619
SN Contact and interaction between and among different racial and ethnic groups.
HN In 1982, this term was created to replace the discontinued term RACE RELATIONS. In 2000, RACE RELATIONS was removed from all records containing it, and replaced with RACIAL AND ETHNIC RELATIONS.
UF Race Relations
B Social Behavior 1967
R Cross Cultural Communication 1997
Cultural Sensitivity 1994
Ethnology 1967
Interracial Family 1988
Interracial Marriage 1973
Interracial Offspring 1988
Multiculturalism 1997
↓ Prejudice 1967
↓ Racial and Ethnic Attitudes 1982
School Integration 1982
↓ Social Discrimination 1982
Social Equality 1973
↓ Social Integration 1982

Racial Differences
HN Term was discontinued in 1982. In 2000, the term was removed from all records containing it, and replaced with RACIAL AND ETHNIC DIFFERENCES, its postable counterpart.
Use Racial and Ethnic Differences

Racial Discrimination
HN Term was discontinued in 1982. From 1982-1993, SOCIAL DISCRIMINATION was used to capture this concept, and then in 1994, RACE AND ETHNIC DISCRIMINATION was created as the new postable terminology. In 2000, RACIAL DISCRIMINATION was removed from all records containing it, and replaced with RACE AND ETHNIC DISCRIMINATION, its postable counterpart.
Use Race and Ethnic Discrimination

Racial Integration
HN Term was discontinued in 1982. In 2000, the term was removed from all records containing it, and replaced with SOCIAL INTEGRATION, its postable counterpart.
Use Social Integration

Racial Segregation (Schools)
Use School Integration

Racism 1973
PN 2463 **SC** 42660
SN Belief that racial differences produce inherent superiority of a particular race.
B Racial and Ethnic Attitudes 1982
R AntiSemitism 1973
Employment Discrimination 1994
Hate Crimes 2003
↓ Prejudice 1967
Race and Ethnic Discrimination 1994
Racial and Ethnic Differences 1982
↓ Social Discrimination 1982
↓ Social Issues 1991

Radial Nerve
Use Spinal Nerves

Radiation 1967
PN 682 **SC** 42680
UF Irradiation
N Laser Irradiation 1973
R Radiation Therapy 1973
↓ Roentgenography 1973

Radiation Therapy 1973
PN 329 **SC** 42690
UF X Ray Therapy
B Physical Treatment Methods 1973
R ↓ Radiation 1967

Radical Movements 1973
PN 110 **SC** 42700
N Political Revolution 1973
R ↓ Social Movements 1967
↓ Terrorism 1982

Radicalism (Political)
Use Political Radicalism

Radio 1973
PN 469 **SC** 42730
B Audiovisual Communications Media 1973
Mass Media 1967
Telecommunications Media 1973
R ↓ News Media 1997

Radiography
Use Roentgenography

Radiology 1973
PN 110 **SC** 42740
B Medical Sciences 1967

Rage
Use Anger

Railroad Trains 1973
PN 220 **SC** 42760
UF Trains (Railroad)
B Ground Transportation 1973
R Public Transportation 1973

Random Sampling 1973
PN 323 **SC** 42780
B Sampling (Experimental) 1973

Range of Motion 2007
PN 56 **SC** 42785
SN Distance and direction by which a joint can be extended or flexed.
HN This term was introduced in April 2007. Relevant records were re-indexed with this term. The posting note reflects the number of records that were re-indexed.
B Motor Processes 1967
R ↓ Joints (Anatomy) 1973

Rank Difference Correlation 1973
PN 32 **SC** 42790
UF Spearman Rho
B Statistical Correlation 1967

Rank Order Correlation 1973
PN 129 **SC** 42800
B Statistical Correlation 1967

Rape 1973
PN 3196 **SC** 42810
B Sexual Abuse 1988
Sexual Intercourse (Human) 1973
Violent Crime 2003
N Acquaintance Rape 1991

Raphe Nuclei 1982
PN 610 **SC** 42815
SN Serotonin synthesizing neurons in and near the median plane of the brain stem lying dorsally in the pons. These nuclei are sometimes grouped with the reticular formation and are thought to function as part of the limbic system.
B Pons 1973
R ↓ Hindbrain 1997
↓ Limbic System 1973
Reticular Formation 1967

Rapid Eye Movement 1971
PN 484 **SC** 42820
UF REM
B Eye Movements 1967
R REM Dream Deprivation 1973
REM Dreams 1973
REM Sleep 1973

Rapid Eye Movement Dreams
Use REM Dreams

Rapid Eye Movement Sleep
Use REM Sleep

Rapid Heart Rate
Use Tachycardia

Rapport
Use Interpersonal Interaction

Rasch Model
Use Item Response Theory

Rat Learning 1967
PN 2347 **SC** 42860
HN Not defined prior to 1982. Use RAT LEARNING or RATS to access references from 1967-1981. From 1982 used for discussions of hypotheses or theories of learning in rats.
B Animal Learning 2003
Learning 1967

Rating 1967
PN 2681 **SC** 42880
SN Measurement technique involving relative evaluation or estimate of characteristics or qualities of a person, process, or thing. Used when rating as a technique is the object of interest.
B Testing 1967
R Halo Effect 1982
Interrater Reliability 1982

Rating Scales 1967
PN 13673 **SC** 42890
B Measurement 1967
N Likert Scales 1994
R Multidimensional Scaling 1982

Ratio Reinforcement
Use Fixed Ratio Reinforcement AND Variable Ratio Reinforcement

Ratiocination
Use Logical Thinking

Rational Emotive Behavior Therapy 2003
PN 1364 **SC** 42914
SN A directive, interpretative, and philosophical therapy developed by Albert Ellis that stresses the reciprocal interactions among cognition, emotion, and behavior and views the goal of treatment as the client's development of rational as opposed to irrational beliefs about his or her problem.
HN In June 2003, this term was created to replace the discontinued term RATIONAL EMOTIVE THERAPY. RATIONAL EMOTIVE THERAPY was removed from all records containing it and replaced with RATIONAL EMOTIVE BEHAVIOR THERAPY.
UF Rational Emotive Therapy
B Psychotherapy 1967
R Cognitive Therapy 1982
Ellis (Albert) 1991
↓ Psychotherapeutic Techniques 1967

Rational Emotive Therapy
HN In June 2003, the term was discontinued and removed from all records containing it, and replaced with RATIONAL EMOTIVE BEHAVIOR THERAPY, its postable counterpart.
Use Rational Emotive Behavior Therapy

Rational Thinking
Use Rationality

Rationality 2005
PN 589 **SC** 42917
SN The state of being reasonable or understanding.
HN This term was introduced in August 2005. Relevant records were re-indexed with this term. The posting note reflects the number of records that were re-indexed.
UF Rational Thinking
R Logical Thinking 1967
↓ Reasoning 1967

Rationalization (Defense Mechanism) 1973
PN 296 **SC** 42920
SN A type of defense mechanism used to explain or justify unacceptable behavior.
B Defense Mechanisms 1967

Rats 1967
PN 74599 **SC** 42930
UF Albino Rats
White Rats
B Rodents 1973
N Norway Rats 1973

Rauwolfia
HN Term was discontinued in 1997. In 2000, the term was removed from all records containing it and replaced with ALKALOIDS, its postable counterpart.
Use Alkaloids

Raven Coloured Progressive Matrices 1973
PN 128 **SC** 42950
B Intelligence Measures 1967

Raven Progressive Matrices 1978
PN 276 **SC** 42960
HN Use RAVENS PROGRESSIVE MATRICES to access references from 1973-1977.
B Intelligence Measures 1967

Raynauds Disease
Use Cardiovascular Disorders

RDC
Use Research Diagnostic Criteria

Reactance
Use Psychological Reactance

Reaction Formation 1973
PN 43 **SC** 42990
SN Defense mechanism that leads to the formation of behaviors and attitudes opposite to the repressed anxiety-inducing behavior or feelings.
B Defense Mechanisms 1967

Reaction Time 1967
PN 11271 **SC** 43000
SN Minimal time interval between the onset of a stimulus and the beginning of a subject's response to that stimulus. Compare RESPONSE LATENCY.
UF Response Lag
Response Speed
Response Time
RT (Response)
Speed (Response)
B Response Parameters 1973
R Cognitive Processing Speed 1997
Conceptual Tempo 1985

Reactive Attachment Disorder
Use Attachment Disorders

Reactive Depression 1973
PN 280 **SC** 43020
B Major Depression 1988

Reactive Psychosis 1973
PN 219 **SC** 43030
SN A type of psychotic disorder that results from a traumatic experience. Usually symptoms are severe but temporary.
UF Reactive Schizophrenia
Traumatic Psychosis

Reactive Psychosis — (cont'd)
B Psychosis 1967

Reactive Schizophrenia
Use Reactive Psychosis AND Schizophrenia

Readability 1978
PN 526 SC 43045
SN Textual difficulty or other qualitative aspects of reading material that facilitate comprehension. May include clarity of graphic displays.
B Written Language 1967
R ↓ Legibility 1978
↓ Reading 1967
Reading Comprehension 1973
Reading Materials 1973

Readaptation
Use Adaptation

Readiness Potential
Use Contingent Negative Variation

Readiness to Change 2007
PN 256 SC 43075
SN Commitment and motivation to make a behavioral or lifestyle change.
HN This term was introduced in April 2007. Relevant records were re-indexed with this term. The posting note reflects the number of records that were re-indexed.
UF Change Readiness
Motivation to Change
R Behavior Change 1973
↓ Behavior Modification 1973
Lifestyle Changes 1997
Motivational Interviewing 2007
Stages of Change 2007

Reading 1967
PN 6954 SC 43080
N Braille 1978
Oral Reading 1973
Remedial Reading 1973
Silent Reading 1973
R Dyslexia 1973
Initial Teaching Alphabet 1973
Proofreading 1988
Readability 1978
Reading Ability 1973
Reading Achievement 1973
Reading Comprehension 1973
Reading Development 1997
↓ Reading Disabilities 1967
Reading Education 1973
Reading Materials 1973
Reading Readiness 1973
↓ Reading Skills 1973
Reading Speed 1973
Sight Vocabulary 1973

Reading Ability 1973
PN 4728 SC 43090
SN Perceptual and intellectual capacity or efficiency in reading.
B Cognitive Ability 1973
R Academic Aptitude 1973
↓ Reading 1967
Reading Development 1997
↓ Reading Skills 1973

Reading Achievement 1973
PN 3919 SC 43100
B Academic Achievement 1967
R ↓ Reading 1967

Reading Aloud
Use Oral Reading

Reading Comprehension 1973
PN 6575 SC 43110
B Reading Skills 1973
Verbal Comprehension 1985
R Readability 1978
↓ Reading 1967

Reading Development 1997
PN 1255 SC 43115
R ↓ Language Development 1967
↓ Literacy 1973
Phonological Awareness 2004
↓ Reading 1967
Reading Ability 1973
Reading Readiness 1973
↓ Reading Skills 1973

Reading Disabilities 1967
PN 3791 SC 43120
B Disabilities 2003
Learning Disorders 1967
N Dyslexia 1973
R ↓ Alexia 1982
Educational Diagnosis 1978
↓ Reading 1967

Reading Education 1973
PN 4507 SC 43130
B Language Arts Education 1973
R Braille 1978
Braille Instruction 1973
Initial Teaching Alphabet 1973
↓ Literacy 1973
Literacy Programs 1997
Phonics 1973
↓ Reading 1967
Remedial Reading 1973

Reading Materials 1973
PN 1388 SC 43140
UF Basal Readers
B Instructional Media 1967
R ↓ Books 1973
Braille 1978
Readability 1978
↓ Reading 1967
Text Structure 1982
↓ Textbooks 1978

Reading Measures 1973
PN 848 SC 43150
B Measurement 1967
N Metropolitan Readiness Tests 1978

Reading Readiness 1973
PN 427 SC 43160
SN Developmental level at which language skills; cognitive, perceptual and motor abilities; experience; and interest combine to enable a child to profit from specific reading activities. Compare SCHOOL READINESS.
R Phonological Awareness 2004
↓ Reading 1967
Reading Development 1997

Reading Skills 1973
PN 2805 SC 43170
SN Proficiency in reading developed through practice and influenced by ability. Includes word recognition, pronunciation, and comprehension.
B Ability 1967
N Reading Comprehension 1973
Reading Speed 1973
R ↓ Literacy 1973
Literacy Programs 1997
↓ Reading 1967
Reading Ability 1973
Reading Development 1997
Sight Vocabulary 1973
Word Recognition 1988

Reading Speed 1973
PN 854 SC 43180
B Reading Skills 1973
R ↓ Reading 1967

Readjustment (Psychosocial)
Use Psychosocial Readjustment

Readmission (Hospital)
Use Hospital Admission

Readmission (Psychiatric Hospital)
Use Psychiatric Hospital Readmission

Realism (Philosophy) 1973
PN 352 SC 43220
B Philosophies 1967

Reality 1973
PN 1960 SC 43230
R ↓ Metaphysics 1973
Reality Testing 1973
Reality Therapy 1973

Reality Testing 1973
PN 315 SC 43240
SN Cognitive process of evaluation and judgment for differentiation between objective perceptions originating outside of the self and subjective stimuli or fantasies.
R ↓ Cognitive Processes 1967
↓ Personality Processes 1967
Reality 1973

Reality Therapy 1973
PN 506 SC 43250
SN Method of psychotherapeutic treatment based on assumption of client's personal responsibility for his/her behavior. Therapist actively guides client to accurate self-perception for fulfillment of needs of self-worth and respect for others.
B Psychotherapy 1967
R ↓ Psychotherapeutic Techniques 1967
Reality 1973

Reasoning 1967
PN 7273 SC 43260
B Thinking 1967
N Case Based Reasoning 2003
↓ Inductive Deductive Reasoning 1973
R Analogy 1991
Cognitive Hypothesis Testing 1982
Critical Thinking 2006
Declarative Knowledge 1997
Dialectics 1973
Heuristics 2003
↓ Intelligence 1967
↓ Problem Solving 1967

Reasoning — (cont'd)
Procedural Knowledge 1997
Rationality 2005

Rebelliousness 2003
PN 51 **SC** 43265
HN This term was introduced in June 2003. Relevant records were re-indexed with this term. The posting note reflects the number of records that were re-indexed.
B Personality Traits 1967
R Acting Out 1967
↓ Behavior Problems 1967
Nonconformity (Personality) 1973

Recall (Learning) 1967
PN 12080 **SC** 43290
B Retention 1967
N Cued Recall 1994
Free Recall 1973
Serial Recall 1994
R ↓ Memory 1967
Memory Training 1994
Reminiscence 1985

Recency Effect 1973
PN 413 **SC** 43298
SN Component of the serial position effect which is manifested by a greater ease in learning items which occur at the end of a series rather than those toward the middle.
B Serial Position Effect 1982
R ↓ Learning 1967
Primacy Effect 1973

Receptive Fields 1985
PN 323 **SC** 43299
SN Spatially discrete patterns of peripheral and central neuronal innervation of sensory mechanisms.
B Nervous System 1967
N Cutaneous Receptive Fields 1985
Visual Receptive Fields 1982
R ↓ Afferent Pathways 1982
Neural Plasticity 1994
Sensory Neglect 1994
↓ Sensory Neurons 1973

Receptor Binding 1985
PN 3566 **SC** 43297
SN Affinity processes occurring between chemical substances and specific cellular sites in the body (e.g., blood platelet or neural receptor binding of an adrenergic drug). Consider also NEURAL RECEPTORS.
B Neurochemistry 1973
Neurophysiology 1973
R Adrenergic Receptors 2003
Cholinergic Receptors 2003
↓ Neural Receptors 1973

Receptors (Adrenergic)
Use Adrenergic Receptors

Receptors (Cholinergic)
Use Cholinergic Receptors

Receptors (Neural)
Use Neural Receptors

Recessiveness (Genetic)
Use Genetic Recessiveness

Recidivism 1973
PN 2447 **SC** 43320
SN Repetition or recurrence of previous condition or behavior pattern (e.g., behavior disorder or criminal or delinquent behavior), especially when recurrence leads to recommitment or a subsequent conviction.
B Antisocial Behavior 1971
R Criminal Record 2006
↓ Criminals 1967

Reciprocal Inhibition Therapy 1973
PN 77 **SC** 43330
SN Form of behavior therapy which seeks to evoke one response in order to bring about a suppression or decrease in the strength of a simultaneous response. Used to weaken unadaptive habits, particularly anxiety responses.
B Behavior Therapy 1967
R Counterconditioning 1973
Systematic Desensitization Therapy 1973

Reciprocity 1973
PN 1230 **SC** 43340
B Social Behavior 1967
R Retaliation 1991

Recognition (Learning) 1967
PN 8708 **SC** 43350
B Retention 1967
N Object Recognition 1997
R Matching to Sample 1994
Memory Training 1994
Word Recognition 1988

Reconstruction (Learning) 1973
PN 163 **SC** 43360
SN Recalling memorized items in the order in which they were originally presented. Compare FREE RECALL.
B Retention 1967

Reconstructive Psychotherapy
Use Psychotherapy

Recorders (Tape)
Use Tape Recorders

Recovery (Disorders) 1973
PN 4929 **SC** 43390
R ↓ Disorders 1967
↓ Drug Abstinence 1994
Illness Behavior 1982
↓ Mental Disorders 1967
↓ Physical Disorders 1997
Postsurgical Complications 1973
Relapse Prevention 1994
↓ Remission (Disorders) 1973
Sobriety 1988
↓ Treatment Outcomes 1982

Recreation 1967
PN 2821 **SC** 43400
UF Play
N Athletic Participation 1973
Baseball 1973
Basketball 1973
Camping 1973
Childrens Recreational Games 1973
Clubs (Social Organizations) 1973
Dance 1973
Doll Play 1973
Football 1973

Recreation — (cont'd)
↓ Gambling 1973
Judo 1973
Martial Arts 1985
Soccer 1994
Summer Camps (Recreation) 1973
Swimming 1973
Television Viewing 1973
Tennis 1973
Traveling 1973
Vacationing 1973
Weightlifting 1994
R ↓ Childhood Play Behavior 1978
Computer Games 1988
Daily Activities 1994
↓ Games 1967
Hobbies 1988
Holidays 1988
Leisure Time 1973
Relaxation 1973
↓ Sports 1967
Tourism 2003
↓ Toys 1973
Wilderness Experience 1991

Recreation Areas 1973
PN 428 **SC** 43410
UF Parks (Recreational)
N Playgrounds 1973
R ↓ Community Facilities 1973
↓ Environmental Planning 1982
Urban Planning 1973

Recreation Therapy 1973
PN 612 **SC** 43420
UF Activity Therapy
Gymnastic Therapy
B Creative Arts Therapy 1994
R Art Therapy 1973
Dance Therapy 1973
Horticulture Therapy 2007
Movement Therapy 1997
Music Therapy 1973
↓ Psychotherapy 1967
Therapeutic Camps 1978

Recreational Day Camps
Use Summer Camps (Recreation)

Recruitment (Military)
Use Military Recruitment

Recruitment (Personnel)
Use Personnel Recruitment

Recruitment (Teachers)
Use Teacher Recruitment

Recurrence (Disorders)
Use Relapse (Disorders)

Recurrent Depression 1994
PN 357 **SC** 43465
SN Depression that reoccurs periodically.
B Major Depression 1988
R Relapse (Disorders) 1973
Seasonal Affective Disorder 1991

Recycling
Use Conservation (Ecological Behavior)

Red Blood Cells
Use Erythrocytes

Red Nucleus
Use Mesencephalon

Reductionism 1973
PN 330 **SC** 43480
UF Atomism
Elementarism
B Philosophies 1967
R Positivism (Philosophy) 1997

Reemployment 1991
PN 394 **SC** 43485
SN Returning to work following a period of absence, e.g., unemployment or retirement.
UF Job Reentry
Return to Work
R ↓ Employment Status 1982
Job Search 1985
Occupational Choice 1967
↓ Personnel 1967
Retirement 1973
Unemployment 1967

Reenactments
Use Enactments

Reentry Students 1985
PN 361 **SC** 43495
SN Persons reentering school or an educational program after an extended absence; for example, middle-aged adults enrolled in undergraduate programs.
B Students 1967
R ↓ Adult Education 1973
Adult Learning 1997
↓ College Students 1967
↓ Continuing Education 1985
High School Students 1967
↓ School Dropouts 1967

Reference Groups 1994
PN 190 **SC** 43497
SN Social groups used as sources for personal and behavioral identification, motivation, and evaluation of one's own status.
B Social Groups 1973
R Ethnic Identity 1973
↓ Group Dynamics 1967
Group Identity 2007
↓ Interpersonal Influences 1967
↓ Peer Relations 1967
↓ Self Concept 1967
↓ Social Identity 1988
↓ Social Influences 1967
Social Support 2004
↓ Socialization 1967

Referral (Professional)
Use Professional Referral

Referral (Self)
Use Self Referral

Reflectiveness 1997
PN 553 **SC** 43505
HN Use IMPULSIVENESS to access references from 1985-1996.
B Cognitive Style 1967
R Conceptual Tempo 1985
Impulsiveness 1973
Introspection 1973
Reminiscence 1985
Self Monitoring (Personality) 1985
Self Perception 1967

Reflexes 1971
PN 2144 **SC** 43530
SN Simple automatic involuntary neuromuscular responses to stimuli.
UF Unconditioned Reflex
B Physiology 1967
N Achilles Tendon Reflex 1973
Acoustic Reflex 1973
Babinski Reflex 1973
Eyeblink Reflex 1973
Flexion Reflex 1973
Hoffmanns Reflex 1973
Nystagmus 1973
Ocular Accommodation 1982
Orienting Reflex 1967
Startle Reflex 1967
Yawning 1988
R Instinctive Behavior 1982
Muscle Contractions 1973
Muscle Tone 1985
Parkinsonism 1994

Reformatories 1973
PN 70 **SC** 43540
SN Specific type of correctional institution to which young or first offenders are committed for training and reformation.
B Correctional Institutions 1973
R Prisons 1967

Refraction Errors 1973
PN 137 **SC** 43550
B Errors 1967
Eye Disorders 1973
Light Refraction 1982
N Myopia 1973
R Amblyopia 1973
↓ Genetic Disorders 1973
Ocular Accommodation 1982

Reframing
Use Paradoxical Techniques

Refugees 1988
PN 1840 **SC** 43555
SN Uprooted, homeless, voluntary or involuntary migrants who flee their native country, usually to escape danger or persecution because of their race, religion, or political views, and who no longer possess protection of their former government.
HN Use HUMAN MIGRATION to access references from 1982-1987.
UF Political Refugees
B Human Migration 1973
R Immigration 1973
↓ Social Processes 1967

Refusal (Treatment)
Use Treatment Refusal

Regional Differences 2001
PN 713 **SC** 43558
SN Used for comparisons between similar populations whose attributes differ primarily due to their geographical region of residence. Used for comparisons both within and across countries. Compare CROSS CULTURAL DIFFERENCES.
UF Geographical Differences
R Cross Cultural Differences 1967
Geography 1973
↓ Group Differences 2007
↓ Sociocultural Factors 1967

Regression (Defense Mechanism) 1967
PN 648 **SC** 43560
B Defense Mechanisms 1967

Regression Analysis
Use Statistical Regression

Regression Artifact
Use Statistical Regression

Regurgitation
Use Vomiting

Rehabilitation 1967
PN 8256 **SC** 43580
SN Treatment designed to restore or bring a client to a condition of health or useful and constructive activity. Used for populations including sensory handicapped, retarded, delinquent, criminal, or disordered. Use a more specific term if possible.
B Treatment 1967
N Cognitive Rehabilitation 1985
Criminal Rehabilitation 2004
↓ Drug Rehabilitation 1973
↓ Neuropsychological Rehabilitation 1997
Occupational Therapy 1967
Physical Therapy 1973
↓ Psychosocial Rehabilitation 1973
R Activities of Daily Living 1991
Adaptive Behavior 1991
Animal Assisted Therapy 1994
Deinstitutionalization 1982
Disability Management 1991
Habilitation 1991
↓ Health Care Services 1978
Independent Living Programs 1991
↓ Intervention 2003
↓ Mainstreaming 1991
Partial Hospitalization 1985
↓ Rehabilitation Centers 1973
Rehabilitation Counseling 1978
Self Care Skills 1978
↓ Support Groups 1991
↓ Twelve Step Programs 1997
Wilderness Experience 1991

Rehabilitation (Drug)
Use Drug Rehabilitation

Rehabilitation (Psychosocial)
Use Psychosocial Rehabilitation

Rehabilitation (Vocational)
Use Vocational Rehabilitation

Rehabilitation Centers 1973
PN 367 **SC** 43620
N Sheltered Workshops 1967
R ↓ Community Facilities 1973
↓ Rehabilitation 1967

Rehabilitation Counseling 1978
PN 949 **SC** 43624
B Counseling 1967
R ↓ Alcohol Rehabilitation 1982
↓ Drug Rehabilitation 1973
↓ Psychosocial Rehabilitation 1973
↓ Rehabilitation 1967
Rehabilitation Education 1997
↓ Vocational Rehabilitation 1967
Work Adjustment Training 1991

Rehabilitation Counselors 1978
PN 893 **SC** 43626
B Counselors 1967
R Rehabilitation Education 1997
↓ Social Workers 1973

Rehabilitation Education 1997
PN 178 **SC** 43627
SN Graduate education to train students in rehabilitation processes or counseling in such areas as drug rehabilitation, vocational rehabilitation, or occupational rehabilitation.
B Graduate Education 1973
R Counselor Education 1973
Rehabilitation Counseling 1978
Rehabilitation Counselors 1978

Rehearsal
Use Practice

Reinforcement 1967
PN 7954 **SC** 43630
SN Presentation of a reinforcer contingent on the performance of some behavior. Also, the reinforcing event or object itself (i.e., the reinforcer), which, when made to follow the performance of some behavior, results in a change in the frequency of occurrence of that behavior. Compare REWARDS and INCENTIVES.
N Differential Reinforcement 1973
Negative Reinforcement 1973
Noncontingent Reinforcement 1988
↓ Positive Reinforcement 1973
Primary Reinforcement 1973
↓ Punishment 1967
Reinforcement Amounts 1973
↓ Reinforcement Schedules 1967
↓ Rewards 1967
Secondary Reinforcement 1967
Self Reinforcement 1973
↓ Social Reinforcement 1967
R Autoshaping 1978
Behavioral Contrast 1978
↓ Biofeedback 1973
↓ Conditioning 1967
Delay of Gratification 1978
Extinction (Learning) 1967
↓ Feedback 1967
↓ Learning 1967
↓ Motivation 1967
↓ Operant Conditioning 1967
↓ Self Stimulation 1967
Vicarious Experiences 1973

Reinforcement (Vicarious)
Use Vicarious Experiences

Reinforcement Amounts 1973
PN 1059 **SC** 43640
B Reinforcement 1967
R Reinforcement Delay 1985

Reinforcement Delay 1985
PN 502 **SC** 43645
SN Time delay between the occurrence of a conditioned response and the administration of reinforcement in an operant conditioning paradigm. Consider INTERSTIMULUS INTERVAL for classical conditioning studies.
UF Delayed Reinforcement
B Reinforcement Schedules 1967
R Delay of Gratification 1978
Delayed Alternation 1994
Interstimulus Interval 1967

Reinforcement Delay — (cont'd)
Reinforcement Amounts 1973
↓ Stimulus Intervals 1973

Reinforcement Schedules 1967
PN 5372 **SC** 43650
UF Continuous Reinforcement
Intermittent Reinforcement
Partial Reinforcement
Schedules (Reinforcement)
B Reinforcement 1967
N Concurrent Reinforcement Schedules 1988
Fixed Interval Reinforcement 1973
Fixed Ratio Reinforcement 1973
Reinforcement Delay 1985
Variable Interval Reinforcement 1973
Variable Ratio Reinforcement 1973

Reinnervation
Use Neural Development

Rejection (Social)
Use Social Acceptance

Relapse (Disorders) 1973
PN 3384 **SC** 43660
SN Recurrence of symptoms after apparent cure or period of improvement.
UF Recurrence (Disorders)
R ↓ Disorders 1967
Expressed Emotion 1991
↓ Mental Disorders 1967
↓ Physical Disorders 1997
Postsurgical Complications 1973
Recurrent Depression 1994
Relapse Prevention 1994
↓ Treatment Outcomes 1982

Relapse Prevention 1994
PN 1038 **SC** 43670
B Prevention 1973
R Maintenance Therapy 1997
Preventive Medicine 1973
Primary Mental Health Prevention 1973
Recovery (Disorders) 1973
Relapse (Disorders) 1973
↓ Remission (Disorders) 1973
↓ Treatment 1967
↓ Treatment Outcomes 1982

Relationship Quality 2004
PN 760 **SC** 43674
SN Used for spouses, couples, friends, or family members.
HN This term was introduced in June 2004. Relevant records were re-indexed with this term. The posting note reflects the number of records that were re-indexed.
R Friendship 1967
↓ Interpersonal Relationships 2004
Marital Satisfaction 1988
↓ Relationship Satisfaction 2001

Relationship Satisfaction 2001
PN 851 **SC** 43675
SN Used for satisfaction in relationships, including those between married and unmarried individuals, same-sex couples, relatives, and friends.
UF Interpersonal Relationship Satisfaction
B Satisfaction 1973
N Marital Satisfaction 1988
R ↓ Family Relations 1967
Friendship 1967
↓ Interpersonal Interaction 1967

Relationship Satisfaction — (cont'd)
↓ Interpersonal Relationships 2004
Male Female Relations 1988
Relationship Quality 2004
↓ Relationship Termination 1997
Role Satisfaction 1994

Relationship Termination 1997
PN 372 **SC** 43680
SN Voluntary or involuntary ending of a relationship.
UF Breakup (Relationship)
N ↓ Marital Separation 1973
R Abandonment 1997
Attachment Disorders 2001
Friendship 1967
↓ Human Courtship 1973
Male Female Relations 1988
Marital Conflict 1973
↓ Marital Relations 1967
Marital Satisfaction 1988
↓ Peer Relations 1967
↓ Relationship Satisfaction 2001
Romance 1997
Separation Anxiety 1973
↓ Separation Reactions 1997
Social Dating 1973

Relationship Therapy 1973
PN 129 **SC** 43690
SN Psychotherapeutic approach in which the relationship between the therapist and client serves as the basis for the therapy. The therapist provides a supportive setting in which the client can grow and develop and gradually reach differentiation from the therapist and come to perceive his/her own self as separate and distinct.
B Psychotherapy 1967

Relativism 1997
PN 120 **SC** 43694
B Philosophies 1967
R Dogmatism 1978
Epistemology 1973
Existentialism 1967
↓ Metaphysics 1973
Physics 1973

Relaxation 1973
PN 1385 **SC** 43697
SN Tranquil and restful state, activity, or pasttime of lessened muscle tension, stress, or attention.
R Guided Imagery 2001
Leisure Time 1973
Muscle Relaxation 1973
↓ Recreation 1967
Yoga 1973

Relaxation Therapy 1978
PN 2523 **SC** 43700
SN Therapy emphasizing relaxation and teaching a person or patient how to relax in order to reduce psychological tensions.
UF Muscle Relaxation Therapy
B Treatment 1967
N Progressive Relaxation Therapy 1978
R Anxiety Management 1997
Autogenic Training 1973
↓ Behavior Modification 1973
Guided Imagery 2001
↓ Hypnotherapy 1973
Meditation 1973
Muscle Relaxation 1973
Posthypnotic Suggestions 1994
↓ Psychotherapeutic Techniques 1967

Relaxation Therapy — (cont'd)
Systematic Desensitization Therapy 1973

Relearning 1973
PN 165 **SC** 43710
B Learning 1967
R ↓ Memory 1967

Reliability (Statistical)
HN Term was discontinued in 1973. In 2000, the term was removed from all records containing it, and replaced with STATISTICAL RELIABILITY, its postable counterpart.
Use Statistical Reliability

Reliability (Test)
Use Test Reliability

Religion 1967
PN 6320 **SC** 43740
SN Conceptually broad term. Use a more specific term if possible.
R Asceticism 1973
↓ Religious Beliefs 1973
Religious Buildings 1973
Religious Conversion 2006
Religious Education 1973
Religious Experiences 1997
↓ Religious Literature 1973
↓ Religious Organizations 1991
↓ Religious Personnel 1973
↓ Religious Practices 1973
↓ Religious Prejudices 1973
Spirituality 1988
Theology 2003

Religiosity 1973
PN 3194 **SC** 43750
SN Degree of one's religious involvement, devotion to religious beliefs, or adherence to religious observances.
B Religious Beliefs 1973
R Religious Fundamentalism 2003
Spirituality 1988

Religious Affiliation 1973
PN 1589 **SC** 43760
B Religious Beliefs 1973
N ↓ Buddhism 1973
↓ Christianity 1973
Hinduism 1973
Islam 1973
Judaism 1967
Shamanism 1973
Sikhism 2004
R ↓ Membership 2007
Religious Fundamentalism 2003
↓ Religious Groups 1997
↓ Religious Practices 1973
Theology 2003

Religious Beliefs 1973
PN 5783 **SC** 43770
UF Beliefs (Religion)
N Atheism 1973
God Concepts 1973
Religiosity 1973
↓ Religious Affiliation 1973
Religious Fundamentalism 2003
Sin 1973

Religious Beliefs — (cont'd)
R Agnosticism 2007
Asceticism 1973
↓ Attitudes 1967
Bible 1973
Cultism 1973
Death Attitudes 1973
↓ Ethics 1967
Evil 2003
Existentialism 1967
Forgiveness 1988
Morality 1967
Mysticism 1967
Occultism 1978
Religion 1967
Religious Conversion 2006
Religious Education 1973
Religious Experiences 1997
↓ Religious Literature 1973
↓ Religious Practices 1973
↓ Religious Prejudices 1973
Soul 2004
Spirit Possession 1997
Spirituality 1988
Superstitions 1973
Theology 2003
Witchcraft 1973

Religious Buildings 1973
PN 234 **SC** 43780
UF Churches
B Facilities 2006
R ↓ Architecture 1973
↓ Community Facilities 1973
Religion 1967

Religious Conversion 2006
PN 58 **SC** 43785
SN Changing one's religious beliefs and affiliation.
HN This term was introduced in May 2006. Relevant records were re-indexed with this term. The posting note reflects the number of records that were re-indexed.
R Missionaries 1973
Religion 1967
↓ Religious Beliefs 1973
Religious Experiences 1997
↓ Religious Groups 1997

Religious Education 1973
PN 657 **SC** 43790
B Education 1967
R Private School Education 1973
Religion 1967
↓ Religious Beliefs 1973
↓ Religious Personnel 1973
Seminaries 1973

Religious Experiences 1997
PN 504 **SC** 43795
R Cultism 1973
Mysticism 1967
↓ Parapsychological Phenomena 1973
Religion 1967
↓ Religious Beliefs 1973
Religious Conversion 2006
Spirituality 1988

Religious Fundamentalism 2003
PN 312 **SC** 43796
SN Conservative religious beliefs and practices that emphasize literal interpretation of scriptures and strict adherence to traditional principles and practices.
HN In June 2003, this term was created to replace the discontinued term FUNDAMENTALISM (RELIGIOUS). FUNDAMENTALISM (RELIGIOUS) was removed from all records containing it and replaced with RELIGIOUS FUNDAMENTALISM.
UF Fundamentalism (Religious)
B Religious Beliefs 1973
R Conservatism 1973
Religiosity 1973
↓ Religious Affiliation 1973

Religious Groups 1997
PN 370 **SC** 43797
SN Groups and their members sharing common religious beliefs and belonging to the same religious affiliation.
N Buddhists 1997
↓ Christians 1997
Hindus 1997
Jews 1997
Muslims 1997
Sikhs 2004
R ↓ Clergy 1973
↓ Racial and Ethnic Groups 2001
↓ Religious Affiliation 1973
Religious Conversion 2006
↓ Religious Organizations 1991
↓ Religious Practices 1973

Religious Literature 1973
PN 201 **SC** 43800
N Bible 1973
R ↓ Literature 1967
Religion 1967
↓ Religious Beliefs 1973
Theology 2003

Religious Occupations
Use Religious Personnel

Religious Organizations 1991
PN 410 **SC** 43815
SN Any type of agency, organization, or institution operated by religious groups or persons. Includes, but not limited to, church, social service, educational, fraternal, recreational, missionary, or rehabilitation organizations.
B Organizations 1967
N Faith Based Organizations 2007
R Religion 1967
↓ Religious Groups 1997

Religious Personnel 1973
PN 405 **SC** 43820
UF Religious Occupations
B Personnel 1967
N ↓ Clergy 1973
Evangelists 1973
Lay Religious Personnel 1973
Missionaries 1973
Nuns 1973
Seminarians 1973
R ↓ Professional Personnel 1978
Religion 1967
Religious Education 1973

Religious Practices 1973
PN 2052 **SC** 43830
UF Rites (Religion)
Rituals (Religion)
Worship
N Asceticism 1973
Confession (Religion) 1973
Faith Healing 1973
Meditation 1973
Prayer 1973
Yoga 1973
R Circumcision 2001
Glossolalia 1973
Mysticism 1967
Religion 1967
↓ Religious Affiliation 1973
↓ Religious Beliefs 1973
↓ Religious Groups 1997

Religious Prejudices 1973
PN 81 **SC** 43840
B Prejudice 1967
N AntiSemitism 1973
R Hate Crimes 2003
Religion 1967
↓ Religious Beliefs 1973

REM
Use Rapid Eye Movement

REM Dream Deprivation 1973
PN 27 **SC** 43860
B Deprivation 1967
R Rapid Eye Movement 1971

REM Dreams 1973
PN 127 **SC** 43870
UF Rapid Eye Movement Dreams
B Dreaming 1967
R ↓ Eye Movements 1967
Lucid Dreaming 1994
Rapid Eye Movement 1971
REM Sleep 1973

REM Sleep 1973
PN 2519 **SC** 43880
UF Paradoxical Sleep
Rapid Eye Movement Sleep
B Sleep 1967
R ↓ Eye Movements 1967
Lucid Dreaming 1994
Rapid Eye Movement 1971
REM Dreams 1973

Remarriage 1985
PN 629 **SC** 43885
B Marriage 1967
R Divorce 1973
↓ Marital Status 1973
Stepfamily 1991

Remedial Education 1985
PN 676 **SC** 43887
SN Specialized instruction designed to raise academic competence of students with below-normal achievement or learning difficulties. Compare COMPENSATORY EDUCATION.
B Education 1967
N Remedial Reading 1973
R Compensatory Education 1973
Educational Therapy 1997
Special Education 1967

Remedial Reading 1973
PN 905 **SC** 43890
SN Specialized instruction designed to correct faulty reading habits or to improve imperfectly learned reading skills.
B Reading 1967
Remedial Education 1985
R Educational Placement 1978
Reading Education 1973

Remembering
Use Retention

Reminiscence 1985
PN 926 **SC** 43905
SN Process of recalling past experiences.
B Memory 1967
R Anniversary Events 1994
Autobiographical Memory 1994
Early Memories 1985
Enactments 1997
Forgetting 1973
Homesickness 1994
Life Review 1991
↓ Recall (Learning) 1967
Reflectiveness 1997
↓ Retention 1967

Remission (Disorders) 1973
PN 1111 **SC** 43910
SN Diminution or disappearance of symptoms.
N Spontaneous Remission 1973
Symptom Remission 1973
R ↓ Disorders 1967
↓ Mental Disorders 1967
↓ Physical Disorders 1997
Recovery (Disorders) 1973
Relapse Prevention 1994
↓ Treatment Outcomes 1982

Renal Diseases
Use Kidney Diseases

Renal Transplantation
Use Organ Transplantation

Repairmen
Use Technical Service Personnel

Repeated Measures 1985
PN 364 **SC** 43935
SN Experimental design in which the subjects serve in all experimental, treatment, or control conditions.
UF Within Subjects Design
B Experimental Design 1967
Testing 1967
R Posttesting 1973
Pretesting 1973

Repetition (Compulsive)
Use Repetition Compulsion

Repetition Compulsion 2005
PN 217 **SC** 43939
SN The unconscious need or impulse to repeat or reenact traumatic experiences over and over in an attempt to deal with them.
HN In August 2005, this term was created to replace the discontinued term COMPULSIVE REPETITION. COMPULSIVE REPETITION was removed from all records containing it, and was replaced with REPETITION COMPULSION, its postable counterpart.
UF Compulsive Repetition
Repetition (Compulsive)

Repetition Compulsion — (cont'd)
B Compulsions 1973
R Enactments 1997
Rumination (Cognitive Process) 2001
Stereotyped Behavior 1973

Repetitive Transcranial Magnetic Stimulation
Use Transcranial Magnetic Stimulation

Replication (Experimental)
Use Experimental Replication

Repressed Memory 1997
PN 579 **SC** 43955
B Memory 1967
R Age Regression (Hypnotic) 1988
↓ Amnesia 1967
Early Memories 1985
Emotional Trauma 1967
False Memory 1997
Repression (Defense Mechanism) 1967

Repression (Defense Mechanism) 1967
PN 1053 **SC** 43960
B Defense Mechanisms 1967
R Repressed Memory 1997
Suppression (Defense Mechanism) 1973

Repression Sensitization 1973
PN 291 **SC** 43968
SN Personality continuum which characterizes individual's defensive response to threat, with avoidance (repression or denial) at one extreme and approach (worry or intellectualization) at the other.
UF Sensitization Repression
B Personality Traits 1967

Repression Sensitization Scale 1973
PN 28 **SC** 43970
B Nonprojective Personality Measures 1973

Reproductive Technology 1988
PN 691 **SC** 43975
UF Artificial Insemination
In Vitro Fertilization
Test Tube Babies
B Biotechnology 2007
R Cloning 2003
Eugenics 1973
Fertilization 1973
↓ Genetic Engineering 1994
↓ Genetics 1967
↓ Pregnancy 1967
Prenatal Diagnosis 1988
Selective Breeding 1973
↓ Sexual Reproduction 1973

Reptiles 1967
PN 109 **SC** 43980
B Vertebrates 1973
N Crocodilians 1973
Lizards 1973
Snakes 1973
Turtles 1973

Republican Party
Use Political Parties

Reputation 1997
PN 330 **SC** 43995
R Credibility 1973
Fame 1985
Morality 1967
Popularity 1988

Reputation — (cont'd)
Social Approval 1967
Social Cognition 1994
↓ Social Perception 1967
↓ Status 1967

Research
Use Experimentation

Research and Development 2007
PN 250 **SC** 44005
SN A multi-phase process in which knowledge is acquired and then applied to the development of new products or services.
HN This term was introduced in April 2007. Relevant records were re-indexed with this term. The posting note reflects the number of records that were re-indexed.
R Innovation 2007
Knowledge Transfer 2007
Product Design 1997

Research Design
Use Experimental Design

Research Diagnostic Criteria 1994
PN 60 **SC** 44013
SN Used when the Research Diagnostic Criteria or its revisions are the focus of the reference. Not used for specific psychodiagnostic categories.
HN Use PSYCHODIAGNOSTIC TYPOLOGIES to access references prior to 1994.
UF RDC
B Psychodiagnostic Typologies 1967
R ↓ Diagnosis 1967
Diagnostic and Statistical Manual 1994
International Classification of Diseases 2001
↓ Mental Disorders 1967
↓ Psychodiagnosis 1967

Research Dropouts
Use Experimental Attrition

Research Methods
Use Methodology

Research Setting 2001
PN 179 **SC** 44024
UF Experimental Environment
Experimental Setting
B Experimentation 1967
R Behavioral Ecology 1997
↓ Environment 1967
↓ Experimental Design 1967
Experimental Laboratories 1973

Research Subjects
Use Experimental Subjects

Resentment
Use Hostility

Reserpine 1967
PN 345 **SC** 44040
UF Serpasil
B Alkaloids 1973
Antihypertensive Drugs 1973
Neuroleptic Drugs 1973
Sedatives 1973
Sympatholytic Drugs 1973

Residence Halls
Use Dormitories

Residency (Medical)
Use Medical Residency

Residential Care Attendants
Use Attendants (Institutions)

Residential Care Institutions 1973
PN 6171 **SC** 44080
SN Facilities where individuals or patients live and receive appropriate treatment or care.
UF Institutions (Residential Care)
B Facilities 2006
N Halfway Houses 1973
↓ Hospitals 1967
Nursing Homes 1973
Orphanages 1973
R Assisted Living 2003
Group Homes 1982
Institution Visitation 1973
Institutional Schools 1978
Institutionalized Mentally Retarded 1973
Psychiatric Units 1991
Retirement Communities 1997
↓ Treatment Facilities 1973

Resilience (Psychological) 2003
PN 2164 **SC** 44085
HN In June 2003, this term replaced the discontinued term HARDINESS. HARDINESS was removed from all records containing it and replaced with RESILIENCE (PSYCHOLOGICAL). Use PSYCHOLOGICAL ENDURANCE to access references from 1991-1996.
UF Hardiness
B Personality Traits 1967
R Adaptability (Personality) 1973
Coping Behavior 1967
↓ Emotional Adjustment 1973
Emotional Stability 1973
Protective Factors 2007
Psychological Endurance 1973
Psychological Stress 1973

Resistance 1997
PN 938 **SC** 44087
N Psychotherapeutic Resistance 1973
R Assertiveness 1973
Avoidance 1967
Coercion 1994
↓ Compliance 1973
Independence (Personality) 1973
Obedience 1973
School Refusal 1994
Temptation 1973
Treatment Refusal 1994

Resistance (Psychotherapeutic)
Use Psychotherapeutic Resistance

Resocialization (Psychosocial)
Use Psychosocial Readjustment

Resonance
Use Vibration

Resource Allocation 1997
PN 945 **SC** 44125
UF Allocation of Resources
R Cost Containment 1991
↓ Costs and Cost Analysis 1973
Distributive Justice 2003
↓ Economics 1985

Resource Allocation — (cont'd)
Egalitarianism 1985
Equity (Payment) 1978
↓ Equity (Social) 1978
Finance 2007
Funding 1988
Human Capital 2003
Money 1967
Reward Allocation 1988

Resource Teachers 1973
PN 112 **SC** 44130
SN Teachers with special competencies who supplement regular curricula or programs or who assist other teachers in specified areas.
B Teachers 1967
R Special Education Teachers 1973

Respiration 1967
PN 3083 **SC** 44140
UF Breathing
R Artificial Respiration 1973
Carbon Dioxide 1973
↓ Respiration Stimulating Drugs 1973
↓ Respiratory Distress 1973
↓ Respiratory System 1973
↓ Respiratory Tract Disorders 1973
Yawning 1988

Respiration Stimulating Drugs 1973
PN 15 **SC** 44160
B Drugs 1967
N Caffeine 1973
R Respiration 1967

Respiratory Distress 1973
PN 206 **SC** 44170
B Symptoms 1967
N ↓ Apnea 1973
↓ Dyspnea 1973
Hyperventilation 1973
R Anoxia 1973
Respiration 1967

Respiratory System 1973
PN 200 **SC** 44180
B Anatomical Systems 1973
N Bronchi 1973
Diaphragm (Anatomy) 1973
↓ Larynx 1973
Lung 1973
↓ Nose 1973
Pharynx 1973
Thorax 1973
Trachea 1973
R Artificial Respiration 1973
Respiration 1967

Respiratory Tract Disorders 1973
PN 728 **SC** 44190
B Physical Disorders 1997
N ↓ Apnea 1973
Bronchial Disorders 1973
↓ Dyspnea 1973
Hay Fever 1973
Hyperventilation 1973
Laryngeal Disorders 1973
↓ Lung Disorders 1973
Pharyngeal Disorders 1973
R Artificial Respiration 1973
Influenza 1973
Poliomyelitis 1973
Respiration 1967

Respite Care 1988
PN 296 **SC** 44195
SN Provision of care, relief, or support to caregivers of physically or mentally disabled persons.
R Caregiver Burden 1994
Caregivers 1988
Home Care 1985

Respondent Conditioning
Use Classical Conditioning

Response Amplitude 1973
PN 971 **SC** 44210
UF Amplitude (Response)
B Response Parameters 1973

Response Bias 1967
PN 2584 **SC** 44220
SN Tendency to respond with different styles or criteria as a result of motivational or physical influences. Response bias frequently serves as a source of measurement error in psychophysical, personality, and other types of measurement.
UF Bias (Response)
R Cultural Test Bias 1973
↓ Measurement 1967
Predisposition 1973
↓ Test Bias 1985
Test Taking 1985

Response Consistency
Use Response Variability

Response Cost 1997
PN 41 **SC** 44228
SN Punishment procedure in which positive reinforcer is lost when a specified behavior is performed.
B Behavior Therapy 1967
Punishment 1967
R Token Economy Programs 1973

Response Duration 1973
PN 505 **SC** 44230
UF Duration (Response)
B Response Parameters 1973

Response Frequency 1973
PN 2074 **SC** 44240
SN Number of responses measured during a fixed time period.
UF Frequency (Response)
Response Rate
B Response Parameters 1973
R Behavioral Contrast 1978
Interresponse Time 1973

Response Generalization 1973
PN 482 **SC** 44250
SN Learning phenomenon in which an emitted response is functionally identical to the originally-conditioned response but which, unlike the conditioned response, was never specifically conditioned. Compare GENERALIZATION (LEARNING) and STIMULUS GENERALIZATION.
UF Generalization (Response)
B Generalization (Learning) 1982
Response Parameters 1973

Response Inhibition 2004
PN 428 **SC** 44255
SN The inhibition of response to certain stimuli.
HN This term was introduced in June 2004. Relevant records were re-indexed with this term. The posting note reflects the number of records that were re-indexed.

Response Inhibition — (cont'd)
B Response Parameters 1973

Response Lag
Use Reaction Time

Response Latency 1967
PN 2727 **SC** 44270
SN Duration of the interval between a stimulus and the onset of the elicited response. Compare REACTION TIME.
UF Latency (Response)
B Response Parameters 1973
R Behavioral Contrast 1978
Cognitive Processing Speed 1997

Response Parameters 1973
PN 1598 **SC** 44280
UF Parameters (Response)
N Interresponse Time 1973
Reaction Time 1967
Response Amplitude 1973
Response Duration 1973
Response Frequency 1973
Response Generalization 1973
Response Inhibition 2004
Response Latency 1967
Response Probability 1973
Response Set 1967
Response Variability 1973
R ↓ Responses 1967

Response Probability 1973
PN 241 **SC** 44290
B Probability 1967
Response Parameters 1973

Response Rate
Use Response Frequency

Response Set 1967
PN 703 **SC** 44300
SN Cognitive state of concentration or behavioral readiness to respond. Also, deliberate or inadvertent style or tendency to respond to test items in characteristic ways (e.g., with socially desirable answers) that detract from the validity of the obtained measures.
UF Set (Response)
B Response Parameters 1973

Response Speed
Use Reaction Time

Response Time
Use Reaction Time

Response Variability 1973
PN 851 **SC** 44330
UF Response Consistency
Variability (Response)
B Response Parameters 1973
R Delayed Alternation 1994
Spontaneous Alternation 1982

Responses 1967
PN 4511 **SC** 44340
N ↓ Conditioned Responses 1967
↓ Emotional Responses 1967
Mediated Responses 1967
Orienting Responses 1967
Unconditioned Responses 1973

Responses — (cont'd)
R ↓ Response Parameters 1973

Responsibility 1973
PN 3686 **SC** 44345
B Social Behavior 1967
N Accountability 1988
Criminal Responsibility 1991
Social Responsibility 2007
R Blame 1994
Conscientiousness 1997
Professional Liability 1985

Restlessness 1973
PN 220 **SC** 44350
B Emotional States 1973
Symptoms 1967
R Agitation 1991
Akathisia 1991
Hyperkinesis 1973

Restraint (Physical)
Use Physical Restraint

Restricted Environmental Stimulation
Use Stimulus Deprivation

Retail Stores
Use Retailing

Retailing 1991
PN 1060 **SC** 44362
UF Retail Stores
N Electronic Retailing 2007
R ↓ Advertising 1967
Brand Names 1978
↓ Business 1967
↓ Consumer Behavior 1967
↓ Electronic Commerce 2006
↓ Marketing 1973
↓ Quality of Services 1997
Sales Personnel 1973
Self Employment 1994
Shopping 1997
Shopping Centers 1973

Retaliation 1991
PN 256 **SC** 44364
HN Use RECIPROCITY to access references from 1973-1990.
UF Revenge
B Social Behavior 1967
R ↓ Aggressive Behavior 1967
Attack Behavior 1973
Hostility 1967
↓ Interpersonal Interaction 1967
Reciprocity 1973

Retardation (Mental)
Use Mental Retardation

Retarded Speech Development 1973
PN 164 **SC** 44390
SN Speech development that is below normal for a specific age level.
UF Delayed Speech
B Delayed Development 1973
Speech Development 1973
R Language Delay 1988
↓ Speech Disorders 1967

Retention 1967
PN 6164 **SC** 44400
SN Persistence of a learned act, information, or experience as measured by reproduction, recall, recognition, or relearning. Consider also LONG TERM MEMORY or SHORT TERM MEMORY. Used for both human and animal populations.
UF Remembering
N ↓ Recall (Learning) 1967
↓ Recognition (Learning) 1967
Reconstruction (Learning) 1973
R Forgetting 1973
↓ Interference (Learning) 1967
↓ Learning 1967
↓ Memory 1967
Memory Training 1994
Reminiscence 1985
↓ Retention Measures 1973

Retention (School)
Use School Retention

Retention Measures 1973
PN 166 **SC** 44410
B Measurement 1967
N Wechsler Memory Scale 1988
R ↓ Retention 1967

Reticular Formation 1967
PN 595 **SC** 44420
SN Network of nerve fibers and cells situated primarily in the brain stem, involved in everyday actions such as sleeping, walking, and lying down. It also regulates consciousness and wakefulness.
B Brain Stem 1973
Neural Pathways 1982
R ↓ Lemniscal System 1985
Locus Ceruleus 1982
Raphe Nuclei 1982

Retina 1967
PN 1957 **SC** 44430
SN Light sensitive membrane lining the inner eyeball that is connected to the brain by the optic nerve.
B Eye (Anatomy) 1967
N Cones (Eye) 1973
Ganglion Cells (Retina) 1985
Rods (Eye) 1973
R Retinal Eccentricity 1991

Retinal Eccentricity 1991
PN 206 **SC** 44435
R ↓ Retina 1967
Retinal Image 1973
Spatial Organization 1973
↓ Visual Perception 1967
Visual Receptive Fields 1982
↓ Visual Thresholds 1973

Retinal Ganglion Cells
Use Ganglion Cells (Retina)

Retinal Image 1973
PN 778 **SC** 44450
UF Image (Retinal)
R ↓ Eye (Anatomy) 1967
Retinal Eccentricity 1991

Retinal Vessels
Use Arteries (Anatomy)

Retirement 1973
PN 1903 **SC** 44470
R Employment History 1978
↓ Employment Status 1982
Job Security 1978
↓ Personnel 1967
Personnel Termination 1973
Reemployment 1991
Retirement Communities 1997
Unemployment 1967

Retirement Communities 1997
PN 145 **SC** 44473
B Communities 1967
Housing 1973
R Aging in Place 2007
Group Homes 1982
↓ Living Arrangements 1991
Nursing Homes 1973
↓ Residential Care Institutions 1973
Retirement 1973

Retroactive Inhibition 1973
PN 597 **SC** 44480
SN The theory that learning new material can interfere with the retention of previously learned material. Also, the actual retroactive interference itself.
UF Inhibition (Retroactive)
B Interference (Learning) 1967
Latent Inhibition 1997

Retrograde Amnesia 2003
PN 387 **SC** 58073
SN Memory loss for events and experiences that occurred before the incident that produced the amnesia.
HN This term was introduced in June 2003. Relevant records were re-indexed with this term. The posting note reflects the number of records that were re-indexed.
B Amnesia 1967
R Anterograde Amnesia 2003
Global Amnesia 1997

Retrospective Studies 1997
PN 276 **SC** 44481
SN Used in records discussing issues involved in the process of conducting studies which utilize data about experiences or events that occurred in the past, usually to study etiologic hypotheses or causative factors related to a disorder, behavior, or phenomenon.
HN From 1997-2000, the term was also used as a document type identifier; however, this usage has been discontinued due to the advent of Form/Content Type field identifiers. References from 1997-2000 can be accessed using either RETROSPECTIVE STUDIES or the Retrospective Studies Form/Content Type field identifier.
R ↓ Longitudinal Studies 1973
Prospective Studies 1997

Rett Syndrome 1994
PN 304 **SC** 44482
B Pervasive Developmental Disorders 2001
Syndromes 1973
R Aspergers Syndrome 1991
↓ Brain Disorders 1967
↓ Mental Disorders 1967
↓ Mental Retardation 1967
↓ Physical Disorders 1997

Return to Home
Use Empty Nest

Return to Work
Use Reemployment

Revenge
Use Retaliation

Reversal Shift Learning 1967
PN 765 **SC** 44490
SN Experimental technique for demonstration of mediating processes in concept formation which assesses ability to learn to reverse responses in stimulus discrimination task, so that the subject is required to respond to a formerly negative stimulus and not to respond to the formerly positive discriminative stimulus.
B Discrimination Learning 1982

Review (of Literature)
HN Term was discontinued in 1973. In 2000, the term was removed from all records containing it, and replaced with LITERATURE REVIEW, its postable counterpart.
Use Literature Review

Revolutions (Political)
Use Political Revolution

Reward Allocation 1988
PN 252 **SC** 44515
R ↓ Justice 1973
Resource Allocation 1997
↓ Rewards 1967
↓ Social Perception 1967

Rewards 1967
PN 4361 **SC** 44520
SN Events or objects subjectively deemed to be pleasant to a recipient. Compare INCENTIVES, REINFORCEMENT, and POSITIVE REINFORCEMENT.
B Reinforcement 1967
N External Rewards 1973
Internal Rewards 1973
Monetary Rewards 1973
Preferred Rewards 1973
R Awards (Merit) 2005
Delay of Gratification 1978
Delayed Alternation 1994
↓ Incentives 1967
Professional Recognition 2005
Reward Allocation 1988

Rh Incompatibility 1973
PN 8 **SC** 44530
UF Erythroblastosis Fetalis
Incompatibility (Rh)
B Blood and Lymphatic Disorders 1973
Genetic Disorders 1973
Immunologic Disorders 1973
R ↓ Neonatal Disorders 1973

Rheoencephalography 1973
PN 19 **SC** 44540
SN Technique used to measure blood flow amount and circulation.
B Encephalography 1973
Medical Diagnosis 1973
R ↓ Electroencephalography 1967

Rhetoric 1991
PN 903 **SC** 44545
B Communication Skills 1973
Language 1967
R ↓ Communication 1967
Creative Writing 1994

Rhetoric — (cont'd)
Debates 1997
Discourse Analysis 1997
Hermeneutics 1991
↓ Oral Communication 1985
↓ Persuasive Communication 1967
↓ Written Communication 1985

Rheumatic Fever 1973
PN 44 **SC** 44550
R ↓ Bacterial Disorders 1973
↓ Heart Disorders 1973
Rheumatoid Arthritis 1973

Rheumatism
Use Arthritis

Rheumatoid Arthritis 1973
PN 1097 **SC** 44570
B Arthritis 1973
R Rheumatic Fever 1973

Rhodopsin 1985
PN 17 **SC** 44575
SN A red pigment localized in the outer segments of rod cells in the retina.
B Pigments 1973
R Rods (Eye) 1973

Rhombencephalon
Use Hindbrain

Rhyme 2004
PN 175 **SC** 58081
HN This term was introduced in June 2004. Relevant records were re-indexed with this term. The posting note reflects the number of records that were re-indexed.
R Phonological Awareness 2004
↓ Phonology 1973
Poetry 1973
Words (Phonetic Units) 1967

Rhythm 1991
PN 647 **SC** 44577
N Speech Rhythm 1973
R ↓ Auditory Perception 1967
↓ Music 1967
Music Perception 1997
Pattern Discrimination 1967
↓ Perception 1967
Speech Perception 1967
Tempo 1997

Rhythm Method 1973
PN 6 **SC** 44580
B Birth Control 1971

Ribonucleic Acid 1973
PN 969 **SC** 44600
UF RNA (Ribonucleic Acid)
B Nucleic Acids 1973
R Gene Expression 2004

Right Brain
HN In August 2005, this term was discontinued and removed from all records containing it, and was replaced with RIGHT HEMISPHERE, its postable counterpart.
Use Right Hemisphere

Right Hemisphere 2005
PN 1213 **SC** 44612
SN Used only when the right hemisphere of the brain is the focus of the document.
HN In August 2005, this term was created to replace the discontinued term RIGHT BRAIN. RIGHT BRAIN was removed from all records containing it, and was replaced with RIGHT HEMISPHERE, its postable counterpart.
UF Right Brain
B Cerebral Cortex 1967
R ↓ Brain 1967
↓ Cerebral Dominance 1973
Corpus Callosum 1973
Interhemispheric Interaction 1985
↓ Lateral Dominance 1967
Left Hemisphere 2005
Ocular Dominance 1973

Right to Treatment 1997
PN 38 **SC** 44615
B Client Rights 1988
R Advocacy 1985
↓ Commitment (Psychiatric) 1973
Deinstitutionalization 1982
Involuntary Treatment 1994
Self Referral 1991

Rigidity (Muscles)
Use Muscle Contractions

Rigidity (Personality) 1967
PN 284 **SC** 44620
B Personality Traits 1967
R Openness to Experience 1997

Riots 1973
PN 178 **SC** 44640
B Collective Behavior 1967
Conflict 1967
R ↓ Violence 1973

Risk Analysis
HN In June 2004, this term was discontinued and removed from all records containing it, and replaced with RISK ASSESSMENT, its postable counterpart.
Use Risk Assessment

Risk Assessment 2004
PN 3400 **SC** 58083
HN In June 2004, this term was created to replace the discontinued term RISK ANALYSIS. RISK ANALYSIS was removed from all records containing it and replaced with RISK ASSESSMENT.
UF Risk Analysis
B Evaluation 1967
R At Risk Populations 1985
↓ Decision Making 1967
Risk Factors 2001
Risk Management 1997

Risk Factors 2001
PN 11091 **SC** 44642
SN Personal behaviors or lifestyles, environmental effects, or inborn characteristics which epidemiological evidence has shown to be associated with the increased rate of a behavior or health-related condition.
R At Risk Populations 1985
Causality 2005
Metabolic Syndrome 2007
Predisposition 1973
Protective Factors 2007
Psychosocial Factors 1988

Risk Factors — (cont'd)
Risk Assessment 2004
↓ Sociocultural Factors 1967
Susceptibility (Disorders) 1973
↓ Symptoms 1967

Risk Management 1997
PN 1278 **SC** 44644
SN Reducing and preventing loss, damage, harm, or danger to a business, group, or individual through safety and protective measures. Used for clinical and nonclinical environments.
B Management 1967
R Accident Prevention 1973
↓ Costs and Cost Analysis 1973
Emergency Preparedness 2007
↓ Harm Reduction 2003
↓ Insurance 1973
↓ Legal Processes 1973
↓ Prevention 1973
Professional Liability 1985
Protective Factors 2007
Risk Assessment 2004
↓ Risk Taking 1967
↓ Safety 1967

Risk Perception 1997
PN 2192 **SC** 44646
SN Awareness of, or attitudes toward, potential risk. Primarily used for risk associated with disease or behavior.
B Perception 1967
R Hazards 1973
↓ Prevention 1973
↓ Risk Taking 1967
↓ Safety 1967
Sexual Risk Taking 1997

Risk Populations
Use At Risk Populations

Risk Taking 1967
PN 5793 **SC** 44650
B Personality Traits 1967
Social Behavior 1967
N ↓ Gambling 1973
Sexual Risk Taking 1997
R Choice Shift 1994
Risk Management 1997
Risk Perception 1997

Risky Shift
Use Choice Shift

Risperidone 1997
PN 1879 **SC** 44657
B Neuroleptic Drugs 1973

Ritalin
Use Methylphenidate

Ritanserin 1997
PN 67 **SC** 44665
B Serotonin Antagonists 1973

Rites (Nonreligious) 1973
PN 840 **SC** 44670
UF Rituals (Nonreligious)
R Cannibalism 2003
Cosmetic Techniques 2001
↓ Rites of Passage 1973
Traditions 2007

Rites (Religion)
Use Religious Practices

Rites of Passage 1973
PN 217 **SC** 44690
B Sociocultural Factors 1967
N Birth Rites 1973
Death Rites 1973
Initiation Rites 1973
Marriage Rites 1973
R Circumcision 2001
↓ Developmental Stages 1973
Ethnography 1973
Rites (Nonreligious) 1973
Taboos 1973

Rituals (Nonreligious)
Use Rites (Nonreligious)

Rituals (Religion)
Use Religious Practices

Rivalry 1973
PN 133 **SC** 44720
B Interpersonal Interaction 1967
R Competition 1967

RNA (Ribonucleic Acid)
Use Ribonucleic Acid

Road Rage
Use Aggressive Driving Behavior

Robbery
Use Theft

Robins 1973
PN 57 **SC** 44750
B Birds 1967

Robotics 1985
PN 901 **SC** 44755
UF Robots
R ↓ Artificial Intelligence 1982
↓ Computers 1967
Cybernetics 1967
↓ Expert Systems 1991

Robots
Use Robotics

Rock Music 1991
PN 173 **SC** 44757
B Music 1967

Rocking (Body)
Use Body Rocking

Rod and Frame Test 1973
PN 135 **SC** 44770
B Nonprojective Personality Measures 1973
Perceptual Measures 1973

Rodents 1973
PN 1488 **SC** 44780
B Mammals 1973
N Beavers 1973
Chinchillas 1973
Gerbils 1973
Guinea Pigs 1967
Hamsters 1973
Mice 1973
Minks 1973
↓ Rats 1967

Rodents — (cont'd)
Squirrels 1973
Voles 2004

Rods (Eye) 1973
PN 321 **SC** 44790
SN Photosensitive receptors located in the retina that are responsive to faint light and which enable night vision.
B Photoreceptors 1973
Retina 1967
R Rhodopsin 1985

Roentgenography 1973
PN 193 **SC** 44800
UF Radiography
X Ray Diagnosis
B Medical Diagnosis 1973
Neuroimaging 2003
N Angiography 1973
Mammography 1994
Pneumoencephalography 1973
R ↓ Encephalography 1973
↓ Radiation 1967
↓ Tomography 1988

Rogerian Therapy
Use Client Centered Therapy

Rogers (Carl) 1991
PN 202 **SC** 44805
SN Identifies biographical or autobiographical studies and discussions of Rogers's works.
R Client Centered Therapy 1967
↓ Humanistic Psychology 1985
↓ Humanistic Psychotherapy 2003
↓ Psychologists 1967

Rohypnol
Use Flunitrazepam

Rokeach Dogmatism Scale 1973
PN 31 **SC** 44810
B Nonprojective Personality Measures 1973
Personality Measures 1967

Role (Counselor)
Use Counselor Role

Role Conflicts 1973
PN 2773 **SC** 44830
UF Role Strain
R Conflict of Interest 2005
Family Work Relationship 1997
Role Satisfaction 1994
↓ Roles 1967

Role Expectations 1973
PN 1239 **SC** 44840
SN Functional patterns or types of behavior expected from an individual in a specific social or professional position or situation.
B Expectations 1967
R Role Satisfaction 1994
↓ Roles 1967

Role Models 1982
PN 655 **SC** 44845
SN Real or theoretical persons consciously or unconsciously perceived as being a standard for emulation in one or more of their roles.
R Heroes 2007
Imitation (Learning) 1967

Role Models — (cont'd)
Role Perception 1973
↓ Roles 1967
Significant Others 1991
↓ Social Influences 1967

Role Perception 1973
PN 2542 **SC** 44850
SN Views or understanding of one's own or others' function or behavior in particular situations.
B Perception 1967
R Professional Identity 1991
Role Models 1982
Role Satisfaction 1994
Role Taking 1982
↓ Roles 1967

Role Playing 1967
PN 1702 **SC** 44860
SN Psychological or behavioral enactment of social roles other than one's own, typically seen in child's play, or used as an experimental, instructional, or psychotherapeutic technique. Compare ROLE TAKING.
R ↓ Childhood Play Behavior 1978
Psychodrama 1967
↓ Psychotherapeutic Techniques 1967
Role Taking 1982
↓ Roles 1967

Role Satisfaction 1994
PN 181 **SC** 44863
B Satisfaction 1973
R Job Satisfaction 1967
Life Satisfaction 1985
Marital Satisfaction 1988
↓ Relationship Satisfaction 2001
Role Conflicts 1973
Role Expectations 1973
Role Perception 1973
↓ Roles 1967
↓ Self Concept 1967

Role Strain
Use Role Conflicts

Role Taking 1982
PN 894 **SC** 44865
SN Perceiving, understanding, or experiencing the social, emotional or physical aspects of a situation from a standpoint of another person or persons. Compare ROLE PLAYING.
HN Use EGOCENTRISM to access references from 1978-1981.
UF Perspective Taking
R Egocentrism 1978
Role Perception 1973
Role Playing 1967
↓ Roles 1967
Symbolic Interactionism 1988

Roles 1967
PN 6213 **SC** 44870
N Counselor Role 1973
Parental Role 1973
Sex Roles 1967
Therapist Role 1978
R Role Conflicts 1973
Role Expectations 1973
Role Models 1982
Role Perception 1973
Role Playing 1967
Role Satisfaction 1994
Role Taking 1982

Roman Catholicism 1973
PN 898 **SC** 44880
UF Catholicism (Roman)
B Christianity 1973
R Catholics 1997

Romance 1997
PN 1282 **SC** 44883
R Affection 1973
Couples 1982
↓ Human Courtship 1973
Human Mate Selection 1988
Intimacy 1973
Love 1973
↓ Marital Relations 1967
↓ Marriage 1967
↓ Psychosexual Behavior 1967
↓ Relationship Termination 1997
Significant Others 1991
Social Dating 1973

Roommates 1973
PN 167 **SC** 44890
SN Individuals residing in common abodes.
R Cohabitation 1973
↓ Living Arrangements 1991

Rorschach Test 1967
PN 3373 **SC** 44900
B Projective Personality Measures 1973

Rosenzweig Picture Frustration Study 1967
PN 59 **SC** 44910
B Projective Personality Measures 1973

Rotary Pursuit 1967
PN 219 **SC** 44920
B Tracking 1967
R ↓ Attention 1967

Rotation Methods (Statistical)
Use Statistical Rotation

Rotational Behavior 1994
PN 218 **SC** 44935
SN Used primarily for animal populations.
UF Body Rotation
B Motor Processes 1967
R Activity Level 1982

ROTC Students 1973
PN 72 **SC** 44940
B College Students 1967
Military Personnel 1967
R Volunteer Military Personnel 1973

Rote Learning 1973
PN 163 **SC** 44950
SN Verbatim memorization of information which requires no understanding.
R ↓ Memory 1967

Rotter Incomplete Sentences Blank 1973
PN 24 **SC** 44960
B Projective Personality Measures 1973

Rotter Internal External Locus of Control Scale 2001
PN 158 **SC** 44971
HN In 2000, the truncated term ROTTER INTERN EXTERN LOCUS CONT SCAL (which was used from 1973-2000) was deleted, removed from all records containing it, and replaced with its expanded form ROTTER INTERNAL EXTERNAL LOCUS OF CONTROL SCALE.
B Nonprojective Personality Measures 1973

RT (Response)
Use Reaction Time

Rubella 1973
PN 68 **SC** 45000
UF German Measles
B Viral Disorders 1973
R Measles 1973

Rule Learning
Use Cognitive Hypothesis Testing

Rumination (Cognitive Process) 2001
PN 234 **SC** 45007
SN Constant preoccupation with particular thoughts which may provoke anxiety and distress. Can be associated with obsessive compulsive disorder and depression.
B Cognitive Processes 1967
R ↓ Cognitions 1985
Concentration 1982
Repetition Compulsion 2005
↓ Thought Disturbances 1973
Thought Suppression 2003

Rumination (Eating) 2001
PN 12 **SC** 45008
SN Behavior characterized by regurgitating partially digested food and chewing it again. Often used to describe an eating disorder of infancy or early childhood.
R ↓ Eating Disorders 1997
Food Intake 1967
Vomiting 1973

Rumors
Use Gossip

Runaway Behavior 1973
PN 487 **SC** 45015
B Antisocial Behavior 1971
R Missing Children 2007
Shelters 1991

Running 1973
PN 895 **SC** 45020
B Motor Performance 1973

Runways (Maze)
Use Maze Pathways

Rural Development
Use Community Development

Rural Environments 1967
PN 6755 **SC** 45040
B Social Environments 1973
R Community Development 1997

Saccadic Eye Movements
Use Eye Movements

Saccharin 1973
PN 557 **SC** 45050
R ↓ Sugars 1973

SAD
Use Seasonal Affective Disorder

Sadism 1973
PN 154 **SC** 45070
B Sadomasochism 1973
N Sexual Sadism 1973
R ↓ Masochism 1973

Sadness 1973
PN 787 **SC** 45090
UF Melancholy
B Emotional States 1973
R Depression (Emotion) 1967
Homesickness 1994
↓ Separation Reactions 1997

Sadomasochism 1973
PN 214 **SC** 45100
SN Derivation of pleasure from infliction of physical or mental pain on others and oneself, with presence of high degree of destructiveness.
N ↓ Masochism 1973
↓ Sadism 1973
R ↓ Mental Disorders 1967
↓ Sadomasochistic Personality 1973

Sadomasochistic Personality 1973
PN 18 **SC** 45110
B Personality Disorders 1967
N Masochistic Personality 1973
R ↓ Sadomasochism 1973

Safe Sex 2003
PN 409 **SC** 45115
SN Sexual behavior or practices which reduce one's risk of pregnancy or transmission of HIV and other sexually transmitted diseases.
HN This term was introduced in June 2003. Relevant records were re-indexed with this term. The posting note reflects the number of records that were re-indexed.
B Health Behavior 1982
Psychosexual Behavior 1967
R AIDS 2006
AIDS Prevention 1994
↓ Birth Control 1971
Condoms 1991
↓ HIV 2006
↓ Pregnancy 1967
Sex Education 1973
↓ Sexual Intercourse (Human) 1973
Sexual Risk Taking 1997

Safety 1967
PN 2870 **SC** 45120
N ↓ Aviation Safety 1973
Highway Safety 1973
Occupational Safety 1973
Transportation Safety 2007
Water Safety 1973
R Accident Prevention 1973
Accident Proneness 1973
↓ Accidents 1967
Fire Prevention 1973
↓ Hazardous Materials 1991
Hazards 1973
↓ Injuries 1973
↓ Prevention 1973
Protective Factors 2007
Risk Management 1997
Risk Perception 1997
↓ Safety Devices 1973
Warning Labels 1997
↓ Warnings 1997

Safety Belts 1973
PN 383 **SC** 45130
UF Seat Belts
B Safety Devices 1973
R ↓ Driving Behavior 1967
↓ Transportation Accidents 1973

Safety Devices 1973
PN 354 **SC** 45140
UF Helmets
N Safety Belts 1973
R Hazards 1973
↓ Safety 1967
Warning Labels 1997
↓ Warnings 1997

Safety Warnings
Use Warnings

Saint John's Wort
Use Hypericum Perforatum

Salamanders 1973
PN 271 **SC** 45150
B Amphibia 1973
R Larvae 1973

Salaries 1973
PN 1934 **SC** 45160
UF Pay
Wages
R Bonuses 1973
Economic Security 2007
↓ Employee Benefits 1973
Equity (Payment) 1978
Income (Economic) 1973
↓ Income Level 1973
↓ Professional Fees 1978

Sales Personnel 1973
PN 1533 **SC** 45170
UF Insurance Agents
B Business and Industrial Personnel 1967
White Collar Workers 1973
R ↓ Retailing 1991
↓ Service Personnel 1991

Salience (Stimulus)
Use Stimulus Salience

Saliva 1973
PN 587 **SC** 45200
B Body Fluids 1973
R Salivation 1973

Salivary Glands 1973
PN 76 **SC** 45210
B Glands 1967
R ↓ Digestive System 1967
Mouth (Anatomy) 1967

Salivation 1973
PN 279 **SC** 45220
B Secretion (Gland) 1973
R Digestion 1973
Saliva 1973

Salmon 1973
PN 103 **SC** 45230
B Fishes 1967

Saltiness
Use Taste Perception

Same Sex Education 2003
PN 70 **SC** 45242
HN This term was introduced in June 2003. Relevant records were re-indexed with this term. The posting note reflects the number of records that were re-indexed.
UF Single Sex Education
B Academic Environment 1973
Single Sex Environments 2001
R Coeducation 1973

Same Sex Environments
Use Single Sex Environments

Same Sex Marriage 2007
PN 46 **SC** 45244
SN A long-term, intimate, stable, and in some jurisdictions legally recognized relationship between two people of the same sex.
HN This term was introduced in April 2007. Relevant records were re-indexed with this term. The posting note reflects the number of records that were re-indexed.
B Marriage 1967
R Civil Law 1994
↓ Civil Rights 1978
↓ Homosexuality 1967
↓ Sexual Orientation 1997

Sample Size 1997
PN 312 **SC** 45245
B Statistical Sample Parameters 1973
R ↓ Sampling (Experimental) 1973

Sampling (Experimental) 1973
PN 1057 **SC** 45250
SN Systematic selection of part of a larger population of individual responses, individuals, or groups for use in empirical study or research. Results about the entire population are then generalized from this smaller sample.
N Biased Sampling 1973
Random Sampling 1973
R Data Collection 1982
↓ Experimental Design 1967
↓ Experimentation 1967
↓ Population (Statistics) 1973
Sample Size 1997
↓ Statistical Analysis 1967
Statistical Power 1991
Statistical Reliability 1973
↓ Statistical Samples 1973
↓ Statistical Variables 1973

Sanatoriums 1973
PN 18 **SC** 45260
SN Formerly, an institution for the treatment and convalescence of individuals with chronic diseases, such as rheumatism, tuberculosis, neurological disorders, or mental disorders.
UF Sanitariums
B Hospitals 1967
R Nursing Homes 1973
Psychiatric Hospitals 1967

Sanitariums
Use Sanatoriums

Sarcomas
Use Neoplasms

SAT
Use College Entrance Examination Board Scholastic Aptitude Test

Satiation 1967
PN 1053 **SC** 45280
SN Primarily limited to gratification or satisfaction of a physiologically-based motivation (e.g., need for food and water) but may also refer to gratification of a psychic goal or motivation. Consider also SATISFACTION or NEED SATISFACTION for the latter concept.
R ↓ Appetite 1973
↓ Motivation 1967

Satisfaction 1973
PN 5768 **SC** 45290
UF Fulfillment
N Client Satisfaction 1994
Consumer Satisfaction 1994
Job Satisfaction 1967
Life Satisfaction 1985
Marital Satisfaction 1988
Need Satisfaction 1973
↓ Relationship Satisfaction 2001
Role Satisfaction 1994
Sexual Satisfaction 1994
R Dissatisfaction 1973
Physical Comfort 1982

Saturation (Color)
Use Color Saturation

Savants 2001
PN 155 **SC** 45297
HN In 2000, this term was created to replace the discontinued term IDIOT SAVANTS. IDIOT SAVANTS was removed from all records and replaced with SAVANTS.
UF Idiot Savants
R Gifted 1967
↓ Mental Disorders 1967
↓ Mental Retardation 1967

Scaffolding 2005
PN 178 **SC** 45298
SN A supportive teaching technique in which assistance is modified based on the learner's progress.
HN This term was introduced in August 2005. Relevant records were re-indexed with this term. The posting note reflects the number of records that were re-indexed.
B Teaching Methods 1967

Scaling (Testing) 1967
PN 1736 **SC** 45360
B Testing 1967
Testing Methods 1967
R Magnitude Estimation 1991
Multidimensional Scaling 1982

Scalp (Anatomy) 1973
PN 81 **SC** 45370
B Anatomy 1967
R Hair 1973
Head (Anatomy) 1973
Skin (Anatomy) 1967

Scalp Disorders
Use Skin Disorders

Scent Marking (Animal)
Use Animal Scent Marking

Schedules (Learning)
Use Learning Schedules

Schedules (Reinforcement)
Use Reinforcement Schedules

Scheduling (Work)
Use Work Scheduling

Schema 1988
PN 3315 **SC** 45425
SN Cognitive structure used for comprehension, perception, and interpretation of stimuli.
UF Scripts
B Cognitive Processes 1967
R Accommodation (Cognitive Process) 2007
Assimilation (Cognitive Process) 2007
↓ Cognitions 1985
Cognitive Maps 1982
↓ Cognitive Style 1967
Conceptual Imagery 1973
Mental Models 2003
Perceptual Style 1973
Social Cognition 1994

Schizoaffective Disorder 1994
PN 1779 **SC** 45427
SN Mental disorder characterized by the presence of both affective disorder and schizophrenia-like symptoms.
B Mental Disorders 1967
R ↓ Affective Disorders 2001
↓ Schizophrenia 1967

Schizoid Personality Disorder 1973
PN 517 **SC** 45430
SN Personality disorder characterized by alienation, shyness, oversensitivity, seclusiveness, egocentricity, avoidance of intimate relationships, autistic thinking, and withdrawal from and lack of response to the environment.
B Personality Disorders 1967
R ↓ Schizophrenia 1967
Schizotypal Personality Disorder 1991

Schizophrenia 1967
PN 46204 **SC** 45440
HN In 1988, this term replaced the terms CHRONIC SCHIZOPHRENIA, PSEUDOPSYCHOPATHIC SCHIZOPHRENIA, and SIMPLE SCHIZOPHRENIA. In 2000, these terms were removed from all records containing them, and replaced with SCHIZOPHRENIA.
UF Chronic Schizophrenia
Dementia Praecox
Pseudopsychopathic Schizophrenia
Reactive Schizophrenia
Schizophrenia (Residual Type)
Simple Schizophrenia
B Psychosis 1967
N Acute Schizophrenia 1973
Catatonic Schizophrenia 1973
Childhood Schizophrenia 1967
Paranoid Schizophrenia 1967
Process Schizophrenia 2005
Schizophrenia (Disorganized Type) 1973
Schizophreniform Disorder 1994
Undifferentiated Schizophrenia 1973
R Anhedonia 1985
Catalepsy 1973
Delusions 1967
Expressed Emotion 1991
Fragmentation (Schizophrenia) 1973
Positive and Negative Symptoms 1997
Schizoaffective Disorder 1994
Schizoid Personality Disorder 1973
Schizotypal Personality Disorder 1991

Schizophrenia (Disorganized Type) 1973
PN 162 **SC** 45445
HN In 2000, the term's status changed from non-postable to postable. HEBEPHRENIC SCHIZOPHRENIA was removed from all records containing it, and replaced with SCHIZOPHRENIA (DISORGANIZED TYPE).
UF Hebephrenic Schizophrenia
B Schizophrenia 1967

Schizophrenia (Residual Type)
Use Schizophrenia

Schizophreniform Disorder 1994
PN 252 **SC** 45447
HN Use ACUTE SCHIZOPHRENIA to access references from 1988-1993.
B Schizophrenia 1967

Schizophrenogenic Family 1967
PN 313 **SC** 45450
B Family 1967
Family Structure 1973
R Double Bind Interaction 1973
Dysfunctional Family 1991
↓ Mental Disorders 1967
Schizophrenogenic Mothers 1973

Schizophrenogenic Mothers 1973
PN 41 **SC** 45460
B Mothers 1967
R Double Bind Interaction 1973
Mother Child Relations 1967
Schizophrenogenic Family 1967

Schizotypal Personality Disorder 1991
PN 787 **SC** 45465
SN Personality disorder characterized by eccentric thoughts and appearance, inappropriate affect and behavior, extreme social anxiety, and limited interpersonal interaction.
HN Consider using SCHIZOID PERSONALITY to access references from 1973-1990.
B Personality Disorders 1967
R Schizoid Personality Disorder 1973
↓ Schizophrenia 1967

Scholarships
Use Educational Financial Assistance

Scholastic Achievement
Use Academic Achievement

Scholastic Aptitude
Use Academic Aptitude

Scholastic Aptitude Test
Use College Entrance Examination Board Scholastic Aptitude Test

School Accreditation
Use Educational Program Accreditation

School Achievement
Use Academic Achievement

School Adjustment 1967
PN 4349 **SC** 45510
SN Process of adjusting to school environment and to the role of a student.
UF Student Adjustment
B Adjustment 1967
R Adjustment Disorders 1994
↓ Education 1967
School Transition 1997

School Administration
Use Educational Administration

School Administrators 1973
PN 2788 **SC** 45530
UF Administrators (School)
Educational Administrators
B Educational Personnel 1973
N School Principals 1973
School Superintendents 1973
R Boards of Education 1978
↓ Management Personnel 1973

School and College Ability Test
HN Term was discontinued in 1997. In 2000, the term was removed from all records containing it, and replaced with APTITUDE MEASURES, its postable counterpart.
Use Aptitude Measures

School Attendance 1973
PN 1410 **SC** 45560
SN Regular presence of students in school or classes or absenteeism due to factors other than truancy. Compare SCHOOL ENROLLMENT.
UF Attendance (School)
R ↓ Education 1967
↓ School Enrollment 1973
School Refusal 1994
School Retention 1994
Student Attrition 1991
Tardiness 2003

School Based Intervention 2003
PN 1992 **SC** 45563
SN Intervening with an individual or group of individuals in a school setting for the purpose of influencing or reorienting one's behavior or approach to learning.
HN This term was introduced in June 2003. Relevant records were re-indexed with this term. The posting note reflects the number of records that were re-indexed.
UF Educational Intervention
B Intervention 2003
R Early Intervention 1982
↓ Educational Programs 1973
School Counseling 1982
Student Personnel Services 1978

School Club Membership 1973
PN 44 **SC** 45570
B Extracurricular Activities 1973
Membership 2007

School Counseling 1982
PN 3955 **SC** 45579
SN Counseling services provided by counselors or teacher counselors in order to help school, college, or university students cope with adjustment problems. Compare EDUCATIONAL COUNSELING.
UF Guidance Counseling
School Guidance
B Counseling 1967
R ↓ Education 1967
Educational Therapy 1997
↓ Mental Health Services 1978
School Based Intervention 2003
School Counselors 1973
Student Personnel Services 1978

School Counselors 1973
PN 2323 **SC** 45580
B Counselors 1967
Educational Personnel 1973

School Counselors — (cont'd)
R School Counseling 1982
School Psychologists 1973
Vocational Counselors 1973

School Dropouts 1967
PN 1556 **SC** 45590
B Dropouts 1973
N College Dropouts 1973
R ↓ Education 1967
Reentry Students 1985
School Refusal 1994
School Retention 1994
Student Attrition 1991

School Engagement
Use Student Engagement

School Enrollment 1973
PN 613 **SC** 45600
SN Number of students registered to attend school, college or university. Also, the act of enrolling in school. Compare SCHOOL ATTENDANCE.
UF Enrollment (School)
Matriculation
N School Expulsion 1973
School Suspension 1973
Student Attrition 1991
R ↓ Dropouts 1973
↓ Education 1967
School Attendance 1973
School Retention 1994
School Truancy 1973

School Environment 1973
PN 6205 **SC** 45610
SN School characteristics, including overall social and physical atmosphere or school climate.
UF Educational Environment
B Academic Environment 1973
N College Environment 1973
R Classroom Environment 1973
↓ Education 1967
Learning Environment 2004
↓ School Facilities 1973
School Violence 2003
↓ Schools 1967

School Expulsion 1973
PN 91 **SC** 45620
UF Expulsion (School)
B School Enrollment 1973
R School Suspension 1973
Student Attrition 1991

School Facilities 1973
PN 181 **SC** 45630
B Facilities 2006
N Campuses 1973
↓ Classrooms 1967
Dormitories 1973
↓ Educational Laboratories 1973
Learning Centers (Educational) 1973
School Libraries 1973
R ↓ Education 1967
Playgrounds 1973
↓ School Environment 1973
↓ Schools 1967

School Federal Aid
Use Educational Financial Assistance

School Financial Assistance
Use Educational Financial Assistance

School Graduation 1991
PN 232 **SC** 45653
SN Completion of a course of study resulting in the award or acceptance of a diploma or degree.
UF Graduation (School)
R ↓ Academic Achievement 1967
College Graduates 1982
↓ Education 1967
Educational Attainment Level 1997
Educational Degrees 1973
High School Graduates 1978
↓ Higher Education 1973
School to Work Transition 1994
School Transition 1997

School Guidance
Use School Counseling

School Integration 1982
PN 813 **SC** 45658
SN Incorporation of students of different racial, ethnic, or other types of groups into the same school.
HN In 1982, this term was created to replace the discontinued term SCHOOL INTEGRATION (RACIAL). In 2000, SCHOOL INTEGRATION (RACIAL) was removed from all records containing it, and replaced with SCHOOL INTEGRATION.
UF Racial Segregation (Schools)
School Integration (Racial)
B Social Integration 1982
R ↓ Activism 2003
↓ Education 1967
Equal Education 1978
Mainstreaming (Educational) 1978
Racial and Ethnic Relations 1982

School Integration (Racial)
HN Term was discontinued in 1982. In 2000, the term was removed from all records containing it, and replaced with SCHOOL INTEGRATION, its postable counterpart.
Use School Integration

School Learning 1967
PN 6319 **SC** 45670
SN Learning in an academic environment. For educational performance use ACADEMIC ACHIEVEMENT or one of its narrower terms.
B Learning 1967
R ↓ Academic Achievement 1967
Cooperative Learning 1994
↓ Education 1967
↓ Experiential Learning 1997
Mastery Learning 1985
Metacognition 1991

School Leavers 1988
PN 106 **SC** 45675
SN British term referring to persons who have recently left school, generally after the completion of a basic education program and satisfaction of government requirements.
R ↓ Educational Background 1967
School Retention 1994
Student Attrition 1991

School Libraries 1973
PN 112 **SC** 45680
UF Libraries (School)
B Libraries 1982
School Facilities 1973

School Nurses 1973
PN 254 **SC** 45690
B Educational Personnel 1973
Nurses 1967

School Organization
Use Educational Administration

School Phobia 1973
PN 302 **SC** 45710
B Phobias 1967
R School Refusal 1994
Separation Anxiety 1973
Student Attitudes 1967

School Principals 1973
PN 2705 **SC** 45720
B School Administrators 1973

School Psychologists 1973
PN 2326 **SC** 45730
SN Psychologists usually associated with elementary or secondary schools who provide counseling, testing, or diagnostic services to students, teachers, or parents.
B Educational Psychologists 1973
Mental Health Personnel 1967
R School Counselors 1973

School Psychology 1973
PN 1945 **SC** 45740
SN Branch of psychology that emphasizes training and certification of school psychologists.
B Educational Psychology 1967

School Readiness 1973
PN 697 **SC** 45750
SN Developmental level at which a child is prepared to adjust to school and the student role. Compare READING READINESS.
R ↓ Education 1967
Project Head Start 1973

School Refusal 1994
PN 199 **SC** 45755
SN Unwillingness of students to attend school or classes.
R ↓ Resistance 1997
School Attendance 1973
↓ School Dropouts 1967
School Phobia 1973
School Truancy 1973
Separation Anxiety 1973
Student Attitudes 1967

School Retention 1994
PN 373 **SC** 45757
SN Retention of students in school or educational programs.
UF Retention (School)
R School Attendance 1973
↓ School Dropouts 1967
↓ School Enrollment 1973
School Leavers 1988
School Truancy 1973
Student Attrition 1991
↓ Students 1967

School Superintendents 1973
PN 508 **SC** 45760
SN Administrators who coordinate and direct the operations and activities of a school system at the district, city, or state level.

School Superintendents — (cont'd)
UF Superintendents (School)
B School Administrators 1973

School Suspension 1973
PN 211 SC 45770
SN Temporary, forced withdrawal of a student from school, usually for disciplinary reasons.
UF Suspension (School)
B School Enrollment 1973
R Classroom Discipline 1973
School Expulsion 1973

School to Work Transition 1994
PN 537 SC 45775
SN Transition following school graduation or termination and entry into the work force. Used for normal and disordered populations.
R College Graduates 1982
↓ Education 1967
Educational Attainment Level 1997
High School Graduates 1978
↓ Mainstreaming 1991
Occupational Adjustment 1973
School Graduation 1991
↓ Vocational Rehabilitation 1967

School Transition 1997
PN 507 SC 45777
SN Movement or advancement from one grade, school, or program to the next.
R ↓ Academic Achievement 1967
↓ Education 1967
Grade Level 1994
School Adjustment 1967
School Graduation 1991

School Truancy 1973
PN 283 SC 45780
SN Student's deliberate, often chronic absence from school without an accepted medical or other justifiable reason.
B Truancy 1973
R ↓ Education 1967
↓ School Enrollment 1973
School Refusal 1994
School Retention 1994

School Violence 2003
PN 508 SC 45783
HN This term was introduced in June 2003. Relevant records were re-indexed with this term. The posting note reflects the number of records that were re-indexed.
B Violence 1973
R ↓ Academic Environment 1973
Bullying 2003
Classroom Environment 1973
↓ School Environment 1973

Schools 1967
PN 6613 SC 45790
N Boarding Schools 1988
Charter Schools 2006
↓ Colleges 1967
Elementary Schools 1973
Graduate Schools 1973
High Schools 1973
Institutional Schools 1978
Junior High Schools 1973
Kindergartens 1973

Schools — (cont'd)
Middle Schools 2003
Military Schools 1973
Nongraded Schools 1973
Nursery Schools 1973
Seminaries 1973
Technical Schools 1973
R ↓ Community Facilities 1973
↓ Education 1967
↓ School Environment 1973
↓ School Facilities 1973

Sciatic Nerve
Use Spinal Nerves

SCID
Use Structured Clinical Interview

Science Achievement 1997
PN 339 SC 45815
B Academic Achievement 1967
R Mathematics Achievement 1973
Mathematics Education 1973
Science Education 1973

Science Education 1973
PN 4938 SC 45820
B Curriculum 1967
R Science Achievement 1997

Sciences 1967
PN 5097 SC 45825
N ↓ Biology 1967
↓ Chemistry 1967
Cognitive Science 2003
Eugenics 1973
Geography 1973
↓ Mathematics 1982
↓ Medical Sciences 1967
↓ Neurosciences 1973
Physics 1973
Psychobiology 1982
↓ Social Sciences 1967
R Nanotechnology 2007
↓ Technology 1973

Scientific Communication 1973
PN 15392 SC 45830
SN Formal or informal communication among professionals.
UF Communication (Professional)
Newsletters (Professional)
Professional Communication
Professional Newsletters
B Communication 1967
R ↓ Interpersonal Communication 1973
Psychological Terminology 1973
↓ Terminology 1991

Scientific Methods
Use Experimental Methods

Scientists 1967
PN 1956 SC 45850
SN Conceptually broad term. Use a more specific term if possible.
B Professional Personnel 1978
R ↓ Aerospace Personnel 1973
Anthropologists 1973
↓ Business and Industrial Personnel 1967

Scientists — (cont'd)
Engineers 1967
Mathematicians 1973
↓ Medical Personnel 1967
Physicists 1973
↓ Psychologists 1967
Sociologists 1973

Sclera
Use Eye (Anatomy)

Sclerosis (Nervous System) 1973
PN 516 SC 45870
SN Hardening of an anatomical structure in the nervous system (often a vessel or nerve) due to an overgrowth of fibrous tissues, or inflammation or disease of the interstitial tissue.
B Nervous System Disorders 1967
N Multiple Sclerosis 1973
R ↓ Neuromuscular Disorders 1973
↓ Paralysis 1973

Scopolamine 1973
PN 1359 SC 45880
UF Hyoscine
Scopolamine Hydrobromide
B Alkaloids 1973
Amines 1973
Cholinergic Blocking Drugs 1973
CNS Depressant Drugs 1973
Sedatives 1973
R Bromides 1973

Scopolamine Hydrobromide
Use Scopolamine

Score Equating 1985
PN 333 SC 45895
SN Techniques, procedures, or methods used to allow comparison of scores obtained from various editions of the same test or from different tests measuring the same trait.
UF Test Equating
R Cutting Scores 1985
↓ Scoring (Testing) 1973
Standard Scores 1985

Scores (Test)
Use Test Scores

Scoring (Testing) 1973
PN 2471 SC 45910
SN Assignment of numerical values or other types of codes, or the application of comments to test results in order to evaluate a test performance in reference to some established standard or other criterion. Compare GRADING (EDUCATIONAL) or TEST SCORES.
B Testing 1967
N Cutting Scores 1985
R Error of Measurement 1985
Grading (Educational) 1973
Score Equating 1985
Standard Scores 1985
Statistical Weighting 1985
Test Interpretation 1985
↓ Test Scores 1967

Scotopic Stimulation 1973
PN 147 SC 45940
SN Presentation of light at intensity levels characteristic of nighttime illumination, activating rod photoreceptors in the retina.

Scotopic Stimulation — (cont'd)
B Illumination 1967
R Photopic Stimulation 1973

Scratching 1973
PN 96 SC 45950
B Symptoms 1967
R Pruritus 1973

Screening 1982
PN 3145 SC 45960
SN Preliminary use of testing procedures or instruments to identify individuals at risk for a particular problem, or in need of a more thorough evaluation, or to determine an individual's suitability for a specific treatment, education, or occupation.
B Measurement 1967
N Drug Usage Screening 1988
↓ Health Screening 1997
Job Applicant Screening 1973
R Biological Markers 1991
↓ Diagnosis 1967
Diagnostic Interview Schedule 1991
↓ Educational Measurement 1967
Educational Placement 1978
Geriatric Assessment 1997
Health Promotion 1991
Intake Interview 1994
Misdiagnosis 1997
↓ Personnel Selection 1967
↓ Psychiatric Evaluation 1997
↓ Screening Tests 1982
Symptom Checklists 1991

Screening Tests 1982
PN 2956 SC 45980
B Measurement 1967
N Psychological Screening Inventory 1973
R General Health Questionnaire 1991
↓ Psychiatric Evaluation 1997
↓ Screening 1982

Scripts
Use Schema

Sculpturing 1973
PN 93 SC 45990
B Art 1967

Sea Gulls 1973
PN 209 SC 46010
UF Gulls
B Birds 1967

Seals (Animal) 1973
PN 191 SC 46020
B Mammals 1973

Seasonal Affective Disorder 1991
PN 720 SC 46025
SN A mood disorder characterized by major depression that recurs the same time every year, typically in the winter months.
UF SAD
Winter Depression
B Affective Disorders 2001
R ↓ Major Depression 1988
Phototherapy 1991
Recurrent Depression 1994

Seasonal Variations 1973
PN 2022 SC 46030
SN Periodic changes in behavioral, psychological, or physiological responses in relation to seasonal changes. Used for human or animal populations.
UF Seasonality
B Environmental Effects 1973
R ↓ Biological Rhythms 1967
↓ Temperature Effects 1967

Seasonality
Use Seasonal Variations

Seat Belts
Use Safety Belts

Seclusion (Patient)
Use Patient Seclusion

Secobarbital 1973
PN 54 SC 46040
UF Seconal
B Barbiturates 1967
Hypnotic Drugs 1973
Sedatives 1973

Seconal
Use Secobarbital

Second Language Education
Use Foreign Language Education

Second Order Conditioning
Use Higher Order Conditioning

Secondary Education 1973
PN 1947 SC 46060
SN Education provided by comprehensive schools, grammar schools, junior high or high schools, typically for grades 7-12.
B Education 1967
R High School Education 2003
High Schools 1973
Junior High Schools 1973

Secondary Reinforcement 1967
PN 407 SC 46070
SN Presentation of a secondary reinforcer. Also, objects or events which acquire reinforcing properties only through having been consistently paired or associated with other reinforcers. Also known as conditioned reinforcers. Compare INTERNAL REWARDS.
UF Token Reinforcement
B Reinforcement 1967
R Conditioned Stimulus 1973

Secondhand Smoking
Use Passive Smoking

Secrecy 1994
PN 240 SC 46075
R Anonymity 1973
↓ Deception 1967
Privacy 1973
Self Disclosure 1973

Secretarial Personnel 1973
PN 169 SC 46080
B Business and Industrial Personnel 1967
White Collar Workers 1973
R Clerical Personnel 1973

Secretarial Skills
Use Clerical Secretarial Skills

Secretion (Gland) 1973
PN 214 SC 46100
B Physiology 1967
N ↓ Endocrine Gland Secretion 1973
Lactation 1973
Salivation 1973
Sweating 1973
R ↓ Endocrine Disorders 1973

Sectioning (Lesion)
Use Lesions

Security (Emotional)
Use Emotional Security

Sedatives 1973
PN 680 SC 46130
HN In 1997, this term replaced the discontinued term PHENAGLYCODOL. In 2000, PHENAGLYCODOL was removed from all records and replaced with SEDATIVES.
UF Phenaglycodol
B Drugs 1967
N Alprazolam 1988
Amobarbital 1973
Atropine 1973
Barbital 1973
Chloral Hydrate 1973
Chlorpromazine 1967
Clozapine 1991
Flurazepam 1982
Glutethimide 1973
Haloperidol 1973
Heroin 1973
Hexobarbital 1973
Meperidine 1973
Meprobamate 1973
Methaqualone 1973
Molindone 1982
Nitrazepam 1978
Pentobarbital 1973
Phenobarbital 1973
Promethazine 1973
Reserpine 1967
Scopolamine 1973
Secobarbital 1973
Thalidomide 1973
Thiopental 1973
Triazolam 1988
R ↓ Analgesic Drugs 1973
↓ Anesthetic Drugs 1973
↓ Anticonvulsive Drugs 1973
↓ Antiemetic Drugs 1973
↓ Antihistaminic Drugs 1973
↓ Antihypertensive Drugs 1973
↓ Barbiturates 1967
↓ Benzodiazepines 1978
↓ CNS Depressant Drugs 1973
↓ Hypnotic Drugs 1973
↓ Tranquilizing Drugs 1967

Seduction 1994
PN 138 SC 46133
B Psychosexual Behavior 1967

Seeing Eye Dogs
Use Mobility Aids

Segregation (Racial)
Use Social Integration

Seizures 2005
PN 3842 **SC** 46145
SN The disruption of motor and sensory functions due to sudden and abnormal electrical discharge of brain cells.
HN In August 2005, this term replaced the discontinued term CONVULSIONS. CONVULSIONS was removed from all records containing it, and was replaced with SEIZURES, its postable counterpart.
UF Convulsions
B Nervous System Disorders 1967
Symptoms 1967
N Audiogenic Seizures 1978
↓ Epileptic Seizures 1973
Grand Mal Seizures 2006
Petit Mal Seizures 2006
R ↓ Anticonvulsive Drugs 1973
↓ Brain Disorders 1967
Experimental Epilepsy 1978
Hydrocephalus 2006
↓ Spasms 1973

Selection (Personnel)
Use Personnel Selection

Selection (Therapist)
Use Therapist Selection

Selection Tests 1973
PN 589 **SC** 46170
SN Tests developed to assess specific traits or skills with the purpose of screening or selecting individuals for occupational or educational placement.
B Measurement 1967
N Psychological Screening Inventory 1973

Selective Attention 1973
PN 3659 **SC** 46175
SN Focusing of awareness on a limited range of stimuli. Compare DIVIDED ATTENTION.
B Attention 1967
R Concentration 1982
Distraction 1978
Divided Attention 1973
↓ Monitoring 1973
Sensory Gating 1991
Vigilance 1967

Selective Breeding 1973
PN 403 **SC** 46180
SN Systematic approach to the development of genotype-dependent differences in a physical or behavioral trait. Compare ANIMAL BREEDING, ANIMAL DOMESTICATION, and EUGENICS.
B Animal Breeding 1973
R Animal Domestication 1978
Eugenics 1973
↓ Genetic Engineering 1994
↓ Genetics 1967
Reproductive Technology 1988

Selective Mutism
Use Elective Mutism

Self Acceptance
Use Self Perception

Self Actualization 1973
PN 2467 **SC** 46190
SN According to A. Maslow's theory, the process of striving to fulfull one's talents, capacities, and potentialities for maximum self realization, ideally with integration of physical, social, intellectual, and emotional needs.

Self Actualization — (cont'd)
UF Actualization (Self)
Self Realization
R Affective Education 1982
↓ Human Potential Movement 1982
Maslow (Abraham Harold) 1991
↓ Personality 1967
Self Determination 1994
↓ Self Help Techniques 1982

Self Administration (Drugs)
Use Drug Self Administration

Self Analysis 1994
PN 193 **SC** 46195
SN A psychotherapist's application of psychoanalytic principles to his or her personal feelings, drives, and behaviors.
B Psychoanalysis 1967
R Personal Therapy 1991
Psychoanalytic Training 1973

Self Assessment
Use Self Evaluation

Self Care Skills 1978
PN 2298 **SC** 46215
SN Skills such as personal hygiene, feeding, independent housekeeping, public transportation use, which are often taught in rehabilitation programs for persons with mental, physical, or emotional handicaps.
UF Independent Living
B Ability 1967
R Activities of Daily Living 1991
Adaptive Behavior 1991
Aging in Place 2007
Child Self Care 1988
Daily Activities 1994
Hygiene 1994
Independent Living Programs 1991
↓ Rehabilitation 1967
↓ Skill Learning 1973
Special Education 1967

Self Concept 1967
PN 26387 **SC** 46220
UF Ideal Self
Identity (Personal)
Self Image
N Academic Self Concept 1997
Self Confidence 1994
Self Esteem 1973
R Affective Education 1982
Ego Identity 1991
Ethnic Identity 1973
↓ Gender Identity 1985
Identity Crisis 1973
Identity Formation 2004
↓ Personality 1967
Professional Identity 1991
Reference Groups 1994
Role Satisfaction 1994
Self Congruence 1978
Self Criticism 2003
Self Perception 1967
↓ Social Identity 1988
Symbolic Interactionism 1988

Self Confidence 1994
PN 1114 **SC** 46230
HN Use SELF ESTEEM to access references from 1973-1993.

Self Confidence — (cont'd)
UF Confidence (Self)
B Self Concept 1967
R Academic Self Concept 1997
Self Efficacy 1985
Self Esteem 1973
Self Perception 1967

Self Congruence 1978
PN 364 **SC** 46235
SN State of harmony between actual and ideal selves, or congruence between experience, personality, and self-concept.
R ↓ Self Concept 1967

Self Consciousness
Use Self Perception

Self Control 1973
PN 4594 **SC** 46240
SN The ability to repress or the practice of repressing one's behavior, impulsive reactions, emotions, or desires.
UF Control (Self)
Willpower
B Personality Traits 1967
R Anger Control 1997
↓ Emotional Control 1973
Emotional Regulation 2007
↓ Helplessness 1997
↓ Impulse Control Disorders 1997
Internal External Locus of Control 1967
Self Regulation 2003
Temptation 1973

Self Criticism 2003
PN 198 **SC** 46242
HN This term was introduced in June 2003. Relevant records were re-indexed with this term. The posting note reflects the number of records that were re-indexed.
B Criticism 1973
R Perfectionism 1988
↓ Self Concept 1967
Self Esteem 1973
Self Evaluation 1967
Self Monitoring 1982

Self Defeating Behavior 1988
PN 245 **SC** 46243
SN Behavior that blocks one's own goals and wishes, e.g., the tendency to compete so aggressively that one cannot hold a job.
B Behavior 1967
R ↓ Self Destructive Behavior 1985
Self Handicapping Strategy 1988

Self Defense 1985
PN 202 **SC** 46245
SN Protecting one's self or property against crime.
UF Personal Defense
R ↓ Crime 1967
↓ Crime Victims 1982
Martial Arts 1985
Self Preservation 1997
↓ Violence 1973

Self Destructive Behavior 1985
PN 2200 **SC** 46244
UF Self Injurious Behavior
B Behavior 1967
N Attempted Suicide 1973
Head Banging 1973
Self Inflicted Wounds 1973

Self Destructive Behavior — (cont'd)
Self Mutilation 1973
↓ Suicide 1967
R ↓ Behavior Disorders 1971
Borderline Personality Disorder 2001
↓ Masochism 1973
Masochistic Personality 1973
Self Defeating Behavior 1988
Trichotillomania 2003

Self Determination 1994
PN 954 **SC** 46246
SN The power of individuals to determine their own destiny or actions.
R Empowerment 1991
↓ Helplessness 1997
Independence (Personality) 1973
Individualism 2007
Individuality 1973
Internal External Locus of Control 1967
Self Actualization 1973
↓ Self Management 1985
Volition 1988
World View 1988

Self Directed Learning
Use Individualized Instruction

Self Disclosure 1973
PN 4184 **SC** 46250
UF Disclosure (Self)
R Anonymity 1973
↓ Interpersonal Communication 1973
Legal Confession 2003
↓ Personality 1967
Secrecy 1994
Self Expression 2006

Self Efficacy 1985
PN 7665 **SC** 46255
SN Cognitive mechanism based on expectations or beliefs about one's ability to perform actions necessary to produce a given effect. Also, a theoretical component of behavior change in various therapeutic treatments.
UF Efficacy Expectations
R Academic Self Concept 1997
↓ Expectations 1967
↓ Helplessness 1997
Instrumentality 1991
Self Confidence 1994
Self Evaluation 1967
Self Fulfilling Prophecies 1997
Self Perception 1967

Self Employment 1994
PN 90 **SC** 46257
B Employment Status 1982
R ↓ Business 1967
Entrepreneurship 1991
Ownership 1985
↓ Retailing 1991
Small Businesses 2007

Self Esteem 1973
PN 15451 **SC** 46260
UF Self Respect
B Self Concept 1967
R Self Confidence 1994
Self Criticism 2003
Self Perception 1967

Self Evaluation 1967
PN 5909 **SC** 46270
UF Self Assessment
B Evaluation 1967
R ↓ Personality 1967
Self Criticism 2003
Self Efficacy 1985
↓ Self Management 1985
Self Monitoring 1982
Self Report 1982
Social Comparison 1985

Self Examination (Medical) 1988
PN 331 **SC** 46273
SN Self examination for detection of medical conditions or disorders, e.g., breast or testicular cancer. Also used for self administration of medical diagnostic procedures.
UF Breast Examination
R Cancer Screening 1997
↓ Health Behavior 1982
Physical Examination 1988

Self Expression 2006
PN 93 **SC** 58095
SN Communicating one's personality and individuality through various means, including verbal communication, art, creative writing, music, dance, or drama.
HN This term was introduced in May 2006. Relevant records were re-indexed with this term. The posting note reflects the number of records that were re-indexed.
R Art Therapy 1973
Assertiveness 1973
Cosmetic Techniques 2001
Creative Writing 1994
Creativity 1967
Dance 1973
Dance Therapy 1973
Individual Differences 1967
Individualism 2007
Individuality 1973
↓ Interpersonal Communication 1973
Self Disclosure 1973

Self Fulfilling Prophecies 1997
PN 95 **SC** 46271
SN Expectations or predictions that turn out just as one prophesized. The fulfillment of expectations is usually due to behavior that optimizes the outcome.
UF Pygmalion Effect
R Attribution 1973
↓ Expectations 1967
↓ Prediction 1967
Self Efficacy 1985
Social Cognition 1994
↓ Social Perception 1967

Self Handicapping Strategy 1988
PN 207 **SC** 46274
SN Conscious or unconscious efforts to lessen one's chances of performing well at a task in which one is ego-involved and fears failure so that poor performance or lack of ability may be attributed to circumstance.
R Fear of Success 1978
Self Defeating Behavior 1988

Self Help Techniques 1982
PN 2353 **SC** 46275
SN Techniques, materials, or processes designed to assist individuals in solving their own problems. Consider also SUPPORT GROUPS.

Self Help Techniques — (cont'd)
N ↓ Self Management 1985
R ↓ Behavior Modification 1973
↓ Community Services 1967
Group Counseling 1973
↓ Psychotherapeutic Techniques 1967
Self Actualization 1973
Self Monitoring 1982
Self Referral 1991
↓ Support Groups 1991
↓ Treatment 1967
↓ Twelve Step Programs 1997

Self Hypnosis
Use Autohypnosis

Self Image
Use Self Concept

Self Inflicted Wounds 1973
PN 628 **SC** 46290
SN Any injury to body tissue (including bones) resulting from self directed physical violence. Compare SELF MUTILATION.
B Self Destructive Behavior 1985
Wounds 1973
R Self Mutilation 1973

Self Injurious Behavior
Use Self Destructive Behavior

Self Instruction
Use Individualized Instruction

Self Instructional Training 1985
PN 231 **SC** 46294
SN Cognitive technique for overcoming cognitive deficits in areas such as problem solving, verbal mediation, and information seeking. Overt verbalizations of thought processes are modeled for and imitated by the client. Covert self-verbalizations follow which result in the client gaining verbal control over behavior.
B Cognitive Techniques 1985
Self Management 1985
Training 2006
R Cognitive Therapy 1982

Self Management 1985
PN 2577 **SC** 46295
SN Self-regulated modification and/or maintenance of behavior by self-governing of behavioral consequences. Used with disordered or normal populations of all ages.
B Behavior Modification 1973
Management 1967
Self Help Techniques 1982
N Self Instructional Training 1985
R Centering 1991
Cognitive Therapy 1982
Self Determination 1994
Self Evaluation 1967
Self Monitoring 1982
Self Regulation 2003
Self Reinforcement 1973
Time Management 1994

Self Managing Work Teams 2001
PN 66 **SC** 46299
SN Autonomous groups of employees who share the responsibility for and have been given the authority to oversee and control all work processes.
B Management Methods 1973
Work Teams 2001

Self Managing Work Teams — (cont'd)
R Organizational Structure 1967
Participative Management 1988

Self Medication 1991
PN 285 **SC** 46298
SN Medicating one's self without the advice or consent of a physician. Not to be confused with DRUG SELF ADMINISTRATION.
R ↓ Drug Therapy 1967
↓ Drugs 1967
Nonprescription Drugs 1991
Prescription Drugs 1991

Self Monitoring 1982
PN 1729 **SC** 46296
SN Systematic observation and recording of one's own behavior usually for the purpose of changing the behavior by means of behavior modification techniques.
UF Self Observation
B Monitoring 1973
R ↓ Behavior Modification 1973
Observation Methods 1967
Self Criticism 2003
Self Evaluation 1967
↓ Self Help Techniques 1982
↓ Self Management 1985
Self Regulation 2003
Self Report 1982

Self Monitoring (Personality) 1985
PN 593 **SC** 46297
SN The process of subjectively observing and comparing one's own behaviors and expressions with those of others in social interactions for the purpose of regulating and controlling one's own verbal and nonverbal behaviors.
R Conscientiousness 1997
Impression Management 1978
Introspection 1973
↓ Personality 1967
Reflectiveness 1997
Self Perception 1967
Self Regulation 2003
Social Comparison 1985
↓ Social Interaction 1967

Self Mutilation 1973
PN 857 **SC** 46300
SN Act of inflicting permanent physical damage to oneself, such as cutting off or destroying a limb or other part of the body. Compare SELF INFLICTED WOUNDS.
UF Autotomy
Mutilation (Self)
B Behavior Disorders 1971
Self Destructive Behavior 1985
R Cosmetic Techniques 2001
Self Inflicted Wounds 1973

Self Observation
Use Self Monitoring

Self Perception 1967
PN 14558 **SC** 46310
SN Physical and social awareness and perceptions of oneself.
UF Self Acceptance
Self Consciousness
B Perception 1967
R Academic Self Concept 1997
Aging (Attitudes Toward) 1985
Body Awareness 1982

Self Perception — (cont'd)
Ingroup Outgroup 1997
Introspection 1973
Mirror Image 1991
↓ Personality 1967
↓ Personality Theory 1967
Reflectiveness 1997
↓ Self Concept 1967
Self Confidence 1994
Self Efficacy 1985
Self Esteem 1973
Self Monitoring (Personality) 1985
Self Reference 1994
Self Report 1982

Self Preservation 1997
PN 210 **SC** 46312
UF Survival Instinct
R Death Instinct 1988
Instinctive Behavior 1982
Self Defense 1985
Theory of Evolution 1967

Self Psychology 1988
PN 1779 **SC** 46315
SN Psychological theory and approach to psychotherapy focusing on interpretation of behavior in reference to self. Includes the psychoanalytic concept of an individual's need to organize the psyche into a cohesive whole, the self.
B Psychology 1967
R ↓ Humanistic Psychology 1985
Mirroring 1997
Object Relations 1982
↓ Personality Theory 1967
↓ Psychoanalytic Theory 1967

Self Realization
Use Self Actualization

Self Reference 1994
PN 259 **SC** 46323
R ↓ Interpersonal Communication 1973
Self Perception 1967
↓ Social Perception 1967

Self Referral 1991
PN 127 **SC** 46325
SN Act of directing oneself to an agency, service, or professional for assessment, diagnosis, treatment, or consultation.
UF Referral (Self)
R ↓ Commitment (Psychiatric) 1973
↓ Health Behavior 1982
Health Care Seeking Behavior 1997
↓ Health Care Services 1978
Health Care Utilization 1985
↓ Help Seeking Behavior 1978
Professional Referral 1973
Right to Treatment 1997
↓ Self Help Techniques 1982

Self Regulated Learning 2003
PN 303 **SC** 46328
SN Approach to learning that involves self adjustment, self monitoring, strategy use, and goal setting.
HN This term was introduced in June 2003. Relevant records were re-indexed with this term. The posting note reflects the number of records that were re-indexed.
B Learning 1967
R Discovery Teaching Method 1973
Individualized Instruction 1973
↓ Learning Strategies 1991

Self Regulated Learning — (cont'd)
Self Regulation 2003

Self Regulation 2003
PN 1726 **SC** 46327
SN Process of adjusting one's behavior to achieve or avoid a particular outcome.
HN This term was introduced in June 2003. Relevant records were re-indexed with this term. The posting note reflects the number of records that were re-indexed.
R Emotional Regulation 2007
Self Control 1973
↓ Self Management 1985
Self Monitoring 1982
Self Monitoring (Personality) 1985
Self Regulated Learning 2003

Self Reinforcement 1973
PN 1457 **SC** 46330
SN Used for human and animal populations.
B Reinforcement 1967
R ↓ Self Management 1985
↓ Self Stimulation 1967

Self Report 1982
PN 7086 **SC** 46335
SN Method for obtaining information through the elicitation of overt verbal responses, oral or written, from the subject/client by the use of questions or directives. Used only when self-report is discussed in reference to methodological considerations.
B Methodology 1967
R Likert Scales 1994
Self Evaluation 1967
Self Monitoring 1982
Self Perception 1967

Self Respect
Use Self Esteem

Self Stimulation 1967
PN 2175 **SC** 46350
B Stimulation 1967
N Brain Self Stimulation 1985
R Electrical Brain Stimulation 1973
↓ Operant Conditioning 1967
↓ Reinforcement 1967
Self Reinforcement 1973
Stereotyped Behavior 1973

Self Talk 1988
PN 514 **SC** 46355
SN Vocalized or unvocalized speech that is directed to oneself or an imaginary recipient.
UF Inner Speech
B Oral Communication 1985
R Ellis (Albert) 1991
↓ Psychotherapeutic Techniques 1967
Subvocalization 1973

Selfishness 1973
PN 152 **SC** 46360
B Personality Traits 1967
R Narcissism 1967

Semantic Differential 1967
PN 907 **SC** 46370
SN Technique or test which uses subjective ratings of an idea, concept, or object by means of scaling opposite adjectives in order to study connotative meaning. Also used to assess interactions between people and situations and for attitude assessment.

Semantic Differential — (cont'd)
R ↓ Attitude Measures 1967
Likert Scales 1994
↓ Measurement 1967

Semantic Generalization 1973
PN 189 **SC** 46380
SN Conditioning of a reaction to a nonverbal stimulus and subsequent generalization of the response to verbal signs representative of the original stimulus. The types include generalization from object to sign, from sign to sign, and from sign to object.
UF Generalization (Semantic)
B Cognitive Processes 1967
R Cognitive Generalization 1967
Connotations 1973

Semantic Memory 1988
PN 1616 **SC** 46385
SN Organized knowledge about words, their meanings, and their relations.
B Verbal Memory 1994
R ↓ Lexical Access 1988
Lexical Decision 1988
Semantic Priming 1994
↓ Semantics 1967

Semantic Priming 1994
PN 920 **SC** 46387
B Priming 1988
R Contextual Associations 1967
Cues 1967
Semantic Memory 1988
↓ Semantics 1967

Semantics 1967
PN 7824 **SC** 46390
SN Linguistic science dealing with the relations between language symbols (words, expressions, phrases) and the objects or concepts to which they refer. Also includes the study of changes in the meanings of words. Used for the discipline or the specific semantic characteristics of linguistic symbols.
B Grammar 1967
N Antonyms 1973
Homonyms 1973
Synonyms 1973
R Discourse Analysis 1997
Metaphor 1982
Morphology (Language) 1973
↓ Phonology 1973
↓ Priming 1988
Semantic Memory 1988
Semantic Priming 1994
↓ Syntax 1971
↓ Verbal Meaning 1973
↓ Vocabulary 1967
Words (Phonetic Units) 1967

Semicircular Canals 1973
PN 85 **SC** 46400
B Vestibular Apparatus 1967

Seminarians 1973
PN 219 **SC** 46410
B Religious Personnel 1973
Students 1967

Seminaries 1973
PN 41 **SC** 46420
SN Institutions for training for ministry, priesthood, or rabbinate.

Seminaries — (cont'd)
B Schools 1967
R Religious Education 1973

Semiotics 1985
PN 618 **SC** 46425
SN Analysis of signs and symbols, especially their syntactic, semantic, and pragmatic functions in language.
N Pragmatics 1985
R Hermeneutics 1991
↓ Linguistics 1973
Symbolism 1967

Senile Dementia 1973
PN 969 **SC** 46440
SN Progressive abnormally accelerated deterioration of mental faculties and emotional stability in old age.
UF Dementia (Senile)
B Dementia 1985
Syndromes 1973
N Senile Psychosis 1973
R Alzheimers Disease 1973
Cerebral Arteriosclerosis 1973
Physiological Aging 1967
↓ Presenile Dementia 1973
Progressive Supranuclear Palsy 1997

Senile Psychosis 1973
PN 20 **SC** 46450
SN Psychosis occurring in old age that is associated with degeneration of the brain.
B Psychosis 1967
Senile Dementia 1973

Sensation
Use Perception

Sensation Seeking 1978
PN 1366 **SC** 46477
SN Need for novel experience or stimulation in order to reach optimal levels of arousal. Limited to human populations.
UF Novelty Seeking
Stimulation Seeking (Personality)
B Personality Traits 1967
R Extraversion 1967

Sensation Seeking Scale 1973
PN 98 **SC** 46480
B Personality Measures 1967

Sense Organ Disorders 1973
PN 52 **SC** 46490
B Physical Disorders 1997
Sensory System Disorders 2001
N Anosmia 1973
↓ Ear Disorders 1973
Taste Disorders 2001
↓ Vision Disorders 1982
R Anesthesia (Feeling) 1973
↓ Sense Organs 1973

Sense Organs 1973
PN 230 **SC** 46500
B Anatomy 1967
N ↓ Ear (Anatomy) 1967
↓ Eye (Anatomy) 1967
Taste Buds 1973
R ↓ Sense Organ Disorders 1973
↓ Sensory System Disorders 2001
Taste Disorders 2001

Sensitivity (Drugs)
Use Drug Sensitivity

Sensitivity (Personality) 1967
PN 1634 **SC** 46520
UF Insensitivity (Personality)
B Personality Traits 1967
R Perceptiveness (Personality) 1973

Sensitivity Training 1973
PN 1131 **SC** 46530
SN Group training that focuses on interpersonal relations within the group and enhancement of self-confidence, self-perception, behavioral skills, and role flexibility.
B Human Potential Movement 1982
Training 2006
R Communication Skills Training 1982
Consciousness Raising Groups 1978
Cultural Sensitivity 1994
↓ Encounter Group Therapy 1973
↓ Group Dynamics 1967
↓ Group Psychotherapy 1967
Human Relations Training 1978
Marathon Group Therapy 1973
↓ Personnel Training 1967
Social Skills Training 1982

Sensitization 2005
PN 454 **SC** 46505
SN The process of becoming more sensitive or responsive to a given stimulus.
HN This term was introduced in August 2005. Relevant records were re-indexed with this term. The posting note reflects the number of records that were re-indexed.
UF Behavioral Sensitization
R Drug Sensitivity 1973

Sensitization (Protein)
Use Anaphylactic Shock

Sensitization Repression
Use Repression Sensitization

Sensorially Handicapped
HN The term was discontinued in 1997, when the term SENSORIALLY DISABLED was created to capture this concept. In 2000, with the deletion of the term SENSORIALLY DISABLED, SENSORIALLY HANDICAPPED was made a nonpostable term for the new postable term SENSORY SYSTEM DISORDERS. SENSORIALLY HANDICAPPED and SENSORIALLY DISABLED were removed from all records containing them and replaced with SENSORY SYSTEM DISORDERS.
Use Sensory System Disorders

Sensorimotor Development
Use Perceptual Motor Development

Sensorimotor Measures 1973
PN 415 **SC** 46550
UF Perceptual Motor Measures
B Measurement 1967
R ↓ Perceptual Measures 1973

Sensorimotor Processes
Use Perceptual Motor Processes

Sensorineural Hearing Loss
Use Hearing Disorders

Sensory Adaptation 1967
PN 2382 **SC** 46560
SN Change in sensitivity of sensory systems or components as a result of ongoing or prolonged stimulation.
UF Adaptation (Sensory)
B Adaptation 1967
Thresholds 1967
N Dark Adaptation 1973
Light Adaptation 1982
Orienting Reflex 1967
Orienting Responses 1967
R Habituation 1967
Interocular Transfer 1985
Sensory Integration 1991

Sensory Deprivation 1967
PN 1289 **SC** 46570
SN Restriction of sensory or environmental stimulation through surgical or other techniques. Used primarily for animal populations. Consider STIMULUS DEPRIVATION for human populations.
B Stimulus Deprivation 1973

Sensory Disabilities (Attitudes Toward) 2001
PN 140 **SC** 46576
HN In 2000, the truncated terms SENSORY DISABILITIES (ATTIT TOWARD) (which was used from 1997-2000) and SENSORY HANDICAPS (ATTIT TOWARD) (which was used from 1973-1996) were deleted, removed from all records containing them, and replaced with the expanded form SENSORY DISABILITIES (ATTITUDES TOWARD).
UF Sensory Handicaps (Attitudes Toward)
B Disabled (Attitudes Toward) 1997
R Disability Discrimination 1997

Sensory Feedback 1973
PN 556 **SC** 46580
SN Return of afferent neural signals or information from sensory receptors. Sensory feedback may function in the regulation of behavior in general but is especially important in the control of bodily movement. Use a more specific term if possible.
B Feedback 1967
Perceptual Stimulation 1973
N ↓ Auditory Feedback 1973
Visual Feedback 1973

Sensory Gating 1991
PN 540 **SC** 46585
SN The internal process of blocking one or more sensory stimuli while attention is focused on another sensory stimuli or sensory channel.
UF Gating (Sensory)
B Perception 1967
R ↓ Awareness 1967
↓ Evoked Potentials 1967
↓ Perceptual Stimulation 1973
Prepulse Inhibition 1997
Selective Attention 1973

Sensory Handicaps (Attitudes Toward)
HN The term was discontinued in 1997, when the term SENSORY DISABILITIES (ATTIT TOWARD) was created to capture this concept. In 2000, these two truncated terms were deleted and replaced with their expanded forms: SENSORY HANDICAPS (ATTITUDES TOWARD) and SENSORY DISABILITIES (ATTITUDES TOWARD). The truncated versions of the terms were removed from all records containing them, and replaced with SENSORY DISABILITIES (ATTITUDES TOWARD), the valid postable version of the term.
Use Sensory Disabilities (Attitudes Toward)

Sensory Integration 1991
PN 984 **SC** 46595
SN Neural processes of organizing sensory inputs from the environment and producing an adaptive response. In treatment, the environment's sensory input is manipulated to facilitate environmental interaction.
UF Intersensory Integration
B Intersensory Processes 1978
Perceptual Motor Processes 1967
R ↓ Sensory Adaptation 1967
↓ Treatment 1967

Sensory Neglect 1994
PN 1103 **SC** 46597
UF Perceptual Neglect
Spatial Neglect
Visual Neglect
R ↓ Perception 1967
↓ Perceptual Distortion 1982
↓ Perceptual Disturbances 1973
↓ Receptive Fields 1985

Sensory Neurons 1973
PN 1496 **SC** 46610
SN Neurons that conduct sensory impulses to the central nervous system.
UF Afferent Neurons
B Neurons 1973
N Auditory Neurons 1973
Baroreceptors 1973
Chemoreceptors 1973
Mechanoreceptors 1973
Nociceptors 1985
↓ Photoreceptors 1973
Proprioceptors 1973
Taste Buds 1973
Thermoreceptors 1973
R ↓ Afferent Pathways 1982
↓ Receptive Fields 1985
Taste Disorders 2001

Sensory Pathways
Use Afferent Pathways

Sensory Preconditioning
Use Preconditioning

Sensory System Disorders 2001
PN 249 **SC** 46599
SN Disorders of the sense organs or of the somatosensory system.
HN The term SENSORIALLY HANDICAPPED was used to represent this concept from 1994-1996, and SENSORIALLY DISABLED was used from 1997-2000. In 2000, SENSORY SYSTEM DISORDERS was created to replace the discontinued and deleted term SENSORIALLY DISABLED. SENSORIALLY DISABLED and SENSORIALLY HANDICAPPED were removed from all records containing them and replaced with SENSORY SYSTEM DISORDERS.
UF Sensorially Handicapped
B Physical Disorders 1997
N ↓ Sense Organ Disorders 1973
Somatosensory Disorders 2001
R ↓ Sense Organs 1973
Somatosensory Cortex 1973
Synesthesia 2003

Sentence Completion Tests 1991
PN 75 **SC** 46617
B Personality Measures 1967
Projective Personality Measures 1973
R Cloze Testing 1973

Sentence Comprehension 1973
PN 2493 **SC** 46620
B Verbal Comprehension 1985

Sentence Structure 1973
PN 2252 **SC** 46630
SN Specific characteristics of a sentence's construction, including such aspects as its syntax, length, and complexity. Compare SYNTAX.
R ↓ Prosody 1991
↓ Syntax 1971
Text Structure 1982

Sentences 1967
PN 2530 **SC** 46640
SN Grammatically and syntactically arranged words that constitute a grammatically complete and meaningful unit.
B Language 1967

Sentencing
Use Adjudication

Separation (Marital)
Use Marital Separation

Separation Anxiety 1973
PN 1034 **SC** 46660
SN Anxiety caused by separation from a significant person or object. It is typically experienced by children when separated from their primary caregiver.
B Anxiety Disorders 1997
Separation Reactions 1997
R Abandonment 1997
Attachment Behavior 1985
Attachment Disorders 2001
Attachment Theory 2007
↓ Relationship Termination 1997
School Phobia 1973
School Refusal 1994
Stranger Reactions 1988

Separation Individuation 1982
PN 1676 **SC** 46665
SN Normal process begun in infancy of disengagement from one's mother and development of a separate, individual identity. Limited to human populations.
B Personality Development 1967
R Attachment Behavior 1985
↓ Childhood Development 1967
Mother Child Relations 1967
Object Relations 1982
Transitional Objects 1985

Separation Reactions 1997
PN 336 **SC** 46670
N Separation Anxiety 1973
R Abandonment 1997
Alienation 1971
Anaclitic Depression 1973
Apathy 1973
Attachment Behavior 1985
Attachment Disorders 2001
Depression (Emotion) 1967

Separation Reactions — (cont'd)
Disappointment 1973
Distress 1973
Emotional Trauma 1967
Grief 1973
Homesickness 1994
↓ Relationship Termination 1997
Sadness 1973
Withdrawal (Defense Mechanism) 1973

Septal Nuclei 1982
PN 684 **SC** 46676
SN Subcallosal nuclei that form an integral part of the limbic system. These nuclei contribute to the medial forebrain bundle and have processes synapsing in the hippocampus.
UF Septum
B Limbic System 1973
R Fornix 1982
Hippocampus 1967
Medial Forebrain Bundle 1982
Nucleus Accumbens 1982

Septum
Use Septal Nuclei

Sequential Learning 1973
PN 681 **SC** 46690
SN Type of learning in which a particular task is completed before the next task is given. The learning of each subsequent task is dependent on the previous task completed.
B Learning 1967
R Mastery Learning 1985

Serial Anticipation (Learning) 1973
PN 162 **SC** 46700
SN Learning paradigm which involves the initial presentation of a list of items or a series of events with a short interval between the items or elements in the series. Upon subsequent presentation of the list/series, the subject attempts to guess or anticipate the next item/element in the sequence. Thus, each item/element serves as a cue for the recall of the next. Compare FREE RECALL.
UF Anticipation (Serial Learning)
B Serial Learning 1967
R ↓ Verbal Learning 1967

Serial Homicide 2003
PN 71 **SC** 46715
HN This term was introduced in June 2003. Relevant records were re-indexed with this term. The posting note reflects the number of records that were re-indexed.
UF Serial Murder
B Homicide 1967

Serial Learning 1967
PN 1534 **SC** 46720
SN Learning, usually memorization, of items in a list according to a prescribed order.
B Learning 1967
N Serial Anticipation (Learning) 1973
R ↓ Serial Position Effect 1982
Serial Recall 1994
↓ Verbal Learning 1967

Serial Murder
Use Serial Homicide

Serial Position Effect 1982
PN 388 **SC** 46724
SN Effect of the relative position of an item in a series on the rate of learning that item.

Serial Position Effect — (cont'd)
N Primacy Effect 1973
Recency Effect 1973
R ↓ Learning 1967
Learning Rate 1973
↓ Serial Learning 1967
Serial Recall 1994

Serial Recall 1994
PN 411 **SC** 46727
B Recall (Learning) 1967
R Forgetting 1973
Free Recall 1973
↓ Memory 1967
↓ Serial Learning 1967
↓ Serial Position Effect 1982

Seriousness 1973
PN 40 **SC** 46730
B Personality Traits 1967

Serotonin 1973
PN 8189 **SC** 46740
UF Hydroxytryptamine (5-)
B Amines 1973
Neurotransmitters 1985
Vasoconstrictor Drugs 1973
R ↓ Adrenergic Drugs 1973
Serotonin Agonists 1988
↓ Serotonin Antagonists 1973
↓ Serotonin Metabolites 1978
↓ Serotonin Precursors 1978

Serotonin Agonists 1988
PN 1638 **SC** 46745
B Drugs 1967
R Buspirone 1991
Serotonin 1973
↓ Serotonin Antagonists 1973

Serotonin Antagonists 1973
PN 2251 **SC** 46750
UF Methysergide
B Drugs 1967
N Dihydroxytryptamine 1991
Lysergic Acid Diethylamide 1967
Mianserin 1982
Molindone 1982
Parachlorophenylalanine 1978
Ritanserin 1997
Tetrabenazine 1973
R ↓ Decarboxylase Inhibitors 1982
Serotonin 1973
Serotonin Agonists 1988
↓ Serotonin Precursors 1978
↓ Serotonin Reuptake Inhibitors 1997

Serotonin Metabolites 1978
PN 185 **SC** 46754
B Metabolites 1973
N Hydroxyindoleacetic Acid (5-) 1985
R Serotonin 1973
↓ Serotonin Precursors 1978

Serotonin Norepinephrine Reuptake Inhibitors 2007
PN 42 **SC** 46755
SN Antidepressant drugs used in the treatment of affective and other mental disorders that act upon both serotonin and norepinephrine neurotransmitters.
HN This term was introduced in April 2007. Relevant records were re-indexed with this term. The posting note reflects the number of records that were re-indexed.

Serotonin Norepinephrine Reuptake Inhibitors — (cont'd)
UF Dual Reuptake Inhibitors
SNRI
B Antidepressant Drugs 1971
Neurotransmitter Uptake Inhibitors 2007
N Venlafaxine 2003
R ↓ Serotonin Reuptake Inhibitors 1997

Serotonin Precursors 1978
PN 100 **SC** 46756
N ↓ Tryptophan 1973
R Serotonin 1973
↓ Serotonin Antagonists 1973
↓ Serotonin Metabolites 1978

Serotonin Reuptake Inhibitors 1997
PN 2298 **SC** 46758
HN Consider using SEROTONIN ANTAGONISTS to access references from 1973-1996.
B Neurotransmitter Uptake Inhibitors 2007
N Chlorimipramine 1973
Citalopram 1997
Fluoxetine 1991
Fluvoxamine 1994
Paroxetine 1994
Zimeldine 1988
R ↓ Serotonin Antagonists 1973
↓ Serotonin Norepinephrine Reuptake Inhibitors 2007

Serpasil
Use Reserpine

Sertraline 1997
PN 765 **SC** 46765
B Antidepressant Drugs 1971

Serum (Blood)
Use Blood Serum

Serum Albumin 1973
PN 61 **SC** 46780
B Blood Proteins 1973

Service Learning 2007
PN 300 **SC** 46783
SN A teaching method that promotes learning through community or public service, usually integrated with regular classroom instruction.
HN This term was introduced in April 2007. Relevant records were re-indexed with this term. The posting note reflects the number of records that were re-indexed.
B Experiential Learning 1997
Teaching Methods 1967
R Community Involvement 2003
↓ Learning Strategies 1991
↓ Nontraditional Education 1982

Service Personnel 1991
PN 717 **SC** 46785
SN Employees who have direct contact with the public; generally nonprofessional and nonsales personnel. Includes hotel, airline, and restaurant personnel, but does not include health care personnel.
B Business and Industrial Personnel 1967
N Domestic Service Personnel 1973
Technical Service Personnel 1973
R Child Care Workers 1978
↓ Nonprofessional Personnel 1982
Sales Personnel 1973
↓ Technical Personnel 1978

Service Quality
Use Quality of Services

Servicemen
Use Military Personnel

Set (Response)
Use Response Set

Severe Mental Retardation 2001
PN 2278 **SC** 46800
SN IQ 20-34.
HN In 2000, this term replaced the discontinued and deleted term SEVERELY MENTALLY RETARDED. SEVERELY MENTALLY RETARDED was removed from all records containing it and replaced with SEVERE MENTAL RETARDATION.
B Mental Retardation 1967

Severity (Disorders) 1982
PN 6824 **SC** 46824
SN Degree of severity of mental or physical disorder.
R ↓ Chronic Illness 1991
↓ Chronic Mental Illness 1997
Chronicity (Disorders) 1982
↓ Diagnosis 1967
↓ Disorders 1967
↓ Mental Disorders 1967
↓ Physical Disorders 1997
Prognosis 1973

Sex 1967
PN 1384 **SC** 46950
SN Conceptually broad term referring to the structural, functional, or behavioral characteristics of males and females of a given species. Use a more specific term if possible. For comparisons of the sexes use HUMAN SEX DIFFERENCES or ANIMAL SEX DIFFERENCES.
R Animal Sex Differences 1967
↓ Animal Sexual Behavior 1985
↓ Genital Disorders 1967
↓ Human Sex Differences 1967
Pornography 1973
↓ Psychosexual Behavior 1967
Psychosexual Development 1982
Sex Change 1988
Sex Chromosomes 1973
Sex Discrimination 1978
Sex Drive 1973
Sex Education 1973
↓ Sex Hormones 1973
↓ Sex Offenses 1982
Sex Recognition 1997
↓ Sex Role Attitudes 1978
Sex Therapy 1978
Sexual Attitudes 1973
Sexual Development 1973
Sexual Harassment 1985
↓ Sexual Reproduction 1973
Sexuality 1973

Sex Change 1988
PN 245 **SC** 46828
UF Sexual Reassignment
B Surgery 1971
R Sex 1967
Transsexualism 1973

Sex Chromosome Disorders 1973
PN 187 **SC** 46830
B Chromosome Disorders 1973
N Klinefelters Syndrome 1973
R Fragile X Syndrome 1994
↓ Sex Linked Hereditary Disorders 1973

Sex Chromosomes 1973
PN 136 **SC** 46840
B Chromosomes 1973
R Sex 1967

Sex Differences (Animal)
Use Animal Sex Differences

Sex Differences (Human)
Use Human Sex Differences

Sex Differentiation Disorders
Use Genital Disorders

Sex Discrimination 1978
PN 1436 **SC** 46875
SN Prejudiced and differential treatment on the basis of sex rather than on the basis of merit.
B Social Discrimination 1982
R Affirmative Action 1985
↓ Civil Rights 1978
Employment Discrimination 1994
↓ Prejudice 1967
Sex 1967
Sexism 1988

Sex Drive 1973
PN 497 **SC** 46880
B Motivation 1967
R Hypersexuality 1973
Inhibited Sexual Desire 1997
Libido 1973
Sex 1967
↓ Sexual Arousal 1978

Sex Education 1973
PN 1774 **SC** 46890
B Family Life Education 1997
Health Education 1973
R Safe Sex 2003
Sex 1967

Sex Hormones 1973
PN 952 **SC** 46900
B Hormones 1967
N ↓ Androgens 1973
↓ Estrogens 1973
Progesterone 1973
R ↓ Gonadotropic Hormones 1973
Luteinizing Hormone 1978
Sex 1967

Sex Linked Developmental Differences 1973
PN 1397 **SC** 46920
SN Differential variation between males and females in specified areas of development. Limited to human populations.
B Human Sex Differences 1967
R Adolescent Development 1973
↓ Development 1967
Heterosexuality 1973
↓ Human Females 1973
↓ Human Males 1973
↓ Physical Development 1973
↓ Psychogenesis 1973
↓ Psychosexual Behavior 1967
Sexual Development 1973

Sex Linked Hereditary Disorders 1973
PN 150 **SC** 46930
SN Disorders occurring in either sex and which are transmitted by genes in the sex chromosomes.
B Genetic Disorders 1973
N Fragile X Syndrome 1994
Hemophilia 1973
Testicular Feminization Syndrome 1973
Turners Syndrome 1973
R ↓ Sex Chromosome Disorders 1973

Sex Offenses 1982
PN 3720 **SC** 46933
B Crime 1967
N ↓ Sexual Abuse 1988
R Incest 1973
↓ Paraphilias 1988
Pedophilia 1973
Pornography 1973
Sex 1967
Sexual Harassment 1985

Sex Recognition 1997
PN 75 **SC** 46934
R Animal Sex Differences 1967
↓ Human Sex Differences 1967
Sex 1967

Sex Role Attitudes 1978
PN 7593 **SC** 46935
SN Attitudes toward culturally- or socially-prescribed patterns of behavior for males and females.
UF Gender Role Attitudes
Sex Role Stereotyping
B Attitudes 1967
N Sexism 1988
R Feminism 1978
Matriarchy 1973
Patriarchy 1973
Sex 1967
Sex Roles 1967
Stereotyped Attitudes 1967

Sex Role Stereotyping
Use Sex Role Attitudes

Sex Roles 1967
PN 12132 **SC** 46940
SN Behavioral patterns in a given society which are deemed appropriate to one sex or the other.
UF Gender Roles
B Psychosexual Behavior 1967
Roles 1967
R Androgyny 1982
↓ Division of Labor 1988
Femininity 1967
↓ Gender Identity 1985
Masculinity 1967
Matriarchy 1973
Nontraditional Careers 1985
Patriarchy 1973
↓ Sex Role Attitudes 1978
Social Norms 1985

Sex Therapy 1978
PN 1344 **SC** 46945
SN Treatment of specific sexual function disturbances or therapy aimed at improving sexual relationships.
B Treatment 1967
R Couples Therapy 1994
↓ Marriage Counseling 1973
Sex 1967

Sexism 1988
PN 855 **SC** 46955
B Sex Role Attitudes 1978
R Employment Discrimination 1994
↓ Prejudice 1967
Sex Discrimination 1978
Stereotyped Attitudes 1967

Sexual Abstinence 1973
PN 232 **SC** 46960
UF Abstinence (Sexual)
Celibacy
B Psychosexual Behavior 1967
R ↓ Birth Control 1971
Virginity 1973

Sexual Abuse 1988
PN 11144 **SC** 46965
B Antisocial Behavior 1971
Sex Offenses 1982
N Incest 1973
↓ Rape 1973
R ↓ Abuse Reporting 1997
Anatomically Detailed Dolls 1991
↓ Child Abuse 1971
Domestic Violence 2006
Elder Abuse 1988
↓ Paraphilias 1988
↓ Partner Abuse 1991
Patient Abuse 1991
Pedophilia 1973
Physical Abuse 1991
Professional Client Sexual Relations 1994
Sexual Harassment 1985
↓ Violent Crime 2003

Sexual Addiction 1997
PN 308 **SC** 46967
UF Compulsivity (Sexual)
Sexual Compulsivity
B Addiction 1973
R Hypersexuality 1973
↓ Paraphilias 1988
Promiscuity 1973
↓ Psychosexual Behavior 1967

Sexual Arousal 1978
PN 1452 **SC** 46970
SN Physiological and/or emotional state of sexual excitation.
UF Arousal (Sexual)
B Psychosexual Behavior 1967
N Eroticism 1973
R Inhibited Sexual Desire 1997
Physiological Arousal 1967
Sex Drive 1973
Sexual Attraction 2003
Sexual Fantasy 1997
Sexual Satisfaction 1994

Sexual Attitudes 1973
PN 3976 **SC** 46980
SN Opinions or beliefs about sexual development and behavior.
B Attitudes 1967
R ↓ Psychosexual Behavior 1967
Psychosexual Development 1982
Sex 1967
Sexual Attraction 2003
↓ Sexual Orientation 1997
Sexual Risk Taking 1997
Sexual Satisfaction 1994

Sexual Attraction 2003
PN 190 **SC** 46984
HN This term was introduced in June 2003. Relevant records were re-indexed with this term. The posting note reflects the number of records that were re-indexed.
B Interpersonal Attraction 1967
R Physical Attractiveness 1973
↓ Psychosexual Behavior 1967
↓ Sexual Arousal 1978
Sexual Attitudes 1973
↓ Sexual Orientation 1997

Sexual Behavior
Use Psychosexual Behavior

Sexual Boundary Violations
Use Professional Client Sexual Relations

Sexual Compulsivity
Use Sexual Addiction

Sexual Delinquency
Use Promiscuity

Sexual Development 1973
PN 1080 **SC** 47010
HN Prior to 1982 used for maturation of cognitive, emotional, and physical aspects of sexuality in humans or animals. From 1982 consider PSYCHOSEXUAL DEVELOPMENT for references on cognitive and emotional aspects.
UF Pubescence
B Physical Development 1973
R Adolescent Development 1973
Heterosexuality 1973
↓ Psychogenesis 1973
↓ Psychosexual Behavior 1967
Psychosexual Development 1982
Sex 1967
Sex Linked Developmental Differences 1973

Sexual Deviations
HN In 2000, the term was discontinued and removed from all records containing it, and replaced with PARAPHILIAS, its postable counterpart.
Use Paraphilias

Sexual Disorders (Physiological)
Use Genital Disorders

Sexual Fantasy 1997
PN 186 **SC** 47035
B Fantasy 1997
R Erotomania 1997
Fantasy (Defense Mechanism) 1967
↓ Psychosexual Behavior 1967
↓ Sexual Arousal 1978
Sexuality 1973

Sexual Fetishism
Use Fetishism

Sexual Function Disturbances 1973
PN 3202 **SC** 47050
B Psychosexual Behavior 1967
N Dyspareunia 1973
Erectile Dysfunction 2006
Female Sexual Dysfunction 2005
Inhibited Sexual Desire 1997
Premature Ejaculation 1973
Vaginismus 1973
R ↓ Mental Disorders 1967
↓ Physical Disorders 1997

Sexual Function Disturbances — (cont'd)
↓ Somatoform Disorders 2001
↓ Urogenital Disorders 1973

Sexual Harassment 1985
PN 1451 **SC** 47055
SN Physical or psychological sexual threats or attempts to willfully subject a person to involuntary sexual activity usually for the purpose of social control.
UF Harassment (Sexual)
B Harassment 2001
R Professional Client Sexual Relations 1994
Sex 1967
↓ Sex Offenses 1982
↓ Sexual Abuse 1988
Victimization 1973

Sexual Identity (Gender)
Use Gender Identity

Sexual Intercourse (Human) 1973
PN 1402 **SC** 47060
UF Coitus
Copulation
Intercourse (Sexual)
B Psychosexual Behavior 1967
N Dyspareunia 1973
Extramarital Intercourse 1973
Incest 1973
Premarital Intercourse 1973
↓ Rape 1973
R Disease Transmission 2004
Female Orgasm 1973
↓ Male Orgasm 1973
Safe Sex 2003
Sexual Partners 2003
↓ Sexual Reproduction 1973
Sexual Satisfaction 1994

Sexual Masochism 1973
PN 69 **SC** 47070
B Masochism 1973
Paraphilias 1988
R Fetishism 1973
Masochistic Personality 1973
Sexual Sadism 1973

Sexual Orientation 1997
PN 1642 **SC** 47072
N Bisexuality 1973
Heterosexuality 1973
↓ Homosexuality 1967
R ↓ Gender Identity 1985
↓ Gender Identity Disorder 1997
Hate Crimes 2003
Homosexuality (Attitudes Toward) 1982
↓ Psychosexual Behavior 1967
Same Sex Marriage 2007
Sexual Attitudes 1973
Sexual Attraction 2003

Sexual Partners 2003
PN 702 **SC** 58061
HN This term was introduced in June 2003. Relevant records were re-indexed with this term. The posting note reflects the number of records that were re-indexed.
R ↓ Psychosexual Behavior 1967
↓ Sexual Intercourse (Human) 1973
Sexual Risk Taking 1997

Sexual Reassignment
Use Sex Change

Sexual Receptivity (Animal)
Use Animal Sexual Receptivity

Sexual Reproduction 1973
PN 2037 **SC** 47090
B Physiology 1967
N Fertility 1988
R ↓ Animal Breeding 1973
Animal Mate Selection 1982
↓ Animal Mating Behavior 1967
↓ Birth 1967
Fertilization 1973
↓ Genetics 1967
↓ Pregnancy 1967
Reproductive Technology 1988
Sex 1967
↓ Sexual Intercourse (Human) 1973
Sperm 1973

Sexual Risk Taking 1997
PN 3104 **SC** 47095
B Psychosexual Behavior 1967
Risk Taking 1967
R AIDS Prevention 1994
↓ Pregnancy 1967
Risk Perception 1997
Safe Sex 2003
Sexual Attitudes 1973
Sexual Partners 2003
↓ Sexually Transmitted Diseases 2003

Sexual Sadism 1973
PN 85 **SC** 47100
B Paraphilias 1988
Sadism 1973
R Fetishism 1973
Sexual Masochism 1973

Sexual Satisfaction 1994
PN 427 **SC** 47110
B Satisfaction 1973
R ↓ Orgasm 1973
↓ Psychosexual Behavior 1967
↓ Sexual Arousal 1978
Sexual Attitudes 1973
↓ Sexual Intercourse (Human) 1973
Sexuality 1973

Sexuality 1973
PN 5594 **SC** 47120
B Personality Traits 1967
R Affection 1973
Psychosexual Development 1982
Sex 1967
Sexual Fantasy 1997
Sexual Satisfaction 1994

Sexually Transmitted Diseases 2003
PN 1659 **SC** 47125
HN In June 2003, this term replaced the discontinued term VENEREAL DISEASES. VENEREAL DISEASES was removed from all records containing it and replaced with SEXUALLY TRANSMITTED DISEASES.
UF Diseases (Venereal)
Venereal Diseases
B Infectious Disorders 1973
N AIDS 2006
Gonorrhea 1973
Herpes Genitalis 1988

Sexually Transmitted Diseases — (cont'd)
↓ HIV 2006
↓ Syphilis 1973
R Condoms 1991
Disease Transmission 2004
Sexual Risk Taking 1997
↓ Urogenital Disorders 1973

Shamanism 1973
PN 320 **SC** 47130
B Religious Affiliation 1973
R Cultism 1973
Ethnology 1967
Faith Healing 1973
Folk Medicine 1973
Transcultural Psychiatry 1973
↓ Treatment 1967
Witchcraft 1973

Shame 1994
PN 1374 **SC** 47140
HN Use GUILT to access references from 1973-1993.
B Emotional States 1973
R ↓ Anxiety 1967
Blame 1994
Embarrassment 1973
↓ Fear 1967
Guilt 1967
Morality 1967

Shape Perception
Use Form and Shape Perception

Shared Paranoid Disorder
Use Folie A Deux

Sharing (Social Behavior) 1978
PN 587 **SC** 47155
B Prosocial Behavior 1982
R Altruism 1973
Charitable Behavior 1973
Needle Sharing 1994

Sheep 1973
PN 803 **SC** 47170
B Mammals 1973

Sheltered Workshops 1967
PN 361 **SC** 47180
SN Places which provide handicapped individuals with job training and work experience.
B Rehabilitation Centers 1973
R ↓ Community Facilities 1973
Supported Employment 1994

Shelters 1991
PN 528 **SC** 47185
B Housing 1973
R Battered Females 1988
↓ Community Facilities 1973
↓ Community Services 1967
Domestic Violence 2006
↓ Government Programs 1973
Group Homes 1982
↓ Homeless 1988
↓ Living Arrangements 1991
Protective Services 1997

Shelters — (cont'd)
Runaway Behavior 1973
↓ Social Services 1982

Shifts (Workday)
Use Workday Shifts

Shock 1967
PN 3138 **SC** 47200
B Symptoms 1967
R Anaphylactic Shock 1973
Electrical Injuries 1973
↓ Electrical Stimulation 1973
↓ Electroconvulsive Shock 1967
↓ Injuries 1973
↓ Shock Therapy 1973
Shock Units 1973
Syncope 1973

Shock Therapy 1973
PN 59 **SC** 47210
B Physical Treatment Methods 1973
N Electroconvulsive Shock Therapy 1967
Insulin Shock Therapy 1973
R ↓ Alternative Medicine 1997
↓ Aversion Therapy 1973
Electrosleep Treatment 1978
Shock 1967

Shock Units 1973
PN 29 **SC** 47220
B Stimulators (Apparatus) 1973
R Shock 1967

Shoplifting 1973
PN 145 **SC** 47230
B Theft 1973

Shopping 1997
PN 499 **SC** 47240
HN Use CONSUMER BEHAVIOR to access references prior to 1997.
B Consumer Behavior 1967
R ↓ Electronic Commerce 2006
Electronic Retailing 2007
↓ Retailing 1991
Shopping Centers 1973

Shopping Centers 1973
PN 193 **SC** 47250
B Community Facilities 1973
R ↓ Consumer Behavior 1967
↓ Retailing 1991
Shopping 1997

Short Term Memory 1967
PN 10092 **SC** 47260
SN Retention of information for very brief periods, usually seconds; also referred to as working memory. Consider also RETENTION.
UF Working Memory
B Memory 1967
N Iconic Memory 1985
R Chunking 2004

Short Term Potentiation
Use Postactivation Potentials

Short Term Psychotherapy
Use Brief Psychotherapy

Shoulder (Anatomy) 1973
PN 168 **SC** 47290
B Joints (Anatomy) 1973
R Arm (Anatomy) 1973

Shuttle Box Grids
HN Term was discontinued in 1997. In 2000, the term was removed from all records containing it, and replaced with SHUTTLE BOXES, its postable counterpart.
Use Shuttle Boxes

Shuttle Box Hurdles
HN Term was discontinued in 1997. In 2000, the term was removed from all records containing it, and replaced with SHUTTLE BOXES, its postable counterpart.
Use Shuttle Boxes

Shuttle Boxes 1973
PN 96 **SC** 47320
HN In 1997, this term replaced the discontinued terms SHUTTLE BOX GRIDS and SHUTTLE BOX HURDLES. In 2000, these terms were removed from all records containing them, and replaced with SHUTTLE BOXES.
UF Shuttle Box Grids
Shuttle Box Hurdles
B Apparatus 1967

Shyness
Use Timidity

Siamese Twins
HN In June 2003, this term was discontinued and removed from all records containing it, and was replaced with CONJOINED TWINS, its postable counterpart.
Use Conjoined Twins

Sibling Relations 1973
PN 1726 **SC** 47350
B Family Relations 1967

Siblings 1967
PN 3219 **SC** 47360
B Family Members 1973
N Brothers 1973
↓ Multiple Births 1973
Sisters 1973

Sick Leave
Use Employee Leave Benefits

Sickle Cell Disease 1994
PN 346 **SC** 47380
B Blood and Lymphatic Disorders 1973
Genetic Disorders 1973
R Anemia 1973

Side Effects (Drug) 1973
PN 13958 **SC** 47390
SN Acute or chronic and often undesirable effects of drugs occurring in addition to the intended or therapeutic objective.
HN In 1982, this term replaced the discontinued term DRUG ADVERSE REACTIONS. In 2000, DRUG ADVERSE REACTIONS was removed from all records containing it, and replaced with SIDE EFFECTS (DRUG).
UF Drug Adverse Reactions
B Side Effects (Treatment) 1988
N ↓ Drug Addiction 1967
Drug Allergies 1973
↓ Drug Dependency 1973

Side Effects (Drug) — (cont'd)
Drug Sensitivity 1973
R Akathisia 1991
↓ Drug Therapy 1967
Drug Tolerance 1973
↓ Drugs 1967
Neuroleptic Malignant Syndrome 1988
Tardive Dyskinesia 1988

Side Effects (Treatment) 1988
PN 1241 **SC** 47392
SN Acute or chronic and often undesirable effects of treatment other than drug therapy occurring in addition to the intended or therapeutic objective. For side effects of drug therapy use SIDE EFFECTS (DRUG).
UF Iatrogenic Effects
N ↓ Side Effects (Drug) 1973
R ↓ Treatment 1967
↓ Treatment Outcomes 1982

Sight Vocabulary 1973
PN 165 **SC** 47400
SN Words that one recognizes immediately while reading.
B Vocabulary 1967
R ↓ Reading 1967
↓ Reading Skills 1973
Word Recognition 1988

Sign Language 1973
PN 1814 **SC** 47410
SN System of hand gestures for communication in which the gestures function as words.
B Language 1967
Manual Communication 1978
R Fingerspelling 1973

Sign Rank Test
Use Wilcoxon Sign Rank Test

Sign Test 1973
PN 6 **SC** 47430
B Nonparametric Statistical Tests 1967
R Statistical Significance 1973

Signal Detection (Perception) 1967
PN 3343 **SC** 47440
SN Psychophysical technique that permits the estimation of the bias of the observer as well as the detectability of the signal (i.e., stimulus) in any sensory modality. Compare THRESHOLDS.
UF Detection (Signal)
R ↓ Attention 1967
↓ Perception 1967
↓ Psychophysical Measurement 1967
Threshold Determination 1973
Visual Search 1982

Signal Intensity
Use Stimulus Intensity

Significance (Statistical)
Use Statistical Significance

Significant Others 1991
PN 820 **SC** 47465
SN Includes teachers, peers, family members, friends, and unmarried persons or couples.
R Couples 1982
↓ Family Members 1973
Friendship 1967
Homosexual Parents 1994
Mentor 1985

Significant Others — (cont'd)
Peers 1978
Role Models 1982
Romance 1997
Social Support 2004
↓ Spouses 1973

Sikhism 2004
PN 10 **SC** 47466
SN A monotheistic religion founded in 16th century India that combines elements of Hinduism and Islam.
HN This term was introduced in June 2004. Relevant records were re-indexed with this term. The posting note reflects the number of records that were re-indexed.
B Religious Affiliation 1973
R Sikhs 2004

Sikhs 2004
PN 18 **SC** 47467
HN This term was introduced in June 2004. Relevant records were re-indexed with this term. The posting note reflects the number of records that were re-indexed.
B Religious Groups 1997
R Sikhism 2004

Sildenafil 2006
PN 101 **SC** 47469
HN This term was introduced in May 2006. Relevant records were re-indexed with this term. The posting note reflects the number of records that were re-indexed.
UF Viagra
B Enzyme Inhibitors 1985

Silence 2003
PN 301 **SC** 47468
HN This term was introduced in June 2003. Relevant records were re-indexed with this term. The posting note reflects the number of records that were re-indexed.
R ↓ Auditory Stimulation 1967
↓ Nonverbal Communication 1971

Silent Reading 1973
PN 318 **SC** 47470
B Reading 1967

Similarity (Stimulus)
Use Stimulus Similarity

Simile
Use Figurative Language

Simple Schizophrenia
HN Term was discontinued in 1988. In 2000, the term was removed from all records containing it, and replaced with SCHIZOPHRENIA, its postable counterpart.
Use Schizophrenia

Simulation 1967
PN 4001 **SC** 47510
UF Modeling
Simulators
N ↓ Computer Simulation 1973
Flight Simulation 1973
Heuristic Modeling 1973
Markov Chains 1973
↓ Mathematical Modeling 1973
Simulation Games 1973
↓ Stochastic Modeling 1973

Simulation — (cont'd)
R Game Theory 1967

Simulation Games 1973
PN 549 SC 47520
B Games 1967
Simulation 1967
R Computer Games 1988
↓ Computer Simulation 1973

Simulators
Use Simulation

Sin 1973
PN 126 SC 47540
B Religious Beliefs 1973
R Evil 2003

Sincerity 1973
PN 93 SC 47550
UF Genuineness
B Personality Traits 1967
R ↓ Deception 1967
Dishonesty 1973

Singing 1997
PN 289 SC 47552
SN Use ANIMAL VOCALIZATIONS for singing in animal populations.
B Oral Communication 1985
R ↓ Music 1967
Music Perception 1997
↓ Vocalization 1967
↓ Voice 1973

Single Cell Organisms
Use Microorganisms

Single Fathers 1994
PN 58 SC 47554
HN Use SINGLE PARENTS to access references from 1978-1993.
B Fathers 1967
Single Parents 1978
R Single Persons 1973

Single Mothers 1994
PN 551 SC 47555
HN Use SINGLE PARENTS to access references from 1978-1993.
B Mothers 1967
Single Parents 1978
R Single Persons 1973
Unwed Mothers 1973
Working Women 1978

Single Parents 1978
PN 1158 SC 47556
SN Parents rearing children alone.
B Parents 1967
N Single Fathers 1994
Single Mothers 1994
R ↓ Family Structure 1973
↓ Marital Status 1973
Never Married 1994
↓ Parental Absence 1973
Single Persons 1973
Unwed Mothers 1973

Single Persons 1973
PN 509 SC 47560
SN Persons who are not married.

Single Persons — (cont'd)
R Living Alone 1994
↓ Marital Status 1973
Never Married 1994
Single Fathers 1994
Single Mothers 1994
↓ Single Parents 1978

Single Sex Education
Use Same Sex Education

Single Sex Environments 2001
PN 93 SC 47565
SN Used for both human and animal populations. Use only when gender is pertinent to the focus of the study.
UF Female Only Environments
Male Only Environments
Same Sex Environments
B Environment 1967
N Same Sex Education 2003
R ↓ Academic Environment 1973
↓ Animal Environments 1967
Animal Sex Differences 1967
Coeducation 1973
Home Environment 1973
↓ Human Sex Differences 1967
↓ Living Arrangements 1991

Sisters 1973
PN 280 SC 47570
B Human Females 1973
Siblings 1967

Sixteen Personality Factors Questionnaire 2001
PN 442 SC 47591
HN In 2000, the truncated term SIXTEEN PERSONALITY FACTORS QUESTION (which was used from 1973-2000) was deleted, removed from all records containing it, and replaced with its expanded form SIXTEEN PERSONALITY FACTORS QUESTIONNAIRE.
B Nonprojective Personality Measures 1973

Size 1973
PN 1108 SC 47610
SN Relative physical dimensions of objects or stimuli.
B Stimulus Parameters 1967
N ↓ Body Size 1985
Brain Size 1973
Family Size 1973
↓ Group Size 1967
Litter Size 1985
Size Constancy 1985
↓ Size Discrimination 1967

Size (Apparent)
Use Apparent Size

Size (Group)
Use Group Size

Size Constancy 1985
PN 55 SC 47635
SN The tendency for the perceived size of stimuli to remain constant despite objective changes in context and stimulus parameters.
B Perceptual Constancy 1985
Size 1973

Size Constancy — (cont'd)
R ↓ Size Discrimination 1967

Size Discrimination 1967
PN 989 SC 47640
B Size 1973
Spatial Perception 1967
N Apparent Size 1973
R Linear Perspective 1982
Size Constancy 1985

Skeletomuscular Disorders
Use Musculoskeletal Disorders

Skepticism 2004
PN 93 SC 47670
HN This term was introduced in June 2004. Relevant records were re-indexed with this term. The posting note reflects the number of records that were re-indexed.
R Agnosticism 2007
↓ Criticism 1973
Cynicism 1973
Negativism 1973
Pessimism 1973
Uncertainty 1991

Skewed Distribution 1973
PN 143 SC 47680
UF Poisson Distribution
B Frequency Distribution 1973

Skill Learning 1973
PN 2887 SC 47690
B Learning 1967
N Fine Motor Skill Learning 1973
Gross Motor Skill Learning 1973
R Communication Skills Training 1982
Habilitation 1991
↓ Perceptual Learning 2006
↓ Perceptual Motor Learning 1967
Self Care Skills 1978
Social Skills Training 1982

Skilled Industrial Workers 1973
PN 316 SC 47700
SN Blue collar workers who perform skilled labor in an industrial setting.
B Blue Collar Workers 1973
Business and Industrial Personnel 1967

Skills
Use Ability

Skin (Anatomy) 1967
PN 1114 SC 47720
UF Epithelium
B Tissues (Body) 1973
R Absorption (Physiological) 1973
Cosmetic Techniques 2001
Epithelial Cells 1973
Hair 1973
Head (Anatomy) 1973
Scalp (Anatomy) 1973

Skin Cancer Screening
Use Cancer Screening

Skin Conduction
Use Skin Resistance

Skin Disorders 1973
PN 727 **SC** 47740
UF Scalp Disorders
B Physical Disorders 1997
N Allergic Skin Disorders 1973
Alopecia 1973
↓ Dermatitis 1973
Herpes Simplex 1973
Lupus 1973
Pruritus 1973
R Albinism 1973
↓ Somatoform Disorders 2001
Sweating 1973
↓ Tuberculosis 1973

Skin Electrical Properties 1973
PN 114 **SC** 47750
SN General electrodermal characteristics and responses as measured on the skin surface. Use a more specific term if possible.
B Electrophysiology 1973
N Skin Potential 1973
↓ Skin Resistance 1973

Skin Potential 1973
PN 114 **SC** 47760
SN Degree of electrical charge of the skin.
B Electrophysiology 1973
Skin Electrical Properties 1973
R Galvanic Skin Response 1967
↓ Skin Resistance 1973

Skin Resistance 1973
PN 1558 **SC** 47770
SN Resistance of the skin to the flow of electric current; reciprocal of skin conductance.
UF Skin Conduction
B Skin Electrical Properties 1973
N Basal Skin Resistance 1973
R Galvanic Skin Response 1967
Skin Potential 1973

Skin Temperature 1973
PN 671 **SC** 47780
B Body Temperature 1973

Skinner (Burrhus Frederic) 1991
PN 372 **SC** 47785
SN Identifies biographical or autobiographical studies and discussions of Skinner's works.
R Behaviorism 1967
↓ Operant Conditioning 1967
↓ Psychologists 1967
Skinner Boxes 1973

Skinner Boxes 1973
PN 29 **SC** 47790
B Apparatus 1967
R Skinner (Burrhus Frederic) 1991

Skull 1973
PN 60 **SC** 47800
B Musculoskeletal System 1973

Slang 1973
PN 71 **SC** 47810
B Vocabulary 1967
R Ethnolinguistics 1973
Nonstandard English 1973

Sleep 1967
PN 8182 **SC** 47820
N Napping 1994
NREM Sleep 1973
REM Sleep 1973
R ↓ Consciousness Disturbances 1973
↓ Consciousness States 1971
Dream Content 1973
↓ Dreaming 1967
Lucid Dreaming 1994
Nocturnal Teeth Grinding 1973
Polysomnography 2003
Sleep Apnea 1991
Sleep Deprivation 1967
↓ Sleep Disorders 1973
Sleep Onset 1973
Sleep Talking 1973
Sleep Treatment 1973
Sleep Wake Cycle 1985
Sleepiness 2007

Sleep Apnea 1991
PN 559 **SC** 47825
SN Temporary absence of breathing or prolonged respiratory failure occurring during sleep.
B Apnea 1973
R ↓ Neonatal Disorders 1973
↓ Sleep 1967
↓ Sleep Disorders 1973
Sudden Infant Death 1982

Sleep Deprivation 1967
PN 1857 **SC** 47830
B Deprivation 1967
R ↓ Sleep 1967
↓ Sleep Disorders 1973
Sleepiness 2007

Sleep Disorders 1973
PN 2960 **SC** 47840
UF Night Terrors
B Consciousness Disturbances 1973
N Hypersomnia 1994
Insomnia 1973
Kleine Levin Syndrome 2001
Narcolepsy 1973
Sleepwalking 1973
R Hypnagogic Hallucinations 1973
↓ Mental Disorders 1967
↓ Physical Disorders 1997
Polysomnography 2003
↓ Sleep 1967
Sleep Apnea 1991
Sleep Deprivation 1967

Sleep Inducing Drugs
Use Hypnotic Drugs

Sleep Monitoring
Use Polysomnography

Sleep Onset 1973
PN 906 **SC** 47860
R Napping 1994
↓ Sleep 1967
Sleepiness 2007

Sleep Talking 1973
PN 21 **SC** 47870
B Consciousness Disturbances 1973
R ↓ Sleep 1967

Sleep Treatment 1973
PN 95 **SC** 47880
SN Prolonged sleep or rest used in the treatment of mental disorders. Such sleep may be induced by drugs, hypnosis, or other means. For sleep withdrawal therapy, which is the deprivation of sleep for therapeutic purposes, use SLEEP DEPRIVATION.
B Narcoanalysis 1973
R ↓ Drug Therapy 1967
Electrosleep Treatment 1978
↓ Sleep 1967

Sleep Wake Cycle 1985
PN 1908 **SC** 47885
B Biological Rhythms 1967
R Napping 1994
↓ Sleep 1967
Sleepiness 2007
Wakefulness 1973

Sleepiness 2007
PN 378 **SC** 47886
SN Difficulty maintaining a state of wakefulness.
HN This term was introduced in April 2007. Relevant records were re-indexed with this term. The posting note reflects the number of records that were re-indexed.
UF Drowsiness
B Consciousness States 1971
R Fatigue 1967
↓ Sleep 1967
Sleep Deprivation 1967
Sleep Onset 1973
Sleep Wake Cycle 1985

Sleeplessness
Use Insomnia

Sleepwalking 1973
PN 202 **SC** 47890
HN In 1982, this term replaced the discontinued term SOMNAMBULISM. In 2000, SOMNAMBULISM was removed from all records containing it, and replaced with SLEEPWALKING.
UF Somnambulism
B Sleep Disorders 1973

Slosson Intelligence Test 2001
PN 71 **SC** 47901
HN In 2000, the truncated term SLOSSON INTELLIGENCE TEST FOR CHILD (which was used from 1991-2000) was deleted, removed from all records containing it, and replaced with its new form SLOSSON INTELLIGENCE TEST.
B Intelligence Measures 1967

Slow Learners
HN In 2000, the term was discontinued and removed from all records containing it, and replaced with BORDERLINE MENTAL RETARDATION, its postable counterpart.
Use Borderline Mental Retardation

Slow Wave Sleep
Use NREM Sleep

Slums
Use Poverty Areas

Small Businesses 2007
PN 239 **SC** 47935
SN A business establishment generally consisting of fewer than 500 employees that is a privately owned corporation, partnership, or sole proprietorship.
HN This term was introduced in April 2007. Relevant records were re-indexed with this term. The posting note reflects the number of records that were re-indexed.
B Business 1967
R Entrepreneurship 1991
Ownership 1985
Self Employment 1994

Smell Perception
Use Olfactory Perception

Smiles 1973
PN 419 **SC** 47950
B Facial Expressions 1967
R Laughter 1978

Smokeless Tobacco 1994
PN 231 **SC** 47960
UF Chewing Tobacco
Snuff
Tobacco (Smokeless)
R ↓ CNS Stimulating Drugs 1973
Nicotine 1973
Nicotine Withdrawal 1997
↓ Tobacco Smoking 1967

Smoking (Tobacco)
Use Tobacco Smoking

Smoking Cessation 1988
PN 4185 **SC** 47980
SN Used for cigarette smoking rehabilitation programs or stopping the habit of smoking.
HN Use DRUG REHABILITATION and TOBACCO SMOKING to access references prior to 1988.
R ↓ Drug Abstinence 1994
↓ Drug Rehabilitation 1973
Nicotine Withdrawal 1997
↓ Tobacco Smoking 1967

Snails 1973
PN 581 **SC** 47990
UF Aplysia
B Mollusca 1973

Snake Phobia
Use Ophidiophobia

Snakes 1973
PN 421 **SC** 48010
B Reptiles 1967

SNRI
Use Serotonin Norepinephrine Reuptake Inhibitors

Snuff
Use Smokeless Tobacco

Sobriety 1988
PN 837 **SC** 48020
UF Alcohol Abstinence
B Drug Abstinence 1994
R Alcohol Drinking Attitudes 1973
↓ Alcohol Rehabilitation 1982
Alcohol Withdrawal 1994
↓ Alcoholism 1967
Detoxification 1973
↓ Drug Rehabilitation 1973
Recovery (Disorders) 1973

Soccer 1994
PN 333 **SC** 48025
B Recreation 1967
Sports 1967

Sociability 1973
PN 514 **SC** 48030
B Personality Traits 1967
R Extraversion 1967
Gregariousness 1973

Social Acceptance 1967
PN 2914 **SC** 48040
SN Degree to which an individual is incorporated by others in their activities or is welcomed to interact with others informally. Limited to human populations.
UF Acceptance (Social)
Rejection (Social)
Social Rejection
B Social Behavior 1967
R ↓ Membership 2007
Need for Approval 1997
Peer Pressure 1994
Popularity 1988
Social Approval 1967
Stigma 1991
↓ Tolerance 1973

Social Adaptation
Use Social Adjustment

Social Adjustment 1973
PN 7166 **SC** 48060
UF Adaptation (Social)
Maladjustment (Social)
Social Adaptation
Social Maladjustment
B Adjustment 1967
Social Behavior 1967
R Adjustment Disorders 1994

Social Anxiety 1985
PN 1579 **SC** 48065
SN Apprehension or fear of social interaction or social situations in general. Compare SOCIAL PHOBIA.
B Anxiety 1967
R ↓ Anxiety Disorders 1997
Avoidant Personality Disorder 1994
↓ Fear 1967
↓ Social Interaction 1967
↓ Social Isolation 1967
Speech Anxiety 1985

Social Anxiety Disorder
Use Social Phobia

Social Approval 1967
PN 1882 **SC** 48070
SN Favorable direct or indirect judgment by member or members of a given social group of another member or members, based on conduct, physical makeup, or other characteristics.
UF Approval (Social)
B Social Behavior 1967
Social Influences 1967
R ↓ Criticism 1973
Likability 1988
Need for Approval 1997
Peer Pressure 1994
Popularity 1988
Reputation 1997
Social Acceptance 1967
↓ Social Reinforcement 1967

Social Approval — (cont'd)
Stigma 1991

Social Behavior 1967
PN 9132 **SC** 48080
B Behavior 1967
N ↓ Activism 2003
↓ Aggressive Behavior 1967
↓ Animal Social Behavior 1967
Competition 1967
↓ Compliance 1973
Conformity (Personality) 1967
Contagion 1988
↓ Criticism 1973
↓ Gambling 1973
↓ Help Seeking Behavior 1978
Interspecies Interaction 1991
↓ Involvement 1973
↓ Leadership 1967
Leadership Style 1973
Militancy 1973
Nurturance 1985
↓ Organizational Behavior 1978
↓ Prosocial Behavior 1982
Racial and Ethnic Relations 1982
Reciprocity 1973
↓ Responsibility 1973
Retaliation 1991
↓ Risk Taking 1967
Social Acceptance 1967
Social Adjustment 1973
Social Approval 1967
Social Cognition 1994
Social Demonstrations 1973
Social Drinking 1973
Social Facilitation 1973
↓ Social Interaction 1967
Social Loafing 2003
↓ Social Perception 1967
↓ Social Reinforcement 1967
Social Responsibility 2007
Social Skills 1978
R ↓ Antisocial Behavior 1971
Dominance Hierarchy 1973
Equity (Payment) 1978
↓ Equity (Social) 1978
Impression Management 1978
Informants 1988
Personal Space 1973
Privacy 1973
Psychodynamics 1973
Social Change 1967
↓ Social Influences 1967

Social Capital 2004
PN 563 **SC** 48085
SN Investing in social relationships by establishing trust, norms, and networks to create social cohesion and facilitate cooperative communities.
HN This term was introduced in June 2004. Relevant records were re-indexed with this term. The posting note reflects the number of records that were re-indexed.
B Social Processes 1967
R Human Capital 2003
↓ Social Networks 1994

Social Casework 1967
PN 6942 **SC** 48090
UF Social Work
B Treatment 1967
R ↓ Case Management 1991
Child Welfare 1988
↓ Counseling 1967

Social Casework — (cont'd)
↓ Family Therapy 1967
↓ Health Care Services 1978
↓ Mental Health Services 1978
Outreach Programs 1997
Protective Services 1997
↓ Social Services 1982

Social Caseworkers
Use Social Workers

Social Change 1967
PN 5636 **SC** 48110
UF Change (Social)
R ↓ Activism 2003
↓ Fads and Fashions 1973
Future 1991
Modernization 2003
↓ Social Behavior 1967
↓ Social Influences 1967
↓ Social Movements 1967
↓ Social Processes 1967
↓ Social Programs 1973
Social Responsibility 2007
Trends 1991

Social Class 1967
PN 3538 **SC** 48120
B Social Structure 1967
Socioeconomic Status 1967
N Lower Class 1973
Middle Class 1973
Upper Class 1973
R Disadvantaged 1967
↓ Income Level 1973
↓ Socioeconomic Class Attitudes 1973

Social Class Attitudes
Use Socioeconomic Class Attitudes

Social Clubs (Therapeutic)
Use Therapeutic Social Clubs

Social Cognition 1994
PN 4245 **SC** 48143
SN Cognitive processes and activity that accompany and mediate social interaction.
B Cognitive Processes 1967
Social Behavior 1967
R ↓ Communication Skills 1973
↓ Interpersonal Interaction 1967
Reputation 1997
Schema 1988
Self Fulfilling Prophecies 1997
↓ Social Interaction 1967
↓ Social Perception 1967
Social Skills Training 1982

Social Comparison 1985
PN 1708 **SC** 48145
SN Subjective evaluation of personal characteristics (e.g., ability level, personality traits, accomplishments) of oneself or another person in relation to the perceived characteristics of others.
B Social Perception 1967
R Self Evaluation 1967
Self Monitoring (Personality) 1985
↓ Social Influences 1967

Social Competence
Use Social Skills

Social Control 1988
PN 1070 **SC** 48148
SN Power of institutions, organizations, or laws of society to influence or regulate behavior or attitudes of groups or individuals. Consider POWER to access references that describe the control an individual has over other persons.
UF Control (Social)
B Social Processes 1967
R ↓ Emotional Control 1973
↓ Social Influences 1967

Social Dating 1973
PN 1972 **SC** 48150
UF Dating (Social)
B Human Courtship 1973
Interpersonal Interaction 1967
R Acquaintance Rape 1991
Couples 1982
Friendship 1967
Male Female Relations 1988
Premarital Intercourse 1973
↓ Relationship Termination 1997
Romance 1997

Social Demonstrations 1973
PN 136 **SC** 48160
UF Demonstrations (Social)
Picketing
B Social Behavior 1967
R ↓ Activism 2003
↓ Collective Behavior 1967
↓ Political Participation 1988
↓ Social Movements 1967
Student Activism 1973

Social Density 1978
PN 651 **SC** 48165
SN Number of animals or humans per given space unit. For specifically high density conditions use CROWDING.
UF Density (Social)
Population Density
R Crowding 1978
Overpopulation 1973
Personal Space 1973
↓ Population 1973
↓ Social Environments 1973

Social Deprivation 1973
PN 450 **SC** 48170
SN Limited access to society's resources due to poverty, neglect, social discrimination, or other disadvantage. For a lack of social contact use SOCIAL ISOLATION. Consider also CULTURAL DEPRIVATION.
B Social Processes 1967
Stimulus Deprivation 1973
N ↓ Social Isolation 1967
R Cultural Deprivation 1973
Disadvantaged 1967
↓ Homeless 1988

Social Desirability 1967
PN 1779 **SC** 48180
UF Desirability (Social)
B Social Influences 1967
R Need for Approval 1997

Social Development
Use Psychosocial Development

Social Dilemma 2003
PN 188 **SC** 48184
SN Situation where an individual's self-interest creates a potentially negative outcome for the rest of the group members.
HN This term was introduced in June 2003. Relevant records were re-indexed with this term. The posting note reflects the number of records that were re-indexed.
B Social Processes 1967
R Choice Behavior 1967
Prisoners Dilemma Game 1973
↓ Social Issues 1991

Social Discrimination 1982
PN 1695 **SC** 48185
SN Prejudiced and differential treatment based on religion, sex, race, ethnicity, disability, or other personal characteristics rather than on the basis of merit. Use a more specific term if possible.
UF Discrimination (Social)
B Discrimination 1967
Social Issues 1991
N Age Discrimination 1994
Disability Discrimination 1997
Employment Discrimination 1994
Race and Ethnic Discrimination 1994
Sex Discrimination 1978
R Affirmative Action 1985
↓ Civil Rights 1978
Racial and Ethnic Relations 1982
Racism 1973
↓ Social Integration 1982
Stereotyped Attitudes 1967
Stigma 1991

Social Drinking 1973
PN 628 **SC** 48190
SN Consumption of alcoholic beverages in social settings.
B Alcohol Drinking Patterns 1967
Social Behavior 1967
R Binge Drinking 2006

Social Environments 1973
PN 3873 **SC** 48200
B Environment 1967
N ↓ Academic Environment 1973
↓ Animal Environments 1967
↓ Communities 1967
Home Environment 1973
Poverty Areas 1973
Rural Environments 1967
Suburban Environments 1967
Towns 1973
Urban Environments 1967
↓ Working Conditions 1973
R Cultural Deprivation 1973
↓ Environmental Effects 1973
Social Density 1978

Social Equality 1973
PN 1846 **SC** 48210
UF Equality (Social)
B Social Issues 1991
R Affirmative Action 1985
↓ Civil Rights 1978
Equal Education 1978
↓ Human Rights 1978
↓ Justice 1973
Racial and Ethnic Relations 1982
↓ Social Integration 1982
↓ Social Justice 2006

Social Facilitation 1973
PN 581 **SC** 48220
SN Process whereby activity is increased in the presence of conspecifics.
UF Facilitation (Social)
B Social Behavior 1967
R ↓ Social Influences 1967
Social Loafing 2003

Social Groups 1973
PN 2054 **SC** 48230
UF Cadres
Cliques
Groups (Social)
N Dyads 1973
Ingroup Outgroup 1997
Minority Groups 1967
Reference Groups 1994
R ↓ Social Networks 1994

Social Identity 1988
PN 4672 **SC** 48235
SN An aspect of self image based on in-group preference or ethnocentrism and a perception of belonging to a social or cultural group.
N Professional Identity 1991
R Ethnic Identity 1973
Ethnocentrism 1973
Group Identity 2007
Identity Formation 2004
Ingroup Outgroup 1997
Minority Groups 1967
Reference Groups 1994
↓ Self Concept 1967

Social Immobility
Use Social Mobility

Social Influences 1967
PN 8082 **SC** 48250
UF Influences (Social)
N Coercion 1994
↓ Criticism 1973
Enabling 1997
Ethnic Values 1973
↓ Interpersonal Influences 1967
↓ Power 1967
↓ Prejudice 1967
Propaganda 1973
Social Approval 1967
Social Desirability 1967
Social Norms 1985
Social Values 1973
Superstitions 1973
Taboos 1973
R Authority 1967
↓ Ethics 1967
Mentor 1985
Popularity 1988
Psychosocial Factors 1988
Reference Groups 1994
Role Models 1982
↓ Social Behavior 1967
Social Change 1967
Social Comparison 1985
Social Control 1988
Social Facilitation 1973
Social Loafing 2003
↓ Social Movements 1967
↓ Social Reinforcement 1967

Social Integration 1982
PN 1837 **SC** 48258
SN Process of uniting diverse groups (e.g., racial, ethnic, religious, or disabled) of a society or organization.
HN In 1982, this term was created to replace the discontinued term RACIAL INTEGRATION. In 2000, RACIAL INTEGRATION was removed from all records containing it, and replaced with SOCIAL INTEGRATION.
UF Desegregation
Integration (Racial)
Racial Integration
Segregation (Racial)
B Social Issues 1991
Social Processes 1967
N School Integration 1982
R ↓ Activism 2003
↓ Civil Rights 1978
↓ Mainstreaming 1991
Racial and Ethnic Relations 1982
↓ Social Discrimination 1982
Social Equality 1973

Social Interaction 1967
PN 11555 **SC** 48260
UF Interaction (Social)
B Social Behavior 1967
N Encouragement 1973
↓ Interpersonal Interaction 1967
Nonviolence 1991
Peace 1988
Physical Contact 1982
Teasing 2003
Victimization 1973
R ↓ Aggressive Behavior 1967
Communities of Practice 2007
↓ Conflict Resolution 1982
Forgiveness 1988
Psychodynamics 1973
Self Monitoring (Personality) 1985
Social Anxiety 1985
Social Cognition 1994
↓ Social Networks 1994
Social Support 2004
Symbolic Interactionism 1988

Social Isolation 1967
PN 3916 **SC** 48270
SN Voluntary or involuntary absence of contact with others. Used for human or animal populations.
UF Isolation (Social)
B Social Deprivation 1973
Stimulus Deprivation 1973
N Patient Seclusion 1994
R Animal Maternal Deprivation 1988
Social Anxiety 1985

Social Issues 1991
PN 3566 **SC** 48275
SN Social concerns, including but not limited to problems or conditions perceived to have social causes, definitions, consequences, or possible solutions.
UF Social Problems
N ↓ Crime 1967
↓ Homeless 1988
↓ Human Rights 1978
Peace 1988
Poverty 1973
↓ Social Discrimination 1982

Social Issues — (cont'd)
Social Equality 1973
↓ Social Integration 1982
Unemployment 1967
↓ War 1967
R Adolescent Pregnancy 1988
Censorship 1978
↓ Civil Rights 1978
↓ Drug Abuse 1973
↓ Justice 1973
↓ Legal Processes 1973
Political Issues 1973
Racism 1973
Social Dilemma 2003
↓ Social Movements 1967
↓ Social Processes 1967
↓ Social Programs 1973

Social Justice 2006
PN 298 **SC** 48277
SN Refers to a society based on fairness and equality for its members regardless of social status.
HN This term was introduced in May 2006. Relevant records were re-indexed with this term. The posting note reflects the number of records that were re-indexed.
B Justice 1973
Social Processes 1967
N Distributive Justice 2003
R ↓ Civil Rights 1978
Social Equality 1973
Social Responsibility 2007

Social Learning 1973
PN 2253 **SC** 48280
B Learning 1967
Learning Strategies 1991
N Imitation (Learning) 1967
Imprinting 1967
R Communities of Practice 2007
Observational Learning 1973
↓ Social Reinforcement 1967

Social Loafing 2003
PN 89 **SC** 48284
SN Tendency of individuals to exert less effort on a task when working together in a group than when working alone.
HN This term was introduced in June 2003. Relevant records were re-indexed with this term. The posting note reflects the number of records that were re-indexed.
B Social Behavior 1967
R Group Participation 1973
Social Facilitation 1973
↓ Social Influences 1967

Social Maladjustment
Use Social Adjustment

Social Marketing 2007
PN 171 **SC** 48295
SN The use of commercial marketing concepts and strategies to influence the behavior of target audiences and to promote positive social change that benefits society.
HN This term was introduced in April 2007. Relevant records were re-indexed with this term. The posting note reflects the number of records that were re-indexed.

Social Marketing — (cont'd)
B Marketing 1973
R Health Promotion 1991

Social Mobility 1967
PN 514 SC 48300
SN Change in social status by an individual or a group.
UF Mobility (Social)
Social Immobility
Upward Mobility
B Social Processes 1967

Social Movements 1967
PN 1600 SC 48310
N Black Power Movement 1973
Civil Rights Movement 1973
Homosexual Liberation Movement 1973
Womens Liberation Movement 1973
R ↓ Civil Rights 1978
Coalition Formation 1973
↓ Human Rights 1978
Peace 1988
↓ Political Participation 1988
↓ Radical Movements 1973
Social Change 1967
Social Demonstrations 1973
↓ Social Influences 1967
↓ Social Issues 1991
↓ Social Programs 1973

Social Networks 1994
PN 2382 SC 48313
SN A formal or informal linkage, association, or network of individuals or groups that share common interests, contacts, knowledge, or resources. Compare SOCIAL SUPPORT and SUPPORT GROUPS.
UF Networks (Social)
N Online Social Networks 2007
R Ingroup Outgroup 1997
↓ Interpersonal Interaction 1967
Professional Networking 2004
Social Capital 2004
↓ Social Groups 1973
↓ Social Interaction 1967
Social Support 2004
Sociograms 1973
↓ Sociometry 1991
↓ Support Groups 1991

Social Norms 1985
PN 2928 SC 48315
SN Rules for social conduct, or standards which comprise a cultural definition of desirable or acceptable behavior. Also, patterns or traits seen as typical in the behavior of a social group.
UF Norms (Social)
B Social Influences 1967
R Sex Roles 1967
Social Values 1973

Social Perception 1967
PN 19073 SC 48320
SN Awareness of social phenomena, including attitudes or behaviors of persons or groups, especially as they relate to one's self.
UF Interpersonal Perception
B Perception 1967
Social Behavior 1967
N Attribution 1973
Impression Formation 1978
Social Comparison 1985

Social Perception — (cont'd)
R Anonymity 1973
Blame 1994
Credibility 1973
Face Perception 1985
Fame 1985
Halo Effect 1982
Impression Management 1978
Ingroup Outgroup 1997
Labeling 1978
Likability 1988
Perceptiveness (Personality) 1973
Popularity 1988
Reputation 1997
Reward Allocation 1988
Self Fulfilling Prophecies 1997
Self Reference 1994
Social Cognition 1994
Stereotyped Attitudes 1967
Stigma 1991
Stranger Reactions 1988
Theory of Mind 2001

Social Phobia 1985
PN 1950 SC 48325
SN Extreme apprehension or fear of social interaction or social situations in general. Compare SOCIAL ANXIETY.
UF Social Anxiety Disorder
B Phobias 1967
R Avoidant Personality Disorder 1994

Social Problems
Use Social Issues

Social Processes 1967
PN 4870 SC 48330
N Anomie 1978
Coalition Formation 1973
↓ Human Migration 1973
Immigration 1973
Industrialization 1973
Modernization 2003
Social Capital 2004
Social Control 1988
↓ Social Deprivation 1973
Social Dilemma 2003
↓ Social Integration 1982
↓ Social Justice 2006
Social Mobility 1967
↓ Socialization 1967
↓ Status 1967
Urbanization 1973
R Equity (Payment) 1978
↓ Equity (Social) 1978
↓ Human Rights 1978
↓ Political Processes 1973
Refugees 1988
Social Change 1967
↓ Social Issues 1991
↓ Sociocultural Factors 1967
Trends 1991

Social Programs 1973
PN 916 SC 48340
N Needle Exchange Programs 2001
Outreach Programs 1997
R ↓ Housing 1973
Human Services 2007
Integrated Services 1997
↓ Program Development 1991
Social Change 1967

Social Programs — (cont'd)
↓ Social Issues 1991
↓ Social Movements 1967
↓ Social Services 1982

Social Psychiatry 1967
PN 335 SC 48350
SN Branch of psychiatry concerned with the role of ecological, social, cultural, and economic factors in the etiology, incidence, and manifestations of mental disorders. Differentiate from COMMUNITY PSYCHIATRY, which emphasizes the practical and clinical applications of social psychiatry.
B Psychiatry 1967
R Social Psychology 1967

Social Psychologists 1973
PN 309 SC 48360
B Psychologists 1967
R Industrial Psychologists 1973
Sociologists 1973

Social Psychology 1967
PN 7193 SC 48370
SN Branch of psychology concerned with the study of individuals in groups and the interpersonal interactions within and between groups.
B Applied Psychology 1973
R Folk Psychology 1997
Social Psychiatry 1967

Social Reinforcement 1967
PN 1400 SC 48380
B Reinforcement 1967
Social Behavior 1967
N Nonverbal Reinforcement 1973
↓ Verbal Reinforcement 1973
R Enabling 1997
Encouragement 1973
Eye Contact 1973
Social Approval 1967
↓ Social Influences 1967
↓ Social Learning 1973

Social Rejection
Use Social Acceptance

Social Responsibility 2007
PN 546 SC 48387
SN The responsibility of an organization, business, individual, or other entity to make decisions and take actions that will benefit the welfare of society.
HN This term was introduced in April 2007. Relevant records were re-indexed with this term. The posting note reflects the number of records that were re-indexed.
B Responsibility 1973
Social Behavior 1967
R ↓ Ethics 1967
Social Change 1967
↓ Social Justice 2006

Social Sciences 1967
PN 4148 SC 48390
SN Group of scientific disciplines which study social institutions, their functioning, and the interpersonal relationships and behavior of individuals of those institutions.
B Sciences 1967
N Anthropology 1967
↓ Behavioral Sciences 1997
↓ Economics 1985
↓ Sociology 1967

Social Sciences — (cont'd)
R Theoretical Orientation 1982

Social Security 1988
PN 289 SC 48392
SN Government program providing for economic security and social welfare of individuals or families upon retirement, death, or disability. Used for US and non-US programs.
B Government Programs 1973
Insurance 1973
R Disability Evaluation 1988
Medicaid 1994
Medicare 1988

Social Services 1982
PN 4249 SC 48393
SN Activities designed to promote social welfare, usually associated with government or a helping organization (e.g., a church).
N ↓ Community Services 1967
Outreach Programs 1997
Protective Services 1997
R Child Welfare 1988
Faith Based Organizations 2007
↓ Government Programs 1973
↓ Health Care Services 1978
Human Services 2007
Integrated Services 1997
Literacy Programs 1997
↓ Mental Health Services 1978
Shelters 1991
Social Casework 1967
↓ Social Programs 1973
↓ Support Groups 1991

Social Skills 1978
PN 7528 SC 48395
UF Competence (Social)
Interpersonal Competence
Social Competence
B Ability 1967
Social Behavior 1967
R Adaptive Behavior 1991
Affective Education 1982
↓ Competence 1982
Listening (Interpersonal) 1997
Male Female Relations 1988
Social Skills Training 1982

Social Skills Training 1982
PN 3032 SC 48397
SN Instruction, usually group oriented, to increase quality and capability of interpersonal interaction.
B Training 2006
R Assertiveness Training 1978
↓ Behavior Modification 1973
Communication Skills Training 1982
Human Relations Training 1978
Sensitivity Training 1973
↓ Skill Learning 1973
Social Cognition 1994
Social Skills 1978

Social Stigma
Use Stigma

Social Stress 1973
PN 1230 SC 48400
B Stress 1967

Social Structure 1967
PN 3146 SC 48410
B Society 1967
N Caste System 1967
↓ Social Class 1967
R Dominance Hierarchy 1973
↓ Status 1967

Social Studies Education 1978
PN 736 SC 48415
SN Social sciences education in elementary, junior high, and high schools. Includes history, current events, and political science.
B Curriculum 1967

Social Support 2004
PN 17724 SC 48416
SN Family members or friends who provide social, emotional, or psychological support or comfort to an individual. Consider also SUPPORT GROUPS.
HN In June 2004, this term was created to replace the discontinued term SOCIAL SUPPORT NETWORKS. SOCIAL SUPPORT NETWORKS was removed from all records containing it and replaced with SOCIAL SUPPORT.
UF Social Support Networks
B Assistance (Social Behavior) 1973
R ↓ Family Relations 1967
Friendship 1967
Reference Groups 1994
Significant Others 1991
↓ Social Interaction 1967
↓ Social Networks 1994
↓ Support Groups 1991

Social Support Networks
HN In June 2004, this term was discontinued and removed from all records containing it, and was replaced with SOCIAL SUPPORT, its postable counterpart.
Use Social Support

Social Values 1973
PN 2661 SC 48420
B Social Influences 1967
Values 1967
R Anomie 1978
Evil 2003
Individualism 2007
Morality 1967
Social Norms 1985
↓ Society 1967

Social Work
Use Social Casework

Social Work Education 1973
PN 1616 SC 48440
B Education 1967

Social Workers 1973
PN 5085 SC 48450
UF Caseworkers
Social Caseworkers
B Personnel 1967
N Psychiatric Social Workers 1973
R ↓ Counselors 1967
↓ Health Personnel 1994
↓ Law Enforcement Personnel 1973
↓ Mental Health Personnel 1967

Social Workers — (cont'd)
↓ Psychologists 1967
Rehabilitation Counselors 1978
Sociologists 1973
↓ Therapists 1967
Vocational Counselors 1973

Socialism 1973
PN 374 SC 48460
B Political Economic Systems 1973

Socialization 1967
PN 5659 SC 48470
SN Process by which individuals acquire social skills and other characteristics necessary to function effectively in society or in a particular group.
B Social Processes 1967
N Political Socialization 1988
R Reference Groups 1994

Socially Disadvantaged
Use Disadvantaged

Society 1967
PN 4705 SC 48490
B Culture (Anthropological) 1967
N ↓ Social Structure 1967
↓ Socioeconomic Status 1967
R Popular Culture 2003
Social Values 1973

Sociobiology 1982
PN 722 SC 48495
SN Systematic study of the biological basis of all aspects of social behavior. Used for both human and animal populations.
B Biology 1967
Sociology 1967
R Behavioral Genetics 1994
Evolutionary Psychology 2003

Sociocultural Factors 1967
PN 20480 SC 48500
UF Cultural Factors
N Cross Cultural Differences 1967
Cultural Deprivation 1973
↓ Culture Change 1967
Ethnic Identity 1973
Ethnic Values 1973
↓ Rites of Passage 1973
R ↓ Childrearing Practices 1967
Cross Cultural Psychology 1997
Cultism 1973
Cultural Sensitivity 1994
↓ Culture (Anthropological) 1967
↓ Culture Bound Syndromes 2004
Ethnography 1973
Ethnology 1967
↓ Family Structure 1973
Kinship Structure 1973
Multiculturalism 1997
Psychosocial Factors 1988
Race (Anthropological) 1973
↓ Racial and Ethnic Groups 2001
Regional Differences 2001
Risk Factors 2001
↓ Social Processes 1967

Socioeconomic Class Attitudes 1973
PN 392 SC 48510
SN Attitudes of, not toward, members of a particular socioeconomic class.
UF Class Attitudes
Social Class Attitudes

Socioeconomic Class Attitudes — (cont'd)
B Attitudes 1967
N Lower Class Attitudes 1973
Middle Class Attitudes 1973
Upper Class Attitudes 1973
R ↓ Social Class 1967
↓ Socioeconomic Status 1967

Socioeconomic Status 1967
PN 11959 **SC** 48520
SN The combination of one's social class and income level. Includes socioeconomic differences between individuals or groups.
B Society 1967
Status 1967
N Family Socioeconomic Level 1973
↓ Income Level 1973
Lower Class 1973
↓ Social Class 1967
R Disadvantaged 1967
Economic Security 2007
Income (Economic) 1973
Poverty 1973
↓ Socioeconomic Class Attitudes 1973

Socioenvironmental Therapy
Use Milieu Therapy

Sociograms 1973
PN 57 **SC** 48530
SN Diagrams in which interactions between group members are analyzed on the basis of mutual attractions or antipathies.
B Sociometry 1991
R ↓ Measurement 1967
↓ Social Networks 1994

Sociolinguistics 1985
PN 801 **SC** 48535
SN The study of the sociological aspects of language, concerned with the part language plays in maintaining the social roles in a community.
B Linguistics 1973
R Code Switching 1988
Ethnolinguistics 1973
Metalinguistics 1994
↓ Sociology 1967
Symbolic Interactionism 1988

Sociologists 1973
PN 276 **SC** 48540
B Professional Personnel 1978
R Anthropologists 1973
↓ Counselors 1967
Scientists 1967
Social Psychologists 1973
↓ Social Workers 1973

Sociology 1967
PN 3674 **SC** 48550
B Social Sciences 1967
N Sociobiology 1982
R ↓ Behavioral Sciences 1997
Sociolinguistics 1985
Symbolic Interactionism 1988

Sociometric Tests 1967
PN 460 **SC** 48560
SN Tests or techniques used to identify preferences, likes, or dislikes of group members with respect to each other, as well as to identify various patterns of group structure or interaction.

Sociometric Tests — (cont'd)
B Measurement 1967
Sociometry 1991

Sociometry 1991
PN 303 **SC** 48565
SN Used for the scientific discipline or the sociometric processes and properties themselves.
N Sociograms 1973
Sociometric Tests 1967
R ↓ Collective Behavior 1967
↓ Group Dynamics 1967
↓ Organizational Behavior 1978
↓ Peer Relations 1967
↓ Social Networks 1994

Sociopath
Use Antisocial Personality Disorder

Sociopathology
Use Antisocial Behavior

Sociotherapy 1973
PN 118 **SC** 48580
SN Any therapy in which the main emphasis is on socioenvironmental and interpersonal factors. Sometimes used to refer to a therapeutic community.
B Treatment 1967
R Milieu Therapy 1988
Therapeutic Community 1967

Sodium 1973
PN 1187 **SC** 48590
B Metallic Elements 1973
N Sodium Ions 1973
R Hyponatremia 1997

Sodium Ions 1973
PN 107 **SC** 48610
B Electrolytes 1973
Sodium 1973

Sodium Lactate
Use Lactic Acid

Sodium Pentobarbital
Use Pentobarbital

Solution Focused Therapy 2004
PN 182 **SC** 48621
SN Approach to psychotherapy that focuses on solutions instead of problems.
HN This term was introduced in June 2004. Relevant records were re-indexed with this term. The posting note reflects the number of records that were re-indexed.
B Psychotherapy 1967
R Brief Psychotherapy 1967
↓ Problem Solving 1967

Solvent Abuse
Use Inhalant Abuse

Solvents 1982
PN 359 **SC** 48625
SN Substances that react chemically with a solid to bring it into solution. Also, liquids that dissolve another substance (solute) without any change in chemical composition.
N Toluene 1991
R ↓ Acids 1973
↓ Alcohols 1967
↓ Inhalant Abuse 1985

Somatization 1994
PN 1328 **SC** 57430
SN Process of organically manifesting and expressing cognitive and emotional disturbances through bodily symptoms. Primarily used in nonclinical contexts.
R ↓ Conversion Disorder 2001
Hypochondriasis 1973
Hysterical Paralysis 1973
Illness Behavior 1982
Somatization Disorder 2001
↓ Somatoform Disorders 2001
Somatoform Pain Disorder 1997
↓ Symptoms 1967

Somatization Disorder 2001
PN 126 **SC** 48627
SN Pattern of recurring polysymptomatic somatic complaints resulting in medical treatment or impaired daily function. Usually begins before age 30 and extends over a period of years.
HN Consider PSYCHOSOMATIC DISORDERS to access records from 1967-2000.
B Somatoform Disorders 2001
R Psychosomatic Medicine 1978
Somatization 1994

Somatoform Disorders 2001
PN 5674 **SC** 48628
SN Disorders characterized by bodily symptoms caused by psychological factors.
HN Consider PSYCHOSOMATIC DISORDERS to access references from 1967-2000.
UF Psychophysiologic Disorders
Psychosomatic Disorders
N Body Dysmorphic Disorder 2001
↓ Conversion Disorder 2001
Hypochondriasis 1973
Neurasthenia 2005
Neurodermatitis 1973
Somatization Disorder 2001
Somatoform Pain Disorder 1997
R Anorexia Nervosa 1973
Asthma 1967
Bulimia 1985
↓ Dyspnea 1973
↓ Endocrine Disorders 1973
↓ Gastrointestinal Disorders 1973
Hay Fever 1973
↓ Headache 1973
Hyperphagia 1973
Hyperventilation 1973
Illness Behavior 1982
Irritable Bowel Syndrome 1991
Malingering 1973
Migraine Headache 1973
Munchausen Syndrome 1994
Myofascial Pain 1991
Obesity 1973
Psychosomatic Medicine 1978
↓ Sexual Function Disturbances 1973
↓ Skin Disorders 1973
Somatization 1994
↓ Symptoms 1967
↓ Urinary Function Disorders 1973
↓ Urogenital Disorders 1973

Somatoform Pain Disorder 1997
PN 424 **SC** 48629
HN In 1997, this term was created to replace the discontinued term PSYCHOGENIC PAIN. In 2000, PSYCHOGENIC PAIN was removed from all records containing it, and replaced with SOMATOFORM PAIN DISORDER.

Somatoform Pain Disorder — (cont'd)
UF Pain (Psychogenic)
Pain Disorder
Psychogenic Pain
B Pain 1967
Somatoform Disorders 2001
R Chronic Pain 1985
↓ Conversion Disorder 2001
Hypochondriasis 1973
Pain Management 1994
Somatization 1994

Somatosensory Cortex 1973
PN 1179 SC 48630
SN Area in the postcentral gyrus that receives and processes touch sensations.
UF Cortex (Somatosensory)
B Parietal Lobe 1973
R ↓ Sensory System Disorders 2001

Somatosensory Disorders 2001
PN 291 SC 48635
SN Disorders of sensory information received from the skin and deep tissue of the body that are associated with impaired or abnormal somatic sensation. Such disorders may affect proprioception; tactile, thermal, and pressure sensation; and pain perception.
UF Hyperalgesia
Hyperesthesia
Hypesthesia
Paresthesia
B Sensory System Disorders 2001
R ↓ Nervous System Disorders 1967
↓ Pain Perception 1973
Pressure Sensation 1973
↓ Somesthetic Perception 1967
Temperature Perception 1973

Somatosensory Evoked Potentials 1973
PN 1228 SC 48640
SN Measured electrical response of the cerebral cortex to somatosensory stimulation of peripheral nerves.
UF Motor Evoked Potentials
B Evoked Potentials 1967

Somatostatin 1991
PN 209 SC 48645
SN A polypeptide produced primarily by the hypothalamus which inhibits the release of various other hormones, including somatotropin and gastrointestinal hormones.
UF Growth Hormone Inhibitor
B Neuropeptides 2003
Peptides 1973
R ↓ Hormones 1967
Somatotropin 1973

Somatotropin 1973
PN 897 SC 48650
UF Growth Hormone
B Neuropeptides 2003
Pituitary Hormones 1973
R Somatostatin 1991

Somatotypes 1973
PN 236 SC 48660
SN Body types as derived from any of various classifications of body build and which usually imply a correlation with personality characteristics.
UF Body Types
R ↓ Overweight 2007
↓ Personality 1967

Somatotypes — (cont'd)
↓ Physical Appearance 1982
Physique 1967

Somesthetic Perception 1967
PN 1074 SC 48670
SN Awareness of bodily condition or stimuli, including kinesthetic and cutaneous perception.
B Perception 1967
N ↓ Cutaneous Sense 1967
Kinesthetic Perception 1967
↓ Pain Perception 1973
Temperature Perception 1973
Weight Perception 1967
R Body Awareness 1982
↓ Labyrinth Disorders 1973
Pressure Sensation 1973
Somatosensory Disorders 2001

Somesthetic Stimulation 1973
PN 822 SC 48680
UF Vestibular Stimulation
B Perceptual Stimulation 1973
N ↓ Tactual Stimulation 1973
R Weightlessness 1967

Somnambulism
HN Term was discontinued in 1982. In 2000, the term was removed from all records containing it, and replaced with SLEEPWALKING, its postable counterpart.
Use Sleepwalking

Sonar 1973
PN 57 SC 48700
B Apparatus 1967

Songs
Use Music

Sons 1973
PN 1236 SC 48710
B Family Members 1973
Human Males 1973
Offspring 1988

Sorority Membership 1973
PN 167 SC 48720
SN Belonging to a club traditionally restricted to females. Used also for sorority organizations.
B Extracurricular Activities 1973
Membership 2007

Sorting (Cognition)
Use Classification (Cognitive Process)

Soul 2004
PN 400 SC 48735
HN This term was introduced in June 2004. Relevant records were re-indexed with this term. The posting note reflects the number of records that were re-indexed.
R Human Body 2003
Mind 1991
↓ Religious Beliefs 1973
Spirituality 1988

Sound
Use Auditory Stimulation

Sound Localization
Use Auditory Localization

Sound Pressure Level
Use Loudness

Sound Waves
Use Acoustics

Source Monitoring 2004
PN 170 SC 48768
SN The cognitive capacity to differentiate between experienced memories and to be able to attribute them to the particular source.
HN This term was introduced in June 2004. Relevant records were re-indexed with this term. The posting note reflects the number of records that were re-indexed.
B Monitoring 1973
R False Memory 1997
↓ Memory 1967

Sourness
Use Taste Perception

South Asian Cultural Groups 2004
PN 519 SC 48780
SN Cultural groups from the subcontinent of India, including Bangladesh, Nepal, Pakistan, Sri Lanka, Maldives, and Bhutan.
HN This term was introduced in June 2004. Relevant records were re-indexed with this term. The posting note reflects the number of records that were re-indexed.
B Asians 1982

South East Asian Cultural Groups
Use Southeast Asian Cultural Groups

Southeast Asian Cultural Groups 2004
PN 200 SC 48785
SN Cultural groups from countries south of China and east of India, including Brunei, Cambodia, Laos, Vietnam, Thailand, Singapore, Malaysia, Indonesia, Philippines, Myanmar, and East Timor.
HN This term was introduced in June 2004. Relevant records were re-indexed with this term. The posting note reflects the number of records that were re-indexed.
UF South East Asian Cultural Groups
B Asians 1982
N Vietnamese Cultural Groups 1997

Spacecraft 1973
PN 72 SC 48820
R Air Transportation 1973
Astronauts 1973

Spaceflight 1967
PN 397 SC 48830
B Aviation 1967
R Acceleration Effects 1973
Decompression Effects 1973
↓ Gravitational Effects 1967
Weightlessness 1967

Spanish Americans
HN In 1982, this term was created to replace the discontinued term SPANISH AMERICANS. In 2000, SPANISH AMERICANS was removed from all records containing it, and replaced with HISPANICS.
Use Hispanics

Spasms 1973
PN 175 SC 48850
B Movement Disorders 1985
Symptoms 1967
N Muscle Spasms 1973
R ↓ Anticonvulsive Drugs 1973
↓ Antispasmodic Drugs 1973
↓ Pain 1967

Spasms — (cont'd)
↓ Seizures 2005

Spatial Ability 1982
PN 2742 **SC** 48855
SN Potential or actual performance on tasks involving mental manipulation of objects or judgments of spatial relationships with respect to actual or imagined bodily orientation.
B Cognitive Ability 1973
Nonverbal Ability 1988
N ↓ Visuospatial Ability 1997
R ↓ Cognitive Processes 1967
Mental Rotation 1991
Spatial Imagery 1982
Spatial Learning 1994
Spatial Orientation (Perception) 1973

Spatial Discrimination
Use Spatial Perception

Spatial Distortion 1973
PN 235 **SC** 48870
SN Alterations of an organism's normal spatial perception in any sensory modality. Distortions may be induced by such means as optical lenses, prisms, mirror displays or images, and left-right inversion of sound stimuli.
B Illusions (Perception) 1967
Perceptual Distortion 1982
Spatial Perception 1967
R Prismatic Stimulation 1973

Spatial Frequency 1982
PN 1872 **SC** 48872
SN Number of alternating cycles (e.g., patterns of vertical stripes of light and dark light) occurring in a specified visual angle as, for example, in sine wave or square wave displays.
B Stimulus Parameters 1967
R Temporal Frequency 1985
↓ Visual Displays 1973
↓ Visual Stimulation 1973

Spatial Imagery 1982
PN 609 **SC** 48875
SN Mental representation of spatial relationships.
B Imagery 1967
R Cognitive Maps 1982
Mental Rotation 1991
↓ Spatial Ability 1982
↓ Spatial Memory 1988
Spatial Organization 1973
Spatial Orientation (Perception) 1973

Spatial Learning 1994
PN 1560 **SC** 48876
B Learning 1967
R Maze Learning 1967
↓ Spatial Ability 1982
↓ Spatial Memory 1988
↓ Spatial Perception 1967

Spatial Memory 1988
PN 2781 **SC** 48877
B Memory 1967
N Visuospatial Memory 1997
R Cognitive Maps 1982
Direction Perception 1997
Eidetic Imagery 1973
Spatial Imagery 1982
Spatial Learning 1994
↓ Visual Memory 1994

Spatial Neglect
Use Sensory Neglect

Spatial Organization 1973
PN 3878 **SC** 48880
SN Perception of spatial relationships. Also, the actual pattern or physical arrangement of objects or stimuli, including the dimensions of proximity, continuation, and relative position.
B Spatial Perception 1967
R Cognitive Maps 1982
Direction Perception 1997
Mental Rotation 1991
Retinal Eccentricity 1991
Spatial Imagery 1982

Spatial Orientation (Perception) 1973
PN 5217 **SC** 48890
SN Ability to perceive or orient oneself or external stimuli in space with respect to environmentally or egocentrically defined reference points.
UF Orientation (Spatial)
B Perceptual Orientation 1973
Spatial Perception 1967
R Cognitive Maps 1982
Equilibrium 1973
Kinesthetic Perception 1967
↓ Spatial Ability 1982
Spatial Imagery 1982

Spatial Perception 1967
PN 6411 **SC** 48900
UF Spatial Discrimination
B Perception 1967
N ↓ Depth Perception 1967
Direction Perception 1997
↓ Distance Perception 1973
↓ Motion Perception 1967
↓ Size Discrimination 1967
Spatial Distortion 1973
Spatial Organization 1973
Spatial Orientation (Perception) 1973
R Figure Ground Discrimination 1973
Mental Rotation 1991
Spatial Learning 1994
Visual Acuity 1982

Spearman Brown Test 1973
PN 19 **SC** 48910
B Statistical Tests 1973
R Statistical Reliability 1973

Spearman Rho
Use Rank Difference Correlation

Special Education 1967
PN 15990 **SC** 48930
SN Educational programs and services for students with disabilities or gifted students whose characteristics and educational needs differ from those who can be taught through standard methods and materials.
B Education 1967
Educational Programs 1973
R Ability Grouping 1973
Adaptive Behavior 1991
Early Intervention 1982
Educational Placement 1978
Educational Therapy 1997
Individual Education Programs 2006
↓ Mainstreaming 1991
Mainstreaming (Educational) 1978
↓ Remedial Education 1985
Self Care Skills 1978
Special Needs 1994

Special Education Students 1973
PN 4793 **SC** 49010
B Students 1967
R Grade Level 1994

Special Education Teachers 1973
PN 2387 **SC** 49020
B Teachers 1967
R Resource Teachers 1973

Special Needs 1994
PN 1452 **SC** 49025
SN Unspecified disorder, disability, or other problem that requires special services or intervention practices. Use a more specific term if possible.
R ↓ Disorders 1967
Early Intervention 1982
Individual Education Programs 2006
↓ Mainstreaming 1991
↓ Mental Disorders 1967
↓ Needs 1967
Needs Assessment 1985
↓ Physical Disorders 1997
Special Education 1967

Specialization (Academic)
Use Academic Specialization

Specialization (Professional)
Use Professional Specialization

Species Differences 1982
PN 2372 **SC** 49035
SN Anatomical, physiological, and/or behavioral variations between members of different species. May be used for comparisons between human and animal populations. Compare ANIMAL STRAIN DIFFERENCES.
HN Consider COMPARATIVE PSYCHOLOGY to access references from 1967-1981.
R ↓ Animals 1967
↓ Genetics 1967
Interspecies Interaction 1991

Species Recognition 1985
PN 501 **SC** 49037
SN Ability of members of a given species to identify and recognize other members of the same species.
B Animal Ethology 1967
R Conspecifics 2003
Imprinting 1967
Instinctive Behavior 1982
Kinship Recognition 1988

Spectral Sensitivity
Use Color Perception

Speech
Use Oral Communication

Speech and Hearing Measures 1973
PN 718 **SC** 49060
SN Consider also AUDIOLOGY and AUDIOMETRY.
UF Hearing Measures
Speech Measures
B Measurement 1967
R ↓ Perceptual Measures 1973

Speech Anxiety 1985
PN 453 **SC** 49065
SN Anxiety or fear associated with actual or anticipated oral communication with others.
UF Communication Apprehension
Fear of Public Speaking

Speech Anxiety — (cont'd)
B Anxiety 1967
R ↓ Anxiety Disorders 1997
Communication Barriers 2006
↓ Communication Disorders 1982
↓ Interpersonal Communication 1973
Public Speaking 1973
Social Anxiety 1985

Speech Characteristics 1973
PN 4993 SC 49070
B Oral Communication 1985
N Articulation (Speech) 1967
Pronunciation 1973
Speech Pauses 1973
Speech Pitch 1973
Speech Rate 1973
Speech Rhythm 1973
R Acoustics 1997
Inflection 1973
↓ Prosody 1991

Speech Development 1973
PN 2055 SC 49080
B Psychomotor Development 1973
N Retarded Speech Development 1973
R ↓ Cognitive Development 1973
↓ Language Development 1967

Speech Disorders 1967
PN 2944 SC 49090
HN The term SPEECH HANDICAPPED was also used to represent this concept from 1973-1996, and SPEECH DISABLED was used from 1997-2000. In 2000, SPEECH DISORDERS replaced the discontinued and deleted term SPEECH DISABLED. SPEECH DISABLED and SPEECH HANDICAPPED were removed from all records containing them and replaced with SPEECH DISORDERS.
UF Speech Handicapped
B Communication Disorders 1982
N ↓ Articulation Disorders 1973
Dysphonia 1973
Stuttering 1967
R Apraxia 1973
↓ Augmentative Communication 1994
Cleft Palate 1967
↓ Language Disorders 1982
Retarded Speech Development 1973

Speech Handicapped
HN The term was discontinued in 1997, when the term SPEECH DISABLED was created to capture this concept. In 2000, with the deletion of the term SPEECH DISABLED, SPEECH HANDICAPPED was made a nonpostable term for the new postable term SPEECH DISORDERS. SPEECH HANDICAPPED and SPEECH DISABLED were removed from all records containing them and replaced with SPEECH DISORDERS.
Use Speech Disorders

Speech Measures
Use Speech and Hearing Measures

Speech Pauses 1973
PN 316 SC 49120
B Speech Characteristics 1973

Speech Perception 1967
PN 6670 SC 49130
B Auditory Perception 1967
R Automated Speech Recognition 1994
Lipreading 1973

Speech Perception — (cont'd)
↓ Rhythm 1991
Word Recognition 1988

Speech Pitch 1973
PN 416 SC 49140
B Pitch (Frequency) 1967
Speech Characteristics 1973

Speech Processing (Mechanical) 1973
PN 306 SC 49150
N Automated Speech Recognition 1994
Compressed Speech 1973
Filtered Speech 1973
Synthetic Speech 1973
R ↓ Auditory Stimulation 1967
↓ Verbal Communication 1967

Speech Rate 1973
PN 765 SC 49160
UF Accelerated Speech
B Speech Characteristics 1973
R Tempo 1997
Verbal Fluency 1973

Speech Rhythm 1973
PN 224 SC 49170
B Rhythm 1991
Speech Characteristics 1973
R Tempo 1997

Speech Therapists 1973
PN 611 SC 49180
B Allied Health Personnel 2007
Therapists 1967
R ↓ Educational Personnel 1973

Speech Therapy 1967
PN 2775 SC 49190
B Treatment 1967
R ↓ Augmentative Communication 1994
↓ Communication Disorders 1982

Speechreading
Use Lipreading

Speed
Use Velocity

Speed (Response)
Use Reaction Time

Spelling 1973
PN 2338 SC 49220
SN Instruction, ability, or performance in the formation of words from letters according to accepted orthographic standards.
B Language 1967
Language Arts Education 1973
R Orthography 1973

Sperm 1973
PN 353 SC 49230
B Cells (Biology) 1973
R ↓ Sexual Reproduction 1973

Sperm Donation
Use Tissue Donation

Spider Phobia
Use Phobias

Spiders
Use Arachnida

Spina Bifida 1978
PN 443 SC 49245
SN Birth defect involving inadequate closure of the bony casement of the spinal cord, through which the spinal membranes, with or without spinal cord tissue, may protrude.
UF Meningomyelocele
Myelomeningocele
B Congenital Disorders 1973
R Anencephaly 1973

Spinal Column 1973
PN 126 SC 49250
UF Spine
B Musculoskeletal System 1973
R Bones 1973
↓ Spinal Cord 1973

Spinal Cord 1973
PN 1569 SC 49260
B Central Nervous System 1967
N Dorsal Horns 1985
Dorsal Roots 1973
Extrapyramidal Tracts 1973
Lumbar Spinal Cord 1973
Pyramidal Tracts 1973
Spinothalamic Tracts 1973
Ventral Roots 1973
R Spinal Column 1973

Spinal Cord Injuries 1973
PN 1242 SC 49270
B Injuries 1973
N Whiplash 1997
R ↓ Central Nervous System Disorders 1973
Hemiplegia 1978
↓ Neuromuscular Disorders 1973
↓ Paralysis 1973
Paraplegia 1978
Quadriplegia 1985

Spinal Fluid
Use Cerebrospinal Fluid

Spinal Ganglia 1973
PN 63 SC 49290
SN Sensory ganglia located on the dorsal root of each spinal nerve containing cell bodies of sensory neurons.
B Ganglia 1973

Spinal Nerves 1973
PN 623 SC 49300
UF Brachial Plexus
Cauda Equina
Cervical Plexus
Femoral Nerve
Lumbrosacral Plexus
Median Nerve
Musculocutaneous Nerve
Nerves (Spinal)
Obturator Nerve
Phrenic Nerve
Radial Nerve
Sciatic Nerve
Thoracic Nerves
Ulnar Nerve
B Peripheral Nervous System 1973

Spine
Use Spinal Column

Spinothalamic Tracts 1973
PN 71 **SC** 49310
SN Sensory pathways of the spinal cord consisting of two main parts. The anterior part carries impulses relating to touch, while the lateral part carries impulses relating to pain and temperature.
B Afferent Pathways 1982
Lemniscal System 1985
Spinal Cord 1973

Spiperone
Use Spiroperidol

Spirit Possession 1997
PN 113 **SC** 49314
UF Demonic Possession
R Occultism 1978
↓ Parapsychological Phenomena 1973
↓ Religious Beliefs 1973

Spirituality 1988
PN 5311 **SC** 49315
SN Degree of involvement or state of awareness or devotion to a higher being or life philosophy. Not always related to conventional religious beliefs.
R Religion 1967
Religiosity 1973
↓ Religious Beliefs 1973
Religious Experiences 1997
Soul 2004

Spiroperidol 1991
PN 45 **SC** 49317
UF Spiperone
B Neuroleptic Drugs 1973

Spleen 1973
PN 92 **SC** 49320
R ↓ Cardiovascular System 1967

Split Brain
Use Commissurotomy

Split Personality
Use Dissociative Identity Disorder

Spontaneous Abortion 1971
PN 404 **SC** 49350
UF Abortion (Spontaneous)
Miscarriage
R Induced Abortion 1971

Spontaneous Alternation 1982
PN 216 **SC** 49352
SN Instinctive successive alternation of responses between alternatives in a situation involving discrete choices or exploration.
R Animal Exploratory Behavior 1973
Delayed Alternation 1994
Instinctive Behavior 1982
↓ Learning 1967
Response Variability 1973

Spontaneous Recovery (Learning) 1973
PN 149 **SC** 49357
SN Recurrence of a conditioned response following experimental extinction. The response is weaker than when originally conditioned and will extinguish rapidly if not reinforced.
B Learning 1967
Memory 1967

Spontaneous Recovery (Learning) — (cont'd)
R ↓ Conditioning 1967

Spontaneous Remission 1973
PN 88 **SC** 49360
B Remission (Disorders) 1973
R ↓ Psychotherapy 1967
↓ Treatment 1967

Sport Performance
Use Athletic Performance

Sport Psychology 1982
PN 1434 **SC** 49365
SN Branch of psychology that investigates and applies psychological and physiological principles relating to athletic activity. Also used for psychological processes and their manifestations in such activity.
B Applied Psychology 1973

Sport Training
Use Athletic Training

Sports 1967
PN 4579 **SC** 49370
N Baseball 1973
Basketball 1973
Football 1973
Judo 1973
Martial Arts 1985
Soccer 1994
Swimming 1973
Tennis 1973
Weightlifting 1994
R ↓ Athletes 1973
Athletic Participation 1973
Athletic Performance 1991
Athletic Training 1991
Coaches 1988
College Athletes 1994
↓ Recreation 1967
Sports (Attitudes Toward) 2004
Sports Spectators 1997
↓ Teams 1988
Wilderness Experience 1991

Sports (Attitudes Toward) 2004
PN 106 **SC** 49371
SN Used for the attitudes of participants and spectators of sports.
HN This term was introduced in June 2004. Relevant records were re-indexed with this term. The posting note reflects the number of records that were re-indexed.
UF Sportsmanship
Sportspersonship
B Attitudes 1967
R ↓ Athletes 1973
↓ Sports 1967
Sports Spectators 1997

Sports Spectators 1997
PN 205 **SC** 49373
UF Fans (Sports)
B Audiences 1967
R ↓ Sports 1967
Sports (Attitudes Toward) 2004

Sportsmanship
Use Sports (Attitudes Toward)

Sportspersonship
Use Sports (Attitudes Toward)

Spouse Abuse
Use Partner Abuse

Spouses 1973
PN 8282 **SC** 49380
SN Married persons.
UF Married Couples
Mates (Humans)
B Family Members 1973
N Husbands 1973
Wives 1973
R Couples 1982
Inlaws 1997
↓ Parents 1967
Significant Others 1991

Spreading Depression 1967
PN 179 **SC** 49390
SN Cerebral cortex cellular depolarization and a depressed electrical activity in depolarized cortical areas resulting from application of intense localized electrical stimulation or local application of a chemical or localized trauma to the cerebral cortex.
B Brain Stimulation 1967

Squirrels 1973
PN 405 **SC** 49400
B Rodents 1973

St. John's Wort
Use Hypericum Perforatum

Stability (Emotional)
Use Emotional Stability

Stage Plays
Use Theatre

Stages of Change 2007
PN 423 **SC** 49433
SN Theoretical model that suggests there are five stages involved in changing a behavior.
HN This term was introduced in April 2007. Relevant records were re-indexed with this term. The posting note reflects the number of records that were re-indexed.
R Behavior Change 1973
↓ Behavior Modification 1973
Lifestyle Changes 1997
Motivational Interviewing 2007
Readiness to Change 2007

Stalking 2001
PN 274 **SC** 49435
SN Willful, malicious, and repeated nonconsensual contact with and harassing of another individual.
B Harassment 2001
R ↓ Crime 1967
↓ Perpetrators 1988
Victimization 1973

Stammering
HN Term was discontinued in 1982. In 2000, the term was removed from all records containing it, and replaced with STUTTERING, its postable counterpart.
Use Stuttering

Standard Deviation 1973
PN 176 **SC** 49450
B Variability Measurement 1973
R Error of Measurement 1985
↓ Frequency Distribution 1973
Homogeneity of Variance 2003
Standard Scores 1985

Standard Error of Measurement
Use Error of Measurement

Standard Scores 1985
PN 139 **SC** 49455
SN Test scores measuring the distance of individual scores from the mean of the normative group, expressed in terms of the standard deviation.
UF Deviation IQ
Stanines
Z Scores
B Test Scores 1967
R Mean 1973
Score Equating 1985
↓ Scoring (Testing) 1973
Standard Deviation 1973

Standardization (Test)
Use Test Standardization

Standardized Tests 1985
PN 746 **SC** 49465
SN Tests with established norms, administration and scoring procedures, and validity and reliability data.
B Measurement 1967
R Educational Standards 2007
Test Norms 1973
Test Standardization 1973

Standards (Professional)
Use Professional Standards

Stanford Achievement Test 1973
PN 63 **SC** 49480
B Achievement Measures 1967

Stanford Binet Intelligence Scale 1967
PN 435 **SC** 49490
B Intelligence Measures 1967

Stanines
Use Standard Scores

Stapedius Reflex
Use Acoustic Reflex

Starfish
Use Echinodermata

Startle Reflex 1967
PN 1762 **SC** 49510
B Reflexes 1971
R Acoustic Reflex 1973
Alarm Responses 1973
Eyeblink Reflex 1973
Prepulse Inhibition 1997

Starvation 1973
PN 178 **SC** 49520
B Nutritional Deficiencies 1973
R Food Deprivation 1967
Hunger 1967

State Board Examinations
Use Professional Examinations

State Dependent Learning 1982
PN 146 **SC** 49525
SN Learning phenomenon wherein the transfer of a response that was learned in the context of specific internal or external cues is dependent on the constancy of the stimulus complex in the new situation to which the behavior is to transfer.
UF Drug Dissociation
B Learning 1967

State Hospitals
Use Psychiatric Hospitals

State Trait Anxiety Inventory 1973
PN 242 **SC** 49540
B Nonprojective Personality Measures 1973

Statistical Analysis 1967
PN 9900 **SC** 49550
SN Application of statistical procedures to the interpretation of numerical data.
B Analysis 1967
N ↓ Central Tendency Measures 1973
Cluster Analysis 1973
Confidence Limits (Statistics) 1973
Consistency (Measurement) 1973
Effect Size (Statistical) 1985
Error of Measurement 1985
↓ Frequency Distribution 1973
Fuzzy Set Theory 1991
Goodness of Fit 1988
Interaction Analysis (Statistics) 1973
Meta Analysis 1985
↓ Multivariate Analysis 1982
Predictability (Measurement) 1973
↓ Statistical Correlation 1967
Statistical Data 1982
↓ Statistical Estimation 1985
Statistical Norms 1971
↓ Statistical Probability 1967
↓ Statistical Regression 1985
Statistical Reliability 1973
Statistical Significance 1973
↓ Statistical Tests 1973
Statistical Validity 1973
Statistical Weighting 1985
Time Series 1985
↓ Variability Measurement 1973
R Conjoint Measurement 1994
↓ Experimental Design 1967
↓ Experimentation 1967
↓ Hypothesis Testing 1973
↓ Mathematics (Concepts) 1967
↓ Measurement 1967
↓ Population (Statistics) 1973
↓ Prediction Errors 1973
Psychometrics 1967
Quantitative Methods 2003
↓ Sampling (Experimental) 1973
↓ Statistical Measurement 1973
↓ Statistical Variables 1973
Uncertainty 1991

Statistical Correlation 1967
PN 3922 **SC** 49560
UF Correlation (Statistical)
Pearson Product Moment Correlation Coefficient
B Statistical Analysis 1967
N Linear Regression 1973
Logistic Regression 2003
Nonlinear Regression 1973
Phi Coefficient 1973
Point Biserial Correlation 1973
Rank Difference Correlation 1973
Rank Order Correlation 1973
Tetrachoric Correlation 1973
R ↓ Experimentation 1967
↓ Factor Analysis 1967
Multiple Regression 1982
↓ Multivariate Analysis 1982
Statistical Data 1982
↓ Statistical Regression 1985
Statistical Significance 1973
Statistical Validity 1973
↓ Statistical Variables 1973
↓ Variability Measurement 1973

Statistical Data 1982
PN 1343 **SC** 49564
SN Sets of quantitative values that summarize, through mathematical operation, or express the parameters that represent a population or some other sample (e.g., response frequency).
B Statistical Analysis 1967
R Data Collection 1982
Graphical Displays 1985
Quantitative Methods 2003
↓ Statistical Correlation 1967
↓ Statistical Measurement 1973
Statistical Tables 1982
↓ Statistical Variables 1973
Time Series 1985

Statistical Estimation 1985
PN 1781 **SC** 49567
SN Any inferential mathematical derivation of an estimate of a parameter from one or more samples. Includes interval estimation.
UF Parameter Estimation
B Estimation 1967
Statistical Analysis 1967
N Least Squares 1985
Magnitude Estimation 1991
Maximum Likelihood 1985
R Error of Measurement 1985
Predictability (Measurement) 1973

Statistical Measurement 1973
PN 905 **SC** 49570
SN Process of or products derived from the collection or manipulation of statistical data in order to derive basic summarizing quantitative values which describe a set of measurements.
B Measurement 1967
N ↓ Central Tendency Measures 1973
Conjoint Measurement 1994
↓ Frequency Distribution 1973
Homogeneity of Variance 2003
Predictability (Measurement) 1973
Statistical Norms 1971
↓ Statistical Probability 1967
↓ Variability Measurement 1973
R Confidence Limits (Statistics) 1973
Data Collection 1982
Error of Measurement 1985
Graphical Displays 1985
Quantitative Methods 2003
↓ Statistical Analysis 1967
Statistical Data 1982
Statistical Significance 1973
↓ Statistical Tests 1973

Statistical Norms 1971
PN 365 **SC** 49580
UF Norms (Statistical)
B Statistical Analysis 1967
Statistical Measurement 1973
R ↓ Statistical Sample Parameters 1973

Statistical Power 1991
PN 401 **SC** 49585
SN The ability of a statistic to reject a false hypothesis.
B Statistical Probability 1967
R ↓ Hypothesis Testing 1973
↓ Prediction Errors 1973
↓ Sampling (Experimental) 1973
Statistical Significance 1973
↓ Statistical Tests 1973
Type I Errors 1973
Type II Errors 1973

Statistical Probability 1967
PN 1583 **SC** 49590
UF Bayes Theorem
B Chance (Fortune) 1973
Probability 1967
Statistical Analysis 1967
Statistical Measurement 1973
N Binomial Distribution 1973
Statistical Power 1991
R Fuzzy Set Theory 1991

Statistical Regression 1985
PN 845 **SC** 49595
SN Statistical comparison of the frequency distributions of one variable while the other(s) are held constant for the purpose of discovering predictive and functional relationships between variables.
HN Use ANALYSIS OF VARIANCE or more specific terms prior to 1985.
UF Regression Analysis
Regression Artifact
B Statistical Analysis 1967
N Linear Regression 1973
Logistic Regression 2003
Multiple Regression 1982
Nonlinear Regression 1973
R Analysis of Variance 1967
Causal Analysis 1994
Least Squares 1985
↓ Multivariate Analysis 1982
↓ Statistical Correlation 1967

Statistical Reliability 1973
PN 2885 **SC** 49600
HN In 1973, this term was created to replace the discontinued term RELIABILITY (STATISTICAL). In 2000, RELIABILITY (STATISTICAL) was removed from all records containing it, and replaced with STATISTICAL RELIABILITY.
UF Reliability (Statistical)
B Statistical Analysis 1967
R Consistency (Measurement) 1973
↓ Experimentation 1967
Interrater Reliability 1982
↓ Population (Statistics) 1973
↓ Prediction Errors 1973
↓ Sampling (Experimental) 1973
Spearman Brown Test 1973
Statistical Validity 1973

Statistical Rotation 1973
PN 95 **SC** 49610
UF Rotation Methods (Statistical)
B Factor Analysis 1967
N Oblique Rotation 1973
↓ Orthogonal Rotation 1973
R Factor Structure 1985

Statistical Sample Parameters 1973
PN 500 **SC** 49620
SN Quantities and qualities describing a statistical population.
B Statistical Samples 1973
N Sample Size 1997
R Binomial Distribution 1973
Confidence Limits (Statistics) 1973
Normal Distribution 1973
Statistical Norms 1971

Statistical Samples 1973
PN 374 **SC** 49630
SN Portion of a population taken as representative of the whole population.
B Population (Statistics) 1973
N ↓ Statistical Sample Parameters 1973
R ↓ Sampling (Experimental) 1973

Statistical Significance 1973
PN 902 **SC** 49640
UF Significance (Statistical)
B Statistical Analysis 1967
R Chi Square Test 1973
Confidence Limits (Statistics) 1973
Effect Size (Statistical) 1985
↓ Factor Analysis 1967
Goodness of Fit 1988
↓ Hypothesis Testing 1973
Sign Test 1973
↓ Statistical Correlation 1967
↓ Statistical Measurement 1973
Statistical Power 1991
↓ Statistical Tests 1973
T Test 1973

Statistical Tables 1982
PN 208 **SC** 49647
SN Systematically organized displays of statistical values or distributions or summary data derived from statistical calculation. The table of critical values of the F distribution is an example of the first category, and a contingency table showing test score means as related to the variables of sex and age is an example of the second category.
R Statistical Data 1982
↓ Statistical Variables 1973

Statistical Tests 1973
PN 833 **SC** 49650
SN Specific mathematical techniques used to analyze data in order to assess the probability that a set of results could have occurred by chance and hence to test for the probable correctness of empirical hypotheses.
UF Tests (Statistical)
B Statistical Analysis 1967
N ↓ Nonparametric Statistical Tests 1967
↓ Parametric Statistical Tests 1973
Spearman Brown Test 1973
R Confidence Limits (Statistics) 1973
↓ Statistical Measurement 1973
Statistical Power 1991
Statistical Significance 1973

Statistical Validity 1973
PN 13546 **SC** 49660
HN In 2000, this term became the postable counterpart for the terms FACTORIAL VALIDITY and PREDICTIVE VALIDITY. These terms were removed from all records containing them and replaced with STATISTICAL VALIDITY.
UF Factorial Validity
Predictive Validity
Validity (Statistical)
B Statistical Analysis 1967
R Consistency (Measurement) 1973
↓ Experimentation 1967
↓ Prediction Errors 1973
↓ Statistical Correlation 1967
Statistical Reliability 1973
↓ Statistical Variables 1973

Statistical Variables 1973
PN 1108 **SC** 49670
N Dependent Variables 1973
Independent Variables 1973
R ↓ Experimental Design 1967
↓ Experimentation 1967
↓ Population (Statistics) 1973
↓ Prediction Errors 1973
↓ Sampling (Experimental) 1973
↓ Statistical Analysis 1967
↓ Statistical Correlation 1967
Statistical Data 1982
Statistical Tables 1982
Statistical Validity 1973

Statistical Weighting 1985
PN 231 **SC** 49671
SN A coefficient or mathematical constant that determines the relative contribution of a statistic to a total numeric value. Also, the process of assigning such statistical weights.
UF Weight (Statistics)
B Statistical Analysis 1967
R Item Analysis (Statistical) 1973
↓ Scoring (Testing) 1973
Test Interpretation 1985
↓ Test Scores 1967

Statistics 1982
PN 2365 **SC** 49672
SN Subdiscipline of mathematics that deals with the gathering and evaluation of numerical data for making inferences from the data.
B Mathematics 1982

Status 1967
PN 2589 **SC** 49675
SN General term used to indicate relative social position or rank.
B Social Processes 1967
N Occupational Status 1978
↓ Socioeconomic Status 1967
R Authority 1967
↓ Dominance 1967
Fame 1985
Reputation 1997
↓ Social Structure 1967

Stealing
Use Theft

Stelazine
Use Trifluoperazine

Stellate Ganglion
Use Autonomic Ganglia

Stem Cells 2006
PN 131 **SC** 49715
SN Undifferentiated cells that have the capacity to reproduce themselves and differentiate into specialized cell types.
HN This term was introduced in May 2006. Relevant records were re-indexed with this term. The posting note reflects the number of records that were re-indexed.
B Cells (Biology) 1973
R Embryo 1973

Stepchildren 1973
PN 337 **SC** 49720
B Family Members 1973
R ↓ Family Structure 1973
Stepfamily 1991

Stepfamily 1991
PN 527 **SC** 49725
B Family 1967
Family Structure 1973
R Family of Origin 1991
Remarriage 1985
Stepchildren 1973
Stepparents 1973

Stepparents 1973
PN 599 **SC** 49730
B Parents 1967
R ↓ Family Structure 1973
Stepfamily 1991

Stereopsis
Use Stereoscopic Vision

Stereoscopic Presentation 1973
PN 230 **SC** 49750
SN Simultaneous presentation of separate two-dimensional pictures (taken from slightly different angles) to each eye of one subject, resulting in a perception of depth.
B Stimulus Presentation Methods 1973
Visual Stimulation 1973

Stereoscopic Vision 1973
PN 1043 **SC** 49760
UF Stereopsis
B Depth Perception 1967
Visual Perception 1967

Stereotaxic Atlas 1973
PN 1253 **SC** 49770
UF Brain Mapping
Brain Maps
R ↓ Stereotaxic Techniques 1973

Stereotaxic Techniques 1973
PN 175 **SC** 49780
SN Methods, procedures, or apparatus which permit precise spatial positioning of electrodes or other probes into the brain for experimental or surgical purposes.
B Surgery 1971
N ↓ Brain Stimulation 1967
Chemical Brain Stimulation 1973
Electrical Brain Stimulation 1973
R Afferent Stimulation 1973
↓ Nervous System 1967
Stereotaxic Atlas 1973

Stereotyped Attitudes 1967
PN 7229 **SC** 49790
SN Oversimplified, rigid, often negative preconceptions of individuals, groups, or social classes who identify with a particular ethnicity, gender, religion, sexual orientation, or other group. Compare STIGMA.
UF Stereotyping
B Attitudes 1967
R Ageism 2003
↓ Disabled (Attitudes Toward) 1997
↓ Discrimination 1967
Homosexuality (Attitudes Toward) 1982
Labeling 1978
↓ Prejudice 1967
↓ Racial and Ethnic Attitudes 1982
↓ Sex Role Attitudes 1978
Sexism 1988
↓ Social Discrimination 1982
↓ Social Perception 1967
Stigma 1991

Stereotyped Behavior 1973
PN 2614 **SC** 49795
SN Highly repetitive, often non-functional, rhythmic behaviors that occur at a high frequency. Used for animal or disordered human populations.
B Behavior 1967
R ↓ Animal Ethology 1967
↓ Pervasive Developmental Disorders 2001
Repetition Compulsion 2005
↓ Self Stimulation 1967
↓ Symptoms 1967

Stereotyping
Use Stereotyped Attitudes

Sterility 1973
PN 58 **SC** 49810
B Infertility 1973
R ↓ Gynecological Disorders 1973
Hermaphroditism 1973
↓ Hypogonadism 1973
↓ Male Genital Disorders 1973
Testicular Feminization Syndrome 1973
Turners Syndrome 1973

Sterilization (Sex) 1973
PN 177 **SC** 49820
N ↓ Castration 1967
Hysterectomy 1973
Tubal Ligation 1973
Vasectomy 1973
R ↓ Birth Control 1971
Eugenics 1973
↓ Family Planning 1973

Steroids 1973
PN 1414 **SC** 49830
B Drugs 1967
N Cholesterol 1973
↓ Corticosteroids 1973
Progesterone 1973
R ↓ Anti Inflammatory Drugs 1982
Antiandrogens 1982
Antiestrogens 1982
Antineoplastic Drugs 1982
↓ Hormones 1967
↓ Lipids 1973

Sticklebacks 1973
PN 251 **SC** 49840
B Fishes 1967

Stigma 1991
PN 2002 **SC** 49843
SN Perception of a distinguishing personal characteristic or condition, e.g., a physical or psychological disorder, race, or religion, which carries or is believed to carry a physical, psychological, or social disadvantage.
UF Social Stigma
R ↓ Attitudes 1967
Labeling 1978
↓ Prejudice 1967
Social Acceptance 1967
Social Approval 1967
↓ Social Discrimination 1982
↓ Social Perception 1967
Stereotyped Attitudes 1967

Stimulants of CNS
Use CNS Stimulating Drugs

Stimulation 1967
PN 1950 **SC** 49850
N Afferent Stimulation 1973
Aversive Stimulation 1973
↓ Brain Stimulation 1967
↓ Electrical Stimulation 1973
↓ Perceptual Stimulation 1973
↓ Self Stimulation 1967
Subliminal Stimulation 1985
Verbal Stimuli 1982
R ↓ Biofeedback 1973
Conditioned Stimulus 1973
↓ Conditioning 1967
↓ Feedback 1967
Stimulus Ambiguity 1967
Stimulus Change 1973
Stimulus Control 1967
↓ Stimulus Deprivation 1973
Stimulus Discrimination 1973
Stimulus Generalization 1967
↓ Stimulus Parameters 1967
↓ Stimulus Presentation Methods 1973
Unconditioned Stimulus 1973

Stimulation Seeking (Personality)
Use Sensation Seeking

Stimulators (Apparatus) 1973
PN 58 **SC** 49860
B Apparatus 1967
N Shock Units 1973
R Electrodes 1967
Vibrators (Apparatus) 1973

Stimulus (Unconditioned)
Use Unconditioned Stimulus

Stimulus Ambiguity 1967
PN 1123 **SC** 49890
UF Ambiguity (Stimulus)
R ↓ Stimulation 1967
Stimulus Generalization 1967
Stroop Effect 1988

Stimulus Attenuation 1973
PN 178 **SC** 49900
SN Controlled, progressive, or otherwise manipulated reduction in the intensity, clarity, salience, or other such distinguishing qualities of a stimulus.

Stimulus Attenuation — (cont'd)
B Stimulus Parameters 1967
R Fading (Conditioning) 1982

Stimulus Change 1973
PN 671 SC 49910
R ↓ Stimulation 1967

Stimulus Complexity 1971
PN 1960 SC 49920
UF Complexity (Stimulus)
B Stimulus Parameters 1967

Stimulus Control 1967
PN 1519 SC 49930
SN Change in the probability of occurrence of a conditioned response as a direct function of the onset, offset, or changes in a conditioned stimulus.
R ↓ Discrimination Learning 1982
↓ Stimulation 1967
Stimulus Generalization 1967

Stimulus Deprivation 1973
PN 194 SC 49940
UF Restricted Environmental Stimulation
B Deprivation 1967
N Food Deprivation 1967
Sensory Deprivation 1967
↓ Social Deprivation 1973
↓ Social Isolation 1967
Water Deprivation 1967
R ↓ Stimulation 1967

Stimulus Discrimination 1973
PN 2497 SC 49950
B Discrimination 1967
R Behavioral Contrast 1978
↓ Discrimination Learning 1982
Fading (Conditioning) 1982
↓ Stimulation 1967
Stimulus Generalization 1967

Stimulus Duration 1973
PN 3019 SC 49960
UF Duration (Stimulus)
Exposure Time (Stimulus)
B Stimulus Parameters 1967

Stimulus Frequency 1973
PN 1605 SC 49980
SN Number of stimulus presentations within a given trial or per unit time.
UF Frequency (Stimulus)
B Stimulus Parameters 1967
R Temporal Frequency 1985

Stimulus Generalization 1967
PN 964 SC 49990
SN Responding in a similar manner to different stimuli which have some common physical property. Also known as primary generalization. Compare GENERALIZATION (LEARNING) and RESPONSE GENERALIZATION.
UF Generalization (Stimulus)
B Generalization (Learning) 1982
R ↓ Stimulation 1967
Stimulus Ambiguity 1967
Stimulus Control 1967
Stimulus Discrimination 1973

Stimulus Intensity 1967
PN 3622 SC 50000
UF Intensity (Stimulus)
Signal Intensity
B Stimulus Parameters 1967
R Luminance 1982

Stimulus Intervals 1973
PN 1447 SC 50010
SN Temporal intervals between stimuli presented in any sensory modality. Use INTERSTIMULUS INTERVAL in conditioning contexts.
B Stimulus Parameters 1967
N Interstimulus Interval 1967
Intertrial Interval 1973
R Reinforcement Delay 1985

Stimulus Novelty 1973
PN 2650 SC 50020
SN New, unexpected, or unfamiliar quality of a stimulus.
UF Novel Stimuli
B Stimulus Parameters 1967
R Neophobia 1985

Stimulus Offset 1985
PN 107 SC 50023
B Stimulus Parameters 1967

Stimulus Onset 1982
PN 752 SC 50025
B Stimulus Parameters 1967

Stimulus Parameters 1967
PN 7477 SC 50030
SN Applied when quantifiable or descriptive characteristics of stimuli in a study are emphasized. Use a more specific term if possible.
UF Parameters (Stimulus)
N ↓ Size 1973
Spatial Frequency 1982
Stimulus Attenuation 1973
Stimulus Complexity 1971
Stimulus Duration 1973
Stimulus Frequency 1973
Stimulus Intensity 1967
↓ Stimulus Intervals 1973
Stimulus Novelty 1973
Stimulus Offset 1985
Stimulus Onset 1982
Stimulus Salience 1973
Stimulus Similarity 1967
Stimulus Variability 1973
Temporal Frequency 1985
R Acoustics 1997
↓ Stimulation 1967

Stimulus Pattern
Use Stimulus Variability

Stimulus Presentation Methods 1973
PN 2968 SC 50050
SN Methodological, procedural, or technical aspects of stimulus presentation. Use a more specific term if possible, e.g., VISUAL STIMULATION for visual stimulus presentation.
B Experimental Methods 1967
N Stereoscopic Presentation 1973
Tachistoscopic Presentation 1973
R Pictorial Stimuli 1978
↓ Stimulation 1967
Verbal Stimuli 1982

Stimulus Salience 1973
PN 1174 SC 50060
SN Relative prominence or distinctiveness of a stimulus.
UF Salience (Stimulus)
B Stimulus Parameters 1967
R Isolation Effect 1973

Stimulus Similarity 1967
PN 2523 SC 50070
SN Conceptual or physical resemblance of two or more stimuli.
UF Similarity (Stimulus)
B Stimulus Parameters 1967

Stimulus Variability 1973
PN 1737 SC 50080
UF Stimulus Pattern
Variability (Stimulus)
B Stimulus Parameters 1967

Stipends
Use Educational Financial Assistance

Stochastic Modeling 1973
PN 816 SC 50100
SN Statistical modeling for sequences of events whose probabilities are constantly changing.
B Simulation 1967
N Markov Chains 1973
R Chaos Theory 1997
Information Theory 1967
↓ Mathematical Modeling 1973
Time Series 1985

Stomach 1973
PN 172 SC 50120
B Gastrointestinal System 1973

Storytelling 1988
PN 2028 SC 50125
B Verbal Communication 1967
R Creative Writing 1994
Folklore 1991
Myths 1967
Narrative Therapy 2006
Narratives 1997

Storytelling Technique
Use Mutual Storytelling Technique

Strabismus 1973
PN 231 SC 50140
UF Crossed Eyes
B Eye Disorders 1973
R Amblyopia 1973
Eye Convergence 1982

Strain Differences (Animal)
Use Animal Strain Differences

Stranger Reactions 1988
PN 353 SC 50148
SN Emotional or behavioral responses to unfamiliar persons. Used for all age groups.
UF Fear of Strangers
Xenophobia
B Interpersonal Interaction 1967
R Attachment Behavior 1985
↓ Emotional Responses 1967
Familiarity 1967
↓ Fear 1967
Separation Anxiety 1973
↓ Social Perception 1967

Strategies 1967
PN 10185 **SC** 50150
SN Methods, techniques, or tactics used in accomplishing a given goal or task.
N ↓ Learning Strategies 1991
R ↓ Cognitive Processes 1967
Guessing 1973
Heuristics 2003
↓ Learning 1967
Note Taking 1991

Strategies (Learning)
Use Learning Strategies

Strength (Physical)
Use Physical Strength

Stress 1967
PN 26885 **SC** 50170
SN Refers to the emotional, psychological, or physical effects as well as the sources of agitation, strain, tension, or pressure. Compare DISTRESS. Used for both human and animal populations.
N Chronic Stress 2004
Environmental Stress 1973
Financial Strain 2005
Occupational Stress 1973
Physiological Stress 1967
Psychological Stress 1973
Social Stress 1973
Stress Reactions 1973
R Adjustment Disorders 1994
↓ Adrenal Cortex Hormones 1973
↓ Anxiety 1967
Caregiver Burden 1994
↓ Crises 1971
↓ Deprivation 1967
Diathesis Stress Model 2005
↓ Disasters 1973
Distress 1973
↓ Endurance 1973
Family Crises 1973
Identity Crisis 1973
Natural Disasters 1973
Organizational Crises 1973
Stress Management 1985

Stress Management 1985
PN 2771 **SC** 50175
SN Techniques or services designed to alleviate the effects and/or causes of stress.
B Management 1967
R Anxiety Management 1997
↓ Behavior Modification 1973
↓ Cognitive Techniques 1985
↓ Stress 1967
↓ Treatment 1967

Stress Reactions 1973
PN 7773 **SC** 50180
SN Reactions to stressful events in everyday life or in experimental settings. Differentiate from POSTTRAUMATIC STRESS DISORDER which refers to reactions that seriously impair a person's functioning.
UF Crisis (Reactions to)
B Stress 1967
R Acute Stress Disorder 2003
Adjustment Disorders 1994
Cardiovascular Reactivity 1994
Coronary Prone Behavior 1982
Posttraumatic Stress Disorder 1985
Psychological Endurance 1973

Striate Cortex
Use Visual Cortex

Striatum 2003
PN 888 **SC** 50187
SN Part of the corpus striatum that includes the caudate nucleus and putamen. For STRIATE CORTEX use VISUAL CORTEX.
HN This term was introduced in June 2003. Relevant records were re-indexed with this term. The posting note reflects the number of records that were reindexed.
UF Neostriatum
B Basal Ganglia 1973
N Caudate Nucleus 1973
Putamen 1985
R Globus Pallidus 1973

Strikes 1973
PN 166 **SC** 50190
R Labor Management Relations 1967

Stroboscopic Movement
Use Apparent Movement

Stroke (Cerebrum)
Use Cerebrovascular Accidents

Strong Vocational Interest Blank 1967
PN 242 **SC** 50220
B Occupational Interest Measures 1973

Stroop Color Word Test 1973
PN 508 **SC** 50250
B Perceptual Measures 1973
R Stroop Effect 1988

Stroop Effect 1988
PN 705 **SC** 50255
SN Interference in information or perceptual processing due to presentation of stimuli that are contradictory in different dimensions as a measure of cognitive control, e.g., stimulus word "red" printed in the color green.
R Cognitive Discrimination 1973
↓ Interference (Learning) 1967
↓ Perceptual Discrimination 1973
Stimulus Ambiguity 1967
Stroop Color Word Test 1973

Structural Equation Modeling 1994
PN 1256 **SC** 50257
B Mathematical Modeling 1973
R Causal Analysis 1994
↓ Factor Analysis 1967
Factor Structure 1985

Structuralism 1973
PN 363 **SC** 50260
B History of Psychology 1967
Psychological Theories 2001

Structured Clinical Interview 2001
PN 130 **SC** 50263
UF SCID
B Interview Schedules 2001
Psychodiagnostic Interview 1973
R ↓ Mental Disorders 1967
↓ Psychodiagnosis 1967
↓ Psychodiagnostic Typologies 1967
↓ Psychological Assessment 1997

Structured Overview
Use Advance Organizers

Strychnine 1973
PN 141 **SC** 50270
B Alkaloids 1973
Analeptic Drugs 1973

Student Activism 1973
PN 273 **SC** 50280
UF Activism (Student)
Protest (Student)
Student Protest
B Activism 2003
R Social Demonstrations 1973

Student Adjustment
Use School Adjustment

Student Admission Criteria 1973
PN 961 **SC** 50290
UF Admission Criteria (Student)
R Academic Aptitude 1973
↓ Education 1967
↓ Entrance Examinations 1973

Student Attitudes 1967
PN 20129 **SC** 50300
SN Attitudes of, not toward, students.
B Attitudes 1967
Student Characteristics 1982
R ↓ Education 1967
School Phobia 1973
School Refusal 1994

Student Attrition 1991
PN 193 **SC** 50301
SN Reduction in students enrolled in school as a result of transfers or dropouts.
B School Enrollment 1973
R School Attendance 1973
↓ School Dropouts 1967
School Expulsion 1973
School Leavers 1988
School Retention 1994
↓ Students 1967

Student Characteristics 1982
PN 4423 **SC** 50303
SN Distinguishing traits or qualities of a student.
N Student Attitudes 1967
R ↓ Education 1967
↓ Students 1967

Student Engagement 2006
PN 148 **SC** 50304
SN Degree to which students are interested and involved in learning, school or classroom activities, and/or school-related extracurricular activities.
HN This term was introduced in May 2006. Relevant records were re-indexed with this term. The posting note reflects the number of records that were reindexed.
UF Academic Engagement
School Engagement
R ↓ Involvement 1973
↓ Participation 1973
Teacher Student Interaction 1973
Time On Task 1988

Student Personnel Services 1978
PN 1810 **SC** 50305
SN Services offered by schools, colleges, or universities related to health, housing, employment, or other student concerns.
R ↓ Counseling 1967
↓ Education 1967

Student Personnel Services — (cont'd)
Educational Counseling 1967
Educational Financial Assistance 1973
↓ Mental Health Services 1978
Occupational Guidance 1967
School Based Intervention 2003
School Counseling 1982

Student Protest
Use Student Activism

Student Records 1978
PN 92 **SC** 50315
UF Academic Records
R ↓ Education 1967

Student Teachers 1973
PN 1620 **SC** 50320
SN Students engaged in practice teaching under the supervision of a cooperating master teacher as partial fulfillment of an education degree.
B Teachers 1967
R Cooperating Teachers 1978
Education Students 1982
Preservice Teachers 1982

Student Teaching 1973
PN 340 **SC** 50330
SN Practice of college students teaching under the supervision of a regular teacher in a real school situation. Part of the graduation requirement for education majors.
B Teacher Education 1967
R Cooperating Teachers 1978
Preservice Teachers 1982

Students 1967
PN 9283 **SC** 50340
SN Persons attending school. Use a more specific term if possible.
N Business Students 1973
Classmates 1973
↓ College Students 1967
Dental Students 1973
↓ Elementary School Students 1967
Graduate Students 1967
High School Students 1967
International Students 2007
Junior High School Students 1971
Kindergarten Students 1973
Law Students 1978
Medical Students 1967
Postgraduate Students 1973
↓ Preschool Students 1982
Reentry Students 1985
Seminarians 1973
Special Education Students 1973
Transfer Students 1973
Vocational School Students 1973
R ↓ Education 1967
School Retention 1994
Student Attrition 1991
↓ Student Characteristics 1982

Students T Test
Use T Test

Studies (Followup)
Use Followup Studies

Studies (Longitudinal)
Use Longitudinal Studies

Study Abroad 2007
PN 171 **SC** 50375
HN In April 2007, this term was created to replace the discontinued term FOREIGN STUDY. FOREIGN STUDY was removed from all records containing it, and was replaced with STUDY ABROAD.
UF Foreign Study
International Study
B Educational Programs 1973
R International Students 2007
Tourism 2003

Study Habits 1973
PN 2040 **SC** 50380
UF Study Skills
R Advance Organizers 1985
↓ Education 1967
Homework 1988
↓ Learning Strategies 1991
Note Taking 1991
Test Taking 1985
Time Management 1994

Study Skills
Use Study Habits

Stuttering 1967
PN 2763 **SC** 50390
HN In 1982, this term replaced the discontinued term STAMMERING. In 2000, STAMMERING was removed from all records containing it, and replaced with STUTTERING.
UF Stammering
B Speech Disorders 1967

Subconscious 1973
PN 268 **SC** 50410
B Psychoanalytic Personality Factors 1973

Subcortical Lesions
Use Brain Lesions

Subculture (Anthropological) 1973
PN 688 **SC** 50430
UF Hippies
B Culture (Anthropological) 1967
R Cosmetic Techniques 2001
Popular Culture 2003

Subcutaneous Injections 1973
PN 79 **SC** 50440
B Injections 1973

Subjectivity 1994
PN 1508 **SC** 50450
HN Use OBJECTIVITY to access references from 1973-1993.
B Personality Traits 1967
R Objectivity 1973

Sublimation 1973
PN 198 **SC** 50460
B Defense Mechanisms 1967

Subliminal Perception 1973
PN 449 **SC** 50470
SN Perceptual response to a stimulus that is below the threshold for conscious detection.

Subliminal Perception — (cont'd)
B Perception 1967
R Subliminal Stimulation 1985

Subliminal Stimulation 1985
PN 361 **SC** 50475
SN Below-threshold stimulation.
B Stimulation 1967
R Subliminal Perception 1973

Submarines 1973
PN 51 **SC** 50480
B Water Transportation 1973

Submissiveness
Use Obedience

Submucous Plexus
Use Autonomic Ganglia

Substance Abuse
Use Drug Abuse

Substance Abuse Prevention
Use Drug Abuse Prevention

Substance P 1985
PN 397 **SC** 50527
B Neuropeptides 2003
Neurotransmitters 1985
R Neurokinins 1997

Substantia Nigra 1994
PN 324 **SC** 50530
HN Use MESENCEPHALON to access references from 1973-1993.
B Basal Ganglia 1973
Mesencephalon 1973

Subtests 1973
PN 1429 **SC** 50540
B Measurement 1967
R ↓ Testing Methods 1967

Subtypes (Disorders) 2004
PN 707 **SC** 50545
SN Subtypes of a particular disorder, e.g., Bulimia Nervosa Purging Type or Non-purging Type.
HN This term was introduced in June 2004. Relevant records were re-indexed with this term. The posting note reflects the number of records that were re-indexed.
R Diagnostic and Statistical Manual 1994
↓ Disorders 1967
↓ Psychodiagnostic Typologies 1967

Suburban Environments 1967
PN 689 **SC** 50550
B Social Environments 1973

Subvocalization 1973
PN 101 **SC** 50555
SN Covert speech behavior that involves movement of the tongue, mouth, and larynx without producing audible sounds.
B Vocalization 1967
R Self Talk 1988

Success
Use Achievement

Successive Contrast
Use Afterimage

Succinylcholine 1973
PN 17 **SC** 50580
B Muscle Relaxing Drugs 1973
R ↓ Choline 1973

Sucking 1978
PN 466 **SC** 50585
B Motor Processes 1967
R Animal Drinking Behavior 1973
Animal Feeding Behavior 1973
↓ Drinking Behavior 1978
Food Intake 1967
Weaning 1973

Sudden Infant Death 1982
PN 294 **SC** 50587
SN Unexpected death of an apparently healthy infant during sleep.
UF Crib Death
R ↓ Apnea 1973
↓ Death and Dying 1967
Sleep Apnea 1991
↓ Syndromes 1973

Suffering 1973
PN 1006 **SC** 50590
B Emotional States 1973
R Distress 1973
Grief 1973
↓ Pain 1967
Torture 1988

Suffocation
Use Anoxia

Sugars 1973
PN 1143 **SC** 50600
B Carbohydrates 1973
N ↓ Glucose 1973
R Saccharin 1973

Suggestibility 1967
PN 1284 **SC** 50610
B Consciousness Disturbances 1973
Personality Traits 1967
R Catalepsy 1973
False Memory 1997
↓ Hysteria 1967
↓ Interpersonal Influences 1967
Posthypnotic Suggestions 1994

Suicidal Ideation 1991
PN 2693 **SC** 50605
SN Thoughts of or an unusual preoccupation with suicide.
B Ideation 1973
R Attempted Suicide 1973
↓ Suicide 1967

Suicide 1967
PN 12431 **SC** 50620
B Self Destructive Behavior 1985
N Assisted Suicide 1997
R Attempted Suicide 1973
↓ Death and Dying 1967
↓ Mental Disorders 1967
Psychological Autopsy 1988
Suicidal Ideation 1991
Suicide Prevention 1973

Suicide (Attempted)
Use Attempted Suicide

Suicide Prevention 1973
PN 1932 **SC** 50640
B Crisis Intervention 1973
Prevention 1973
R Attempted Suicide 1973
↓ Suicide 1967
Suicide Prevention Centers 1973

Suicide Prevention Centers 1973
PN 108 **SC** 50650
B Community Facilities 1973
Crisis Intervention Services 1973
Mental Health Programs 1973
R Community Mental Health Centers 1973
Hot Line Services 1973
↓ Prevention 1973
Suicide Prevention 1973

Sulpiride 1973
PN 470 **SC** 50660
B Antidepressant Drugs 1971
Antiemetic Drugs 1973
Dopamine Antagonists 1982
Neuroleptic Drugs 1973

Summer Camps (Recreation) 1973
PN 177 **SC** 50670
UF Day Camps (Recreation)
Recreational Day Camps
B Recreation 1967
R Camping 1973
Vacationing 1973

Superego 1973
PN 574 **SC** 50690
B Psychoanalytic Personality Factors 1973
N Conscience 1967

Superintendents (School)
Use School Superintendents

Superior Colliculus 1973
PN 744 **SC** 50700
B Mesencephalon 1973

Superiority (Emotional)
Use Emotional Superiority

Superstitions 1973
PN 235 **SC** 50720
B Social Influences 1967
R Astrology 1973
↓ Attitudes 1967
Irrational Beliefs 1982
↓ Parapsychological Phenomena 1973
↓ Religious Beliefs 1973
Taboos 1973

Supervising Teachers
Use Cooperating Teachers

Supervision (Professional)
Use Professional Supervision

Supervisor Employee Interaction 1997
PN 994 **SC** 50729
UF Employee Supervisor Interaction
Manager Employee Interaction
B Employee Interaction 1988
R Groupware 2003
↓ Human Resource Management 2003
Labor Management Relations 1967
↓ Management Methods 1973
↓ Management Personnel 1973

Supervisor Employee Interaction — (cont'd)
Mentor 1985
Psychological Contracts 2003

Supervisors
Use Management Personnel

Supply and Demand 2004
PN 156 **SC** 50735
HN This term was introduced in June 2004. Relevant records were re-indexed with this term. The posting note reflects the number of records that were re-indexed.
R ↓ Consumer Behavior 1967
↓ Economics 1985
Labor Market 2007

Supply Chain Management 2007
PN 13 **SC** 50737
SN Oversight or coordination of the supply chain process that enables the delivery of products to the consumer.
HN This term was introduced in April 2007. Relevant records were re-indexed with this term. The posting note reflects the number of records that were re-indexed.
R ↓ Business 1967
Business Management 1973
Supply Chains 2007

Supply Chains 2007
PN 32 **SC** 50738
SN The process by which materials, information, and finances move from supplier to manufacturer to wholesaler to retailer to consumer.
HN This term was introduced in April 2007. Relevant records were re-indexed with this term. The posting note reflects the number of records that were re-indexed.
R ↓ Business 1967
Product Design 1997
Supply Chain Management 2007

Support Groups 1991
PN 2310 **SC** 50740
SN Groups, organizations, or institutions providing social and emotional support to an individual. Compare SOCIAL NETWORKS and SELF HELP TECHNIQUES.
HN Consider SOCIAL SUPPORT NETWORKS to access references from 1982-1990.
N ↓ Twelve Step Programs 1997
R ↓ Community Services 1967
↓ Counseling 1967
Employee Assistance Programs 1985
Group Counseling 1973
↓ Group Psychotherapy 1967
↓ Mental Health Services 1978
Outreach Programs 1997
↓ Rehabilitation 1967
↓ Self Help Techniques 1982
↓ Social Networks 1994
↓ Social Services 1982
Social Support 2004

Supported Employment 1994
PN 539 **SC** 50745
SN Competitive employment in an integrated setting for persons with disabilities who require ongoing support to perform their jobs.
B Vocational Rehabilitation 1967
R Community Mental Health Services 1978
Disabled Personnel 1997

Supported Employment — (cont'd)
Employability 1973
↓ Employee Skills 1973
↓ Employment Status 1982
↓ Human Resource Management 2003
Independent Living Programs 1991
Sheltered Workshops 1967
Work Adjustment Training 1991

Supportive Psychotherapy 1997
PN 236 **SC** 50750
SN Psychotherapy aimed at supporting or reinforcing strengths and coping mechanisms, rather than interpreting or uncovering deeper psychological conflicts. May entail guidance, reassurance, advice, encouragement, and assistance.
HN Use PSYCHOTHERAPY to access references from 1973-1996.
B Psychotherapy 1967
R Expressive Psychotherapy 1973

Suppression (Conditioned)
Use Conditioned Suppression

Suppression (Defense Mechanism) 1973
PN 236 **SC** 50770
B Defense Mechanisms 1967
R Forgetting 1973
Repression (Defense Mechanism) 1967

Surgeons 1973
PN 228 **SC** 50780
UF Neurosurgeons
B Physicians 1967
R Gynecologists 1973
Neurologists 1973
Obstetricians 1978
Pathologists 1973

Surgery 1971
PN 3463 **SC** 50790
UF Operation (Surgery)
B Medical Sciences 1967
Physical Treatment Methods 1973
N ↓ Amputation 1973
Circumcision 2001
Cochlear Implants 1994
Colostomy 1973
Dental Surgery 1973
↓ Endocrine Gland Surgery 1973
Heart Surgery 1973
Hysterectomy 1973
Induced Abortion 1971
↓ Neurosurgery 1973
Organ Transplantation 1973
Plastic Surgery 1973
Sex Change 1988
↓ Stereotaxic Techniques 1973
Vasectomy 1973
R Afferent Stimulation 1973
Biopsy 1973
↓ Lesions 1967
Postsurgical Complications 1973

Surgical Complications
Use Postsurgical Complications

Surgical Patients 1973
PN 2027 **SC** 50810
B Patients 1967

Surrogate Parents (Humans) 1973
PN 174 **SC** 50820
B Parents 1967
R Foster Parents 1973

Surveys 1967
PN 3746 **SC** 50830
B Measurement 1967
N Consumer Surveys 1973
Mail Surveys 1994
Telephone Surveys 1994
R Data Collection 1982
Likert Scales 1994
↓ Methodology 1967
Needs Assessment 1985
↓ Questionnaires 1967

Survival Instinct
Use Self Preservation

Survivors 1994
PN 3103 **SC** 50850
SN Family members, significant others, or individuals surviving traumatic life events.
N Holocaust Survivors 1988

Susceptibility (Disorders) 1973
PN 2952 **SC** 50880
SN Vulnerability to mental or physical disorders due to genetic, immunologic, or other characteristics. Consider also PREDISPOSITION.
UF Vulnerability (Disorders)
R At Risk Populations 1985
Biological Markers 1991
Coronary Prone Behavior 1982
Diathesis Stress Model 2005
↓ Disorders 1967
↓ Mental Disorders 1967
↓ Physical Disorders 1997
Predisposition 1973
Premorbidity 1978
Risk Factors 2001

Susceptibility (Hypnotic)
Use Hypnotic Susceptibility

Suspension (School)
Use School Suspension

Suspicion 1973
PN 242 **SC** 50910
UF Distrust
B Emotional States 1973
R Doubt 1973
Uncertainty 1991

Sustained Attention 1997
PN 461 **SC** 50915
SN Focusing or attending to one or more stimuli over an extended period.
B Attention 1967
N Attention Span 1973
Concentration 1982
Vigilance 1967

Swallowing 1988
PN 202 **SC** 50920
B Motor Processes 1967
R Digestion 1973
Dysphagia 2003

Swallowing — (cont'd)
↓ Ingestion 2001

Sweat 1973
PN 52 **SC** 50930
UF Perspiration
B Body Fluids 1973
R Sweating 1973

Sweating 1973
PN 98 **SC** 50940
B Secretion (Gland) 1973
R ↓ Skin Disorders 1973
Sweat 1973

Sweetness
Use Taste Perception

Swimming 1973
PN 918 **SC** 50970
B Motor Processes 1967
Recreation 1967
Sports 1967

Syllables 1973
PN 1383 **SC** 50990
B Phonology 1973
R Consonants 1973
Phonetics 1967
Vowels 1973

Syllogistic Reasoning
Use Inductive Deductive Reasoning

Symbiosis (Biological)
Use Biological Symbiosis

Symbiotic Infantile Psychosis 1973
PN 23 **SC** 51020
B Childhood Psychosis 1967
R Childhood Schizophrenia 1967
Mother Child Relations 1967

Symbolic Interactionism 1988
PN 551 **SC** 51025
SN Sociological theory that assumes that self concept is created through interpretation of symbolic gestures, words, actions, and appearances expressed by others during social interaction.
R Role Taking 1982
↓ Self Concept 1967
↓ Social Interaction 1967
Sociolinguistics 1985
↓ Sociology 1967

Symbolism 1967
PN 3482 **SC** 51030
R ↓ Communication 1967
↓ Figurative Language 1985
↓ Language 1967
Metaphor 1982
↓ Semiotics 1985

Sympathectomy 1973
PN 57 **SC** 51050
B Neurosurgery 1973
R ↓ Psychosurgery 1973

Sympathetic Nervous System 1973
PN 584 **SC** 51060
B Autonomic Nervous System 1967
N Baroreceptors 1973
R ↓ Adrenergic Blocking Drugs 1973
↓ Adrenergic Drugs 1973

Sympathetic Nervous System — (cont'd)
↓ Sympatholytic Drugs 1973
↓ Sympathomimetic Drugs 1973

Sympatholytic Drugs 1973
PN 28 **SC** 51080
UF Antiadrenergic Drugs
B Drugs 1967
N Hydralazine 1973
Reserpine 1967
R ↓ Adrenergic Blocking Drugs 1973
↓ Sympathetic Nervous System 1973
↓ Sympathomimetic Drugs 1973

Sympathomimetic Amines 1973
PN 13 **SC** 51090
B Amines 1973
Sympathomimetic Drugs 1973
N ↓ Amphetamine 1967
↓ Catecholamines 1973
Dextroamphetamine 1973
Ephedrine 1973
Methoxamine 1973
Phenmetrazine 1973
Tyramine 1973

Sympathomimetic Drugs 1973
PN 99 **SC** 51100
B Drugs 1967
N Fenfluramine 1973
Isoproterenol 1973
↓ Sympathomimetic Amines 1973
R ↓ Adrenergic Drugs 1973
Prostaglandins 1982
↓ Sympathetic Nervous System 1973
↓ Sympatholytic Drugs 1973

Sympathy 1973
PN 274 **SC** 51110
B Emotional States 1973

Symptom Checklists 1991
PN 422 **SC** 51124
B Measurement 1967
R ↓ Diagnosis 1967
Health Complaints 1997
Psychiatric Symptoms 1997
↓ Screening 1982
↓ Symptoms 1967

Symptom Prescription
Use Paradoxical Techniques

Symptom Remission 1973
PN 208 **SC** 51130
B Remission (Disorders) 1973
R Psychiatric Symptoms 1997
↓ Symptoms 1967

Symptoms 1967
PN 23562 **SC** 51140
N Acting Out 1967
Anhedonia 1985
Anoxia 1973
Aphagia 1973
Apraxia 1973
↓ Asthenia 1973
Ataxia 1973
Aura 1973
Automatism 1973
Body Rocking 1973
Catalepsy 1973
Catatonia 1973

Symptoms — (cont'd)
Coma 1973
Delirium 1973
Depersonalization 1973
Distractibility 1973
↓ Dyskinesia 1973
↓ Dyspnea 1973
Extrapyramidal Symptoms 1994
Fatigue 1967
↓ Headache 1973
Hematoma 1973
↓ Hemorrhage 1973
Hyperglycemia 1985
Hyperkinesis 1973
Hyperphagia 1973
Hyperthermia 1973
Hyperventilation 1973
Hypoglycemia 1973
Hypothermia 1973
Insomnia 1973
Nausea 1973
↓ Pain 1967
Positive and Negative Symptoms 1997
Prodrome 2004
Pruritus 1973
Psychiatric Symptoms 1997
↓ Respiratory Distress 1973
Restlessness 1973
Scratching 1973
↓ Seizures 2005
Shock 1967
↓ Spasms 1973
Syncope 1973
Tics 1973
Tremor 1973
↓ Underweight 1973
Vertigo 1973
Vomiting 1973
R Akathisia 1991
↓ Behavior Disorders 1971
Binge Eating 1991
Capgras Syndrome 1985
↓ Digestive System Disorders 1973
↓ Disorders 1967
↓ Eating Disorders 1997
Fecal Incontinence 1973
Female Sexual Dysfunction 2005
Health Complaints 1997
Hypersomnia 1994
Inflammation 2004
↓ Mental Disorders 1967
Metabolic Syndrome 2007
↓ Movement Disorders 1985
↓ Nervous System Disorders 1967
Parkinsonism 1994
↓ Physical Disorders 1997
Physiological Correlates 1967
Risk Factors 2001
Somatization 1994
↓ Somatoform Disorders 2001
Stereotyped Behavior 1973
Symptom Checklists 1991
Symptom Remission 1973
Urinary Incontinence 1973
Wandering Behavior 1991

Synapses 1973
PN 2556 **SC** 51150
B Nerve Endings 1973
R Neurotransmission 2003

Synaptic Plasticity
Use Neural Plasticity

Synaptic Transmission
Use Neurotransmission

Syncope 1973
PN 131 **SC** 51160
SN A temporary loss of consciousness and postural tone due to reduced blood flow to the brain.
UF Fainting
B Blood Pressure Disorders 1973
Symptoms 1967
R Shock 1967
Vertigo 1973

Syndromes 1973
PN 5877 **SC** 51170
N Addisons Disease 1973
AIDS 2006
Aspergers Syndrome 1991
Battered Child Syndrome 1973
Capgras Syndrome 1985
Chronic Fatigue Syndrome 1997
Creutzfeldt Jakob Syndrome 1994
Crying Cat Syndrome 1973
↓ Culture Bound Syndromes 2004
Cushings Syndrome 1973
Delirium Tremens 1973
Downs Syndrome 1967
Fetal Alcohol Syndrome 1985
Fragile X Syndrome 1994
Irritable Bowel Syndrome 1991
Kleine Levin Syndrome 2001
Klinefelters Syndrome 1973
Menieres Disease 1973
Metabolic Syndrome 2007
Neuroleptic Malignant Syndrome 1988
↓ Organic Brain Syndromes 1973
Prader Willi Syndrome 1991
Premenstrual Syndrome 2003
Rett Syndrome 1994
↓ Senile Dementia 1973
Testicular Feminization Syndrome 1973
Turners Syndrome 1973
Wernickes Syndrome 1973
Williams Syndrome 2003
R ↓ Disorders 1967
↓ Epidemics 2001
↓ Mental Disorders 1967
Myofascial Pain 1991
↓ Physical Disorders 1997
Sudden Infant Death 1982

Synesthesia 2003
PN 143 **SC** 51172
SN Condition in which experiences that normally arouse sensation in one particular sensory modality also arouse sensation in another (e.g., colors may be experienced as odor).
HN This term was introduced in June 2003. Relevant records were re-indexed with this term. The posting note reflects the number of records that were re-indexed.
B Intersensory Processes 1978
R ↓ Sensory System Disorders 2001

Synonyms 1973
PN 130 **SC** 51190
B Semantics 1967
Vocabulary 1967

Synonyms — (cont'd)
R Words (Phonetic Units) 1967

Syntax 1971
PN 4309 **SC** 51220
SN Study and rules of the relation of morphemes to one another as expressions of ideas and as structural components of sentences; the study and science of sentence construction; and, the actual grouping and specific combination and relationship of words in a sentence. Compare GRAMMAR and SENTENCE STRUCTURE.
B Grammar 1967
N ↓ Form Classes (Language) 1973
R Discourse Analysis 1997
Inflection 1973
Morphology (Language) 1973
↓ Phonology 1973
Phrases 1973
↓ Semantics 1967
Sentence Structure 1973
Transformational Generative Grammar 1973

Synthetic Speech 1973
PN 398 **SC** 51230
SN Sounds having similar characteristics and functional properties of natural speech but which are made by means other than natural vocalization mechanisms (e.g., computer-generated speech sounds).
B Speech Processing (Mechanical) 1973

Syphilis 1973
PN 119 **SC** 51240
B Sexually Transmitted Diseases 2003
N Neurosyphilis 1973
R ↓ Congenital Disorders 1973
General Paresis 1973

Systematic Desensitization Therapy 1973
PN 1639 **SC** 51250
UF Desensitization (Systematic)
B Behavior Therapy 1967
Exposure Therapy 1997
R Progressive Relaxation Therapy 1978
Reciprocal Inhibition Therapy 1973
↓ Relaxation Therapy 1978

Systems 1967
PN 1194 **SC** 51270
SN Conceptually broad term referring to interrelated elements acting as or constituting a unified whole. Use a more specific term if possible.
N ↓ Anatomical Systems 1973
Caste System 1973
↓ Communication Systems 1973
↓ Expert Systems 1991
Human Machine Systems 1997
↓ Information Systems 1991
Number Systems 1973
↓ Political Economic Systems 1973
R ↓ Computer Software 1967
↓ Computers 1967
Human Machine Systems Design 1997
Person Environment Fit 1991
Systems Analysis 1973
↓ Systems Design 2003
Systems Theory 1988

Systems Analysis 1973
PN 736 **SC** 51260
B Analysis 1967
R Computer Programming 2001
Human Machine Systems 1997
Human Machine Systems Design 1997
↓ Systems 1967
↓ Systems Design 2003
Systems Theory 1988
Task Analysis 1967

Systems Design 2003
PN 274 **SC** 51262
SN A process of defining the hardware and software architecture, components, modules, interfaces, and data for a system to satisfy specified requirements.
HN This term was introduced in June 2003. Relevant records were re-indexed with this term. The posting note reflects the number of records that were re-indexed.
N Human Machine Systems Design 1997
R Computer Programming 2001
↓ Systems 1967
Systems Analysis 1973

Systems Theory 1988
PN 3582 **SC** 51265
SN Examination of organizations, structures, or procedures from a macroscopic perspective that integrates constituent parts into a whole.
B Theories 1967
R Biopsychosocial Approach 1991
↓ Systems 1967
Systems Analysis 1973

Systolic Pressure 1973
PN 384 **SC** 51280
B Blood Pressure 1967

Szondi Test 1973
PN 55 **SC** 51290
B Projective Personality Measures 1973

T Groups
Use Human Relations Training

T Mazes 1973
PN 125 **SC** 51310
B Mazes 1967

T Test 1973
PN 163 **SC** 51320
UF Students T Test
B Parametric Statistical Tests 1973
R ↓ Central Tendency Measures 1973
Statistical Significance 1973

Tabes Dorsalis
Use Neurosyphilis

Taboos 1973
PN 224 **SC** 51330
B Social Influences 1967
R Animism 1973
Cannibalism 2003
Ethnology 1967
↓ Rites of Passage 1973
Superstitions 1973
Transcultural Psychiatry 1973

Tachistoscopes 1973
PN 44 **SC** 51340
SN Apparatus used in experimental studies for presentation of visual stimuli for controlled stimulus intervals, intensities, and durations.
B Apparatus 1967

Tachistoscopic Presentation 1973
PN 477 **SC** 51350
B Stimulus Presentation Methods 1973
Visual Stimulation 1973

Tachycardia 1973
PN 110 **SC** 51360
SN General term describing any excessive or abnormally rapid heart action.
UF Rapid Heart Rate
B Arrhythmias (Heart) 1973
R Hyperthyroidism 1973

Tactual Discrimination
Use Tactual Perception

Tactual Displays 1973
PN 119 **SC** 51380
SN Materials or apparatus designed to present information or patterns by means of touch or manipulation. Also, any information or patterns conveyed by such means.
B Displays 1967
Tactual Stimulation 1973

Tactual Maps
Use Mobility Aids

Tactual Perception 1967
PN 2670 **SC** 51390
SN Awareness of the qualities or characteristics of objects, substances, or surfaces by means of touch.
UF Tactual Discrimination
Touch
B Cutaneous Sense 1967
N Texture Perception 1982
Vibrotactile Thresholds 1973
R Anesthesia (Feeling) 1973
Braille 1978
Physical Contact 1982

Tactual Stimulation 1973
PN 1574 **SC** 51400
SN Perceptual arousal or excitation of an organism by means of touch.
B Somesthetic Stimulation 1973
N Massage 2001
Tactual Displays 1973

Tailored Testing
Use Adaptive Testing

Talent
Use Ability

Talented
Use Gifted

Tantrums 1973
PN 99 **SC** 51440
B Behavior Problems 1967
R ↓ Anger 1967
↓ Emotional Control 1973

Tape Recorders 1973
PN 101 **SC** 51450
UF Recorders (Tape)
B Apparatus 1967
N Videotape Recorders 1973

Tardiness 2003
PN 42 **SC** 51455
HN This term was introduced in June 2003. Relevant records were re-indexed with this term. The posting note reflects the number of records that were re-indexed.
UF Lateness
R Employee Absenteeism 1973
School Attendance 1973

Tardive Dyskinesia 1988
PN 1217 **SC** 51460
SN Abnormal involuntary movements caused by the long term use of neuroleptic drugs.
B Dyskinesia 1973
R ↓ Drug Therapy 1967
↓ Neuroleptic Drugs 1973
↓ Side Effects (Drug) 1973

Task Analysis 1967
PN 2039 **SC** 51470
B Analysis 1967
R Constant Time Delay 1997
Job Analysis 1967
Systems Analysis 1973
Task Complexity 1973

Task Complexity 1973
PN 5219 **SC** 51480
UF Complexity (Task)
Task Difficulty
R Dual Task Performance 2006
Task Analysis 1967

Task Difficulty
Use Task Complexity

Taste Aversion Conditioning
Use Aversion Conditioning

Taste Buds 1973
PN 246 **SC** 51500
B Sense Organs 1973
Sensory Neurons 1973
Tongue 1973
R Chemoreceptors 1973
Taste Disorders 2001

Taste Discrimination
Use Taste Perception

Taste Disorders 2001
PN 11 **SC** 51515
SN Disorders involving abnormal gustatory function or perception.
B Sense Organ Disorders 1973
R Anosmia 1973
Chemoreceptors 1973
↓ Sense Organs 1973
↓ Sensory Neurons 1973
Taste Buds 1973
↓ Tongue 1973

Taste Perception 1967
PN 4220 **SC** 51520
UF Bitterness
Gustatory Perception
Saltiness

Taste Perception — (cont'd)
Sourness
Sweetness
Taste Discrimination
B Perception 1967
R ↓ Olfactory Perception 1967

Taste Stimulation 1967
PN 1008 **SC** 51530
B Perceptual Stimulation 1973

Tattoos
Use Cosmetic Techniques

Taurine 1982
PN 75 **SC** 51545
SN Suspected neurotransmitter or membrane stabilizer located in the posterior pituitary gland as well as other mammalian tissue.
B Acids 1973
R Bile 1973

Taxation 1985
PN 311 **SC** 51547
R ↓ Economy 1973
Government 1967
Income (Economic) 1973

Taxonomies 1973
PN 5018 **SC** 51550
UF Classification Systems
Typologies (General)
R Ontologies 2007
↓ Psychodiagnostic Typologies 1967

Tay Sachs Disease 2003
PN 30 **SC** 51560
HN In June 2003, this term replaced the discontinued term AMAUROTIC FAMILIAL IDIOCY. AMAUROTIC FAMILIAL IDIOCY was removed from all records containing it and replaced with TAY SACHS DISEASE.
UF Amaurotic Familial Idiocy
Familial Idiocy (Amaurotic)
B Brain Disorders 1967
Genetic Disorders 1973
Lipid Metabolism Disorders 1973
Mental Retardation 1967
Neonatal Disorders 1973

Taylor Manifest Anxiety Scale 1973
PN 36 **SC** 51570
B Nonprojective Personality Measures 1973

Tea
Use Beverages (Nonalcoholic)

Teacher Accreditation
Use Accreditation (Education Personnel)

Teacher Aides 1973
PN 181 **SC** 51600
SN Paraprofessional school personnel who assist teachers in the instructional process or other classroom duties.
B Educational Personnel 1973
Paraprofessional Personnel 1973

Teacher Attitudes 1967
PN 11697 **SC** 51610
SN Attitudes of, not toward, teachers.
B Attitudes 1967
Teacher Characteristics 1973

Teacher Attitudes — (cont'd)
N Teacher Expectations 1978
R Parent School Relationship 1982
Teacher Personality 1973
Teacher Student Interaction 1973

Teacher Characteristics 1973
PN 5624 **SC** 51615
UF Teacher Effectiveness
N ↓ Teacher Attitudes 1967
Teacher Personality 1973
R ↓ Education 1967
Teacher Effectiveness Evaluation 1978
Teacher Expectations 1978
Teacher Student Interaction 1973
↓ Teachers 1967
↓ Teaching 1967

Teacher Education 1967
PN 5763 **SC** 51620
UF Teacher Training
B Education 1967
N Inservice Teacher Education 1973
Student Teaching 1973
R Cooperating Teachers 1978
Education Students 1982
Practicum Supervision 1978
Preservice Teachers 1982

Teacher Effectiveness
Use Teacher Characteristics

Teacher Effectiveness Evaluation 1978
PN 1674 **SC** 51625
SN Techniques, materials, or the procedural aspects of judging teachers' performance by peers, students, or others based on stated criteria.
HN Use PERSONNEL EVALUATION and TEACHERS (or a more specific term, e.g., COLLEGE TEACHERS) to access references from 1973-1977.
B Personnel Evaluation 1973
R Course Evaluation 1978
Educational Quality 1997
↓ Teacher Characteristics 1973

Teacher Expectations 1978
PN 833 **SC** 51627
B Expectations 1967
Teacher Attitudes 1967
R ↓ Teacher Characteristics 1973
Teacher Student Interaction 1973

Teacher Personality 1973
PN 534 **SC** 51630
B Teacher Characteristics 1973
R ↓ Personality 1967
↓ Teacher Attitudes 1967
Teacher Student Interaction 1973

Teacher Recruitment 1973
PN 83 **SC** 51640
SN Process of attracting candidates to the teaching profession or finding teachers to fill vacancies.
UF Recruitment (Teachers)
B Personnel Recruitment 1973

Teacher Student Interaction 1973
PN 6390 **SC** 51650
R Classroom Discipline 1973
↓ Education 1967
Student Engagement 2006
↓ Teacher Attitudes 1967
↓ Teacher Characteristics 1973
Teacher Expectations 1978

Teacher Student Interaction — (cont'd)
Teacher Personality 1973

Teacher Tenure 1973
PN 163 **SC** 51670
UF Tenure (Teacher)
B Occupational Tenure 1973
R ↓ Education 1967

Teacher Training
Use Teacher Education

Teachers 1967
PN 12923 **SC** 51690
UF Classroom Teachers
Instructors
Tutors
B Educational Personnel 1973
N College Teachers 1973
Cooperating Teachers 1978
Elementary School Teachers 1973
High School Teachers 1973
Junior High School Teachers 1973
Middle School Teachers 2003
Preschool Teachers 1985
Preservice Teachers 1982
Resource Teachers 1973
Special Education Teachers 1973
Student Teachers 1973
Vocational Education Teachers 1988
R ↓ Teacher Characteristics 1973

Teaching 1967
PN 9506 **SC** 51700
UF Classroom Instruction
Instruction
Pedagogy
N ↓ Instructional Media 1967
↓ Teaching Methods 1967
R Bilingual Education 1978
Cooperative Learning 1994
Course Evaluation 1978
↓ Education 1967
↓ Teacher Characteristics 1973

Teaching Machines 1973
PN 106 **SC** 51730
SN Mechanical, electronic, or electrically controlled apparatus for the presentation of programed instructional material or texts for independent, self-paced education. Compare COMPUTER ASSISTED INSTRUCTION.
B Instructional Media 1967
R ↓ Computer Assisted Instruction 1973
Programmed Instruction 2001

Teaching Methods 1967
PN 24106 **SC** 51740
B Teaching 1967
N Advance Organizers 1985
↓ Audiovisual Instruction 1973
↓ Computer Assisted Instruction 1973
Directed Discussion Method 1973
Discovery Teaching Method 1973
Educational Field Trips 1973
↓ Experiential Learning 1997
Group Instruction 1973
Individualized Instruction 1973
Lecture Method 1973
Lesson Plans 1973
Montessori Method 1973
Nondirected Discussion Method 1973
Open Classroom Method 1973
Programmed Instruction 2001

Teaching Methods — (cont'd)
Scaffolding 2005
Service Learning 2007
Team Teaching Method 1973
↓ Tutoring 1973
R Collaborative Learning 2007
Constant Time Delay 1997
Cooperative Learning 1994
↓ Education 1967
Educational Therapy 1997
Home Schooling 1994
Initial Teaching Alphabet 1973
Mastery Learning 1985
↓ Nontraditional Education 1982
↓ Prompting 1997
Questioning 1982

Team Teaching Method 1973
PN 200 **SC** 51750
B Teaching Methods 1967
R Open Classroom Method 1973
↓ Teams 1988

Teams 1988
PN 3286 **SC** 51751
N ↓ Work Teams 2001
R Athletic Performance 1991
Athletic Training 1991
Collaborative Learning 2007
College Athletes 1994
Cooperative Learning 1994
↓ Group Dynamics 1967
Interdisciplinary Treatment Approach 1973
↓ Management Methods 1973
↓ Personnel 1967
↓ Sports 1967
Team Teaching Method 1973

Teasing 2003
PN 126 **SC** 51752
SN To annoy, taunt, or joke with in a manner that is considered either petty, harassing, or playful.
HN This term was introduced in June 2003. Relevant records were re-indexed with this term. The posting note reflects the number of records that were re-indexed.
B Social Interaction 1967
R Bullying 2003
Jokes 1973
↓ Peer Relations 1967
Victimization 1973

Technical Education Teachers
Use Vocational Education Teachers

Technical Personnel 1978
PN 468 **SC** 51755
B Business and Industrial Personnel 1967
N Technical Service Personnel 1973
R ↓ Service Personnel 1991

Technical Schools 1973
PN 196 **SC** 51760
SN Schools that teach specific job skills, usually at the postsecondary level, often emphasizing underlying sciences and supporting mathematics as well as skills, methods, materials, and processes of a specialized field of technology.

Technical Schools — (cont'd)
UF Vocational Schools
B Schools 1967

Technical Service Personnel 1973
PN 147 **SC** 51770
UF Repairmen
B Service Personnel 1991
Technical Personnel 1978
R ↓ Blue Collar Workers 1973
↓ Business and Industrial Personnel 1967
↓ Nonprofessional Personnel 1982

Technological Innovation
Use Innovation

Technology 1973
PN 8072 **SC** 51805
N Assistive Technology 2007
↓ Biotechnology 2007
↓ Information Technology 2007
Nanotechnology 2007
Nuclear Technology 1985
Technology Transfer 2007
R Digital Divide 2007
↓ Electronic Communication 2001
Groupware 2003
Industrialization 1973
Innovation 2007
↓ Sciences 1967

Technology Transfer 2007
PN 98 **SC** 58113
SN Process by which technology is shared among industries, universities, or other public, and private sectors.
HN This term was introduced in April 2007. Relevant records were re-indexed with this term. The posting note reflects the number of records that were re-indexed.
B Technology 1973
R Information Dissemination 2005
Information Services 1988
Knowledge Management 2005

Teenage Fathers
Use Adolescent Fathers

Teenage Mothers
Use Adolescent Mothers

Teenage Pregnancy
Use Adolescent Pregnancy

Teeth (Anatomy) 1973
PN 310 **SC** 51820
B Digestive System 1967
R Mouth (Anatomy) 1967

Teeth Grinding
Use Bruxism

Tegmentum 1991
PN 729 **SC** 51835
UF Ventral Tegmental Area
B Mesencephalon 1973
N Periaqueductal Gray 1985

Telecommunications Media 1973
PN 785 **SC** 51840
B Communications Media 1973
N Radio 1973
Telephone Systems 1973
↓ Television 1967

Telecommunications Media — (cont'd)
Television Advertising 1973
R Distance Education 2003
Internet 2001
Online Therapy 2003
Telecommuting 2003
Teleconferencing 1997
Telemedicine 2003
Telemetry 1973

Telecommuting 2003
PN 85 **SC** 51842
SN Working at home via computer and telecommunications media.
HN This term was introduced in June 2003. Relevant records were re-indexed with this term. The posting note reflects the number of records that were re-indexed.
UF Work at Home
R Commuting (Travel) 1985
↓ Telecommunications Media 1973
Teleconferencing 1997
Virtual Teams 2007
↓ Working Conditions 1973

Teleconferencing 1997
PN 370 **SC** 51845
SN Communication between persons remote from one another by means of a telecommunication system with audio and/or visual links.
UF Computer Conferencing
R Groupware 2003
↓ Telecommunications Media 1973
Telecommuting 2003
Telephone Systems 1973
↓ Television 1967
Virtual Classrooms 2007
Virtual Teams 2007

Telehealth
Use Telemedicine

Telekinesis
Use Psychokinesis

Telemedicine 2003
PN 529 **SC** 51858
SN Provision of health care via various forms of telecommunications media.
HN This term was introduced in June 2003. Relevant records were re-indexed with this term. The posting note reflects the number of records that were re-indexed.
UF Telehealth
B Health Care Delivery 1978
R Computer Assisted Diagnosis 1973
Computer Assisted Therapy 2007
Computer Mediated Communication 2003
↓ Health Care Services 1978
Health Knowledge 1994
Internet 2001
↓ Telecommunications Media 1973
↓ Therapeutic Processes 1978

Telemetry 1973
PN 70 **SC** 51860
SN Process of measuring and transmitting quantitative information and recording at a remote location.

Telemetry — (cont'd)
R ↓ Telecommunications Media 1973

Telencephalon 1973
PN 454 **SC** 51870
B Forebrain 1985
N ↓ Basal Ganglia 1973
↓ Cerebral Cortex 1967

Telepathy 1973
PN 209 **SC** 51880
B Parapsychological Phenomena 1973
R ↓ Extrasensory Perception 1967

Telephone Hot Lines
Use Hot Line Services

Telephone Surveys 1994
PN 233 **SC** 51895
B Surveys 1967
R ↓ Consumer Research 1973
Consumer Surveys 1973
Mail Surveys 1994
↓ Methodology 1967
↓ Questionnaires 1967
Telephone Systems 1973

Telephone Systems 1973
PN 1118 **SC** 51900
B Communication Systems 1973
Telecommunications Media 1973
R Teleconferencing 1997
Telephone Surveys 1994

Teletherapy
Use Online Therapy

Televised Instruction 1973
PN 208 **SC** 51910
B Audiovisual Instruction 1973
R Educational Audiovisual Aids 1973
Educational Television 1967

Television 1967
PN 2808 **SC** 51920
B Audiovisual Communications Media 1973
Mass Media 1967
Telecommunications Media 1973
N Closed Circuit Television 1973
Educational Television 1967
Television Advertising 1973
R ↓ Apparatus 1967
↓ News Media 1997
Teleconferencing 1997
Video Display Units 1985

Television Advertising 1973
PN 1095 **SC** 51930
UF Commercials
B Advertising 1967
Audiovisual Communications Media 1973
Telecommunications Media 1973
Television 1967
R Public Service Announcements 2004

Television Viewing 1973
PN 2672 **SC** 51940
B Recreation 1967

Temperament
Use Personality

Temperature (Body)
Use Body Temperature

Temperature Effects 1967
PN 1576 **SC** 51990
UF Thermal Factors
B Environmental Effects 1973
N Cold Effects 1973
Heat Effects 1973
R Atmospheric Conditions 1973
Pollution 1973
Seasonal Variations 1973
Thermal Acclimatization 1973

Temperature Perception 1973
PN 433 **SC** 52000
B Somesthetic Perception 1967
R Somatosensory Disorders 2001

Tempo 1997
PN 191 **SC** 52005
R ↓ Music 1967
Music Perception 1997
↓ Rhythm 1991
Speech Rate 1973
Speech Rhythm 1973
↓ Time Perception 1967

Temporal Frequency 1985
PN 943 **SC** 52015
SN Number of alternating cycles (e.g., patterns of vertical stripes of light and dark light) occurring during a specified time interval. Usually expressed in terms of cycles per second (Hz) as, for example, in sine or square wave visual displays.
B Stimulus Parameters 1967
R Spatial Frequency 1982
Stimulus Frequency 1973
↓ Visual Displays 1973
↓ Visual Stimulation 1973

Temporal Lobe 1973
PN 4909 **SC** 52010
B Cerebral Cortex 1967
N Auditory Cortex 1967

Temporal Spatial Concept Scale
HN Term was discontinued in 1997. In 2000, the term was removed from all records containing it, and replaced with INTELLIGENCE MEASURES, its postable counterpart.
Use Intelligence Measures

Temporomandibular Joint Syndrome
Use Musculoskeletal Disorders

Temptation 1973
PN 183 **SC** 52030
B Motivation 1967
R ↓ Incentives 1967
Peer Pressure 1994
↓ Resistance 1997
Self Control 1973

Tendons 1973
PN 33 **SC** 52050
B Musculoskeletal System 1973

Tennessee Self Concept Scale 1973
PN 51 **SC** 52060
B Nonprojective Personality Measures 1973

Tennis 1973
PN 287 **SC** 52070
B Recreation 1967
Sports 1967

Tension Headache
Use Muscle Contraction Headache

Tenure (Occupational)
Use Occupational Tenure

Tenure (Teacher)
Use Teacher Tenure

Teratogens 1988
PN 333 **SC** 52105
SN Drugs or other agents that cause developmental malformations.
B Hazardous Materials 1991
R ↓ Congenital Disorders 1973
↓ Drugs 1967
↓ Prenatal Development 1973
Prenatal Exposure 1991
Thalidomide 1973
↓ Toxicity 1973
↓ Toxins 2007

Terminal Cancer 1973
PN 724 **SC** 52110
B Neoplasms 1967
R ↓ Death and Dying 1967
Terminally Ill Patients 1973

Terminally Ill Patients 1973
PN 2806 **SC** 52120
UF Dying Patients
B Patients 1967
R Advance Directives 1994
Assisted Suicide 1997
↓ Death and Dying 1967
Hospice 1982
Life Sustaining Treatment 1997
Palliative Care 1991
Terminal Cancer 1973

Terminology 1991
PN 1083 **SC** 52125
SN Definitions, analysis, evaluation, or review of individual terms or nomenclature in any field.
N Psychological Terminology 1973
R Concepts 1967
Ontologies 2007
Scientific Communication 1973

Terminology (Psychological)
Use Psychological Terminology

Territoriality 1967
PN 2314 **SC** 52140
SN Behavioral patterns characteristic of defense or occupation of a territory. Used for both human and animal populations.
UF Habitat Selection
B Animal Ethology 1967
R ↓ Animal Aggressive Behavior 1973
Animal Courtship Displays 1973
Animal Dominance 1973
Animal Homing 1991
Animal Scent Marking 1985
Boundaries (Psychological) 1997

Terror Management Theory 2006
PN 39 **SC** 52145
SN A theory that contends that humans cope and manage fear and anxiety associated with death by adopting a strong cultural world view, i.e., adhering to

Terror Management Theory — (cont'd)
the standards and values of the culture. This coping mechanism is thought to promote self-esteem and reduce the anxiety of death.
HN This term was introduced in May 2006. Relevant records were re-indexed with this term. The posting note reflects the number of records that were re-indexed.
B Theories 1967
R ↓ Death and Dying 1967
↓ Terrorism 1982
World View 1988

Terrorism 1982
PN 2629 **SC** 52150
SN Violence or threats of violence in order to achieve political, economic, or social goals.
B Antisocial Behavior 1971
Violent Crime 2003
N Bioterrorism 2007
R ↓ Crime 1967
Emergency Preparedness 2007
Hostages 1988
Political Revolution 1973
↓ Radical Movements 1973
Terror Management Theory 2006
↓ Violence 1973

Test Administration 1973
PN 2383 **SC** 52180
SN Instructions, timing, preparation of test materials, testing conditions, mode of presentation, and other factors involved in the administration of tests.
UF Administration (Test)
B Testing 1967
R Group Testing 1973
Individual Testing 1973
↓ Testing Methods 1967

Test Anxiety 1967
PN 2225 **SC** 52190
SN Fear or tension in anticipation of formal examination frequently resulting in performance decrement and contributing to measurement error.
B Anxiety 1967
R ↓ Anxiety Disorders 1997
Test Taking 1985

Test Bias 1985
PN 656 **SC** 52196
SN Any significant differential performance on tests by different populations (e.g., males versus females) as a result of test characteristics which are irrelevant to the variable or construct being measured.
UF Item Bias
B Test Construction 1973
Testing 1967
N Cultural Test Bias 1973
R Error of Measurement 1985
Response Bias 1967

Test Bias (Cultural)
Use Cultural Test Bias

Test Coaching 1997
PN 49 **SC** 52205
R ↓ Practice 1967
Test Taking 1985
↓ Testing 1967
Testwiseness 1978
↓ Tutoring 1973

Test Construction 1973
PN 15362 **SC** 52210
SN Planning, selection, writing, editing, and statistical analysis of test items, and design of instructions for test administration and scoring.
N Content Analysis (Test) 1967
Difficulty Level (Test) 1973
Item Analysis (Test) 1967
Item Content (Test) 1973
↓ Test Bias 1985
Test Forms 1988
Test Items 1973
Test Reliability 1973
Test Standardization 1973
Test Validity 1973
R Adaptive Testing 1985
↓ Experimental Design 1967
↓ Measurement 1967

Test Difficulty
Use Difficulty Level (Test)

Test Equating
Use Score Equating

Test Forms 1988
PN 2508 **SC** 52214
SN Includes different versions or schedules of a test.
B Test Construction 1973
Testing 1967
R Item Content (Test) 1973

Test Interpretation 1985
PN 1525 **SC** 52215
SN Judgment and explanation of the significance, meaning, application, or limitation of an assessment instrument and an obtained score or scores.
B Testing 1967
R Cultural Test Bias 1973
Cutting Scores 1985
Psychometrics 1967
↓ Scoring (Testing) 1973
Statistical Weighting 1985
↓ Test Scores 1967
Test Validity 1973

Test Items 1973
PN 1685 **SC** 52220
B Test Construction 1973
Testing 1967
R Item Analysis (Statistical) 1973
Item Analysis (Test) 1967
Item Content (Test) 1973

Test Normalization
Use Test Standardization

Test Norms 1973
PN 1767 **SC** 52240
UF Norms (Test)
R ↓ Measurement 1967
Standardized Tests 1985

Test Reliability 1973
PN 20470 **SC** 52250
SN Consistency, dependability, and reproducibility of test scores, expressed as a reliability coefficient.
UF Internal Consistency
Reliability (Test)
B Test Construction 1973
Testing 1967
R Error of Measurement 1985
Interrater Reliability 1982
Test Standardization 1973

Test Scores 1967
PN 5172 **SC** 52260
SN Quantitative values or evaluations assigned to describe test performance of individuals. Compare SCORING (TESTING) and GRADING (EDUCATIONAL).
UF Scores (Test)
N Cutting Scores 1985
Intelligence Quotient 1967
Standard Scores 1985
R Classical Test Theory 2003
Error of Measurement 1985
Item Response Theory 1985
↓ Measurement 1967
↓ Scoring (Testing) 1973
Statistical Weighting 1985
Test Interpretation 1985

Test Standardization 1973
PN 1111 **SC** 52270
UF Normalization (Test)
Standardization (Test)
Test Normalization
B Test Construction 1973
Testing 1967
R Standardized Tests 1985
Test Reliability 1973
Test Validity 1973

Test Taking 1985
PN 909 **SC** 52275
SN Strategies, attitudes, behaviors, or other factors associated with taking any type of test.
R Cheating 1973
Guessing 1973
Response Bias 1967
Study Habits 1973
Test Anxiety 1967
Test Coaching 1997
↓ Testing 1967
Testwiseness 1978

Test Tube Babies
Use Reproductive Technology

Test Validity 1973
PN 30306 **SC** 52280
SN Extent to which a test measures what it was designed to measure.
UF Concept Validity
Concurrent Validity
Construct Validity
Content Validity
Convergent Validity
Criterion Related Validity
Discriminant Validity
Validity (Test)
B Test Construction 1973
Testing 1967
R Test Interpretation 1985
Test Standardization 1973

Testes 1973
PN 242 **SC** 52290
B Gonads 1973
Male Genitalia 1973

Testes Disorders
Use Endocrine Sexual Disorders

Testicular Feminization Syndrome 1973
PN 11 **SC** 52310
SN Occurs when an individual who is genetically male (has an X and Y chromosome) is unresponsive to androgen. As a result, the individual exhibits some or all of the phenotypic characteristics of a female.
UF Androgen Insensitivity Syndrome
Feminization Syndrome (Testicular)
B Endocrine Sexual Disorders 1973
Male Genital Disorders 1973
Sex Linked Hereditary Disorders 1973
Syndromes 1973
R Hermaphroditism 1973
Sterility 1973

Testimony (Expert)
Use Expert Testimony

Testing 1967
PN 4695 **SC** 52330
SN Administration of tests, and analysis and interpretation of test scores in order to measure differences between individuals or between test performances of the same individual on different occasions.
B Measurement 1967
N Classical Test Theory 2003
Computer Assisted Testing 1988
Content Analysis (Test) 1967
Difficulty Level (Test) 1973
↓ Educational Measurement 1967
Item Analysis (Test) 1967
Item Content (Test) 1973
Item Response Theory 1985
Rating 1967
Repeated Measures 1985
Scaling (Testing) 1967
↓ Scoring (Testing) 1973
Test Administration 1973
↓ Test Bias 1985
Test Forms 1988
Test Interpretation 1985
Test Items 1973
Test Reliability 1973
Test Standardization 1973
Test Validity 1973
R ↓ Neuropsychological Assessment 1982
Psychometrics 1967
Test Coaching 1997
Test Taking 1985
Testwiseness 1978

Testing (Job Applicants)
Use Job Applicant Screening

Testing Methods 1967
PN 1432 **SC** 52370
N Adaptive Testing 1985
Cloze Testing 1973
Essay Testing 1973
Forced Choice (Testing Method) 1967
Multiple Choice (Testing Method) 1973
Q Sort Testing Technique 1967
Scaling (Testing) 1967
R ↓ Measurement 1967
Posttesting 1973
Pretesting 1973
Subtests 1973
Test Administration 1973

Testosterone 1973
PN 2895 **SC** 52380
B Androgens 1973

Tests
Use Measurement

Tests (Achievement)
Use Achievement Measures

Tests (Aptitude)
Use Aptitude Measures

Tests (Intelligence)
Use Intelligence Measures

Tests (Personality)
Use Personality Measures

Tests (Statistical)
Use Statistical Tests

Testwiseness 1978
PN 118 **SC** 52415
SN High degree of sophistication in test-taking skills resulting in advantage over others with same knowledge or ability.
R ↓ Measurement 1967
Test Coaching 1997
Test Taking 1985
↓ Testing 1967

Tetrabenazine 1973
PN 47 **SC** 52430
B Neuroleptic Drugs 1973
Serotonin Antagonists 1973

Tetrachoric Correlation 1973
PN 21 **SC** 52450
B Statistical Correlation 1967

Tetrahydrocannabinol 1973
PN 818 **SC** 52470
B Cannabinoids 1982
R ↓ Cannabis 1973
↓ Hallucinogenic Drugs 1967
Hashish 1973
Marijuana 2003

Text Structure 1982
PN 2389 **SC** 52473
SN Arrangement of sentence or paragraph segments, concepts, or physical format of reading material.
R Discourse Analysis 1997
↓ Prose 1973
Reading Materials 1973
Sentence Structure 1973
↓ Verbal Communication 1967

Textbooks 1978
PN 1612 **SC** 52475
SN Books focusing on principles of a specific subject and used as basis of instruction. Use BOOK to access references that are in themselves textbooks. Use TEXTBOOKS when textbooks are the object of discussion or study (e.g., analyses of best format for textbook chapters).
B Books 1973
Instructional Media 1967

Textbooks — (cont'd)
N Programmed Textbooks 2001
R Reading Materials 1973

Texture Perception 1982
PN 812 **SC** 52485
SN Perception of the surface characteristics (frequently patterned) or appearance of objects or substances, usually through the visual or haptic senses.
B Tactual Perception 1967
Visual Perception 1967
R Pattern Discrimination 1967

Thalamic Nuclei 1973
PN 751 **SC** 52500
B Thalamus 1967

Thalamotomy 1973
PN 36 **SC** 52510
B Psychosurgery 1973

Thalamus 1967
PN 1699 **SC** 52520
B Diencephalon 1973
N Geniculate Bodies (Thalamus) 1973
Thalamic Nuclei 1973
R ↓ Basal Ganglia 1973

Thalidomide 1973
PN 28 **SC** 52530
SN A sedative drug that was used (primarily with pregnant women) until it was discovered it produced fetal malformations when taken during pregnancy.
B Amines 1973
Hypnotic Drugs 1973
Sedatives 1973
R ↓ Drug Induced Congenital Disorders 1973
Prenatal Exposure 1991
Teratogens 1988

Thanatology
Use Death Education

Thanatos
Use Death Instinct

Thankfulness
Use Gratitude

Theatre 1973
PN 496 **SC** 52540
UF Stage Plays
B Arts 1973
N Drama 1973

Theft 1973
PN 673 **SC** 52550
UF Robbery
Stealing
B Crime 1967
N Shoplifting 1973

Thematic Apperception Test 1967
PN 730 **SC** 52560
B Projective Personality Measures 1973

Theology 2003
PN 401 **SC** 52570
SN Study of religious beliefs, practices, and experience, as well as the relationship between God and the world.
HN Use RELIGION to access references from 1973 to June 2003.

Theology — (cont'd)
B Humanities 2003
R God Concepts 1973
Religion 1967
↓ Religious Affiliation 1973
↓ Religious Beliefs 1973
↓ Religious Literature 1973

Theophylline 1973
PN 103 **SC** 52580
B Alkaloids 1973
Diuretics 1973
Enzyme Inhibitors 1985
Heart Rate Affecting Drugs 1973
Muscle Relaxing Drugs 1973
R ↓ Analeptic Drugs 1973
Vasodilation 1973

Theoretical Interpretation 1988
PN 1206 **SC** 52582
SN Description or analysis of any particular event, condition, or process from a specific psychological perspective. Usually used in conjunction with other index terms, e.g., humanistic psychology.
UF Psychological Interpretation
N Psychoanalytic Interpretation 1967
R ↓ Theories 1967

Theoretical Orientation 1982
PN 4557 **SC** 52584
SN Adherence to a particular school of thought, theoretical movement, or practice in a scientific or other area of knowledge.
UF Eclectic Psychology
Professional Orientation
R ↓ Clinical Methods Training 1973
↓ Psychology Education 1978
↓ Psychotherapy 1967
↓ Social Sciences 1967
↓ Theories 1967
↓ Therapist Characteristics 1973

Theories 1967
PN 34807 **SC** 52590
SN Conceptually broad term referring to the systematic deductive derivation of secondary principles explaining observed phenomena. Use a more specific term if possible.
N Activity Theory 2003
Chaos Theory 1997
Classical Test Theory 2003
Communication Theory 1973
Constructivism 1994
↓ Darwinism 1973
Decision Theory 2003
Fuzzy Set Theory 1991
Game Theory 1967
Information Theory 1967
Item Response Theory 1985
Learning Theory 1967
↓ Psychological Theories 2001
Systems Theory 1988
Terror Management Theory 2006
Theories of Education 1973
Theory of Evolution 1967
Utility Theory 2004
R ↓ Experimentation 1967
↓ History of Psychology 1967
↓ Hypothesis Testing 1973
↓ Theoretical Interpretation 1988
Theoretical Orientation 1982
Theory Formulation 1973
Theory Verification 1973

Theories of Education 1973
PN 1034 **SC** 52587
SN Principles and supporting data concerning the educational process, with application for educational practice.
UF Educational Theory
B Theories 1967
R ↓ Education 1967

Theory Formulation 1973
PN 1830 **SC** 52600
SN Advancement of propositions and formulation of hypotheses concerning description, explanation, or interpretation of facts. Applies both to principles of theory formulation and presentation of new theories.
R Grounded Theory 2004
↓ Hypothesis Testing 1973
↓ Methodology 1967
↓ Theories 1967
Theory Verification 1973

Theory of Evolution 1967
PN 5181 **SC** 52610
SN Theories explaining the origins of living organisms and the process by which they evolved into their present forms. For C. Darwin's theory of evolution, use DARWINISM.
UF Evolution (Theory of)
B Theories 1967
R ↓ Darwinism 1973
Evolutionary Economics 2007
Evolutionary Psychology 2003
Mimicry (Biology) 2003
Natural Selection 1997
Self Preservation 1997

Theory of Mind 2001
PN 1220 **SC** 52615
SN Ability to attribute mental states, cognitions, attitudes, beliefs, and emotions to oneself and other individuals. Used for both human and animal populations.
UF Mind Blindness
R Autism 1967
↓ Cognitive Development 1973
↓ Comprehension 1967
False Beliefs 2007
Mind 1991
↓ Social Perception 1967

Theory Verification 1973
PN 1779 **SC** 52620
SN Process of proving or disproving theoretical assumptions using empirical data. Applies both to principles of theory testing and their applications.
UF Verification (of Theories)
R ↓ Hypothesis Testing 1973
↓ Methodology 1967
↓ Theories 1967
Theory Formulation 1973

Therapeutic Abortion
Use Induced Abortion

Therapeutic Alliance 1994
PN 1439 **SC** 52633
UF Working Alliance
B Psychotherapeutic Processes 1967
R Psychotherapeutic Transference 1967
↓ Treatment 1967

Therapeutic Camps 1978
PN 168 **SC** 52635
SN Camps, usually for children, staffed by mental health personnel and offering treatment programs as well as outdoor activities fostering personal growth and accomplishment.
UF Camps (Therapeutic)
B Treatment Facilities 1973
R Recreation Therapy 1973
Wilderness Experience 1991

Therapeutic Community 1967
PN 1916 **SC** 52640
SN Institutional or residential treatment setting emphasizing social and environmental factors in therapy and management and rehabilitation, usually of psychiatric or drug rehabilitation patients.
B Group Psychotherapy 1967
Psychiatric Hospital Programs 1967
R Milieu Therapy 1988
Sociotherapy 1973

Therapeutic Devices (Medical)
Use Medical Therapeutic Devices

Therapeutic Environment 2001
PN 285 **SC** 52621
UF Treatment Environment
B Environment 1967
N ↓ Facility Environment 1988
R Milieu Therapy 1988
↓ Therapeutic Processes 1978
↓ Treatment Facilities 1973

Therapeutic Outcomes
Use Treatment Outcomes

Therapeutic Processes 1978
PN 10124 **SC** 52655
SN Experiential, attitudinal, emotional, or behavioral phenomena occurring during the course of treatment. Applies to the patient or therapist (i.e., nurse, doctor, etc.) individually or to their interaction.
UF Dentist Patient Interaction
Nurse Patient Interaction
Physician Patient Interaction
N ↓ Psychotherapeutic Processes 1967
R Client Education 1985
Dual Relationships 2003
Patient Abuse 1991
Patient Violence 1994
Professional Client Sexual Relations 1994
Telemedicine 2003
↓ Therapeutic Environment 2001
Therapist Selection 1994
↓ Treatment 1967
↓ Treatment Outcomes 1982
Treatment Termination 1982

Therapeutic Social Clubs 1973
PN 92 **SC** 52660
SN Associations of persons, usually patients or former patients, who engage in regular social activities stressing self-help and psychosocial rehabilitation.
UF Social Clubs (Therapeutic)
B Psychosocial Rehabilitation 1973
R ↓ Treatment 1967

Therapeutic Techniques (Psychotherapy)
Use Psychotherapeutic Techniques

Therapist Attitudes 1978
PN 1697 **SC** 52680
SN Attitudes of, not toward, therapists.

Therapist Attitudes — (cont'd)
B Health Personnel Attitudes 1985
Therapist Characteristics 1973
N Psychotherapist Attitudes 1973
R Psychologist Attitudes 1991
Therapist Role 1978

Therapist Characteristics 1973
PN 4161 **SC** 52690
SN Traits or qualities of therapists, including but not limited to effectiveness, experience level, and personality.
UF Therapist Effectiveness
Therapist Experience
Therapist Personality
N ↓ Therapist Attitudes 1978
R ↓ Cross Cultural Treatment 1994
Theoretical Orientation 1982
Therapist Selection 1994
↓ Therapists 1967

Therapist Effectiveness
Use Therapist Characteristics

Therapist Experience
Use Therapist Characteristics

Therapist Patient Interaction
Use Psychotherapeutic Processes

Therapist Patient Sexual Relations
Use Professional Client Sexual Relations

Therapist Personality
Use Therapist Characteristics

Therapist Role 1978
PN 1327 **SC** 52735
B Roles 1967
R Counselor Role 1973
Psychotherapist Attitudes 1973
↓ Therapist Attitudes 1978

Therapist Selection 1994
PN 37 **SC** 52737
SN Motivational and judgmental processes involved in the decision to choose a particular therapist or counselor.
UF Selection (Therapist)
R Choice Behavior 1967
↓ Client Attitudes 1982
Patient Selection 1997
↓ Therapeutic Processes 1978
↓ Therapist Characteristics 1973
↓ Therapists 1967
↓ Treatment 1967

Therapist Trainees 1973
PN 1143 **SC** 52740
UF Psychotherapist Trainees
R Counselor Trainees 1973
↓ Therapists 1967

Therapists 1967
PN 4016 **SC** 52750
SN Conceptually broad term referring to persons trained in the treatment of problems including mental disorders and behavior disorders. Use a more specific term if possible.
B Professional Personnel 1978
N Occupational Therapists 1973
Physical Therapists 1973
↓ Psychotherapists 1973
Speech Therapists 1973

Therapists — (cont'd)
R Clinicians 1973
↓ Counselors 1967
↓ Health Personnel 1994
↓ Mental Health Personnel 1967
↓ Social Workers 1973
↓ Therapist Characteristics 1973
Therapist Selection 1994
Therapist Trainees 1973

Therapy
Use Treatment

Therapy (Drug)
Use Drug Therapy

Thermal Acclimatization 1973
PN 77 **SC** 52830
SN Adjustment to ambient temperature ranges that may be different from the organism's typical experience or that may be typical but cyclical in nature (e.g., seasonal changes in temperature). Compare THERMOREGULATION (BODY).
UF Acclimatization (Thermal)
B Adaptation 1967
Physiology 1967
R Atmospheric Conditions 1973
Environmental Stress 1973
Physiological Stress 1967
↓ Temperature Effects 1967
Thermoregulation (Body) 1973

Thermal Factors
Use Temperature Effects

Thermoreceptors 1973
PN 59 **SC** 52840
B Nerve Endings 1973
Neural Receptors 1973
Sensory Neurons 1973

Thermoregulation (Body) 1973
PN 733 **SC** 52850
SN Homeostatic behavioral or physiological responses that maintain body temperature within a viable range. Compare THERMAL ACCLIMATIZATION.
B Body Temperature 1973
R Hyperthermia 1973
Hypothermia 1973
↓ Metabolism 1967
Thermal Acclimatization 1973

Theta Rhythm 1973
PN 510 **SC** 52860
SN Electrically measured impulses or waves of low amplitude and a frequency of 4-7 cycles per second observable in the electroencephalogram during stage 1 sleep.
B Electrical Activity 1967
Electroencephalography 1967

Thigh 1973
PN 20 **SC** 52870
B Anatomy 1967
R Leg (Anatomy) 1973

Thinking 1967
PN 6714 **SC** 52880
SN Cognitive process involved in the manipulation of concepts and ideas.
B Cognitive Processes 1967
N ↓ Abstraction 1967
Autistic Thinking 1973

Thinking — (cont'd)
Critical Thinking 2006
Divergent Thinking 1973
Logical Thinking 1967
Magical Thinking 1973
↓ Reasoning 1967
R ↓ Intelligence 1967

Thiopental 1973
PN 41 SC 52890
UF Pentothal
B Barbiturates 1967
General Anesthetics 1973
Hypnotic Drugs 1973
Sedatives 1973

Thioridazine 1973
PN 347 SC 52900
UF Mellaril
B Phenothiazine Derivatives 1973

Thiothixene 1973
PN 104 SC 52910
B Tranquilizing Drugs 1967

Third World Countries
Use Developing Countries

Thirst 1967
PN 349 SC 52920
B Motivation 1967
R Animal Drinking Behavior 1973
↓ Drinking Behavior 1978
↓ Fluid Intake 1985
Water Deprivation 1967

Thoracic Nerves
Use Spinal Nerves

Thorax 1973
PN 175 SC 52960
UF Chest
B Musculoskeletal System 1973
Respiratory System 1973
R Diaphragm (Anatomy) 1973

Thorazine
Use Chlorpromazine

Thought Content
Use Cognitions

Thought Control
Use Brainwashing

Thought Disturbances 1973
PN 1368 SC 52980
SN Disturbances of thinking that affect thought content, language, and/or communication marked by delusions, incoherence, and profound loosening of associations.
N Autistic Thinking 1973
Confabulation 1973
Delusions 1967
Fantasies (Thought Disturbances) 1967
Fragmentation (Schizophrenia) 1973
Judgment Disturbances 1973
Magical Thinking 1973
↓ Memory Disorders 1973
Obsessions 1967
Perseveration 1967
R Cognitive Impairment 2003
Mental Confusion 1973

Thought Disturbances — (cont'd)
↓ Mental Disorders 1967
Rumination (Cognitive Process) 2001

Thought Suppression 2003
PN 175 SC 52984
SN Active process of attempting not to think about a particular thought or event.
HN This term was introduced in June 2003. Relevant records were re-indexed with this term. The posting note reflects the number of records that were re-indexed.
B Cognitive Processes 1967
R ↓ Cognitions 1985
Rumination (Cognitive Process) 2001

Threat 1967
PN 3038 SC 52990
R Bullying 2003
Coercion 1994
↓ Harassment 2001
↓ Punishment 1967
Threat Postures 1973

Threat Postures 1973
PN 120 SC 53000
B Animal Aggressive Behavior 1973
Animal Defensive Behavior 1982
R Animal Predatory Behavior 1978
Threat 1967

Threshold Determination 1973
PN 469 SC 53010
SN Methods and apparatus used in the measurement of both absolute and difference thresholds for any sensory modality.
R ↓ Psychophysical Measurement 1967
Signal Detection (Perception) 1967
↓ Thresholds 1967

Thresholds 1967
PN 1814 SC 53020
SN The minimal level (e.g., intensity) of stimulation, the minimal difference between any stimuli, or the minimal stimulus change that is perceptually detectable or to which a sensory receptor or other neuron will respond. Compare SIGNAL DETECTION (PERCEPTION).
UF Differential Limen
Limen
N Auditory Thresholds 1973
Olfactory Thresholds 1973
Pain Thresholds 1973
↓ Sensory Adaptation 1967
Vibrotactile Thresholds 1973
↓ Visual Thresholds 1973
R ↓ Perceptual Measures 1973
Threshold Determination 1973

Thromboses 1973
PN 104 SC 53040
B Cardiovascular Disorders 1967
N Coronary Thromboses 1973
R Embolisms 1973

Thumb 1973
PN 41 SC 53050
B Fingers (Anatomy) 1973

Thumbsucking 1973
PN 81 SC 53060
B Habits 1967
R ↓ Behavior Disorders 1971

Thymoleptic Drugs
Use Tranquilizing Drugs

Thyroid Disorders 1973
PN 252 SC 53090
B Endocrine Disorders 1973
N Goiters 1973
Hyperthyroidism 1973
Hypothyroidism 1973
Thyrotoxicosis 1973
R ↓ Endocrine Sexual Disorders 1973
↓ Pituitary Disorders 1973

Thyroid Extract
HN Term was discontinued in 1997. In 2000, the term was removed from all records containing it, and replaced with THYROID HORMONES, its postable counterpart.
Use Thyroid Hormones

Thyroid Gland 1973
PN 146 SC 53110
B Endocrine Glands 1973

Thyroid Hormones 1973
PN 430 SC 53120
HN In 1997, this term replaced the discontinued term THYROID EXTRACT. In 2000, THYROID EXTRACT was removed from all records containing it, and replaced with THYROID HORMONES.
UF Thyroid Extract
B Hormones 1967
N Thyroxine 1973
Triiodothyronine 1973

Thyroid Stimulating Hormone
Use Thyrotropin

Thyroidectomy 1973
PN 33 SC 53140
B Endocrine Gland Surgery 1973

Thyrotoxicosis 1973
PN 38 SC 53150
SN A disorder caused by an overactive thyroid gland.
B Thyroid Disorders 1973
Toxic Disorders 1973
R ↓ Encephalopathies 1982
Hyperthyroidism 1973
Toxic Psychoses 1973

Thyrotropic Hormone
Use Thyrotropin

Thyrotropin 1973
PN 864 SC 53170
UF Thyroid Stimulating Hormone
Thyrotropic Hormone

Thyrotropin — (cont'd)
B Neuropeptides 2003
Pituitary Hormones 1973
R Hypothyroidism 1973

Thyroxine 1973
PN 275 SC 53180
B Thyroid Hormones 1973
R Hypothyroidism 1973

Tic Doloureux
Use Trigeminal Neuralgia

Tics 1973
PN 756 SC 53200
SN Repetitive, involuntary, or habitual contractions of a specific group of muscles, e.g., continual throat clearing, eyeblinking, or grimacing.
B Movement Disorders 1985
Symptoms 1967
R Tourette Syndrome 2006

Tigers
Use Felids

Time 1967
PN 6987 SC 53210
SN Continuum in which events or experiences are expressed in terms of the past, the present, and the future. For effects of time-of-day or season consider also SEASONAL VARIATIONS and BIOLOGICAL RHYTHMS or their associated terms.
N Interresponse Time 1973
R Future 1991
Time Disorientation 1973
Time Management 1994
↓ Time Perception 1967
Time Perspective 1978
Trends 1991

Time Disorientation 1973
PN 106 SC 53230
UF Disorientation (Time)
B Consciousness Disturbances 1973
R ↓ Time 1967

Time Estimation 1967
PN 1279 SC 53240
SN Estimation of duration or passage of time.
B Estimation 1967
Time Perception 1967
R Time Management 1994

Time Limited Psychotherapy
Use Brief Psychotherapy

Time Management 1994
PN 408 SC 51435
UF Time Planning Style
Time Scheduling
Time Utilization
B Management 1967
R ↓ Learning Strategies 1991
↓ Self Management 1985
Study Habits 1973
↓ Time 1967
Time Estimation 1967
Time On Task 1988
↓ Time Perception 1967
Time Perspective 1978

Time On Task 1988
PN 712 SC 53244
SN Period of active involvement in a learning or production activity.
R ↓ Attention 1967
↓ Learning 1967
Student Engagement 2006
Time Management 1994

Time Out 1985
PN 186 SC 53245
SN Removal of the availability of gratification and reinforcement for any behavior following the occurrence of an undesired response. Has application in therapeutic, experimental, educational, and childrearing contexts.
B Behavior Modification 1973
Operant Conditioning 1967
R Omission Training 1985

Time Perception 1967
PN 2580 SC 53250
SN Perception of duration, simultaneity, or succession in the passage of time.
HN Prior to the introduction of TIME PERSPECTIVE in 1978, TIME PERCEPTION was used for this concept also.
B Perception 1967
N Time Estimation 1967
R Tempo 1997
↓ Time 1967
Time Management 1994
Time Perspective 1978

Time Perspective 1978
PN 1296 SC 53255
SN Mental representation of temporal relationships or the capacity to remember events in their actual chronology. Also, one's outlook on the past, present, and/or future in relation to subjective qualities of time passage.
HN To access references prior to 1978 use TIME PERCEPTION.
R ↓ Perceptual Orientation 1973
↓ Time 1967
Time Management 1994
↓ Time Perception 1967

Time Planning Style
Use Time Management

Time Scheduling
Use Time Management

Time Series 1985
PN 589 SC 53257
SN A set of observational data ordered in time, typically with observations made at regular intervals.
B Statistical Analysis 1967
R Statistical Data 1982
↓ Stochastic Modeling 1973

Time Utilization
Use Time Management

Timers (Apparatus) 1973
PN 57 SC 53260
B Apparatus 1967

Timidity 1973
PN 758 SC 53270
UF Shyness
B Personality Traits 1967

Tinnitus 1973
PN 299 SC 53280
SN A condition characterized by a buzzing or ringing noise in one's ear.
B Ear Disorders 1973

Tiredness
Use Fatigue

Tissue Donation 1991
PN 495 SC 53295
SN Donation of organs, blood, sperm, or other tissues for medical use.
UF Blood Donation
Organ Donation
Plasma Donation
Sperm Donation
R Blood Transfusion 1973
Charitable Behavior 1973
Neural Transplantation 1985
Organ Transplantation 1973

Tissues (Body) 1973
PN 262 SC 53300
B Anatomy 1967
N ↓ Connective Tissues 1973
↓ Membranes 1973
↓ Nerve Tissues 1973
Skin (Anatomy) 1967
R Histology 1973
↓ Muscles 1967

Toads 1973
PN 224 SC 53320
B Amphibia 1973
R Larvae 1973

Tobacco (Drug)
Use Nicotine

Tobacco (Smokeless)
Use Smokeless Tobacco

Tobacco Smoking 1967
PN 12040 SC 53340
UF Cigarette Smoking
Smoking (Tobacco)
B Drug Usage 1971
Habits 1967
N Passive Smoking 2006
R Carcinogens 1973
Nicotine 1973
Nicotine Withdrawal 1997
Prenatal Exposure 1991
Smokeless Tobacco 1994
Smoking Cessation 1988

Toes (Anatomy)
Use Feet (Anatomy)

Tofranil
Use Imipramine

Toilet Training 1973
PN 156 **SC** 53400
B Childrearing Practices 1967
Training 2006

Token Economy Programs 1973
PN 705 **SC** 53410
SN Group treatment based on operant conditioning in which elements in a patient's environment are arranged so that reinforcement is made contingent on the patient's behavior. When the desired behavior occurs, a token is given which may be exchanged for a reinforcing agent (e.g., goods or services).
B Contingency Management 1973
R ↓ Psychiatric Hospital Programs 1967
Response Cost 1997

Token Reinforcement
Use Secondary Reinforcement

Tolerance 1973
PN 672 **SC** 53440
B Personality Traits 1967
N Tolerance for Ambiguity 1967
R Agreeableness 1997
Openness to Experience 1997
Social Acceptance 1967

Tolerance (Drug)
Use Drug Tolerance

Tolerance for Ambiguity 1967
PN 505 **SC** 53460
SN Willingness to accept situations having conflicting or multiple interpretations or outcomes.
UF Ambiguity (Tolerance)
B Tolerance 1973

Toluene 1991
PN 76 **SC** 53465
B Solvents 1982

Tomography 1988
PN 3199 **SC** 53470
UF CAT Scan
Positron Emission Tomography
B Medical Diagnosis 1973
Neuroimaging 2003
N Magnetic Resonance Imaging 1994
R Computer Assisted Diagnosis 1973
↓ Roentgenography 1973

Tone (Frequency)
Use Pitch (Frequency)

Tongue 1973
PN 510 **SC** 53490
B Digestive System 1967
N Taste Buds 1973
R Mouth (Anatomy) 1967
Taste Disorders 2001

Tonic Immobility 1978
PN 384 **SC** 53495
SN Adaptive escape or alarm response in certain species in which the animal adopts a motionless posture as if feigning death.
B Motor Processes 1967
R Alarm Responses 1973
↓ Animal Defensive Behavior 1982

Tonic-Clonic Seizures
Use Grand Mal Seizures

Tool Use 1991
PN 415 **SC** 53497
SN Used for human or animal populations.
UF Animal Tool Use
B Motor Processes 1967
R ↓ Animal Ethology 1967

Top Level Managers 1973
PN 2374 **SC** 53500
SN Executives in business or industry who are responsible for the major strategic and policy decisions.
UF Executives
B Management Personnel 1973
R Middle Level Managers 1973

Topography 1973
PN 357 **SC** 53510
B Ecological Factors 1973

Torticollis 1973
PN 100 **SC** 53520
SN A symptom characterized by continuous, spasmodic contractions of the neck muscles.
UF Wryneck
B Movement Disorders 1985
Muscular Disorders 1973

Tortoises
Use Turtles

Torture 1988
PN 524 **SC** 53535
B Antisocial Behavior 1971
R ↓ Aggressive Behavior 1967
Coercion 1994
Persecution 1973
Prisoner Abuse 2007
Suffering 1973
Victimization 1973
↓ Violence 1973

Totalitarianism 1973
PN 95 **SC** 53540
B Political Economic Systems 1973

Touch
Use Tactual Perception

Touching
Use Physical Contact

Tourette Syndrome 2006
PN 1626 **SC** 53556
SN Tourette Syndrome is a neurological disorder characterized by involuntary movements and vocalizations, called tics, occurring many times a day over a period of more than one year. Symptoms have a marked effect on social, occupational, and other areas of functioning.
HN In May 2006, this term replaced the discontinued term GILLES DE LA TOURETTE DISORDER. GILLES DE LA TOURETTE DISORDER was removed from all records containing it and replaced with TOURETTE SYNDROME, its postable counterpart.
UF Gilles de la Tourette Disorder
B Neuromuscular Disorders 1973
R Echolalia 1973
Tics 1973

Tourism 2003
PN 472 **SC** 53558
HN This term was introduced in June 2003. Relevant records were re-indexed with this term. The posting note reflects the number of records that were re-indexed.
R Holidays 1988
↓ Recreation 1967
Study Abroad 2007
Traveling 1973
Vacationing 1973

Towns 1973
PN 157 **SC** 53560
B Social Environments 1973

Toxic Disorders 1973
PN 605 **SC** 53570
HN In August 2005, this term replaced the discontinued term BARBITURATE POISONING. BARBITURATE POISONING was removed from all records containing it, and was and replaced with TOXIC DISORDERS, its postable counterpart.
UF Barbiturate Poisoning
Intoxication
Poisoning
B Physical Disorders 1997
N Acute Alcoholic Intoxication 1973
Carbon Monoxide Poisoning 1973
↓ Drug Induced Congenital Disorders 1973
Lead Poisoning 1973
Mercury Poisoning 1973
Narcosis 1973
Neuroleptic Malignant Syndrome 1988
Thyrotoxicosis 1973
Toxic Encephalopathies 1973
Toxic Hepatitis 1973
Toxic Psychoses 1973
R ↓ Alcohol Intoxication 1973
↓ Alcoholism 1967
↓ Dermatitis 1973
↓ Digestive System Disorders 1973
↓ Gastrointestinal Disorders 1973
Hyponatremia 1997
↓ Liver Disorders 1973
↓ Mental Disorders 1967
↓ Neurotoxins 1982
↓ Toxicity 1973
Toxicomania 1973

Toxic Encephalopathies 1973
PN 110 **SC** 53580
B Encephalopathies 1982
Toxic Disorders 1973
R Acute Alcoholic Intoxication 1973
Chronic Alcoholic Intoxication 1973
Toxic Psychoses 1973

Toxic Hepatitis 1973
PN 17 **SC** 53590
B Hepatitis 1973
Toxic Disorders 1973

Toxic Psychoses 1973
PN 151 **SC** 53600
SN Psychotic states or conditions resulting from ingestion of toxic agents or by the presence of toxins within the body. Compare EXPERIMENTAL PSYCHOSIS.
B Organic Brain Syndromes 1973
Psychosis 1967
Toxic Disorders 1973
R ↓ Alcohol Intoxication 1973
↓ Alcoholic Psychosis 1973

Toxic Psychoses — (cont'd)
Thyrotoxicosis 1973
Toxic Encephalopathies 1973

Toxic Waste
Use Hazardous Materials

Toxicity 1973
PN 1342 **SC** 53610
N Neurotoxicity 2003
R ↓ Drugs 1967
↓ Hazardous Materials 1991
↓ Neurotoxins 1982
Teratogens 1988
↓ Toxic Disorders 1973
↓ Toxins 2007

Toxicomania 1973
PN 18 **SC** 53620
SN Pathological desire to consume poisons.
R Pica 1973
↓ Toxic Disorders 1973

Toxins 2007
PN 659 **SC** 53630
SN A biologically produced substance considered poisonous.
HN In April 2007, this term replaced the discontinued term POISONS. POISONS was removed from all records containing it, and was replaced with TOXINS.
UF Poisons
B Hazardous Materials 1991
N ↓ Neurotoxins 1982
R Carbon Monoxide 1973
↓ Insecticides 1973
Prenatal Exposure 1991
Teratogens 1988
↓ Toxicity 1973

Toy Selection 1973
PN 215 **SC** 53650
R ↓ Childhood Play Behavior 1978
↓ Toys 1973

Toys 1973
PN 607 **SC** 53660
N Anatomically Detailed Dolls 1991
Educational Toys 1973
R ↓ Childhood Play Behavior 1978
Childrens Recreational Games 1973
Computer Games 1988
↓ Games 1967
↓ Recreation 1967
Toy Selection 1973

Trachea 1973
PN 56 **SC** 53680
B Respiratory System 1973

Tracking 1967
PN 662 **SC** 53700
SN Following the movement of a moving stimulus or the contours (or shape) of a stationary target by means of direct physical contact or through any sensory modality. Used for human or animal populations.
B Perceptual Motor Processes 1967
N Rotary Pursuit 1967
Visual Tracking 1973
R ↓ Attention 1967
↓ Monitoring 1973
Motor Skills 1973
↓ Perceptual Learning 2006

Tracking — (cont'd)
↓ Perceptual Localization 1967
↓ Perceptual Motor Learning 1967

Tractotomy 1973
PN 27 **SC** 53710
B Neurosurgery 1973
R ↓ Psychosurgery 1973

Trade (Business)
Use Commerce

Traditionalism
Use Conservatism

Traditions 2007
PN 743 **SC** 53725
SN A set of social customs or other ethnic or family practices handed down from generation to generation.
HN This term was introduced in April 2007. Relevant records were re-indexed with this term. The posting note reflects the number of records that were re-indexed.
UF Customs
R Anniversary Events 1994
↓ Culture (Anthropological) 1967
Ethnography 1973
Folklore 1991
Holidays 1988
Marriage Rites 1973
Rites (Nonreligious) 1973

Traffic Accidents (Motor)
Use Motor Traffic Accidents

Trainable Mentally Retarded
HN In 2000, the term was discontinued, and removed from all records containing it, and replaced with MODERATE MENTAL RETARDATION, its postable counterpart.
Use Moderate Mental Retardation

Training 2006
PN 268 **SC** 53770
SN Instruction and practice focused on acquiring specific skills and knowledge.
HN In May 2006, TRAINING changed status from nonpostable to postable. Relevant records were re-indexed with this term. The posting note reflects the number of records that were re-indexed.
N Assertiveness Training 1978
Athletic Training 1991
Autogenic Training 1973
Biofeedback Training 1978
Childbirth Training 1978
↓ Clinical Methods Training 1973
Communication Skills Training 1982
Computer Training 1994
Human Relations Training 1978
Memory Training 1994
Military Training 1973
Motivation Training 1973
Parent Training 1978
↓ Personnel Training 1967
Self Instructional Training 1985
Sensitivity Training 1973
Social Skills Training 1982
Toilet Training 1973
Work Adjustment Training 1991
R Career Development 1985
Career Education 1978
↓ Continuing Education 1985
↓ Education 1967

Training (Athletic)
Use Athletic Training

Training (Clinical Methods)
Use Clinical Methods Training

Training (Clinical Psychology Graduate)
Use Clinical Psychology Graduate Training

Training (Community Mental Health)
Use Community Mental Health Training

Training (Graduate Psychology)
Use Graduate Psychology Education

Training (Mental Health Inservice)
Use Mental Health Inservice Training

Training (Motivation)
Use Motivation Training

Training (Personnel)
Use Personnel Training

Training (Psychiatric)
Use Psychiatric Training

Training (Psychoanalytic)
Use Psychoanalytic Training

Training (Psychotherapy)
Use Psychotherapy Training

Trains (Railroad)
Use Railroad Trains

Tranquilizing Drugs 1967
PN 2477 **SC** 53900
UF Antianxiety Drugs
Anxiety Reducing Drugs
Anxiolytic Drugs
Ataractic Drugs
Ataraxic Drugs
Thymoleptic Drugs
B Drugs 1967
N Amitriptyline 1973
Benactyzine 1973
Doxepin 1994
Haloperidol 1973
Meprobamate 1973
↓ Minor Tranquilizers 1973
↓ Neuroleptic Drugs 1973
↓ Phenothiazine Derivatives 1973
Pimozide 1973
Thiothixene 1973
R ↓ Anticonvulsive Drugs 1973
↓ Antiemetic Drugs 1973
↓ Antihypertensive Drugs 1973
↓ Benzodiazepines 1978
↓ Dopamine Antagonists 1982
↓ Muscle Relaxing Drugs 1973
↓ Narcotic Drugs 1973
↓ Sedatives 1973

Transactional Analysis 1973
PN 1216 **SC** 53910
SN Type of psychotherapy developed by E. Berne based on the theory that all interactions between individuals reflect the inner relationships of the "Parent," "Adult," and "Child" ego states.
B Human Potential Movement 1982
Psychotherapy 1967
R ↓ Group Psychotherapy 1967
↓ Psychoanalysis 1967

Transaminases 1973
PN 47 **SC** 53920
UF Aminotransferases
B Transferases 1973

Transcranial Magnetic Stimulation 2003
PN 882 **SC** 53925
SN Noninvasive therapeutic technique for stimulating the brain.
HN This term was introduced in June 2003. Relevant records were re-indexed with this term. The posting note reflects the number of records that were re-indexed.
UF Repetitive Transcranial Magnetic Stimulation
B Brain Stimulation 1967
Physical Treatment Methods 1973
R Magnetism 1985

Transcultural Psychiatry 1973
PN 622 **SC** 53930
SN Comparative study of mental illness and mental health among various societies or cultures, including epidemiology and symptomatology.
UF Comparative Psychiatry
Cultural Psychiatry
B Psychiatry 1967
R ↓ Alternative Medicine 1997
Cross Cultural Psychology 1997
↓ Cross Cultural Treatment 1994
↓ Culture Bound Syndromes 2004
Ethnology 1967
Folk Medicine 1973
Folk Psychology 1997
Myths 1967
Shamanism 1973
Taboos 1973

Transducers 1973
PN 36 **SC** 53940
B Apparatus 1967

Transfer (Learning) 1967
PN 3751 **SC** 53950
SN Effect of previous learning on the acquisition of new material or skills as a function of the relative similarity between the prior and current learning situations. Compare GENERALIZATION (LEARNING).
B Learning 1967
N Negative Transfer 1973
Positive Transfer 1973
R ↓ Generalization (Learning) 1982

Transfer Students 1973
PN 179 **SC** 53955
SN Students transferring from one school or educational program to another.
B Students 1967
R Grade Level 1994

Transferases 1973
PN 399 **SC** 53960
B Enzymes 1973
N Transaminases 1973

Transference (Psychotherapeutic)
Use Psychotherapeutic Transference

Transformational Generative Grammar 1973
PN 140 **SC** 53980
SN Transformational grammar relates the deep syntactic structures of a language to the surface structures by means of transformational rules. Generative grammar represents, through abstract formulas, all and only the grammatical utterances of a language.

Transformational Generative Grammar — (cont'd)
B Grammar 1967
R ↓ Syntax 1971

Transformational Leadership 2003
PN 430 **SC** 53985
SN A style of leadership that motivates and transforms followers to transcend their self-interests and personal goals to work for a common goal.
HN This term was introduced in June 2003. Relevant records were re-indexed with this term. The posting note reflects the number of records that were re-indexed.
UF Charismatic Leadership
B Leadership 1967
R Charisma 1988
Leadership Style 1973
↓ Management 1967

Transfusion (Blood)
Use Blood Transfusion

Transgendered
Use Transsexualism

Transgenerational Patterns 1991
PN 1230 **SC** 54005
SN Patterns of behavior (e.g., adolescent pregnancy, drug abuse, or child abuse) appearing in successive generations.
UF Intergenerational Transmission
R Children of Alcoholics 2003
↓ Family 1967
↓ Family Relations 1967
Family Resemblance 1991
Generation Gap 1973
Intergenerational Relations 1988
↓ Parent Child Relations 1967
Trends 1991

Transistors (Apparatus)
HN Term was discontinued in 1997. In 2000, the term was removed from all records containing it, and replaced with APPARATUS, its postable counterpart.
Use Apparatus

Transitional Objects 1985
PN 317 **SC** 54015
SN Psychoanalytic concept referring to any material object having a special value that serves an anxiety-reducing function. Such attachment is a normal phenomenon during transition from one phase to another in separation-individuation.
R ↓ Childhood Development 1967
Object Relations 1982
Separation Individuation 1982

Translocation (Chromosome) 1973
PN 54 **SC** 54020
B Chromosome Disorders 1973
R ↓ Genetics 1967
Mutations 1973

Transnational Corporations
Use Multinational Corporations

Transpersonal Psychology 1988
PN 572 **SC** 54025
SN Subdiscipline of humanistic psychology which studies higher states of consciousness and transcendental experiences.

Transpersonal Psychology — (cont'd)
B Humanistic Psychology 1985

Transplants (Organ)
Use Organ Transplantation

Transportation 1973
PN 364 **SC** 54040
N Air Transportation 1973
↓ Ground Transportation 1973
Public Transportation 1973
↓ Water Transportation 1973
R Commuting (Travel) 1985
↓ Transportation Accidents 1973
Transportation Safety 2007

Transportation Accidents 1973
PN 218 **SC** 54050
UF Bicycle Accidents
B Accidents 1967
N Air Traffic Accidents 1973
Motor Traffic Accidents 1973
R Accident Prevention 1973
Air Traffic Control 1973
↓ Aviation Safety 1973
Highway Safety 1973
Safety Belts 1973
↓ Transportation 1973
Transportation Safety 2007

Transportation Safety 2007
PN 12 **SC** 54055
HN This term was introduced in April 2007. Relevant records were re-indexed with this term. The posting note reflects the number of records that were re-indexed.
UF Bicycle Safety
B Safety 1967
R Accident Prevention 1973
↓ Transportation 1973
↓ Transportation Accidents 1973

Transposition (Cognition) 1973
PN 61 **SC** 54060
SN Condition in learning in which subjects react to relationships between stimuli rather than to each stimulus itself.
B Cognitive Processes 1967

Transracial Adoption
Use Interracial Adoption

Transsexualism 1973
PN 1476 **SC** 54070
SN The urge to belong to the opposite sex that may include surgical procedures to modify the sex organs in order to appear as the opposite sex.
UF Transgendered
B Gender Identity 1985
Gender Identity Disorder 1997
Psychosexual Behavior 1967
R Bisexuality 1973
↓ Homosexuality 1967
Sex Change 1988
Transvestism 1973

Transvestism 1973
PN 342 **SC** 54080
SN The act of dressing like and adopting the behavior of the opposite sex, often for sexual gratification.
B Paraphilias 1988
Psychosexual Behavior 1967
R Bisexuality 1973
Fetishism 1973

Transvestism — (cont'd)
↓ Gender Identity Disorder 1997
↓ Homosexuality 1967
Transsexualism 1973

Tranylcypromine 1973
PN 194 **SC** 54090
B Antidepressant Drugs 1971
Monoamine Oxidase Inhibitors 1973

Trauma 2006
PN 752 **SC** 54095
SN Physical or psychological damage caused by a painful event or injury. Use a more specific term if possible.
HN This term was introduced in May 2006. Relevant records were re-indexed with this term. The posting note reflects the number of records that were re-indexed.
N Birth Trauma 1973
Emotional Trauma 1967
↓ Injuries 1973
↓ Traumatic Brain Injury 1997
R Posttraumatic Stress Disorder 1985

Trauma (Emotional)
Use Emotional Trauma

Trauma (Physical)
Use Injuries

Traumatic Brain Injury 1997
PN 3839 **SC** 54115
SN Brain injury resulting from an accident, surgery, or other trauma.
HN Consider BRAIN DAMAGE or BRAIN DAMAGED to access references prior to 1997.
UF Brain Injury (Traumatic)
B Brain Damage 1967
Trauma 2006
N Brain Concussion 1973
R ↓ Head Injuries 1973
↓ Neuropsychological Assessment 1982

Traumatic Neurosis 1973
PN 242 **SC** 54130
HN Use TRAUMATIC NEUROSIS or STRESS REACTIONS to access references to POSTTRAUMATIC STRESS DISORDER from 1973-1984.
B Neurosis 1967
R Posttraumatic Stress Disorder 1985

Traumatic Psychosis
Use Reactive Psychosis

Traveling 1973
PN 583 **SC** 54150
B Recreation 1967
R Commuting (Travel) 1985
Tourism 2003
Vacationing 1973

Trazodone 1988
PN 280 **SC** 54152
B Antidepressant Drugs 1971
Piperazines 1994

Treatment 1967
PN 33624 **SC** 54190
SN Conceptually broad term referring to psychological or physical measures designed to ameliorate or cure an abnormal or undesirable condition. Use a more specific term if possible.

Treatment — (cont'd)
UF Therapy
N Aftercare 1973
↓ Alternative Medicine 1997
↓ Behavior Modification 1973
Bibliotherapy 1973
↓ Cognitive Techniques 1985
Computer Assisted Therapy 2007
↓ Creative Arts Therapy 1994
↓ Crisis Intervention Services 1973
↓ Cross Cultural Treatment 1994
Disease Management 2007
↓ Health Care Services 1978
Interdisciplinary Treatment Approach 1973
Involuntary Treatment 1994
Life Sustaining Treatment 1997
Medical Treatment (General) 1973
Milieu Therapy 1988
Movement Therapy 1997
Multimodal Treatment Approach 1991
Online Therapy 2003
↓ Outpatient Treatment 1967
Pain Management 1994
Partial Hospitalization 1985
Personal Therapy 1991
↓ Physical Treatment Methods 1973
Preventive Medicine 1973
↓ Psychotherapeutic Techniques 1967
↓ Psychotherapy 1967
↓ Rehabilitation 1967
↓ Relaxation Therapy 1978
Sex Therapy 1978
Social Casework 1967
Sociotherapy 1973
Speech Therapy 1967
Treatment Guidelines 2001
R Caregivers 1988
↓ Case Management 1991
↓ Client Rights 1988
Client Transfer 1997
Client Treatment Matching 1997
↓ Clinics 1967
Cost Containment 1991
↓ Counseling 1967
Court Referrals 1994
Death Education 1982
Early Intervention 1982
Euthanasia 1973
Health Care Costs 1994
↓ Health Care Delivery 1978
Health Care Seeking Behavior 1997
↓ Intervention 2003
Life Review 1991
↓ Medical Records 1978
Mental Health Program Evaluation 1973
Patient Abuse 1991
Patient History 1973
Physical Restraint 1982
Posttreatment Followup 1973
↓ Prescribing (Drugs) 1991
↓ Prevention 1973
Prognosis 1973
↓ Psychiatry 1967
Psychoeducation 1994
Psychosocial Readjustment 1973
Quality of Care 1988
Relapse Prevention 1994
↓ Self Help Techniques 1982
Sensory Integration 1991
Shamanism 1973
↓ Side Effects (Treatment) 1988
Spontaneous Remission 1973

Treatment — (cont'd)
Stress Management 1985
Therapeutic Alliance 1994
↓ Therapeutic Processes 1978
Therapeutic Social Clubs 1973
Therapist Selection 1994
Treatment Compliance 1982
↓ Treatment Duration 1988
Treatment Effectiveness Evaluation 1973
↓ Treatment Facilities 1973
↓ Treatment Outcomes 1982
↓ Treatment Planning 1997
↓ Treatment Resistant Disorders 1994
Treatment Termination 1982
Treatment Withholding 1988
↓ Twelve Step Programs 1997

Treatment Barriers 2005
PN 269 **SC** 58085
SN A broad term used to describe anything that deters one from seeking or receiving health or mental health services.
HN This term was introduced in August 2005. Relevant records were re-indexed with this term. The posting note reflects the number of records that were re-indexed.
UF Barriers (Treatment)
Health Care Barriers
Mental Health Care Barriers
R ↓ Client Attitudes 1982
Client Participation 1997
Health Attitudes 1985
↓ Health Care Delivery 1978
Health Care Seeking Behavior 1997
Health Care Utilization 1985
Health Service Needs 1997
Treatment Compliance 1982
Treatment Dropouts 1978
Treatment Refusal 1994

Treatment Client Matching
Use Client Treatment Matching

Treatment Compliance 1982
PN 6254 **SC** 54153
SN Adherence by a patient or client to professional advice or a systematic plan of treatment.
UF Client Compliance
Medical Regimen Compliance
B Compliance 1973
R ↓ Client Attitudes 1982
Client Education 1985
Client Participation 1997
↓ Client Rights 1988
Disease Management 2007
Illness Behavior 1982
Informed Consent 1985
Involuntary Treatment 1994
↓ Treatment 1967
Treatment Barriers 2005
Treatment Dropouts 1978
↓ Treatment Duration 1988
Treatment Refusal 1994
Treatment Withholding 1988

Treatment Dropouts 1978
PN 1600 **SC** 54155
SN Persons who drop out of treatment, or discontinuation of treatment without the consent of the person in charge of treatment or before scheduled termination. Compare TREATMENT TERMINATION.
UF Client Dropouts
Patient Dropouts

Treatment Dropouts — (cont'd)
B Dropouts 1973
R Involuntary Treatment 1994
Psychotherapeutic Outcomes 1973
Treatment Barriers 2005
Treatment Compliance 1982
↓ Treatment Duration 1988
↓ Treatment Outcomes 1982
Treatment Refusal 1994
Treatment Termination 1982

Treatment Duration 1988
PN 2301 **SC** 54157
SN Length of hospital or institutional stay and length or number of treatment or therapy sessions. Used for any treatment modality.
UF Length of Stay
N Long Term Care 1994
R ↓ Case Management 1991
Maintenance Therapy 1997
↓ Treatment 1967
Treatment Compliance 1982
Treatment Dropouts 1978
↓ Treatment Outcomes 1982
↓ Treatment Planning 1997
Treatment Termination 1982

Treatment Effectiveness Evaluation 1973
PN 8195 **SC** 54160
SN Methodology or procedures for assessment of treatment success in relation to previously established goals or other criteria. Also used for formal evaluations themselves. For effectiveness of particular treatment modes, use the specific type of treatment (e.g., DRUG THERAPY). For efficacy of treatment for a particular disorder, use the specific disorder (e.g., MANIA) and the specific type of treatment.
UF Evaluation (Treatment Effectiveness)
B Evaluation 1967
R Clinical Audits 2007
Clinical Trials 2004
Mental Health Program Evaluation 1973
Psychotherapeutic Outcomes 1973
↓ Treatment 1967
↓ Treatment Outcomes 1982

Treatment Environment
Use Therapeutic Environment

Treatment Facilities 1973
PN 658 **SC** 54170
B Facilities 2006
N ↓ Clinics 1967
Community Mental Health Centers 1973
Halfway Houses 1973
↓ Hospitals 1967
Nursing Homes 1973
Therapeutic Camps 1978
R ↓ Crisis Intervention Services 1973
↓ Facility Admission 1988
↓ Facility Discharge 1988
↓ Facility Environment 1988
↓ Health Care Administration 1997
Institutional Schools 1978
↓ Residential Care Institutions 1973
↓ Therapeutic Environment 2001
↓ Treatment 1967

Treatment Guidelines 2001
PN 1347 **SC** 54175
B Treatment 1967
R Client Treatment Matching 1997
Clinical Governance 2007

Treatment Guidelines — (cont'd)
↓ Professional Standards 1973
↓ Quality of Services 1997
↓ Treatment Planning 1997

Treatment Methods (Physical)
Use Physical Treatment Methods

Treatment Outcomes 1982
PN 13664 **SC** 54185
SN Limited to treatment results that are a function of unique or specifically-described circumstances or characteristics (e.g., race) of the clients/patients, the treatment provider, or the treatment itself. For effectiveness of particular treatment modes, use the specific type of treatment (e.g., DRUG THERAPY). For efficacy of treatment for a particular disorder, use the specific disorder (e.g., MANIA) and the specific type of treatment.
UF Outcomes (Treatment)
Therapeutic Outcomes
N Psychotherapeutic Outcomes 1973
R Client Treatment Matching 1997
Mental Health Program Evaluation 1973
Postsurgical Complications 1973
↓ Psychotherapeutic Processes 1967
Recovery (Disorders) 1973
Relapse (Disorders) 1973
Relapse Prevention 1994
↓ Remission (Disorders) 1973
↓ Side Effects (Treatment) 1988
↓ Therapeutic Processes 1978
↓ Treatment 1967
Treatment Dropouts 1978
↓ Treatment Duration 1988
Treatment Effectiveness Evaluation 1973
Treatment Termination 1982

Treatment Planning 1997
PN 1940 **SC** 54189
UF Patient Care Planning
N Discharge Planning 1994
R Aftercare 1973
↓ Case Management 1991
↓ Client Characteristics 1973
Client Treatment Matching 1997
Clinical Judgment (Not Diagnosis) 1973
Disease Management 2007
↓ Health Care Delivery 1978
↓ Managed Care 1994
Needs Assessment 1985
Posttreatment Followup 1973
↓ Treatment 1967
↓ Treatment Duration 1988
Treatment Guidelines 2001

Treatment Refusal 1994
PN 417 **SC** 54186
SN Patient or client refusal of or resistance to medical, psychological, or psychiatric treatment. Consider TREATMENT WITHHOLDING for life sustaining contexts.
UF Refusal (Treatment)
R Advance Directives 1994
Assisted Suicide 1997
↓ Client Rights 1988
Client Transfer 1997
Informed Consent 1985
Involuntary Treatment 1994
Life Sustaining Treatment 1997
Psychotherapeutic Resistance 1973
↓ Resistance 1997
Treatment Barriers 2005
Treatment Compliance 1982

Treatment Refusal — (cont'd)
Treatment Dropouts 1978
Treatment Termination 1982
Treatment Withholding 1988

Treatment Resistant Depression 1994
PN 767 **SC** 57440
UF Tricyclic Resistant Depression
B Major Depression 1988
Treatment Resistant Disorders 1994
R ↓ Drug Therapy 1967

Treatment Resistant Disorders 1994
PN 1286 **SC** 57445
SN Used for any disorder that is resistant to any type of psychological or medical treatment.
N Treatment Resistant Depression 1994
R ↓ Chronic Mental Illness 1997
↓ Mental Disorders 1967
↓ Physical Disorders 1997
↓ Treatment 1967

Treatment Seeking Behavior
Use Health Care Seeking Behavior

Treatment Termination 1982
PN 1288 **SC** 54187
SN Completion of medical or psychological/behavioral treatment programs. Compare TREATMENT DROPOUTS.
R Client Transfer 1997
Discharge Planning 1994
↓ Hospital Discharge 1973
Psychiatric Hospital Discharge 1978
↓ Therapeutic Processes 1978
↓ Treatment 1967
Treatment Dropouts 1978
↓ Treatment Duration 1988
↓ Treatment Outcomes 1982
Treatment Refusal 1994
Treatment Withholding 1988

Treatment Withholding 1988
PN 336 **SC** 54188
SN Limiting or restricting medical treatment for seriously ill persons. Includes do-not-resuscitate orders. Compare TREATMENT TERMINATION.
R Advance Directives 1994
Assisted Suicide 1997
↓ Client Rights 1988
↓ Death and Dying 1967
Euthanasia 1973
↓ Human Rights 1978
Informed Consent 1985
Life Sustaining Treatment 1997
↓ Treatment 1967
Treatment Compliance 1982
Treatment Refusal 1994
Treatment Termination 1982

Tremor 1973
PN 469 **SC** 54200
B Movement Disorders 1985
Symptoms 1967
R ↓ Antitremor Drugs 1973
Parkinsonism 1994
Parkinsons Disease 1973

Trends 1991
PN 3769 **SC** 54204
SN Used specifically for analysis of past, present, or future patterns in technology, economics, and social or developmental processes.

Trends — (cont'd)
R ↓ Fads and Fashions 1973
Future 1991
↓ History 1973
Popular Culture 2003
Social Change 1967
↓ Social Processes 1967
↓ Time 1967
Transgenerational Patterns 1991

Triadic Therapy
Use Conjoint Therapy

Trial and Error Learning 1973
PN 93 **SC** 54210
B Learning 1967
Learning Strategies 1991

Triazolam 1988
PN 294 **SC** 54215
UF Halcion
B Hypnotic Drugs 1973
Sedatives 1973

Tribes 1973
PN 629 **SC** 54220
R Alaska Natives 1997
American Indians 1967
↓ Racial and Ethnic Groups 2001

Trichotillomania 2003
PN 430 **SC** 54225
SN Excessive pulling of one's own hair.
HN In June 2003, this term replaced the discontinued term HAIR PULLING. HAIR PULLING was removed from all records containing it and replaced with TRICHOTILLOMANIA.
UF Hair Pulling
B Habits 1967
R ↓ Behavior Disorders 1971
↓ Self Destructive Behavior 1985

Tricyclic Antidepressant Drugs 1997
PN 441 **SC** 54226
B Antidepressant Drugs 1971
N Amitriptyline 1973
Chlorimipramine 1973
Desipramine 1973
Doxepin 1994
Imipramine 1973
Maprotiline 1982
Nortriptyline 1994
R ↓ Adrenergic Blocking Drugs 1973
↓ Lithium 1973
↓ Monoamine Oxidase Inhibitors 1973

Tricyclic Resistant Depression
Use Treatment Resistant Depression

Trifluoperazine 1973
PN 123 **SC** 54230
UF Stelazine
B Phenothiazine Derivatives 1973

Triflupromazine
HN Term discontinued in 1997. In 2000, the term was removed from all records containing it, and replaced with PHENOTHIAZINE DERIVATIVES, its postable counterpart.
Use Phenothiazine Derivatives

Trigeminal Nerve 1973
PN 290 **SC** 54250
B Cranial Nerves 1973

Trigeminal Neuralgia 1973
PN 105 **SC** 54260
SN A disorder characterized by sudden, intense recurrences of pain involving the trigeminal nerve.
UF Tic Doloureux
B Neuralgia 1973

Trigonum Cerebrale
Use Fornix

Trihexyphenidyl 1973
PN 68 **SC** 54270
B Amines 1973
Antispasmodic Drugs 1973
Antitremor Drugs 1973
Cholinergic Blocking Drugs 1973

Triiodothyronine 1973
PN 173 **SC** 54280
B Thyroid Hormones 1973

Triplets 1973
PN 52 **SC** 54310
B Multiple Births 1973

Trisomy 1973
PN 96 **SC** 54320
B Chromosome Disorders 1973

Trisomy 21
HN In August 2005, this term was discontinued and removed from all records containing it, and was replaced with DOWNS SYNDROME, its postable counterpart.
Use Downs Syndrome

Trochlear Nerve
Use Cranial Nerves

Truancy 1973
PN 115 **SC** 54360
N School Truancy 1973

Trucks
Use Motor Vehicles

True False Tests
Use Forced Choice (Testing Method)

Trust (Social Behavior) 1967
PN 2773 **SC** 54370
B Prosocial Behavior 1982
R Hope 1991

Tryptamine 1973
PN 120 **SC** 54380
B Amines 1973
Vasoconstrictor Drugs 1973

Tryptophan 1973
PN 1292 **SC** 54390
B Amino Acids 1973
Serotonin Precursors 1978
N Hydroxytryptophan (5-) 1991

Tubal Ligation 1973
PN 52 **SC** 54400
B Birth Control 1971
Sterilization (Sex) 1973

Tuberculosis 1973
PN 249 **SC** 54410
B Bacterial Disorders 1973
N Pulmonary Tuberculosis 1973
R ↓ Antitubercular Drugs 1973
Lupus 1973
↓ Musculoskeletal Disorders 1973
↓ Nervous System Disorders 1967
↓ Skin Disorders 1973

Tubocurarine 1973
PN 15 **SC** 54420
B Alkaloids 1973
Muscle Relaxing Drugs 1973
R Curare 1973

Tumor Necrosis Factor 2006
PN 94 **SC** 54425
SN A protein with the ability to kill tumor cells, activate white blood cells, and mediate inflammation.
HN This term was introduced in May 2006. Relevant records were re-indexed with this term. The posting note reflects the number of records that were re-indexed.
B Cytokines 2003

Tumors
Use Neoplasms

Tunnel Vision 1973
PN 18 **SC** 54440
SN Disorder characterized by severe limitation or total lack of peripheral vision.
B Eye Disorders 1973
R ↓ Vision 1967

Turners Syndrome 1973
PN 213 **SC** 54460
B Hypogonadism 1973
Neonatal Disorders 1973
Sex Linked Hereditary Disorders 1973
Syndromes 1973
R Hermaphroditism 1973
Sterility 1973

Turnover
Use Employee Turnover

Turtles 1973
PN 266 **SC** 54480
UF Tortoises
B Reptiles 1967

Tutoring 1973
PN 1023 **SC** 54490
B Teaching Methods 1967
N Peer Tutoring 1973
R Individualized Instruction 1973
Test Coaching 1997

Tutors
Use Teachers

Twelve Step Programs 1997
PN 307 **SC** 54505
UF Gamblers Anonymous
Narcotics Anonymous
B Support Groups 1991
N Alcoholics Anonymous 1973
R ↓ Drug Rehabilitation 1973
Group Counseling 1973
↓ Group Psychotherapy 1967
↓ Mental Health Services 1978
↓ Psychotherapeutic Techniques 1967

Twelve Step Programs — (cont'd)
↓ Rehabilitation 1967
↓ Self Help Techniques 1982
↓ Treatment 1967

Twins 1967
PN 2514 **SC** 54510
B Multiple Births 1973
N Conjoined Twins 2003
Heterozygotic Twins 1973
Monozygotic Twins 1973
R Family Resemblance 1991
↓ Genetics 1967

Tympanic Membrane
Use Middle Ear

Type A Personality
Use Coronary Prone Behavior

Type B Personality
Use Coronary Prone Behavior

Type I Errors 1973
PN 409 **SC** 54530
B Prediction Errors 1973
R Statistical Power 1991

Type II Errors 1973
PN 105 **SC** 54540
B Prediction Errors 1973
R Statistical Power 1991

Typing 1991
PN 122 **SC** 54550
HN Use CLERICAL SECRETARIAL SKILLS to access references from 1973-1990.
R Clerical Secretarial Skills 1973
Keyboards 1985
Word Processing 1991

Typists
Use Clerical Personnel

Typologies (General)
Use Taxonomies

Typologies (Psychodiagnostic)
Use Psychodiagnostic Typologies

Tyramine 1973
PN 95 **SC** 54580
B Adrenergic Drugs 1973
Sympathomimetic Amines 1973
Vasoconstrictor Drugs 1973
R ↓ Ergot Derivatives 1973

Tyrosine 1973
PN 544 **SC** 54590
B Amino Acids 1973
N Alpha Methylparatyrosine 1978
R Melanin 1973

Ulcerative Colitis 1973
PN 187 **SC** 54620
B Colitis 1973

Ulcers (Gastrointestinal)
Use Gastrointestinal Ulcers

Ulnar Nerve
Use Spinal Nerves

Ultrasound 1973
PN 459 **SC** 54650
SN Sound waves with frequencies above the range of human hearing.
B Pitch (Frequency) 1967

Uncertainty 1991
PN 1899 **SC** 54655
SN May be used for uncertainty reduction processes; uncertainty in decision making, choice, or judgment; or in statistical contexts.
R ↓ Chance (Fortune) 1973
Chaos Theory 1997
Choice Behavior 1967
↓ Decision Making 1967
Doubt 1973
Impression Management 1978
↓ Judgment 1967
Skepticism 2004
↓ Statistical Analysis 1967
Suspicion 1973

Unconditioned Reflex
Use Reflexes

Unconditioned Responses 1973
PN 193 **SC** 54680
B Classical Conditioning 1967
Responses 1967

Unconditioned Stimulus 1973
PN 1494 **SC** 54690
UF Stimulus (Unconditioned)
B Conditioning 1967
R ↓ Classical Conditioning 1967
↓ Operant Conditioning 1967
Primary Reinforcement 1973
↓ Stimulation 1967

Unconscious (Personality Factor) 1967
PN 2612 **SC** 54700
B Psychoanalytic Personality Factors 1973
R Archetypes 1991
Death Instinct 1988
Free Association 1994
Id 1973
Mind 1991

Underachievement (Academic)
Use Academic Underachievement

Underage Drinking 2007
PN 46 **SC** 54712
HN This term was introduced in April 2007. Relevant records were re-indexed with this term. The posting note reflects the number of records that were re-indexed.
R ↓ Alcohol Abuse 1988
↓ Alcohol Drinking Patterns 1967
Peer Pressure 1994

Underdeveloped Countries
Use Developing Countries

Undergraduate Degrees
Use Educational Degrees

Undergraduate Education 1978
PN 1859 **SC** 54725
UF College Education
B Higher Education 1973

Undergraduates
Use College Students

Underprivileged
Use Disadvantaged

Understanding
Use Comprehension

Underwater Effects 1973
PN 223 **SC** 54760
B Environmental Effects 1973
R Decompression Effects 1973
↓ Gravitational Effects 1967

Underweight 1973
PN 102 **SC** 54770
B Body Weight 1967
Symptoms 1967
N Anorexia Nervosa 1973
R Diets 1978
↓ Eating Disorders 1997
Hyperthyroidism 1973
↓ Nutritional Deficiencies 1973

Undifferentiated Schizophrenia 1973
PN 107 **SC** 54780
SN A form of schizophrenia in which patients exhibit prominent psychotic symptoms but fail to meet the criteria for the other schizophrenia subtypes (catatonic, disorganized, or paranoid).
B Schizophrenia 1967

Unemployment 1967
PN 2088 **SC** 54790
B Employment Status 1982
Social Issues 1991
R Employment History 1978
Job Search 1985
Job Security 1978
↓ Personnel 1967
Personnel Termination 1973
Reemployment 1991
Retirement 1973

Unipolar Depression
HN Use DEPRESSION (EMOTION) to access references from 1982-1987.
Use Major Depression

Universities
Use Colleges

Unskilled Industrial Workers 1973
PN 95 **SC** 54880
SN Blue collar workers who perform unskilled labor in an industrial setting.
B Blue Collar Workers 1973

Unwed Mothers 1973
PN 298 **SC** 54890
SN Consider also ADOLESCENT MOTHERS.
B Mothers 1967
R Never Married 1994
Premarital Intercourse 1973
Single Mothers 1994
↓ Single Parents 1978

Upper Class 1973
PN 152 **SC** 54900
B Social Class 1967

Upper Class Attitudes 1973
PN 13 **SC** 54910
SN Attitudes of, not toward, the upper class.

Upper Class Attitudes — (cont'd)
B Socioeconomic Class Attitudes 1973

Upper Income Level 1973
PN 90 SC 54920
B Income Level 1973

Upward Bound 1973
PN 51 SC 54930
SN U.S. Government educational and counseling program for disadvantaged high school and college students.
B Educational Programs 1973
Government Programs 1973
R Compensatory Education 1973
Government 1967

Upward Mobility
Use Social Mobility

Urban Development
Use Community Development

Urban Environments 1967
PN 9986 SC 54940
UF Cities
Inner City
B Social Environments 1973
R Community Development 1997
Ghettoes 1973
Urban Planning 1973

Urban Planning 1973
PN 312 SC 54960
B Environmental Planning 1982
R ↓ Architecture 1973
Built Environment 2007
Community Development 1997
↓ Community Facilities 1973
↓ Environment 1967
↓ Recreation Areas 1973
Urban Environments 1967

Urbanization 1973
PN 261 SC 54970
B Social Processes 1967
R Industrialization 1973
Modernization 2003

Uric Acid 1973
PN 77 SC 55010
B Acids 1973

Urinalysis 1973
PN 282 SC 55020
B Medical Diagnosis 1973
R Drug Usage Screening 1988

Urinary Function Disorders 1973
PN 226 SC 55040
B Urogenital Disorders 1973
N Urinary Incontinence 1973
R ↓ Somatoform Disorders 2001

Urinary Incontinence 1973
PN 1156 SC 55050
UF Bedwetting
Enuresis
Incontinence (Urinary)
B Urinary Function Disorders 1973
R ↓ Behavior Disorders 1971
↓ Symptoms 1967

Urination 1967
PN 292 SC 55070
UF Micturition
B Excretion 1967
N Diuresis 1973
R ↓ Diuretics 1973

Urine 1973
PN 1005 SC 55080
B Body Fluids 1973

Urogenital Disorders 1973
PN 326 SC 55090
B Physical Disorders 1997
N ↓ Genital Disorders 1967
↓ Gynecological Disorders 1973
Kidney Diseases 1988
↓ Urinary Function Disorders 1973
R ↓ Sexual Function Disturbances 1973
↓ Sexually Transmitted Diseases 2003
↓ Somatoform Disorders 2001
↓ Urogenital System 1973

Urogenital System 1973
PN 82 SC 55100
B Anatomical Systems 1973
N Bladder 1973
↓ Female Genitalia 1973
↓ Gonads 1973
Kidneys 1973
↓ Male Genitalia 1973
R ↓ Urogenital Disorders 1973

Usability (Systems)
Use Human Factors Engineering

Uterus 1973
PN 103 SC 55110
B Female Genitalia 1973
N Cervix 1973
R Placenta 1973

Utility Theory 2004
PN 143 SC 55113
SN Theory asserting that rational choices are made based on logical analysis of the subjective value of the outcomes.
HN This term was introduced in June 2004. Relevant records were re-indexed with this term. The posting note reflects the number of records that were re-indexed.
B Theories 1967
R Choice Behavior 1967
↓ Decision Making 1967

Utilization (Health Care)
Use Health Care Utilization

Utilization Reviews 2007
PN 63 SC 55117
SN A formal review of the necessity and quality of services provided in a hospital or clinic by an individual provider. Conducted by a specially appointed committee, a utilization review often addresses whether the level of service provided is the most appropriate to the severity of the presenting problem.
HN This term was introduced in April 2007. Relevant records were re-indexed with this term. The posting note reflects the number of records that were re-indexed.
R ↓ Health Care Administration 1997
Health Care Costs 1994

Utilization Reviews — (cont'd)
Health Care Utilization 1985
↓ Health Insurance 1973
↓ Managed Care 1994
Needs Assessment 1985
Quality of Care 1988

Vacation Benefits
Use Employee Leave Benefits

Vacationing 1973
PN 315 SC 55130
B Recreation 1967
R Camping 1973
Holidays 1988
Summer Camps (Recreation) 1973
Tourism 2003
Traveling 1973

Vaccination
Use Immunization

Vagina 1973
PN 291 SC 55150
B Female Genitalia 1973

Vaginismus 1973
PN 112 SC 55160
B Sexual Function Disturbances 1973
R Dyspareunia 1973
Female Sexual Dysfunction 2005

Vagotomy 1973
PN 153 SC 55170
B Neurosurgery 1973

Vagus Nerve 1973
PN 424 SC 55180
B Cranial Nerves 1973
Parasympathetic Nervous System 1973
R ↓ Heart 1967

Validity (Statistical)
Use Statistical Validity

Validity (Test)
Use Test Validity

Valium
Use Diazepam

Valproic Acid 1991
PN 770 SC 55215
B Anticonvulsive Drugs 1973

Values 1967
PN 8150 SC 55220
SN Qualities, principles or behaviors considered to be morally or intrinsically valuable or desirable. Use a more specific term if possible.
UF Mores
N Ethnic Values 1973
Personal Values 1973
Social Values 1973
R ↓ Ethics 1967
Integrity 1997
Morality 1967
World View 1988

Valves (Heart)
Use Heart Valves

Vandalism 1978
PN 130 **SC** 55235
SN Willful or malicious destruction or defacement of public or private property.
B Crime 1967

Vane Kindergarten Test
HN Term discontinued in 1997. In 2000, the term was removed from all records containing it, and replaced with INTELLIGENCE MEASURES, its postable counterpart.
Use Intelligence Measures

Variability (Response)
Use Response Variability

Variability (Stimulus)
Use Stimulus Variability

Variability Measurement 1973
PN 415 **SC** 55270
B Statistical Analysis 1967
Statistical Measurement 1973
N Analysis of Covariance 1973
Analysis of Variance 1967
Interaction Variance 1973
Standard Deviation 1973
R ↓ Central Tendency Measures 1973
F Test 1973
↓ Statistical Correlation 1967

Variable Interval Reinforcement 1973
PN 792 **SC** 55280
UF Interval Reinforcement
B Reinforcement Schedules 1967

Variable Ratio Reinforcement 1973
PN 207 **SC** 55290
UF Ratio Reinforcement
B Reinforcement Schedules 1967

Variance Homogeneity
HN In June 2003, the term was discontinued and removed from all records containing it, and was replaced with HOMOGENEITY of VARIANCE, its postable counterpart.
Use Homogeneity of Variance

Varimax Rotation 1973
PN 64 **SC** 55330
B Orthogonal Rotation 1973

Vascular Dementia 1997
PN 1096 **SC** 55333
SN A step-like deteriorating form of dementia that is a result of multiple cerebral infarctions.
HN In August 2005, this term replaced the discontinued term MULTI INFARCT DEMENTIA. MULTI INFARCT DEMENTIA was removed from all records containing it, and was replaced with VASCULAR DEMENTIA, its postable counterpart.
UF Dementia (Multi Infarct)
Multi Infarct Dementia
B Dementia 1985
R ↓ Cerebrovascular Disorders 1973

Vascular Disorders
Use Cardiovascular Disorders

Vasectomy 1973
PN 93 **SC** 55350
B Birth Control 1971
Sterilization (Sex) 1973
Surgery 1971

Vasoconstriction 1973
PN 124 **SC** 55360
R ↓ Blood Pressure Disorders 1973
Epinephrine 1967

Vasoconstrictor Drugs 1973
PN 36 **SC** 55370
UF Pressors (Drugs)
Vasopressor Drugs
B Drugs 1967
N ↓ Amphetamine 1967
Angiotensin 1973
Bufotenine 1973
Dihydroergotamine 1973
Ephedrine 1973
Methamphetamine 1973
Methoxamine 1973
Norepinephrine 1973
Serotonin 1973
Tryptamine 1973
Tyramine 1973
R ↓ Blood Pressure 1967
↓ Heart Rate Affecting Drugs 1973
↓ Vasodilator Drugs 1973
Vasopressin 1973

Vasodilation 1973
PN 106 **SC** 55380
R ↓ Blood Pressure Disorders 1973
Epinephrine 1967
↓ Muscle Relaxing Drugs 1973
Theophylline 1973

Vasodilator Drugs 1973
PN 201 **SC** 55390
B Drugs 1967
N Nicotinic Acid 1973
Verapamil 1991
R ↓ Antihypertensive Drugs 1973
↓ Blood Pressure 1967
Channel Blockers 1991
↓ Heart Rate Affecting Drugs 1973
↓ Vasoconstrictor Drugs 1973

Vasopressin 1973
PN 1083 **SC** 55400
B Neuropeptides 2003
Pituitary Hormones 1973
R ↓ Vasoconstrictor Drugs 1973

Vasopressor Drugs
Use Vasoconstrictor Drugs

Veins (Anatomy) 1973
PN 49 **SC** 55420
B Blood Vessels 1973

Velocity 1973
PN 1654 **SC** 55430
UF Speed
R Vibration 1967

Venereal Diseases
HN In June 2003, the term was discontinued and removed from all records containing it, and was replaced with SEXUALLY TRANSMITTED DISEASES.
Use Sexually Transmitted Diseases

Venlafaxine 2003
PN 545 **SC** 55450
HN This term was introduced in June 2003. Relevant records were re-indexed with this term. The posting note reflects the number of records that were re-indexed.
B Antidepressant Drugs 1971
Serotonin Norepinephrine Reuptake Inhibitors 2007

Ventral Roots 1973
PN 41 **SC** 55460
B Spinal Cord 1973

Ventral Striatum
Use Basal Ganglia

Ventral Tegmental Area
Use Tegmentum

Ventricles (Cerebral)
Use Cerebral Ventricles

Ventricles (Heart)
Use Heart Ventricles

Ventricular Fibrillation
Use Fibrillation (Heart)

Venture Capital 2007
PN 14 **SC** 55493
SN A type of financial investment in which an individual or group takes on a high degree of risk in funding a start-up company or other business venture. Investors typically gain partial ownership of the company and profit substantially if the company succeeds.
HN This term was introduced in April 2007. Relevant records were re-indexed with this term. The posting note reflects the number of records that were re-indexed.
B Business Investments 2007
R Entrepreneurship 1991
Finance 2007
Funding 1988

Verapamil 1991
PN 86 **SC** 55495
B Heart Rate Affecting Drugs 1973
Vasodilator Drugs 1973
R Channel Blockers 1991

Verbal Ability 1967
PN 3540 **SC** 55500
B Cognitive Ability 1973
R Academic Aptitude 1973
Language Proficiency 1988
Metalinguistics 1994
↓ Oral Communication 1985
Proofreading 1988
↓ Verbal Communication 1967
↓ Verbal Memory 1994
Writing Skills 1985
↓ Written Communication 1985

Verbal Abuse 2003
PN 101 **SC** 55504
SN Written or spoken words that are excessively critical, insulting, and/or intimidating.
HN This term was introduced in June 2003. Relevant records were re-indexed with this term. The posting note reflects the number of records that were re-indexed.
B Antisocial Behavior 1971
R ↓ Child Abuse 1971
Elder Abuse 1988

Verbal Abuse — (cont'd)
Emotional Abuse 1991
↓ Partner Abuse 1991
Patient Abuse 1991
Physical Abuse 1991

Verbal Communication 1967
PN 11323 **SC** 55520
SN Communication through spoken or written language. Use narrower terms if possible.
B Communication 1967
N Articulation (Speech) 1967
Conversation 1973
↓ Handwriting 1967
Language Proficiency 1988
↓ Manual Communication 1978
Narratives 1997
↓ Oral Communication 1985
Pragmatics 1985
Storytelling 1988
↓ Written Communication 1985
R ↓ Communication Skills 1973
Discourse Analysis 1997
↓ Grammar 1967
↓ Language 1967
↓ Language Development 1967
↓ Linguistics 1973
Metalinguistics 1994
Neurolinguistics 1991
↓ Speech Processing (Mechanical) 1973
Text Structure 1982
Verbal Ability 1967
↓ Vocabulary 1967
↓ Vocalization 1967

Verbal Comprehension 1985
PN 1651 **SC** 55525
B Comprehension 1967
N Listening Comprehension 1973
Reading Comprehension 1973
Sentence Comprehension 1973

Verbal Conditioning
Use Verbal Learning

Verbal Fluency 1973
PN 2274 **SC** 55540
SN Ability to produce and manipulate words in thought or speech.
UF Fluency
R Language Proficiency 1988
↓ Oral Communication 1985
Speech Rate 1973

Verbal Learning 1967
PN 4189 **SC** 55550
SN Acquisition, retention, and retrieval of verbal stimulus materials such as nonsense syllables, words, or sentences. Compare LANGUAGE DEVELOPMENT.
UF Conditioning (Verbal)
Verbal Conditioning
B Learning 1967
N Nonsense Syllable Learning 1967
Paired Associate Learning 1967
R Isolation Effect 1973
Serial Anticipation (Learning) 1973
↓ Serial Learning 1967
↓ Verbal Memory 1994

Verbal Meaning 1973
PN 919 **SC** 55560
SN Connotative or denotative meaning associated with any verbally informative unit (e.g., morpheme, word, sentence, or phrase).
B Meaning 1967
N Word Meaning 1973
R ↓ Figurative Language 1985
↓ Semantics 1967

Verbal Memory 1994
PN 1510 **SC** 55565
B Memory 1967
N Semantic Memory 1988
R ↓ Lexical Access 1988
Lexical Decision 1988
Verbal Ability 1967
↓ Verbal Learning 1967

Verbal Reinforcement 1973
PN 727 **SC** 55570
B Social Reinforcement 1967
N Praise 1973

Verbal Stimuli 1982
PN 1408 **SC** 55575
SN Aural or visual presentation of syllables or words or nonword letter combinations.
B Stimulation 1967
R ↓ Stimulus Presentation Methods 1973

Verbal Tests 1973
PN 207 **SC** 55580
SN Tests designed to assess verbal ability or in which performance depends upon verbal ability.
B Measurement 1967

Verbalization
Use Oral Communication

Verbs 1973
PN 1795 **SC** 55600
B Form Classes (Language) 1973

Verdict Determination
Use Adjudication

Vergence Movements
Use Eye Convergence

Verification (of Theories)
Use Theory Verification

Vernier Acuity
Use Visual Acuity

Vertebrates 1973
PN 432 **SC** 55620
B Animals 1967
N ↓ Amphibia 1973
↓ Birds 1967
↓ Fishes 1967
↓ Mammals 1973
Pigs 1973
↓ Reptiles 1967
R ↓ Invertebrates 1973

Vertigo 1973
PN 303 **SC** 55630
UF Dizziness
B Symptoms 1967
R ↓ Labyrinth Disorders 1973
Menieres Disease 1973
Syncope 1973

Vestibular Apparatus 1967
PN 874 **SC** 55660
SN Major organ of equilibrium which acts as a sensory receptor that detects the position and changes in the position of the head in space.
B Ear (Anatomy) 1967
N Semicircular Canals 1973
R ↓ Labyrinth (Anatomy) 1973
↓ Labyrinth Disorders 1973

Vestibular Disorders
Use Labyrinth Disorders

Vestibular Nystagmus
Use Nystagmus

Vestibular Stimulation
Use Somesthetic Stimulation

Vestibulocochlear Nerve
Use Acoustic Nerve

Veterans (Military)
Use Military Veterans

Veterinary Medicine 1973
PN 104 **SC** 55680
B Medical Sciences 1967

Viagra
Use Sildenafil

Vibration 1967
PN 587 **SC** 55690
UF Resonance
R Velocity 1973

Vibrators (Apparatus) 1973
PN 23 **SC** 55700
B Apparatus 1967
R ↓ Stimulators (Apparatus) 1973

Vibrotactile Thresholds 1973
PN 376 **SC** 55710
SN The minimal level of vibratory stimulation, the minimal difference between any such stimuli, or the minimal vibratory stimulus change that is tactually perceptible.
B Tactual Perception 1967
Thresholds 1967
R ↓ Perceptual Measures 1973

Vicarious Experiences 1973
PN 405 **SC** 55713
UF Reinforcement (Vicarious)
Vicarious Reinforcement
B Experiences (Events) 1973
R Imagination 1967
↓ Reinforcement 1967

Vicarious Reinforcement
Use Vicarious Experiences

Victimization 1973
PN 9235 **SC** 55716
SN Process or state of having been personally subjected to crime, deception, fraud, or other detrimental circumstances as a result of the deeds of others.
B Social Interaction 1967
R Bullying 2003
↓ Crime 1967
↓ Crime Victims 1982
Criminal Profiling 2007
Erotomania 1997
↓ Harassment 2001

Victimization — (cont'd)
Hate Crimes 2003
Human Trafficking 2007
↓ Perpetrators 1988
Persecution 1973
Sexual Harassment 1985
Stalking 2001
Teasing 2003
Torture 1988
↓ Violent Crime 2003

Video Display Terminals
Use Video Display Units

Video Display Units 1985
PN 729 **SC** 55718
SN Electronic devices used to present information or stimulation through visual means.
HN Use VISUAL DISPLAYS to access references from 1973-1984.
UF Cathode Ray Tubes
CRT
Video Display Terminals
B Computer Peripheral Devices 1985
Visual Displays 1973
R ↓ Television 1967
↓ Visual Stimulation 1973

Video Games
Use Computer Games

Videotape Instruction 1973
PN 757 **SC** 55720
SN Audiovisual teaching method which employs presentation of feedback as an aid to learning.
B Audiovisual Instruction 1973
R Educational Audiovisual Aids 1973

Videotape Recorders 1973
PN 129 **SC** 55730
SN Device for recording on magnetic tape and having varied applications (e.g., teaching aid, analysis of research data).
B Tape Recorders 1973

Videotapes 1973
PN 1871 **SC** 55740
SN Audiovisual tape recordings used in both noneducational and educational settings.
B Audiovisual Communications Media 1973
R Digital Video 2007

Vietnamese Cultural Groups 1997
PN 207 **SC** 57748
HN Use ASIANS to access references from 1982-1996.
B Asians 1982
Southeast Asian Cultural Groups 2004

Vigilance 1967
PN 1807 **SC** 55750
SN Intentional and conscious alertness characterized by a readiness to respond to environmental changes. Compare ATTENTION.
B Attention 1967
Monitoring 1973
Sustained Attention 1997
R Attention Span 1973
Selective Attention 1973

Vineland Social Maturity Scale 1973
PN 45 **SC** 55760
B Nonprojective Personality Measures 1973

Violence 1973
PN 13202 **SC** 55770
B Antisocial Behavior 1971
Conflict 1967
N Domestic Violence 2006
Intimate Partner Violence 2007
Patient Violence 1994
School Violence 2003
↓ Violent Crime 2003
Workplace Violence 2007
R Coercion 1994
Dangerousness 1988
Hate Crimes 2003
Nonviolence 1991
↓ Partner Abuse 1991
Physical Abuse 1991
Riots 1973
Self Defense 1985
↓ Terrorism 1982
Torture 1988
↓ War 1967

Violent Crime 2003
PN 418 **SC** 55773
HN This term was introduced in June 2003. Relevant records were re-indexed with this term. The posting note reflects the number of records that were re-indexed.
B Crime 1967
Violence 1973
N Domestic Violence 2006
↓ Homicide 1967
Physical Abuse 1991
Political Assassination 1973
↓ Rape 1973
↓ Terrorism 1982
R Arson 1985
↓ Child Abuse 1971
Kidnapping 1988
↓ Sexual Abuse 1988
Victimization 1973

Viral Disorders 1973
PN 561 **SC** 55780
B Infectious Disorders 1973
N ↓ Encephalitis 1973
Epstein Barr Viral Disorder 1994
Herpes Genitalis 1988
Herpes Simplex 1973
↓ HIV 2006
Influenza 1973
Measles 1973
Poliomyelitis 1973
Rubella 1973
R Chronic Fatigue Syndrome 1997
Pneumonia 1973

Virginity 1973
PN 146 **SC** 55810
B Psychosexual Behavior 1967
R Premarital Intercourse 1973
Sexual Abstinence 1973

Virtual Classrooms 2007
PN 25 **SC** 55812
SN Interactive classrooms that utilize computer mediated communication between teachers and students.
HN This term was introduced in April 2007. Relevant records were re-indexed with this term. The posting note reflects the number of records that were re-indexed.
B Classrooms 1967
R Classroom Environment 1973
Computer Mediated Communication 2003
Distance Education 2003
Learning Environment 2004
↓ Nontraditional Education 1982
Teleconferencing 1997

Virtual Markets
Use Electronic Commerce

Virtual Reality 1997
PN 1535 **SC** 55815
B Computer Simulation 1973
R ↓ Computer Applications 1973
Human Machine Systems 1997

Virtual Teams 2007
PN 98 **SC** 55817
SN Project or work teams comprised of individuals located remotely from each other, who interact via electronic communication technology.
HN This term was introduced in April 2007. Relevant records were re-indexed with this term. The posting note reflects the number of records that were re-indexed.
B Work Teams 2001
R Computer Mediated Communication 2003
↓ Electronic Communication 2001
Telecommuting 2003
Teleconferencing 1997

Vision 1967
PN 4405 **SC** 55820
N Linear Perspective 1982
↓ Visual Perception 1967
R Tunnel Vision 1973
Visual Cortex 1967
Visual Evoked Potentials 1973
Visual Hallucinations 1973
Visual Tracking 1973

Vision Disorders 1982
PN 3728 **SC** 55825
SN Disorders involving the visual system, including visual neural pathways.
HN The term VISUALLY HANDICAPPED was also used to represent this concept from 1967-1996, and VISUALLY DISABLED was used from 1997-2000. In 2000, VISION DISORDERS replaced the discontinued and deleted term VISUALLY DISABLED. VISUALLY DISABLED and VISUALLY HANDICAPPED were removed from all records containing them, and replaced with VISION DISORDERS.
UF Visual Impairment
Visually Handicapped
B Physical Disorders 1997
Sense Organ Disorders 1973
N ↓ Blind 1967
↓ Eye Disorders 1973
Hemianopia 1973

Vision Disturbances (Hysterical)
Use Hysterical Vision Disturbances

Visions (Mysticism)
Use Mysticism

Visitation (Institution)
Use Institution Visitation

Visitation Rights
Use Child Visitation

Visual Acuity 1982
PN 1343 **SC** 55897
SN The ability or capacity of an observer to perceive fine detail.
HN Consider VISUAL THRESHOLDS or VISUAL DISCRIMINATION to access references prior to 1982.
UF Vernier Acuity
B Visual Perception 1967
R Pattern Discrimination 1967
↓ Spatial Perception 1967

Visual Attention 2004
PN 1188 **SC** 58080
HN This term was introduced in June 2004. Relevant records were re-indexed with this term. The posting note reflects the number of records that were re-indexed.
B Attention 1967
R Eye Fixation 1982
↓ Visual Perception 1967

Visual Contrast 1985
PN 1591 **SC** 55898
SN Perceived difference in color, brightness, or other qualities of two or more simultaneously or successively presented visual stimuli despite a lack of objective differences.
B Visual Perception 1967
N Brightness Contrast 1985
Color Contrast 1985

Visual Cortex 1967
PN 4249 **SC** 55900
UF Cortex (Visual)
Striate Cortex
B Occipital Lobe 1973
R ↓ Vision 1967
Visual Receptive Fields 1982

Visual Discrimination 1967
PN 7363 **SC** 55910
SN Ability to recognize quantitative or qualitative differences between visual shapes, forms, and patterns.
HN Use VISUAL DISCRIMINATION or VISUAL THRESHOLDS to access references on visual acuity prior to 1982.
B Perceptual Discrimination 1973
Visual Perception 1967
R Visual Search 1982
Visual Tracking 1973

Visual Displays 1973
PN 3429 **SC** 55920
SN Presentation of visual information in the form of charts, graphs, maps, signs, symbols, or patterns.
HN Prior to 1985, used for visual devices such as cathode-ray tubes or instrument panels. From 1985, consider also VIDEO DISPLAY UNITS, INSTRUMENT CONTROLS, or GRAPHICAL DISPLAYS.
B Displays 1967
Visual Stimulation 1973
N Video Display Units 1985
R ↓ Computer Peripheral Devices 1985
Pictorial Stimuli 1978

Visual Displays — (cont'd)
Spatial Frequency 1982
Temporal Frequency 1985

Visual Evoked Potentials 1973
PN 3318 **SC** 55930
B Evoked Potentials 1967
R ↓ Vision 1967

Visual Feedback 1973
PN 705 **SC** 55940
SN Return of information on specified behavioral functions or parameters by means of visual stimulation. Such stimulation may serve to regulate or control subsequent behavior, cognition, perception, or performance.
B Sensory Feedback 1973
Visual Stimulation 1973

Visual Field 1967
PN 4021 **SC** 55950
R Eye Fixation 1982
Fovea 1982
Peripheral Vision 1988
↓ Visual Perception 1967

Visual Fixation
Use Eye Fixation

Visual Hallucinations 1973
PN 479 **SC** 55960
B Hallucinations 1967
R ↓ Vision 1967

Visual Impairment
Use Vision Disorders

Visual Masking 1973
PN 1238 **SC** 55970
SN Changes in perceptual sensitivity to a visual stimulus due to the presence of a second stimulus in close temporal proximity.
B Masking 1967
R ↓ Visual Stimulation 1973

Visual Memory 1994
PN 1284 **SC** 55973
B Memory 1967
N Visuospatial Memory 1997
R Eidetic Imagery 1973
↓ Spatial Memory 1988
↓ Visual Perception 1967

Visual Neglect
Use Sensory Neglect

Visual Perception 1967
PN 23657 **SC** 55980
B Perception 1967
Vision 1967
N Autokinetic Illusion 1967
Binocular Vision 1967
↓ Brightness Perception 1973
↓ Color Perception 1967
Dark Adaptation 1973
Eye Fixation 1982
Face Perception 1985
Foveal Vision 1988
Interocular Transfer 1985
Monocular Vision 1973
Peripheral Vision 1988
Stereoscopic Vision 1973
Texture Perception 1982

Visual Perception — (cont'd)
Visual Acuity 1982
↓ Visual Contrast 1985
Visual Discrimination 1967
↓ Visual Thresholds 1973
↓ Visuospatial Ability 1997
R ↓ Eye (Anatomy) 1967
↓ Eye Disorders 1973
Lipreading 1973
Mirror Image 1991
Retinal Eccentricity 1991
Visual Attention 2004
Visual Field 1967
↓ Visual Memory 1994
Visual Receptive Fields 1982
Visual Tracking 1973

Visual Perspective
Use Linear Perspective

Visual Receptive Fields 1982
PN 762 **SC** 55985
SN Area of the retina which, when stimulated, affects a specific ganglion cell or lateral geniculate body cell, with zones in each field responding in a complementary way to various properties of visual stimuli such as color or onset/offset. Also, those zones in visual cortex which respond in a complementary way to straight-edge orientation-specific stimuli.
B Receptive Fields 1985
R Geniculate Bodies (Thalamus) 1973
↓ Neurons 1973
↓ Photoreceptors 1973
Retinal Eccentricity 1991
Visual Cortex 1967
↓ Visual Perception 1967

Visual Search 1982
PN 2601 **SC** 55987
SN Perceptual processes associated with detecting and/or locating specified visual targets which are usually not continuously visible. Compare VISUAL TRACKING.
R Cognitive Discrimination 1973
↓ Eye Movements 1967
Pattern Discrimination 1967
Signal Detection (Perception) 1967
Visual Discrimination 1967
↓ Visual Thresholds 1973

Visual Spatial Ability
Use Visuospatial Ability

Visual Spatial Memory
Use Visuospatial Memory

Visual Stimulation 1973
PN 10188 **SC** 55990
B Perceptual Stimulation 1973
N Dichoptic Stimulation 1982
↓ Illumination 1967
Prismatic Stimulation 1973
Stereoscopic Presentation 1973
Tachistoscopic Presentation 1973
↓ Visual Displays 1973
Visual Feedback 1973
R ↓ Color 1967
Linear Perspective 1982
Pictorial Stimuli 1978
Spatial Frequency 1982
Temporal Frequency 1985
Video Display Units 1985
Visual Masking 1973

Visual Thresholds 1973
PN 2542 **SC** 56000
SN The minimal level of stimulation, the minimal difference between any stimuli, or the minimal stimulus change that is visually detectable.
UF Luminance Threshold
Photic Threshold
B Thresholds 1967
Visual Perception 1967
N Critical Flicker Fusion Threshold 1967
R Dark Adaptation 1973
Light Adaptation 1982
Luminance 1982
↓ Perceptual Measures 1973
Retinal Eccentricity 1991
Visual Search 1982

Visual Tracking 1973
PN 1677 **SC** 56010
SN Perceptual processes associated with following a specified visual target with the eyes along its path of movement. Usually involves a continuously visible target. Compare VISUAL SEARCH.
B Tracking 1967
R ↓ Vision 1967
Visual Discrimination 1967
↓ Visual Perception 1967

Visualization
Use Imagery

Visually Handicapped
HN The term was discontinued in 1997, when the term VISUALLY DISABLED was created to capture this concept. In 2000, with the deletion of the term VISUALLY DISABLED, VISUALLY HANDICAPPED was made a nonpostable term for the postable term VISION DISORDERS. VISUALLY DISABLED and VISUALLY HANDICAPPED were removed from all records containing them and replaced with VISION DISORDERS.
Use Vision Disorders

Visuospatial Ability 1997
PN 1576 **SC** 56025
UF Visual Spatial Ability
B Spatial Ability 1982
Visual Perception 1967
N Visuospatial Memory 1997

Visuospatial Memory 1997
PN 594 **SC** 56027
UF Visual Spatial Memory
B Spatial Memory 1988
Visual Memory 1994
Visuospatial Ability 1997

Vitamin C
Use Ascorbic Acid

Vitamin Deficiency Disorders 1973
PN 218 **SC** 56040
B Nutritional Deficiencies 1973
N Pellagra 1973
Wernickes Syndrome 1973

Vitamin Deficiency Disorders — (cont'd)
R ↓ Vitamins 1973

Vitamin Therapy 1978
PN 340 **SC** 56045
B Drug Therapy 1967
R ↓ Vitamins 1973

Vitamins 1973
PN 791 **SC** 56050
N Ascorbic Acid 1973
↓ Choline 1973
Folic Acid 1973
Nicotinamide 1973
Nicotinic Acid 1973
R ↓ Antioxidants 2004
Dietary Supplements 2001
↓ Drugs 1967
↓ Vitamin Deficiency Disorders 1973
Vitamin Therapy 1978

Vocabulary 1967
PN 3113 **SC** 56060
UF Words (Vocabulary)
B Language 1967
N Anagrams 1973
Antonyms 1973
Homographs 1973
Homonyms 1973
Neologisms 1973
Sight Vocabulary 1973
Slang 1973
Synonyms 1973
R ↓ Semantics 1967
↓ Verbal Communication 1967

Vocal Cords 1973
PN 83 **SC** 56070
B Larynx 1973

Vocalization 1967
PN 1036 **SC** 56075
SN Production of sounds by means of vocal cord vibrations.
N ↓ Animal Vocalizations 1973
Crying 1973
Laughter 1978
Subvocalization 1973
↓ Voice 1973
R ↓ Animal Communication 1967
↓ Communication 1967
↓ Oral Communication 1985
Singing 1997
↓ Verbal Communication 1967

Vocalization (Infant)
Use Infant Vocalization

Vocalizations (Animal)
Use Animal Vocalizations

Vocational Adjustment
Use Occupational Adjustment

Vocational Aspirations
Use Occupational Aspirations

Vocational Choice
Use Occupational Choice

Vocational Counseling
Use Occupational Guidance

Vocational Counselors 1973
PN 339 **SC** 56140
SN Persons engaged in career guidance, usually in social service, school, government agency, industrial, or employment center settings.
B Counselors 1967
R Mentor 1985
Occupational Guidance 1967
School Counselors 1973
↓ Social Workers 1973

Vocational Education 1973
PN 1760 **SC** 56150
SN Formal training in or out of school, designed to teach skills and knowledge required for occupational proficiency, especially for paraprofessional, trade, or clerical occupations.
UF Industrial Arts Education
B Curriculum 1967
N Cooperative Education 1982
R ↓ Occupations 1967

Vocational Education Teachers 1988
PN 61 **SC** 56155
UF Technical Education Teachers
B Teachers 1967

Vocational Evaluation 1991
PN 228 **SC** 56157
SN Assessment of vocational aptitude, job skills, and performance potential using simulated or real work experiences and measures. Used for disabled or disordered populations.
B Evaluation 1967
Vocational Rehabilitation 1967
R Disability Management 1991
Employability 1973
↓ Employee Skills 1973
Work Adjustment Training 1991

Vocational Guidance
Use Occupational Guidance

Vocational Interests
Use Occupational Interests

Vocational Maturity 1978
PN 1000 **SC** 56175
SN Ability to make age-appropriate vocational decisions and choices, usually predictive of good vocational adjustment.
UF Career Maturity
Maturity (Vocational)
R Occupational Attitudes 1973
Occupational Choice 1967
Occupational Interests 1967
Occupational Preference 1973
↓ Occupations 1967

Vocational Mobility
Use Occupational Mobility

Vocational Preference
Use Occupational Preference

Vocational Rehabilitation 1967
PN 3946 **SC** 56210
SN Planning and providing necessary services required for successful job placement and subsequent vocational adjustment of handicapped clients.
UF Rehabilitation (Vocational)
B Psychosocial Rehabilitation 1973
N Supported Employment 1994
Vocational Evaluation 1991
Work Adjustment Training 1991

Vocational Rehabilitation — (cont'd)
R Disability Management 1991
Rehabilitation Counseling 1978
School to Work Transition 1994

Vocational School Students 1973
PN 389 SC 56220
B Students 1967

Vocational Schools
Use Technical Schools

Vocations
Use Occupations

Voice 1973
PN 1341 SC 56250
B Vocalization 1967
N Crying 1973
Infant Vocalization 1973
R ↓ Communication 1967
↓ Oral Communication 1985
Singing 1997

Voice Disorders
Use Dysphonia

Voles 2004
PN 69 SC 56255
HN Use RODENTS to access references from 1973 to June 2004.
B Rodents 1973

Volition 1988
PN 1115 SC 56257
SN Process of deciding on a course of action voluntarily or without direct external influence.
UF Free Will
R Choice Behavior 1967
↓ Decision Making 1967
Determinism 1997
Freedom 1978
Self Determination 1994

Volt Meters
HN Term discontinued in 1997. In 2000, the term was removed from all records containing it, and replaced with APPARATUS, its postable counterpart.
Use Apparatus

Volunteer Civilian Personnel
HN In June 2003, the term was discontinued and removed from all records containing it, and was replaced with VOLUNTEERS, its postable counterpart.
Use Volunteers

Volunteer Military Personnel 1973
PN 38 SC 56290
SN Persons who enter military service voluntarily.
B Military Personnel 1967
R Commissioned Officers 1973
↓ Enlisted Military Personnel 1973
National Guard Personnel 1973
ROTC Students 1973
Volunteers 2003

Volunteer Personnel
HN In June 2003, the term was discontinued and removed from all records containing it, and was replaced with VOLUNTEERS, its postable counterpart.
Use Volunteers

Volunteerism
Use Volunteers

Volunteers 2003
PN 1762 SC 56303
SN Individuals who willingly undertake a service.
HN In June 2003, this term was created to replace the discontinued terms VOLUNTEER PERSONNEL and VOLUNTEER CIVILIAN PERSONNEL. VOLUNTEER PERSONNEL and VOLUNTEER CIVILIAN PERSONNEL were removed from all records containing them and replaced with VOLUNTEERS.
UF Volunteer Civilian Personnel
Volunteer Personnel
Volunteerism
R ↓ Assistance (Social Behavior) 1973
Charitable Behavior 1973
Community Involvement 2003
Cooperation 1967
↓ Prosocial Behavior 1982
Volunteer Military Personnel 1973

Volunteers (Experiment)
Use Experimental Subjects

Vomeronasal Sense 1982
PN 205 SC 56327
SN Perceptual system activated by chemical stimuli which trigger vomeronasal nerve activity.
R Chemoreceptors 1973
↓ Olfactory Perception 1967

Vomit Inducing Drugs
Use Emetic Drugs

Vomiting 1973
PN 603 SC 56340
UF Regurgitation
B Gastrointestinal Disorders 1973
Symptoms 1967
R ↓ Antiemetic Drugs 1973
↓ Emetic Drugs 1973
Nausea 1973
Purging (Eating Disorders) 2003
Rumination (Eating) 2001

Voting Behavior 1973
PN 1374 SC 56350
B Behavior 1967
Political Participation 1988
Political Processes 1973
R ↓ Political Attitudes 1973
Political Elections 1973
Political Issues 1973
Political Psychology 1997

Vowels 1973
PN 1410 SC 56360
B Letters (Alphabet) 1973
Phonology 1973
R ↓ Phonemes 1973
Syllables 1973
Words (Phonetic Units) 1967

Voyeurism 1973
PN 88 SC 56370
B Paraphilias 1988
R Exhibitionism 1973

Vulnerability (Disorders)
Use Susceptibility (Disorders)

Vygotsky (Lev) 1991
PN 631 SC 56375
SN Identifies biographical or autobiographical studies and discussions of Vygotsky's works. Sometimes spelled Vigotsky or Vygotski.
R Activity Theory 2003
↓ Language Development 1967
Psycholinguistics 1967
↓ Psychologists 1967

Wages
Use Salaries

Wakefulness 1973
PN 1433 SC 56410
B Consciousness States 1971
R Sleep Wake Cycle 1985

Walk In Clinics 1973
PN 63 SC 56430
SN Facilities in hospitals or other community locations which typically provide immediate access to counseling and referral; are often staffed by volunteers and nondegreed counselors and focus on minority, indigent, or youthful populations.
B Clinics 1967
R ↓ Crisis Intervention Services 1973
Psychiatric Clinics 1973

Walking 1973
PN 1161 SC 56440
B Motor Performance 1973

Wandering Behavior 1991
PN 93 SC 56450
SN Aimless activity usually resulting from a confused mental state.
B Behavior 1967
Motor Processes 1967
R Mental Confusion 1973
Place Disorientation 1973
↓ Symptoms 1967

War 1967
PN 5176 SC 56460
B Conflict 1967
Social Issues 1991
N Nuclear War 1985
R Bioterrorism 2007
Combat Experience 1991
Foreign Policy Making 1973
↓ Government Policy Making 1973
National Security 2006
Peace 1988
↓ Violence 1973

Warning Labels 1997
PN 69 SC 56464
B Warnings 1997
R Accident Prevention 1973
↓ Accidents 1967
Consumer Protection 1973
Hazards 1973
↓ Safety 1967
↓ Safety Devices 1973

Warning Signs
Use Warnings

Warnings 1997
PN 381 SC 56470
UF Safety Warnings
Warning Signs

Warnings — (cont'd)
N Warning Labels 1997
R Accident Prevention 1973
↓ Accidents 1967
Consumer Protection 1973
Hazards 1973
↓ Safety 1967
↓ Safety Devices 1973

Wasps 1982
PN 426 SC 56475
SN Any of numerous social or solitary winged hymenopterous insects.
B Insects 1967
R Larvae 1973

Water Deprivation 1967
PN 768 SC 56480
SN Absence of ad libitum water access. In experimental settings, water deprivation is used to achieve a definable level of motivation within the organism.
B Deprivation 1967
Stimulus Deprivation 1973
R Dehydration 1988
Thirst 1967

Water Intake 1967
PN 2169 SC 56490
SN Ingestion of water. Frequently used as an objective measure of physiological or motivational state or learning. Used for human or animal populations.
B Drinking Behavior 1978
Fluid Intake 1985
R Animal Drinking Behavior 1973
Dehydration 1988

Water Safety 1973
PN 147 SC 56500
SN Programs or activities for accident prevention in aquatic environments.
B Safety 1967

Water Transportation 1973
PN 193 SC 56510
B Transportation 1973
N Submarines 1973

Watson (John Broadus) 1991
PN 60 SC 56515
SN Identifies biographical or autobiographical studies and discussions of Watson's works.
R Behaviorism 1967
↓ Psychologists 1967

Weaning 1973
PN 397 SC 56520
SN Process of acclimating an infant or child to a substitute for the mother's milk. Used for human or animal populations.
B Childrearing Practices 1967
Eating Behavior 2004
R Breast Feeding 1973
Sucking 1978

Weapons 1978
PN 709 SC 56525
N Firearms 2003
R Bioterrorism 2007

Weather
Use Atmospheric Conditions

Web Based Mental Health Services
Use Online Therapy

Web Sites
Use Websites

Websites 2007
PN 328 SC 58114
SN Files located on the World Wide Web that are produced by using certain programming languages such as HTML and are comprised of various connected Web pages.
HN This term was introduced in April 2007. Relevant records were re-indexed with this term. The posting note reflects the number of records that were re-indexed.
UF Web Sites
R Information Dissemination 2005
Internet 2001

Wechsler Adult Intelligence Scale 1967
PN 1951 SC 56530
B Intelligence Measures 1967

Wechsler Bellevue Intelligence Scale 1967
PN 73 SC 56540
B Intelligence Measures 1967

Wechsler Intelligence Scale for Children 2001
PN 2493 SC 56551
HN In 2000, the truncated term WECHSLER INTELLIGENCE SCALE CHILDREN (which was used from 1967-2000) was deleted, removed from all records containing it, and replaced with its expanded form WECHSLER INTELLIGENCE SCALE FOR CHILDREN.
B Intelligence Measures 1967

Wechsler Memory Scale 1988
PN 290 SC 56553
B Neuropsychological Assessment 1982
Retention Measures 1973

Wechsler Preschool Primary Scale 1988
PN 117 SC 56555
B Intelligence Measures 1967

Weight (Body)
Use Body Weight

Weight (Statistics)
Use Statistical Weighting

Weight Control 1985
PN 2228 SC 56565
SN Deliberate regulation of one's weight through diet, exercise, or other means. Also, the relative weight change resulting from such regulation practices. Used for human populations only.
R Aerobic Exercise 1988
↓ Body Weight 1967
Diets 1978
↓ Exercise 1973
Food Intake 1967
↓ Health Behavior 1982
Obesity (Attitudes Toward) 1997

Weight Perception 1967
PN 374 SC 56570
SN Awareness of mass or weight.
B Somesthetic Perception 1967

Weightlessness 1967
PN 80 SC 56580
B Gravitational Effects 1967
R ↓ Somesthetic Stimulation 1973
Spaceflight 1967

Weightlifting 1994
PN 122 SC 56585
B Exercise 1973
Recreation 1967
Sports 1967

Welfare Reform 2007
PN 270 SC 56601
SN Political movement to change the way social welfare programs are governed and administered.
HN This term was introduced in April 2007. Relevant records were re-indexed with this term. The posting note reflects the number of records that were re-indexed.
B Government Policy Making 1973
R Child Welfare 1988
Community Welfare Services 1973
Welfare Services (Government) 1973

Welfare Services (Government) 1973
PN 1521 SC 56600
B Government Programs 1973
R Community Welfare Services 1973
Government 1967
Human Services 2007
Medicaid 1994
Welfare Reform 2007

Well Being 1994
PN 9407 SC 56603
R ↓ Adjustment 1967
↓ Health 1973
Life Changes 2004
Life Satisfaction 1985
Lifestyle Changes 1997
↓ Mental Health 1967
Positive Psychology 2003
↓ Quality of Life 1985

Wellness
Use Health

Wernickes Syndrome 1973
PN 151 SC 56630
SN Use APHASIA for Wernickes aphasia.
B Alcoholic Hallucinosis 1973
Encephalopathies 1982
Syndromes 1973
Vitamin Deficiency Disorders 1973
R Korsakoffs Psychosis 1973

Whales 1985
PN 124 SC 56665
B Mammals 1973
N Dolphins 1973
Porpoises 1973

Wheelchairs
Use Mobility Aids

Whiplash 1997
PN 150 SC 56669
SN Soft tissue injury of cervical spine due to sudden hyperextension or hyperflexion or hyperrotation of neck or limbs.
UF Cervical Sprain Syndrome
B Spinal Cord Injuries 1973
R ↓ Head Injuries 1973

Whistleblowing
Use Informants

White Betz A B Scale
HN Term discontinued in 1997. In 2000, the term was removed from all records containing it, and replaced with NONPROJECTIVE PERSONALITY MEASURES, its postable counterpart.
Use Nonprojective Personality Measures

White Blood Cells
Use Leucocytes

White Collar Workers 1973
PN 628 **SC** 56690
SN Individuals employed in technical, professional, sales, administrative, or clerical positions.
B Business and Industrial Personnel 1967
N Accountants 1973
Clerical Personnel 1973
↓ Management Personnel 1973
Sales Personnel 1973
Secretarial Personnel 1973

White Noise 1973
PN 408 **SC** 56700
SN Noise composed of random mixture of sounds of different wavelengths.
B Auditory Stimulation 1967

White Rats
Use Rats

Whites 1982
PN 13129 **SC** 56720
HN In 1982, this term was created to replace the discontinued term CAUCASIANS. In 2000, CAUCASIANS was removed from all records and replaced with WHITES.
UF Caucasians
B Racial and Ethnic Groups 2001
N Anglos 1988
R Race (Anthropological) 1973

Wholistic Health
Use Holistic Health

Wide Range Achievement Test 1973
PN 176 **SC** 56730
B Achievement Measures 1967

Widowers 1973
PN 499 **SC** 56740
B Human Males 1973
R ↓ Family 1967
↓ Marital Status 1973
↓ Parental Absence 1973

Widows 1973
PN 1048 **SC** 56750
B Human Females 1973
R ↓ Family 1967
↓ Marital Status 1973
↓ Parental Absence 1973

Wilcoxon Sign Rank Test 1973
PN 20 **SC** 56760
UF Sign Rank Test
B Nonparametric Statistical Tests 1967

Wilderness Experience 1991
PN 206 **SC** 56763
SN Outdoor environment and activities used to promote experiential learning or to treat and rehabilitate individuals with physical, emotional, or behavioral problems.

Wilderness Experience — (cont'd)
UF Outward Bound
R Management Training 1973
↓ Psychotherapeutic Techniques 1967
↓ Recreation 1967
↓ Rehabilitation 1967
↓ Sports 1967
Therapeutic Camps 1978

Williams Syndrome 2003
PN 319 **SC** 56764
SN A genetic disorder with onset in infancy that is characterized by supravalvular aortic stenosis, mental retardation, elfin facies, and hypercalcemia.
HN This term was introduced in June 2003. Relevant records were re-indexed with this term. The posting note reflects the number of records that were re-indexed.
B Chromosome Disorders 1973
Genetic Disorders 1973
Syndromes 1973
R ↓ Heart Disorders 1973
↓ Mental Retardation 1967

Willpower
Use Self Control

Wilson Patterson Conservatism Scale 1973
PN 17 **SC** 56780
B Attitude Measures 1967

Wine 1973
PN 111 **SC** 56810
B Alcoholic Beverages 1973

Winnicottian Theory
Use Object Relations

Winter Depression
Use Seasonal Affective Disorder

Wisconsin Card Sorting Test 1994
PN 285 **SC** 56835
B Neuropsychological Assessment 1982

Wisdom 1994
PN 457 **SC** 56837
R ↓ Intelligence 1967
↓ Judgment 1967
↓ Knowledge Level 1978

Witchcraft 1973
PN 173 **SC** 56840
R Ethnology 1967
Faith Healing 1973
Mysticism 1967
Occultism 1978
↓ Parapsychology 1967
↓ Religious Beliefs 1973
Shamanism 1973

Withdrawal (Defense Mechanism) 1973
PN 309 **SC** 56860
SN Psychoanalytic term describing the escape from or avoidance of emotionally or psychologically painful situations.
B Defense Mechanisms 1967
R ↓ Separation Reactions 1997

Withdrawal (Drug)
Use Drug Withdrawal

Within Subjects Design
Use Repeated Measures

Witnesses 1985
PN 2363 **SC** 56885
SN Persons giving evidence in a court of law or observing traumatic events in a nonlegal context. Also used for analog studies of eyewitness identification performance, perception of witness credibility, and other studies of witness characteristics having legal implications.
UF Eyewitnesses
R Cross Examination 2005
↓ Legal Evidence 1991
↓ Legal Testimony 1982

Wives 1973
PN 2718 **SC** 56900
B Human Females 1973
Spouses 1973

Wolves 1973
PN 169 **SC** 56910
B Canids 1997

Women
Use Human Females

Women Centered Psychology
Use Psychology of Women

Womens Liberation Movement 1973
PN 553 **SC** 56920
B Social Movements 1967
R ↓ Activism 2003
Feminism 1978

Woodcock Johnson Psychoeducational Battery 2001
PN 73 **SC** 56926
HN In 2001, the truncated term WOODCOCK JOHNSON PSYCHOED BATTERY (which was used from 1994-2000) was deleted, removed from all records containing it, and replaced with its expanded form WOODCOCK JOHNSON PSYCHOEDUCATIONAL BATTERY.
B Achievement Measures 1967
R Educational Diagnosis 1978

Word Associations 1967
PN 2161 **SC** 56930
UF Associations (Word)
R ↓ Associative Processes 1967
↓ Cognitive Processes 1967
Paired Associate Learning 1967

Word Blindness
Use Alexia

Word Deafness
Use Aphasia

Word Frequency 1973
PN 1202 **SC** 56970
SN Statistical probability of the occurrence of a given word in a given natural language.
R Contextual Associations 1967

Word Meaning 1973
PN 3031 **SC** 56980
SN Connotative or denotative significance of a word.
B Verbal Meaning 1973
R Connotations 1973
Contextual Associations 1967
↓ Lexical Access 1988
Lexical Decision 1988

Word Origins
Use Etymology

Word Processing 1991
PN 278 **SC** 56993
SN Use of computer software to compose, edit, and produce text.
B Computer Software 1967
Data Processing 1967
R Clerical Secretarial Skills 1973
↓ Computer Applications 1973
↓ Information Systems 1991
Typing 1991

Word Recognition 1988
PN 4483 **SC** 56995
R ↓ Associative Processes 1967
Human Information Storage 1973
Phonological Awareness 2004
↓ Reading Skills 1973
↓ Recognition (Learning) 1967
Sight Vocabulary 1973
Speech Perception 1967
Words (Phonetic Units) 1967

Words (Form Classes)
Use Form Classes (Language)

Words (Phonetic Units) 1967
PN 9432 **SC** 57020
SN Spoken or written symbolic representation of an idea, frequently viewed as the smallest grammatically independent unit.
R Antonyms 1973
Consonants 1973
Etymology 1973
↓ Grammar 1967
Homographs 1973
Homonyms 1973
↓ Lexical Access 1988
Lexical Decision 1988
Morphology (Language) 1973
Neologisms 1973
Rhyme 2004
↓ Semantics 1967
Synonyms 1973
Vowels 1973
Word Recognition 1988

Words (Vocabulary)
Use Vocabulary

Work (Attitudes Toward) 1973
PN 3989 **SC** 57037
SN General work values. Use EMPLOYEE ATTITUDES for specific job situations and OCCUPATIONAL ATTITUDES for specific careers.
UF Work Ethic
B Attitudes 1967
R ↓ Employee Attitudes 1967
Employer Attitudes 1973
Family Work Relationship 1997
Job Involvement 1978
Occupational Attitudes 1973
↓ Personnel 1967
Professionalism 2003
Workaholism 2004

Work Addiction
Use Workaholism

Work Adjustment Training 1991
PN 73 **SC** 57045
SN Training or programs to help disabled individuals increase work productivity, handle day-to-day demands of competitive employment, develop work tolerance, and encourage interpersonal work relationships.
B Training 2006
Vocational Rehabilitation 1967
R ↓ Adjustment 1967
Occupational Adjustment 1973
Rehabilitation Counseling 1978
Supported Employment 1994
Vocational Evaluation 1991

Work at Home
Use Telecommuting

Work Environments
Use Working Conditions

Work Ethic
Use Work (Attitudes Toward)

Work Family Relationship
Use Family Work Relationship

Work Load 1982
PN 1391 **SC** 57055
SN Amount of work or working time expected from, assigned to, or performed by an individual.
B Job Characteristics 1985
R ↓ Division of Labor 1988
Human Channel Capacity 1973
Job Analysis 1967
↓ Job Performance 1967
Work Scheduling 1973
↓ Working Conditions 1973

Work Related Illnesses 1994
PN 482 **SC** 57057
SN Includes both physical and mental illnesses, injuries, or disorders. Consider OCCUPATIONAL STRESS for work related stress.
R Industrial Accidents 1973
↓ Mental Disorders 1967
Occupational Exposure 1988
Occupational Safety 1973
Occupational Stress 1973
↓ Physical Disorders 1997
Workers' Compensation Insurance 2003
↓ Working Conditions 1973

Work Rest Cycles 1973
PN 155 **SC** 57060
SN Strictly scheduled periods of working and resting based on observations that any increase in number of working hours beyond an optimal point diminishes production and efficiency.
B Working Conditions 1973
R Work Scheduling 1973
Workaholism 2004

Work Satisfaction
Use Job Satisfaction

Work Scheduling 1973
PN 696 **SC** 57070
SN Individual or organizational distribution of workload or work hours. Consider also WORKDAY SHIFTS.
UF Flextime
Scheduling (Work)

Work Scheduling — (cont'd)
R ↓ Management Methods 1973
Work Load 1982
Work Rest Cycles 1973

Work Stress
Use Occupational Stress

Work Study Programs
Use Educational Programs

Work Teams 2001
PN 1205 **SC** 57077
B Teams 1988
N Self Managing Work Teams 2001
Virtual Teams 2007
R Groupware 2003
↓ Management 1967
↓ Management Methods 1973
Organizational Structure 1967

Work Week Length 1973
PN 102 **SC** 57080
SN Actual number of hours or workdays an employee is required to work during a consecutive 7-day period.
B Working Conditions 1973

Workaholism 2004
PN 103 **SC** 57085
SN Compulsive or excessive need to work.
HN This term was introduced in June 2004. Relevant records were re-indexed with this term. The posting note reflects the number of records that were re-indexed.
UF Work Addiction
R ↓ Addiction 1973
↓ Employee Characteristics 1988
Occupational Stress 1973
Work (Attitudes Toward) 1973
Work Rest Cycles 1973

Workday Shifts 1973
PN 862 **SC** 57090
SN Regularly scheduled daily working hours or scheduled working shifts with core hours being in morning, evening, or late night/predawn. Consider also WORK SCHEDULING.
UF Shifts (Workday)
B Working Conditions 1973

Workers
Use Personnel

Workers' Compensation Insurance 2003
PN 284 **SC** 57103
SN Insurance providing medical benefits for employees injured in work-related accidents and providing continued income during disability.
HN In June 2003, this term was created to update the spelling from the discontinued term WORKMEN'S COMPENSATION INSURANCE, which was removed from all records containing it, and replaced with WORKERS' COMPENSATION INSURANCE.
UF Workmen's Compensation Insurance
B Employee Benefits 1973
Employee Health Insurance 1973
R Disabled Personnel 1997
Work Related Illnesses 1994

Workforce Diversity
Use Diversity in the Workplace

Working Alliance
Use Therapeutic Alliance

Working Conditions 1973
PN 9042 **SC** 57120
SN Factors which contribute to the global milieu of the workplace. Includes physical environment characteristics, job content and work load, and psychosocial factors such as personnel composition, norms, attitudes, motivation, and employee services.
UF Factory Environments
Office Environment
Work Environments
B Social Environments 1973
N Job Enrichment 1973
Noise Levels (Work Areas) 1973
Occupational Safety 1973
Work Rest Cycles 1973
Work Week Length 1973
Workday Shifts 1973
Working Space 1973
R Disabled Personnel 1997
Family Work Relationship 1997
Groupware 2003
Human Factors Engineering 1973
Occupational Exposure 1988
Organizational Climate 1973
Person Environment Fit 1991
↓ Personnel 1967
Quality of Work Life 1988
Telecommuting 2003
Work Load 1982
Work Related Illnesses 1994
Workplace Violence 2007

Working Memory
Use Short Term Memory

Working Space 1973
PN 149 **SC** 57130
SN Physical characteristics of job setting, including such factors as amount of space, noise level, or lighting conditions.
B Working Conditions 1973

Working Women 1978
PN 3874 **SC** 57135
B Human Females 1973
R Dual Careers 1982
↓ Employment Status 1982
↓ Family 1967
Family Work Relationship 1997
↓ Occupations 1967
↓ Personnel 1967
Single Mothers 1994

Workmen's Compensation Insurance
HN In June 2003, this term was discontinued and removed from all records containing it, and replaced with WORKERS' COMPENSATION INSURANCE, its postable counterpart.
Use Workers' Compensation Insurance

Workplace Diversity
Use Diversity in the Workplace

Workplace Violence 2007
PN 143 **SC** 57147
SN Physical attack or assault occurring in the work setting that involves aggressive, threatening, or intimidating behavior or damaged property.
HN This term was introduced in April 2007. Relevant records were re-indexed with this term. The posting note reflects the number of records that were re-indexed.

Workplace Violence — (cont'd)
B Violence 1973
R ↓ Working Conditions 1973

World View 1988
PN 1875 **SC** 57150
UF Philosophy of Life
R ↓ Attitudes 1967
Self Determination 1994
Terror Management Theory 2006
↓ Values 1967

World Wide Web (WWW)
Use Internet

Worms 1967
PN 211 **SC** 57160
B Invertebrates 1973
N Earthworms 1973
Planarians 1973

Worry
Use Anxiety

Worship
Use Religious Practices

Wounds 1973
PN 115 **SC** 57180
B Injuries 1973
N Self Inflicted Wounds 1973
R Burns 1973
Electrical Injuries 1973
↓ Head Injuries 1973

Wrist 1973
PN 184 **SC** 57190
B Joints (Anatomy) 1973
R Arm (Anatomy) 1973
Hand (Anatomy) 1967

Writers 1991
PN 1215 **SC** 57195
UF Authors
B Artists 1973
R Drama 1973
↓ Literature 1967

Writing (Creative)
HN Use LITERATURE to access references from 1973-1993.
Use Creative Writing

Writing (Cursive)
Use Cursive Writing

Writing (Handwriting)
Use Handwriting

Writing Skills 1985
PN 3092 **SC** 57225
SN Proficiency in writing as developed through practice and influenced by ability.
B Communication Skills 1973
R ↓ Literacy 1973
Literacy Programs 1997
Verbal Ability 1967
↓ Written Communication 1985

Written Communication 1985
PN 5058 **SC** 57227
SN Expression of information in written form.

Written Communication — (cont'd)
B Verbal Communication 1967
N Creative Writing 1994
R Note Taking 1991
Proofreading 1988
Rhetoric 1991
Verbal Ability 1967
Writing Skills 1985

Written Language 1967
PN 2058 **SC** 57230
SN System of signs and symbols used to convey information.
B Language 1967
N ↓ Alphabets 1973
↓ Handwriting 1967
Numbers (Numerals) 1967
Paragraphs 1973
Readability 1978
R ↓ Legibility 1978
Orthography 1973

Wryneck
Use Torticollis

X Rated Materials
Use Pornography

X Ray Diagnosis
Use Roentgenography

X Ray Therapy
Use Radiation Therapy

Xenophobia
Use Stranger Reactions

Xylocaine
Use Lidocaine

Yawning 1988
PN 151 **SC** 57300
B Reflexes 1971
R Respiration 1967

Yoga 1973
PN 432 **SC** 57310
B Exercise 1973
Religious Practices 1973
R Relaxation 1973

Yohimbine 1988
PN 291 **SC** 57315
B Adrenergic Blocking Drugs 1973

Z Scores
Use Standard Scores

Zen Buddhism 1973
PN 208 **SC** 57370
B Buddhism 1973

Zidovudine 1994
PN 77 **SC** 57371
UF Azidothymidine
AZT
B Antiviral Drugs 1994
R AIDS 2006
↓ HIV 2006

Zimeldine 1988
PN 47 **SC** 57373
B Antidepressant Drugs 1971
Serotonin Reuptake Inhibitors 1997

Zinc 1985
PN 199 **SC** 57375
B Electrolytes 1973
Metallic Elements 1973

Zoo Environment
Use Animal Captivity

Zoology 1973
PN 46 **SC** 57380
B Biology 1967

Zulliger Z Test 1973
PN 17 **SC** 57390
B Projective Personality Measures 1973

Zungs Self Rating Depression Scale 1973
PN 83 **SC** 57400
B Nonprojective Personality Measures 1973

ROTATED ALPHABETICAL TERMS SECTION

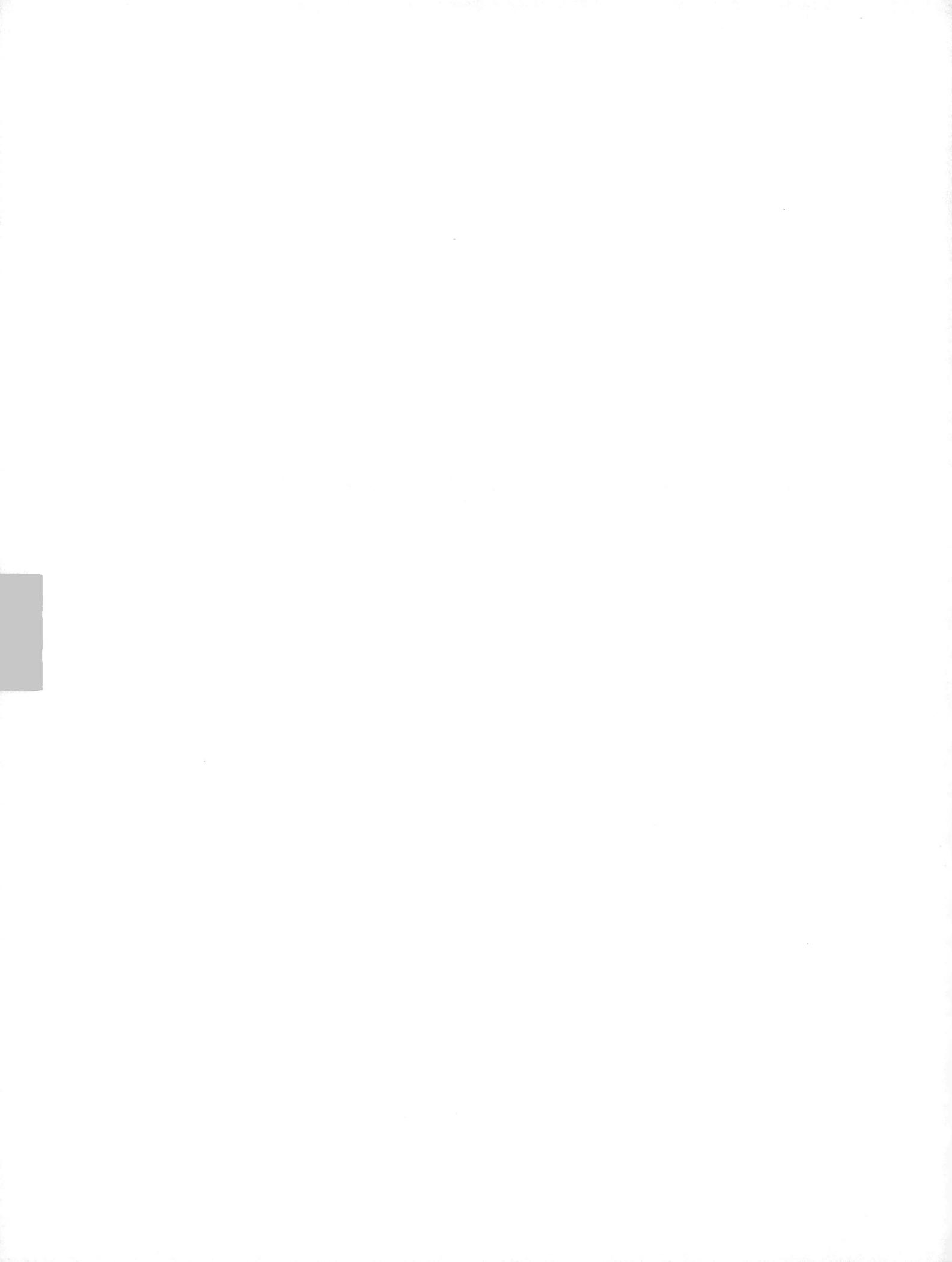

ROTATED ALPHABETICAL TERMS SECTION

Abandonment
Abdomen
Abdominal Wall
Abducens Nerve
Nerve (Abducens) *USE Abducens Nerve*
Child Abduction *USE Kidnapping*
Illinois Test of Psycholinguistic **Abilities**
Ability
Ability Grouping
Ability Level
Ability Tests *USE Aptitude Measures*
Artistic **Ability**
Cognitive **Ability**
Henmon Nelson Tests of Mental Ability *USE Intelligence Measures*
Learning **Ability**
Mathematical **Ability**
Musical **Ability**
Nonverbal **Ability**
Numerical Ability *USE Mathematical Ability*
Reading **Ability**
School and College Ability Test *USE Aptitude Measures*
Spatial **Ability**
Verbal **Ability**
Visual Spatial Ability *USE Visuospatial Ability*
Visuospatial **Ability**
Ablation *USE Lesions*
Brain Ablation *USE Brain Lesions*
Abnormal Psychology
Aboriginal Populations
USE Indigenous Populations
Abortion (Induced) *USE Induced Abortion*
Abortion (Spontaneous)
USE Spontaneous Abortion
Abortion Laws
Elective Abortion *USE Induced Abortion*
Induced **Abortion**
Spontaneous **Abortion**
Therapeutic Abortion *USE Induced Abortion*
Maslow **(Abraham** Harold)
Abreaction *USE Catharsis*
Study **Abroad**
Absence Seizures *USE Petit Mal Seizures*
Father **Absence**
Mother **Absence**
Parental **Absence**
Absenteeism (Employee)
USE Employee Absenteeism
Employee **Absenteeism**
Absorption (Physiological)
Abstinence (Drugs) *USE Drug Abstinence*
Abstinence (Sexual)
USE Sexual Abstinence
Alcohol Abstinence *USE Sobriety*
Drug **Abstinence**
Sexual **Abstinence**
Abstraction
Abuse of Power
Abuse Potential (Drugs)
USE Drug Abuse Liability
Abuse Reporting
Alcohol **Abuse**
Child **Abuse**
Child **Abuse** Reporting
Client Abuse *USE Patient Abuse*
Drug **Abuse**
Drug **Abuse** Liability
Drug **Abuse** Prevention
Elder **Abuse**
Emotional **Abuse**
Inhalant **Abuse**
Multidrug Abuse *USE Polydrug Abuse*
Partner **Abuse**
Patient **Abuse**
Physical **Abuse**
Polydrug **Abuse**
Prisoner **Abuse**
Psychological Abuse *USE Emotional Abuse*
Sexual **Abuse**
Solvent Abuse *USE Inhalant Abuse*
Spouse Abuse *USE Partner Abuse*
Substance Abuse *USE Drug Abuse*
Substance Abuse Prevention
USE Drug Abuse Prevention
Verbal **Abuse**
Academic Achievement
Academic Achievement Motivation
Academic Achievement Prediction
Academic Aptitude
Academic Engagement
USE Student Engagement
Academic Environment
Academic Failure
Academic Grade Level *USE Grade Level*
Academic Overachievement
Academic Records *USE Student Records*
Academic Self Concept
Academic Specialization
Academic Standards
USE Educational Standards
Academic Underachievement
Aptitude (Academic) *USE Academic Aptitude*
College **Academic** Achievement
Overachievement (Academic)
USE Academic Overachievement
Specialization (Academic) *USE Academic Specialization*
Underachievement (Academic)
USE Academic Underachievement
Acalculia
Accelerated Speech *USE Speech Rate*
Acceleration Effects
Acceptance (Social)
USE Social Acceptance
Self Acceptance *USE Self Perception*
Social **Acceptance**
Lexical **Access**
Accessory Nerve *USE Cranial Nerves*
Nerve (Accessory) *USE Cranial Nerves*
Accident Prevention
Accident Proneness
Accidents
Air Traffic **Accidents**
Automobile Accidents *USE Motor Traffic Accidents*
Bicycle Accidents *USE Transportation Accidents*
Cerebrovascular **Accidents**
Home **Accidents**
Industrial **Accidents**
Motor Traffic **Accidents**
Pedestrian **Accidents**
Traffic Accidents (Motor)
USE Motor Traffic Accidents
Transportation **Accidents**
Acclimatization (Thermal)
USE Thermal Acclimatization
Thermal **Acclimatization**
Accommodation (Cognitive Process)
Accommodation (Disabilities)
Eye Accommodation
USE Ocular Accommodation
Ocular **Accommodation**
Accomplishment *USE Achievement*
Accountability
Accountants
Certified Public Accountants *USE Accountants*
Accreditation (Education Personnel)
Accreditation (Educational Programs)
USE Educational Program Accreditation
Educational Program **Accreditation**
Hospital **Accreditation**
School Accreditation
USE Educational Program Accreditation
Teacher Accreditation
USE Accreditation (Education Personnel)
Acculturation
Nucleus **Accumbens**

Acetaldehyde
Acetazolamide
Acetic Aldehyde *USE Acetaldehyde*
Acetylcholine
Acetylcholine Receptors
USE Cholinergic Receptors
Acetylcholinesterase
Acetylsalicylic Acid *USE Aspirin*
Aches *USE Pain*
Achievement
Achievement Measures
Achievement Motivation
Achievement Potential
Academic **Achievement**
Academic **Achievement** Motivation
Academic **Achievement** Prediction
Attainment (Achievement) *USE Achievement*
College Academic **Achievement**
Mathematics **Achievement**
Need Achievement *USE Achievement Motivation*
Potential (Achievement) *USE Achievement Potential*
Reading **Achievement**
Scholastic Achievement *USE Academic Achievement*
School Achievement *USE Academic Achievement*
Science **Achievement**
Stanford **Achievement** Test
Tests (Achievement) *USE Achievement Measures*
Wide Range **Achievement** Test
Achilles Tendon Reflex
Achromatic Color
Acetylsalicylic Acid *USE Aspirin*
Ascorbic **Acid**
Aspartic **Acid**
Deoxyribonucleic Acid *USE DNA*
Dihydroxyphenylacetic **Acid**
Folic **Acid**
Gamma Aminobutyric **Acid**
Gamma Aminobutyric **Acid** Agonists
Gamma Aminobutyric **Acid** Antagonists
Glutamic **Acid**
Homovanillic **Acid**
Hydroxyindoleacetic **Acid** (5-)
Ibotenic **Acid**
Kainic **Acid**
Lactic **Acid**
Lysergic **Acid** Diethylamide
Nicotinic **Acid**
Nicotinic Acid Amide *USE Nicotinamide*
Ribonucleic **Acid**
RNA (Ribonucleic Acid) *USE Ribonucleic Acid*
Uric **Acid**
Valproic **Acid**
Acids
Amino **Acids**
Fatty **Acids**
Nucleic **Acids**
Acoustic Nerve
Acoustic Reflex
Acoustic Stimuli *USE Auditory Stimulation*
Nerve (Acoustic) *USE Acoustic Nerve*
Acoustics
Acquaintance Rape
Acquired Immune Deficiency Syndrome
USE AIDS
Acquisitions (Organizational)
USE Mergers and Acquisitions
Corporate Acquisitions *USE Mergers and Acquisitions*
Mergers and **Acquisitions**
Acrophobia
ACTH (Hormone) *USE Corticotropin*
ACTH Releasing Factor
USE Corticotropin Releasing Factor
Acting Out
Affirmative **Action**
Active Avoidance
USE Avoidance Conditioning
Active Duty *USE Military Duty Status*

Active Living
Activism
Activism (Student) *USE Student Activism*
Student **Activism**
Activist Movements *USE Activism*
Activities of Daily Living
Daily **Activities**
Extracurricular **Activities**
Activity Level
Activity Theory
Activity Therapy *USE Recreation Therapy*
Electrical **Activity**
Physical **Activity**
Actualization (Self) *USE Self Actualization*
Self **Actualization**
Auditory **Acuity**
Hearing Acuity *USE Auditory Acuity*
Vernier Acuity *USE Visual Acuity*
Visual **Acuity**
Acupuncture
Acute Alcoholic Intoxication
Acute Paranoid Disorder
USE Paranoia (Psychosis)
Acute Psychosis
Acute Psychotic Episode
USE Acute Psychosis
Acute Schizophrenia
Acute Stress Disorder
Psychotic Episode (Acute) *USE Acute Psychosis*
Adaptability (Personality)
Adaptation
Adaptation (Dark) *USE Dark Adaptation*
Adaptation (Environmental)
USE Environmental Adaptation
Adaptation (Light) *USE Light Adaptation*
Adaptation (Sensory)
USE Sensory Adaptation
Adaptation (Social) *USE Social Adjustment*
Dark **Adaptation**
Environmental **Adaptation**
Light **Adaptation**
Sensory **Adaptation**
Social Adaptation *USE Social Adjustment*
Kirton **Adaption** Innovation Inventory
Adaptive Behavior
Adaptive Testing
Computer Adaptive Testing *USE Adaptive Testing*
Addiction
Alcohol Addiction *USE Alcoholism*
Drug **Addiction**
Heroin **Addiction**
Hospital Addiction Syndrome
USE Munchausen Syndrome
Internet **Addiction**
Sexual **Addiction**
Work Addiction *USE Workaholism*
Addisons Disease
Food **Additives**
Adenosine
Cyclic **Adenosine** Monophosphate
ADHD
USE Attention Deficit Disorder with Hyperactivity
Gough **Adjective** Check List
Adjectives
Adjudication
Adjunctive Behavior
Adjustment
Adjustment Disorders
Emotional **Adjustment**
Marital Adjustment *USE Marital Relations*
Occupational **Adjustment**
Personal Adjustment *USE Emotional Adjustment*
Psychological Adjustment *USE Emotional Adjustment*
School **Adjustment**
Social **Adjustment**
Student Adjustment *USE School Adjustment*

ROTATED ALPHABETICAL TERMS SECTION

Vocational Adjustment *USE Occupational Adjustment*
Work **Adjustment** Training
Adler (Alfred)
Adlerian Psychotherapy
Individual Psychotherapy (Adlerian) *USE Adlerian Psychotherapy*
Administration (Test)
USE Test Administration
Drug Self **Administration**
Drug **Administration** Methods
Educational **Administration**
Health Care **Administration**
Hospital **Administration**
School Administration
USE Educational Administration
Self Administration (Drugs)
USE Drug Self Administration
Test **Administration**
Administrators (School)
USE School Administrators
Administrators *USE Management Personnel*
Educational Administrators *USE School Administrators*
School **Administrators**
Admission (Hospital)
USE Hospital Admission
Admission (Psychiatric Hospital)
USE Psychiatric Hospital Admission
Admission Criteria (Student)
USE Student Admission Criteria
Facility **Admission**
Hospital **Admission**
Psychiatric Hospital **Admission**
Student **Admission** Criteria
Adolescent Attitudes
Adolescent Development
Adolescent Fathers
Adolescent Mothers
Adolescent Pregnancy
Adolescent Psychiatry
Adolescent Psychology
Adolescent Psychopathology
Adolescent Psychotherapy
Adopted Children
Adoptees
Adoption (Child)
Interracial **Adoption**
Transracial Adoption *USE Interracial Adoption*
Adoptive Parents
Adrenal Cortex Hormones
Adrenal Cortex Steroids
USE Corticosteroids
Adrenal Gland Disorders
Adrenal Gland Secretion
Adrenal Glands
Adrenal Medulla Hormones
Hypothalamic Pituitary **Adrenal** Axis
Hypothalamo Pituitary Adrenal System
USE Hypothalamic Pituitary Adrenal Axis
Adrenalectomy
Adrenaline *USE Epinephrine*
Adrenaline Receptors
USE Adrenergic Receptors
Adrenergic Blocking Drugs
Adrenergic Drugs
Adrenergic Nerves
Adrenergic Receptors
Nerves (Adrenergic) *USE Adrenergic Nerves*
Receptors (Adrenergic) *USE Adrenergic Receptors*
Adrenoceptors *USE Adrenergic Receptors*
Adrenocorticotropin *USE Corticotropin*
Adrenolytic Drugs *USE Adrenergic Drugs*
Adult Attitudes
Adult Children of Alcoholics
USE Children of Alcoholics
Adult Children *USE Adult Offspring*
Adult Day Care
Adult Development
Adult Education
Adult Learning
Adult Offspring
Leiter Adult Intelligence Scale
USE Intelligence Measures
Offenders (Adult) *USE Criminals*
Wechsler **Adult** Intelligence Scale
Adultery *USE Extramarital Intercourse*
Advance Directives
Advance Organizers
Adventitious Disorders
Adventitiously Handicapped
USE Adventitious Disorders
Adverbs
Drug Adverse Reactions *USE Side Effects (Drug)*
Advertising
Television **Advertising**
Advocacy
Child Advocacy *USE Advocacy*
Aerobic Exercise
Aerospace Personnel
Aesthetic Preferences
Aesthetics
Aetiology *USE Etiology*
Affairs (Sexual)
USE Extramarital Intercourse
Affect Regulation
USE Emotional Regulation
CNS **Affecting** Drugs
Heart Rate **Affecting** Drugs
Affection
Affective Disorders
Affective Disturbances
USE Affective Disorders
Affective Education
Affective Psychosis
Bipolar Affective Disorder *USE Bipolar Disorder*
Seasonal **Affective** Disorder
Afferent Neurons *USE Sensory Neurons*
Afferent Pathways
Afferent Stimulation
Afferentation *USE Afferent Stimulation*
Affiliation Motivation
Need for Affiliation *USE Affiliation Motivation*
Religious **Affiliation**
Affirmative Action
African Americans *USE Blacks*
African Cultural Groups
Africans *USE African Cultural Groups*
After School Programs
Aftercare
Aftereffect (Perceptual)
USE Perceptual Aftereffect
Perceptual **Aftereffect**
Afterimage
Age Differences
Age Discrimination
Age Regression (Hypnotic)
Developmental **Age** Groups
Intelligence Age *USE Mental Age*
Mental **Age**
Aged (Attitudes Toward)
Ageism
Agencies (Groups) *USE Organizations*
Government **Agencies**
County Agricultural Agents *USE Agricultural Extension Workers*
Insurance Agents *USE Sales Personnel*
Intelligent **Agents**
Aggressive Behavior
Aggressive Driving Behavior
Animal **Aggressive** Behavior
Passive **Aggressive** Personality Disorder
Aggressiveness
Agility (Physical) *USE Physical Agility*
Physical **Agility**
Aging
Aging (Attitudes Toward)

Amantadine
Amatadine *USE Amantadine*
Amaurotic Familial Idiocy *USE Tay Sachs Disease*
Familial Idiocy (Amaurotic) *USE Tay Sachs Disease*
Ambidexterity *USE Handedness*
Ambiguity (Stimulus) *USE Stimulus Ambiguity*
Ambiguity (Tolerance) *USE Tolerance for Ambiguity*
Stimulus **Ambiguity**
Tolerance for **Ambiguity**
Ambition *USE Aspirations*
Ambivalence
Amblyopia
Ambulatory Care *USE Outpatient Treatment*
Amenorrhea
Amentia *USE Mental Retardation*
American Indians
American Psychological Association
American Psychological Association Divisions
Indians (American) *USE American Indians*
African Americans *USE Blacks*
Asian Americans *USE Asians*
Cuban Americans *USE Hispanics*
Japanese **Americans**
Mexican **Americans**
Native Americans *USE American Indians*
Puerto Rican Americans *USE Hispanics*
Spanish Americans *USE Hispanics*
Nicotinic Acid Amide *USE Nicotinamide*
Amine Oxidase Inhibitors
Amines
Sympathomimetic **Amines**
Amino Acids
Gamma **Aminobutyric** Acid
Gamma **Aminobutyric** Acid Agonists
Gamma **Aminobutyric** Acid Antagonists
Aminotransferases *USE Transaminases*
Amitriptyline
Amnesia
Anterograde **Amnesia**
Global **Amnesia**
Retrograde **Amnesia**
Amniocentesis *USE Prenatal Diagnosis*
Amniotic Fluid
Amobarbital
Amobarbital Sodium *USE Amobarbital*
Reinforcement **Amounts**
Amphetamine
Amphetamine (d-) *USE Dextroamphetamine*
Amphetamine (dl-) *USE Amphetamine*
Amphetamine Sulfate *USE Amphetamine*
Amphibia
Amplifiers (Apparatus)
Amplitude (Response) *USE Response Amplitude*
Response **Amplitude**
Amputation
Amygdala
Amygdaloid Body *USE Amygdala*
Amygdaloid Nucleus *USE Amygdala*
Amytal *USE Amobarbital*
Anabolism *USE Biosynthesis*
Anabolites *USE Metabolites*
Anaclitic Depression
Anagram Problem Solving
Anagrams
Analeptic Drugs
Analgesia
Analgesic Drugs
Analog Computers
Miller **Analogies** Test
Analogy
Analysis
Analysis of Covariance
Analysis of Variance
Behavior **Analysis**
Causal **Analysis**
Cluster **Analysis**
Cohort **Analysis**
Confirmatory Factor Analysis *USE Factor Analysis*
Content **Analysis**
Content **Analysis** (Test)
Costs and Cost **Analysis**
Discourse **Analysis**
Dream **Analysis**
Error **Analysis**
Factor **Analysis**
Functional **Analysis**
Interaction **Analysis** (Statistics)
Item **Analysis** (Statistical)
Item **Analysis** (Test)
Job **Analysis**
Linkage Analysis *USE Genetic Linkage*
Meta **Analysis**
Multivariate **Analysis**
Path **Analysis**
Regression Analysis *USE Statistical Regression*
Risk Analysis *USE Risk Assessment*
Self **Analysis**
Statistical **Analysis**
Systems **Analysis**
Task **Analysis**
Transactional **Analysis**
Analysts *USE Psychoanalysts*
Analytic Psychology *USE Jungian Psychology*
Analytical Psychotherapy
Neural **Analyzers**
Anankastic Personality *USE Obsessive Compulsive Personality Disorder*
Anaphylactic Shock
Anatomical Systems
Anatomically Detailed Dolls
Anatomy
Arm **(Anatomy)**
Arteries **(Anatomy)**
Back **(Anatomy)**
Capillaries **(Anatomy)**
Diaphragm **(Anatomy)**
Ear **(Anatomy)**
Elbow **(Anatomy)**
Eye **(Anatomy)**
Face **(Anatomy)**
Feet **(Anatomy)**
Fingers **(Anatomy)**
Hand **(Anatomy)**
Head **(Anatomy)**
Heels (Anatomy) *USE Feet (Anatomy)*
Joints **(Anatomy)**
Labyrinth **(Anatomy)**
Leg **(Anatomy)**
Mouth **(Anatomy)**
Neck **(Anatomy)**
Palm **(Anatomy)**
Scalp **(Anatomy)**
Shoulder **(Anatomy)**
Skin **(Anatomy)**
Teeth **(Anatomy)**
Toes (Anatomy) *USE Feet (Anatomy)*
Veins **(Anatomy)**
Ancestors
Androgen Antagonists *USE Antiandrogens*
Androgen Insensitivity Syndrome *USE Testicular Feminization Syndrome*
Androgens
Androgyny
Anemia
Anencephaly
Anesthesia (Feeling)

Anesthesiology
Anesthetic Drugs
Ether **(Anesthetic)**
Ethyl Ether (Anesthetic) *USE Ether (Anesthetic)*
General **Anesthetics**
Local **Anesthetics**
Aneurysms
Anger
Anger Control
Anger Management *USE Anger Control*
Angina Pectoris
Angiography
Angiotensin
Cerebellopontile Angle *USE Cerebellum*
Anglos
Angst *USE Anxiety*
Anguish *USE Distress*
Anhedonia
Carbonic Anhydrase *USE Enzymes*
Animal Aggressive Behavior
Animal Assisted Therapy
Animal Behavior *USE Animal Ethology*
Animal Biological Rhythms
Animal Breeding
Animal Captivity
Animal Circadian Rhythms
Animal Coloration
Animal Communication
Animal Courtship Behavior
Animal Courtship Displays
Animal Defensive Behavior
Animal Development
Animal Distress Calls
Animal Division of Labor
Animal Domestication
Animal Dominance
Animal Drinking Behavior
Animal Emotionality
Animal Environments
Animal Escape Behavior
Animal Ethology
Animal Exploratory Behavior
Animal Feeding Behavior
Animal Foraging Behavior
Animal Grooming Behavior
Animal Hoarding Behavior
Animal Homing
Animal Human Interaction
USE Interspecies Interaction
Animal Innate Behavior
USE Instinctive Behavior
Animal Instinctive Behavior
USE Instinctive Behavior
Animal Learning
Animal Licking Behavior *USE Licking*
Animal Locomotion
Animal Mate Selection
Animal Maternal Behavior
Animal Maternal Deprivation
Animal Mating Behavior
Animal Models
Animal Motivation
Animal Navigation
USE Migratory Behavior (Animal)
Animal Nocturnal Behavior
Animal Open Field Behavior
Animal Parental Behavior
Animal Paternal Behavior
Animal Play
Animal Predatory Behavior
Animal Rearing
Animal Scent Marking
Animal Sex Differences
Animal Sexual Behavior
Animal Sexual Receptivity
Animal Social Behavior
Animal Strain Differences
Animal Tool Use *USE Tool Use*
Animal Vocalizations
Animal Welfare
Biological Clocks (Animal) *USE Animal Biological Rhythms*
Breeding (Animal) *USE Animal Breeding*
Captivity (Animal) *USE Animal Captivity*
Circadian Rhythms (Animal) *USE Animal Circadian Rhythms*
Coitus (Animal) *USE Animal Mating Behavior*
Copulation (Animal) *USE Animal Mating Behavior*
Courtship Displays (Animal) *USE Animal Courtship Displays*
Courtship (Animal) *USE Animal Courtship Behavior*
Daily Biological Rhythms (Animal) *USE Animal Circadian Rhythms*
Defensive Behavior (Animal) *USE Animal Defensive Behavior*
Distress Calls (Animal) *USE Animal Distress Calls*
Division of Labor (Animal) *USE Animal Division of Labor*
Domestication (Animal) *USE Animal Domestication*
Dominance (Animal) *USE Animal Dominance*
Drinking Behavior (Animal) *USE Animal Drinking Behavior*
Emotionality (Animal) *USE Animal Emotionality*
Escape Behavior (Animal) *USE Animal Escape Behavior*
Ethology (Animal) *USE Animal Ethology*
Feeding Behavior (Animal) *USE Animal Feeding Behavior*
Foraging (Animal) *USE Animal Foraging Behavior*
Grooming Behavior (Animal) *USE Animal Grooming Behavior*
Habitats (Animal) *USE Animal Environments*
Hoarding Behavior (Animal) *USE Animal Hoarding Behavior*
Homing (Animal) *USE Animal Homing*
Human Animal Interaction
USE Interspecies Interaction
Infants **(Animal)**
Innate Behavior (Animal) *USE Instinctive Behavior*
Lordosis (Animal) *USE Animal Sexual Receptivity*
Maternal Behavior (Animal) *USE Animal Maternal Behavior*
Mating Behavior (Animal) *USE Animal Mating Behavior*
Migratory Behavior **(Animal)**
Neonates (Animal) *USE Infants (Animal)*
Nocturnal Behavior (Animal) *USE Animal Nocturnal Behavior*
Open Field Behavior (Animal) *USE Animal Open Field Behavior*
Parental Behavior (Animal) *USE Animal Parental Behavior*
Play (Animal) *USE Animal Play*
Predatory Behavior (Animal) *USE Animal Predatory Behavior*
Scent Marking (Animal) *USE Animal Scent Marking*
Seals **(Animal)**
Sex Differences (Animal) *USE Animal Sex Differences*
Sexual Receptivity (Animal) *USE Animal Sexual Receptivity*
Strain Differences (Animal) *USE Animal Strain Differences*
Vocalizations (Animal) *USE Animal Vocalizations*
Animals
Female **Animals**
Male **Animals**
Animism
Ankle
Anniversary Events
Anniversary Reactions
USE Anniversary Events
Public Service **Announcements**
Annual Leave
USE Employee Leave Benefits
Anodynes *USE Analgesic Drugs*
Anomie
Anonymity
Alcoholics **Anonymous**
Gamblers Anonymous *USE Twelve Step Programs*
Narcotics Anonymous *USE Twelve Step Programs*
Anorexia Nervosa
Anorexigenic Drugs
USE Appetite Depressing Drugs
Anosmia
Anosognosia
ANOVA (Statistics)
USE Analysis of Variance
Anoxia
Antabuse *USE Disulfiram*
Antagonism *USE Hostility*
Antagonists (CNS Depressant Drugs)
USE Analeptic Drugs
Androgen Antagonists *USE Antiandrogens*

ROTATED ALPHABETICAL TERMS SECTION

Benzodiazepine **Antagonists**
CNS Depressant Drug Antagonists *USE Analeptic Drugs*
Dopamine **Antagonists**
Estrogen Antagonists *USE Antiestrogens*
GABA Antagonists *USE Gamma Aminobutyric Acid Antagonists*
Gamma Aminobutyric Acid **Antagonists**
Narcotic **Antagonists**
Opiate Antagonists *USE Narcotic Antagonists*
Opioid Antagonists *USE Narcotic Antagonists*
Serotonin **Antagonists**
Anterograde Amnesia
Culture **(Anthropological)**
Race **(Anthropological)**
Subculture **(Anthropological)**
Anthropologists
Anthropology
Anti Inflammatory Drugs
Antiadrenergic Drugs *USE Sympatholytic Drugs*
Antiandrogens
Antianxiety Drugs *USE Tranquilizing Drugs*
Antibiotics
Antibodies
Anticholinergic Drugs *USE Cholinergic Blocking Drugs*
Anticholinesterase Drugs *USE Cholinesterase Inhibitors*
Anticipation (Serial Learning) *USE Serial Anticipation (Learning)*
Serial **Anticipation** (Learning)
Anticoagulant Drugs
Anticonvulsive Drugs
Antidepressant Drugs
Tricyclic **Antidepressant** Drugs
Antiemetic Drugs
Antiepileptic Drugs *USE Anticonvulsive Drugs*
Antiestrogens
Antigens
Antihistaminic Drugs
Antihypertensive Drugs
Antinauseant Drugs *USE Antiemetic Drugs*
Antineoplastic Drugs
Antioxidants
Antiparkinsonian Drugs *USE Antitremor Drugs*
Antipathy *USE Aversion*
Antipsychotic Drugs *USE Neuroleptic Drugs*
Antipyretic Drugs *USE Anti Inflammatory Drugs*
Antischizophrenic Drugs *USE Neuroleptic Drugs*
AntiSemitism
Antisocial Behavior
Antisocial Personality Disorder
Antispasmodic Drugs
Antitremor Drugs
Antitubercular Drugs
Antiviral Drugs
Antonyms
Ants
Anxiety
Anxiety Disorders
Anxiety Management
Anxiety Neurosis *USE Anxiety Disorders*
Anxiety Reducing Drugs *USE Tranquilizing Drugs*
Castration **Anxiety**
Childrens Manifest **Anxiety** Scale
Computer **Anxiety**
Death **Anxiety**
Generalized **Anxiety** Disorder
Mathematics **Anxiety**
Performance **Anxiety**
Separation **Anxiety**
Social **Anxiety**
Social Anxiety Disorder *USE Social Phobia*
Speech **Anxiety**
State Trait **Anxiety** Inventory
Taylor Manifest **Anxiety** Scale
Test **Anxiety**
Anxiolytic Drugs *USE Tranquilizing Drugs*
Anxiousness *USE Anxiety*
Aorta
APA *USE American Psychological Association*
APA Divisions *USE American Psychological Association Divisions*
Apathy
Apes *USE Primates (Nonhuman)*
Aphagia
Aphasia
Aphrodisiacs
Aplysia *USE Snails*
Apnea
Sleep **Apnea**
Apolipoproteins
Apomorphine
Apomorphine Hydrochloride *USE Apomorphine*
Apoplexy *USE Cerebrovascular Accidents*
Apoptosis
Apparatus
Amplifiers **(Apparatus)**
Cage **Apparatus**
Experimental Apparatus *USE Apparatus*
Generators **(Apparatus)**
Incubators **(Apparatus)**
Labyrinth (Apparatus) *USE Mazes*
Stimulators **(Apparatus)**
Timers **(Apparatus)**
Transistors (Apparatus) *USE Apparatus*
Vestibular **Apparatus**
Vibrators **(Apparatus)**
Apparent Distance
Apparent Movement
Apparent Size
Size (Apparent) *USE Apparent Size*
Physical **Appearance**
Apperception
Childrens **Apperception** Test
Thematic **Apperception** Test
Appetite
Appetite Depressing Drugs
Appetite Disorders *USE Eating Disorders*
Job **Applicant** Attitudes
Job **Applicant** Interviews
Job **Applicant** Screening
Job **Applicants**
Testing (Job Applicants) *USE Job Applicant Screening*
Computer **Applications**
Applied Psychology
Cognitive **Appraisal**
Apprehension *USE Anxiety*
Communication Apprehension *USE Speech Anxiety*
Apprenticeship
Biopsychosocial **Approach**
Interdisciplinary Treatment **Approach**
Multidisciplinary Treatment Approach *USE Interdisciplinary Treatment Approach*
Multimodal Treatment **Approach**
Approval (Social) *USE Social Approval*
Need for **Approval**
Social **Approval**
Apraxia
Aptitude (Academic) *USE Academic Aptitude*
Aptitude *USE Ability*
Aptitude Measures

ROTATED ALPHABETICAL TERMS SECTION

Academic **Aptitude**
Armed Services Vocational **Aptitude** Battery
College Entrance Examination Board Scholastic **Aptitude** Test
Differential **Aptitude** Tests
General **Aptitude** Test Battery
Mechanical **Aptitude**
Preliminary Scholastic Aptitude Test *USE College Entrance Examination Board Scholastic Aptitude Test*
Scholastic Aptitude *USE Academic Aptitude*
Scholastic Aptitude Test *USE College Entrance Examination Board Scholastic Aptitude Test*
Tests (Aptitude) *USE Aptitude Measures*
Cerebral Aqueduct *USE Cerebral Ventricles*
Arabs
Arachnida
Arachnophobia *USE Phobias*
Archetypes
Architects
Architecture
Broca's **Area**
Preoptic **Area**
Ventral Tegmental Area *USE Tegmentum*
Noise Levels (Work **Areas)**
Poverty **Areas**
Recreation **Areas**
Arecoline
Arecoline Hydrobromide *USE Arecoline*
Arguments
Arithmetic *USE Mathematics*
Arm (Anatomy)
Armed Services Vocational Aptitude Battery
Army Personnel
Arousal (Physiological) *USE Physiological Arousal*
Arousal (Sexual) *USE Sexual Arousal*
Physiological **Arousal**
Sexual **Arousal**
Living **Arrangements**
Arrest (Law) *USE Legal Arrest*
Cardiac Arrest *USE Heart Disorders*
Legal **Arrest**
Arrhythmias (Heart)
Arson
Art
Art Education
Art Therapy
Body Art *USE Cosmetic Techniques*
Painting **(Art)**
Photographic **Art**
Arterial Pulse
Pulse (Arterial) *USE Arterial Pulse*
Arteries (Anatomy)
Carotid **Arteries**
Arteriosclerosis
Cerebral **Arteriosclerosis**
Arthritis
Rheumatoid **Arthritis**
Arthropoda
Articulation (Speech)
Articulation Disorders
Regression Artifact *USE Statistical Regression*
Artificial Insemination *USE Reproductive Technology*
Artificial Intelligence
Artificial Limbs *USE Prostheses*
Artificial Pacemakers
Artificial Respiration
Pacemakers (Artificial) *USE Artificial Pacemakers*
Artistic Ability
Artists
Arts
Creative **Arts** Therapy
Industrial Arts Education *USE Vocational Education*
Language **Arts** Education
Martial **Arts**
Performing Arts *USE Arts*
Artwork *USE Art*
Asbestos *USE Hazardous Materials*
Asceticism
Ascorbic Acid
Asian Americans *USE Asians*
South East Asian Cultural Groups *USE Southeast Asian Cultural Groups*
South **Asian** Cultural Groups
Southeast **Asian** Cultural Groups
Asians
Aspartic Acid
Aspergers Syndrome
Asphyxia *USE Anoxia*
Aspiration Level
Aspirations
Career Aspirations *USE Occupational Aspirations*
Educational **Aspirations**
Occupational **Aspirations**
Vocational Aspirations *USE Occupational Aspirations*
Aspirin
Assassination (Political) *USE Political Assassination*
Political **Assassination**
Assertiveness
Assertiveness Training
Assessment (Cognitive) *USE Cognitive Assessment*
Assessment (Psychological) *USE Psychological Assessment*
Assessment *USE Measurement*
Assessment Centers
Assessment Criteria *USE Evaluation Criteria*
Behavioral **Assessment**
Cognitive **Assessment**
Curriculum Based **Assessment**
Geriatric **Assessment**
Kaufman **Assessment** Battery for Children
Needs **Assessment**
Neuropsychological **Assessment**
Personality Assessment *USE Personality Measures*
Psychological **Assessment**
Risk **Assessment**
Self Assessment *USE Self Evaluation*
Assimilation (Cognitive Process)
Assimilation (Cultural) *USE Acculturation*
Cultural Assimilation *USE Acculturation*
Assistance (Social Behavior)
Assistance Seeking (Professional) *USE Health Care Utilization*
Educational Financial **Assistance**
Employee **Assistance** Programs
Financial Assistance (Educational) *USE Educational Financial Assistance*
School Financial Assistance *USE Educational Financial Assistance*
Assisted Living
Assisted Suicide
Animal **Assisted** Therapy
Computer **Assisted** Design
Computer **Assisted** Diagnosis
Computer **Assisted** Instruction
Computer **Assisted** Language Learning
Computer **Assisted** Testing
Computer **Assisted** Therapy
Instruction (Computer Assisted) *USE Computer Assisted Instruction*
Assistive Devices *USE Assistive Technology*
Assistive Technology
Paired **Associate** Learning
Association (Free) *USE Free Association*
American Psychological **Association**
American Psychological **Association** Divisions
Free **Association**
Associationism

Associations (Contextual)
USE Contextual Associations
Associations (Groups) *USE Organizations*
Associations (Word)
USE Word Associations
Contextual **Associations**
Loosening of Associations
USE Fragmentation (Schizophrenia)
Word **Associations**
Associative Processes
Assortative Mating
Assortive Mating *USE Assortative Mating*
Asthenia
Asthenic Personality
USE Personality Disorders
Asthma
Astrology
Astronauts
ASVAB
USE Armed Services Vocational Aptitude Battery
Asylums *USE Psychiatric Hospitals*
Ataractic Drugs *USE Tranquilizing Drugs*
Ataraxic Drugs *USE Tranquilizing Drugs*
Ataxia
Atheism
Atherosclerosis
Athetosis
Athletes
College **Athletes**
Athletic Participation
Athletic Performance
Athletic Training
Training (Athletic) *USE Athletic Training*
Stereotaxic **Atlas**
Atmospheric Conditions
Atomism *USE Reductionism*
Atria (Heart) *USE Heart Auricles*
Atrial Fibrillation *USE Fibrillation (Heart)*
Atrophy (Cerebral) *USE Cerebral Atrophy*
Atrophy (Muscular) *USE Muscular Atrophy*
Cerebral **Atrophy**
Cortical Atrophy *USE Cerebral Atrophy*
Muscular **Atrophy**
Atropine
Attachment Behavior
Attachment Disorders
Attachment Theory
Reactive Attachment Disorder
USE Attachment Disorders
Attack Behavior
Panic **Attack**
Heart Attacks *USE Heart Disorders*
Attainment (Achievement)
USE Achievement
Attainment Level (Education)
USE Educational Attainment Level
Educational **Attainment** Level
Attempted Suicide
Suicide (Attempted) *USE Attempted Suicide*
Attendance (School)
USE School Attendance
School **Attendance**
Attendants (Institutions)
Flight Attendants *USE Aerospace Personnel*
Hospital Attendants *USE Attendants (Institutions)*
Residential Care Attendants *USE Attendants (Institutions)*
Attention
Attention Deficit Disorder
Attention Deficit Disorder with Hyperactivity
Attention Span
Divided **Attention**
Selective **Attention**
Sustained **Attention**
Visual **Attention**
Stimulus **Attenuation**
Attitude Change
Attitude Formation
Attitude Measurement
Attitude Measures
Attitude Similarity
Minnesota Teacher Attitude Inventory *USE Attitude Measures*
Opinion Attitude and Interest Survey
USE Attitude Measures
Attitudes
Adolescent **Attitudes**
Adult **Attitudes**
Aged **(Attitudes** Toward)
Aging **(Attitudes** Toward)
AIDS **(Attitudes** Toward)
Alcohol Drinking **Attitudes**
Birth Control Attitudes *USE Family Planning Attitudes*
Child **Attitudes**
Childrearing **Attitudes**
Class Attitudes
USE Socioeconomic Class Attitudes
Client **Attitudes**
Community **Attitudes**
Computer **Attitudes**
Consumer **Attitudes**
Counselor **Attitudes**
Death **Attitudes**
Disabled **(Attitudes** Toward)
Drinking Attitudes *USE Alcohol Drinking Attitudes*
Drug Usage **Attitudes**
Eating **Attitudes**
Employee **Attitudes**
Employer **Attitudes**
Environmental **Attitudes**
Family Planning **Attitudes**
Female **Attitudes**
Gender Role Attitudes *USE Sex Role Attitudes*
Handicapped (Attitudes Toward)
USE Disabled (Attitudes Toward)
Health Personnel **Attitudes**
Health **Attitudes**
Homosexuality **(Attitudes** Toward)
Job Applicant **Attitudes**
Lower Class **Attitudes**
Male **Attitudes**
Marriage **Attitudes**
Mental Illness **(Attitudes** Toward)
Mental Retardation **(Attitudes** Toward)
Middle Class **Attitudes**
Obesity **(Attitudes** Toward)
Occupational **Attitudes**
Parental **Attitudes**
Patient Attitudes *USE Client Attitudes*
Physical Disabilities **(Attitudes** Toward)
Physical Handicaps (Attitudes Toward)
USE Physical Disabilities (Attitudes Toward)
Physical Illness **(Attitudes** Toward)
Political **Attitudes**
Psychologist **Attitudes**
Psychotherapist **Attitudes**
Public Attitudes *USE Public Opinion*
Race Attitudes *USE Racial and Ethnic Attitudes*
Racial and Ethnic **Attitudes**
Sensory Disabilities **(Attitudes** Toward)
Sensory Handicaps (Attitudes Toward)
USE Sensory Disabilities (Attitudes Toward)
Sex Role **Attitudes**
Sexual **Attitudes**
Social Class Attitudes
USE Socioeconomic Class Attitudes
Socioeconomic Class **Attitudes**
Sports **(Attitudes** Toward)
Stereotyped **Attitudes**
Student **Attitudes**
Teacher **Attitudes**
Therapist **Attitudes**
Upper Class **Attitudes**

Work **(Attitudes** Toward)
Attorneys
Attraction (Interpersonal)
USE Interpersonal Attraction
Interpersonal **Attraction**
Sexual **Attraction**
Physical **Attractiveness**
Attribution
Attrition (Experimental)
USE Experimental Attrition
Attrition (Military) *USE Military Attrition*
Experimental **Attrition**
Military **Attrition**
Student **Attrition**
Atypical Depression
Atypical Disorders
Atypical Paranoid Disorder
USE Paranoia (Psychosis)
Atypical Somatoform Disorder
USE Body Dysmorphic Disorder
Audiences
Audiogenic Seizures
Audiology
Audiometers
Audiometry
Bekesy Audiometry *USE Audiometry*
Bone Conduction **Audiometry**
Audiotapes
Audiovisual Aids (Educational)
USE Educational Audiovisual Aids
Audiovisual Communications Media
Audiovisual Instruction
Educational **Audiovisual** Aids
Audition *USE Auditory Perception*
Auditory Acuity
Auditory Cortex
Auditory Discrimination
Auditory Displays
Auditory Evoked Potentials
Auditory Feedback
Auditory Hallucinations
Auditory Localization
Auditory Masking
Auditory Nerve *USE Acoustic Nerve*
Auditory Neurons
Auditory Perception
Auditory Stimulation
Auditory Thresholds
Cortex (Auditory) *USE Auditory Cortex*
Delayed **Auditory** Feedback
Clinical **Audits**
Medical Audits *USE Clinical Audits*
Drug **Augmentation**
Augmentative Communication
Aura
Intra Aural Muscle Reflex *USE Acoustic Reflex*
Aurally Handicapped
USE Hearing Disorders
Auricles (Heart) *USE Heart Auricles*
Heart **Auricles**
Auricular Fibrillation *USE Fibrillation (Heart)*
Authoritarianism
Authoritarianism (Parental)
USE Parenting Style
Authoritarianism Rebellion Scale
USE Nonprojective Personality Measures
Parental Authoritarianism *USE Parenting Style*
Authority
Authors *USE Writers*
Autism
Autism Spectrum Disorders
USE Pervasive Developmental Disorders
Early Infantile Autism *USE Autism*
Autistic Children *USE Autism*
Autistic Psychopathy
USE Aspergers Syndrome
Autistic Thinking

Autobiographical Memory
Autobiography
Autoeroticism
Autogenic Training
Autohypnosis
Autoimmune Disorders
USE Immunologic Disorders
Autokinetic Illusion
Illusion (Autokinetic) *USE Autokinetic Illusion*
Automated Information Coding
Automated Information Processing
Automated Information Retrieval
Automated Information Storage
Automated Speech Recognition
Information Processing (Automated)
USE Automated Information Processing
Information Retrieval (Automated)
USE Automated Information Retrieval
Automatic Speaker Recognition
USE Automated Speech Recognition
Automation
Automatism
Automobile Accidents
USE Motor Traffic Accidents
Automobile Safety *USE Highway Safety*
Automobiles
Autonomic Ganglia
Autonomic Nervous System
Autonomic Nervous System Disorders
Postganglionic Autonomic Fibers *USE Autonomic Ganglia*
Preganglionic Autonomic Fibers *USE Autonomic Ganglia*
Autonomy (Government)
Autonomy (Personality)
USE Independence (Personality)
Autopsy
Psychological **Autopsy**
Autoregulation *USE Homeostasis*
Autoshaping
Autosome Disorders
Autosomes
Autotomy *USE Self Mutilation*
Auxiliary Health Workers
USE Allied Health Personnel
Gradepoint Average *USE Academic Achievement*
Aversion
Aversion Conditioning
Aversion Therapy
Odor Aversion Conditioning
USE Aversion Conditioning
Taste Aversion Conditioning
USE Aversion Conditioning
Aversive Stimulation
Aviation
Aviation Personnel
USE Aerospace Personnel
Aviation Safety
Aviators *USE Aircraft Pilots*
Avoidance
Avoidance Conditioning
Active Avoidance *USE Avoidance Conditioning*
Conditioning (Avoidance) *USE Avoidance Conditioning*
Passive Avoidance *USE Avoidance Conditioning*
Avoidant Personality Disorder
Awards (Jury)
Awards (Merit)
Damage Awards *USE Awards (Jury)*
Awareness
Body **Awareness**
Phonemic Awareness *USE Phonological Awareness*
Phonological **Awareness**
Hypothalamic Pituitary Adrenal **Axis**
Axons
Azidothymidine *USE Zidovudine*
AZT *USE Zidovudine*
Type B Personality
USE Coronary Prone Behavior

ROTATED ALPHABETICAL TERMS SECTION

White Betz A B Scale
USE Nonprojective Personality Measures
Babbling *USE Infant Vocalization*
Bush Babies *USE Lemurs*
Test Tube Babies *USE Reproductive Technology*
Babinski Reflex
Baboons
Babysitting *USE Child Care*
Back (Anatomy)
Back Pain
Background (Family)
USE Family Background
Educational **Background**
Educational Background (Parents)
USE Parent Educational Background
Family **Background**
Parent Educational **Background**
Backward Masking *USE Masking*
Baclofen
Bacteria *USE Microorganisms*
Bacterial Disorders
Bacterial Meningitis
Balance (Motor Processes)
USE Equilibrium
Baldness *USE Alopecia*
Ballet *USE Dance*
Head **Banging**
Banking
Bannister Repertory Grid
Baptists *USE Protestants*
Barbital
Barbiturate Poisoning *USE Toxic Disorders*
Barbiturates
Bargaining
Barium
Barometric Pressure
USE Atmospheric Conditions
Baroreceptors
Epstein **Barr** Viral Disorder
Blood Brain **Barrier**
Barriers (Treatment)
USE Treatment Barriers
Communication **Barriers**
Health Care Barriers *USE Treatment Barriers*
Mental Health Care Barriers *USE Treatment Barriers*
Treatment **Barriers**
Basal Ganglia
Basal Magnocellular Cholinergic Nucleus
USE Nucleus Basalis Magnocellularis
Basal Metabolism
Basal Readers *USE Reading Materials*
Basal Skin Resistance
Nucleus **Basalis** Magnocellularis
Nucleus Basalis of Meynert
USE Nucleus Basalis Magnocellularis
Baseball
Case **Based** Reasoning
Computer Based Training
USE Computer Assisted Instruction
Curriculum **Based** Assessment
Evidence Based Medicine
USE Evidence Based Practice
Evidence **Based** Practice
Faith **Based** Organizations
Knowledge Based Systems *USE Expert Systems*
School **Based** Intervention
Web Based Mental Health Services
USE Online Therapy
Basic Skills Testing
USE Minimum Competency Tests
Iowa Tests of **Basic** Skills
Basketball
Bass (Fish)
Bats
Battered Child Syndrome
Battered Females
Battered Women *USE Battered Females*

Armed Services
Vocational Aptitude **Battery**
General Aptitude Test **Battery**
Halstead Reitan
Neuropsychological **Battery**
Kaufman Assessment **Battery** for Children
Luria Nebraska
Neuropsychological **Battery**
Woodcock Johnson
Psychoeducational **Battery**
Bayes Theorem *USE Statistical Probability*
Bayley Scales of Infant Development
Heart Beat *USE Heart Rate*
Beavers
Beck Depression Inventory
Bedwetting *USE Urinary Incontinence*
Beer
Bees
Beetles
Behavior
Behavior Analysis
Behavior Change
Behavior Contracting
Behavior Disorders
Behavior Modification
Behavior Problems
Behavior Therapy
Adaptive **Behavior**
Adjunctive **Behavior**
Aggressive Driving **Behavior**
Aggressive **Behavior**
Agonistic Behavior *USE Aggressive Behavior*
Animal Aggressive **Behavior**
Animal Courtship **Behavior**
Animal Defensive **Behavior**
Animal Drinking **Behavior**
Animal Escape **Behavior**
Animal Exploratory **Behavior**
Animal Feeding **Behavior**
Animal Foraging **Behavior**
Animal Grooming **Behavior**
Animal Hoarding **Behavior**
Animal Innate Behavior *USE Instinctive Behavior*
Animal Instinctive Behavior *USE Instinctive Behavior*
Animal Licking Behavior *USE Licking*
Animal Maternal **Behavior**
Animal Mating **Behavior**
Animal Nocturnal **Behavior**
Animal Open Field **Behavior**
Animal Parental **Behavior**
Animal Paternal **Behavior**
Animal Predatory **Behavior**
Animal Sexual **Behavior**
Animal Social **Behavior**
Animal Behavior *USE Animal Ethology*
Antisocial **Behavior**
Assistance (Social **Behavior)**
Attachment **Behavior**
Attack **Behavior**
Charitable **Behavior**
Child **Behavior** Checklist
Childhood Play **Behavior**
Choice **Behavior**
Civic Behavior *USE Community Involvement*
Classroom **Behavior**
Classroom **Behavior** Modification
Cognitive **Behavior** Therapy
Collective **Behavior**
Conservation (Ecological **Behavior)**
Consumer **Behavior**
Coping **Behavior**
Coronary Prone **Behavior**
Criminal **Behavior**
Defensive Behavior (Animal)
USE Animal Defensive Behavior
Deviant Behavior *USE Antisocial Behavior*
Disruptive Behavior *USE Behavior Problems*

Drinking **Behavior**
Drinking Behavior (Animal) *USE Animal Drinking Behavior*
Driving **Behavior**
Eating **Behavior**
Escape Behavior (Animal) *USE Animal Escape Behavior*
Exploratory **Behavior**
Feeding Behavior (Animal) *USE Animal Feeding Behavior*
Fundamental Interpersonal Relation Orientation **Behavior** Ques
Grooming Behavior (Animal) *USE Animal Grooming Behavior*
Health Care Seeking **Behavior**
Health **Behavior**
Help Seeking **Behavior**
Helping Behavior *USE Assistance (Social Behavior)*
Hoarding **Behavior**
Hoarding Behavior (Animal) *USE Animal Hoarding Behavior*
Humanitarian Behavior *USE Prosocial Behavior*
Illness **Behavior**
Innate Behavior (Animal) *USE Instinctive Behavior*
Instinctive **Behavior**
Maternal Behavior (Animal) *USE Animal Maternal Behavior*
Maternal Behavior (Human) *USE Mother Child Relations*
Mating Behavior (Animal) *USE Animal Mating Behavior*
Migratory **Behavior** (Animal)
Modeling Behavior *USE Imitation (Learning)*
Nocturnal Behavior (Animal) *USE Animal Nocturnal Behavior*
Open Field Behavior (Animal) *USE Animal Open Field Behavior*
Organizational **Behavior**
Parental Behavior (Animal) *USE Animal Parental Behavior*
Planned **Behavior**
Play Behavior (Childhood) *USE Childhood Play Behavior*
Predatory Behavior (Animal) *USE Animal Predatory Behavior*
Prosocial **Behavior**
Psychosexual **Behavior**
Rational Emotive **Behavior** Therapy
Rotational **Behavior**
Runaway **Behavior**
Self Defeating **Behavior**
Self Destructive **Behavior**
Self Injurious Behavior *USE Self Destructive Behavior*
Sexual Behavior *USE Psychosexual Behavior*
Sharing (Social **Behavior)**
Social **Behavior**
Stereotyped **Behavior**
Treatment Seeking Behavior *USE Health Care Seeking Behavior*
Trust (Social **Behavior)**
Voting **Behavior**
Wandering **Behavior**
Behavioral Assessment
Behavioral Contrast
Behavioral Ecology
Behavioral Economics
Behavioral Genetics
Behavioral Health *USE Health Care Psychology*
Behavioral Medicine *USE Health Care Psychology*
Behavioral Sciences
Behavioral Sensitization *USE Sensitization*
Behaviorism
Well **Being**
Bekesy Audiometry *USE Audiometry*
Beliefs (Nonreligious) *USE Attitudes*
Beliefs (Religion) *USE Religious Beliefs*
False **Beliefs**
Irrational **Beliefs**
Religious **Beliefs**
Wechsler **Bellevue** Intelligence Scale
Safety **Belts**
Seat Belts *USE Safety Belts*
Bem Sex Role Inventory
Bemegride
Benactyzine
Benadryl *USE Diphenhydramine*
Bender Gestalt Test
Employee Leave **Benefits**
Employee **Benefits**
Vacation Benefits *USE Employee Leave Benefits*
Benign Neoplasms
Benton Revised Visual Retention Test
Benzedrine *USE Amphetamine*
Benzodiazepine Agonists
Benzodiazepine Antagonists
Benzodiazepines
Bereavement *USE Grief*
Beta Blockers *USE Adrenergic Blocking Drugs*
Between Groups Design
White Betz A B Scale *USE Nonprojective Personality Measures*
Beverages (Alcoholic) *USE Alcoholic Beverages*
Beverages (Nonalcoholic)
Alcoholic **Beverages**
Bias (Experimenter) *USE Experimenter Bias*
Bias (Response) *USE Response Bias*
Bias Crimes *USE Hate Crimes*
Cognitive **Bias**
Cultural Test **Bias**
Experimenter **Bias**
Hindsight **Bias**
Item Bias *USE Test Bias*
Response **Bias**
Test **Bias**
Test Bias (Cultural) *USE Cultural Test Bias*
Biased Sampling
Bible
Bibliotherapy
Bicuculline
Bicycle Accidents *USE Transportation Accidents*
Bicycle Safety *USE Transportation Safety*
Spina **Bifida**
Big Five Personality Model *USE Five Factor Personality Model*
Bile
Bilingual Education
Bilingualism
Double **Bind** Interaction
Receptor **Binding**
Stanford **Binet** Intelligence Scale
Binge Drinking
Binge Eating
Binocular Vision
Binomial Distribution
Bioavailability
Biochemical Markers *USE Biological Markers*
Biochemistry
Biodata *USE Biographical Data*
Bioequivalence *USE Bioavailability*
Bioethics
Biofeedback
Biofeedback Training
EEG Biofeedback *USE Neurofeedback*
Biographical Data
Biographical Inventories
Biography
Bioinformatics

ROTATED ALPHABETICAL TERMS SECTION

Biological Clocks (Animal)
USE Animal Biological Rhythms
Biological Family
Biological Markers
Biological Psychiatry
Biological Rhythms
Biological Symbiosis
Animal **Biological** Rhythms
Daily Biological Rhythms (Animal)
USE Animal Circadian Rhythms
Human **Biological** Rhythms
Symbiosis (Biological) *USE Biological Symbiosis*
Biology
Cells **(Biology)**
Hybrids **(Biology)**
Mimicry **(Biology)**
Biopsy
Biopsychosocial Approach
Biopsychosocial Model
USE Biopsychosocial Approach
Biosynthesis
Biotechnology
Bioterrorism
Bipolar Affective Disorder
USE Bipolar Disorder
Bipolar Disorder
Bipolar Mood Disorder
USE Bipolar Disorder
Biracial Children *USE Interracial Offspring*
Birds
Birth
Birth Control
Birth Control Attitudes
USE Family Planning Attitudes
Birth Injuries
Birth Order
Birth Parents *USE Biological Family*
Birth Rate
Birth Rites
Birth Trauma
Birth Weight
Diaphragms **(Birth** Control)
Home Birth *USE Midwifery*
Injuries (Birth) *USE Birth Injuries*
Low Birth Weight *USE Birth Weight*
Premature **Birth**
Multiple **Births**
Point **Biserial** Correlation
Bisexuality
Nail **Biting**
Bitterness *USE Taste Perception*
Black Power Movement
Blackbirds
Blacks
Blacky Pictures Test
USE Projective Personality Measures
Bladder
Blame
Rotter Incomplete Sentences **Blank**
Strong Vocational Interest **Blank**
Blind
Deaf **Blind**
Color **Blindness**
Hysterical Blindness
USE Hysterical Vision Disturbances
Mind Blindness *USE Theory of Mind*
Word Blindness *USE Alexia*
Blink Reflex *USE Eyeblink Reflex*
Block Design Test (Kohs)
USE Kohs Block Design Test
Kohs **Block** Design Test
Beta Blockers *USE Adrenergic Blocking Drugs*
Calcium Channel Blockers *USE Channel Blockers*
Channel **Blockers**
Adrenergic **Blocking** Drugs
Cholinergic **Blocking** Drugs
Ganglion **Blocking** Drugs

Neuromuscular Blocking Drugs
USE Muscle Relaxing Drugs
Blood
Blood Alcohol Concentration
Blood and Lymphatic Disorders
Blood Brain Barrier
Blood Cells
Blood Circulation
Blood Coagulation
Blood Disorders
USE Blood and Lymphatic Disorders
Blood Donation *USE Tissue Donation*
Blood Flow
Blood Glucose *USE Blood Sugar*
Blood Groups
Blood Plasma
Blood Platelets
Blood Pressure
Blood Pressure Disorders
Blood Proteins
Blood Serum
Blood Sugar
Blood Transfusion
Blood Vessels
Blood Volume
Cerebral **Blood** Flow
Circulation (Blood) *USE Blood Circulation*
Coagulation (Blood) *USE Blood Coagulation*
Plasma (Blood) *USE Blood Plasma*
Platelets (Blood) *USE Blood Platelets*
Red Blood Cells *USE Erythrocytes*
Serum (Blood) *USE Blood Serum*
Transfusion (Blood) *USE Blood Transfusion*
White Blood Cells *USE Leucocytes*
Blue Collar Workers
College Entrance Examination **Board** Scholastic Aptitude Test
State Board Examinations
USE Professional Examinations
Boarding Schools
Boards of Education
Dementia with Lewy **Bodies**
Geniculate **Bodies** (Thalamus)
Mammillary Bodies (Hypothalamic) *USE Hypothalamus*
Body Art *USE Cosmetic Techniques*
Body Awareness
Body Dysmorphic Disorder
Body Fluids
Body Height
Body Image
Body Image Disturbances
Body Language
Body Mass Index
Body Rocking
Body Rotation *USE Rotational Behavior*
Body Size
Body Sway Testing
Body Temperature
Body Types *USE Somatotypes*
Body Weight
Amygdaloid Body *USE Amygdala*
Height (Body) *USE Body Height*
Human **Body**
Lewy Body Disease
USE Dementia with Lewy Bodies
Mind Body *USE Dualism*
Out of **Body** Experiences
Pineal **Body**
Rocking (Body) *USE Body Rocking*
Temperature (Body) *USE Body Temperature*
Thermoregulation **(Body)**
Tissues **(Body)**
Weight (Body) *USE Body Weight*
Bombesin
Bonding (Emotional)
USE Attachment Behavior
Bone Conduction Audiometry
Bone Disorders

Bone Marrow
Bones
Bonobos
Bonuses
Books
Borderline Mental Retardation
Borderline Personality Disorder
Borderline States
Boredom
Plants **(Botanical)**
Botany
Bottle Feeding
Culture **Bound** Syndromes
Outward Bound *USE Wilderness Experience*
Upward **Bound**
Boundaries (Psychological)
Boundary Violations (Sexual)
USE Professional Client Sexual Relations
Sexual Boundary Violations
USE Professional Client Sexual Relations
Bourgeois *USE Middle Class*
Bowel Disorders *USE Colon Disorders*
Irritable **Bowel** Syndrome
Shuttle Box Grids *USE Shuttle Boxes*
Shuttle Box Hurdles *USE Shuttle Boxes*
Shuttle **Boxes**
Skinner **Boxes**
Boys *USE Human Males*
Brachial Plexus *USE Spinal Nerves*
Bradycardia
Bradykinesia
Braille
Braille Instruction
Brain
Brain Ablation *USE Brain Lesions*
Brain Concussion
Brain Damage
Brain Development
Brain Disorders
Brain Growth *USE Brain Development*
Brain Injury (Traumatic)
USE Traumatic Brain Injury
Brain Lesions
Brain Mapping *USE Stereotaxic Atlas*
Brain Maps *USE Stereotaxic Atlas*
Brain Metabolism *USE Neurochemistry*
Brain Neoplasms
Brain Self Stimulation
Brain Size
Brain Stem
Brain Stimulation
Brain Volume *USE Brain Size*
Brain Weight
Blood **Brain** Barrier
Chemical **Brain** Stimulation
Concussion (Brain) *USE Brain Concussion*
Decortication **(Brain)**
Electrical **Brain** Stimulation
Left Brain *USE Left Hemisphere*
Minimal Brain Disorders
USE Attention Deficit Disorder with Hyperactivity
Monoamines (Brain) *USE Catecholamines*
Organic **Brain** Syndromes
Right Brain *USE Right Hemisphere*
Split Brain *USE Commissurotomy*
Traumatic **Brain** Injury
Brainstorming
Brainwashing
Brand Names
Brand Preferences
Bravery *USE Courage*
Nervous Breakdown *USE Mental Disorders*
Breakthrough (Psychotherapeutic)
USE Psychotherapeutic Breakthrough

Psychotherapeutic **Breakthrough**
Breakup (Relationship)
USE Relationship Termination
Breast
Breast Cancer Screening
USE Cancer Screening
Breast Examination
USE Self Examination (Medical)
Breast Feeding
Breast Neoplasms
Breathing *USE Respiration*
Breeding (Animal) *USE Animal Breeding*
Animal **Breeding**
Selective **Breeding**
Brief Psychotherapy
Brief Reactive Psychosis
USE Acute Psychosis
Myers **Briggs** Type Indicator
Bright Light Therapy *USE Phototherapy*
Brightness Constancy
Brightness Contrast
Brightness Perception
Watson (John **Broadus)**
Broca's Area
Lithium Bromide *USE Bromides*
Bromides
Bromocriptine
Bronchi
Bronchial Disorders
Brothers
Spearman **Brown** Test
Bruxism
Buddhism
Zen **Buddhism**
Buddhists
Budgerigars
Budgets
Taste **Buds**
Bufotenine
Nest **Building**
Buildings *USE Facilities*
Religious **Buildings**
Built Environment
Olfactory **Bulb**
Bulimia
Bulls *USE Cattle*
Bullying
Medial Forebrain **Bundle**
Bupropion
Caregiver **Burden**
Government Bureaucracy *USE Government*
Burnout *USE Occupational Stress*
Burns
Skinner **(Burrhus** Frederic)
Buses *USE Motor Vehicles*
Bush Babies *USE Lemurs*
Business
Business and Industrial Personnel
Business Education
Business Innovation *USE Innovation*
Business Investments
Business Management
Business Networking
USE Professional Networking
Business Organizations
Business Students
Exchange (Business) *USE Commerce*
Investments (Business) *USE Business Investments*
Trade (Business) *USE Commerce*
Small **Businesses**
Businessmen
USE Business and Industrial Personnel
Buspirone
Butterflies
Butyrylperazine
USE Phenothiazine Derivatives
Buying *USE Consumer Behavior*

Cadres *USE Social Groups*
Caffeine
Cage Apparatus
Calcium
Calcium Channel Blockers
USE Channel Blockers
Calcium Ions
Calculators *USE Digital Computers*
Calculus
California F Scale
California Psychological Inventory
CALL
USE Computer Assisted Language Learning
Corpus **Callosum**
Animal Distress **Calls**
Distress Calls (Animal) *USE Animal Distress Calls*
Calories
Cameras
Campaigns (Political)
USE Political Campaigns
Political **Campaigns**
Camping
Camps (Therapeutic)
USE Therapeutic Camps
Concentration **Camps**
Day Camps (Recreation)
USE Summer Camps (Recreation)
Recreational Day Camps *USE Summer Camps (Recreation)*
Summer **Camps** (Recreation)
Therapeutic **Camps**
Campuses
Ear Canal *USE External Ear*
Semicircular **Canals**
Canaries
Cancer Screening
Breast Cancer Screening *USE Cancer Screening*
Prostate Cancer Screening *USE Cancer Screening*
Skin Cancer Screening *USE Cancer Screening*
Terminal **Cancer**
Cancers *USE Neoplasms*
Candidates (Political)
USE Political Candidates
Political **Candidates**
Canids
Cannabinoids
Cannabis
Hemp (Cannabis) *USE Cannabis*
Cannibalism
Canonical Correlation
USE Multivariate Analysis
Human Channel **Capacity**
Capgras Syndrome
Capillaries (Anatomy)
Capital Punishment
Human **Capital**
Punishment (Capital) *USE Capital Punishment*
Social **Capital**
Venture **Capital**
Capitalism
Capsaicin
Captivity (Animal) *USE Animal Captivity*
Animal **Captivity**
Captopril
Carbachol
Carbamazepine
Carbidopa
Carbohydrate Metabolism
Carbohydrates
Carbon
Carbon Dioxide
Carbon Monoxide
Carbon Monoxide Poisoning
Lithium **Carbonate**
Carbonic Anhydrase *USE Enzymes*
Carboxyhemoglobinemia
USE Carbon Monoxide Poisoning
Carcinogens
Carcinomas *USE Neoplasms*
Wisconsin **Card** Sorting Test
Cardiac Arrest *USE Heart Disorders*
Cardiac Disorders *USE Heart Disorders*
Cardiac Rate *USE Heart Rate*
Cardiac Surgery *USE Heart Surgery*
Cardiography
Cardiology
Cardiotonic Drugs *USE Drugs*
Cardiovascular Disorders
Cardiovascular Reactivity
Cardiovascular System
Adult Day **Care**
Ambulatory Care *USE Outpatient Treatment*
Child Day **Care**
Child Self **Care**
Child **Care**
Child **Care** Workers
Continuity of Care *USE Continuum of Care*
Continuum of **Care**
Day Care (Child) *USE Child Day Care*
Day Care (Treatment)
USE Partial Hospitalization
Day **Care** Centers
Elder **Care**
End of Life Care *USE Palliative Care*
Foster **Care**
Health **Care** Administration
Health Care Barriers *USE Treatment Barriers*
Health **Care** Costs
Health **Care** Delivery
Health **Care** Economics
Health **Care** Policy
Health Care Professionals *USE Health Personnel*
Health **Care** Psychology
Health **Care** Reform
Health **Care** Seeking Behavior
Health **Care** Services
Health **Care** Utilization
Home **Care**
Home **Care** Personnel
Institutions (Residential Care) *USE Residential Care Institutions*
Intensive **Care**
Long Term **Care**
Managed **Care**
Medical Care Costs *USE Health Care Costs*
Mental Health Care Barriers *USE Treatment Barriers*
Mental Health Care Costs *USE Health Care Costs*
Mental Health Care Policy *USE Health Care Policy*
Palliative **Care**
Patient Care Planning *USE Treatment Planning*
Prenatal **Care**
Primary Health **Care**
Quality of **Care**
Residential Care Attendants
USE Attendants (Institutions)
Residential **Care** Institutions
Respite **Care**
Self **Care** Skills
Utilization (Health Care) *USE Health Care Utilization*
Career Aspirations
USE Occupational Aspirations
Career Change
Career Choice *USE Occupational Choice*
Career Counseling
USE Occupational Guidance
Career Development
Career Education
Career Exploration *USE Career Education*
Career Goals
USE Occupational Aspirations
Career Guidance
USE Occupational Guidance
Career Maturity *USE Vocational Maturity*
Career Preference
USE Occupational Preference

Career Transitions *USE Career Development*
Careers *USE Occupations*
Dual **Careers**
Nontraditional **Careers**
Caregiver Burden
Caregivers
Family Caregivers *USE Caregivers*
Jung **(Carl)**
Rogers **(Carl)**
Carotid Arteries
Carp
Cartoons (Humor)
Case Based Reasoning
Case History *USE Patient History*
Case Management
Case Report
Social **Casework**
Caseworkers *USE Social Workers*
Social Caseworkers *USE Social Workers*
Caste System
Castration
Castration Anxiety
Male **Castration**
Cat Learning
CAT Scan *USE Tomography*
Crying **Cat** Syndrome
Catabolism
Catabolites *USE Metabolites*
Catalepsy
Catamnesis *USE Posttreatment Followup*
Cataplexy
Cataracts
Catatonia
Catatonic Schizophrenia
Catecholamines
Categorizing *USE Classification (Cognitive Process)*
Catharsis
Catheterization
Cathexis
Cathode Ray Tubes *USE Video Display Units*
Catholicism (Roman) *USE Roman Catholicism*
Roman **Catholicism**
Catholics
Cats
Cattell Culture Fair Intelligence Test *USE Culture Fair Intelligence Test*
Cattle
Caucasians *USE Whites*
Cauda Equina *USE Spinal Nerves*
Caudate Nucleus
Causal Analysis
Causality
Causation *USE Causality*
Cause Effect Relationships *USE Causality*
Cecotrophy *USE Coprophagia*
Celebrities
Celebrity *USE Fame*
Celiac Plexus *USE Autonomic Ganglia*
Celibacy *USE Sexual Abstinence*
Cell Nucleus
Sickle **Cell** Disease
Single Cell Organisms *USE Microorganisms*
Cells (Biology)
Blood **Cells**
Connective Tissue **Cells**
Epithelial **Cells**
Ganglion **Cells** (Retina)
Natural Killer **Cells**
Nerve Cells *USE Neurons*
Purkinje **Cells**
Red Blood Cells *USE Erythrocytes*
Retinal Ganglion Cells *USE Ganglion Cells (Retina)*
Stem **Cells**
White Blood Cells *USE Leucocytes*
Censorship
Client **Centered** Therapy
Person Centered Psychotherapy *USE Client Centered Therapy*
Women Centered Psychology *USE Psychology of Women*
Centering
Assessment **Centers**
Community Mental Health **Centers**
Day Care **Centers**
Growth Centers *USE Human Potential Movement*
Learning **Centers** (Educational)
Mental Health Centers (Community) *USE Community Mental Health Centers*
Rehabilitation **Centers**
Shopping **Centers**
Suicide Prevention **Centers**
Central Nervous System
Central Nervous System Disorders
Central Nervous System Drugs *USE CNS Affecting Drugs*
Central Tendency Measures
Central Vision *USE Foveal Vision*
CER (Conditioning) *USE Conditioned Emotional Responses*
Cerebellar Cortex *USE Cerebellum*
Cerebellar Nuclei *USE Cerebellum*
Cerebellopontile Angle *USE Cerebellum*
Cerebellum
Cerebral Aqueduct *USE Cerebral Ventricles*
Cerebral Arteriosclerosis
Cerebral Atrophy
Cerebral Blood Flow
Cerebral Cortex
Cerebral Dominance
Cerebral Hemorrhage
Cerebral Ischemia
Cerebral Lesions *USE Brain Lesions*
Cerebral Palsy
Cerebral Vascular Disorders *USE Cerebrovascular Disorders*
Cerebral Ventricles
Atrophy (Cerebral) *USE Cerebral Atrophy*
Cortex (Cerebral) *USE Cerebral Cortex*
Ventricles (Cerebral) *USE Cerebral Ventricles*
Trigonum Cerebrale *USE Fornix*
Cerebrospinal Fluid
Cerebrovascular Accidents
Cerebrovascular Disorders
Stroke (Cerebrum) *USE Cerebrovascular Accidents*
Certification (Professional) *USE Professional Certification*
Certification Examinations *USE Professional Examinations*
Professional **Certification**
Certified Public Accountants *USE Accountants*
Locus **Ceruleus**
Cervical Plexus *USE Spinal Nerves*
Cervical Sprain Syndrome *USE Whiplash*
Cervix
Smoking **Cessation**
Supply **Chain** Management
Markov **Chains**
Supply **Chains**
Chance (Fortune)
Change (Organizational) *USE Organizational Change*
Change (Social) *USE Social Change*
Change Readiness *USE Readiness to Change*
Attitude **Change**
Behavior **Change**
Career **Change**
Culture **Change**
Job Change *USE Career Change*

ROTATED ALPHABETICAL TERMS SECTION

Motivation to Change *USE Readiness to Change*
Opinion Change *USE Attitude Change*
Organizational **Change**
Personality **Change**
Readiness to **Change**
Sex **Change**
Social **Change**
Stages of **Change**
Stimulus **Change**
Life **Changes**
Lifestyle **Changes**
Channel Blockers
Calcium Channel Blockers *USE Channel Blockers*
Human **Channel** Capacity
Chaos Theory
Chaplains
Character *USE Personality*
Character Development *USE Personality Development*
Character Disorders *USE Personality Disorders*
Character Formation *USE Personality Development*
Client **Characteristics**
Counselor **Characteristics**
Demographic **Characteristics**
Employee **Characteristics**
Group **Characteristics**
Job **Characteristics**
Organizational **Characteristics**
Parental **Characteristics**
Patient Characteristics *USE Client Characteristics*
Population Characteristics *USE Demographic Characteristics*
Speech **Characteristics**
Student **Characteristics**
Teacher **Characteristics**
Therapist **Characteristics**
Charisma
Charismatic Leadership *USE Transformational Leadership*
Charitable Behavior
Charter Schools
Cri du Chat Syndrome *USE Crying Cat Syndrome*
Cheating
Gough Adjective **Check** List
Mooney Problem **Check** List
Child Behavior **Checklist**
Symptom **Checklists**
Chemical Brain Stimulation
Chemical Elements
Chemicals
Chemistry
Chemoreceptors
Chemotherapy
Chess
Chest *USE Thorax*
Chewing Tobacco *USE Smokeless Tobacco*
Chi Square Test
Optic **Chiasm**
Chicanos *USE Mexican Americans*
Chickens
Child Abduction *USE Kidnapping*
Child Abuse
Child Abuse Reporting
Child Advocacy *USE Advocacy*
Child Attitudes
Child Behavior Checklist
Child Care
Child Care Workers
Child Custody
Child Day Care
Child Discipline
Child Guidance Clinics
Child Labor
Child Maltreatment *USE Child Abuse*
Child Molestation *USE Pedophilia*
Child Neglect
Child Psychiatric Clinics *USE Child Guidance Clinics*
Child Psychiatry
Child Psychology
Child Psychopathology
Child Psychotherapy
Child Self Care
Child Support
Child Visitation
Child Welfare
Adoption **(Child)**
Battered **Child** Syndrome
Day Care (Child) *USE Child Day Care*
Discipline (Child) *USE Child Discipline*
Father **Child** Communication
Father **Child** Relations
Mother **Child** Communication
Mother **Child** Relations
Parent **Child** Communication
Parent **Child** Relations
Childbirth (Natural) *USE Natural Childbirth*
Childbirth *USE Birth*
Childbirth Training
Labor **(Childbirth)**
Natural **Childbirth**
Childhood Development
Childhood Memories *USE Early Memories*
Childhood Neurosis
Childhood Play Behavior
Childhood Play Development
Childhood Psychosis
Childhood Schizophrenia
Early **Childhood** Development
Play Behavior (Childhood) *USE Childhood Play Behavior*
Play Development (Childhood) *USE Childhood Play Development*
Childlessness
Childrearing Attitudes
Childrearing Practices
Children of Alcoholics
Adopted **Children**
Adult Children *USE Adult Offspring*
Adult Children of Alcoholics *USE Children of Alcoholics*
Autistic Children *USE Autism*
Biracial Children *USE Interracial Offspring*
Exceptional Children (Gifted) *USE Gifted*
Exceptional Children (Handicapped) *USE Disorders*
Foster **Children**
Grown Children *USE Adult Offspring*
Illegitimate **Children**
Kaufman Assessment Battery for **Children**
Latchkey Children *USE Child Self Care*
Missing **Children**
Only **Children**
Wechsler Intelligence Scale for **Children**
Childrens Apperception Test
Childrens Manifest Anxiety Scale
Childrens Recreational Games
Chimpanzees
Pygmy Chimpanzees *USE Bonobos*
Chinchillas
Chinese Cultural Groups
Chiroptera *USE Bats*
Chloral Hydrate
Chloralose *USE Hypnotic Drugs*
Chlordiazepoxide
Chloride Ions
Choline Chloride *USE Choline*
Chlorimipramine
Chlorisondamine *USE Amines*
Chlorophenylpiperazine *USE Piperazines*
Chlorpromazine
Chlorprothixene
Choice Behavior
Choice Shift

Career Choice *USE Occupational Choice*
Forced **Choice** (Testing Method)
Multiple **Choice** (Testing Method)
Occupational **Choice**
Vocational Choice *USE Occupational Choice*
Cholecystokinin
Cholesterol
Choline
Choline Chloride *USE Choline*
Cholinergic Blocking Drugs
Cholinergic Drugs
Cholinergic Nerves
Cholinergic Receptors
Basal Magnocellular Cholinergic Nucleus
USE Nucleus Basalis Magnocellularis
Nerves (Cholinergic) *USE Cholinergic Nerves*
Receptors (Cholinergic) *USE Cholinergic Receptors*
Cholinesterase
Cholinesterase Inhibitors
Cholinoceptors *USE Cholinergic Receptors*
Cholinolytic Drugs
USE Cholinergic Blocking Drugs
Cholinomimetic Drugs
Chorda Tympani Nerve *USE Facial Nerve*
Chorea
Huntingtons Chorea *USE Huntingtons Disease*
Choroid *USE Eye (Anatomy)*
Choroid Plexus *USE Cerebral Ventricles*
Christianity
Christians
Chromaticity
Chromosome Disorders
Deletion **(Chromosome)**
Sex **Chromosome** Disorders
Translocation **(Chromosome)**
Chromosomes
Sex **Chromosomes**
Chronic Alcoholic Intoxication
Chronic Fatigue Syndrome
Chronic Illness
Chronic Mental Illness
Chronic Pain
Chronic Psychosis
Chronic Schizophrenia *USE Schizophrenia*
Chronic Stress
Chronicity (Disorders)
Chunking
Churches *USE Religious Buildings*
Cichlids
Cigarette Smoking *USE Tobacco Smoking*
Cimetidine
Cinema *USE Films*
Gyrus **Cinguli**
Circadian Rhythms (Animal)
USE Animal Circadian Rhythms
Circadian Rhythms (Human)
USE Human Biological Rhythms
Animal **Circadian** Rhythms
Quality Circles *USE Participative Management*
Closed **Circuit** Television
Circulation (Blood) *USE Blood Circulation*
Blood **Circulation**
Circulatory Disorders
USE Cardiovascular Disorders
Circumcision
Cirrhosis (Liver)
Citalopram
Cities *USE Urban Environments*
Citizen Participation
USE Community Involvement
Citizenship
Inner City *USE Urban Environments*
Civic Behavior
USE Community Involvement
Civil Law
Civil Rights
Civil Rights Movement
Civil Servants *USE Government Personnel*
Volunteer Civilian Personnel *USE Volunteers*
Clairvoyance
Class Attitudes
USE Socioeconomic Class Attitudes
Class Size
Lower **Class**
Lower **Class** Attitudes
Middle **Class**
Middle **Class** Attitudes
Social **Class**
Social Class Attitudes
USE Socioeconomic Class Attitudes
Socioeconomic **Class** Attitudes
Upper **Class**
Upper **Class** Attitudes
Form **Classes** (Language)
Words (Form Classes) *USE Form Classes (Language)*
Classical Conditioning
Classical Test Theory
Conditioning (Classical) *USE Classical Conditioning*
Classification (Cognitive Process)
Classification Systems *USE Taxonomies*
International **Classification** of Diseases
Psychiatric Classifications (Taxonomies)
USE Psychodiagnostic Typologies
Classmates
Classroom Behavior
Classroom Behavior Modification
Classroom Discipline
Classroom Environment
Classroom Instruction *USE Teaching*
Classroom Management
Classroom Teachers *USE Teachers*
Discipline (Classroom) *USE Classroom Discipline*
Open **Classroom** Method
Classrooms
Virtual **Classrooms**
Claustrophobia
Cleft Palate
Clergy
Clerical Personnel
Clerical Secretarial Skills
Client Abuse *USE Patient Abuse*
Client Attitudes
Client Centered Therapy
Client Characteristics
Client Compliance
USE Treatment Compliance
Client Counselor Interaction
USE Psychotherapeutic Processes
Client Dropouts *USE Treatment Dropouts*
Client Education
Client Participation
Client Records
Client Rights
Client Satisfaction
Client Transfer
Client Treatment Matching
Client Violence *USE Patient Violence*
Counselor Client Interaction
USE Psychotherapeutic Processes
Professional **Client** Sexual Relations
Treatment Client Matching
USE Client Treatment Matching
Clients
Climate (Meteorological)
USE Atmospheric Conditions
Climate (Organizational)
USE Organizational Climate
Organizational **Climate**
Climax (Sexual) *USE Orgasm*
Clinical Audits
Clinical Governance
Clinical Judgment (Medical Diagnosis)
USE Medical Diagnosis
Clinical Judgment (Not Diagnosis)

Collective Hysteria *USE Mass Hysteria*
Collective Unconscious
Collectivism
College Academic Achievement
College Athletes
College Degrees *USE Educational Degrees*
College Dropouts
College Education
USE Undergraduate Education
College Entrance Examination Board Scholastic Aptitude Test
College Environment
College Graduates
College Major
USE Academic Specialization
College Students
College Teachers
Community **College** Students
Junior **College** Students
School and College Ability Test *USE Aptitude Measures*
Colleges
Community **Colleges**
Junior Colleges *USE Colleges*
Inferior **Colliculus**
Superior **Colliculus**
Colon Disorders
Color
Color Blindness
Color Constancy
Color Contrast
Color Perception
Color Pyramid Test
USE Projective Personality Measures
Color Saturation
Achromatic **Color**
Eye **Color**
Saturation (Color) *USE Color Saturation*
Stroop **Color** Word Test
Animal **Coloration**
Colostomy
Raven **Coloured** Progressive Matrices
Spinal **Column**
Coma
Combat Experience
Comfort (Physical) *USE Physical Comfort*
Physical **Comfort**
Commerce
Electronic **Commerce**
Commercialization
Commercials *USE Television Advertising*
Commissioned Officers
Officers (Commissioned)
USE Commissioned Officers
Hippocampal Commissure *USE Fornix*
Commissurotomy
Commitment
Commitment (Outpatient)
USE Outpatient Commitment
Commitment (Psychiatric)
Organizational **Commitment**
Outpatient **Commitment**
Communes
Communicable Diseases
USE Infectious Disorders
Communication
Communication (Privileged)
USE Privileged Communication
Communication (Professional)
USE Scientific Communication
Communication Apprehension
USE Speech Anxiety
Communication Barriers
Communication Disorders
Communication Skills
Communication Skills Training
Communication Systems
Communication Theory
Animal **Communication**
Augmentative **Communication**
Computer Mediated **Communication**
Cross Cultural **Communication**
Electronic **Communication**
Facilitated Communication
USE Augmentative Communication
Father Child **Communication**
Intercultural Communication
USE Cross Cultural Communication
Interethnic Communication
USE Cross Cultural Communication
Interpersonal **Communication**
Manual **Communication**
Mother Child **Communication**
Nonverbal **Communication**
Oral **Communication**
Parent Child **Communication**
Persuasive **Communication**
Privileged **Communication**
Professional Communication
USE Scientific Communication
Scientific **Communication**
Verbal **Communication**
Written **Communication**
Communications Media
Audiovisual **Communications** Media
Media (Communications)
USE Communications Media
Printed **Communications** Media
Communicative Competence
USE Communication Skills
Communism
Communities
Communities of Practice
Retirement **Communities**
Community Attitudes
Community College Students
Community Colleges
Community Development
Community Facilities
Community Involvement
Community Mental Health
Community Mental Health Centers
Community Mental Health Services
Community Mental Health Training
Community Psychiatry
Community Psychology
Community Services
Community Welfare Services
Mental Health Centers (Community)
USE Community Mental Health Centers
Mental Health Training (Community)
USE Community Mental Health Training
Therapeutic **Community**
Training (Community Mental Health)
USE Community Mental Health Training
Commuting (Travel)
Comorbidity
Companies *USE Business Organizations*
Comparative Psychiatry
USE Transcultural Psychiatry
Comparative Psychology
Social **Comparison**
Compatibility (Interpersonal)
USE Interpersonal Compatibility
Interpersonal **Compatibility**
Compensation (Defense Mechanism)
Workers' **Compensation** Insurance
Workmen's Compensation Insurance
USE Workers' Compensation Insurance
Compensatory Education
Competence
Competence (Social) *USE Social Skills*
Communicative Competence *USE Communication Skills*
Interpersonal Competence *USE Social Skills*
Professional **Competence**

Social Competence *USE Social Skills*
Competency to Stand Trial
Minimum **Competency** Tests
Competition
Health **Complaints**
Complementary Medicine
USE Alternative Medicine
Sentence **Completion** Tests
AIDS Dementia **Complex**
Electra **Complex**
Oedipal **Complex**
Complexity (Cognitive)
USE Cognitive Complexity
Complexity (Stimulus)
USE Stimulus Complexity
Complexity (Task) *USE Task Complexity*
Cognitive **Complexity**
Stimulus **Complexity**
Task **Complexity**
Compliance
Client Compliance *USE Treatment Compliance*
Medical Regimen Compliance *USE Treatment Compliance*
Treatment **Compliance**
Obstetrical **Complications**
Postsurgical **Complications**
Surgical Complications
USE Postsurgical Complications
Comprehension
Comprehension Tests
Listening **Comprehension**
Number **Comprehension**
Reading **Comprehension**
Sentence **Comprehension**
Verbal **Comprehension**
Compressed Speech
Repetition **Compulsion**
Compulsions
Compulsive Gambling
USE Pathological Gambling
Compulsive Neurosis
USE Obsessive Compulsive Disorder
Compulsive Personality Disorder
USE Obsessive Compulsive Personality Disorder
Compulsive Repetition
USE Repetition Compulsion
Obsessive **Compulsive** Disorder
Obsessive Compulsive Neurosis
USE Obsessive Compulsive Disorder
Obsessive **Compulsive** Personality Disorder
Repetition (Compulsive) *USE Repetition Compulsion*
Compulsivity (Sexual)
USE Sexual Addiction
Sexual Compulsivity *USE Sexual Addiction*
Computer Adaptive Testing
USE Adaptive Testing
Computer Anxiety
Computer Applications
Computer Assisted Design
Computer Assisted Diagnosis
Computer Assisted Instruction
Computer Assisted Language Learning
Computer Assisted Testing
Computer Assisted Therapy
Computer Attitudes
Computer Based Training
USE Computer Assisted Instruction
Computer Conferencing
USE Teleconferencing
Computer Games
Computer Literacy
Computer Mediated Communication
Computer Peripheral Devices
Computer Programming
Computer Programming Languages
Computer Programs
USE Computer Software
Computer Searching
Computer Simulation
Computer Software
Computer Supported Cooperative Work
USE Groupware
Computer Training
Human **Computer** Interaction
Human Computer Interface
USE Human Computer Interaction
Instruction (Computer Assisted)
USE Computer Assisted Instruction
Programming Languages (Computer)
USE Computer Programming Languages
Programming (Computer) *USE Computer Programming*
Computerized Databases *USE Databases*
Computers
Analog **Computers**
Digital **Computers**
Personal Computers *USE Microcomputers*
Concentration
Concentration Camps
Blood Alcohol **Concentration**
Concept Formation
Concept Learning *USE Concept Formation*
Concept Validity *USE Test Validity*
Academic Self **Concept**
Conservation **(Concept)**
Self **Concept**
Temporal Spatial Concept Scale *USE Intelligence Measures*
Tennessee Self **Concept** Scale
Concepts
God **Concepts**
Mathematics **(Concepts)**
Conceptual Imagery
Conceptual Tempo
Imagery (Conceptual) *USE Conceptual Imagery*
Conceptualization *USE Concept Formation*
Concurrent Reinforcement Schedules
Concurrent Tasks
USE Dual Task Performance
Concurrent Validity *USE Test Validity*
Concussion (Brain) *USE Brain Concussion*
Brain **Concussion**
Conditioned Emotional Responses
Conditioned Fear
Conditioned Inhibition
USE Conditioned Suppression
Conditioned Place Preference
USE Place Conditioning
Conditioned Reflex
USE Conditioned Responses
Conditioned Responses
Conditioned Stimulus
Conditioned Suppression
Suppression (Conditioned) *USE Conditioned Suppression*
Conditioning
Conditioning (Avoidance)
USE Avoidance Conditioning
Conditioning (Classical)
USE Classical Conditioning
Conditioning (Escape)
USE Escape Conditioning
Conditioning (Eyelid)
USE Eyelid Conditioning
Conditioning (Operant)
USE Operant Conditioning
Conditioning (Verbal) *USE Verbal Learning*
Aversion **Conditioning**
Avoidance **Conditioning**
CER (Conditioning)
USE Conditioned Emotional Responses
Classical **Conditioning**
Escape **Conditioning**
Eyelid **Conditioning**
Fading **(Conditioning)**
Higher Order **Conditioning**
Instrumental Conditioning *USE Operant Conditioning*

Odor Aversion Conditioning *USE Aversion Conditioning*
Operant **Conditioning**
Pavlovian Conditioning *USE Classical Conditioning*
Place **Conditioning**
Respondent Conditioning *USE Classical Conditioning*
Second Order Conditioning *USE Higher Order Conditioning*
Taste Aversion Conditioning *USE Aversion Conditioning*
Verbal Conditioning *USE Verbal Learning*
Atmospheric **Conditions**
Mental Disorders due to General Medical **Conditions**
Working **Conditions**
Condoms
Conduct Disorder
Bone **Conduction** Audiometry
Skin Conduction *USE Skin Resistance*
Cones (Eye)
Cones (Retina) *USE Cones (Eye)*
Confabulation
Computer Conferencing *USE Teleconferencing*
Confession (Legal) *USE Legal Confession*
Confession (Religion)
Legal **Confession**
Confidence (Self) *USE Self Confidence*
Confidence Limits (Statistics)
Self **Confidence**
Confidentiality of Information *USE Privileged Communication*
Confirmatory Factor Analysis *USE Factor Analysis*
Conflict
Conflict of Interest
Conflict Resolution
Family **Conflict**
Marital **Conflict**
Role **Conflicts**
Conformity (Personality)
Confusion (Mental) *USE Mental Confusion*
Mental **Confusion**
Congenital Disorders
Drug Induced **Congenital** Disorders
Congenitally Handicapped *USE Congenital Disorders*
Self **Congruence**
Conjoined Twins
Conjoint Measurement
Conjoint Therapy
Connectionism
Connective Tissue Cells
Connective Tissues
Connotations
Consanguineous Marriage
Conscience
Conscientiousness
Conscious (Personality Factor)
Consciousness Disturbances
Consciousness Raising Groups
Consciousness States
Self Consciousness *USE Self Perception*
Informed **Consent**
Conservation (Concept)
Conservation (Ecological Behavior)
Conservatism
Conservatism (Political) *USE Political Conservatism*
Political **Conservatism**
Wilson Patterson **Conservatism** Scale
Conservatorship *USE Guardianship*
Consistency (Measurement)
Internal Consistency *USE Test Reliability*
Response Consistency *USE Response Variability*
Consonants
Conspecifics
Brightness **Constancy**
Color **Constancy**
Perceptual **Constancy**
Size **Constancy**
Constant Time Delay
Constipation
Construct Validity *USE Test Validity*
Personal Construct Theory *USE Personality Theory*
Laborers (Construction and Industry) *USE Blue Collar Workers*
Test **Construction**
Constructionism *USE Constructivism*
Constructivism
Consultation (Professional) *USE Professional Consultation*
Consultation Liaison Psychiatry
Mental Health Consultation *USE Professional Consultation*
Professional **Consultation**
Consumer Attitudes
Consumer Behavior
Consumer Education
Consumer Fraud *USE Fraud*
Consumer Product Design *USE Product Design*
Consumer Protection
Consumer Psychology
Consumer Research
Consumer Satisfaction
Consumer Surveys
Contact Lenses
Eye **Contact**
Physical **Contact**
Contagion
Cost **Containment**
Content Analysis
Content Analysis (Test)
Content Validity *USE Test Validity*
Dream **Content**
Emotional **Content**
Item **Content** (Test)
Thought Content *USE Cognitions*
Contextual Associations
Associations (Contextual) *USE Contextual Associations*
Contiguity (Cognitive) *USE Cognitive Contiguity*
Cognitive **Contiguity**
Contingency Management
Contingent Negative Variation
Continuing Education
Continuity of Care *USE Continuum of Care*
Continuous Reinforcement *USE Reinforcement Schedules*
Continuum of Care
Contour *USE Form and Shape Perception*
Contour Perception *USE Form and Shape Perception*
Contraception *USE Birth Control*
Contraceptive Devices
Oral **Contraceptives**
Contracting Out *USE Outsourcing*
Behavior **Contracting**
Muscle **Contraction** Headache
Muscle **Contractions**
Contracts (Psychological) *USE Psychological Contracts*
Psychological **Contracts**
Behavioral **Contrast**
Brightness **Contrast**
Color **Contrast**
Successive Contrast *USE Afterimage*
Visual **Contrast**
Monetary Contributions *USE Fundraising*
Control (Emotional) *USE Emotional Control*
Control (Locus of) *USE Internal External Locus of Control*
Control (Self) *USE Self Control*
Control (Social) *USE Social Control*
Control Groups *USE Experiment Controls*
Air Traffic **Control**
Anger **Control**
Birth **Control**

ROTATED ALPHABETICAL TERMS SECTION

Birth Control Attitudes *USE Family Planning Attitudes*
Diaphragms (Birth **Control)**
Emotional **Control**
Gun **Control** Laws
Health Locus of Control *USE Health Attitudes*
Impulse **Control** Disorders
Internal External Locus of **Control**
Locus of Control *USE Internal External Locus of Control*
Population Control *USE Birth Control*
Quality **Control**
Rotter Internal External Locus of **Control** Scale
Self **Control**
Social **Control**
Stimulus **Control**
Thought Control *USE Brainwashing*
Weight **Control**
Controls (Instrument) *USE Instrument Controls*
Experiment **Controls**
Instrument **Controls**
Eye **Convergence**
Convergent Thinking *USE Inductive Deductive Reasoning*
Convergent Validity *USE Test Validity*
Conversation
Conversion Disorder
Conversion Hysteria *USE Conversion Disorder*
Conversion Neurosis *USE Conversion Disorder*
Hysterical Neurosis (Conversion) *USE Conversion Disorder*
Religious **Conversion**
Conviction (Criminal) *USE Criminal Conviction*
Criminal **Conviction**
Convulsions *USE Seizures*
Cooperating Teachers
Cooperation
Cooperative Education
Cooperative Learning
Cooperative Therapy *USE Cotherapy*
Computer Supported Cooperative Work *USE Groupware*
Coordination (Motor) *USE Motor Coordination*
Coordination (Perceptual Motor) *USE Perceptual Motor Coordination*
Motor **Coordination**
Perceptual Motor **Coordination**
Coping Behavior
Copper
Coprophagia
Copulation (Animal) *USE Animal Mating Behavior*
Copulation *USE Sexual Intercourse (Human)*
Lumbar Spinal **Cord**
Spinal **Cord**
Spinal **Cord** Injuries
Vocal **Cords**
Cornea
Coronary Disorders *USE Cardiovascular Disorders*
Coronary Heart Disease *USE Heart Disorders*
Coronary Prone Behavior
Coronary Thromboses
Coronary Vessels *USE Arteries (Anatomy)*
Corporal Punishment *USE Punishment*
Corporate Acquisitions *USE Mergers and Acquisitions*
Corporations *USE Business Organizations*
Multinational **Corporations**
Transnational Corporations *USE Multinational Corporations*
Job **Corps**
Peace **Corps**
Corpus Callosum
Corpus Striatum *USE Basal Ganglia*
Correctional Institutions
Institutions (Correctional) *USE Correctional Institutions*
Corrective Lenses *USE Optical Aids*
Personality **Correlates**
Physiological **Correlates**
Psychological Correlates *USE Psychodynamics*
Correlation (Statistical) *USE Statistical Correlation*
Canonical Correlation *USE Multivariate Analysis*
Pearson Product Moment Correlation Coefficient *USE Statistical Correlation*
Point Biserial **Correlation**
Rank Difference **Correlation**
Rank Order **Correlation**
Statistical **Correlation**
Tetrachoric **Correlation**
Cortex (Auditory) *USE Auditory Cortex*
Cortex (Cerebral) *USE Cerebral Cortex*
Cortex (Motor) *USE Motor Cortex*
Cortex (Somatosensory) *USE Somatosensory Cortex*
Cortex (Visual) *USE Visual Cortex*
Adrenal **Cortex** Hormones
Adrenal Cortex Steroids *USE Corticosteroids*
Auditory **Cortex**
Cerebellar Cortex *USE Cerebellum*
Cerebral **Cortex**
Motor **Cortex**
Prefrontal **Cortex**
Somatosensory **Cortex**
Striate Cortex *USE Visual Cortex*
Visual **Cortex**
Organ of Corti *USE Cochlea*
Cortical Atrophy *USE Cerebral Atrophy*
Cortical Evoked Potentials *USE Evoked Potentials*
Corticoids *USE Corticosteroids*
Corticospinal Tracts *USE Pyramidal Tracts*
Corticosteroids
Corticosterone
Corticotropin
Corticotropin Releasing Factor
Cortisol *USE Hydrocortisone*
Cortisone
Cosmetic Techniques
Cost Containment
Cost Effectiveness *USE Costs and Cost Analysis*
Costs and **Cost** Analysis
Response **Cost**
Costs and Cost Analysis
Health Care **Costs**
Medical Care Costs *USE Health Care Costs*
Mental Health Care Costs *USE Health Care Costs*
Cotherapy
Counselees *USE Clients*
Counseling
Counseling (Group) *USE Group Counseling*
Counseling Psychologists
Counseling Psychology
Career Counseling *USE Occupational Guidance*
Cross Cultural **Counseling**
Educational **Counseling**
Family Counseling *USE Family Therapy*
Genetic **Counseling**
Group **Counseling**
Guidance Counseling *USE School Counseling*
Individual Counseling *USE Individual Psychotherapy*
Internet Counseling *USE Online Therapy*
Marriage **Counseling**
Pastoral **Counseling**
Peer **Counseling**
Premarital **Counseling**
Psychotherapeutic **Counseling**

ROTATED ALPHABETICAL TERMS SECTION

Rehabilitation **Counseling**
School **Counseling**
Vocational Counseling *USE Occupational Guidance*
Counselor Attitudes
Counselor Characteristics
Counselor Client Interaction *USE Psychotherapeutic Processes*
Counselor Education
Counselor Effectiveness *USE Counselor Characteristics*
Counselor Personality *USE Counselor Characteristics*
Counselor Role
Counselor Trainees
Client Counselor Interaction *USE Psychotherapeutic Processes*
Role (Counselor) *USE Counselor Role*
Counselors
Rehabilitation **Counselors**
School **Counselors**
Vocational **Counselors**
Over the Counter Drugs *USE Nonprescription Drugs*
Counterconditioning
Countertransference
Countries
Developed **Countries**
Developing **Countries**
Third World Countries *USE Developing Countries*
Underdeveloped Countries *USE Developing Countries*
County Agricultural Agents *USE Agricultural Extension Workers*
Couples
Couples Therapy
Married Couples *USE Spouses*
Courage
Course Evaluation
Course Objectives *USE Educational Objectives*
Course of Illness *USE Disease Course*
Disease **Course**
Disorder Course *USE Disease Course*
Life Course *USE Life Span*
Court Ordered Treatment *USE Court Referrals*
Court Referrals
Juvenile Court *USE Adjudication*
Courts *USE Adjudication*
Courtship (Animal) *USE Animal Courtship Behavior*
Courtship (Human) *USE Human Courtship*
Courtship Displays (Animal) *USE Animal Courtship Displays*
Animal **Courtship** Behavior
Animal **Courtship** Displays
Human **Courtship**
Cousins
Analysis of **Covariance**
Covert Sensitization
Least Preferred **Coworker** Scale
Cows *USE Cattle*
Coyotes *USE Canids*
Crabs
Crack Cocaine
Crafts
Cramps (Muscle) *USE Muscular Disorders*
Muscle Cramps *USE Muscular Disorders*
Cranial Nerves
Nerves (Cranial) *USE Cranial Nerves*
Craving
Crayfish
Creative Arts Therapy
Creative Writing
Writing (Creative) *USE Creative Writing*
Creativity
Creativity Measurement
Credibility
Creutzfeldt Jakob Syndrome
Aircraft Crew *USE Aerospace Personnel*
Cri du Chat Syndrome *USE Crying Cat Syndrome*
Crib Death *USE Sudden Infant Death*
Crime
Crime Prevention
Crime Victims
Violent **Crime**
Bias Crimes *USE Hate Crimes*
Hate **Crimes**
Criminal Behavior
Criminal Conviction
Criminal History *USE Criminal Record*
Criminal Interrogation *USE Interrogation*
Criminal Justice
Criminal Law
Criminal Profiling
Criminal Record
Criminal Rehabilitation
Criminal Responsibility
Conviction (Criminal) *USE Criminal Conviction*
Criminality *USE Criminal Behavior*
Criminally Insane *USE Mentally Ill Offenders*
Criminals
Female **Criminals**
Male **Criminals**
Criminology
Crises
Family **Crises**
Organizational **Crises**
Crisis (Reactions to) *USE Stress Reactions*
Crisis Intervention
Crisis Intervention Services
Identity **Crisis**
Admission Criteria (Student) *USE Student Admission Criteria*
Assessment Criteria *USE Evaluation Criteria*
Evaluation **Criteria**
Research Diagnostic **Criteria**
Student Admission **Criteria**
Criterion Referenced Tests
Criterion Related Validity *USE Test Validity*
Critical Flicker Fusion Threshold
Critical Incident Debriefing *USE Debriefing (Psychological)*
Critical Period
Critical Scores *USE Cutting Scores*
Critical Thinking
Criticism
Self **Criticism**
CRM *USE Customer Relationship Management*
Crocodilians
Cross Cultural Communication
Cross Cultural Counseling
Cross Cultural Differences
Cross Cultural Psychology
Cross Cultural Treatment
Cross Disciplinary Research *USE Interdisciplinary Research*
Cross Examination
Crossed Eyes *USE Strabismus*
Crowding
Marlowe **Crowne** Social Desirability Scale
CRT *USE Video Display Units*
Cruelty
Crustacea
Crying
Crying Cat Syndrome
Cuban Americans *USE Hispanics*
Cued Recall
Cues
Cultism
Cultural Assimilation *USE Acculturation*
Cultural Deprivation

ROTATED ALPHABETICAL TERMS SECTION

Cultural Differences
USE Cross Cultural Differences
Cultural Factors *USE Sociocultural Factors*
Cultural Familial Mental Retardation
USE Psychosocial Mental Retardation
Cultural Pluralism *USE Multiculturalism*
Cultural Psychiatry
USE Transcultural Psychiatry
Cultural Sensitivity
Cultural Test Bias
African **Cultural** Groups
Assimilation (Cultural) *USE Acculturation*
Chinese **Cultural** Groups
Cross **Cultural** Communication
Cross **Cultural** Counseling
Cross **Cultural** Differences
Cross **Cultural** Psychology
Cross **Cultural** Treatment
Japanese **Cultural** Groups
Korean **Cultural** Groups
South Asian **Cultural** Groups
South East Asian Cultural Groups
USE Southeast Asian Cultural Groups
Southeast Asian **Cultural** Groups
Test Bias (Cultural) *USE Cultural Test Bias*
Vietnamese **Cultural** Groups
Culturally Disadvantaged
USE Cultural Deprivation
Culture (Anthropological)
Culture Bound Syndromes
Culture Change
Culture Fair Intelligence Test
Culture Shock
Culture Specific Syndromes
USE Culture Bound Syndromes
Cattell Culture Fair Intelligence Test
USE Culture Fair Intelligence Test
Mass Culture *USE Popular Culture*
Organizational Culture *USE Organizational Climate*
Popular **Culture**
Curare
Curiosity
Curricular Field Experience
Curriculum
Curriculum Based Assessment
Curriculum Development
Cursive Writing
Writing (Cursive) *USE Cursive Writing*
Cushings Syndrome
Child **Custody**
Joint **Custody**
Customer Relationship Management
Customer Satisfaction
USE Consumer Satisfaction
Customs *USE Traditions*
Cutaneous Receptive Fields
Cutaneous Sense
Cutting Scores
Cybercounseling *USE Online Therapy*
Cybernetics
Lunar Synodic **Cycle**
Menstrual **Cycle**
Sleep Wake **Cycle**
Work Rest **Cycles**
Cyclic Adenosine Monophosphate
Cycloheximide
Cyclothymic Disorder
USE Cyclothymic Personality
Cyclothymic Personality
Cynicism
Cysteine
Cystic Fibrosis
Cytochrome Oxidase
Cytokines
Cytology
Cytoplasm
Daily Activities

Daily Biological Rhythms (Animal)
USE Animal Circadian Rhythms
Activities of **Daily** Living
Damage Awards *USE Awards (Jury)*
Brain **Damage**
Dance
Dance Therapy
Dangerousness
Dark Adaptation
Adaptation (Dark) *USE Dark Adaptation*
Darwinism
Data Collection
Data Pooling *USE Meta Analysis*
Data Processing
Biographical **Data**
Statistical **Data**
Databases
Computerized Databases *USE Databases*
Online Databases *USE Databases*
Date Rape *USE Acquaintance Rape*
Dating (Social) *USE Social Dating*
Social **Dating**
Daughters
Day Camps (Recreation)
USE Summer Camps (Recreation)
Day Care (Child) *USE Child Day Care*
Day Care (Treatment)
USE Partial Hospitalization
Day Care Centers
Day Hospital *USE Partial Hospitalization*
Adult **Day** Care
Child **Day** Care
Recreational Day Camps
USE Summer Camps (Recreation)
Daydreaming
DDT (Insecticide)
Deaf
Deaf Blind
Word Deafness *USE Aphasia*
Drug Dealing *USE Illegal Drug Distribution*
Deanol *USE Antidepressant Drugs*
Death and Dying
Death Anxiety
Death Attitudes
Death Education
Death Instinct
Death Penalty *USE Capital Punishment*
Death Rate *USE Mortality Rate*
Death Rites
Crib Death *USE Sudden Infant Death*
Near **Death** Experiences
Parental **Death**
Sudden Infant **Death**
Debates
Political Debates *USE Debates*
Presidential Debates *USE Debates*
Debriefing (Experimental)
Debriefing (Psychological)
Critical Incident Debriefing *USE Debriefing (Psychological)*
Psychological Debriefing *USE Debriefing (Psychological)*
Debt *USE Financial Strain*
Decarboxylase Inhibitors
Decarboxylases
Memory **Decay**
Decentralization
Deception
Decerebration
Decision Making
Decision Support Systems
Decision Theory
Group **Decision** Making
Lexical **Decision**
Management **Decision** Making
Legal **Decisions**
Declarative Knowledge
Decoding *USE Human Information Storage*
Decompression Effects

Decortication (Brain)
Deductive Reasoning
USE Inductive Deductive Reasoning
Inductive **Deductive** Reasoning
Deer
Self **Defeating** Behavior
Defecation
Defendants
Defense Mechanisms
Compensation **(Defense** Mechanism)
Displacement **(Defense** Mechanism)
Fantasy **(Defense** Mechanism)
Identification **(Defense** Mechanism)
Insanity **Defense**
Isolation **(Defense** Mechanism)
Personal Defense *USE Self Defense*
Projection **(Defense** Mechanism)
Rationalization **(Defense** Mechanism)
Regression **(Defense** Mechanism)
Repression **(Defense** Mechanism)
Self **Defense**
Suppression **(Defense** Mechanism)
Withdrawal **(Defense** Mechanism)
Defensive Behavior (Animal)
USE Animal Defensive Behavior
Animal **Defensive** Behavior
Defensiveness
Oppositional **Defiant** Disorder
Nutritional **Deficiencies**
Acquired Immune Deficiency Syndrome *USE AIDS*
Mental Deficiency *USE Mental Retardation*
Protein **Deficiency** Disorders
Vitamin **Deficiency** Disorders
Attention **Deficit** Disorder
Attention **Deficit** Disorder with Hyperactivity
Cognitive Deficits *USE Cognitive Impairment*
Deformity *USE Physical Disfigurement*
Degrees (Educational)
USE Educational Degrees
College Degrees *USE Educational Degrees*
Educational **Degrees**
Graduate Degrees *USE Educational Degrees*
Undergraduate Degrees *USE Educational Degrees*
Dehydration
Lactate **Dehydrogenase**
Dehydrogenases
Alcohol **Dehydrogenases**
Deinstitutionalization
Deja Vu *USE Consciousness States*
Delay of Gratification
Constant Time **Delay**
Language **Delay**
Reinforcement **Delay**
Delayed Alternation
Delayed Auditory Feedback
Delayed Development
Delayed Feedback
Delayed Parenthood
Delayed Reinforcement
USE Reinforcement Delay
Delayed Speech
USE Retarded Speech Development
Deletion (Chromosome)
Delinquency (Juvenile)
USE Juvenile Delinquency
Female **Delinquency**
Juvenile **Delinquency**
Male **Delinquency**
Sexual Delinquency *USE Promiscuity*
Delirium
Delirium Tremens
Health Care **Delivery**
Delta Rhythm
Delusions
Supply and **Demand**
Dementia
Dementia (Multi Infarct)
USE Vascular Dementia
Dementia (Presenile)
USE Presenile Dementia
Dementia (Senile) *USE Senile Dementia*
Dementia of Alzheimers Type
USE Alzheimers Disease
Dementia Paralytica *USE General Paresis*
Dementia Praecox *USE Schizophrenia*
Dementia with Lewy Bodies
AIDS **Dementia** Complex
Multi Infarct Dementia *USE Vascular Dementia*
Presenile **Dementia**
Senile **Dementia**
Vascular **Dementia**
Democracy
Democratic Party *USE Political Parties*
Demographic Characteristics
Demonic Possession *USE Spirit Possession*
Demonstrations (Social)
USE Social Demonstrations
Social **Demonstrations**
Dendrites
Denial
Density (Social) *USE Social Density*
Population Density *USE Social Density*
Social **Density**
Dental Education
Dental Students
Dental Surgery
Dental Treatment
Dentist Patient Interaction
USE Therapeutic Processes
Dentistry
Dentists
Deoxycorticosterone
Deoxyglucose
Deoxyribonucleic Acid *USE DNA*
Alcohol Dependence *USE Alcoholism*
Field **Dependence**
Dependency (Drug) *USE Drug Dependency*
Dependency (Personality)
Drug **Dependency**
Dependent Personality Disorder
Dependent Variables
State **Dependent** Learning
Depersonalization
Deployment (Military)
USE Military Deployment
Military **Deployment**
Antagonists (CNS Depressant Drugs) *USE Analeptic Drugs*
CNS Depressant Drug Antagonists
USE Analeptic Drugs
CNS **Depressant** Drugs
Appetite **Depressing** Drugs
Depression (Emotion)
Agitated Depression *USE Major Depression*
Anaclitic **Depression**
Atypical **Depression**
Beck **Depression** Inventory
Endogenous **Depression**
Major **Depression**
Manic Depression *USE Bipolar Disorder*
Postnatal Depression *USE Postpartum Depression*
Postpartum **Depression**
Puerperal Depression *USE Postpartum Depression*
Reactive **Depression**
Recurrent **Depression**
Spreading **Depression**
Treatment Resistant **Depression**
Tricyclic Resistant Depression
USE Treatment Resistant Depression
Unipolar Depression *USE Major Depression*
Winter Depression
USE Seasonal Affective Disorder
Zungs Self Rating **Depression** Scale

Depressive Reaction (Neurotic) *USE Major Depression*
Manic Depressive Psychosis *USE Bipolar Disorder*
Neurotic Depressive Reaction *USE Major Depression*
Psychotic Depressive Reaction *USE Major Depression*
Deprivation
Animal Maternal **Deprivation**
Cultural **Deprivation**
Food **Deprivation**
REM Dream **Deprivation**
Sensory **Deprivation**
Sleep **Deprivation**
Social **Deprivation**
Stimulus **Deprivation**
Water **Deprivation**
Depth Perception
Depth Psychology
Ergot **Derivatives**
Opium Derivatives *USE Opiates*
Phenothiazine **Derivatives**
Dermatitis
Dermatomes *USE Cutaneous Receptive Fields*
Desegregation *USE Social Integration*
Desensitization (Systematic) *USE Systematic Desensitization Therapy*
Eye Movement **Desensitization** Therapy
Systematic **Desensitization** Therapy
Desertion *USE Abandonment*
Design (Experimental) *USE Experimental Design*
Design (Man Machine Systems) *USE Human Machine Systems Design*
Between Groups **Design**
Block Design Test (Kohs) *USE Kohs Block Design Test*
Computer Assisted **Design**
Consumer Product Design *USE Product Design*
Environmental Design *USE Environmental Planning*
Experimental **Design**
Human Machine Systems **Design**
Interior **Design**
Kohs Block **Design** Test
Man Machine Systems Design *USE Human Machine Systems Design*
Product **Design**
Research Design *USE Experimental Design*
Systems **Design**
Within Subjects Design *USE Repeated Measures*
Memory for **Designs** Test
Desipramine
Desirability (Social) *USE Social Desirability*
Edwards Social **Desirability** Scale
Marlowe Crowne Social **Desirability** Scale
Social **Desirability**
Hypoactive Sexual Desire Disorder *USE Inhibited Sexual Desire*
Inhibited Sexual **Desire**
Desires *USE Motivation*
Self **Destructive** Behavior
Anatomically **Detailed** Dolls
Detection (Signal) *USE Signal Detection (Perception)*
Signal **Detection** (Perception)
Detention (Legal) *USE Legal Detention*
Legal **Detention**
Self **Determination**
Threshold **Determination**
Verdict Determination *USE Adjudication*
Determinism
Detoxification
Kupfer Detre Self Rating Scale *USE Nonprojective Personality Measures*
Folie A **Deux**
Developed Countries

Developing Countries
Development
Adolescent **Development**
Adult **Development**
Animal **Development**
Bayley Scales of Infant **Development**
Brain **Development**
Career **Development**
Character Development *USE Personality Development*
Childhood Play **Development**
Childhood **Development**
Cognitive **Development**
Community **Development**
Curriculum **Development**
Delayed **Development**
Early Childhood **Development**
Economic **Development**
Ego **Development**
Emotional **Development**
Group **Development**
Human **Development**
Infant **Development**
Intellectual **Development**
Language **Development**
Management Development *USE Career Development*
Moral **Development**
Motor **Development**
Neonatal **Development**
Neural **Development**
Organizational **Development**
Perceptual Motor **Development**
Perceptual **Development**
Personality **Development**
Personnel Development *USE Personnel Training*
Physical **Development**
Play Development (Childhood) *USE Childhood Play Development*
Precocious **Development**
Prenatal **Development**
Professional **Development**
Program **Development**
Psychological Development *USE Psychogenesis*
Psychomotor **Development**
Psychosexual **Development**
Psychosocial **Development**
Reading **Development**
Research and **Development**
Retarded Speech **Development**
Rural Development *USE Community Development*
Sensorimotor Development *USE Perceptual Motor Development*
Sexual **Development**
Social Development *USE Psychosocial Development*
Speech **Development**
Urban Development *USE Community Development*
Developmental Age Groups
Developmental Differences *USE Age Differences*
Developmental Disabilities
Developmental Measures
Developmental Psychology
Developmental Stages
Frostig **Developmental** Test of Visual Perception
Pervasive **Developmental** Disorders
Prenatal **Developmental** Stages
Sex Linked **Developmental** Differences
Deviant Behavior *USE Antisocial Behavior*
Deviation IQ *USE Standard Scores*
Standard **Deviation**
Deviations (Sexual) *USE Paraphilias*
Sexual Deviations *USE Paraphilias*
Devices (Experimental) *USE Apparatus*
Assistive Devices *USE Assistive Technology*
Computer Peripheral **Devices**
Contraceptive **Devices**
Intrauterine **Devices**

Medical Therapeutic **Devices**
Safety **Devices**
Therapeutic Devices (Medical)
USE Medical Therapeutic Devices
Dexamethasone
Dexamethasone Suppression Test
Dexamphetamine *USE Dextroamphetamine*
Dexedrine *USE Dextroamphetamine*
Dexterity (Physical) *USE Physical Dexterity*
Physical **Dexterity**
Dextroamphetamine
Diabetes
Diabetes Insipidus
Diabetes Mellitus
Diacetylmorphine *USE Heroin*
Diagnosis
Diagnosis Related Groups
Clinical Judgment (Medical Diagnosis) *USE Medical Diagnosis*
Clinical Judgment (Not **Diagnosis)**
Computer Assisted **Diagnosis**
Differential **Diagnosis**
Dual **Diagnosis**
Educational **Diagnosis**
Medical **Diagnosis**
Prenatal **Diagnosis**
X Ray Diagnosis *USE Roentgenography*
Diagnostic and Statistical Manual
Diagnostic Interview Schedule
Research **Diagnostic** Criteria
Dialect
Dialectics
Dialysis
Diaphragm (Anatomy)
Diaphragms (Birth Control)
Diarrhea
Diastolic Pressure
Diathesis Stress Model
Diazepam
Dichoptic Stimulation
Dichotic Stimulation
Dieldrin *USE Insecticides*
Diencephalon
Dietary Restraint
Dietary Supplements
Lysergic Acid **Diethylamide**
Diets
Rank **Difference** Correlation
Age **Differences**
Animal Sex **Differences**
Animal Strain **Differences**
Cross Cultural **Differences**
Cultural Differences *USE Cross Cultural Differences*
Developmental Differences *USE Age Differences*
Ethnic Differences
USE Racial and Ethnic Differences
Gender Differences *USE Human Sex Differences*
Geographical Differences *USE Regional Differences*
Group **Differences**
Human Sex **Differences**
Individual **Differences**
Racial and Ethnic **Differences**
Racial Differences
USE Racial and Ethnic Differences
Regional **Differences**
Sex Linked Developmental **Differences**
Sex Differences (Animal)
USE Animal Sex Differences
Sex Differences (Human)
USE Human Sex Differences
Species **Differences**
Strain Differences (Animal)
USE Animal Strain Differences
Differential Aptitude Tests
Differential Diagnosis
Differential Limen *USE Thresholds*
Differential Personality Inventory
USE Nonprojective Personality Measures
Differential Reinforcement
Semantic **Differential**
Sex Differentiation Disorders
USE Genital Disorders
Difficulty Level (Test)
Task Difficulty *USE Task Complexity*
Test Difficulty *USE Difficulty Level (Test)*
Digestion
Digestive System
Digestive System Disorders
Digit Span Testing
Digital Computers
Digital Divide
Digital Video
Digits (Mathematics)
USE Numbers (Numerals)
Dihydroergotamine
Dihydroxyphenylacetic Acid
Dihydroxytryptamine
Dilantin *USE Diphenylhydantoin*
Dilation (Pupil) *USE Pupil Dilation*
Pupil **Dilation**
Prisoners **Dilemma** Game
Social **Dilemma**
Carbon **Dioxide**
Diphenhydramine
Diphenylhydantoin
Diphenylhydantoin Sodium
USE Diphenylhydantoin
Diptera
Directed Discussion Method
Directed Reverie Therapy
USE Guided Imagery
Self Directed Learning
USE Individualized Instruction
Direction Perception
Advance **Directives**
Disabilities
Accommodation **(Disabilities)**
Developmental **Disabilities**
Learning **Disabilities**
Multiple **Disabilities**
Physical **Disabilities** (Attitudes Toward)
Reading **Disabilities**
Sensory **Disabilities** (Attitudes Toward)
Disability Discrimination
Disability Evaluation
Disability Laws
Disability Management
Disabled (Attitudes Toward)
Disabled Personnel
Disadvantaged
Culturally Disadvantaged *USE Cultural Deprivation*
Economically Disadvantaged *USE Disadvantaged*
Socially Disadvantaged *USE Disadvantaged*
Disappointment
Disaster Planning
USE Emergency Preparedness
Disaster Preparedness
USE Emergency Preparedness
Natural Disaster Preparedness
USE Emergency Preparedness
Disasters
Natural **Disasters**
Discharge Planning
Facility **Discharge**
Hospital **Discharge**
Psychiatric Hospital **Discharge**
Cross Disciplinary Research
USE Interdisciplinary Research
Discipline (Child) *USE Child Discipline*
Discipline (Classroom)
USE Classroom Discipline
Child **Discipline**
Classroom **Discipline**
Disclosure (Experimental)
USE Debriefing (Experimental)

Disclosure (Self) *USE Self Disclosure*
Self **Disclosure**
Discourse Analysis
Discovery Teaching Method
Discriminant Validity *USE Test Validity*
Discrimination
Discrimination (Cognitive) *USE Cognitive Discrimination*
Discrimination (Social) *USE Social Discrimination*
Discrimination Learning
Age **Discrimination**
Auditory **Discrimination**
Cognitive **Discrimination**
Disability **Discrimination**
Distance Discrimination *USE Distance Perception*
Drug **Discrimination**
Employment **Discrimination**
Ethnic Discrimination *USE Race and Ethnic Discrimination*
Figure Ground **Discrimination**
Job Discrimination *USE Employment Discrimination*
Loudness **Discrimination**
Minority Group Discrimination *USE Race and Ethnic Discrimination*
Odor **Discrimination**
Pattern **Discrimination**
Perceptual **Discrimination**
Pitch **Discrimination**
Race and Ethnic **Discrimination**
Racial Discrimination *USE Race and Ethnic Discrimination*
Sex **Discrimination**
Size **Discrimination**
Social **Discrimination**
Spatial Discrimination *USE Spatial Perception*
Stimulus **Discrimination**
Tactual Discrimination *USE Tactual Perception*
Taste Discrimination *USE Taste Perception*
Visual **Discrimination**
Discriminative Learning *USE Discrimination Learning*
Discriminative Stimulus *USE Conditioned Stimulus*
Discussion (Group) *USE Group Discussion*
Directed **Discussion** Method
Group **Discussion**
Nondirected **Discussion** Method
Disease Course
Disease Management
Disease Outbreaks *USE Epidemics*
Disease Transmission
Addisons **Disease**
Alzheimer Disease *USE Alzheimers Disease*
Alzheimers **Disease**
Coronary Heart Disease *USE Heart Disorders*
Duchennes Disease *USE Muscular Disorders*
Huntingtons **Disease**
Lewy Body Disease *USE Dementia with Lewy Bodies*
Menieres **Disease**
Parkinsons **Disease**
Picks **Disease**
Raynauds Disease *USE Cardiovascular Disorders*
Sickle Cell **Disease**
Tay Sachs **Disease**
Diseases (Venereal) *USE Sexually Transmitted Diseases*
Communicable Diseases *USE Infectious Disorders*
International Classification of **Diseases**
Kidney **Diseases**
Neurodegenerative **Diseases**
Renal Diseases *USE Kidney Diseases*
Sexually Transmitted **Diseases**
Venereal Diseases *USE Sexually Transmitted Diseases*
Physical **Disfigurement**
Disgust
Dishonesty
Dislike *USE Aversion*
Disorder Course *USE Disease Course*
Acute Paranoid Disorder *USE Paranoia (Psychosis)*
Acute Stress **Disorder**
Antisocial Personality **Disorder**
Attention Deficit **Disorder**
Attention Deficit **Disorder** with Hyperactivity
Atypical Paranoid Disorder *USE Paranoia (Psychosis)*
Atypical Somatoform Disorder *USE Body Dysmorphic Disorder*
Avoidant Personality **Disorder**
Bipolar Affective Disorder *USE Bipolar Disorder*
Bipolar Mood Disorder *USE Bipolar Disorder*
Bipolar **Disorder**
Body Dysmorphic **Disorder**
Borderline Personality **Disorder**
Compulsive Personality Disorder *USE Obsessive Compulsive Personality Disorder*
Conduct **Disorder**
Conversion **Disorder**
Cyclothymic Disorder *USE Cyclothymic Personality*
Dependent Personality **Disorder**
Dissociative Identity **Disorder**
Dysthymic **Disorder**
Epstein Barr Viral **Disorder**
Explosive **Disorder**
Gender Identity **Disorder**
Generalized Anxiety **Disorder**
Gilles de la Tourette Disorder *USE Tourette Syndrome*
Histrionic Personality **Disorder**
Hypoactive Sexual Desire Disorder *USE Inhibited Sexual Desire*
Intermittent Explosive Disorder *USE Explosive Disorder*
Narcissistic Personality **Disorder**
Obsessive Compulsive Personality **Disorder**
Obsessive Compulsive **Disorder**
Oppositional Defiant **Disorder**
Pain Disorder *USE Somatoform Pain Disorder*
Panic **Disorder**
Paranoid Personality **Disorder**
Paranoid Disorder *USE Paranoia (Psychosis)*
Passive Aggressive Personality **Disorder**
PKU (Hereditary Disorder) *USE Phenylketonuria*
Posttraumatic Stress **Disorder**
Premenstrual Dysphoric **Disorder**
Reactive Attachment Disorder *USE Attachment Disorders*
Schizoaffective **Disorder**
Schizoid Personality **Disorder**
Schizophreniform **Disorder**
Schizotypal Personality **Disorder**
Seasonal Affective **Disorder**
Shared Paranoid Disorder *USE Folie A Deux*
Social Anxiety Disorder *USE Social Phobia*
Somatization **Disorder**
Somatoform Pain **Disorder**
Disorders
Adjustment **Disorders**
Adrenal Gland **Disorders**
Adventitious **Disorders**
Affective **Disorders**
Allergic Skin **Disorders**
Allergic **Disorders**
Anxiety **Disorders**
Appetite Disorders *USE Eating Disorders*
Articulation **Disorders**
Attachment **Disorders**
Atypical **Disorders**
Autism Spectrum Disorders *USE Pervasive Developmental Disorders*
Autoimmune Disorders *USE Immunologic Disorders*
Autonomic Nervous System **Disorders**
Autosome **Disorders**
Bacterial **Disorders**
Behavior **Disorders**
Blood and Lymphatic **Disorders**
Blood Pressure **Disorders**

Blood Disorders
USE Blood and Lymphatic Disorders
Bone **Disorders**
Bowel Disorders *USE Colon Disorders*
Brain **Disorders**
Bronchial **Disorders**
Cardiac Disorders *USE Heart Disorders*
Cardiovascular **Disorders**
Central Nervous System **Disorders**
Cerebral Vascular Disorders *USE Cerebrovascular Disorders*
Cerebrovascular **Disorders**
Character Disorders *USE Personality Disorders*
Chromosome **Disorders**
Chronicity **(Disorders)**
Circulatory Disorders *USE Cardiovascular Disorders*
Colon **Disorders**
Communication **Disorders**
Congenital **Disorders**
Coronary Disorders *USE Cardiovascular Disorders*
Digestive System **Disorders**
Dissociative **Disorders**
Drug Induced Congenital **Disorders**
Ear **Disorders**
Eating **Disorders**
Endocrine Sexual **Disorders**
Endocrine **Disorders**
Eye **Disorders**
Factitious **Disorders**
Gastrointestinal **Disorders**
Genetic **Disorders**
Genital **Disorders**
Gynecological **Disorders**
Hearing **Disorders**
Heart **Disorders**
Hematologic Disorders
USE Blood and Lymphatic Disorders
Hepatic Disorders *USE Liver Disorders*
Hereditary Disorders *USE Genetic Disorders*
Hypophysis Disorders *USE Pituitary Disorders*
Immunologic **Disorders**
Impulse Control **Disorders**
Infectious **Disorders**
Joint **Disorders**
Karyotype Disorders *USE Chromosome Disorders*
Labyrinth **Disorders**
Language **Disorders**
Laryngeal **Disorders**
Learning **Disorders**
Lipid Metabolism **Disorders**
Liver **Disorders**
Lung **Disorders**
Lymphatic Disorders
USE Blood and Lymphatic Disorders
Male Genital **Disorders**
Memory **Disorders**
Menstrual **Disorders**
Mental **Disorders**
Mental **Disorders** due to General Medical Conditions
Metabolism **Disorders**
Minimal Brain Disorders
USE Attention Deficit Disorder with Hyperactivity
Mood Disorders *USE Affective Disorders*
Motor Disorders *USE Nervous System Disorders*
Movement **Disorders**
Muscular **Disorders**
Musculoskeletal **Disorders**
Neonatal **Disorders**
Nervous System **Disorders**
Neurological Disorders *USE Nervous System Disorders*
Neuromuscular **Disorders**
Onset **(Disorders)**
Ovary Disorders *USE Endocrine Sexual Disorders*
Parasitic **Disorders**
Parathyroid **Disorders**
Peripheral Nerve Disorders *USE Peripheral Neuropathy*
Personality **Disorders**
Pervasive Developmental **Disorders**
Pharyngeal **Disorders**
Physical **Disorders**
Pituitary **Disorders**
Protein Deficiency **Disorders**
Psychiatric Disorders *USE Mental Disorders*
Psychophysiologic Disorders *USE Somatoform Disorders*
Psychosomatic Disorders *USE Somatoform Disorders*
Pulmonary Disorders *USE Lung Disorders*
Purging (Eating **Disorders)**
Recovery **(Disorders)**
Recurrence (Disorders) *USE Relapse (Disorders)*
Relapse **(Disorders)**
Remission **(Disorders)**
Respiratory Tract **Disorders**
Scalp Disorders *USE Skin Disorders*
Sense Organ **Disorders**
Sensory System **Disorders**
Severity **(Disorders)**
Sex Chromosome **Disorders**
Sex Differentiation Disorders *USE Genital Disorders*
Sex Linked Hereditary **Disorders**
Sexual Disorders (Physiological)
USE Genital Disorders
Skeletomuscular Disorders *USE Musculoskeletal Disorders*
Skin **Disorders**
Sleep **Disorders**
Somatoform **Disorders**
Somatosensory **Disorders**
Speech **Disorders**
Subtypes **(Disorders)**
Susceptibility **(Disorders)**
Taste **Disorders**
Testes Disorders *USE Endocrine Sexual Disorders*
Thyroid **Disorders**
Toxic **Disorders**
Treatment Resistant **Disorders**
Urinary Function **Disorders**
Urogenital **Disorders**
Vascular Disorders *USE Cardiovascular Disorders*
Vestibular Disorders *USE Labyrinth Disorders*
Viral **Disorders**
Vision **Disorders**
Vitamin Deficiency **Disorders**
Voice Disorders *USE Dysphonia*
Vulnerability (Disorders) *USE Susceptibility (Disorders)*
Schizophrenia **(Disorganized** Type)
Disorientation (Place)
USE Place Disorientation
Disorientation (Time)
USE Time Disorientation
Place **Disorientation**
Time **Disorientation**
Displacement (Defense Mechanism)
Video Display Terminals *USE Video Display Units*
Video **Display** Units
Displays
Animal Courtship **Displays**
Auditory **Displays**
Courtship Displays (Animal)
USE Animal Courtship Displays
Graphical **Displays**
Tactual **Displays**
Visual **Displays**
Disposition *USE Personality*
Disruptive Behavior
USE Behavior Problems
Dissatisfaction
Information **Dissemination**
Dissociation
Drug Dissociation *USE State Dependent Learning*
Hysterical Neurosis (Dissociation) *USE Dissociative Disorders*
Dissociative Disorders
Dissociative Identity Disorder
Dissociative Neurosis
USE Dissociative Disorders

ROTATED ALPHABETICAL TERMS SECTION

Dissociative Patterns *USE Dissociative Disorders*
Dissonance (Cognitive) *USE Cognitive Dissonance*
Cognitive **Dissonance**
Distance Discrimination *USE Distance Perception*
Distance Education
Distance Learning *USE Distance Education*
Distance Perception
Apparent **Distance**
Interpersonal Distance *USE Personal Space*
Distortion (Perceptual) *USE Perceptual Distortion*
Perceptual **Distortion**
Spatial **Distortion**
Distractibility
Distraction
Distress
Distress Calls (Animal) *USE Animal Distress Calls*
Animal **Distress** Calls
Respiratory **Distress**
Distributed Practice
Distribution (Frequency) *USE Frequency Distribution*
Binomial **Distribution**
Frequency **Distribution**
Gaussian Distribution *USE Normal Distribution*
Illegal Drug **Distribution**
Normal **Distribution**
Poisson Distribution *USE Skewed Distribution*
Skewed **Distribution**
Distributive Justice
Distrust *USE Suspicion*
Affective Disturbances *USE Affective Disorders*
Body Image **Disturbances**
Consciousness **Disturbances**
Emotional **Disturbances**
Fantasies (Thought **Disturbances)**
Hysterical Vision **Disturbances**
Judgment **Disturbances**
Perceptual **Disturbances**
Sexual Function **Disturbances**
Thought **Disturbances**
Vision Disturbances (Hysterical) *USE Hysterical Vision Disturbances*
Emotionally Disturbed *USE Emotional Disturbances*
Disulfiram
Diuresis
Diuretics
Diurnal Variations *USE Human Biological Rhythms*
Divergent Thinking
Diversity
Diversity in the Workplace
Workforce Diversity *USE Diversity in the Workplace*
Workplace Diversity *USE Diversity in the Workplace*
Digital **Divide**
Divided Attention
Division of Labor
Division of Labor (Animal) *USE Animal Division of Labor*
Animal **Division** of Labor
American Psychological Association **Divisions**
APA Divisions *USE American Psychological Association Divisions*
Physical Divisions (Geographic) *USE Geography*
Political Divisions (Geographic) *USE Geography*
Divorce
Divorced Persons
Dizygotic Twins *USE Heterozygotic Twins*
Dizziness *USE Vertigo*
Amphetamine (dl-) *USE Amphetamine*
Hyoscyamine (dl-) *USE Atropine*

DNA
Doctors *USE Physicians*
Dogmatism
Rokeach **Dogmatism** Scale
Dogs
Seeing Eye Dogs *USE Mobility Aids*
Doll Play
Anatomically Detailed **Dolls**
Tic Doloureux *USE Trigeminal Neuralgia*
Dolphins
Domestic Service Personnel
Domestic Violence
Domestication (Animal) *USE Animal Domestication*
Animal **Domestication**
Dominance
Dominance (Animal) *USE Animal Dominance*
Dominance Hierarchy
Animal **Dominance**
Cerebral **Dominance**
Eye Dominance *USE Ocular Dominance*
Genetic **Dominance**
Lateral **Dominance**
Ocular **Dominance**
Domination *USE Authoritarianism*
Blood Donation *USE Tissue Donation*
Organ Donation *USE Tissue Donation*
Plasma Donation *USE Tissue Donation*
Sperm Donation *USE Tissue Donation*
Tissue **Donation**
DOPA
L Dopa *USE Levodopa*
DOPAC *USE Dihydroxyphenylacetic Acid*
Dopamine
Dopamine Agonists
Dopamine Antagonists
Dopamine Metabolites
Dormitories
Dorsal Horns
Dorsal Roots
Tabes Dorsalis *USE Neurosyphilis*
Drug **Dosages**
Double Bind Interaction
Doubt
Doves
Down Syndrome *USE Downs Syndrome*
Downs Syndrome
Downsizing
Doxepin
Draftees
Drama
Drama Therapy *USE Psychodrama*
Draw A Man Test *USE Human Figures Drawing*
Goodenough Harris **Draw** A Person Test
Drawing
Human Figures **Drawing**
Dream Analysis
Dream Content
Dream Interpretation *USE Dream Analysis*
Dream Recall
REM **Dream** Deprivation
Dreaming
Lucid **Dreaming**
Rapid Eye Movement Dreams *USE REM Dreams*
REM **Dreams**
DRGs *USE Diagnosis Related Groups*
Drinking (Alcohol) *USE Alcohol Drinking Patterns*
Drinking Attitudes *USE Alcohol Drinking Attitudes*
Drinking Behavior
Drinking Behavior (Animal) *USE Animal Drinking Behavior*
Alcohol **Drinking** Attitudes
Alcohol **Drinking** Patterns

Animal **Drinking** Behavior
Binge **Drinking**
Problem Drinking *USE Alcohol Abuse*
Social **Drinking**
Underage **Drinking**
Drive *USE Motivation*
Sex **Drive**
Driver Education
Driver Safety *USE Highway Safety*
Drivers
Driving Behavior
Driving Under the Influence
Aggressive **Driving** Behavior
Drunk Driving *USE Driving Under the Influence*
Dropouts
Client Dropouts *USE Treatment Dropouts*
College **Dropouts**
Patient Dropouts *USE Treatment Dropouts*
Potential **Dropouts**
Research Dropouts *USE Experimental Attrition*
School **Dropouts**
Treatment **Dropouts**
Drosophila
Drowsiness *USE Sleepiness*
Drug Abstinence
Drug Abuse
Drug Abuse Liability
Drug Abuse Prevention
Drug Addiction
Drug Administration Methods
Drug Adverse Reactions *USE Side Effects (Drug)*
Drug Allergies
Drug Augmentation
Drug Dealing *USE Illegal Drug Distribution*
Drug Dependency
Drug Discrimination
Drug Dissociation *USE State Dependent Learning*
Drug Dosages
Drug Education
Drug Effects *USE Drugs*
Drug Induced Congenital Disorders
Drug Induced Hallucinations
Drug Industry *USE Pharmaceutical Industry*
Drug Interactions
Drug Laws
Drug Legalization
Drug Overdoses
Drug Potentiation *USE Drug Interactions*
Drug Rehabilitation
Drug Self Administration
Drug Sensitivity
Drug Synergism *USE Drug Interactions*
Drug Testing *USE Drug Usage Screening*
Drug Therapy
Drug Tolerance
Drug Trafficking *USE Illegal Drug Distribution*
Drug Usage
Drug Usage Attitudes
Drug Usage Screening
Drug Withdrawal
Drug Withdrawal Effects *USE Drug Withdrawal*
CNS Depressant Drug Antagonists *USE Analeptic Drugs*
Dependency (Drug) *USE Drug Dependency*
Ecstasy (Drug) *USE Methylenedioxymethamphetamine*
Illegal **Drug** Distribution
Intravenous **Drug** Usage
IV Drug Usage *USE Intravenous Drug Usage*
LSD (Drug) *USE Lysergic Acid Diethylamide*
Rehabilitation (Drug) *USE Drug Rehabilitation*
Side Effects **(Drug)**
Therapy (Drug) *USE Drug Therapy*
Tobacco (Drug) *USE Nicotine*
Tolerance (Drug) *USE Drug Tolerance*
Withdrawal (Drug) *USE Drug Withdrawal*
Drugs
Abstinence (Drugs) *USE Drug Abstinence*
Abuse Potential (Drugs) *USE Drug Abuse Liability*
Adrenergic Blocking **Drugs**
Adrenergic **Drugs**
Adrenolytic Drugs *USE Adrenergic Drugs*
Analeptic **Drugs**
Analgesic **Drugs**
Anesthetic **Drugs**
Anorexigenic Drugs *USE Appetite Depressing Drugs*
Antagonists (CNS Depressant Drugs) *USE Analeptic Drugs*
Anti Inflammatory **Drugs**
Antiadrenergic Drugs *USE Sympatholytic Drugs*
Antianxiety Drugs *USE Tranquilizing Drugs*
Anticholinergic Drugs *USE Cholinergic Blocking Drugs*
Anticholinesterase Drugs *USE Cholinesterase Inhibitors*
Anticoagulant **Drugs**
Anticonvulsive **Drugs**
Antidepressant **Drugs**
Antiemetic **Drugs**
Antiepileptic Drugs *USE Anticonvulsive Drugs*
Antihistaminic **Drugs**
Antihypertensive **Drugs**
Antinauseant Drugs *USE Antiemetic Drugs*
Antineoplastic **Drugs**
Antiparkinsonian Drugs *USE Antitremor Drugs*
Antipsychotic Drugs *USE Neuroleptic Drugs*
Antipyretic Drugs *USE Anti Inflammatory Drugs*
Antischizophrenic Drugs *USE Neuroleptic Drugs*
Antispasmodic **Drugs**
Antitremor **Drugs**
Antitubercular **Drugs**
Antiviral **Drugs**
Anxiety Reducing Drugs *USE Tranquilizing Drugs*
Anxiolytic Drugs *USE Tranquilizing Drugs*
Appetite Depressing **Drugs**
Ataractic Drugs *USE Tranquilizing Drugs*
Ataraxic Drugs *USE Tranquilizing Drugs*
Cardiotonic Drugs *USE Drugs*
Central Nervous System Drugs *USE CNS Affecting Drugs*
Cholinergic Blocking **Drugs**
Cholinergic **Drugs**
Cholinolytic Drugs *USE Cholinergic Blocking Drugs*
Cholinomimetic **Drugs**
CNS Affecting **Drugs**
CNS Depressant **Drugs**
CNS Stimulating **Drugs**
Cognition Enhancing Drugs *USE Nootropic Drugs*
Emetic **Drugs**
Ganglion Blocking **Drugs**
Hallucinogenic **Drugs**
Heart Rate Affecting **Drugs**
Hypnotic **Drugs**
Memory Enhancing Drugs *USE Nootropic Drugs*
Muscarinic Drugs *USE Cholinergic Drugs*
Muscle Relaxing **Drugs**
Narcoanalytic Drugs *USE Drugs*
Narcotic **Drugs**
Neuroleptic **Drugs**
Neuromuscular Blocking Drugs *USE Muscle Relaxing Drugs*
Nonprescription **Drugs**
Nootropic **Drugs**
Over the Counter Drugs *USE Nonprescription Drugs*
Pain Relieving Drugs *USE Analgesic Drugs*
Parasympatholytic Drugs *USE Antispasmodic Drugs*
Parasympathomimetic Drugs *USE Cholinomimetic Drugs*
Potentiation (Drugs) *USE Drug Interactions*
Prescribing **(Drugs)**
Prescription **Drugs**
Pressors (Drugs) *USE Vasoconstrictor Drugs*
Psychedelic Drugs *USE Hallucinogenic Drugs*
Psychoactive Drugs *USE Drugs*
Psychostimulant Drugs *USE CNS Stimulating Drugs*
Psychotomimetic **Drugs**
Psychotropic Drugs *USE Drugs*

Respiration Stimulating **Drugs**
Self Administration (Drugs) *USE Drug Self Administration*
Sensitivity (Drugs) *USE Drug Sensitivity*
Sleep Inducing Drugs *USE Hypnotic Drugs*
Sympatholytic **Drugs**
Sympathomimetic **Drugs**
Thymoleptic Drugs *USE Tranquilizing Drugs*
Tranquilizing **Drugs**
Tricyclic Antidepressant **Drugs**
Vasoconstrictor **Drugs**
Vasodilator **Drugs**
Vasopressor Drugs *USE Vasoconstrictor Drugs*
Vomit Inducing Drugs *USE Emetic Drugs*
Drunk Driving
USE Driving Under the Influence
Drunkenness *USE Alcohol Intoxication*
DSM *USE Diagnostic and Statistical Manual*
Dual Careers
Dual Diagnosis
Dual Relationships
Dual Reuptake Inhibitors
USE Serotonin Norepinephrine Reuptake Inhibitors
Dual Task Performance
Dual Task Procedure
USE Dual Task Performance
Dualism
Duchennes Disease
USE Muscular Disorders
Ducks
Mental Disorders **due** to General Medical Conditions
Duodenum *USE Intestines*
Duration (Response)
USE Response Duration
Duration (Stimulus) *USE Stimulus Duration*
Response **Duration**
Stimulus **Duration**
Treatment **Duration**
Job Duties *USE Job Characteristics*
Duty to Warn
Active Duty *USE Military Duty Status*
Military **Duty** Status
Dwarfism (Pituitary) *USE Hypopituitarism*
Pituitary Dwarfism *USE Hypopituitarism*
Dyads
Dying *USE Death and Dying*
Dying Patients *USE Terminally Ill Patients*
Death and **Dying**
Dynamics (Group) *USE Group Dynamics*
Family Dynamics *USE Family Relations*
Group **Dynamics**
Intergroup **Dynamics**
Dynorphins
Dysarthria
Dyscalculia *USE Acalculia*
Cognitive Dysfunction *USE Cognitive Impairment*
Erectile **Dysfunction**
Executive Dysfunction *USE Cognitive Impairment*
Female Sexual **Dysfunction**
Dysfunctional Family
Dyskinesia
Tardive **Dyskinesia**
Dyslexia
Dysmenorrhea
Dysmetria *USE Ataxia*
Body **Dysmorphic** Disorder
Dysmorphophobia
USE Body Dysmorphic Disorder
Dyspareunia
Dysphagia
Dysphasia
Dysphonia
Dysphoria *USE Major Depression*
Postnatal Dysphoria *USE Postpartum Depression*
Premenstrual **Dysphoric** Disorder
Dyspnea
Dyspraxia *USE Movement Disorders*
Dysthymia *USE Dysthymic Disorder*
Dysthymic Disorder
Dystonia *USE Muscular Disorders*
Dystrophy (Muscular)
USE Muscular Dystrophy
Muscular **Dystrophy**
E-Commerce *USE Electronic Commerce*
E-Tailing *USE Electronic Retailing*
E-Therapy *USE Online Therapy*
Eagerness *USE Enthusiasm*
Ear (Anatomy)
Ear Canal *USE External Ear*
Ear Disorders
Ear Ossicles *USE Middle Ear*
External **Ear**
Inner Ear *USE Labyrinth (Anatomy)*
Middle **Ear**
Early Childhood Development
Early Experience
Early Infantile Autism *USE Autism*
Early Intervention
Early Memories
Earthworms
South East Asian Cultural Groups
USE Southeast Asian Cultural Groups
Eating *USE Eating Behavior*
Eating Attitudes
Eating Behavior
Eating Disorders
Eating Habits *USE Eating Behavior*
Eating Patterns *USE Eating Behavior*
Binge **Eating**
Purging **(Eating** Disorders)
Rumination **(Eating)**
Retinal **Eccentricity**
Echinodermata
Echoencephalography
Echolalia
Echolocation
Eclectic Psychology
USE Theoretical Orientation
Eclectic Psychotherapy
Ecological Factors
Ecological Psychology
Conservation **(Ecological** Behavior)
Ecology
Behavioral **Ecology**
Economic Development
Economic Security
Income **(Economic)**
Political **Economic** Systems
Economically Disadvantaged
USE Disadvantaged
Economics
Behavioral **Economics**
Evolutionary **Economics**
Health Care **Economics**
Health Economics *USE Health Care Economics*
Home **Economics**
Pharmaceutical Economics *USE Pharmacoeconomics*
Economy
Knowledge **Economy**
Token **Economy** Programs
ECS Therapy
USE Electroconvulsive Shock Therapy
Ecstasy (Drug)
USE Methylenedioxymethamphetamine
ECT (Therapy)
USE Electroconvulsive Shock Therapy
Eczema
Educable Mentally Retarded
USE Mild Mental Retardation
Education
Education Students
Accreditation **(Education** Personnel)
Adult **Education**
Affective **Education**

ROTATED ALPHABETICAL TERMS SECTION

Alcohol Education *USE Drug Education*
Art **Education**
Attainment Level (Education)
USE Educational Attainment Level
Bilingual **Education**
Boards of **Education**
Business **Education**
Career **Education**
Client **Education**
College Education *USE Undergraduate Education*
Compensatory **Education**
Consumer **Education**
Continuing **Education**
Cooperative **Education**
Counselor **Education**
Death **Education**
Dental **Education**
Distance **Education**
Driver **Education**
Drug **Education**
Elementary **Education**
Environmental **Education**
Equal **Education**
Family Life **Education**
Foreign Language **Education**
Graduate Psychology **Education**
Graduate **Education**
Health **Education**
High School **Education**
Higher **Education**
Humanistic Education *USE Affective Education*
Individual **Education** Programs
Industrial Arts Education *USE Vocational Education*
Inservice Teacher **Education**
Language Arts **Education**
Marriage and Family Education *USE Family Life Education*
Mathematics **Education**
Medical **Education**
Middle School **Education**
Multicultural **Education**
Music **Education**
Nontraditional **Education**
Nursing **Education**
Paraprofessional **Education**
Parochial School Education *USE Private School Education*
Patient Education *USE Client Education*
Physical **Education**
Preschool **Education**
Private School **Education**
Psychology **Education**
Public School **Education**
Quality of Education *USE Educational Quality*
Reading **Education**
Rehabilitation **Education**
Religious **Education**
Remedial **Education**
Same Sex **Education**
Science **Education**
Second Language Education
USE Foreign Language Education
Secondary **Education**
Sex **Education**
Single Sex Education *USE Same Sex Education*
Social Studies **Education**
Social Work **Education**
Special **Education**
Special **Education** Students
Special **Education** Teachers
Teacher **Education**
Technical Education Teachers
USE Vocational Education Teachers
Theories of **Education**
Undergraduate **Education**
Vocational **Education**
Vocational **Education** Teachers
Educational Administration
Educational Administrators
USE School Administrators
Educational Aspirations
Educational Attainment Level
Educational Audiovisual Aids
Educational Background
Educational Background (Parents)
USE Parent Educational Background
Educational Counseling
Educational Degrees
Educational Diagnosis
Educational Environment
USE School Environment
Educational Field Trips
Educational Financial Assistance
Educational Guidance
USE Educational Counseling
Educational Incentives
Educational Inequality
USE Equal Education
Educational Intervention
USE School Based Intervention
Educational Laboratories
Educational Measurement
Educational Objectives
Educational Personnel
Educational Placement
Educational Process *USE Education*
Educational Program Accreditation
Educational Program Evaluation
Educational Program Planning
Educational Programs
Educational Psychologists
Educational Psychology
Educational Quality
Educational Reform
Educational Standards
Educational Supervision
USE Professional Supervision
Educational Television
Educational Theory
USE Theories of Education
Educational Therapy
Educational Toys
Accreditation (Educational Programs)
USE Educational Program Accreditation
Audiovisual Aids (Educational)
USE Educational Audiovisual Aids
Degrees (Educational) *USE Educational Degrees*
Field Trips (Educational) *USE Educational Field Trips*
Field Work (Educational)
USE Curricular Field Experience
Financial Assistance (Educational)
USE Educational Financial Assistance
Grading **(Educational)**
Guidance (Educational) *USE Educational Counseling*
Inclusion (Educational)
USE Mainstreaming (Educational)
Individualized Educational Plans
USE Individual Education Programs
Laboratories (Educational) *USE Educational Laboratories*
Learning Centers **(Educational)**
Mainstreaming **(Educational)**
Parent **Educational** Background
Placement (Educational) *USE Educational Placement*
Program Evaluation (Educational)
USE Educational Program Evaluation
Program Planning (Educational)
USE Educational Program Planning
Edwards Personal Preference Schedule
Edwards Social Desirability Scale
EEG (Electrophysiology)
USE Electroencephalography
EEG Biofeedback *USE Neurofeedback*
Effect Size (Statistical)
Cause Effect Relationships *USE Causality*
Generation **Effect** (Learning)

Halo **Effect**
Isolation **Effect**
Magnitude of Effect (Statistical)
USE Effect Size (Statistical)
Primacy **Effect**
Pygmalion Effect *USE Self Fulfilling Prophecies*
Recency **Effect**
Serial Position **Effect**
Stroop **Effect**
Cost Effectiveness *USE Costs and Cost Analysis*
Counselor Effectiveness
USE Counselor Characteristics
Evaluation (Treatment Effectiveness)
USE Treatment Effectiveness Evaluation
Organizational **Effectiveness**
Parent Effectiveness Training *USE Parent Training*
Teacher Effectiveness *USE Teacher Characteristics*
Teacher **Effectiveness** Evaluation
Therapist Effectiveness *USE Therapist Characteristics*
Treatment **Effectiveness** Evaluation
Acceleration **Effects**
Altitude **Effects**
Cold **Effects**
Decompression **Effects**
Drug Withdrawal Effects *USE Drug Withdrawal*
Drug Effects *USE Drugs*
Environmental **Effects**
Framing **Effects**
Gravitational **Effects**
Heat **Effects**
Iatrogenic Effects *USE Side Effects (Treatment)*
Noise **Effects**
Practice Effects *USE Practice*
Side **Effects** (Drug)
Side **Effects** (Treatment)
Temperature **Effects**
Underwater **Effects**
Efferent Pathways
Efficacy Expectations *USE Self Efficacy*
Self **Efficacy**
Efficiency (Employee)
USE Employee Efficiency
Employee **Efficiency**
Effort *USE Energy Expenditure*
Egalitarianism
Ego
Ego Development
Ego Identity
Egocentrism
Egotism
Eidetic Imagery
Ejaculation *USE Male Orgasm*
Premature **Ejaculation**
EKG (Electrophysiology)
USE Electrocardiography
Elavil *USE Amitriptyline*
Elbow (Anatomy)
Elder Abuse
Elder Care
Elected Government Officials
USE Government Personnel
Elections (Political) *USE Political Elections*
Political **Elections**
Elective Abortion *USE Induced Abortion*
Elective Mutism
Electra Complex
Electric Fishes
Electrical Activity
Electrical Brain Stimulation
Electrical Injuries
Electrical Stimulation
Skin **Electrical** Properties
Electro Oculography
Electrocardiography
Electroconvulsive Shock
Electroconvulsive Shock Therapy
Electrodermal Response
USE Galvanic Skin Response
Electrodes
Electroencephalography
Electrolytes
Electromyography
Electronic Commerce
Electronic Communication
Electronic Mail
USE Computer Mediated Communication
Electronic Retailing
Electronystagmography
Electrophysiology
EEG (Electrophysiology)
USE Electroencephalography
EKG (Electrophysiology)
USE Electrocardiography
EMG (Electrophysiology) *USE Electromyography*
EOG (Electrophysiology)
USE Electro Oculography
GSR (Electrophysiology)
USE Galvanic Skin Response
Electroplethysmography
Electroretinography
Electroshock Therapy
USE Electroconvulsive Shock Therapy
Electrosleep Treatment
Elementarism *USE Reductionism*
Elementary Education
Elementary School Students
Elementary School Teachers
Elementary Schools
Chemical **Elements**
Metallic **Elements**
Nonmetallic Elements *USE Chemical Elements*
Elephants
Elimination (Excretion) *USE Excretion*
Ellis (Albert)
Email
USE Computer Mediated Communication
Embarrassment
Embedded Figures Testing
Embolisms
Embryo
EMDR
USE Eye Movement Desensitization Therapy
Emergency Preparedness
Emergency Services
Emetic Drugs
EMG (Electrophysiology)
USE Electromyography
Nocturnal **Emission**
Positron Emission Tomography *USE Tomography*
Emotion Focused Therapy
Depression **(Emotion)**
Expressed **Emotion**
Emotional Abuse
Emotional Adjustment
Emotional Content
Emotional Control
Emotional Development
Emotional Disturbances
Emotional Expressiveness
USE Emotionality (Personality)
Emotional Immaturity
Emotional Inferiority
Emotional Insecurity
USE Emotional Security
Emotional Instability
Emotional Intelligence
Emotional Maladjustment
USE Emotional Adjustment
Emotional Maturity
Emotional Needs *USE Psychological Needs*

Emotional Regulation
Emotional Responses
Emotional Restraint *USE Emotional Control*
Emotional Security
Emotional Stability
Emotional States
Emotional Superiority
Emotional Trauma
Bonding (Emotional) *USE Attachment Behavior*
Conditioned **Emotional** Responses
Control (Emotional) *USE Emotional Control*
Immaturity (Emotional) *USE Emotional Immaturity*
Inferiority (Emotional) *USE Emotional Inferiority*
Insecurity (Emotional) *USE Emotional Security*
Instability (Emotional) *USE Emotional Instability*
Maladjustment (Emotional) *USE Emotional Adjustment*
Maturity (Emotional) *USE Emotional Maturity*
Security (Emotional) *USE Emotional Security*
Stability (Emotional) *USE Emotional Stability*
Superiority (Emotional) *USE Emotional Superiority*
Trauma (Emotional) *USE Emotional Trauma*
Emotionality (Animal) *USE Animal Emotionality*
Emotionality (Personality)
Animal **Emotionality**
Emotionally Disturbed *USE Emotional Disturbances*
Emotionally Focused Therapy *USE Emotion Focused Therapy*
Emotions
Rational **Emotive** Behavior Therapy
Rational Emotive Therapy *USE Rational Emotive Behavior Therapy*
Empathy
Emphysema (Pulmonary) *USE Pulmonary Emphysema*
Pulmonary **Emphysema**
Empirical Methods
Employability
Employee Absenteeism
Employee Assistance Programs
Employee Attitudes
Employee Benefits
Employee Characteristics
Employee Efficiency
Employee Health Insurance
Employee Interaction
Employee Leave Benefits
Employee Motivation
Employee Pension Plans
Employee Productivity
Employee Recognition *USE Professional Recognition*
Employee Selection *USE Personnel Selection*
Employee Skills
Employee Supervisor Interaction *USE Supervisor Employee Interaction*
Employee Termination *USE Personnel Termination*
Employee Turnover
Absenteeism (Employee) *USE Employee Absenteeism*
Efficiency (Employee) *USE Employee Efficiency*
Manager Employee Interaction *USE Supervisor Employee Interaction*
Pension Plans (Employee) *USE Employee Pension Plans*
Productivity (Employee) *USE Employee Productivity*
Supervisor **Employee** Interaction
Employees *USE Personnel*
Employer Attitudes
Employment *USE Employment Status*
Employment Discrimination
Employment History
Employment Interviews *USE Job Applicant Interviews*
Employment Processes *USE Personnel Recruitment*
Employment Status
Employment Tests
Part Time Employment *USE Employment Status*
Self **Employment**
Supported **Employment**
Empowerment
Empty Nest
Enabling
Enactments
Encephalitis
Encephalography
Encephalography (Air) *USE Pneumoencephalography*
Air Encephalography *USE Pneumoencephalography*
Encephalomyelitis
Encephalopathies
Toxic **Encephalopathies**
Encoding *USE Human Information Storage*
Encopresis *USE Fecal Incontinence*
Encounter Group Therapy
Encouragement
End of Life Care *USE Palliative Care*
Nerve **Endings**
Endocrine Disorders
Endocrine Gland Secretion
Endocrine Gland Surgery
Endocrine Glands
Endocrine Neoplasms
Endocrine Sexual Disorders
Endocrine System
Endocrinology
Endogamous Marriage
Endogenous Depression
Endogenous Opiates
Opioids (Endogenous) *USE Endogenous Opiates*
Endorphins
Endurance
Physical **Endurance**
Psychological **Endurance**
Energy Expenditure
Law **Enforcement**
Law **Enforcement** Personnel
Academic Engagement *USE Student Engagement*
School Engagement *USE Student Engagement*
Student **Engagement**
Engineering Psychology
Genetic **Engineering**
Human Factors **Engineering**
Knowledge **Engineering**
Engineers
English as Second Language
Limited English Proficiency *USE Language Proficiency*
Nonstandard **English**
Fertility **Enhancement**
Cognition Enhancing Drugs *USE Nootropic Drugs*
Memory Enhancing Drugs *USE Nootropic Drugs*
Enjoyment *USE Pleasure*
Enkephalins
Enlisted Military Personnel
Enlistment (Military) *USE Military Enlistment*
Military **Enlistment**
Job **Enrichment**
Enrollment (School) *USE School Enrollment*
School **Enrollment**
Enteropeptidase *USE Kinases*
Multinational Enterprises *USE Multinational Corporations*
Enthusiasm
Entrance Examinations
College **Entrance** Examination Board Scholastic Aptitude Test
Entrapment Games
Entrepreneurship
Enuresis *USE Urinary Incontinence*
Environment
Academic **Environment**

Built **Environment**
Classroom **Environment**
College **Environment**
Educational Environment *USE School Environment*
Experimental Environment *USE Research Setting*
Facility **Environment**
Family Environment *USE Home Environment*
Home **Environment**
Hospital **Environment**
Learning **Environment**
Office Environment *USE Working Conditions*
Person **Environment** Fit
School **Environment**
Therapeutic **Environment**
Treatment Environment *USE Therapeutic Environment*
Zoo Environment *USE Animal Captivity*
Environmental Adaptation
Environmental Attitudes
Environmental Design *USE Environmental Planning*
Environmental Education
Environmental Effects
Environmental Planning
Environmental Psychology
Environmental Stress
Environmental Therapy *USE Milieu Therapy*
Environmental Tobacco Smoke *USE Passive Smoking*
Adaptation (Environmental) *USE Environmental Adaptation*
Restricted Environmental Stimulation *USE Stimulus Deprivation*
Animal **Environments**
Factory Environments *USE Working Conditions*
Female Only Environments *USE Single Sex Environments*
Male Only Environments *USE Single Sex Environments*
Rural **Environments**
Same Sex Environments *USE Single Sex Environments*
Single Sex **Environments**
Social **Environments**
Suburban **Environments**
Urban **Environments**
Work Environments *USE Working Conditions*
Envy *USE Jealousy*
Penis **Envy**
Enzyme Inhibitors
Enzymes
EOG (Electrophysiology) *USE Electro Oculography*
Ependyma *USE Cerebral Ventricles*
Ephedrine
Epidemic Hysteria *USE Mass Hysteria*
Epidemics
Epidemiology
Epilepsy
Experimental **Epilepsy**
Epileptic Seizures
Epinephrine
Episcopalians *USE Protestants*
Acute Psychotic Episode *USE Acute Psychosis*
Psychotic Episode (Acute) *USE Acute Psychosis*
Episodic Memory
Epistemology
Epithelial Cells
Epithelium *USE Skin (Anatomy)*
Epstein Barr Viral Disorder
Equal Education
Equality (Social) *USE Social Equality*
Social **Equality**
Score **Equating**
Test Equating *USE Score Equating*
Structural **Equation** Modeling
Equilibrium
Cauda Equina *USE Spinal Nerves*

Equipment *USE Apparatus*
Equity (Payment)
Equity (Social)
High School Equivalency *USE Adult Education*
Erectile Dysfunction
Erection (Penis)
Ergonomics *USE Human Factors Engineering*
Ergot Derivatives
Erikson **(Erik)**
Erikson (Erik)
Eroticism
Erotomania
Error Analysis
Error of Measurement
Error Variance *USE Error of Measurement*
Measurement Error *USE Error of Measurement*
Standard Error of Measurement *USE Error of Measurement*
Trial and **Error** Learning
Errors
Prediction **Errors**
Refraction **Errors**
Type I **Errors**
Type II **Errors**
Erythroblastosis Fetalis *USE Rh Incompatibility*
Erythrocytes
Escape *USE Avoidance*
Escape Behavior (Animal) *USE Animal Escape Behavior*
Escape Conditioning
Animal **Escape** Behavior
Conditioning (Escape) *USE Escape Conditioning*
Eserine *USE Physostigmine*
Eskimos *USE Inuit*
ESL *USE English as Second Language*
Esophagus
ESP (Parapsychology) *USE Extrasensory Perception*
Essay Testing
Essential Hypertension
Self **Esteem**
Esterases
Estimation
Magnitude **Estimation**
Parameter Estimation *USE Statistical Estimation*
Statistical **Estimation**
Time **Estimation**
Estradiol
Estrogen Antagonists *USE Antiestrogens*
Estrogen Replacement Therapy *USE Hormone Therapy*
Estrogens
Estrone
Estrus
Ethanal *USE Acetaldehyde*
Ethanol
Ether (Anesthetic)
Ethyl Ether (Anesthetic) *USE Ether (Anesthetic)*
Work Ethic *USE Work (Attitudes Toward)*
Ethics
Experimental **Ethics**
Medical Ethics *USE Bioethics*
Professional **Ethics**
Ethnic Differences *USE Racial and Ethnic Differences*
Ethnic Discrimination *USE Race and Ethnic Discrimination*
Ethnic Groups *USE Racial and Ethnic Groups*
Ethnic Identity
Ethnic Sensitivity *USE Cultural Sensitivity*
Ethnic Values
Race and **Ethnic** Discrimination
Racial and **Ethnic** Attitudes
Racial and **Ethnic** Differences

Racial and **Ethnic** Groups
Racial and **Ethnic** Relations
Ethnicity *USE Ethnic Identity*
Ethnocentrism
Ethnography
Ethnolinguistics
Ethnology
Ethology (Animal) *USE Animal Ethology*
Animal **Ethology**
Ethyl Alcohol *USE Ethanol*
Ethyl Ether (Anesthetic)
USE Ether (Anesthetic)
Ethylaldehyde *USE Acetaldehyde*
Etiology
Etiopathogenesis *USE Etiology*
Etymology
Eugenics
Euphoria
Eustachian Tube *USE Middle Ear*
Euthanasia
Evaluation
Evaluation (Psychiatric)
USE Psychiatric Evaluation
Evaluation (Treatment Effectiveness)
USE Treatment Effectiveness Evaluation
Evaluation Criteria
Course **Evaluation**
Disability **Evaluation**
Educational Program **Evaluation**
Forensic **Evaluation**
Mental Health Program **Evaluation**
Peer **Evaluation**
Personnel **Evaluation**
Program **Evaluation**
Program Evaluation (Educational)
USE Educational Program Evaluation
Program Evaluation (Mental Health)
USE Mental Health Program Evaluation
Psychiatric **Evaluation**
Self **Evaluation**
Teacher Effectiveness **Evaluation**
Treatment Effectiveness **Evaluation**
Vocational **Evaluation**
Evangelists
Event Related Potentials
USE Evoked Potentials
Anniversary **Events**
Experiences **(Events)**
Evidence Based Medicine
USE Evidence Based Practice
Evidence Based Practice
Legal **Evidence**
Evil
Evoked Potentials
Auditory **Evoked** Potentials
Cortical Evoked Potentials *USE Evoked Potentials*
Motor Evoked Potentials
USE Somatosensory Evoked Potentials
Olfactory **Evoked** Potentials
Somatosensory **Evoked** Potentials
Visual **Evoked** Potentials
Evolution (Theory of)
USE Theory of Evolution
Theory of **Evolution**
Evolutionary Economics
Evolutionary Psychology
Breast Examination
USE Self Examination (Medical)
College Entrance **Examination** Board Scholastic Aptitude Test
Cross **Examination**
Eye Examination
USE Ophthalmologic Examination
Graduate Record **Examination**
Mini Mental State **Examination**
Ophthalmologic **Examination**
Physical **Examination**
Self **Examination** (Medical)

Certification Examinations
USE Professional Examinations
Entrance **Examinations**
Licensure Examinations
USE Professional Examinations
Professional **Examinations**
State Board Examinations
USE Professional Examinations
Exceptional Children (Gifted) *USE Gifted*
Exceptional Children (Handicapped)
USE Disorders
Exchange (Business) *USE Commerce*
Information Exchange *USE Communication*
Needle **Exchange** Programs
Excitation (Physiological)
USE Physiological Arousal
Excretion
Elimination (Excretion) *USE Excretion*
Executive Dysfunction
USE Cognitive Impairment
Executive Functioning *USE Cognitive Ability*
Executives *USE Top Level Managers*
Exercise
Aerobic **Exercise**
Physical Exercise *USE Exercise*
Exhaustion *USE Fatigue*
Exhibitionism
Existential Therapy
Existentialism
Exogamous Marriage
Expatriates
Life **Expectancy**
Expectant Fathers
Expectant Mothers
Expectant Parents
Expectations
Efficacy Expectations *USE Self Efficacy*
Experimenter **Expectations**
Parental **Expectations**
Role **Expectations**
Teacher **Expectations**
Energy **Expenditure**
Experience (Practice) *USE Practice*
Experience Level
Experience Level (Job)
USE Job Experience Level
Combat **Experience**
Curricular Field **Experience**
Early **Experience**
Job **Experience** Level
Openness to **Experience**
Therapist Experience *USE Therapist Characteristics*
Wilderness **Experience**
Experiences (Events)
Experiences (Life) *USE Life Experiences*
First **Experiences**
Life **Experiences**
Near Death **Experiences**
Out of Body **Experiences**
Psychedelic **Experiences**
Religious **Experiences**
Vicarious **Experiences**
Experiential Learning
Experiential Psychotherapy
Experiment Controls
Experiment Volunteers
USE Experimental Subjects
Field Experiment *USE Observation Methods*
Volunteers (Experiment) *USE Experimental Subjects*
Experimental Apparatus *USE Apparatus*
Experimental Attrition
Experimental Design
Experimental Environment
USE Research Setting
Experimental Epilepsy
Experimental Ethics
Experimental Instructions

ROTATED ALPHABETICAL TERMS SECTION

Experimental Laboratories
Experimental Methods
Experimental Neurosis
Experimental Psychologists
Experimental Psychology
Experimental Psychosis
Experimental Replication
Experimental Setting *USE Research Setting*
Experimental Subjects
Attrition (Experimental) *USE Experimental Attrition*
Debriefing **(Experimental)**
Design (Experimental) *USE Experimental Design*
Devices (Experimental) *USE Apparatus*
Disclosure (Experimental) *USE Debriefing (Experimental)*
Instructions (Experimental) *USE Experimental Instructions*
Laboratories (Experimental) *USE Experimental Laboratories*
Quasi **Experimental** Methods
Replication (Experimental) *USE Experimental Replication*
Sampling **(Experimental)**
Experimentation
Experimenter Bias
Experimenter Expectations
Bias (Experimenter) *USE Experimenter Bias*
Experimenters
Expert Systems
Expert Testimony
Testimony (Expert) *USE Expert Testimony*
Expertise *USE Experience Level*
Explicit Memory
Career Exploration *USE Career Education*
Exploratory Behavior
Animal **Exploratory** Behavior
Explosive Disorder
Explosive Personality *USE Explosive Disorder*
Intermittent Explosive Disorder *USE Explosive Disorder*
Exposure Therapy
Exposure Time (Stimulus) *USE Stimulus Duration*
Fetal Exposure *USE Prenatal Exposure*
Occupational **Exposure**
Prenatal **Exposure**
Expressed Emotion
Gene **Expression**
Self **Expression**
Expressions (Facial) *USE Facial Expressions*
Facial **Expressions**
Expressive Psychotherapy
Emotional Expressiveness *USE Emotionality (Personality)*
Expulsion (School) *USE School Expulsion*
School **Expulsion**
Extended Family
Extension Workers (Agricultural) *USE Agricultural Extension Workers*
Agricultural **Extension** Workers
External Ear
External Rewards
Internal **External** Locus of Control
Rotter Internal **External** Locus of Control Scale
Externalization
Extinction (Learning)
Thyroid Extract *USE Thyroid Hormones*
Extracurricular Activities
Extradimensional Shift Learning *USE Nonreversal Shift Learning*
Extramarital Intercourse
Extrapyramidal Motor System *USE Extrapyramidal Tracts*
Extrapyramidal Symptoms
Extrapyramidal System *USE Extrapyramidal Tracts*
Extrapyramidal Tracts
Extrasensory Perception
Extraversion
Extrinsic Motivation
Extrinsic Rewards *USE External Rewards*
Extroversion *USE Extraversion*
Eye (Anatomy)
Eye Accommodation *USE Ocular Accommodation*
Eye Color
Eye Contact
Eye Convergence
Eye Disorders
Eye Dominance *USE Ocular Dominance*
Eye Examination *USE Ophthalmologic Examination*
Eye Fixation
Eye Movement Desensitization Therapy
Eye Movements
Cones **(Eye)**
Iris **(Eye)**
Lens **(Eye)**
Nonrapid Eye Movement Sleep *USE NREM Sleep*
Pupil **(Eye)**
Rapid **Eye** Movement
Rapid Eye Movement Dreams *USE REM Dreams*
Rapid Eye Movement Sleep *USE REM Sleep*
Rods **(Eye)**
Saccadic Eye Movements *USE Eye Movements*
Seeing Eye Dogs *USE Mobility Aids*
Eyeblink Reflex
Eyelid Conditioning
Conditioning (Eyelid) *USE Eyelid Conditioning*
Crossed Eyes *USE Strabismus*
Eyewitnesses *USE Witnesses*
Eysenck Personality Inventory
F Test
California **F** Scale
Face (Anatomy)
Face Perception
Face Recognition *USE Face Perception*
Lips **(Face)**
Facial Expressions
Facial Features
Facial Muscles
Facial Nerve
Expressions (Facial) *USE Facial Expressions*
Nerve (Facial) *USE Facial Nerve*
Facilitated Communication *USE Augmentative Communication*
Facilitation (Social) *USE Social Facilitation*
Social **Facilitation**
Facilities
Community **Facilities**
Maximum Security **Facilities**
School **Facilities**
Treatment **Facilities**
Facility Admission
Facility Discharge
Facility Environment
Facility Readmission *USE Facility Admission*
Factitious Disorders
Factor Analysis
Factor Structure
ACTH Releasing Factor *USE Corticotropin Releasing Factor*
Confirmatory Factor Analysis *USE Factor Analysis*
Conscious (Personality **Factor)**
Corticotropin Releasing **Factor**
Five **Factor** Personality Model
Nerve Growth **Factor**
Tumor Necrosis **Factor**
Unconscious (Personality **Factor)**
Factorial Validity *USE Statistical Validity*
Cultural Factors *USE Sociocultural Factors*
Ecological **Factors**
Human **Factors** Engineering

Immunologic **Factors**
Personality Factors (Psychoanalytic)
USE Psychoanalytic Personality Factors
Personality Factors *USE Personality Traits*
Protective **Factors**
Psychoanalytic Personality **Factors**
Psychosocial **Factors**
Risk **Factors**
Sixteen Personality **Factors** Questionnaire
Sociocultural **Factors**
Thermal Factors *USE Temperature Effects*
Factory Environments
USE Working Conditions
Factual Knowledge
USE Declarative Knowledge
Faculty *USE Educational Personnel*
Fading (Conditioning)
Fads and Fashions
Failure
Failure to Thrive
Academic **Failure**
Fainting *USE Syncope*
Cattell Culture Fair Intelligence Test
USE Culture Fair Intelligence Test
Culture **Fair** Intelligence Test
Fairbairnian Theory *USE Object Relations*
Fairy Tales *USE Folklore*
Faith Based Organizations
Faith Healing
Faking
Falls
False Beliefs
False Memory
False Pregnancy *USE Pseudocyesis*
Pregnancy (False) *USE Pseudocyesis*
True False Tests
USE Forced Choice (Testing Method)
Fame
Familial Idiocy (Amaurotic)
USE Tay Sachs Disease
Amaurotic Familial Idiocy *USE Tay Sachs Disease*
Cultural Familial Mental Retardation
USE Psychosocial Mental Retardation
Familiarity
Family
Family Background
Family Caregivers *USE Caregivers*
Family Conflict
Family Counseling *USE Family Therapy*
Family Crises
Family Dynamics *USE Family Relations*
Family Environment
USE Home Environment
Family Intervention
Family Life Education
Family Life *USE Family Relations*
Family Medicine
Family Members
Family of Origin
Family Physicians
Family Planning
Family Planning Attitudes
Family Preservation
Family Relations
Family Resemblance
Family Reunification
Family Size
Family Socioeconomic Level
Family Structure
Family Systems Model
USE Family Systems Theory
Family Systems Theory
Family Therapy
Family Violence *USE Domestic Violence*
Family Work Relationship
Background (Family) *USE Family Background*
Biological **Family**
Dysfunctional **Family**
Extended **Family**
Interethnic **Family**
Interracial **Family**
Job Family Relationship
USE Family Work Relationship
Marriage and Family Education
USE Family Life Education
Natural Family *USE Biological Family*
Nuclear **Family**
Schizophrenogenic **Family**
Work Family Relationship
USE Family Work Relationship
Fans (Sports) *USE Sports Spectators*
Fantasies (Thought Disturbances)
Fantasy
Fantasy (Defense Mechanism)
Guided Fantasy *USE Guided Imagery*
Sexual **Fantasy**
Laborers (Farm) *USE Agricultural Workers*
Migrant **Farm** Workers
Farmers *USE Agricultural Workers*
Fascism
Fads and **Fashions**
Fat Metabolism *USE Lipid Metabolism*
Fatalism
Father Absence
Father Child Communication
Father Child Relations
Fathers
Adolescent **Fathers**
Expectant **Fathers**
Single **Fathers**
Teenage Fathers *USE Adolescent Fathers*
Fatigue
Chronic **Fatigue** Syndrome
Fatty Acids
Fear
Fear of Public Speaking
USE Speech Anxiety
Fear of Strangers *USE Stranger Reactions*
Fear of Success
Fear Survey Schedule
Conditioned **Fear**
Facial **Features**
Fecal Incontinence
Incontinence (Fecal) *USE Fecal Incontinence*
School Federal Aid
USE Educational Financial Assistance
Fee for Service
Feedback
Auditory **Feedback**
Delayed Auditory **Feedback**
Delayed **Feedback**
Sensory **Feedback**
Visual **Feedback**
Feeding Behavior (Animal)
USE Animal Feeding Behavior
Feeding Practices *USE Eating Behavior*
Animal **Feeding** Behavior
Bottle **Feeding**
Breast **Feeding**
Anesthesia **(Feeling)**
Feelings *USE Emotions*
Professional **Fees**
Feet (Anatomy)
Felids
Felonies *USE Crime*
Female Animals
Female Attitudes
Female Criminals
Female Delinquency
Female Genital Mutilation
USE Circumcision
Female Genitalia
Female Homosexuality *USE Lesbianism*

ROTATED ALPHABETICAL TERMS SECTION

Female Only Environments
USE Single Sex Environments
Female Orgasm
Female Sexual Dysfunction
Genitalia (Female) *USE Female Genitalia*
Male **Female** Relations
Females (Human) *USE Human Females*
Battered **Females**
Human **Females**
Femininity
Feminism
Feminist Psychology
Feminist Therapy
Feminization Syndrome (Testicular)
USE Testicular Feminization Syndrome
Testicular **Feminization** Syndrome
Femoral Nerve *USE Spinal Nerves*
Fenfluramine
Fentanyl
Fertility
Fertility Enhancement
Fertilization
In Vitro Fertilization *USE Reproductive Technology*
Fetal Alcohol Syndrome
Fetal Exposure *USE Prenatal Exposure*
Erythroblastosis Fetalis *USE Rh Incompatibility*
Fetishism
Sexual Fetishism *USE Fetishism*
Fetus
Fever *USE Hyperthermia*
Hay **Fever**
Rheumatic **Fever**
Postganglionic Autonomic Fibers *USE Autonomic Ganglia*
Preganglionic Autonomic Fibers *USE Autonomic Ganglia*
Fibrillation (Heart)
Atrial Fibrillation *USE Fibrillation (Heart)*
Auricular Fibrillation *USE Fibrillation (Heart)*
Ventricular Fibrillation *USE Fibrillation (Heart)*
Fibromyalgia
Cystic **Fibrosis**
Fiction *USE Literature*
Marital Fidelity *USE Monogamy*
Field Dependence
Field Experiment
USE Observation Methods
Field Instruction
USE Curricular Field Experience
Field Trips (Educational)
USE Educational Field Trips
Field Work (Educational)
USE Curricular Field Experience
Animal Open **Field** Behavior
Curricular **Field** Experience
Educational **Field** Trips
Open Field Behavior (Animal)
USE Animal Open Field Behavior
Visual **Field**
Cutaneous Receptive **Fields**
Receptive **Fields**
Visual Receptive **Fields**
Fire **Fighters**
Fighting *USE Aggressive Behavior*
Figurative Language
Figure Ground Discrimination
Figures of Speech
USE Figurative Language
Embedded **Figures** Testing
Human **Figures** Drawing
Perceptual Fill *USE Perceptual Closure*
Films
Filtered Noise
Filtered Speech
Finance
Financial Assistance (Educational)
USE Educational Financial Assistance
Financial Problems *USE Financial Strain*
Financial Security *USE Economic Security*
Financial Services
Financial Strain
Financial Stress *USE Financial Strain*
Educational **Financial** Assistance
School Financial Assistance
USE Educational Financial Assistance
Fine Motor Skill Learning
Finger Tapping
Fingers (Anatomy)
Fingerspelling
Fire Fighters
Fire Prevention
Firearms
Firesetting *USE Arson*
FIRO-B
USE Fundamental Interpersonal Relation Orientation Behavior Ques
First Experiences
First Language *USE Native Language*
Bass **(Fish)**
Fishes
Electric **Fishes**
Goodness of **Fit**
Person Environment **Fit**
Physical **Fitness**
Five Factor Personality Model
Big Five Personality Model
USE Five Factor Personality Model
Fixation (Psychoanalytic)
Fixation (Psychological)
Eye **Fixation**
Ocular Fixation *USE Eye Fixation*
Visual Fixation *USE Eye Fixation*
Fixed Interval Reinforcement
Fixed Ratio Reinforcement
Flashbacks *USE Hallucinations*
Flexibility (Personality)
USE Adaptability (Personality)
Flexion Reflex
Flextime *USE Work Scheduling*
Flicker Fusion Frequency
USE Critical Flicker Fusion Threshold
Critical **Flicker** Fusion Threshold
Flies *USE Diptera*
Flight Attendants
USE Aerospace Personnel
Flight Instrumentation
Flight Simulation
Instrumentation (Flight) *USE Flight Instrumentation*
Flooding Therapy *USE Implosive Therapy*
Blood **Flow**
Cerebral Blood **Flow**
Fluency *USE Verbal Fluency*
Verbal **Fluency**
Fluid Intake
Amniotic **Fluid**
Cerebrospinal **Fluid**
Spinal Fluid *USE Cerebrospinal Fluid*
Body **Fluids**
Flunitrazepam
Fluoxetine
Fluphenazine
Flurazepam
Fluvoxamine
Fruit Fly *USE Drosophila*
Emotion **Focused** Therapy
Emotionally Focused Therapy
USE Emotion Focused Therapy
Solution **Focused** Therapy
Focusing (Visual)
USE Ocular Accommodation
Folic Acid
Folie A Deux
Folk Medicine
Folk Psychology
Folklore
Folktales *USE Folklore*

Follicle Stimulating Hormone
Project **Follow** Through
Followup (Posttreatment) *USE Posttreatment Followup*
Followup Studies
Posttreatment **Followup**
Studies (Followup) *USE Followup Studies*
Food
Food Additives
Food Allergies
Food Deprivation
Food Intake
Food Preferences
Football
Foraging (Animal) *USE Animal Foraging Behavior*
Animal **Foraging** Behavior
Air **Force** Personnel
Forced Choice (Testing Method)
Forebrain
Medial **Forebrain** Bundle
Foreign Language Education
Foreign Language Learning
Foreign Language Translation
Foreign Languages
Foreign Nationals *USE Expatriates*
Foreign Organizations
Foreign Policy Making
Foreign Students *USE International Students*
Foreign Study *USE Study Abroad*
Foreign Workers
Policy Making (Foreign) *USE Foreign Policy Making*
Foremen (Industrial) *USE Industrial Foremen*
Industrial **Foremen**
Forensic Evaluation
Forensic Psychiatry
Forensic Psychology
Forgetting
Forgiveness
Form and Shape Perception
Form Classes (Language)
Form Perception *USE Form and Shape Perception*
Words (Form Classes) *USE Form Classes (Language)*
Attitude **Formation**
Character Formation *USE Personality Development*
Coalition **Formation**
Concept **Formation**
Identity **Formation**
Impression **Formation**
Reaction **Formation**
Reticular **Formation**
Test **Forms**
Theory **Formulation**
Fornix
FORTRAN *USE Computer Programming Languages*
Chance **(Fortune)**
Forward Masking *USE Masking*
Foster Care
Foster Children
Foster Homes *USE Foster Care*
Foster Parents
Fovea
Foveal Vision
Fowl *USE Birds*
Foxes
Fragile X Syndrome
Fragmentation (Schizophrenia)
Frail *USE Health Impairments*
Rod and **Frame** Test
Framing Effects
Frankness *USE Honesty*
Fraternal Twins *USE Heterozygotic Twins*
Fraternity Membership
Fraud
Consumer Fraud *USE Fraud*
Skinner (Burrhus **Frederic)**
Free Association
Free Recall
Free Will *USE Volition*
Association (Free) *USE Free Association*
Freedom
Frequency (Pitch) *USE Pitch (Frequency)*
Frequency (Response) *USE Response Frequency*
Frequency (Stimulus) *USE Stimulus Frequency*
Frequency Distribution
Distribution (Frequency) *USE Frequency Distribution*
Flicker Fusion Frequency *USE Critical Flicker Fusion Threshold*
Pitch **(Frequency)**
Response **Frequency**
Spatial **Frequency**
Stimulus **Frequency**
Temporal **Frequency**
Tone (Frequency) *USE Pitch (Frequency)*
Word **Frequency**
Freud (Sigmund)
Freudian Psychoanalytic School
Psychoanalytic School (Freudian) *USE Freudian Psychoanalytic School*
Friendship
Frigidity *USE Female Sexual Dysfunction*
Frogs
Frontal Lobe
Frostig Developmental Test of Visual Perception
Fruit Fly *USE Drosophila*
Frustration
Rosenzweig Picture **Frustration** Study
Fugue Reaction
Self **Fulfilling** Prophecies
Fulfillment *USE Satisfaction*
Sexual **Function** Disturbances
Urinary **Function** Disorders
Functional Analysis
Functional Knowledge *USE Procedural Knowledge*
Functional Status *USE Ability Level*
Functionalism
Cognitive Functioning *USE Cognitive Ability*
Executive Functioning *USE Cognitive Ability*
Intellectual Functioning *USE Cognitive Ability*
Level of Functioning *USE Ability Level*
Job Functions *USE Job Characteristics*
Fundamental Interpersonal Relation Orientation Behavior Ques
Fundamentalism (Religious) *USE Religious Fundamentalism*
Religious **Fundamentalism**
Funding
Fundraising
Funerals *USE Death Rites*
Furniture
Critical Flicker **Fusion** Threshold
Flicker Fusion Frequency *USE Critical Flicker Fusion Threshold*
Future
Fuzzy Logic
Fuzzy Set Theory
GABA Agonists *USE Gamma Aminobutyric Acid Agonists*
GABA Antagonists *USE Gamma Aminobutyric Acid Antagonists*
Galanin *USE Peptides*
Galantamine *USE Galanthamine*
Galanthamine
Galvanic Skin Response

ROTATED ALPHABETICAL TERMS SECTION

Gamblers Anonymous
USE Twelve Step Programs
Gambling
Compulsive Gambling *USE Pathological Gambling*
Pathological **Gambling**
Game Theory
Prisoners Dilemma **Game**
Games
Childrens Recreational **Games**
Computer **Games**
Entrapment **Games**
Non Zero Sum **Games**
Simulation **Games**
Video Games *USE Computer Games*
Gamma Aminobutyric Acid
Gamma Aminobutyric Acid Agonists
Gamma Aminobutyric Acid Antagonists
Gamma Globulin
Ganglia
Autonomic **Ganglia**
Basal **Ganglia**
Spinal **Ganglia**
Ganglion Blocking Drugs
Ganglion Cells (Retina)
Retinal Ganglion Cells *USE Ganglion Cells (Retina)*
Stellate Ganglion *USE Autonomic Ganglia*
Gangrene *USE Necrosis*
Gangs (Juvenile) *USE Juvenile Gangs*
Juvenile **Gangs**
Ganser Syndrome *USE Factitious Disorders*
Generation **Gap**
Gardening Therapy
USE Horticulture Therapy
Gastrointestinal Disorders
Gastrointestinal System
Gastrointestinal Ulcers
Ulcers (Gastrointestinal)
USE Gastrointestinal Ulcers
Gastropods *USE Mollusca*
Gating (Sensory) *USE Sensory Gating*
Sensory **Gating**
Gaussian Distribution
USE Normal Distribution
Gay Liberation Movement
USE Homosexual Liberation Movement
Gay Males *USE Male Homosexuality*
Gay Parents *USE Homosexual Parents*
Gazing *USE Eye Fixation*
Geese
Gender Differences
USE Human Sex Differences
Gender Identity
Gender Identity Disorder
Gender Role Attitudes
USE Sex Role Attitudes
Gender Roles *USE Sex Roles*
Sexual Identity (Gender) *USE Gender Identity*
Gene Expression
General Anesthetics
General Aptitude Test Battery
General Health Questionnaire
General Paresis
General Practitioners
Medical Treatment **(General)**
Mental Disorders due to **General** Medical Conditions
Paresis (General) *USE General Paresis*
Typologies (General) *USE Taxonomies*
Generalization (Cognitive)
USE Cognitive Generalization
Generalization (Learning)
Generalization (Response)
USE Response Generalization
Generalization (Semantic)
USE Semantic Generalization
Generalization (Stimulus)
USE Stimulus Generalization
Cognitive **Generalization**
Response **Generalization**
Semantic **Generalization**
Stimulus **Generalization**
Generalized Anxiety Disorder
Generation Effect (Learning)
Generation Gap
Transformational **Generative** Grammar
Generativity
Generators (Apparatus)
Genes
Genetic Counseling
Genetic Disorders
Genetic Dominance
Genetic Engineering
Genetic Linkage
Genetic Recessiveness
Genetic Screening *USE Genetic Testing*
Genetic Testing
Recessiveness (Genetic) *USE Genetic Recessiveness*
Genetics
Behavioral **Genetics**
Population **Genetics**
Geniculate Bodies (Thalamus)
Lateral Geniculate Nucleus
USE Geniculate Bodies (Thalamus)
Medial Geniculate Nucleus
USE Geniculate Bodies (Thalamus)
Genital Disorders
Genital Herpes *USE Herpes Genitalis*
Female Genital Mutilation *USE Circumcision*
Male **Genital** Disorders
Genitalia (Female) *USE Female Genitalia*
Genitalia (Male) *USE Male Genitalia*
Female **Genitalia**
Male **Genitalia**
Herpes **Genitalis**
Geniuses *USE Gifted*
Genocide
Genome
Human Genome *USE Genome*
Genotypes
Genuineness *USE Sincerity*
Geographic Regions *USE Geography*
Physical Divisions (Geographic) *USE Geography*
Political Divisions (Geographic) *USE Geography*
Geographical Differences
USE Regional Differences
Geographical Mobility
Mobility (Geographical) *USE Geographical Mobility*
Geography
Physical Geography *USE Geography*
Geomagnetism *USE Magnetism*
Geometry
Gerbils
Geriatric Assessment
Geriatric Patients
Geriatric Psychiatry
Geriatric Psychology *USE Geropsychology*
Geriatric Psychotherapy
Geriatrics
German Measles *USE Rubella*
Gerontology
Geropsychology
Gestalt Psychology
Gestalt Therapy
Bender **Gestalt** Test
Gestation *USE Pregnancy*
Gestures
Ghettoes
Ghettos *USE Ghettoes*
Gifted
Exceptional Children (Gifted) *USE Gifted*
Intellectually Gifted *USE Gifted*
Gilles de la Tourette Disorder
USE Tourette Syndrome
Gipsies *USE Gypsies*
Girls *USE Human Females*

Adrenal **Gland** Disorders
Adrenal **Gland** Secretion
Endocrine **Gland** Secretion
Endocrine **Gland** Surgery
Pituitary **Gland**
Pituitary Gland Surgery *USE Hypophysectomy*
Secretion **(Gland)**
Thyroid **Gland**
Glands
Adrenal **Glands**
Endocrine **Glands**
Mammary **Glands**
Parathyroid **Glands**
Salivary **Glands**
Glaucoma
Global Amnesia
Globalization
Gamma **Globulin**
Globulins
Globus Pallidus
Glossolalia
Glossopharyngeal Nerve
USE Cranial Nerves
Glucagon
Glucocorticoids
Glucose
Glucose Metabolism
Blood Glucose *USE Blood Sugar*
Glue Sniffing
Glutamate *USE Glutamic Acid*
Glutamate Receptors
Glutamic Acid
Glutamine
Glutethimide
Glycine
Glycogen
Glycoproteins *USE Globulins*
Goal Orientation
Goal Setting
Goals
Career Goals *USE Occupational Aspirations*
Organizational Goals *USE Organizational Objectives*
Goats
God Concepts
Goiters
Goldfish
Gonadotropic Hormones
Gonadotropin *USE Gonadotropic Hormones*
Gonads
Gonorrhea
Goodenough Harris Draw A Person Test
Goodness of Fit
Gorillas
Gossip
Gough Adjective Check List
Clinical **Governance**
Government
Government Agencies
Government Bureaucracy *USE Government*
Government Personnel
Government Policy Making
Government Programs
Autonomy **(Government)**
Elected Government Officials
USE Government Personnel
Law **(Government)**
Policy Making (Government)
USE Government Policy Making
Programs (Government) *USE Government Programs*
Welfare Services **(Government)**
Grade Level
Academic Grade Level *USE Grade Level*
Gradepoint Average
USE Academic Achievement
Grading (Educational)
Graduate Degrees
USE Educational Degrees

Graduate Education
Graduate Psychology Education
Graduate Record Examination
Graduate Schools
Graduate Students
Clinical Psychology **Graduate** Training
Training (Clinical Psychology Graduate)
USE Clinical Psychology Graduate Training
Training (Graduate Psychology)
USE Graduate Psychology Education
College **Graduates**
High School **Graduates**
Graduation (School)
USE School Graduation
School **Graduation**
Alcohol (Grain) *USE Ethanol*
Grammar
Grammar Schools
USE Elementary Schools
Transformational Generative **Grammar**
Grand Mal Seizures
Grandchildren
Grandiosity
Grandparents
Great Grandparents *USE Ancestors*
Graphical Displays
Graphology *USE Handwriting*
Grasping
Grasshoppers
Gratefulness *USE Gratitude*
Delay of **Gratification**
Gratitude
Myasthenia **Gravis**
Gravitational Effects
Periaqueductal **Gray**
Great Grandparents *USE Ancestors*
Gregariousness
Bannister Repertory **Grid**
Shuttle Box Grids *USE Shuttle Boxes*
Grief
Grimaces
Nocturnal Teeth **Grinding**
Teeth Grinding *USE Bruxism*
Grooming Behavior (Animal)
USE Animal Grooming Behavior
Animal **Grooming** Behavior
Gross Motor Skill Learning
Ground Transportation
Figure **Ground** Discrimination
Grounded Theory
Group Characteristics
Group Cohesion
Group Counseling
Group Decision Making
Group Development
Group Differences
Group Discussion
Group Dynamics
Group Health Plans
USE Health Maintenance Organizations
Group Homes
Group Identity
Group Instruction
Group Participation
Group Performance
Group Problem Solving
Group Psychotherapy
Group Size
Group Structure
Group Testing
Group Therapy *USE Group Psychotherapy*
Cohesion (Group) *USE Group Cohesion*
Counseling (Group) *USE Group Counseling*
Discussion (Group) *USE Group Discussion*
Dynamics (Group) *USE Group Dynamics*
Encounter **Group** Therapy

ROTATED ALPHABETICAL TERMS SECTION

Marathon **Group** Therapy
Minority Group Discrimination *USE Race and Ethnic Discrimination*
Size (Group) *USE Group Size*
Ability **Grouping**
Groups (Organizations) *USE Organizations*
Groups (Social) *USE Social Groups*
African Cultural **Groups**
Agencies (Groups) *USE Organizations*
Associations (Groups) *USE Organizations*
Between **Groups** Design
Blood **Groups**
Chinese Cultural **Groups**
Consciousness Raising **Groups**
Control Groups *USE Experiment Controls*
Developmental Age **Groups**
Diagnosis Related **Groups**
Ethnic Groups *USE Racial and Ethnic Groups*
Japanese Cultural **Groups**
Korean Cultural **Groups**
Minority **Groups**
Racial and Ethnic **Groups**
Reference **Groups**
Religious **Groups**
Social **Groups**
South Asian Cultural **Groups**
South East Asian Cultural Groups *USE Southeast Asian Cultural Groups*
Southeast Asian Cultural **Groups**
Support **Groups**
T Groups *USE Human Relations Training*
Vietnamese Cultural **Groups**
Groupware
Grown Children *USE Adult Offspring*
Growth *USE Development*
Growth Centers *USE Human Potential Movement*
Growth Hormone Inhibitor *USE Somatostatin*
Growth Hormone *USE Somatotropin*
Brain Growth *USE Brain Development*
Nerve **Growth** Factor
Personal Growth Techniques *USE Human Potential Movement*
Physical Growth *USE Physical Development*
GSR (Electrophysiology) *USE Galvanic Skin Response*
Guanethidine
Guanosine
Coast **Guard** Personnel
National **Guard** Personnel
Guardianship
Guessing
Guest Workers *USE Foreign Workers*
Guidance (Educational) *USE Educational Counseling*
Guidance (Occupational) *USE Occupational Guidance*
Guidance Counseling *USE School Counseling*
Career Guidance *USE Occupational Guidance*
Child **Guidance** Clinics
Educational Guidance *USE Educational Counseling*
Occupational **Guidance**
School Guidance *USE School Counseling*
Vocational Guidance *USE Occupational Guidance*
Guided Fantasy *USE Guided Imagery*
Guided Imagery
Treatment **Guidelines**
Guilt
Guinea Pigs
Gulls *USE Sea Gulls*
Sea **Gulls**
Gun Control Laws
Guns *USE Firearms*
Gustatory Perception *USE Taste Perception*

Gymnastic Therapy *USE Recreation Therapy*
Gynecological Disorders
Gynecologists
Gynecology
Gypsies
Gyrus Cinguli
Habilitation
Habitat Selection *USE Territoriality*
Habitats (Animal) *USE Animal Environments*
Habits
Eating Habits *USE Eating Behavior*
Study **Habits**
Habituation
Hair
Hair Loss *USE Alopecia*
Hair Pulling *USE Trichotillomania*
Halcion *USE Triazolam*
Halfway Houses
Residence Halls *USE Dormitories*
Hallucinations
Auditory **Hallucinations**
Drug Induced **Hallucinations**
Hypnagogic **Hallucinations**
Visual **Hallucinations**
Hallucinogenic Drugs
Hallucinosis
Alcoholic **Hallucinosis**
Halo Effect
Haloperidol
Halstead Reitan Neuropsychological Battery
Hamsters
Hand (Anatomy)
Handedness
Handicapped (Attitudes Toward) *USE Disabled (Attitudes Toward)*
Adventitiously Handicapped *USE Adventitious Disorders*
Aurally Handicapped *USE Hearing Disorders*
Congenitally Handicapped *USE Congenital Disorders*
Exceptional Children (Handicapped) *USE Disorders*
Multiply Handicapped *USE Multiple Disabilities*
Orthopedically Handicapped *USE Physical Disorders*
Physically Handicapped *USE Physical Disorders*
Sensorially Handicapped *USE Sensory System Disorders*
Speech Handicapped *USE Speech Disorders*
Visually Handicapped *USE Vision Disorders*
Self **Handicapping** Strategy
Handicaps *USE Disabilities*
Physical Handicaps (Attitudes Toward) *USE Physical Disabilities (Attitudes Toward)*
Sensory Handicaps (Attitudes Toward) *USE Sensory Disabilities (Attitudes Toward)*
Handicrafts *USE Crafts*
Handwriting
Handwriting Legibility
Legibility (Handwriting) *USE Handwriting Legibility*
Printing **(Handwriting)**
Writing (Handwriting) *USE Handwriting*
Happiness
Haptic Perception *USE Cutaneous Sense*
Harassment
Harassment (Sexual) *USE Sexual Harassment*
Sexual **Harassment**
Hardiness *USE Resilience (Psychological)*
Harm Reduction
Maslow (Abraham **Harold)**
Goodenough **Harris** Draw A Person Test
Hashish
Hate
Hate Crimes
Hawaii Natives
Native Hawaiians *USE Hawaii Natives*

Hay Fever
Hazardous Materials
Hazards
Head (Anatomy)
Head Banging
Head Injuries
Head Start *USE Project Head Start*
Closed Head Injuries *USE Head Injuries*
Project **Head** Start
Headache
Migraine **Headache**
Muscle Contraction **Headache**
Tension Headache
USE Muscle Contraction Headache
Faith **Healing**
Psychic Healing *USE Faith Healing*
Health
Health Attitudes
Health Behavior
Health Care Administration
Health Care Barriers
USE Treatment Barriers
Health Care Costs
Health Care Delivery
Health Care Economics
Health Care Policy
Health Care Professionals
USE Health Personnel
Health Care Psychology
Health Care Reform
Health Care Seeking Behavior
Health Care Services
Health Care Utilization
Health Complaints
Health Economics
USE Health Care Economics
Health Education
Health Impairments
Health Insurance
Health Knowledge
Health Locus of Control
USE Health Attitudes
Health Maintenance Organizations
Health Personnel
Health Personnel Attitudes
Health Promotion
Health Psychology
USE Health Care Psychology
Health Screening
Health Service Needs
Health Service Utilization
USE Health Care Utilization
Allied **Health** Personnel
Auxiliary Health Workers
USE Allied Health Personnel
Behavioral Health *USE Health Care Psychology*
Community Mental **Health**
Community Mental **Health** Centers
Community Mental **Health** Services
Community Mental **Health** Training
Employee **Health** Insurance
General **Health** Questionnaire
Group Health Plans
USE Health Maintenance Organizations
Holistic **Health**
Home Health Aides *USE Home Care Personnel*
Inservice Training (Mental Health)
USE Mental Health Inservice Training
Mental **Health**
Mental Health Care Barriers
USE Treatment Barriers
Mental Health Care Costs *USE Health Care Costs*
Mental Health Care Policy *USE Health Care Policy*
Mental Health Centers (Community)
USE Community Mental Health Centers
Mental Health Consultation
USE Professional Consultation
Mental **Health** Inservice Training
Mental **Health** Parity
Mental **Health** Personnel
Mental **Health** Personnel Supply
Mental **Health** Program Evaluation
Mental **Health** Programs
Mental Health Service Needs
USE Health Service Needs
Mental **Health** Services
Mental Health Training (Community)
USE Community Mental Health Training
Physical **Health**
Primary Mental **Health** Prevention
Primary **Health** Care
Program Evaluation (Mental Health)
USE Mental Health Program Evaluation
Programs (Mental Health) *USE Mental Health Programs*
Public **Health**
Public **Health** Service Nurses
Public **Health** Services
Training (Community Mental Health)
USE Community Mental Health Training
Training (Mental Health Inservice)
USE Mental Health Inservice Training
Utilization (Health Care) *USE Health Care Utilization*
Web Based Mental Health Services *USE Online Therapy*
Wholistic Health *USE Holistic Health*
Hearing Acuity *USE Auditory Acuity*
Hearing Aids
Hearing Disorders
Hearing Impaired (Partially)
USE Partially Hearing Impaired
Hearing Measures
USE Speech and Hearing Measures
Partially **Hearing** Impaired
Sensorineural Hearing Loss *USE Hearing Disorders*
Speech and **Hearing** Measures
Heart
Heart Attacks *USE Heart Disorders*
Heart Auricles
Heart Beat *USE Heart Rate*
Heart Disorders
Heart Rate
Heart Rate Affecting Drugs
Heart Surgery
Heart Transplants
USE Organ Transplantation
Heart Valves
Heart Ventricles
Arrhythmias **(Heart)**
Atria (Heart) *USE Heart Auricles*
Auricles (Heart) *USE Heart Auricles*
Coronary Heart Disease *USE Heart Disorders*
Fibrillation **(Heart)**
Rapid Heart Rate *USE Tachycardia*
Valves (Heart) *USE Heart Valves*
Ventricles (Heart) *USE Heart Ventricles*
Heartbeat *USE Heart Rate*
Heat Effects
Hebephrenic Schizophrenia
USE Schizophrenia (Disorganized Type)
Hedonism
Heels (Anatomy) *USE Feet (Anatomy)*
Height (Body) *USE Body Height*
Body **Height**
Helicopters
Helium
Helmets *USE Safety Devices*
Help Seeking Behavior
Self **Help** Techniques
Helping Behavior
USE Assistance (Social Behavior)
Helplessness
Helplessness (Learned)
USE Learned Helplessness
Learned **Helplessness**

Hematologic Disorders
USE Blood and Lymphatic Disorders
Hematoma
Hemianopia
Hemianopsia *USE Hemianopia*
Hemiopia *USE Hemianopia*
Hemiplegia
Left **Hemisphere**
Right **Hemisphere**
Hemispherectomy
Hemispheric Specialization
USE Lateral Dominance
Hemodialysis
Hemoglobin
Hemophilia
Hemorrhage
Cerebral **Hemorrhage**
Hemp (Cannabis) *USE Cannabis*
Henmon Nelson Tests of Mental Ability
USE Intelligence Measures
Heparin
Hepatic Disorders *USE Liver Disorders*
Hepatitis
Toxic **Hepatitis**
Medicinal **Herbs** and Plants
Hereditary Disorders
USE Genetic Disorders
PKU (Hereditary Disorder) *USE Phenylketonuria*
Sex Linked **Hereditary** Disorders
Heredity *USE Genetics*
Heritability
Hermaphroditism
Hermeneutics
Heroes
Heroin
Heroin Addiction
Herpes Genitalis
Herpes Simplex
Genital Herpes *USE Herpes Genitalis*
Heterogeneity of Variance
USE Homogeneity of Variance
Heterosexism
USE Homosexuality (Attitudes Toward)
Heterosexual Interaction
USE Male Female Relations
Heterosexuality
Heterozygotic Twins
Heuristic Modeling
Heuristics
Hexamethonium
Hexobarbital
Hibernation
Dominance **Hierarchy**
High Risk Populations
USE At Risk Populations
High School Education
High School Equivalency
USE Adult Education
High School Graduates
High School Personality Questionnaire
High School Students
High School Teachers
High Schools
Junior **High** School Students
Junior **High** School Teachers
Junior **High** Schools
Higher Education
Higher Order Conditioning
Highway Safety
Hindbrain
Hindsight Bias
Hinduism
Hindus
Hippies *USE Subculture (Anthropological)*
Hippocampal Commissure *USE Fornix*
Hippocampus
Hips
Hiring *USE Personnel Selection*
Hispanics
Histamine
Histidine
Histology
History
History of Psychology
Case History *USE Patient History*
Criminal History *USE Criminal Record*
Employment **History**
Medical History *USE Patient History*
Patient **History**
Psychiatric History *USE Patient History*
Histrionic Personality Disorder
HIV
HIV Testing
HMO
USE Health Maintenance Organizations
Hoarding Behavior
Hoarding Behavior (Animal)
USE Animal Hoarding Behavior
Animal **Hoarding** Behavior
Hobbies
Hoffmanns Reflex
Holidays
Holistic Health
Holocaust
Holocaust Survivors
Holtzman Inkblot Technique
Homatropine *USE Alkaloids*
Home Accidents
Home Birth *USE Midwifery*
Home Care
Home Care Personnel
Home Economics
Home Environment
Home Health Aides
USE Home Care Personnel
Home Reared Mentally Retarded
Home Schooling
Home Visiting Programs
Return to Home *USE Empty Nest*
Work at Home *USE Telecommuting*
Homebound
Homeless
Homeless Mentally Ill
Mentally Ill Homeless *USE Homeless Mentally Ill*
Homemakers
Homemaking *USE Household Management*
Homeopathic Medicine
USE Alternative Medicine
Homeostasis
Foster Homes *USE Foster Care*
Group **Homes**
Nursing **Homes**
Homesickness
Homework
Homicide
Serial **Homicide**
Homing (Animal) *USE Animal Homing*
Animal **Homing**
Homogeneity of Variance
Variance Homogeneity *USE Homogeneity of Variance*
Homographs
Homonyms
Homophobia
USE Homosexuality (Attitudes Toward)
Homosexual Liberation Movement
Homosexual Parents
Homosexuality
Homosexuality (Attitudes Toward)
Female Homosexuality *USE Lesbianism*
Male **Homosexuality**
Homovanillic Acid
Honesty
Honors *USE Awards (Merit)*
Hope

Hopelessness
Hormone Therapy
ACTH (Hormone) *USE Corticotropin*
Follicle Stimulating **Hormone**
Growth Hormone *USE Somatotropin*
Growth Hormone Inhibitor *USE Somatostatin*
Luteinizing **Hormone**
Melanocyte Stimulating **Hormone**
Parathyroid **Hormone**
Thyroid Stimulating Hormone *USE Thyrotropin*
Thyrotropic Hormone *USE Thyrotropin*
Hormones
Adrenal Cortex **Hormones**
Adrenal Medulla **Hormones**
Gonadotropic **Hormones**
Pituitary **Hormones**
Progestational **Hormones**
Sex **Hormones**
Thyroid **Hormones**
Dorsal **Horns**
Horses
Horticulture Therapy
Hospice
Hospital Accreditation
Hospital Addiction Syndrome *USE Munchausen Syndrome*
Hospital Administration
Hospital Admission
Hospital Attendants *USE Attendants (Institutions)*
Hospital Discharge
Hospital Environment
Hospital Programs
Hospital Psychiatric Units *USE Psychiatric Units*
Hospital Staff *USE Medical Personnel*
Admission (Psychiatric Hospital) *USE Psychiatric Hospital Admission*
Admission (Hospital) *USE Hospital Admission*
Day Hospital *USE Partial Hospitalization*
Psychiatric **Hospital** Admission
Psychiatric **Hospital** Discharge
Psychiatric **Hospital** Programs
Psychiatric **Hospital** Readmission
Psychiatric **Hospital** Staff
Readmission (Psychiatric Hospital) *USE Psychiatric Hospital Readmission*
Readmission (Hospital) *USE Hospital Admission*
Hospitalization
Partial **Hospitalization**
Psychiatric **Hospitalization**
Hospitalized Patients
Hospitals
Mental Hospitals *USE Psychiatric Hospitals*
Psychiatric **Hospitals**
State Hospitals *USE Psychiatric Hospitals*
Hostages
Hostility
Hot Line Services
Telephone Hot Lines *USE Hot Line Services*
Household Management
Household Structure *USE Living Arrangements*
Halfway **Houses**
Housewives *USE Homemakers*
Housework *USE Household Management*
Housing
Hue
Human Animal Interaction *USE Interspecies Interaction*
Human Biological Rhythms
Human Body
Human Capital
Human Channel Capacity
Human Computer Interaction
Human Computer Interface *USE Human Computer Interaction*
Human Courtship
Human Development
Human Factors Engineering
Human Females
Human Figures Drawing
Human Genome *USE Genome*
Human Immunodeficiency Virus *USE HIV*
Human Information Processes *USE Cognitive Processes*
Human Information Storage
Human Machine Systems
Human Machine Systems Design
Human Males
Human Mate Selection
Human Migration
Human Nature
Human Potential Movement
Human Relations Training
Human Resource Management
Human Resources *USE Human Resource Management*
Human Rights
Human Services
Human Sex Differences
Human Trafficking
Animal Human Interaction *USE Interspecies Interaction*
Circadian Rhythms (Human) *USE Human Biological Rhythms*
Courtship (Human) *USE Human Courtship*
Females (Human) *USE Human Females*
Information Processes (Human) *USE Cognitive Processes*
Information Storage (Human) *USE Human Information Storage*
Males (Human) *USE Human Males*
Maternal Behavior (Human) *USE Mother Child Relations*
Migration (Human) *USE Human Migration*
Sex Differences (Human) *USE Human Sex Differences*
Sexual Intercourse **(Human)**
Humanism
Humanistic Education *USE Affective Education*
Humanistic Psychology
Humanistic Psychotherapy
Humanitarian Behavior *USE Prosocial Behavior*
Humanities
Mates (Humans) *USE Spouses*
Surrogate Parents **(Humans)**
Humor
Cartoons **(Humor)**
Hunger
Huntingtons Chorea *USE Huntingtons Disease*
Huntingtons Disease
Shuttle Box Hurdles *USE Shuttle Boxes*
Husbands
Hybrids (Biology)
Hydralazine
Chloral **Hydrate**
Arecoline Hydrobromide *USE Arecoline*
Scopolamine Hydrobromide *USE Scopolamine*
Hydrocephalus
Hydrocephaly *USE Hydrocephalus*
Apomorphine Hydrochloride *USE Apomorphine*
Hydrocortisone
Hydrogen
Hydroxydopamine (6-)
Hydroxyindoleacetic Acid (5-)
Hydroxylase Inhibitors
Hydroxylases
Hydroxytryptamine (5-) *USE Serotonin*
Hydroxytryptophan (5-)
Hydroxyzine
Hygiene
Hyoscine *USE Scopolamine*
Hyoscyamine (dl-) *USE Atropine*
Hyperactivity *USE Hyperkinesis*
Attention Deficit Disorder with **Hyperactivity**

Hyperalgesia
USE Somatosensory Disorders
Hypercholesterolemia
USE Metabolism Disorders
Hypercortisolism *USE Cushings Syndrome*
Hyperesthesia
USE Somatosensory Disorders
Hyperglycemia
Hypericum Perforatum
Hyperkinesis
Hypermedia
Hyperparathyroidism
USE Parathyroid Disorders
Hyperphagia
Hypersensitivity (Immunologic)
USE Immunologic Disorders
Hypersexuality
Hypersomnia
Hypertension
Essential **Hypertension**
Hypertext
Hyperthermia
Hyperthyroidism
Hyperventilation
Hypesthesia *USE Somatosensory Disorders*
Hypnagogic Hallucinations
Hypnoanalysis *USE Hypnotherapy*
Hypnosis
Self Hypnosis *USE Autohypnosis*
Hypnotherapists
Hypnotherapy
Hypnotic Drugs
Hypnotic Susceptibility
Age Regression **(Hypnotic)**
Susceptibility (Hypnotic) *USE Hypnotic Susceptibility*
Hypnotists
Hypoactive Sexual Desire Disorder
USE Inhibited Sexual Desire
Hypochondriasis
Hypogastric Plexus
USE Autonomic Ganglia
Hypoglossal Nerve *USE Cranial Nerves*
Hypoglycemia
Hypogonadism
Hypokinesia *USE Bradykinesia*
Hypomania
Hyponatremia
Hypoparathyroidism
USE Parathyroid Disorders
Hypothalamo **Hypophyseal** System
Hypophysectomy
Hypophysis Disorders
USE Pituitary Disorders
Hypopituitarism
Hypotension
Hypothalamic Pituitary Adrenal Axis
Mammillary Bodies (Hypothalamic) *USE Hypothalamus*
Hypothalamo Hypophyseal System
Hypothalamo Pituitary Adrenal System
USE Hypothalamic Pituitary Adrenal Axis
Hypothalamus
Hypothalamus Lesions
Hypothermia
Hypothesis Testing
Hypothesis Testing (Cognitive)
USE Cognitive Hypothesis Testing
Cognitive **Hypothesis** Testing
Null **Hypothesis** Testing
Hypothyroidism
Hypoxia *USE Anoxia*
Hysterectomy
Hysteria
Collective Hysteria *USE Mass Hysteria*
Conversion Hysteria *USE Conversion Disorder*
Epidemic Hysteria *USE Mass Hysteria*
Mass **Hysteria**

Hysterical Blindness
USE Hysterical Vision Disturbances
Hysterical Neurosis (Conversion)
USE Conversion Disorder
Hysterical Neurosis (Dissociation)
USE Dissociative Disorders
Hysterical Paralysis
Hysterical Personality
USE Histrionic Personality Disorder
Hysterical Vision Disturbances
Paralysis (Hysterical) *USE Hysterical Paralysis*
Vision Disturbances (Hysterical)
USE Hysterical Vision Disturbances
Iatrogenic Effects
USE Side Effects (Treatment)
Ibotenic Acid
ICD
USE International Classification of Diseases
Iconic Memory
Id
Ideal Self *USE Self Concept*
Idealism
Ideation
Suicidal **Ideation**
Identical Twins *USE Monozygotic Twins*
Identification (Defense Mechanism)
Projective **Identification**
Identity (Personal) *USE Self Concept*
Identity (Professional)
USE Professional Identity
Identity Crisis
Identity Formation
Dissociative **Identity** Disorder
Ego **Identity**
Ethnic **Identity**
Gender **Identity**
Gender **Identity** Disorder
Group **Identity**
Professional **Identity**
Sexual Identity (Gender) *USE Gender Identity*
Social **Identity**
Amaurotic Familial Idiocy *USE Tay Sachs Disease*
Familial Idiocy (Amaurotic) *USE Tay Sachs Disease*
Idiot Savants *USE Savants*
IEP *USE Individual Education Programs*
Ileum *USE Intestines*
Homeless Mentally **Ill**
Mentally Ill Homeless *USE Homeless Mentally Ill*
Mentally **Ill** Offenders
Terminally **Ill** Patients
Illegal Drug Distribution
Illegitimate Children
Illinois Test of Psycholinguistic Abilities
Illiteracy *USE Literacy*
Illness (Physical) *USE Physical Disorders*
Illness Behavior
Chronic Mental **Illness**
Chronic **Illness**
Course of Illness *USE Disease Course*
Mental **Illness** (Attitudes Toward)
Mental Illness *USE Mental Disorders*
Persistent Mental Illness *USE Chronic Mental Illness*
Physical **Illness** (Attitudes Toward)
Physical Illness *USE Physical Disorders*
Work Related **Illnesses**
Illumination
Illumination Therapy *USE Phototherapy*
Illusion (Autokinetic)
USE Autokinetic Illusion
Autokinetic **Illusion**
Mueller Lyer **Illusion**
Illusions (Perception)
Optical Illusions *USE Illusions (Perception)*
ILP *USE Inductive Logic Programming*
Image (Retinal) *USE Retinal Image*
Body **Image**

ROTATED ALPHABETICAL TERMS SECTION

Body **Image** Disturbances
Mirror **Image**
Retinal **Image**
Self Image *USE Self Concept*
Imagery
Imagery (Conceptual) *USE Conceptual Imagery*
Conceptual **Imagery**
Eidetic **Imagery**
Guided **Imagery**
Spatial **Imagery**
Onomatopoeia and Images Test *USE Projective Personality Measures*
Imagination
Imaginativeness *USE Openness to Experience*
Magnetic Resonance **Imaging**
Imipramine
Imitation (Learning)
Immaturity (Emotional) *USE Emotional Immaturity*
Emotional **Immaturity**
Immersion Programs *USE Foreign Language Education*
Immigrants *USE Immigration*
Immigration
Social Immobility *USE Social Mobility*
Tonic **Immobility**
Immune System
Acquired Immune Deficiency Syndrome *USE AIDS*
Immunization
Human Immunodeficiency Virus *USE HIV*
Immunogens *USE Antigens*
Immunoglobulins
Immunologic Disorders
Immunologic Factors
Hypersensitivity (Immunologic) *USE Immunologic Disorders*
Immunology
Immunopathology *USE Immunology*
Immunoreactivity
Impaired Professionals
Hearing Impaired (Partially) *USE Partially Hearing Impaired*
Partially Hearing **Impaired**
Cognitive **Impairment**
Olfactory Impairment *USE Anosmia*
Visual Impairment *USE Vision Disorders*
Health **Impairments**
Cochlear **Implants**
Implicit Learning
Implicit Memory
Implosive Therapy
Impotence *USE Erectile Dysfunction*
Impression Formation
Impression Management
Imprinting
Improvisation
Impulse Control Disorders
Impulsiveness
Incarceration
Incentives
Educational **Incentives**
Monetary **Incentives**
Incest
Critical Incident Debriefing *USE Debriefing (Psychological)*
Incidental Learning
Inclusion (Educational) *USE Mainstreaming (Educational)*
Income (Economic)
Income Level
Lower **Income** Level
Middle **Income** Level
Upper **Income** Level
Incompatibility (Rh) *USE Rh Incompatibility*
Rh **Incompatibility**
Rotter **Incomplete** Sentences Blank
Incontinence (Fecal) *USE Fecal Incontinence*
Incontinence (Urinary) *USE Urinary Incontinence*
Fecal **Incontinence**
Urinary **Incontinence**
Incorporation (Psychological) *USE Internalization*
Incubators (Apparatus)
Independence (Personality)
Independent Living Programs
Independent Living *USE Self Care Skills*
Independent Party (Political) *USE Political Parties*
Independent Study *USE Individualized Instruction*
Independent Variables
Body Mass **Index**
Indians (American) *USE American Indians*
American **Indians**
Myers Briggs Type **Indicator**
Indifference *USE Apathy*
Indigenous Populations
Individual Counseling *USE Individual Psychotherapy*
Individual Differences
Individual Education Programs
Individual Problem Solving *USE Problem Solving*
Individual Psychology
Individual Psychotherapy
Individual Psychotherapy (Adlerian) *USE Adlerian Psychotherapy*
Individual Testing
Individual Therapy *USE Individual Psychotherapy*
Psychotherapy (Individual) *USE Individual Psychotherapy*
Individualism
Individuality
Individualized Educational Plans *USE Individual Education Programs*
Individualized Instruction
Instruction (Individualized) *USE Individualized Instruction*
Separation **Individuation**
Induced Abortion
Abortion (Induced) *USE Induced Abortion*
Drug **Induced** Congenital Disorders
Drug **Induced** Hallucinations
Sleep Inducing Drugs *USE Hypnotic Drugs*
Vomit Inducing Drugs *USE Emetic Drugs*
Inductive Deductive Reasoning
Inductive Logic Programming
Industrial Accidents
Industrial and Organizational Psychology
Industrial Arts Education *USE Vocational Education*
Industrial Foremen
Industrial Personnel *USE Business and Industrial Personnel*
Industrial Psychologists
Industrial Psychology *USE Industrial and Organizational Psychology*
Industrial Safety *USE Occupational Safety*
Business and **Industrial** Personnel
Foremen (Industrial) *USE Industrial Foremen*
Skilled **Industrial** Workers
Unskilled **Industrial** Workers
Industrialization
Industry *USE Business*
Drug Industry *USE Pharmaceutical Industry*
Laborers (Construction and Industry) *USE Blue Collar Workers*
Pharmaceutical **Industry**
Educational Inequality *USE Equal Education*
Infant Development
Infant Vocalization

Bayley Scales of **Infant** Development
Sudden **Infant** Death
Vocalization (Infant) *USE Infant Vocalization*
Infanticide
Infantile Neurosis *USE Childhood Neurosis*
Infantile Paralysis *USE Poliomyelitis*
Infantile Psychosis *USE Childhood Psychosis*
Early Infantile Autism *USE Autism*
Paralysis (Infantile) *USE Poliomyelitis*
Symbiotic **Infantile** Psychosis
Infantilism
Infants (Animal)
Dementia (Multi Infarct) *USE Vascular Dementia*
Multi Infarct Dementia *USE Vascular Dementia*
Infarctions (Myocardial) *USE Myocardial Infarctions*
Myocardial **Infarctions**
Infections *USE Infectious Disorders*
Infectious Disorders
Inference
Inferior Colliculus
Inferiority (Emotional) *USE Emotional Inferiority*
Emotional **Inferiority**
Infertility
Infidelity
Infirmaries *USE Hospitals*
Inflammation
Anti **Inflammatory** Drugs
Inflection
Self **Inflicted** Wounds
Influence (Interpersonal) *USE Interpersonal Influences*
Driving Under the **Influence**
Parental Influence *USE Parent Child Relations*
Influences (Social) *USE Social Influences*
Interpersonal **Influences**
Social **Influences**
Influenza
Informants
Information
Information (Messages) *USE Messages*
Information Dissemination
Information Exchange *USE Communication*
Information Literacy
Information Processes (Human) *USE Cognitive Processes*
Information Processing (Automated) *USE Automated Information Processing*
Information Processing Model
Information Processing Speed *USE Cognitive Processing Speed*
Information Retrieval (Automated) *USE Automated Information Retrieval*
Information Seeking
Information Services
Information Specialists
Information Storage (Human) *USE Human Information Storage*
Information Systems
Information Technology
Information Theory
Automated **Information** Coding
Automated **Information** Processing
Automated **Information** Retrieval
Automated **Information** Storage
Confidentiality of Information *USE Privileged Communication*
Human Information Processes *USE Cognitive Processes*
Human **Information** Storage
Management Information Systems *USE Information Systems*
Informed Consent
Ingestion
Ingratiation *USE Impression Management*
Ingroup Outgroup
Outgroup Ingroup *USE Ingroup Outgroup*
Inhalant Abuse
Inhibited Sexual Desire
Inhibition (Personality)
Inhibition (Proactive) *USE Proactive Inhibition*
Inhibition (Retroactive) *USE Retroactive Inhibition*
Conditioned Inhibition *USE Conditioned Suppression*
Latent **Inhibition**
Prepulse **Inhibition**
Proactive **Inhibition**
Reciprocal **Inhibition** Therapy
Response **Inhibition**
Retroactive **Inhibition**
Growth Hormone Inhibitor *USE Somatostatin*
Amine Oxidase **Inhibitors**
Cholinesterase **Inhibitors**
Decarboxylase **Inhibitors**
Dual Reuptake Inhibitors *USE Serotonin Norepinephrine Reuptake Inhibitors*
Enzyme **Inhibitors**
Hydroxylase **Inhibitors**
Monoamine Oxidase **Inhibitors**
Neurotransmitter Uptake **Inhibitors**
Serotonin Norepinephrine Reuptake **Inhibitors**
Serotonin Reuptake **Inhibitors**
Initial Teaching Alphabet
Initiation Rites
Initiative
Injections
Intramuscular **Injections**
Intraperitoneal **Injections**
Intravenous **Injections**
Subcutaneous **Injections**
Injuries
Injuries (Birth) *USE Birth Injuries*
Birth **Injuries**
Closed Head Injuries *USE Head Injuries*
Electrical **Injuries**
Head **Injuries**
Spinal Cord **Injuries**
Self Injurious Behavior *USE Self Destructive Behavior*
Brain Injury (Traumatic) *USE Traumatic Brain Injury*
Traumatic Brain **Injury**
Holtzman **Inkblot** Technique
Inlaws
Inmates (Prison) *USE Prisoners*
Innate Behavior (Animal) *USE Instinctive Behavior*
Animal Innate Behavior *USE Instinctive Behavior*
Inner City *USE Urban Environments*
Inner Ear *USE Labyrinth (Anatomy)*
Inner Speech *USE Self Talk*
Innovation
Business Innovation *USE Innovation*
Kirton Adaption **Innovation** Inventory
Organizational Innovation *USE Innovation*
Technological Innovation *USE Innovation*
Innovativeness *USE Creativity*
Inquisitiveness *USE Curiosity*
Criminally Insane *USE Mentally Ill Offenders*
Insanity *USE Mental Disorders*
Insanity Defense
DDT **(Insecticide)**
Insecticides
Insects
Insecurity (Emotional) *USE Emotional Security*
Emotional Insecurity *USE Emotional Security*
Artificial Insemination *USE Reproductive Technology*
Insensitivity (Personality) *USE Sensitivity (Personality)*

Androgen Insensitivity Syndrome
USE Testicular Feminization Syndrome
Inservice Teacher Education
Inservice Training
Inservice Training (Mental Health)
USE Mental Health Inservice Training
Mental Health **Inservice** Training
Training (Mental Health Inservice)
USE Mental Health Inservice Training
Insight
Insight (Psychotherapeutic Process)
Insight Therapy
Diabetes **Insipidus**
Insomnia
Instability (Emotional)
USE Emotional Instability
Emotional **Instability**
Death **Instinct**
Survival Instinct *USE Self Preservation*
Instinctive Behavior
Animal Instinctive Behavior
USE Instinctive Behavior
Institution Visitation
Visitation (Institution) *USE Institution Visitation*
Institutional Release
Institutional Schools
Institutionalization
Institutionalized Mentally Retarded
Institutions (Correctional)
USE Correctional Institutions
Institutions (Residential Care)
USE Residential Care Institutions
Attendants **(Institutions)**
Correctional **Institutions**
Residential Care **Institutions**
Instruction (Computer Assisted)
USE Computer Assisted Instruction
Instruction (Individualized)
USE Individualized Instruction
Instruction (Programmed)
USE Programmed Instruction
Instruction *USE Teaching*
Audiovisual **Instruction**
Braille **Instruction**
Classroom Instruction *USE Teaching*
Computer Assisted **Instruction**
Field Instruction *USE Curricular Field Experience*
Group **Instruction**
Individualized **Instruction**
Programmed **Instruction**
Self Instruction *USE Individualized Instruction*
Televised **Instruction**
Videotape **Instruction**
Instructional Media
Instructional Objectives
USE Educational Objectives
Self **Instructional** Training
Instructions (Experimental)
USE Experimental Instructions
Experimental **Instructions**
Instructors *USE Teachers*
Instrument Controls
Controls (Instrument) *USE Instrument Controls*
Instrumental Conditioning
USE Operant Conditioning
Instrumental Learning
USE Operant Conditioning
Instrumentality
Instrumentation (Flight)
USE Flight Instrumentation
Flight **Instrumentation**
Musical **Instruments**
Insulin
Insulin Resistance Syndrome
USE Metabolic Syndrome
Insulin Shock Therapy
Insurance
Insurance Agents *USE Sales Personnel*
Employee Health **Insurance**
Health **Insurance**
Life **Insurance**
Workers' Compensation **Insurance**
Workmen's Compensation Insurance
USE Workers' Compensation Insurance
Intake Interview
Fluid **Intake**
Food **Intake**
Water **Intake**
Integrated Services
Integration (Racial) *USE Social Integration*
Intersensory Integration *USE Sensory Integration*
Racial Integration *USE Social Integration*
School **Integration**
School Integration (Racial) *USE School Integration*
Sensory **Integration**
Social **Integration**
Integrative Psychotherapy
Integrity
Intellectual Development
Intellectual Functioning
USE Cognitive Ability
Intellectualism
Intellectualization
Intellectually Gifted *USE Gifted*
Intelligence
Intelligence Age *USE Mental Age*
Intelligence Measures
Intelligence Quotient
Artificial **Intelligence**
Cattell Culture Fair Intelligence Test
USE Culture Fair Intelligence Test
Culture Fair **Intelligence** Test
Emotional **Intelligence**
Leiter Adult Intelligence Scale
USE Intelligence Measures
Slosson **Intelligence** Test
Stanford Binet **Intelligence** Scale
Tests (Intelligence) *USE Intelligence Measures*
Wechsler Adult **Intelligence** Scale
Wechsler Bellevue **Intelligence** Scale
Wechsler **Intelligence** Scale for Children
Multiple **Intelligences**
Intelligent Agents
Intelligent Tutoring Systems
Intensity (Stimulus) *USE Stimulus Intensity*
Signal Intensity *USE Stimulus Intensity*
Stimulus **Intensity**
Intensive Care
Intention
Intentional Learning
Interaction (Interpersonal)
USE Interpersonal Interaction
Interaction (Social) *USE Social Interaction*
Interaction Analysis (Statistics)
Interaction Variance
Animal Human Interaction *USE Interspecies Interaction*
Client Counselor Interaction
USE Psychotherapeutic Processes
Counselor Client Interaction
USE Psychotherapeutic Processes
Dentist Patient Interaction *USE Therapeutic Processes*
Double Bind **Interaction**
Employee Supervisor Interaction
USE Supervisor Employee Interaction
Employee **Interaction**
Heterosexual Interaction *USE Male Female Relations*
Human Animal Interaction *USE Interspecies Interaction*
Human Computer **Interaction**
Interhemispheric **Interaction**
Interpersonal **Interaction**
Interspecies **Interaction**
Manager Employee Interaction
USE Supervisor Employee Interaction
Nurse Patient Interaction *USE Therapeutic Processes*

ROTATED ALPHABETICAL TERMS SECTION

Patient Therapist Interaction
USE Psychotherapeutic Processes
Physician Patient Interaction *USE Therapeutic Processes*
Social **Interaction**
Supervisor Employee **Interaction**
Teacher Student **Interaction**
Therapist Patient Interaction
USE Psychotherapeutic Processes
Symbolic **Interactionism**
Drug **Interactions**
Interagency Services
USE Integrated Services
Intercourse (Sexual)
USE Sexual Intercourse (Human)
Extramarital **Intercourse**
Premarital **Intercourse**
Sexual **Intercourse** (Human)
Intercultural Communication
USE Cross Cultural Communication
Interdisciplinary Research
Interdisciplinary Treatment Approach
Interest Inventories
Interest Patterns *USE Interests*
Conflict of **Interest**
Kuder Occupational **Interest** Survey
Occupational **Interest** Measures
Opinion Attitude and Interest Survey *USE Attitude Measures*
Strong Vocational **Interest** Blank
Interests
Occupational **Interests**
Vocational Interests *USE Occupational Interests*
Interethnic Communication
USE Cross Cultural Communication
Interethnic Family
Interethnic Marriage
USE Exogamous Marriage
Human Computer Interface *USE Human Computer Interaction*
Interfaith Marriage
Interference (Learning)
Interferons
Intergenerational Relations
Intergenerational Transmission
USE Transgenerational Patterns
Intergroup Dynamics
Interhemispheric Interaction
Interhemispheric Transfer
USE Interhemispheric Interaction
Interior Design
Interleukins
Intermarriage *USE Exogamous Marriage*
Intermediate School Students
Intermittent Explosive Disorder
USE Explosive Disorder
Intermittent Reinforcement
USE Reinforcement Schedules
Internal Consistency *USE Test Reliability*
Internal External Locus of Control
Internal Rewards
Rotter **Internal** External Locus of Control Scale
Internalization
International Classification of Diseases
International Organizations
International Relations
International Students
International Study *USE Study Abroad*
Internet
Internet Addiction
Internet Counseling *USE Online Therapy*
Internet Shopping
USE Electronic Commerce
Internet Social Networking
USE Online Social Networks
Internet Usage
Internists
Internship (Medical) *USE Medical Internship*
Internship Programs
Clinical Psychology **Internship**
Medical **Internship**
Interobserver Reliability
USE Interrater Reliability
Interocular Transfer
Interpersonal Attraction
Interpersonal Communication
Interpersonal Compatibility
Interpersonal Competence
USE Social Skills
Interpersonal Distance
USE Personal Space
Interpersonal Influences
Interpersonal Interaction
Interpersonal Perception
USE Social Perception
Interpersonal Psychotherapy
Interpersonal Relationship Satisfaction
USE Relationship Satisfaction
Interpersonal Relationships
Interpersonal Therapy
USE Interpersonal Psychotherapy
Attraction (Interpersonal) *USE Interpersonal Attraction*
Compatibility (Interpersonal)
USE Interpersonal Compatibility
Fundamental **Interpersonal** Relation Orientation Behavior Ques
Influence (Interpersonal)
USE Interpersonal Influences
Interaction (Interpersonal)
USE Interpersonal Interaction
Listening **(Interpersonal)**
Dream Interpretation *USE Dream Analysis*
Psychoanalytic **Interpretation**
Psychological Interpretation *USE Theoretical Interpretation*
Test **Interpretation**
Theoretical **Interpretation**
Interracial Adoption
Interracial Family
Interracial Marriage
Interracial Offspring
Interrater Reliability
Interresponse Time
Interrogation
Criminal Interrogation *USE Interrogation*
Legal Interrogation *USE Interrogation*
Police Interrogation *USE Interrogation*
Intersensory Integration
USE Sensory Integration
Intersensory Processes
Intersexuality *USE Hermaphroditism*
Interspecies Interaction
Interstimulus Interval
Intertrial Interval
Interval Reinforcement
USE Fixed Interval Reinforcement
Interval Reinforcement
USE Variable Interval Reinforcement
Fixed **Interval** Reinforcement
Interstimulus **Interval**
Intertrial **Interval**
Variable **Interval** Reinforcement
Stimulus **Intervals**
Intervention
Crisis **Intervention**
Crisis **Intervention** Services
Early **Intervention**
Educational Intervention *USE School Based Intervention*
Family **Intervention**
School Based **Intervention**
Interview Schedules
Diagnostic **Interview** Schedule
Intake **Interview**
Psychodiagnostic **Interview**
Structured Clinical **Interview**
Interviewers
Interviewing
Motivational **Interviewing**

Interviews
Employment Interviews *USE Job Applicant Interviews*
Job Applicant **Interviews**
Intestines
Intimacy
Intimate Partner Violence
Intoxication (Alcohol)
USE Alcohol Intoxication
Intoxication *USE Toxic Disorders*
Acute Alcoholic **Intoxication**
Alcohol **Intoxication**
Chronic Alcoholic **Intoxication**
Intra Aural Muscle Reflex
USE Acoustic Reflex
Intracranial Self Stimulation
USE Brain Self Stimulation
Intramuscular Injections
Intraperitoneal Injections
Intrauterine Devices
Intravenous Drug Usage
Intravenous Injections
Intrinsic Motivation
Intrinsic Rewards *USE Internal Rewards*
Introjection
Introspection
Introversion
Intuition
Inuit
Inventories
Biographical **Inventories**
Interest **Inventories**
Beck Depression **Inventory**
Bem Sex Role **Inventory**
California Psychological **Inventory**
Differential Personality Inventory
USE Nonprojective Personality Measures
Eysenck Personality **Inventory**
Kirton Adaption Innovation **Inventory**
Millon Clinical Multiaxial **Inventory**
Minnesota Multiphasic Personality **Inventory**
Minnesota Teacher Attitude Inventory *USE Attitude Measures*
NEO Personality **Inventory**
Personal Orientation **Inventory**
Psychological Screening **Inventory**
State Trait Anxiety **Inventory**
Invertebrates
Investigation *USE Experimentation*
Maternal Investment *USE Parental Investment*
Parental **Investment**
Paternal Investment *USE Parental Investment*
Investments (Business)
USE Business Investments
Business **Investments**
Involuntary Smoking *USE Passive Smoking*
Involuntary Treatment
Involvement
Community **Involvement**
Job **Involvement**
Parental **Involvement**
Political Involvement *USE Political Participation*
Ions *USE Electrolytes*
Calcium **Ions**
Chloride **Ions**
Magnesium **Ions**
Potassium **Ions**
Sodium **Ions**
Iowa Tests of Basic Skills
Iproniazid
Deviation IQ *USE Standard Scores*
Iris (Eye)
Iron
Irradiation *USE Radiation*
Laser **Irradiation**
Irrational Beliefs
Irritability
Irritable Bowel Syndrome
Ischemia
Cerebral **Ischemia**
Islam
Pacific **Islanders**
Isocarboxazid
Isoenzymes *USE Isozymes*
Isolation (Defense Mechanism)
Isolation (Social) *USE Social Isolation*
Isolation Effect
Social **Isolation**
Isoniazid
Isoproterenol
Isozymes
Political **Issues**
Social **Issues**
Itching *USE Pruritus*
Item Analysis (Statistical)
Item Analysis (Test)
Item Bias *USE Test Bias*
Item Content (Test)
Item Response Theory
Test **Items**
IV Drug Usage
USE Intravenous Drug Usage
Pavlov **(Ivan)**
Jails *USE Prisons*
Creutzfeldt **Jakob** Syndrome
James (William)
Japanese Americans
Japanese Cultural Groups
Jaundice
Jaw
Jealousy
Piaget **(Jean)**
Jews
Job Analysis
Job Applicant Attitudes
Job Applicant Interviews
Job Applicant Screening
Job Applicants
Job Change *USE Career Change*
Job Characteristics
Job Corps
Job Discrimination
USE Employment Discrimination
Job Duties *USE Job Characteristics*
Job Enrichment
Job Experience Level
Job Family Relationship
USE Family Work Relationship
Job Functions *USE Job Characteristics*
Job Involvement
Job Knowledge
Job Mobility *USE Occupational Mobility*
Job Performance
Job Promotion *USE Personnel Promotion*
Job Reentry *USE Reemployment*
Job Satisfaction
Job Search
Job Security
Job Selection *USE Occupational Choice*
Job Status *USE Occupational Status*
Job Stress *USE Occupational Stress*
Job Training *USE Personnel Training*
Experience Level (Job) *USE Job Experience Level*
On the **Job** Training
Testing (Job Applicants)
USE Job Applicant Screening
Jobs *USE Occupations*
Saint John's Wort *USE Hypericum Perforatum*
St. John's Wort *USE Hypericum Perforatum*
Watson **(John** Broadus)
Woodcock **Johnson** Psychoeducational Battery
Joint Custody
Joint Disorders
Temporomandibular Joint Syndrome
USE Musculoskeletal Disorders
Joints (Anatomy)

Jokes
Journalists
Joy *USE Happiness*
Judaism
Judges
Judgment
Judgment Disturbances
Clinical Judgment (Medical Diagnosis) *USE Medical Diagnosis*
Clinical **Judgment** (Not Diagnosis)
Clinical Judgment (Psychodiagnosis) *USE Psychodiagnosis*
Probability **Judgment**
Judo
Jumping
Jung (Carl)
Jungian Psychology
Jungian Psychotherapy *USE Analytical Psychotherapy*
Junior College Students
Junior Colleges *USE Colleges*
Junior High School Students
Junior High School Teachers
Junior High Schools
Juries
Jury Selection
Awards **(Jury)**
Justice
Criminal **Justice**
Distributive **Justice**
Juvenile **Justice**
Procedural **Justice**
Social **Justice**
Juvenile Court *USE Adjudication*
Juvenile Delinquency
Juvenile Gangs
Juvenile Justice
Delinquency (Juvenile) *USE Juvenile Delinquency*
Gangs (Juvenile) *USE Juvenile Gangs*
Offenders (Juvenile) *USE Juvenile Delinquency*
Kainic Acid
Kangaroos
Karate *USE Martial Arts*
Karyotype Disorders *USE Chromosome Disorders*
Kaufman Assessment Battery for Children
Ketamine
Keyboards
Keypunch Operators *USE Clerical Personnel*
Kibbutz
Kidnapping
Kidney Diseases
Kidney Transplants *USE Organ Transplantation*
Kidneys
Natural **Killer** Cells
Mercy Killing *USE Euthanasia*
Mouse Killing *USE Muricide*
Kinases
Kindergarten Students
Vane Kindergarten Test *USE Intelligence Measures*
Kindergartens
Kindling
Kinesics *USE Body Language*
Kinesthetic Perception
Kinship
Kinship Recognition
Kinship Structure
Kirton Adaption Innovation Inventory
Kleine Levin Syndrome
Kleptomania
Klinefelters Syndrome
Knee
Knowledge Based Systems *USE Expert Systems*
Knowledge Economy
Knowledge Engineering
Knowledge Level
Knowledge Management
Knowledge of Results
Knowledge Transfer
Declarative **Knowledge**
Factual Knowledge *USE Declarative Knowledge*
Functional Knowledge *USE Procedural Knowledge*
Health **Knowledge**
Job **Knowledge**
Practical Knowledge *USE Procedural Knowledge*
Procedural **Knowledge**
Kohlberg (Lawrence)
Kohs Block Design Test
Block Design Test (Kohs) *USE Kohs Block Design Test*
Korean Cultural Groups
Koro
Korsakoffs Psychosis
Alcoholic Korsakoffs Syndrome *USE Korsakoffs Psychosis*
Kuder Occupational Interest Survey
Kuder Preference Record
Kupfer Detre Self Rating Scale *USE Nonprojective Personality Measures*
Kwashiorkor
L Dopa *USE Levodopa*
Labeling
Warning **Labels**
Labor (Childbirth)
Labor Management Relations
Labor Market
Labor Relations *USE Labor Management Relations*
Labor Union Members
Labor Unions
Animal Division of **Labor**
Child **Labor**
Division of **Labor**
Division of Labor (Animal) *USE Animal Division of Labor*
Laboratories (Educational) *USE Educational Laboratories*
Laboratories (Experimental) *USE Experimental Laboratories*
Educational **Laboratories**
Experimental **Laboratories**
Language **Laboratories**
Laborers (Construction and Industry) *USE Blue Collar Workers*
Laborers (Farm) *USE Agricultural Workers*
Labyrinth (Anatomy)
Labyrinth (Apparatus) *USE Mazes*
Labyrinth Disorders
Lactate Dehydrogenase
Sodium Lactate *USE Lactic Acid*
Lactation
Lactic Acid
Response Lag *USE Reaction Time*
Language
Language Alternation *USE Code Switching*
Language Arts Education
Language Delay
Language Development
Language Disorders
Language Laboratories
Language Proficiency
Body **Language**
Computer Assisted **Language** Learning
English as Second **Language**
Figurative **Language**
First Language *USE Native Language*
Foreign **Language** Education
Foreign **Language** Learning
Foreign **Language** Translation
Form Classes **(Language)**
Morphology **(Language)**

Native **Language**
Second Language Education *USE Foreign Language Education*
Sign **Language**
Written **Language**
Computer Programming **Languages**
Foreign **Languages**
Programming Languages (Computer) *USE Computer Programming Languages*
Larvae
Laryngeal Disorders
Larynx
Laser Irradiation
Latchkey Children *USE Child Self Care*
Latency (Response) *USE Response Latency*
Response **Latency**
Lateness *USE Tardiness*
Latent Inhibition
Latent Learning
Latent Trait Theory *USE Item Response Theory*
Lateral Dominance
Lateral Geniculate Nucleus *USE Geniculate Bodies (Thalamus)*
Latinos/Latinas *USE Hispanics*
Laughter
Law (Government)
Law Enforcement
Law Enforcement Personnel
Law Students
Arrest (Law) *USE Legal Arrest*
Civil **Law**
Criminal **Law**
Kohlberg **(Lawrence)**
Laws
Abortion **Laws**
Disability **Laws**
Drug **Laws**
Gun Control **Laws**
Marijuana **Laws**
Lawsuits *USE Litigation*
Lawyers *USE Attorneys*
Lay Religious Personnel
Lead (Metal)
Lead Poisoning
Leadership
Leadership Qualities
Leadership Style
Charismatic Leadership *USE Transformational Leadership*
Transformational **Leadership**
Learned Helplessness
Helplessness (Learned) *USE Learned Helplessness*
Slow Learners *USE Borderline Mental Retardation*
Learning
Learning Ability
Learning Centers (Educational)
Learning Disabilities
Learning Disorders
Learning Environment
Learning Organizations *USE Organizational Learning*
Learning Rate
Learning Schedules
Learning Strategies
Learning Style *USE Cognitive Style*
Learning Theory
Adult **Learning**
Animal **Learning**
Anticipation (Serial Learning) *USE Serial Anticipation (Learning)*
Cat **Learning**
Collaborative **Learning**
Computer Assisted Language **Learning**
Concept Learning *USE Concept Formation*
Cooperative **Learning**
Discrimination **Learning**
Discriminative Learning *USE Discrimination Learning*
Distance Learning *USE Distance Education*
Experiential **Learning**
Extinction **(Learning)**
Extradimensional Shift Learning *USE Nonreversal Shift Learning*
Fine Motor Skill **Learning**
Foreign Language **Learning**
Generalization **(Learning)**
Generation Effect **(Learning)**
Gross Motor Skill **Learning**
Imitation **(Learning)**
Implicit **Learning**
Incidental **Learning**
Instrumental Learning *USE Operant Conditioning*
Intentional **Learning**
Interference **(Learning)**
Latent **Learning**
Machine **Learning**
Mastery **Learning**
Maze **Learning**
Mnemonic **Learning**
Motor Skill Learning *USE Perceptual Motor Learning*
Nonreversal Shift **Learning**
Nonsense Syllable **Learning**
Nonverbal **Learning**
Observational **Learning**
Organizational **Learning**
Paired Associate **Learning**
Perceptual Motor **Learning**
Perceptual **Learning**
Probability **Learning**
Rat **Learning**
Recall **(Learning)**
Recognition **(Learning)**
Reconstruction **(Learning)**
Reversal Shift **Learning**
Rote **Learning**
Rule Learning *USE Cognitive Hypothesis Testing*
Schedules (Learning) *USE Learning Schedules*
School **Learning**
Self Directed Learning *USE Individualized Instruction*
Self Regulated **Learning**
Sequential **Learning**
Serial Anticipation **(Learning)**
Serial **Learning**
Service **Learning**
Skill **Learning**
Social **Learning**
Spatial **Learning**
Spontaneous Recovery **(Learning)**
State Dependent **Learning**
Strategies (Learning) *USE Learning Strategies*
Transfer **(Learning)**
Trial and Error **Learning**
Verbal **Learning**
Least Preferred Coworker Scale
Least Squares
Annual Leave *USE Employee Leave Benefits*
Employee **Leave** Benefits
Sick Leave *USE Employee Leave Benefits*
School **Leavers**
Lecithin
Lecture Method
Left Brain *USE Left Hemisphere*
Left Hemisphere
Leg (Anatomy)
Legal Arrest
Legal Confession
Legal Decisions
Legal Detention
Legal Evidence
Legal Interrogation *USE Interrogation*
Legal Liability (Professional) *USE Professional Liability*
Legal Personnel
Legal Processes

ROTATED ALPHABETICAL TERMS SECTION

Legal Psychology
USE Forensic Psychology
Legal Testimony
Confession (Legal) *USE Legal Confession*
Detention (Legal) *USE Legal Detention*
Legalization (Marihuana)
USE Marijuana Legalization
Drug **Legalization**
Marijuana **Legalization**
Legibility
Legibility (Handwriting)
USE Handwriting Legibility
Handwriting **Legibility**
Legislative Processes
Leisure Time
Leiter Adult Intelligence Scale
USE Intelligence Measures
Lemniscal System
Lemurs
Length of Stay *USE Treatment Duration*
Work Week **Length**
Lens (Eye)
Contact **Lenses**
Corrective Lenses *USE Optical Aids*
Leptin
Lesbian Parents *USE Homosexual Parents*
Lesbianism
Sectioning (Lesion) *USE Lesions*
Lesions
Brain **Lesions**
Cerebral Lesions *USE Brain Lesions*
Hypothalamus **Lesions**
Neural **Lesions**
Subcortical Lesions *USE Brain Lesions*
Lesson Plans
Letters (Alphabet)
Leucine
Leucocytes
Leukemias
Leukocytes *USE Leucocytes*
Leukotomy *USE Psychosurgery*
Vygotsky **(Lev)**
Level of Functioning *USE Ability Level*
Ability **Level**
Academic Grade Level *USE Grade Level*
Activity **Level**
Aspiration **Level**
Attainment Level (Education)
USE Educational Attainment Level
Difficulty **Level** (Test)
Educational Attainment **Level**
Experience **Level**
Experience Level (Job) *USE Job Experience Level*
Family Socioeconomic **Level**
Grade **Level**
Income **Level**
Job Experience **Level**
Knowledge **Level**
Lower Income **Level**
Middle Income **Level**
Middle **Level** Managers
Sound Pressure Level *USE Loudness*
Top **Level** Managers
Upper Income **Level**
Noise **Levels** (Work Areas)
Kleine **Levin** Syndrome
Levodopa
Lewy Body Disease
USE Dementia with Lewy Bodies
Dementia with **Lewy** Bodies
Lexical Access
Lexical Decision
Drug Abuse **Liability**
Legal Liability (Professional)
USE Professional Liability
Professional **Liability**
Consultation **Liaison** Psychiatry

Liberalism
Liberalism (Political)
USE Political Liberalism
Political **Liberalism**
Gay Liberation Movement
USE Homosexual Liberation Movement
Homosexual **Liberation** Movement
Womens **Liberation** Movement
Libido
Librarians
Libraries
Libraries (School) *USE School Libraries*
School **Libraries**
Librium *USE Chlordiazepoxide*
Licensing (Professional)
USE Professional Licensing
Professional **Licensing**
Licensure Examinations
USE Professional Examinations
Licking
Animal Licking Behavior *USE Licking*
Lidocaine
Life Changes
Life Course *USE Life Span*
Life Expectancy
Life Experiences
Life Insurance
Life Review
Life Satisfaction
Life Span
Life Sustaining Treatment
Life Transitions *USE Life Changes*
End of Life Care *USE Palliative Care*
Experiences (Life) *USE Life Experiences*
Family Life *USE Family Relations*
Family **Life** Education
Philosophy of Life *USE World View*
Quality of Work **Life**
Quality of **Life**
Lifesaving *USE Artificial Respiration*
Lifestyle
Lifestyle Changes
Tubal **Ligation**
Light *USE Illumination*
Light Adaptation
Light Refraction
Light Therapy *USE Phototherapy*
Adaptation (Light) *USE Light Adaptation*
Bright Light Therapy *USE Phototherapy*
Likability
Maximum **Likelihood**
Likert Scales
Liking *USE Affection*
Limbic System
Artificial Limbs *USE Prostheses*
Phantom **Limbs**
Limen *USE Thresholds*
Differential Limen *USE Thresholds*
Limited English Proficiency
USE Language Proficiency
Time Limited Psychotherapy
USE Brief Psychotherapy
Confidence **Limits** (Statistics)
Allport Vernon Lindzey Study Values
USE Attitude Measures
Hot **Line** Services
Linear Perspective
Linear Regression
Telephone Hot Lines *USE Hot Line Services*
Linguistics
Linkage Analysis *USE Genetic Linkage*
Genetic **Linkage**
Sex **Linked** Developmental Differences
Sex **Linked** Hereditary Disorders
Lions *USE Felids*
Lipid Metabolism
Lipid Metabolism Disorders

Lipids
Lipoproteins
Lipreading
Lips (Face)
Liquor
Gough Adjective Check **List**
Mooney Problem Check **List**
Listening (Interpersonal)
Listening *USE Auditory Perception*
Listening Comprehension
Literacy
Literacy Programs
Computer **Literacy**
Information **Literacy**
Literature
Literature Review
Religious **Literature**
Review (of Literature) *USE Literature Review*
Lithium
Lithium Bromide *USE Bromides*
Lithium Carbonate
Litigation
Litter Size
Liver
Liver Disorders
Cirrhosis **(Liver)**
Living Alone
Living Arrangements
Living Wills *USE Advance Directives*
Active **Living**
Activities of Daily **Living**
Assisted **Living**
Independent Living *USE Self Care Skills*
Independent **Living** Programs
Lizards
Cognitive Load *USE Human Channel Capacity*
Mental Load *USE Human Channel Capacity*
Work **Load**
Social **Loafing**
Frontal **Lobe**
Occipital **Lobe**
Optic **Lobe**
Parietal **Lobe**
Temporal **Lobe**
Lobectomy *USE Psychosurgery*
Lobotomy *USE Psychosurgery*
Local Anesthetics
Localization (Perceptual)
USE Perceptual Localization
Localization (Sound)
USE Auditory Localization
Auditory **Localization**
Perceptual **Localization**
Sound Localization *USE Auditory Localization*
Quantitative Trait **Loci**
Locomotion
Animal **Locomotion**
Locus Ceruleus
Locus of Control
USE Internal External Locus of Control
Control (Locus of)
USE Internal External Locus of Control
Health Locus of Control *USE Health Attitudes*
Internal External **Locus** of Control
Rotter Internal External **Locus** of Control Scale
Logic (Philosophy)
Fuzzy **Logic**
Inductive **Logic** Programming
Logical Thinking
Logistic Models
USE Item Response Theory
Logistic Regression
Logotherapy
Loneliness
Long Term Care
Long Term Memory
Long Term Potentiation
USE Postactivation Potentials
Longevity *USE Life Expectancy*
Longitudinal Studies
Studies (Longitudinal) *USE Longitudinal Studies*
Loosening of Associations
USE Fragmentation (Schizophrenia)
Lorazepam
Lordosis (Animal)
USE Animal Sexual Receptivity
Hair Loss *USE Alopecia*
Sensorineural Hearing Loss *USE Hearing Disorders*
Loudness
Loudness Discrimination
Loudness Perception
Love
Low Birth Weight *USE Birth Weight*
Lower Class
Lower Class Attitudes
Lower Income Level
Loxapine
Loyalty
LSD (Drug)
USE Lysergic Acid Diethylamide
Lucid Dreaming
Luck *USE Chance (Fortune)*
Lumbar Spinal Cord
Lumbrosacral Plexus *USE Spinal Nerves*
Luminance
Luminance Threshold
USE Brightness Perception
Luminance Threshold
USE Visual Thresholds
Lunar Synodic Cycle
Lung
Lung Disorders
Lupus
Luria Nebraska Neuropsychological Battery
Luteinizing Hormone
Lutherans *USE Protestants*
Mueller **Lyer** Illusion
Lying *USE Deception*
Lymphatic Disorders
USE Blood and Lymphatic Disorders
Blood and **Lymphatic** Disorders
Lymphocytes
Lysergic Acid Diethylamide
Machiavellianism
Machine Learning
Design (Man Machine Systems)
USE Human Machine Systems Design
Human **Machine** Systems
Human **Machine** Systems Design
Man Machine Systems Design
USE Human Machine Systems Design
Man Machine Systems
USE Human Machine Systems
Teaching **Machines**
Magazines
Magical Thinking
Magnesium
Magnesium Ions
Magnet Schools
USE Nontraditional Education
Magnetic Resonance Imaging
Repetitive Transcranial Magnetic Stimulation
USE Transcranial Magnetic Stimulation
Transcranial **Magnetic** Stimulation
Magnetism
Magnetoencephalography
Magnitude Estimation
Magnitude of Effect (Statistical)
USE Effect Size (Statistical)
Basal Magnocellular Cholinergic Nucleus
USE Nucleus Basalis Magnocellularis
Nucleus Basalis **Magnocellularis**
Maids *USE Domestic Service Personnel*

ROTATED ALPHABETICAL TERMS SECTION

Mail Surveys
Electronic Mail
USE Computer Mediated Communication
Mainstreaming
Mainstreaming (Educational)
Maintenance Therapy
Health **Maintenance** Organizations
Methadone **Maintenance**
Major Depression
Major Tranquilizers *USE Neuroleptic Drugs*
College Major *USE Academic Specialization*
Decision **Making**
Foreign Policy **Making**
Government Policy **Making**
Group Decision **Making**
Management Decision **Making**
Organizational Policy Making *USE Policy Making*
Policy **Making**
Policy Making (Foreign)
USE Foreign Policy Making
Policy Making (Government)
USE Government Policy Making
Grand **Mal** Seizures
Petit **Mal** Seizures
Maladjustment (Emotional)
USE Emotional Adjustment
Maladjustment (Social)
USE Social Adjustment
Emotional Maladjustment *USE Emotional Adjustment*
Social Maladjustment *USE Social Adjustment*
Malaria
Male Animals
Male Attitudes
Male Castration
Male Criminals
Male Delinquency
Male Female Relations
Male Genital Disorders
Male Genitalia
Male Homosexuality
Male Only Environments
USE Single Sex Environments
Male Orgasm
Genitalia (Male) *USE Male Genitalia*
Males (Human) *USE Human Males*
Gay Males *USE Male Homosexuality*
Human **Males**
Malignant Neoplasms *USE Neoplasms*
Neuroleptic **Malignant** Syndrome
Malingering
Malnutrition *USE Nutritional Deficiencies*
Malpractice *USE Professional Liability*
Child Maltreatment *USE Child Abuse*
Mammals
Mammary Glands
Mammary Neoplasms
USE Breast Neoplasms
Mammillary Bodies (Hypothalamic)
USE Hypothalamus
Mammography
Man Machine Systems Design
USE Human Machine Systems Design
Man Machine Systems
USE Human Machine Systems
Design (Man Machine Systems)
USE Human Machine Systems Design
Draw A Man Test *USE Human Figures Drawing*
Managed Care
Management
Management Decision Making
Management Development
USE Career Development
Management Information Systems
USE Information Systems
Management Methods
Management Personnel
Management Planning
Management Training
Anger Management *USE Anger Control*
Anxiety **Management**
Business **Management**
Case **Management**
Classroom **Management**
Contingency **Management**
Customer Relationship **Management**
Disability **Management**
Disease **Management**
Household **Management**
Human Resource **Management**
Impression **Management**
Knowledge **Management**
Labor **Management** Relations
Pain **Management**
Participative **Management**
Personnel Management
USE Human Resource Management
Planning (Management) *USE Management Planning*
Risk **Management**
Self **Management**
Stress **Management**
Supply Chain **Management**
Terror **Management** Theory
Time **Management**
Manager Employee Interaction
USE Supervisor Employee Interaction
Middle Level **Managers**
Top Level **Managers**
Self **Managing** Work Teams
Mandibula *USE Jaw*
Mania
Manic Depression *USE Bipolar Disorder*
Manic Depressive Psychosis
USE Bipolar Disorder
Childrens **Manifest** Anxiety Scale
Taylor **Manifest** Anxiety Scale
Mann Whitney U Test
Mannerisms *USE Habits*
Manpower *USE Personnel Supply*
Mantis
Praying Mantis *USE Mantis*
Manual Communication
Diagnostic and Statistical **Manual**
Manufacturing *USE Business*
Maori *USE Indigenous Populations*
MAOs *USE Monoamine Oxidases*
Brain Mapping *USE Stereotaxic Atlas*
Maprotiline
Brain Maps *USE Stereotaxic Atlas*
Cognitive **Maps**
Tactual Maps *USE Mobility Aids*
Marathon Group Therapy
Marihuana *USE Marijuana*
Legalization (Marihuana) *USE Marijuana Legalization*
Marijuana
Marijuana Laws
Marijuana Legalization
Marijuana Usage
Marine Personnel
Marital Adjustment *USE Marital Relations*
Marital Conflict
Marital Fidelity *USE Monogamy*
Marital Relations
Marital Satisfaction
Marital Separation
Marital Status
Marital Therapy *USE Marriage Counseling*
Separation (Marital) *USE Marital Separation*
Biochemical Markers *USE Biological Markers*
Biological **Markers**
Clinical Markers *USE Biological Markers*
Labor **Market**
Marketing
Social **Marketing**

Virtual Markets *USE Electronic Commerce*
Animal Scent **Marking**
Scent Marking (Animal)
USE Animal Scent Marking
Markov Chains
Marlowe Crowne Social Desirability Scale
Marriage
Marriage and Family Education
USE Family Life Education
Marriage Attitudes
Marriage Counseling
Marriage Rites
Marriage Therapy
USE Marriage Counseling
Consanguineous **Marriage**
Endogamous **Marriage**
Exogamous **Marriage**
Interethnic Marriage *USE Exogamous Marriage*
Interfaith **Marriage**
Interracial **Marriage**
Miscegenous Marriage *USE Interracial Marriage*
Same Sex **Marriage**
Married Couples *USE Spouses*
Never **Married**
Bone **Marrow**
Marsupials
Martial Arts
Marxism *USE Communism*
Masculinity
Masking
Auditory **Masking**
Backward Masking *USE Masking*
Forward Masking *USE Masking*
Visual **Masking**
Maslow (Abraham Harold)
Masochism
Sexual **Masochism**
Masochistic Personality
Mass Culture *USE Popular Culture*
Mass Hysteria
Mass Media
Body **Mass** Index
Massage
Massed Practice
Mastectomy
Mastery Learning
Mastery Tests
USE Criterion Referenced Tests
Masticatory Muscles
Masturbation
Matching Test *USE Matching to Sample*
Matching to Sample
Client Treatment **Matching**
Patient Treatment Matching *USE Client Treatment Matching*
Treatment Client Matching *USE Client Treatment Matching*
Mate Selection *USE Animal Mate Selection*
Mate Selection *USE Human Mate Selection*
Mate Swapping
USE Extramarital Intercourse
Animal **Mate** Selection
Human **Mate** Selection
Materialism
Hazardous **Materials**
Reading **Materials**
X Rated Materials *USE Pornography*
Maternal Behavior (Animal)
USE Animal Maternal Behavior
Maternal Behavior (Human)
USE Mother Child Relations
Maternal Investment
USE Parental Investment
Animal **Maternal** Behavior
Animal **Maternal** Deprivation
Mates (Humans) *USE Spouses*
Mathematical Ability
Mathematical Modeling
Mathematical Psychology
Mathematicians
Mathematics
Mathematics (Concepts)
Mathematics Achievement
Mathematics Anxiety
Mathematics Education
Digits (Mathematics) *USE Numbers (Numerals)*
Mating Behavior (Animal)
USE Animal Mating Behavior
Animal **Mating** Behavior
Assortative **Mating**
Assortive Mating *USE Assortative Mating*
Matriarchy
Raven Coloured Progressive **Matrices**
Raven Progressive **Matrices**
Matriculation *USE School Enrollment*
Maturation *USE Human Development*
Maturity (Emotional)
USE Emotional Maturity
Maturity (Physical) *USE Physical Maturity*
Maturity (Vocational)
USE Vocational Maturity
Career Maturity *USE Vocational Maturity*
Emotional **Maturity**
Physical **Maturity**
Vineland Social **Maturity** Scale
Vocational **Maturity**
Maxilla *USE Jaw*
Maximum Likelihood
Maximum Security Facilities
Maze Learning
Maze Pathways
Porteus **Maze** Test
Runways (Maze) *USE Maze Pathways*
Mazes
T **Mazes**
MCPP *USE Piperazines*
MDMA
USE Methylenedioxymethamphetamine
Mealtimes
Mean
Meaning
Nonverbal **Meaning**
Verbal **Meaning**
Word **Meaning**
Meaningfulness
Measles
German Measles *USE Rubella*
Measurement
Measurement Error
USE Error of Measurement
Attitude **Measurement**
Conjoint **Measurement**
Consistency **(Measurement)**
Creativity **Measurement**
Educational **Measurement**
Error of **Measurement**
Pain **Measurement**
Predictability **(Measurement)**
Profiles **(Measurement)**
Psychophysical **Measurement**
Standard Error of Measurement *USE Error of Measurement*
Statistical **Measurement**
Variability **Measurement**
Achievement **Measures**
Aptitude **Measures**
Attitude **Measures**
Central Tendency **Measures**
Developmental **Measures**
Hearing Measures
USE Speech and Hearing Measures
Intelligence **Measures**
Nonprojective Personality **Measures**
Occupational Interest **Measures**
Perceptual Motor Measures *USE Sensorimotor Measures*
Perceptual **Measures**
Personality **Measures**

Mental Disorders
Mental Disorders due to General Medical Conditions
Mental Health
Mental Health Care Barriers *USE Treatment Barriers*
Mental Health Care Costs *USE Health Care Costs*
Mental Health Care Policy *USE Health Care Policy*
Mental Health Centers (Community) *USE Community Mental Health Centers*
Mental Health Consultation *USE Professional Consultation*
Mental Health Inservice Training
Mental Health Parity
Mental Health Personnel
Mental Health Personnel Supply
Mental Health Program Evaluation
Mental Health Programs
Mental Health Service Needs *USE Health Service Needs*
Mental Health Services
Mental Health Training (Community) *USE Community Mental Health Training*
Mental Hospitals *USE Psychiatric Hospitals*
Mental Illness (Attitudes Toward)
Mental Illness *USE Mental Disorders*
Mental Load *USE Human Channel Capacity*
Mental Models
Mental Retardation
Mental Retardation (Attitudes Toward)
Mental Rotation
Borderline **Mental** Retardation
Chronic **Mental** Illness
Community **Mental** Health
Community **Mental** Health Centers
Community **Mental** Health Services
Community **Mental** Health Training
Confusion (Mental) *USE Mental Confusion*
Cultural Familial Mental Retardation *USE Psychosocial Mental Retardation*
Henmon Nelson Tests of Mental Ability *USE Intelligence Measures*
Inservice Training (Mental Health) *USE Mental Health Inservice Training*
Mild **Mental** Retardation
Mini **Mental** State Examination
Moderate **Mental** Retardation
Persistent Mental Illness *USE Chronic Mental Illness*
Primary **Mental** Health Prevention
Profound **Mental** Retardation
Program Evaluation (Mental Health) *USE Mental Health Program Evaluation*
Programs (Mental Health) *USE Mental Health Programs*
Psychosocial **Mental** Retardation
Retardation (Mental) *USE Mental Retardation*
Severe **Mental** Retardation
Training (Community Mental Health) *USE Community Mental Health Training*
Training (Mental Health Inservice) *USE Mental Health Inservice Training*
Web Based Mental Health Services *USE Online Therapy*
Mentally Ill Homeless *USE Homeless Mentally Ill*
Mentally Ill Offenders
Educable Mentally Retarded *USE Mild Mental Retardation*
Home Reared **Mentally** Retarded
Homeless **Mentally** Ill
Institutionalized **Mentally** Retarded
Trainable Mentally Retarded *USE Moderate Mental Retardation*
Mentor
Meperidine
Mephenesin *USE Muscle Relaxing Drugs*
Meprobamate
Mercury (Metal)
Mercury Poisoning
Mercy Killing *USE Euthanasia*
Organizational Merger *USE Mergers and Acquisitions*
Mergers and Acquisitions
Awards **(Merit)**
Mescaline
Mesencephalon
Mesoridazine
Messages
Information (Messages) *USE Messages*
Meta Analysis
Metabolic Rates
Metabolic Syndrome
Metabolic Syndrome X *USE Metabolic Syndrome*
Metabolism
Metabolism Disorders
Basal **Metabolism**
Brain Metabolism *USE Neurochemistry*
Carbohydrate **Metabolism**
Fat Metabolism *USE Lipid Metabolism*
Glucose **Metabolism**
Lipid **Metabolism**
Lipid **Metabolism** Disorders
Protein **Metabolism**
Metabolites
Dopamine **Metabolites**
Norepinephrine **Metabolites**
Serotonin **Metabolites**
Metacognition
Lead **(Metal)**
Mercury **(Metal)**
Metalinguistics
Metallic Elements
Metals
Metamemory *USE Metacognition*
Metaphor
Metaphysics
Metapsychology
Climate (Meteorological) *USE Atmospheric Conditions*
Volt Meters *USE Apparatus*
Methadone
Methadone Maintenance
Methamphetamine
Methanol
Methaqualone
Methedrine *USE Methamphetamine*
Methionine
Directed Discussion **Method**
Discovery Teaching **Method**
Forced Choice (Testing **Method)**
Lecture **Method**
Montessori **Method**
Multiple Choice (Testing **Method)**
Nondirected Discussion **Method**
Open Classroom **Method**
Rhythm **Method**
Team Teaching **Method**
Methodists *USE Protestants*
Methodology
Clinical **Methods** Training
Drug Administration **Methods**
Empirical **Methods**
Experimental **Methods**
Management **Methods**
Observation **Methods**
Physical Treatment **Methods**
Psychotherapeutic Methods *USE Psychotherapeutic Techniques*
Qualitative Methods *USE Qualitative Research*
Quantitative **Methods**
Quasi Experimental **Methods**
Research Methods *USE Methodology*

Rotation Methods (Statistical)
USE Statistical Rotation
Scientific Methods *USE Experimental Methods*
Stimulus Presentation **Methods**
Teaching **Methods**
Testing **Methods**
Training (Clinical Methods) *USE Clinical Methods Training*
Treatment Methods (Physical)
USE Physical Treatment Methods
Methohexital
Methoxamine
Methoxyhydroxyphenylglycol (3,4)
Methyl Alcohol *USE Methanol*
Methylatropine *USE Atropine*
Methyldiphenylhydramine
USE Orphenadrine
Methyldopa
Methylenedioxymethamphetamine
Methylmorphine *USE Codeine*
Alpha **Methylparatyrosine**
Methylphenidate
Methylphenyltetrahydropyridine
Alpha Methyltyrosine
USE Alpha Methylparatyrosine
Methysergide *USE Serotonin Antagonists*
Metrazole *USE Pentylenetetrazol*
Metronomes
Metropolitan Readiness Tests
Mexican Americans
Nucleus Basalis of Meynert
USE Nucleus Basalis Magnocellularis
MHPG
USE Methoxyhydroxyphenylglycol (3,4)
Mianserin
Mice
Microcephaly
Microcomputers
Microcounseling
Microorganisms
Microscopes
Micturition *USE Urination*
Midazolam
Midbrain *USE Mesencephalon*
Middle Class
Middle Class Attitudes
Middle Ear
Middle Income Level
Middle Level Managers
Middle School Education
Middle School Students
Middle School Teachers
Middle Schools
Midwifery
Migraine Headache
Migrant Farm Workers
Migration (Human) *USE Human Migration*
Human **Migration**
Migratory Behavior (Animal)
Mild Mental Retardation
Milieu Therapy
Militancy
Military Attrition
Military Deployment
Military Duty Status
Military Enlistment
Military Medical Personnel
Military Officers
USE Commissioned Officers
Military Personnel
Military Psychologists
Military Psychology
Military Recruitment
Military Reserves *USE Military Duty Status*
Military Schools
Military Training
Military Veterans
Attrition (Military) *USE Military Attrition*
Deployment (Military) *USE Military Deployment*
Enlisted **Military** Personnel
Enlistment (Military) *USE Military Enlistment*
Recruitment (Military) *USE Military Recruitment*
Veterans (Military) *USE Military Veterans*
Volunteer **Military** Personnel
Miller Analogies Test
Millon Clinical Multiaxial Inventory
Mimicry (Biology)
Mind
Mind Blindness *USE Theory of Mind*
Mind Body *USE Dualism*
Theory of **Mind**
Mindfulness
Mini Mental State Examination
Minimal Brain Disorders
USE Attention Deficit Disorder with Hyperactivity
Minimum Competency Tests
Ministers (Religion)
Minks
Minnesota Multiphasic Personality Inventory
Minnesota Teacher Attitude Inventory
USE Attitude Measures
Minor Tranquilizers
Minority Group Discrimination
USE Race and Ethnic Discrimination
Minority Groups
Mirror Image
Mirroring
Misanthropy
Misarticulation *USE Articulation Disorders*
Misbehavior *USE Behavior Problems*
Miscarriage *USE Spontaneous Abortion*
Miscegenous Marriage
USE Interracial Marriage
Misconduct *USE Behavior Problems*
Misdemeanors *USE Crime*
Misdiagnosis
Misogyny *USE Misanthropy*
Missing Children
Missionaries
Mistakes *USE Errors*
MMPI
USE Minnesota Multiphasic Personality Inventory
Mnemonic Learning
Mobility (Geographical)
USE Geographical Mobility
Mobility (Occupational)
USE Occupational Mobility
Mobility (Social) *USE Social Mobility*
Mobility Aids
Geographical **Mobility**
Job Mobility *USE Occupational Mobility*
Occupational **Mobility**
Physical **Mobility**
Social **Mobility**
Upward Mobility *USE Social Mobility*
Vocational Mobility *USE Occupational Mobility*
Moclobemide
Big Five Personality Model *USE Five Factor Personality Model*
Biopsychosocial Model *USE Biopsychosocial Approach*
Diathesis Stress **Model**
Family Systems Model *USE Family Systems Theory*
Five Factor Personality **Model**
Information Processing **Model**
Medical **Model**
Rasch Model *USE Item Response Theory*
Modeling *USE Simulation*
Modeling Behavior *USE Imitation (Learning)*
Heuristic **Modeling**
Mathematical **Modeling**
Stochastic **Modeling**
Structural Equation **Modeling**
Models
Animal **Models**

Logistic Models *USE Item Response Theory*
Mental **Models**
Role **Models**
Moderate Mental Retardation
Modernization
Behavior **Modification**
Classroom Behavior **Modification**
Child Molestation *USE Pedophilia*
Molindone
Mollusca
Pearson Product Moment Correlation Coefficient
USE Statistical Correlation
Monetary Contributions *USE Fundraising*
Monetary Incentives
Monetary Rewards
Money
Mongolism *USE Downs Syndrome*
Monitoring
Self **Monitoring**
Self **Monitoring** (Personality)
Sleep Monitoring *USE Polysomnography*
Source **Monitoring**
Monkeys
Monoamine Oxidase Inhibitors
Monoamine Oxidases
Monoamines (Brain) *USE Catecholamines*
Monocular Vision
Monogamy
Monolingualism
Cyclic Adenosine **Monophosphate**
Monotony
Carbon **Monoxide**
Carbon **Monoxide** Poisoning
Monozygotic Twins
Montessori Method
Mood Disorders *USE Affective Disorders*
Bipolar Mood Disorder *USE Bipolar Disorder*
Moodiness
Moods *USE Emotional States*
Mooney Problem Check List
Moral Development
Morale
Morality
Morals *USE Morality*
Mores *USE Values*
Morita Therapy
Morphemes
Morphine
Morphology
Morphology (Language)
Mortality *USE Death and Dying*
Mortality Rate
Mosaicism *USE Chromosome Disorders*
Moslems *USE Muslims*
Mother Absence
Mother Child Communication
Mother Child Relations
Mothers
Adolescent **Mothers**
Expectant **Mothers**
Schizophrenogenic **Mothers**
Single **Mothers**
Teenage Mothers *USE Adolescent Mothers*
Unwed **Mothers**
Moths
Motion Parallax
Motion Perception
Motion Pictures *USE Films*
Motion Sickness
Range of **Motion**
Motivation
Motivation to Change
USE Readiness to Change
Motivation Training
Academic Achievement **Motivation**
Achievement **Motivation**
Affiliation **Motivation**
Animal **Motivation**
Employee **Motivation**
Extrinsic **Motivation**
Intrinsic **Motivation**
Training (Motivation) *USE Motivation Training*
Motivational Interviewing
Motor Coordination
Motor Cortex
Motor Development
Motor Disorders
USE Nervous System Disorders
Motor Evoked Potentials
USE Somatosensory Evoked Potentials
Motor Neurons
Motor Pathways *USE Efferent Pathways*
Motor Performance
Motor Processes
Motor Skill Learning
USE Perceptual Motor Learning
Motor Skills
Motor Traffic Accidents
Motor Vehicles
Balance (Motor Processes) *USE Equilibrium*
Coordination (Perceptual Motor) *USE Perceptual Motor Coordination*
Coordination (Motor) *USE Motor Coordination*
Cortex (Motor) *USE Motor Cortex*
Extrapyramidal Motor System *USE Extrapyramidal Tracts*
Fine **Motor** Skill Learning
Gross **Motor** Skill Learning
Perceptual **Motor** Coordination
Perceptual **Motor** Development
Perceptual **Motor** Learning
Perceptual Motor Measures
USE Sensorimotor Measures
Perceptual **Motor** Processes
Traffic Accidents (Motor) *USE Motor Traffic Accidents*
Motorcycles *USE Motor Vehicles*
Mourning *USE Grief*
Mouse Killing *USE Muricide*
Mouth (Anatomy)
Movement Disorders
Movement Perception
USE Motion Perception
Movement Therapy
Apparent **Movement**
Black Power **Movement**
Civil Rights **Movement**
Eye **Movement** Desensitization Therapy
Gay Liberation Movement
USE Homosexual Liberation Movement
Homosexual Liberation **Movement**
Human Potential **Movement**
Nonrapid Eye Movement Sleep *USE NREM Sleep*
Rapid Eye **Movement**
Rapid Eye Movement Dreams *USE REM Dreams*
Rapid Eye Movement Sleep *USE REM Sleep*
Stroboscopic Movement *USE Apparent Movement*
Womens Liberation **Movement**
Activist Movements *USE Activism*
Eye **Movements**
Radical **Movements**
Saccadic Eye Movements *USE Eye Movements*
Social **Movements**
Vergence Movements *USE Eye Convergence*
Movies *USE Films*
MPTP *USE Methylphenyltetrahydropyridine*
MRI *USE Magnetic Resonance Imaging*
Nasal **Mucosa**
Olfactory **Mucosa**
Mucus
Mueller Lyer Illusion
Multi Infarct Dementia
USE Vascular Dementia
Dementia (Multi Infarct) *USE Vascular Dementia*
Millon Clinical **Multiaxial** Inventory
Multicultural Education
Multiculturalism

ROTATED ALPHABETICAL TERMS SECTION

Multidimensional Scaling
Multidisciplinary Research *USE Interdisciplinary Research*
Multidisciplinary Treatment Approach *USE Interdisciplinary Treatment Approach*
Multidrug Abuse *USE Polydrug Abuse*
Multilingualism
Multimodal Treatment Approach
Multinational Corporations
Multinational Enterprises *USE Multinational Corporations*
Multinational Organizations *USE Multinational Corporations*
Minnesota **Multiphasic** Personality Inventory
Multiple Births
Multiple Choice (Testing Method)
Multiple Disabilities
Multiple Intelligences
Multiple Personality *USE Dissociative Identity Disorder*
Multiple Regression
Multiple Sclerosis
Multiple Therapy *USE Cotherapy*
Multiply Handicapped *USE Multiple Disabilities*
Multivariate Analysis
Munchausen Syndrome
Munchausen Syndrome by Proxy
Murder *USE Homicide*
Serial Murder *USE Serial Homicide*
Muricide
Muscarinic Drugs *USE Cholinergic Drugs*
Muscarinic Receptors *USE Cholinergic Receptors*
Muscimol
Muscle Contraction Headache
Muscle Contractions
Muscle Cramps *USE Muscular Disorders*
Muscle Relaxation
Muscle Relaxation Therapy *USE Relaxation Therapy*
Muscle Relaxing Drugs
Muscle Spasms
Muscle Tone
Cramps (Muscle) *USE Muscular Disorders*
Intra Aural Muscle Reflex *USE Acoustic Reflex*
Muscles
Facial **Muscles**
Masticatory **Muscles**
Oculomotor **Muscles**
Rigidity (Muscles) *USE Muscle Contractions*
Muscular Atrophy
Muscular Disorders
Muscular Dystrophy
Atrophy (Muscular) *USE Muscular Atrophy*
Dystrophy (Muscular) *USE Muscular Dystrophy*
Musculocutaneous Nerve *USE Spinal Nerves*
Musculoskeletal Disorders
Musculoskeletal System
Museums
Music
Music Education
Music Perception
Music Therapy
Rock **Music**
Musical Ability
Musical Instruments
Musicians
Muslims
Mutations
Mutilation (Self) *USE Self Mutilation*
Female Genital Mutilation *USE Circumcision*
Self **Mutilation**
Mutism
Elective **Mutism**
Selective Mutism *USE Elective Mutism*
Mutual Storytelling Technique
Myasthenia
Myasthenia Gravis
Myelin Sheath
Myelitis
Myelomeningocele *USE Spina Bifida*
Myenteric Plexus *USE Autonomic Ganglia*
Myers Briggs Type Indicator
Myocardial Infarctions
Infarctions (Myocardial) *USE Myocardial Infarctions*
Myocardium
Myoclonus
Myofascial Pain
Myopia
Myotonia
Mysticism
Visions (Mysticism) *USE Mysticism*
Myths
Myxedema *USE Hypothyroidism*
N-Methyl-D-Aspartate
Nabilone *USE Cannabinoids*
NAch *USE Achievement Motivation*
Nail Biting
Nalorphine
Naloxone
Naltrexone
Names
Brand **Names**
Naming
Nanotechnology
Napping
Narcissism
Narcissistic Personality Disorder
Narcoanalysis
Narcoanalytic Drugs *USE Drugs*
Narcolepsy
Narcosis
Narcotic Agonists
Narcotic Antagonists
Narcotic Drugs
Narcotics Anonymous *USE Twelve Step Programs*
Narrative Therapy
Narratives
Nasal Mucosa
National Guard Personnel
National Security
Nationalism
Foreign Nationals *USE Expatriates*
Native Alaskans *USE Alaska Natives*
Native Americans *USE American Indians*
Native Hawaiians *USE Hawaii Natives*
Native Language
Natives *USE Indigenous Populations*
Alaska **Natives**
Hawaii **Natives**
Natural Childbirth
Natural Disaster Preparedness *USE Emergency Preparedness*
Natural Disasters
Natural Family *USE Biological Family*
Natural Killer Cells
Natural Selection
Childbirth (Natural) *USE Natural Childbirth*
Naturalistic Observation *USE Observation Methods*
Nature Nurture
Human **Nature**
Nausea
Animal Navigation *USE Migratory Behavior (Animal)*
Navigators (Aircraft) *USE Aerospace Personnel*
Navy Personnel
Nazism *USE Fascism*
Near Death Experiences
Nearsightedness *USE Myopia*

Luria **Nebraska** Neuropsychological Battery
Neck (Anatomy)
Necrosis
Tumor **Necrosis** Factor
Need Achievement
USE Achievement Motivation
Need for Affiliation
USE Affiliation Motivation
Need for Approval
Need for Cognition
Need Satisfaction
Needle Exchange Programs
Needle Sharing
Needs
Needs Assessment
Emotional Needs *USE Psychological Needs*
Health Service **Needs**
Mental Health Service Needs *USE Health Service Needs*
Psychological **Needs**
Special **Needs**
Nefazodone
Negative and Positive Symptoms
USE Positive and Negative Symptoms
Negative Reinforcement
Negative Therapeutic Reaction
Negative Transfer
Contingent **Negative** Variation
Positive and **Negative** Symptoms
Negativism
Child **Neglect**
Perceptual Neglect *USE Sensory Neglect*
Sensory **Neglect**
Spatial Neglect *USE Sensory Neglect*
Visual Neglect *USE Sensory Neglect*
Negotiation
Negroes *USE Blacks*
Neighborhoods
Henmon Nelson Tests of Mental Ability
USE Intelligence Measures
Nembutal *USE Pentobarbital*
NEO Personality Inventory
NeoFreudian School
USE Neopsychoanalytic School
Neologisms
Neonatal Development
Neonatal Disorders
Neonatal Period
Neonates (Animal) *USE Infants (Animal)*
Neonaticide *USE Infanticide*
Neophobia
Neoplasms
Benign **Neoplasms**
Brain **Neoplasms**
Breast **Neoplasms**
Endocrine **Neoplasms**
Malignant Neoplasms *USE Neoplasms*
Mammary Neoplasms *USE Breast Neoplasms*
Nervous System **Neoplasms**
Neopsychoanalytic School
Neostigmine
Neostriatum *USE Striatum*
Nepotism
Nerve (Abducens) *USE Abducens Nerve*
Nerve (Accessory) *USE Cranial Nerves*
Nerve (Acoustic) *USE Acoustic Nerve*
Nerve (Facial) *USE Facial Nerve*
Nerve Cells *USE Neurons*
Nerve Endings
Nerve Growth Factor
Nerve Tissues
Abducens **Nerve**
Accessory Nerve *USE Cranial Nerves*
Acoustic **Nerve**
Auditory Nerve *USE Acoustic Nerve*
Chorda Tympani Nerve *USE Facial Nerve*
Cochlear Nerve *USE Acoustic Nerve*
Facial **Nerve**
Femoral Nerve *USE Spinal Nerves*
Glossopharyngeal Nerve *USE Cranial Nerves*
Hypoglossal Nerve *USE Cranial Nerves*
Median Nerve *USE Spinal Nerves*
Musculocutaneous Nerve *USE Spinal Nerves*
Obturator Nerve *USE Spinal Nerves*
Oculomotor Nerve *USE Cranial Nerves*
Olfactory **Nerve**
Optic **Nerve**
Peripheral Nerve Disorders
USE Peripheral Neuropathy
Phrenic Nerve *USE Spinal Nerves*
Radial Nerve *USE Spinal Nerves*
Sciatic Nerve *USE Spinal Nerves*
Trigeminal **Nerve**
Trochlear Nerve *USE Cranial Nerves*
Ulnar Nerve *USE Spinal Nerves*
Vagus **Nerve**
Vestibulocochlear Nerve *USE Acoustic Nerve*
Nerves (Adrenergic)
USE Adrenergic Nerves
Nerves (Cholinergic)
USE Cholinergic Nerves
Nerves (Cranial) *USE Cranial Nerves*
Nerves (Peripheral)
USE Peripheral Nervous System
Nerves (Spinal) *USE Spinal Nerves*
Adrenergic **Nerves**
Cholinergic **Nerves**
Cranial **Nerves**
Spinal **Nerves**
Thoracic Nerves *USE Spinal Nerves*
Anorexia **Nervosa**
Nervous Breakdown *USE Mental Disorders*
Nervous System
Nervous System Disorders
Nervous System Neoplasms
Nervous System Plasticity
USE Neural Plasticity
Autonomic **Nervous** System
Autonomic **Nervous** System Disorders
Central **Nervous** System
Central **Nervous** System Disorders
Central Nervous System Drugs
USE CNS Affecting Drugs
Parasympathetic **Nervous** System
Peripheral **Nervous** System
Sclerosis **(Nervous** System)
Sympathetic **Nervous** System
Nervousness
Nest Building
Empty **Nest**
Business Networking *USE Professional Networking*
Internet Social Networking *USE Online Social Networks*
Professional **Networking**
Networks (Social) *USE Social Networks*
Neural **Networks**
Online Social **Networks**
Social Support Networks *USE Social Support*
Social **Networks**
Neural Analyzers
Neural Development
Neural Lesions
Neural Networks
Neural Pathways
Neural Plasticity
Neural Receptors
Neural Regeneration
USE Neural Development
Neural Transmission
USE Neurotransmission
Neural Transplantation
Receptors (Neural) *USE Neural Receptors*
Neuralgia
Trigeminal **Neuralgia**
Neurasthenia
Neuroanatomy

Neurobiology
Neurochemistry
Neurocognition
Neurodegenerative Diseases
Neurodermatitis
Neuroendocrinology
Neurofeedback
Neuroimaging
Neuroinfections *USE Infectious Disorders*
Neuroinfections
USE Nervous System Disorders
Neurokinins
Neuroleptic Drugs
Neuroleptic Malignant Syndrome
Neurolinguistic Programming
Neurolinguistics
Neurological Disorders
USE Nervous System Disorders
Neurologists
Neurology
Neuromuscular Blocking Drugs
USE Muscle Relaxing Drugs
Neuromuscular Disorders
Neurons
Afferent Neurons *USE Sensory Neurons*
Auditory **Neurons**
Motor **Neurons**
Sensory **Neurons**
Neuropathologists *USE Neurologists*
Neuropathology
Neuropathy *USE Nervous System Disorders*
Peripheral **Neuropathy**
Neuropeptide Y
Neuropeptides
Neurophysiology
Neuropsychiatrists *USE Psychiatrists*
Neuropsychiatry
Neuropsychological Assessment
Neuropsychological Rehabilitation
Halstead Reitan **Neuropsychological** Battery
Luria Nebraska **Neuropsychological** Battery
Neuropsychology
Neuroreceptors *USE Neural Receptors*
Neurosciences
Neurosis
Anxiety Neurosis *USE Anxiety Disorders*
Childhood **Neurosis**
Compulsive Neurosis
USE Obsessive Compulsive Disorder
Conversion Neurosis *USE Conversion Disorder*
Dissociative Neurosis *USE Dissociative Disorders*
Experimental **Neurosis**
Hysterical Neurosis (Conversion)
USE Conversion Disorder
Hysterical Neurosis (Dissociation)
USE Dissociative Disorders
Infantile Neurosis *USE Childhood Neurosis*
Obsessive Compulsive Neurosis
USE Obsessive Compulsive Disorder
Obsessive Neurosis
USE Obsessive Compulsive Disorder
Occupational **Neurosis**
Phobic Neurosis *USE Phobias*
Traumatic **Neurosis**
Neurosurgeons *USE Surgeons*
Neurosurgery
Neurosyphilis
Neurotensin
Neurotic Depressive Reaction
USE Major Depression
Depressive Reaction (Neurotic) *USE Major Depression*
Neuroticism
Neurotoxicity
Neurotoxins
Neurotransmission
Neurotransmitter Uptake Inhibitors
Neurotransmitters

Neutrality (Psychotherapeutic)
USE Psychotherapeutic Neutrality
Psychotherapeutic **Neutrality**
Never Married
News Media
Newsletters (Professional)
USE Scientific Communication
Professional Newsletters *USE Scientific Communication*
Newspapers
NGOs
Niacin *USE Nicotinic Acid*
Niacinamide *USE Nicotinamide*
Nialamide
Nicotinamide
Nicotine
Nicotine Withdrawal
Nicotinic Acid
Nicotinic Acid Amide *USE Nicotinamide*
Nicotinic Receptors
USE Cholinergic Receptors
Nictitating Membrane
Night Terrors *USE Sleep Disorders*
Nightmares
Substantia **Nigra**
Nihilism
Nitrazepam
Nitric Oxide
Nitrogen
NMDA *USE N-Methyl-D-Aspartate*
Nociception *USE Pain Perception*
Nociceptors
Nocturnal Behavior (Animal)
USE Animal Nocturnal Behavior
Nocturnal Emission
Nocturnal Teeth Grinding
Animal **Nocturnal** Behavior
Noise (Sound) *USE Auditory Stimulation*
Noise Effects
Noise Levels (Work Areas)
Filtered **Noise**
White **Noise**
Nomenclature (Psychological)
USE Psychological Terminology
Nomifensine
Non-governmental Organizations
USE NGOs
Non Zero Sum Games
Beverages **(Nonalcoholic)**
Noncommissioned Officers
Officers (Noncommissioned)
USE Noncommissioned Officers
Nonconformity (Personality)
Noncontingent Reinforcement
Nondirected Discussion Method
Nondirective Therapy
USE Client Centered Therapy
Nongovernmental Organizations
USE NGOs
Nongraded Schools
Primates **(Nonhuman)**
Nonlinear Regression
Nonmetallic Elements
USE Chemical Elements
Nonparametric Statistical Tests
Nonprescription Drugs
Nonprofessional Personnel
Nonprofit Organizations
Nonprojective Personality Measures
Nonrapid Eye Movement Sleep
USE NREM Sleep
Beliefs (Nonreligious) *USE Attitudes*
Rites **(Nonreligious)**
Rituals (Nonreligious) *USE Rites (Nonreligious)*
NonREM Sleep *USE NREM Sleep*
Nonreversal Shift Learning
Nonsense Syllable Learning
Nonstandard English

Nontraditional Careers
Nontraditional Education
Nonverbal Ability
Nonverbal Communication
Nonverbal Learning
Nonverbal Meaning
Nonverbal Reinforcement
Nonviolence
Nootropic Drugs
Noradrenaline *USE Norepinephrine*
Norepinephrine
Norepinephrine Metabolites
Serotonin **Norepinephrine** Reuptake Inhibitors
Normal Distribution
Normalization (Test) *USE Test Standardization*
Test Normalization *USE Test Standardization*
Norms (Social) *USE Social Norms*
Norms (Statistical) *USE Statistical Norms*
Norms (Test) *USE Test Norms*
Social **Norms**
Statistical **Norms**
Test **Norms**
Nortriptyline
Norway Rats
Nose
Note Taking
Nouns
Novel Stimuli *USE Stimulus Novelty*
Novelty Seeking *USE Sensation Seeking*
Stimulus **Novelty**
Novocaine *USE Procaine*
NREM Sleep
Nuclear Family
Nuclear Technology
Nuclear War
Cerebellar Nuclei *USE Cerebellum*
Raphe **Nuclei**
Septal **Nuclei**
Thalamic **Nuclei**
Nucleic Acids
Nucleotides
Nucleus Accumbens
Nucleus Basalis Magnocellularis
Nucleus Basalis of Meynert *USE Nucleus Basalis Magnocellularis*
Amygdaloid Nucleus *USE Amygdala*
Basal Magnocellular Cholinergic Nucleus *USE Nucleus Basalis Magnocellularis*
Caudate **Nucleus**
Cell **Nucleus**
Lateral Geniculate Nucleus *USE Geniculate Bodies (Thalamus)*
Medial Geniculate Nucleus *USE Geniculate Bodies (Thalamus)*
Red Nucleus *USE Mesencephalon*
Nudity
Null Hypothesis Testing
Number Comprehension
Number Systems
Numbers (Numerals)
Numbers **(Numerals)**
Numerical Ability *USE Mathematical Ability*
Numerosity Perception
Nuns
Nurse Patient Interaction *USE Therapeutic Processes*
Nursery School Students
Nursery Schools
Nurses
Psychiatric **Nurses**
Public Health Service **Nurses**
School **Nurses**
Nursing
Nursing Education
Nursing Homes
Nursing Students
Nurturance
Nature **Nurture**
Nutrition
Nutritional Deficiencies
Nutritional Supplements *USE Dietary Supplements*
Nymphomania *USE Hypersexuality*
Nystagmus
Optokinetic Nystagmus *USE Nystagmus*
Vestibular Nystagmus *USE Nystagmus*
Obedience
Obesity
Obesity (Attitudes Toward)
Object Permanence
Object Recognition
Object Relations
Objective Referenced Tests *USE Criterion Referenced Tests*
Objectives (Organizational) *USE Organizational Objectives*
Objectives *USE Goals*
Course Objectives *USE Educational Objectives*
Educational **Objectives**
Instructional Objectives *USE Educational Objectives*
Organizational **Objectives**
Objectivity
Transitional **Objects**
Oblique Rotation
Medulla **Oblongata**
Obscenity
Observation Methods
Naturalistic Observation *USE Observation Methods*
Self Observation *USE Self Monitoring*
Observational Learning
Observers
Obsessions
Obsessive Compulsive Disorder
Obsessive Compulsive Neurosis *USE Obsessive Compulsive Disorder*
Obsessive Compulsive Personality Disorder
Obsessive Neurosis *USE Obsessive Compulsive Disorder*
Obstetrical Complications
Obstetricians
Obstetrics
Obturator Nerve *USE Spinal Nerves*
Occipital Lobe
Occultism
Occupation (Parental) *USE Parental Occupation*
Parental **Occupation**
Occupational Adjustment
Occupational Aspirations
Occupational Attitudes
Occupational Choice
Occupational Exposure
Occupational Guidance
Occupational Interest Measures
Occupational Interests
Occupational Mobility
Occupational Neurosis
Occupational Preference
Occupational Safety
Occupational Status
Occupational Stress
Occupational Success
Occupational Success Prediction
Occupational Tenure
Occupational Therapists
Occupational Therapy
Guidance (Occupational) *USE Occupational Guidance*
Kuder **Occupational** Interest Survey
Mobility (Occupational) *USE Occupational Mobility*
Prestige (Occupational) *USE Occupational Status*
Tenure (Occupational) *USE Occupational Tenure*
Occupations
Religious Occupations *USE Religious Personnel*
Octopus
Ocular Accommodation

ROTATED ALPHABETICAL TERMS SECTION

Ocular Dominance
Ocular Fixation *USE Eye Fixation*
Electro **Oculography**
Oculomotor Muscles
Oculomotor Nerve *USE Cranial Nerves*
Oculomotor Response *USE Eye Movements*
Odor Aversion Conditioning *USE Aversion Conditioning*
Odor Discrimination
Oedipal Complex
Offender Profiling *USE Criminal Profiling*
Offenders (Adult) *USE Criminals*
Offenders (Juvenile) *USE Juvenile Delinquency*
Mentally Ill **Offenders**
Sex **Offenses**
Office Environment *USE Working Conditions*
Officers (Commissioned) *USE Commissioned Officers*
Officers (Noncommissioned) *USE Noncommissioned Officers*
Commissioned **Officers**
Military Officers *USE Commissioned Officers*
Noncommissioned **Officers**
Parole **Officers**
Probation **Officers**
Elected Government Officials *USE Government Personnel*
Stimulus **Offset**
Offshoring *USE Outsourcing*
Offspring
Offspring of Alcoholics *USE Children of Alcoholics*
Adult **Offspring**
Alcoholic Offspring *USE Children of Alcoholics*
Interracial **Offspring**
Olanzapine
Olfactory Bulb
Olfactory Evoked Potentials
Olfactory Impairment *USE Anosmia*
Olfactory Mucosa
Olfactory Nerve
Olfactory Perception
Olfactory Stimulation
Olfactory Thresholds
Oligophrenia (Phenylpyruvic) *USE Phenylketonuria*
Oligophrenia *USE Mental Retardation*
Omission Training
Omnipotence
Online Databases *USE Databases*
Online Retailing *USE Electronic Retailing*
Online Searching *USE Computer Searching*
Online Shopping *USE Electronic Commerce*
Online Social Networks
Online Therapy
Only Children
Female Only Environments *USE Single Sex Environments*
Male Only Environments *USE Single Sex Environments*
Onomatopoeia and Images Test *USE Projective Personality Measures*
Onset (Disorders)
Sleep **Onset**
Stimulus **Onset**
Ontogeny *USE Development*
Ontologies
Ontology (Philosophy)
Open Classroom Method
Open Field Behavior (Animal) *USE Animal Open Field Behavior*
Open Universities *USE Nontraditional Education*
Animal **Open** Field Behavior
Openmindedness
Openness to Experience
Operant Conditioning
Conditioning (Operant) *USE Operant Conditioning*
Operation (Surgery) *USE Surgery*
Keypunch Operators *USE Clerical Personnel*
Ophidiophobia
Ophthalmologic Examination
Ophthalmology
Opiate Agonists *USE Narcotic Agonists*
Opiate Antagonists *USE Narcotic Antagonists*
Opiates
Endogenous **Opiates**
Opinion (Public) *USE Public Opinion*
Opinion Attitude and Interest Survey *USE Attitude Measures*
Opinion Change *USE Attitude Change*
Opinion Questionnaires *USE Attitude Measures*
Opinion Surveys *USE Attitude Measures*
Public **Opinion**
Opinions *USE Attitudes*
Opioid Antagonists *USE Narcotic Antagonists*
Opioids (Endogenous) *USE Endogenous Opiates*
Opioids *USE Opiates*
Opium Alkaloids *USE Alkaloids*
Opium Alkaloids *USE Opiates*
Opium Derivatives *USE Opiates*
Opossums
Oppositional Defiant Disorder
Optic Chiasm
Optic Lobe
Optic Nerve
Optic Tract
Optical Aids
Optical Illusions *USE Illusions (Perception)*
Optimism
Optokinetic Nystagmus *USE Nystagmus*
Optometrists
Optometry
Oral Communication
Oral Contraceptives
Oral Reading
Birth **Order**
Higher **Order** Conditioning
Pecking Order *USE Animal Dominance*
Rank **Order** Correlation
Second Order Conditioning *USE Higher Order Conditioning*
Court Ordered Treatment *USE Court Referrals*
Organ Donation *USE Tissue Donation*
Organ of Corti *USE Cochlea*
Organ Transplantation
Sense **Organ** Disorders
Transplants (Organ) *USE Organ Transplantation*
Organic Brain Syndromes
Organic Therapies *USE Physical Treatment Methods*
Single Cell Organisms *USE Microorganisms*
School Organization *USE Educational Administration*
Spatial **Organization**
Organizational Behavior
Organizational Change
Organizational Characteristics
Organizational Climate
Organizational Commitment
Organizational Crises
Organizational Culture *USE Organizational Climate*
Organizational Development
Organizational Effectiveness
Organizational Goals *USE Organizational Objectives*
Organizational Innovation *USE Innovation*

Organizational Learning
Organizational Merger
USE Mergers and Acquisitions
Organizational Objectives
Organizational Performance
USE Organizational Effectiveness
Organizational Policy Making
USE Policy Making
Organizational Psychology
USE Industrial and Organizational Psychology
Organizational Structure
Acquisitions (Organizational)
USE Mergers and Acquisitions
Change (Organizational)
USE Organizational Change
Climate (Organizational)
USE Organizational Climate
Industrial and **Organizational** Psychology
Objectives (Organizational)
USE Organizational Objectives
Organizations
Business **Organizations**
Clubs (Social **Organizations)**
Faith Based **Organizations**
Foreign **Organizations**
Groups (Organizations) *USE Organizations*
Health Maintenance **Organizations**
International **Organizations**
Learning Organizations *USE Organizational Learning*
Multinational Organizations
USE Multinational Corporations
Non-governmental Organizations *USE NGOs*
Nongovernmental Organizations *USE NGOs*
Nonprofit **Organizations**
Professional **Organizations**
Religious **Organizations**
Advance **Organizers**
Sense **Organs**
Orgasm
Female **Orgasm**
Male **Orgasm**
Orientation (Perceptual)
USE Perceptual Orientation
Orientation (Spatial)
USE Spatial Orientation (Perception)
Fundamental Interpersonal Relation **Orientation** Behavior Ques
Goal **Orientation**
Perceptual **Orientation**
Personal **Orientation** Inventory
Professional Orientation *USE Theoretical Orientation*
Sexual **Orientation**
Spatial **Orientation** (Perception)
Theoretical **Orientation**
Psychoanalytically Oriented Psychotherapy
USE Psychodynamic Psychotherapy
Orienting Reflex
Orienting Responses
Family of **Origin**
Originality *USE Creativity*
Word Origins *USE Etymology*
Orphanages
Orphans
Orphenadrine
Orthogonal Rotation
Orthography
Orthopedically Handicapped
USE Physical Disorders
Orthopsychiatry
Oscilloscopes
Ear Ossicles *USE Middle Ear*
Osteopathic Medicine
Osteopathy *USE Osteopathic Medicine*
Osteoporosis
Significant **Others**
Otosclerosis *USE Ear Disorders*

Out of Body Experiences
Acting **Out**
Contracting Out *USE Outsourcing*
Time **Out**
Disease Outbreaks *USE Epidemics*
Outcomes (Psychotherapeutic)
USE Psychotherapeutic Outcomes
Outcomes (Treatment)
USE Treatment Outcomes
Psychotherapeutic **Outcomes**
Therapeutic Outcomes *USE Treatment Outcomes*
Treatment **Outcomes**
Outgroup Ingroup *USE Ingroup Outgroup*
Ingroup **Outgroup**
Outpatient Commitment
Outpatient Psychiatric Clinics
USE Psychiatric Clinics
Outpatient Treatment
Commitment (Outpatient) *USE Outpatient Commitment*
Outpatients
Outreach Programs
Outsourcing
Outward Bound
USE Wilderness Experience
Ovariectomy
Ovaries
Ovary Disorders
USE Endocrine Sexual Disorders
Over the Counter Drugs
USE Nonprescription Drugs
Overachievement (Academic)
USE Academic Overachievement
Academic **Overachievement**
Overcorrection
Drug **Overdoses**
Overlearning
Overpopulation
Structured Overview *USE Advance Organizers*
Overweight
Ovulation
Owls
Ownership
Oxazepam
Amine **Oxidase** Inhibitors
Cytochrome **Oxidase**
Monoamine **Oxidase** Inhibitors
Oxidases
Monoamine **Oxidases**
Nitric **Oxide**
Oxidopamine *USE Hydroxydopamine (6-)*
Oxilapine *USE Loxapine*
Oxygen
Oxygenation
Oxytocin
Pacemakers (Artificial)
USE Artificial Pacemakers
Artificial **Pacemakers**
Pacific Islanders
Pacifism
Pain
Pain (Psychogenic)
USE Somatoform Pain Disorder
Pain Disorder
USE Somatoform Pain Disorder
Pain Management
Pain Measurement
Pain Perception
Pain Receptors *USE Nociceptors*
Pain Relieving Drugs *USE Analgesic Drugs*
Pain Thresholds
Back **Pain**
Chronic **Pain**
Myofascial **Pain**
Psychogenic Pain *USE Somatoform Pain Disorder*
Somatoform **Pain** Disorder
Painting (Art)
Paired Associate Learning

Cleft **Palate**
Palestinians *USE Arabs*
Palliative Care
Globus **Pallidus**
Palm (Anatomy)
Palsy *USE Paralysis*
Cerebral **Palsy**
Progressive Supranuclear **Palsy**
Pancreas
Pancreozymin *USE Cholecystokinin*
Pandemics
Panic
Panic Attack
Panic Disorder
Pantherine *USE Muscimol*
Papaverine
Parachlorophenylalanine
Paradigmatic Techniques
USE Paradoxical Techniques
Paradoxical Sleep *USE REM Sleep*
Paradoxical Techniques
Paragraphs
Paraldehyde *USE Anticonvulsive Drugs*
Paralegal Personnel *USE Legal Personnel*
Motion **Parallax**
Paralysis
Paralysis (Hysterical)
USE Hysterical Paralysis
Paralysis (Infantile) *USE Poliomyelitis*
Paralysis Agitans *USE Parkinsons Disease*
Hysterical **Paralysis**
Infantile Paralysis *USE Poliomyelitis*
Dementia Paralytica *USE General Paresis*
Paramedical Personnel
USE Allied Health Personnel
Paramedical Sciences
Parameter Estimation
USE Statistical Estimation
Parameters (Response)
USE Response Parameters
Parameters (Stimulus)
USE Stimulus Parameters
Response **Parameters**
Statistical Sample **Parameters**
Stimulus **Parameters**
Parametric Statistical Tests
Paranoia
Paranoia (Psychosis)
Paranoid Disorder
USE Paranoia (Psychosis)
Paranoid Personality Disorder
Paranoid Schizophrenia
Acute Paranoid Disorder
USE Paranoia (Psychosis)
Atypical Paranoid Disorder
USE Paranoia (Psychosis)
Shared Paranoid Disorder *USE Folie A Deux*
Paraphilias
Paraplegia
Paraprofessional Education
Paraprofessional Personnel
Parapsychological Phenomena
Parapsychology
ESP (Parapsychology)
USE Extrasensory Perception
Parasitic Disorders
Parasitism *USE Biological Symbiosis*
Parasuicide *USE Attempted Suicide*
Parasympathetic Nervous System
Parasympatholytic Drugs
USE Antispasmodic Drugs
Parasympathomimetic Drugs
USE Cholinomimetic Drugs
Parathion
Parathyroid Disorders
Parathyroid Glands
Parathyroid Hormone

Parent Child Communication
Parent Child Relations
Parent Educational Background
Parent Effectiveness Training
USE Parent Training
Parent School Relationship
Parent Training
Parental Absence
Parental Attitudes
Parental Authoritarianism
USE Parenting Style
Parental Behavior (Animal)
USE Animal Parental Behavior
Parental Characteristics
Parental Death
Parental Expectations
Parental Influence
USE Parent Child Relations
Parental Investment
Parental Involvement
Parental Occupation
Parental Participation
USE Parental Involvement
Parental Permissiveness
Parental Role
Animal **Parental** Behavior
Authoritarianism (Parental) *USE Parenting Style*
Occupation (Parental) *USE Parental Occupation*
Permissiveness (Parental) *USE Parental Permissiveness*
Parenthood Status
Delayed **Parenthood**
Parenting Skills
Parenting Style
Parents
Adoptive **Parents**
Birth Parents *USE Biological Family*
Educational Background (Parents)
USE Parent Educational Background
Expectant **Parents**
Foster **Parents**
Gay Parents *USE Homosexual Parents*
Homosexual **Parents**
Lesbian Parents *USE Homosexual Parents*
Single **Parents**
Surrogate **Parents** (Humans)
Paresis (General) *USE General Paresis*
General **Paresis**
Paresthesia *USE Somatosensory Disorders*
Pargyline
Parietal Lobe
Mental Health **Parity**
Parkinsonism
Parkinsons Disease
Parks (Recreational) *USE Recreation Areas*
Parochial School Education
USE Private School Education
Parole
Parole Officers
Parolees *USE Parole*
Paroxetine
Paroxysmal Sleep *USE Narcolepsy*
Part Time Employment
USE Employment Status
Partial Hospitalization
Partial Reinforcement
USE Reinforcement Schedules
Partially Hearing Impaired
Partially Sighted
Hearing Impaired (Partially) *USE Partially Hearing Impaired*
Participation
Athletic **Participation**
Citizen Participation *USE Community Involvement*
Client **Participation**
Group **Participation**
Parental Participation *USE Parental Involvement*
Patient Participation *USE Client Participation*
Political **Participation**

Participative Management
Political **Parties**
Partner Abuse
Intimate **Partner** Violence
Sexual **Partners**
Parturition *USE Birth*
Democratic Party *USE Political Parties*
Independent Party (Political) *USE Political Parties*
Republican Party *USE Political Parties*
Rites of **Passage**
Passive Aggressive Personality Disorder
Passive Avoidance
USE Avoidance Conditioning
Passive Smoking
Passiveness
Pastoral Counseling
Pastors *USE Ministers (Religion)*
Patents
Paternal Investment
USE Parental Investment
Animal **Paternal** Behavior
Path Analysis
Pathogenesis *USE Etiology*
Pathological Gambling
Pathologists
Pathology
Pathophysiology
Afferent **Pathways**
Efferent **Pathways**
Maze **Pathways**
Motor Pathways *USE Efferent Pathways*
Neural **Pathways**
Sensory Pathways *USE Afferent Pathways*
Patient Abuse
Patient Attitudes *USE Client Attitudes*
Patient Care Planning
USE Treatment Planning
Patient Characteristics
USE Client Characteristics
Patient Dropouts *USE Treatment Dropouts*
Patient Education *USE Client Education*
Patient History
Patient Participation
USE Client Participation
Patient Records *USE Client Records*
Patient Rights *USE Client Rights*
Patient Satisfaction *USE Client Satisfaction*
Patient Seclusion
Patient Selection
Patient Therapist Interaction
USE Psychotherapeutic Processes
Patient Therapist Sexual Relations
USE Professional Client Sexual Relations
Patient Transfer *USE Client Transfer*
Patient Treatment Matching
USE Client Treatment Matching
Patient Violence
Dentist Patient Interaction
USE Therapeutic Processes
Nurse Patient Interaction
USE Therapeutic Processes
Physician Patient Interaction
USE Therapeutic Processes
Seclusion (Patient) *USE Patient Seclusion*
Therapist Patient Interaction
USE Psychotherapeutic Processes
Therapist Patient Sexual Relations
USE Professional Client Sexual Relations
Patients
Dying Patients *USE Terminally Ill Patients*
Geriatric **Patients**
Hospitalized **Patients**
Medical **Patients**
Psychiatric **Patients**
Surgical **Patients**
Terminally Ill **Patients**
Patriarchy
Pattern Discrimination
Stimulus Pattern *USE Stimulus Variability*
Alcohol Drinking **Patterns**
Dissociative Patterns *USE Dissociative Disorders*
Eating Patterns *USE Eating Behavior*
Interest Patterns *USE Interests*
Transgenerational **Patterns**
Wilson **Patterson** Conservatism Scale
Speech **Pauses**
Pavlov (Ivan)
Pavlovian Conditioning
USE Classical Conditioning
Pay *USE Salaries*
Equity **(Payment)**
PCP *USE Phencyclidine*
Peabody Picture Vocabulary Test
Peace
Peace Corps
Peacekeeping
Pearson Product Moment Correlation Coefficient *USE Statistical Correlation*
Pecking Order *USE Animal Dominance*
Angina **Pectoris**
Pedagogy *USE Teaching*
Pederasty *USE Pedophilia*
Pedestrian Accidents
Pedestrians
Pediatricians
Pediatrics
Pedophilia
Peer Counseling
Peer Evaluation
Peer Pressure
Peer Relations
Peer Review *USE Peer Evaluation*
Peer Tutoring
Peers
Pellagra
Pemoline
Death Penalty *USE Capital Punishment*
Penguins
Penicillins
Penis
Penis Envy
Erection **(Penis)**
Penitentiaries *USE Prisons*
Penology
Pension Plans (Employee)
USE Employee Pension Plans
Employee **Pension** Plans
Pensions *USE Employee Pension Plans*
Pentazocine
Pentobarbital
Sodium Pentobarbital *USE Pentobarbital*
Pentothal *USE Thiopental*
Pentylenetetrazol
Pentylenetetrazole *USE Pentylenetetrazol*
Peptic Ulcers *USE Gastrointestinal Ulcers*
Peptides
Perception
Auditory **Perception**
Brightness **Perception**
Color **Perception**
Contour Perception
USE Form and Shape Perception
Depth **Perception**
Direction **Perception**
Distance **Perception**
Extrasensory **Perception**
Face **Perception**
Form and Shape **Perception**
Form Perception
USE Form and Shape Perception
Frostig Developmental Test of Visual **Perception**

Gustatory Perception *USE Taste Perception*
Haptic Perception *USE Cutaneous Sense*
Illusions **(Perception)**
Interpersonal Perception *USE Social Perception*
Kinesthetic **Perception**
Loudness **Perception**
Motion **Perception**
Movement Perception *USE Motion Perception*
Music **Perception**
Numerosity **Perception**
Olfactory **Perception**
Pain **Perception**
Pitch **Perception**
Risk **Perception**
Role **Perception**
Self **Perception**
Shape Perception *USE Form and Shape Perception*
Signal Detection **(Perception)**
Smell Perception *USE Olfactory Perception*
Social **Perception**
Somesthetic **Perception**
Spatial Orientation **(Perception)**
Spatial **Perception**
Speech **Perception**
Subliminal **Perception**
Tactual **Perception**
Taste **Perception**
Temperature **Perception**
Texture **Perception**
Time **Perception**
Visual **Perception**
Weight **Perception**
Perceptiveness (Personality)
Perceptual Aftereffect
Perceptual Closure
Perceptual Constancy
Perceptual Development
Perceptual Discrimination
Perceptual Distortion
Perceptual Disturbances
Perceptual Fill *USE Perceptual Closure*
Perceptual Learning
Perceptual Localization
Perceptual Measures
Perceptual Motor Coordination
Perceptual Motor Development
Perceptual Motor Learning
Perceptual Motor Measures *USE Sensorimotor Measures*
Perceptual Motor Processes
Perceptual Neglect *USE Sensory Neglect*
Perceptual Orientation
Perceptual Stimulation
Perceptual Style
Aftereffect (Perceptual) *USE Perceptual Aftereffect*
Closure (Perceptual) *USE Perceptual Closure*
Coordination (Perceptual Motor) *USE Perceptual Motor Coordination*
Distortion (Perceptual) *USE Perceptual Distortion*
Localization (Perceptual) *USE Perceptual Localization*
Orientation (Perceptual) *USE Perceptual Orientation*
Perfectionism
Hypericum **Perforatum**
Performance
Performance Anxiety
Performance Tests
Athletic **Performance**
Dual Task **Performance**
Group **Performance**
Job **Performance**
Motor **Performance**
Organizational Performance *USE Organizational Effectiveness*
Sport Performance *USE Athletic Performance*
Performing Arts *USE Arts*
Periaqueductal Gray
Perinatal Period
Critical **Period**
Neonatal **Period**
Perinatal **Period**
Postnatal **Period**
Peripheral Nerve Disorders *USE Peripheral Neuropathy*
Peripheral Nervous System
Peripheral Neuropathy
Peripheral Vision
Computer **Peripheral** Devices
Nerves (Peripheral) *USE Peripheral Nervous System*
Object **Permanence**
Permissiveness (Parental) *USE Parental Permissiveness*
Parental **Permissiveness**
Perpetrators
Perphenazine
Persecution
Perseverance *USE Persistence*
Perseveration
Persistence
Persistent Mental Illness *USE Chronic Mental Illness*
Person Centered Psychotherapy *USE Client Centered Therapy*
Person Environment Fit
Goodenough Harris Draw A **Person** Test
Personal Adjustment *USE Emotional Adjustment*
Personal Computers *USE Microcomputers*
Personal Construct Theory *USE Personality Theory*
Personal Defense *USE Self Defense*
Personal Growth Techniques *USE Human Potential Movement*
Personal Orientation Inventory
Personal Relationships *USE Interpersonal Relationships*
Personal Space
Personal Therapy
Personal Values
Edwards **Personal** Preference Schedule
Identity (Personal) *USE Self Concept*
Personality
Personality Assessment *USE Personality Measures*
Personality Change
Personality Correlates
Personality Development
Personality Disorders
Personality Factors (Psychoanalytic) *USE Psychoanalytic Personality Factors*
Personality Factors *USE Personality Traits*
Personality Measures
Personality Processes
Personality Tests *USE Personality Measures*
Personality Theory
Personality Traits
Adaptability **(Personality)**
Anankastic Personality *USE Obsessive Compulsive Personality Disorder*
Antisocial **Personality** Disorder
Asthenic Personality *USE Personality Disorders*
Autonomy (Personality) *USE Independence (Personality)*
Avoidant **Personality** Disorder
Big Five Personality Model *USE Five Factor Personality Model*
Borderline **Personality** Disorder
Compulsive Personality Disorder *USE Obsessive Compulsive Personality Disorder*
Conformity **(Personality)**

Phenothiazine Derivatives
Phenotypes
Phenoxybenzamine
Phenylalanine
Phenylethylamines *USE Phenethylamines*
Phenylketonuria
Oligophrenia (Phenylpyruvic) *USE Phenylketonuria*
Phenytoin *USE Diphenylhydantoin*
Pheromones
Phi Coefficient
Philanthropy *USE Charitable Behavior*
Philosophies
Philosophy of Life *USE World View*
Logic **(Philosophy)**
Ontology **(Philosophy)**
Positivism **(Philosophy)**
Realism **(Philosophy)**
School **Phobia**
Snake Phobia *USE Ophidiophobia*
Social **Phobia**
Spider Phobia *USE Phobias*
Phobias
Phobic Neurosis *USE Phobias*
Phonemes
Phonemic Awareness
USE Phonological Awareness
Words **(Phonetic** Units)
Phonetics
Phonics
Phonological Awareness
Phonology
Phosphatases
Phosphatides
Phospholipids *USE Phosphatides*
Phosphorus
Phosphorylases
Photic Threshold *USE Illumination*
Photic Threshold *USE Visual Thresholds*
Photographic Art
Photographic Memory *USE Eidetic Imagery*
Photographs
Photopic Stimulation
Photoreceptors
Phototherapy
Phrases
Phrenic Nerve *USE Spinal Nerves*
Phylogenesis
Physical Abuse
Physical Activity
Physical Agility
Physical Appearance
Physical Attractiveness
Physical Comfort
Physical Contact
Physical Development
Physical Dexterity
Physical Disabilities (Attitudes Toward)
Physical Disfigurement
Physical Disorders
Physical Divisions (Geographic)
USE Geography
Physical Education
Physical Endurance
Physical Examination
Physical Exercise *USE Exercise*
Physical Fitness
Physical Geography *USE Geography*
Physical Growth
USE Physical Development
Physical Handicaps (Attitudes Toward)
USE Physical Disabilities (Attitudes Toward)
Physical Health
Physical Illness (Attitudes Toward)
Physical Illness *USE Physical Disorders*
Physical Maturity
Physical Mobility
Physical Restraint
Physical Strength
Physical Therapists
Physical Therapy
Physical Trauma *USE Injuries*
Physical Treatment Methods
Agility (Physical) *USE Physical Agility*
Comfort (Physical) *USE Physical Comfort*
Dexterity (Physical) *USE Physical Dexterity*
Illness (Physical) *USE Physical Disorders*
Maturity (Physical) *USE Physical Maturity*
Restraint (Physical) *USE Physical Restraint*
Strength (Physical) *USE Physical Strength*
Trauma (Physical) *USE Injuries*
Treatment Methods (Physical) *USE Physical Treatment Methods*
Physically Handicapped
USE Physical Disorders
Physician Patient Interaction
USE Therapeutic Processes
Physicians
Family **Physicians**
Physicists
Physics
Physiological Aging
Physiological Arousal
Physiological Correlates
Physiological Psychology
Physiological Stress
Absorption **(Physiological)**
Aging (Physiological) *USE Physiological Aging*
Arousal (Physiological) *USE Physiological Arousal*
Excitation (Physiological) *USE Physiological Arousal*
Sexual Disorders (Physiological) *USE Genital Disorders*
Physiology
Physiotherapy *USE Physical Therapy*
Physique
Physostigmine
Piaget (Jean)
Piagetian Tasks
Piano *USE Musical Instruments*
Pica
Picketing *USE Social Demonstrations*
Picks Disease
Picrotoxin
Pictorial Stimuli
Peabody **Picture** Vocabulary Test
Rosenzweig **Picture** Frustration Study
Blacky Pictures Test
USE Projective Personality Measures
Motion Pictures *USE Films*
Piercings *USE Cosmetic Techniques*
Pigeons
Pigments
Pigs
Guinea **Pigs**
Pilocarpine
Pilots (Aircraft) *USE Aircraft Pilots*
Aircraft **Pilots**
Pimozide
Pineal Body
Pinealectomy
Piperazines
Pipradrol
Piracetam
Pitch (Frequency)
Pitch Discrimination
Pitch Perception
Frequency (Pitch) *USE Pitch (Frequency)*
Speech **Pitch**
Pituitary Disorders
Pituitary Dwarfism *USE Hypopituitarism*
Pituitary Gland
Pituitary Gland Surgery
USE Hypophysectomy
Pituitary Hormones
Dwarfism (Pituitary) *USE Hypopituitarism*
Hypothalamic **Pituitary** Adrenal Axis

ROTATED ALPHABETICAL TERMS SECTION

Hypothalamo Pituitary Adrenal System
USE Hypothalamic Pituitary Adrenal Axis
PKU (Hereditary Disorder)
USE Phenylketonuria
Place Conditioning
Place Disorientation
Aging in **Place**
Conditioned Place Preference *USE Place Conditioning*
Disorientation (Place) *USE Place Disorientation*
Placebo
Placement (Educational)
USE Educational Placement
Placement (Personnel)
USE Personnel Placement
Educational **Placement**
Personnel **Placement**
Placenta
Planarians
Planned Behavior
Planning (Management)
USE Management Planning
Disaster Planning *USE Emergency Preparedness*
Discharge **Planning**
Educational Program **Planning**
Environmental **Planning**
Family **Planning**
Family **Planning** Attitudes
Management **Planning**
Patient Care Planning *USE Treatment Planning*
Program Planning (Educational)
USE Educational Program Planning
Program Planning *USE Program Development*
Time Planning Style *USE Time Management*
Treatment **Planning**
Urban **Planning**
Employee Pension **Plans**
Group Health Plans
USE Health Maintenance Organizations
Individualized Educational Plans *USE Individual Education Programs*
Lesson **Plans**
Pension Plans (Employee)
USE Employee Pension Plans
Plants (Botanical)
Medicinal Herbs and **Plants**
Plasma (Blood) *USE Blood Plasma*
Plasma Donation *USE Tissue Donation*
Blood **Plasma**
Plastic Surgery
Nervous System Plasticity *USE Neural Plasticity*
Neural **Plasticity**
Synaptic Plasticity *USE Neural Plasticity*
Platelets (Blood) *USE Blood Platelets*
Blood **Platelets**
Play (Animal) *USE Animal Play*
Play *USE Recreation*
Play Behavior (Childhood)
USE Childhood Play Behavior
Play Development (Childhood)
USE Childhood Play Development
Play Therapy
Animal **Play**
Childhood **Play** Behavior
Childhood **Play** Development
Doll **Play**
Pretend **Play**
Playgrounds
Role **Playing**
Stage Plays *USE Theatre*
Pleasure
Plethysmography
Brachial Plexus *USE Spinal Nerves*
Celiac Plexus *USE Autonomic Ganglia*
Cervical Plexus *USE Spinal Nerves*
Choroid Plexus *USE Cerebral Ventricles*
Hypogastric Plexus *USE Autonomic Ganglia*
Lumbrosacral Plexus *USE Spinal Nerves*
Myenteric Plexus *USE Autonomic Ganglia*
Submucous Plexus *USE Autonomic Ganglia*
Cultural Pluralism *USE Multiculturalism*
PMS *USE Premenstrual Syndrome*
Pneumoencephalography
Pneumonia
Poetry
Poetry Therapy
Point Biserial Correlation
Poisoning *USE Toxic Disorders*
Barbiturate Poisoning *USE Toxic Disorders*
Carbon Monoxide **Poisoning**
Lead **Poisoning**
Mercury **Poisoning**
Poisons *USE Toxins*
Poisson Distribution
USE Skewed Distribution
Police Interrogation *USE Interrogation*
Police Personnel
Policy Making
Policy Making (Foreign)
USE Foreign Policy Making
Policy Making (Government)
USE Government Policy Making
Foreign **Policy** Making
Government **Policy** Making
Health Care **Policy**
Mental Health Care Policy *USE Health Care Policy*
Organizational Policy Making *USE Policy Making*
Public Policy *USE Government Policy Making*
Poliomyelitis
Political Assassination
Political Attitudes
Political Campaigns
Political Candidates
Political Conservatism
Political Debates *USE Debates*
Political Divisions (Geographic)
USE Geography
Political Economic Systems
Political Elections
Political Involvement
USE Political Participation
Political Issues
Political Liberalism
Political Participation
Political Parties
Political Processes
Political Psychology
Political Radicalism
Political Refugees *USE Refugees*
Political Revolution
Political Socialization
Assassination (Political) *USE Political Assassination*
Campaigns (Political) *USE Political Campaigns*
Candidates (Political) *USE Political Candidates*
Conservatism (Political) *USE Political Conservatism*
Elections (Political) *USE Political Elections*
Independent Party (Political) *USE Political Parties*
Liberalism (Political) *USE Political Liberalism*
Radicalism (Political) *USE Political Radicalism*
Revolutions (Political) *USE Political Revolution*
Politicians
Politics
Pollution
Polydipsia
Polydrug Abuse
Polygamy
Polygraphs
Polymorphism
Polyphagia *USE Hyperphagia*
Polypharmacy
Polysomnography
Pons
Data Pooling *USE Meta Analysis*
Popular Culture
Popularity
Population

ROTATED ALPHABETICAL TERMS SECTION

Population (Statistics)
Population Characteristics
USE Demographic Characteristics
Population Control *USE Birth Control*
Population Density *USE Social Density*
Population Genetics
Population Shifts *USE Human Migration*
Aboriginal Populations *USE Indigenous Populations*
At Risk **Populations**
High Risk Populations *USE At Risk Populations*
Indigenous **Populations**
Risk Populations *USE At Risk Populations*
Pornography
Porphyria
Porpoises
Porteus Maze Test
Serial **Position** Effect
Positive and Negative Symptoms
Positive Psychology
Positive Reinforcement
Positive Transfer
Negative and Positive Symptoms
USE Positive and Negative Symptoms
Positivism
Positivism (Philosophy)
Positron Emission Tomography
USE Tomography
Possession *USE Ownership*
Demonic Possession *USE Spirit Possession*
Spirit **Possession**
Postactivation Potentials
Postganglionic Autonomic Fibers
USE Autonomic Ganglia
Postgraduate Students
Postgraduate Training
Posthypnotic Suggestions
Postmodernism
Postnatal Depression
USE Postpartum Depression
Postnatal Dysphoria
USE Postpartum Depression
Postnatal Period
Postpartum Depression
Postpartum Psychosis
Postsurgical Complications
Posttesting
Posttraumatic Stress Disorder
Posttreatment Followup
Followup (Posttreatment)
USE Posttreatment Followup
Posture
Threat **Postures**
Potassium
Potassium Ions
Potential (Achievement)
USE Achievement Potential
Potential Dropouts
Abuse Potential (Drugs) *USE Drug Abuse Liability*
Achievement **Potential**
Human **Potential** Movement
Readiness Potential *USE Contingent Negative Variation*
Skin **Potential**
Auditory Evoked **Potentials**
Cortical Evoked Potentials *USE Evoked Potentials*
Event Related Potentials *USE Evoked Potentials*
Evoked **Potentials**
Motor Evoked Potentials
USE Somatosensory Evoked Potentials
Olfactory Evoked **Potentials**
Postactivation **Potentials**
Somatosensory Evoked **Potentials**
Visual Evoked **Potentials**
Potentiation (Drugs) *USE Drug Interactions*
Drug Potentiation *USE Drug Interactions*
Long Term Potentiation *USE Postactivation Potentials*
Short Term Potentiation *USE Postactivation Potentials*
Poverty
Poverty Areas
Power
Abuse of **Power**
Black **Power** Movement
Statistical **Power**
Practical Knowledge
USE Procedural Knowledge
Practice
Practice Effects *USE Practice*
Clinical **Practice**
Communities of **Practice**
Distributed **Practice**
Evidence Based **Practice**
Experience (Practice) *USE Practice*
Massed **Practice**
Private **Practice**
Childrearing **Practices**
Feeding Practices *USE Eating Behavior*
Religious **Practices**
Practicum Supervision
General **Practitioners**
Prader Willi Syndrome
Dementia Praecox *USE Schizophrenia*
Pragmatics
Pragmatism
Praise
Prayer
Praying Mantis *USE Mantis*
Precocious Development
Precognition
Preconditioning
Sensory Preconditioning *USE Preconditioning*
Serotonin **Precursors**
Predatory Behavior (Animal)
USE Animal Predatory Behavior
Animal **Predatory** Behavior
Predelinquent Youth
Predictability (Measurement)
Prediction
Prediction Errors
Academic Achievement **Prediction**
Occupational Success **Prediction**
Predictive Validity *USE Statistical Validity*
Predisposition
Prednisolone
Preference Measures
Career Preference *USE Occupational Preference*
Conditioned Place Preference *USE Place Conditioning*
Edwards Personal **Preference** Schedule
Kuder **Preference** Record
Occupational **Preference**
Vocational Preference *USE Occupational Preference*
Preferences
Aesthetic **Preferences**
Brand **Preferences**
Food **Preferences**
Preferred Rewards
Least **Preferred** Coworker Scale
Prefrontal Cortex
Preganglionic Autonomic Fibers
USE Autonomic Ganglia
Pregnancy
Pregnancy (False) *USE Pseudocyesis*
Adolescent **Pregnancy**
False Pregnancy *USE Pseudocyesis*
Teenage Pregnancy *USE Adolescent Pregnancy*
Prejudice
Religious **Prejudices**
Preliminary Scholastic Aptitude Test
USE College Entrance Examination Board Scholastic Aptitude Test
Premarital Counseling
Premarital Intercourse
Premature Birth
Premature Ejaculation
Premenstrual Dysphoric Disorder
Premenstrual Syndrome

Premenstrual Tension
USE Premenstrual Syndrome
Premorbidity
Prenatal Care
Prenatal Development
Prenatal Developmental Stages
Prenatal Diagnosis
Prenatal Exposure
Preoptic Area
Disaster Preparedness
USE Emergency Preparedness
Emergency **Preparedness**
Natural Disaster Preparedness
USE Emergency Preparedness
Prepulse Inhibition
Presbyterians *USE Protestants*
Preschool Education
Preschool Students
Preschool Teachers
Wechsler **Preschool** Primary Scale
Prescribing (Drugs)
Prescription Drugs
Prescription Privileges
Symptom Prescription *USE Paradoxical Techniques*
Presenile Dementia
Dementia (Presenile) *USE Presenile Dementia*
Stereoscopic **Presentation**
Stimulus **Presentation** Methods
Tachistoscopic **Presentation**
Family **Preservation**
Self **Preservation**
Preservice Teachers
Presidential Debates *USE Debates*
Pressoreceptors *USE Baroreceptors*
Pressors (Drugs)
USE Vasoconstrictor Drugs
Pressure Sensation
Barometric Pressure *USE Atmospheric Conditions*
Blood **Pressure**
Blood **Pressure** Disorders
Diastolic **Pressure**
Peer **Pressure**
Sound Pressure Level *USE Loudness*
Systolic **Pressure**
Prestige (Occupational)
USE Occupational Status
Pretend Play
Pretesting
Pretraining (Therapy) *USE Client Education*
Prevention
Accident **Prevention**
AIDS **Prevention**
Crime **Prevention**
Drug Abuse **Prevention**
Fire **Prevention**
Primary Mental Health **Prevention**
Relapse **Prevention**
Substance Abuse Prevention *USE Drug Abuse Prevention*
Suicide **Prevention**
Suicide **Prevention** Centers
Preventive Medicine
Price *USE Costs and Cost Analysis*
Pride
Priests
Primacy Effect
Primal Therapy
Primary Health Care
Primary Mental Health Prevention
Primary Reinforcement
Primary School Students
Primary Schools *USE Elementary Schools*
Wechsler Preschool **Primary** Scale
Primates (Nonhuman)
Primidone
Priming
Semantic **Priming**
Primipara

School **Principals**
Printed Communications Media
Printing (Handwriting)
Prismatic Stimulation
Prison Personnel
Prison Record *USE Criminal Record*
Inmates (Prison) *USE Prisoners*
Prisoner Abuse
Prisoners
Prisoners Dilemma Game
Prisoners of War
Prisons
Privacy
Private Practice
Private School Education
Private Sector
Privileged Communication
Communication (Privileged) *USE Privileged Communication*
Prescription **Privileges**
Proactive Inhibition
Inhibition (Proactive) *USE Proactive Inhibition*
Probability
Probability Judgment
Probability Learning
Response **Probability**
Statistical **Probability**
Probation
Probation Officers
Probenecid
Problem Drinking *USE Alcohol Abuse*
Problem Solving
Anagram **Problem** Solving
Group **Problem** Solving
Individual Problem Solving *USE Problem Solving*
Mooney **Problem** Check List
Behavior **Problems**
Financial Problems *USE Financial Strain*
Social Problems *USE Social Issues*
Procaine
Procedural Justice
Procedural Knowledge
Dual Task Procedure *USE Dual Task Performance*
Process Psychosis
USE Process Schizophrenia
Process Schizophrenia
Accommodation (Cognitive **Process)**
Assimilation (Cognitive **Process)**
Classification (Cognitive **Process)**
Educational Process *USE Education*
Insight (Psychotherapeutic **Process)**
Rumination (Cognitive **Process)**
Associative **Processes**
Balance (Motor Processes) *USE Equilibrium*
Cognitive **Processes**
Employment Processes *USE Personnel Recruitment*
Human Information Processes *USE Cognitive Processes*
Information Processes (Human)
USE Cognitive Processes
Intersensory **Processes**
Legal **Processes**
Legislative **Processes**
Motor **Processes**
Perceptual Motor **Processes**
Personality **Processes**
Political **Processes**
Psychomotor Processes *USE Perceptual Motor Processes*
Psychotherapeutic **Processes**
Sensorimotor Processes *USE Perceptual Motor Processes*
Social **Processes**
Therapeutic **Processes**
Automated Information **Processing**
Cognitive **Processing** Speed
Data **Processing**
Information Processing (Automated)
USE Automated Information Processing
Information **Processing** Model

Information Processing Speed
USE Cognitive Processing Speed
Speech **Processing** (Mechanical)
Word **Processing**
Prochlorperazine
Procrastination
Prodrome
Product Design
Consumer Product Design *USE Product Design*
Pearson Product Moment Correlation Coefficient
USE Statistical Correlation
Productivity
Productivity (Employee)
USE Employee Productivity
Employee **Productivity**
Profanity
Professional Certification
Professional Client Sexual Relations
Professional Communication
USE Scientific Communication
Professional Competence
Professional Consultation
Professional Development
Professional Ethics
Professional Examinations
Professional Fees
Professional Identity
Professional Liability
Professional Licensing
Professional Networking
Professional Newsletters
USE Scientific Communication
Professional Organizations
Professional Orientation
USE Theoretical Orientation
Professional Personnel
Professional Recognition
Professional Referral
Professional Specialization
Professional Standards
Professional Supervision
Assistance Seeking (Professional) *USE Health Care Utilization*
Certification (Professional)
USE Professional Certification
Communication (Professional)
USE Scientific Communication
Consultation (Professional)
USE Professional Consultation
Identity (Professional) *USE Professional Identity*
Legal Liability (Professional) *USE Professional Liability*
Licensing (Professional) *USE Professional Licensing*
Newsletters (Professional)
USE Scientific Communication
Referral (Professional) *USE Professional Referral*
Specialization (Professional)
USE Professional Specialization
Standards (Professional) *USE Professional Standards*
Supervision (Professional) *USE Professional Supervision*
Professionalism
Health Care Professionals *USE Health Personnel*
Impaired **Professionals**
Professors *USE College Teachers*
Language **Proficiency**
Limited English Proficiency *USE Language Proficiency*
Profiles (Measurement)
Criminal **Profiling**
Offender Profiling *USE Criminal Profiling*
Profound Mental Retardation
Progestational Hormones
Progesterone
Progestins *USE Progestational Hormones*
Prognosis
Program Development
Program Evaluation
Program Evaluation (Educational)
USE Educational Program Evaluation
Program Evaluation (Mental Health)
USE Mental Health Program Evaluation
Program Planning (Educational)
USE Educational Program Planning
Program Planning
USE Program Development
Educational **Program** Accreditation
Educational **Program** Evaluation
Educational **Program** Planning
Mental Health **Program** Evaluation
Programmed Instruction
Programmed Textbooks
Instruction (Programmed) *USE Programmed Instruction*
Programming (Computer)
USE Computer Programming
Programming Languages (Computer)
USE Computer Programming Languages
Computer **Programming**
Computer **Programming** Languages
Inductive Logic **Programming**
Neurolinguistic **Programming**
Programs (Government)
USE Government Programs
Programs (Mental Health)
USE Mental Health Programs
Accreditation (Educational Programs)
USE Educational Program Accreditation
After School **Programs**
Computer Programs *USE Computer Software*
Educational **Programs**
Employee Assistance **Programs**
Government **Programs**
Home Visiting **Programs**
Hospital **Programs**
Immersion Programs *USE Foreign Language Education*
Independent Living **Programs**
Individual Education **Programs**
Internship **Programs**
Literacy **Programs**
Mental Health **Programs**
Needle Exchange **Programs**
Outreach **Programs**
Psychiatric Hospital **Programs**
Social **Programs**
Token Economy **Programs**
Twelve Step **Programs**
Work Study Programs *USE Educational Programs*
Progressive Relaxation Therapy
Progressive Supranuclear Palsy
Raven Coloured **Progressive** Matrices
Raven **Progressive** Matrices
Project Follow Through
Project Head Start
Projection (Defense Mechanism)
Projective Identification
Projective Personality Measures
Projective Techniques
Projective Testing Technique
Projective Tests *USE Projective Techniques*
Prolactin
Proline
Prolixin *USE Fluphenazine*
Promazine
Promethazine
Promiscuity
Health **Promotion**
Job Promotion *USE Personnel Promotion*
Personnel **Promotion**
Prompting
Coronary **Prone** Behavior
Accident **Proneness**
Pronouns
Pronunciation
Proofreading
Propaganda
Propanolol *USE Propranolol*
Skin Electrical **Properties**

	Property *USE Ownership*
Self Fulfilling	**Prophecies**
	Propranolol
	Proprioceptors
	Prose
	Prosencephalon *USE Forebrain*
	Proserine *USE Neostigmine*
	Prosocial Behavior
	Prosody
	Prosopagnosia
	Prospective Studies
	Prostaglandins
	Prostate
	Prostate Cancer Screening *USE Cancer Screening*
	Prostheses
	Prostitution
Consumer	**Protection**
	Protective Factors
	Protective Services
	Protein Deficiency Disorders
	Protein Metabolism
	Protein Sensitization *USE Anaphylactic Shock*
Sensitization	(Protein) *USE Anaphylactic Shock*
	Proteinases
	Proteins
Blood	**Proteins**
	Protest (Student) *USE Student Activism*
Student	Protest *USE Student Activism*
	Protestantism
	Protestants
	Protozoa
Munchausen Syndrome by	**Proxy**
	Prozac *USE Fluoxetine*
	Pruritus
	Pseudocyesis
	Pseudodementia
	Pseudohermaphroditism *USE Hermaphroditism*
	Pseudomemory *USE False Memory*
	Pseudopregnancy *USE Pseudocyesis*
	Pseudopsychopathic Schizophrenia *USE Schizophrenia*
	Psilocybin
	Psyche *USE Mind*
	Psychedelic Drugs *USE Hallucinogenic Drugs*
	Psychedelic Experiences
	Psychiatric Aides
	Psychiatric Classifications (Taxonomies) *USE Psychodiagnostic Typologies*
	Psychiatric Clinics
	Psychiatric Disorders *USE Mental Disorders*
	Psychiatric Evaluation
	Psychiatric History *USE Patient History*
	Psychiatric Hospital Admission
	Psychiatric Hospital Discharge
	Psychiatric Hospital Programs
	Psychiatric Hospital Readmission
	Psychiatric Hospital Staff
	Psychiatric Hospitalization
	Psychiatric Hospitals
	Psychiatric Nurses
	Psychiatric Patients
	Psychiatric Report *USE Psychological Report*
	Psychiatric Residency *USE Medical Residency*
	Psychiatric Residency *USE Psychiatric Training*
	Psychiatric Social Workers
	Psychiatric Symptoms
	Psychiatric Training
	Psychiatric Units
Admission	(Psychiatric Hospital) *USE Psychiatric Hospital Admission*
Child	Psychiatric Clinics *USE Child Guidance Clinics*
Commitment	**(Psychiatric)**
Evaluation	(Psychiatric) *USE Psychiatric Evaluation*
Hospital	Psychiatric Units *USE Psychiatric Units*
Outpatient	Psychiatric Clinics *USE Psychiatric Clinics*
Readmission	(Psychiatric Hospital) *USE Psychiatric Hospital Readmission*
Training	(Psychiatric) *USE Psychiatric Training*
	Psychiatrists
	Psychiatry
Adolescent	**Psychiatry**
Biological	**Psychiatry**
Child	**Psychiatry**
Community	**Psychiatry**
Comparative	Psychiatry *USE Transcultural Psychiatry*
Consultation Liaison	**Psychiatry**
Cultural	Psychiatry *USE Transcultural Psychiatry*
Forensic	**Psychiatry**
Geriatric	**Psychiatry**
Social	**Psychiatry**
Transcultural	**Psychiatry**
	Psychic Healing *USE Faith Healing*
	Psychoactive Drugs *USE Drugs*
	Psychoanalysis
	Psychoanalysts
	Psychoanalytic Interpretation
	Psychoanalytic Personality Factors
	Psychoanalytic School (Freudian) *USE Freudian Psychoanalytic School*
	Psychoanalytic Theory
	Psychoanalytic Therapy *USE Psychoanalysis*
	Psychoanalytic Training
Fixation	**(Psychoanalytic)**
Freudian	**Psychoanalytic** School
Personality Factors	(Psychoanalytic) *USE Psychoanalytic Personality Factors*
Training	(Psychoanalytic) *USE Psychoanalytic Training*
	Psychoanalytically Oriented Psychotherapy *USE Psychodynamic Psychotherapy*
	Psychobiology
	Psychodiagnosis
Clinical Judgment	(Psychodiagnosis) *USE Psychodiagnosis*
	Psychodiagnostic Interview
	Psychodiagnostic Typologies
Typologies	(Psychodiagnostic) *USE Psychodiagnostic Typologies*
	Psychodrama
	Psychodynamic Psychotherapy
	Psychodynamics
	Psychoeducation
Woodcock Johnson	**Psychoeducational** Battery
	Psychogalvanic Reflex *USE Galvanic Skin Response*
	Psychogenesis
	Psychogenic Pain *USE Somatoform Pain Disorder*
Pain	(Psychogenic) *USE Somatoform Pain Disorder*
	Psychohistory
	Psychoimmunology *USE Psychoneuroimmunology*
	Psychokinesis
Illinois Test of	**Psycholinguistic** Abilities
	Psycholinguistics
	Psychological Abuse *USE Emotional Abuse*
	Psychological Adjustment *USE Emotional Adjustment*
	Psychological Assessment
	Psychological Autopsy
	Psychological Contracts
	Psychological Correlates *USE Psychodynamics*

Psychological Debriefing
USE Debriefing (Psychological)
Psychological Development
USE Psychogenesis
Psychological Endurance
Psychological Interpretation
USE Theoretical Interpretation
Psychological Needs
Psychological Reactance
Psychological Report
Psychological Screening Inventory
Psychological Stress
Psychological Terminology
Psychological Testing *USE Psychometrics*
Psychological Theories
American **Psychological** Association
American **Psychological** Association Divisions
Assessment (Psychological)
USE Psychological Assessment
Boundaries **(Psychological)**
California **Psychological** Inventory
Contracts (Psychological)
USE Psychological Contracts
Debriefing **(Psychological)**
Fixation **(Psychological)**
Incorporation (Psychological) *USE Internalization*
Nomenclature (Psychological)
USE Psychological Terminology
Resilience **(Psychological)**
Terminology (Psychological)
USE Psychological Terminology
Psychologist Attitudes
Psychologists
Clinical **Psychologists**
Counseling **Psychologists**
Educational **Psychologists**
Experimental **Psychologists**
Industrial **Psychologists**
Military **Psychologists**
School **Psychologists**
Social **Psychologists**
Psychology
Psychology Education
Psychology of Women
Abnormal **Psychology**
Adolescent **Psychology**
Analytic Psychology *USE Jungian Psychology*
Applied **Psychology**
Child **Psychology**
Clinical **Psychology**
Clinical **Psychology** Graduate Training
Clinical **Psychology** Internship
Cognitive **Psychology**
Community **Psychology**
Comparative **Psychology**
Consumer **Psychology**
Counseling **Psychology**
Cross Cultural **Psychology**
Depth **Psychology**
Developmental **Psychology**
Eclectic Psychology *USE Theoretical Orientation*
Ecological **Psychology**
Educational **Psychology**
Engineering **Psychology**
Environmental **Psychology**
Evolutionary **Psychology**
Experimental **Psychology**
Feminist **Psychology**
Folk **Psychology**
Forensic **Psychology**
Geriatric Psychology *USE Geropsychology*
Gestalt **Psychology**
Graduate **Psychology** Education
Health Care **Psychology**
Health Psychology *USE Health Care Psychology*
History of **Psychology**
Humanistic **Psychology**
Individual **Psychology**
Industrial and Organizational **Psychology**
Industrial Psychology
USE Industrial and Organizational Psychology
Jungian **Psychology**
Legal Psychology *USE Forensic Psychology*
Mathematical **Psychology**
Medical **Psychology**
Military **Psychology**
Organizational Psychology
USE Industrial and Organizational Psychology
Physiological **Psychology**
Political **Psychology**
Positive **Psychology**
School **Psychology**
Self **Psychology**
Social **Psychology**
Sport **Psychology**
Training (Clinical Psychology Graduate)
USE Clinical Psychology Graduate Training
Training (Graduate Psychology)
USE Graduate Psychology Education
Transpersonal **Psychology**
Women Centered Psychology *USE Psychology of Women*
Psychometrics
Psychomotor Development
Psychomotor Processes
USE Perceptual Motor Processes
Psychoneuroendocrinology
Psychoneuroimmunology
Psychoneurosis *USE Neurosis*
Psychopath
USE Antisocial Personality Disorder
Psychopathology
Adolescent **Psychopathology**
Child **Psychopathology**
Psychopathy
Autistic Psychopathy *USE Aspergers Syndrome*
Psychopharmacology
Psychophysical Measurement
Psychophysics
Psychophysiologic Disorders
USE Somatoform Disorders
Psychophysiology
Toxic **Psychoses**
Psychosexual Behavior
Psychosexual Development
Psychosis
Acute **Psychosis**
Affective **Psychosis**
Alcoholic **Psychosis**
Brief Reactive Psychosis *USE Acute Psychosis*
Childhood **Psychosis**
Chronic **Psychosis**
Experimental **Psychosis**
Infantile Psychosis *USE Childhood Psychosis*
Korsakoffs **Psychosis**
Manic Depressive Psychosis *USE Bipolar Disorder*
Paranoia **(Psychosis)**
Postpartum **Psychosis**
Process Psychosis *USE Process Schizophrenia*
Puerperal Psychosis *USE Postpartum Psychosis*
Reactive **Psychosis**
Senile **Psychosis**
Symbiotic Infantile **Psychosis**
Traumatic Psychosis *USE Reactive Psychosis*
Psychosocial Development
Psychosocial Factors
Psychosocial Mental Retardation
Psychosocial Readjustment
Psychosocial Rehabilitation
Psychosocial Resocialization
USE Psychosocial Readjustment

Readjustment (Psychosocial)
USE Psychosocial Readjustment
Rehabilitation (Psychosocial)
USE Psychosocial Rehabilitation
Resocialization (Psychosocial)
USE Psychosocial Readjustment
Psychosomatic Disorders
USE Somatoform Disorders
Psychosomatic Medicine
Psychostimulant Drugs
USE CNS Stimulating Drugs
Psychosurgery
Psychotherapeutic Breakthrough
Psychotherapeutic Counseling
Psychotherapeutic Methods
USE Psychotherapeutic Techniques
Psychotherapeutic Neutrality
Psychotherapeutic Outcomes
Psychotherapeutic Processes
Psychotherapeutic Resistance
Psychotherapeutic Techniques
Psychotherapeutic Transference
Breakthrough (Psychotherapeutic)
USE Psychotherapeutic Breakthrough
Insight **(Psychotherapeutic** Process)
Neutrality (Psychotherapeutic)
USE Psychotherapeutic Neutrality
Outcomes (Psychotherapeutic)
USE Psychotherapeutic Outcomes
Resistance (Psychotherapeutic)
USE Psychotherapeutic Resistance
Transference (Psychotherapeutic)
USE Psychotherapeutic Transference
Psychotherapist Attitudes
Psychotherapist Trainees
USE Therapist Trainees
Psychotherapists
Psychotherapy
Psychotherapy (Individual)
USE Individual Psychotherapy
Psychotherapy Training
Adlerian **Psychotherapy**
Adolescent **Psychotherapy**
Analytical **Psychotherapy**
Brief **Psychotherapy**
Child **Psychotherapy**
Eclectic **Psychotherapy**
Experiential **Psychotherapy**
Expressive **Psychotherapy**
Geriatric **Psychotherapy**
Group **Psychotherapy**
Humanistic **Psychotherapy**
Individual **Psychotherapy**
Individual Psychotherapy (Adlerian)
USE Adlerian Psychotherapy
Integrative **Psychotherapy**
Interpersonal **Psychotherapy**
Jungian Psychotherapy
USE Analytical Psychotherapy
Person Centered Psychotherapy
USE Client Centered Therapy
Psychoanalytically Oriented Psychotherapy
USE Psychodynamic Psychotherapy
Psychodynamic **Psychotherapy**
Reconstructive Psychotherapy *USE Psychotherapy*
Short Term Psychotherapy *USE Brief Psychotherapy*
Supportive **Psychotherapy**
Therapeutic Techniques (Psychotherapy)
USE Psychotherapeutic Techniques
Time Limited Psychotherapy *USE Brief Psychotherapy*
Training (Psychotherapy)
USE Psychotherapy Training
Psychotic Depressive Reaction
USE Major Depression
Psychotic Episode (Acute)
USE Acute Psychosis
Psychotic Symptoms
USE Psychiatric Symptoms
Acute Psychotic Episode *USE Acute Psychosis*
Psychoticism
Psychotomimetic Drugs
Psychotropic Drugs *USE Drugs*
PTA *USE Parent School Relationship*
PTSD *USE Posttraumatic Stress Disorder*
Puberty
Pubescence *USE Sexual Development*
Public Attitudes *USE Public Opinion*
Public Health
Public Health Service Nurses
Public Health Services
Public Opinion
Public Policy
USE Government Policy Making
Public Relations
Public School Education
Public Sector
Public Service Announcements
Public Speaking
Public Transportation
Public Welfare Services
USE Community Welfare Services
Certified Public Accountants *USE Accountants*
Fear of Public Speaking *USE Speech Anxiety*
Opinion (Public) *USE Public Opinion*
Puerperal Depression
USE Postpartum Depression
Puerperal Psychosis
USE Postpartum Psychosis
Puerto Rican Americans *USE Hispanics*
Hair Pulling *USE Trichotillomania*
Pulmonary Disorders *USE Lung Disorders*
Pulmonary Emphysema
Pulmonary Tuberculosis
Emphysema (Pulmonary) *USE Pulmonary Emphysema*
Pulse (Arterial) *USE Arterial Pulse*
Arterial **Pulse**
Punishment
Punishment (Capital)
USE Capital Punishment
Capital **Punishment**
Corporal Punishment *USE Punishment*
Pupil (Eye)
Pupil Dilation
Dilation (Pupil) *USE Pupil Dilation*
Purging (Eating Disorders)
Purkinje Cells
Puromycin
Rotary **Pursuit**
Putamen
Pygmalion Effect
USE Self Fulfilling Prophecies
Pygmy Chimpanzees *USE Bonobos*
Color Pyramid Test
USE Projective Personality Measures
Pyramidal Tracts
Pyromania
Q Sort Testing Technique
Cochran Q Test *USE Nonparametric Statistical Tests*
Quaalude *USE Methaqualone*
Quadriplegia
Quails
Qualitative Methods
USE Qualitative Research
Qualitative Research
Leadership **Qualities**
Quality Circles
USE Participative Management
Quality Control
Quality of Care
Quality of Education
USE Educational Quality
Quality of Life
Quality of Services

Quality of Work Life
Educational **Quality**
Relationship **Quality**
Service Quality *USE Quality of Services*
Quantitative Methods
Quantitative Research *USE Quantitative Methods*
Quantitative Trait Loci
Quasi Experimental Methods
Fundamental Interpersonal Relation Orientation Behavior **Ques**
Questioning
General Health **Questionnaire**
High School Personality **Questionnaire**
Sixteen Personality Factors **Questionnaire**
Questionnaires
Opinion Questionnaires *USE Attitude Measures*
Quetiapine
Quinidine *USE Alkaloids*
Quinine
Quinpirole
Intelligence **Quotient**
Rabbis
Rabbits
Race (Anthropological)
Race and Ethnic Discrimination
Race Attitudes *USE Racial and Ethnic Attitudes*
Race Relations *USE Racial and Ethnic Relations*
Racial and Ethnic Attitudes
Racial and Ethnic Differences
Racial and Ethnic Groups
Racial and Ethnic Relations
Racial Differences *USE Racial and Ethnic Differences*
Racial Discrimination *USE Race and Ethnic Discrimination*
Racial Integration *USE Social Integration*
Racial Segregation (Schools) *USE School Integration*
Integration (Racial) *USE Social Integration*
School Integration (Racial) *USE School Integration*
Segregation (Racial) *USE Social Integration*
Racism
Radial Nerve *USE Spinal Nerves*
Radiation
Radiation Therapy
Radical Movements
Radicalism (Political) *USE Political Radicalism*
Political **Radicalism**
Radio
Radiography *USE Roentgenography*
Radiology
Rage *USE Anger*
Road Rage *USE Aggressive Driving Behavior*
Railroad Trains
Trains (Railroad) *USE Railroad Trains*
Consciousness **Raising** Groups
Random Sampling
Range of Motion
Wide **Range** Achievement Test
Rank Difference Correlation
Rank Order Correlation
Sign Rank Test *USE Wilcoxon Sign Rank Test*
Wilcoxon Sign **Rank** Test
Rape
Acquaintance **Rape**
Date Rape *USE Acquaintance Rape*
Raphe Nuclei
Rapid Eye Movement
Rapid Eye Movement Dreams *USE REM Dreams*
Rapid Eye Movement Sleep *USE REM Sleep*
Rapid Heart Rate *USE Tachycardia*
Rapport *USE Interpersonal Interaction*
Rasch Model *USE Item Response Theory*
Rat Learning
Birth **Rate**
Cardiac Rate *USE Heart Rate*
Death Rate *USE Mortality Rate*
Heart **Rate**
Heart **Rate** Affecting Drugs
Learning **Rate**
Mortality **Rate**
Rapid Heart Rate *USE Tachycardia*
Response Rate *USE Response Frequency*
Speech **Rate**
X Rated Materials *USE Pornography*
Metabolic **Rates**
Rating
Rating Scales
Kupfer Detre Self Rating Scale *USE Nonprojective Personality Measures*
Zungs Self **Rating** Depression Scale
Ratio Reinforcement *USE Fixed Ratio Reinforcement*
Ratio Reinforcement *USE Variable Ratio Reinforcement*
Fixed **Ratio** Reinforcement
Variable **Ratio** Reinforcement
Ratiocination *USE Logical Thinking*
Rational Emotive Behavior Therapy
Rational Emotive Therapy *USE Rational Emotive Behavior Therapy*
Rational Thinking *USE Rationality*
Rationality
Rationalization (Defense Mechanism)
Rats
Albino Rats *USE Rats*
Norway **Rats**
White Rats *USE Rats*
Rauwolfia *USE Alkaloids*
Raven Coloured Progressive Matrices
Raven Progressive Matrices
Cathode Ray Tubes *USE Video Display Units*
X Ray Diagnosis *USE Roentgenography*
X Ray Therapy *USE Radiation Therapy*
Raynauds Disease *USE Cardiovascular Disorders*
RDC *USE Research Diagnostic Criteria*
Reactance *USE Psychological Reactance*
Psychological **Reactance**
Reaction Formation
Reaction Time
Depressive Reaction (Neurotic) *USE Major Depression*
Fugue **Reaction**
Negative Therapeutic **Reaction**
Neurotic Depressive Reaction *USE Major Depression*
Psychotic Depressive Reaction *USE Major Depression*
Anniversary Reactions *USE Anniversary Events*
Crisis (Reactions to) *USE Stress Reactions*
Drug Adverse Reactions *USE Side Effects (Drug)*
Separation **Reactions**
Stranger **Reactions**
Stress **Reactions**
Reactive Attachment Disorder *USE Attachment Disorders*
Reactive Depression
Reactive Psychosis
Reactive Schizophrenia *USE Reactive Psychosis*
Reactive Schizophrenia *USE Schizophrenia*
Brief Reactive Psychosis *USE Acute Psychosis*
Cardiovascular **Reactivity**
Readability
Readaptation *USE Adaptation*
Basal Readers *USE Reading Materials*
Readiness Potential *USE Contingent Negative Variation*
Readiness to Change
Change Readiness *USE Readiness to Change*

Metropolitan **Readiness** Tests
Reading **Readiness**
School **Readiness**
Reading
Reading Ability
Reading Achievement
Reading Aloud *USE Oral Reading*
Reading Comprehension
Reading Development
Reading Disabilities
Reading Education
Reading Materials
Reading Measures
Reading Readiness
Reading Skills
Reading Speed
Oral **Reading**
Remedial **Reading**
Silent **Reading**
Readjustment (Psychosocial) *USE Psychosocial Readjustment*
Psychosocial **Readjustment**
Readmission (Hospital) *USE Hospital Admission*
Readmission (Psychiatric Hospital) *USE Psychiatric Hospital Readmission*
Facility Readmission *USE Facility Admission*
Psychiatric Hospital **Readmission**
Realism (Philosophy)
Reality
Reality Testing
Reality Therapy
Virtual **Reality**
Self Realization *USE Self Actualization*
Home **Reared** Mentally Retarded
Animal **Rearing**
Reasoning
Case Based **Reasoning**
Deductive Reasoning *USE Inductive Deductive Reasoning*
Inductive Deductive **Reasoning**
Syllogistic Reasoning *USE Inductive Deductive Reasoning*
Sexual Reassignment *USE Sex Change*
Authoritarianism Rebellion Scale *USE Nonprojective Personality Measures*
Rebelliousness
Recall (Learning)
Cued **Recall**
Dream **Recall**
Free **Recall**
Serial **Recall**
Recency Effect
Receptive Fields
Cutaneous **Receptive** Fields
Visual **Receptive** Fields
Animal Sexual **Receptivity**
Sexual Receptivity (Animal) *USE Animal Sexual Receptivity*
Receptor Binding
Receptors (Adrenergic) *USE Adrenergic Receptors*
Receptors (Cholinergic) *USE Cholinergic Receptors*
Receptors (Neural) *USE Neural Receptors*
Acetylcholine Receptors *USE Cholinergic Receptors*
Adrenaline Receptors *USE Adrenergic Receptors*
Adrenergic **Receptors**
Cholinergic **Receptors**
Glutamate **Receptors**
Muscarinic Receptors *USE Cholinergic Receptors*
Neural **Receptors**
Nicotinic Receptors *USE Cholinergic Receptors*
Pain Receptors *USE Nociceptors*
Recessiveness (Genetic) *USE Genetic Recessiveness*
Genetic **Recessiveness**

Recidivism
Reciprocal Inhibition Therapy
Reciprocity
Recognition (Learning)
Automated Speech **Recognition**
Automatic Speaker Recognition *USE Automated Speech Recognition*
Employee Recognition *USE Professional Recognition*
Face Recognition *USE Face Perception*
Kinship **Recognition**
Object **Recognition**
Professional **Recognition**
Sex **Recognition**
Species **Recognition**
Word **Recognition**
Reconstruction (Learning)
Reconstructive Psychotherapy *USE Psychotherapy*
Criminal **Record**
Graduate **Record** Examination
Kuder Preference **Record**
Prison Record *USE Criminal Record*
Recorders (Tape) *USE Tape Recorders*
Tape **Recorders**
Videotape **Recorders**
Academic Records *USE Student Records*
Client **Records**
Medical **Records**
Patient Records *USE Client Records*
Student **Records**
Recovery (Disorders)
Spontaneous **Recovery** (Learning)
Recreation
Recreation Areas
Recreation Therapy
Day Camps (Recreation) *USE Summer Camps (Recreation)*
Summer Camps **(Recreation)**
Recreational Day Camps *USE Summer Camps (Recreation)*
Childrens **Recreational** Games
Parks (Recreational) *USE Recreation Areas*
Recruitment (Military) *USE Military Recruitment*
Recruitment (Personnel) *USE Personnel Recruitment*
Recruitment (Teachers) *USE Teacher Recruitment*
Military **Recruitment**
Personnel **Recruitment**
Teacher **Recruitment**
Recurrence (Disorders) *USE Relapse (Disorders)*
Recurrent Depression
Recycling *USE Conservation (Ecological Behavior)*
Red Blood Cells *USE Erythrocytes*
Red Nucleus *USE Mesencephalon*
Anxiety Reducing Drugs *USE Tranquilizing Drugs*
Harm **Reduction**
Reductionism
Reemployment
Reenactments *USE Enactments*
Reentry Students
Job Reentry *USE Reemployment*
Reference Groups
Self **Reference**
Criterion **Referenced** Tests
Objective Referenced Tests *USE Criterion Referenced Tests*
Referral (Professional) *USE Professional Referral*
Referral (Self) *USE Self Referral*
Professional **Referral**
Self **Referral**
Court **Referrals**
Reflectiveness

Achilles Tendon **Reflex**
Acoustic **Reflex**
Babinski **Reflex**
Blink Reflex *USE Eyeblink Reflex*
Conditioned Reflex *USE Conditioned Responses*
Eyeblink **Reflex**
Flexion **Reflex**
Hoffmanns **Reflex**
Intra Aural Muscle Reflex *USE Acoustic Reflex*
Orienting **Reflex**
Psychogalvanic Reflex *USE Galvanic Skin Response*
Stapedius Reflex *USE Acoustic Reflex*
Startle **Reflex**
Unconditioned Reflex *USE Reflexes*
Reflexes
Educational **Reform**
Health Care **Reform**
Welfare **Reform**
Reformatories
Refraction Errors
Light **Refraction**
Reframing *USE Paradoxical Techniques*
Refugees
Political Refugees *USE Refugees*
Refusal (Treatment) *USE Treatment Refusal*
School **Refusal**
Treatment **Refusal**
Neural Regeneration *USE Neural Development*
Medical Regimen Compliance
USE Treatment Compliance
Regional Differences
Geographic Regions *USE Geography*
Regression (Defense Mechanism)
Regression Analysis
USE Statistical Regression
Regression Artifact
USE Statistical Regression
Age **Regression** (Hypnotic)
Linear **Regression**
Logistic **Regression**
Multiple **Regression**
Nonlinear **Regression**
Statistical **Regression**
Self **Regulated** Learning
Affect Regulation *USE Emotional Regulation*
Emotional **Regulation**
Self **Regulation**
Regurgitation *USE Vomiting*
Rehabilitation
Rehabilitation (Drug)
USE Drug Rehabilitation
Rehabilitation (Psychosocial)
USE Psychosocial Rehabilitation
Rehabilitation (Vocational)
USE Vocational Rehabilitation
Rehabilitation Centers
Rehabilitation Counseling
Rehabilitation Counselors
Rehabilitation Education
Alcohol **Rehabilitation**
Cognitive **Rehabilitation**
Criminal **Rehabilitation**
Drug **Rehabilitation**
Neuropsychological **Rehabilitation**
Psychosocial **Rehabilitation**
Vocational **Rehabilitation**
Rehearsal *USE Practice*
Reinforcement
Reinforcement (Vicarious)
USE Vicarious Experiences
Reinforcement Amounts
Reinforcement Delay
Reinforcement Schedules
Concurrent **Reinforcement** Schedules
Continuous Reinforcement
USE Reinforcement Schedules
Delayed Reinforcement *USE Reinforcement Delay*
Differential **Reinforcement**
Fixed Interval **Reinforcement**
Fixed Ratio **Reinforcement**
Intermittent Reinforcement
USE Reinforcement Schedules
Interval Reinforcement
USE Fixed Interval Reinforcement
Interval Reinforcement
USE Variable Interval Reinforcement
Negative **Reinforcement**
Noncontingent **Reinforcement**
Nonverbal **Reinforcement**
Partial Reinforcement
USE Reinforcement Schedules
Positive **Reinforcement**
Primary **Reinforcement**
Ratio Reinforcement
USE Fixed Ratio Reinforcement
Ratio Reinforcement
USE Variable Ratio Reinforcement
Schedules (Reinforcement)
USE Reinforcement Schedules
Secondary **Reinforcement**
Self **Reinforcement**
Social **Reinforcement**
Token Reinforcement
USE Secondary Reinforcement
Variable Interval **Reinforcement**
Variable Ratio **Reinforcement**
Verbal **Reinforcement**
Vicarious Reinforcement *USE Vicarious Experiences*
Reinnervation *USE Neural Development*
Halstead **Reitan** Neuropsychological Battery
Rejection (Social) *USE Social Acceptance*
Social Rejection *USE Social Acceptance*
Relapse (Disorders)
Relapse Prevention
Criterion Related Validity *USE Test Validity*
Diagnosis **Related** Groups
Event Related Potentials *USE Evoked Potentials*
Work **Related** Illnesses
Fundamental Interpersonal **Relation** Orientation Behavior Ques
Family **Relations**
Father Child **Relations**
Human **Relations** Training
Intergenerational **Relations**
International **Relations**
Labor Management **Relations**
Labor Relations
USE Labor Management Relations
Male Female **Relations**
Marital **Relations**
Mother Child **Relations**
Object **Relations**
Parent Child **Relations**
Patient Therapist Sexual Relations
USE Professional Client Sexual Relations
Peer **Relations**
Professional Client Sexual **Relations**
Public **Relations**
Race Relations *USE Racial and Ethnic Relations*
Racial and Ethnic **Relations**
Sibling **Relations**
Therapist Patient Sexual Relations
USE Professional Client Sexual Relations
Relationship Quality
Relationship Satisfaction
Relationship Termination
Relationship Therapy
Breakup (Relationship) *USE Relationship Termination*
Customer **Relationship** Management
Family Work **Relationship**
Interpersonal Relationship Satisfaction
USE Relationship Satisfaction
Job Family Relationship *USE Family Work Relationship*

Parent School **Relationship**
Work Family Relationship *USE Family Work Relationship*
Cause Effect Relationships *USE Causality*
Dual **Relationships**
Interpersonal **Relationships**
Personal Relationships
USE Interpersonal Relationships
Relativism
Relaxation
Relaxation Therapy
Muscle **Relaxation**
Muscle Relaxation Therapy
USE Relaxation Therapy
Progressive **Relaxation** Therapy
Muscle **Relaxing** Drugs
Relearning
Institutional **Release**
ACTH Releasing Factor
USE Corticotropin Releasing Factor
Corticotropin **Releasing** Factor
Reliability (Statistical)
USE Statistical Reliability
Reliability (Test) *USE Test Reliability*
Interobserver Reliability *USE Interrater Reliability*
Interrater **Reliability**
Statistical **Reliability**
Test **Reliability**
Pain Relieving Drugs *USE Analgesic Drugs*
Religion
Beliefs (Religion) *USE Religious Beliefs*
Confession **(Religion)**
Ministers **(Religion)**
Rites (Religion) *USE Religious Practices*
Rituals (Religion) *USE Religious Practices*
Religiosity
Religious Affiliation
Religious Beliefs
Religious Buildings
Religious Conversion
Religious Education
Religious Experiences
Religious Fundamentalism
Religious Groups
Religious Literature
Religious Occupations
USE Religious Personnel
Religious Organizations
Religious Personnel
Religious Practices
Religious Prejudices
Fundamentalism (Religious) *USE Religious Fundamentalism*
Lay **Religious** Personnel
REM *USE Rapid Eye Movement*
REM Dream Deprivation
REM Dreams
REM Sleep
Remarriage
Remedial Education
Remedial Reading
Remembering *USE Retention*
Reminiscence
Remission (Disorders)
Spontaneous **Remission**
Symptom **Remission**
Renal Diseases *USE Kidney Diseases*
Renal Transplantation
USE Organ Transplantation
Repairmen
USE Technical Service Personnel
Repeated Measures
Bannister **Repertory** Grid
Repetition (Compulsive)
USE Repetition Compulsion
Repetition Compulsion
Compulsive Repetition *USE Repetition Compulsion*
Repetitive Transcranial Magnetic Stimulation
USE Transcranial Magnetic Stimulation

Estrogen Replacement Therapy
USE Hormone Therapy
Replication (Experimental)
USE Experimental Replication
Experimental **Replication**
Case **Report**
Psychiatric Report *USE Psychological Report*
Psychological **Report**
Self **Report**
Abuse **Reporting**
Child Abuse **Reporting**
Repressed Memory
Repression (Defense Mechanism)
Repression Sensitization
Repression Sensitization Scale
Sensitization Repression *USE Repression Sensitization*
Sexual **Reproduction**
Reproductive Technology
Reptiles
Republican Party *USE Political Parties*
Reputation
Research *USE Experimentation*
Research and Development
Research Design *USE Experimental Design*
Research Diagnostic Criteria
Research Dropouts
USE Experimental Attrition
Research Methods *USE Methodology*
Research Setting
Research Subjects
USE Experimental Subjects
Consumer **Research**
Cross Disciplinary Research *USE Interdisciplinary Research*
Interdisciplinary **Research**
Multidisciplinary Research *USE Interdisciplinary Research*
Qualitative **Research**
Quantitative Research *USE Quantitative Methods*
Family **Resemblance**
Resentment *USE Hostility*
Reserpine
Military Reserves *USE Military Duty Status*
Residence Halls *USE Dormitories*
Residency (Medical)
USE Medical Residency
Medical **Residency**
Psychiatric Residency *USE Medical Residency*
Psychiatric Residency *USE Psychiatric Training*
Residential Care Attendants
USE Attendants (Institutions)
Residential Care Institutions
Institutions (Residential Care)
USE Residential Care Institutions
Schizophrenia (Residual Type) *USE Schizophrenia*
Resilience (Psychological)
Resistance
Resistance (Psychotherapeutic)
USE Psychotherapeutic Resistance
Basal Skin **Resistance**
Insulin Resistance Syndrome
USE Metabolic Syndrome
Psychotherapeutic **Resistance**
Skin **Resistance**
Treatment **Resistant** Depression
Treatment **Resistant** Disorders
Tricyclic Resistant Depression
USE Treatment Resistant Depression
Resocialization (Psychosocial)
USE Psychosocial Readjustment
Psychosocial Resocialization
USE Psychosocial Readjustment
Conflict **Resolution**
Resonance *USE Vibration*
Magnetic **Resonance** Imaging
Resource Allocation
Resource Teachers
Human **Resource** Management
Allocation of Resources *USE Resource Allocation*

ROTATED ALPHABETICAL TERMS SECTION

Human Resources *USE Human Resource Management*
Self Respect *USE Self Esteem*
Respiration
Respiration Stimulating Drugs
Artificial **Respiration**
Respiratory Distress
Respiratory System
Respiratory Tract Disorders
Respite Care
Respondent Conditioning *USE Classical Conditioning*
Response Amplitude
Response Bias
Response Consistency *USE Response Variability*
Response Cost
Response Duration
Response Frequency
Response Generalization
Response Inhibition
Response Lag *USE Reaction Time*
Response Latency
Response Parameters
Response Probability
Response Rate *USE Response Frequency*
Response Set
Response Speed *USE Reaction Time*
Response Time *USE Reaction Time*
Response Variability
Amplitude (Response) *USE Response Amplitude*
Bias (Response) *USE Response Bias*
Duration (Response) *USE Response Duration*
Electrodermal Response *USE Galvanic Skin Response*
Frequency (Response) *USE Response Frequency*
Galvanic Skin **Response**
Generalization (Response) *USE Response Generalization*
Item **Response** Theory
Latency (Response) *USE Response Latency*
Oculomotor Response *USE Eye Movements*
Parameters (Response) *USE Response Parameters*
RT (Response) *USE Reaction Time*
Set (Response) *USE Response Set*
Speed (Response) *USE Reaction Time*
Variability (Response) *USE Response Variability*
Responses
Alarm **Responses**
Conditioned Emotional **Responses**
Conditioned **Responses**
Emotional **Responses**
Mediated **Responses**
Orienting **Responses**
Unconditioned **Responses**
Responsibility
Criminal **Responsibility**
Social **Responsibility**
Work **Rest** Cycles
Restlessness
Restraint (Physical) *USE Physical Restraint*
Dietary **Restraint**
Emotional Restraint *USE Emotional Control*
Physical **Restraint**
Restricted Environmental Stimulation *USE Stimulus Deprivation*
Cognitive **Restructuring**
Knowledge of **Results**
Retail Stores *USE Retailing*
Retailing
Electronic **Retailing**
Online Retailing *USE Electronic Retailing*
Retaliation
Retardation (Mental) *USE Mental Retardation*
Borderline Mental **Retardation**
Cultural Familial Mental Retardation *USE Psychosocial Mental Retardation*
Mental **Retardation**
Mental **Retardation** (Attitudes Toward)
Mild Mental **Retardation**
Moderate Mental **Retardation**
Profound Mental **Retardation**
Psychosocial Mental **Retardation**
Severe Mental **Retardation**
Retarded Speech Development
Educable Mentally Retarded *USE Mild Mental Retardation*
Home Reared Mentally **Retarded**
Institutionalized Mentally **Retarded**
Trainable Mentally Retarded *USE Moderate Mental Retardation*
Retention
Retention (School) *USE School Retention*
Retention Measures
Benton Revised Visual **Retention** Test
School **Retention**
Reticular Formation
Retina
Cones (Retina) *USE Cones (Eye)*
Ganglion Cells **(Retina)**
Retinal Eccentricity
Retinal Ganglion Cells *USE Ganglion Cells (Retina)*
Retinal Image
Retinal Vessels *USE Arteries (Anatomy)*
Image (Retinal) *USE Retinal Image*
Retirement
Retirement Communities
Automated Information **Retrieval**
Information Retrieval (Automated) *USE Automated Information Retrieval*
Retroactive Inhibition
Inhibition (Retroactive) *USE Retroactive Inhibition*
Retrograde Amnesia
Retrospective Studies
Rett Syndrome
Return to Home *USE Empty Nest*
Return to Work *USE Reemployment*
Family **Reunification**
Dual Reuptake Inhibitors *USE Serotonin Norepinephrine Reuptake Inhibitors*
Serotonin Norepinephrine **Reuptake** Inhibitors
Serotonin **Reuptake** Inhibitors
Revenge *USE Retaliation*
Directed Reverie Therapy *USE Guided Imagery*
Reversal Shift Learning
Review (of Literature) *USE Literature Review*
Life **Review**
Literature **Review**
Peer Review *USE Peer Evaluation*
Utilization **Reviews**
Benton **Revised** Visual Retention Test
Political **Revolution**
Revolutions (Political) *USE Political Revolution*
Reward Allocation
Rewards
External **Rewards**
Extrinsic Rewards *USE External Rewards*
Internal **Rewards**
Intrinsic Rewards *USE Internal Rewards*
Monetary **Rewards**
Preferred **Rewards**
Rh Incompatibility
Incompatibility (Rh) *USE Rh Incompatibility*
Rheoencephalography
Rhetoric
Rheumatic Fever
Rheumatism *USE Arthritis*
Rheumatoid Arthritis
Spearman Rho *USE Rank Difference Correlation*
Rhodopsin
Rhombencephalon *USE Hindbrain*
Rhyme
Rhythm

Rhythm Method
Alpha **Rhythm**
Delta **Rhythm**
Speech **Rhythm**
Theta **Rhythm**
Animal Biological **Rhythms**
Animal Circadian **Rhythms**
Biological **Rhythms**
Circadian Rhythms (Animal)
USE Animal Circadian Rhythms
Circadian Rhythms (Human)
USE Human Biological Rhythms
Daily Biological Rhythms (Animal)
USE Animal Circadian Rhythms
Human Biological **Rhythms**
Ribonucleic Acid
RNA (Ribonucleic Acid) *USE Ribonucleic Acid*
Puerto Rican Americans *USE Hispanics*
Right Brain *USE Right Hemisphere*
Right Hemisphere
Right to Treatment
Civil **Rights**
Civil **Rights** Movement
Client **Rights**
Human **Rights**
Patient Rights *USE Client Rights*
Visitation Rights *USE Child Visitation*
Rigidity (Muscles) *USE Muscle Contractions*
Rigidity (Personality)
Riots
Risk Analysis *USE Risk Assessment*
Risk Assessment
Risk Factors
Risk Management
Risk Perception
Risk Populations *USE At Risk Populations*
Risk Taking
At **Risk** Populations
High Risk Populations *USE At Risk Populations*
Sexual **Risk** Taking
Risky Shift *USE Choice Shift*
Risperidone
Ritalin *USE Methylphenidate*
Ritanserin
Rites (Nonreligious)
Rites (Religion) *USE Religious Practices*
Rites of Passage
Birth **Rites**
Death **Rites**
Initiation **Rites**
Marriage **Rites**
Rituals (Nonreligious)
USE Rites (Nonreligious)
Rituals (Religion) *USE Religious Practices*
Rivalry
RNA (Ribonucleic Acid)
USE Ribonucleic Acid
Road Rage
USE Aggressive Driving Behavior
Robbery *USE Theft*
Robins
Robotics
Robots *USE Robotics*
Rock Music
Rocking (Body) *USE Body Rocking*
Body **Rocking**
Rod and Frame Test
Rodents
Rods (Eye)
Roentgenography
Rogerian Therapy
USE Client Centered Therapy
Rogers (Carl)
Rohypnol *USE Flunitrazepam*
Rokeach Dogmatism Scale
Role (Counselor) *USE Counselor Role*
Role Conflicts
Role Expectations
Role Models
Role Perception
Role Playing
Role Satisfaction
Role Strain *USE Role Conflicts*
Role Taking
Bem Sex **Role** Inventory
Counselor **Role**
Gender Role Attitudes *USE Sex Role Attitudes*
Parental **Role**
Sex **Role** Attitudes
Sex Role Stereotyping *USE Sex Role Attitudes*
Therapist **Role**
Roles
Gender Roles *USE Sex Roles*
Sex **Roles**
Roman Catholicism
Catholicism (Roman) *USE Roman Catholicism*
Romance
Roommates
Dorsal **Roots**
Ventral **Roots**
Rorschach Test
Rosenzweig Picture Frustration Study
Rotary Pursuit
Rotation Methods (Statistical)
USE Statistical Rotation
Body Rotation *USE Rotational Behavior*
Mental **Rotation**
Oblique **Rotation**
Orthogonal **Rotation**
Statistical **Rotation**
Varimax **Rotation**
Rotational Behavior
ROTC Students
Rote Learning
Rotter Incomplete Sentences Blank
Rotter Internal External Locus of Control Scale
RT (Response) *USE Reaction Time*
Rubella
Rule Learning
USE Cognitive Hypothesis Testing
Rumination (Cognitive Process)
Rumination (Eating)
Rumors *USE Gossip*
Runaway Behavior
Running
Runways (Maze) *USE Maze Pathways*
Rural Development
USE Community Development
Rural Environments
Saccadic Eye Movements
USE Eye Movements
Saccharin
Tay **Sachs** Disease
SAD *USE Seasonal Affective Disorder*
Sadism
Sexual **Sadism**
Sadness
Sadomasochism
Sadomasochistic Personality
Safe Sex
Safety
Safety Belts
Safety Devices
Safety Warnings *USE Warnings*
Automobile Safety *USE Highway Safety*
Aviation **Safety**
Bicycle Safety *USE Transportation Safety*
Driver Safety *USE Highway Safety*
Highway **Safety**
Industrial Safety *USE Occupational Safety*
Occupational **Safety**
Transportation **Safety**
Water **Safety**

School Counseling
School Counselors
School Dropouts
School Engagement *USE Student Engagement*
School Enrollment
School Environment
School Expulsion
School Facilities
School Federal Aid *USE Educational Financial Assistance*
School Financial Assistance *USE Educational Financial Assistance*
School Graduation
School Guidance *USE School Counseling*
School Integration
School Integration (Racial) *USE School Integration*
School Learning
School Leavers
School Libraries
School Nurses
School Organization *USE Educational Administration*
School Phobia
School Principals
School Psychologists
School Psychology
School Readiness
School Refusal
School Retention
School Superintendents
School Suspension
School to Work Transition
School Transition
School Truancy
School Violence
Administrators (School) *USE School Administrators*
After **School** Programs
Attendance (School) *USE School Attendance*
Elementary **School** Students
Elementary **School** Teachers
Enrollment (School) *USE School Enrollment*
Expulsion (School) *USE School Expulsion*
Freudian Psychoanalytic **School**
Graduation (School) *USE School Graduation*
High **School** Education
High School Equivalency *USE Adult Education*
High **School** Graduates
High **School** Personality Questionnaire
High **School** Students
High **School** Teachers
Intermediate **School** Students
Junior High **School** Students
Junior High **School** Teachers
Libraries (School) *USE School Libraries*
Middle **School** Education
Middle **School** Students
Middle **School** Teachers
NeoFreudian School *USE Neopsychoanalytic School*
Neopsychoanalytic **School**
Nursery **School** Students
Parent **School** Relationship
Parochial School Education *USE Private School Education*
Primary **School** Students
Private **School** Education
Psychoanalytic School (Freudian) *USE Freudian Psychoanalytic School*
Public **School** Education
Retention (School) *USE School Retention*
Superintendents (School) *USE School Superintendents*
Suspension (School) *USE School Suspension*
Vocational **School** Students
Home **Schooling**
Schools
Alternative Schools *USE Nontraditional Education*
Boarding **Schools**
Charter **Schools**
Elementary **Schools**
Graduate **Schools**
Grammar Schools *USE Elementary Schools*
High **Schools**
Institutional **Schools**
Junior High **Schools**
Magnet Schools *USE Nontraditional Education*
Middle **Schools**
Military **Schools**
Nongraded **Schools**
Nursery **Schools**
Primary Schools *USE Elementary Schools*
Racial Segregation (Schools) *USE School Integration*
Technical **Schools**
Vocational Schools *USE Technical Schools*
Sciatic Nerve *USE Spinal Nerves*
SCID *USE Structured Clinical Interview*
Science Achievement
Science Education
Cognitive **Science**
Medicine (Science of) *USE Medical Sciences*
Sciences
Behavioral **Sciences**
Medical **Sciences**
Paramedical **Sciences**
Social **Sciences**
Scientific Communication
Scientific Methods *USE Experimental Methods*
Scientists
Sclera *USE Eye (Anatomy)*
Sclerosis (Nervous System)
Multiple **Sclerosis**
Scopolamine
Scopolamine Hydrobromide *USE Scopolamine*
Score Equating
Scores (Test) *USE Test Scores*
Critical Scores *USE Cutting Scores*
Cutting **Scores**
Standard **Scores**
Test **Scores**
Z Scores *USE Standard Scores*
Scoring (Testing)
Scotopic Stimulation
Scratching
Screening
Screening Tests
Breast Cancer Screening *USE Cancer Screening*
Cancer **Screening**
Drug Usage **Screening**
Genetic Screening *USE Genetic Testing*
Health **Screening**
Job Applicant **Screening**
Prostate Cancer Screening *USE Cancer Screening*
Psychological **Screening** Inventory
Skin Cancer Screening *USE Cancer Screening*
Scripts *USE Schema*
Sculpturing
Sea Gulls
Seals (Animal)
Job **Search**
Visual **Search**
Computer **Searching**
Online Searching *USE Computer Searching*
Seasonal Affective Disorder
Seasonal Variations
Seasonality *USE Seasonal Variations*
Seat Belts *USE Safety Belts*
Seclusion (Patient) *USE Patient Seclusion*
Patient **Seclusion**
Secobarbital
Seconal *USE Secobarbital*
Second Language Education *USE Foreign Language Education*

ROTATED ALPHABETICAL TERMS SECTION

Second Order Conditioning *USE Higher Order Conditioning*
English as **Second** Language
Secondary Education
Secondary Reinforcement
Secondhand Smoking *USE Passive Smoking*
Secrecy
Secretarial Personnel
Secretarial Skills *USE Clerical Secretarial Skills*
Clerical **Secretarial** Skills
Secretion (Gland)
Adrenal Gland **Secretion**
Endocrine Gland **Secretion**
Sectioning (Lesion) *USE Lesions*
Private **Sector**
Public **Sector**
Security (Emotional) *USE Emotional Security*
Economic **Security**
Emotional **Security**
Financial Security *USE Economic Security*
Job **Security**
Maximum **Security** Facilities
National **Security**
Social **Security**
Sedatives
Seduction
Seeing Eye Dogs *USE Mobility Aids*
Assistance Seeking (Professional) *USE Health Care Utilization*
Health Care **Seeking** Behavior
Help **Seeking** Behavior
Information **Seeking**
Novelty Seeking *USE Sensation Seeking*
Sensation **Seeking**
Sensation **Seeking** Scale
Stimulation Seeking (Personality) *USE Sensation Seeking*
Treatment Seeking Behavior *USE Health Care Seeking Behavior*
Segregation (Racial) *USE Social Integration*
Racial Segregation (Schools) *USE School Integration*
Seizures
Absence Seizures *USE Petit Mal Seizures*
Audiogenic **Seizures**
Epileptic **Seizures**
Grand Mal **Seizures**
Petit Mal **Seizures**
Tonic-Clonic Seizures *USE Grand Mal Seizures*
Selection (Personnel) *USE Personnel Selection*
Selection (Therapist) *USE Therapist Selection*
Selection Tests
Animal Mate **Selection**
Employee Selection *USE Personnel Selection*
Habitat Selection *USE Territoriality*
Human Mate **Selection**
Job Selection *USE Occupational Choice*
Jury **Selection**
Mate Selection *USE Animal Mate Selection*
Mate Selection *USE Human Mate Selection*
Natural **Selection**
Patient **Selection**
Personnel **Selection**
Therapist **Selection**
Toy **Selection**
Selective Attention
Selective Breeding
Selective Mutism *USE Elective Mutism*
Self Acceptance *USE Self Perception*
Self Actualization
Self Administration (Drugs) *USE Drug Self Administration*
Self Analysis
Self Assessment *USE Self Evaluation*
Self Care Skills
Self Concept
Self Confidence
Self Congruence
Self Consciousness *USE Self Perception*
Self Control
Self Criticism
Self Defeating Behavior
Self Defense
Self Destructive Behavior
Self Determination
Self Directed Learning *USE Individualized Instruction*
Self Disclosure
Self Efficacy
Self Employment
Self Esteem
Self Evaluation
Self Examination (Medical)
Self Expression
Self Fulfilling Prophecies
Self Handicapping Strategy
Self Help Techniques
Self Hypnosis *USE Autohypnosis*
Self Image *USE Self Concept*
Self Inflicted Wounds
Self Injurious Behavior *USE Self Destructive Behavior*
Self Instruction *USE Individualized Instruction*
Self Instructional Training
Self Management
Self Managing Work Teams
Self Medication
Self Monitoring
Self Monitoring (Personality)
Self Mutilation
Self Observation *USE Self Monitoring*
Self Perception
Self Preservation
Self Psychology
Self Realization *USE Self Actualization*
Self Reference
Self Referral
Self Regulated Learning
Self Regulation
Self Reinforcement
Self Report
Self Respect *USE Self Esteem*
Self Stimulation
Self Talk
Academic **Self** Concept
Actualization (Self) *USE Self Actualization*
Brain **Self** Stimulation
Child **Self** Care
Confidence (Self) *USE Self Confidence*
Control (Self) *USE Self Control*
Disclosure (Self) *USE Self Disclosure*
Drug **Self** Administration
Ideal Self *USE Self Concept*
Intracranial Self Stimulation *USE Brain Self Stimulation*
Kupfer Detre Self Rating Scale *USE Nonprojective Personality Measures*
Mutilation (Self) *USE Self Mutilation*
Referral (Self) *USE Self Referral*
Tennessee **Self** Concept Scale
Zungs **Self** Rating Depression Scale
Selfishness
Semantic Differential
Semantic Generalization
Semantic Memory
Semantic Priming
Generalization (Semantic) *USE Semantic Generalization*
Semantics
Semicircular Canals

Seminarians
Seminaries
Semiotics
Senile Dementia
Senile Psychosis
Dementia (Senile) *USE Senile Dementia*
Sensation *USE Perception*
Sensation Seeking
Sensation Seeking Scale
Pressure **Sensation**
Sense Organ Disorders
Sense Organs
Cutaneous **Sense**
Vomeronasal **Sense**
Sensitivity (Drugs) *USE Drug Sensitivity*
Sensitivity (Personality)
Sensitivity Training
Cultural **Sensitivity**
Drug **Sensitivity**
Ethnic Sensitivity *USE Cultural Sensitivity*
Spectral Sensitivity *USE Color Perception*
Sensitization
Sensitization (Protein)
USE Anaphylactic Shock
Sensitization Repression
USE Repression Sensitization
Behavioral Sensitization *USE Sensitization*
Covert **Sensitization**
Protein Sensitization *USE Anaphylactic Shock*
Repression **Sensitization**
Repression **Sensitization** Scale
Sensorially Handicapped
USE Sensory System Disorders
Sensorimotor Development
USE Perceptual Motor Development
Sensorimotor Measures
Sensorimotor Processes
USE Perceptual Motor Processes
Sensorineural Hearing Loss
USE Hearing Disorders
Sensory Adaptation
Sensory Deprivation
Sensory Disabilities (Attitudes Toward)
Sensory Feedback
Sensory Gating
Sensory Handicaps (Attitudes Toward)
USE Sensory Disabilities (Attitudes Toward)
Sensory Integration
Sensory Neglect
Sensory Neurons
Sensory Pathways *USE Afferent Pathways*
Sensory Preconditioning
USE Preconditioning
Sensory System Disorders
Adaptation (Sensory) *USE Sensory Adaptation*
Gating (Sensory) *USE Sensory Gating*
Sentence Completion Tests
Sentence Comprehension
Sentence Structure
Sentences
Rotter Incomplete **Sentences** Blank
Sentencing *USE Adjudication*
Separation (Marital) *USE Marital Separation*
Separation Anxiety
Separation Individuation
Separation Reactions
Marital **Separation**
Septal Nuclei
Septum *USE Septal Nuclei*
Sequential Learning
Serial Anticipation (Learning)
Serial Homicide
Serial Learning
Serial Murder *USE Serial Homicide*
Serial Position Effect
Serial Recall
Anticipation (Serial Learning)
USE Serial Anticipation (Learning)
Time **Series**
Seriousness
Serotonin
Serotonin Agonists
Serotonin Antagonists
Serotonin Metabolites
Serotonin Norepinephrine Reuptake Inhibitors
Serotonin Precursors
Serotonin Reuptake Inhibitors
Serpasil *USE Reserpine*
Sertraline
Serum (Blood) *USE Blood Serum*
Serum Albumin
Blood **Serum**
Civil Servants *USE Government Personnel*
Service Learning
Service Personnel
Service Quality *USE Quality of Services*
Domestic **Service** Personnel
Fee for **Service**
Health **Service** Needs
Health Service Utilization
USE Health Care Utilization
Mental Health Service Needs *USE Health Service Needs*
Public Health **Service** Nurses
Public **Service** Announcements
Technical **Service** Personnel
Servicemen *USE Military Personnel*
Armed **Services** Vocational Aptitude Battery
Community Mental Health **Services**
Community Welfare **Services**
Community **Services**
Crisis Intervention **Services**
Emergency **Services**
Financial **Services**
Health Care **Services**
Hot Line **Services**
Human **Services**
Information **Services**
Integrated **Services**
Interagency Services *USE Integrated Services*
Mental Health **Services**
Protective **Services**
Public Health **Services**
Public Welfare Services *USE Community Welfare Services*
Quality of **Services**
Social **Services**
Student Personnel **Services**
Web Based Mental Health Services *USE Online Therapy*
Welfare **Services** (Government)
Set (Response) *USE Response Set*
Fuzzy **Set** Theory
Response **Set**
Experimental Setting *USE Research Setting*
Goal **Setting**
Research **Setting**
Severe Mental Retardation
Severity (Disorders)
Sex
Sex Change
Sex Chromosome Disorders
Sex Chromosomes
Sex Differences (Animal)
USE Animal Sex Differences
Sex Differences (Human)
USE Human Sex Differences
Sex Differentiation Disorders
USE Genital Disorders
Sex Discrimination
Sex Drive
Sex Education
Sex Hormones
Sex Linked Developmental Differences
Sex Linked Hereditary Disorders

Sex Offenses
Sex Recognition
Sex Role Attitudes
Sex Role Stereotyping
USE Sex Role Attitudes
Sex Roles
Sex Therapy
Animal **Sex** Differences
Bem **Sex** Role Inventory
Human **Sex** Differences
Safe **Sex**
Same **Sex** Education
Same Sex Environments
USE Single Sex Environments
Same **Sex** Marriage
Single Sex Education *USE Same Sex Education*
Single **Sex** Environments
Sterilization **(Sex)**
Sexism
Sexual Abstinence
Sexual Abuse
Sexual Addiction
Sexual Arousal
Sexual Attitudes
Sexual Attraction
Sexual Behavior
USE Psychosexual Behavior
Sexual Boundary Violations
USE Professional Client Sexual Relations
Sexual Compulsivity *USE Sexual Addiction*
Sexual Delinquency *USE Promiscuity*
Sexual Development
Sexual Deviations *USE Paraphilias*
Sexual Disorders (Physiological)
USE Genital Disorders
Sexual Fantasy
Sexual Fetishism *USE Fetishism*
Sexual Function Disturbances
Sexual Harassment
Sexual Identity (Gender)
USE Gender Identity
Sexual Intercourse (Human)
Sexual Masochism
Sexual Orientation
Sexual Partners
Sexual Reassignment *USE Sex Change*
Sexual Receptivity (Animal)
USE Animal Sexual Receptivity
Sexual Reproduction
Sexual Risk Taking
Sexual Sadism
Sexual Satisfaction
Abstinence (Sexual) *USE Sexual Abstinence*
Affairs (Sexual) *USE Extramarital Intercourse*
Animal **Sexual** Behavior
Animal **Sexual** Receptivity
Arousal (Sexual) *USE Sexual Arousal*
Boundary Violations (Sexual)
USE Professional Client Sexual Relations
Climax (Sexual) *USE Orgasm*
Compulsivity (Sexual) *USE Sexual Addiction*
Deviations (Sexual) *USE Paraphilias*
Endocrine **Sexual** Disorders
Female **Sexual** Dysfunction
Harassment (Sexual) *USE Sexual Harassment*
Hypoactive Sexual Desire Disorder
USE Inhibited Sexual Desire
Inhibited **Sexual** Desire
Intercourse (Sexual) *USE Sexual Intercourse (Human)*
Patient Therapist Sexual Relations
USE Professional Client Sexual Relations
Perversions (Sexual) *USE Paraphilias*
Professional Client **Sexual** Relations
Therapist Patient Sexual Relations
USE Professional Client Sexual Relations
Sexuality
Sexually Transmitted Diseases
Shamanism
Shame
Shape Perception
USE Form and Shape Perception
Form and **Shape** Perception
Shared Paranoid Disorder
USE Folie A Deux
Sharing (Social Behavior)
Needle **Sharing**
Myelin **Sheath**
Sheep
Sheltered Workshops
Shelters
Choice **Shift**
Extradimensional Shift Learning
USE Nonreversal Shift Learning
Nonreversal **Shift** Learning
Reversal **Shift** Learning
Risky Shift *USE Choice Shift*
Shifts (Workday) *USE Workday Shifts*
Population Shifts *USE Human Migration*
Workday **Shifts**
Shock
Shock Therapy
Shock Units
Anaphylactic **Shock**
Culture **Shock**
Electroconvulsive **Shock**
Electroconvulsive **Shock** Therapy
Insulin **Shock** Therapy
Shoplifting
Shopping
Shopping Centers
Internet Shopping *USE Electronic Commerce*
Online Shopping *USE Electronic Commerce*
Short Term Memory
Short Term Potentiation
USE Postactivation Potentials
Short Term Psychotherapy
USE Brief Psychotherapy
Shoulder (Anatomy)
Shuttle Box Grids *USE Shuttle Boxes*
Shuttle Box Hurdles *USE Shuttle Boxes*
Shuttle Boxes
Shyness *USE Timidity*
Siamese Twins *USE Conjoined Twins*
Sibling Relations
Siblings
Sick Leave *USE Employee Leave Benefits*
Sickle Cell Disease
Motion **Sickness**
Side Effects (Drug)
Side Effects (Treatment)
Sight Vocabulary
Partially **Sighted**
Freud **(Sigmund)**
Sign Language
Sign Rank Test
USE Wilcoxon Sign Rank Test
Sign Test
Wilcoxon **Sign** Rank Test
Signal Detection (Perception)
Signal Intensity *USE Stimulus Intensity*
Detection (Signal) *USE Signal Detection (Perception)*
Significance (Statistical)
USE Statistical Significance
Statistical **Significance**
Significant Others
Warning Signs *USE Warnings*
Sikhism
Sikhs
Sildenafil

Silence
Silent Reading
Similarity (Stimulus)
USE Stimulus Similarity
Attitude **Similarity**
Stimulus **Similarity**
Simile *USE Figurative Language*
Simple Schizophrenia *USE Schizophrenia*
Herpes **Simplex**
Simulation
Simulation Games
Computer **Simulation**
Flight **Simulation**
Simulators *USE Simulation*
Sin
Sincerity
Singing
Single Cell Organisms *USE Microorganisms*
Single Fathers
Single Mothers
Single Parents
Single Persons
Single Sex Education
USE Same Sex Education
Single Sex Environments
Sisters
Web Sites *USE Websites*
Sixteen Personality Factors Questionnaire
Size
Size (Apparent) *USE Apparent Size*
Size (Group) *USE Group Size*
Size Constancy
Size Discrimination
Apparent **Size**
Body **Size**
Brain **Size**
Class **Size**
Effect **Size** (Statistical)
Family **Size**
Group **Size**
Litter **Size**
Sample **Size**
Skeletomuscular Disorders
USE Musculoskeletal Disorders
Skepticism
Skewed Distribution
Skill Learning
Fine Motor **Skill** Learning
Gross Motor **Skill** Learning
Motor Skill Learning
USE Perceptual Motor Learning
Skilled Industrial Workers
Skills *USE Ability*
Basic Skills Testing
USE Minimum Competency Tests
Clerical Secretarial **Skills**
Communication **Skills**
Communication **Skills** Training
Employee **Skills**
Iowa Tests of Basic **Skills**
Motor **Skills**
Parenting **Skills**
Reading **Skills**
Secretarial Skills *USE Clerical Secretarial Skills*
Self Care **Skills**
Social **Skills**
Social **Skills** Training
Study Skills *USE Study Habits*
Writing **Skills**
Skin (Anatomy)
Skin Cancer Screening
USE Cancer Screening
Skin Conduction *USE Skin Resistance*
Skin Disorders
Skin Electrical Properties
Skin Potential
Skin Resistance
Skin Temperature
Allergic **Skin** Disorders
Basal **Skin** Resistance
Galvanic **Skin** Response
Skinner (Burrhus Frederic)
Skinner Boxes
Skull
Slang
Sleep
Sleep Apnea
Sleep Deprivation
Sleep Disorders
Sleep Inducing Drugs *USE Hypnotic Drugs*
Sleep Monitoring *USE Polysomnography*
Sleep Onset
Sleep Talking
Sleep Treatment
Sleep Wake Cycle
Nonrapid Eye Movement Sleep *USE NREM Sleep*
NonREM Sleep *USE NREM Sleep*
NREM **Sleep**
Paradoxical Sleep *USE REM Sleep*
Paroxysmal Sleep *USE Narcolepsy*
Rapid Eye Movement Sleep *USE REM Sleep*
REM **Sleep**
Slow Wave Sleep *USE NREM Sleep*
Sleepiness
Sleeplessness *USE Insomnia*
Sleepwalking
Slosson Intelligence Test
Slow Learners
USE Borderline Mental Retardation
Slow Wave Sleep *USE NREM Sleep*
Slums *USE Poverty Areas*
Small Businesses
Smell Perception *USE Olfactory Perception*
Smiles
Environmental Tobacco Smoke *USE Passive Smoking*
Smokeless Tobacco
Tobacco (Smokeless) *USE Smokeless Tobacco*
Smoking (Tobacco) *USE Tobacco Smoking*
Smoking Cessation
Cigarette Smoking *USE Tobacco Smoking*
Involuntary Smoking *USE Passive Smoking*
Passive **Smoking**
Secondhand Smoking *USE Passive Smoking*
Tobacco **Smoking**
Snails
Snake Phobia *USE Ophidiophobia*
Snakes
Glue **Sniffing**
SNRI
USE Serotonin Norepinephrine Reuptake Inhibitors
Snuff *USE Smokeless Tobacco*
Sobriety
Soccer
Sociability
Social Acceptance
Social Adaptation *USE Social Adjustment*
Social Adjustment
Social Anxiety
Social Anxiety Disorder *USE Social Phobia*
Social Approval
Social Behavior
Social Capital
Social Casework
Social Caseworkers *USE Social Workers*
Social Change
Social Class
Social Class Attitudes
USE Socioeconomic Class Attitudes
Social Clubs (Therapeutic)
USE Therapeutic Social Clubs
Social Cognition
Social Comparison
Social Competence *USE Social Skills*

Social Control
Social Dating
Social Demonstrations
Social Density
Social Deprivation
Social Desirability
Social Development
USE Psychosocial Development
Social Dilemma
Social Discrimination
Social Drinking
Social Environments
Social Equality
Social Facilitation
Social Groups
Social Identity
Social Immobility *USE Social Mobility*
Social Influences
Social Integration
Social Interaction
Social Isolation
Social Issues
Social Justice
Social Learning
Social Loafing
Social Maladjustment
USE Social Adjustment
Social Marketing
Social Mobility
Social Movements
Social Networks
Social Norms
Social Perception
Social Phobia
Social Problems *USE Social Issues*
Social Processes
Social Programs
Social Psychiatry
Social Psychologists
Social Psychology
Social Reinforcement
Social Rejection *USE Social Acceptance*
Social Responsibility
Social Sciences
Social Security
Social Services
Social Skills
Social Skills Training
Social Stigma *USE Stigma*
Social Stress
Social Structure
Social Studies Education
Social Support
Social Support Networks
USE Social Support
Social Values
Social Work Education
Social Work *USE Social Casework*
Social Workers
Acceptance (Social) *USE Social Acceptance*
Adaptation (Social) *USE Social Adjustment*
Animal **Social** Behavior
Approval (Social) *USE Social Approval*
Assistance **(Social** Behavior)
Change (Social) *USE Social Change*
Clubs **(Social** Organizations)
Competence (Social) *USE Social Skills*
Control (Social) *USE Social Control*
Dating (Social) *USE Social Dating*
Demonstrations (Social) *USE Social Demonstrations*
Density (Social) *USE Social Density*
Desirability (Social) *USE Social Desirability*
Discrimination (Social) *USE Social Discrimination*
Edwards **Social** Desirability Scale
Equality (Social) *USE Social Equality*
Equity **(Social)**
Facilitation (Social) *USE Social Facilitation*
Groups (Social) *USE Social Groups*
Influences (Social) *USE Social Influences*
Interaction (Social) *USE Social Interaction*
Internet Social Networking
USE Online Social Networks
Isolation (Social) *USE Social Isolation*
Maladjustment (Social) *USE Social Adjustment*
Marlowe Crowne **Social** Desirability Scale
Mobility (Social) *USE Social Mobility*
Networks (Social) *USE Social Networks*
Norms (Social) *USE Social Norms*
Online **Social** Networks
Psychiatric **Social** Workers
Rejection (Social) *USE Social Acceptance*
Sharing **(Social** Behavior)
Therapeutic **Social** Clubs
Trust **(Social** Behavior)
Vineland **Social** Maturity Scale
Socialism
Socialization
Political **Socialization**
Socially Disadvantaged
USE Disadvantaged
Society
Sociobiology
Sociocultural Factors
Socioeconomic Class Attitudes
Socioeconomic Status
Family **Socioeconomic** Level
Socioenvironmental Therapy
USE Milieu Therapy
Sociograms
Sociolinguistics
Sociologists
Sociology
Sociometric Tests
Sociometry
Sociopath
USE Antisocial Personality Disorder
Sociopathology *USE Antisocial Behavior*
Sociotherapy
Sodium
Sodium Ions
Sodium Lactate *USE Lactic Acid*
Sodium Pentobarbital *USE Pentobarbital*
Amobarbital Sodium *USE Amobarbital*
Diphenylhydantoin Sodium *USE Diphenylhydantoin*
Computer **Software**
Solution Focused Therapy
Solvent Abuse *USE Inhalant Abuse*
Solvents
Anagram Problem **Solving**
Group Problem **Solving**
Individual Problem Solving *USE Problem Solving*
Problem **Solving**
Somatization
Somatization Disorder
Somatoform Disorders
Somatoform Pain Disorder
Atypical Somatoform Disorder
USE Body Dysmorphic Disorder
Somatosensory Cortex
Somatosensory Disorders
Somatosensory Evoked Potentials
Cortex (Somatosensory)
USE Somatosensory Cortex
Somatostatin
Somatotropin
Somatotypes
Somesthetic Perception
Somesthetic Stimulation
Somnambulism *USE Sleepwalking*
Sonar
Songs *USE Music*
Sons
Sorority Membership
Q **Sort** Testing Technique

ROTATED ALPHABETICAL TERMS SECTION

Sorting (Cognition) *USE Classification (Cognitive Process)*
Wisconsin Card **Sorting** Test
Soul
Sound *USE Auditory Stimulation*
Sound Localization *USE Auditory Localization*
Sound Pressure Level *USE Loudness*
Sound Waves *USE Acoustics*
Localization (Sound) *USE Auditory Localization*
Noise (Sound) *USE Auditory Stimulation*
Source Monitoring
Sourness *USE Taste Perception*
South Asian Cultural Groups
South East Asian Cultural Groups *USE Southeast Asian Cultural Groups*
Southeast Asian Cultural Groups
Personal **Space**
Working **Space**
Spacecraft
Spaceflight
Attention **Span**
Digit **Span** Testing
Life **Span**
Spanish Americans *USE Hispanics*
Spasms
Muscle **Spasms**
Spatial Ability
Spatial Discrimination *USE Spatial Perception*
Spatial Distortion
Spatial Frequency
Spatial Imagery
Spatial Learning
Spatial Memory
Spatial Neglect *USE Sensory Neglect*
Spatial Organization
Spatial Orientation (Perception)
Spatial Perception
Orientation (Spatial) *USE Spatial Orientation (Perception)*
Temporal Spatial Concept Scale *USE Intelligence Measures*
Visual Spatial Ability *USE Visuospatial Ability*
Visual Spatial Memory *USE Visuospatial Memory*
Automatic Speaker Recognition *USE Automated Speech Recognition*
Fear of Public Speaking *USE Speech Anxiety*
Public **Speaking**
Spearman Brown Test
Spearman Rho *USE Rank Difference Correlation*
Special Education
Special Education Students
Special Education Teachers
Special Needs
Information **Specialists**
Specialization (Academic) *USE Academic Specialization*
Specialization (Professional) *USE Professional Specialization*
Academic **Specialization**
Hemispheric Specialization *USE Lateral Dominance*
Professional **Specialization**
Species Differences
Species Recognition
Culture Specific Syndromes *USE Culture Bound Syndromes*
Sports **Spectators**
Spectral Sensitivity *USE Color Perception*
Autism Spectrum Disorders *USE Pervasive Developmental Disorders*
Speech *USE Oral Communication*
Speech and Hearing Measures
Speech Anxiety
Speech Characteristics
Speech Development
Speech Disorders
Speech Handicapped *USE Speech Disorders*
Speech Measures *USE Speech and Hearing Measures*
Speech Pauses
Speech Perception
Speech Pitch
Speech Processing (Mechanical)
Speech Rate
Speech Rhythm
Speech Therapists
Speech Therapy
Accelerated Speech *USE Speech Rate*
Articulation **(Speech)**
Automated **Speech** Recognition
Compressed **Speech**
Delayed Speech *USE Retarded Speech Development*
Figures of Speech *USE Figurative Language*
Filtered **Speech**
Inner Speech *USE Self Talk*
Retarded **Speech** Development
Synthetic **Speech**
Speechreading *USE Lipreading*
Speed (Response) *USE Reaction Time*
Speed *USE Velocity*
Cognitive Processing **Speed**
Information Processing Speed *USE Cognitive Processing Speed*
Reading **Speed**
Response Speed *USE Reaction Time*
Spelling
Sperm
Sperm Donation *USE Tissue Donation*
Spider Phobia *USE Phobias*
Spiders *USE Arachnida*
Spina Bifida
Spinal Column
Spinal Cord
Spinal Cord Injuries
Spinal Fluid *USE Cerebrospinal Fluid*
Spinal Ganglia
Spinal Nerves
Lumbar **Spinal** Cord
Nerves (Spinal) *USE Spinal Nerves*
Spine *USE Spinal Column*
Spinothalamic Tracts
Spiperone *USE Spiroperidol*
Spirit Possession
Spirituality
Spiroperidol
Spleen
Split Brain *USE Commissurotomy*
Split Personality *USE Dissociative Identity Disorder*
Spontaneous Abortion
Spontaneous Alternation
Spontaneous Recovery (Learning)
Spontaneous Remission
Abortion (Spontaneous) *USE Spontaneous Abortion*
Sport Performance *USE Athletic Performance*
Sport Psychology
Sport Training *USE Athletic Training*
Sports
Sports (Attitudes Toward)
Sports Spectators
Fans (Sports) *USE Sports Spectators*
Sportsmanship *USE Sports (Attitudes Toward)*
Sportspersonship *USE Sports (Attitudes Toward)*
Spouse Abuse *USE Partner Abuse*
Spouses
Cervical Sprain Syndrome *USE Whiplash*
Spreading Depression
Chi **Square** Test

Least **Squares**
Squirrels
St. John's Wort *USE Hypericum Perforatum*
Stability (Emotional)
USE Emotional Stability
Emotional **Stability**
Hospital Staff *USE Medical Personnel*
Psychiatric Hospital **Staff**
Stage Plays *USE Theatre*
Stages of Change
Developmental **Stages**
Prenatal Developmental **Stages**
Stalking
Stammering *USE Stuttering*
Competency to **Stand** Trial
Standard Deviation
Standard Error of Measurement
USE Error of Measurement
Standard Scores
Standardization (Test)
USE Test Standardization
Test **Standardization**
Standardized Tests
Standards (Professional)
USE Professional Standards
Academic Standards *USE Educational Standards*
Educational **Standards**
Professional **Standards**
Stanford Achievement Test
Stanford Binet Intelligence Scale
Stanines *USE Standard Scores*
Stapedius Reflex *USE Acoustic Reflex*
Starfish *USE Echinodermata*
Head Start *USE Project Head Start*
Project Head **Start**
Startle Reflex
Starvation
State Board Examinations
USE Professional Examinations
State Dependent Learning
State Hospitals *USE Psychiatric Hospitals*
State Trait Anxiety Inventory
Mini Mental **State** Examination
Borderline **States**
Consciousness **States**
Emotional **States**
Statistical Analysis
Statistical Correlation
Statistical Data
Statistical Estimation
Statistical Measurement
Statistical Norms
Statistical Power
Statistical Probability
Statistical Regression
Statistical Reliability
Statistical Rotation
Statistical Sample Parameters
Statistical Samples
Statistical Significance
Statistical Tables
Statistical Tests
Statistical Validity
Statistical Variables
Statistical Weighting
Correlation (Statistical) *USE Statistical Correlation*
Diagnostic and **Statistical** Manual
Effect Size **(Statistical)**
Item Analysis **(Statistical)**
Magnitude of Effect (Statistical) *USE Effect Size (Statistical)*
Nonparametric **Statistical** Tests
Norms (Statistical) *USE Statistical Norms*
Parametric **Statistical** Tests
Reliability (Statistical) *USE Statistical Reliability*
Rotation Methods (Statistical) *USE Statistical Rotation*
Significance (Statistical) *USE Statistical Significance*
Tests (Statistical) *USE Statistical Tests*

Validity (Statistical) *USE Statistical Validity*
Statistics
ANOVA (Statistics) *USE Analysis of Variance*
Confidence Limits **(Statistics)**
Interaction Analysis **(Statistics)**
Population **(Statistics)**
Weight (Statistics) *USE Statistical Weighting*
Status
Employment **Status**
Functional Status *USE Ability Level*
Job Status *USE Occupational Status*
Marital **Status**
Military Duty **Status**
Occupational **Status**
Parenthood **Status**
Socioeconomic **Status**
Length of Stay *USE Treatment Duration*
Stealing *USE Theft*
Stelazine *USE Trifluoperazine*
Stellate Ganglion *USE Autonomic Ganglia*
Stem Cells
Brain **Stem**
Twelve **Step** Programs
Stepchildren
Stepfamily
Stepparents
Stereopsis *USE Stereoscopic Vision*
Stereoscopic Presentation
Stereoscopic Vision
Stereotaxic Atlas
Stereotaxic Techniques
Stereotyped Attitudes
Stereotyped Behavior
Stereotyping *USE Stereotyped Attitudes*
Sex Role Stereotyping *USE Sex Role Attitudes*
Sterility
Sterilization (Sex)
Steroids
Adrenal Cortex Steroids *USE Corticosteroids*
Sticklebacks
Stigma
Social Stigma *USE Stigma*
Stimulants of CNS
USE CNS Stimulating Drugs
CNS **Stimulating** Drugs
Follicle **Stimulating** Hormone
Melanocyte **Stimulating** Hormone
Respiration **Stimulating** Drugs
Thyroid Stimulating Hormone *USE Thyrotropin*
Stimulation
Stimulation Seeking (Personality)
USE Sensation Seeking
Afferent **Stimulation**
Auditory **Stimulation**
Aversive **Stimulation**
Brain Self **Stimulation**
Brain **Stimulation**
Chemical Brain **Stimulation**
Dichoptic **Stimulation**
Dichotic **Stimulation**
Electrical Brain **Stimulation**
Electrical **Stimulation**
Intracranial Self Stimulation *USE Brain Self Stimulation*
Olfactory **Stimulation**
Perceptual **Stimulation**
Photopic **Stimulation**
Prismatic **Stimulation**
Repetitive Transcranial Magnetic Stimulation
USE Transcranial Magnetic Stimulation
Restricted Environmental Stimulation *USE Stimulus Deprivation*
Scotopic **Stimulation**
Self **Stimulation**
Somesthetic **Stimulation**
Subliminal **Stimulation**
Tactual **Stimulation**
Taste **Stimulation**
Transcranial Magnetic **Stimulation**

Vestibular Stimulation *USE Somesthetic Stimulation*
Visual **Stimulation**
Stimulators (Apparatus)
Acoustic Stimuli *USE Auditory Stimulation*
Novel Stimuli *USE Stimulus Novelty*
Pictorial **Stimuli**
Verbal **Stimuli**
Stimulus (Unconditioned)
USE Unconditioned Stimulus
Stimulus Ambiguity
Stimulus Attenuation
Stimulus Change
Stimulus Complexity
Stimulus Control
Stimulus Deprivation
Stimulus Discrimination
Stimulus Duration
Stimulus Frequency
Stimulus Generalization
Stimulus Intensity
Stimulus Intervals
Stimulus Novelty
Stimulus Offset
Stimulus Onset
Stimulus Parameters
Stimulus Pattern *USE Stimulus Variability*
Stimulus Presentation Methods
Stimulus Salience
Stimulus Similarity
Stimulus Variability
Ambiguity (Stimulus) *USE Stimulus Ambiguity*
Complexity (Stimulus) *USE Stimulus Complexity*
Conditioned **Stimulus**
Discriminative Stimulus *USE Conditioned Stimulus*
Duration (Stimulus) *USE Stimulus Duration*
Exposure Time (Stimulus) *USE Stimulus Duration*
Frequency (Stimulus) *USE Stimulus Frequency*
Generalization (Stimulus) *USE Stimulus Generalization*
Intensity (Stimulus) *USE Stimulus Intensity*
Parameters (Stimulus) *USE Stimulus Parameters*
Salience (Stimulus) *USE Stimulus Salience*
Similarity (Stimulus) *USE Stimulus Similarity*
Unconditioned **Stimulus**
Variability (Stimulus) *USE Stimulus Variability*
Stipends
USE Educational Financial Assistance
Stochastic Modeling
Stomach
Automated Information **Storage**
Human Information **Storage**
Information Storage (Human)
USE Human Information Storage
Retail Stores *USE Retailing*
Storytelling
Storytelling Technique
USE Mutual Storytelling Technique
Mutual **Storytelling** Technique
Strabismus
Strain Differences (Animal)
USE Animal Strain Differences
Animal **Strain** Differences
Financial **Strain**
Role Strain *USE Role Conflicts*
Stranger Reactions
Fear of Strangers *USE Stranger Reactions*
Strategies
Strategies (Learning)
USE Learning Strategies
Learning **Strategies**
Self Handicapping **Strategy**
Strength (Physical) *USE Physical Strength*
Physical **Strength**
Stress
Stress Management
Stress Reactions
Acute **Stress** Disorder
Chronic **Stress**

Diathesis **Stress** Model
Environmental **Stress**
Financial Stress *USE Financial Strain*
Job Stress *USE Occupational Stress*
Occupational **Stress**
Physiological **Stress**
Posttraumatic **Stress** Disorder
Psychological **Stress**
Social **Stress**
Work Stress *USE Occupational Stress*
Striate Cortex *USE Visual Cortex*
Striatum
Corpus Striatum *USE Basal Ganglia*
Ventral Striatum *USE Basal Ganglia*
Strikes
Stroboscopic Movement
USE Apparent Movement
Stroke (Cerebrum)
USE Cerebrovascular Accidents
Strong Vocational Interest Blank
Stroop Color Word Test
Stroop Effect
Structural Equation Modeling
Structuralism
Factor **Structure**
Family **Structure**
Group **Structure**
Household Structure *USE Living Arrangements*
Kinship **Structure**
Organizational **Structure**
Sentence **Structure**
Social **Structure**
Text **Structure**
Structured Clinical Interview
Structured Overview
USE Advance Organizers
Strychnine
Student Activism
Student Adjustment
USE School Adjustment
Student Admission Criteria
Student Attitudes
Student Attrition
Student Characteristics
Student Engagement
Student Personnel Services
Student Protest *USE Student Activism*
Student Records
Student Teachers
Student Teaching
Activism (Student) *USE Student Activism*
Admission Criteria (Student) *USE Student Admission Criteria*
Protest (Student) *USE Student Activism*
Teacher **Student** Interaction
Students
Students T Test *USE T Test*
Business **Students**
College **Students**
Community College **Students**
Dental **Students**
Education **Students**
Elementary School **Students**
Foreign Students *USE International Students*
Graduate **Students**
High School **Students**
Intermediate School **Students**
International **Students**
Junior College **Students**
Junior High School **Students**
Kindergarten **Students**
Law **Students**
Medical **Students**
Middle School **Students**
Nursery School **Students**
Nursing **Students**
Postgraduate **Students**
Preschool **Students**

Primary School **Students**
Reentry **Students**
ROTC **Students**
Special Education **Students**
Transfer **Students**
Vocational School **Students**
Studies (Followup) *USE Followup Studies*
Studies (Longitudinal) *USE Longitudinal Studies*
Followup **Studies**
Longitudinal **Studies**
Prospective **Studies**
Retrospective **Studies**
Social **Studies** Education
Study Abroad
Study Habits
Study Skills *USE Study Habits*
Allport Vernon Lindzey Study Values *USE Attitude Measures*
Foreign Study *USE Study Abroad*
Independent Study *USE Individualized Instruction*
International Study *USE Study Abroad*
Rosenzweig Picture Frustration **Study**
Work Study Programs *USE Educational Programs*
Stuttering
Cognitive **Style**
Leadership **Style**
Learning Style *USE Cognitive Style*
Parenting **Style**
Perceptual **Style**
Time Planning Style *USE Time Management*
Subconscious
Subcortical Lesions *USE Brain Lesions*
Subculture (Anthropological)
Subcutaneous Injections
Subjectivity
Experimental **Subjects**
Research Subjects *USE Experimental Subjects*
Within Subjects Design *USE Repeated Measures*
Sublimation
Subliminal Perception
Subliminal Stimulation
Submarines
Submissiveness *USE Obedience*
Submucous Plexus *USE Autonomic Ganglia*
Substance Abuse Prevention *USE Drug Abuse Prevention*
Substance Abuse *USE Drug Abuse*
Substance P
Substantia Nigra
Subtests
Subtypes (Disorders)
Suburban Environments
Subvocalization
Success *USE Achievement*
Fear of **Success**
Occupational **Success**
Occupational **Success** Prediction
Successive Contrast *USE Afterimage*
Succinylcholine
Sucking
Sudden Infant Death
Suffering
Suffocation *USE Anoxia*
Blood **Sugar**
Sugars
Suggestibility
Posthypnotic **Suggestions**
Suicidal Ideation
Suicide
Suicide (Attempted) *USE Attempted Suicide*
Suicide Prevention
Suicide Prevention Centers
Assisted **Suicide**
Attempted **Suicide**
Amphetamine Sulfate *USE Amphetamine*
Codeine Sulfate *USE Codeine*

Sulpiride
Non Zero **Sum** Games
Summer Camps (Recreation)
Superego
Superintendents (School) *USE School Superintendents*
School **Superintendents**
Superior Colliculus
Superiority (Emotional) *USE Emotional Superiority*
Emotional **Superiority**
Superstitions
Supervising Teachers *USE Cooperating Teachers*
Supervision (Professional) *USE Professional Supervision*
Clinical Supervision *USE Professional Supervision*
Educational Supervision *USE Professional Supervision*
Practicum **Supervision**
Professional **Supervision**
Supervisor Employee Interaction
Employee Supervisor Interaction *USE Supervisor Employee Interaction*
Supervisors *USE Management Personnel*
Dietary **Supplements**
Nutritional Supplements *USE Dietary Supplements*
Supply and Demand
Supply Chain Management
Supply Chains
Medical Personnel **Supply**
Mental Health Personnel **Supply**
Personnel **Supply**
Support Groups
Child **Support**
Decision **Support** Systems
Social **Support**
Social Support Networks *USE Social Support*
Supported Employment
Computer Supported Cooperative Work *USE Groupware*
Supportive Psychotherapy
Suppression (Conditioned) *USE Conditioned Suppression*
Suppression (Defense Mechanism)
Conditioned **Suppression**
Dexamethasone **Suppression** Test
Thought **Suppression**
Progressive **Supranuclear** Palsy
Surgeons
Surgery
Cardiac Surgery *USE Heart Surgery*
Dental **Surgery**
Endocrine Gland **Surgery**
Heart **Surgery**
Operation (Surgery) *USE Surgery*
Pituitary Gland Surgery *USE Hypophysectomy*
Plastic **Surgery**
Surgical Complications *USE Postsurgical Complications*
Surgical Patients
Surrogate Parents (Humans)
Fear **Survey** Schedule
Kuder Occupational Interest **Survey**
Opinion Attitude and Interest Survey *USE Attitude Measures*
Surveys
Consumer **Surveys**
Mail **Surveys**
Opinion Surveys *USE Attitude Measures*
Telephone **Surveys**
Survival Instinct *USE Self Preservation*
Survivors
Holocaust **Survivors**
Susceptibility (Disorders)
Susceptibility (Hypnotic) *USE Hypnotic Susceptibility*
Hypnotic **Susceptibility**

ROTATED ALPHABETICAL TERMS SECTION

Suspension (School)
USE School Suspension
School **Suspension**
Suspicion
Sustained Attention
Life **Sustaining** Treatment
Swallowing
Mate Swapping *USE Extramarital Intercourse*
Body **Sway** Testing
Sweat
Sweating
Sweetness *USE Taste Perception*
Swimming
Code **Switching**
Nonsense **Syllable** Learning
Syllables
Syllogistic Reasoning
USE Inductive Deductive Reasoning
Symbiosis (Biological)
USE Biological Symbiosis
Biological **Symbiosis**
Symbiotic Infantile Psychosis
Symbolic Interactionism
Symbolism
Sympathectomy
Sympathetic Nervous System
Sympatholytic Drugs
Sympathomimetic Amines
Sympathomimetic Drugs
Sympathy
Symptom Checklists
Symptom Prescription
USE Paradoxical Techniques
Symptom Remission
Symptoms
Extrapyramidal **Symptoms**
Negative and Positive Symptoms
USE Positive and Negative Symptoms
Positive and Negative **Symptoms**
Psychiatric **Symptoms**
Psychotic Symptoms *USE Psychiatric Symptoms*
Synapses
Synaptic Plasticity *USE Neural Plasticity*
Synaptic Transmission
USE Neurotransmission
Syncope
Acquired Immune Deficiency Syndrome *USE AIDS*
Alcoholic Korsakoffs Syndrome *USE Korsakoffs Psychosis*
Androgen Insensitivity Syndrome
USE Testicular Feminization Syndrome
Aspergers **Syndrome**
Battered Child **Syndrome**
Capgras **Syndrome**
Cervical Sprain Syndrome *USE Whiplash*
Chronic Fatigue **Syndrome**
Creutzfeldt Jakob **Syndrome**
Cri du Chat Syndrome *USE Crying Cat Syndrome*
Crying Cat **Syndrome**
Cushings **Syndrome**
Down Syndrome *USE Downs Syndrome*
Downs **Syndrome**
Feminization Syndrome (Testicular)
USE Testicular Feminization Syndrome
Fetal Alcohol **Syndrome**
Fragile X **Syndrome**
Ganser Syndrome *USE Factitious Disorders*
Hospital Addiction Syndrome *USE Munchausen Syndrome*
Insulin Resistance Syndrome *USE Metabolic Syndrome*
Irritable Bowel **Syndrome**
Kleine Levin **Syndrome**
Klinefelters **Syndrome**
Metabolic **Syndrome**
Metabolic Syndrome X *USE Metabolic Syndrome*
Munchausen **Syndrome**
Munchausen **Syndrome** by Proxy
Neuroleptic Malignant **Syndrome**
Prader Willi **Syndrome**
Premenstrual **Syndrome**
Rett **Syndrome**
Temporomandibular Joint Syndrome *USE Musculoskeletal Disorders*
Testicular Feminization **Syndrome**
Tourette **Syndrome**
Turners **Syndrome**
Wernickes **Syndrome**
Williams **Syndrome**
Syndromes
Culture Bound **Syndromes**
Culture Specific Syndromes *USE Culture Bound Syndromes*
Organic Brain **Syndromes**
Drug Synergism *USE Drug Interactions*
Synesthesia
Lunar **Synodic** Cycle
Synonyms
Syntax
Synthetic Speech
Syphilis
Autonomic Nervous **System**
Autonomic Nervous **System** Disorders
Cardiovascular **System**
Caste **System**
Central Nervous **System**
Central Nervous **System** Disorders
Central Nervous System Drugs *USE CNS Affecting Drugs*
Digestive **System**
Digestive **System** Disorders
Endocrine **System**
Extrapyramidal Motor System *USE Extrapyramidal Tracts*
Extrapyramidal System *USE Extrapyramidal Tracts*
Gastrointestinal **System**
Hypothalamo Hypophyseal **System**
Hypothalamo Pituitary Adrenal System
USE Hypothalamic Pituitary Adrenal Axis
Immune **System**
Lemniscal **System**
Limbic **System**
Musculoskeletal **System**
Nervous **System**
Nervous **System** Disorders
Nervous **System** Neoplasms
Nervous System Plasticity *USE Neural Plasticity*
Parasympathetic Nervous **System**
Peripheral Nervous **System**
Respiratory **System**
Sclerosis (Nervous **System)**
Sensory **System** Disorders
Sympathetic Nervous **System**
Urogenital **System**
Systematic Desensitization Therapy
Desensitization (Systematic)
USE Systematic Desensitization Therapy
Systems
Systems Analysis
Systems Design
Systems Theory
Anatomical **Systems**
Classification Systems *USE Taxonomies*
Communication **Systems**
Decision Support **Systems**
Design (Man Machine Systems)
USE Human Machine Systems Design
Expert **Systems**
Family Systems Model
USE Family Systems Theory
Family **Systems** Theory
Human Machine **Systems**
Human Machine **Systems** Design
Information **Systems**
Intelligent Tutoring **Systems**
Knowledge Based Systems *USE Expert Systems*
Man Machine Systems *USE Human Machine Systems*
Man Machine Systems Design
USE Human Machine Systems Design
Management Information Systems *USE Information Systems*
Number **Systems**

ROTATED ALPHABETICAL TERMS SECTION

Political Economic **Systems**
Telephone **Systems**
Usability (Systems) *USE Human Factors Engineering*
Systolic Pressure
Szondi Test
T Groups *USE Human Relations Training*
T Mazes
T Test
Students T Test *USE T Test*
Tabes Dorsalis *USE Neurosyphilis*
Statistical **Tables**
Taboos
Tachistoscopes
Tachistoscopic Presentation
Tachycardia
Tactual Discrimination
USE Tactual Perception
Tactual Displays
Tactual Maps *USE Mobility Aids*
Tactual Perception
Tactual Stimulation
Tailored Testing *USE Adaptive Testing*
Note **Taking**
Perspective Taking *USE Role Taking*
Risk **Taking**
Role **Taking**
Sexual Risk **Taking**
Test **Taking**
Talent *USE Ability*
Talented *USE Gifted*
Fairy Tales *USE Folklore*
Self **Talk**
Sleep **Talking**
Tantrums
Tape Recorders
Recorders (Tape) *USE Tape Recorders*
Finger **Tapping**
Tardiness
Tardive Dyskinesia
Task Analysis
Task Complexity
Task Difficulty *USE Task Complexity*
Complexity (Task) *USE Task Complexity*
Dual **Task** Performance
Dual Task Procedure
USE Dual Task Performance
Time On **Task**
Concurrent Tasks *USE Dual Task Performance*
Piagetian **Tasks**
Taste Aversion Conditioning
USE Aversion Conditioning
Taste Buds
Taste Discrimination *USE Taste Perception*
Taste Disorders
Taste Perception
Taste Stimulation
Tattoos *USE Cosmetic Techniques*
Taurine
Taxation
Taxonomies
Psychiatric Classifications (Taxonomies)
USE Psychodiagnostic Typologies
Tay Sachs Disease
Taylor Manifest Anxiety Scale
Tea *USE Beverages (Nonalcoholic)*
Teacher Accreditation
USE Accreditation (Education Personnel)
Teacher Aides
Teacher Attitudes
Teacher Characteristics
Teacher Education
Teacher Effectiveness Evaluation
Teacher Effectiveness
USE Teacher Characteristics
Teacher Expectations
Teacher Personality
Teacher Recruitment
Teacher Student Interaction
Teacher Tenure
Teacher Training *USE Teacher Education*
Inservice **Teacher** Education
Minnesota Teacher Attitude Inventory
USE Attitude Measures
Tenure (Teacher) *USE Teacher Tenure*
Teachers
Classroom Teachers *USE Teachers*
College **Teachers**
Cooperating **Teachers**
Elementary School **Teachers**
High School **Teachers**
Junior High School **Teachers**
Middle School **Teachers**
Preschool **Teachers**
Preservice **Teachers**
Recruitment (Teachers) *USE Teacher Recruitment*
Resource **Teachers**
Special Education **Teachers**
Student **Teachers**
Supervising Teachers *USE Cooperating Teachers*
Technical Education Teachers
USE Vocational Education Teachers
Vocational Education **Teachers**
Teaching
Teaching Machines
Teaching Methods
Discovery **Teaching** Method
Initial **Teaching** Alphabet
Student **Teaching**
Team **Teaching** Method
Team Teaching Method
Teams
Self Managing Work **Teams**
Virtual **Teams**
Work **Teams**
Teasing
Technical Education Teachers
USE Vocational Education Teachers
Technical Personnel
Technical Schools
Technical Service Personnel
Holtzman Inkblot **Technique**
Mutual Storytelling **Technique**
Projective Testing **Technique**
Q Sort Testing **Technique**
Storytelling Technique
USE Mutual Storytelling Technique
Cognitive **Techniques**
Cosmetic **Techniques**
Paradigmatic Techniques *USE Paradoxical Techniques*
Paradoxical **Techniques**
Personal Growth Techniques
USE Human Potential Movement
Projective **Techniques**
Psychotherapeutic **Techniques**
Self Help **Techniques**
Stereotaxic **Techniques**
Therapeutic Techniques (Psychotherapy)
USE Psychotherapeutic Techniques
Technological Innovation *USE Innovation*
Technology
Technology Transfer
Assistive **Technology**
Information **Technology**
Nuclear **Technology**
Reproductive **Technology**
Teenage Fathers *USE Adolescent Fathers*
Teenage Mothers *USE Adolescent Mothers*
Teenage Pregnancy
USE Adolescent Pregnancy
Teeth (Anatomy)
Teeth Grinding *USE Bruxism*
Nocturnal **Teeth** Grinding
Ventral Tegmental Area *USE Tegmentum*
Tegmentum

Telecommunications Media
Telecommuting
Teleconferencing
Telehealth *USE Telemedicine*
Telekinesis *USE Psychokinesis*
Telemedicine
Telemetry
Telencephalon
Telepathy
Telephone Hot Lines *USE Hot Line Services*
Telephone Surveys
Telephone Systems
Teletherapy *USE Online Therapy*
Televised Instruction
Television
Television Advertising
Television Viewing
Closed Circuit **Television**
Educational **Television**
Temperament *USE Personality*
Temperature (Body)
USE Body Temperature
Temperature Effects
Temperature Perception
Body **Temperature**
Skin **Temperature**
Tempo
Conceptual **Tempo**
Temporal Frequency
Temporal Lobe
Temporal Spatial Concept Scale
USE Intelligence Measures
Temporomandibular Joint Syndrome
USE Musculoskeletal Disorders
Temptation
Central **Tendency** Measures
Achilles **Tendon** Reflex
Tendons
Tennessee Self Concept Scale
Tennis
Tension Headache
USE Muscle Contraction Headache
Premenstrual Tension *USE Premenstrual Syndrome*
Tenure (Occupational)
USE Occupational Tenure
Tenure (Teacher) *USE Teacher Tenure*
Occupational **Tenure**
Teacher **Tenure**
Teratogens
Long **Term** Care
Long **Term** Memory
Long Term Potentiation
USE Postactivation Potentials
Short **Term** Memory
Short Term Potentiation
USE Postactivation Potentials
Short Term Psychotherapy
USE Brief Psychotherapy
Terminal Cancer
Terminally Ill Patients
Video Display Terminals *USE Video Display Units*
Employee Termination *USE Personnel Termination*
Personnel **Termination**
Relationship **Termination**
Treatment **Termination**
Terminology
Terminology (Psychological)
USE Psychological Terminology
Psychological **Terminology**
Territoriality
Terror Management Theory
Terrorism
Night Terrors *USE Sleep Disorders*
Test Administration
Test Anxiety
Test Bias
Test Bias (Cultural) *USE Cultural Test Bias*
Test Coaching
Test Construction
Test Difficulty *USE Difficulty Level (Test)*
Test Equating *USE Score Equating*
Test Forms
Test Interpretation
Test Items
Test Normalization
USE Test Standardization
Test Norms
Test Reliability
Test Scores
Test Standardization
Test Taking
Test Tube Babies
USE Reproductive Technology
Test Validity
Administration (Test) *USE Test Administration*
Bender Gestalt **Test**
Benton Revised Visual Retention **Test**
Blacky Pictures Test *USE Projective Personality Measures*
Block Design Test (Kohs) *USE Kohs Block Design Test*
Cattell Culture Fair Intelligence Test *USE Culture Fair Intelligence Test*
Chi Square **Test**
Childrens Apperception **Test**
Classical **Test** Theory
Cochran Q Test *USE Nonparametric Statistical Tests*
College Entrance Examination
Board Scholastic Aptitude **Test**
Color Pyramid Test *USE Projective Personality Measures*
Content Analysis **(Test)**
Cultural **Test** Bias
Culture Fair Intelligence **Test**
Dexamethasone Suppression **Test**
Difficulty Level **(Test)**
Draw A Man Test *USE Human Figures Drawing*
F **Test**
Frostig Developmental **Test** of Visual Perception
General Aptitude **Test** Battery
Goodenough Harris Draw A Person **Test**
Illinois **Test** of Psycholinguistic Abilities
Item Analysis **(Test)**
Item Content **(Test)**
Kohs Block Design **Test**
Mann Whitney U **Test**
Matching Test *USE Matching to Sample*
Memory for Designs **Test**
Miller Analogies **Test**
Normalization (Test) *USE Test Standardization*
Norms (Test) *USE Test Norms*
Onomatopoeia and Images Test *USE Projective Personality Measures*
Peabody Picture Vocabulary **Test**
Porteus Maze **Test**
Preliminary Scholastic Aptitude Test
USE College Entrance Examination Board Scholastic Aptitude Test
Reliability (Test) *USE Test Reliability*
Rod and Frame **Test**
Rorschach **Test**
Scholastic Aptitude Test
USE College Entrance Examination Board Scholastic Aptitude Test
School and College Ability Test *USE Aptitude Measures*
Scores (Test) *USE Test Scores*
Sign Rank Test *USE Wilcoxon Sign Rank Test*
Sign **Test**
Slosson Intelligence **Test**
Spearman Brown **Test**
Standardization (Test) *USE Test Standardization*
Stanford Achievement **Test**
Stroop Color Word **Test**
Students T Test *USE T Test*
Szondi **Test**
T **Test**
Thematic Apperception **Test**
Validity (Test) *USE Test Validity*
Vane Kindergarten Test *USE Intelligence Measures*

Wide Range Achievement **Test**
Wilcoxon Sign Rank **Test**
Wisconsin Card Sorting **Test**
Zulliger Z **Test**
Testes
Testes Disorders
USE Endocrine Sexual Disorders
Testicular Feminization Syndrome
Feminization Syndrome (Testicular)
USE Testicular Feminization Syndrome
Testimony (Expert) *USE Expert Testimony*
Expert **Testimony**
Legal **Testimony**
Testing
Testing (Job Applicants)
USE Job Applicant Screening
Testing Methods
Adaptive **Testing**
AIDS Testing *USE HIV Testing*
Basic Skills Testing *USE Minimum Competency Tests*
Body Sway **Testing**
Cloze **Testing**
Cognitive Hypothesis **Testing**
Computer Adaptive Testing *USE Adaptive Testing*
Computer Assisted **Testing**
Digit Span **Testing**
Drug Testing *USE Drug Usage Screening*
Embedded Figures **Testing**
Essay **Testing**
Forced Choice **(Testing** Method)
Genetic **Testing**
Group **Testing**
HIV **Testing**
Hypothesis **Testing**
Hypothesis Testing (Cognitive)
USE Cognitive Hypothesis Testing
Individual **Testing**
Multiple Choice **(Testing** Method)
Null Hypothesis **Testing**
Projective **Testing** Technique
Psychological Testing *USE Psychometrics*
Q Sort **Testing** Technique
Reality **Testing**
Scaling **(Testing)**
Scoring **(Testing)**
Tailored Testing *USE Adaptive Testing*
Testosterone
Tests (Achievement)
USE Achievement Measures
Tests (Aptitude) *USE Aptitude Measures*
Tests (Intelligence)
USE Intelligence Measures
Tests (Personality)
USE Personality Measures
Tests (Statistical) *USE Statistical Tests*
Tests *USE Measurement*
Ability Tests *USE Aptitude Measures*
Comprehension **Tests**
Criterion Referenced **Tests**
Differential Aptitude **Tests**
Employment **Tests**
Henmon Nelson Tests of Mental Ability
USE Intelligence Measures
Iowa **Tests** of Basic Skills
Mastery Tests *USE Criterion Referenced Tests*
Metropolitan Readiness **Tests**
Minimum Competency **Tests**
Nonparametric Statistical **Tests**
Objective Referenced Tests *USE Criterion Referenced Tests*
Parametric Statistical **Tests**
Performance **Tests**
Personality Tests *USE Personality Measures*
Projective Tests *USE Projective Techniques*
Screening **Tests**
Selection **Tests**
Sentence Completion **Tests**
Sociometric **Tests**

Standardized **Tests**
Statistical **Tests**
True False Tests *USE Forced Choice (Testing Method)*
Verbal **Tests**
Testwiseness
Tetrabenazine
Tetrachoric Correlation
Tetrahydrocannabinol
Text Structure
Textbooks
Programmed **Textbooks**
Texture Perception
Thalamic Nuclei
Thalamotomy
Thalamus
Geniculate Bodies **(Thalamus)**
Thalidomide
Thanatology *USE Death Education*
Thanatos *USE Death Instinct*
Thankfulness *USE Gratitude*
Theatre
Theft
Thematic Apperception Test
Theology
Theophylline
Bayes Theorem *USE Statistical Probability*
Theoretical Interpretation
Theoretical Orientation
Theories
Theories of Education
Psychological **Theories**
Verification (of Theories) *USE Theory Verification*
Theory Formulation
Theory of Evolution
Theory of Mind
Theory Verification
Activity **Theory**
Attachment **Theory**
Chaos **Theory**
Classical Test **Theory**
Communication **Theory**
Decision **Theory**
Educational Theory *USE Theories of Education*
Evolution (Theory of) *USE Theory of Evolution*
Fairbairnian Theory *USE Object Relations*
Family Systems **Theory**
Fuzzy Set **Theory**
Game **Theory**
Grounded **Theory**
Information **Theory**
Item Response **Theory**
Latent Trait Theory *USE Item Response Theory*
Learning **Theory**
Personal Construct Theory *USE Personality Theory*
Personality **Theory**
Psychoanalytic **Theory**
Systems **Theory**
Terror Management **Theory**
Utility **Theory**
Winnicottian Theory *USE Object Relations*
Therapeutic Abortion *USE Induced Abortion*
Therapeutic Alliance
Therapeutic Camps
Therapeutic Community
Therapeutic Devices (Medical)
USE Medical Therapeutic Devices
Therapeutic Environment
Therapeutic Outcomes
USE Treatment Outcomes
Therapeutic Processes
Therapeutic Social Clubs
Therapeutic Techniques (Psychotherapy)
USE Psychotherapeutic Techniques
Camps (Therapeutic) *USE Therapeutic Camps*
Medical **Therapeutic** Devices
Negative **Therapeutic** Reaction
Social Clubs (Therapeutic) *USE Therapeutic Social Clubs*

Organic Therapies *USE Physical Treatment Methods*
Therapist Attitudes
Therapist Characteristics
Therapist Effectiveness *USE Therapist Characteristics*
Therapist Experience *USE Therapist Characteristics*
Therapist Patient Interaction *USE Psychotherapeutic Processes*
Therapist Patient Sexual Relations *USE Professional Client Sexual Relations*
Therapist Personality *USE Therapist Characteristics*
Therapist Role
Therapist Selection
Therapist Trainees
Patient Therapist Interaction *USE Psychotherapeutic Processes*
Patient Therapist Sexual Relations *USE Professional Client Sexual Relations*
Selection (Therapist) *USE Therapist Selection*
Therapists
Occupational **Therapists**
Physical **Therapists**
Speech **Therapists**
Therapy (Drug) *USE Drug Therapy*
Therapy *USE Treatment*
Activity Therapy *USE Recreation Therapy*
Animal Assisted **Therapy**
Art **Therapy**
Aversion **Therapy**
Behavior **Therapy**
Bright Light Therapy *USE Phototherapy*
Client Centered **Therapy**
Cognitive Behavior **Therapy**
Cognitive **Therapy**
Computer Assisted **Therapy**
Conjoint **Therapy**
Cooperative Therapy *USE Cotherapy*
Couples **Therapy**
Creative Arts **Therapy**
Dance **Therapy**
Directed Reverie Therapy *USE Guided Imagery*
Drama Therapy *USE Psychodrama*
Drug **Therapy**
ECS Therapy *USE Electroconvulsive Shock Therapy*
ECT (Therapy) *USE Electroconvulsive Shock Therapy*
Educational **Therapy**
Electroconvulsive Shock **Therapy**
Electroshock Therapy *USE Electroconvulsive Shock Therapy*
Emotion Focused **Therapy**
Emotionally Focused Therapy *USE Emotion Focused Therapy*
Encounter Group **Therapy**
Environmental Therapy *USE Milieu Therapy*
Estrogen Replacement Therapy *USE Hormone Therapy*
Existential **Therapy**
Exposure **Therapy**
Eye Movement Desensitization **Therapy**
Family **Therapy**
Feminist **Therapy**
Flooding Therapy *USE Implosive Therapy*
Gardening Therapy *USE Horticulture Therapy*
Gestalt **Therapy**
Group Therapy *USE Group Psychotherapy*
Gymnastic Therapy *USE Recreation Therapy*
Hormone **Therapy**
Horticulture **Therapy**
Illumination Therapy *USE Phototherapy*
Implosive **Therapy**
Individual Therapy *USE Individual Psychotherapy*
Insight **Therapy**
Insulin Shock **Therapy**
Interpersonal Therapy *USE Interpersonal Psychotherapy*
Light Therapy *USE Phototherapy*
Maintenance **Therapy**
Marathon Group **Therapy**
Marital Therapy *USE Marriage Counseling*
Marriage Therapy *USE Marriage Counseling*
Milieu **Therapy**
Morita **Therapy**
Movement **Therapy**
Multiple Therapy *USE Cotherapy*
Muscle Relaxation Therapy *USE Relaxation Therapy*
Music **Therapy**
Narrative **Therapy**
Nondirective Therapy *USE Client Centered Therapy*
Occupational **Therapy**
Online **Therapy**
Personal **Therapy**
Persuasion **Therapy**
Pet Therapy *USE Animal Assisted Therapy*
Physical **Therapy**
Play **Therapy**
Poetry **Therapy**
Pretraining (Therapy) *USE Client Education*
Primal **Therapy**
Progressive Relaxation **Therapy**
Psychoanalytic Therapy *USE Psychoanalysis*
Radiation **Therapy**
Rational Emotive Behavior **Therapy**
Rational Emotive Therapy *USE Rational Emotive Behavior Therapy*
Reality **Therapy**
Reciprocal Inhibition **Therapy**
Recreation **Therapy**
Relationship **Therapy**
Relaxation **Therapy**
Rogerian Therapy *USE Client Centered Therapy*
Sex **Therapy**
Shock **Therapy**
Socioenvironmental Therapy *USE Milieu Therapy*
Solution Focused **Therapy**
Speech **Therapy**
Systematic Desensitization **Therapy**
Triadic Therapy *USE Conjoint Therapy*
Vitamin **Therapy**
X Ray Therapy *USE Radiation Therapy*
Thermal Acclimatization
Thermal Factors *USE Temperature Effects*
Acclimatization (Thermal) *USE Thermal Acclimatization*
Thermoreceptors
Thermoregulation (Body)
Theta Rhythm
Thigh
Thinking
Autistic **Thinking**
Convergent Thinking *USE Inductive Deductive Reasoning*
Critical **Thinking**
Divergent **Thinking**
Logical **Thinking**
Magical **Thinking**
Rational Thinking *USE Rationality*
Thiopental
Thioridazine
Thiothixene
Third World Countries *USE Developing Countries*
Thirst
Thoracic Nerves *USE Spinal Nerves*
Thorax
Thorazine *USE Chlorpromazine*
Thought Content *USE Cognitions*
Thought Control *USE Brainwashing*
Thought Disturbances
Thought Suppression
Fantasies **(Thought** Disturbances)
Threat
Threat Postures

Threshold Determination
Critical Flicker Fusion **Threshold**
Luminance Threshold *USE Brightness Perception*
Luminance Threshold *USE Visual Thresholds*
Photic Threshold *USE Illumination*
Photic Threshold *USE Visual Thresholds*
Thresholds
Auditory **Thresholds**
Olfactory **Thresholds**
Pain **Thresholds**
Vibrotactile **Thresholds**
Visual **Thresholds**
Failure to **Thrive**
Thromboses
Coronary **Thromboses**
Project Follow **Through**
Thumb
Thumbsucking
Thymoleptic Drugs *USE Tranquilizing Drugs*
Thyroid Disorders
Thyroid Extract *USE Thyroid Hormones*
Thyroid Gland
Thyroid Hormones
Thyroid Stimulating Hormone
USE Thyrotropin
Thyroidectomy
Thyrotoxicosis
Thyrotropic Hormone *USE Thyrotropin*
Thyrotropin
Thyroxine
Tic Douloureux *USE Trigeminal Neuralgia*
Tics
Tigers *USE Felids*
Time
Time Disorientation
Time Estimation
Time Limited Psychotherapy
USE Brief Psychotherapy
Time Management
Time On Task
Time Out
Time Perception
Time Perspective
Time Planning Style
USE Time Management
Time Scheduling *USE Time Management*
Time Series
Time Utilization *USE Time Management*
Constant **Time** Delay
Disorientation (Time) *USE Time Disorientation*
Exposure Time (Stimulus) *USE Stimulus Duration*
Interresponse **Time**
Leisure **Time**
Part Time Employment *USE Employment Status*
Reaction **Time**
Response Time *USE Reaction Time*
Timers (Apparatus)
Timidity
Tinnitus
Tiredness *USE Fatigue*
Tissue Donation
Connective **Tissue** Cells
Tissues (Body)
Connective **Tissues**
Nerve **Tissues**
Toads
Tobacco (Drug) *USE Nicotine*
Tobacco (Smokeless)
USE Smokeless Tobacco
Tobacco Smoking
Chewing Tobacco *USE Smokeless Tobacco*
Environmental Tobacco Smoke *USE Passive Smoking*
Smokeless **Tobacco**
Smoking (Tobacco) *USE Tobacco Smoking*
Toes (Anatomy) *USE Feet (Anatomy)*
Tofranil *USE Imipramine*
Toilet Training

Token Economy Programs
Token Reinforcement
USE Secondary Reinforcement
Tolerance
Tolerance (Drug) *USE Drug Tolerance*
Tolerance for Ambiguity
Ambiguity (Tolerance) *USE Tolerance for Ambiguity*
Drug **Tolerance**
Toluene
Tomography
Positron Emission Tomography *USE Tomography*
Tone (Frequency) *USE Pitch (Frequency)*
Muscle **Tone**
Tongue
Tonic-Clonic Seizures
USE Grand Mal Seizures
Tonic Immobility
Tool Use
Animal Tool Use *USE Tool Use*
Top Level Managers
Topography
Torticollis
Tortoises *USE Turtles*
Torture
Totalitarianism
Touch *USE Tactual Perception*
Touching *USE Physical Contact*
Tourette Syndrome
Gilles de la Tourette Disorder *USE Tourette Syndrome*
Tourism
Aged (Attitudes **Toward)**
Aging (Attitudes **Toward)**
AIDS (Attitudes **Toward)**
Disabled (Attitudes **Toward)**
Handicapped (Attitudes Toward) *USE Disabled (Attitudes Toward)*
Homosexuality (Attitudes **Toward)**
Mental Illness (Attitudes **Toward)**
Mental Retardation (Attitudes **Toward)**
Obesity (Attitudes **Toward)**
Physical Disabilities (Attitudes **Toward)**
Physical Handicaps (Attitudes Toward)
USE Physical Disabilities (Attitudes Toward)
Physical Illness (Attitudes **Toward)**
Sensory Disabilities (Attitudes **Toward)**
Sensory Handicaps (Attitudes Toward)
USE Sensory Disabilities (Attitudes Toward)
Sports (Attitudes **Toward)**
Work (Attitudes **Toward)**
Towns
Toxic Disorders
Toxic Encephalopathies
Toxic Hepatitis
Toxic Psychoses
Toxic Waste *USE Hazardous Materials*
Toxicity
Toxicomania
Toxins
Toy Selection
Toys
Educational **Toys**
Memory **Trace**
Trachea
Tracking
Visual **Tracking**
Optic **Tract**
Respiratory **Tract** Disorders
Tractotomy
Corticospinal Tracts *USE Pyramidal Tracts*
Extrapyramidal **Tracts**
Pyramidal **Tracts**
Spinothalamic **Tracts**
Trade (Business) *USE Commerce*
Traditionalism *USE Conservatism*
Traditions

Traffic Accidents (Motor) *USE Motor Traffic Accidents*
Air **Traffic** Accidents
Air **Traffic** Control
Motor **Traffic** Accidents
Drug Trafficking *USE Illegal Drug Distribution*
Human **Trafficking**
Trainable Mentally Retarded *USE Moderate Mental Retardation*
Counselor **Trainees**
Psychotherapist Trainees *USE Therapist Trainees*
Therapist **Trainees**
Training
Training (Athletic) *USE Athletic Training*
Training (Clinical Methods) *USE Clinical Methods Training*
Training (Clinical Psychology Graduate) *USE Clinical Psychology Graduate Training*
Training (Community Mental Health) *USE Community Mental Health Training*
Training (Graduate Psychology) *USE Graduate Psychology Education*
Training (Mental Health Inservice) *USE Mental Health Inservice Training*
Training (Motivation) *USE Motivation Training*
Training (Personnel) *USE Personnel Training*
Training (Psychiatric) *USE Psychiatric Training*
Training (Psychoanalytic) *USE Psychoanalytic Training*
Training (Psychotherapy) *USE Psychotherapy Training*
Assertiveness **Training**
Athletic **Training**
Autogenic **Training**
Biofeedback **Training**
Childbirth **Training**
Clinical Methods **Training**
Clinical Psychology Graduate **Training**
Communication Skills **Training**
Community Mental Health **Training**
Computer Based Training *USE Computer Assisted Instruction*
Computer **Training**
Human Relations **Training**
Inservice **Training**
Inservice Training (Mental Health) *USE Mental Health Inservice Training*
Job Training *USE Personnel Training*
Management **Training**
Memory **Training**
Mental Health Inservice **Training**
Mental Health Training (Community) *USE Community Mental Health Training*
Military **Training**
Motivation **Training**
Omission **Training**
On the Job **Training**
Parent Effectiveness Training *USE Parent Training*
Parent **Training**
Personnel **Training**
Postgraduate **Training**
Psychiatric **Training**
Psychoanalytic **Training**
Psychotherapy **Training**
Self Instructional **Training**
Sensitivity **Training**
Social Skills **Training**
Sport Training *USE Athletic Training*
Teacher Training *USE Teacher Education*
Toilet **Training**
Work Adjustment **Training**
Trains (Railroad) *USE Railroad Trains*
Railroad **Trains**
Latent Trait Theory *USE Item Response Theory*
Quantitative **Trait** Loci
State **Trait** Anxiety Inventory
Personality **Traits**
Major Tranquilizers *USE Neuroleptic Drugs*
Minor **Tranquilizers**
Tranquilizing Drugs
Transactional Analysis
Transaminases
Transcranial Magnetic Stimulation
Repetitive Transcranial Magnetic Stimulation *USE Transcranial Magnetic Stimulation*
Transcultural Psychiatry
Transducers
Transfer (Learning)
Transfer Students
Client **Transfer**
Interhemispheric Transfer *USE Interhemispheric Interaction*
Interocular **Transfer**
Knowledge **Transfer**
Negative **Transfer**
Patient Transfer *USE Client Transfer*
Positive **Transfer**
Technology **Transfer**
Transferases
Transference (Psychotherapeutic) *USE Psychotherapeutic Transference*
Psychotherapeutic **Transference**
Transformational Generative Grammar
Transformational Leadership
Transfusion (Blood) *USE Blood Transfusion*
Blood **Transfusion**
Transgendered *USE Transsexualism*
Transgenerational Patterns
Transistors (Apparatus) *USE Apparatus*
School to Work **Transition**
School **Transition**
Transitional Objects
Career Transitions *USE Career Development*
Life Transitions *USE Life Changes*
Foreign Language **Translation**
Translocation (Chromosome)
Disease **Transmission**
Intergenerational Transmission *USE Transgenerational Patterns*
Neural Transmission *USE Neurotransmission*
Synaptic Transmission *USE Neurotransmission*
Sexually **Transmitted** Diseases
Transnational Corporations *USE Multinational Corporations*
Transpersonal Psychology
Neural **Transplantation**
Organ **Transplantation**
Renal Transplantation *USE Organ Transplantation*
Transplants (Organ) *USE Organ Transplantation*
Heart Transplants *USE Organ Transplantation*
Kidney Transplants *USE Organ Transplantation*
Transportation
Transportation Accidents
Transportation Safety
Air **Transportation**
Ground **Transportation**
Public **Transportation**
Water **Transportation**
Transposition (Cognition)
Transracial Adoption *USE Interracial Adoption*
Transsexualism
Transvestism
Tranylcypromine
Trauma
Trauma (Emotional) *USE Emotional Trauma*
Trauma (Physical) *USE Injuries*
Birth **Trauma**
Emotional **Trauma**
Physical Trauma *USE Injuries*
Traumatic Brain Injury

Traumatic Neurosis
Traumatic Psychosis *USE Reactive Psychosis*
Brain Injury (Traumatic) *USE Traumatic Brain Injury*
Commuting **(Travel)**
Traveling
Trazodone
Treatment
Treatment Barriers
Treatment Client Matching *USE Client Treatment Matching*
Treatment Compliance
Treatment Dropouts
Treatment Duration
Treatment Effectiveness Evaluation
Treatment Environment *USE Therapeutic Environment*
Treatment Facilities
Treatment Guidelines
Treatment Methods (Physical) *USE Physical Treatment Methods*
Treatment Outcomes
Treatment Planning
Treatment Refusal
Treatment Resistant Depression
Treatment Resistant Disorders
Treatment Seeking Behavior *USE Health Care Seeking Behavior*
Treatment Termination
Treatment Withholding
Barriers (Treatment) *USE Treatment Barriers*
Client **Treatment** Matching
Court Ordered Treatment *USE Court Referrals*
Cross Cultural **Treatment**
Day Care (Treatment) *USE Partial Hospitalization*
Dental **Treatment**
Electrosleep **Treatment**
Evaluation (Treatment Effectiveness) *USE Treatment Effectiveness Evaluation*
Interdisciplinary **Treatment** Approach
Involuntary **Treatment**
Life Sustaining **Treatment**
Medical **Treatment** (General)
Multidisciplinary Treatment Approach *USE Interdisciplinary Treatment Approach*
Multimodal **Treatment** Approach
Outcomes (Treatment) *USE Treatment Outcomes*
Outpatient **Treatment**
Patient Treatment Matching *USE Client Treatment Matching*
Physical **Treatment** Methods
Refusal (Treatment) *USE Treatment Refusal*
Right to **Treatment**
Side Effects **(Treatment)**
Sleep **Treatment**
Delirium **Tremens**
Tremor
Trends
Triadic Therapy *USE Conjoint Therapy*
Trial and Error Learning
Competency to Stand **Trial**
Clinical **Trials**
Triazolam
Tribes
Trichotillomania
Tricyclic Antidepressant Drugs
Tricyclic Resistant Depression *USE Treatment Resistant Depression*
Trifluoperazine
Triflupromazine *USE Phenothiazine Derivatives*
Trigeminal Nerve
Trigeminal Neuralgia
Trigonum Cerebrale *USE Fornix*
Trihexyphenidyl
Triiodothyronine
Triplets
Educational Field **Trips**
Field Trips (Educational) *USE Educational Field Trips*
Trisomy
Trisomy 21 *USE Downs Syndrome*
Trochlear Nerve *USE Cranial Nerves*
Truancy
School **Truancy**
Trucks *USE Motor Vehicles*
True False Tests *USE Forced Choice (Testing Method)*
Trust (Social Behavior)
Tryptamine
Tryptophan
Tubal Ligation
Eustachian Tube *USE Middle Ear*
Test Tube Babies *USE Reproductive Technology*
Tuberculosis
Pulmonary **Tuberculosis**
Cathode Ray Tubes *USE Video Display Units*
Tubocurarine
Tumor Necrosis Factor
Tumors *USE Neoplasms*
Tunnel Vision
Turners Syndrome
Turnover *USE Employee Turnover*
Employee **Turnover**
Personnel Turnover *USE Employee Turnover*
Turtles
Tutoring
Intelligent **Tutoring** Systems
Peer **Tutoring**
Tutors *USE Teachers*
Twelve Step Programs
Twins
Conjoined **Twins**
Dizygotic Twins *USE Heterozygotic Twins*
Fraternal Twins *USE Heterozygotic Twins*
Heterozygotic **Twins**
Identical Twins *USE Monozygotic Twins*
Monozygotic **Twins**
Siamese Twins *USE Conjoined Twins*
Chorda Tympani Nerve *USE Facial Nerve*
Tympanic Membrane *USE Middle Ear*
Type A Personality *USE Coronary Prone Behavior*
Type B Personality *USE Coronary Prone Behavior*
Type I Errors
Type II Errors
Dementia of Alzheimers Type *USE Alzheimers Disease*
Myers Briggs **Type** Indicator
Schizophrenia (Disorganized **Type)**
Schizophrenia (Residual Type) *USE Schizophrenia*
Body Types *USE Somatotypes*
Typing
Typists *USE Clerical Personnel*
Typologies (General) *USE Taxonomies*
Typologies (Psychodiagnostic) *USE Psychodiagnostic Typologies*
Psychodiagnostic **Typologies**
Tyramine
Tyrosine
Mann Whitney **U** Test
Ulcerative Colitis
Ulcers (Gastrointestinal) *USE Gastrointestinal Ulcers*
Gastrointestinal **Ulcers**
Peptic Ulcers *USE Gastrointestinal Ulcers*
Ulnar Nerve *USE Spinal Nerves*
Ultrasound
Uncertainty
Unconditioned Reflex *USE Reflexes*
Unconditioned Responses
Unconditioned Stimulus

Stimulus (Unconditioned)
USE Unconditioned Stimulus
Unconscious (Personality Factor)
Collective **Unconscious**
Driving **Under** the Influence
Underachievement (Academic)
USE Academic Underachievement
Academic **Underachievement**
Underage Drinking
Underdeveloped Countries
USE Developing Countries
Undergraduate Degrees
USE Educational Degrees
Undergraduate Education
Undergraduates *USE College Students*
Underprivileged *USE Disadvantaged*
Understanding *USE Comprehension*
Underwater Effects
Underweight
Undifferentiated Schizophrenia
Unemployment
Labor **Union** Members
Labor **Unions**
Unipolar Depression *USE Major Depression*
Hospital Psychiatric Units *USE Psychiatric Units*
Psychiatric **Units**
Shock **Units**
Video Display **Units**
Words (Phonetic **Units)**
Universities *USE Colleges*
Open Universities *USE Nontraditional Education*
Unskilled Industrial Workers
Unwed Mothers
Upper Class
Upper Class Attitudes
Upper Income Level
Neurotransmitter **Uptake** Inhibitors
Upward Bound
Upward Mobility *USE Social Mobility*
Urban Development
USE Community Development
Urban Environments
Urban Planning
Urbanization
Uric Acid
Urinalysis
Urinary Function Disorders
Urinary Incontinence
Incontinence (Urinary) *USE Urinary Incontinence*
Urination
Urine
Urogenital Disorders
Urogenital System
Usability (Systems)
USE Human Factors Engineering
Drug **Usage**
Drug **Usage** Attitudes
Drug **Usage** Screening
Internet **Usage**
Intravenous Drug **Usage**
IV Drug Usage *USE Intravenous Drug Usage*
Marijuana **Usage**
Animal Tool Use *USE Tool Use*
Tool **Use**
Uterus
Utility Theory
Utilization (Health Care)
USE Health Care Utilization
Utilization Reviews
Health Care **Utilization**
Health Service Utilization *USE Health Care Utilization*
Time Utilization *USE Time Management*
Vacation Benefits
USE Employee Leave Benefits
Vacationing
Vaccination *USE Immunization*
Vagina
Vaginismus
Vagotomy
Vagus Nerve
Validity (Statistical) *USE Statistical Validity*
Validity (Test) *USE Test Validity*
Concept Validity *USE Test Validity*
Concurrent Validity *USE Test Validity*
Construct Validity *USE Test Validity*
Content Validity *USE Test Validity*
Convergent Validity *USE Test Validity*
Criterion Related Validity *USE Test Validity*
Discriminant Validity *USE Test Validity*
Factorial Validity *USE Statistical Validity*
Predictive Validity *USE Statistical Validity*
Statistical **Validity**
Test **Validity**
Valium *USE Diazepam*
Valproic Acid
Values
Allport Vernon Lindzey Study Values *USE Attitude Measures*
Ethnic **Values**
Personal **Values**
Social **Values**
Valves (Heart) *USE Heart Valves*
Heart **Valves**
Vandalism
Vane Kindergarten Test
USE Intelligence Measures
Variability (Response)
USE Response Variability
Variability (Stimulus)
USE Stimulus Variability
Variability Measurement
Response **Variability**
Stimulus **Variability**
Variable Interval Reinforcement
Variable Ratio Reinforcement
Dependent **Variables**
Independent **Variables**
Statistical **Variables**
Variance Homogeneity
USE Homogeneity of Variance
Analysis of **Variance**
Error Variance *USE Error of Measurement*
Heterogeneity of Variance *USE Homogeneity of Variance*
Homogeneity of **Variance**
Interaction **Variance**
Contingent Negative **Variation**
Diurnal Variations *USE Human Biological Rhythms*
Seasonal **Variations**
Varimax Rotation
Vascular Dementia
Vascular Disorders
USE Cardiovascular Disorders
Cerebral Vascular Disorders
USE Cerebrovascular Disorders
Vasectomy
Vasoconstriction
Vasoconstrictor Drugs
Vasodilation
Vasodilator Drugs
Vasopressin
Vasopressor Drugs
USE Vasoconstrictor Drugs
Motor **Vehicles**
Veins (Anatomy)
Velocity
Venereal Diseases
USE Sexually Transmitted Diseases
Diseases (Venereal)
USE Sexually Transmitted Diseases
Venlafaxine
Ventral Roots
Ventral Striatum *USE Basal Ganglia*
Ventral Tegmental Area *USE Tegmentum*
Ventricles (Cerebral)
USE Cerebral Ventricles

ROTATED ALPHABETICAL TERMS SECTION

Ventricles (Heart) *USE Heart Ventricles*
Cerebral **Ventricles**
Heart **Ventricles**
Ventricular Fibrillation *USE Fibrillation (Heart)*
Venture Capital
Verapamil
Verbal Ability
Verbal Abuse
Verbal Communication
Verbal Comprehension
Verbal Conditioning *USE Verbal Learning*
Verbal Fluency
Verbal Learning
Verbal Meaning
Verbal Memory
Verbal Reinforcement
Verbal Stimuli
Verbal Tests
Conditioning (Verbal) *USE Verbal Learning*
Verbalization *USE Oral Communication*
Verbs
Verdict Determination *USE Adjudication*
Vergence Movements *USE Eye Convergence*
Verification (of Theories) *USE Theory Verification*
Theory **Verification**
Vernier Acuity *USE Visual Acuity*
Allport Vernon Lindzey Study Values *USE Attitude Measures*
Vertebrates
Vertigo
Blood **Vessels**
Coronary Vessels *USE Arteries (Anatomy)*
Retinal Vessels *USE Arteries (Anatomy)*
Vestibular Apparatus
Vestibular Disorders *USE Labyrinth Disorders*
Vestibular Nystagmus *USE Nystagmus*
Vestibular Stimulation *USE Somesthetic Stimulation*
Vestibulocochlear Nerve *USE Acoustic Nerve*
Veterans (Military) *USE Military Veterans*
Military **Veterans**
Veterinary Medicine
Viagra *USE Sildenafil*
Vibration
Vibrators (Apparatus)
Vibrotactile Thresholds
Vicarious Experiences
Vicarious Reinforcement *USE Vicarious Experiences*
Reinforcement (Vicarious) *USE Vicarious Experiences*
Victimization
Crime **Victims**
Video Display Terminals *USE Video Display Units*
Video Display Units
Video Games *USE Computer Games*
Digital **Video**
Videotape Instruction
Videotape Recorders
Videotapes
Vietnamese Cultural Groups
World **View**
Television **Viewing**
Vigilance
Vineland Social Maturity Scale
Boundary Violations (Sexual) *USE Professional Client Sexual Relations*
Sexual Boundary Violations *USE Professional Client Sexual Relations*
Violence
Client Violence *USE Patient Violence*
Domestic **Violence**
Family Violence *USE Domestic Violence*
Intimate Partner **Violence**
Patient **Violence**
School **Violence**
Workplace **Violence**
Violent Crime
Viral Disorders
Epstein Barr **Viral** Disorder
Virginity
Virtual Classrooms
Virtual Markets *USE Electronic Commerce*
Virtual Reality
Virtual Teams
Human Immunodeficiency Virus *USE HIV*
Vision
Vision Disorders
Vision Disturbances (Hysterical) *USE Hysterical Vision Disturbances*
Binocular **Vision**
Central Vision *USE Foveal Vision*
Foveal **Vision**
Hysterical **Vision** Disturbances
Monocular **Vision**
Peripheral **Vision**
Stereoscopic **Vision**
Tunnel **Vision**
Visions (Mysticism) *USE Mysticism*
Visitation (Institution) *USE Institution Visitation*
Visitation Rights *USE Child Visitation*
Child **Visitation**
Institution **Visitation**
Home **Visiting** Programs
Visual Acuity
Visual Attention
Visual Contrast
Visual Cortex
Visual Discrimination
Visual Displays
Visual Evoked Potentials
Visual Feedback
Visual Field
Visual Fixation *USE Eye Fixation*
Visual Hallucinations
Visual Impairment *USE Vision Disorders*
Visual Masking
Visual Memory
Visual Neglect *USE Sensory Neglect*
Visual Perception
Visual Perspective *USE Linear Perspective*
Visual Receptive Fields
Visual Search
Visual Spatial Ability *USE Visuospatial Ability*
Visual Spatial Memory *USE Visuospatial Memory*
Visual Stimulation
Visual Thresholds
Visual Tracking
Benton Revised **Visual** Retention Test
Cortex (Visual) *USE Visual Cortex*
Focusing (Visual) *USE Ocular Accommodation*
Frostig Developmental Test of **Visual** Perception
Visualization *USE Imagery*
Visually Handicapped *USE Vision Disorders*
Visuospatial Ability
Visuospatial Memory
Vitamin C *USE Ascorbic Acid*
Vitamin Deficiency Disorders
Vitamin Therapy
Vitamins
In Vitro Fertilization *USE Reproductive Technology*
Vocabulary
Peabody Picture **Vocabulary** Test

ROTATED ALPHABETICAL TERMS SECTION

Sight **Vocabulary**
Words (Vocabulary) *USE Vocabulary*
Vocal Cords
Vocalization
Vocalization (Infant) *USE Infant Vocalization*
Infant **Vocalization**
Vocalizations (Animal)
USE Animal Vocalizations
Animal **Vocalizations**
Vocational Adjustment
USE Occupational Adjustment
Vocational Aspirations
USE Occupational Aspirations
Vocational Choice
USE Occupational Choice
Vocational Counseling
USE Occupational Guidance
Vocational Counselors
Vocational Education
Vocational Education Teachers
Vocational Evaluation
Vocational Guidance
USE Occupational Guidance
Vocational Interests
USE Occupational Interests
Vocational Maturity
Vocational Mobility
USE Occupational Mobility
Vocational Preference
USE Occupational Preference
Vocational Rehabilitation
Vocational School Students
Vocational Schools *USE Technical Schools*
Armed Services **Vocational** Aptitude Battery
Maturity (Vocational) *USE Vocational Maturity*
Rehabilitation (Vocational) *USE Vocational Rehabilitation*
Strong **Vocational** Interest Blank
Vocations *USE Occupations*
Voice
Voice Disorders *USE Dysphonia*
Voles
Volition
Volt Meters *USE Apparatus*
Blood **Volume**
Brain Volume *USE Brain Size*
Volunteer Civilian Personnel
USE Volunteers
Volunteer Military Personnel
Volunteer Personnel *USE Volunteers*
Volunteerism *USE Volunteers*
Volunteers
Volunteers (Experiment)
USE Experimental Subjects
Experiment Volunteers *USE Experimental Subjects*
Vomeronasal Sense
Vomit Inducing Drugs *USE Emetic Drugs*
Vomiting
Voting Behavior
Vowels
Voyeurism
Deja Vu *USE Consciousness States*
Vulnerability (Disorders)
USE Susceptibility (Disorders)
Vygotsky (Lev)
Wages *USE Salaries*
Sleep **Wake** Cycle
Wakefulness
Walk In Clinics
Walking
Abdominal **Wall**
Wandering Behavior
War
Nuclear **War**
Prisoners of **War**
Duty to **Warn**
Warning Labels
Warning Signs *USE Warnings*
Warnings
Safety Warnings *USE Warnings*
Wasps
Toxic Waste *USE Hazardous Materials*
Water Deprivation
Water Intake
Water Safety
Water Transportation
Watson (John Broadus)
Slow Wave Sleep *USE NREM Sleep*
Sound Waves *USE Acoustics*
Weaning
Weapons
Weather *USE Atmospheric Conditions*
Web Based Mental Health Services
USE Online Therapy
Web Sites *USE Websites*
World Wide Web (WWW) *USE Internet*
Websites
Wechsler Adult Intelligence Scale
Wechsler Bellevue Intelligence Scale
Wechsler Intelligence Scale for Children
Wechsler Memory Scale
Wechsler Preschool Primary Scale
Work **Week** Length
Weight (Body) *USE Body Weight*
Weight (Statistics)
USE Statistical Weighting
Weight Control
Weight Perception
Birth **Weight**
Body **Weight**
Brain **Weight**
Low Birth Weight *USE Birth Weight*
Statistical **Weighting**
Weightlessness
Weightlifting
Welfare Reform
Welfare Services (Government)
Animal **Welfare**
Child **Welfare**
Community **Welfare** Services
Public Welfare Services
USE Community Welfare Services
Well Being
Wellness *USE Health*
Wernickes Syndrome
Whales
Wheelchairs *USE Mobility Aids*
Whiplash
Whistleblowing *USE Informants*
White Betz A B Scale
USE Nonprojective Personality Measures
White Blood Cells *USE Leucocytes*
White Collar Workers
White Noise
White Rats *USE Rats*
Whites
Mann **Whitney** U Test
Wholistic Health *USE Holistic Health*
Wide Range Achievement Test
World Wide Web (WWW) *USE Internet*
Widowers
Widows
Wilcoxon Sign Rank Test
Wilderness Experience
Free Will *USE Volition*
Prader **Willi** Syndrome
James **(William)**
Williams Syndrome
Willpower *USE Self Control*
Living Wills *USE Advance Directives*
Wilson Patterson Conservatism Scale
Wine
Winnicottian Theory *USE Object Relations*
Winter Depression
USE Seasonal Affective Disorder

ROTATED ALPHABETICAL TERMS SECTION

Wisconsin Card Sorting Test
Wisdom
Witchcraft
Attention Deficit Disorder **with** Hyperactivity
Dementia **with** Lewy Bodies
Withdrawal (Defense Mechanism)
Withdrawal (Drug) *USE Drug Withdrawal*
Alcohol **Withdrawal**
Drug **Withdrawal**
Drug Withdrawal Effects *USE Drug Withdrawal*
Nicotine **Withdrawal**
Treatment **Withholding**
Within Subjects Design
USE Repeated Measures
Witnesses
Wives
Wolves
Women *USE Human Females*
Women Centered Psychology
USE Psychology of Women
Battered Women *USE Battered Females*
Psychology of **Women**
Working **Women**
Womens Liberation Movement
Woodcock Johnson Psychoeducational Battery
Word Associations
Word Blindness *USE Alexia*
Word Deafness *USE Aphasia*
Word Frequency
Word Meaning
Word Origins *USE Etymology*
Word Processing
Word Recognition
Associations (Word) *USE Word Associations*
Stroop Color **Word** Test
Words (Form Classes)
USE Form Classes (Language)
Words (Phonetic Units)
Words (Vocabulary) *USE Vocabulary*
Work (Attitudes Toward)
Work Addiction *USE Workaholism*
Work Adjustment Training
Work at Home *USE Telecommuting*
Work Environments
USE Working Conditions
Work Ethic *USE Work (Attitudes Toward)*
Work Family Relationship
USE Family Work Relationship
Work Load
Work Related Illnesses
Work Rest Cycles
Work Satisfaction *USE Job Satisfaction*
Work Scheduling
Work Stress *USE Occupational Stress*
Work Study Programs
USE Educational Programs
Work Teams
Work Week Length
Computer Supported Cooperative Work *USE Groupware*
Family **Work** Relationship
Field Work (Educational)
USE Curricular Field Experience
Noise Levels **(Work** Areas)
Quality of **Work** Life
Return to Work *USE Reemployment*
Scheduling (Work) *USE Work Scheduling*
School to **Work** Transition
Self Managing **Work** Teams
Social Work *USE Social Casework*
Social **Work** Education
Workaholism
Workday Shifts
Shifts (Workday) *USE Workday Shifts*
Workers' Compensation Insurance
Workers *USE Personnel*
Agricultural Extension **Workers**
Agricultural **Workers**
Auxiliary Health Workers *USE Allied Health Personnel*
Blue Collar **Workers**
Child Care **Workers**
Extension Workers (Agricultural)
USE Agricultural Extension Workers
Foreign **Workers**
Guest Workers *USE Foreign Workers*
Migrant Farm **Workers**
Psychiatric Social **Workers**
Skilled Industrial **Workers**
Social **Workers**
Unskilled Industrial **Workers**
White Collar **Workers**
Workforce Diversity
USE Diversity in the Workplace
Working Alliance *USE Therapeutic Alliance*
Working Conditions
Working Memory *USE Short Term Memory*
Working Space
Working Women
Workmen's Compensation Insurance
USE Workers' Compensation Insurance
Workplace Diversity
USE Diversity in the Workplace
Workplace Violence
Diversity in the **Workplace**
Sheltered **Workshops**
World View
World Wide Web (WWW) *USE Internet*
Third World Countries *USE Developing Countries*
Worms
Worry *USE Anxiety*
Worship *USE Religious Practices*
Saint John's Wort *USE Hypericum Perforatum*
St. John's Wort *USE Hypericum Perforatum*
Wounds
Self Inflicted **Wounds**
Wrist
Writers
Writing (Creative) *USE Creative Writing*
Writing (Cursive) *USE Cursive Writing*
Writing (Handwriting) *USE Handwriting*
Writing Skills
Creative **Writing**
Cursive **Writing**
Written Communication
Written Language
Wryneck *USE Torticollis*
World Wide Web (WWW) *USE Internet*
X Rated Materials *USE Pornography*
X Ray Diagnosis *USE Roentgenography*
X Ray Therapy *USE Radiation Therapy*
Fragile **X** Syndrome
Xenophobia *USE Stranger Reactions*
Xylocaine *USE Lidocaine*
Yawning
Yoga
Yohimbine
Predelinquent **Youth**
Z Scores *USE Standard Scores*
Zulliger **Z** Test
Zen Buddhism
Non **Zero** Sum Games
Zidovudine
Zimeldine
Zinc
Zoo Environment *USE Animal Captivity*
Zoology
Zulliger Z Test
Zungs Self Rating Depression Scale

TERM CLUSTERS SECTION

Term Cluster/Subcluster Subject Areas

Computers Cluster
- Computer Applications
- Computer Automation
- Computers & Communication
- Computers & Media
- Education & Training
- Equipment
- Human Machine Systems & Engineering
- Information

Disorders Cluster
- Antisocial Behavior & Behavior Disorders
- Diagnosis
- Disorder Characteristics
- Learning Disorders & Mental Retardation
- Physical & Psychosomatic Disorders
- Psychological Disorders
- Speech & Language Disorders
- Symptomatology

Educational Cluster
- Academic Learning & Achievement
- Curricula
- Educational Personnel & Administration
- Educational Testing & Counseling
- Schools & Institutions
- Special Education
- Student Characteristics & Academic Environment
- Student Populations
- Teaching & Teaching Methods

Legal Cluster
- Adjudication
- Criminal Groups
- Criminal Offenses
- Criminal Rehabilitation
- Laws
- Legal Issues
- Legal Personnel
- Legal Processes

Neuropsychology & Neurology Cluster
- Assessment & Diagnosis
- Electrophysiology
- Neuroanatomy
- Neurological Disorders
- Neurological Intervention
- Neurosciences
- Neurotransmitters & Neuroregulators

Occupational & Employment Cluster
- Career Areas
- Employee, Occupational & Job Characteristics
- Occupational Groups
- Organizations & Organizational Behavior
- Personnel Management & Professional Personnel Issues

Statistical Cluster
- Design, Analysis & Interpretation
- Statistical Reliability & Validity
- Statistical Theory & Experimental

Tests & Testing Cluster
- Academic Achievement & Aptitude Measures
- Attitude & Interest Measures
- Developmental Measures
- Intelligence Measures
- Neuropsychological Measures
- Nonprojective Personality Measures
- Perceptual Measures
- Projective Personality Measures
- Testing
- Testing Methods

Treatment Cluster
- Alternative Therapies
- Behavior Modification & Therapy
- Counseling
- Hospitalization & Institutionalization
- Medical & Physical Treatment
- Psychotherapy
- Rehabilitation
- Treatment (General)
- Treatment Facilities

COMPUTERS CLUSTER

- Computer Applications
- Computer Automation
- Computers & Communication
- Computers & Media
- Education & Training
- Equipment
- Human Machine Systems & Engineering
- Information

Computer Applications

Algorithms
Artificial Intelligence
Audiovisual Communications Media
Automated Information Coding
Automated Information Processing
Automated Information Retrieval
Automated Information Storage
Automated Speech Recognition
Computer Applications
Computer Assisted Design
Computer Assisted Diagnosis
Computer Assisted Instruction
Computer Assisted Testing
Computer Assisted Therapy
Computer Games
Computer Programming
Computer Programming Languages
Computer Searching
Computer Simulation
Computer Software
Cybernetics
Data Processing
Databases
Decision Support Systems
Electronic Commerce
Electronic Communication
Electronic Retailing
Error Analysis
Expert Systems
Groupware
Hypermedia
Hypertext
Information Systems
Intelligent Agents
Internet
Internet Usage
Neural Networks
Online Therapy
Word Processing

Computer Automation

Artificial Intelligence
Automated Information Coding
Automated Information Processing
Automated Information Retrieval
Automated Information Storage
Automated Speech Recognition
Automation
Computer Assisted Design
Computer Assisted Diagnosis
Computer Assisted Instruction
Computer Assisted Testing
Cybernetics
Decision Support Systems
Human Machine Systems
Neural Networks
Robotics

Computers & Communication

Audiovisual Communications Media
Communication Systems
Communication Theory
Communications Media
Computer Mediated Communication
Electronic Commerce
Electronic Communication
Electronic Retailing
Groupware
Hot Line Services
Hypermedia
Hypertext
Information Dissemination
Internet
Internet Addiction
Internet Usage
Mass Media
Online Social Networks
Scientific Communication
Technology Transfer
Telecommunications Media
Television Advertising
Virtual Classrooms
Virtual Teams
Websites

Computers & Media

Audiovisual Communications Media
Communications Media
Computer Software
Databases
Electronic Commerce
Electronic Communication
Electronic Retailing
Hot Line Services
Hypermedia
Hypertext
Information Services
Information Systems
Internet
Mass Media
News Media
Telecommunications Media
Televised Instruction
Websites

Education & Training

Computer Assisted Instruction
Computer Assisted Language Learning
Computer Assisted Testing
Computer Literacy
Computer Training
Digital Divide
Educational Television
Teaching Machines
Televised Instruction
Virtual Classrooms
Virtual Teams

Equipment

Analog Computers
Apparatus
Computer Peripheral Devices
Digital Computers
Digital Video
Human Computer Interaction
Keyboards
Microcomputers
Robotics
Video Display Units
Visual Displays

Human Machine Systems & Engineering

Automated Speech Recognition
Computer Peripheral Devices
Decision Support Systems
Human Computer Interaction
Human Factors Engineering
Human Machine Systems
Human Machine Systems Design
Inductive Logic Programming
Instrument Controls
Intelligent Tutoring Systems
Knowledge Engineering
Person Environment Fit
Systems Design
Teaching Machines
Virtual Reality

Information

Automated Information Coding
Automated Information Processing
Automated Information Retrieval
Automated Information Storage
Bioinformatics
Communication Theory
Communications Media
Computer Searching
Data Collection
Data Processing
Databases
Expert Systems
Hot Line Services

Consult Relationship Section for more information

Hypermedia
Hypertext
Information
Information Dissemination
Information Literacy
Information Processing Model
Information Seeking
Information Services
Information Specialists
Information Systems
Information Technology
Information Theory
Internet
Knowledge Management
Mass Media
Ontologies
Telecommunications Media
Websites

DISORDERS CLUSTER

- Antisocial Behavior & Behavior Disorders
- Diagnosis
- Disorder Characteristics
- Learning Disorders & Mental Retardation
- Physical & Psychosomatic Disorders
- Psychological Disorders
- Speech & Language Disorders
- Symptomatology

Antisocial Behavior & Behavior Disorders

Abuse of Power
Acquaintance Rape
Acute Alcoholic Intoxication
Addiction
Aggressive Driving Behavior
Alcohol Abuse
Alcoholism
Antisocial Behavior
Antisocial Personality Disorder
Arson
Attachment Disorders
Attempted Suicide
Attention Deficit Disorder
Attention Deficit Disorder with Hyperactivity
Battered Child Syndrome
Battered Females
Behavior Disorders
Behavior Problems
Binge Drinking
Bullying
Child Abuse
Child Neglect
Chronic Alcoholic Intoxication
Conduct Disorder
Crime
Criminal Behavior
Criminals
Cruelty
Domestic Violence
Driving Under the Influence
Drug Abuse
Drug Addiction
Drug Dependency
Elder Abuse
Emotional Abuse
Erotomania
Exhibitionism
Female Criminals
Female Delinquency
Fetishism
Genocide
Glue Sniffing
Harassment
Hate Crimes
Heroin Addiction
Homicide
Illegal Drug Distribution
Impulse Control Disorders
Incest
Infanticide
Inhalant Abuse
Internet Addiction
Intimate Partner Violence
Intravenous Drug Usage
Juvenile Delinquency
Juvenile Gangs
Kidnapping
Kleptomania
Male Criminals
Male Delinquency
Masochism
Mentally Ill Offenders
Oppositional Defiant Disorder
Paraphilias
Partner Abuse
Pathological Gambling
Patient Abuse
Patient Violence
Pedophilia
Perpetrators
Persecution
Physical Abuse
Polydrug Abuse
Prisoner Abuse
Psychopathy
Pyromania
Rape
Recidivism
Runaway Behavior
Sadism
Sadomasochism
Sadomasochistic Personality
School Truancy
School Violence
Self Destructive Behavior
Self Mutilation
Serial Homicide
Sex Offenses
Sexual Abuse
Sexual Addiction
Sexual Harassment
Sexual Masochism
Sexual Sadism
Shoplifting
Stalking
Suicidal Ideation
Suicide
Tantrums
Terrorism
Theft
Torture
Transvestism
Truancy
Underage Drinking
Vandalism
Verbal Abuse
Victimization
Violence
Violent Crime
Voyeurism
Workplace Violence

Diagnosis

Anatomically Detailed Dolls
Angiography
Biological Markers
Biopsy
Body Mass Index
Cancer Screening
Cardiography
Clinical Judgment (Not Diagnosis)
Cognitive Assessment
Computer Assisted Diagnosis
Dexamethasone Suppression Test
Diagnosis
Diagnosis Related Groups
Diagnostic and Statistical Manual
Diagnostic Interview Schedule
Differential Diagnosis
Drug Usage Screening
Dual Diagnosis
Echoencephalography
Electro Oculography
Electrocardiography
Electroencephalography
Electromyography
Electronystagmography
Electroplethysmography
Electroretinography
Encephalography
General Health Questionnaire
Genetic Testing
Geriatric Assessment

Health Screening
HIV Testing
Intake Interview
International Classification of Diseases
Magnetic Resonance Imaging
Mammography
Medical Diagnosis
Medical Model
Misdiagnosis
Needs Assessment
Neuroimaging
Neuropsychological Assessment
Ophthalmologic Examination
Pain Measurement
Physical Examination
Plethysmography
Pneumoencephalography
Polysomnography
Prenatal Diagnosis
Psychiatric Evaluation
Psychodiagnosis
Psychodiagnostic Interview
Psychodiagnostic Typologies
Psychological Assessment
Research Diagnostic Criteria
Rheoencephalography
Roentgenography
Screening
Structured Clinical Interview
Subtypes (Disorders)
Symptom Checklists
Tomography
Urinalysis

Disorder Characteristics

At Risk Populations
Chronicity (Disorders)
Client Attitudes
Client Characteristics
Comorbidity
Diagnosis
Diathesis Stress Model
Disease Course
Disease Transmission
Dual Diagnosis
Epidemics
Epidemiology
Etiology
Health Complaints
Heritability
Illness Behavior
Mortality Rate
Onset (Disorders)
Pandemics
Pathology
Pathophysiology
Patient History
Positive and Negative Symptoms
Predisposition
Premorbidity
Prodrome
Prognosis
Protective Factors
Psychiatric Symptoms
Recovery (Disorders)
Relapse (Disorders)
Remission (Disorders)
Risk Factors
Seasonal Variations
Severity (Disorders)
Spontaneous Remission
Subtypes (Disorders)
Susceptibility (Disorders)
Symptom Remission
Symptoms
Treatment Resistant Disorders

Learning Disorders & Mental Retardation

Acalculia
Agnosia
Agraphia
Alexia
Anencephaly
Attention Deficit Disorder
Attention Deficit Disorder with Hyperactivity
Autism
Borderline Mental Retardation
Cognitive Impairment
Crying Cat Syndrome
Downs Syndrome
Dyslexia
Dysphasia
Home Reared Mentally Retarded
Hyperkinesis
Institutionalized Mentally Retarded
Learning Disabilities
Learning Disorders
Mental Retardation
Mental Retardation (Attitudes Toward)
Microcephaly
Mild Mental Retardation
Moderate Mental Retardation
Profound Mental Retardation
Psychosocial Mental Retardation
Reading Disabilities
Rett Syndrome
Savants
Severe Mental Retardation
Tay Sachs Disease
Trisomy
Williams Syndrome

Physical & Psychosomatic Disorders

Acalculia
Addisons Disease
Adrenal Gland Disorders
Adventitious Disorders
Agnosia
Agraphia
AIDS
AIDS (Attitudes Toward)
AIDS Dementia Complex
Albinism
Allergic Disorders
Allergic Skin Disorders
Alopecia
Alzheimers Disease
Amblyopia
Amenorrhea
Amnesia
Anaphylactic Shock
Anemia
Anencephaly
Aneurysms
Angina Pectoris
Anorexia Nervosa
Anosmia
Anosognosia
Anterograde Amnesia
Aphagia
Aphasia
Apnea
Apraxia
Arrhythmias (Heart)
Arteriosclerosis
Arthritis
Asthenia
Asthma
Ataxia
Atherosclerosis
Athetosis
Atypical Disorders
Audiogenic Seizures
Autonomic Nervous System Disorders
Autosome Disorders
Back Pain
Bacterial Disorders
Bacterial Meningitis
Benign Neoplasms
Birth Injuries
Blind
Blood and Lymphatic Disorders
Blood Pressure Disorders
Body Dysmorphic Disorder
Bone Disorders
Bradycardia
Bradykinesia
Brain Concussion
Brain Damage
Brain Disorders
Brain Neoplasms
Breast Neoplasms
Bronchial Disorders
Bruxism

Consult Relationship Section for more information

Bulimia
Burns
Carbon Monoxide Poisoning
Cardiovascular Disorders
Catabolism
Catalepsy
Cataplexy
Cataracts
Central Nervous System Disorders
Cerebral Arteriosclerosis
Cerebral Hemorrhage
Cerebral Ischemia
Cerebral Palsy
Cerebrovascular Accidents
Cerebrovascular Disorders
Chorea
Chromosome Disorders
Chronic Fatigue Syndrome
Chronic Illness
Chronic Pain
Chronic Stress
Cirrhosis (Liver)
Cleft Palate
Cognitive Impairment
Colitis
Colon Disorders
Color Blindness
Congenital Disorders
Constipation
Conversion Disorder
Coronary Prone Behavior
Coronary Thromboses
Creutzfeldt Jakob Syndrome
Crying Cat Syndrome
Culture Bound Syndromes
Cushings Syndrome
Cystic Fibrosis
Deaf
Deaf Blind
Delirium Tremens
Dementia
Dementia with Lewy Bodies
Dermatitis
Developmental Disabilities
Diabetes
Diabetes Insipidus
Diabetes Mellitus
Diarrhea
Digestive System Disorders
Disabilities
Disabled (Attitudes Toward)
Disorders
Downs Syndrome
Drug Allergies
Drug Induced Congenital Disorders
Drug Induced Hallucinations
Dysarthria
Dyskinesia
Dysmenorrhea
Dyspareunia
Dysphagia
Dysphasia
Dyspnea
Ear Disorders
Eating Disorders
Eczema
Electrical Injuries
Embolisms
Encephalitis
Encephalomyelitis
Encephalopathies
Endocrine Disorders
Endocrine Neoplasms
Endocrine Sexual Disorders
Epilepsy
Epileptic Seizures
Epstein Barr Viral Disorder
Erectile Dysfunction
Essential Hypertension
Eye Disorders
Failure to Thrive
Fecal Incontinence
Female Sexual Dysfunction
Fetal Alcohol Syndrome
Fibrillation (Heart)
Fibromyalgia
Food Allergies
Fragile X Syndrome
Gastrointestinal Disorders
Gastrointestinal Ulcers
General Paresis
Genetic Disorders
Genital Disorders
Glaucoma
Global Amnesia
Goiters
Gonorrhea
Grand Mal Seizures
Gynecological Disorders
Hay Fever
Head Injuries
Headache
Health Impairments
Hearing Disorders
Heart Disorders
Hematoma
Hemianopia
Hemiplegia
Hemophilia
Hemorrhage
Hepatitis
Hermaphroditism
Herpes Genitalis
Herpes Simplex
HIV
Huntingtons Disease
Hydrocephalus
Hyperglycemia
Hyperkinesis
Hyperphagia
Hypersexuality
Hypersomnia
Hypertension
Hyperthyroidism
Hypochondriasis
Hypoglycemia
Hypogonadism
Hyponatremia
Hypopituitarism
Hypotension
Hypothyroidism
Hysterical Paralysis
Hysterical Vision Disturbances
Immunologic Disorders
Infectious Disorders
Infertility
Influenza
Injuries
Insomnia
Irritable Bowel Syndrome
Ischemia
Jaundice
Joint Disorders
Kidney Diseases
Kleine Levin Syndrome
Klinefelters Syndrome
Korsakoffs Psychosis
Kwashiorkor
Labyrinth Disorders
Laryngeal Disorders
Lead Poisoning
Leukemias
Lipid Metabolism Disorders
Liver Disorders
Lung Disorders
Lupus
Malaria
Male Genital Disorders
Measles
Memory Disorders
Menieres Disease
Meningitis
Menstrual Disorders
Mercury Poisoning
Metabolic Syndrome
Metabolism Disorders
Microcephaly
Migraine Headache
Motion Sickness
Movement Disorders
Multiple Disabilities
Multiple Sclerosis
Munchausen Syndrome
Munchausen Syndrome by Proxy
Muscle Contraction Headache
Muscle Spasms
Muscular Atrophy

Consult Relationship Section for more information

Muscular Disorders
Muscular Dystrophy
Musculoskeletal Disorders
Myasthenia
Myasthenia Gravis
Myelitis
Myocardial Infarctions
Myoclonus
Myofascial Pain
Myopia
Myotonia
Narcolepsy
Narcosis
Necrosis
Neonatal Disorders
Neoplasms
Nervous System Disorders
Nervous System Neoplasms
Neuralgia
Neurasthenia
Neurodegenerative Diseases
Neurodermatitis
Neuroleptic Malignant Syndrome
Neuromuscular Disorders
Neurosyphilis
Nocturnal Teeth Grinding
Nutritional Deficiencies
Nystagmus
Obesity
Obesity (Attitudes Toward)
Obstetrical Complications
Organic Brain Syndromes
Osteoporosis
Pain
Paralysis
Paraplegia
Parasitic Disorders
Parathyroid Disorders
Parkinsonism
Parkinsons Disease
Partially Hearing Impaired
Partially Sighted
Pellagra
Perceptual Disturbances
Peripheral Neuropathy
Petit Mal Seizures
Phantom Limbs
Pharyngeal Disorders
Phenylketonuria
Physical Disabilities (Attitudes Toward)
Physical Disfigurement
Physical Disorders
Physical Illness (Attitudes Toward)
Pica
Picks Disease
Pituitary Disorders
Pneumonia
Poliomyelitis
Porphyria
Prader Willi Syndrome
Premature Ejaculation
Premenstrual Dysphoric Disorder
Premenstrual Syndrome
Presenile Dementia
Progressive Supranuclear Palsy
Prosopagnosia
Protein Deficiency Disorders
Pruritus
Pseudocyesis
Pseudodementia
Pulmonary Emphysema
Pulmonary Tuberculosis
Quadriplegia
Refraction Errors
Respiratory Distress
Respiratory Tract Disorders
Retrograde Amnesia
Rett Syndrome
Rheumatic Fever
Rheumatoid Arthritis
Rubella
Sclerosis (Nervous System)
Seizures
Self Inflicted Wounds
Senile Dementia
Senile Psychosis
Sense Organ Disorders
Sensory Disabilities (Attitudes Toward)
Sensory System Disorders
Sex Chromosome Disorders
Sex Linked Hereditary Disorders
Sexual Function Disturbances
Sexually Transmitted Diseases
Sickle Cell Disease
Skin Disorders
Sleep Apnea
Sleep Disorders
Somatization
Somatoform Disorders
Somatoform Pain Disorder
Somatosensory Disorders
Spasms
Spina Bifida
Spinal Cord Injuries
Sterility
Strabismus
Sudden Infant Death
Syncope
Syndromes
Synesthesia
Syphilis
Tachycardia
Tardive Dyskinesia
Taste Disorders
Tay Sachs Disease
Terminal Cancer
Terminally Ill Patients
Testicular Feminization Syndrome
Thromboses
Thyroid Disorders
Thyrotoxicosis
Tics
Tinnitus
Torticollis
Tourette Syndrome
Toxic Disorders
Toxic Encephalopathies
Toxic Hepatitis
Toxic Psychoses
Toxicomania
Traumatic Brain Injury
Tremor
Trigeminal Neuralgia
Tuberculosis
Tunnel Vision
Turners Syndrome
Ulcerative Colitis
Urinary Function Disorders
Urinary Incontinence
Urogenital Disorders
Vaginismus
Vascular Dementia
Viral Disorders
Vision Disorders
Vitamin Deficiency Disorders
Vomiting
Wernickes Syndrome
Whiplash
Williams Syndrome
Work Related Illnesses
Wounds

Psychological Disorders

Acrophobia
Acute Psychosis
Acute Schizophrenia
Acute Stress Disorder
Adjustment Disorders
Affective Disorders
Affective Psychosis
Agoraphobia
AIDS Dementia Complex
Alcoholic Hallucinosis
Alcoholic Psychosis
Alexithymia
Alzheimers Disease
Amnesia
Anaclitic Depression
Anorexia Nervosa
Antisocial Personality Disorder
Anxiety Disorders
Aspergers Syndrome
Atypical Depression
Atypical Disorders
Auditory Hallucinations
Autism
Avoidant Personality Disorder

Consult Relationship Section for more information

Bipolar Disorder
Body Dysmorphic Disorder
Body Image Disturbances
Borderline Personality Disorder
Borderline States
Bulimia
Capgras Syndrome
Castration Anxiety
Catatonic Schizophrenia
Childhood Neurosis
Childhood Psychosis
Childhood Schizophrenia
Chronic Mental Illness
Chronic Psychosis
Chronic Stress
Claustrophobia
Cognitive Impairment
Confabulation
Consciousness Disturbances
Coprophagia
Creutzfeldt Jakob Syndrome
Culture Bound Syndromes
Cyclothymic Personality
Death Anxiety
Delirium Tremens
Delusions
Dementia
Dementia with Lewy Bodies
Dependent Personality Disorder
Depersonalization
Depression (Emotion)
Dissociative Disorders
Dissociative Identity Disorder
Dysfunctional Family
Dysthymic Disorder
Eating Disorders
Elective Mutism
Electra Complex
Emotional Disturbances
Endogenous Depression
Erotomania
Explosive Disorder
Factitious Disorders
Fantasies (Thought Disturbances)
Fetal Alcohol Syndrome
Fixation (Psychoanalytic)
Fixation (Psychological)
Folie A Deux
Fragmentation (Schizophrenia)
Fugue Reaction
Gender Identity Disorder
Generalized Anxiety Disorder
Global Amnesia
Hallucinations
Hallucinosis
Histrionic Personality Disorder
Homeless Mentally Ill
Hypnagogic Hallucinations
Hypomania
Hysteria
Impulse Control Disorders
Infantilism
Inhibited Sexual Desire
Judgment Disturbances
Koro
Korsakoffs Psychosis
Magical Thinking
Major Depression
Malingering
Mania
Masochistic Personality
Mass Hysteria
Memory Disorders
Mental Disorders
Mental Disorders due to General Medical Conditions
Mental Illness (Attitudes Toward)
Mentally Ill Offenders
Munchausen Syndrome
Munchausen Syndrome by Proxy
Narcissistic Personality Disorder
Neurosis
Obsessive Compulsive Disorder
Obsessive Compulsive Personality Disorder
Occupational Neurosis
Oedipal Complex
Ophidiophobia
Organic Brain Syndromes
Panic Disorder
Paranoia (Psychosis)
Paranoid Personality Disorder
Paranoid Schizophrenia
Paraphilias
Passive Aggressive Personality Disorder
Personality Disorders
Pervasive Developmental Disorders
Phobias
Pica
Picks Disease
Postpartum Depression
Postpartum Psychosis
Posttraumatic Stress Disorder
Presenile Dementia
Process Schizophrenia
Pseudodementia
Psychosis
Reactive Depression
Reactive Psychosis
Recurrent Depression
Repetition Compulsion
Sadomasochistic Personality
Schizoaffective Disorder
Schizoid Personality Disorder
Schizophrenia
Schizophrenia (Disorganized Type)
Schizophreniform Disorder
Schizophrenogenic Family
Schizophrenogenic Mothers
Schizotypal Personality Disorder
School Phobia
Seasonal Affective Disorder
Self Defeating Behavior
Self Destructive Behavior
Self Mutilation
Senile Dementia
Senile Psychosis
Separation Anxiety
Sexual Addiction
Social Anxiety
Social Phobia
Speech Anxiety
Stress Reactions
Symbiotic Infantile Psychosis
Syndromes
Thought Disturbances
Toxic Psychoses
Traumatic Neurosis
Treatment Resistant Depression
Trichotillomania
Undifferentiated Schizophrenia
Vascular Dementia
Visual Hallucinations
Work Related Illnesses

Speech & Language Disorders

Acalculia
Agnosia
Agraphia
Alexia
Anosognosia
Aphasia
Articulation Disorders
Communication Disorders
Dysarthria
Dyslexia
Dysphasia
Dysphonia
Echolalia
Elective Mutism
Glossolalia
Language Delay
Language Disorders
Mutism
Prosopagnosia
Reading Disabilities
Retarded Speech Development
Speech Disorders
Stuttering

Symptomatology

Acting Out
Agitation
Akathisia
Amnesia
Anhedonia

Consult Relationship Section for more information

Anoxia
Anxiety
Aphagia
Apnea
Apraxia
Asthenia
Ataxia
Automatism
Back Pain
Behavior Change
Binge Eating
Body Rocking
Bruxism
Catalepsy
Catatonia
Chronic Pain
Chronic Stress
Cognitive Impairment
Coma
Constipation
Craving
Delirium
Depersonalization
Diarrhea
Dissociation
Distractibility
Drug Withdrawal
Dyskinesia
Dysphagia
Dyspnea
Emotional Disturbances
Extrapyramidal Symptoms
Falls
Fatigue
Fecal Incontinence
Head Banging
Headache
Health Complaints
Hematoma
Hemorrhage
Hoarding Behavior
Hyperglycemia
Hypersomnia
Hypertension
Hyperthermia
Hyperventilation
Hypoglycemia
Hyponatremia
Hypotension
Hypothermia
Inflammation
Insomnia
Mental Confusion
Muscle Spasms
Nail Biting
Nausea
Necrosis
Neurotoxicity
Nicotine Withdrawal
Nocturnal Teeth Grinding
Overweight
Pain
Panic Attack
Parkinsonism
Personality Change
Physiological Correlates
Place Disorientation
Positive and Negative Symptoms
Prodrome
Pruritus
Psychiatric Symptoms
Purging (Eating Disorders)
Respiratory Distress
Restlessness
Scratching
Seizures
Self Destructive Behavior
Shock
Sleepiness
Somatization
Spasms
Symptom Checklists
Symptom Remission
Symptoms
Syncope
Tics
Time Disorientation
Tremor
Urinary Incontinence
Vertigo
Vomiting
Wandering Behavior

EDUCATIONAL CLUSTER

- Academic Learning & Achievement
- Curricula
- Educational Personnel & Administration
- Educational Testing & Counseling
- Schools & Institutions
- Special Education
- Student Characteristics & Academic Environment
- Student Populations
- Teaching & Teaching Methods

Academic Learning & Achievement

Academic Achievement
Academic Achievement Motivation
Academic Achievement Prediction
Academic Aptitude
Academic Failure
Academic Overachievement
Academic Self Concept
Academic Specialization
Academic Underachievement
Adult Learning
Awards (Merit)
Collaborative Learning
College Academic Achievement
Computer Assisted Language Learning
Cooperative Learning
Discrimination Learning
Educational Attainment Level
Experiential Learning
Foreign Language Learning
Generalization (Learning)
Goal Orientation
Grade Level
Incidental Learning
Intentional Learning
Interference (Learning)
Latent Learning
Learning
Learning Ability
Learning Environment
Learning Rate
Learning Schedules
Learning Strategies
Learning Theory
Literacy
Mastery Learning
Mathematics Achievement
Metacognition
Mnemonic Learning
Multiple Intelligences
Nonsense Syllable Learning
Nonverbal Learning
Note Taking
Observational Learning
Overlearning
Paired Associate Learning
Perceptual Learning
Perceptual Motor Learning
Phonological Awareness
Probability Learning
Reading Achievement
Reading Readiness
Reading Skills
Reading Speed
Recall (Learning)
Recognition (Learning)
Reconstruction (Learning)
Relearning
Retention
Rote Learning
School Graduation
School Learning
School Retention
Science Achievement
Self Regulated Learning
Sequential Learning
Serial Anticipation (Learning)
Serial Learning
Service Learning
Skill Learning

Consult Relationship Section for more information

Social Learning
Spatial Learning
State Dependent Learning
Time On Task
Transfer (Learning)
Trial and Error Learning
Verbal Learning
Writing Skills

Curricula

Adult Education
Affective Education
After School Programs
Algebra
Apprenticeship
Art Education
Bilingual Education
Braille Instruction
Business Education
Calculus
Career Education
Clinical Methods Training
Clinical Psychology Graduate Training
Clinical Psychology Internship
Community Mental Health Training
Compensatory Education
Computer Training
Consumer Education
Continuing Education
Cooperative Education
Counselor Education
Curriculum
Curriculum Development
Death Education
Dental Education
Distance Education
Driver Education
Drug Education
Education
Educational Program Accreditation
Educational Program Planning
Educational Programs
Elementary Education
English as Second Language
Environmental Education
Equal Education
Extracurricular Activities
Family Life Education
Foreign Language Education
Geometry
Graduate Education
Graduate Psychology Education
Health Education
High School Education
Higher Education
Home Economics
Home Schooling
Humanities
Inservice Teacher Education
Inservice Training
Internship Programs
Language Arts Education
Literacy Programs
Management Training
Mathematics
Mathematics Education
Medical Education
Medical Internship
Medical Residency
Mental Health Inservice Training
Middle School Education
Military Training
Multicultural Education
Music Education
Nontraditional Education
Nursing Education
On the Job Training
Paraprofessional Education
Parent Training
Personnel Training
Phonics
Physical Education
Postgraduate Training
Preschool Education
Private School Education
Project Follow Through
Project Head Start
Psychiatric Training
Psychoanalytic Training
Psychology Education
Psychotherapy Training
Public School Education
Reading Education
Rehabilitation Education
Religious Education
Remedial Education
Remedial Reading
Same Sex Education
Science Education
Secondary Education
Sex Education
Social Studies Education
Social Work Education
Special Education
Spelling
Sports
Student Teaching
Study Abroad
Teacher Education
Undergraduate Education
Upward Bound
Vocational Education

Educational Personnel & Administration

Accreditation (Education Personnel)
Boards of Education
Budgets
College Teachers
Cooperating Teachers
Educational Administration
Educational Personnel
Educational Program Accreditation
Educational Psychologists
Educational Quality
Educational Reform
Educational Standards
Elementary School Teachers
High School Teachers
Junior High School Teachers
Librarians
Middle School Teachers
Parent School Relationship
Preschool Teachers
Preservice Teachers
Resource Teachers
School Administrators
School Counselors
School Nurses
School Principals
School Psychologists
School Superintendents
Special Education Teachers
Speech Therapists
Student Teachers
Teacher Aides
Teacher Attitudes
Teacher Characteristics
Teacher Education
Teacher Effectiveness Evaluation
Teacher Expectations
Teacher Personality
Teacher Recruitment
Teacher Student Interaction
Teacher Tenure
Teachers
Vocational Counselors
Vocational Education Teachers

Educational Testing & Counseling

Achievement Measures
Adaptive Testing
Aptitude Measures
College Entrance Examination Board
  Scholastic Aptitude Test
Computer Assisted Testing
Course Evaluation
Criterion Referenced Tests
Cultural Test Bias
Curriculum Based Assessment
Educational Counseling
Educational Diagnosis
Educational Financial Assistance
Educational Measurement
Educational Placement
Educational Program Evaluation
Educational Psychology

Consult Relationship Section for more information

Educational Therapy
Entrance Examinations
Essay Testing
Grading (Educational)
Graduate Record Examination
Group Testing
Minimum Competency Tests
Posttesting
School Based Intervention
School Counseling
School Psychology
Student Admission Criteria
Student Personnel Services
Student Records
Teacher Effectiveness Evaluation
Test Coaching
Test Taking
Testing
Testing Methods
Testwiseness
Woodcock Johnson Psychoeducational Battery

Schools & Institutions

Boarding Schools
Campuses
Charter Schools
Classrooms
Colleges
Community Colleges
Dormitories
Educational Laboratories
Elementary Schools
Graduate Schools
High Schools
Institutional Schools
Junior High Schools
Kindergartens
Learning Centers (Educational)
Middle Schools
Military Schools
Nongraded Schools
Nursery Schools
School Facilities
School Libraries
Schools
Seminaries
Technical Schools

Special Education

Acalculia
Accommodation (Disabilities)
Agnosia
Agraphia
Alexia
Anencephaly
Aphasia
Apraxia
Articulation Disorders
Aspergers Syndrome
Assistive Technology
Ataxia
Attention Deficit Disorder
Attention Deficit Disorder with Hyperactivity
Augmentative Communication
Autism
Behavior Disorders
Behavior Modification
Behavior Problems
Blind
Borderline Mental Retardation
Braille Instruction
Classroom Behavior Modification
Cleft Palate
Communication Disorders
Communication Skills Training
Compensatory Education
Crying Cat Syndrome
Deaf
Deaf Blind
Delayed Development
Developmental Disabilities
Downs Syndrome
Dysarthria
Dyskinesia
Dyslexia
Dysphasia
Dysphonia
Ear Disorders
Early Intervention
Echolalia
Educational Placement
Educational Therapy
Emotional Disturbances
Gifted
Hearing Disorders
Home Reared Mentally Retarded
Hyperkinesis
Individual Education Programs
Institutionalized Mentally Retarded
Language Delay
Language Disorders
Learning Disabilities
Learning Disorders
Literacy Programs
Mainstreaming
Mainstreaming (Educational)
Memory Disorders
Mental Retardation
Microcephaly
Mild Mental Retardation
Moderate Mental Retardation
Mutism
Partially Hearing Impaired
Perceptual Disturbances
Pervasive Developmental Disorders
Profound Mental Retardation
Psychosocial Mental Retardation
Reading Disabilities
Remedial Education
Remedial Reading
Retarded Speech Development
Rett Syndrome
Savants
School Based Intervention
Severe Mental Retardation
Social Skills Training
Special Education
Special Education Students
Special Needs
Speech Disorders
Speech Therapy
Stuttering
Tay Sachs Disease
Vision Disorders

Student Characteristics & Academic Environment

Ability Level
Academic Achievement
Academic Achievement Motivation
Academic Aptitude
Academic Environment
Academic Failure
Academic Overachievement
Academic Self Concept
Academic Specialization
Academic Underachievement
Artistic Ability
Athletic Participation
Bullying
Class Size
Classroom Behavior
Classroom Environment
Classroom Management
Classrooms
Coeducation
Cognitive Ability
College Academic Achievement
College Environment
Computer Anxiety
Computer Literacy
Declarative Knowledge
Educational Aspirations
Educational Attainment Level
Educational Background
Educational Degrees
Educational Incentives
Educational Objectives
Fraternity Membership
Goal Orientation
Grade Level
Learning Ability
Learning Environment
Literacy
Mathematical Ability

Consult Relationship Section for more information

Mathematics Anxiety
Musical Ability
Native Language
Nonverbal Ability
Parental Involvement
Performance Anxiety
Phonological Awareness
Pretend Play
Procedural Knowledge
Reading Ability
Reading Comprehension
Reading Skills
Same Sex Education
School Adjustment
School Attendance
School Club Membership
School Enrollment
School Environment
School Expulsion
School Graduation
School Integration
School Phobia
School Readiness
School Refusal
School Retention
School Suspension
School to Work Transition
School Transition
School Truancy
School Violence
Social Loafing
Sorority Membership
Special Needs
Speech Anxiety
Student Activism
Student Attitudes
Student Attrition
Student Characteristics
Student Engagement
Student Records
Study Habits
Tardiness
Teacher Student Interaction
Test Anxiety
Truancy
Verbal Ability
Virtual Classrooms
Writing Skills

Student Populations

Business Students
Classmates
College Athletes
College Dropouts
College Graduates
College Students
Community College Students
Counselor Trainees
Dental Students
Dropouts
Education Students
Elementary School Students
Gifted
Graduate Students
High School Graduates
High School Students
Intermediate School Students
International Students
Junior College Students
Junior High School Students
Kindergarten Students
Law Students
Medical Students
Middle School Students
Nursery School Students
Nursing Students
Postgraduate Students
Potential Dropouts
Preschool Students
Preservice Teachers
Primary School Students
Reentry Students
ROTC Students
School Dropouts
School Leavers
Seminarians
Special Education Students
Student Teachers
Students
Therapist Trainees
Transfer Students
Vocational School Students

Teaching & Teaching Methods

Ability Grouping
Advance Organizers
Apprenticeship
Audiovisual Instruction
Braille Instruction
Classroom Behavior Modification
Classroom Discipline
Classroom Management
Computer Assisted Instruction
Constant Time Delay
Curricular Field Experience
Directed Discussion Method
Discovery Teaching Method
Distance Education
Education
Educational Audiovisual Aids
Educational Field Trips
Educational Incentives
Educational Laboratories
Educational Objectives
Educational Programs
Educational Television
Educational Toys
Experiential Learning
Feedback
Films
Group Discussion
Group Instruction
Home Schooling
Homework
Individualized Instruction
Initial Teaching Alphabet
Instructional Media
Language Laboratories
Learning Strategies
Lecture Method
Lesson Plans
Montessori Method
Nondirected Discussion Method
On the Job Training
Open Classroom Method
Peer Tutoring
Programmed Instruction
Programmed Textbooks
Prompting
Psychoeducation
Reading Materials
Remedial Reading
Scaffolding
School Learning
Self Instructional Training
Sight Vocabulary
Silent Reading
Student Teaching
Teaching
Teaching Machines
Teaching Methods
Team Teaching Method
Televised Instruction
Textbooks
Theories of Education
Tutoring
Videotape Instruction

LEGAL CLUSTER

- Adjudication
- Criminal Groups
- Criminal Offenses
- Criminal Rehabilitation
- Laws
- Legal Issues
- Legal Personnel
- Legal Processes

Adjudication

Adjudication
Awards (Jury)
Capital Punishment
Commitment (Psychiatric)
Competency to Stand Trial
Court Referrals
Crime
Crime Victims

Consult Relationship Section for more information

Criminal Conviction
Criminal Justice
Criminal Record
Criminal Responsibility
Cross Examination
Defendants
Expert Testimony
Forensic Evaluation
Informants
Informed Consent
Insanity Defense
Interrogation
Juries
Jury Selection
Justice
Juvenile Justice
Law Enforcement
Legal Arrest
Legal Decisions
Legal Detention
Legal Evidence
Legal Processes
Legal Testimony
Litigation
Parole
Perpetrators
Polygraphs
Probation
Protective Services
Witnesses

Criminal Groups

Criminals
Defendants
Female Criminals
Female Delinquency
Juvenile Delinquency
Juvenile Gangs
Male Criminals
Male Delinquency
Mentally Ill Offenders
Perpetrators
Predelinquent Youth
Prisoners

Criminal Offenses

Abandonment
Acquaintance Rape
Age Discrimination
Arson
Assisted Suicide
Battered Child Syndrome
Battered Females
Bioterrorism
Child Abuse
Child Neglect
Crime
Criminal Behavior
Disability Discrimination
Domestic Violence
Driving Under the Influence
Elder Abuse
Employment Discrimination
Fraud
Gambling
Genocide
Harassment
Hate Crimes
Homicide
Human Trafficking
Illegal Drug Distribution
Incest
Infanticide
Intimate Partner Violence
Kidnapping
Kleptomania
Partner Abuse
Pathological Gambling
Patient Abuse
Pedophilia
Persecution
Physical Abuse
Political Assassination
Pornography
Prisoner Abuse
Prostitution
Race and Ethnic Discrimination
Rape
Runaway Behavior
School Violence
Serial Homicide
Sex Discrimination
Sex Offenses
Sexual Abuse
Sexual Harassment
Shoplifting
Social Discrimination
Stalking
Terrorism
Theft
Torture
Vandalism
Victimization
Violent Crime

Criminal Rehabilitation

Correctional Institutions
Criminal Rehabilitation
Criminology
Forensic Psychiatry
Forensic Psychology
Incarceration
Institutional Release
Institutional Schools
Institutionalization
Maximum Security Facilities
Parole
Penology
Prisons
Probation
Recidivism
Reformatories

Laws

Abortion Laws
Abuse Reporting
Affirmative Action
Child Abuse Reporting
Child Labor
Civil Law
Criminal Law
Disability Laws
Drug Laws
Equal Education
Government Policy Making
Gun Control Laws
Health Care Policy
Law (Government)
Laws
Legal Decisions
Legislative Processes
Marijuana Laws
Medicare
Mental Health Parity
Same Sex Marriage
Social Security
Taxation

Legal Issues

Affirmative Action
Age Discrimination
Ageism
Assisted Suicide
Capital Punishment
Censorship
Child Care
Child Welfare
Civil Rights
Conflict of Interest
Crime Prevention
Criminal Justice
Criminal Responsibility
Dangerousness
Disability Discrimination
Drug Legalization
Drug Usage Screening
Duty to Warn
Employment Discrimination
Equal Education
Eugenics
Euthanasia
Health Care Reform
HIV Testing
Human Rights
Informed Consent
Life Sustaining Treatment
Marijuana Legalization

Missing Children
Morality
Political Revolution
Privileged Communication
Professional Client Sexual Relations
Professional Liability
Race and Ethnic Discrimination
Refugees
Right to Treatment
Riots
Safety Belts
Safety Devices
Same Sex Marriage
School Integration
School Truancy
Self Defense
Sex Discrimination
Social Discrimination
Social Equality
Social Integration
Surrogate Parents (Humans)
Transportation Safety
Treatment Withholding
Underage Drinking
Victimization
Warning Labels
Welfare Reform

Legal Personnel

Attorneys
Judges
Juries
Law Enforcement Personnel
Law Students
Legal Personnel
Parole Officers
Police Personnel
Prison Personnel
Probation Officers

Legal Processes

Abuse Reporting
Adoption (Child)
Advance Directives
Advocacy
Autopsy
Censorship
Child Abuse Reporting
Child Custody
Child Support
Child Visitation
Child Welfare
Citizenship
Civil Rights
Client Rights
Commitment (Psychiatric)
Conflict of Interest
Conflict Resolution
Consumer Protection
Court Referrals
Crime Prevention
Criminal Profiling
Criminal Record
Criminology
Divorce
Drug Legalization
Forensic Evaluation
Forensic Psychiatry
Forensic Psychology
Foster Care
Guardianship
Immigration
Interracial Adoption
Involuntary Treatment
Joint Custody
Juvenile Justice
Labor Management Relations
Labor Union Members
Labor Unions
Legal Confession
Legal Processes
Litigation
Marijuana Legalization
Marital Separation
Mediation
Outpatient Commitment
Professional Licensing
Protective Services
Psychiatric Evaluation
School Integration
Social Integration
Strikes

NEUROPSYCHOLOGY & NEUROLOGY CLUSTER

- Assessment & Diagnosis
- Electrophysiology
- Neuroanatomy
- Neurological Disorders
- Neurological Intervention
- Neurosciences
- Neurotransmitters & Neuroregulators

Assessment & Diagnosis

Bender Gestalt Test
Echoencephalography
Electroencephalography
Halstead Reitan Neuropsychological Battery
Luria Nebraska Neuropsychological Battery
Magnetic Resonance Imaging
Magnetoencephalography
Memory for Designs Test
Mini Mental State Examination
Neurofeedback
Neuroimaging
Neuropsychological Assessment
Pneumoencephalography
Polysomnography
Rheoencephalography
Wechsler Memory Scale
Wisconsin Card Sorting Test

Electrophysiology

Alpha Rhythm
Auditory Evoked Potentials
Basal Skin Resistance
Contingent Negative Variation
Delta Rhythm
Electrical Activity
Electrical Brain Stimulation
Electroencephalography
Electrophysiology
Evoked Potentials
Galvanic Skin Response
Kindling
Magnetoencephalography
Olfactory Evoked Potentials
Polysomnography
Postactivation Potentials
Skin Electrical Properties
Skin Potential
Skin Resistance
Somatosensory Evoked Potentials
Theta Rhythm
Visual Evoked Potentials

Neuroanatomy

Abducens Nerve
Acoustic Nerve
Adrenergic Nerves
Adrenergic Receptors
Afferent Pathways
Amygdala
Auditory Cortex
Auditory Neurons
Autonomic Ganglia
Autonomic Nervous System
Axons
Baroreceptors
Basal Ganglia
Blood Brain Barrier
Brain
Brain Development
Brain Size
Brain Stem
Brain Weight
Broca's Area
Caudate Nucleus
Central Nervous System
Cerebellum
Cerebral Blood Flow
Cerebral Cortex
Cerebral Dominance
Cerebral Ventricles
Cerebrospinal Fluid

Chemoreceptors
Cholinergic Nerves
Cholinergic Receptors
Cones (Eye)
Corpus Callosum
Cutaneous Receptive Fields
Cutaneous Sense
Dendrites
Diencephalon
Dorsal Horns
Dorsal Roots
Efferent Pathways
Extrapyramidal Tracts
Facial Nerve
Forebrain
Fornix
Fovea
Frontal Lobe
Ganglia
Ganglion Cells (Retina)
Geniculate Bodies (Thalamus)
Globus Pallidus
Glutamate Receptors
Gyrus Cinguli
Hindbrain
Hippocampus
Hypothalamic Pituitary Adrenal Axis
Hypothalamo Hypophyseal System
Hypothalamus
Inferior Colliculus
Interhemispheric Interaction
Lateral Dominance
Left Hemisphere
Lemniscal System
Limbic System
Locus Ceruleus
Lumbar Spinal Cord
Mechanoreceptors
Medial Forebrain Bundle
Medulla Oblongata
Meninges
Mesencephalon
Motor Cortex
Motor Neurons
Myelin Sheath
Nerve Endings
Nerve Growth Factor
Nerve Tissues
Nervous System
Neural Analyzers
Neural Development
Neural Pathways
Neural Plasticity
Neural Receptors
Neurons
Nociceptors
Nucleus Basalis Magnocellularis
Occipital Lobe
Ocular Dominance
Olfactory Bulb
Olfactory Nerve
Optic Chiasm
Optic Lobe
Optic Nerve
Optic Tract
Parasympathetic Nervous System
Parietal Lobe
Periaqueductal Gray
Peripheral Nervous System
Photoreceptors
Pons
Preoptic Area
Proprioceptors
Purkinje Cells
Putamen
Pyramidal Tracts
Raphe Nuclei
Receptive Fields
Receptor Binding
Reticular Formation
Retina
Right Hemisphere
Rods (Eye)
Sense Organs
Sensory Neurons
Septal Nuclei
Somatosensory Cortex
Spinal Column
Spinal Cord
Spinal Ganglia
Spinothalamic Tracts
Striatum
Substantia Nigra
Sympathetic Nervous System
Tegmentum
Telencephalon
Thalamic Nuclei
Thalamus
Trigeminal Nerve
Vagus Nerve
Ventral Roots
Visual Cortex

Neurological Disorders

Acalculia
Agnosia
Agraphia
AIDS Dementia Complex
Alcoholic Hallucinosis
Alcoholic Psychosis
Alexia
Alzheimers Disease
Anencephaly
Anosognosia
Anoxia
Anterograde Amnesia
Aphasia
Apraxia
Ataxia
Athetosis
Audiogenic Seizures
Autonomic Nervous System Disorders
Back Pain
Bacterial Meningitis
Bradykinesia
Brain Concussion
Brain Damage
Brain Disorders
Brain Neoplasms
Catalepsy
Cataplexy
Central Nervous System Disorders
Cerebral Arteriosclerosis
Cerebral Atrophy
Cerebral Hemorrhage
Cerebral Ischemia
Cerebral Palsy
Cerebrovascular Accidents
Cerebrovascular Disorders
Chorea
Chronic Pain
Cognitive Impairment
Coma
Creutzfeldt Jakob Syndrome
Delirium Tremens
Dementia
Dementia with Lewy Bodies
Dysarthria
Dyskinesia
Dyslexia
Dysphasia
Dysphonia
Encephalitis
Encephalomyelitis
Encephalopathies
Epilepsy
Epileptic Seizures
Extrapyramidal Symptoms
General Paresis
Global Amnesia
Grand Mal Seizures
Head Injuries
Headache
Hemianopia
Hemiplegia
Huntingtons Disease
Hydrocephalus
Hyperkinesis
Korsakoffs Psychosis
Memory Disorders
Meningitis
Microcephaly
Migraine Headache
Movement Disorders
Multiple Sclerosis
Muscle Contraction Headache
Muscular Dystrophy

Consult Relationship Section for more information

Myasthenia Gravis
Myelitis
Myofascial Pain
Narcolepsy
Nervous System Disorders
Nervous System Neoplasms
Neuralgia
Neurodegenerative Diseases
Neuroleptic Malignant Syndrome
Neuromuscular Disorders
Neuropathology
Neurosyphilis
Organic Brain Syndromes
Pain
Paralysis
Paraplegia
Parkinsons Disease
Peripheral Neuropathy
Petit Mal Seizures
Picks Disease
Poliomyelitis
Presenile Dementia
Progressive Supranuclear Palsy
Prosopagnosia
Quadriplegia
Retrograde Amnesia
Sclerosis (Nervous System)
Seizures
Senile Dementia
Senile Psychosis
Spasms
Spinal Cord Injuries
Synesthesia
Tardive Dyskinesia
Tics
Torticollis
Tourette Syndrome
Toxic Encephalopathies
Traumatic Brain Injury
Tremor
Trigeminal Neuralgia
Vascular Dementia
Wernickes Syndrome
Williams Syndrome

Neurological Intervention

Afferent Stimulation
Brain Lesions
Brain Self Stimulation
Brain Stimulation
Chemical Brain Stimulation
Commissurotomy
Decerebration
Decortication (Brain)
Electrical Brain Stimulation
Hemispherectomy
Hypothalamus Lesions
Kindling
Neural Lesions
Neural Transplantation
Neurosurgery
Psychosurgery
Stereotaxic Techniques
Sympathectomy
Thalamotomy
Tractotomy
Vagotomy

Neurosciences

Neural Networks
Neuroanatomy
Neurobiology
Neurochemistry
Neurocognition
Neuroendocrinology
Neurolinguistics
Neurology
Neuropathology
Neurophysiology
Neuropsychiatry
Neuropsychology
Neurosciences
Neurosurgery
Psychoneuroendocrinology
Psychoneuroimmunology
Psychopharmacology
Psychosurgery

Neurotransmitters & Neuroregulators

Acetylcholine
Acetylcholinesterase
Adenosine
Alanines
Amino Acids
Angiotensin
Aspartic Acid
Bombesin
Catecholamines
Cholecystokinin
Choline
Cholinesterase
Dihydroxyphenylacetic Acid
Dihydroxytryptamine
Dopamine
Dopamine Metabolites
Dynorphins
Endogenous Opiates
Endorphins
Enkephalins
Epinephrine
Gamma Aminobutyric Acid
Glutamic Acid
Glycine
Histamine
Homovanillic Acid
Hydroxydopamine (6-)
Hydroxyindoleacetic Acid (5-)
Ibotenic Acid
Kainic Acid
Leptin
Melanocyte Stimulating Hormone
Methoxyhydroxyphenylglycol (3,4)
Monoamine Oxidases
Neurokinins
Neuropeptide Y
Neuropeptides
Neurotensin
Neurotoxicity
Neurotoxins
Neurotransmission
Neurotransmitter Uptake Inhibitors
Neurotransmitters
Nitric Oxide
Norepinephrine
Norepinephrine Metabolites
Oxytocin
Peptides
Phenethylamines
Serotonin
Serotonin Metabolites
Serotonin Norepinephrine Reuptake Inhibitors
Somatostatin
Substance P
Taurine
Tryptamine
Tyramine

OCCUPATIONAL & EMPLOYMENT CLUSTER

- Career Areas
- Employee, Occupational & Job Characteristics
- Occupational Groups
- Organizations & Organizational Behavior
- Personnel Management & Professional Personnel Issues

Career Areas

Advertising
Air Traffic Control
Banking
Behavioral Sciences
Business
Business Management
Child Care
Child Day Care
Community Psychology
Computer Programming
Consultation Liaison Psychiatry
Counseling
Cross Cultural Psychology
Data Processing
Education
Educational Administration

Consult Relationship Section for more information

Educational Psychology
Entrepreneurship
Experimental Psychology
Family Therapy
Forensic Psychiatry
Forensic Psychology
Geriatric Psychiatry
Gynecology
Health Care Administration
Health Promotion
Human Factors Engineering
Hypnotherapy
Industrial and Organizational Psychology
Job Corps
Law Enforcement
Marketing
Marriage Counseling
News Media
Nontraditional Careers
Nursing
Obstetrics
Occupational Therapy
Optometry
Paramedical Sciences
Pathology
Peace Corps
Pediatrics
Physical Therapy
Politics
Product Design
Psychiatry
Psychology
Psychotherapy
Public Relations
Rehabilitation
Rehabilitation Counseling
Retailing
School Psychology
Sciences
Self Employment
Social Casework
Social Psychology
Speech Therapy
Sports
Surgery
Teaching
Veterinary Medicine
Vocational Rehabilitation
Zoology

Employee, Occupational & Job Characteristics

Awards (Merit)
Bonuses
Career Change
Child Labor
Clerical Secretarial Skills
Disabled Personnel
Diversity in the Workplace
Division of Labor
Dual Careers
Employability
Employee Absenteeism
Employee Attitudes
Employee Benefits
Employee Characteristics
Employee Efficiency
Employee Health Insurance
Employee Interaction
Employee Leave Benefits
Employee Motivation
Employee Pension Plans
Employee Productivity
Employee Skills
Employee Turnover
Employment History
Employment Status
Family Work Relationship
Health Personnel Attitudes
Impaired Professionals
Income Level
Industrial Accidents
Job Applicant Attitudes
Job Characteristics
Job Enrichment
Job Experience Level
Job Involvement
Job Knowledge
Job Performance
Job Satisfaction
Job Search
Job Security
Labor Market
Labor Union Members
Leadership Qualities
Mentor
Military Attrition
Military Deployment
Military Duty Status
Noise Levels (Work Areas)
Occupational Adjustment
Occupational Aspirations
Occupational Attitudes
Occupational Choice
Occupational Exposure
Occupational Interests
Occupational Mobility
Occupational Neurosis
Occupational Preference
Occupational Safety
Occupational Status
Occupational Stress
Occupational Success
Occupational Tenure
Organizational Characteristics
Organizational Climate
Organizational Commitment
Organizational Learning
Private Practice
Procedural Justice
Professional Competence
Professional Identity
Professional Networking
Professional Recognition
Professional Specialization
Professionalism
Psychological Contracts
Quality of Work Life
Reemployment
Retirement
Salaries
School to Work Transition
Social Loafing
Supervisor Employee Interaction
Supply Chains
Tardiness
Telecommuting
Typing
Unemployment
Virtual Teams
Vocational Maturity
Work (Attitudes Toward)
Work Adjustment Training
Work Load
Work Related Illnesses
Work Rest Cycles
Work Scheduling
Work Week Length
Workaholism
Workday Shifts
Working Conditions
Working Space
Working Women
Workplace Violence

Occupational Groups

Accountants
Aerospace Personnel
Agricultural Extension Workers
Agricultural Workers
Air Force Personnel
Aircraft Pilots
Allied Health Personnel
Anthropologists
Apprenticeship
Architects
Army Personnel
Artists
Astronauts
Athletes
Attendants (Institutions)
Attorneys
Blue Collar Workers
Business and Industrial Personnel
Chaplains
Child Care Workers

Consult Relationship Section for more information

Clergy
Clerical Personnel
Clinical Psychologists
Clinicians
Coaches
Coast Guard Personnel
College Teachers
Commissioned Officers
Cooperating Teachers
Counseling Psychologists
Counselor Trainees
Counselors
Dentists
Disabled Personnel
Domestic Service Personnel
Draftees
Educational Personnel
Educational Psychologists
Elementary School Teachers
Engineers
Enlisted Military Personnel
Evangelists
Experimental Psychologists
Family Physicians
Fire Fighters
Foreign Workers
General Practitioners
Government Personnel
Gynecologists
Health Personnel
High School Teachers
Home Care Personnel
Hypnotherapists
Hypnotists
Industrial Foremen
Industrial Psychologists
Information Specialists
Internists
Interviewers
Job Applicants
Journalists
Judges
Junior High School Teachers
Labor Union Members
Law Enforcement Personnel
Lay Religious Personnel
Legal Personnel
Librarians
Management Personnel
Marine Personnel
Mathematicians
Medical Personnel
Mental Health Personnel
Mentor
Middle Level Managers
Migrant Farm Workers
Military Medical Personnel
Military Personnel
Military Psychologists
Ministers (Religion)
Missionaries
Musicians
National Guard Personnel
Navy Personnel
Neurologists
Noncommissioned Officers
Nonprofessional Personnel
Nuns
Nurses
Obstetricians
Occupational Therapists
Occupations
Optometrists
Paraprofessional Personnel
Parole Officers
Pathologists
Pediatricians
Personnel
Pharmacists
Physical Therapists
Physicians
Physicists
Police Personnel
Politicians
Preschool Teachers
Preservice Teachers
Priests
Prison Personnel
Probation Officers
Professional Personnel
Psychiatric Aides
Psychiatric Hospital Staff
Psychiatric Nurses
Psychiatric Social Workers
Psychiatrists
Psychoanalysts
Psychologists
Psychotherapists
Public Health Service Nurses
Rabbis
Rehabilitation Counselors
Religious Personnel
Resource Teachers
Sales Personnel
School Administrators
School Counselors
School Nurses
School Principals
School Psychologists
School Superintendents
Scientists
Secretarial Personnel
Seminarians
Service Personnel
Skilled Industrial Workers
Social Psychologists
Social Workers
Sociologists
Special Education Teachers
Speech Therapists
Student Teachers
Surgeons
Teacher Aides
Teachers
Technical Personnel
Technical Service Personnel
Therapist Trainees
Therapists
Top Level Managers
Unskilled Industrial Workers
Vocational Counselors
Vocational Education Teachers
Volunteer Military Personnel
Volunteers
White Collar Workers
Working Women
Writers

Organizations & Organizational Behavior

American Psychological Association
American Psychological Association Divisions
Business Organizations
Communities of Practice
Conflict of Interest
Decentralization
Diversity in the Workplace
Division of Labor
Downsizing
Entrepreneurship
Faith Based Organizations
Foreign Organizations
Globalization
Government Agencies
Government Policy Making
Health Care Policy
Health Maintenance Organizations
Innovation
International Organizations
Knowledge Management
Labor Unions
Mergers and Acquisitions
Multinational Corporations
Nepotism
NGOs
Nonprofit Organizations
Organizational Behavior
Organizational Change
Organizational Characteristics
Organizational Climate
Organizational Commitment
Organizational Crises
Organizational Development
Organizational Effectiveness
Organizational Learning
Organizational Objectives

Consult Relationship Section for more information

Organizational Structure
Organizations
Outsourcing
Policy Making
Professional Networking
Professional Organizations
Professional Recognition
Religious Organizations
Research and Development
Self Managing Work Teams
Small Businesses
Teams
Work Teams

Personnel Management & Professional Personnel Issues

Affirmative Action
Age Discrimination
Assessment Centers
Bonuses
Budgets
Career Development
Career Education
Conflict Resolution
Disability Discrimination
Disability Evaluation
Disability Management
Distributive Justice
Diversity in the Workplace
Downsizing
Employee Assistance Programs
Employee Attitudes
Employee Benefits
Employee Health Insurance
Employee Leave Benefits
Employee Pension Plans
Employee Turnover
Employer Attitudes
Employment Discrimination
Employment Tests
Entrepreneurship
Human Capital
Human Resource Management
Inservice Training
Job Analysis
Job Applicant Interviews
Job Applicant Screening
Job Enrichment
Job Search
Labor Management Relations
Labor Market
Leadership
Leadership Qualities
Leadership Style
Management
Management Decision Making
Management Methods
Management Personnel
Management Planning
Management Training
Mediation
Medical Personnel Supply
Mental Health Inservice Training
Mental Health Personnel Supply
Middle Level Managers
Military Recruitment
Military Training
Negotiation
Nepotism
Occupational Guidance
Occupational Success Prediction
On the Job Training
Organizational Learning
Outsourcing
Participative Management
Personnel Evaluation
Personnel Placement
Personnel Promotion
Personnel Recruitment
Personnel Selection
Personnel Supply
Personnel Termination
Personnel Training
Policy Making
Private Practice
Procedural Justice
Professional Certification
Professional Consultation
Professional Development
Professional Ethics
Professional Examinations
Professional Fees
Professional Identity
Professional Liability
Professional Licensing
Professional Recognition
Professional Referral
Professional Specialization
Professional Standards
Professional Supervision
Professionalism
Psychological Contracts
Quality Control
Race and Ethnic Discrimination
Reemployment
Retirement
Salaries
Sex Discrimination
Sexual Harassment
Social Security
Stress Management
Strikes
Supervisor Employee Interaction
Supply Chain Management
Supported Employment
Tardiness
Teacher Recruitment
Telecommuting
Top Level Managers
Transformational Leadership
Unemployment
Vocational Evaluation
Workers' Compensation Insurance

STATISTICAL CLUSTER

- Design, Analysis & Interpretation
- Statistical Reliability & Validity
- Statistical Theory & Experimentation

Design, Analysis & Interpretation

Algorithms
Analysis of Covariance
Analysis of Variance
Between Groups Design
Causal Analysis
Central Tendency Measures
Chi Square Test
Cluster Analysis
Cohort Analysis
Content Analysis
Content Analysis (Test)
Decision Theory
Error Analysis
Error of Measurement
Evaluation Criteria
Experimental Design
F Test
Factor Analysis
Factor Structure
Fuzzy Set Theory
Goodness of Fit
Heuristic Modeling
Homogeneity of Variance
Interaction Analysis (Statistics)
Interaction Variance
Item Analysis (Statistical)
Item Analysis (Test)
Item Response Theory
Least Squares
Linear Regression
Logistic Regression
Mann Whitney U Test
Markov Chains
Mathematical Modeling
Maximum Likelihood
Mean
Median
Meta Analysis
Multidimensional Scaling
Multiple Regression
Multivariate Analysis
Nonlinear Regression
Nonparametric Statistical Tests
Oblique Rotation
Orthogonal Rotation
Parametric Statistical Tests

Consult Relationship Section for more information

Path Analysis
Phi Coefficient
Point Biserial Correlation
Probability
Q Sort Testing Technique
Rank Difference Correlation
Rank Order Correlation
Repeated Measures
Scaling (Testing)
Score Equating
Scoring (Testing)
Sign Test
Spearman Brown Test
Standard Deviation
Standard Scores
Statistical Analysis
Statistical Correlation
Statistical Data
Statistical Estimation
Statistical Measurement
Statistical Norms
Statistical Probability
Statistical Regression
Statistical Reliability
Statistical Rotation
Statistical Significance
Statistical Tables
Statistical Tests
Statistical Validity
Statistical Variables
Statistical Weighting
Stochastic Modeling
Structural Equation Modeling
T Test
Tetrachoric Correlation
Time Series
Variability Measurement
Varimax Rotation
Wilcoxon Sign Rank Test
Zulliger Z Test

Statistical Reliability & Validity

Content Analysis
Content Analysis (Test)
Error Analysis
Error of Measurement
Interrater Reliability
Item Analysis (Statistical)
Item Content (Test)
Statistical Power
Statistical Reliability
Statistical Validity
Test Reliability
Test Validity

Statistical Theory & Experimentation

Biased Sampling
Binomial Distribution
Chaos Theory
Classical Test Theory
Confidence Limits (Statistics)
Conjoint Measurement
Consistency (Measurement)
Cutting Scores
Data Collection
Data Processing
Dependent Variables
Double Bind Interaction
Effect Size (Statistical)
Empirical Methods
Experiment Controls
Experimental Design
Experimental Replication
Experimental Subjects
Experimentation
Experimenter Bias
Followup Studies
Frequency Distribution
Fuzzy Set Theory
Halo Effect
Independent Variables
Knowledge of Results
Longitudinal Studies
Maximum Likelihood
Methodology
Normal Distribution
Null Hypothesis Testing
Population (Statistics)
Prediction Errors
Prospective Studies
Qualitative Research
Quantitative Methods
Quasi Experimental Methods
Random Sampling
Research Setting
Retrospective Studies
Sample Size
Sampling (Experimental)
Skewed Distribution
Statistical Data
Statistical Sample Parameters
Statistical Samples
Statistical Significance
Statistical Tables
Statistical Variables
Statistics
Type I Errors
Type II Errors

TESTS & TESTING CLUSTER

- Academic Achievement & Aptitude Measures
- Attitude & Interest Measures
- Developmental Measures
- Intelligence Measures
- Neuropsychological Measures
- Nonprojective Personality Measures
- Perceptual Measures
- Projective Personality Measures
- Testing
- Testing Methods

Academic Achievement & Aptitude Measures

Achievement Measures
Aptitude Measures
Armed Services Vocational Aptitude Battery
College Entrance Examination Board Scholastic Aptitude Test
Comprehension Tests
Curriculum Based Assessment
Differential Aptitude Tests
Educational Measurement
Entrance Examinations
General Aptitude Test Battery
Graduate Record Examination
Iowa Tests of Basic Skills
Metropolitan Readiness Tests
Minimum Competency Tests
Professional Examinations
Reading Measures
Retention Measures
Stanford Achievement Test
Verbal Tests
Wide Range Achievement Test
Woodcock Johnson Psychoeducational Battery

Attitude & Interest Measures

Attitude Measurement
Attitude Measures
Consumer Surveys
Interest Inventories
Kuder Occupational Interest Survey
Kuder Preference Record
Least Preferred Coworker Scale
Occupational Interest Measures
Preference Measures
Strong Vocational Interest Blank
Wilson Patterson Conservatism Scale

Developmental Measures

Bayley Scales of Infant Development
Developmental Measures

Intelligence Measures

Benton Revised Visual Retention Test
Cognitive Assessment
Creativity Measurement
Culture Fair Intelligence Test
Frostig Developmental Test of Visual Perception
Goodenough Harris Draw A Person Test
Illinois Test of Psycholinguistic Abilities
Intelligence Measures

Consult Relationship Section for more information

Kaufman Assessment Battery for Children
Kohs Block Design Test
Miller Analogies Test
Peabody Picture Vocabulary Test
Porteus Maze Test
Raven Coloured Progressive Matrices
Raven Progressive Matrices
Slosson Intelligence Test
Stanford Binet Intelligence Scale
Verbal Tests
Wechsler Adult Intelligence Scale
Wechsler Bellevue Intelligence Scale
Wechsler Intelligence Scale for Children
Wechsler Memory Scale
Wechsler Preschool Primary Scale

Neuropsychological Measures

Bender Gestalt Test
Benton Revised Visual Retention Test
Body Sway Testing
Halstead Reitan Neuropsychological Battery
Luria Nebraska Neuropsychological Battery
Memory for Designs Test
Mini Mental State Examination
Neuropsychological Assessment
Wechsler Memory Scale
Wisconsin Card Sorting Test

Nonprojective Personality Measures

Bannister Repertory Grid
Beck Depression Inventory
Bem Sex Role Inventory
California F Scale
California Psychological Inventory
Child Behavior Checklist
Childrens Manifest Anxiety Scale
Edwards Personal Preference Schedule
Edwards Social Desirability Scale
Embedded Figures Testing
Eysenck Personality Inventory
Fear Survey Schedule
Fundamental Interpersonal Relation Orientation Behavior Ques
General Health Questionnaire
Gough Adjective Check List
High School Personality Questionnaire
Kirton Adaption Innovation Inventory
Marlowe Crowne Social Desirability Scale
Memory for Designs Test
Millon Clinical Multiaxial Inventory
Minnesota Multiphasic Personality Inventory
Mooney Problem Check List
Myers Briggs Type Indicator
NEO Personality Inventory
Nonprojective Personality Measures
Personal Orientation Inventory
Personality Measures
Psychological Screening Inventory
Repression Sensitization Scale
Rod and Frame Test
Rokeach Dogmatism Scale
Rotter Internal External Locus of Control Scale
Sensation Seeking Scale
Sixteen Personality Factors Questionnaire
State Trait Anxiety Inventory
Taylor Manifest Anxiety Scale
Tennessee Self Concept Scale
Vineland Social Maturity Scale
Zungs Self Rating Depression Scale

Perceptual Measures

Audiometry
Bone Conduction Audiometry
Pain Measurement
Perceptual Measures
Psychophysical Measurement
Rod and Frame Test
Sensorimotor Measures
Speech and Hearing Measures
Stroop Color Word Test

Projective Personality Measures

Bender Gestalt Test
Childrens Apperception Test
Holtzman Inkblot Technique
Human Figures Drawing
Personality Measures
Projective Personality Measures
Projective Techniques
Projective Testing Technique
Rorschach Test
Rosenzweig Picture Frustration Study
Rotter Incomplete Sentences Blank
Sentence Completion Tests
Szondi Test
Thematic Apperception Test
Zulliger Z Test

Testing

Consistency (Measurement)
Content Analysis (Test)
Cultural Test Bias
Cutting Scores
Difficulty Level (Test)
Employment Tests
Evaluation Criteria
Factor Analysis
Factor Structure
Foreign Language Translation
Interview Schedules
Inventories
Item Analysis (Test)
Item Content (Test)
Item Response Theory
Measurement
Performance Tests
Piagetian Tasks
Profiles (Measurement)
Psychometrics
Rating Scales
Score Equating
Scoring (Testing)
Screening Tests
Selection Tests
Semantic Differential
Sociometric Tests
Sociometry
Standard Scores
Standardized Tests
Statistical Validity
Statistical Weighting
Subtests
Test Administration
Test Anxiety
Test Bias
Test Construction
Test Forms
Test Interpretation
Test Items
Test Norms
Test Reliability
Test Scores
Test Standardization
Test Taking
Testing
Testwiseness

Testing Methods

Adaptive Testing
Behavioral Assessment
Biographical Inventories
Body Sway Testing
Clinical Trials
Cloze Testing
Cognitive Assessment
Computer Assisted Testing
Consumer Surveys
Criterion Referenced Tests
Digit Span Testing
Essay Testing
Forced Choice (Testing Method)
Group Testing
Individual Testing
Interview Schedules
Inventories
Likert Scales
Mail Surveys
Matching to Sample

Consult Relationship Section for more information

Multidimensional Scaling
Multiple Choice (Testing Method)
Neuropsychological Assessment
Performance Tests
Posttesting
Pretesting
Psychological Assessment
Q Sort Testing Technique
Questionnaires
Rating Scales
Scaling (Testing)
Screening
Screening Tests
Standardized Tests
Surveys
Symptom Checklists
Telephone Surveys
Testing Methods
Verbal Tests

TREATMENT CLUSTER

- Alternative Therapies
- Behavior Modification & Therapy
- Counseling
- Hospitalization & Institutionalization
- Medical & Physical Treatment
- Psychotherapy
- Rehabilitation
- Treatment (General)
- Treatment Facilities

Alternative Therapies

Acupuncture
Aerobic Exercise
Alternative Medicine
Animal Assisted Therapy
Art Therapy
Autohypnosis
Biofeedback Training
Communication Skills Training
Creative Arts Therapy
Dance Therapy
Dietary Supplements
Encounter Group Therapy
Eye Movement Desensitization Therapy
Faith Healing
Folk Medicine
Guided Imagery
Holistic Health
Horticulture Therapy
Human Relations Training
Hypericum Perforatum
Hypnosis
Hypnotherapy
Imagery
Massage
Medicinal Herbs and Plants
Meditation
Milieu Therapy
Morita Therapy
Motivation Training
Movement Therapy
Music Therapy
Narcoanalysis
Online Therapy
Osteopathic Medicine
Pain Management
Phototherapy
Poetry Therapy
Recreation Therapy
Relaxation Therapy
Role Playing
Self Medication
Sensitivity Training
Sex Therapy
Sleep Treatment
Social Skills Training
Sociotherapy
Stress Management
Support Groups
Therapeutic Camps
Therapeutic Social Clubs
Wilderness Experience

Behavior Modification & Therapy

Anger Control
Anxiety Management
Assertiveness Training
Aversion Therapy
Behavior Contracting
Behavior Modification
Behavior Therapy
Biofeedback Training
Cognitive Behavior Therapy
Cognitive Restructuring
Cognitive Techniques
Cognitive Therapy
Conditioning
Contingency Management
Counterconditioning
Covert Sensitization
Differential Reinforcement
Exposure Therapy
Fading (Conditioning)
Functional Analysis
Harm Reduction
Implosive Therapy
Motivational Interviewing
Omission Training
Operant Conditioning
Overcorrection
Paradoxical Techniques
Progressive Relaxation Therapy
Rational Emotive Behavior Therapy
Reciprocal Inhibition Therapy
Relaxation Therapy
Response Cost
Self Help Techniques
Self Management
Self Monitoring
Sensitization
Stress Management
Systematic Desensitization Therapy
Time Out
Token Economy Programs

Counseling

AIDS Prevention
Clinical Practice
Counseling
Counseling Psychology
Couples Therapy
Crisis Intervention
Crisis Intervention Services
Cross Cultural Counseling
Debriefing (Psychological)
Drug Abuse Prevention
Family Intervention
Family Planning
Feminist Therapy
Genetic Counseling
Group Counseling
Health Promotion
Hot Line Services
Marriage Counseling
Microcounseling
Online Therapy
Pastoral Counseling
Peer Counseling
Premarital Counseling
Psychotherapeutic Counseling
Rehabilitation Counseling
Social Casework
Suicide Prevention
Suicide Prevention Centers

Hospitalization & Institutionalization

Aftercare
Client Transfer
Commitment (Psychiatric)
Continuum of Care
Deinstitutionalization
Discharge Planning
Emergency Services
Facility Admission
Facility Discharge
Hospice
Hospital Admission
Hospital Discharge
Hospital Environment
Hospital Programs
Hospitalization
Hospitalized Patients
Hospitals
Institution Visitation
Institutional Release

Institutionalization
Intensive Care
Outpatient Commitment
Outpatient Treatment
Outpatients
Partial Hospitalization
Patient Seclusion
Psychiatric Hospital Admission
Psychiatric Hospital Discharge
Psychiatric Hospital Programs
Psychiatric Hospital Readmission
Psychiatric Hospitalization
Psychiatric Units
Sanatoriums
Therapeutic Community

Medical & Physical Treatment

Acupuncture
Adolescent Psychiatry
Adrenalectomy
Amputation
Artificial Pacemakers
Artificial Respiration
Biological Psychiatry
Biopsy
Blood Transfusion
Castration
Catheterization
Chemotherapy
Child Psychiatry
Circumcision
Cochlear Implants
Colostomy
Commissurotomy
Community Psychiatry
Computer Assisted Therapy
Dental Surgery
Dental Treatment
Dialysis
Disease Management
Drug Augmentation
Drug Self Administration
Drug Therapy
Electroconvulsive Shock Therapy
Electrosleep Treatment
Endocrine Gland Surgery
Evidence Based Practice
Family Medicine
Fertility Enhancement
Geriatric Psychiatry
Health Care Services
Health Maintenance Organizations
Heart Surgery
Hemispherectomy
Hemodialysis
Hormone Therapy
Hypophysectomy
Hysterectomy
Immunization
Induced Abortion
Insulin Shock Therapy
Intensive Care
Laser Irradiation
Male Castration
Massage
Mastectomy
Medical Therapeutic Devices
Medical Treatment (General)
Mobility Aids
Movement Therapy
Narcoanalysis
Neural Transplantation
Neurosurgery
Organ Transplantation
Orthopsychiatry
Ovariectomy
Pain Management
Phototherapy
Physical Therapy
Physical Treatment Methods
Pinealectomy
Plastic Surgery
Polypharmacy
Postsurgical Complications
Prenatal Care
Prescribing (Drugs)
Prescription Drugs
Preventive Medicine
Primary Health Care
Prostheses
Psychiatric Patients
Psychiatry
Psychosomatic Medicine
Psychosurgery
Public Health Services
Radiation Therapy
Self Medication
Sex Change
Shock Therapy
Sleep Treatment
Stem Cells
Stereotaxic Techniques
Surgery
Surgical Patients
Sympathectomy
Telemedicine
Thalamotomy
Thyroidectomy
Tractotomy
Transcranial Magnetic Stimulation
Tubal Ligation
Vagotomy
Vasectomy
Vitamin Therapy

Psychotherapy

Adlerian Psychotherapy
Adolescent Psychotherapy
Age Regression (Hypnotic)
Analytical Psychotherapy
Autogenic Training
Bibliotherapy
Brief Psychotherapy
Centering
Child Psychotherapy
Client Centered Therapy
Clinical Practice
Cognitive Behavior Therapy
Cognitive Restructuring
Cognitive Techniques
Cognitive Therapy
Conjoint Therapy
Consultation Liaison Psychiatry
Cotherapy
Countertransference
Couples Therapy
Crisis Intervention
Debriefing (Psychological)
Dream Analysis
Eclectic Psychotherapy
Emotion Focused Therapy
Enactments
Encounter Group Therapy
Existential Therapy
Experiential Psychotherapy
Expressive Psychotherapy
Family Therapy
Feminist Therapy
Free Association
Geriatric Psychotherapy
Gestalt Therapy
Group Psychotherapy
Guided Imagery
Humanistic Psychotherapy
Hypnotherapy
Individual Psychotherapy
Insight (Psychotherapeutic Process)
Insight Therapy
Integrative Psychotherapy
Interpersonal Psychotherapy
Logotherapy
Marathon Group Therapy
Marriage Counseling
Mirroring
Morita Therapy
Mutual Storytelling Technique
Narrative Therapy
Negative Therapeutic Reaction
Online Therapy
Paradoxical Techniques
Personal Therapy
Persuasion Therapy
Play Therapy
Primal Therapy
Psychoanalysis
Psychodrama
Psychodynamic Psychotherapy

Consult Relationship Section for more information

Psychotherapeutic Breakthrough
Psychotherapeutic Counseling
Psychotherapeutic Neutrality
Psychotherapeutic Outcomes
Psychotherapeutic Processes
Psychotherapeutic Resistance
Psychotherapeutic Techniques
Psychotherapeutic Transference
Psychotherapy
Rational Emotive Behavior Therapy
Reality Therapy
Relationship Therapy
Self Analysis
Solution Focused Therapy
Supportive Psychotherapy
Therapeutic Alliance
Therapeutic Community
Therapist Selection
Transactional Analysis

Rehabilitation

Activities of Daily Living
Adaptive Behavior
Aftercare
Aging in Place
Alcohol Rehabilitation
Alcoholics Anonymous
Assisted Living
Assistive Technology
Augmentative Communication
Cochlear Implants
Cognitive Rehabilitation
Criminal Rehabilitation
Detoxification
Disability Management
Drug Rehabilitation
Habilitation
Halfway Houses
Harm Reduction
Horticulture Therapy
Independent Living Programs
Mainstreaming
Maintenance Therapy
Memory Training
Methadone Maintenance
Motivational Interviewing
Needle Exchange Programs
Neuropsychological Rehabilitation
Occupational Therapy
Physical Therapy
Prostheses
Psychosocial Rehabilitation
Readiness to Change
Rehabilitation
Rehabilitation Centers
Rehabilitation Counseling
Self Care Skills
Sheltered Workshops
Smoking Cessation
Speech Therapy
Stages of Change
Support Groups
Therapeutic Community
Therapeutic Social Clubs
Twelve Step Programs
Vocational Evaluation
Vocational Rehabilitation
Wilderness Experience
Work Adjustment Training

Treatment (General)

Adolescent Psychiatry
Adult Day Care
Advance Directives
AIDS Prevention
Assisted Suicide
Biological Psychiatry
Biopsychosocial Approach
Caregiver Burden
Caregivers
Case Management
Child Psychiatry
Child Psychology
Childbirth Training
Client Education
Client Participation
Client Records
Client Rights
Client Transfer
Client Treatment Matching
Clinical Audits
Clinical Governance
Clinical Psychology
Community Psychiatry
Computer Assisted Therapy
Continuum of Care
Cross Cultural Treatment
Discharge Planning
Disease Management
Drug Abuse Prevention
Drug Education
Drug Therapy
Early Intervention
Elder Care
Euthanasia
Evidence Based Practice
Family Intervention
Fee for Service
Geriatric Patients
Geriatric Psychiatry
Health Care Costs
Health Care Delivery
Health Care Policy
Health Care Psychology
Health Care Seeking Behavior
Health Care Services
Health Care Utilization
Health Education
Health Insurance
Health Promotion
Health Service Needs
Help Seeking Behavior
Holistic Health
Home Visiting Programs
Hospice
Informed Consent
Integrated Services
Interdisciplinary Treatment Approach
Intervention
Involuntary Treatment
Life Sustaining Treatment
Long Term Care
Maintenance Therapy
Managed Care
Medicaid
Medical Patients
Medical Psychology
Medical Records
Medical Treatment (General)
Medicare
Multimodal Treatment Approach
Nonprescription Drugs
Online Therapy
Optical Aids
Orthopsychiatry
Osteopathic Medicine
Outreach Programs
Palliative Care
Patient Abuse
Patient History
Patient Selection
Patients
Physical Examination
Posttreatment Followup
Prescribing (Drugs)
Prescription Drugs
Prescription Privileges
Primary Mental Health Prevention
Private Practice
Psychiatric Patients
Psychiatry
Psychoeducation
Quality of Care
Quality of Services
Relapse Prevention
Respite Care
Right to Treatment
Self Examination (Medical)
Self Medication
Self Referral
Sex Education
Side Effects (Treatment)
Social Psychiatry
Social Services
Surgical Patients
Telemedicine
Therapeutic Alliance

Therapeutic Processes
Treatment
Treatment Barriers
Treatment Compliance
Treatment Dropouts
Treatment Duration
Treatment Effectiveness Evaluation
Treatment Guidelines
Treatment Outcomes
Treatment Planning
Treatment Refusal
Treatment Termination
Treatment Withholding
Utilization Reviews

Treatment Facilities

Adult Day Care
Assisted Living
Child Guidance Clinics
Clinics
Community Facilities
Community Mental Health Centers
Community Mental Health Services
Day Care Centers
Facility Environment
Group Homes
Halfway Houses
Health Care Services
Health Maintenance Organizations
Home Care
Hospital Environment
Hospitals
Institutional Schools
Intensive Care
Maximum Security Facilities
Mental Health Programs
Mental Health Services
Nursing Homes
Orphanages
Psychiatric Clinics
Psychiatric Hospitals
Psychiatric Units
Public Health Services
Rehabilitation Centers
Residential Care Institutions
Sanatoriums
Shelters
Social Services
Suicide Prevention Centers
Therapeutic Camps
Therapeutic Community
Therapeutic Environment
Treatment Facilities
Walk In Clinics